Almanac
of American
Education
2011

Almanac of American Education

2011

Edited by Deirdre A. Gaquin
and Sarah E. Baltic

Published in the United States of America
by Bernan Press, a wholly owned subsidiary of
The Rowman & Littlefield Publishing Group, Inc.
4501 Forbes Boulevard, Suite 200
Lanham, Maryland 20706

Bernan Press
800-865-3457
info@bernan.com
www.bernan.com

ISBN: 978-1-59888-477-7
E-ISBN: 978-1-59888-478-4

♾™ The paper used in this publication meets the minimum requirements of American National
Standard for Information Sciences—Permanence of Paper for Printed Library Materials,
ANSI/NISO Z39.48-1992.
Manufactured in the United States of America.

Contents

Tables

PART A—NATIONAL EDUCATION STATISTICS

ENROLLMENT TABLES

HISTORICAL ENROLLMENT TABLES

PART B—REGION AND STATE EDUCATION STATISTICS

PART C—COUNTY EDUCATION STATISTICS

Figures

PART C—COUNTY EDUCATION STATISTICS

Preface

This edition of *The Almanac of American Education* serves as a guide to understanding and comparing the quality of education at the national, state, and county levels. Compiled from sources such as the U.S. Census Bureau and the National Center for Education Statistics (NCES), *The Almanac* contains historical and current data, insightful analysis, and useful graphics that paint a compelling picture of the state of education in the United States.

The Almanac is organized into three sections: Part A—National Education Statistics; Part B—Region and State Education Statistics; and Part C—County Education Statistics. Most of the data presented in Part A are no longer available in print form from the Census Bureau. New tables in Part A are excerpted from the *Digest of Education Statistics* from the NCES, providing an overview of higher education in the United States. The data in Parts B and C have been specially tabulated for this publication from data obtained from the NCES, the Census Bureau, and other sources.

The Almanac's contents and coverage allow users to answer—and ask—important questions about education, including:

- What are the nationwide trends in earnings by educational attainment level?
- Is the earnings gap between high school graduates and college graduates growing or shrinking?
- Which states have the highest and lowest high school dropout rates?
- Which states have the largest county-to-county variation in student-teacher ratios?

- Is there a relationship between student poverty rates and county-level expenditures per student?

The data in this volume meet the publication standards of the federal statistical agencies and the few nongovernmental organizations from which they were obtained. Every effort has been made to select accurate, meaningful, and useful data. All statistical data are subject to error arising from sampling variability, reporting errors, incomplete coverage, imputation, and other causes. The responsibility of the editors and publisher of this volume is limited to reasonable care in the reproduction and presentation of data obtained from established sources.

Deirdre A. Gaquin and Sarah E. Baltic edited this edition of *The Almanac of American Education*. Ms. Gaquin has been a data use consultant to private organizations, government agencies, and universities for over 25 years. Prior to that, she was Director of Data Access Services at Data Use & Access Laboratories, a pioneer in private sector distribution of federal statistical data. A former President of the Association of Public Data Users, Ms. Gaquin has served on numerous boards, panels, and task forces concerned with federal statistical data and has worked on four decennial censuses. She holds a Master of Urban Planning (MUP) degree from Hunter College. Ms. Gaquin is also an editor of Bernan Press's *The Who, What, and Where of America: Understanding the Census Results*; *Places, Towns and Townships*; and *County and City Extra*.

Sarah E. Baltic, associate editor with Bernan Press, received her bachelor's degree in magazine journalism from Syracuse University's S.I. Newhouse School of Public Communications and is a former magazine editor with *Voice of Youth Advocates*. Additionally, Ms. Baltic has worked in the publications field as a book acquisitions editor and a freelance magazine writer and editor. She is the editor of *Employment, Hours, and Earnings 2010* and has assisted with the *Social Security Handbook (Large Print Edition)*, *County and City Extra*, *The United States Government Internet Manual*, and *The Almanac of the Unelected*; all published by Bernan Press.

Much appreciation is due to the federal agency personnel who prepared the original data and generously responded to our requests for assistance.

PART A
NATIONAL EDUCATION STATISTICS

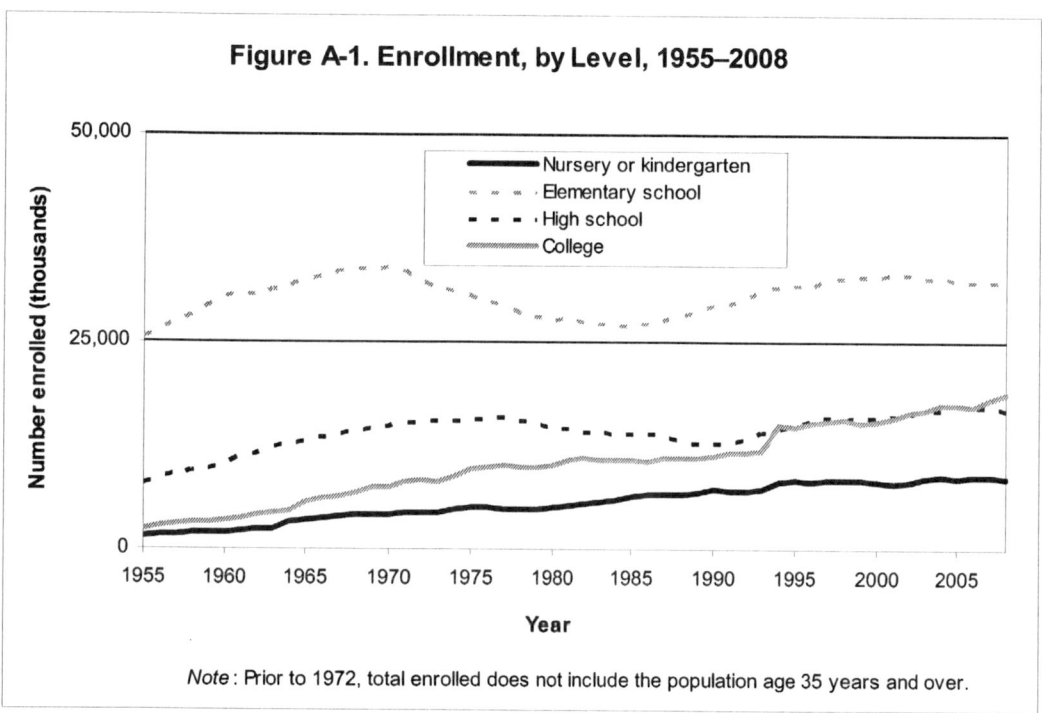

Figure A-1. Enrollment, by Level, 1955–2008

Note: Prior to 1972, total enrolled does not include the population age 35 years and over.

Over 76 million people were enrolled in school in 2008. This number reflected an increase of less than one percent from 2007 and is the highest number ever measured for the nation. Most of the increase in the 21st century has been in college enrollment. Elementary school enrollment has remained at about 32 to 33 million through the decade, similar to the baby boom levels of the 1960s but never quite reaching the nearly 34 million elementary school enrollees of 1970. College enrollment in 2008, however, at 18.6 million, was more than double the levels of the 1970s. (Table A-9)

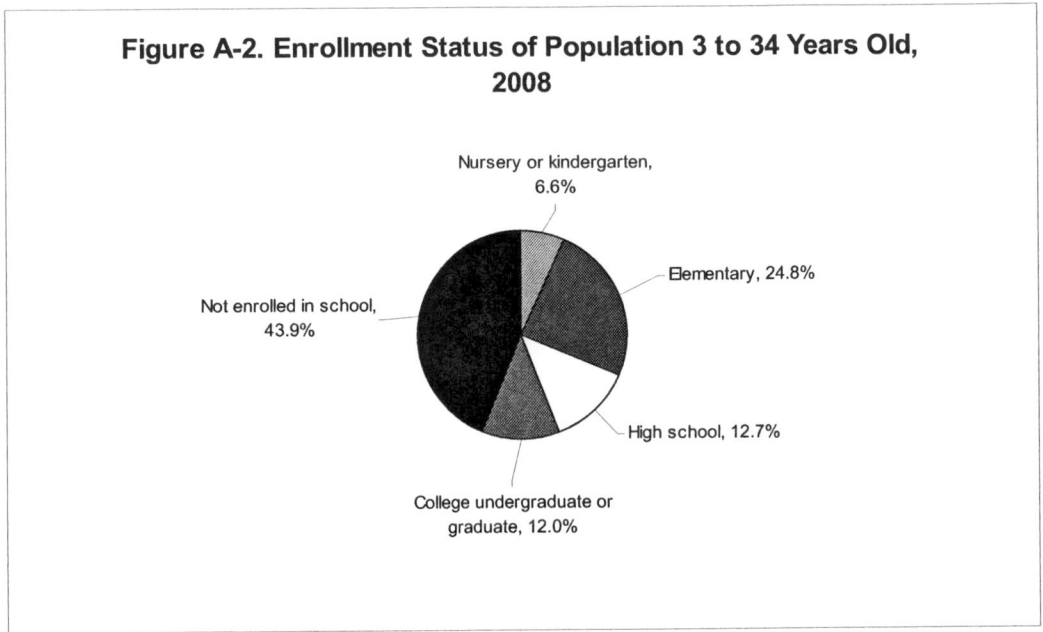

Figure A-2. Enrollment Status of Population 3 to 34 Years Old, 2008

In 2008, 26.6 percent of people age 3 years and over were enrolled in school. For the population 3 to 34 years old, 6.6 percent were enrolled in nursery school or kindergarten, and nearly 25 percent were enrolled in elementary school. Among the population 18 to 24 years old, 45.4 percent were enrolled in school, as were 13.2 percent of 25 to 29 year olds. The proportion of 35 to 44 year olds enrolled in school increased to above 4 percent for the first time. (Table A-1)

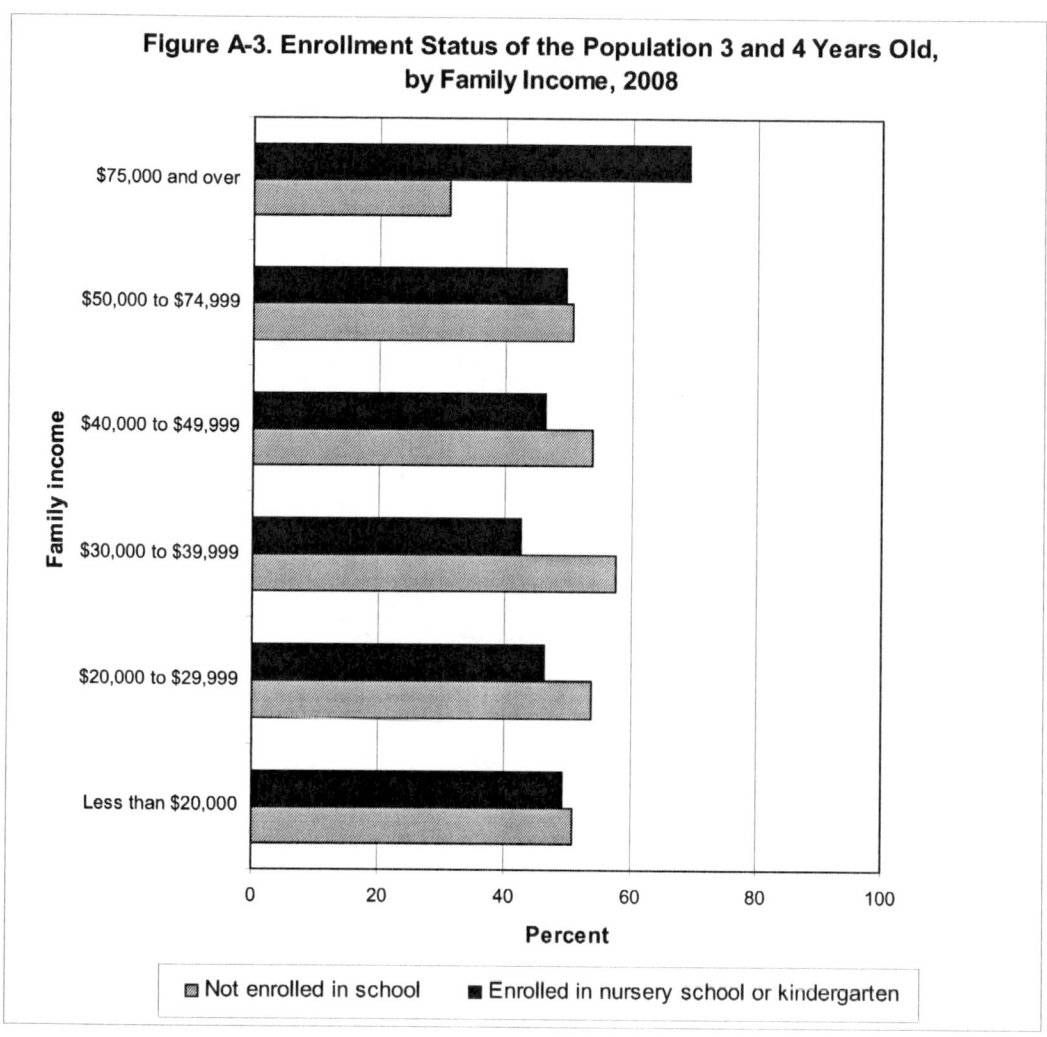

Figure A-3. Enrollment Status of the Population 3 and 4 Years Old, by Family Income, 2008

In 2008, 52.8 percent of all 3- and 4-year-olds were enrolled in nursery school or kindergarten, the lowest proportion since 2001. Approximately 70 percent of children from families with incomes of over $75,000 were enrolled in nursery school or kindergarten, while only 49 percent of 3- and 4-year-olds from families with incomes of less than $20,000 attended school. Private school enrollment declined as grade level increased. Although 43 percent of all nursery school students were enrolled in private school in 2008, only 9.8 percent of elementary school students and 7.9 percent of high school students were enrolled in private schools that year. Nearly 21 percent of college students were enrolled in private institutions. (Table A-3 and A-9)

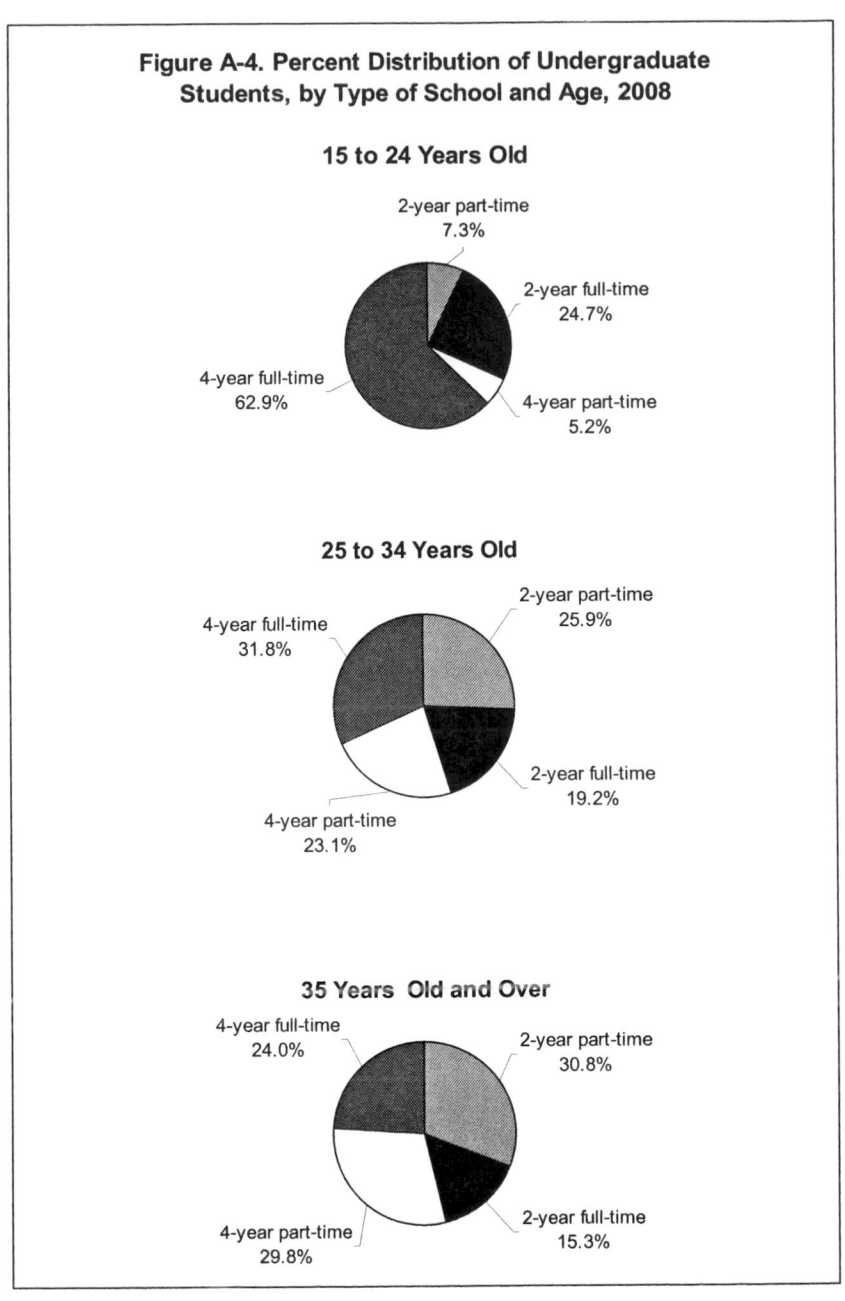

Figure A-4. Percent Distribution of Undergraduate Students, by Type of School and Age, 2008

15 to 24 Years Old

2-year part-time 7.3%
2-year full-time 24.7%
4-year full-time 62.9%
4-year part-time 5.2%

25 to 34 Years Old

2-year part-time 25.9%
4-year full-time 31.8%
2-year full-time 19.2%
4-year part-time 23.1%

35 Years Old and Over

4-year full-time 24.0%
2-year part-time 30.8%
4-year part-time 29.8%
2-year full-time 15.3%

In 2008, more than 18.6 million students 15 years old and over were enrolled in colleges and universities. Almost 15 million of them were undergraduates. Those attending four-year colleges were far more likely to be full-time students (83 percent) than those attending 2-year colleges (64 percent). Younger students were also more likely to attend school full time. Among students 15 to 24 years old, 87.6 percent were enrolled full time, while only 33.4 percent of students 35 years old and over were enrolled full time. Graduate students were evenly divided between full-time and part-time status, with slightly over 50 percent attending school full time. (Table A-5)

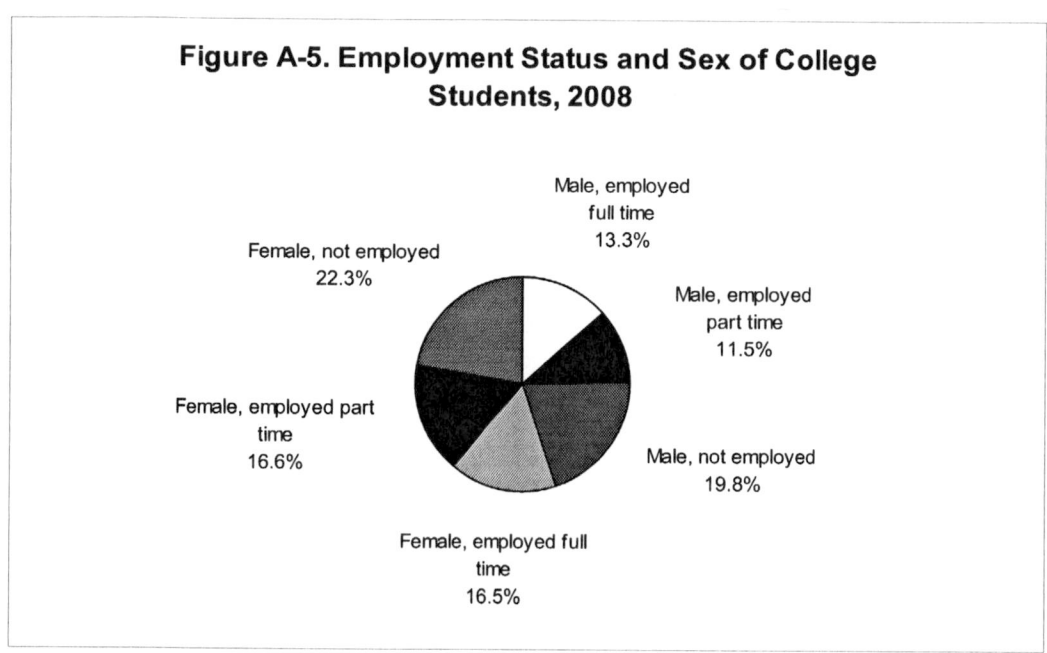

Figure A-5. Employment Status and Sex of College Students, 2008

Male, employed full time 13.3%

Male, employed part time 11.5%

Male, not employed 19.8%

Female, employed full time 16.5%

Female, employed part time 16.6%

Female, not employed 22.3%

In 2008, women made up 55.4 percent of all college students. In contrast, less than 35 percent of all college students in 1960 were women. By the end of the 1970s, the proportion of men and women were equal, and women's share has increased since then. The greatest disparity was among Black college students—63 percent were women. Fifty-two percent of Asian college students were women, making it the race or ethnic group with the most equal enrollment levels for males and females. Among graduate students, women accounted for 57.2 percent of enrollment in 2008. (Table A-15 and Table A-16)

Nearly 60 percent of female college students were employed—either part or full time. In 2008, 55.7 percent of male college students were employed. Among college students who are also enrolled in vocational courses, 60.7 percent were employed, compared with 58 percent for all college students. (Table A-6)

Over the past 30 years, total college enrollment has gradually increased. For Blacks and Hispanics, this increase was substantial. In 1978, approximately 1 million Black students were enrolled in college. By 2008, this number had jumped to almost 2.5 million. For Hispanics, the increase was even more dramatic, partly reflecting the growth in the Hispanic population during those years. From 1978 to 2008, enrollment for Hispanics more than tripled, with numbers rising from 337,000 to nearly 2.3 million. During this same time period, enrollment for Whites increased from 8.5 million college students to 14.4 million. (Table A-9)

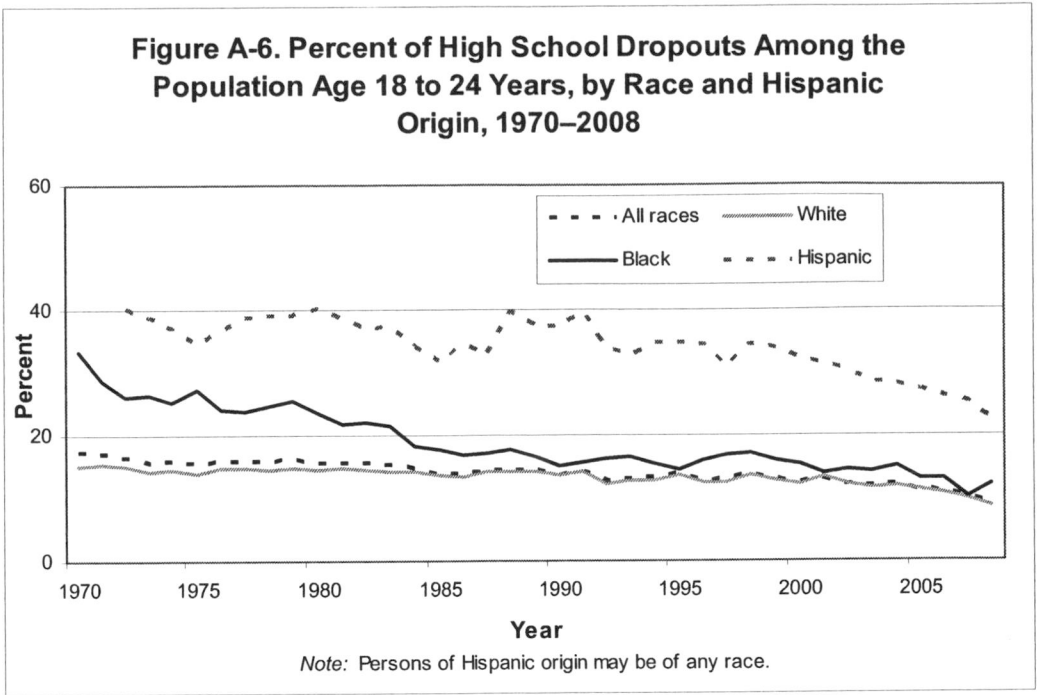

Figure A-6. Percent of High School Dropouts Among the Population Age 18 to 24 Years, by Race and Hispanic Origin, 1970–2008

Note: Persons of Hispanic origin may be of any race.

The high school dropout rate has declined between 1970 and 2008. In 1970, over 17 percent of the population between the ages of 18 and 24 years had dropped out of high school. By 2008, only 9.3 percent of the population had dropped out. While the proportion of dropouts has declined for all races, it declined most dramatically for Blacks. In 1970, approximately 1 out of every 3 Blacks between the ages of 18 and 24 years was a high school dropout. In 2008, only 12.1 percent of Blacks were high school dropouts. Hispanics continue to have the highest dropout rate for the 18 to 24 year-old population at 22.3 percent in 2008. (Table A-13)

In 2008, the high school dropout rate for grades 10 to 12 was 3.3 percent, which was the lowest rate in the past 30 years. For the first time in ten years, the dropout rate for women (3.8) was higher than the rate for men (2.9). The dropout rate for grade 10 was 1.4 percent, compared to 2.3 percent for grade 11 and 7 percent for grade 12. (Table A-12)

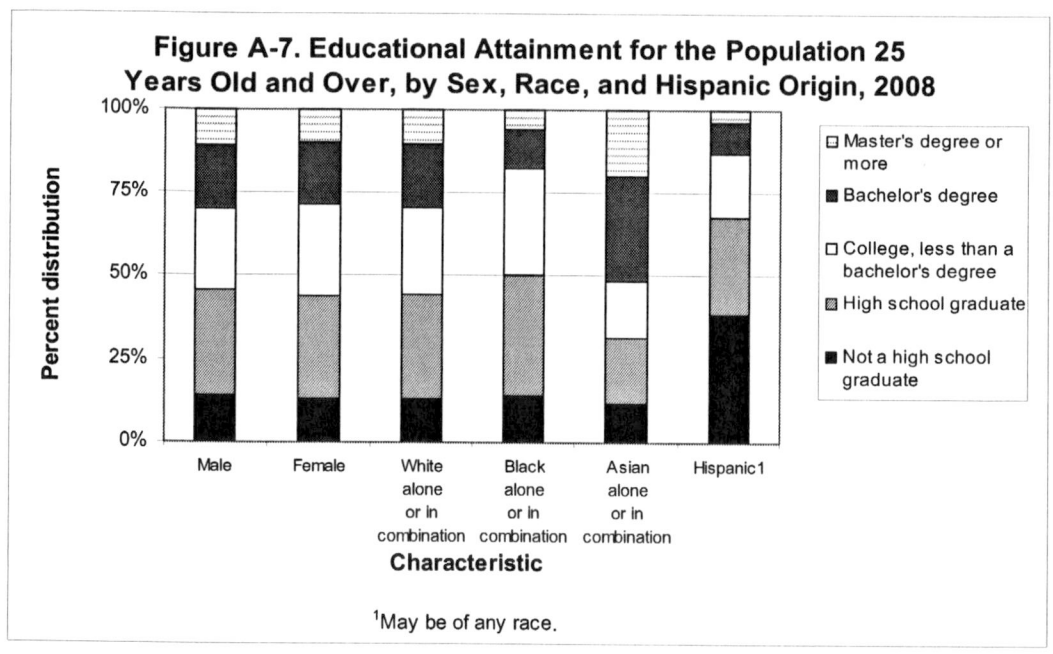

Figure A-7. Educational Attainment for the Population 25 Years Old and Over, by Sex, Race, and Hispanic Origin, 2008

¹May be of any race.

In 2009, almost 87 percent of Americans 25 years old and over were high school graduates and 29.5 percent held a bachelor's degree or more. This marked an increase of 13 percentage points from the 1980 college attainment levels. For people age 25 to 34 years, 88 percent had a high school diploma and 32 percent held a bachelor's degree or more. Women over 25 years of age had slightly higher rates of high school attainment, while men had higher rates of college attainment. Among race and ethnic groups in 2009, Asians had the highest high school graduation rate (88.3 percent), followed by Whites (87.1 percent), Blacks (84.1 percent), and Hispanics (61.9 percent). (Tables A-17, A-18, and A-26)

More than one-third of civilians over 25 years of age in the labor force held a bachelor's degree or more, a proportion higher than that of the general population in 2009. Only 9 percent of this group had not graduated from high school, compared with 13.3 percent of all people over 25 years of age. (Table A-21)

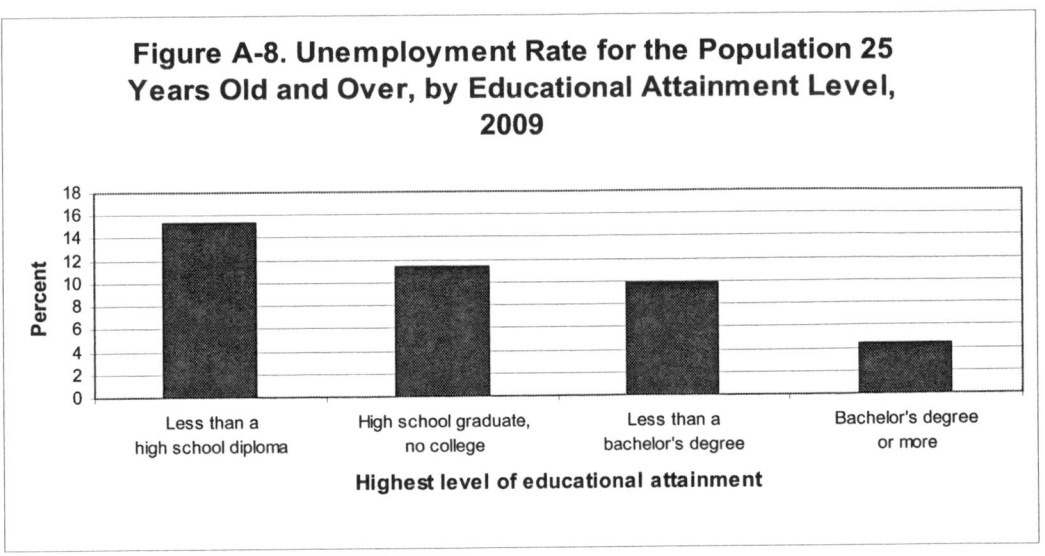

Figure A-8. Unemployment Rate for the Population 25 Years Old and Over, by Educational Attainment Level, 2009

The more education a person had obtained, the less likely he or she was to be unemployed. The unemployment rate declined successively for each level of educational attainment. For people with less than a high school diploma, the unemployment rate was 15.3 percent in 2009. In comparison, the unemployment rate for people with a bachelor's degree or more was only 4.3 percent. The overall unemployment rate in 2009 was 8.0 percent. The unemployment rate for men (9.4) was higher than that of women (6.4). In 2009, the labor force participation rate was 73.8 percent for men, but only 60 percent for women. (Table A-21)

For persons between 18 and 64 years of age, professional and related occupations provided the most jobs. This category includes teachers, lawyers, scientists, artists, doctors, nurses, and other healthcare professionals. More than 70 percent of those employed in professional and related occupations held a bachelor's degree or more. In contrast, less than 10 percent of those employed in farming, forestry, and fishing, construction, production, and transportation occupations had reached this level of educational attainment. Service occupations employed the highest number of people without a high school diploma. (Table A-22)

The educational and health services industry was the largest employer in the United States and employed more than 28.8 million people in 2009. More than half of the people in the education and health services industry held a bachelor's degree or more, and more than 25 percent of workers in this field had a master's degree or more. Mining was the smallest industry in terms of employment, with 679,000 workers. (Table A-23)

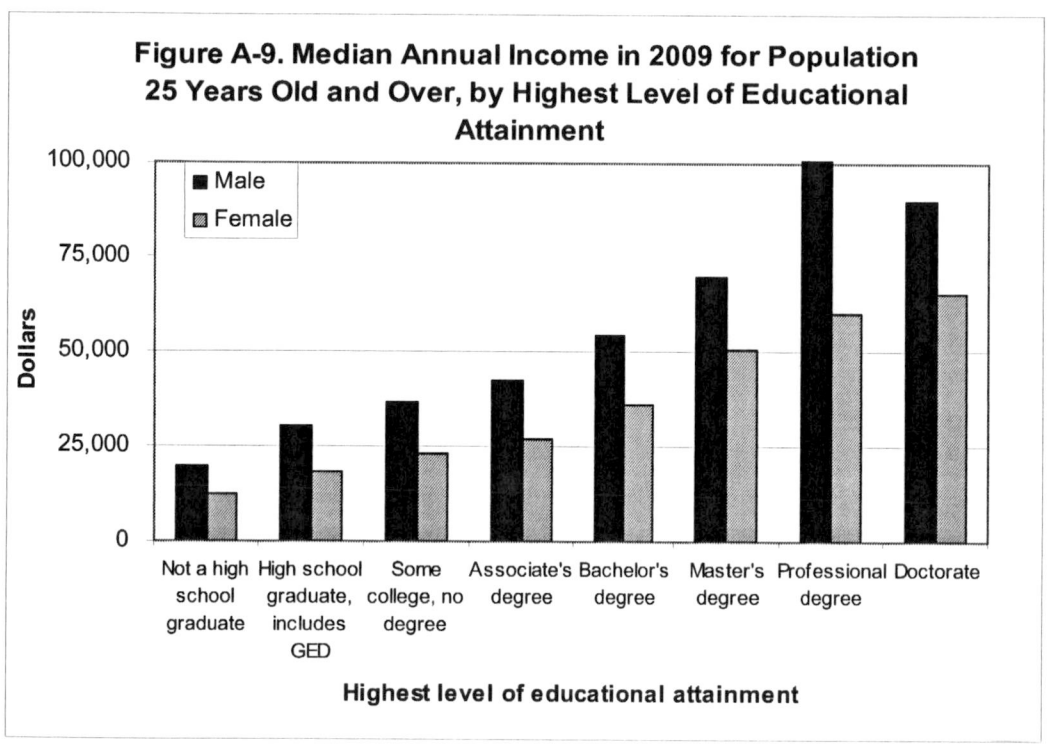

Figure A-9. Median Annual Income in 2009 for Population 25 Years Old and Over, by Highest Level of Educational Attainment

In 2009, the median income from all sources for men 25 years old and over was $36,801, and for women it was $23,159, with half of the men or women earning more than this amount and half earning less. For those who did not finish high school, the median income was $20,776 for men, $11,859 for women. For high school graduates, including GED, median income rose to $30,303 for men and $18,340 for women. Men with bachelor's degrees had a median income of $54,091 while women with bachelor's degrees had a median income of $35,972. Workers with a professional degree had the highest median income, $102,398 for men and $60,259 for women. Men earned more than women at all levels of educational attainment. (Table A-28)

Among workers 18 years old and over, the mean earnings in 2008 were $42,588. Mean earnings represents the average of income from wages, salaries, and self-employment. White males with advanced degrees had the highest mean earnings ($107,099), followed closely by Asian and Hispanic males with advanced degrees ($97,068 and $96,976) and Black males with advanced degrees, at $73,948. Asian women with advanced degrees earned an average of $65,148, more than the averages for similarly educated Black women ($60,430), white women ($59,877) and Hispanic women ($56,175). At the other end of the education spectrum, white men who were not high school graduates earned an average of $25,386, followed by Hispanic men ($24,340), Asian men ($23,814), and Black men ($22,344). Asian women who did not graduate from high school earned an average of $18,395, followed by Hispanic women ($14,960), White women ($14,370), and Black women ($13,976). (Table A-27)

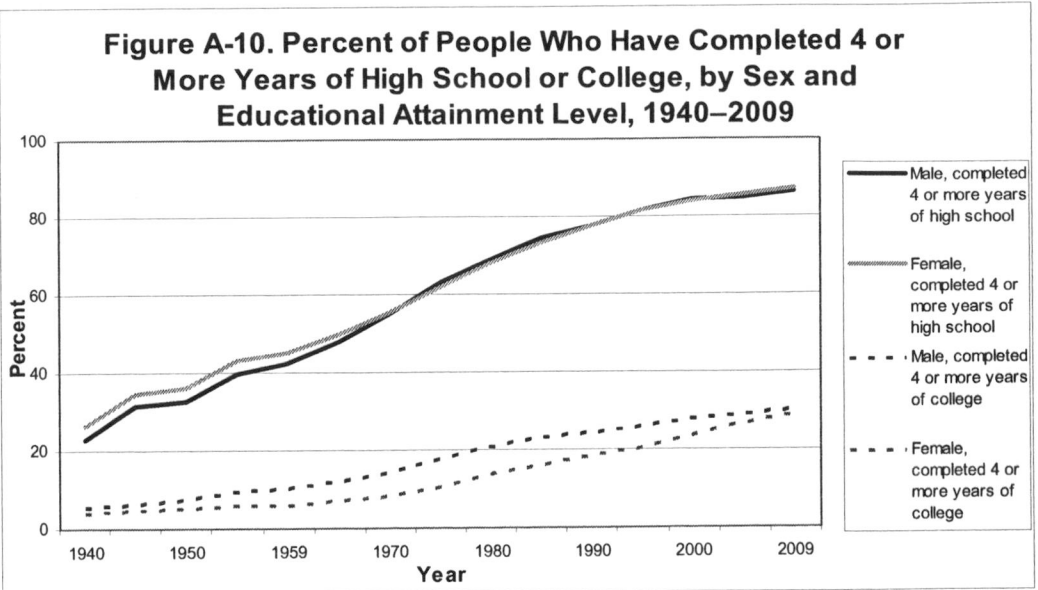

Figure A-10. Percent of People Who Have Completed 4 or More Years of High School or College, by Sex and Educational Attainment Level, 1940–2009

In 1940, only one in four Americans had completed high school. As recently as 1966, less than half of the U.S. population 25 years old and over had high school diplomas. By 2009, 86.7 percent of Americans in this age group were high school graduates. The high school graduation rate for women continued to exceed that of men, just as it had done in every year since 2001.

The percentage of college graduates, which constituted less than 5 percent of the population in 1940, had risen to 9.8 percent by 1966. By 2009, it included 29.5 percent of the population 25 years old and over. In recent years, women have narrowed the gap with men. In 1985, 23.1 percent of men and 16.0 percent of women age 25 years and over had graduated from college. In 2009, 30.1 percent of men and 29.1 percent of women were college graduates. (Table A-26)

In 2009, 69.2 percent of foreign-born people 25 years old and over in the United States were high school graduates. However, this percentage was significantly different among foreign-born people who were naturalized citizens and those who were not citizens. Among those that were not citizens, only 59.4 percent were high school graduates, whereas 80.7 percent of naturalized citizens were high school graduates. Among all foreign-born people, 10.9 percent held master's degrees, as compared to 10.5 percent of U.S. natives. Among the foreign-born, 12.6 percent of naturalized citizens held advanced degrees, compared with 9.4 percent of non-citizens. Among the native-born, 12.2 percent of those with foreign or mixed parents held advanced degrees, compared with 10.3 percent of those with native-born parents. (Table A-24)

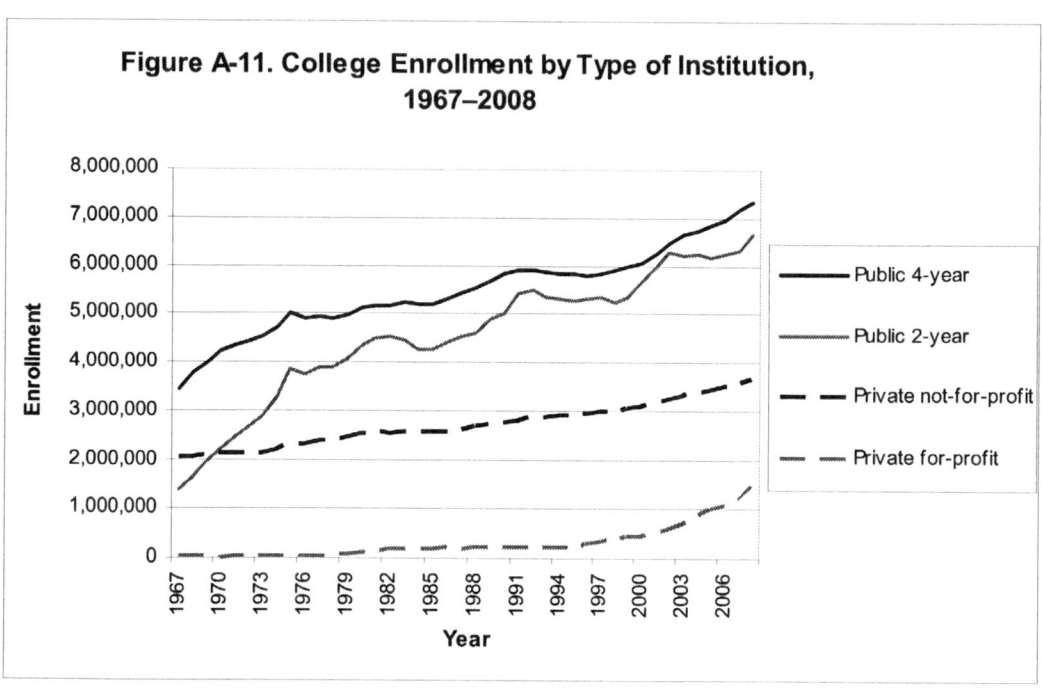

Figure A-11. College Enrollment by Type of Institution, 1967–2008

College enrollment increased by 25 percent between 2000 and 2008, after only an 11 percent increase in the 1990s. In 2008, over 19 million students were enrolled in college, with 14 million (73 percent) of them in public colleges and universities. Enrollment in private for-profit colleges tripled during the decade, enrolling about 1.5 million students in 2008. Public 4-year colleges continued to enroll the most students, increasing by 21 percent to 7.3 million students, while public 2-year colleges grew to 6.6 million students, an increase of 16.6 percent. Private not-for-profit colleges served 3.7 million students, 17.7 percent more than in 2000.

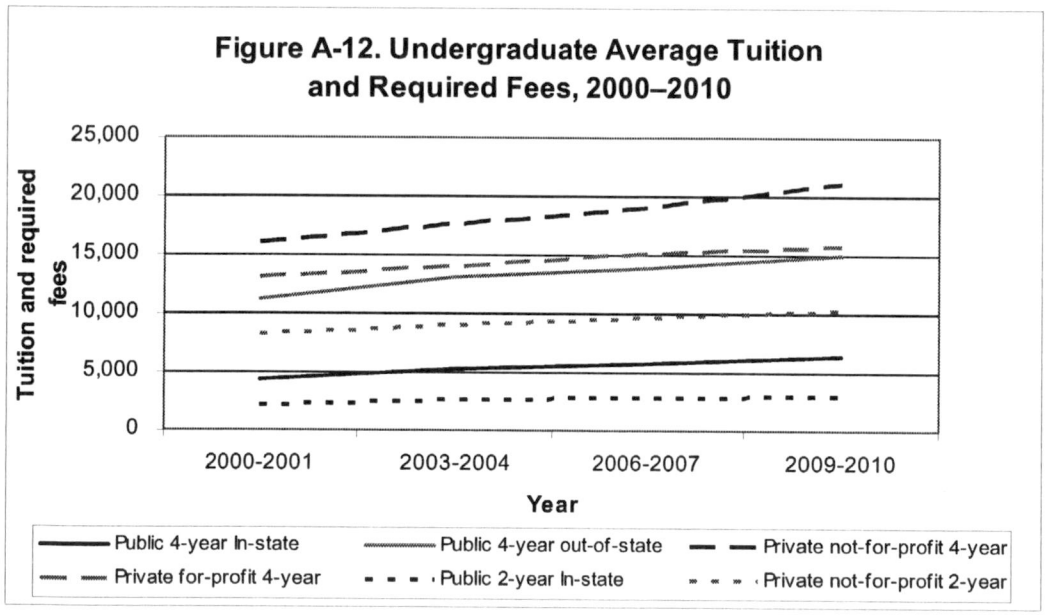

Figure A-12. Undergraduate Average Tuition and Required Fees, 2000–2010

College costs have also increased during the decade. Most expensive are the private not-for-profit colleges—about 1300 of them—whose average tuition and fees have increased by 30.8 percent since 2000. Though much less expensive, the biggest proportional increase has been in-state tuition in the approximately 600 public 4-year colleges and universities where tuition and fees have increased by 46.1 percent. About 1,000 public 2-year colleges have offered the most affordable option through the decade, though even they have increased their tuition and fees by 33.2 percent. The number of for-profit 4-year colleges tripled during the decade. Their tuition and fees were high, but their proportional increase was not as great as the average tuition increases for not-for-profit colleges and public 4-year out-of-state tuitions.

Table A-1.   Enrollment Status of the Population 3 Years Old and Over, by Age, Sex, Race, Hispanic Origin, Foreign Born, and Foreign-Born Parentage, October 2008

(Numbers in thousands, percent.)

Age, sex, race, Hispanic origin, and nativity	Population	Enrolled in school									
		Total		Nursery or kindergarten		Elementary		High school		College undergraduate or graduate	
	Number	Number	Percent	Number	Percent	Number	Percent	Number	Percent	Number	Percent
ALL RACES											
Both Sexes											
.Total	287,347	76,353	26.6	8,661	3.0	32,344	11.3	16,715	5.8	18,632	6.5
.3 and 4 years old	8,445	4,458	52.8	4,458	52.8	-	-	-	-	-	-
.5 and 6 years old	8,161	7,651	93.8	4,160	51.0	3,491	42.8	-	-	-	-
.7 to 9 years old	12,028	11,827	98.3	43	0.4	11,784	98.0	-	-	-	-
.10 to 13 years old	16,024	15,854	98.9	-	-	15,600	97.4	254	1.6	-	-
.14 and 15 years old	8,076	7,965	98.6	-	-	1,323	16.4	6,605	81.8	36	0.5
.16 and 17 years old	8,618	8,202	95.2	-	-	67	0.8	7,930	92.0	205	2.4
.18 and 19 years old	8,492	5,607	66.0	-	-	4	-	1,477	17.4	4,126	48.6
.20 and 21 years old	8,083	4,052	50.1	-	-	10	0.1	121	1.5	3,920	48.5
.22 to 24 years old	12,376	3,488	28.2	-	-	2	-	66	0.5	3,420	27.6
.25 to 29 years old	20,917	2,764	13.2	-	-	18	0.1	89	0.4	2,657	12.7
.30 to 34 years old	19,271	1,407	7.3	-	-	13	0.1	38	0.2	1,356	7.0
.35 to 44 years old	41,520	1,760	4.2	-	-	23	0.1	65	0.2	1,672	4.0
.45 to 54 years old	44,143	970	2.2	-	-	5	-	49	0.1	915	2.1
.55 years old and over	71,192	349	0.5	-	-	4	-	20	-	325	0.5
Male											
.Total	140,480	37,755	26.9	4,463	3.2	16,504	11.7	8,477	6.0	8,311	5.9
.3 and 4 years old	4,294	2,246	52.3	2,246	52.3	-	-	-	-	-	-
.5 and 6 years old	4,157	3,900	93.8	2,195	52.8	1,705	41.0	-	-	-	-
.7 to 9 years old	6,140	6,014	98.0	22	0.4	5,992	97.6	-	-	-	-
.10 to 13 years old	8,208	8,101	98.7	-	-	7,973	97.1	128	1.6	-	-
.14 and 15 years old	4,136	4,096	99.0	-	-	744	18.0	3,328	80.5	24	0.6
.16 and 17 years old	4,389	4,167	94.9	-	-	47	1.1	4,011	91.4	109	2.5
.18 and 19 years old	4,289	2,743	64.0	-	-	4	0.1	830	19.4	1,909	44.5
.20 and 21 years old	4,145	1,964	47.4	-	-	10	0.2	47	1.1	1,908	46.0
.22 to 24 years old	6,125	1,609	26.3	-	-	-	-	43	0.7	1,566	25.6
.25 to 29 years old	10,513	1,273	12.1	-	-	6	0.1	38	0.4	1,229	11.7
.30 to 34 years old	9,600	605	6.3	-	-	4	-	24	0.3	577	6.0
.35 to 44 years old	20,486	616	3.0	-	-	13	0.1	8	-	596	2.9
.45 to 54 years old	21,618	267	1.2	-	-	2	-	11	0.1	254	1.2
.55 years old and over	32,380	153	0.5	-	-	4	-	10	-	139	0.4
Female											
.Total	146,867	38,598	26.3	4,199	2.9	15,840	10.8	8,238	5.6	10,321	7.0
.3 and 4 years old	4,152	2,212	53.3	2,212	53.3	-	-	-	-	-	-
.5 and 6 years old	4,004	3,752	93.7	1,965	49.1	1,786	44.6	-	-	-	-
.7 to 9 years old	5,888	5,812	98.7	21	0.4	5,791	98.4	-	-	-	-
.10 to 13 years old	7,816	7,753	99.2	-	-	7,627	97.6	127	1.6	-	-
.14 and 15 years old	3,941	3,869	98.2	-	-	579	14.7	3,277	83.2	12	0.3
.16 and 17 years old	4,230	4,035	95.4	-	-	21	0.5	3,919	92.6	96	2.3
.18 and 19 years old	4,203	2,864	68.1	-	-	-	-	647	15.4	2,217	52.7
.20 and 21 years old	3,937	2,087	53.0	-	-	-	-	75	1.9	2,013	51.1
.22 to 24 years old	6,251	1,879	30.1	-	-	2	-	23	0.4	1,854	29.7
.25 to 29 years old	10,404	1,491	14.3	-	-	12	0.1	51	0.5	1,428	13.7
.30 to 34 years old	9,670	802	8.3	-	-	9	0.1	14	0.1	779	8.1
.35 to 44 years old	21,034	1,143	5.4	-	-	10	-	57	0.3	1,076	5.1
.45 to 54 years old	22,525	702	3.1	-	-	3	-	38	0.2	661	2.9
.55 years old and over	38,812	196	0.5	-	-	-	-	10	-	186	0.5
WHITE ALONE OR IN COMBINATION											
Both Sexes											
.Total	234,713	60,309	25.7	6889	2.9	25,498	10.9	13,184	5.6	14,738	6.3
.3 and 4 years old	6,648	3,482	52.4	3482	52.4	-	-	-	-	-	-
.5 and 6 years old	6,555	6,161	94.0	3372	51.4	2,789	42.5	-	-	-	-
.7 to 9 years old	9,513	9,346	98.2	34	0.4	9,312	97.9	-	-	-	-
.10 to 13 years old	12,649	12,508	98.9	-	-	12,328	97.5	180	1.4	-	-
.14 and 15 years old	6,402	6,321	98.7	-	-	975	15.2	5,317	83.1	29	0.4
.16 and 17 years old	6,781	6,476	95.5	-	-	45	0.7	6,284	92.7	147	2.2
.18 and 19 years old	6,762	4,534	67.0	-	-	4	0.1	1,089	16.1	3,440	50.9
.20 and 21 years old	6,408	3,267	51.0	-	-	10	0.2	75	1.2	3,181	49.7
.22 to 24 years old	9,951	2,797	28.1	-	-	2	-	57	0.6	2,738	27.5
.25 to 29 years old	16,691	2,062	12.4	-	-	5	-	54	0.3	2,003	12.0
.30 to 34 years old	15,295	969	6.3	-	-	6	-	27	0.2	936	6.1
.35 to 44 years old	33,327	1,333	4.0	-	-	18	0.1	46	0.1	1,270	3.8
.45 to 54 years old	36,456	748	2.1	-	-	5	-	34	0.1	709	1.9
.55 years old and over	61,277	305	0.5	-	-	-	-	20	-	285	0.5

- = Quantity zero or rounds to zero.

Table A-1. Enrollment Status of the Population 3 Years Old and Over, by Age, Sex, Race, Hispanic Origin, Foreign Born, and Foreign-Born Parentage, October 2008—*Continued*

(Numbers in thousands, percent.)

Age, sex, race, Hispanic origin, and nativity	Not enrolled in school					
	Total		High school graduate		Not high school graduate	
	Number	Percent	Number	Percent	Number	Percent
ALL RACES						
Both Sexes						
.Total.............................	210,994	73.4	177,649	61.8	33,345	11.6
.3 and 4 years old..............	3,987	47.2	-	-	3,987	47.2
.5 and 6 years old..............	510	6.2	-	-	510	6.2
.7 to 9 years old.................	201	1.7	-	-	201	1.7
.10 to 13 years old.............	170	1.1	-	-	170	1.1
.14 and 15 years old..........	111	1.4	4	-	107	1.3
.16 and 17 years old..........	416	4.8	108	1.3	308	3.6
.18 and 19 years old..........	2,885	34.0	2,134	25.1	750	8.8
.20 and 21 years old..........	4,031	49.9	3,329	41.2	702	8.7
.22 to 24 years old.............	8,889	71.8	7,639	61.7	1,249	10.1
.25 to 29 years old.............	18,154	86.8	15,709	75.1	2,445	11.7
.30 to 34 years old.............	17,863	92.7	15,659	81.3	2,204	11.4
.35 to 44 years old.............	39,761	95.8	35,147	84.7	4,613	11.1
.45 to 54 years old.............	43,174	97.8	38,663	87.6	4,510	10.2
.55 years old and over........	70,844	99.5	59,256	83.2	11,588	16.3
Male						
.Total.............................	102,725	73.1	85,942	61.2	16,783	11.9
.3 and 4 years old..............	2,048	47.7	-	-	2,048	47.7
.5 and 6 years old..............	257	6.2	-	-	257	6.2
.7 to 9 years old.................	125	2.0	-	-	125	2.0
.10 to 13 years old.............	107	1.3	-	-	107	1.3
.14 and 15 years old..........	40	1.0	-	-	40	1.0
.16 and 17 years old..........	222	5.1	60	1.4	162	3.7
.18 and 19 years old..........	1,546	36.0	1,169	27.3	376	8.8
.20 and 21 years old..........	2,181	52.6	1,812	43.7	369	8.9
.22 to 24 years old.............	4,516	73.7	3,816	62.3	700	11.4
.25 to 29 years old.............	9,240	87.9	7,812	74.3	1,429	13.6
.30 to 34 years old.............	8,995	93.7	7,781	81.0	1,215	12.7
.35 to 44 years old.............	19,870	97.0	17,383	84.9	2,487	12.1
.45 to 54 years old.............	21,351	98.8	18,887	87.4	2,464	11.4
.55 years old and over........	32,227	99.5	27,222	84.1	5,005	15.5
Female						
.Total.............................	108,269	73.7	91,706	62.4	16,562	11.3
.3 and 4 years old..............	1,940	46.7	-	-	1,940	46.7
.5 and 6 years old..............	253	6.3	-	-	253	6.3
.7 to 9 years old.................	75	1.3	-	-	75	1.3
.10 to 13 years old.............	63	0.8	-	-	63	0.8
.14 and 15 years old..........	72	1.8	4	0.1	68	1.7
.16 and 17 years old..........	195	4.6	48	1.1	146	3.5
.18 and 19 years old..........	1,339	31.9	965	23.0	374	8.9
.20 and 21 years old..........	1,850	47.0	1,517	38.5	333	8.5
.22 to 24 years old.............	4,372	69.9	3,823	61.2	549	8.8
.25 to 29 years old.............	8,913	85.7	7,897	75.9	1,016	9.8
.30 to 34 years old.............	8,868	91.7	7,878	81.5	990	10.2
.35 to 44 years old.............	19,891	94.6	17,764	84.5	2,126	10.1
.45 to 54 years old.............	21,823	96.9	19,777	87.8	2,046	9.1
.55 years old and over........	38,616	99.5	32,034	82.5	6,582	17.0
WHITE ALONE OR IN COMBINATION						
Both Sexes						
.Total.............................	174,405	74.3	147,646	62.9	26,759	11.4
.3 and 4 years old..............	3,166	47.6	-	-	3,166	47.6
.5 and 6 years old..............	394	6.0	-	-	394	6.0
.7 to 9 years old.................	167	1.8	-	-	167	1.8
.10 to 13 years old.............	141	1.1	-	-	141	1.1
.14 and 15 years old..........	80	1.3	-	-	80	1.3
.16 and 17 years old..........	306	4.5	82	1.2	223	3.3
.18 and 19 years old..........	2,229	33.0	1,647	24.4	581	8.6
.20 and 21 years old..........	3,140	49.0	2,610	40.7	529	8.3
.22 to 24 years old.............	7,154	71.9	6,193	62.2	961	9.7
.25 to 29 years old.............	14,629	87.6	12,603	75.5	2,027	12.1
.30 to 34 years old.............	14,326	93.7	12,465	81.5	1,861	12.2
.35 to 44 years old.............	31,994	96.0	28,177	84.5	3,817	11.5
.45 to 54 years old.............	35,708	97.9	32,110	88.1	3,597	9.9
.55 years old and over........	60,971	99.5	51,758	84.5	9,213	15.0

- = Quantity zero or rounds to zero.

Table A-1. Enrollment Status of the Population 3 Years Old and Over, by Age, Sex, Race, Hispanic Origin, Foreign Born, and Foreign-Born Parentage, October 2008—*Continued*

(Numbers in thousands, percent.)

| Age, sex, race, Hispanic origin, and nativity | Population | Enrolled in school | | | | | | | | | | |
| | | Total | | Nursery or kindergarten | | Elementary | | High school | | College undergraduate or graduate | |
	Number	Number	Percent	Number	Percent	Number	Percent	Number	Percent	Number	Percent
Male											
.Total..................	115,856	30,058	25.9	3577	3.1	13,041	11.3	6,710	5.8	6,730	5.8
.3 and 4 years old................	3,408	1,774	52.1	1774	52.1	-	-	-	-	-	-
.5 and 6 years old................	3,352	3,138	93.6	1786	53.3	1,351	40.3	-	-	-	-
.7 to 9 years old..................	4,887	4,783	97.9	16	0.3	4,767	97.6	-	-	-	-
.10 to 13 years old..............	6,483	6,397	98.7	-	-	6,315	97.4	82	1.3	-	-
.14 and 15 years old............	3,306	3,274	99.0	-	-	552	16.7	2,702	81.7	20	0.6
.16 and 17 years old............	3,472	3,298	95.0	-	-	31	0.9	3,200	92.2	67	1.9
.18 and 19 years old..........	3,435	2,213	64.4	-	-	4	0.1	601	17.5	1,608	46.8
.20 and 21 years old..........	3,309	1,593	48.1	-	-	10	0.3	33	1.0	1,550	46.9
.22 to 24 years old..............	4,995	1,321	26.4	-	-	-	-	34	0.7	1,286	25.7
.25 to 29 years old..............	8,510	984	11.6	-	-	-	-	17	0.2	966	11.4
.30 to 34 years old..............	7,758	440	5.7	-	-	-	-	14	0.2	426	5.5
.35 to 44 years old..............	16,718	499	3.0	-	-	8	-	6	0.0	484	2.9
.45 to 54 years old..............	18,087	213	1.2	-	-	2	-	11	0.1	200	1.1
.55 years old and over	28,149	133	0.5	-	-	-	-	10	0.0	123	0.4
Female											
.Total..................	118,857	30,251	25.5	3,312	2.8	12,457	10.5	6,473	5.4	8,008	6.7
.3 and 4 years old................	3,241	1,708	52.7	1,708	52.7	-	-	-	-	-	-
.5 and 6 years old................	3,203	3,023	94.4	1,586	49.5	1,438	44.9	-	-	-	-
.7 to 9 years old..................	4,626	4,562	98.6	18	0.4	4,545	98.2	-	-	-	-
.10 to 13 years old..............	6,166	6,110	99.1	-	-	6,013	97.5	97	1.6	-	-
.14 and 15 years old............	3,095	3,048	98.5	-	-	423	13.7	2,616	84.5	9	0.3
.16 and 17 years old............	3,310	3,178	96.0	-	-	14	0.4	3,085	93.2	79	2.4
.18 and 19 years old..........	3,328	2,321	69.7	-	-	-	-	488	14.7	1,833	55.1
.20 and 21 years old..........	3,098	1,674	54.0	-	-	-	-	43	1.4	1,631	52.7
.22 to 24 years old..............	4,956	1,476	29.8	-	-	2	-	23	0.5	1,452	29.3
.25 to 29 years old..............	8,182	1,089	13.2	-	-	5	0.1	37	0.5	1,037	12.7
.30 to 34 years old..............	7,536	529	7.0	-	-	6	0.1	13	0.2	510	6.8
.35 to 44 years old..............	16,610	835	5.0	-	-	10	0.1	39	0.2	786	4.7
.45 to 54 years old..............	18,379	535	2.9	-	-	3	-	23	0.1	509	2.8
.55 years old and over	33,128	173	0.5	-	-	-	-	10	-	163	0.5
BLACK ALONE OR IN COMBINATION											
Both Sexes											
.Total..................	38,028	12,542	33.0	1,444	3.8	5,593	14.7	2,886	7.6	2,619	6.9
.3 and 4 years old................	1,464	797	54.5	797	54.5	-	-	-	-	-	-
.5 and 6 years old................	1,361	1,264	92.9	636	46.7	628	46.1	-	-	-	-
.7 to 9 years old..................	2,052	2,028	98.8	11	0.5	2,017	98.3	-	-	-	-
.10 to 13 years old..............	2,699	2,674	99.1	-	-	2,622	97.1	52	1.9	-	-
.14 and 15 years old............	1,349	1,323	98.1	-	-	292	21.7	1,027	76.1	4	0.3
.16 and 17 years old............	1,467	1,386	94.5	-	-	16	1.1	1,338	91.2	32	2.2
.18 and 19 years old..........	1,431	854	59.7	-	-	-	-	339	23.7	515	36.0
.20 and 21 years old..........	1,334	539	40.4	-	-	-	-	49	3.6	490	36.7
.22 to 24 years old..............	1,767	438	24.8	-	-	-	-	8	0.5	429	24.3
.25 to 29 years old..............	2,976	448	15.1	-	-	9	0.3	39	1.3	400	13.4
.30 to 34 years old..............	2,576	294	11.4	-	-	4	0.2	12	0.5	278	10.8
.35 to 44 years old..............	5,391	306	5.7	-	-	5	0.1	14	0.3	287	5.3
.45 to 54 years old..............	5,369	161	3.0	-	-	-	-	8	0.1	153	2.8
.55 years old and over	6,794	31	0.5	-	-	-	-	-	-	31	0.5
Male											
.Total..................	17,608	5,980	34.0	696	4.0	2,867	16.3	1,435	8.2	983	5.6
.3 and 4 years old................	687	365	53.1	365	53.1	-	-	-	-	-	-
.5 and 6 years old................	669	629	94.0	325	48.7	303	45.4	-	-	-	-
.7 to 9 years old..................	1,053	1,035	98.3	6	0.6	1,029	97.7	-	-	-	-
.10 to 13 years old..............	1,390	1,371	98.7	-	-	1,340	96.4	31	2.3	-	-
.14 and 15 years old............	671	664	99.0	-	-	169	25.2	495	73.8	-	-
.16 and 17 years old............	739	697	94.3	-	-	13	1.8	663	89.7	21	2.8
.18 and 19 years old..........	706	410	58.0	-	-	-	-	191	27.0	219	31.1
.20 and 21 years old..........	637	243	38.1	-	-	-	-	13	2.1	229	36.0
.22 to 24 years old..............	846	192	22.7	-	-	-	-	8	1.0	184	21.8
.25 to 29 years old..............	1,392	153	11.0	-	-	4	0.3	21	1.5	127	9.1
.30 to 34 years old..............	1,168	101	8.6	-	-	4	0.3	12	1.0	85	7.3
.35 to 44 years old..............	2,398	65	2.7	-	-	4	0.2	-	-	61	2.5
.45 to 54 years old..............	2,420	42	1.7	-	-	-	-	-	-	42	1.7
.55 years old and over	2,832	14	0.5	-	-	-	-	-	-	14	0.5

- = Quantity zero or rounds to zero.

Table A-1. Enrollment Status of the Population 3 Years Old and Over, by Age, Sex, Race, Hispanic Origin, Foreign Born, and Foreign-Born Parentage, October 2008—*Continued*

(Numbers in thousands, percent.)

Age, sex, race, Hispanic origin, and nativity	Not enrolled in school					
	Total		High school graduate		Not high school graduate	
	Number	Percent	Number	Percent	Number	Percent
Male						
.Total.................................	85,798	74.1	71,910	62.1	13,888	12.0
.3 and 4 years old...............	1,633	47.9	-	-	1,633	47.9
.5 and 6 years old...............	215	6.4	-	-	215	6.4
.7 to 9 years old.................	103	2.1	-	-	103	2.1
.10 to 13 years old..............	85	1.3	-	-	85	1.3
.14 and 15 years old...........	33	1.0	-	-	33	1.0
.16 and 17 years old...........	174	5.0	53	1.5	121	3.5
.18 and 19 years old...........	1,222	35.6	917	26.7	305	8.9
.20 and 21 years old...........	1,716	51.9	1,413	42.7	303	9.2
.22 to 24 years old..............	3,674	73.6	3,117	62.4	557	11.2
.25 to 29 years old..............	7,526	88.4	6,297	74.0	1,229	14.4
.30 to 34 years old..............	7,319	94.3	6,253	80.6	1,066	13.7
.35 to 44 years old..............	16,219	97.0	14,096	84.3	2,123	12.7
.45 to 54 years old..............	17,863	98.8	15,825	87.5	2,038	11.3
.55 years old and over	28,016	99.5	23,938	85.0	4,088	14.5
Female						
.Total.................................	88,606	74.5	75,736	63.7	12,870	10.8
.3 and 4 years old...............	1,533	47.3	-	-	1,533	47.3
.5 and 6 years old...............	180	5.6	-	-	180	5.6
.7 to 9 years old.................	64	1.4	-	-	64	1.4
.10 to 13 years old..............	56	0.9	-	-	56	0.9
.14 and 15 years old...........	48	1.5	-	-	48	1.5
.16 and 17 years old...........	132	4.0	29	0.9	103	3.1
.18 and 19 years old...........	1,008	30.3	730	21.9	277	8.3
.20 and 21 years old...........	1,424	46.0	1,198	38.7	226	7.3
.22 to 24 years old..............	3,480	70.2	3,085	62.1	404	8.2
.25 to 29 years old..............	7,103	86.8	6,305	77.1	798	9.7
.30 to 34 years old..............	7,008	93.0	6,212	82.4	796	10.6
.35 to 44 years old..............	15,775	95.0	14,081	84.8	1,694	10.2
.45 to 54 years old..............	17,844	97.1	16,285	88.6	1,559	8.5
.55 years old and over	32,955	99.5	27,820	84.0	5,135	15.5
BLACK ALONE OR IN COMBINATION						
Both Sexes						
.Total.................................	25,486	67.0	20,422	53.7	5,065	13.3
.3 and 4 years old...............	666	45.5	-	-	666	45.5
.5 and 6 years old...............	97	7.1	-	-	97	7.1
.7 to 9 years old.................	24	1.2	-	-	24	1.2
.10 to 13 years old..............	25	0.9	-	-	25	0.9
.14 and 15 years old...........	26	1.9	-	-	26	1.9
.16 and 17 years old...........	81	5.5	22	1.5	59	4.0
.18 and 19 years old...........	577	40.3	422	29.5	155	10.8
.20 and 21 years old...........	795	59.6	643	48.2	153	11.4
.22 to 24 years old..............	1,329	75.2	1,089	61.6	240	13.6
.25 to 29 years old..............	2,528	84.9	2,207	74.2	321	10.8
.30 to 34 years old..............	2,282	88.6	2,025	78.6	257	10.0
.35 to 44 years old..............	5,085	94.3	4,524	83.9	561	10.4
.45 to 54 years old..............	5,208	97.0	4,484	83.5	724	13.5
.55 years old and over	6,763	99.5	5,006	73.7	1,757	25.9
Male						
.Total.................................	11,628	66.0	9,325	53.0	2,303	13.1
.3 and 4 years old...............	322	46.9	-	-	322	46.9
.5 and 6 years old...............	40	6.0	-	-	40	6.0
.7 to 9 years old.................	18	1.7	-	-	18	1.7
.10 to 13 years old..............	18	1.3	-	-	18	1.3
.14 and 15 years old...........	7	1.0	-	-	7	1.0
.16 and 17 years old...........	42	5.7	6	0.9	36	4.9
.18 and 19 years old...........	296	42.0	238	33.7	58	8.3
.20 and 21 years old...........	394	61.9	335	52.5	60	9.4
.22 to 24 years old..............	654	77.3	537	63.5	117	13.8
.25 to 29 years old..............	1,238	89.0	1,083	77.8	155	11.2
.30 to 34 years old..............	1,068	91.4	963	82.4	105	9.0
.35 to 44 years old..............	2,333	97.3	2,064	86.1	269	11.2
.45 to 54 years old..............	2,378	98.3	2,012	83.1	366	15.1
.55 years old and over	2,818	99.5	2,086	73.7	732	25.8

- = Quantity zero or rounds to zero.

Table A-1. Enrollment Status of the Population 3 Years Old and Over, by Age, Sex, Race, Hispanic Origin, Foreign Born, and Foreign-Born Parentage, October 2008—*Continued*

(Numbers in thousands, percent.)

Age, sex, race, Hispanic origin, and nativity	Population	Enrolled in school									
		Total		Nursery or kindergarten		Elementary		High school		College undergraduate or graduate	
	Number	Number	Percent	Number	Percent	Number	Percent	Number	Percent	Number	Percent
Female											
.Total..................................	20,420	6,562	32.1	748	3.7	2,726	13.4	1,451	7.1	1,636	8.0
.3 and 4 years old................	776	432	55.7	432	55.7	-	-	-	-	-	-
.5 and 6 years old................	692	635	91.7	311	44.9	325	46.9	-	-	-	-
.7 to 9 years old...................	999	993	99.4	5	0.5	988	98.9	-	-	-	-
.10 to 13 years old...............	1,309	1,303	99.5	-	-	1,282	97.9	21	1.6	-	-
.14 and 15 years old............	678	659	97.2	-	-	123	18.2	532	78.4	4	0.5
.16 and 17 years old............	728	689	94.7	-	-	3	0.5	675	92.7	11	1.6
.18 and 19 years old............	724	444	61.3	-	-	-	-	148	20.5	296	40.8
.20 and 21 years old............	697	296	42.5	-	-	-	-	35	5.0	261	37.4
.22 to 24 years old...............	920	245	26.6	-	-	-	-	-	-	245	26.6
.25 to 29 years old...............	1,584	295	18.6	-	-	5	0.3	18	1.1	272	17.2
.30 to 34 years old...............	1,407	194	13.8	-	-	-	-	-	-	193	13.7
.35 to 44 years old...............	2,993	241	8.0	-	-	-	-	14	0.5	226	7.5
.45 to 54 years old...............	2,950	119	4.0	-	-	-	-	8	0.3	111	3.8
.55 years old and over..........	3,962	17	0.4	-	-	-	-	-	-	17	0.4
ASIAN ALONE OR IN COMBINATION											
Both Sexes											
.Total..................................	13,986	4,122	29.5	454	3.2	1,570	11.2	758	5.4	1,340	9.6
.3 and 4 years old................	445	255	57.4	255	57.4	-	-	-	-	-	-
.5 and 6 years old................	396	367	92.6	198	50.1	168	42.5	-	-	-	-
.7 to 9 years old...................	601	590	98.3	-	0.1	590	98.2	-	-	-	-
.10 to 13 years old...............	771	768	99.6	-	-	750	97.2	18	2.4	-	-
.14 and 15 years old............	374	369	98.8	-	-	47	12.7	319	85.4	3	0.7
.16 and 17 years old............	411	384	93.5	-	-	6	1.5	354	86.1	25	6
.18 and 19 years old............	309	266	85.9	-	-	-	-	52	16.8	214	69.1
.20 and 21 years old............	338	268	79.4	-	-	-	-	3	1	265	78.4
.22 to 24 years old...............	604	260	43	-	-	-	-	1	0.1	259	42.9
.25 to 29 years old...............	1,139	262	23	-	-	3	0.2	-	-	260	22.8
.30 to 34 years old...............	1,273	152	11.9	-	-	3	0.2	-	-	149	11.7
.35 to 44 years old...............	2,535	110	4.4	-	-	-	-	3	0.1	108	4.3
.45 to 54 years old...............	2,065	60	2.9	-	-	-	-	8	0.4	53	2.6
.55 years old and over..........	2,726	10	0.4	-	-	4	0.1	-	-	6	0.2
Male											
.Total..................................	6,742	2,039	30.2	249	3.7	763	11.3	396	5.9	632	9.4
.3 and 4 years old................	246	138	56.1	138	56.1	-	-	-	-	-	-
.5 and 6 years old................	202	187	92.8	111	55	76	37.8	-	-	-	-
.7 to 9 years old...................	288	280	97.3	-	-	280	97.3	-	-	-	-
.10 to 13 years old...............	399	396	99.2	-	-	385	96.4	11	2.8	-	-
.14 and 15 years old............	188	188	100	-	-	15	7.9	170	90.7	3	1.4
.16 and 17 years old............	199	191	96.4	-	-	2	1.3	170	85.5	19	9.7
.18 and 19 years old............	150	135	89.7	-	-	-	-	41	27.6	93	62.1
.20 and 21 years old............	185	137	74.2	-	-	-	-	3	1.8	134	72.4
.22 to 24 years old...............	291	113	39	-	-	-	-	-	-	113	39
.25 to 29 years old...............	550	135	24.5	-	-	-	-	-	-	135	24.5
.30 to 34 years old...............	619	70	11.3	-	-	-	-	-	-	70	11.3
.35 to 44 years old...............	1,227	52	4.3	-	-	-	-	-	-	52	4.3
.45 to 54 years old...............	990	12	1.2	-	-	-	-	-	-	12	1.2
.55 years old and over..........	1,209	4	0.4	-	-	4	0.3	-	-	1	0.1
Female											
.Total..................................	7,244	2,083	28.8	206	2.8	807	11.1	361	5	708	9.8
.3 and 4 years old................	199	118	59.1	118	59.1	-	-	-	-	-	-
.5 and 6 years old................	194	180	92.3	87	45	92	47.4	-	-	-	-
.7 to 9 years old...................	312	310	99.2	-	0.1	309	99	-	-	-	-
.10 to 13 years old...............	372	372	100	-	-	365	98.1	7	1.9	-	-
.14 and 15 years old............	186	181	97.5	-	-	32	17.5	149	80	-	-
.16 and 17 years old............	213	193	90.8	-	-	3	1.6	184	86.7	5	2.5
.18 and 19 years old............	159	131	82.4	-	-	-	-	11	6.6	121	75.8
.20 and 21 years old............	153	131	85.7	-	-	-	-	-	-	131	85.7
.22 to 24 years old...............	313	146	46.8	-	-	-	-	1	0.2	146	46.6
.25 to 29 years old...............	589	128	21.7	-	-	3	0.4	-	-	125	21.2
.30 to 34 years old...............	654	82	12.5	-	-	3	0.5	-	-	79	12.1
.35 to 44 years old...............	1,308	58	4.5	-	-	-	-	3	0.2	56	4.3
.45 to 54 years old...............	1,075	48	4.5	-	-	-	-	8	0.7	41	3.8
.55 years old and over..........	1,516	5	0.4	-	-	-	-	-	-	5	0.4

- = Quantity zero or rounds to zero.

Table A-1. Enrollment Status of the Population 3 Years Old and Over, by Age, Sex, Race, Hispanic Origin, Foreign Born, and Foreign-Born Parentage, October 2008—*Continued*

(Numbers in thousands, percent.)

Age, sex, race, Hispanic origin, and nativity	Not enrolled in school					
	Total		High school graduate		Not high school graduate	
	Number	Percent	Number	Percent	Number	Percent
Female						
.Total..................................	13,858	67.9	11,097	54.3	2,761	13.5
.3 and 4 years old...............	344	44.3	-	-	344	44.3
.5 and 6 years old...............	57	8.3	-	-	57	8.3
.7 to 9 years old..................	6	0.6	-	-	6	0.6
.10 to 13 years old..............	7	0.5	-	-	7	0.5
.14 and 15 years old...........	19	2.8	-	-	19	2.8
.16 and 17 years old...........	39	5.3	16	2.1	23	3.2
.18 and 19 years old...........	280	38.7	184	25.4	96	13.3
.20 and 21 years old...........	401	57.5	308	44.2	93	13.3
.22 to 24 years old..............	675	73.4	551	59.9	124	13.5
.25 to 29 years old..............	1,289	81.4	1,124	71.0	165	10.4
.30 to 34 years old..............	1,214	86.2	1,062	75.4	152	10.8
.35 to 44 years old..............	2,752	92.0	2,460	82.2	292	9.8
.45 to 54 years old..............	2,831	96.0	2,472	83.8	358	12.1
.55 years old and over	3,945	99.6	2,920	73.7	1,025	25.9
ASIAN ALONE OR IN COMBINATION						
Both Sexes						
.Total..................................	9,864	70.5	8,612	61.6	1,252	8.9
.3 and 4 years old...............	189	42.6	-	-	189	42.6
.5 and 6 years old...............	29	7.4	-	-	29	7.4
.7 to 9 years old..................	10	1.7	-	-	10	1.7
.10 to 13 years old..............	3	0.4	-	-	3	0.4
.14 and 15 years old...........	5	1.2	4	1	1	0.2
.16 and 17 years old...........	27	6.5	4	1	22	5.5
.18 and 19 years old...........	43	14.1	37	11.8	7	2.3
.20 and 21 years old...........	69	20.6	61	18	9	2.5
.22 to 24 years old..............	344	57	318	52.6	27	4.4
.25 to 29 years old..............	877	77	810	71.1	67	5.9
.30 to 34 years old..............	1,121	88.1	1,062	83.4	60	4.7
.35 to 44 years old..............	2,425	95.6	2,229	87.9	196	7.7
.45 to 54 years old..............	2,004	97.1	1,844	89.3	161	7.8
.55 years old and over	2,716	99.6	2,245	82.4	471	17.3
Male						
.Total..................................	4,703	69.8	4,219	62.6	484	7.2
.3 and 4 years old...............	108	43.9	-	-	108	43.9
.5 and 6 years old...............	15	7.2	-	-	15	7.2
.7 to 9 years old..................	8	2.7	-	-	8	2.7
.10 to 13 years old..............	3	0.8	-	-	3	0.8
.14 and 15 years old...........	-	-	-	-	-	-
.16 and 17 years old...........	7	3.6	1	0.5	6	3.1
.18 and 19 years old...........	15	10.3	9	6	6	4.3
.20 and 21 years old...........	48	25.8	44	23.9	4	1.9
.22 to 24 years old..............	178	61	166	57.1	11	3.9
.25 to 29 years old..............	415	75.5	392	71.2	24	4.3
.30 to 34 years old..............	549	88.7	519	83.8	30	4.9
.35 to 44 years old..............	1,175	95.7	1,092	89	82	6.7
.45 to 54 years old..............	978	98.8	933	94.3	45	4.5
.55 years old and over	1,205	99.6	1,063	87.9	142	11.8
Female						
.Total..................................	5,161	71.2	4,394	60.7	767	10.6
.3 and 4 years old...............	82	40.9	-	-	82	40.9
.5 and 6 years old...............	15	7.7	-	-	15	7.7
.7 to 9 years old..................	3	0.8	-	-	3	0.8
.10 to 13 years old..............	-	-	-	-	-	-
.14 and 15 years old...........	5	2.5	4	2	1	0.5
.16 and 17 years old...........	20	9.2	3	1.5	16	7.7
.18 and 19 years old...........	28	17.6	28	17.3	-	0.3
.20 and 21 years old...........	22	14.3	17	11	5	3.3
.22 to 24 years old..............	166	53.2	151	48.4	15	4.8
.25 to 29 years old..............	461	78.3	418	71	43	7.3
.30 to 34 years old..............	573	87.5	543	83	29	4.5
.35 to 44 years old..............	1,250	95.5	1,137	86.9	113	8.6
.45 to 54 years old..............	1,026	95.5	910	84.7	116	10.8
.55 years old and over	1,511	99.6	1,182	78	329	21.7

- = Quantity zero or rounds to zero.

Table A-1. Enrollment Status of the Population 3 Years Old and Over, by Age, Sex, Race, Hispanic Origin, Foreign Born, and Foreign-Born Parentage, October 2008—*Continued*

(Numbers in thousands, percent.)

| Age, sex, race, Hispanic origin, and nativity | Population | Enrolled in school | | | | | | | | | |
| | | Total | | Nursery or kindergarten | | Elementary | | High school | | College undergraduate or graduate | |
	Number	Number	Percent	Number	Percent	Number	Percent	Number	Percent	Number	Percent
HISPANIC[1]											
Both Sexes											
.Total..........................	43,763	13,967	31.9	1,805	4.1	6,742	15.4	3,192	7.3	2,227	5.1
.3 and 4 years old................	2,045	892	43.6	892	43.6	-	-	-	-	-	-
.5 and 6 years old................	1,871	1,718	91.8	897	47.9	820	43.8	-	-	-	-
.7 to 9 years old...................	2,591	2,515	97.1	16	0.6	2,499	96.4	-	-	-	-
.10 to 13 years old...............	3,254	3,210	98.6	-	-	3,138	96.4	72	2.2	-	-
.14 and 15 years old............	1,533	1,513	98.7	-	-	267	17.4	1,241	80.9	5	0.4
.16 and 17 years old............	1,544	1,449	93.8	-	-	2	0.1	1,398	90.6	48	3.1
.18 and 19 years old............	1,539	848	55.1	-	-	-	-	320	20.8	528	34.3
.20 and 21 years old............	1,402	450	32.1	-	-	-	-	43	3.0	407	29.0
.22 to 24 years old...............	2,235	443	19.8	-	-	-	-	40	1.8	402	18.0
.25 to 29 years old...............	4,137	381	9.2	-	-	-	-	22	0.5	359	8.7
.30 to 34 years old...............	4,055	171	4.2	-	-	6	0.1	25	0.6	141	3.5
.35 to 44 years old...............	7,006	249	3.6	-	-	9	0.1	22	0.3	217	3.1
.45 to 54 years old...............	5,030	80	1.6	-	-	-	-	3	0.1	77	1.5
.55 years old and over.........	5,519	50	0.9	-	-	-	-	7	0.1	43	0.8
Male											
.Total..........................	22,480	6,996	31.1	899	4.0	3,411	15.2	1,643	7.3	1,042	4.6
.3 and 4 years old................	1,057	428	40.5	428	40.5	-	-	-	-	-	-
.5 and 6 years old................	947	862	91.0	462	48.8	400	42.3	-	-	-	-
.7 to 9 years old...................	1,322	1,279	96.7	9	0.7	1,270	96.0	-	-	-	-
.10 to 13 years old...............	1,668	1,646	98.6	-	-	1,609	96.4	37	2.2	-	-
.14 and 15 years old............	788	777	98.6	-	-	129	16.4	646	82.0	2	0.2
.16 and 17 years old............	797	742	93.1	-	-	-	-	713	89.5	29	3.6
.18 and 19 years old............	779	426	54.7	-	-	-	-	190	24.4	236	30.3
.20 and 21 years old............	730	225	30.8	-	-	-	-	15	2.1	210	28.7
.22 to 24 years old...............	1,166	193	16.6	-	-	-	-	24	2.1	169	14.5
.25 to 29 years old...............	2,264	186	8.2	-	-	-	-	-	-	186	8.2
.30 to 34 years old...............	2,200	90	4.1	-	-	-	-	14	0.6	76	3.5
.35 to 44 years old...............	3,691	82	2.2	-	-	3	0.1	-	-	79	2.1
.45 to 54 years old...............	2,553	27	1.0	-	-	-	-	-	-	27	1.0
.55 years old and over.........	2,519	33	1.3	-	-	-	-	4	0.2	29	1.2
Female											
.Total..........................	21,282	6,971	32.8	906	4.3	3,331	15.7	1,550	7.3	1,185	5.6
.3 and 4 years old................	989	463	46.9	463	46.9	-	-	-	-	-	-
.5 and 6 years old................	924	855	92.6	435	47.1	420	45.5	-	-	-	-
.7 to 9 years old...................	1,269	1,236	97.4	7	0.6	1,229	96.9	-	-	-	-
.10 to 13 years old...............	1,585	1,564	98.7	-	-	1,529	96.4	35	2.2	-	-
.14 and 15 years old............	745	736	98.8	-	-	138	18.5	595	79.8	4	0.5
.16 and 17 years old............	748	707	94.5	-	-	2	0.3	685	91.7	19	2.5
.18 and 19 years old............	760	422	55.5	-	-	-	-	130	17.1	292	38.4
.20 and 21 years old............	672	225	33.5	-	-	-	-	28	4.1	197	29.4
.22 to 24 years old...............	1,069	250	23.4	-	-	-	-	16	1.5	233	21.8
.25 to 29 years old...............	1,873	195	10.4	-	-	-	-	22	1.2	173	9.2
.30 to 34 years old...............	1,855	82	4.4	-	-	6	0.3	11	0.6	65	3.5
.35 to 44 years old...............	3,316	167	5.0	-	-	6	0.2	22	0.7	138	4.2
.45 to 54 years old...............	2,477	53	2.1	-	-	-	-	3	0.1	50	2.0
.55 years old and over.........	3,000	16	0.5	-	-	-	-	3	0.1	13	0.4
FOREIGN-BORN											
Both Sexes											
.Total..........................	37,522	4,778	12.7	160	0.4	1,448	3.9	1,046	2.8	2,124	5.7
.3 and 4 years old................	183	69	37.8	69	37.8	-	-	-	-	-	-
.5 and 6 years old................	218	186	85.1	91	41.5	95	43.6	-	-	-	-
.7 to 9 years old...................	470	462	98.4	-	-	462	98.4	-	-	-	-
.10 to 13 years old...............	765	760	99.3	-	-	734	96.0	26	3.3	-	-
.14 and 15 years old............	422	405	96.1	-	-	109	25.9	290	68.8	6	1.4
.16 and 17 years old............	574	521	90.9	-	-	9	1.5	477	83.2	35	6.2
.18 and 19 years old............	699	412	59.0	-	-	-	-	141	20.1	272	38.9
.20 and 21 years old............	862	357	41.4	-	-	-	-	19	2.2	338	39.3
.22 to 24 years old...............	1,626	389	23.9	-	-	2	0.1	22	1.4	366	22.5
.25 to 29 years old...............	3,682	451	12.3	-	-	3	0.1	20	0.5	429	11.6
.30 to 34 years old...............	4,353	290	6.7	-	-	9	0.2	22	0.5	260	6.0
.35 to 44 years old...............	8,310	313	3.8	-	-	19	0.2	24	0.3	270	3.3
.45 to 54 years old...............	6,809	129	1.9	-	-	3	0.1	4	0.1	122	1.8
.55 years old and over.........	8,550	33	0.4	-	-	4	-	3	-	27	0.3

[1]May be of any race.

- = Quantity zero or rounds to zero.

Table A-1. Enrollment Status of the Population 3 Years Old and Over, by Age, Sex, Race, Hispanic Origin, Foreign Born, and Foreign-Born Parentage, October 2008—*Continued*

(Numbers in thousands, percent.)

Age, sex, race, Hispanic origin, and nativity	Not enrolled in school					
	Total		High school graduate		Not high school graduate	
	Number	Percent	Number	Percent	Number	Percent
HISPANIC[1]						
Both Sexes						
.Total....................	29,796	68.1	17,695	40.4	12,102	27.7
.3 and 4 years old...............	1,154	56.4	-	-	1,154	56.4
.5 and 6 years old...............	153	8.2	-	-	153	8.2
.7 to 9 years old..................	76	2.9	-	-	76	2.9
.10 to 13 years old...............	44	1.4	-	-	44	1.4
.14 and 15 years old...........	20	1.3	-	-	20	1.3
.16 and 17 years old..........	96	6.2	19	1.2	76	5.0
.18 and 19 years old..........	691	44.9	395	25.7	296	19.3
.20 and 21 years old..........	952	67.9	660	47.1	292	20.8
.22 to 24 years old..............	1,793	80.2	1,226	54.8	567	25.4
.25 to 29 years old..............	3,757	90.8	2,450	59.2	1,306	31.6
.30 to 34 years old..............	3,883	95.8	2,511	61.9	1,372	33.8
.35 to 44 years old..............	6,758	96.4	4,345	62.0	2,413	34.4
.45 to 54 years old..............	4,950	98.4	3,156	62.8	1,794	35.7
.55 years old and over........	5,470	99.1	2,932	53.1	2,537	46.0
Male						
.Total....................	15,485	68.9	9,058	40.3	6,427	28.6
.3 and 4 years old...............	628	59.5	-	-	628	59.5
.5 and 6 years old...............	85	9.0	-	-	85	9.0
.7 to 9 years old..................	43	3.3	-	-	43	3.3
.10 to 13 years old...............	23	1.4	-	-	23	1.4
.14 and 15 years old...........	11	1.4	-	-	11	1.4
.16 and 17 years old..........	55	6.9	13	1.6	42	5.2
.18 and 19 years old..........	353	45.3	212	27.2	141	18.1
.20 and 21 years old..........	505	69.2	347	47.5	159	21.7
.22 to 24 years old..............	973	83.4	624	53.5	349	30.0
.25 to 29 years old..............	2,078	91.8	1,280	56.5	798	35.2
.30 to 34 years old..............	2,110	95.9	1,313	59.7	797	36.2
.35 to 44 years old..............	3,609	97.8	2,327	63.1	1,282	34.7
.45 to 54 years old..............	2,526	99.0	1,567	61.4	959	37.6
.55 years old and over........	2,485	98.7	1,375	54.6	1,110	44.1
Female						
.Total....................	14,311	67.2	8,636	40.6	5,675	26.7
.3 and 4 years old...............	525	53.1	-	-	525	53.1
.5 and 6 years old...............	69	7.4	-	-	69	7.4
.7 to 9 years old..................	33	2.6	-	-	33	2.6
.10 to 13 years old...............	21	1.3	-	-	21	1.3
.14 and 15 years old...........	9	1.2	-	-	9	1.2
.16 and 17 years old..........	41	5.5	6	0.8	35	4.7
.18 and 19 years old..........	338	44.5	183	24.0	156	20.5
.20 and 21 years old..........	447	66.5	313	46.7	133	19.8
.22 to 24 years old..............	819	76.6	602	56.3	218	20.3
.25 to 29 years old..............	1,679	89.6	1,170	62.5	509	27.2
.30 to 34 years old..............	1,773	95.6	1,198	64.6	575	31.0
.35 to 44 years old..............	3,149	95.0	2,018	60.9	1,131	34.1
.45 to 54 years old..............	2,424	97.9	1,589	64.2	835	33.7
.55 years old and over........	2,984	99.5	1,557	51.9	1,427	47.6
FOREIGN-BORN						
Both Sexes						
.Total....................	32,743	87.3	22,614	60.3	10,130	27.0
.3 and 4 years old...............	114	62.2	-	-	114	62.2
.5 and 6 years old...............	33	14.9	-	-	33	14.9
.7 to 9 years old..................	8	1.6	-	-	8	1.6
.10 to 13 years old...............	5	0.7	-	-	5	0.7
.14 and 15 years old...........	17	3.9	4	0.9	13	3.0
.16 and 17 years old..........	52	9.1	12	2.1	40	7.0
.18 and 19 years old..........	287	41.0	130	18.6	157	22.4
.20 and 21 years old..........	505	58.6	322	37.4	182	21.2
.22 to 24 years old..............	1,236	76.1	802	49.3	434	26.7
.25 to 29 years old..............	3,231	87.7	2,108	57.3	1,123	30.5
.30 to 34 years old..............	4,063	93.3	2,795	64.2	1,268	29.1
.35 to 44 years old..............	7,997	96.2	5,647	68.0	2,350	28.3
.45 to 54 years old..............	6,680	98.1	4,967	72.9	1,713	25.2
.55 years old and over........	8,516	99.6	5,826	68.1	2,690	31.5

[1]May be of any race.
- = Quantity zero or rounds to zero.

Table A-1. Enrollment Status of the Population 3 Years Old and Over, by Age, Sex, Race, Hispanic Origin, Foreign Born, and Foreign-Born Parentage, October 2008—*Continued*

(Numbers in thousands, percent.)

Age, sex, race, Hispanic origin, and nativity	Population	Enrolled in school									
		Total		Nursery or kindergarten		Elementary		High school		College undergraduate or graduate	
	Number	Number	Percent	Number	Percent	Number	Percent	Number	Percent	Number	Percent
Male											
.Total...............................	18,928	2,390	12.6	90	0.5	730	3.9	549	2.9	1,021	5.4
.3 and 4 years old................	95	32	33.6	32	33.6	-	-	-	-	-	-
.5 and 6 years old................	103	92	89.2	58	56.9	33	32.3	-	-	-	-
.7 to 9 years old..................	234	231	98.9	-	-	231	98.9	-	-	-	-
.10 to 13 years old...............	403	402	99.6	-	-	387	95.9	15	3.7	-	-
.14 and 15 years old............	224	216	96.7	-	-	57	25.7	157	70.3	2	0.7
.16 and 17 years old............	304	277	91.1	-	-	5	1.7	245	80.8	26	8.6
.18 and 19 years old............	363	217	59.9	-	-	-	-	92	25.3	126	34.6
.20 and 21 years old............	465	181	38.9	-	-	-	-	8	1.7	173	37.1
.22 to 24 years old..............	861	171	19.9	-	-	-	-	13	1.5	158	18.4
.25 to 29 years old..............	2,016	252	12.5	-	-	-	-	5	0.2	247	12.3
.30 to 34 years old..............	2,297	134	5.8	-	-	-	-	14	0.6	120	5.2
.35 to 44 years old..............	4,339	118	2.7	-	-	12	0.3	-	-	106	2.4
.45 to 54 years old..............	3,487	48	1.4	-	-	-	-	-	-	48	1.4
.55 years old and over	3,738	20	0.5	-	-	4	0.1	-	-	16	0.4
Female											
.Total...............................	18,594	2,388	12.8	69	0.4	718	3.9	497	2.7	1,103	5.9
.3 and 4 years old................	88	37	42.2	37	42.2	-	-	-	-	-	-
.5 and 6 years old................	115	94	81.4	32	27.8	62	53.7	-	-	-	-
.7 to 9 years old..................	236	231	97.8	-	-	231	97.8	-	-	-	-
.10 to 13 years old...............	362	358	99.1	-	-	347	96.1	11	3.0	-	-
.14 and 15 years old............	198	189	95.4	-	-	52	26.1	133	67.0	4	2.2
.16 and 17 years old............	270	245	90.7	-	-	3	1.3	232	86.0	9	3.4
.18 and 19 years old............	336	195	58.0	-	-	-	-	49	14.5	146	43.5
.20 and 21 years old............	397	176	44.4	-	-	-	-	11	2.7	166	41.7
.22 to 24 years old..............	765	218	28.5	-	-	2	0.2	9	1.2	207	27.1
.25 to 29 years old..............	1,666	199	11.9	-	-	3	0.2	15	0.9	181	10.9
.30 to 34 years old..............	2,056	157	7.6	-	-	9	0.4	8	0.4	140	6.8
.35 to 44 years old..............	3,971	195	4.9	-	-	7	0.2	24	0.6	165	4.1
.45 to 54 years old..............	3,322	81	2.4	-	-	3	0.1	4	0.1	74	2.2
.55 years old and over	4,811	14	0.3	-	-	-	-	3	0.1	11	0.2
CHILDREN OF FOREIGN-BORN PARENTS											
Both Sexes											
.Total...............................	66,556	17,175	25.8	1,946	2.9	7,274	10.9	3,600	5.4	4,355	6.5
.3 and 4 years old................	2,079	977	47.0	977	47.0	-	-	-	-	-	-
.5 and 6 years old................	1,978	1,821	92.0	952	48.1	869	43.9	-	-	-	-
.7 to 9 years old..................	2,758	2,698	97.8	17	0.6	2,681	97.2	-	-	-	-
.10 to 13 years old...............	3,479	3,445	99.0	-	-	3,369	96.8	76	2.2	-	-
.14 and 15 years old............	1,739	1,715	98.6	-	-	301	17.3	1,405	80.8	9	0.5
.16 and 17 years old............	1,809	1,717	94.9	-	-	15	0.8	1,628	90.0	74	4.1
.18 and 19 years old............	1,896	1,261	66.5	-	-	-	-	351	18.5	911	48.0
.20 and 21 years old............	1,727	836	48.4	-	-	-	-	33	1.9	803	46.5
.22 to 24 years old..............	2,975	892	30.0	-	-	2	0.1	22	0.7	868	29.2
.25 to 29 years old..............	5,544	749	13.5	-	-	3	-	23	0.4	723	13.0
.30 to 34 years old..............	5,838	383	6.6	-	-	9	0.2	22	0.4	353	6.0
.35 to 44 years old..............	10,862	426	3.9	-	-	19	0.2	25	0.2	382	3.5
.45 to 54 years old..............	9,038	193	2.1	-	-	3	-	13	0.1	177	2.0
.55 years old and over	14,834	63	0.4	-	-	4	-	3	-	56	0.4
Male											
.Total...............................	33,448	8,757	26.2	1,037	3.1	3,724	11.1	1,885	5.6	2,111	6.3
.3 and 4 years old................	1,070	512	47.8	512	47.8	-	-	-	-	-	-
.5 and 6 years old................	995	921	92.6	518	52.1	403	40.5	-	-	-	-
.7 to 9 years old..................	1,428	1,396	97.7	7	0.5	1,389	97.3	-	-	-	-
.10 to 13 years old...............	1,820	1,800	98.9	-	-	1,752	96.3	48	2.6	-	-
.14 and 15 years old............	888	878	98.9	-	-	157	17.7	717	80.7	4	0.5
.16 and 17 years old............	969	920	94.9	-	-	6	0.7	858	88.5	56	5.7
.18 and 19 years old............	978	649	66.3	-	-	-	-	213	21.8	436	44.6
.20 and 21 years old............	913	413	45.2	-	-	-	-	15	1.7	398	43.5
.22 to 24 years old..............	1,571	425	27.1	-	-	-	-	13	0.8	412	26.2
.25 to 29 years old..............	2,981	407	13.7	-	-	-	-	5	0.2	402	13.5
.30 to 34 years old..............	3,065	183	6.0	-	-	-	-	14	0.4	170	5.5
.35 to 44 years old..............	5,617	153	2.7	-	-	12	0.2	-	-	141	2.5
.45 to 54 years old..............	4,550	66	1.5	-	-	-	-	3	0.1	63	1.4
.55 years old and over	6,603	33	0.5	-	-	4	0.1	-	-	29	0.4

- = Quantity zero or rounds to zero.

Table A-1.   Enrollment Status of the Population 3 Years Old and Over, by Age, Sex, Race, Hispanic Origin, Foreign Born, and Foreign-Born Parentage, October 2008—*Continued*

(Numbers in thousands, percent.)

Age, sex, race, Hispanic origin, and nativity	Not enrolled in school					
	Total		High school graduate		Not high school graduate	
	Number	Percent	Number	Percent	Number	Percent
Male						
.Total..................	16,538	87.4	11,316	59.8	5,222	27.6
.3 and 4 years old...............	63	66.4	-	-	63	66.4
.5 and 6 years old...............	11	10.8	-	-	11	10.8
.7 to 9 years old..................	3	1.1	-	-	3	1.1
.10 to 13 years old..............	2	0.4	-	-	2	0.4
.14 and 15 years old..........	7	3.3	-	-	7	3.3
.16 and 17 years old..........	27	8.9	9	3.0	18	6.0
.18 and 19 years old..........	146	40.1	70	19.2	76	21.0
.20 and 21 years old..........	284	61.1	180	38.8	104	22.3
.22 to 24 years old..............	689	80.1	440	51.1	249	29.0
.25 to 29 years old..............	1,764	87.5	1,105	54.8	659	32.7
.30 to 34 years old..............	2,164	94.2	1,414	61.5	750	32.7
.35 to 44 years old..............	4,221	97.3	2,938	67.7	1,282	29.6
.45 to 54 years old..............	3,439	98.6	2,542	72.9	897	25.7
.55 years old and over........	3,719	99.5	2,618	70.0	1,101	29.5
Female						
.Total..................	16,205	87.2	11,298	60.8	4,908	26.4
.3 and 4 years old...............	51	57.8	-	-	51	57.8
.5 and 6 years old...............	21	18.6	-	-	21	18.6
.7 to 9 years old..................	5	2.2	-	-	5	2.2
.10 to 13 years old..............	3	0.9	-	-	3	0.9
.14 and 15 years old..........	9	4.6	4	1.9	5	2.7
.16 and 17 years old..........	25	9.3	3	1.2	22	8.1
.18 and 19 years old..........	141	42.0	61	18.0	81	24.0
.20 and 21 years old..........	221	55.6	142	35.8	79	19.8
.22 to 24 years old..............	547	71.5	362	47.3	185	24.2
.25 to 29 years old..............	1,467	88.1	1,003	60.2	464	27.9
.30 to 34 years old..............	1,900	92.4	1,382	67.2	518	25.2
.35 to 44 years old..............	3,776	95.1	2,708	68.2	1,068	26.9
.45 to 54 years old..............	3,240	97.6	2,425	73.0	816	24.6
.55 years old and over........	4,798	99.7	3,208	66.7	1,589	33.0
CHILDREN OF FOREIGN-BORN PARENTS						
Both Sexes						
.Total..................	49,380	74.2	36,138	54.3	13,243	19.9
.3 and 4 years old...............	1,102	53.0	-	-	1,102	53.0
.5 and 6 years old...............	157	8.0	-	-	157	8.0
.7 to 9 years old..................	60	2.2	-	-	60	2.2
.10 to 13 years old..............	34	1.0	-	-	34	1.0
.14 and 15 years old..........	25	1.4	4	0.2	21	1.2
.16 and 17 years old..........	92	5.1	19	1.0	73	4.0
.18 and 19 years old..........	635	33.5	388	20.5	247	13.0
.20 and 21 years old..........	891	51.6	641	37.1	250	14.5
.22 to 24 years old..............	2,083	70.0	1,534	51.6	549	18.4
.25 to 29 years old..............	4,795	86.5	3,515	63.4	1,280	23.1
.30 to 34 years old..............	5,454	93.4	4,108	70.4	1,346	23.1
.35 to 44 years old..............	10,436	96.1	7,928	73.0	2,509	23.1
.45 to 54 years old..............	8,844	97.9	6,966	77.1	1,878	20.8
.55 years old and over........	14,771	99.6	11,034	74.4	3,737	25.2
Male						
.Total..................	24,690	73.8	17,955	53.7	6,736	20.1
.3 and 4 years old...............	558	52.2	-	-	558	52.2
.5 and 6 years old...............	73	7.4	-	-	73	7.4
.7 to 9 years old..................	32	2.3	-	-	32	2.3
.10 to 13 years old..............	19	1.1	-	-	19	1.1
.14 and 15 years old..........	10	1.1	-	-	10	1.1
.16 and 17 years old..........	49	5.1	12	1.3	37	3.8
.18 and 19 years old..........	329	33.7	214	21.9	115	11.8
.20 and 21 years old..........	500	54.8	352	38.5	148	16.3
.22 to 24 years old..............	1,146	72.9	818	52.1	328	20.9
.25 to 29 years old..............	2,574	86.3	1,817	60.9	757	25.4
.30 to 34 years old..............	2,881	94.0	2,095	68.4	786	25.6
.35 to 44 years old..............	5,464	97.3	4,123	73.4	1,341	23.9
.45 to 54 years old..............	4,484	98.5	3,495	76.8	989	21.7
.55 years old and over........	6,570	99.5	5,028	76.1	1,542	23.4

- = Quantity zero or rounds to zero.

Table A-1.   Enrollment Status of the Population 3 Years Old and Over, by Age, Sex, Race, Hispanic Origin, Foreign Born, and Foreign-Born Parentage, October 2008—*Continued*

(Numbers in thousands, percent.)

| Age, sex, race, Hispanic origin, and nativity | Population | Enrolled in school | | | | | | | | | | |
| | | Total | | Nursery or kindergarten | | Elementary | | High school | | College undergraduate or graduate | |
	Number	Number	Percent	Number	Percent	Number	Percent	Number	Percent	Number	Percent
Female											
.Total.................................	33,108	8,418	25.4	909	2.7	3,550	10.7	1,715	5.2	2,244	6.8
.3 and 4 years old................	1,009	465	46.1	465	46.1	-	-	-	-	-	-
.5 and 6 years old................	983	899	91.5	434	44.1	466	47.4	-	-	-	-
.7 to 9 years old..................	1,330	1,303	97.9	11	0.8	1,292	97.1	-	-	-	-
.10 to 13 years old...............	1,660	1,645	99.1	-	-	1,617	97.4	28	1.7	-	-
.14 and 15 years old............	851	836	98.3	-	-	144	16.9	688	80.8	4	0.5
.16 and 17 years old............	839	796	94.9	-	-	8	1.0	770	91.7	18	2.2
.18 and 19 years old............	918	613	66.7	-	-	-	-	138	15.0	475	51.7
.20 and 21 years old............	814	423	52.0	-	-	-	-	18	2.2	405	49.8
.22 to 24 years old...............	1,404	467	33.3	-	-	2	0.1	9	0.6	456	32.5
.25 to 29 years old...............	2,563	342	13.3	-	-	3	0.1	18	0.7	321	12.5
.30 to 34 years old...............	2,773	200	7.2	-	-	9	0.3	8	0.3	183	6.6
.35 to 44 years old...............	5,245	272	5.2	-	-	7	0.1	25	0.5	240	4.6
.45 to 54 years old...............	4,487	127	2.8	-	-	3	0.1	10	0.2	113	2.5
.55 years old and over.........	8,231	30	0.4	-	-	-	-	3	-	27	0.3

- = Quantity zero or rounds to zero.

Table A-1. Enrollment Status of the Population 3 Years Old and Over, by Age, Sex, Race, Hispanic Origin, Foreign Born, and Foreign-Born Parentage, October 2008—*Continued*

(Numbers in thousands, percent.)

| Age, sex, race, Hispanic origin, and nativity | Not enrolled in school | | | | | |
| | Total | | High school graduate | | Not high school graduate | |
	Number	Percent	Number	Percent	Number	Percent
Female						
.Total..................................	24,690	74.6	18,183	54.9	6,507	19.7
.3 and 4 years old................	544	53.9	-	-	544	53.9
.5 and 6 years old................	84	8.5	-	-	84	8.5
.7 to 9 years old...................	28	2.1	-	-	28	2.1
.10 to 13 years old...............	15	0.9	-	-	15	0.9
.14 and 15 years old............	15	1.7	4	0.4	11	1.3
.16 and 17 years old............	43	5.1	7	0.8	36	4.3
.18 and 19 years old............	306	33.3	174	18.9	132	14.3
.20 and 21 years old............	391	48.0	289	35.5	102	12.5
.22 to 24 years old..............	937	66.7	716	51.0	221	15.7
.25 to 29 years old..............	2,221	86.7	1,698	66.3	523	20.4
.30 to 34 years old..............	2,573	92.8	2,013	72.6	560	20.2
.35 to 44 years old..............	4,973	94.8	3,805	72.5	1,168	22.3
.45 to 54 years old..............	4,360	97.2	3,471	77.4	889	19.8
.55 years old and over.........	8,201	99.6	6,007	73.0	2,194	26.7

- = Quantity zero or rounds to zero.

Table A-2.   Single Grade of Enrollment and High School Graduation Status for Population 3 Years Old and Over, by Sex, Age (Single Years for 3 to 24 Years), Race, and Hispanic Origin, October 2008

(Numbers in thousands, percent.)

Age, sex, race, and Hispanic origin	Population	Enrolled		Enrolled										
		Number	Percent	Nursery	Kinder-garten	Elementary grades								
						1	2	3	4	5	6	7	8
ALL RACES														
Both Sexes														
Total	287,347	76,353	26.6	4,614	4,047	4,144	4,116	4,082	3,797	4,045	4,070	4,141	3,949
3 years old	4,204	1,655	39.4	1,558	97	-	-	-	-	-	-	-	-
4 years old	4,241	2,804	66.1	2,521	283	-	-	-	-	-	-	-	-
5 years old	4,137	3,764	91.0	492	2,978	246	48	-	-	-	-	-	-
6 years old	4,024	3,887	96.6	44	646	2,975	181	41	-	-	-	-	-
7 years old	4,131	4,056	98.2	-	43	794	2,989	180	50	-	-	-	-
8 years old	3,949	3,883	98.3	-	-	82	783	2,810	161	48	-	-	-
9 years old	3,948	3,888	98.5	-	-	46	79	946	2,550	194	72	-	-
10 years old	3,903	3,846	98.5	-	-	-	37	64	896	2,632	181	37	-
11 years old	3,942	3,897	98.9	-	-	-	-	42	97	974	2,524	186	74
12 years old	4,083	4,038	98.9	-	-	-	-	-	43	137	1,043	2,544	190
13 years old	4,096	4,073	99.4	-	-	-	-	-	-	60	186	1,120	2,533
14 years old	3,948	3,878	98.2	-	-	-	-	-	-	-	53	163	948
15 years old	4,128	4,087	99.0	-	-	-	-	-	-	-	-	12	147
16 years old	4,269	4,151	97.2	-	-	-	-	-	-	-	-	18	33
17 years old	4,349	4,051	93.1	-	-	-	-	-	-	-	2	1	13
18 years old	4,332	3,151	72.7	-	-	-	-	-	-	-	-	-	-
19 years old	4,160	2,456	59.0	-	-	-	-	-	-	-	-	4	-
20 years old	4,007	2,147	53.6	-	-	-	-	-	-	-	-	-	-
21 years old	4,076	1,904	46.7	-	-	-	-	-	-	-	-	10	-
22 years old	4,113	1,398	34.0	-	-	-	-	-	-	-	-	-	-
23 years old	4,212	1,148	27.2	-	-	-	-	-	-	-	-	2	-
24 years old	4,051	942	23.2	-	-	-	-	-	-	-	-	-	-
25 to 29 years old	20,917	2,764	13.2	-	-	-	-	-	-	-	9	9	-
30 to 34 years old	19,271	1,407	7.3	-	-	-	-	-	-	-	-	6	7
35 to 39 years old	20,480	1,027	5.0	-	-	-	-	-	-	-	-	12	3
40 to 44 years old	21,040	733	3.5	-	-	-	-	-	-	-	-	8	-
45 to 49 years old	22,705	566	2.5	-	-	-	-	-	-	-	1	3	-
50 to 54 years old	21,438	404	1.9	-	-	-	-	-	-	-	-	1	-
55 to 59 years old	18,500	209	1.1	-	-	-	-	-	-	-	-	4	-
60 to 64 years old	15,296	95	0.6	-	-	-	-	-	-	-	-	-	-
65 years and over	37,396	45	0.1	-	-	-	-	-	-	-	-	-	-
Male														
Total	140,480	37,755	26.9	2,318	2,145	2,074	2,109	2,092	1,906	2,049	2,140	2,141	1,994
3 years old	2,112	811	38.4	756	55	-	-	-	-	-	-	-	-
4 years old	2,182	1,435	65.8	1,297	138	-	-	-	-	-	-	-	-
5 years old	2,128	1,940	91.2	248	1,551	107	33	-	-	-	-	-	-
6 years old	2,029	1,960	96.6	17	378	1,456	93	15	-	-	-	-	-
7 years old	2,104	2,065	98.2	-	22	439	1,473	99	33	-	-	-	-
8 years old	2,041	2,003	98.2	-	-	43	456	1,400	81	23	-	-	-
9 years old	1,995	1,946	97.5	-	-	28	33	529	1,228	95	33	-	-
10 years old	2,000	1,965	98.2	-	-	-	20	27	489	1,323	81	24	-
11 years old	2,010	1,982	98.6	-	-	-	-	22	51	502	1,290	77	40
12 years old	2,078	2,049	98.6	-	-	-	-	-	24	79	595	1,248	64
13 years old	2,120	2,105	99.3	-	-	-	-	-	-	28	107	639	1,244
14 years old	2,022	2,000	98.9	-	-	-	-	-	-	-	33	96	516
15 years old	2,113	2,096	99.2	-	-	-	-	-	-	-	-	5	94
16 years old	2,166	2,100	97.0	-	-	-	-	-	-	-	-	15	26
17 years old	2,223	2,067	93.0	-	-	-	-	-	-	-	-	-	5
18 years old	2,187	1,558	71.2	-	-	-	-	-	-	-	-	-	-
19 years old	2,102	1,185	56.4	-	-	-	-	-	-	-	-	4	-
20 years old	2,086	1,094	52.4	-	-	-	-	-	-	-	-	-	-
21 years old	2,059	870	42.3	-	-	-	-	-	-	-	-	10	-
22 years old	2,046	607	29.7	-	-	-	-	-	-	-	-	-	-
23 years old	2,088	551	26.4	-	-	-	-	-	-	-	-	-	-
24 years old	1,992	451	22.6	-	-	-	-	-	-	-	-	-	-
25 to 29 years old	10,513	1,273	12.1	-	-	-	-	-	-	-	-	6	-
30 to 34 years old	9,600	605	6.3	-	-	-	-	-	-	-	-	-	4
35 to 39 years old	10,115	371	3.7	-	-	-	-	-	-	-	-	8	-
40 to 44 years old	10,371	245	2.4	-	-	-	-	-	-	-	-	4	-
45 to 49 years old	11,146	170	1.5	-	-	-	-	-	-	-	1	-	-
50 to 54 years old	10,472	97	0.9	-	-	-	-	-	-	-	-	1	-
55 to 59 years old	8,931	80	0.9	-	-	-	-	-	-	-	-	4	-
60 to 64 years old	7,340	46	0.6	-	-	-	-	-	-	-	-	-	-
65 years and over	16,110	27	0.2	-	-	-	-	-	-	-	-	-	-

- = Quantity zero or rounds to zero.

Table A-2. Single Grade of Enrollment and High School Graduation Status for Population 3 Years Old and Over, by Sex, Age (Single Years for 3 to 24 Years), Race, and Hispanic Origin, October 2008—*Continued*

(Numbers in thousands, percent.)

Age, sex, race, and Hispanic origin	Enrolled — High school				Enrolled — Undergraduate college				Enrolled — Graduate school		Not enrolled — H.S. grad	Not enrolled — Not grad	Not enrolled — Number	Not enrolled — Percent
	9	10	11	12	1	2	3	4	1	2+				
ALL RACES														
Both Sexes														
Total....................	4,062	4,195	4,185	4,273	4,588	4,388	3,523	2,456	1,408	2,268	177,649	33,345	210,994	73.4
3 years old	-	-	-	-	-	-	-	-	-	-	-	2,550	2,550	60.6
4 years old	-	-	-	-	-	-	-	-	-	-	-	1,437	1,437	33.9
5 years old	-	-	-	-	-	-	-	-	-	-	-	373	373	9.0
6 years old	-	-	-	-	-	-	-	-	-	-	-	137	137	3.4
7 years old	-	-	-	-	-	-	-	-	-	-	-	75	75	1.8
8 years old	-	-	-	-	-	-	-	-	-	-	-	65	65	1.7
9 years old	-	-	-	-	-	-	-	-	-	-	-	60	60	1.5
10 years old............	-	-	-	-	-	-	-	-	-	-	-	57	57	1.5
11 years old............	-	-	-	-	-	-	-	-	-	-	-	45	45	1.1
12 years old............	80	-	-	-	-	-	-	-	-	-	-	45	45	1.1
13 years old............	163	11	-	-	-	-	-	-	-	-	-	23	23	0.6
14 years old............	2,495	198	21	-	-	3	17	-	-	-	-	70	70	1.8
15 years old............	1,058	2,565	229	39	15	3	17	-	1	-	4	37	41	1.0
16 years old............	177	1,067	2,554	268	27	-	-	-	6	-	26	93	118	2.8
17 years old............	47	219	1,097	2,500	150	16	5	-	-	-	82	216	298	6.9
18 years old............	11	53	141	996	1,819	121	9	-	-	2	843	337	1,180	27.3
19 years old............	4	23	52	197	737	1,276	146	6	8	3	1,291	413	1,704	41.0
20 years old............	-	-	39	44	349	794	863	55	3	-	1,524	336	1,860	46.4
21 years old............	-	3	3	31	138	341	647	675	29	26	1,805	366	2,171	53.3
22 years old............	7	4	7	17	141	243	306	492	126	56	2,285	430	2,715	66.0
23 years old............	2	-	-	15	109	191	201	291	151	186	2,678	387	3,065	72.8
24 years old............	-	12	4	-	96	152	167	211	128	172	2,676	433	3,109	76.8
25 to 29 years old.....	1	13	8	67	390	474	454	301	374	663	15,709	2,445	18,154	86.8
30 to 34 years old.....	3	7	-	28	205	249	236	120	201	346	16,659	2,204	17,863	92.7
35 to 39 years old.....	4	6	1	29	153	209	176	96	109	228	17,179	2,275	19,453	95.0
40 to 44 years old.....	-	9	2	13	91	150	116	83	81	180	17,968	2,339	20,307	96.5
45 to 49 years old.....	4	2	9	11	81	78	87	57	82	151	19,911	2,228	22,139	97.5
50 to 54 years old.....	6	-	7	11	34	55	60	45	75	109	18,752	2,283	21,035	98.1
55 to 59 years old.....	-	-	3	-	29	23	12	13	22	104	16,284	2,008	18,292	98.9
60 to 64 years old.....	-	-	-	-	19	5	20	6	7	36	13,419	1,782	15,201	99.4
65 years and over	-	3	7	6	4	7	2	4	6	5	29,553	7,798	37,351	99.9
Male														
Total....................	2,088	2,145	2,113	2,131	2,132	1,925	1,589	1,091	587	987	85,942	16,783	102,725	73.1
3 years old	-	-	-	-	-	-	-	-	-	-	-	1,301	1,301	61.6
4 years old	-	-	-	-	-	-	-	-	-	-	-	746	746	34.2
5 years old	-	-	-	-	-	-	-	-	-	-	-	188	188	8.8
6 years old	-	-	-	-	-	-	-	-	-	-	-	69	69	3.4
7 years old	-	-	-	-	-	-	-	-	-	-	-	39	39	1.8
8 years old	-	-	-	-	-	-	-	-	-	-	-	37	37	1.8
9 years old	-	-	-	-	-	-	-	-	-	-	-	49	49	2.5
10 years old............	-	-	-	-	-	-	-	-	-	-	-	36	36	1.8
11 years old............	-	-	-	-	-	-	-	-	-	-	-	28	28	1.4
12 years old............	40	-	-	-	-	-	-	-	-	-	-	28	28	1.4
13 years old............	78	9	-	-	-	-	-	-	-	-	-	15	15	0.7
14 years old............	1,226	111	18	-	-	-	-	-	-	-	-	22	22	1.1
15 years old............	572	1,274	106	20	12	3	8	-	1	-	-	17	17	0.8
16 years old............	115	566	1,236	124	16	-	-	-	3	-	15	51	66	3.0
17 years old............	37	117	611	1,205	78	10	2	-	-	-	45	111	156	7.0
18 years old............	11	37	86	529	855	38	2	-	-	-	460	169	629	28.8
19 years old............	-	10	25	132	382	553	71	-	4	3	710	207	917	43.6
20 years old............	-	-	15	25	197	401	430	26	-	-	829	164	993	47.6
21 years old............	-	-	-	6	70	176	315	275	5	11	984	205	1,189	57.7
22 years old............	3	4	3	9	58	97	132	218	56	28	1,189	250	1,439	70.3
23 years old............	2	-	-	15	47	98	96	146	71	78	1,316	221	1,537	73.6
24 years old............	-	4	4	-	36	76	70	132	59	70	1,312	229	1,541	77.4
25 to 29 years old.....	-	5	1	32	189	221	215	130	186	288	7,812	1,429	9,240	87.9
30 to 34 years old.....	2	3	-	19	88	92	99	64	70	164	7,781	1,215	8,995	93.7
35 to 39 years old.....	-	-	-	5	42	61	67	23	42	123	8,465	1,279	9,744	96.3
40 to 44 years old	-	3	-	-	16	48	35	32	41	64	8,918	1,208	10,126	97.6
45 to 49 years old	1	-	4	7	17	25	20	16	23	58	9,720	1,256	10,976	98.5
50 to 54 years old	-	-	-	-	5	16	15	11	13	34	9,167	1,208	10,375	99.1
55 to 59 years old	-	-	-	-	10	4	1	10	3	48	7,853	998	8,851	99.1
60 to 64 years old	-	-	-	-	10	4	9	3	6	13	6,467	826	7,294	99.4
65 years and over	-	3	4	3	4	1	2	4	3	3	12,902	3,181	16,082	99.8

- = Quantity zero or rounds to zero.

Table A-2. Single Grade of Enrollment and High School Graduation Status for Population 3 Years Old and Over, by Sex, Age (Single Years for 3 to 24 Years), Race, and Hispanic Origin, October 2008—*Continued*

(Numbers in thousands, percent.)

Age, sex, race, and Hispanic origin	Population	Enrolled		Enrolled									
				Nursery	Kinder-garten	Elementary grades							
		Number	Percent			1	2	3	4	5	6	7	8
Female													
Total................................	146,867	38,598	26.3	2,296	1,902	2,071	2,007	1,991	1,891	1,996	1,930	2,000	1,955
3 years old	2,092	844	40.3	802	42	-	-	-	-	-	-	-	-
4 years old	2,059	1,369	66.5	1,224	145	-	-	-	-	-	-	-	-
5 years old	2,009	1,824	90.8	244	1,427	139	15	-	-	-	-	-	-
6 years old	1,995	1,927	96.6	27	268	1,519	87	26	-	-	-	-	-
7 years old	2,027	1,991	98.2	-	21	356	1,516	81	17	-	-	-	-
8 years old	1,908	1,880	98.5	-	-	39	326	1,410	80	25	-	-	-
9 years old	1,953	1,942	99.4	-	-	18	46	417	1,322	99	39	-	-
10 years old.......................	1,903	1,882	98.9	-	-	-	16	37	407	1,308	100	13	-
11 years old.......................	1,932	1,915	99.1	-	-	-	-	20	46	472	1,234	108	34
12 years old.......................	2,005	1,989	99.2	-	-	-	-	-	19	59	448	1,297	127
13 years old.......................	1,976	1,968	99.6	-	-	-	-	-	-	33	79	481	1,289
14 years old.......................	1,926	1,878	97.5	-	-	-	-	-	-	-	20	68	432
15 years old.......................	2,014	1,991	98.8	-	-	-	-	-	-	-	-	7	53
16 years old.......................	2,103	2,051	97.5	-	-	-	-	-	-	-	-	3	7
17 years old.......................	2,126	1,984	93.3	-	-	-	-	-	-	-	2	1	7
18 years old.......................	2,145	1,594	74.3	-	-	-	-	-	-	-	-	-	-
19 years old.......................	2,058	1,270	61.7	-	-	-	-	-	-	-	-	-	-
20 years old.......................	1,921	1,053	54.8	-	-	-	-	-	-	-	-	-	-
21 years old.......................	2,017	1,034	51.3	-	-	-	-	-	-	-	-	-	-
22 years old.......................	2,067	791	38.3	-	-	-	-	-	-	-	-	-	-
23 years old.......................	2,124	597	28.1	-	-	-	-	-	-	-	-	2	-
24 years old.......................	2,059	491	23.8	-	-	-	-	-	-	-	-	-	-
25 to 29 years old	10,404	1,491	14.3	-	-	-	-	-	-	-	9	3	-
30 to 34 years old	9,670	802	8.3	-	-	-	-	-	-	-	-	6	3
35 to 39 years old	10,365	656	6.3	-	-	-	-	-	-	-	-	4	3
40 to 44 years old	10,669	488	4.6	-	-	-	-	-	-	-	-	4	-
45 to 49 years old	11,559	396	3.4	-	-	-	-	-	-	-	-	3	-
50 to 54 years old	10,966	307	2.8	-	-	-	-	-	-	-	-	-	-
55 to 59 years old	9,569	129	1.4	-	-	-	-	-	-	-	-	-	-
60 to 64 years old	7,956	49	0.6	-	-	-	-	-	-	-	-	-	-
65 years and over	21,286	18	0.1	-	-	-	-	-	-	-	-	-	-
WHITE ALONE NON-HISPANIC													
Both Sexes													
Total................................	189,639	45,373	23.9	2,710	2,206	2,330	2,325	2,268	2,223	2,210	2,388	2,381	2,223
3 years old	2,208	953	43.2	937	16	-	-	-	-	-	-	-	-
4 years old	2,261	1,551	68.6	1,448	103	-	-	-	-	-	-	-	-
5 years old	2,273	2,106	92.6	307	1,670	109	19	-	-	-	-	-	-
6 years old	2,244	2,180	97.2	17	402	1,670	80	11	-	-	-	-	-
7 years old	2,294	2,262	98.6	-	16	475	1,686	72	14	-	-	-	-
8 years old	2,260	2,230	98.7	-	-	56	478	1,595	82	20	-	-	-
9 years old	2,226	2,203	98.9	-	-	20	40	543	1,517	46	37	-	-
10 years old.......................	2,157	2,127	98.6	-	-	-	21	30	532	1,457	71	16	-
11 years old.......................	2,384	2,363	99.1	-	-	-	-	18	62	606	1,586	68	23
12 years old.......................	2,303	2,276	98.8	-	-	-	-	-	17	49	590	1,536	60
13 years old.......................	2,363	2,344	99.2	-	-	-	-	-	-	33	80	646	1,501
14 years old.......................	2,342	2,310	98.6	-	-	-	-	-	-	-	16	75	555
15 years old.......................	2,418	2,392	98.9	-	-	-	-	-	-	-	-	3	53
16 years old.......................	2,547	2,470	97.0	-	-	-	-	-	-	-	-	8	23
17 years old.......................	2,569	2,437	94.9	-	-	-	-	-	-	-	2	-	7
18 years old.......................	2,680	2,062	76.9	-	-	-	-	-	-	-	-	-	-
19 years old.......................	2,504	1,568	62.6	-	-	-	-	-	-	-	-	4	-
20 years old.......................	2,414	1,402	58.1	-	-	-	-	-	-	-	-	-	-
21 years old.......................	2,563	1,375	53.6	-	-	-	-	-	-	-	-	10	-
22 years old.......................	2,474	901	36.4	-	-	-	-	-	-	-	-	-	-
23 years old.......................	2,608	794	30.4	-	-	-	-	-	-	-	-	2	-
24 years old.......................	2,595	633	24.4	-	-	-	-	-	-	-	-	-	-
25 to 29 years old	12,504	1,661	13.3	-	-	-	-	-	-	-	4	-	-
30 to 34 years old	11,274	782	6.9	-	-	-	-	-	-	-	-	-	-
35 to 39 years old	12,631	590	4.7	-	-	-	-	-	-	-	-	4	-
40 to 44 years old	13,763	486	3.5	-	-	-	-	-	-	-	-	5	-
45 to 49 years old	15,737	363	2.3	-	-	-	-	-	-	-	1	3	-
50 to 54 years old	15,526	298	1.9	-	-	-	-	-	-	-	-	1	-
55 to 59 years old	13,868	161	1.2	-	-	-	-	-	-	-	-	-	-
60 to 64 years old	11,773	59	0.5	-	-	-	-	-	-	-	-	-	-
65 years and over	29,874	34	0.1	-	-	-	-	-	-	-	-	-	-

- = Quantity zero or rounds to zero.

Table A-2.   Single Grade of Enrollment and High School Graduation Status for Population 3 Years Old and Over, by Sex, Age (Single Years for 3 to 24 Years), Race, and Hispanic Origin, October 2008—*Continued*

(Numbers in thousands, percent.)

Age, sex, race, and Hispanic origin	Enrolled										Not enrolled		Not enrolled	
	High school				Undergraduate college				Graduate school		H.S. grad	Not grad		
	9	10	11	12	1	2	3	4	1	2+			Number	Percent
Female														
Total......................	1,974	2,050	2,072	2,143	2,456	2,463	1,934	1,364	822	1,281	91,706	16,562	108,408	73.7
3 years old	-	-	-	-	-	-	-	-	-	-	-	1,249	1,132	55.9
4 years old	-	-	-	-	-	-	-	-	-	-	-	691	670	34.3
5 years old	-	-	-	-	-	-	-	-	-	-	-	185	126	6.3
6 years old	-	-	-	-	-	-	-	-	-	-	-	68	63	3.1
7 years old	-	-	-	-	-	-	-	-	-	-	-	36	40	2.1
8 years old	-	-	-	-	-	-	-	-	-	-	-	28	37	1.9
9 years old	-	-	-	-	-	-	-	-	-	-	-	11	31	1.7
10 years old............	-	-	-	-	-	-	-	-	-	-	-	21	32	1.6
11 years old............	-	-	-	-	-	-	-	-	-	-	-	17	15	0.8
12 years old............	40	-	-	-	-	-	-	-	-	-	-	17	19	0.9
13 years old............	84	2	-	-	-	-	-	-	-	-	-	8	34	1.7
14 years old............	1,269	87	3	-	-	-	-	-	-	-	-	48	17	0.9
15 years old............	486	1,291	122	19	3	-	9	-	-	-	4	20	22	1.1
16 years old............	62	501	1,318	144	11	-	-	-	3	-	11	42	87	4.1
17 years old............	10	101	486	1,294	73	6	3	-	-	-	37	105	164	7.7
18 years old............	-	16	54	467	964	82	7	-	-	2	384	168	532	25.9
19 years old............	4	13	27	65	355	723	74	6	3	-	581	207	816	39.6
20 years old............	-	-	24	19	152	394	433	29	3	-	695	172	894	44.0
21 years old............	-	3	3	25	68	165	332	399	24	15	821	161	963	49.6
22 years old............	4	-	4	7	83	146	175	275	70	28	1,096	180	1,396	67.0
23 years old............	-	-	-	-	62	93	105	146	80	109	1,362	166	1,405	70.2
24 years old............	-	8	-	-	60	76	98	79	68	102	1,365	204	1,565	75.1
25 to 29 years old	1	8	7	35	201	254	239	171	189	375	7,897	1,016	8,816	85.3
30 to 34 years old	0	3	-	10	117	156	137	56	131	182	7,878	990	8,867	92.1
35 to 39 years old	4	6	1	25	112	148	109	73	67	105	8,714	995	9,902	94.4
40 to 44 years old	-	6	2	13	75	102	81	50	39	116	9,050	1,131	10,520	96.2
45 to 49 years old	3	2	5	5	64	53	66	42	59	93	10,191	972	11,143	96.5
50 to 54 years old	6	-	7	11	29	39	45	34	62	75	9,586	1,074	10,459	97.1
55 to 59 years old	-	-	3	-	19	20	11	3	18	56	8,430	1,010	9,319	98.7
60 to 64 years old	-	-	-	-	9	1	11	3	1	23	6,952	956	7,546	99.2
65 years and over	-	-	3	3	-	5	-	-	4	2	16,651	4,617	20,876	99.8
WHITE ALONE NON-HISPANIC														
Both Sexes														
Total......................	2,397	2,413	2,473	2,500	2,915	2,701	2,314	1,815	996	1,583	129,504	14,762	144,266	76.1
3 years old	-	-	-	-	-	-	-	-	-	-	-	1,255	1,255	56.8
4 years old	-	-	-	-	-	-	-	-	-	-	-	710	710	31.4
5 years old	-	-	-	-	-	-	-	-	-	-	-	167	167	7.4
6 years old	-	-	-	-	-	-	-	-	-	-	-	63	63	2.8
7 years old	-	-	-	-	-	-	-	-	-	-	-	32	32	1.4
8 years old	-	-	-	-	-	-	-	-	-	-	-	29	29	1.3
9 years old	-	-	-	-	-	-	-	-	-	-	-	24	24	1.1
10 years old............	-	-	-	-	-	-	-	-	-	-	-	31	31	1.4
11 years old............	-	-	-	-	-	-	-	-	-	-	-	21	21	0.9
12 years old............	23	-	-	-	-	-	-	-	-	-	-	27	27	1.2
13 years old............	81	2	-	-	-	-	-	-	-	-	-	19	19	0.8
14 years old............	1,569	81	14	-	-	-	-	-	-	-	-	32	32	1.4
15 years old............	604	1,601	89	17	13	3	7	-	1	-	-	26	26	1.1
16 years old............	78	606	1,616	124	12	-	-	-	3	-	19	58	77	3.0
17 years old............	18	79	661	1,590	71	10	-	-	-	-	47	86	132	5.1
18 years old............	7	15	62	590	1,301	79	9	-	-	-	478	140	618	23.1
19 years old............	-	16	8	78	469	910	69	6	4	3	780	156	936	37.4
20 years old............	-	-	13	9	198	474	665	41	3	-	883	129	1,012	41.9
21 years old............	-	-	-	11	81	196	485	551	23	18	1,067	121	1,188	46.4
22 years old............	4	-	-	4	82	125	186	369	93	37	1,438	136	1,574	63.6
23 years old............	2	-	-	7	60	112	124	215	121	151	1,693	121	1,814	69.6
24 years old............	-	-	-	-	73	93	84	155	99	129	1,805	157	1,962	75.6
25 to 29 years old	1	4	-	28	206	239	258	201	258	463	10,118	725	10,843	86.7
30 to 34 years old	-	1	-	2	110	130	138	75	125	201	9,961	531	10,492	93.1
35 to 39 years old	-	-	-	9	86	142	102	46	64	137	11,366	674	12,041	95.3
40 to 44 years old	-	7	-	10	54	84	80	59	61	126	12,503	775	13,278	96.5
45 to 49 years old	4	-	7	7	43	48	51	38	54	108	14,469	905	15,374	97.7
50 to 54 years old	6	-	-	8	22	36	41	39	59	85	14,282	947	15,229	98.1
55 to 59 years old	-	-	-	-	21	13	2	9	22	94	12,813	893	13,706	98.8
60 to 64 years old	-	-	-	-	12	2	11	6	4	23	10,822	892	11,714	99.5
65 years and over	-	3	3	6	-	5	2	4	5	5	24,960	4,880	29,840	99.9

- = Quantity zero or rounds to zero.

Table A-2. Single Grade of Enrollment and High School Graduation Status for Population 3 Years Old and Over, by Sex, Age (Single Years for 3 to 24 Years), Race, and Hispanic Origin, October 2008—*Continued*

(Numbers in thousands, percent.)

Age, sex, race, and Hispanic origin	Population	Enrolled		Enrolled										
		Number	Percent	Nursery	Kinder-garten	Elementary grades								
						1	2	3	4	5	6	7	8
Male														
Total	92,729	22,561	24.3	1,418	1,182	1,188	1,176	1,173	1,132	1,077	1,286	1,224	1,166
3 years old	1,125	481	42.8	469	12	-	-	-	-	-	-	-	-
4 years old	1,172	832	71.0	776	56	-	-	-	-	-	-	-	-
5 years old	1,171	1,084	92.6	170	853	53	8	-	-	-	-	-	-
6 years old	1,162	1,126	96.9	2	254	829	36	4	-	-	-	-	-
7 years old	1,167	1,152	98.7	-	7	273	822	41	9	-	-	-	-
8 years old	1,155	1,137	98.4	-	-	29	283	775	44	6	-	-	-
9 years old	1,144	1,124	98.2	-	-	5	14	327	732	24	22	-	-
10 years old	1,066	1,050	98.5	-	-	-	13	17	296	687	25	12	-
11 years old	1,248	1,232	98.7	-	-	-	-	9	39	312	826	31	15
12 years old	1,186	1,167	98.4	-	-	-	-	-	11	27	344	752	22
13 years old	1,213	1,202	99.1	-	-	-	-	-	-	22	52	349	746
14 years old	1,200	1,193	99.4	-	-	-	-	-	-	-	16	49	327
15 years old	1,265	1,250	98.8	-	-	-	-	-	-	-	-	3	34
16 years old	1,305	1,262	96.7	-	-	-	-	-	-	-	-	8	18
17 years old	1,291	1,218	94.3	-	-	-	-	-	-	-	-	-	3
18 years old	1,385	1,032	74.6	-	-	-	-	-	-	-	-	-	-
19 years old	1,264	737	58.3	-	-	-	-	-	-	-	-	4	-
20 years old	1,278	712	55.7	-	-	-	-	-	-	-	-	-	-
21 years old	1,293	635	49.1	-	-	-	-	-	-	-	-	10	-
22 years old	1,235	407	33.0	-	-	-	-	-	-	-	-	-	-
23 years old	1,332	401	30.1	-	-	-	-	-	-	-	-	-	-
24 years old	1,245	301	24.2	-	-	-	-	-	-	-	-	-	-
25 to 29 years old	6,217	783	12.6	-	-	-	-	-	-	-	-	-	-
30 to 34 years old	5,575	347	6.2	-	-	-	-	-	-	-	-	-	-
35 to 39 years old	6,246	219	3.5	-	-	-	-	-	-	-	-	4	-
40 to 44 years old	6,812	192	2.8	-	-	-	-	-	-	-	-	1	-
45 to 49 years old	7,784	104	1.3	-	-	-	-	-	-	-	1	-	-
50 to 54 years old	7,653	81	1.1	-	-	-	-	-	-	-	-	1	-
55 to 59 years old	6,819	57	0.8	-	-	-	-	-	-	-	-	-	-
60 to 64 years old	5,699	25	0.4	-	-	-	-	-	-	-	-	-	-
65 years and over	13,019	17	0.1	-	-	-	-	-	-	-	-	-	-
Female														
Total	96,910	22,811	23.5	1,291	1,024	1,142	1,149	1,095	1,092	1,133	1,102	1,157	1,057
3 years old	1,083	472	43.6	468	4	-	-	-	-	-	-	-	-
4 years old	1,089	719	66.0	671	47	-	-	-	-	-	-	-	-
5 years old	1,102	1,021	92.7	137	817	57	11	-	-	-	-	-	-
6 years old	1,082	1,054	97.5	15	147	840	45	7	-	-	-	-	-
7 years old	1,127	1,110	98.5	-	9	202	863	32	5	-	-	-	-
8 years old	1,104	1,093	99.0	-	-	27	196	820	37	14	-	-	-
9 years old	1,082	1,079	99.7	-	-	16	26	215	785	22	15	-	-
10 years old	1,091	1,077	98.7	-	-	-	8	12	235	771	46	4	-
11 years old	1,136	1,131	99.6	-	-	-	-	9	23	294	760	38	8
12 years old	1,117	1,109	99.3	-	-	-	-	-	7	22	247	783	38
13 years old	1,149	1,142	99.4	-	-	-	-	-	-	11	28	297	755
14 years old	1,142	1,116	97.8	-	-	-	-	-	-	-	-	26	228
15 years old	1,153	1,141	99.0	-	-	-	-	-	-	-	-	-	18
16 years old	1,242	1,208	97.3	-	-	-	-	-	-	-	-	-	6
17 years old	1,278	1,220	95.4	-	-	-	-	-	-	-	2	-	4
18 years old	1,296	1,030	79.5	-	-	-	-	-	-	-	-	-	-
19 years old	1,240	831	67.0	-	-	-	-	-	-	-	-	-	-
20 years old	1,136	691	60.8	-	-	-	-	-	-	-	-	-	-
21 years old	1,270	740	58.3	-	-	-	-	-	-	-	-	-	-
22 years old	1,239	494	39.8	-	-	-	-	-	-	-	-	-	-
23 years old	1,276	393	30.8	-	-	-	-	-	-	-	-	2	-
24 years old	1,351	333	24.6	-	-	-	-	-	-	-	-	-	-
25 to 29 years old	6,286	878	14.0	-	-	-	-	-	-	-	4	-	-
30 to 34 years old	5,699	435	7.6	-	-	-	-	-	-	-	-	-	-
35 to 39 years old	6,385	371	5.8	-	-	-	-	-	-	-	-	-	-
40 to 44 years old	6,951	294	4.2	-	-	-	-	-	-	-	-	4	-
45 to 49 years old	7,952	259	3.3	-	-	-	-	-	-	-	-	3	-
50 to 54 years old	7,874	217	2.8	-	-	-	-	-	-	-	-	-	-
55 to 59 years old	7,049	104	1.5	-	-	-	-	-	-	-	-	-	-
60 to 64 years old	6,073	34	0.6	-	-	-	-	-	-	-	-	-	-
65 years and over	16,855	17	0.1	-	-	-	-	-	-	-	-	-	-

- = Quantity zero or rounds to zero.

Table A-2. Single Grade of Enrollment and High School Graduation Status for Population 3 Years Old and Over, by Sex, Age (Single Years for 3 to 24 Years), Race, and Hispanic Origin, October 2008—Continued

(Numbers in thousands, percent.)

Age, sex, race, and Hispanic origin	Enrolled										Not enrolled		Not enrolled	
	High school				Undergraduate college				Graduate school		H.S. grad	Not grad	Number	Percent
	9	10	11	12	1	2	3	4	1	2+				
Male														
Total......................	1,209	1,231	1,272	1,223	1,381	1,204	1,061	825	447	684	62,659	7,509	70,167	75.7
3 years old	-	-	-	-	-	-	-	-	-	-	-	644	644	57.2
4 years old	-	-	-	-	-	-	-	-	-	-	-	340	340	29.0
5 years old	-	-	-	-	-	-	-	-	-	-	-	87	87	7.4
6 years old	-	-	-	-	-	-	-	-	-	-	-	36	36	3.1
7 years old	-	-	-	-	-	-	-	-	-	-	-	15	15	1.3
8 years old	-	-	-	-	-	-	-	-	-	-	-	18	18	1.6
9 years old	-	-	-	-	-	-	-	-	-	-	-	20	20	1.8
10 years old.............	-	-	-	-	-	-	-	-	-	-	-	16	16	1.5
11 years old.............	-	-	-	-	-	-	-	-	-	-	-	16	16	1.3
12 years old.............	11	-	-	-	-	-	-	-	-	-	-	19	19	1.6
13 years old.............	31	2	-	-	-	-	-	-	-	-	-	11	11	0.9
14 years old.............	744	47	11	-	-	-	-	-	-	-	-	7	7	0.6
15 years old.............	343	791	48	12	10	3	5	-	1	-	-	15	15	1.2
16 years old.............	55	326	783	65	7	-	-	-	-	-	11	32	43	3.3
17 years old.............	15	40	385	744	27	4	-	-	-	-	28	45	73	5.7
18 years old.............	7	13	36	308	640	27	2	-	-	-	267	86	352	25.4
19 years old.............	-	6	-	48	259	392	21	-	3	3	442	84	527	41.7
20 years old.............	-	-	7	4	104	245	336	15	-	-	499	68	567	44.3
21 years old.............	-	-	-	4	42	98	249	224	5	3	580	78	659	50.9
22 years old.............	-	-	-	2	37	48	79	176	43	23	747	81	828	67.0
23 years old.............	2	-	-	7	35	63	52	120	59	64	856	74	931	69.9
24 years old.............	-	-	-	-	27	49	41	96	44	43	871	73	944	75.8
25 to 29 years old	-	-	-	16	85	127	122	83	147	202	5,003	431	5,434	87.4
30 to 34 years old	-	-	-	-	46	47	58	43	54	100	4,945	282	5,228	93.8
35 to 39 years old	-	-	-	3	26	40	39	10	28	69	5,630	396	6,027	96.5
40 to 44 years old	-	3	-	-	16	33	28	26	29	55	6,172	449	6,620	97.2
45 to 49 years old	1	-	4	7	9	13	13	9	12	36	7,119	561	7,680	98.7
50 to 54 years old	-	-	-	-	4	13	11	11	13	27	7,024	548	7,572	98.9
55 to 59 years old	-	-	-	-	3	-	-	7	3	44	6,268	493	6,762	99.2
60 to 64 years old	-	-	-	-	3	1	3	3	3	11	5,250	425	5,675	99.6
65 years and over	-	3	-	3	-	-	2	4	3	3	10,946	2,056	13,002	99.9
Female														
Total......................	1,188	1,182	1,201	1,277	1,534	1,497	1,254	990	549	899	66,845	7,254	74,098	76.5
3 years old	-	-	-	-	-	-	-	-	-	-	-	611	611	56.4
4 years old	-	-	-	-	-	-	-	-	-	-	-	370	370	34.0
5 years old	-	-	-	-	-	-	-	-	-	-	-	81	81	7.3
6 years old	-	-	-	-	-	-	-	-	-	-	-	28	28	2.5
7 years old	-	-	-	-	-	-	-	-	-	-	-	17	17	1.5
8 years old	-	-	-	-	-	-	-	-	-	-	-	11	11	1.0
9 years old	-	-	-	-	-	-	-	-	-	-	-	3	3	0.3
10 years old.............	-	-	-	-	-	-	-	-	-	-	-	14	14	1.3
11 years old.............	-	-	-	-	-	-	-	-	-	-	-	5	5	0.4
12 years old.............	12	-	-	-	-	-	-	-	-	-	-	8	8	0.7
13 years old.............	50	-	-	-	-	-	-	-	-	-	-	7	7	0.6
14 years old.............	825	34	3	-	-	-	-	-	-	-	-	26	26	2.2
15 years old.............	262	810	41	5	3	-	2	-	-	-	-	11	11	1.0
16 years old.............	23	280	833	58	5	-	-	-	3	-	8	26	33	2.7
17 years old.............	3	39	277	846	44	5	-	-	-	-	18	40	59	4.6
18 years old.............	-	2	26	281	661	52	7	-	-	-	211	54	266	20.5
19 years old.............	-	10	8	30	210	518	48	6	1	-	338	72	409	33.0
20 years old.............	-	-	6	5	93	229	329	26	3	-	384	61	446	39.2
21 years old.............	-	-	-	7	40	98	236	327	17	15	487	43	530	41.7
22 years old.............	4	-	-	3	45	77	107	194	49	15	691	54	745	60.2
23 years old.............	-	-	-	-	25	50	73	95	62	87	837	46	883	69.2
24 years old.............	-	-	-	-	46	44	43	59	54	87	934	84	1,018	75.4
25 to 29 years old	-	4	-	11	121	111	136	119	111	261	5,115	294	5,409	86.0
30 to 34 years old	-	1	-	2	64	83	80	33	71	101	5,016	249	5,265	92.4
35 to 39 years old	-	-	-	6	60	101	63	37	36	68	5,736	278	6,014	94.2
40 to 44 years old	-	4	-	10	38	51	51	34	32	71	6,331	326	6,657	95.8
45 to 49 years old	3	-	3	-	33	35	39	29	41	72	7,349	344	7,694	96.7
50 to 54 years old	6	-	-	8	18	23	30	27	46	59	7,258	399	7,657	97.2
55 to 59 years old	-	-	-	-	17	13	2	3	18	50	6,545	400	6,945	98.5
60 to 64 years old	-	-	-	-	9	1	8	3	1	12	5,572	467	6,039	99.4
65 years and over	-	-	3	3	-	5	-	-	3	2	14,014	2,824	16,838	99.9

- = Quantity zero or rounds to zero.

Table A-2. Single Grade of Enrollment and High School Graduation Status for Population 3 Years Old and Over, by Sex, Age (Single Years for 3 to 24 Years), Race, and Hispanic Origin, October 2008—*Continued*

(Numbers in thousands, percent.)

Age, sex, race, and Hispanic origin	Population	Enrolled		Enrolled									
				Nursery	Kinder-garten	Elementary grades							
		Number	Percent			1	2	3	4	5	6	7	8
BLACK ALONE													
Both Sexes													
Total..............................	35,994	11,421	31.7	706	601	627	634	626	577	641	664	621	604
3 years old	658	270	41.1	236	35	-	-	-	-	-	-	-	-
4 years old	666	453	68.0	379	74	-	-	-	-	-	-	-	-
5 years old	614	559	91.1	84	425	29	22	-	-	-	-	-	-
6 years old	568	541	95.3	8	59	448	23	4	-	-	-	-	-
7 years old	639	631	98.9	-	9	129	447	33	14	-	-	-	-
8 years old	575	564	98.1	-	-	11	115	411	23	4	-	-	-
9 years old	624	622	99.7	-	-	10	21	161	388	33	8	-	-
10 years old.....................	617	607	98.5	-	-	-	6	11	131	415	39	6	-
11 years old.....................	557	549	98.6	-	-	-	-	6	18	126	342	38	19
12 years old.....................	604	597	98.9	-	-	-	-	-	3	48	179	305	39
13 years old.....................	649	648	99.9	-	-	-	-	-	-	16	78	202	323
14 years old.....................	598	578	96.7	-	-	-	-	-	-	-	14	51	168
15 years old.....................	644	638	99.1	-	-	-	-	-	-	-	-	-	45
16 years old.....................	652	635	97.4	-	-	-	-	-	-	-	-	10	5
17 years old.....................	698	636	91.2	-	-	-	-	-	-	-	-	-	2
18 years old.....................	715	458	64.2	-	-	-	-	-	-	-	-	-	-
19 years old.....................	620	332	53.4	-	-	-	-	-	-	-	-	-	-
20 years old.....................	654	320	48.9	-	-	-	-	-	-	-	-	-	-
21 years old.....................	604	188	31.0	-	-	-	-	-	-	-	-	-	-
22 years old.....................	597	198	33.1	-	-	-	-	-	-	-	-	-	-
23 years old.....................	591	121	20.5	-	-	-	-	-	-	-	-	-	-
24 years old.....................	483	97	20.1	-	-	-	-	-	-	-	-	-	-
25 to 29 years old	2,839	418	14.7	-	-	-	-	-	-	-	5	4	-
30 to 34 years old	2,457	282	11.5	-	-	-	-	-	-	-	-	-	4
35 to 39 years old	2,553	198	7.7	-	-	-	-	-	-	-	-	4	-
40 to 44 years old	2,625	101	3.8	-	-	-	-	-	-	-	-	-	-
45 to 49 years old	2,749	98	3.6	-	-	-	-	-	-	-	-	-	-
50 to 54 years old	2,489	53	2.1	-	-	-	-	-	-	-	-	-	-
55 to 59 years old	1,909	15	0.8	-	-	-	-	-	-	-	-	-	-
60 to 64 years old	1,566	14	0.9	-	-	-	-	-	-	-	-	-	-
65 years and over	3,182	-	-	-	-	-	-	-	-	-	-	-	-
Male													
Total..............................	16,595	5,419	32.7	307	319	332	320	317	268	347	353	339	294
3 years old	312	119	38.1	98	21	-	-	-	-	-	-	-	-
4 years old	313	215	68.5	170	44	-	-	-	-	-	-	-	-
5 years old	307	288	93.9	35	226	7	20	-	-	-	-	-	-
6 years old	275	268	97.4	3	23	230	12	-	-	-	-	-	-
7 years old	334	329	98.7	-	6	81	217	15	11	-	-	-	-
8 years old	308	300	97.4	-	-	4	62	222	12	-	-	-	-
9 years old	298	296	99.3	-	-	10	9	76	182	15	4	-	-
10 years old.....................	311	304	97.8	-	-	-	-	-	52	224	25	3	-
11 years old.....................	298	294	98.6	-	-	-	-	3	8	79	183	11	11
12 years old.....................	308	302	97.9	-	-	-	-	-	2	27	91	148	15
13 years old.....................	323	322	99.7	-	-	-	-	-	-	3	41	131	133
14 years old.....................	303	296	97.7	-	-	-	-	-	-	-	9	30	98
15 years old.....................	319	319	100.0	-	-	-	-	-	-	-	-	-	27
16 years old.....................	322	312	97.0	-	-	-	-	-	-	-	-	7	5
17 years old.....................	351	321	91.3	-	-	-	-	-	-	-	-	-	2
18 years old.....................	336	208	62.0	-	-	-	-	-	-	-	-	-	-
19 years old.....................	317	170	53.5	-	-	-	-	-	-	-	-	-	-
20 years old.....................	326	156	47.9	-	-	-	-	-	-	-	-	-	-
21 years old.....................	283	74	26.2	-	-	-	-	-	-	-	-	-	-
22 years old.....................	284	91	32.1	-	-	-	-	-	-	-	-	-	-
23 years old.....................	249	46	18.5	-	-	-	-	-	-	-	-	-	-
24 years old.....................	251	45	17.9	-	-	-	-	-	-	-	-	-	-
25 to 29 years old	1,323	140	10.6	-	-	-	-	-	-	-	-	4	-
30 to 34 years old	1,097	94	8.5	-	-	-	-	-	-	-	-	-	4
35 to 39 years old	1,130	43	3.8	-	-	-	-	-	-	-	-	4	-
40 to 44 years old	1,174	17	1.5	-	-	-	-	-	-	-	-	-	-
45 to 49 years old	1,244	29	2.3	-	-	-	-	-	-	-	-	-	-
50 to 54 years old	1,128	9	0.8	-	-	-	-	-	-	-	-	-	-
55 to 59 years old	856	-	-	-	-	-	-	-	-	-	-	-	-
60 to 64 years old	682	12	1.8	-	-	-	-	-	-	-	-	-	-
65 years and over	1,232	-	-	-	-	-	-	-	-	-	-	-	-

- = Quantity zero or rounds to zero.

Table A-2. Single Grade of Enrollment and High School Graduation Status for Population 3 Years Old and Over, by Sex, Age (Single Years for 3 to 24 Years), Race, and Hispanic Origin, October 2008—*Continued*

(Numbers in thousands, percent.)

Age, sex, race, and Hispanic origin	Enrolled										Not enrolled		Not enrolled	
	High school				Undergraduate college				Graduate school		H.S. grad	Not grad		
	9	10	11	12	1	2	3	4	1	2+			Number	Percent
BLACK ALONE														
Both Sexes														
Total......................	614	682	600	743	697	676	506	241	155	206	19,786	4,787	24,573	68.3
3 years old	-	-	-	-	-	-	-	-	-	-	-	388	388	58.9
4 years old	-	-	-	-	-	-	-	-	-	-	-	213	213	32.0
5 years old	-	-	-	-	-	-	-	-	-	-	-	55	55	8.9
6 years old	-	-	-	-	-	-	-	-	-	-	-	27	27	4.7
7 years old	-	-	-	-	-	-	-	-	-	-	-	7	7	1.1
8 years old	-	-	-	-	-	-	-	-	-	-	-	11	11	1.9
9 years old	-	-	-	-	-	-	-	-	-	-	-	2	2	0.3
10 years old.............	-	-	-	-	-	-	-	-	-	-	-	9	9	1.5
11 years old.............	-	-	-	-	-	-	-	-	-	-	-	8	8	1.4
12 years old.............	23	-	-	-	-	-	-	-	-	-	-	7	7	1.1
13 years old.............	29	-	-	-	-	-	-	-	-	-	-	1	1	0.1
14 years old.............	296	50	-	-	-	-	-	-	-	-	-	20	20	3.3
15 years old.............	202	336	41	10	-	-	4	-	-	-	-	6	6	0.9
16 years old.............	48	196	322	54	2	-	-	-	-	-	5	11	17	2.6
17 years old.............	14	61	171	358	27	4	-	-	-	-	16	45	62	8.8
18 years old.............	-	19	30	195	207	8	-	-	-	-	186	70	256	35.8
19 years old.............	-	-	16	51	95	142	27	-	-	-	214	74	289	46.6
20 years old.............	-	-	18	22	83	113	76	8	-	-	267	67	334	51.1
21 years old.............	-	1	-	4	11	64	59	48	-	-	339	78	417	69.0
22 years old.............	-	-	-	7	45	35	48	56	3	4	330	70	399	66.9
23 years old.............	-	-	-	1	23	33	25	16	5	19	384	87	470	79.5
24 years old.............	-	-	-	-	6	21	26	16	18	10	318	68	386	79.9
25 to 29 years old......	-	9	-	23	69	102	90	26	52	37	2,117	304	2,421	85.3
30 to 34 years old......	-	3	-	5	50	68	59	19	33	40	1,938	237	2,175	88.5
35 to 39 years old......	-	3	-	10	40	24	37	29	18	33	2,113	243	2,356	92.3
40 to 44 years old......	-	2	-	-	8	37	14	12	7	20	2,243	281	2,524	96.2
45 to 49 years old......	-	2	2	4	17	10	22	9	9	23	2,334	317	2,650	96.4
50 to 54 years old......	-	-	-	-	10	11	10	3	6	13	2,071	364	2,436	97.9
55 to 59 years old......	-	-	-	-	2	3	8	-	-	2	1,583	310	1,894	99.2
60 to 64 years old......	-	-	-	-	4	-	3	-	3	4	1,246	306	1,552	99.1
65 years and over	-	-	-	-	-	-	-	-	-	-	2,080	1,102	3,182	100.0
Male														
Total......................	323	334	298	349	267	259	188	100	46	59	9,017	2,159	11,176	67.3
3 years old	-	-	-	-	-	-	-	-	-	-	-	194	194	61.9
4 years old	-	-	-	-	-	-	-	-	-	-	-	99	99	31.5
5 years old	-	-	-	-	-	-	-	-	-	-	-	19	19	6.1
6 years old	-	-	-	-	-	-	-	-	-	-	-	7	7	2.6
7 years old	-	-	-	-	-	-	-	-	-	-	-	4	4	1.3
8 years old	-	-	-	-	-	-	-	-	-	-	-	8	8	2.6
9 years old	-	-	-	-	-	-	-	-	-	-	-	2	2	0.7
10 years old.............	-	-	-	-	-	-	-	-	-	-	-	7	7	2.2
11 years old.............	-	-	-	-	-	-	-	-	-	-	-	4	4	1.4
12 years old.............	17	-	-	-	-	-	-	-	-	-	-	6	6	2.1
13 years old.............	14	-	-	-	-	-	-	-	-	-	-	1	1	0.3
14 years old.............	137	22	-	-	-	-	-	-	-	-	-	7	7	2.3
15 years old.............	115	155	19	3	-	-	-	-	-	-	-	-	-	-
16 years old.............	30	98	155	17	2	-	-	-	-	-	2	7	10	3.0
17 years old.............	11	36	81	172	16	4	-	-	-	-	4	26	31	8.7
18 years old.............	-	16	24	91	77	-	-	-	-	-	109	19	128	38.0
19 years old.............	-	-	14	28	45	64	18	-	-	-	114	34	148	46.5
20 years old.............	-	-	4	9	51	47	37	8	-	-	144	26	170	52.1
21 years old.............	-	-	-	-	1	35	19	18	-	-	182	26	209	73.8
22 years old.............	-	-	-	7	20	17	22	26	-	-	166	27	193	67.9
23 years old.............	-	-	-	1	-	19	9	13	-	4	165	38	203	81.5
24 years old.............	-	-	-	-	-	11	6	8	11	9	167	39	206	82.1
25 to 29 years old......	-	5	-	16	30	31	29	13	11	1	1,035	147	1,183	89.4
30 to 34 years old......	-	3	-	5	14	19	18	13	5	12	906	97	1,004	91.5
35 to 39 years old......	-	-	-	-	8	-	16	-	6	8	969	118	1,087	96.2
40 to 44 years old......	-	-	-	-	-	3	3	1	7	3	1,023	134	1,157	98.5
45 to 49 years old......	-	-	-	-	-	6	4	-	2	16	1,055	161	1,216	97.7
50 to 54 years old......	-	-	-	-	-	1	4	-	-	4	931	187	1,118	99.2
55 to 59 years old......	-	-	-	-	-	-	-	-	-	-	732	124	856	100.0
60 to 64 years old......	-	-	-	-	4	-	3	-	3	2	527	143	670	98.2
65 years and over	-	-	-	-	-	-	-	-	-	-	786	446	1,232	100.0

- = Quantity zero or rounds to zero.

Table A-2.   Single Grade of Enrollment and High School Graduation Status for Population 3 Years Old and Over, by Sex, Age (Single Years for 3 to 24 Years), Race, and Hispanic Origin, October 2008—*Continued*

(Numbers in thousands, percent.)

Age, sex, race, and Hispanic origin	Population	Enrolled		Enrolled									
						Elementary grades							
		Number	Percent	Nursery	Kinder-garten	1	2	3	4	5	6	7	8
Female													
Total..............................	19,398	6,002	30.9	399	282	296	313	309	308	295	312	281	309
3 years old	345	151	43.8	138	14	-	-	-	-	-	-	-	-
4 years old	353	238	67.5	208	30	-	-	-	-	-	-	-	-
5 years old	307	271	88.4	49	199	21	2	-	-	-	-	-	-
6 years old	292	273	93.4	5	36	218	11	3	-	-	-	-	-
7 years old	305	302	99.0	-	3	49	229	18	3	-	-	-	-
8 years old	267	264	99.0	-	-	7	53	190	10	4	-	-	-
9 years old	325	325	100.0	-	-	-	12	85	206	19	4	-	-
10 years old.......................	306	303	99.2	-	-	-	6	11	79	191	14	3	-
11 years old.......................	258	254	98.5	-	-	-	-	3	10	48	159	27	8
12 years old.......................	296	295	99.9	-	-	-	-	-	-	21	88	156	24
13 years old.......................	326	326	100.0	-	-	-	-	-	-	13	37	71	190
14 years old.......................	296	282	95.6	-	-	-	-	-	-	-	5	20	69
15 years old.......................	326	320	98.2	-	-	-	-	-	-	-	-	-	17
16 years old.......................	331	323	97.8	-	-	-	-	-	-	-	-	3	-
17 years old.......................	346	315	91.0	-	-	-	-	-	-	-	-	-	-
18 years old.......................	378	250	66.1	-	-	-	-	-	-	-	-	-	-
19 years old.......................	303	162	53.4	-	-	-	-	-	-	-	-	-	-
20 years old.......................	328	164	49.8	-	-	-	-	-	-	-	-	-	-
21 years old.......................	322	114	35.3	-	-	-	-	-	-	-	-	-	-
22 years old.......................	313	107	34.1	-	-	-	-	-	-	-	-	-	-
23 years old.......................	343	75	21.9	-	-	-	-	-	-	-	-	-	-
24 years old.......................	233	52	22.5	-	-	-	-	-	-	-	-	-	-
25 to 29 years old	1,516	277	18.3	-	-	-	-	-	-	-	5	-	-
30 to 34 years old	1,360	188	13.8	-	-	-	-	-	-	-	-	-	-
35 to 39 years old	1,424	155	10.9	-	-	-	-	-	-	-	-	-	-
40 to 44 years old	1,450	83	5.7	-	-	-	-	-	-	-	-	-	-
45 to 49 years old	1,504	70	4.6	-	-	-	-	-	-	-	-	-	-
50 to 54 years old	1,361	43	3.2	-	-	-	-	-	-	-	-	-	-
55 to 59 years old	1,052	15	1.4	-	-	-	-	-	-	-	-	-	-
60 to 64 years old	884	2	0.2	-	-	-	-	-	-	-	-	-	-
65 years and over	1,949	-	-	-	-	-	-	-	-	-	-	-	-
ASIAN ALONE													
Both Sexes													
Total..............................	12,953	3,545	27.4	205	144	155	172	176	153	191	165	181	163
3 years old	156	77	49.2	73	3	-	-	-	-	-	-	-	-
4 years old	193	118	61.1	107	11	-	-	-	-	-	-	-	-
5 years old	166	148	89.5	20	104	25	-	-	-	-	-	-	-
6 years old	153	141	92.1	5	26	100	10	-	-	-	-	-	-
7 years old	162	160	98.6	-	-	19	134	6	-	-	-	-	-
8 years old	176	173	98.3	-	-	11	23	132	6	-	-	-	-
9 years old	182	177	97.1	-	-	-	5	34	126	11	-	-	-
10 years old.......................	163	162	99.3	-	-	-	-	3	18	115	26	-	-
11 years old.......................	172	172	100.0	-	-	-	-	-	-	57	92	21	2
12 years old.......................	171	170	99.7	-	-	-	-	-	2	8	34	111	15
13 years old.......................	168	167	99.1	-	-	-	-	-	-	-	5	37	108
14 years old.......................	143	143	100.0	-	-	-	-	-	-	-	7	3	32
15 years old.......................	157	153	97.6	-	-	-	-	-	-	-	-	-	2
16 years old.......................	174	168	96.7	-	-	-	-	-	-	-	-	-	3
17 years old.......................	176	155	88.1	-	-	-	-	-	-	-	-	-	-
18 years old.......................	118	110	93.7	-	-	-	-	-	-	-	-	-	-
19 years old.......................	142	111	78.4	-	-	-	-	-	-	-	-	-	-
20 years old.......................	149	123	82.4	-	-	-	-	-	-	-	-	-	-
21 years old.......................	155	123	79.9	-	-	-	-	-	-	-	-	-	-
22 years old.......................	169	94	55.7	-	-	-	-	-	-	-	-	-	-
23 years old.......................	207	77	37.2	-	-	-	-	-	-	-	-	-	-
24 years old.......................	173	66	37.9	-	-	-	-	-	-	-	-	-	-
25 to 29 years old	1,057	248	23.4	-	-	-	-	-	-	-	-	3	-
30 to 34 years old	1,211	140	11.5	-	-	-	-	-	-	-	-	3	-
35 to 39 years old	1,332	78	5.9	-	-	-	-	-	-	-	-	-	-
40 to 44 years old	1,090	25	2.3	-	-	-	-	-	-	-	-	-	-
45 to 49 years old	1,072	32	3.0	-	-	-	-	-	-	-	-	-	-
50 to 54 years old	902	25	2.7	-	-	-	-	-	-	-	-	-	-
55 to 59 years old	797	7	0.9	-	-	-	-	-	-	-	-	4	-
60 to 64 years old	562	2	0.4	-	-	-	-	-	-	-	-	-	-
65 years and over	1,307	-	-	-	-	-	-	-	-	-	-	-	-

- = Quantity zero or rounds to zero.

Table A-2. Single Grade of Enrollment and High School Graduation Status for Population 3 Years Old and Over, by Sex, Age (Single Years for 3 to 24 Years), Race, and Hispanic Origin, October 2008—*Continued*

(Numbers in thousands, percent.)

Age, sex, race, and Hispanic origin	Enrolled										Not enrolled		Not enrolled	
	High school				Undergraduate college				Graduate school		H.S. grad	Not grad		
	9	10	11	12	1	2	3	4	1	2+			Number	Percent
Female														
Total......................	290	348	302	394	429	417	319	142	109	147	10,769	2,628	13,397	69.1
3 years old	-	-	-	-	-	-	-	-	-	-	-	194	194	56.2
4 years old	-	-	-	-	-	-	-	-	-	-	-	115	115	32.5
5 years old	-	-	-	-	-	-	-	-	-	-	-	36	36	11.6
6 years old	-	-	-	-	-	-	-	-	-	-	-	19	19	6.6
7 years old	-	-	-	-	-	-	-	-	-	-	-	3	3	1.0
8 years old	-	-	-	-	-	-	-	-	-	-	-	3	3	1.0
9 years old	-	-	-	-	-	-	-	-	-	-	-	-	-	-
10 years old.............	-	-	-	-	-	-	-	-	-	-	-	3	3	0.8
11 years old.............	-	-	-	-	-	-	-	-	-	-	-	4	4	1.5
12 years old.............	6	-	-	-	-	-	-	-	-	-	-	-	-	0.1
13 years old.............	15	-	-	-	-	-	-	-	-	-	-	-	-	-
14 years old.............	159	28	-	-	-	-	-	-	-	-	-	13	13	4.4
15 years old.............	88	182	22	7	-	-	4	-	-	-	-	6	6	1.8
16 years old.............	19	98	167	37	-	-	-	-	-	-	3	4	7	2.2
17 years old.............	4	25	89	186	11	-	-	-	-	-	12	19	31	9.0
18 years old.............	-	3	6	104	129	7	-	-	-	-	77	51	128	33.9
19 years old.............	-	-	2	23	50	78	9	-	-	-	101	40	141	46.6
20 years old.............	-	-	14	13	32	66	39	-	-	-	123	41	165	50.2
21 years old.............	-	1	-	3	10	29	40	31	-	-	157	51	208	64.7
22 years old.............	-	-	-	-	25	18	27	30	3	4	164	42	206	65.9
23 years old.............	-	-	-	-	23	14	16	3	5	15	219	49	268	78.1
24 years old.............	-	-	-	-	6	10	20	7	7	1	152	28	180	77.5
25 to 29 years old......	-	4	-	7	39	71	60	13	42	36	1,081	157	1,238	81.7
30 to 34 years old......	-	-	-	-	35	49	41	6	28	28	1,032	140	1,172	86.2
35 to 39 years old......	-	3	-	10	32	24	21	29	11	25	1,144	125	1,269	89.1
40 to 44 years old......	-	2	-	-	8	35	10	11	-	18	1,220	147	1,367	94.3
45 to 49 years old......	-	2	2	4	17	4	18	9	7	7	1,279	156	1,435	95.4
50 to 54 years old......	-	-	-	-	10	10	6	3	6	8	1,141	177	1,318	96.8
55 to 59 years old......	-	-	-	-	2	3	8	-	-	2	851	186	1,037	98.6
60 to 64 years old......	-	-	-	-	-	-	-	-	-	2	719	162	882	99.8
65 years and over	-	-	-	-	-	-	-	-	-	-	1,293	656	1,949	100.0
ASIAN ALONE														
Both Sexes														
Total......................	126	164	162	168	211	234	222	132	144	277	8,217	1,191	9,408	72.6
3 years old	-	-	-	-	-	-	-	-	-	-	-	79	79	50.8
4 years old	-	-	-	-	-	-	-	-	-	-	-	75	75	38.9
5 years old	-	-	-	-	-	-	-	-	-	-	-	17	17	10.5
6 years old	-	-	-	-	-	-	-	-	-	-	-	12	12	7.9
7 years old	-	-	-	-	-	-	-	-	-	-	-	2	2	1.4
8 years old	-	-	-	-	-	-	-	-	-	-	-	3	3	1.7
9 years old	-	-	-	-	-	-	-	-	-	-	-	5	5	2.9
10 years old.............	-	-	-	-	-	-	-	-	-	-	-	1	1	0.7
11 years old.............	-	-	-	-	-	-	-	-	-	-	-	-	-	-
12 years old.............	-	-	-	-	-	-	-	-	-	-	-	-	-	0.3
13 years old.............	14	2	-	-	-	-	-	-	-	-	-	1	1	0.9
14 years old.............	81	20	-	-	-	-	-	-	-	-	-	-	-	-
15 years old.............	18	105	22	5	-	-	3	-	-	-	4	-	4	2.4
16 years old.............	9	27	100	29	-	-	-	-	-	-	1	5	6	3.3
17 years old.............	-	8	28	92	22	3	-	-	-	-	3	18	21	11.9
18 years old.............	4	-	2	24	67	11	-	-	-	2	6	2	7	6.3
19 years old.............	-	2	2	15	27	50	12	-	3	-	25	5	31	21.6
20 years old.............	-	-	-	-	17	53	51	3	-	-	22	5	26	17.6
21 years old.............	-	-	-	-	8	23	50	28	6	8	27	4	31	20.1
22 years old.............	-	-	-	1	6	19	12	22	30	3	69	6	75	44.3
23 years old.............	-	-	-	-	11	10	11	21	20	5	121	9	130	62.8
24 years old.............	-	-	-	-	1	8	28	8	5	15	96	11	107	62.1
25 to 29 years old......	-	-	-	-	31	27	34	28	19	106	746	64	810	76.6
30 to 34 years old......	-	-	-	-	-	20	10	11	31	64	1,014	57	1,071	88.5
35 to 39 years old......	-	-	-	3	11	8	-	7	14	36	1,179	75	1,253	94.1
40 to 44 years old......	-	-	-	-	3	1	-	-	4	18	951	114	1,065	97.7
45 to 49 years old......	-	-	-	1	7	1	8	-	8	7	964	76	1,040	97.0
50 to 54 years old......	-	-	7	-	-	1	3	4	3	8	795	82	878	97.3
55 to 59 years old......	-	-	-	-	-	-	1	-	-	3	699	91	789	99.1
60 to 64 years old......	-	-	-	-	-	-	-	-	-	2	481	78	559	99.6
65 years and over	-	-	-	-	-	-	-	-	-	-	1,014	293	1,307	100.0

- = Quantity zero or rounds to zero.

Table A-2. Single Grade of Enrollment and High School Graduation Status for Population 3 Years Old and Over, by Sex, Age (Single Years for 3 to 24 Years), Race, and Hispanic Origin, October 2008—*Continued*

(Numbers in thousands, percent.)

Age, sex, race, and Hispanic origin	Population	Enrolled		Nursery	Kinder-garten	Enrolled								
						Elementary grades								
		Number	Percent			1	2	3	4	5	6	7	8
Male														
Total..............................	6,230	1,741	27.9	122	72	76	85	70	73	90	90	82	85
3 years old	91	43	47.2	43	-	-	-	-	-	-	-	-	-
4 years old	111	67	60.1	64	3	-	-	-	-	-	-	-	-
5 years old	91	84	92.5	11	55	18	-	-	-	-	-	-	-
6 years old	72	65	89.3	4	15	42	4	-	-	-	-	-	-
7 years old	76	74	97.1	-	-	9	60	4	-	-	-	-	-
8 years old	78	77	97.6	-	-	7	19	47	3	-	-	-	-
9 years old	92	88	95.9	-	-	-	2	15	66	5	-	-	-
10 years old........................	75	73	98.5	-	-	-	-	3	3	51	16	-	-
11 years old........................	91	91	100.0	-	-	-	-	-	-	29	53	9	-
12 years old........................	68	67	99.3	-	-	-	-	-	-	5	16	47	-
13 years old........................	109	108	98.6	-	-	-	-	-	-	-	3	23	71
14 years old........................	72	72	100.0	-	-	-	-	-	-	-	3	-	11
15 years old........................	76	76	100.0	-	-	-	-	-	-	-	-	-	-
16 years old........................	81	80	98.7	-	-	-	-	-	-	-	-	-	2
17 years old........................	96	90	93.7	-	-	-	-	-	-	-	-	-	-
18 years old........................	67	64	96.3	-	-	-	-	-	-	-	-	-	-
19 years old........................	61	50	81.1	-	-	-	-	-	-	-	-	-	-
20 years old........................	85	63	74.2	-	-	-	-	-	-	-	-	-	-
21 years old........................	81	60	74.1	-	-	-	-	-	-	-	-	-	-
22 years old........................	80	36	45.4	-	-	-	-	-	-	-	-	-	-
23 years old........................	79	27	34.7	-	-	-	-	-	-	-	-	-	-
24 years old........................	94	32	34.3	-	-	-	-	-	-	-	-	-	-
25 to 29 years old	523	132	25.2	-	-	-	-	-	-	-	-	-	-
30 to 34 years old	591	61	10.3	-	-	-	-	-	-	-	-	-	-
35 to 39 years old	651	49	7.6	-	-	-	-	-	-	-	-	-	-
40 to 44 years old	523	-	-	-	-	-	-	-	-	-	-	-	-
45 to 49 years old	501	5	1.0	-	-	-	-	-	-	-	-	-	-
50 to 54 years old	438	3	0.7	-	-	-	-	-	-	-	-	-	-
55 to 59 years old	331	4	1.3	-	-	-	-	-	-	-	-	4	-
60 to 64 years old	289	-	-	-	-	-	-	-	-	-	-	-	-
65 years and over	558	-	-	-	-	-	-	-	-	-	-	-	-
Female														
Total..............................	6,722	1,804	26.8	83	71	79	87	106	81	101	74	98	78
3 years old	65	34	52.0	30	3	-	-	-	-	-	-	-	-
4 years old	82	51	62.5	43	8	-	-	-	-	-	-	-	-
5 years old	75	64	85.8	9	49	7	-	-	-	-	-	-	-
6 years old	81	76	94.7	1	11	59	6	-	-	-	-	-	-
7 years old	86	86	100.0	-	-	10	74	2	-	-	-	-	-
8 years old	97	96	98.8	-	-	4	4	85	3	-	-	-	-
9 years old	90	89	98.4	-	-	-	3	19	60	6	-	-	-
10 years old........................	89	89	100.0	-	-	-	-	-	15	64	9	-	-
11 years old........................	81	81	100.0	-	-	-	-	-	-	28	40	12	2
12 years old........................	103	103	100.0	-	-	-	-	-	2	3	19	64	15
13 years old........................	59	59	100.0	-	-	-	-	-	-	-	3	14	37
14 years old........................	71	71	100.0	-	-	-	-	-	-	-	4	3	21
15 years old........................	80	77	95.3	-	-	-	-	-	-	-	-	-	-
16 years old........................	93	88	95.1	-	-	-	-	-	-	-	-	-	-
17 years old........................	80	66	81.4	-	-	-	-	-	-	-	-	-	3
18 years old........................	51	46	90.2	-	-	-	-	-	-	-	-	-	-
19 years old........................	80	61	76.4	-	-	-	-	-	-	-	-	-	-
20 years old........................	64	60	93.1	-	-	-	-	-	-	-	-	-	-
21 years old........................	73	63	86.3	-	-	-	-	-	-	-	-	-	-
22 years old........................	90	58	64.8	-	-	-	-	-	-	-	-	-	-
23 years old........................	128	50	38.7	-	-	-	-	-	-	-	-	-	-
24 years old........................	79	33	42.1	-	-	-	-	-	-	-	-	-	-
25 to 29 years old	534	116	21.7	-	-	-	-	-	-	-	-	3	-
30 to 34 years old	619	79	12.7	-	-	-	-	-	-	-	-	3	-
35 to 39 years old	680	29	4.2	-	-	-	-	-	-	-	-	-	-
40 to 44 years old	567	25	4.5	-	-	-	-	-	-	-	-	-	-
45 to 49 years old	571	27	4.7	-	-	-	-	-	-	-	-	-	-
50 to 54 years old	464	21	4.6	-	-	-	-	-	-	-	-	-	-
55 to 59 years old	466	3	0.7	-	-	-	-	-	-	-	-	-	-
60 to 64 years old	273	2	0.9	-	-	-	-	-	-	-	-	-	-
65 years and over	749	-	-	-	-	-	-	-	-	-	-	-	-

- = Quantity zero or rounds to zero.

Table A-2. Single Grade of Enrollment and High School Graduation Status for Population 3 Years Old and Over, by Sex, Age (Single Years for 3 to 24 Years), Race, and Hispanic Origin, October 2008—*Continued*

(Numbers in thousands, percent.)

Age, sex, race, and Hispanic origin	Enrolled										Not enrolled		Not enrolled	
	High school				Undergraduate college				Graduate school		H.S. grad	Not grad	Number	Percent
	9	10	11	12	1	2	3	4	1	2+				
Male														
Total......................	70	85	80	94	107	121	93	53	46	148	4,031	459	4,489	72.1
3 years old	-	-	-	-	-	-	-	-	-	-	-	48	48	52.8
4 years old	-	-	-	-	-	-	-	-	-	-	-	44	44	39.9
5 years old	-	-	-	-	-	-	-	-	-	-	-	7	7	7.5
6 years old	-	-	-	-	-	-	-	-	-	-	-	8	8	10.7
7 years old	-	-	-	-	-	-	-	-	-	-	-	2	2	2.9
8 years old	-	-	-	-	-	-	-	-	-	-	-	2	2	2.4
9 years old	-	-	-	-	-	-	-	-	-	-	-	4	4	4.1
10 years old.............	-	-	-	-	-	-	-	-	-	-	-	1	1	1.5
11 years old.............	-	-	-	-	-	-	-	-	-	-	-	-	-	-
12 years old.............	-	-	-	-	-	-	-	-	-	-	-	-	-	0.7
13 years old.............	8	2	-	-	-	-	-	-	-	-	-	1	1	1.4
14 years old.............	49	9	-	-	-	-	-	-	-	-	-	-	-	-
15 years old.............	5	57	9	2	-	-	3	-	-	-	-	-	-	-
16 years old.............	3	11	52	11	-	-	-	-	-	-	1	-	1	1.3
17 years old.............	-	6	16	49	17	3	-	-	-	-	-	6	6	6.3
18 years old.............	4	-	-	20	36	3	-	-	-	-	1	2	2	3.7
19 years old.............	-	-	2	12	11	17	7	-	1	-	7	5	12	18.9
20 years old.............	-	-	-	-	7	31	22	3	-	8	18	4	22	25.8
21 years old.............	-	-	-	-	8	14	18	13	-	8	21	-	21	25.9
22 years old.............	-	-	-	-	-	14	3	6	12	1	41	3	44	54.6
23 years old.............	-	-	-	-	4	3	5	6	6	5	47	4	51	65.3
24 years old.............	-	-	-	-	1	4	10	5	2	10	58	4	62	65.7
25 to 29 years old......	-	-	-	-	16	12	22	13	8	61	369	23	391	74.8
30 to 34 years old......	-	-	-	-	-	12	4	5	11	29	501	29	530	89.7
35 to 39 years old......	-	-	-	-	4	8	-	3	4	31	567	35	602	92.4
40 to 44 years old......	-	-	-	-	-	-	-	-	-	-	478	45	523	100.0
45 to 49 years old......	-	-	-	-	4	1	-	-	-	-	475	21	496	99.0
50 to 54 years old......	-	-	-	-	-	-	-	-	-	3	411	23	434	99.3
55 to 59 years old......	-	-	-	-	-	-	1	-	-	-	300	27	327	98.7
60 to 64 years old......	-	-	-	-	-	-	-	-	-	-	256	33	289	100.0
65 years and over	-	-	-	-	-	-	-	-	-	-	480	78	558	100.0
Female														
Total......................	56	79	83	74	104	113	129	79	99	129	4,186	732	4,919	73.2
3 years old	-	-	-	-	-	-	-	-	-	-	-	31	31	48.0
4 years old	-	-	-	-	-	-	-	-	-	-	-	31	31	37.5
5 years old	-	-	-	-	-	-	-	-	-	-	-	11	11	14.2
6 years old	-	-	-	-	-	-	-	-	-	-	-	4	4	5.3
7 years old	-	-	-	-	-	-	-	-	-	-	-	-	-	-
8 years old	-	-	-	-	-	-	-	-	-	-	-	1	1	1.2
9 years old	-	-	-	-	-	-	-	-	-	-	-	1	1	1.6
10 years old.............	-	-	-	-	-	-	-	-	-	-	-	-	-	-
11 years old.............	-	-	-	-	-	-	-	-	-	-	-	-	-	-
12 years old.............	-	-	-	-	-	-	-	-	-	-	-	-	-	-
13 years old.............	6	-	-	-	-	-	-	-	-	-	-	-	-	-
14 years old.............	32	11	-	-	-	-	-	-	-	-	-	-	-	-
15 years old.............	12	48	13	3	-	-	-	-	-	-	4	-	4	4.7
16 years old.............	6	16	48	18	-	-	-	-	-	-	-	5	5	4.9
17 years old.............	-	2	12	43	5	-	-	-	-	-	3	12	15	18.6
18 years old.............	-	-	2	3	30	8	-	-	-	2	5	-	5	9.8
19 years old.............	-	2	-	2	16	33	5	-	2	-	18	-	19	23.6
20 years old.............	-	-	-	-	10	21	29	-	-	-	3	1	4	6.9
21 years old.............	-	-	-	-	-	9	32	16	6	-	6	4	10	13.7
22 years old.............	-	-	-	1	6	5	10	16	18	3	29	3	32	35.2
23 years old.............	-	-	-	-	7	7	7	15	14	-	73	5	79	61.3
24 years old.............	-	-	-	-	-	4	19	3	3	5	39	7	46	57.9
25 to 29 years old......	-	-	-	-	15	16	12	16	11	45	377	41	418	78.3
30 to 34 years old......	-	-	-	-	-	8	6	6	20	35	512	28	541	87.3
35 to 39 years old......	-	-	-	3	7	1	-	4	10	5	612	39	651	95.8
40 to 44 years old......	-	-	-	-	3	1	-	-	4	18	473	69	542	95.5
45 to 49 years old......	-	-	-	1	3	-	8	-	8	7	489	55	544	95.3
50 to 54 years old......	-	-	7	-	-	1	3	4	3	4	384	59	443	95.4
55 to 59 years old......	-	-	-	-	-	-	-	-	-	3	399	64	463	99.3
60 to 64 years old......	-	-	-	-	-	-	-	-	-	2	226	45	271	99.1
65 years and over	-	-	-	-	-	-	-	-	-	-	534	215	749	100.0

- = Quantity zero or rounds to zero.

Table A-2.   Single Grade of Enrollment and High School Graduation Status for Population 3 Years Old and Over, by Sex, Age (Single Years for 3 to 24 Years), Race, and Hispanic Origin, October 2008—*Continued*

(Numbers in thousands, percent.)

Age, sex, race, and Hispanic origin	Population	Enrolled		Nursery	Kinder-garten	Enrolled							
		Number	Percent			Elementary grades							
						1	2	3	4	5	6	7	8
HISPANIC[1]													
Both Sexes													
Total...........................	43,763	13,967	31.9	844	961	914	886	892	746	877	765	836	825
3 years old	1,031	291	28.2	247	44	-	-	-	-	-	-	-	-
4 years old	1,014	601	59.2	511	90	-	-	-	-	-	-	-	-
5 years old	958	838	87.5	76	677	75	10	-	-	-	-	-	-
6 years old	913	880	96.3	10	134	658	53	25	-	-	-	-	-
7 years old	933	903	96.8	-	16	161	652	55	19	-	-	-	-
8 years old	843	821	97.4	-	-	4	153	594	48	22	-	-	-
9 years old	815	791	97.1	-	-	16	13	176	457	103	26	-	-
10 years old.....................	865	849	98.2	-	-	-	6	25	190	565	47	16	-
11 years old.....................	722	707	97.8	-	-	-	-	17	14	147	443	55	31
12 years old.....................	899	888	98.8	-	-	-	-	-	17	31	212	520	73
13 years old.....................	767	766	99.8	-	-	-	-	-	-	9	25	200	493
14 years old.....................	756	740	97.9	-	-	-	-	-	-	-	13	26	170
15 years old.....................	777	773	99.5	-	-	-	-	-	-	-	-	7	50
16 years old.....................	779	763	97.9	-	-	-	-	-	-	-	-	-	1
17 years old.....................	765	686	89.6	-	-	-	-	-	-	-	-	1	-
18 years old.....................	741	465	62.7	-	-	-	-	-	-	-	-	-	-
19 years old.....................	798	383	48.0	-	-	-	-	-	-	-	-	-	-
20 years old.....................	706	262	37.1	-	-	-	-	-	-	-	-	-	-
21 years old.....................	696	188	27.0	-	-	-	-	-	-	-	-	-	-
22 years old.....................	779	175	22.5	-	-	-	-	-	-	-	-	-	-
23 years old.....................	712	129	18.2	-	-	-	-	-	-	-	-	-	-
24 years old.....................	744	138	18.5	-	-	-	-	-	-	-	-	-	-
25 to 29 years old	4,137	381	9.2	-	-	-	-	-	-	-	-	-	-
30 to 34 years old	4,055	171	4.2	-	-	-	-	-	-	-	-	3	3
35 to 39 years old	3,730	150	4.0	-	-	-	-	-	-	-	-	4	3
40 to 44 years old	3,276	99	3.0	-	-	-	-	-	-	-	-	3	-
45 to 49 years old	2,820	60	2.1	-	-	-	-	-	-	-	-	-	-
50 to 54 years old	2,210	20	0.9	-	-	-	-	-	-	-	-	-	-
55 to 59 years old	1,692	21	1.2	-	-	-	-	-	-	-	-	-	-
60 to 64 years old	1,197	19	1.6	-	-	-	-	-	-	-	-	-	-
65 years and over	2,631	10	0.4	-	-	-	-	-	-	-	-	-	-
Male													
Total...........................	22,480	6,996	31.1	405	495	444	472	463	371	479	371	427	384
3 years old	516	137	26.5	117	20	-	-	-	-	-	-	-	-
4 years old	541	292	53.9	253	38	-	-	-	-	-	-	-	-
5 years old	495	428	86.5	31	360	29	8	-	-	-	-	-	-
6 years old	453	434	96.0	4	67	321	31	10	-	-	-	-	-
7 years old	480	463	96.5	-	9	77	336	31	10	-	-	-	-
8 years old	445	436	97.9	-	-	3	84	312	20	16	-	-	-
9 years old	398	380	95.6	-	-	14	9	93	207	51	7	-	-
10 years old.....................	495	484	97.6	-	-	-	4	6	120	324	20	10	-
11 years old.....................	325	318	97.9	-	-	-	-	10	3	66	203	23	14
12 years old.....................	447	444	99.4	-	-	-	-	-	11	19	121	255	28
13 years old.....................	401	399	99.6	-	-	-	-	-	-	4	14	119	236
14 years old.....................	386	377	97.7	-	-	-	-	-	-	-	6	14	73
15 years old.....................	402	400	99.4	-	-	-	-	-	-	-	-	3	33
16 years old.....................	389	380	97.7	-	-	-	-	-	-	-	-	-	-
17 years old.....................	408	362	88.8	-	-	-	-	-	-	-	-	-	-
18 years old.....................	371	224	60.4	-	-	-	-	-	-	-	-	-	-
19 years old.....................	408	202	49.5	-	-	-	-	-	-	-	-	-	-
20 years old.....................	362	140	38.7	-	-	-	-	-	-	-	-	-	-
21 years old.....................	368	85	23.0	-	-	-	-	-	-	-	-	-	-
22 years old.....................	414	63	15.3	-	-	-	-	-	-	-	-	-	-
23 years old.....................	379	62	16.4	-	-	-	-	-	-	-	-	-	-
24 years old.....................	373	67	18.1	-	-	-	-	-	-	-	-	-	-
25 to 29 years old	2,264	186	8.2	-	-	-	-	-	-	-	-	-	-
30 to 34 years old	2,200	90	4.1	-	-	-	-	-	-	-	-	-	-
35 to 39 years old	1,975	55	2.8	-	-	-	-	-	-	-	-	-	-
40 to 44 years old	1,716	27	1.6	-	-	-	-	-	-	-	-	3	-
45 to 49 years old	1,446	25	1.7	-	-	-	-	-	-	-	-	-	-
50 to 54 years old	1,107	2	0.2	-	-	-	-	-	-	-	-	-	-
55 to 59 years old	822	14	1.7	-	-	-	-	-	-	-	-	-	-
60 to 64 years old	569	9	1.6	-	-	-	-	-	-	-	-	-	-
65 years and over	1,128	10	0.9	-	-	-	-	-	-	-	-	-	-

[1]May be of any race.
- = Quantity zero or rounds to zero.

Table A-2. Single Grade of Enrollment and High School Graduation Status for Population 3 Years Old and Over, by Sex, Age (Single Years for 3 to 24 Years), Race, and Hispanic Origin, October 2008—*Continued*

(Numbers in thousands, percent.)

Age, sex, race, and Hispanic origin	Enrolled										Not enrolled		Not enrolled	
	High school				Undergraduate college				Graduate school		H.S. grad	Not grad	Number	Percent
	9	10	11	12	1	2	3	4	1	2+				
HISPANIC[1]														
Both Sexes														
Total......................	814	815	820	743	687	633	432	228	75	173	17,695	12,102	29,796	681
3 years old	-	-	-	-	-	-	-	-	-	-	-	740	740	71.8
4 years old	-	-	-	-	-	-	-	-	-	-	-	413	413	40.8
5 years old	-	-	-	-	-	-	-	-	-	-	-	120	120	12.5
6 years old	-	-	-	-	-	-	-	-	-	-	-	34	34	3.7
7 years old	-	-	-	-	-	-	-	-	-	-	-	30	30	3.2
8 years old	-	-	-	-	-	-	-	-	-	-	-	22	22	2.6
9 years old	-	-	-	-	-	-	-	-	-	-	-	24	24	2.9
10 years old	-	-	-	-	-	-	-	-	-	-	-	16	16	1.8
11 years old.............	-	-	-	-	-	-	-	-	-	-	-	16	16	2.2
12 years old.............	33	-	-	-	-	-	-	-	-	-	-	11	11	1.2
13 years old.............	35	4	-	-	-	-	-	-	-	-	-	2	2	0.2
14 years old.............	478	45	7	-	-	-	-	-	-	-	-	16	16	2.1
15 years old.............	197	444	66	3	2	-	4	-	-	-	-	4	4	0.5
16 years old.............	44	207	432	64	13	-	-	-	3	-	-	16	16	2.1
17 years old.............	14	71	202	365	26	-	5	-	-	-	19	60	79	10.4
18 years old.............	-	16	42	169	219	19	-	-	-	-	153	124	277	37.3
19 years old.............	4	3	32	54	127	130	34	-	-	-	242	172	414	52.0
20 years old.............	-	-	8	9	49	134	59	3	-	-	315	129	444	62.9
21 years old.............	-	3	3	20	38	36	55	33	-	-	345	163	508	73.0
22 years old.............	3	4	7	5	6	51	52	38	3	7	391	212	604	77.5
23 years old.............	-	-	-	6	13	36	36	28	3	6	427	156	583	81.8
24 years old.............	-	12	4	-	18	25	32	32	-	15	408	199	606	81.5
25 to 29 years old	-	-	7	15	80	93	61	45	33	48	2,450	1,306	3,757	90.8
30 to 34 years old......	2	3	-	19	42	22	25	12	8	32	2,511	1,372	3,883	95.8
35 to 39 years old......	4	3	1	9	14	30	33	13	10	27	2,320	1,261	3,581	96.0
40 to 44 years old......	-	-	2	3	20	23	20	9	3	16	2,026	1,152	3,177	97.0
45 to 49 years old......	-	-	-	-	8	15	3	11	11	13	1,843	917	2,760	97.9
50 to 54 years old......	-	-	-	3	-	7	6	-	-	3	1,313	877	2,190	99.1
55 to 59 years old......	-	-	3	-	7	7	-	4	-	-	991	681	1,671	98.8
60 to 64 years old......	-	-	-	-	3	3	7	-	-	7	708	469	1,178	98.4
65 years and over	-	-	4	-	4	1	-	-	-	-	1,233	1,388	2,621	99.6
Male														
Total......................	420	442	392	388	339	265	228	99	32	79	9,058	6,427	15,485	68.9
3 years old	-	-	-	-	-	-	-	-	-	-	-	379	379	73.5
4 years old	-	-	-	-	-	-	-	-	-	-	-	249	249	46.1
5 years old	-	-	-	-	-	-	-	-	-	-	-	67	67	13.5
6 years old	-	-	-	-	-	-	-	-	-	-	-	18	18	4.0
7 years old	-	-	-	-	-	-	-	-	-	-	-	17	17	3.5
8 years old	-	-	-	-	-	-	-	-	-	-	-	9	9	2.1
9 years old	-	-	-	-	-	-	-	-	-	-	-	18	18	4.4
10 years old.............	-	-	-	-	-	-	-	-	-	-	-	12	12	2.4
11 years old.............	-	-	-	-	-	-	-	-	-	-	-	7	7	2.1
12 years old.............	11	-	-	-	-	-	-	-	-	-	-	3	3	0.6
13 years old.............	22	4	-	-	-	-	-	-	-	-	-	1	1	0.4
14 years old.............	244	33	7	-	-	-	-	-	-	-	-	9	9	2.3
15 years old.............	101	234	24	3	2	-	-	-	-	-	-	2	2	0.6
16 years old.............	26	116	201	26	7	-	-	-	3	-	-	9	9	2.3
17 years old.............	11	36	108	187	17	-	2	-	-	-	13	33	46	11.2
18 years old.............	-	8	22	97	92	5	-	-	-	-	83	64	147	39.6
19 years old.............	-	3	15	44	61	56	22	-	-	-	129	77	206	50.5
20 years old.............	-	-	3	9	35	62	30	-	-	-	159	63	222	61.3
21 years old.............	-	-	-	3	20	13	30	19	-	-	188	96	283	77.0
22 years old.............	3	4	3	1	1	14	28	11	-	-	215	136	351	84.7
23 years old.............	-	-	-	6	8	13	27	4	2	3	217	100	317	83.6
24 years old.............	-	4	4	-	7	12	13	20	-	8	192	114	305	81.9
25 to 29 years old	-	-	-	-	49	47	37	22	16	16	1,280	798	2,078	91.8
30 to 34 years old......	2	-	-	11	23	14	20	-	-	19	1,313	797	2,110	95.9
35 to 39 years old......	-	-	-	-	4	11	10	10	-	21	1,198	721	1,919	97.2
40 to 44 years old......	-	-	-	-	-	8	3	3	3	6	1,129	560	1,689	98.4
45 to 49 years old......	-	-	-	-	-	-	3	7	9	6	906	515	1,421	98.3
50 to 54 years old......	-	-	-	-	-	2	-	-	-	-	661	444	1,106	99.8
55 to 59 years old......	-	-	-	-	7	4	-	4	-	-	468	340	808	98.3
60 to 64 years old......	-	-	-	-	3	3	3	-	-	-	345	215	560	98.4
65 years and over	-	-	4	-	4	1	-	-	-	-	562	556	1,118	99.1

[1]May be of any race.
- = Quantity zero or rounds to zero.

Table A-2. Single Grade of Enrollment and High School Graduation Status for Population 3 Years Old and Over, by Sex, Age (Single Years for 3 to 24 Years), Race, and Hispanic Origin, October 2008—*Continued*

(Numbers in thousands, percent.)

Age, sex, race, and Hispanic origin	Population	Enrolled		Nursery	Kinder-garten	Enrolled								
						Elementary grades								
		Number	Percent			1	2	3	4	5	6	7	8
Female													
Total..............................	21,282	6,971	32.8	440	466	470	414	429	375	398	394	409	441
3 years old	515	154	29.9	131	24	-	-	-	-	-	-	-	-
4 years old	474	309	65.3	258	51	-	-	-	-	-	-	-	-
5 years old	463	410	88.5	45	317	46	2	-	-	-	-	-	-
6 years old	461	445	96.7	6	67	336	21	15	-	-	-	-	-
7 years old	454	440	97.0	-	7	85	316	24	9	-	-	-	-
8 years old	398	385	96.7	-	-	1	68	282	28	6	-	-	-
9 years old	417	411	98.5	-	-	3	4	84	250	52	19	-	-
10 years old.......................	369	365	98.9	-	-	-	2	18	71	241	27	6	-
11 years old.......................	397	388	97.8	-	-	-	-	7	12	82	240	32	16
12 years old.......................	452	444	98.2	-	-	-	-	-	7	12	92	266	45
13 years old.......................	367	366	99.9	-	-	-	-	-	-	5	11	80	257
14 years old.......................	370	363	98.0	-	-	-	-	-	-	-	6	12	97
15 years old.......................	375	374	99.6	-	-	-	-	-	-	-	-	4	17
16 years old.......................	390	383	98.1	-	-	-	-	-	-	-	-	-	1
17 years old.......................	357	323	90.5	-	-	-	-	-	-	-	-	1	-
18 years old.......................	370	241	65.0	-	-	-	-	-	-	-	-	-	-
19 years old.......................	390	181	46.5	-	-	-	-	-	-	-	-	-	-
20 years old.......................	344	122	35.4	-	-	-	-	-	-	-	-	-	-
21 years old.......................	327	103	31.5	-	-	-	-	-	-	-	-	-	-
22 years old.......................	365	112	30.7	-	-	-	-	-	-	-	-	-	-
23 years old.......................	333	67	20.2	-	-	-	-	-	-	-	-	-	-
24 years old.......................	372	71	19.0	-	-	-	-	-	-	-	-	-	-
25 to 29 years old	1,873	195	10.4	-	-	-	-	-	-	-	-	-	-
30 to 34 years old	1,855	82	4.4	-	-	-	-	-	-	-	-	3	3
35 to 39 years old	1,756	95	5.4	-	-	-	-	-	-	-	-	4	3
40 to 44 years old	1,560	72	4.6	-	-	-	-	-	-	-	-	-	-
45 to 49 years old	1,375	35	2.5	-	-	-	-	-	-	-	-	-	-
50 to 54 years old	1,102	18	1.6	-	-	-	-	-	-	-	-	-	-
55 to 59 years old	870	6	0.7	-	-	-	-	-	-	-	-	-	-
60 to 64 years old	628	10	1.6	-	-	-	-	-	-	-	-	-	-
65 years and over	1,503	-	-	-	-	-	-	-	-	-	-	-	-

- = Quantity zero or rounds to zero.

Table A-2. Single Grade of Enrollment and High School Graduation Status for Population 3 Years Old and Over, by Sex, Age (Single Years for 3 to 24 Years), Race, and Hispanic Origin, October 2008—_Continued_

(Numbers in thousands, percent.)

Age, sex, race, and Hispanic origin	Enrolled										Not enrolled		Not enrolled	
	High school				Undergraduate college				Graduate school		H.S. grad	Not grad		
	9	10	11	12	1	2	3	4	1	2+			Number	Percent
Female														
Total......................	394	372	428	355	348	368	204	129	43	94	8,636	5,675	14,311	67.2
3 years old	-	-	-	-	-	-	-	-	-	-	-	361	361	70.1
4 years old	-	-	-	-	-	-	-	-	-	-	-	164	164	34.7
5 years old	-	-	-	-	-	-	-	-	-	-	-	53	53	11.5
6 years old	-	-	-	-	-	-	-	-	-	-	-	15	15	3.3
7 years old	-	-	-	-	-	-	-	-	-	-	-	14	14	3.0
8 years old	-	-	-	-	-	-	-	-	-	-	-	13	13	3.3
9 years old	-	-	-	-	-	-	-	-	-	-	-	6	6	1.5
10 years old.............	-	-	-	-	-	-	-	-	-	-	-	4	4	1.1
11 years old.............	-	-	-	-	-	-	-	-	-	-	-	9	9	2.2
12 years old.............	23	-	-	-	-	-	-	-	-	-	-	8	8	1.8
13 years old.............	12	-	-	-	-	-	-	-	-	-	-	-	-	0.1
14 years old.............	235	12	-	-	-	-	-	-	-	-	-	7	7	2.0
15 years old.............	96	210	42	-	-	-	4	-	-	-	-	2	2	0.4
16 years old.............	18	90	230	37	6	-	-	-	-	-	-	7	7	1.9
17 years old.............	3	35	94	178	10	-	3	-	-	-	6	28	34	9.5
18 years old.............	-	8	20	72	127	14	-	-	-	-	69	60	130	35.0
19 years old.............	4	-	16	10	66	74	12	-	-	-	113	95	209	53.5
20 years old.............	-	-	4	-	14	72	29	3	-	-	156	66	223	64.6
21 years old.............	-	3	3	17	18	22	25	14	-	-	157	67	224	68.5
22 years old.............	-	-	4	4	5	38	24	28	3	7	176	77	253	69.3
23 years old.............	-	-	-	-	5	23	9	25	2	3	209	56	265	79.8
24 years old.............	-	8	-	-	11	13	19	12	-	7	216	85	301	81.0
25 to 29 years old	-	-	7	15	31	45	24	23	17	32	1,170	509	1,679	89.6
30 to 34 years old	-	3	-	8	19	8	5	12	8	12	1,198	575	1,773	95.6
35 to 39 years old	4	3	1	9	10	19	23	3	10	6	1,121	540	1,661	94.6
40 to 44 years old	-	-	2	3	20	15	16	6	-	10	896	591	1,488	95.4
45 to 49 years old	-	-	-	-	8	15	-	4	2	7	938	402	1,340	97.5
50 to 54 years old	-	-	-	3	-	6	6	-	-	3	652	433	1,084	98.4
55 to 59 years old	-	-	3	-	-	4	-	-	-	-	522	341	864	99.3
60 to 64 years old	-	-	-	-	-	-	3	-	-	7	363	255	618	98.4
65 years and over	-	-	-	-	-	-	-	-	-	-	672	831	1,503	100.0

- = Quantity zero or rounds to zero.

Table A-3. Nursery and Primary School Enrollment of Population 3 to 6 Years Old, by Control of School, Attendance Status, Age, Race, Hispanic Origin, Mother's Labor Force Status and Education, and Family Income, October 2008

(Numbers in thousands.)

| Characteristic | Total | Not enrolled | Enrolled in nursery school | | | | | | | | |
| | | | Total | | | Public | | | Private | | |
			Total	Part-day	Full-day	Total	Part-day	Full-day	Total	Part-day	Full-day
3 to 6 Years Old											
Total	16,607	4,497	4,614	2,400	2,214	2,632	1,393	1,239	1,982	1,007	975
Race											
White alone	12,645	3,434	3,479	1,954	1,525	1,830	1,036	794	1,649	917	731
White alone non-Hispanic	8,985	2,195	2,710	1,520	1,190	1,213	673	540	1,497	847	650
Black alone	2,506	682	706	225	481	548	200	347	158	25	134
Asian alone	667	184	205	103	102	110	72	38	95	32	64
Hispanic[1]	3,916	1,307	844	472	372	668	395	273	177	77	99
Labor force status of mother											
Children not living with mother	1,252	435	275	113	162	205	96	109	70	17	53
Mother employed part-time	2,423	500	809	496	313	396	222	174	413	274	139
Mother employed full-time	6,553	1,546	1,958	784	1,174	1,102	536	566	856	248	608
Mother unemployed	828	256	196	106	90	140	60	80	56	45	10
Mother not in the labor force	5,552	1,761	1,377	901	476	790	479	311	588	422	165
Education of mother											
Children not living with mother	1,252	435	275	113	162	205	96	109	70	17	53
Elementary: 0 to 8 years	758	315	124	85	39	114	79	35	9	6	3
High School: 9 to 11 years	1,466	552	341	177	164	307	163	144	34	14	20
High school graduate	4,009	1,174	978	454	524	705	344	361	273	110	163
Some college or associate's degree	4,427	1,129	1,255	657	598	736	386	350	519	271	248
Bachelor's degree or more	4,695	892	1,642	915	728	564	325	240	1,078	590	488
Family income											
Less than $20,000	2,655	810	700	324	376	603	287	316	98	37	61
$20,000 to $29,999	1,593	482	360	201	159	292	170	122	67	31	37
$30,000 to $39,999	1,687	580	399	193	207	309	149	159	91	43	47
$40,000 to $49,999	1,181	372	297	169	129	219	130	90	78	39	39
$50,000 to $74,999	2,606	720	692	369	323	343	204	139	348	164	184
$75,000 and over	4,260	706	1,465	805	661	458	239	219	1,007	565	442
Not reported	2,625	827	701	341	360	407	213	194	293	127	166
3 and 4 Years Old											
Total	8,445	3,987	4,079	2,117	1,961	2,281	1,195	1,086	1,798	922	876
Race											
White alone	6,376	3,058	3,073	1,719	1,354	1,584	881	703	1,488	838	650
White alone non-Hispanic	4,469	1,965	2,385	1,345	1,040	1,038	575	463	1,347	770	577
Black alone	1,324	601	614	193	422	470	168	302	144	25	120
Asian alone	349	154	180	96	84	90	66	24	90	30	60
Hispanic[1]	2,045	1,154	758	407	351	593	333	260	166	74	91
Labor force status of mother											
Children not living with mother	676	389	259	101	157	192	87	105	67	14	53
Mother employed part-time	1,248	468	733	464	269	348	204	145	385	260	125
Mother employed full-time	3,217	1,365	1,721	682	1,038	942	448	494	779	235	544
Mother unemployed	413	226	169	88	80	123	53	70	45	35	10
Mother not in the labor force	2,891	1,539	1,197	781	416	675	403	272	522	378	144
Education of mother											
Children not living with mother	676	389	259	101	157	192	87	105	67	14	53
Elementary: 0 to 8 years	400	256	114	76	37	106	71	35	8	6	2
High School: 9 to 11 years	848	502	300	155	145	268	143	125	32	12	20
High school graduate	1,984	1,030	851	393	458	615	301	314	236	92	144
Some college or associate's degree	2,178	1,017	1,089	564	526	624	312	312	465	252	213
Bachelor's degree or more	2,360	794	1,467	828	639	477	282	195	990	546	444
Family income											
Less than $20,000	1,429	727	623	290	333	539	256	283	84	33	50
$20,000 to $29,999	801	431	310	169	141	256	144	113	54	25	28
$30,000 to $39,999	933	537	356	173	182	272	135	137	84	39	45
$40,000 to $49,999	622	335	256	138	118	186	104	83	70	34	36
$50,000 to $74,999	1,279	645	592	308	284	274	157	117	318	151	168
$75,000 and over	2,018	621	1,333	738	595	399	205	194	934	533	401
Not reported	1,363	691	608	301	307	354	194	160	255	107	147

[1]May be of any race.
- = Quantity zero or rounds to zero.

Table A-3. Nursery and Primary School Enrollment of Population 3 to 6 Years Old, by Control of School, Attendance Status, Age, Race, Hispanic Origin, Mother's Labor Force Status and Education, and Family Income, October 2008—*Continued*

(Numbers in thousands.)

Characteristic	Enrolled in kindergarten									Enrolled in elementary school		
	Total			Public			Private			Total	Public	Private
	Total	Part-day	Full-day	Total	Part-day	Full-day	Total	Part-day	Full-day			
3 to 6 Years Old												
Total	4,004	1,127	2,876	3,544	998	2,547	460	130	330	3,491	3,164	328
Race												
White alone	3,089	928	2,161	2,719	814	1,905	370	114	256	2,643	2,385	258
White alone non-Hispanic	2,191	649	1,542	1,871	545	1,326	320	104	216	1,890	1,646	244
Black alone	592	115	477	542	108	434	50	7	43	525	480	46
Asian alone	144	52	92	119	43	76	24	9	15	134	116	19
Hispanic[1]	945	293	652	894	283	611	51	10	41	820	803	17
Labor force status of mother												
Children not living with mother	276	75	202	260	72	188	16	3	13	265	245	21
Mother employed part-time	616	199	417	544	178	365	72	21	51	499	443	56
Mother employed full-time	1,561	393	1,168	1,360	357	1,003	200	35	165	1,489	1,322	166
Mother unemployed	213	40	173	212	40	172	1	-	1	163	154	9
Mother not in the labor force	1,338	421	917	1,168	351	818	170	71	99	1,075	1,000	75
Education of mother												
Children not living with mother	276	75	202	260	72	188	16	3	13	265	245	21
Elementary: 0 to 8 years	157	51	106	156	51	104	1	-	1	162	155	7
High School: 9 to 11 years	295	64	231	285	64	221	10	-	10	278	270	8
High school graduate	990	261	729	920	235	685	70	26	44	867	801	67
Some college or associate's degree	1,073	287	786	963	244	719	110	43	67	971	901	69
Bachelor's degree or more	1,212	390	823	960	331	629	252	58	194	949	793	155
Family income												
Less than $20,000	587	142	445	573	140	432	14	2	12	558	533	25
$20,000 to $29,999	398	88	310	389	88	301	9	-	9	353	332	21
$30,000 to $39,999	360	120	240	338	113	224	22	6	15	348	332	15
$40,000 to $49,999	289	67	222	253	55	198	36	12	24	222	204	18
$50,000 to $74,999	643	191	452	566	169	397	77	22	55	551	513	38
$75,000 and over	1,126	329	796	888	261	627	237	68	170	964	801	163
Not reported	601	191	411	538	171	367	64	20	44	496	448	48
3 and 4 Years Old												
Total	380	158	222	324	132	192	56	26	30	-	-	-
Race												
White alone	245	125	120	208	101	106	38	24	14	-	-	-
White alone non-Hispanic	119	38	81	89	22	66	30	16	14	-	-	-
Black alone	109	25	84	95	25	70	14	-	14	-	-	-
Asian alone	14	7	8	12	5	8	2	2	-	-	-	-
Hispanic[1]	133	89	44	124	82	43	9	8	1	-	-	-
Labor force status of mother												
Children not living with mother	28	13	15	25	13	12	3	-	3	-	-	-
Mother employed part-time	47	23	24	42	18	24	5	5	-	-	-	-
Mother employed full-time	131	40	91	101	29	72	30	11	19	-	-	-
Mother unemployed	19	4	15	18	4	14	1	-	1	-	-	-
Mother not in the labor force	155	78	77	138	68	70	17	10	7	-	-	-
Education of mother												
Children not living with mother	28	13	15	25	13	12	3	-	3	-	-	-
Elementary: 0 to 8 years	30	22	7	30	22	7	-	-	-	-	-	-
High School: 9 to 11 years	47	16	31	47	16	31	-	-	-	-	-	-
High school graduate	103	36	67	99	32	67	4	4	1	-	-	-
Some college or associate's degree	72	23	50	58	13	45	14	10	4	-	-	-
Bachelor's degree or more	100	48	52	65	36	30	34	12	22	-	-	-
Family income												
Less than $20,000	80	25	54	78	25	52	2	-	2	-	-	-
$20,000 to $29,999	60	30	30	59	30	29	1	-	1	-	-	-
$30,000 to $39,999	40	24	16	37	24	13	3	1	2	-	-	-
$40,000 to $49,999	31	12	19	25	7	17	6	4	2	-	-	-
$50,000 to $74,999	42	19	24	35	12	24	7	7	-	-	-	-
$75,000 and over	64	19	45	34	9	25	30	11	19	-	-	-
Not reported	64	29	35	56	25	31	8	3	4	-	-	-

[1] May be of any race.
- = Quantity zero or rounds to zero.

Table A-3. Nursery and Primary School Enrollment of Population 3 to 6 Years Old, by Control of School, Attendance Status, Age, Race, Hispanic Origin, Mother's Labor Force Status and Education, and Family Income, October 2008—*Continued*

(Numbers in thousands.)

| Characteristic | Total | Not enrolled | Enrolled in nursery school | | | | | | | | |
| | | | Total | | | Public | | | Private | | |
			Total	Part-day	Full-day	Total	Part-day	Full-day	Total	Part-day	Full-day
5 Years Old											
Total	4,137	373	492	266	226	329	190	139	163	76	87
Race											
White alone	3,173	279	379	221	158	229	147	82	149	74	76
White alone non-Hispanic	2,273	167	307	166	141	165	95	69	143	71	72
Black alone	614	55	84	33	51	73	33	40	11	-	11
Asian alone	166	17	20	7	13	19	6	13	1	1	-
Hispanic[1]	958	120	76	59	17	69	56	13	7	3	4
Labor force status of mother											
Children not living with mother	294	35	16	12	4	13	9	4	3	2	-
Mother employed part-time	596	21	65	29	37	39	15	24	27	14	13
Mother employed full-time	1,622	125	216	97	118	153	87	66	63	10	53
Mother unemployed	220	24	27	17	10	17	7	10	10	10	-
Mother not in the labor force	1,405	168	168	111	57	108	72	36	60	39	21
Education of mother											
Children not living with mother	294	35	16	12	4	13	9	4	3	2	-
Elementary: 0 to 8 years	158	47	9	8	-	9	8	-	-	-	-
High School: 9 to 11 years	321	39	40	22	19	39	20	19	1	1	-
High school graduate	1,025	113	113	53	60	76	35	41	37	18	19
Some college or associate's degree	1,138	65	153	91	63	106	75	32	47	16	31
Bachelor's degree or more	1,203	74	161	80	80	86	42	44	75	38	36
Family income											
Less than $20,000	576	59	69	31	38	57	28	29	13	4	9
$20,000 to $29,999	414	38	43	29	14	33	23	9	10	5	5
$30,000 to $39,999	390	32	36	19	17	29	15	14	7	4	2
$40,000 to $49,999	314	30	41	31	10	33	26	7	8	5	3
$50,000 to $74,999	661	58	94	61	33	66	47	20	27	14	14
$75,000 and over	1,114	65	120	59	61	57	32	25	63	27	36
Not reported	667	92	88	36	52	54	19	35	35	17	17
6 Years Old											
Total	4,024	137	44	17	27	23	8	14	21	9	13
Race											
White alone	3,096	97	28	14	14	17	8	8	11	6	5
White alone non-Hispanic	2,244	63	17	8	9	10	2	8	7	6	1
Black alone	568	27	8	-	8	5	-	5	3	-	3
Asian alone	153	12	5	-	5	1	-	1	4	-	4
Hispanic[1]	913	34	10	6	4	6	6	-	4	-	4
Labor force status of mother											
Children not living with mother	283	11	-	-	-	-	-	-	-	-	-
Mother employed part-time	578	11	10	3	7	9	3	6	1	-	1
Mother employed full-time	1,713	56	21	4	17	7	1	6	14	3	11
Mother unemployed	194	6	-	-	-	-	-	-	-	-	-
Mother not in the labor force	1,256	54	13	10	3	7	4	3	6	6	-
Education of mother											
Children not living with mother	283	11	-	-	-	-	-	-	-	-	-
Elementary: 0 to 8 years	201	12	1	-	1	-	-	-	1	-	1
High School: 9 to 11 years	296	11	1	-	1	1	-	1	-	-	-
High school graduate	1,000	30	14	7	7	14	7	7	-	-	-
Some college or associate's degree	1,112	48	12	3	9	6	-	6	6	3	3
Bachelor's degree or more	1,132	24	15	7	8	1	1	-	14	6	8
Family income											
Less than $20,000	650	24	8	3	5	7	3	4	1	-	1
$20,000 to $29,999	377	13	6	3	3	3	3	-	3	-	3
$30,000 to $39,999	364	11	8	-	8	8	-	8	-	-	-
$40,000 to $49,999	246	7	-	-	-	-	-	-	-	-	-
$50,000 to $74,999	666	18	5	-	5	3	-	3	3	-	3
$75,000 and over	1,128	19	12	8	4	2	2	-	10	6	4
Not reported	594	43	4	3	1	-	-	-	4	3	1

[1]May be of any race.
- = Quantity zero or rounds to zero.

Table A-3. Nursery and Primary School Enrollment of Population 3 to 6 Years Old, by Control of School, Attendance Status, Age, Race, Hispanic Origin, Mother's Labor Force Status and Education, and Family Income, October 2008—*Continued*

(Numbers in thousands.)

Characteristic	Enrolled in kindergarten									Enrolled in elementary school		
	Total			Public			Private			Total	Public	Private
	Total	Part-day	Full-day	Total	Part-day	Full-day	Total	Part-day	Full-day			
5 Years Old												
Total	2,978	772	2,206	2,659	697	1,962	320	76	244	294	273	22
Race												
White alone	2,314	637	1,677	2,055	570	1,485	259	66	193	202	186	16
White alone non-Hispanic	1,670	475	1,195	1,445	411	1,033	225	64	161	128	115	14
Black alone	425	77	348	389	71	318	36	7	29	51	46	5
Asian alone	104	33	70	92	31	61	12	2	9	25	24	-
Hispanic[1]	677	167	510	644	165	479	34	2	32	85	83	2
Labor force status of mother												
Children not living with mother	214	50	164	207	49	158	7	-	6	28	24	4
Mother employed part-time	471	142	329	426	134	291	46	8	37	39	39	-
Mother employed full-time	1,165	278	887	1,021	262	759	144	16	128	117	104	14
Mother unemployed	161	33	128	161	33	128	-	-	-	8	8	-
Mother not in the labor force	967	269	699	844	218	626	123	51	72	102	98	4
Education of mother												
Children not living with mother	214	50	164	207	49	158	7	-	6	28	24	4
Elementary: 0 to 8 years	95	21	74	93	21	73	1	-	1	7	7	-
High School: 9 to 11 years	202	39	163	192	39	154	10	-	10	40	40	-
High school graduate	723	171	552	680	155	525	42	16	27	76	76	-
Some college or associate's degree	839	220	619	760	194	566	79	26	54	80	73	8
Bachelor's degree or more	906	272	634	725	238	487	180	34	147	62	52	10
Family income												
Less than $20,000	394	83	311	382	81	300	12	2	10	54	54	-
$20,000 to $29,999	302	53	249	294	53	240	8	-	8	31	31	-
$30,000 to $39,999	272	82	191	256	79	177	16	3	13	50	50	-
$40,000 to $49,999	220	50	170	196	42	154	24	8	16	23	21	2
$50,000 to $74,999	481	133	348	427	123	304	54	11	44	29	29	-
$75,000 and over	860	237	623	691	194	498	169	44	125	69	58	11
Not reported	449	134	315	413	125	288	35	8	27	38	30	8
6 Years Old												
Total	646	198	448	562	169	393	84	29	56	3,197	2,891	306
Race												
White alone	530	167	363	457	143	314	73	24	49	2,441	2,199	243
White alone non-Hispanic	402	135	267	337	111	226	64	24	40	1,761	1,531	230
Black alone	59	13	46	59	13	46	-	-	-	475	434	40
Asian alone	26	12	14	15	7	7	11	4	6	110	92	18
Hispanic[1]	134	36	98	126	36	89	8	-	8	735	720	15
Labor force status of mother												
Children not living with mother	34	12	23	28	9	19	6	2	4	237	220	17
Mother employed part-time	98	34	64	76	26	50	22	8	14	460	404	56
Mother employed full-time	265	74	191	238	66	172	27	9	18	1,371	1,218	153
Mother unemployed	33	3	30	33	3	30	-	-	-	155	147	9
Mother not in the labor force	216	75	141	186	65	121	29	10	20	973	902	71
Education of mother												
Children not living with mother	34	12	23	28	9	19	6	2	4	237	220	17
Elementary: 0 to 8 years	32	8	24	32	8	24	-	-	-	155	147	7
High School: 9 to 11 years	46	10	36	46	10	36	-	-	-	238	230	8
High school graduate	164	54	111	141	47	94	23	6	17	791	725	67
Some college or associate's degree	162	45	117	145	37	108	17	8	9	890	828	62
Bachelor's degree or more	207	69	137	169	58	112	37	12	25	886	741	145
Family income												
Less than $20,000	114	34	80	114	34	80	-	-	-	504	479	25
$20,000 to $29,999	36	5	31	36	5	31	-	-	-	322	301	21
$30,000 to $39,999	47	13	34	44	11	34	3	3	-	297	282	15
$40,000 to $49,999	39	6	33	33	6	27	6	-	6	200	184	16
$50,000 to $74,999	120	39	81	104	35	69	16	4	12	522	484	38
$75,000 and over	201	72	129	163	59	104	38	13	25	895	743	152
Not reported	89	28	61	68	20	48	21	8	13	458	418	40

[1] May be of any race.

- = Quantity zero or rounds to zero.

Table A-4. Current Grade for People 15 to 24 Years Old Enrolled in School, and Highest Grade Completed for People with Selected Enrollment and Completion Status, by Sex, Age, Race and Hispanic Origin, October 2008

(Numbers in thousands.)

Age, sex, race, and Hispanic origin	Enrolled							Not enrolled						Not enrolled last year
	Current grade							Enrolled last year						
								Highest grade completed						
	Less than 9th grade	9th grade	10th grade	11th grade	12th grade	College (graduated this year)	Other college	Less than 9th grade	9th grade	10th grade	11th or 12th, no diploma	New HS graduate	Other	
ALL RACES														
Both Sexes														
Total	242	1,306	3,946	4,127	4,106	2,170	9,537	24	56	96	237	989	2,214	12,644
15 years old	159	1,058	2,565	229	39	9	27	3	3	7	-	-	-	27
16 years old	51	177	1,067	2,554	268	22	11	10	16	41	7	15	1	29
17 years old	16	47	219	1,097	2,500	125	47	1	16	29	73	47	13	119
18 years old	-	11	53	141	996	1,489	461	3	12	4	90	522	75	475
19 years old	4	4	23	52	197	408	1,767	4	2	11	27	241	284	1,135
20 to 24 years old	12	8	19	53	107	117	7,223	3	7	3	41	164	1,842	10,859
Male														
Total	160	740	2,010	2,087	2,066	1,087	4,429	23	25	60	89	560	987	6,738
15 years old	99	572	1,274	106	20	6	17	3	3	-	-	-	-	11
16 years old	41	115	566	1,236	124	14	4	9	8	19	5	7	1	18
17 years old	5	37	117	611	1,205	64	27	1	6	26	33	30	6	54
18 years old	-	11	37	86	529	706	189	3	7	4	25	294	31	264
19 years old	4	-	10	25	132	224	789	4	1	8	13	148	136	607
20 to 24 years old	10	4	8	22	56	72	3,402	3	-	3	13	80	813	5,785
Female														
Total	82	566	1,935	2,040	2,041	1,084	5,108	1	31	36	149	430	1,227	5,906
15 years old	60	486	1,291	122	19	2	10	-	-	7	-	-	-	17
16 years old	10	62	501	1,318	144	8	7	1	8	23	2	8	-	11
17 years old	11	10	101	486	1,294	61	20	-	10	3	40	17	7	65
18 years old	-	-	16	54	467	783	272	-	5	-	65	227	44	210
19 years old	-	4	13	27	65	184	977	-	2	3	14	93	147	528
20 to 24 years old	2	4	12	32	51	45	3,822	-	7	-	28	84	1,029	5,074
WHITE ALONE														
Total	169	950	3,026	3,171	3,045	1,794	7,518	20	31	79	137	736	1,755	9,759
15 years old	110	789	2,015	152	21	9	20	3	3	7	-	-	-	16
16 years old	32	109	795	2,004	177	20	11	6	12	34	2	8	1	29
17 years old	11	32	148	845	1,916	81	30	1	6	22	41	39	6	93
18 years old	-	7	31	101	740	1,268	346	3	4	4	56	382	40	368
19 years old	4	4	19	34	127	331	1,408	4	2	9	14	185	200	897
20 to 24 years old	12	8	19	35	64	85	5,703	3	4	2	23	122	1,508	8,355
WHITE ALONE NON-HISPANIC														
Total	112	713	2,316	2,449	2,429	1,508	6,507	8	22	57	77	592	1,513	7,070
15 years old	56	604	1,601	89	17	9	16	3	3	5	-	-	-	14
16 years old	31	78	606	1,616	124	11	5	2	12	30	1	8	1	23
17 years old	9	18	79	661	1,590	64	17	-	3	14	12	28	4	71
18 years old	-	7	15	62	590	1,091	297	3	-	2	42	309	31	232
19 years old	4	-	16	8	78	273	1,189	-	1	6	7	140	149	633
20 to 24 years old	12	5	-	13	31	60	4,984	-	4	-	15	106	1,328	6,097
BLACK ALONE														
Total	61	265	612	598	701	235	1,150	3	22	7	84	193	286	2,039
15 years old	45	202	336	41	10	-	4	-	-	-	-	-	-	6
16 years old	14	48	196	322	54	2	-	3	4	-	4	5	-	-
17 years old	2	14	61	171	358	20	11	-	10	7	18	4	7	15
18 years old	-	-	19	30	195	141	74	-	8	-	32	103	32	81
19 years old	-	-	-	16	51	47	217	-	-	-	13	48	64	164
20 to 24 years old	-	-	1	19	34	25	845	-	-	-	17	32	183	1,774

- = Quantity zero or rounds to zero.

Table A-4. Current Grade for People 15 to 24 Years Old Enrolled in School, and Highest Grade Completed for People with Selected Enrollment and Completion Status, by Sex, Age, Race and Hispanic Origin, October 2008—*Continued*

(Numbers in thousands.)

Age, sex, race, and Hispanic origin	Enrolled							Not enrolled						Not enrolled last year
	Current grade							Enrolled last year						
								Highest grade completed						
	Less than 9th grade	9th grade	10th grade	11th grade	12th grade	College (graduated this year)	Other college	Less than 9th grade	9th grade	10th grade	11th or 12th, no diploma	New HS graduate	Other	
ASIAN ALONE														
Total......................	6	31	142	155	165	84	598	-	-	5	12	11	101	309
15 years old..............	-	18	105	22	5	-	3	-	-	-	-	-	-	4
16 years old..............	2	9	27	100	29	-	-	-	-	5	-	1	-	-
17 years old..............	3	-	8	28	92	20	4	-	-	-	12	3	-	6
18 years old..............	-	4	-	2	24	46	35	-	-	-	-	2	3	1
19 years old..............	-	-	2	2	15	19	73	-	-	-	-	1	5	24
20 to 24 years old.......	-	-	-	-	1	-	483	-	-	-	-	3	93	274
HISPANIC[1]														
Total......................	60	262	760	795	695	292	1,099	12	16	22	63	165	291	2,966
15 years old..............	57	197	444	66	3	-	5	-	-	2	-	-	-	2
16 years old..............	1	44	207	432	64	9	7	5	-	4	2	-	-	6
17 years old..............	1	14	71	202	365	17	15	1	3	8	29	11	5	22
18 years old..............	-	-	16	42	169	183	55	-	8	3	15	88	12	151
19 years old..............	-	4	3	32	54	58	232	4	2	3	6	50	55	294
20 to 24 years old.......	-	3	19	22	40	26	784	3	3	2	11	16	219	2,491

[1]May be of any race.
- = Quantity zero or rounds to zero.

Table A-5.   Type of College and Year Enrolled for College Students 15 Years Old and Over, by Age, Sex, Race, Attendance Status, Control of School, and Enrollment Status, October 2008

(Numbers in thousands.)

Characteristic	Total enrolled	Undergraduate college								Graduate school	
		All colleges				Two-year college		Four-year college			
		1st year	2nd year	3rd year	4th year	1st year	2nd or higher	1st year	2nd or higher	1st year	2nd or higher
BOTH SEXES											
Full-Time Students											
Total	13,245	3,485	3,242	2,658	1,994	1,498	1,899	1,987	5,994	697	1,170
Age											
15–19 years old	4,020	2,514	1,304	176	6	971	479	1,542	1,007	15	6
20–24 years old	6,161	600	1,383	1,908	1,571	283	934	317	3,928	340	359
25–34 years old	2,091	255	340	369	276	170	296	85	689	252	599
35 years old and over	972	116	214	205	140	74	189	42	370	90	206
Race											
White alone....................	10,256	2,709	2,454	2,082	1,653	1,176	1,483	1,533	4,706	516	843
White alone non-Hispanic ...	8,925	2,310	2,038	1,813	1,509	953	1,167	1,356	4,192	480	776
Black alone	1,690	522	467	336	172	225	272	297	703	85	109
Asian alone....................	917	167	189	178	118	62	85	105	400	76	188
Hispanic[1]	1,434	432	432	295	160	240	331	192	556	39	77
Employment Status											
Full time	2,007	349	425	400	264	167	335	183	754	206	363
Part time.......................	4,305	924	1,147	951	829	505	742	419	2,185	120	334
Not employed	6,932	2,211	1,669	1,307	901	826	822	1,385	3,055	371	473
Control of School											
Public	10,541	2,978	2,690	2,109	1,539	1,402	1,795	1,577	4,543	477	748
Private	2,703	507	551	549	455	97	104	410	1,451	220	422
Disability Status											
Any disability..................	314	92	60	71	60	45	63	47	128	4	28
No disability	12,930	3,393	3,182	2,587	1,934	1,453	1,837	1,940	5,866	693	1,142
Part-Time Students											
Total	5,387	1,103	1,147	866	462	769	1,178	334	1,296	711	1,098
Age											
15–19 years old	347	234	112	1	-	185	96	49	18	-	-
20–24 years old	1,179	233	338	277	153	153	357	80	410	97	82
25–34 years old	1,922	341	383	321	145	223	406	118	444	323	409
35 years old and over	1,939	296	313	267	164	209	320	87	425	292	607
Race											
White alone....................	4,149	840	859	627	369	570	879	270	977	550	904
White alone non-Hispanic ...	3,400	605	663	501	306	397	676	208	795	517	807
Black alone	791	175	209	171	69	128	215	47	233	70	97
Asian alone....................	303	43	45	44	14	39	59	4	44	68	88
Hispanic[1]	793	255	200	137	68	189	211	67	195	36	97
Employment Status											
Full time	3,547	590	613	583	299	412	663	178	832	573	889
Part time.......................	941	232	286	172	98	159	284	73	272	65	88
Not employed	899	281	248	110	65	198	231	83	192	74	121
Control of School											
Public	4,197	967	1,000	713	343	704	1,106	263	951	498	676
Private	1,190	136	147	153	118	65	72	71	345	214	422
Disability Status											
Any disability..................	227	61	60	27	16	33	57	27	46	33	31
No disability	5,160	1,043	1,087	839	445	736	1,121	307	1,250	678	1,068

[1]May be of any race.
- = Quantity zero or rounds to zero.

Table A-5. Type of College and Year Enrolled for College Students 15 Years Old and Over, by Age, Sex, Race, Attendance Status, Control of School, and Enrollment Status, October 2008—*Continued*

(Numbers in thousands.)

Characteristic	Total enrolled	Undergraduate college								Graduate school	
		All colleges				Two-year college		Four-year college			
		1st year	2nd year	3rd year	4th year	1st year	2nd or higher	1st year	2nd or higher	1st year	2nd or higher
MALE											
Full-Time Students											
Total	6,100	1,666	1,439	1,218	896	688	799	979	2,754	325	555
Age											
15–19 years old	1,888	1,223	570	83	-	443	201	780	452	9	3
20–24 years old	2,973	314	676	922	736	160	455	154	1,879	157	167
25–34 years old	932	107	144	166	119	73	107	34	322	113	282
35 years old and over	307	22	49	47	40	11	36	11	101	47	102
Race											
White alone	4,728	1,320	1,052	965	757	549	625	771	2,149	250	384
White alone non-Hispanic	4,156	1,138	913	826	697	456	499	682	1,937	231	351
Black alone	714	219	215	143	72	86	104	133	327	31	34
Asian alone	469	89	93	82	52	34	39	55	187	33	120
Hispanic[1]	629	198	156	153	65	100	139	98	235	18	39
Employment Status											
Full time	912	157	204	179	105	75	147	83	341	106	161
Part time	1,827	389	477	413	330	189	308	200	912	60	157
Not employed	3,362	1,120	758	626	462	424	344	696	1,502	159	237
Control of School											
Public	4,890	1,426	1,204	976	698	654	761	772	2,117	237	350
Private	1,210	240	235	242	198	34	38	206	637	89	205
Disability Status											
Any disability	155	42	31	34	25	16	34	25	56	3	20
No disability	5,945	1,624	1,409	1,184	871	671	766	953	2,699	322	535
Part-Time Students											
Total	2,211	466	485	371	195	322	522	144	529	261	432
Age											
15–19 years old	154	119	35	-	-	98	33	21	2	-	-
20–24 years old	501	94	171	120	61	60	182	34	170	35	20
25–34 years old	874	170	169	148	75	100	196	70	195	143	170
35 years old and over	682	83	111	102	59	64	111	19	161	84	242
Race											
White alone	1,843	377	400	301	162	259	420	118	444	230	373
White alone non-Hispanic	1,446	243	292	235	128	161	319	82	336	216	333
Black alone	205	48	44	45	28	33	68	16	49	15	25
Asian alone	98	17	28	12	1	13	21	4	20	12	27
Hispanic[1]	414	141	109	76	35	100	105	40	114	14	40
Employment Status											
Full time	1,574	291	284	247	147	206	322	86	356	234	371
Part time	319	73	109	74	23	50	112	23	93	16	24
Not employed	318	101	93	50	26	66	88	36	80	11	37
Control of School											
Public	1,718	415	431	313	135	299	493	116	386	169	255
Private	493	50	54	58	61	23	30	28	143	92	178
Disability Status											
Any disability	99	29	23	9	6	9	20	20	18	19	13
No disability	2,112	437	462	362	190	313	502	124	512	242	420

[1]May be of any race.
- = Quantity zero or rounds to zero.

Table A-5. Type of College and Year Enrolled for College Students 15 Years Old and Over, by Age, Sex, Race, Attendance Status, Control of School, and Enrollment Status, October 2008—*Continued*

(Numbers in thousands.)

| Characteristic | Total enrolled | Undergraduate college | | | | | | | | Graduate school | |
| | | All colleges | | | | Two-year college | | Four-year college | | | |
		1st year	2nd year	3rd year	4th year	1st year	2nd or higher	1st year	2nd or higher	1st year	2nd or higher
FEMALE											
Full-Time Students											
Total	7,145	1,819	1,802	1,439	1,098	811	1,100	1,008	3,239	372	615
Age											
15–19 years old	2,132	1,291	734	93	6	528	278	763	555	6	2
20–24 years old	3,188	286	707	985	835	123	479	163	2,049	183	192
25–34 years old	1,160	148	196	203	157	97	189	51	366	139	317
35 years old and over	665	94	166	158	99	63	154	32	269	43	104
Race											
White alone	5,528	1,389	1,402	1,117	896	627	858	761	2,557	266	458
White alone non-Hispanic	4,768	1,171	1,125	987	812	497	668	674	2,255	248	425
Black alone	977	303	252	193	100	139	168	164	377	54	75
Asian alone	448	78	96	97	66	28	46	50	213	43	68
Hispanic[1]	805	233	276	142	95	140	192	93	321	21	38
Employment Status											
Full time	1,095	192	222	220	159	92	188	100	413	100	202
Part time	2,478	535	670	537	499	316	434	219	1,273	60	177
Not employed	3,571	1,092	910	682	439	402	478	690	1,553	211	236
Control of School											
Public	5,651	1,552	1,487	1,133	841	748	1,034	805	2,426	240	398
Private	1,493	266	316	307	257	63	66	204	813	131	217
Disability Status											
Any disability	160	50	29	37	35	29	29	21	72	-	8
No disability	6,985	1,769	1,773	1,402	1,062	782	1,071	987	3,167	371	607
Part-Time Students											
Total	3,176	638	661	495	267	448	656	190	767	450	666
Age											
15–19 years old	194	115	77	1	-	87	63	28	16	-	-
20–24 years old	678	139	167	156	92	93	175	45	240	62	62
25–34 years old	1,048	171	215	173	70	123	209	48	248	180	240
35 years old and over	1,258	213	202	165	105	144	209	69	263	208	365
Race											
White alone	2,306	463	459	325	207	311	459	152	533	320	531
White alone non-Hispanic	1,953	362	372	267	178	236	357	126	459	301	474
Black alone	586	127	165	126	41	95	148	31	185	55	72
Asian alone	205	26	17	32	13	26	38	-	24	56	61
Hispanic[1]	380	115	92	61	33	88	105	26	81	22	57
Employment Status											
Full time	1,973	299	329	336	152	207	341	92	476	338	518
Part time	622	159	177	98	75	108	172	50	178	49	64
Not employed	581	180	155	61	39	133	143	47	112	62	84
Control of School											
Public	2,479	552	569	400	209	405	613	147	564	329	422
Private	697	86	93	95	58	43	43	43	202	121	244
Disability Status											
Any disability	129	32	37	18	11	24	37	8	29	14	18
No disability	3,048	606	624	477	256	423	619	182	738	436	648

[1]May be of any race.
- = Quantity zero or rounds to zero.

Table A-6. Employment Status and Enrollment in Vocational[1] Courses for the Population 15 Years Old and Over, by Sex, Age, Educational Attainment, and College Enrollment, October 2008

(Numbers in thousands, percent.)

Characteristic	Total	Enrolled in Vocational courses		Employed full time	Enrolled in Vocational courses		Employed part time	Enrolled in Vocational courses		Not employed	Enrolled in Vocational courses	
	Total	Number	Percent	Total	Number	Percent	Total	Number	Percent	Total	Number	Percent
Both Sexes												
Total..............................	238,740	3,999	1.7	120,169	2,325	1.9	25,951	578	2.2	92,620	1,095	1.2
Age												
15 to 19 years old............	21,238	327	1.5	1,559	39	2.5	4,219	66	1.6	15,459	222	1.4
20 to 24 years old............	20,459	639	3.1	9,114	236	2.6	4,370	129	3.0	6,975	274	3.9
25 to 34 years old............	40,188	975	2.4	27,510	653	2.4	3,734	123	3.3	8,944	199	2.2
35 to 44 years old............	41,520	819	2.0	29,470	611	2.1	3,767	94	2.5	8,283	113	1.4
45 to 64 years old............	77,940	1,115	1.4	48,988	752	1.5	7,192	133	1.8	21,760	230	1.1
65 years and over............	37,396	123	0.3	3,529	34	1.0	2,668	33	1.2	31,199	56	0.2
Educational attainment												
Not a high school graduate ..	42,290	217	0.5	10,310	76	0.7	4,431	35	0.8	27,549	106	0.4
High school graduate only ...	70,959	852	1.2	35,150	407	1.2	6,883	105	1.5	28,925	339	1.2
Some college or associate's												
degree..........................	64,004	1,575	2.5	33,706	831	2.5	9,036	260	2.9	21,262	485	2.3
Bachelor's degree or more...	61,488	1,355	2.2	41,003	1,011	2.5	5,601	179	3.2	14,884	165	1.1
College enrollment												
Enrolled in college	18,632	1,114	6.0	5,554	455	8.2	5,246	221	4.2	7,831	437	5.6
Not enrolled in college........	220,108	2,885	1.3	114,615	1,869	1.6	20,705	357	1.7	84,788	658	0.8
Male												
Total..............................	115,660	1,875	1.6	68,572	1,278	1.9	8,971	149	1.7	38,117	448	1.2
Age												
15 to 19 years old............	10,791	188	1.7	920	31	3.3	1,854	27	1.5	8,017	131	1.6
20 to 24 years old............	10,271	271	2.6	4,972	133	2.7	1,901	35	1.8	3,398	103	3.0
25 to 34 years old............	20,114	470	2.3	16,003	367	2.3	1,164	33	2.9	2,947	70	2.4
35 to 44 years old............	20,486	381	1.9	17,248	331	1.9	780	16	2.1	2,459	35	1.4
45 to 64 years old............	37,889	518	1.4	27,340	403	1.5	1,926	27	1.4	8,624	88	1.0
65 years and over............	16,110	46	0.3	2,089	14	0.7	1,348	11	0.8	12,672	21	0.2
Educational attainment												
Not a high school graduate....	21,305	110	0.5	7,114	60	0.8	1,907	8	0.4	12,284	42	0.3
High school graduate only ...	34,931	391	1.1	21,248	228	1.1	2,387	21	0.9	11,297	142	1.3
Some college or associate's												
degree	29,276	726	2.5	17,734	436	2.5	3,020	90	3.0	8,522	200	2.3
Bachelor's degree or more	30,148	648	2.1	22,476	554	2.5	1,658	30	1.8	6,014	64	1.1
College enrollment												
Enrolled in college	8,311	508	6.1	2,486	241	9.7	2,146	73	3.4	3,679	195	5.3
Not enrolled in college........	107,349	1,366	1.3	66,086	1,037	1.6	6,825	77	1.1	34,438	253	0.7
Female												
Total..............................	123,080	2,124	1.7	51,598	1,047	2.0	16,980	429	2.5	54,502	648	1.2
Age												
15 to 19 years old............	10,447	139	1.3	639	9	1.4	2,366	40	1.7	7,442	91	1.2
20 to 24 years old............	10,188	368	3.6	4,142	103	2.5	2,469	94	3.8	3,577	171	4.8
25 to 34 years old............	20,074	505	2.5	11,507	285	2.5	2,570	90	3.5	5,997	130	2.2
35 to 44 years old............	21,034	437	2.1	12,222	281	2.3	2,988	78	2.6	5,824	79	1.4
45 to 64 years old............	40,051	597	1.5	21,648	349	1.6	5,267	106	2.0	13,136	142	1.1
65 years and over............	21,286	77	0.4	1,439	20	1.4	1,321	22	1.6	18,526	35	0.2
Educational attainment												
Not a high school graduate	20,985	107	0.5	3,196	16	0.5	2,524	26	1.0	15,264	65	0.4
High school graduate only.....	36,028	461	1.3	13,903	179	1.3	4,496	85	1.9	17,629	197	1.1
Some college or associate's												
degree..........................	34,729	850	2.4	15,972	395	2.5	6,017	170	2.8	12,740	285	2.2
Bachelor's degree or more	31,340	707	2.3	18,527	458	2.5	3,943	148	3.8	8,870	101	1.1
College enrollment												
Enrolled in college	10,321	605	5.9	3,069	214	7.0	3,100	148	4.8	4,152	242	5.8
Not enrolled in college........	112,759	1,518	1.3	48,529	832	1.7	13,880	280	2.0	50,350	405	0.8

[1]People enrolled in vocational courses are not considered to be enrolled in school for all tables.
- = Quantity zero or rounds to zero.

Table A-7. Enrollment Status of High School Graduates 15 to 24 Years Old, by Type of School, Attendance Status, and Sex, October 2008

(Numbers in thousands.)

Characteristic	Total	Enrolled in college or vocational school						Not enrolled	
		2-year college		4-year college		Graduate school	Vocational school	Employed	Not employed
		Full time	Part time	Full time	Part time				
All Races									
Both sexes	24,859	2,649	770	6,773	555	898	337	3,384	9,493
Graduated this year	3,160	755	115	1,263	32	5	50	405	534
Graduated earlier	21,699	1,894	654	5,510	523	893	287	2,979	8,959
Male	12,356	1,252	369	3,259	226	391	151	1,667	5,040
Graduated this year	1,647	346	64	664	10	2	22	235	303
Graduated earlier	10,709	907	305	2,594	216	388	129	1,432	4,737
Female	12,503	1,397	400	3,514	329	507	186	1,717	4,453
Graduated this year	1,513	409	51	599	22	3	29	170	231
Graduated earlier	10,990	988	349	2,915	307	504	157	1,547	4,222
White Alone									
Both sexes	19,547	2,132	616	5,346	459	718	265	2,329	7,680
Graduated this year	2,530	655	97	1,005	32	5	34	268	434
Graduated earlier	17,016	1,477	519	4,342	428	713	231	2,061	7,246
Male	9,771	1,019	311	2,571	203	308	129	1,167	4,063
Graduated this year	1,339	302	58	546	10	2	17	169	234
Graduated earlier	8,433	717	253	2,026	193	306	111	998	3,829
Female	9,775	1,114	305	2,775	256	410	137	1,162	3,617
Graduated this year	1,192	353	39	459	22	3	17	99	200
Graduated earlier	8,584	761	266	2,316	235	407	120	1,063	3,417
White Alone, Non-Hispanic									
Both sexes	16,199	1,697	448	4,808	351	685	208	1,773	6,229
Graduated this year	2,099	525	67	898	14	2	31	202	359
Graduated earlier	14,100	1,171	380	3,910	337	683	177	1,571	5,871
Male	8,118	829	217	2,335	144	292	114	937	3,250
Graduated this year	1,128	248	45	490	4	2	14	128	196
Graduated earlier	6,990	581	172	1,845	140	290	100	810	3,054
Female	8,081	868	231	2,473	208	393	94	836	2,979
Graduated this year	972	277	22	408	10	-	17	75	162
Graduated earlier	7,110	591	209	2,065	198	393	77	761	2,817
Black Alone									
Both sexes	3,430	334	109	801	67	59	42	791	1,228
Graduated this year	428	69	15	151	-	-	15	97	82
Graduated earlier	3,002	266	94	650	67	59	26	694	1,146
Male	1,667	146	36	395	14	24	12	394	645
Graduated this year	218	27	4	68	-	-	4	56	58
Graduated earlier	1,449	119	32	327	14	24	8	338	587
Female	1,763	188	72	406	53	35	29	397	582
Graduated this year	210	41	11	83	-	-	11	40	23
Graduated earlier	1,553	147	62	323	53	35	18	357	559
Asian Alone									
Both sexes	1,051	122	25	422	9	99	25	82	268
Graduated this year	96	16	1	67	-	-	-	5	6
Graduated earlier	956	106	24	355	9	99	25	77	261
Male	508	63	11	193	2	46	9	27	158
Graduated this year	49	12	1	32	-	-	-	1	3
Graduated earlier	459	51	10	160	2	46	9	26	155
Female	543	59	14	230	7	53	16	55	110
Graduated this year	47	4	-	35	-	-	-	4	4
Graduated earlier	497	55	14	195	7	53	16	51	106
Hispanic[1]									
Both sexes	3,672	450	179	591	116	37	61	640	1,599
Graduated this year	458	130	32	110	18	3	3	82	80
Graduated earlier	3,215	320	147	480	99	34	58	558	1,519
Male	1,832	198	100	263	60	16	18	266	912
Graduated this year	221	54	13	56	6	-	3	47	41
Graduated earlier	1,612	144	86	207	54	16	15	219	870
Female	1,840	252	79	328	56	21	43	374	687
Graduated this year	237	76	18	54	12	3	-	35	39
Graduated earlier	1,603	176	61	273	44	18	43	340	649

[1]May be of any race.
- = Quantity zero or rounds to zero.

Table A-8. Enrollment Status for Families with Children 5 to 24 Years Old, by Control of School, Race, Type of Family, and Family Income, October 2008

(Numbers in thousands.)

Characteristic	Total	Families with no dependents[1] 5 to 24 years old	Kindergarten, elementary, and high school enrollment status				College enrollment status		
			None enrolled in elementary or high school	Public only	Public and private	Private only	None enrolled in college	One enrolled in college	Two or more enrolled in college
All Races									
All families....................	79,983	40,810	7,510	28,376	708	2,578	32,881	5,399	893
Less than $20,000.......	8,833	3,964	756	3,900	68	144	4,484	349	36
$20,000 to $74,999	33,668	17,538	2,975	12,134	180	841	13,878	2,002	250
$75,000 and over........	21,780	10,613	2,295	7,338	322	1,211	8,717	2,042	408
Not reported..............	15,701	8,695	1,483	5,004	137	382	5,802	1,006	199
Married-couple families.....	59,394	33,577	4,494	18,793	522	2,009	21,371	3,754	692
Less than $20,000.......	3,740	2,363	174	1,131	14	58	1,288	77	12
$20,000 to $74,999	24,366	14,287	1,574	7,809	118	578	8,662	1,247	169
$75,000 and over........	19,743	9,843	1,867	6,650	298	1,085	7,783	1,756	361
Not reported..............	11,545	7,084	878	3,202	92	288	3,637	673	150
Unmarried householder[2]....	20,589	7,233	3,017	9,584	186	569	11,510	1,645	201
Less than $20,000.......	5,093	1,601	582	2,769	55	86	3,196	272	24
$20,000 to $74,999	9,303	3,251	1,401	4,325	63	263	5,216	755	81
$75,000 and over........	2,037	770	429	688	24	126	934	286	47
Not reported..............	4,157	1,611	605	1,802	45	94	2,164	333	48
White Alone									
All families....................	64,876	34,508	5,925	21,835	532	2,075	25,363	4,284	720
Less than $20,000.......	6,005	2,875	511	2,483	39	99	2,924	190	17
$20,000 to $74,999	27,435	14,957	2,308	9,386	134	649	10,707	1,586	185
$75,000 and over........	19,024	9,476	1,944	6,309	266	1,030	7,457	1,727	364
Not reported..............	12,411	7,201	1,163	3,656	94	297	4,275	781	154
Married-couple families.....	50,840	29,348	3,761	15,623	422	1,686	17,791	3,128	572
Less than $20,000.......	2,978	1,897	136	884	14	48	1,020	55	7
$20,000 to $74,999	20,754	12,485	1,287	6,409	93	480	7,140	1,004	125
$75,000 and over........	17,417	8,853	1,615	5,783	247	919	6,735	1,507	322
Not reported..............	9,691	6,114	723	2,547	68	239	2,896	563	118
Unmarried householder[2]....	14,036	5,160	2,164	6,213	110	388	7,572	1,156	148
Less than $20,000.......	3,027	977	375	1,599	25	51	1,903	136	11
$20,000 to $74,999	6,681	2,472	1,021	2,978	41	170	3,567	582	60
$75,000 and over........	1,608	623	329	526	19	111	722	221	42
Not reported..............	2,720	1,087	439	1,110	26	58	1,379	218	36
White Alone Non-Hispanic									
All families....................	54,363	30,697	4,859	16,484	441	1,881	19,512	3,551	603
Less than $20,000.......	3,885	2,133	304	1,343	27	78	1,620	118	14
$20,000 to $74,999	22,156	13,074	1,786	6,638	101	558	7,764	1,190	127
$75,000 and over........	17,647	8,930	1,811	5,699	234	973	6,778	1,600	339
Not reported..............	10,676	6,561	959	2,804	79	272	3,349	643	123
Married-couple families.....	43,885	26,698	3,193	12,087	351	1,557	14,042	2,654	491
Less than $20,000.......	1,933	1,435	69	382	7	40	457	34	7
$20,000 to $74,999	17,074	11,183	991	4,415	68	417	5,074	732	85
$75,000 and over........	16,268	8,383	1,530	5,265	216	873	6,181	1,402	301
Not reported..............	8,611	5,696	602	2,025	61	227	2,331	485	99
Unmarried householder[2]....	10,478	4,000	1,667	4,397	90	324	5,470	897	112
Less than $20,000.......	1,952	697	235	961	20	38	1,163	84	7
$20,000 to $74,999	5,082	1,890	794	2,223	33	141	2,691	458	43
$75,000 and over........	1,379	546	280	433	19	100	597	198	38
Not reported..............	2,065	865	357	779	19	45	1,018	157	24

[1]Unmarried (or married with spouse absent) child, grandchild, brother/sister or other relative.
[2]No spouse present.
- = Quantity zero or rounds to zero.

Table A-8. Enrollment Status for Families with Children 5 to 24 Years Old, by Control of School, Race, Type of Family, and Family Income, October 2008—*Continued*

(Numbers in thousands.)

Characteristic	Total	Families with no dependents[1] 5 to 24 years old	Families with dependents[1] 5 to 24 years old						
			Kindergarten, elementary, and high school enrollment status				College enrollment status		
			None enrolled in elementary or high school	Public only	Public and private	Private only	None enrolled in college	One enrolled in college	Two or more enrolled in college
Black Alone									
All families....................	9,691	3,774	1,038	4,461	108	310	5,152	672	93
Less than $20,000......	2,208	827	205	1,116	22	38	1,245	120	16
$20,000 to $74,999	4,102	1,614	459	1,882	21	126	2,179	275	33
$75,000 and over........	1,194	416	168	484	34	92	620	138	20
Not reported..............	2,187	918	206	980	30	54	1,108	138	23
Married-couple families.....	4,582	2,255	398	1,706	57	166	1,936	332	58
Less than $20,000.......	480	303	31	140	-	5	159	12	5
$20,000 to $74,999	2,097	1,047	173	807	13	56	875	157	17
$75,000 and over........	958	359	112	380	29	78	465	114	20
Not reported..............	1,047	546	81	378	16	26	437	49	15
Unmarried householder[2]....	5,109	1,519	641	2,755	50	144	3,215	340	35
Less than $20,000......	1,728	524	174	975	22	33	1,086	108	11
$20,000 to $74,999	2,005	567	286	1,075	8	70	1,305	118	16
$75,000 and over........	236	56	56	104	5	14	155	25	-
Not reported..............	1,140	372	124	602	15	27	670	89	8
Asian Alone									
All families....................	3,562	1,716	362	1,285	45	154	1,447	335	64
Less than $20,000.......	276	142	17	109	4	4	103	31	-
$20,000 to $74,999	1,228	577	112	475	14	51	537	87	28
$75,000 and over........	1,253	574	148	437	17	77	515	144	20
Not reported..............	805	423	85	264	11	22	292	73	16
Married-couple families.....	2,863	1,417	257	1,030	31	128	1,159	231	56
Less than $20,000......	162	111	1	46	-	4	41	10	-
$20,000 to $74,999	933	460	70	363	6	34	394	56	24
$75,000 and over........	1,121	505	121	402	17	76	487	112	17
Not reported..............	647	340	66	219	8	14	238	54	15
Unmarried householder[2]	700	299	105	255	14	26	288	104	9
Less than $20,000.......	115	31	17	63	4	-	62	22	-
$20,000 to $74,999	295	116	42	112	7	17	143	31	4
$75,000 and over........	132	68	27	35	-	1	28	32	3
Not reported..............	158	83	19	45	3	8	54	20	1
Hispanic[3]									
All families....................	11,282	4,042	1,176	5,747	102	215	6,341	780	119
Less than $20,000.......	2,290	778	229	1,243	15	24	1,430	79	3
$20,000 to $74,999	5,672	2,014	570	2,952	36	99	3,175	425	58
$75,000 and over........	1,462	571	153	637	36	66	734	132	25
Not reported..............	1,858	679	224	915	15	25	1,003	144	33
Married-couple families.....	7,372	2,806	612	3,738	75	140	3,994	489	83
Less than $20,000.......	1,123	487	80	542	7	8	611	24	-
$20,000 to $74,999	3,924	1,395	318	2,118	25	68	2,207	281	41
$75,000 and over........	1,200	486	90	537	36	52	588	105	21
Not reported..............	1,124	438	124	542	7	13	587	78	22
Unmarried householder[2]....	3,910	1,236	564	2,008	27	75	2,347	291	35
Less than $20,000.......	1,167	291	150	701	9	16	818	55	3
$20,000 to $74,999	1,748	619	252	834	11	32	968	144	17
$76,000 and over........	262	85	62	100	-	14	146	27	4
Not reported..............	734	241	100	373	7	13	416	66	11

[1]Unmarried (or married with spouse absent) child, grandchild, brother/sister or other relative.
[2]No spouse present.
[3]May be of any race.
- = Quantity zero or rounds to zero.

Table A-9. School Enrollment of the Population 3 Years Old and Over, by Level and Control of School, Race, and Hispanic Origin, October 1955–2008

(Numbers in thousands.)

Year, race, and Hispanic origin	Total enrolled	Nursery school			Kindergarten			Elementary school		
		Total	Public	Private	Total	Public	Private	Total	Public	Private
All Races										
2008	76,353	4,614	2,632	1,982	4,047	3,578	469	32,344	29,162	3,182
2007	75,967	4,628	2,570	2,058	4,132	3,656	476	32,169	29,052	3,117
2006	75,197	4,688	2,519	2,169	4,039	3,552	487	32,089	28,975	3,113
2005	75,780	4,603	2,480	2,123	3,912	3,349	563	32,438	29,072	3,366
2004	75,461	4,739	2,487	2,252	3,992	3,417	575	32,556	29,166	3,389
2003	74,911	4,928	2,567	2,361	3,719	3,098	622	32,565	29,204	3,361
2002	74,046	4,471	2,246	2,225	3,571	2,976	594	33,132	29,658	3,474
2001	73,124	4,289	2,161	2,128	3,737	3,145	591	33,166	29,800	3,366
2000	72,214	4,401	2,217	2,184	3,832	3,173	659	32,898	29,378	3,520
1999	72,395	4,578	2,269	2,309	3,825	3,167	658	32,873	29,264	3,609
1998	72,109	4,577	2,265	2,313	3,828	3,128	700	32,573	29,124	3,449
1997	72,031	4,500	2,254	2,246	3,933	3,271	663	32,369	29,308	3,061
1996	70,297	4,212	1,868	2,344	4,034	3,353	681	31,515	28,153	3,362
1995	69,769	4,399	2,012	2,387	3,877	3,174	704	31,815	28,384	3,431
1994[3]	69,272	4,259	1,940	2,319	3,863	3,278	585	31,512	28,131	3,381
1993[r]	64,414	3,032	1,258	1,774	4,275	3,589	686	31,219	28,278	2,941
1993	62,730	3,018	1,230	1,788	4,180	3,499	681	30,604	27,688	2,914
1992	62,082	2,899	1,098	1,801	4,130	3,507	623	30,165	27,066	3,102
1991	61,276	2,933	1,094	1,839	4,152	3,531	621	29,591	26,632	2,958
1990	60,588	3,401	1,212	2,188	3,899	3,332	567	29,265	26,591	2,674
1989	59,236	2,877	971	1,906	3,868	3,293	575	28,637	25,897	2,740
1988	58,847	2,639	838	1,770	3,958	3,420	538	28,223	25,443	2,778
1987	58,691	2,587	848	1,739	4,018	3,423	595	27,524	24,760	2,765
1986	58,153	2,554	835	1,719	3,961	3,328	633	27,121	24,163	2,958
1985	58,014	2,491	854	1,637	3,815	3,221	594	26,866	23,803	3,063
1984	57,313	2,354	761	1,593	3,484	2,953	531	26,838	24,120	2,718
1983	57,745	2,350	809	1,541	3,361	2,706	656	27,198	24,203	2,994
1982	57,905	2,153	729	1,423	3,299	2,746	553	27,412	24,381	3,031
1981	58,390	2,058	663	1,396	3,161	2,616	545	27,795	24,758	3,037
1980	57,348	1,987	633	1,354	3,176	2,690	486	27,449	24,398	3,051
1979	57,854	1,869	636	1,233	3,025	2,593	432	27,865	24,756	3,109
1978	58,616	1,824	587	1,237	2,989	2,493	496	28,490	25,252	3,238
1977	60,013	1,618	562	1,056	3,191	2,665	526	29,234	25,983	3,251
1976	60,482	1,526	476	1,050	3,490	2,962	528	29,774	26,698	3,075
1975	60,969	1,748	574	1,174	3,393	2,851	542	30,446	27,166	3,279
1974	60,259	1,607	423	1,184	3,252	2,726	526	31,126	27,956	3,169
1973	59,392	1,324	400	924	3,074	2,582	493	31,469	28,201	3,268
1972	60,142	1,283	402	881	3,135	2,636	499	32,242	28,693	3,549
1971	61,106	1,066	317	749	3,263	2,689	574	33,507	29,829	3,678
1970	60,357	1,096	333	763	3,183	2,647	536	33,950	30,001	3,949
1969	59,913	860	245	615	3,276	2,682	594	33,788	29,825	3,964
1968	58,791	816	262	554	3,268	2,709	559	33,761	29,527	4,234
1967	57,656	713	230	484	3,312	2,678	635	33,440	28,877	4,562
1966	56,167	688	215	473	3,115	2,527	588	32,916	28,208	4,706
1965	54,701	520	127	393	3,057	2,439	618	32,474	27,596	4,878
1964	52,490	471	91	380	2,830	2,349	481	31,734	26,811	4,923
1963	50,356	...	...	...	2,340	1,936	404	31,245	26,502	4,742
1962	48,704	...	...	...	2,319	1,914	405	30,661	26,148	4,513
1961	47,708	...	...	...	2,299	1,926	373	30,718	26,221	4,497
1960	46,260	...	...	...	2,092	1,691	401	30,349	25,814	4,535
1959	44,370	...	...	...	2,032	1,678	354	29,382	24,680	4,702
1958	42,900	...	...	...	1,991	1,569	422	28,184	23,800	4,385
1957	41,166	...	...	...	1,824	1,471	353	27,248	23,076	4,172
1956	39,353	...	...	...	1,758	1,566	192	26,169	22,474	3,695
1955	37,426	...	...	...	1,628	1,365	263	25,458	22,078	3,379
White Alone										
2008	58,244	3,479	1,830	1,649	3,121	2,748	373	24,552	21,986	2,565
2007	58,021	3,545	1,880	1,665	3,223	2,836	387	24,431	21,869	2,562
2006	57,419	3,624	1,815	1,809	3,084	2,701	382	24,472	21,923	2,549
2005	58,013	3,542	1,767	1,775	3,056	2,611	445	24,562	21,858	2,795
2004	57,585	3,566	1,703	1,863	3,043	2,571	472	24,773	21,889	2,883
2003[1]	57,391	3,909	1,918	1,990	2,866	2,367	499	24,711	21,893	2,818
2002	57,501	3,473	1,613	1,860	2,760	2,240	520	25,625	22,703	2,922
2001	56,649	3,278	1,484	1,794	2,893	2,394	499	25,729	22,848	2,881
2000	56,344	3,392	1,539	1,853	2,998	2,453	545	25,562	22,538	3,024

Note: Data shown for 1955 to 1966 for the Black population are for Black and Other races.
[1]Starting in 2003 respondents could identify more than one race. Except as noted, the race data in this table from 2003 onward represent those respondents who indicated only one race category.
[3]Prior to 1994, total enrolled does not include the 35 years old and over population.
r = Revised, controlled to 1990 census based population estimates; previous 1993 data controlled to 1980 census based population estimates.
... = Not available.

Table A-9. School Enrollment of the Population 3 Years Old and Over, by Level and Control of School, Race, and Hispanic Origin, October 1955–2008—*Continued*

(Numbers in thousands.)

Year, race, and Hispanic origin	High school			College			
	Total	Public	Private	Total	Public	Private	Full time
All Races							
2008	16,715	15,397	1,319	18,632	14,739	3,893	13,245
2007	17,082	15,804	1,278	17,956	14,072	3,884	12,656
2006	17,149	15,617	1,532	17,232	13,466	3,766	12,070
2005	17,354	15,934	1,420	17,472	13,435	4,037	12,237
2004	16,791	15,498	1,293	17,383	13,652	3,731	11,990
2003	17,062	15,785	1,276	16,638	13,109	3,529	11,490
2002	16,374	15,064	1,310	16,497	12,834	3,664	11,141
2001	16,059	14,830	1,230	15,873	12,421	3,452	10,404
2000	15,770	14,431	1,339	15,314	12,008	3,305	10,159
1999	15,916	14,638	1,278	15,203	11,659	3,544	10,112
1998	15,584	14,299	1,285	15,547	11,984	3,563	10,184
1997	15,793	14,634	1,159	15,436	12,091	3,345	10,236
1996	15,309	14,113	1,197	15,226	12,014	3,212	9,839
1995	14,963	13,750	1,213	14,715	11,372	3,343	9,544
1994[3]	14,616	13,539	1,077	15,022	11,694	3,329	9,573
1993[r]	13,989	12,985	1,004	11,901	9,440	2,461	8,706
1993	13,522	12,542	977	11,409	9,031	2,374	8,308
1992	13,219	12,268	952	11,671	9,282	2,386	8,503
1991	13,010	12,069	945	11,589	9,078	2,511	8,461
1990	12,719	11,818	903	11,306	8,889	2,417	8,154
1989	12,786	11,980	806	11,066	8,576	2,490	7,905
1988	13,093	12,095	998	10,937	8,663	2,278	7,771
1987	13,647	12,577	1,070	10,915	8,556	2,361	7,560
1986	13,912	12,746	1,166	10,605	8,153	2,452	7,507
1985	13,979	12,764	1,215	10,863	8,379	2,483	7,720
1984	13,777	12,721	1,057	10,859	8,467	2,392	7,822
1983	14,010	12,792	1,218	10,825	8,185	2,640	7,711
1982	14,123	13,004	1,118	10,919	8,354	2,565	7,736
1981	14,642	13,523	1,119	10,734	8,159	2,576	7,569
1980	14,556	...	...	10,180	...	...	7,147
1979	15,116	13,994	1,122	9,978	7,699	2,280	7,010
1978	15,475	14,231	1,244	9,838	7,427	2,410	6,979
1977	15,753	14,505	1,248	10,217	7,925	2,292	7,196
1976	15,742	14,541	1,201	9,950	7,739	2,211	7,176
1975	15,683	14,503	1,180	9,697	7,704	1,994	7,105
1974	15,447	14,275	1,172	8,827	6,905	1,922	6,351
1973	15,347	14,162	1,184	8,179	6,224	1,955	6,089
1972	15,169	14,015	1,155	8,313	6,337	1,976	6,314
1971	15,183	14,057	1,126	8,087	6,271	1,816	6,204
1970	14,715	13,545	1,170	7,413	5,699	1,714	5,763
1969	14,553	13,400	1,153	7,435	5,439	1,995	5,810
1968	14,145	12,793	1,352	6,801	4,948	1,854	5,357
1967	13,790	12,498	1,292	6,401	4,540	1,861	4,976
1966	13,364	11,985	1,377	6,085	4,178	1,908	4,847
1965	12,975	11,517	1,457	5,675	3,840	1,835	4,414
1964	12,812	11,403	1,410	4,643	3,025	1,618	3,556
1963	12,438	11,186	1,251	4,336	2,897	1,439	3,260
1962	11,516	10,431	1,085	4,208	2,820	1,388	3,237
1961	10,959	9,817	1,141	3,731	2,376	1,354	2,902
1960	10,249	9,215	1,033	3,570	2,307	1,262	2,681
1959	9,616	8,571	1,045	3,340	2,120	1,220	2,464
1958	9,482	8,485	998	3,242	2,088	1,155	...
1957	8,956	8,059	897	3,138	2,054	1,084	...
1956	8,543	7,668	875	2,883	1,824	1,059	...
1955	7,961	7,181	780	2,379	1,515	864	...
White Alone							
2008	12,687	11,585	1,103	14,405	11,432	2,973	10,256
2007	12,986	11,886	1,100	13,835	10,855	2,979	9,696
2006	12,966	11,694	1,273	13,273	10,338	2,936	9,236
2005	13,296	12,109	1,187	13,466	10,303	3,163	9,392
2004	12,823	11,684	1,138	13,381	10,478	2,904	9,257
2003[1]	13,036	11,939	1,097	12,870	10,101	2,769	8,855
2002	12,862	11,730	1,132	12,781	9,774	3,007	8,613
2001	12,540	11,473	1,067	12,208	9,503	2,705	7,909
2000	12,392	11,259	1,133	11,999	9,364	2,636	7,945

Note: Data shown for 1955 to 1966 for the Black population are for Black and Other races.
[1] Starting in 2003 respondents could identify more than one race. Except as noted, the race data in this table from 2003 onward represent those respondents who indicated only one race category.
[3] Prior to 1994, total enrolled does not include the 35 years old and over population.
r = Revised, controlled to 1990 census based population estimates; previous 1993 data controlled to 1980 census based population estimates.
... = Not available.

Table A-9.   School Enrollment of the Population 3 Years Old and Over, by Level and Control of School, Race, and Hispanic Origin, October 1955–2008—*Continued*

(Numbers in thousands.)

Year, race, and Hispanic origin	Total enrolled	Nursery school			Kindergarten			Elementary school		
		Total	Public	Private	Total	Public	Private	Total	Public	Private
1999	56,713	3,590	1,571	2,019	2,956	2,422	534	25,628	22,552	3,076
1998	56,515	3,549	1,598	1,951	2,933	2,356	577	25,489	22,547	2,942
1997	56,587	3,489	1,572	1,917	3,078	2,532	546	25,289	22,679	2,610
1996	55,378	3,284	1,314	1,970	3,163	2,596	567	24,692	21,785	2,907
1995	55,186	3,553	1,435	2,118	3,032	2,440	592	24,963	22,010	2,954
1994[3]	54,823	3,376	1,330	2,046	3,010	2,505	505	24,786	21,903	2,883
1993[r]	51,034	2,434	851	1,583	3,323	2,730	593	24,637	22,078	2,559
1993	49,985	2,447	843	1,604	3,273	2,681	592	24,249	21,714	2,535
1992	49,713	2,387	785	1,602	3,256	2,727	529	23,932	21,213	2,718
1991	49,156	2,447	810	1,637	3,274	2,766	508	23,547	20,948	2,599
1990	48,897	2,830	869	1,961	3,081	2,609	472	23,343	20,984	2,359
1989	47,923	2,393	712	1,681	3,118	2,611	506	22,867	20,468	2,399
1988	47,672	2,234	651	1,583	3,192	2,722	471	22,541	20,086	2,455
1987	47,471	2,204	630	1,574	3,120	2,591	529	22,037	19,538	2,498
1986	47,267	2,144	601	1,543	3,161	2,589	572	21,761	19,090	2,671
1985	47,452	2,087	617	1,470	3,060	2,545	515	21,593	18,817	2,776
1984	46,941	1,915	543	1,372	2,788	2,319	469	21,730	19,282	2,449
1983	47,423	1,932	563	1,369	2,769	2,181	588	22,054	19,340	2,714
1982	47,662	1,783	504	1,279	2,677	2,189	489	22,297	19,583	2,713
1981	48,169	1,685	447	1,238	2,597	2,130	467	22,663	19,924	2,739
1980	47,673	1,637	432	1,205	2,595	2,172	423	22,510	19,743	2,768
1979	48,225	1,537	428	1,110	2,437	2,069	368	22,959	20,174	2,785
1978	48,843	1,456	351	1,105	2,452	2,009	444	23,524	20,551	2,973
1977	50,151	1,314	372	942	2,611	2,153	458	24,262	21,312	2,950
1976	50,761	1,246	318	929	2,881	2,423	457	24,776	21,947	2,829
1975	51,430	1,432	392	1,040	2,845	2,363	483	25,412	22,351	3,059
1974	50,992	1,340	293	1,048	2,745	2,268	477	26,051	23,063	2,990
1973	50,617	1,087	242	845	2,584	2,139	445	26,531	23,506	3,025
1972	51,314	1,079	285	794	2,633	2,185	448	27,185	23,869	3,316
1971	52,081	888	225	664	2,735	2,207	527	28,187	24,720	3,466
1970	51,719	893	198	695	2,706	2,233	473	28,638	24,923	3,715
1969	51,465	676	136	539	2,803	2,289	515	28,572	24,803	3,768
1968	50,608	664	163	501	2,775	2,272	504	28,634	24,580	4,054
1967	49,721	564	134	429	2,840	2,254	587	28,415	24,044	4,371
1966	48,620	564	127	437	2,693	2,163	530	28,012	23,469	4,542
1965	47,451	451	93	358	2,648	2,086	562	27,679	22,976	4,703
1964	44,850	...	...	...	2,157	1,795	362	27,099	22,381	4,718
1963	43,815	...	...	...	2,064	1,699	365	26,709	22,181	4,527
1962	42,501	...	...	...	2,025	1,667	358	26,272	21,922	4,350
1961	42,498	...	...	...	1,968	1,618	350	26,294	22,014	4,281
1960	40,348	...	...	...	1,849	1,485	364	26,035	21,696	4,339
1959	38,857	...	...	...	1,758	1,434	324	25,395	20,854	4,541
1958	37,662	...	...	...	1,769	1,383	386	24,380	20,178	4,203
1957	36,132	...	...	...	1,595	1,258	337	23,610	19,595	4,015
1956	34,641	...	...	...	1,544	1,364	180	22,740	19,186	3,554
1955	32,929	...	...	...	1,484	1,244	240	22,185	18,947	3,238
White Alone Non-Hispanic										
2008	45,373	2,710	1,213	1,497	2,206	1,884	323	18,349	16,029	2,320
2007	45,334	2,711	1,225	1,486	2,279	1,929	351	18,306	15,998	2,307
2006	45,386	2,769	1,152	1,616	2,288	1,940	348	18,622	16,322	2,301
2005	46,338	2,810	1,211	1,599	2,308	1,936	372	18,858	16,335	2,523
2004	46,095	2,840	1,153	1,687	2,325	1,917	408	19,093	16,437	2,646
2003[1]	46,440	3,184	1,382	1,802	2,245	1,804	440	19,252	16,735	2,517
2002	46,725	2,881	1,172	1,709	2,065	1,585	480	20,124	17,495	2,628
2001	46,110	2,725	1,054	1,671	2,203	1,781	422	20,298	17,693	2,605
2000	46,660	2,854	1,149	1,705	2,346	1,846	500	20,574	17,747	2,827
1999	47,292	3,044	1,146	1,898	2,307	1,839	468	20,779	17,960	2,819
1998	47,386	2,964	1,136	1,828	2,336	1,790	547	20,806	18,107	2,699
1997	47,776	2,956	1,143	1,813	2,456	1,970	486	20,839	18,426	2,413
1996	46,947	2,767	922	1,845	2,590	2,081	509	20,447	17,808	2,639
1995	48,019	3,104	1,129	1,975	2,551	2,047	504	21,256	18,518	2,738
1994[3]	47,679	3,024	1,090	1,934	2,522	2,059	462	21,170	18,555	2,615
1993	43,827	2,277	720	1,557	2,779	2,239	540	20,961	18,617	2,344

Note: Data shown for 1955 to 1966 for the Black population are for Black and Other races.
[1]Starting in 2003 respondents could identify more than one race. Except as noted, the race data in this table from 2003 onward represent those respondents who indicated only one race category.
[3]Prior to 1994, total enrolled does not include the 35 years old and over population.
r = Revised, controlled to 1990 census based population estimates; previous 1993 data controlled to 1980 census based population estimates.
... = Not available.

Table A-9. School Enrollment of the Population 3 Years Old and Over, by Level and Control of School, Race, and Hispanic Origin, October 1955–2008—*Continued*

(Numbers in thousands.)

Year, race, and Hispanic origin	High school			College			
	Total	Public	Private	Total	Public	Private	Full time
1999	12,487	11,374	1,113	12,053	9,185	2,868	7,886
1998	12,142	11,013	1,130	12,401	9,518	2,883	8,012
1997	12,290	11,287	1,003	12,442	9,713	2,729	8,127
1996	12,052	10,999	1,053	12,188	9,567	2,622	7,849
1995	11,617	10,574	1,042	12,021	9,311	2,711	7,773
1994[3]	11,430	10,514	916	12,222	9,472	2,751	7,722
1993[r]	10,960	10,124	836	9,685	7,695	1,990	6,996
1993	10,651	9,834	819	9,366	7,428	1,940	6,739
1992	10,480	9,648	833	9,658	7,653	2,001	6,985
1991	10,309	9,467	841	9,579	7,464	2,118	6,919
1990	10,177	9,370	807	9,466	7,411	2,056	6,776
1989	10,172	9,443	730	9,374	7,219	2,158	6,658
1988	10,462	9,571	890	9,245	7,302	1,940	6,488
1987	10,967	10,019	947	9,143	7,113	2,034	6,275
1986	11,259	10,229	1,030	8,943	6,821	2,122	6,253
1985	11,378	10,258	1,120	9,334	7,131	2,203	6,597
1984	11,240	10,266	974	9,269	7,163	2,105	6,672
1983	11,425	10,339	1,086	9,242	6,949	2,293	6,532
1982	11,577	10,541	1,036	9,328	7,102	2,227	6,579
1981	12,062	11,035	1,027	9,162	6,906	2,256	6,452
1980	12,056	...	...	8,875	...	...	6,212
1979	12,583	11,549	1,033	8,709	6,672	2,037	6,058
1978	12,897	11,741	1,156	8,514	6,368	2,145	5,974
1977	13,152	11,980	1,172	8,812	6,743	2,069	6,165
1976	13,214	12,093	1,121	8,644	6,657	1,987	6,170
1975	13,224	12,112	1,112	8,516	6,724	1,792	6,183
1974	13,073	11,966	1,107	7,781	6,049	1,732	5,575
1973	13,091	11,967	1,124	7,324	5,550	1,773	5,408
1972	12,959	11,876	1,083	7,458	5,644	1,814	5,678
1971	12,998	11,937	1,061	7,273	5,624	1,650	5,560
1970	12,723	11,599	1,124	6,759	5,168	1,591	5,221
1969	12,588	11,502	1,085	6,827	4,967	1,860	5,307
1968	12,280	11,007	1,272	6,255	4,501	1,753	4,919
1967	11,997	10,769	1,228	5,905	4,155	1,750	4,604
1966	11,643	10,312	1,329	5,708	3,914	1,795	4,556
1965	11,356	9,961	1,395	5,317	3,568	1,749	4,111
1964	11,257	9,898	1,359	4,338	2,798	1,540	...
1963	10,994	9,782	1,212	4,050	2,680	1,370	...
1962	10,270	9,217	1,053	3,934	2,620	1,314	...
1961	9,737	8,635	1,102	3,498	2,205	1,293	...
1960	9,122	8,124	999	3,342	2,126	1,215	...
1959	8,586	7,572	1,014	3,118	1,960	1,158	...
1958	8,484	7,501	982	3,030	1,928	1,101	...
1957	7,995	7,121	874	2,932	1,924	1,006	...
1956	7,670	6,825	845	2,687	1,704	983	...
1955	7,036	6,303	733	2,224	1,429	795	...
White Alone Non-Hispanic							
2008	9,783	8,798	986	12,324	9,630	2,694	8,925
2007	10,171	9,204	966	11,867	9,141	2,726	8,379
2006	10,222	9,072	1,150	11,485	8,821	2,664	8,105
2005	10,647	9,566	1,081	11,715	8,852	2,863	8,246
2004	10,266	9,144	1,029	11,571	8,928	2,643	8,082
2003[1]	10,463	9,473	990	11,295	8,742	2,553	7,810
2002	10,419	9,388	1,031	11,236	8,488	2,749	7,673
2001	10,281	9,331	950	10,602	8,133	2,469	6,980
2000	10,250	9,222	1,029	10,636	8,202	2,434	7,105
1999	10,344	9,314	1,030	10,818	8,158	2,660	7,162
1998	10,170	9,131	1,039	11,109	8,435	2,674	7,251
1997	10,280	9,358	922	11,245	8,688	2,558	7,378
1996	10,107	9,148	959	11,034	8,584	2,450	7,178
1995	10,084	9,094	991	11,024	8,439	2,585	7,194
1994[3]	9,786	8,951	835	11,178	8,568	2,610	7,152
1993	9,216	8,449	767	8,594	6,772	1,822	6,247

Note: Data shown for 1955 to 1966 for the Black population are for Black and Other races.
[1]Starting in 2003 respondents could identify more than one race. Except as noted, the race data in this table from 2003 onward represent those respondents who indicated only one race category.
[3]Prior to 1994, total enrolled does not include the 35 years old and over population.
r = Revised, controlled to 1990 census based population estimates; previous 1993 data controlled to 1980 census based population estimates.
... = Not available.

Table A-9. School Enrollment of the Population 3 Years Old and Over, by Level and Control of School, Race, and Hispanic Origin, October 1955–2008—*Continued*

(Numbers in thousands.)

Year, race, and Hispanic origin	Total enrolled	Nursery school			Kindergarten			Elementary school		
		Total	Public	Private	Total	Public	Private	Total	Public	Private
Black Alone										
2008	11,421	706	548	158	601	545	56	4,993	4,665	329
2007	11,475	700	485	215	605	548	56	4,926	4,572	353
2006	11,400	715	513	202	608	536	71	4,952	4,608	344
2005	11,384	719	542	177	538	486	52	5,106	4,747	359
2004	11,540	825	600	224	596	535	61	5,159	4,905	254
2003[1]	11,408	697	484	212	558	495	63	5,245	4,942	302
2002	11,703	725	503	221	598	543	55	5,545	5,210	335
2001	11,630	787	537	250	605	536	69	5,478	5,160	318
2000	11,503	726	531	195	629	547	82	5,481	5,133	347
1999	11,282	729	569	160	632	558	74	5,388	5,002	386
1998	11,411	761	528	233	689	592	97	5,332	5,031	301
1997	11,270	796	582	214	632	571	61	5,332	5,049	284
1996	10,851	702	459	243	634	545	89	5,171	4,846	325
1995	10,753	663	478	185	653	564	89	5,185	4,845	340
1994[3]	10,702	721	513	208	662	603	59	5,086	4,709	378
1993[r]	9,786	433	320	113	721	649	72	5,009	4,733	276
1993	9,470	414	307	107	687	618	69	4,865	4,599	266
1992	9,150	374	250	124	688	625	63	4,730	4,494	234
1991	9,031	360	244	117	676	598	79	4,672	4,445	229
1990	8,854	431	283	148	636	574	62	4,627	4,428	199
1989	8,707	366	216	150	601	557	44	4,528	4,296	232
1988	8,609	286	168	118	591	547	44	4,538	4,289	250
1987	8,712	277	164	113	699	658	41	4,402	4,206	194
1986	8,556	315	200	115	647	600	47	4,326	4,134	193
1985	8,444	332	212	120	625	562	63	4,307	4,131	175
1984	8,226	340	179	161	563	513	51	4,123	3,947	177
1983	8,199	326	215	111	476	427	48	4,153	3,964	189
1982	8,262	305	192	113	508	463	45	4,194	3,974	220
1981	8,350	284	182	102	474	412	62	4,291	4,087	204
1980	8,251	294	180	115	490	440	50	4,259	4,058	202
1979	8,317	278	185	95	497	443	54	4,296	4,053	243
1978	8,416	312	210	102	451	414	38	4,356	4,154	202
1977	8,564	250	171	78	496	447	50	4,387	4,166	221
1976	8,518	226	146	80	542	482	60	4,430	4,256	175
1975	8,400	276	171	105	468	426	42	4,509	4,344	165
1974	8,215	227	121	106	463	416	47	4,585	4,455	131
1973	7,834	210	146	64	423	391	32	4,473	4,277	196
1972	7,959	185	113	72	448	402	46	4,573	4,382	191
1971	8,179	151	90	61	464	422	42	4,877	4,712	165
1970	7,829	178	129	49	426	374	53	4,868	4,668	200
1969	7,680	170	102	68	425	361	64	4,785	4,633	151
1968	7,448	132	89	43	448	397	51	4,716	4,569	146
1967	7,196	140	92	47	418	375	44	4,618	4,444	173
1966	7,547	125	88	37	420	364	56	4,904	4,739	165
1965	7,252	72	37	35	407	353	54	4,796	4,620	176
1964	6,807	...	...	...	312	275	37	4,634	4,430	205
1963	6,541	...	...	...	276	237	39	4,536	4,321	215
1962	6,203	...	...	...	294	247	47	4,389	4,226	163
1961	6,210	...	...	...	331	308	23	4,424	4,207	216
1960	5,910	...	...	...	243	206	37	4,313	4,118	195
1959	5,513	...	...	...	274	244	30	3,987	3,826	161
1958	5,238	...	...	...	222	186	36	3,804	3,621	182
1957	5,034	...	...	...	229	213	16	3,638	3,483	155
1956	4,712	...	...	...	214	202	12	3,429	3,287	142
1955	4,498	...	...	...	144	121	23	3,273	3,131	142
Asian[2]										
2008	3,545	205	110	95	144	119	24	1,356	1,168	188
2007	3,470	171	77	94	137	112	25	1,421	1,305	115
2006	3,287	143	65	78	162	149	13	1,235	1,105	130
2005	3,377	185	80	105	138	99	39	1,228	1,137	91
2004	3,409	165	72	93	164	152	12	1,239	1,153	86
2003[1]	3,312	138	56	82	122	93	29	1,258	1,122	136
2002	3,787	217	85	132	157	137	20	1,431	1,237	195
2001	3,803	161	91	70	181	161	20	1,409	1,263	146
2000	3,442	222	91	132	152	124	28	1,350	1,257	93
1999	3,621	205	96	109	195	148	47	1,461	1,343	118

Note: Data shown for 1955 to 1966 for the Black population are for Black and Other races.

[1] Starting in 2003 respondents could identify more than one race. Except as noted, the race data in this table from 2003 onward represent those respondents who indicated only one race category.

[2] The data shown prior to 2003 consists of those identifying themselves as "Asian or Pacific Islanders."

[3] Prior to 1994, total enrolled does not include the 35 years old and over population.

r = Revised, controlled to 1990 census based population estimates; previous 1993 data controlled to 1980 census based population estimates.

... = Not available.

Table A-9. School Enrollment of the Population 3 Years Old and Over, by Level and Control of School, Race, and Hispanic Origin, October 1955–2008—*Continued*

(Numbers in thousands.)

Year, race, and Hispanic origin	High school			College			
	Total	Public	Private	Total	Public	Private	Full time
Black Alone	2,639	2,524	115	2,481	1,975	506	1,690
2008..........................	2,743	2,627	116	2,501	1,968	533	1,683
2007..........................	2,792	2,628	165	2,334	1,816	518	1,628
2006..........................	2,723	2,592	131	2,298	1,800	498	1,526
2005..........................	2,660	2,584	76	2,301	1,831	470	1,504
2004..........................	2,765	2,691	74	2,144	1,773	371	1,416
2003[1]..........................	2,558	2,451	107	2,278	1,868	410	1,468
2002..........................	2,531	2,412	119	2,230	1,766	463	1,475
2001..........................	2,502	2,350	152	2,164	1,721	443	1,351
2000..........................	2,536	2,427	109	1,998	1,587	411	1,372
1999..........................	2,614	2,515	99	2,016	1,595	421	1,284
1998..........................	2,605	2,516	89	1,903	1,546	357	1,280
1997..........................	2,443	2,338	105	1,901	1,519	381	1,179
1996..........................	2,481	2,370	111	1,772	1,353	419	1,117
1995..........................	2,434	2,313	121	1,800	1,439	361	1,147
1994[3]..........................	2,317	2,197	120	1,305	1,006	299	951
1993[r]..........................	2,244	2,128	115	1,261	973	288	914
1993..........................	2,152	2,072	72	1,217	980	237	904
1992..........................	2,100	2,044	56	1,220	1,004	217	900
1991..........................	1,975	1,909	65	1,188	963	227	869
1990..........................	2,069	2,027	42	1,139	932	208	833
1989..........................	2,079	2,016	62	1,114	894	220	801
1988..........................	2,140	2,056	84	1,193	977	218	852
1987..........................	2,130	2,040	91	1,138	896	242	859
1986..........................	2,131	2,068	63	1,049	860	190	767
1985..........................	2,061	2,002	59	1,138	918	220	810
1984..........................	2,143	2,057	86	1,102	858	245	806
1983..........................	2,128	2,073	55	1,127	865	263	800
1982..........................	2,168	2,102	65	1,133	898	235	815
1981..........................	2,200	...	...	1,007	...	...	723
1980..........................	2,245	2,171	74	1,002	814	188	748
1979..........................	2,276	2,211	65	1,020	822	199	753
1978..........................	2,327	2,269	59	1,103	916	187	803
1977..........................	2,258	2,187	71	1,062	887	175	817
1976..........................	2,199	2,140	59	948	782	166	742
1975..........................	2,125	2,072	54	814	659	155	589
1974..........................	2,044	1,988	56	685	537	147	536
1973..........................	2,025	1,971	54	727	582	145	525
1972..........................	2,006	1,951	55	680	532	148	534
1971..........................	1,834	1,794	41	522	422	100	427
1970..........................	1,808	1,751	57	492	372	120	401
1969..........................	1,718	1,656	62	434	359	75	338
1968..........................	1,651	1,605	46	370	280	90	271
1967..........................	1,721	1,673	48	282	...	...	210
1966..........................	1,619	1,556	62	358	272	86	218
1965..........................	1,556	1,505	51	306	227	78	...
1964..........................	1,444	1,404	39	286	217	69	...
1963..........................	1,246	1,214	32	274	200	74	...
1962..........................	1,222	1,182	39	233	171	61	...
1961..........................	1,127	1,092	34	227	180	46	...
1960..........................	1,030	999	31	222	160	62	...
1959..........................	998	981	17	212	160	53	...
1958..........................	961	939	22	206	132	74	...
1957..........................	873	843	30	196	120	76	...
1956..........................	926	878	48	155	86	69	...
1955..........................							
Asian[2]	620	564	56	1,220	918	301	917
2008..........................	638	616	23	1,103	841	261	896
2007..........................	663	611	51	1,084	862	223	866
2006..........................	642	596	46	1,184	904	279	948
2005..........................	650	619	31	1,191	928	263	881
2004..........................	632	585	47	1,162	833	328	901
2003[1]..........................	723	664	59	1,258	1,040	218	951
2002..........................	771	736	35	1,280	1,026	254	921
2001..........................	668	622	46	1,049	831	218	792
2000..........................	719	666	53	1,041	779	261	787
1999..........................	650	599	51	1,016	783	233	821

Note: Data shown for 1955 to 1966 for the Black population are for Black and Other races.
[1] Starting in 2003 respondents could identify more than one race. Except as noted, the race data in this table from 2003 onward represent those respondents who indicated only one race category.
[2] The data shown prior to 2003 consists of those identifying themselves as "Asian or Pacific Islanders."
[3] Prior to 1994, total enrolled does not include the 35 years old and over population.
r = Revised, controlled to 1990 census based population estimates; previous 1993 data controlled to 1980 census based population estimates.
... = Not available.

Table A-9.   School Enrollment of the Population 3 Years Old and Over, by Level and Control of School, Race, and Hispanic Origin, October 1955–2008—*Continued*

(Numbers in thousands.)

Year, race, and Hispanic origin	Total enrolled	Nursery school Total	Nursery school Public	Nursery school Private	Kindergarten Total	Kindergarten Public	Kindergarten Private	Elementary school Total	Elementary school Public	Elementary school Private
1998	3,386	196	77	118	145	120	25	1,380	1,190	189
1997	3,261	168	59	108	161	110	51	1,329	1,186	144
1996	3,258	183	63	120	177	158	19	1,255	1,144	111
1995	1,863	76	28	47	75	62	13	697	622	74
1994[3]	2,057	76	27	50	74	60	14	785	707	78
1993	2,321	100	38	62	139	125	14	1,012	930	82
Hispanic[4]										
2008	13,967	844	668	177	961	910	51	6,742	6,450	292
2007	13,708	905	711	194	990	954	37	6,582	6,299	284
2006	13,111	911	707	205	846	798	48	6,394	6,109	285
2005	12,809	797	601	196	804	725	79	6,330	5,991	339
2004	12,509	787	591	196	769	699	70	6,184	5,895	290
2003	11,929	768	561	206	694	633	61	5,974	5,651	322
2002	11,544	637	476	161	727	688	39	5,909	5,585	324
2001	11,163	593	452	141	728	641	87	5,779	5,478	301
2000	10,163	574	419	154	687	639	48	5,224	5,012	213
1999	9,936	585	458	127	666	594	73	5,088	4,829	259
1998	9,528	618	492	126	639	608	31	4,831	4,568	262
1997	9,220	548	436	112	648	589	59	4,644	4,427	217
1996	8,818	533	403	130	602	539	63	4,443	4,162	281
1995	8,563	510	350	160	558	465	93	4,434	4,165	269
1994[3]	8,183	400	278	122	559	516	43	4,162	3,848	314
1993[r]	7,651	231	169	62	639	576	63	4,027	3,779	248
1993	6,689	194	142	52	538	484	53	3,534	3,317	217
1992	6,598	209	139	70	554	493	60	3,525	3,271	252
1991	6,306	215	146	69	552	525	27	3,461	3,240	221
1990	6,072	242	153	88	475	446	29	3,301	3,107	197
1989	5,722	181	95	86	404	382	21	3,219	3,031	188
1988	5,588	151	111	40	461	445	16	3,160	2,954	207
1987	5,619	226	138	88	439	399	39	3,048	2,861	187
1986	5,513	179	114	65	465	421	44	2,995	2,787	208
1985	5,070	168	105	63	364	315	49	2,803	2,607	196
1984	4,284	117	78	39	293	267	26	2,384	2,218	166
1983	4,618	108	60	48	335	285	50	2,548	2,323	225
1982	4,478	83	46	37	329	291	37	2,501	2,276	225
1981	4,551	131	68	63	306	282	24	2,474	2,239	235
1980	4,263	146	70	75	263	234	30	2,363	2,134	228
1979	3,608	89	50	39	226	210	16	1,934	1,745	189
1978	3,455	87	47	39	231	198	33	1,893	1,704	188
1977	3,516	75	30	46	220	206	14	1,874	1,654	220
1976	3,623	68	38	30	262	242	20	1,934	1,768	165
1975	3,741	85	47	39	235	218	17	2,062	1,858	204
1974	3,620	85	37	48	225	207	18	2,040	1,780	260
1973	3,171	68	41	27	171	165	6	1,884	1,712	172
1972	3,257	61	43	18	241	227	14	1,879	1,705	173
White Alone or in Combination										
2008	60,309	3,642	1,927	1,715	3,247	2,863	385	25,498	22,849	2,649
2007	59,896	3,689	1,959	1,730	3,339	2,946	393	25,321	22,689	2,632
2006	59,391	3,765	1,895	1,871	3,213	2,820	393	25,424	22,809	2,615
2005	60,035	3,642	1,819	1,823	3,179	2,715	463	25,682	22,794	2,888
2004	59,427	3,682	1,762	1,920	3,169	2,670	498	25,691	22,682	3,009
2003	59,184	4,039	1,989	2,050	3,002	2,477	525	25,581	22,686	2,895
Black Alone or in Combination										
2008	12,542	776	589	187	668	609	59	5,593	5,225	368
2007	12,401	788	546	242	673	617	57	5,395	5,030	365
2006	12,261	801	568	234	678	607	71	5,365	5,002	363
2005	12,118	763	563	200	593	531	62	5,504	5,122	382
2004	12,303	864	622	242	676	606	70	5,540	5,251	289
2003	12,144	787	526	262	637	559	78	5,604	5,276	327
Asian Alone or in Combination										
2008	4,122	267	143	123	188	156	32	1,570	1,351	219
2007	4,025	219	94	125	179	151	28	1,664	1,513	151
2006	3,849	189	78	111	203	181	22	1,497	1,331	166
2005	3,964	220	94	126	159	118	41	1,495	1,362	133
2004	3,943	208	82	127	191	169	21	1,497	1,350	148
2003	3,817	164	73	90	148	111	38	1,507	1,346	161

Note: Data shown for 1955 to 1966 for the Black population are for Black and Other races.
[3] Prior to 1994, total enrolled does not include the 35 years old and over population.
[4] May be of any race.
r = Revised, controlled to 1990 census based population estimates; previous 1993 data controlled to 1980 census based population estimates.
… = Not available.

Table A-9. School Enrollment of the Population 3 Years Old and Over, by Level and Control of School, Race, and Hispanic Origin, October 1955–2008—*Continued*

(Numbers in thousands.)

Year, race, and Hispanic origin	High school			College			
	Total	Public	Private	Total	Public	Private	Full time
1998............................	656	600	57	947	712	235	721
1997............................	644	606	38	999	816	183	710
1996............................	399	375	24	617	470	147	456
1995............................	399	365	34	723	548	174	530
1994³...........................	428	390	37	641	519	122	542
1993............................							
Hispanic⁴	3,192	3,066	126	2,227	1,919	308	1,434
2008............................	3,058	2,902	156	2,172	1,888	284	1,459
2007............................	2,990	2,856	134	1,968	1,664	304	1,246
2006............................	2,937	2,824	113	1,942	1,625	316	1,255
2005............................	2,793	2,685	108	1,975	1,676	299	1,276
2004............................	2,779	2,667	112	1,714	1,480	235	1,139
2003............................	2,614	2,513	101	1,656	1,374	283	1,004
2002............................	2,363	2,246	117	1,700	1,445	255	1,005
2001............................	2,253	2,144	108	1,426	1,219	207	873
2000............................	2,290	2,200	91	1,307	1,093	214	765
1999............................	2,077	1,978	98	1,363	1,137	226	801
1998............................	2,119	2,035	84	1,260	1,079	181	797
1997............................	2,018	1,922	96	1,223	1,031	192	708
1996............................	1,854	1,772	83	1,207	1,037	170	709
1995............................	1,874	1,781	92	1,187	1,019	169	640
1994³...........................	1,722	1,653	69	1,029	872	157	686
1993ʳ...........................	1,556	1,496	60	867	731	134	573
1993............................	1,494	1,435	59	813	710	104	487
1992............................	1,357	1,299	61	721	607	115	481
1991............................	1,437	1,374	64	617	515	100	380
1990............................	1,278	1,231	48	642	557	82	416
1989............................	1,163	1,113	49	654	592	60	414
1988............................	1,239	1,160	80	668	551	115	414
1987............................	1,197	1,116	81	677	540	137	418
1986............................	1,156	1,090	167	579	464	116	381
1985............................	966	909	57	524	433	91	356
1984............................	1,104	1,027	77	523	441	82	335
1983............................	1,072	995	77	493	398	96	312
1982............................	1,130	1,056	74	510	398	112	343
1981............................	1,048	...	...	443	...	...	294
1980............................	920	875	45	440	365	75	314
1979............................	868	825	43	377	315	62	231
1978............................	928	836	92	418	357	60	287
1977............................	932	867	65	427	354	73	297
1976............................	948	886	61	411	358	53	287
1975............................	916	858	59	354	297	57	247
1974............................	758	707	51	290	247	43	201
1973............................	834	784	50	242	213	29	178
1972............................							
White Alone or in Combination	13,184	12,050	1,133	14,738	11,692	3,046	10,511
2008............................	13,433	12,302	1,131	14,114	11,058	3,056	9,912
2007............................	13,425	12,115	1,309	13,564	10,569	2,995	9,433
2006............................	13,741	12,516	1,225	13,791	10,561	3,230	9,618
2005............................	13,218	12,047	1,170	13,668	10,711	2,957	9,468
2004............................	13,398	12,267	1,131	13,164	10,366	2,798	9,048
2003............................							
Black Alone or in Combination	2,886	2,769	118	2,619	2,065	554	1,779
2008............................	2,915	2,792	122	2,630	2,059	571	1,774
2007............................	2,971	2,798	174	2,444	1,907	537	1,702
2006............................	2,870	2,729	141	2,387	1,866	521	1,585
2005............................	2,811	2,762	85	2,412	1,922	490	1,591
2004............................	2,889	2,800	89	2,227	1,846	381	1,482
2003............................							
Asian Alone or in Combination							
2008............................	758	690	68	1,340	1,009	331	1,009
2007............................	760	718	42	1,204	917	287	988
2006............................	806	743	63	1,154	918	235	900
2005............................	792	726	67	1,297	993	305	1,036
2004............................	786	743	43	1,260	980	281	936
2003............................	736	674	62	1,262	925	337	965

Note: Data shown for 1955 to 1966 for the Black population are for Black and Other races.
³Prior to 1994, total enrolled does not include the 35 years old and over population.
⁴May be of any race.
r = Revised, controlled to 1990 census based population estimates; previous 1993 data controlled to 1980 census based population estimates.
... = Not available.

Table A-10.   Percent of the Population 3 Years Old and Over Enrolled in School, by Age, Sex, Race, and Hispanic Origin, October 1947–2008

(Percent.)

Year, sex, race, and Hispanic origin	Total enrolled 3 to 34 years old	Total enrolled 3 years old and over	3 and 4 years old	5 and 6 years old	7 to 9 years old	10 to 13 years old	14 and 15 years old	16 and 17 years old	18 and 19 years old	20 and 21 years old	22 to 24 years old	25 to 29 years old	30 to 34 years old	35 years old and over
ALL RACES														
Both Sexes														
2008	56.2	26.6	52.8	93.8	98.3	98.9	98.6	95.2	66.0	50.1	28.2	13.2	7.3	2.0
2007	56.1	26.6	54.5	94.7	98.1	98.6	98.7	94.3	66.8	48.4	27.3	12.4	7.2	1.9
2006	56.2	26.7	55.7	94.6	98.2	98.3	98.3	94.5	65.5	47.5	26.7	11.7	7.2	1.9
2005	56.5	27.1	53.6	95.4	98.6	98.6	98.0	95.1	67.6	48.7	27.3	11.9	6.9	2.0
2004	56.2	27.2	54.0	95.4	98.1	98.6	98.5	94.5	64.4	48.9	26.3	13.0	6.6	2.0
2003	56.2	27.2	55.1	94.5	98.1	98.4	97.5	94.9	64.5	48.3	27.8	11.8	6.8	1.9
2002	56.1	27.3	54.5	95.2	98.0	98.5	98.4	94.3	63.3	47.8	25.6	12.1	6.6	2.1
2001	55.7	27.2	52.2	95.3	98.2	98.4	98.1	93.4	61.0	45.5	25.1	11.7	6.8	2.0
2000	55.9	27.5	52.1	95.6	98.1	98.3	98.7	92.8	61.2	44.1	24.6	11.4	6.7	1.9
1999	56.0	27.7	54.2	96.0	98.5	98.8	98.2	93.6	60.6	45.3	24.5	11.1	6.2	2.1
1998	55.8	27.9	52.1	95.6	98.8	99.0	98.4	93.9	62.2	44.8	24.9	11.9	6.6	2.1
1997	55.6	28.3	52.6	96.6	98.8	99.3	98.9	94.3	61.5	45.9	26.4	11.8	5.7	2.3
1996	54.1	27.8	48.3	94.0	97.2	98.1	98.0	92.8	61.5	44.4	24.8	11.9	6.1	2.3
1995	53.7	27.8	48.7	96.0	98.7	99.1	98.9	93.6	59.4	44.9	23.2	11.6	6.0	2.2
1994	53.3	27.9	47.3	96.7	99.3	99.4	98.8	94.4	60.2	44.9	24.1	10.8	6.7	2.3
1993r	51.9	...	40.1	95.3	99.5	99.5	98.9	93.9	61.4	42.6	23.5	10.2	5.9	...
1993	51.8	26.9	40.4	95.4	99.5	99.5	98.9	94.0	61.6	42.7	23.6	10.2	5.9	2.2
1992	51.4	26.9	39.7	95.5	99.4	99.4	99.1	94.1	61.4	44.0	23.7	9.8	6.1	2.1
1991	50.7	26.9	40.5	95.4	99.6	99.7	98.8	93.3	59.6	42.0	22.2	10.2	6.2	2.2
1990	50.2	26.8	44.4	96.5	99.7	99.6	99.0	92.5	57.3	39.7	21.0	9.7	5.8	2.1
1989	49.1	26.4	39.1	95.2	99.2	99.4	98.8	92.7	56.0	38.5	19.9	9.3	5.7	2.0
1988	48.7	26.5	38.2	96.0	99.6	99.7	98.9	91.6	55.7	39.1	18.3	8.3	5.9	2.1
1987	48.6	26.6	38.3	95.1	99.6	99.5	98.6	91.7	55.6	38.7	17.5	9.0	5.9	1.8
1986	48.2	26.6	39.0	95.3	99.3	99.1	97.6	92.3	54.6	33.0	17.9	8.8	6.0	1.8
1985	48.3	26.8	38.9	96.1	99.1	99.3	98.1	91.7	51.6	35.3	16.9	9.2	6.1	1.7
1984	47.9	26.6	36.3	94.5	99.0	99.4	97.8	91.5	50.1	33.9	17.3	9.1	6.3	1.5
1983	48.4	27.1	37.6	95.4	98.9	99.4	98.3	91.7	50.4	32.5	16.6	9.6	6.4	1.7
1982	48.6	27.4	36.4	95.0	99.2	99.1	98.5	90.6	47.8	34.0	16.8	9.6	6.3	1.6
1981	48.9	27.9	36.0	94.0	99.2	99.3	98.0	90.6	49.0	31.6	16.5	9.0	6.9	1.7
1980	49.7	28.2	36.7	95.7	99.1	99.4	98.2	89.0	46.4	31.0	16.3	9.3	6.5	1.6
1979	50.3	28.7	35.1	95.8	99.2	99.1	98.1	89.2	45.0	30.2	15.8	9.6	6.4	1.7
1978	51.2	29.3	34.2	95.3	99.3	99.0	98.4	89.1	45.4	29.5	16.3	9.4	6.4	1.6
1977	52.5	...	32.0	95.8	99.5	99.4	98.5	88.9	46.2	31.8	16.5	10.8	6.9	...
1976	53.1	31.7	31.3	95.5	99.2	99.2	98.2	89.1	46.2	32.0	17.1	10.0	6.0	3.9
1975	53.7	...	31.5	94.7	99.3	99.3	98.2	89.0	46.9	31.2	16.2	10.1	6.6	...
1974	53.6	...	28.8	94.2	99.1	99.5	97.9	87.9	43.1	30.2	15.1	9.6	5.7	...
1973	53.5	...	24.2	92.5	99.1	99.2	97.5	88.3	42.9	30.1	14.5	8.5	4.5	...
1972	54.9	...	24.4	91.9	99.0	99.3	97.6	88.9	46.3	31.4	14.8	8.6	4.6	...
1971	56.2	...	21.2	91.6	99.1	99.2	98.6	90.2	49.2	32.2	15.4	8.0	4.9	...
1970	56.4	...	20.5	89.5	99.3	99.2	98.1	90.0	47.7	31.9	14.9	7.5	4.2	...
1969	57.0	...	16.1	88.4	99.3	99.1	98.1	89.7	50.2	34.1	15.4	7.9	4.8	...
1968	56.7	...	15.7	87.6	99.1	99.1	98.0	90.2	50.4	31.2	13.8	7.0	3.9	...
1967	56.6	...	14.2	87.4	99.4	99.1	98.2	88.8	47.6	33.3	13.6	6.6	4.0	...
1966	56.1	...	12.5	85.1	99.3	99.3	98.6	88.5	47.2	29.9	13.2	6.5	2.7	...
1965	55.5	...	10.6	84.4	99.3	99.4	98.9	87.4	46.3	27.6	13.2	6.1	3.2	...
1964	54.5	...	9.5	83.3	99.0	99.0	98.6	87.7	41.6	26.3	9.9	5.2	2.6	...
1963	58.5	...	...	82.7	99.4	99.3	98.4	87.1	40.9	25.0	11.4	4.9	2.5	...
1962	57.8	...	...	82.2	99.2	99.3	98.0	84.3	41.8	23.0	10.3	5.0	2.6	...
1961	56.8	...	...	81.7	99.4	99.3	97.6	83.6	38.0	21.5	8.4	4.4	2.0	...
1960	56.4	...	...	80.7	99.6	99.5	97.8	82.6	38.4	19.4	8.7	4.9	2.4	...
1959	55.5	...	...	80.0	99.4	99.4	97.5	82.9	36.8	18.8	8.6	5.1	2.2	...
1958	54.8	...	...	80.4	99.5	99.5	96.9	80.6	37.6	------13.4------		5.7	2.2	...
1957	53.6	...	...	78.6	99.5	99.5	97.1	80.5	34.9	------14.0------		5.5	1.8	...
1956	52.3	...	...	77.6	99.4	99.2	96.9	78.4	35.4	------12.8------		5.1	1.9	...
1955	50.8	...	...	78.1	99.2	99.2	95.9	77.4	31.5	------11.1------		4.2	1.6	...
1954	50.0	...	...	77.3	99.2	99.5	95.8	78.0	32.4	------11.2------		4.1	1.5	...
1953	48.8	...	...	55.7	99.4	99.4	96.5	74.7	31.2	------11.1------		2.9	1.7	...
1952	46.8	...	...	54.7	98.7	98.9	96.2	73.4	28.7	------9.5------		2.6	1.1	...
1951	45.4	...	...	54.5	99.0	99.2	94.8	75.1	26.3	------8.3------		2.5	...	...

Note: Data for 1947 to 1953 exclude kindergarten. Nursery school was first collected in 1964. Data shown for 1947 to 1966 for the Black population are for Black and other races.

r = Revised, controlled to 1990 census based population estimates; previous 1993 data controlled to 1980 census based population estimates.

... = Not available.

Table A-10.   Percent of the Population 3 Years Old and Over Enrolled in School, by Age, Sex, Race, and Hispanic Origin, October 1947–2008—*Continued*

(Percent.)

Year, sex, race, and Hispanic origin	Total enrolled 3 to 34 years old	Total enrolled 3 years old and over	Age											
			3 and 4 years old	5 and 6 years old	7 to 9 years old	10 to 13 years old	14 and 15 years old	16 and 17 years old	18 and 19 years old	20 and 21 years old	22 to 24 years old	25 to 29 years old	30 to 34 years old	35 years old and over
1950..............	44.2	...	...	58.2	98.9	98.6	94.7	71.3	29.4	------9.0------		3.0	...	...
1949..............	43.9	...	...	59.3	98.5	98.7	93.5	69.5	25.3	------9.2------		3.8	1.1	...
1948..............	43.1	...	...	56.0	98.3	98.0	92.7	71.2	26.9	------9.7------		2.6	0.9	...
1947..............	42.3	...	...	58.0	98.4	98.6	91.6	67.6	24.3	------10.2------		3.0	1.0	...
Male														
2008..............	55.6	26.9	52.3	93.8	98.0	98.7	99.0	94.9	64.0	47.4	26.3	12.1	6.3	1.4
2007..............	55.4	26.9	54.4	94.0	98.1	98.4	98.4	94.4	66.3	43.7	25.4	10.2	6.4	1.5
2006..............	55.5	27.0	56.0	94.4	98.1	98.2	98.2	94.1	63.6	44.0	25.0	10.4	5.9	1.5
2005..............	55.8	27.4	52.8	94.8	98.2	98.4	97.5	95.1	66.5	45.3	25.2	9.6	5.9	1.5
2004..............	55.0	27.6	54.7	95.5	97.8	98.5	98.7	94.9	60.3	46.6	24.1	11.5	5.6	1.6
2003..............	55.9	27.8	55.9	94.7	97.9	98.3	97.5	95.0	62.4	43.4	26.1	10.8	6.3	1.5
2002..............	55.8	27.9	54.6	95.3	98.1	98.3	98.4	94.0	61.8	44.8	23.8	10.7	5.5	1.7
2001..............	55.4	27.8	51.6	95.2	98.5	98.1	98.1	93.0	58.9	44.0	23.8	10.3	5.7	1.5
2000..............	55.8	28.0	50.8	95.1	98.0	98.3	98.7	92.7	58.3	41.0	23.9	10.0	5.6	1.5
1999..............	56.6	28.6	53.3	95.9	98.3	98.7	98.0	93.7	60.3	44.7	23.6	10.7	5.8	1.6
1998..............	55.9	28.6	53.3	95.2	98.7	99.0	98.3	93.5	60.1	42.7	24.6	10.9	5.5	1.6
1997..............	55.8	28.8	51.9	96.7	98.6	99.4	99.1	94.2	60.6	44.4	25.4	11.7	4.7	1.6
1996..............	54.4	28.5	46.9	93.8	97.2	98.0	98.5	93.2	60.8	43.9	25.2	11.4	4.9	1.8
1995..............	54.3	28.7	49.4	95.3	98.9	99.1	99.0	94.5	59.5	44.7	22.8	11.0	5.4	1.8
1994..............	53.7	28.7	47.6	97.0	99.2	99.4	98.8	94.3	60.4	42.7	24.2	10.5	5.9	1.7
1993ʳ............	52.6	...	41.1	95.5	99.5	99.6	99.0	94.9	61.1	42.3	25.3	9.6	5.2	...
1993..............	52.6	27.9	41.5	95.5	99.5	99.6	99.0	95.0	61.6	42.6	25.5	9.6	5.2	1.6
1992..............	51.9	27.7	40.3	95.7	99.5	99.5	99.2	95.4	61.6	41.7	23.8	9.1	5.2	1.5
1991..............	51.5	27.9	39.9	95.0	99.7	99.8	99.1	93.7	59.8	41.8	24.0	10.6	5.6	1.6
1990..............	50.9	27.7	43.9	96.5	99.7	99.6	99.1	92.7	58.2	40.3	22.3	9.2	4.8	1.5
1989..............	49.7	27.3	38.8	95.1	99.3	99.2	99.2	93.2	56.6	37.3	20.4	9.3	5.0	1.4
1988..............	49.6	27.6	38.3	95.9	99.6	99.7	98.9	92.1	56.2	39.0	20.5	8.1	5.5	1.5
1987..............	49.9	27.9	40.0	95.7	99.7	99.7	98.7	92.3	57.9	41.2	18.7	9.1	5.0	1.3
1986..............	49.3	27.8	38.8	96.0	99.4	98.9	97.6	92.3	57.1	33.4	19.0	9.4	5.6	1.3
1985..............	49.2	27.9	36.8	95.3	99.1	99.2	98.3	92.4	52.2	36.5	18.8	9.4	5.4	1.3
1984..............	49.1	28.0	35.9	94.0	98.8	99.3	97.5	91.8	52.4	36.2	20.1	9.6	5.8	1.1
1983..............	49.7	28.6	38.1	95.1	98.8	99.3	98.4	91.8	50.4	35.2	19.4	10.7	5.8	1.2
1982..............	49.7	28.8	36.4	94.7	99.2	99.0	98.7	91.3	48.9	35.2	18.5	10.1	5.6	1.2
1981..............	50.2	29.3	36.8	94.2	98.9	99.2	98.2	90.7	50.5	32.1	19.2	9.6	6.2	1.2
1980..............	50.9	29.6	37.8	95.0	99.0	99.4	98.7	89.1	47.0	32.6	17.8	9.8	5.9	1.2
1979..............	51.8	30.2	34.6	96.3	99.0	98.9	98.3	90.8	46.6	31.6	17.6	10.4	6.0	1.3
1978..............	52.9	31.0	34.0	95.1	99.1	99.8	98.4	89.5	47.8	31.7	19.1	10.9	6.5	1.3
1977..............	54.3	...	32.1	94.7	99.5	99.2	98.7	90.0	48.4	34.6	19.7	12.6	7.1	...
1976..............	55.1	33.6	30.9	95.6	98.9	99.1	98.6	90.5	48.2	33.6	20.7	13.0	6.8	3.6
1975..............	56.0	...	30.6	94.3	99.2	98.9	98.4	90.7	49.9	35.3	20.0	13.1	7.7	...
1974..............	56.0	...	28.1	94.4	99.1	99.3	98.0	88.6	45.8	34.8	19.4	12.7	6.7	...
1973..............	56.1	...	24.5	92.2	99.0	99.2	97.9	89.4	47.9	34.4	19.1	11.8	5.6	...
1972..............	57.8	...	24.4	91.7	98.9	99.3	97.7	90.2	51.2	37.3	21.3	12.1	5.8	...
1971..............	59.3	...	20.0	90.9	99.0	98.8	98.7	91.7	55.4	38.9	23.3	11.9	6.3	...
1970..............	59.7	...	21.2	88.9	99.3	98.8	98.2	91.3	54.4	42.7	21.2	11.0	5.3	...
1969..............	60.5	...	15.5	87.7	99.0	98.9	98.1	91.6	59.4	46.5	22.9	11.4	5.9	...
1968..............	60.4	...	15.4	87.3	98.9	98.9	98.2	91.7	60.4	45.0	20.5	10.8	5.0	...
1967..............	60.0	...	14.2	86.6	99.4	98.9	98.3	91.0	56.3	44.3	21.0	9.9	5.4	...
1966..............	59.7	...	12.3	84.5	99.2	99.1	98.7	89.9	57.8	41.4	21.3	9.6	3.8	...
1965..............	58.8	...	10.2	84.4	99.3	99.3	99.0	88.0	55.6	37.6	21.1	9.4	4.5	...
1964..............	57.5	...	8.9	83.4	98.7	98.9	99.0	89.8	50.9	34.4	16.1	8.1	3.6	...
1963..............	62.3	...	...	82.7	99.2	99.0	98.7	89.4	51.0	33.6	19.5	7.8	3.7	...
1962..............	61.7	...	...	82.6	99.1	99.2	98.7	87.1	51.2	31.3	17.7	8.5	3.9	...
1961..............	60.4	...	...	82.0	99.5	99.2	98.1	84.7	48.6	29.5	13.9	7.1	2.9	...
1960..............	60.0	...	...	80.8	99.6	99.4	97.9	84.5	47.8	27.1	15.0	8.4	3.7	...
1959..............	59.1	...	...	79.5	99.2	99.4	97.8	84.8	45.6	28.3	13.7	8.9	3.3	...
1958..............	58.7	...	...	80.6	99.6	99.4	96.9	83.8	47.5	------21.0------		9.5	2.9	...
1957..............	57.5	...	...	78.3	99.4	99.6	98.0	82.8	43.3	------21.3------		9.5	2.6	...
1956..............	56.3	...	...	77.1	99.2	99.1	97.1	79.9	45.1	------20.6------		8.9	2.7	...
1955..............	54.9	...	...	78.1	99.1	99.4	95.7	81.1	42.5	------18.1------		7.0	2.1	...

Note: Data for 1947 to 1953 exclude kindergarten. Nursery school was first collected in 1964. Data shown for 1947 to 1966 for the Black population are for Black and other races.

r = Revised, controlled to 1990 census based population estimates; previous 1993 data controlled to 1980 census based population estimates.
... = Not available.

Table A-10.   Percent of the Population 3 Years Old and Over Enrolled in School, by Age, Sex, Race, and Hispanic Origin, October 1947–2008—*Continued*

(Percent.)

Year, sex, race, and Hispanic origin	Total enrolled 3 to 34 years old	Total enrolled 3 years old and over	Age											
			3 and 4 years old	5 and 6 years old	7 to 9 years old	10 to 13 years	14 and 15 years old	16 and 17 years old	18 and 19 years old	20 and 21 years old	22 to 24 years old	25 to 29 years old	30 to 34 years old	35 years old and over
1954	54.0	...	...	76.3	99.0	99.4	96.1	80.9	40.6	------19.1------		6.7	1.9	...
1953	50.2	...	...	55.0	99.3	99.1	96.4	76.5	37.7	------18.5------		5.5	2.0	...
1952	49.4	...	...	54.8	98.6	98.9	96.2	73.9	37.2	------16.9------		4.7	1.7	...
1951	56.8	...	...	55.1	99.1	99.1	95.1	74.3	32.4	------14.3------		4.2	...	...
1950	54.8	...	...	56.8	98.8	98.7	95.2	72.8	35.7	------14.3------		5.9	...	...
1949	45.8	...	...	60.1	98.5	98.6	93.9	70.8	31.6	------15.4------		6.8	1.9	...
1948	44.8	...	...	55.1	99.5	98.1	92.0	72.1	34.3	------16.5------		5.1	1.5	...
1947	44.3	...	...	57.4	98.5	98.7	90.3	67.6	31.4	------17.0------		5.8	1.7	...
Female														
2008	56.7	26.3	53.3	93.7	98.7	99.2	98.2	95.4	68.1	53.0	30.1	14.3	8.3	2.5
2007	56.8	26.3	54.7	95.3	98.1	98.7	99.0	94.1	67.2	53.3	29.2	14.7	7.9	2.4
2006	56.6	26.3	55.4	94.8	98.3	98.4	98.4	95.0	67.4	51.1	28.5	13.0	8.5	2.3
2005	57.2	26.8	54.4	96.1	99.0	98.9	98.4	95.1	68.8	52.3	29.2	14.2	7.9	2.4
2004	56.5	26.8	53.2	95.3	98.5	98.7	98.3	94.1	68.5	51.3	28.4	14.4	7.7	2.5
2003	56.4	26.6	54.1	94.4	98.3	98.6	97.5	94.8	66.6	52.9	29.5	12.8	7.3	2.2
2002	56.4	26.8	54.4	95.1	97.9	98.7	98.5	94.7	65.0	50.9	27.3	13.5	7.7	2.5
2001	55.9	26.7	52.9	95.4	97.8	98.8	98.2	93.8	63.2	46.9	26.5	13.0	7.9	2.5
2000	56.0	26.9	53.4	96.1	98.2	98.3	98.6	92.9	64.2	47.3	25.3	12.7	7.7	2.3
1999	55.5	27.0	55.2	96.1	98.7	98.9	98.3	93.5	60.9	45.8	25.4	11.4	6.6	2.4
1998	55.6	27.3	50.9	95.9	98.8	99.1	98.5	94.3	64.4	47.2	25.2	12.9	7.7	2.6
1997	55.4	27.6	53.2	96.4	99.1	99.3	98.7	94.4	62.4	47.4	27.4	11.9	6.6	2.9
1996	53.8	27.1	49.8	94.3	97.3	98.2	97.5	92.4	62.2	44.8	24.5	12.5	7.3	2.8
1995	53.2	27.0	48.1	96.8	98.5	99.1	98.8	92.6	59.2	45.1	23.6	12.2	6.5	2.7
1994	52.9	27.2	46.9	96.4	99.5	99.4	98.7	94.4	60.0	47.0	23.9	11.1	7.5	2.8
1993r	51.1	...	39.0	95.2	99.4	99.5	98.7	92.8	61.7	42.8	21.7	10.8	6.6	...
1993	51.0	25.9	39.3	95.2	99.4	99.5	98.7	92.9	61.7	42.9	21.8	10.8	6.6	2.6
1992	51.0	26.1	39.1	95.2	99.2	99.2	99.1	92.7	61.2	46.1	23.6	10.5	7.0	2.6
1991	49.9	26.0	41.1	95.8	99.5	99.6	98.4	92.8	59.4	42.2	20.4	9.8	6.8	2.8
1990	49.5	25.9	44.9	96.4	99.6	99.7	98.9	92.4	56.3	39.2	19.9	10.2	6.9	2.7
1989	48.4	25.5	39.5	95.2	99.2	99.6	98.4	92.2	55.5	39.7	19.5	9.3	6.4	2.5
1988	47.7	25.5	38.1	96.0	99.6	99.7	98.8	91.2	55.2	39.1	16.2	8.6	6.4	2.6
1987	47.4	25.3	36.6	94.5	99.5	99.2	98.4	91.1	53.4	36.4	16.5	9.0	6.7	2.2
1986	47.1	25.4	39.0	94.6	99.2	99.3	97.5	92.3	52.1	32.7	16.8	8.2	6.4	2.2
1985	47.4	25.7	41.2	97.0	99.2	99.4	97.9	90.9	51.0	34.1	15.1	9.1	6.8	2.1
1984	46.6	25.3	36.7	95.1	99.3	99.4	98.2	91.2	48.0	31.7	14.6	8.6	6.7	1.9
1983	47.0	25.7	36.9	95.8	99.0	99.5	98.2	91.6	50.3	29.9	13.9	8.5	7.0	2.0
1982	47.5	26.1	36.4	95.3	99.2	99.3	98.3	89.9	46.8	32.9	15.1	9.0	6.9	1.9
1981	47.7	26.6	35.2	93.8	99.5	99.4	97.7	90.5	47.5	31.2	13.9	8.4	7.5	2.0
1980	48.5	26.9	35.5	96.4	99.2	99.4	97.7	88.8	45.8	29.5	14.9	8.8	7.0	1.9
1979	49.0	27.3	35.6	95.2	99.4	99.4	97.9	87.6	43.4	28.9	14.1	8.8	6.7	2.0
1978	49.5	27.8	34.5	95.5	99.5	99.2	98.4	88.8	43.0	27.5	13.6	7.9	6.2	2.0
1977	50.7	...	32.0	96.9	99.5	99.6	98.3	87.7	44.0	29.1	13.6	9.1	6.7	...
1976	51.0	29.8	31.6	95.5	99.4	99.3	97.8	87.7	44.4	30.6	13.8	7.3	5.2	4.2
1975	51.5	...	32.4	95.2	99.5	99.6	98.0	87.2	44.2	27.4	12.6	7.2	5.6	...
1974	51.3	...	29.5	93.9	99.2	99.7	97.9	87.1	40.7	26.0	11.1	6.7	4.6	...
1973	50.9	...	23.8	92.9	99.3	99.2	97.1	87.2	38.2	26.3	10.2	5.4	3.6	...
1972	52.0	...	24.4	92.2	99.1	99.4	97.5	87.6	41.8	26.3	8.9	5.3	3.6	...
1971	53.2	...	22.4	92.3	99.2	99.5	98.5	88.7	43.4	26.8	8.4	4.4	3.6	...
1970	53.2	...	19.8	90.2	99.3	99.5	98.0	88.6	41.6	23.6	9.4	4.3	3.1	...
1969	53.6	...	16.8	89.1	99.6	99.4	98.2	87.7	41.8	25.3	9.1	4.6	3.8	...
1968	53.2	...	16.1	88.0	99.3	99.3	97.8	88.7	41.3	21.5	8.3	3.4	2.9	...
1967	53.3	...	14.1	88.2	99.5	99.3	98.2	86.7	40.3	24.9	7.4	3.6	2.8	...
1966	52.7	...	12.7	85.7	99.4	99.5	98.4	87.1	37.7	20.9	6.6	3.6	1.7	...
1965	52.3	...	10.9	84.4	99.3	99.5	98.7	86.9	37.7	19.5	6.5	3.1	2.1	...
1964	51.5	...	10.2	83.2	99.3	99.2	98.2	85.6	33.7	19.5	4.4	2.6	1.6	...
1963	54.9	...	...	82.6	99.6	99.6	98.0	84.8	32.3	17.8	4.4	2.4	1.5	...
1962	54.0	...	...	81.7	99.3	99.4	97.3	81.5	33.7	16.1	3.9	1.8	1.4	...
1961	53.4	...	...	81.4	99.3	99.4	97.2	82.4	28.6	14.9	3.7	1.9	1.2	...
1960	52.8	...	...	80.6	99.6	99.5	97.6	80.6	30.0	13.1	3.4	1.8	1.2	...
1959	52.0	...	...	80.5	99.6	99.5	97.1	81.0	29.2	11.1	4.4	1.7	1.3	...

Note: Data for 1947 to 1953 exclude kindergarten. Nursery school was first collected in 1964. Data shown for 1947 to 1966 for the Black population are for Black and other races.
r = Revised, controlled to 1990 census based population estimates; previous 1993 data controlled to 1980 census based population estimates.
... = Not available.

Table A-10. Percent of the Population 3 Years Old and Over Enrolled in School, by Age, Sex, Race, and Hispanic Origin, October 1947–2008—*Continued*

(Percent.)

Year, sex, race, and Hispanic origin	Total enrolled 3 to 34 years old	Total enrolled 3 years old and over	Age											
			3 and 4 years old	5 and 6 years old	7 to 9 years old	10 to 13 years old	14 and 15 years old	16 and 17 years old	18 and 19 years old	20 and 21 years old	22 to 24 years old	25 to 29 years old	30 to 34 years old	35 years old and over
1958.............	51.0	...	...	80.2	99.4	99.5	96.9	77.3	29.4	------7.3------		2.2	1.5	...
1957.............	50.0	...	...	79.0	99.6	99.5	96.2	78.1	28.1	------8.2------		1.9	1.1	...
1956.............	48.7	...	...	78.2	99.5	99.4	96.8	76.9	27.4	------6.8------		1.7	1.2	...
1955.............	47.0	...	...	78.1	99.3	99.0	96.1	73.8	22.5	------6.1------		1.8	1.1	...
1954.............	46.3	...	...	78.3	99.5	99.7	95.4	75.2	25.4	------6.0------		1.7	1.1	...
1953.............	43.0	...	...	56.6	99.5	99.7	96.6	72.9	25.9	------6.4------		0.5	1.4	...
1952.............	41.9	...	...	54.6	98.9	98.9	96.6	72.9	22.1	------4.9------		0.6	0.7	...
1951.............	49.1	...	...	54.0	98.9	99.3	94.5	75.4	21.3	------4.3------		1.0	...	...
1950.............	48.4	...	...	59.5	99.0	98.4	94.3	69.8	24.3	------4.6------		0.4	...	...
1949.............	39.2	...	...	58.4	98.5	98.8	93.1	68.2	19.9	------3.7------		1.1	0.4	...
1948.............	38.4	...	...	56.8	98.2	97.8	93.5	70.3	20.3	------3.4------		0.4	0.4	...
1947.............	38.0	...	...	58.7	98.4	98.5	92.8	67.5	18.5	------3.9------		0.4	0.3	...
WHITE ALONE														
Both Sexes														
2008.............	55.5	25.3	52.0	94.0	98.2	98.9	98.7	95.4	67.1	51.2	28.1	12.3	6.2	1.8
2007.............	55.5	25.3	54.1	94.8	98.0	98.7	98.7	94.6	67.1	50.1	26.3	11.5	6.6	1.8
2006.............	55.5	25.3	55.6	95.0	98.4	98.4	98.4	95.0	64.9	48.2	25.5	11.3	6.7	1.7
2005.............	55.9	25.7	54.2	95.3	98.6	98.7	98.3	95.4	68.0	49.3	26.0	11.3	6.2	1.8
2004	55.5	25.7	52.8	95.5	98.1	98.3	98.5	94.2	64.9	49.3	25.3	12.2	6.4	1.8
2003¹...........	55.4	25.8	55.3	94.7	98.0	98.4	97.3	95.0	64.4	48.2	26.7	11.0	6.2	1.8
2002.............	55.4	26.0	53.9	95.1	98.0	98.5	98.5	94.6	63.8	47.4	24.6	11.4	5.9	2.0
2001.............	54.8	25.8	51.7	94.8	98.3	98.7	98.2	93.5	60.4	45.9	23.3	10.7	6.0	1.8
2000.............	55.1	26.1	50.2	95.3	98.2	98.3	98.4	92.8	61.3	44.9	23.7	10.4	6.0	1.8
1999.............	55.2	26.4	53.7	95.6	98.5	98.8	98.2	93.5	60.5	45.6	24.1	10.5	5.8	1.9
1998.............	55.0	26.6	50.7	95.4	98.8	99.1	98.6	94.1	61.9	44.8	24.1	11.0	6.2	2.0
1997.............	54.8	26.8	50.9	96.8	98.8	99.3	90.0	94.5	61.5	46.4	25.8	11.3	5.4	2.2
1996.............	53.4	26.4	47.9	94.8	97.1	98.2	98.0	92.8	62.5	44.9	24.6	11.3	5.7	2.2
1995.............	53.2	26.6	49.6	96.2	98.9	99.0	98.8	93.7	59.3	46.2	23.1	11.5	5.5	2.1
1994.............	52.6	26.6	47.0	96.6	99.2	99.3	98.7	94.3	60.9	46.2	23.5	10.4	6.6	2.2
1993ʳ...........	51.2	...	40.4	95.4	99.5	99.5	98.9	93.9	61.4	43.7	23.1	9.7	5.9	...
1993.............	51.1	25.7	40.8	95.5	99.5	99.5	98.9	94.1	61.7	44.0	23.3	9.8	5.9	2.1
1992.............	50.7	...	40.1	95.4	99.4	99.3	99.2	94.2	61.7	45.3	23.3	9.6	6.0	...
1991.............	50.0	...	41.3	95.3	99.6	99.7	98.7	93.3	59.7	43.2	21.7	9.9	6.0	...
1990.............	49.5	...	44.9	96.5	99.7	99.6	99.1	92.5	57.1	41.0	20.2	9.9	5.9	...
1989.............	48.4	...	39.4	95.2	99.2	99.4	98.8	92.3	56.4	39.5	20.0	9.4	5.6	...
1988.............	48.0	...	38.9	96.1	99.7	99.7	98.8	91.4	55.8	40.2	18.6	8.2	5.9	...
1987.............	47.7	...	38.2	94.8	99.6	99.4	98.5	91.8	55.3	39.6	17.3	8.7	5.7	...
1986.............	47.7	...	39.1	95.3	99.3	97.8	99.0	92.2	55.3	33.9	17.7	9.1	6.2	...
1985.............	47.8	...	38.6	96.4	99.3	99.3	98.1	91.6	52.4	36.1	17.0	9.2	5.9	...
1984.............	47.3	...	36.0	94.6	99.0	99.4	97.8	91.2	51.1	34.3	17.2	9.1	6.2	...
1983.............	47.7	...	37.6	95.7	98.9	99.3	98.4	91.4	50.9	33.4	16.4	9.4	6.1	...
1982.............	47.9	...	35.9	94.9	99.2	99.2	98.6	90.3	47.9	35.1	16.2	9.6	6.2	...
1981.............	48.2	...	35.6	93.9	99.3	99.3	98.1	90.4	48.5	32.6	16.2	8.5	6.1	...
1980.............	48.9	...	36.3	95.8	99.0	99.4	98.3	88.6	46.3	31.9	16.4	9.2	6.3	...
1979.............	49.6	...	33.9	95.8	99.2	99.2	98.2	89.0	44.5	31.1	15.7	9.7	6.3	...
1978.............	50.3	...	32.7	95.4	99.3	99.0	98.4	88.7	44.9	29.6	16.1	9.4	6.2	...
1977.............	51.6	...	31.1	95.6	99.5	99.4	98.5	88.5	45.5	31.8	16.3	10.6	6.6	...
1976.............	52.3	...	30.4	95.8	99.1	99.2	98.1	89.1	45.4	32.5	17.0	10.0	5.7	...
1975.............	53.1	...	30.9	94.8	99.4	99.3	98.3	89.3	46.5	31.8	16.8	10.0	6.6	...
1974.............	53.0	...	28.6	94.4	99.2	99.4	98.1	87.9	42.6	30.7	15.2	9.6	5.5	...
1973.............	53.1	...	23.2	93.0	99.1	99.3	97.6	88.3	43.4	31.3	14.6	8.7	4.5	...
1972.............	54.4	...	23.8	92.2	99.1	99.3	97.6	88.9	46.6	32.6	15.0	8.7	4.5	...
1971.............	55.8	...	20.9	91.9	99.1	99.2	98.7	90.5	49.4	32.7	15.9	8.1	4.8	...
1970.............	56.2	...	19.9	90.3	99.3	99.1	98.2	90.6	48.7	33.1	15.7	7.7	4.2	...
1969.............	56.8	...	15.1	89.2	99.4	99.2	98.2	90.2	50.9	35.4	16.2	8.2	5.0	...
1968.............	56.6	...	15.0	88.5	99.1	99.1	98.1	90.8	50.9	32.8	14.5	7.4	3.9	...
1967.............	56.5	...	13.3	88.2	99.5	99.2	98.5	89.5	48.4	34.7	14.1	6.7	4.1	...
1966.............	56.1	...	12.3	85.7	99.3	99.3	98.8	89.0	48.2	32.2	14.0	6.9	2.7	...
1965.............	55.5	...	10.3	85.3	99.4	99.4	99.0	87.8	47.1	29.4	14.1	6.5	3.2	...

Note: Data for 1947 to 1953 exclude kindergarten. Nursery school was first collected in 1964. Data shown for 1947 to 1966 for the Black population are for Black and other races.

¹Starting in 2003 respondents could identify more than one race. Except as noted, the race data in this table from 2003 onward represent those respondents who indicated only one race category.

r = Revised, controlled to 1990 census based population estimates; previous 1993 data controlled to 1980 census based population estimates.

... = Not available.

Table A-10.   Percent of the Population 3 Years Old and Over Enrolled in School, by Age, Sex, Race, and Hispanic Origin, October 1947–2008—*Continued*

(Percent.)

Year, sex, race, and Hispanic origin	Total enrolled 3 to 34 years old	Total enrolled 3 years old and over	3 and 4 years old	5 and 6 years old	7 to 9 years old	10 to 13 years old	14 and 15 years old	16 and 17 years old	18 and 19 years old	20 and 21 years old	22 to 24 years old	25 to 29 years old	30 to 34 years old	35 years old and over
1964	54.4	...	9.3	84.0	99.0	99.0	98.8	88.3	42.3	27.8	10.6	5.4	2.6	...
1963	58.4	...	...	83.7	99.5	99.3	98.5	87.8	41.0	26.2	12.2	5.2	2.6	...
1962	57.9	...	...	83.2	99.3	99.4	98.2	85.9	43.0	24.1	10.9	5.2	2.7	...
1961	56.9	...	...	82.2	99.6	99.5	98.0	84.5	39.0	22.4	9.0	4.6	2.1	...
1960	56.4	...	...	82.0	99.7	99.5	98.1	83.3	38.9	20.6	9.3	5.2	2.6	...
1959	55.5	...	...	81.0	99.5	99.5	97.9	83.8	37.3	19.9	8.9	5.4	2.3	...
1958	54.9	...	...	81.4	-----99.6-----		----90.0-----		38.1	------14.1------		5.9	2.3	...
1957	53.7	...	...	79.3	-----99.7-----		----90.1-----		34.6	------14.7------		5.7	1.9	...
1956	52.5	...	...	78.4	-----99.4-----		----89.2-----		35.9	------13.4------		5.4	2.1	...
1955	50.8	...	...	79.2	-----99.3-----		----87.5-----		32.1	------11.6------		4.2	1.6	...
1954	50.2	...	...	78.6	-----99.6-----		----88.3-----		33.6	------12.0------		4.0	1.5	...
1953	46.6	...	...	67.1	-----99.7-----		----86.4-----		31.7	------11.9------		3.1	1.8	...
1952	45.4	...	...	54.8	-----99.1-----		----86.1-----		28.9	-------9.8------		2.7	1.2	...
1951	52.8	...	...	54.5	-----99.3-----		----86.3-----		26.9	-------8.8------		2.8	...	...
1950	51.6	...	...	----------89.0----------			----84.4-----		30.5	-------9.5------		3.0	...	...
1949	42.6	...	...	----------88.8----------			----83.0-----		25.9	-------9.6------		4.0	1.2	...
1948	41.8	...	...	----------87.8----------			----83.9-----		27.3	------10.0------		2.8	0.9	...
1947	41.2	...	...	----------88.7----------			----80.2-----		24.8	------10.5------		3.0	1.1	...
Male														
2008	54.8	25.5	51.8	93.8	97.9	98.7	99.0	94.9	64.3	48.4	26.5	11.5	5.5	1.3
2007	54.4	25.4	52.9	94.1	97.9	98.6	98.3	94.5	66.4	44.6	24.2	9.6	5.7	1.4
2006	54.6	25.5	55.9	94.8	98.3	98.4	98.2	94.7	62.7	43.8	24.0	10.2	5.5	1.3
2005	54.9	25.9	53.1	94.6	98.2	98.6	98.3	95.1	66.1	45.1	24.4	8.9	5.5	1.4
2004	54.8	26.0	53.4	95.8	97.9	98.2	98.8	94.5	60.0	46.0	23.3	11.2	5.5	1.4
2003[1]	54.8	26.2	56.2	95.0	97.6	98.2	97.2	95.3	61.7	43.2	25.6	9.9	5.6	1.4
2002	54.9	26.5	54.0	95.0	98.0	98.3	98.4	94.2	62.5	44.1	23.5	10.2	5.0	1.6
2001	54.3	26.2	51.8	94.7	98.6	98.4	98.0	92.8	58.2	43.6	21.5	9.8	5.0	1.4
2000	54.8	26.5	49.1	94.8	97.8	98.3	98.4	93.1	58.5	41.8	23.2	9.5	4.9	1.4
1999	55.5	27.1	53.5	95.4	98.5	98.6	98.2	93.1	60.0	44.5	23.7	10.3	5.4	1.5
1998	54.9	27.1	52.4	94.9	98.8	99.1	98.7	93.3	59.7	42.1	24.5	10.2	5.2	1.6
1997	54.7	27.3	50.4	97.4	98.5	99.4	99.1	94.2	60.0	45.0	24.9	10.8	4.3	1.5
1996	53.3	27.0	46.5	94.6	96.9	98.0	98.6	93.0	60.9	43.6	25.4	10.6	4.3	1.7
1995	53.5	27.3	49.6	95.5	99.0	99.0	98.8	94.2	59.4	46.3	22.7	11.3	5.0	1.7
1994	52.7	27.2	46.2	97.0	99.1	99.3	98.7	94.3	61.3	43.4	23.6	9.9	5.8	1.7
1993[r]	51.6	...	41.2	95.1	99.5	99.5	98.9	95.0	60.1	44.4	24.5	9.1	5.2	...
1993	51.6	26.4	41.7	95.2	99.5	99.5	99.0	95.1	60.6	44.8	24.9	9.1	5.2	1.5
1992	50.8	...	39.8	95.1	99.5	99.5	99.0	99.5	60.7	44.0	23.6	8.6	5.2	...
1991	50.4	...	40.6	94.9	99.7	99.8	98.9	94.2	58.4	42.4	23.3	10.0	5.4	...
1990	50.0	...	44.9	96.7	99.7	99.6	99.2	92.3	57.3	41.2	21.8	9.4	4.9	...
1989	48.9	...	38.7	95.4	99.3	99.2	99.3	92.6	57.3	39.3	20.4	9.3	5.0	...
1988	48.7	...	39.0	96.1	99.7	99.6	98.9	91.6	56.5	40.9	20.7	7.8	5.4	...
1987	48.8	...	39.8	95.2	99.6	99.7	98.8	92.5	57.3	42.1	18.4	8.6	5.0	...
1986	48.6	...	39.3	95.6	99.4	99.0	99.1	92.1	57.5	34.2	19.2	9.6	5.7	...
1985	48.5	...	37.3	95.7	99.3	99.2	98.2	92.5	51.9	37.2	19.0	9.5	5.4	...
1984	48.3	...	35.8	94.1	98.7	99.3	97.6	91.5	52.6	36.3	20.2	9.2	5.4	...
1983	48.9	...	38.2	95.1	98.8	99.3	98.3	91.6	50.7	36.6	19.2	10.4	5.6	...
1982	48.9	...	36.3	94.8	99.2	99.1	98.8	91.0	48.5	36.5	18.0	10.2	5.4	...
1981	49.2	...	36.8	94.3	99.1	99.2	98.3	90.5	49.2	33.3	19.1	9.1	5.5	...
1980	50.0	...	38.0	95.2	98.8	99.4	98.7	88.8	47.5	33.7	18.2	9.6	5.6	...
1979	50.7	...	33.5	96.3	99.0	99.0	98.3	90.3	46.1	32.2	17.6	10.5	5.9	...
1978	51.9	...	33.1	95.3	99.2	98.9	98.3	88.9	47.2	32.0	19.2	10.9	6.4	...
1977	53.3	...	31.7	94.3	99.6	99.3	98.7	89.5	47.7	34.7	19.4	12.6	6.8	...
1976	54.2	...	29.9	95.8	98.8	99.1	98.5	90.6	46.9	34.2	20.4	12.9	6.5	...
1975	55.4	...	30.8	94.3	99.2	99.0	98.5	91.0	49.6	36.3	20.5	13.1	7.5	...
1974	55.2	...	27.7	94.8	99.1	99.2	98.2	88.2	45.5	35.0	19.2	12.8	6.4	...
1973	55.6	...	23.5	92.7	99.0	99.3	98.0	89.4	48.4	35.7	19.6	12.1	5.4	...
1972	57.3	...	23.4	91.7	98.9	99.2	97.7	90.4	51.5	38.4	21.6	12.5	5.8	...
1971	59.0	...	20.1	91.2	99.0	98.9	98.9	92.0	55.9	39.7	24.6	12.1	6.2	...
1970	59.6	...	20.7	89.7	99.3	98.8	98.3	92.2	56.0	45.0	22.6	11.2	5.4	...
1969	60.5	...	14.5	88.5	99.1	98.9	98.2	92.2	60.9	48.9	24.2	12.2	6.2	...

Note: Data for 1947 to 1953 exclude kindergarten. Nursery school was first collected in 1964. Data shown for 1947 to 1966 for the Black population are for Black and other races.

[1]Starting in 2003 respondents could identify more than one race. Except as noted, the race data in this table from 2003 onward represent those respondents who indicated only one race category.

r = Revised, controlled to 1990 census based population estimates; previous 1993 data controlled to 1980 census based population estimates.

... = Not available.

Table A-10.   Percent of the Population 3 Years Old and Over Enrolled in School, by Age, Sex, Race, and Hispanic Origin, October 1947–2008—_Continued_

(Percent.)

Year, sex, race, and Hispanic origin	Total enrolled 3 to 34 years old	Total enrolled 3 years old and over	3 and 4 years old	5 and 6 years old	7 to 9 years old	10 to 13 years old	14 and 15 years old	16 and 17 years old	18 and 19 years old	20 and 21 years old	22 to 24 years old	25 to 29 years old	30 to 34 years old	35 years old and over
1968	60.4	...	14.8	87.9	99.0	99.0	98.2	92.1	61.5	47.8	21.9	11.4	5.0	...
1967	60.0	...	13.6	87.5	99.5	99.0	98.5	91.4	57.2	46.9	22.0	10.5	5.4	...
1966	59.8	...	12.2	85.0	99.2	99.1	98.8	90.3	59.0	44.9	23.0	10.3	3.8	...
1965	59.0	...	10.4	84.8	99.3	99.3	99.1	88.6	56.6	39.9	23.3	10.0	4.5	...
1964	57.6	...	8.8	84.0	98.8	98.9	99.0	90.4	52.4	36.6	17.7	8.3	3.6	...
1963	62.3	...	...	84.1	99.4	99.0	98.8	89.8	51.6	35.2	21.1	8.2	3.8	...
1962	61.9	...	...	83.9	99.1	99.3	98.7	88.5	52.7	33.7	18.8	8.9	4.2	...
1961	60.4	...	...	82.6	99.7	99.4	98.3	85.5	49.6	31.1	15.0	7.5	3.1	...
1960	60.3	...	...	82.3	99.7	99.5	98.1	85.2	49.5	29.2	16.3	8.9	4.0	...
1959	59.2	...	...	80.1	99.3	99.4	98.1	85.9	47.1	30.8	14.1	9.5	3.4	...
1958	58.8	...	...	81.5	------99.6------		----91.1-----		48.1	------22.3------		9.9	3.0	...
1957	57.7	...	...	79.1	------99.7------		----91.9-----		44.0	------22.9------		9.9	2.7	...
1956	56.5	...	...	78.2	------99.4------		----90.1-----		46.4	------21.8------		9.3	2.9	...
1955	54.9	...	...	79.0	------99.4------		----89.1-----		43.9	------19.3------		7.1	2.2	...
1954	54.3	...	...	78.0	------99.4------		----89.6-----		43.3	------20.5------		6.5	1.9	...
1953	50.5	...	...	56.8	------99.4------		----87.9-----		38.1	------20.3------		5.7	2.2	...
1952	49.4	...	...	55.2	------99.1------		----87.0-----		38.3	------17.8------		5.0	1.6	...
1951	56.8	...	...	55.4	------99.3------		----86.6-----		33.8	------14.9------		4.2	...	...
1950	54.7	...	...	----------88.6----------			----85.0-----		37.3	------14.6------		5.9	...	...
1949	45.9	...	...	----------89.1----------			----84.1-----		32.1	------15.7------		7.1	2.0	...
1948	45.3	...	...	----------87.6----------			----84.4-----		35.9	------17.2------		5.3	1.5	...
1947	44.4	...	...	----------88.6----------			----79.6-----		32.6	------17.4------		5.9	1.8	...
Female														
2008	56.3	25.1	52.3	94.2	98.6	99.1	98.5	95.9	69.9	54.3	29.8	13.1	6.9	2.3
2007	56.7	25.2	55.4	95.6	98.1	98.8	99.2	94.7	67.8	55.7	28.5	13.6	7.6	2.2
2006	56.3	25.1	55.3	95.2	98.5	98.5	98.7	95.3	67.2	52.6	27.1	12.4	8.0	2.1
2005	57.0	25.6	55.4	96.0	98.9	98.8	98.4	95.7	70.1	53.8	27.7	13.8	7.0	2.2
2004	56.2	25.4	52.0	95.2	98.4	98.5	98.2	93.9	69.8	52.6	27.4	13.3	7.2	2.2
2003[1]	55.9	25.4	54.3	94.4	98.4	98.6	97.4	94.8	67.3	53.1	27.8	12.1	6.8	2.1
2002	55.8	25.6	53.7	95.1	98.0	98.7	98.5	95.0	65.1	50.8	25.7	12.7	6.9	2.3
2001	55.3	25.4	51.5	94.9	97.9	98.9	98.4	94.3	62.7	48.2	25.1	11.7	7.0	2.2
2000	55.4	25.7	51.4	95.8	98.5	98.4	98.3	92.5	64.2	48.2	24.2	11.3	7.1	2.2
1999	55.0	25.8	53.9	95.8	98.7	98.9	98.3	93.8	60.9	46.8	24.5	10.7	6.3	2.3
1998	55.0	26.0	49.0	96.0	98.8	99.2	98.5	94.9	64.2	47.9	23.8	11.9	7.2	2.4
1997	54.9	26.3	51.3	96.2	99.1	99.2	98.6	94.8	63.1	47.9	26.7	11.8	6.4	2.8
1996	53.5	25.9	49.3	95.0	97.4	98.3	97.3	92.7	64.1	46.1	23.6	12.0	7.1	2.6
1995	52.9	25.8	49.6	96.9	98.8	99.1	98.8	93.3	59.2	46.0	23.6	11.7	6.0	2.6
1994	52.6	26.0	47.9	96.1	99.4	99.4	98.8	94.4	60.5	49.0	23.5	11.0	7.4	2.7
1993[1]	50.7	...	39.5	95.7	99.5	99.5	98.9	92.8	62.8	43.0	21.7	10.4	6.5	...
1993	50.6	24.9	39.9	95.8	99.5	99.5	98.9	93.0	62.9	43.3	21.8	10.4	6.5	2.6
1992	50.5	...	40.4	95.7	99.2	99.1	99.4	92.8	62.7	46.6	22.9	10.6	6.7	...
1991	49.5	...	42.0	95.7	99.5	99.6	98.5	92.5	60.9	43.9	20.2	9.7	6.7	...
1990	49.0	...	44.8	96.4	99.7	99.7	98.9	92.8	57.0	40.9	18.7	10.4	6.9	...
1989	47.8	...	40.2	94.9	99.2	99.6	98.1	92.1	55.6	39.7	19.6	9.6	6.3	...
1988	47.2	...	38.8	96.1	99.6	99.8	98.8	91.1	55.1	39.6	16.5	8.6	6.3	...
1987	46.7	...	36.4	94.4	99.5	99.2	98.3	91.0	53.3	37.3	16.2	8.7	6.4	...
1986	46.8	...	39.0	94.9	99.1	99.3	98.8	92.2	53.0	33.7	16.2	8.7	6.7	...
1985	47.0	...	39.9	97.1	99.3	99.3	97.9	90.8	52.9	35.0	15.0	9.0	6.4	...
1984	46.3	...	36.1	95.2	99.3	99.4	98.0	91.0	49.6	32.3	14.2	8.9	6.9	...
1983	46.6	...	36.0	96.5	99.0	99.4	98.4	91.2	51.1	30.5	13.6	8.5	6.7	...
1982	46.9	...	35.5	95.0	99.2	99.4	98.4	89.6	47.4	33.7	14.5	9.0	6.9	...
1981	47.1	...	34.3	93.5	99.5	99.4	97.8	90.4	47.8	31.9	13.4	7.9	6.7	...
1980	47.9	...	34.6	96.4	99.2	99.4	97.8	88.4	45.1	30.2	14.8	8.9	7.0	...
1979	48.4	...	34.4	95.3	99.5	99.5	98.1	87.7	43.0	30.0	13.9	9.0	6.7	...
1978	48.7	...	32.2	95.6	99.5	99.2	98.5	88.4	42.7	27.4	13.0	7.9	6.0	...
1977	49.9	...	30.5	96.9	99.5	99.6	98.4	87.4	43.4	29.0	13.3	8.8	6.3	...
1976	50.4	...	31.0	95.8	99.5	99.3	97.6	87.7	44.0	30.9	13.7	7.1	4.8	...
1975	50.9	...	30.9	95.3	99.5	99.6	98.1	87.5	43.5	27.5	12.2	7.0	5.7	...
1974	50.9	...	29.5	94.0	99.3	99.7	97.9	87.6	39.9	26.6	11.4	6.5	4.6	...
1973	50.5	...	22.9	93.2	99.3	99.3	97.1	87.3	38.7	27.4	9.9	5.4	3.6	...

Note: Data for 1947 to 1953 exclude kindergarten. Nursery school was first collected in 1964. Data shown for 1947 to 1966 for the Black population are for Black and other races.
[1] Starting in 2003 respondents could identify more than one race. Except as noted, the race data in this table from 2003 onward represent those respondents who indicated only one race category.
r = Revised, controlled to 1990 census based population estimates; previous 1993 data controlled to 1980 census based population estimates.
... = Not available.

Table A-10. Percent of the Population 3 Years Old and Over Enrolled in School, by Age, Sex, Race, and Hispanic Origin, October 1947–2008—*Continued*

(Percent.)

Year, sex, race, and Hispanic origin	Total enrolled 3 to 34 years old	Total enrolled 3 years old and over	Age											
			3 and 4 years old	5 and 6 years old	7 to 9 years old	10 to 13 years old	14 and 15 years old	16 and 17 years old	18 and 19 years old	20 and 21 years old	22 to 24 years old	25 to 29 years old	30 to 34 years old	35 years old and over
1972.............	51.5	...	24.4	92.7	99.2	99.4	97.5	87.3	41.9	27.5	8.9	5.1	3.2	...
1971.............	52.6	...	21.7	92.6	99.3	99.5	98.4	88.9	43.2	27.0	8.1	4.3	3.5	...
1970.............	52.9	...	19.1	90.9	99.3	99.5	98.1	89.0	41.8	24.1	9.7	4.4	3.1	...
1969.............	53.2	...	15.8	89.8	99.6	99.5	98.2	88.2	41.8	25.8	9.4	4.5	3.7	...
1968.............	52.9	...	15.2	89.0	99.3	99.3	98.0	89.4	41.3	22.3	8.2	3.7	2.8	...
1967.............	53.0	...	13.1	89.0	99.6	99.4	98.5	87.4	41.0	25.6	7.5	3.3	2.9	...
1966.............	52.5	...	12.4	86.4	99.5	99.5	98.7	87.6	38.6	22.3	6.6	3.9	1.7	...
1965.............	52.2	...	10.3	85.7	99.4	99.5	98.9	87.0	38.3	20.9	6.3	3.2	2.0	...
1964.............	51.3	...	9.9	83.9	99.2	99.1	98.6	86.1	33.7	20.3	4.5	2.6	1.6	...
1963.............	54.7	...	...	83.8	99.7	99.5	98.2	85.7	32.1	18.6	4.4	2.4	1.5	...
1962.............	54.0	...	...	82.4	99.5	99.5	97.6	83.3	34.6	16.3	4.1	1.8	1.4	...
1961.............	53.4	...	...	81.7	99.5	99.5	97.7	83.5	29.7	15.3	3.8	2.1	1.3	...
1960.............	52.7	...	...	81.6	99.7	99.6	98.1	81.4	29.7	13.5	3.5	1.8	1.2	...
1959.............	52.0	...	...	81.9	99.7	99.6	97.7	81.6	28.8	11.1	4.6	1.7	1.3	...
1958.............	51.1	...	...	81.2	------99.6------		----88.9-----		29.9	-------7.5------		2.2	1.6	...
1957.............	49.8	...	...	79.5	------99.7-------		----88.2-----		27.0	-------8.3------		1.7	1.1	...
1956.............	48.6	...	...	78.6	------99.5-----		----88.2-----		27.3	-------7.0------		1.8	1.3	...
1955.............	46.9	...	...	79.5	------99.3-----		----85.9-----		22.4	-------6.2------		1.5	1.0	...
1954.............	46.4	...	...	79.1	------99.8-----		----87.0-----		25.3	-------6.4------		1.7	1.1	...
1953.............	42.9	...	...	57.4	------99.9-----		----84.9-----		26.5	-------6.5------		0.6	1.5	...
1952.............	41.7	...	...	54.3	------99.1-----		----85.3-----		21.1	-------4.3------		0.6	0.7	...
1951.............	49.0	...	...	53.6	------99.4-----		----86.0-----		21.7	-------4.3------		0.9	...	...
1950.............	48.6	...	...	----------89.4----------			----83.7-----		24.2	-------4.8------		0.4	...	...
1949.............	39.4	...	...	----------88.6----------			----81.9-----		20.5	-------3.8------		1.2	0.4	...
1948.............	38.4	...	...	----------87.9----------			----83.4-----		19.7	-------3.5------		0.4	0.4	...
1947.............	38.1	...	...	----------88.9----------			----80.8-----		18.3	-------4.1------		0.4	0.4	...
WHITE ALONE NON-HISPANIC														
Both Sexes														
2008.............	56.7	23.9	56.0	94.9	98.8	98.9	98.8	95.9	70.0	55.8	30.3	13.3	6.9	1.8
2007.............	56.6	23.9	56.3	95.0	98.6	98.6	98.8	95.6	69.7	54.5	28.4	12.5	7.4	1.8
2006.............	56.8	24.0	58.2	95.6	98.5	98.6	98.4	95.9	67.9	52.9	27.4	12.5	7.4	1.7
2005.............	57.6	24.6	58.5	95.9	99.0	99.0	98.6	96.1	71.6	54.4	27.8	12.5	6.9	1.8
2004.............	56.9	24.5	56.0	96.2	98.3	98.6	98.5	95.1	68.1	54.0	27.0	13.5	6.7	1.8
2003[1].............	57.0	24.7	58.8	95.8	98.2	98.5	97.5	95.6	67.9	51.8	29.4	12.5	6.8	1.8
2002.............	56.8	24.9	57.8	95.3	98.1	98.6	98.6	95.3	67.1	53.1	27.3	12.2	6.3	1.9
2001.............	56.2	24.7	55.1	95.3	98.5	98.8	98.2	94.6	64.2	50.8	25.5	11.7	6.4	1.8
2000.............	56.0	25.0	54.6	95.5	98.4	98.5	98.9	94.0	63.9	49.2	24.9	11.1	6.1	1.8
1999.............	56.2	25.4	58.6	96.0	98.5	98.9	98.4	94.5	64.1	50.0	26.3	10.9	5.9	1.9
1998.............	55.9	25.6	54.0	96.1	98.8	99.2	98.9	95.1	66.6	49.2	26.1	11.5	6.3	2.0
1997.............	55.6	25.9	54.9	96.9	98.9	99.2	98.9	95.1	64.1	49.9	27.8	12.2	5.6	2.2
1996.............	54.0	25.5	50.3	96.1	97.3	98.3	98.2	93.6	65.5	48.9	25.9	11.8	5.8	2.2
1995.............	53.8	25.9	52.3	96.6	99.0	99.0	98.8	94.4	61.8	49.7	24.4	12.3	5.7	2.1
1994.............	54.5	25.9	50.1	96.7	99.2	99.3	99.2	95.1	62.6	50.1	24.9	10.8	6.7	2.2
1993.............	51.4	25.0	43.1	95.7	99.5	99.5	99.1	95.0	63.6	46.1	24.9	10.2	6.0	2.1

Note: Data for 1947 to 1953 exclude kindergarten. Nursery school was first collected in 1964. Data shown for 1947 to 1966 for the Black population are for Black and other races.
[1]Starting in 2003 respondents could identify more than one race. Except as noted, the race data in this table from 2003 onward represent those respondents who indicated only one race category.
... = Not available.

Table A-10.   Percent of the Population 3 Years Old and Over Enrolled in School, by Age, Sex, Race, and Hispanic Origin, October 1947–2008—*Continued*

(Percent.)

Year, sex, race, and Hispanic origin	Total enrolled 3 to 34 years old	Total enrolled 3 years old and over	Age											
			3 and 4 years old	5 and 6 years old	7 to 9 years old	10 to 13 years old	14 and 15 years old	16 and 17 years old	18 and 19 years old	20 and 21 years old	22 to 24 years old	25 to 29 years old	30 to 34 years old	35 years old and over
Male														
2008	56.5	24.3	57.2	94.7	98.5	98.7	99.1	95.5	66.8	52.4	29.1	12.6	6.2	1.3
2007	56.0	24.2	53.8	94.0	98.5	98.5	98.3	95.2	69.3	49.9	26.9	10.6	6.7	1.3
2006	56.4	24.4	58.3	95.9	98.5	98.6	97.9	95.5	65.4	49.2	26.2	11.9	6.3	1.3
2005	57.1	24.9	56.8	95.4	98.9	99.1	98.4	95.9	69.8	50.5	26.4	10.2	6.5	1.3
2004	56.7	25.0	57.2	96.2	98.2	98.4	98.7	95.6	63.8	50.6	25.1	12.7	6.2	1.4
2003¹	57.1	25.4	60.6	96.2	97.7	98.2	97.4	96.1	65.4	47.9	28.9	11.7	6.3	1.4
2002	56.8	25.5	57.8	94.9	98.1	98.5	98.5	95.2	66.3	49.2	27.6	11.1	5.5	1.6
2001	56.0	25.2	54.4	94.8	98.8	98.4	97.8	94.0	62.7	49.1	23.7	10.8	5.3	1.3
2000	55.8	25.5	54.1	94.5	98.1	98.2	98.8	94.7	61.2	45.8	25.0	10.5	4.7	1.4
1999	56.7	26.2	59.2	96.1	98.4	98.7	98.2	94.3	63.7	48.9	26.8	10.7	5.8	1.5
1998	55.7	26.3	54.8	95.5	98.8	99.0	99.0	94.4	65.2	46.4	27.4	10.9	5.3	1.6
1997	55.9	26.5	54.9	97.4	98.8	99.3	99.0	94.5	63.3	48.5	27.5	12.0	4.6	1.5
1996	54.2	26.1	48.0	95.5	97.2	98.1	98.8	93.5	63.7	48.7	27.3	11.4	4.3	1.6
1995	54.2	26.6	51.1	95.9	99.0	99.0	98.9	95.0	61.9	50.0	24.1	12.2	5.0	1.6
1994	53.5	26.6	49.0	97.1	99.2	99.4	99.4	95.4	62.5	47.6	25.5	10.3	6.0	1.6
1993	52.2	25.9	44.1	95.4	99.5	99.6	99.3	96.2	62.5	47.0	26.7	9.9	5.2	1.5
Female														
2008	57.0	23.5	54.8	95.0	99.1	99.2	98.4	96.3	73.4	59.5	31.5	14.0	7.6	2.2
2007	57.3	23.7	58.9	96.0	98.8	98.7	99.2	96.0	70.1	59.2	29.9	14.4	8.0	2.2
2006	57.1	23.7	58.1	95.3	98.6	98.5	99.0	96.2	70.5	56.5	28.7	13.2	8.5	2.1
2005	58.0	24.3	60.3	96.3	99.0	98.8	98.7	96.3	73.5	58.5	29.1	14.7	7.4	2.2
2004	57.1	24.1	54.7	96.2	98.5	98.7	98.3	94.5	72.5	57.4	28.8	14.4	7.2	2.1
2003¹	57.0	24.1	56.9	95.3	98.6	98.8	97.6	95.1	70.3	55.6	29.9	13.2	7.3	2.1
2002	56.8	24.3	57.7	95.6	98.0	98.6	98.6	95.5	67.9	57.0	27.0	13.4	7.2	2.2
2001	56.4	24.2	55.9	95.9	98.3	99.1	98.6	95.3	65.8	52.4	27.3	12.5	7.4	2.2
2000	56.1	24.6	55.2	96.4	98.6	98.8	99.0	93.3	66.7	52.7	24.8	11.8	7.4	2.1
1999	55.7	24.7	57.9	96.0	98.5	99.1	98.6	94.8	64.6	51.1	25.7	11.0	6.1	2.3
1998	55.7	25.0	53.1	96.7	98.7	99.3	98.8	95.7	68.0	52.2	24.8	12.1	7.3	2.4
1997	55.2	25.4	55.0	96.4	99.0	99.1	98.8	95.7	64.9	51.3	28.1	12.4	6.6	2.9
1996	53.8	25.0	52.9	96.7	97.3	98.6	97.7	93.7	67.3	49.0	24.5	12.1	7.3	2.6
1995	53.4	25.1	53.5	97.4	98.9	99.0	98.7	93.8	61.8	49.3	24.8	12.3	6.3	2.5
1994	52.9	25.3	51.3	96.3	99.3	99.3	98.9	94.8	62.7	52.4	24.3	11.4	7.3	2.7
1993	50.6	24.3	42.0	96.0	99.5	99.5	98.9	93.7	64.8	45.2	23.1	10.5	6.7	2.6
BLACK ALONE														
Both Sexes														
2008	57.8	31.7	54.6	93.1	98.9	99.0	97.9	94.2	59.2	40.3	24.9	14.7	11.5	2.8
2007	58.4	32.2	58.5	94.0	98.2	97.9	99.0	93.4	61.7	38.7	28.0	15.0	9.4	3.0
2006	58.1	32.3	59.2	92.6	97.1	97.2	97.5	93.3	64.7	39.1	27.2	11.8	8.6	3.1
2005	58.4	32.7	52.2	95.9	98.6	98.6	95.8	93.1	62.8	37.6	28.0	11.7	10.0	3.1
2004	59.0	33.4	59.6	94.1	97.5	99.4	99.0	95.7	59.2	40.0	25.1	14.3	7.2	3.3
2003¹	59.2	33.4	55.5	94.4	98.3	98.2	97.9	94.3	61.9	41.4	27.4	12.2	8.6	2.8
2002	59.6	34.1	57.5	95.7	98.1	98.1	98.2	93.3	57.7	43.5	23.5	13.6	9.8	3.1
2001	59.5	34.3	58.8	96.0	97.8	97.0	97.6	92.1	59.6	37.2	26.0	12.2	11.5	3.2
2000	59.0	34.0	59.9	96.3	97.5	98.4	99.6	91.4	57.2	36.6	24.2	14.3	9.6	2.6
1999	58.1	33.7	56.3	97.5	98.2	98.7	98.2	93.3	57.4	39.4	21.7	10.4	7.8	2.5
1998	58.9	34.6	58.5	95.3	98.7	98.6	98.9	92.9	60.2	39.2	21.5	13.6	8.5	2.6
1997	58.4	34.6	60.0	95.8	99.2	99.4	99.2	93.4	58.2	35.9	25.4	10.7	6.5	2.8
1996	56.2	33.8	49.9	90.5	97.4	97.4	98.9	92.1	52.8	37.0	21.0	13.7	7.1	3.0
1995	56.1	33.9	47.5	95.5	97.7	99.2	99.0	92.9	57.4	37.4	19.9	10.0	7.8	2.7
1994	56.4	34.4	51.9	97.2	99.7	99.6	99.2	95.4	54.0	34.9	22.6	10.5	7.2	2.9
1993r	53.8	…	39.8	94.5	99.0	99.8	98.5	94.8	57.6	30.1	18.0	10.4	5.5	…
1993	53.6	32.4	39.8	94.6	99.0	99.8	98.5	94.7	57.7	30.0	18.1	10.4	5.5	2.6
1992	53.0	…	38.6	95.9	99.4	99.7	99.4	93.0	56.2	33.3	20.3	7.9	5.3	…
1991	52.5	…	37.2	95.8	99.6	100.0	99.1	91.7	55.6	30.0	18.2	8.7	6.5	…
1990	51.9	…	41.6	96.3	99.9	99.9	99.2	91.7	55.2	28.4	20.0	6.1	4.4	…
1989	51.3	…	38.9	94.9	99.0	99.4	99.4	93.7	50.2	30.7	17.2	6.4	4.9	…
1988	50.6	…	33.4	95.5	99.7	99.7	98.9	91.5	50.3	28.1	13.2	7.2	5.6	…

Note: Data for 1947 to 1953 exclude kindergarten. Nursery school was first collected in 1964. Data shown for 1947 to 1966 for the Black population are for Black and other races.

¹Starting in 2003 respondents could identify more than one race. Except as noted, the race data in this table from 2003 onward represent those respondents who indicated only one race category.

r = Revised, controlled to 1990 census based population estimates; previous 1993 data controlled to 1980 census based population estimates.

… = Not available.

Table A-10.   Percent of the Population 3 Years Old and Over Enrolled in School, by Age, Sex, Race, and Hispanic Origin, October 1947–2008—*Continued*

(Percent.)

Year, sex, race, and Hispanic origin	Total enrolled 3 to 34 years old	Total enrolled 3 years old and over	3 and 4 years old	5 and 6 years old	7 to 9 years old	10 to 13 years old	14 and 15 years old	16 and 17 years old	18 and 19 years old	20 and 21 years old	22 to 24 years old	25 to 29 years old	30 to 34 years old	35 years old and over
1987...............	51.7	...	36.8	95.8	99.7	99.8	98.3	91.5	53.2	28.7	15.0	9.3	6.0	...
1986...............	51.6	...	38.6	95.4	99.8	99.0	98.3	93.9	50.7	25.6	17.1	8.0	6.2	...
1985...............	50.9	...	42.7	95.7	98.4	99.5	97.9	91.7	44.1	27.7	13.7	7.5	5.9	...
1984...............	50.1	...	38.2	94.1	99.5	99.3	97.9	92.4	44.3	27.7	15.7	7.4	5.1	...
1983...............	50.8	...	36.2	94.7	99.1	99.7	97.8	92.6	46.1	23.4	15.6	7.4	6.5	...
1982...............	51.6	...	38.6	95.4	99.2	98.9	98.1	91.6	43.6	24.3	17.0	7.8	7.6	...
1981...............	52.5	...	36.7	94.5	98.8	99.4	97.1	91.3	48.2	23.4	14.7	8.4	7.0	...
1980...............	53.9	...	38.2	95.4	99.4	99.4	97.9	90.6	45.7	23.4	13.6	8.8	6.8	...
1979...............	55.0	...	40.8	96.0	99.4	98.7	97.4	90.8	46.6	23.7	15.0	7.9	6.8	...
1978...............	56.3	...	41.3	93.9	99.5	98.9	98.5	91.2	46.2	25.6	15.0	8.7	7.9	...
1977...............	57.7	...	35.2	96.5	99.3	99.0	98.8	90.8	48.3	29.5	15.2	11.3	9.0	...
1976...............	57.9	...	34.5	94.0	99.3	98.8	99.0	89.0	50.4	28.2	16.4	9.4	8.1	...
1975...............	57.7	...	33.5	94.3	99.3	99.2	97.4	86.9	47.1	27.1	14.2	9.4	7.1	...
1974...............	57.3	...	29.1	92.8	99.2	99.8	97.0	87.1	44.0	23.4	12.1	8.9	6.9	...
1973...............	55.8	...	28.9	89.9	99.2	99.0	96.7	87.7	37.8	20.5	12.4	6.1	5.0	...
1972...............	57.8	...	28.3	90.0	98.7	99.3	97.4	89.5	42.8	22.0	13.1	6.5	5.9	...
1971...............	58.6	...	21.5	89.8	99.0	98.8	98.4	89.2	46.6	27.3	11.4	6.2	5.2	...
1970...............	57.4	...	22.7	84.9	99.3	99.3	97.6	85.7	40.1	22.8	8.0	4.8	3.4	...
1969...............	57.8	...	21.2	84.1	98.8	99.1	97.9	85.8	44.5	23.3	8.6	4.3	3.4	...
1968...............	57.4	...	18.7	82.7	99.2	99.0	97.7	86.4	45.4	18.2	7.9	3.1	3.3	...
1967...............	56.8	...	17.7	82.2	99.1	98.7	86.1	84.1	40.7	21.2	7.2	5.0	2.4	...
1966...............	55.5	...	13.7	80.8	99.2	99.2	97.4	85.2	37.7	11.6	6.1	2.3	2.3	...
1965...............	55.6	...	11.8	79.1	98.9	99.3	98.1	83.9	39.6	12.8	6.2	2.1	2.4	...
1964...............	54.5	...	10.5	80.3	99.0	99.0	96.9	82.4	35.6	14.0	3.8	3.1	2.9	...
1963...............	58.8	...	...	76.6	98.5	99.5	97.6	82.0	39.8	16.2	5.5	3.3	2.0	...
1962...............	57.1	...	...	76.0	98.6	98.8	97.1	73.2	33.4	14.9	6.1	3.8	1.5	...
1961...............	56.8	...	...	79.1	98.0	98.3	95.1	76.8	30.6	15.9	4.3	2.4	1.1	...
1960...............	55.9	...	...	73.3	99.3	99.0	95.9	76.9	34.6	11.9	4.4	2.9	1.0	...
1959...............	55.1	...	...	74.3	98.9	99.1	93.9	76.3	33.6	11.6	6.3	2.8	1.3	...
1958...............	54.0	...	...	73.9	------98.8-----		----82.8-----		34.3	------8.7------		3.9	1.3	...
1957...............	53.5	...	...	74.3	------98.2-----		----84.8-----		36.7	------8.8------		4.6	1.2	...
1956...............	51.5	...	...	72.8	------98.4-----		----81.2-----		31.8	------8.7------		3.1	0.7	...
1955...............	50.7	...	...	71.1	------98.2-----		----82.8-----		27.6	------7.2------		4.9	1.8	...
1954...............	48.6	...	...	68.8	------98.0-----		----78.8-----		24.0	------5.8------		4.8	1.4	...
1953...............	45.5	...	...	46.3	------97.3-----		----82.3-----		27.6	------5.4------		1.7	0.8	...
1952...............	46.4	...	...	54.0	------96.4-----		----77.3-----		------------------6.3--------------------					...
1951...............	53.4	...	...	54.9	------97.3-----		----77.1-----		20.8	------6.2------		2.7	...	...
1950...............	51.2	...	...	--------------86.8----------			----75.5-----		23.3	------6.3------		3.0	...	...
1949...............	40.9	...	...	--------------83.7----------			----69.5-----		20.0	------6.2------		1.8	0.5	...
1948...............	39.2	...	...	-------------80.1----------			----66.8-----		24.6	------6.3------		1.5	0.6	...
1947...............	41.0	...	...	-------------84.8----------			----71.9-----		20.2	------6.9------		2.5	0.5	...
Male														
2008...............	58.0	32.7	53.3	95.5	98.5	98.5	98.9	94.0	57.9	37.8	23.2	10.6	8.5	1.5
2007...............	59.5	33.9	59.6	93.9	98.3	97.2	99.2	95.2	61.9	37.8	28.0	10.4	9.4	2.0
2006...............	58.7	33.7	56.6	93.5	97.2	96.8	97.7	91.8	63.9	38.0	24.2	9.3	6.9	2.5
2005...............	58.9	34.0	54.0	94.8	97.7	97.7	93.6	93.6	67.2	35.1	23.4	9.3	6.3	2.4
2004...............	59.2	34.6	61.1	93.7	96.7	99.2	98.8	96.5	58.1	37.8	20.2	8.7	4.0	2.2
2003[1]...............	60.0	34.9	56.5	92.4	98.8	98.1	98.3	94.0	61.5	34.3	23.5	9.7	7.4	1.9
2002...............	60.2	35.4	57.5	96.2	99.1	97.9	97.6	92.9	54.9	39.5	16.6	10.1	7.5	2.1
2001...............	60.1	35.7	55.4	95.6	98.3	96.0	99.0	93.2	57.3	36.2	22.7	8.2	8.3	2.3
2000...............	59.5	35.3	57.6	95.8	98.3	98.7	99.6	89.1	52.4	30.5	21.8	11.3	8.3	2.2
1999...............	59.9	35.8	53.0	98.4	97.7	99.0	97.9	94.4	60.3	42.3	16.1	9.0	6.5	2.0
1998...............	60.1	36.2	57.8	95.0	98.5	98.6	97.7	93.9	58.2	40.7	15.1	12.6	5.6	1.8
1997...............	59.5	36.2	57.3	94.2	98.7	99.1	99.6	93.9	56.7	34.1	21.5	10.5	5.6	2.0
1996...............	57.8	35.7	47.0	90.1	98.1	97.2	98.1	93.7	55.2	39.0	18.6	12.8	5.4	2.4
1995...............	58.3	36.2	51.5	94.7	98.2	99.5	99.6	95.2	59.1	36.1	20.3	6.1	6.7	2.3
1994...............	58.4	36.5	56.8	97.1	99.6	99.5	99.7	95.3	53.4	33.7	21.3	10.8	5.7	2.1
1993[r]...............	56.0	...	41.6	96.8	99.3	100.0	99.0	96.1	63.4	23.7	19.6	10.4	3.1	...
1993...............	55.8	34.8	41.7	96.9	99.3	100.0	99.0	96.0	63.6	23.9	19.6	10.3	3.1	2.0
1992...............	54.8	...	41.3	97.6	99.9	99.7	99.9	94.5	60.7	27.1	18.7	7.6	3.3	...

Note: Data for 1947 to 1953 exclude kindergarten. Nursery school was first collected in 1964. Data shown for 1947 to 1966 for the Black population are for Black and other races.
[1]Starting in 2003 respondents could identify more than one race. Except as noted, the race data in this table from 2003 onward represent those respondents who indicated only one race category.
r = Revised, controlled to 1990 census based population estimates; previous 1993 data controlled to 1980 census based population estimates.
... = Not available.

Table A-10. Percent of the Population 3 Years Old and Over Enrolled in School, by Age, Sex, Race, and Hispanic Origin, October 1947–2008—Continued

(Percent.)

Year, sex, race, and Hispanic origin	Total enrolled 3 to 34 years old	Total enrolled 3 years old and over	3 and 4 years old	5 and 6 years old	7 to 9 years old	10 to 13 years old	14 and 15 years old	16 and 17 years old	18 and 19 years old	20 and 21 years old	22 to 24 years old	25 to 29 years old	30 to 34 years old	35 years old and over
1991	54.5	...	35.2	95.4	99.8	100.0	100.0	90.4	62.2	30.1	19.3	8.6	4.8	...
1990	53.9	...	38.3	96.1	99.9	99.9	99.7	93.2	60.7	31.1	20.0	4.6	2.3	...
1989	52.6	...	40.2	92.9	98.9	98.8	99.3	95.6	51.0	23.2	15.5	5.5	3.2	...
1988	52.4	...	34.5	96.0	99.6	100.0	99.1	93.2	49.7	20.7	14.7	6.3	4.1	...
1987	54.0	...	39.0	97.4	100.0	99.8	98.1	91.8	58.7	30.3	15.5	8.4	3.4	...
1986	53.8	...	38.7	97.1	99.6	98.8	98.4	94.7	54.1	25.4	17.3	7.1	5.9	...
1985	52.6	...	34.6	94.6	98.2	99.1	98.2	91.8	49.5	29.7	13.2	6.9	5.7	...
1984	52.6	...	37.2	92.8	99.5	99.1	96.9	93.2	48.6	29.7	17.5	5.7	3.9	...
1983	52.9	...	37.1	95.8	98.9	99.4	98.4	91.8	46.6	23.5	17.2	9.1	6.6	...
1982	53.2	...	37.4	93.9	99.3	98.4	97.8	92.2	46.5	20.9	17.4	8.5	7.1	...
1981	54.5	...	34.8	94.5	98.5	99.2	97.3	92.1	51.9	20.6	14.7	8.4	5.6	...
1980	56.1	...	36.6	94.1	99.5	99.4	98.5	90.8	42.8	23.0	13.3	10.6	7.3	...
1979	57.8	...	40.4	96.6	99.0	98.4	98.5	94.6	48.0	26.9	14.6	8.1	6.3	...
1978	58.7	...	37.9	93.2	99.4	98.8	99.0	92.8	50.5	25.2	14.7	9.5	7.8	...
1977	60.3	...	32.4	96.0	99.1	98.6	99.0	92.5	50.5	31.0	18.5	12.1	9.2	...
1976	61.1	...	36.3	94.4	99.5	98.8	99.5	90.9	54.9	28.0	18.7	11.0	8.8	...
1975	60.3	...	29.5	94.6	99.3	99.0	97.6	88.2	49.9	28.7	14.7	11.8	8.6	...
1974	60.7	...	30.3	91.8	99.5	99.6	96.1	90.1	46.1	27.7	16.0	10.4	9.7	...
1973	58.6	...	29.2	89.0	99.2	99.1	96.9	89.0	43.5	24.5	13.9	6.9	6.5	...
1972	60.9	...	32.1	90.8	98.4	99.4	97.6	88.9	47.7	27.1	18.4	7.3	5.2	...
1971	60.4	...	19.0	88.7	99.1	98.1	97.7	90.0	50.7	31.3	12.9	8.5	6.4	...
1970	59.5	...	22.3	84.2	99.2	99.1	98.0	85.4	41.3	27.8	9.6	6.1	3.6	...
1969	60.0	...	21.3	83.1	98.3	98.9	98.0	87.4	49.5	28.4	10.7	2.8	2.9	...
1968	60.0	...	16.9	84.1	98.8	98.4	98.5	88.5	53.1	23.4	7.5	5.2	3.4	...
1967	59.2	...	17.0	81.0	99.0	98.3	96.5	86.7	48.6	24.5	9.0	3.5	3.5	...
1966	58.1	...	12.7	80.0	99.1	99.0	98.2	87.4	46.3	14.4	9.1	2.6	2.7	...
1965	57.7	...	9.5	81.0	99.3	99.4	98.7	82.2	47.5	18.5	4.3	2.6	2.3	...
1964	56.8	...	9.4	80.7	98.2	98.7	98.8	84.3	39.9	14.2	3.8	3.5	4.0	...
1963	61.9	...	...	74.3	97.7	99.2	98.2	85.9	46.5	21.7	7.1	4.7	2.7	...
1962	60.4	...	...	74.5	98.9	98.6	99.1	77.1	40.3	15.0	10.1	5.8	1.7	...
1961	60.0	...	...	78.7	98.4	97.6	96.6	78.6	41.7	19.9	6.1	4.0	1.9	...
1960	58.3	...	...	71.8	99.4	98.7	97.0	79.1	36.9	13.7	6.3	3.9	1.0	...
1959	58.0	...	...	76.0	98.7	99.1	95.8	76.3	35.5	12.5	10.6	4.5	1.8	...
1958	58.0	...	...	74.2	----98.8---		------87.6-----		43.4	------11.8-----		6.3	2.4	...
1957	55.9	...	...	73.1	----98.2---		------84.7-----		38.5	------10.3-----		6.0	1.2	...
1956	54.3	...	...	70.4	----97.6---		------81.3-----		36.8	------12.5-----		5.3	0.9	...
1955	54.4	...	...	72.8	----98.2---		------85.2-----		32.9	------9.8-----		6.2	1.9	...
1954	52.0	...	...	64.7	----97.5---		------82.8-----		21.6	------10.1-----		7.9	1.9	...
1953	47.8	...	...	41.6	----97.1---		------79.1-----		34.6	------5.8-----		3.3	0.9	...
1952	49.7	...	...	51.4	----96.0--		------72.5-----		------------------6.0----------------					...
1951	56.9	...	...	52.8	----98.0---		------74.9-----		23.6	------9.0-----		4.3	...	...
1950	56.0	...	...	------87.0------			------79.3-----		19.9	------11.1-----		6.1	...	...
1949	45.0	...	...	------83.1----------			------68.8-----		26.1	------11.8-----		3.3	1.1	...
1948	40.4	...	...	------78.9----------			------63.9-----		24.0	------11.8-----		2.5	1.4	...
1947	45.1	...	...	------84.6----------			------72.6-----		20.7	------12.3-----		5.1	0.8	...
Female														
2008	57.6	30.9	55.8	90.8	99.4	99.4	96.9	94.4	60.5	42.6	26.3	18.3	13.8	3.8
2007	57.4	30.8	57.3	94.2	98.1	98.6	98.8	91.7	61.6	39.5	27.9	18.9	9.4	3.8
2006	57.6	31.1	61.5	91.7	96.9	97.6	97.2	94.7	65.4	40.2	30.0	14.0	9.9	3.6
2005	57.9	31.5	50.6	97.1	99.5	99.5	98.0	92.5	58.5	40.1	31.8	13.8	13.0	3.6
2004	58.7	32.3	57.7	94.5	98.2	99.6	99.1	94.8	60.2	41.9	29.5	19.0	9.8	4.2
2003[1]	58.4	32.1	54.5	96.4	97.7	98.3	97.5	94.6	62.2	47.4	30.8	14.2	9.6	3.5
2002	59.1	33.0	57.4	95.2	97.2	98.3	98.8	93.7	60.6	47.1	28.8	16.3	11.7	3.8
2001	58.9	33.1	62.1	96.5	97.2	98.1	96.2	91.0	62.0	37.9	29.0	15.3	14.0	3.9
2000	58.7	32.9	62.3	96.8	96.8	98.2	99.6	93.8	61.5	41.3	26.4	16.5	10.7	2.9
1999	56.5	32.0	59.1	96.5	98.7	98.6	98.5	92.1	54.7	36.9	25.9	11.5	8.9	2.9
1998	57.8	33.2	59.1	95.6	98.9	98.7	100.0	91.8	62.2	37.8	26.2	14.4	10.9	3.2
1997	57.4	33.3	62.9	97.2	99.8	99.7	98.9	92.9	59.6	37.3	28.7	10.8	7.2	3.5
1996	54.7	32.2	52.6	90.8	96.7	97.6	99.6	90.4	50.5	35.5	23.2	14.4	8.6	3.5

Note: Data for 1947 to 1953 exclude kindergarten. Nursery school was first collected in 1964. Data shown for 1947 to 1966 for the Black population are for Black and other races.
[1] Starting in 2003 respondents could identify more than one race. Except as noted, the race data in this table from 2003 onward represent those respondents who indicated only one race category.
r = Revised, controlled to 1990 census based population estimates; previous 1993 data controlled to 1980 census based population estimates.
... = Not available.

Table A-10.　Percent of the Population 3 Years Old and Over Enrolled in School, by Age, Sex, Race, and Hispanic Origin, October 1947–2008—*Continued*

(Percent.)

Year, sex, race, and Hispanic origin	Total enrolled 3 to 34 years old	Total enrolled 3 years old and over	Age											
			3 and 4 years old	5 and 6 years old	7 to 9 years old	10 to 13 years old	14 and 15 years old	16 and 17 years old	18 and 19 years old	20 and 21 years old	22 to 24 years old	25 to 29 years old	30 to 34 years old	35 years old and over
1995	54.1	31.9	43.6	96.3	97.2	99.0	98.3	90.4	55.9	38.5	19.5	13.0	8.7	3.0
1994	54.4	32.5	47.0	97.2	99.7	99.7	98.6	95.5	54.6	35.9	23.6	10.3	8.5	3.4
1993ʳ	51.6	...	37.9	92.0	98.7	99.7	97.9	93.4	52.0	35.3	16.6	10.5	7.4	...
1993	51.6	30.4	37.8	92.1	98.7	99.7	97.9	93.4	51.9	35.1	16.7	10.5	7.5	3.0
1992	51.3	...	35.8	94.1	98.9	99.6	98.8	91.5	51.8	38.6	21.6	8.2	6.9	...
1991	50.6	...	39.5	96.1	99.5	100.0	98.2	93.1	49.4	29.9	17.3	8.8	7.9	...
1990	50.1	...	45.0	96.5	99.8	99.8	98.7	90.2	50.0	26.0	20.1	7.3	6.2	...
1989	50.1	...	37.6	97.1	99.2	99.9	99.5	91.7	49.4	37.3	18.6	7.1	6.3	...
1988	49.0	...	32.3	94.9	99.8	99.3	98.6	89.8	50.9	34.3	11.9	7.9	6.9	...
1987	49.6	...	34.4	94.1	99.3	99.7	98.6	91.2	48.2	27.4	14.6	10.0	8.1	...
1986	49.5	...	38.6	93.7	100.0	99.3	98.2	93.1	47.6	25.7	16.9	8.6	6.5	...
1985	49.4	...	50.2	97.1	98.7	99.9	97.6	91.6	39.0	26.0	14.1	7.9	6.1	...
1984	47.8	...	39.2	95.3	99.5	99.4	99.0	91.7	40.3	25.9	14.1	8.8	6.2	...
1983	48.8	...	35.2	93.6	99.3	100.0	97.1	93.4	45.7	23.3	14.2	6.0	6.5	...
1982	50.2	...	39.8	97.0	99.1	99.5	98.3	91.0	41.0	27.2	16.6	7.2	8.0	...
1981	50.6	...	38.7	94.4	99.1	99.6	97.0	90.5	44.9	25.7	14.7	8.4	8.1	...
1980	52.0	...	39.7	96.7	99.3	99.3	97.4	90.4	48.2	23.7	13.9	7.4	6.5	...
1979	52.5	...	41.2	95.5	99.7	99.0	96.4	87.1	45.4	21.1	15.3	7.7	7.3	...
1978	54.1	...	44.8	94.7	99.6	99.1	98.0	89.6	42.4	26.0	15.2	8.1	8.0	...
1977	55.4	...	38.1	97.0	99.4	99.4	98.5	89.1	46.3	28.2	12.6	10.7	8.9	...
1976	55.0	...	32.6	93.6	99.1	98.8	98.4	87.0	46.4	28.4	14.5	8.1	7.6	...
1975	55.3	...	37.6	93.9	99.3	99.4	97.2	85.6	44.7	25.8	13.8	7.5	5.9	...
1974	54.2	...	28.0	93.8	98.9	100.0	97.9	84.2	42.1	20.1	9.0	7.7	4.8	...
1973	53.3	...	28.5	90.9	99.2	98.9	96.5	86.4	32.8	17.3	11.1	5.5	3.8	...
1972	54.9	...	24.5	89.1	99.0	99.3	97.3	90.1	38.7	17.9	8.5	5.9	6.5	...
1971	56.9	...	24.1	90.9	98.9	99.4	99.0	88.4	43.1	24.1	10.1	4.2	4.2	...
1970	55.5	...	23.2	85.7	99.5	99.5	97.2	85.9	38.9	18.9	6.7	3.6	3.3	...
1969	55.8	...	21.1	85.0	99.4	99.2	97.7	84.3	40.1	19.6	6.9	5.5	3.7	...
1968	54.9	...	20.5	81.3	99.7	99.5	96.9	84.3	38.6	14.5	8.3	1.5	3.2	...
1967	54.6	...	18.5	83.4	99.2	99.0	95.8	81.6	34.0	18.5	5.6	6.1	1.5	...
1966	53.2	...	14.7	81.6	99.3	99.4	96.5	83.1	30.3	9.3	3.6	2.0	2.0	...
1965	53.6	...	14.1	77.3	98.6	99.2	97.6	85.6	32.5	8.0	7.8	1.7	2.4	...
1964	52.5	...	11.7	79.9	99.9	99.3	95.0	80.6	31.7	13.7	3.8	2.8	2.0	...
1963	56.0	...	...	79.0	99.2	99.8	96.9	78.2	33.9	11.5	4.3	2.2	1.5	...
1962	54.1	...	...	77.5	98.3	99.1	95.2	69.5	27.3	14.9	3.0	2.2	1.3	...
1961	53.8	...	...	79.5	97.6	99.0	93.5	75.1	20.6	12.4	2.7	1.0	0.4	...
1960	53.7	...	...	74.9	99.1	99.3	94.8	74.7	32.2	10.4	2.8	2.1	1.0	...
1959	52.4	...	...	72.5	99.2	99.1	92.0	76.4	31.9	10.8	2.7	1.4	1.0	...
1958	50.3	...	...	73.7	------98.7------		----78.1----		26.4	------6.0------		1.9	0.4	...
1957	51.3	...	...	75.6	------98.2------		----85.0----		35.1	------7.6------		3.5	1.1	...
1956	49.0	...	...	75.2	------99.1------		----81.1----		27.5	------5.7------		1.3	0.6	...
1955	47.4	...	...	69.4	------98.1------		----80.5----		23.1	------5.5------		3.8	1.7	...
1954	45.6	...	...	73.0	------98.6------		----74.7----		25.7	------2.9------		2.3	0.9	...
1953	43.5	...	...	51.1	------97.6------		----85.5----		21.6	------5.0------		0.3	0.7	...
1952	43.6	...	...	56.3	------97.0------		----82.3----		------------------------6.4------------------------					...
1951	50.3	...	...	57.1	------96.5------		----79.2----		17.9	------4.3------		1.5	...	...
1950	47.0	...	...	--------------86.5--------------			----71.9----		25.7	------3.0------		0.6	...	...
1949	37.3	...	...	--------------84.5--------------			----70.0----		14.5	------1.9------		0.7	-	...
1948	38.2	...	...	--------------81.3--------------			----69.6----		25.2	------2.7------		0.6	-	...
1947	37.3	...	...	--------------84.9--------------			----71.3----		19.9	------2.5------		0.3	0.3	...

Note: Data for 1947 to 1953 exclude kindergarten. Nursery school was first collected in 1964. Data shown for 1947 to 1966 for the Black population are for Black and other races.

r = Revised, controlled to 1990 census based population estimates; previous 1993 data controlled to 1980 census based population estimates.

... = Not available.

Table A-10. Percent of the Population 3 Years Old and Over Enrolled in School, by Age, Sex, Race, and Hispanic Origin, October 1947–2008—*Continued*

(Percent.)

Year, sex, race, and Hispanic origin	Total enrolled 3 to 34 years old	Total enrolled 3 years old and over	Age 3 and 4 years old	5 and 6 years old	7 to 9 years old	10 to 13 years old	14 and 15 years old	16 and 17 years old	18 and 19 years old	20 and 21 years old	22 to 24 years old	25 to 29 years old	30 to 34 years old	35 years old and over
ASIAN[2]														
Both Sexes														
2008	57.3	27.4	55.8	90.8	98	99.5	98.7	92.4	85.4	81.1	43.1	23.4	11.5	2.4
2007	55.6	26.9	53.4	94.3	98.2	99.2	99.8	92.6	86.5	66.5	47.4	19.0	9.9	1.7
2006	54.7	26.9	48.3	96.7	99.1	99.2	99.5	92.2	83.0	74.7	44.8	17.8	8.7	2.2
2005	55.6	28.2	55.0	94.7	99.5	97.6	98.8	98.3	88.3	80.5	42.7	21.0	9.3	2.2
2004	56.8	29.3	58.3	97.2	99.9	99.1	97.5	98.6	82.6	79.7	46.8	21.5	9.5	2.6
2003[1]	56.8	29.3	54.5	89.4	99.0	99.3	99.0	97.6	87.3	79.8	48.1	22.5	9.2	2.2
2002	57.3	30.8	56.1	95.6	96.9	98.8	98.4	94.9	78.9	72.8	49.5	18.3	8.3	2.4
2001	57.7	31.7	41.9	99.4	96.3	99.6	98.4	95.7	84.0	72.6	50.8	22.6	7.8	2.2
2000	58.3	32.6	56.0	97.6	97.8	97.6	99.6	98.4	78.8	66.2	45.3	18.7	8.9	2.8
1999	60.9	34.3	55.8	98.9	99.6	100.0	95.8	97.3	78.5	61.7	45.6	20.3	7.8	3.0
1998	59.9	34.2	53.4	97.9	97.9	98.1	95.3	95.6	83.3	70.6	49.0	21.3	8.7	2.6
1997	60.6	34.6	60.2	94.0	97.7	100.0	99.4	94.7	80.2	73.2	41.8	24.2	9.6	2.7
1996	58.6	35.0	50.4	95.7	98.9	99.3	96.8	94.3	78.3	65.8	39.5	18.6	9.9	3.6
1995	57.3	32.5	42.1	95.9	99.5	99.8	100.0	95.9	83.1	63.4	46.7	21.2	11.1	3.2
1994	60.9	33.1	42.3	97.8	99.5	99.7	100.0	97.3	81.8	67.4	53.5	23.8	8.4	2.7
1993	62.2	34.7	39.6	97.1	99.7	100.0	99.9	91.1	82.5	76.1	55.3	21.0	8.6	3.4
Male														
2008	57.1	27.9	54.2	91.1	96.8	99.1	100.0	96.0	89.0	74.1	38.0	25.2	10.3	1.9
2007	57.2	28.6	56.7	96.9	99.0	99.0	99.7	93.5	91.8	67.6	46.0	18.1	10.3	1.9
2006	55.5	28.3	56.7	96.8	98.3	98.8	99.4	91.0	79.7	76.1	42.2	16.3	8.5	2.4
2005	56.9	29.7	53.2	96.8	99.8	96.9	97.8	97.8	85.2	84.0	42.6	21.1	10.3	2.0
2004	59.3	31.9	58.3	96.0	99.7	99.8	96.5	99.0	85.9	84.2	49.8	24.1	11.4	2.9
2003[1]	59.6	31.8	53.3	90.8	97.9	99.9	97.8	100.0	90.4	77.0	47.8	28.9	11.9	2.3
2002	58.7	32.3	54.1	97.7	95.6	98.4	99.5	94.3	80.0	70.2	50.1	20.6	9.5	2.4
2001	59.1	33.6	35.9	99.6	96.0	100.0	97.1	94.5	83.3	74.9	58.9	22.9	10.6	1.7
2000	60.5	35.0	56.0	96.8	99.5	97.0	99.3	97.8	75.5	67.2	49.1	16.0	10.2	2.7
1999	62.0	35.8	53.5	97.9	99.2	100.0	93.7	98.7	74.4	59.6	50.5	21.4	10.6	3.1
1998	60.8	35.2	51.5	100.0	97.9	98.5	95.0	96.8	74.8	68.0	51.3	21.4	11.1	2.2
1997	63.4	36.6	61.3	89.7	99.4	100.0	98.6	95.5	88.2	71.6	46.9	31.0	10.6	2.5
1996	62.1	38.0	51.0	94.0	99.0	99.6	97.9	93.7	81.0	70.7	37.3	24.4	14.4	3.6
1995	60.0	35.6	38.0	94.5	98.9	99.6	100.0	96.9	81.9	60.3	47.8	24.8	15.7	3.5
1994	64.7	35.8	45.5	98.2	99.0	100.0	100.0	96.9	81.5	70.9	57.0	31.3	10.7	2.1
1993	65.9	37.9	43.0	95.9	99.8	99.9	100.0	93.4	79.4	78.5	65.4	21.0	11.2	3.4
Female														
2008	57.4	26.8	57.8	90.4	99.0	100.0	97.5	88.7	81.8	89.5	47.5	21.7	12.7	2.9
2007	54.0	25.3	49.1	91.9	97.3	99.5	100.0	91.7	81.0	65.4	48.5	19.8	9.6	1.5
2006	53.8	25.6	39.1	96.5	100.0	99.5	99.0	93.3	87.3	72.9	47.0	19.1	8.9	2.0
2005	54.4	26.8	56.8	92.3	99.3	98.3	100.0	98.8	91.7	75.9	42.9	20.9	8.4	2.4
2004	54.1	26.9	58.4	99.1	100.0	98.2	98.5	98.1	79.0	74.7	43.9	19.1	7.6	2.4
2003[1]	54.0	27.1	55.8	87.4	100.0	98.4	100.0	94.9	84.6	82.5	48.3	16.6	6.7	2.1
2002	56.1	29.5	58.1	93.4	97.9	99.2	97.5	95.5	77.9	75.8	48.9	16.1	7.2	2.3
2001	56.2	29.9	47.7	99.1	96.6	99.2	100.0	97.2	84.6	70.0	42.5	22.3	5.1	2.6
2000	56.0	30.4	55.9	98.6	96.2	98.2	100.0	99.1	82.0	65.1	41.7	20.6	7.5	2.9
1999	59.8	32.9	57.8	100.0	100.0	100.0	97.6	95.8	82.0	63.7	42.2	19.4	5.2	2.9
1998	59.0	33.2	55.0	95.6	97.8	97.7	95.6	94.4	91.5	73.6	46.6	21.2	6.5	3.0
1997	57.9	32.7	59.5	98.4	95.5	100.0	100.0	93.8	71.6	74.3	36.5	17.4	8.8	2.9
1996	54.9	32.0	49.5	97.9	98.8	99.0	95.5	95.0	75.4	80.8	42.2	13.5	6.1	3.7
1995	54.5	29.6	46.0	98.1	100.0	100.0	100.0	94.8	84.4	67.0	46.2	17.8	6.8	3.1
1994	57.3	30.6	39.0	97.4	100.0	99.4	100.0	97.7	81.9	64.2	49.3	16.9	6.7	3.2
1993	58.6	31.9	36.1	98.5	99.6	100.0	99.8	88.7	87.0	74.5	43.4	20.9	6.3	3.4

Note: Data for 1947 to 1953 exclude kindergarten. Nursery school was first collected in 1964. Data shown for 1947 to 1966 for the Black population are for Black and other races.

[1] Starting in 2003 respondents could identify more than one race. Except as noted, the race data in this table from 2003 onward represent those respondents who indicated only one race category.

[2] The data shown prior to 2003 consists of those identifying themselves as "Asian or Pacific Islanders."

r = Revised, controlled to 1990 census based population estimates; previous 1993 data controlled to 1980 census based population estimates.

… = Not available.

Table A-10.   Percent of the Population 3 Years Old and Over Enrolled in School, by Age, Sex, Race, and Hispanic Origin, October 1947–2008—*Continued*

(Percent.)

Year, sex, race, and Hispanic origin	Total enrolled 3 to 34 years old	Total enrolled 3 years old and over	Age												
			3 and 4 years old	5 and 6 years old	7 to 9 years old	10 to 13 years old	14 and 15 years old	16 and 17 years old	18 and 19 years old	20 and 21 years old	22 to 24 years old	25 to 29 years old	30 to 34 years old	35 years old and over
HISPANIC[4]														
Both Sexes														
2008...............	51.9	31.9	43.6	91.8	97.1	98.6	98.7	93.8	55.1	32.1	19.8	9.2	4.2	2.2
2007...............	51.7	32.1	48.2	94.3	96.3	99.0	98.4	90.6	57.2	32.3	18.8	8.3	4.5	2.1
2006...............	51.3	31.9	48.8	93.4	98.1	98.2	98.4	91.1	53.4	30.6	17.9	7.3	5.3	1.8
2005...............	50.9	32.1	43.0	93.8	97.4	97.9	97.3	92.6	54.3	30.0	19.5	7.8	4.2	2.0
2004...............	50.7	32.4	43.9	93.9	97.2	97.5	99.0	89.2	43.9	30.6	17.2	6.7	3.3	1.5
2003...............	49.6	31.6	43.7	91.6	97.5	98.3	96.7	92.1	50.5	33.7	16.1	6.2	4.6	1.8
2002...............	49.9	32.3	41.0	94.4	97.9	98.1	98.1	90.9	50.6	24.6	15.3	8.4	4.4	2.4
2001...............	49.5	32.4	39.7	93.6	97.4	98.3	97.8	88.2	45.5	27.9	15.5	7.7	4.4	2.5
2000...............	51.3	32.6	35.9	94.3	97.5	97.4	96.2	87.0	49.5	26.1	18.2	7.4	5.6	2.0
1999...............	51.1	32.9	36.9	93.9	99.0	98.3	97.6	88.1	44.5	22.6	15.0	9.1	5.6	2.3
1998...............	50.4	32.6	36.7	98.2	98.8	99.1	96.8	89.1	40.3	25.6	16.3	8.7	5.5	2.3
1997...............	50.8	32.7	36.6	96.6	98.6	99.6	98.4	91.1	49.4	28.9	16.4	7.3	3.7	1.8
1996...............	50.3	32.8	38.1	89.5	96.6	97.6	96.6	88.7	47.0	25.3	17.6	8.6	5.0	2.5
1995...............	49.7	32.9	36.9	93.9	98.5	99.2	98.9	88.2	46.1	27.1	15.6	7.1	4.7	2.7
1994...............	49.0	32.6	30.8	96.1	99.2	99.4	96.1	88.3	51.4	24.9	15.1	8.1	5.7	2.7
1993ʳ...............	48.6	...	26.8	93.6	99.6	99.2	97.6	88.1	50.0	31.8	13.8	7.7	5.1	...
1993...............	48.9	31.6	26.8	93.8	99.6	99.2	97.6	88.3	50.0	31.8	13.7	7.7	5.1	1.9
1992...............	49.2	...	28.8	96.0	99.5	99.1	98.8	87.2	53.7	30.1	14.5	6.7	6.0	...
1991...............	47.9	...	30.6	92.4	99.9	99.4	97.2	82.6	47.9	26.4	11.6	6.9	5.9	...
1990...............	47.4	...	29.8	94.8	99.6	99.2	99.0	85.4	44.1	27.2	9.9	6.3	3.1	...
1989...............	45.8	...	23.8	92.8	98.0	99.3	96.5	86.4	44.6	18.8	12.0	6.6	3.5	...
1988...............	46.0	...	24.5	95.7	99.6	99.8	98.8	78.8	44.1	16.7	12.1	5.8	6.2	...
1987...............	47.2	...	30.7	93.0	99.2	99.4	97.6	87.1	39.1	26.5	12.3	7.5	4.9	...
1986...............	48.2	...	28.8	93.7	99.4	99.3	97.2	84.0	46.0	21.4	13.7	9.2	5.6	...
1985...............	47.7	...	27.0	94.5	98.4	99.4	96.1	84.5	41.8	24.0	11.6	8.6	5.6	...
1984...............	47.7	...	24.2	93.9	98.7	99.4	94.9	85.7	39.9	28.1	11.3	6.6	7.5	...
1983...............	49.3	...	23.5	95.1	98.5	99.7	96.0	88.6	44.3	24.0	12.5	7.1	5.7	...
1982...............	49.4	...	21.8	92.2	98.7	98.8	96.9	85.5	39.2	22.7	10.4	8.2	4.4	...
1981...............	49.0	...	24.5	90.4	99.2	99.1	94.0	82.8	37.8	20.6	12.3	8.0	4.7	...
1980...............	49.8	...	28.5	94.5	98.4	99.7	94.3	81.8	37.8	19.5	11.7	6.9	4.1	...
1979...............	48.6	...	22.5	92.5	98.7	99.0	96.3	82.3	39.9	22.6	10.0	7.8	7.1	...
1978...............	48.3	...	22.5	91.4	99.5	98.0	95.2	83.0	35.7	16.8	11.8	8.0	4.1	...
1977...............	50.8	...	19.5	93.7	99.0	99.3	97.6	83.6	40.6	23.1	10.8	9.3	5.6	...
1976...............	51.8	...	22.2	95.0	97.5	99.1	95.4	81.3	45.2	24.0	14.8	7.9	2.7	...
1975...............	54.8	...	27.3	92.1	99.6	99.2	95.6	86.2	44.0	27.5	14.1	8.3	4.1	...
1974...............	54.3	...	25.3	92.1	98.8	99.2	96.1	78.3	45.2	23.2	11.3	6.7	2.2	...
1973...............	52.8	...	18.8	90.7	98.7	99.1	94.4	80.2	39.2	21.5	10.0	6.8	1.3	...
1972...............	53.0	...	20.5	90.0	98.7	99.1	96.7	83.9	41.4	17.0	9.9	5.2	3.5	...
Male														
2008...............	50.0	31.1	40.5	91.0	96.7	98.6	98.6	93.1	54.7	30.8	16.6	8.2	4.1	1.6
2007...............	49.4	31.1	50.7	94.1	96.4	99.0	97.8	91.1	55.2	24.6	14.4	6.7	3.1	1.8
2006...............	49.0	30.9	49.1	91.7	97.7	97.9	99.0	91.7	51.5	24.1	16.0	5.4	3.5	1.2
2005...............	48.4	31.0	43.0	92.4	96.0	97.2	97.8	92.5	51.8	25.2	17.5	5.6	2.6	1.6
2004...............	48.5	31.5	43.8	93.9	97.2	97.5	99.0	89.2	43.9	30.6	17.2	6.7	3.3	1.5
2003	47.3	30.8	42.9	91.3	97.5	98.4	96.7	90.4	47.0	27.2	13.3	4.9	3.8	1.3
2002...............	48.1	31.9	41.7	95.1	97.8	97.6	98.2	88.8	48.4	24.5	11.5	7.0	3.1	2.2
2001...............	48.4	32.2	42.9	94.9	97.9	98.6	98.4	87.8	40.0	24.4	14.6	6.5	3.5	2.2
2000...............	50.5	32.5	31.9	95.4	96.6	98.4	96.9	85.7	48.0	24.2	15.2	5.1	5.7	1.4
1999...............	50.3	32.9	33.5	92.8	98.8	98.5	98.1	87.9	45.3	21.5	11.2	8.6	3.9	2.0
1998...............	49.0	32.4	44.9	92.8	98.8	99.3	97.0	88.0	33.7	24.6	12.9	6.9	4.7	1.8
1997...............	49.0	32.3	35.5	97.7	97.7	99.8	99.5	92.5	45.4	27.6	14.0	5.9	2.7	1.6
1996...............	49.2	33.0	39.6	91.0	95.4	97.9	98.0	90.4	46.8	19.5	16.2	6.8	4.3	2.6
1995...............	49.1	33.1	40.8	93.6	98.8	98.8	98.4	88.4	47.4	24.8	14.8	5.6	4.5	2.1
1994...............	48.0	32.5	32.6	96.5	98.6	99.3	94.6	86.6	54.2	23.7	14.0	7.1	4.2	2.3
1993ʳ...............	46.6	...	26.9	93.4	99.8	98.8	96.9	88.7	47.8	31.6	13.0	5.5	5.4	...
1993...............	47.4	31.5	27.0	93.6	99.8	98.8	96.9	89.1	47.7	31.6	12.8	5.5	5.4	1.5
1992...............	47.9	...	24.9	96.5	100.0	99.2	98.1	89.2	52.6	24.3	13.8	5.3	3.5	...

Note: Data for 1947 to 1953 exclude kindergarten. Nursery school was first collected in 1964. Data shown for 1947 to 1966 for the Black population are for Black and other races.
[4]May be of any race.
r = Revised, controlled to 1990 census based population estimates; previous 1993 data controlled to 1980 census based population estimates.
... = Not available.

Table A-10.   Percent of the Population 3 Years Old and Over Enrolled in School, by Age, Sex, Race, and Hispanic Origin, October 1947–2008—*Continued*

(Percent.)

Year, sex, race, and Hispanic origin	Total enrolled 3 to 34 years old	Total enrolled 3 years old and over	Age												
			3 and 4 years old	5 and 6 years old	7 to 9 years old	10 to 13 years old	14 and 15 years old	16 and 17 years old	18 and 19 years old	20 and 21 years old	22 to 24 years old	25 to 29 years old	30 to 34 years old	35 years old and over
1991..............	46.4	...	30.7	92.3	99.8	99.7	97.8	83.6	42.1	20.8	9.9	6.8	3.3	...
1990..............	47.1	...	27.3	95.6	99.5	99.0	99.1	85.5	40.7	21.7	11.2	4.6	4.0	...
1989..............	45.8	...	21.3	92.5	97.7	98.6	98.0	88.7	44.2	17.1	12.2	7.3	4.1	...
1988..............	46.2	...	27.9	96.7	99.2	100.0	98.1	80.9	44.7	21.6	12.5	4.5	5.0	...
1987..............	47.8	...	30.5	92.8	99.7	100.0	98.1	90.9	42.3	30.1	11.4	7.8	5.1	...
1986..............	47.3	...	29.4	93.0	100.0	99.4	96.8	85.0	45.8	19.2	13.0	9.1	4.4	...
1985..............	47.5	...	26.4	95.3	98.9	99.1	96.2	88.9	38.6	20.3	12.6	8.7	3.8	...
1984..............	48.6	...	20.0	93.6	98.2	100.0	95.7	85.1	38.8	27.5	12.3	8.2	4.0	...
1983..............	50.7	...	25.0	91.9	98.8	99.6	97.8	88.2	40.4	26.2	15.1	6.9	4.6	...
1982..............	50.4	...	25.2	90.3	99.6	98.4	96.8	87.8	39.7	21.6	11.2	10.8	3.1	...
1981..............	49.6	...	25.5	89.6	98.8	99.0	92.3	84.5	36.0	24.4	11.4	8.3	4.3	...
1980..............	49.9	...	30.1	94.0	97.7	99.4	96.7	81.5	36.9	21.4	10.7	6.8	6.2	...
1979..............	51.0	...	22.8	93.8	98.7	99.0	96.6	85.1	42.6	24.0	12.4	8.7	6.1	...
1978..............	50.5	...	22.6	93.2	99.1	97.8	94.0	80.4	40.0	18.1	13.6	9.5	4.4	...
1977..............	54.2	...	23.2	91.4	100.0	98.7	99.1	89.4	43.1	22.8	16.0	13.1	6.4	...
1976..............	55.0	...	22.1	94.6	97.4	98.5	97.3	85.5	46.3	27.1	18.6	11.4	5.6	...
1975..............	58.1	...	26.7	89.7	99.6	98.8	97.4	88.3	51.9	31.3	15.9	11.9	7.2	...
1974..............	56.0	...	23.5	93.1	98.3	98.5	97.9	78.6	46.8	22.3	14.5	8.4	7.4	...
1973..............	55.5	...	23.1	92.4	99.1	99.1	96.5	86.6	45.8	23.8	10.8	9.9	6.7	...
1972..............	54.7	...	20.4	90.3	98.8	99.1	98.1	87.8	40.5	20.0	13.9	5.8	2.5	...
Female														
2008..............	53.9	32.8	46.9	92.6	97.4	98.7	98.8	94.5	55.5	33.5	23.4	10.4	4.4	2.7
2007..............	54.3	33.1	45.6	94.5	96.2	99.0	99.1	90.0	59.2	41.0	23.7	10.3	6.1	2.3
2006..............	53.9	33.1	48.5	95.3	98.5	98.6	97.7	90.4	55.4	37.5	20.1	9.7	7.3	2.3
2005..............	58.0	33.3	43.0	95.3	98.8	98.6	96.7	92.6	57.2	35.3	21.8	10.4	6.1	2.4
2004..............	53.1	33.3	44.0	92.2	97.9	97.5	97.5	91.3	56.9	34.0	22.0	9.7	7.5	2.8
2003..............	52.2	32.5	44.7	92.0	97.5	98.2	96.8	93.8	54.4	41.1	19.4	7.9	5.6	2.2
2002..............	51.8	32.8	40.3	93.8	98.1	98.7	97.9	92.8	53.2	24.6	20.2	9.9	6.0	2.7
2001..............	50.6	32.6	36.3	92.4	96.9	98.1	97.2	88.7	51.1	31.6	16.7	9.1	5.3	2.8
2000..............	52.2	32.8	40.0	93.1	98.4	96.4	95.4	88.3	51.1	28.1	21.6	9.5	5.5	2.6
1999..............	52.1	32.8	40.5	95.0	99.3	98.0	96.9	88.3	43.6	23.6	19.2	9.5	7.3	2.7
1998..............	51.9	32.8	34.3	93.7	98.8	98.9	96.7	90.5	46.8	26.8	20.0	10.6	6.5	2.8
1997..............	52.7	33.0	37.7	95.7	99.6	99.5	97.3	89.6	53.9	30.4	19.2	8.8	4.9	2.0
1996..............	51.4	32.7	36.8	87.8	97.9	97.4	95.0	86.9	47.2	31.1	19.3	10.5	5.7	2.5
1995..............	50.3	32.7	32.7	94.3	98.2	99.6	99.4	88.0	44.8	29.2	16.6	8.7	4.9	3.2
1994..............	50.2	32.7	28.9	95.7	99.8	99.4	97.6	90.2	48.6	26.4	16.5	9.1	7.3	3.0
1993ʳ.............	50.7	...	26.7	93.9	99.4	99.6	98.2	87.3	51.9	31.9	14.7	10.2	4.7	...
1993..............	50.6	31.6	26.7	93.9	99.4	99.6	98.2	87.4	51.9	32.0	14.5	10.2	4.8	2.2
1992..............	50.6	...	32.7	95.4	99.0	99.1	99.6	85.0	54.9	35.6	15.4	8.2	6.0	...
1991..............	49.5	...	30.5	92.6	100.0	99.2	96.6	81.5	53.7	32.0	13.6	7.0	5.9	...
1990..............	47.7	...	32.3	93.9	99.7	99.4	98.8	85.3	47.2	33.1	8.4	8.1	3.1	...
1989..............	45.9	...	26.5	93.3	98.3	100.0	95.1	83.7	45.0	20.8	11.9	5.8	3.5	...
1988..............	45.8	...	20.7	94.6	100.0	99.6	99.6	76.6	43.5	11.2	11.5	7.2	6.2	...
1987..............	46.5	...	30.8	93.2	98.7	98.9	97.1	82.6	36.2	22.0	13.2	7.3	4.9	...
1986..............	49.0	...	28.2	94.4	98.7	99.2	97.5	83.0	46.2	23.7	14.5	9.2	5.6	...
1985..............	47.9	...	27.7	93.7	98.0	99.7	96.0	80.0	44.7	27.4	10.4	8.6	5.6	...
1984..............	46.8	...	28.2	94.2	99.2	98.7	94.0	86.3	40.8	28.7	10.4	4.9	7.5	...
1983..............	48.0	...	22.0	98.3	98.1	99.8	94.1	89.1	47.6	21.7	10.1	7.4	5.7	...
1982..............	48.4	...	16.3	93.9	97.8	99.2	97.1	82.8	38.7	23.7	9.7	5.7	4.4	...
1981..............	48.4	...	23.4	91.3	99.6	99.3	95.7	80.8	39.4	16.8	13.1	7.7	4.7	...
1980..............	49.8	...	26.6	94.9	99.0	99.9	92.1	82.2	38.8	17.6	12.6	6.9	4.1	...
1979..............	46.3	...	22.3	91.1	98.7	98.9	95.9	79.5	37.1	21.5	7.8	7.0	7.1	...
1978..............	46.2	...	22.5	89.4	100.0	98.2	96.6	86.2	31.9	15.7	10.1	6.5	4.1	...
1977..............	47.6	...	15.8	96.3	97.9	99.5	95.9	77.4	38.5	23.4	6.2	5.9	5.6	...
1976..............	48.8	...	22.3	95.5	97.6	99.7	93.6	77.6	44.2	21.4	12.1	4.8	2.7	...
1975..............	51.7	...	27.9	94.4	99.5	99.7	93.8	84.0	37.1	24.3	12.5	5.3	4.1	...
1974..............	52.5	...	27.4	91.1	99.2	100.0	94.1	77.9	43.7	23.9	8.4	4.9	2.2	...
1973..............	50.1	...	14.0	88.9	98.3	99.1	92.5	74.9	32.9	19.4	9.2	3.9	1.3	...
1972..............	51.4	...	20.5	89.7	98.5	99.0	95.4	80.0	42.4	14.6	6.8	4.7	3.5	...

Note: Data for 1947 to 1953 exclude kindergarten. Nursery school was first collected in 1964. Data shown for 1947 to 1966 for the Black population are for Black and other races.
r = Revised, controlled to 1990 census based population estimates; previous 1993 data controlled to 1980 census based population estimates.
... = Not available.

Table A-10. Percent of the Population 3 Years Old and Over Enrolled in School, by Age, Sex, Race, and Hispanic Origin, October 1947–2008—*Continued*

(Percent.)

Year, sex, race, and Hispanic origin	Total enrolled 3 to 34 years old	Total enrolled 3 years old and over	Age											
			3 and 4 years old	5 and 6 years old	7 to 9 years old	10 to 13 years old	14 and 15 years old	16 and 17 years old	18 and 19 years old	20 and 21 years old	22 to 24 years old	25 to 29 years old	30 to 34 years old	35 years old and over
WHITE ALONE OR IN COMBINATION														
Both Sexes														
2008...............	55.9	25.7	52.4	94	98.2	98.9	98.7	95.5	67	51	28.1	12.4	6.3	1.8
2007...............	55.7	25.7	54.0	94.8	98.0	98.7	98.7	94.6	67.1	49.7	26.2	16.2	9.4	1.8
2006...............	55.8	25.7	55.5	94.8	98.4	98.5	98.4	94.9	65.0	47.9	25.6	11.4	6.8	1.7
2005...............	56.2	26.1	53.9	95.3	98.6	98.7	98.3	95.3	67.7	49.3	26.2	11.3	6.2	1.8
2004...............	55.7	26.1	52.7	95.5	98.2	98.4	98.5	94.0	64.8	49.4	25.2	12.2	6.4	1.8
2003...............	55.6	26.1	55.2	94.8	98.0	98.4	97.4	95.0	64.2	48.3	26.8	11.0	6.3	1.7
Male														
2008...............	55.2	25.9	52.1	93.6	97.9	98.7	99.0	95.0	64.4	48.1	26.4	11.6	5.7	1.3
2007...............	54.6	25.8	53.2	94.0	97.9	98.6	98.3	94.4	66.4	44.1	24.0	12.9	9.4	1.4
2006...............	54.9	25.9	56.0	94.5	98.3	98.4	98.2	94.7	62.7	43.5	24.1	10.3	5.6	1.3
2005...............	55.2	26.2	52.6	94.7	98.2	98.6	98.3	95.2	65.7	45.1	24.6	8.9	5.4	1.4
2004...............	55.0	26.3	53.4	95.8	98.0	98.2	98.8	94.3	59.9	46.5	23.2	11.1	5.5	1.4
2003...............	55.0	26.5	55.9	95.2	97.7	98.2	97.3	95.1	61.6	43.4	25.5	9.8	5.7	1.4
Female														
2008...............	56.6	25.5	52.7	94.4	98.6	99.1	98.5	96.0	69.7	54.0	29.8	13.2	7	2.3
2007...............	56.9	25.6	54.9	95.6	98.1	98.7	99.2	94.9	67.9	55.5	28.4	19.2	9.4	2.2
2006...............	56.6	25.5	55.0	95.2	98.5	98.5	98.6	95.2	67.3	52.4	27.1	12.4	8.1	2.1
2005...............	57.4	26.0	55.3	96.0	98.9	98.8	98.4	95.5	70.0	53.8	27.9	13.8	7.1	2.3
2004...............	56.5	25.8	51.9	95.3	98.4	98.5	98.2	93.8	69.7	52.4	27.1	13.4	7.3	2.2
2003...............	56.3	25.7	54.4	94.5	98.3	98.7	97.5	94.9	66.8	53.1	28.1	12.2	7.0	2.1
BLACK ALONE OR IN COMBINATION														
Both Sexes														
2008...............	58.8	33.0	54.5	92.9	98.8	99.1	98.1	94.5	59.7	40.4	24.8	15.1	11.4	2.8
2007...............	59.0	33.2	58.2	94.2	98.2	98.0	99.1	93.7	62.0	38.1	27.3	15.3	9.6	3.0
2006...............	58.8	33.3	59.0	92.4	96.9	97.2	97.4	93.2	64.9	38.9	27.8	11.9	8.9	3.2
2005...............	59.0	33.5	51.3	96.1	98.5	98.6	95.9	92.9	62.5	38.1	27.8	11.7	9.9	3.1
2004...............	59.6	34.3	58.6	94.5	97.4	99.4	98.6	95.3	59.7	40.8	25.3	14.8	7.0	3.3
2003...............	59.8	34.2	56.5	94.6	98.1	98.3	98.0	94.2	60.9	42.1	27.2	12.4	8.4	2.8
Male														
2008...............	58.8	34.0	53.1	94.0	98.3	98.7	99.0	94.3	58.0	38.1	22.7	11.0	8.6	1.6
2007...............	60.1	35.0	60.5	93.9	98.1	97.5	99.2	95.2	61.5	37.8	27.8	10.7	9.7	2.0
2006...............	59.5	34.8	57.0	92.5	97.0	97.1	97.8	91.9	64.1	38.8	25.6	9.5	7.0	2.5
2005...............	59.2	34.6	52.5	95.1	97.5	97.9	93.8	93.8	66.2	34.9	23.9	9.3	6.1	2.3
2004...............	59.7	35.3	59.9	93.9	96.8	99.2	98.8	96.3	57.9	38.2	21.0	9.3	3.9	2.2
2003...............	60.6	35.7	57.6	93.2	98.8	98.2	98.3	93.8	61.1	35.6	23.4	9.4	7.2	1.9
Female														
2008...............	58.8	32.1	55.7	91.7	99.4	99.5	97.2	94.7	61.3	42.5	26.6	18.6	13.8	3.8
2007...............	57.9	31.7	55.7	94.5	98.2	98.4	98.9	92.2	62.6	38.5	26.8	19.4	9.5	3.8
2006...............	58.2	32.0	60.9	92.3	96.9	97.4	97.0	94.6	65.6	39.0	29.8	14.0	10.5	3.6
2005...............	58.8	32.4	50.0	97.1	99.4	99.3	97.8	92.0	59.1	41.3	31.1	13.8	12.8	3.7
2004...............	59.6	33.4	57.0	95.0	98.1	99.6	98.4	94.2	61.3	43.1	29.3	19.3	9.5	4.2
2003...............	59.1	32.9	55.3	95.9	97.3	98.4	97.6	94.5	60.7	47.5	30.7	14.7	9.4	3.5

Note: Data for 1947 to 1953 exclude kindergarten. Nursery school was first collected in 1964. Data shown for 1947 to 1966 for the Black population are for Black and other races.

... = Not available.

Table A-10.   Percent of the Population 3 Years Old and Over Enrolled in School, by Age, Sex, Race, and Hispanic Origin, October 1947–2008—*Continued*

(Percent.)

Year, sex, race, and Hispanic origin	Total enrolled 3 to 34 years old	Total enrolled 3 years old and over	Age											
			3 and 4 years old	5 and 6 years old	7 to 9 years old	10 to 13 years old	14 and 15 years old	16 and 17 years old	18 and 19 years old	20 and 21 years old	22 to 24 years old	25 to 29 years old	30 to 34 years old	35 years old and over
ASIAN ALONE OR IN COMBINATION														
Both Sexes														
2008..............	59.2	29.5	57.4	92.6	98.3	99.6	98.8	93.5	85.9	79.4	43.0	23.0	11.9	2.5
2007..............	57.0	28.8	54.1	93.9	98.4	99.3	99.7	93.4	86.3	64.3	45.9	19.6	9.5	1.8
2006..............	56.3	29.0	51.5	94.6	99.0	99.3	99.6	92.0	82.3	72.2	43.1	17.3	8.8	2.2
2005..............	57.6	30.5	54.4	95.5	99.6	97.5	98.7	98.2	86.2	77.1	44.4	20.9	9.4	2.3
2004..............	58.5	31.4	57.7	97.6	99.9	99.2	98.0	97.1	79.9	77.7	46.2	20.8	9.3	2.7
2003..............	58.2	31.3	51.4	89.3	99.2	99.4	99.1	95.7	87.1	77.0	48.1	21.6	9.4	2.2
Male														
2008..............	59.4	30.2	56.1	92.8	97.3	99.2	100	96.4	89.7	74.2	39	24.5	11.3	2
2007..............	58.6	30.4	58.9	95.4	99.1	99.1	99.7	93.5	90.6	62.7	47.0	19.5	9.8	2.1
2006..............	57.0	30.2	60.4	94.7	98.2	99.0	0.0	90.1	78.1	74.6	43.0	14.9	8.5	2.4
2005..............	58.3	31.7	51.1	97.4	99.7	96.5	98.0	97.3	83.6	82.1	42.2	20.2	9.9	2.0
2004..............	60.8	33.9	57.2	96.5	99.8	99.9	97.1	96.9	83.5	83.6	49.6	23.0	10.9	2.9
2003..............	60.2	33.4	49.3	91.9	98.2	99.9	98.2	95.9	89.6	74.0	47.3	27.9	12.1	2.4
Female														
2008..............	58.9	28.8	59.1	92.3	99.2	100	97.5	90.8	82.4	85.7	46.8	21.7	12.5	2.9
2007..............	55.5	27.4	48.3	92.5	97.6	99.5	99.7	93.2	82.2	66.1	45.0	19.7	9.2	1.5
2006..............	55.7	27.9	41.4	94.5	100.0	99.6	99.1	93.6	87.8	69.4	43.2	19.4	9.0	2.1
2005..............	57.0	29.3	57.5	93.2	99.5	98.5	99.7	99.1	89.2	71.2	46.2	21.6	8.9	2.5
2004..............	56.1	29.0	58.4	99.2	99.9	98.5	98.9	97.2	76.3	71.5	42.9	18.8	7.8	2.5
2003..............	56.2	29.3	54.2	86.0	100.0	98.7	100.0	95.4	85.1	79.7	48.8	15.8	6.9	2.1

Note: Data for 1947 to 1953 exclude kindergarten. Nursery school was first collected in 1964. Data shown for 1947 to 1966 for the Black population are for Black and other races.
... = Not available.

Table A-11. The Population 6 to 17 Years Old Enrolled Below Modal Grade, 1971–2008

(Numbers in thousands, percent.)

Year, sex, race, and Hispanic origin	Percent below modal grade				Dropout rate, 15 to 17 years old	Population in age group			
	6 to 8 years old	9 to 11 years old	12 to 14 years old	15 to 17 years old		6 to 8 years old	9 to 11 years old	12 to 14 years old	15 to 17 years old
ALL RACES									
Both Sexes									
2008	19.8	27.0	31.0	30.5	2.7	12,104	11,793	12,128	12,746
2007	20.1	26.2	27.9	30.0	2.9	12,011	11,805	12,398	12,857
2006	20.1	26.1	27.9	30.5	3.0	11,776	11,902	12,473	12,926
2005	20.7	25.4	28.3	30.6	2.8	11,784	11,998	12,689	13,204
2004	21.7	25.4	28.2	32.0	3.5	11,799	12,034	12,870	12,766
2003	21.3	28.1	28.8	30.6	3.2	11,866	12,124	12,951	12,753
2002	18.0	25.5	27.1	30.1	3.3	12,029	12,421	12,592	12,187
2001	18.6	23.7	25.9	29.7	3.8	11,972	12,738	12,357	12,031
2000	19.2	24.0	27.8	30.2	4.3	12,079	12,713	12,003	11,933
1999	17.4	25.3	26.5	30.8	4.0	12,159	12,537	11,921	12,048
1998	19.0	23.8	26.7	31.9	3.8	12,165	11,960	11,600	11,314
1997	18.6	24.2	28.5	32.1	3.6	12,325	11,866	11,650	11,953
1996	17.9	23.3	28.8	31.0	4.8	12,191	11,845	11,653	11,617
1995	17.5	25.6	30.8	32.8	4.1	11,728	11,812	11,582	11,401
1994	18.9	26.2	31.3	30.9	3.8	11,601	11,528	11,462	10,560
1993ʳ	18.7	28.1	31.0	32.3	3.8	11,363	11,283	10,981	10,247
1993	18.7	28.0	30.8	32.0	3.7	11,363	11,283	10,981	10,247
1992	19.4	28.4	30.9	30.5	3.6	11,260	11,183	10,723	10,114
1991	21.2	26.9	29.6	30.0	4.6	11,120	11,099	10,440	9,923
1990	21.5	27.6	31.0	30.1	4.7	11,015	10,914	10,152	9,912
1989	21.4	29.0	31.8	28.0	4.5	11,007	10,673	9,928	10,020
1988	20.4	28.4	28.7	26.2	5.1	10,906	10,350	9,869	10,379
1987	20.9	26.7	27.6	24.8	5.1	10,702	10,053	9,795	10,944
1986	19.2	26.5	27.3	25.8	4.9	10,389	9,959	9,908	11,149
1985	17.9	24.9	25.7	25.5	5.1	10,076	9,673	10,442	11,024
1984	16.6	23.9	27.0	24.6	5.3	9,707	9,594	10,858	10,711
1983	15.4	24.4	24.8	23.7	5.2	9,605	9,730	11,123	10,768
1982	16.6	22.8	23.9	23.0	5.4	9,492	10,169	10,989	11,131
1981	14.4	23.3	23.0	23.8	6.1	9,519	10,657	10,712	11,757
1980	14.3	20.3	22.6	22.5	6.6	9,350	10,681	10,537	11,835
1979	13.0	20.2	20.3	21.6	6.5	9,804	10,545	10,886	12,190
1978	12.4	19.5	19.2	21.8	6.5	10,246	10,448	11,391	12,346
1977	10.7	18.9	18.9	21.2	6.4	10,449	10,537	11,826	12,472
1976	10.6	18.1	19.8	22.2	6.3	10,334	10,872	12,137	12,550
1975	11.1	17.4	21.3	22.5	6.4	10,256	11,343	12,372	12,531
1974	10.3	17.8	21.7	21.6	7.1	10,343	11,789	12,415	12,566
1973	10.7	18.4	21.5	21.3	7.1	10,614	11,946	12,542	12,309
1972	10.7	19.6	21.9	22.3	6.6	11,119	12,152	12,451	12,283
1971	11.1	19.7	22.0	22.5	5.7	11,938	12,648	12,429	11,906
Male									
2008	22.0	28.3	34.0	33.3	2.8	6,174	6,005	6,220	6,502
2007	23.0	28.1	29.8	33.7	2.9	6,159	6,031	6,310	6,572
2006	21.7	28.2	31.1	35.0	3.3	5,991	6,115	6,374	6,574
2005	23.2	28.6	30.7	34.3	3.0	6,014	6,126	6,523	6,645
2004	23.9	28.2	31.7	36.8	3.5	6,075	6,120	6,685	6,395
2003	23.9	32.0	31.8	35.1	3.4	6,198	6,331	6,426	6,569
2002	20.3	29.2	31.0	35.6	3.5	6,156	6,349	6,436	6,210
2001	22.1	26.1	28.7	34.0	4.3	6,147	6,540	6,311	6,182
2000	22.1	27.2	31.3	34.3	4.5	6,181	6,504	6,148	6,136
1999	18.8	28.9	30.2	36.2	3.9	6,211	6,471	6,048	6,195
1998	21.4	26.6	30.4	37.4	4.1	6,234	6,125	5,897	5,791
1997	21.9	27.7	33.4	37.8	3.7	6,295	6,112	5,932	6,126
1996	20.7	26.0	33.9	36.9	4.5	6,268	6,043	5,934	5,985
1995	20.2	28.0	35.2	38.5	3.5	5,999	6,027	5,930	5,840
1994	21.1	28.0	35.6	35.7	3.9	5,894	6,026	5,874	5,640
1993ʳ	21.2	32.1	35.4	40.3	3.3	5,837	5,736	5,629	5,262
1993	21.1	32.0	35.0	38.7	3.1	5,837	5,736	5,629	5,262
1992	21.6	32.6	37.0	35.2	2.7	5,738	5,742	5,502	5,166
1991	24.0	30.7	34.7	35.5	4.3	5,674	5,704	5,343	5,085
1990	23.9	32.0	36.2	35.3	4.6	5,629	5,603	5,200	5,078
1989	25.1	32.9	36.7	33.4	4.3	5,632	5,472	5,088	5,151
1988	23.5	33.2	33.7	30.6	4.8	5,580	5,298	5,065	5,286
1987	23.7	31.8	31.8	29.2	4.6	5,496	5,147	5,036	5,535
1986	22.9	30.4	32.2	30.2	4.9	5,311	5,113	5,066	5,697
1985	20.6	28.3	29.0	30.2	4.9	5,159	4,946	5,340	5,623

r = Revised, controlled to 1990 census based population estimates; previous 1993 data controlled to 1980 census based population estimates.

Table A-11. The Population 6 to 17 Years Old Enrolled Below Modal Grade, 1971–2008—*Continued*

(Numbers in thousands, percent.)

Year, sex, race, and Hispanic origin	Percent below modal grade				Dropout rate, 15 to 17 years old	Population in age group			
	6 to 8 years old	9 to 11 years old	12 to 14 years old	15 to 17 years old		6 to 8 years old	9 to 11 years old	12 to 14 years old	15 to 17 years old
1984	18.8	27.7	31.1	30.2	5.5	4,963	4,905	5,521	5,469
1983	17.8	28.7	30.3	28.5	5.3	4,913	4,974	5,690	5,463
1982	19.2	26.4	28.0	27.9	5.2	4,852	5,198	5,566	5,688
1981	17.2	27.9	25.6	28.1	6.2	4,866	5,447	5,510	5,914
1980	16.4	23.4	27.3	26.8	6.4	4,774	5,453	5,282	6,067
1979	15.5	23.4	24.1	27.4	5.9	5,004	5,379	5,555	6,174
1978	14.7	22.9	22.9	26.2	6.7	5,227	5,326	5,797	6,265
1977	12.5	22.4	22.6	25.3	6.1	5,327	5,371	6,044	6,297
1976	12.5	20.9	23.4	27.5	5.7	5,265	5,540	6,185	6,356
1975	12.6	21.2	25.8	26.8	5.7	5,223	5,782	6,336	6,309
1974	12.2	21.2	25.9	26.3	7.0	5,267	6,011	6,329	6,352
1973	12.8	20.8	25.2	26.4	6.8	5,403	6,082	6,397	6,215
1972	12.5	23.3	26.8	26.8	6.2	5,662	6,188	6,322	6,232
1971	13.5	22.8	26.1	27.2	5.0	6,088	6,440	6,293	6,019
Female									
2008	17.5	25.6	27.7	27.7	2.4	5,930	5,787	5,908	6,244
2007	17.2	24.1	25.9	26.2	2.9	5,852	5,773	6,088	6,285
2006	18.4	23.9	24.6	25.9	2.6	5,785	5,787	6,099	6,352
2005	18.2	22.0	25.8	26.8	2.6	5,769	5,872	6,167	6,559
2004	19.4	22.5	24.4	27.1	3.5	5,724	5,914	6,185	6,371
2003	18.5	23.8	25.8	25.8	3.0	5,668	5,793	6,524	6,184
2002	15.6	21.7	23.0	24.4	3.1	5,872	6,072	6,156	5,977
2001	14.9	21.3	23.0	25.2	3.3	5,825	6,197	6,046	5,849
2000	16.1	20.6	24.2	25.8	4.2	5,897	6,209	5,855	5,797
1999	16.1	21.6	22.7	25.1	4.2	5,948	6,066	5,872	5,852
1998	16.5	20.9	22.8	26.2	3.5	5,931	5,835	5,703	5,523
1997	15.1	20.4	23.3	26.1	3.5	6,030	5,754	5,718	5,827
1996	14.9	20.4	23.4	24.7	5.3	5,923	5,802	5,719	5,632
1995	14.6	23.1	26.0	26.7	4.4	5,728	5,786	5,653	5,552
1994	16.5	24.2	26.7	24.8	3.6	5,705	5,644	5,666	5,384
1993¹	16.3	24.0	26.4	26.4	4.4	5,526	5,545	5,353	4,984
1993	16.1	23.9	26.2	24.9	4.3	5,526	5,545	5,353	4,984
1992	17.1	23.5	24.6	25.6	4.5	5,523	5,441	5,220	4,947
1991	18.2	22.8	24.6	24.2	5.1	5,445	5,395	5,098	4,838
1990	19.1	23.2	25.7	24.7	4.7	5,387	5,312	4,951	4,834
1989	18.1	22.6	26.6	22.3	4.6	5,375	5,201	4,840	4,869
1988	17.3	23.6	23.4	21.7	5.4	5,327	5,052	4,803	5,093
1987	17.8	21.5	23.2	20.2	5.6	5,206	4,906	4,759	5,408
1986	15.2	22.4	22.1	21.1	4.9	5,078	4,846	4,842	5,452
1985	15.1	21.4	22.1	20.6	5.5	4,917	4,727	5,102	5,401
1984	14.2	19.8	22.9	18.7	5.1	4,744	4,689	5,337	5,242
1983	12.9	19.9	19.1	18.6	5.2	4,692	4,756	5,433	5,305
1982	13.8	19.0	19.7	17.9	5.7	4,640	4,971	5,423	5,443
1981	11.6	18.4	20.1	19.6	6.1	4,653	5,210	5,202	5,843
1980	12.1	17.0	17.8	18.0	6.7	4,576	5,228	5,255	5,768
1979	10.4	16.9	16.4	15.6	7.1	4,800	5,166	5,331	6,016
1978	10.1	16.0	15.3	17.2	6.4	5,019	5,122	5,594	6,081
1977	8.9	15.2	15.0	17.1	6.6	5,122	5,166	5,782	6,175
1976	8.6	15.1	16.0	16.8	7.0	5,069	5,332	5,952	6,194
1975	9.4	13.5	16.7	18.2	7.2	5,033	5,561	6,036	6,222
1974	8.3	14.4	17.4	16.8	7.1	5,076	5,778	6,086	6,214
1973	8.7	15.8	16.5	16.1	7.4	5,211	5,864	6,145	6,094
1972	8.9	15.7	17.0	17.7	7.1	5,457	5,964	6,129	6,051
1971	8.7	12.3	17.8	17.6	6.5	5,850	6,208	6,136	5,887
WHITE ALONE									
Both Sexes									
2008	20.3	27.1	29.4	29.7	2.6	9,288	8,967	9,250	9,658
2007	21.3	26.2	27.6	28.3	2.8	9,118	9,021	9,432	9,834
2006	20.6	25.5	26.8	29.9	3.0	8,981	9,074	9,542	9,813
2005	21.4	23.8	28.0	29.5	2.6	8,929	9,194	9,680	10,131
2004	22.4	25.6	27.6	30.7	3.8	9,051	9,173	9,853	9,784
2003¹	21.5	27.6	28.3	29.4	3.2	9,102	9,112	9,875	9,889
2002	18.1	25.7	26.2	29.6	3.1	9,230	9,682	9,832	9,520
2001	19.2	22.7	25.2	28.9	3.8	9,330	9,826	9,651	9,480
2000	19.4	23.7	26.3	29.7	4.5	9,404	9,937	9,368	9,449
1999	18.3	24.6	25.8	30.0	4.2	9,539	9,768	9,323	9,428

¹Starting in 2003 respondents could identify more than one race. Except as noted, the race data in this table from 2003 onward represent those respondents who indicated only one race category.

r = Revised, controlled to 1990 census based population estimates; previous 1993 data controlled to 1980 census based population estimates.

Table A-11.   The Population 6 to 17 Years Old Enrolled Below Modal Grade, 1971–2008—*Continued*

(Numbers in thousands, percent.)

Year, sex, race, and Hispanic origin	Percent below modal grade				Dropout rate, 15 to 17 years old	Population in age group			
	6 to 8 years old	9 to 11 years old	12 to 14 years old	15 to 17 years old		6 to 8 years old	9 to 11 years old	12 to 14 years old	15 to 17 years old
1998..............................	19.5	23.5	25.8	30.5	3.8	9,481	9,413	9,130	8,926
1997..............................	18.8	24.0	27.9	30.3	3.5	9,555	9,390	9,167	9,352
1996..............................	18.1	22.6	27.6	30.1	4.9	9,458	9,420	9,184	9,135
1995..............................	17.7	24.9	29.2	31.0	3.9	9,221	9,340	9,130	8,933
1994..............................	19.4	25.8	30.1	29.6	3.7	9,087	9,261	9,121	8,668
1993ʳ.............................	18.8	27.3	29.4	31.2	3.9	9,018	8,967	8,728	8,160
1993..............................	18.7	27.2	29.2	29.7	3.6	9,074	9,017	8,783	8,159
1992..............................	19.5	27.5	29.6	28.1	3.5	8,956	8,996	8,520	8,031
1991..............................	21.3	25.7	27.7	27.2	4.7	8,874	8,840	8,328	7,903
1990..............................	21.9	26.8	28.4	27.3	4.6	8,860	8,752	8,140	7,909
1989..............................	22.4	26.8	29.9	25.7	4.6	8,858	8,527	7,994	8,026
1988..............................	21.0	27.6	27.2	23.9	5.4	8,758	8,323	7,929	8,353
1987..............................	21.1	25.9	26.0	22.7	5.1	8,606	8,117	7,846	8,887
1986..............................	19.1	25.1	25.3	23.7	5.0	8,395	8,000	8,054	9,037
1985..............................	18.0	23.3	23.3	23.0	5.3	8,136	7,840	8,429	9,045
1984..............................	16.3	22.1	24.7	22.7	5.6	7,915	7,781	8,827	8,853
1983..............................	15.5	22.4	23.1	21.1	5.4	7,821	7,906	9,152	8,831
1982..............................	16.4	21.8	22.1	21.1	5.6	7,729	8,294	9,035	9,184
1981..............................	14.7	22.2	21.0	21.6	6.1	7,782	8,741	8,813	9,762
1980..............................	14.1	19.0	21.1	19.3	6.7	7,635	8,823	8,739	10,132
1979..............................	12.9	18.4	18.5	19.4	6.5	8,041	8,747	9,026	10,239
1978..............................	12.4	18.0	17.9	19.3	6.8	8,460	8,686	9,522	10,358
1977..............................	10.6	17.7	17.5	19.3	6.6	8,675	8,771	9,918	10,510
1976..............................	10.5	17.2	18.7	19.7	6.3	8,612	9,066	10,187	10,622
1975..............................	11.0	16.0	20.0	20.4	6.3	8,566	9,486	10,466	10,583
1974..............................	10.2	16.5	19.7	19.4	6.9	8,656	9,912	10,508	10,678
1973..............................	10.6	17.3	19.9	19.1	7.0	8,929	10,117	10,704	10,481
1972..............................	10.3	18.2	20.1	20.0	6.6	9,359	10,313	10,606	10,506
1971..............................	10.5	18.3	20.4	19.9	5.5	9,988	10,692	10,682	10,231
Male									
2008..............................	22.5	29.3	32.6	32.9	2.7	4,764	4,568	4,748	4,966
2007..............................	24.3	28.4	29.5	31.8	2.9	4,671	4,620	4,851	5,022
2006..............................	22.5	27.0	29.8	34.2	3.3	4,596	4,652	4,900	5,011
2005..............................	24.3	27.4	31.0	33.2	2.7	4,576	4,715	4,995	5,116
2004	24.9	28.0	31.4	35.2	3.8	4,706	4,647	5,168	4,905
2003¹.............................	24.4	31.6	31.2	34.0	3.4	4,785	4,795	4,961	5,026
2002..............................	21.7	29.5	30.4	34.7	3.2	4,737	4,965	5,044	4,875
2001..............................	22.7	25.3	28.3	32.8	4.4	4,789	5,040	4,949	4,862
2000..............................	22.5	27.6	29.6	34.0	4.4	4,815	5,094	4,798	4,861
1999..............................	19.9	28.2	29.7	35.8	4.2	4,883	5,009	4,777	4,851
1998..............................	21.9	26.4	30.2	36.2	4.4	4,851	4,823	4,686	4,571
1997..............................	22.3	27.8	32.7	37.0	3.8	4,897	4,819	4,702	4,821
1996..............................	20.8	25.9	32.3	36.5	4.5	4,849	4,836	4,706	4,694
1995..............................	20.5	28.0	33.4	36.5	3.8	4,727	4,797	4,680	4,592
1994..............................	22.0	27.9	34.4	35.2	4.0	4,659	4,758	4,679	4,457
1993ʳ.............................	21.4	31.8	33.8	37.6	3.2	4,625	4,601	4,476	4,178
1993..............................	21.4	31.6	33.6	36.1	3.1	4,662	4,614	4,485	4,178
1992..............................	21.5	31.8	35.8	32.4	2.8	4,602	4,607	4,359	4,115
1991..............................	24.4	29.1	32.5	32.5	4.2	4,556	4,568	4,270	4,047
1990..............................	24.6	31.3	33.3	32.6	4.8	4,555	4,482	4,186	4,054
1989..............................	26.0	32.1	35.0	30.8	4.6	4,544	4,378	4,112	4,107
1988..............................	24.7	32.8	32.2	28.8	5.1	4,493	4,272	4,062	4,281
1987..............................	24.6	30.5	30.4	26.6	4.5	4,415	4,167	4,069	4,504
1986..............................	22.9	28.9	30.1	27.9	5.2	4,307	4,108	4,125	4,624
1985..............................	21.1	26.5	26.7	28.0	4.9	4,175	4,024	4,307	4,634
1984..............................	18.1	25.8	28.7	28.1	5.8	4,061	3,994	4,501	4,542
1983..............................	18.1	26.3	28.0	26.3	5.6	4,002	4,054	4,697	4,481
1982..............................	19.3	26.2	26.2	26.1	5.3	3,956	4,260	4,591	4,711
1981..............................	17.3	26.9	24.2	25.4	6.3	3,990	4,480	4,556	4,937
1980..............................	16.3	21.9	25.7	23.9	6.7	3,907	4,517	4,399	5,066
1979..............................	15.4	20.8	22.3	24.8	6.2	4,114	4,475	4,616	5,201
1978..............................	14.7	21.2	22.0	23.1	7.2	4,328	4,441	4,843	5,287
1977..............................	12.5	21.1	21.2	23.5	6.3	4,436	4,484	5,079	5,325
1976..............................	12.6	20.2	22.1	24.8	5.6	4,402	4,632	5,200	5,398
1975..............................	12.9	19.7	24.7	24.7	5.4	4,376	4,848	5,385	5,332
1974..............................	12.1	19.5	23.7	23.8	7.0	4,422	5,066	5,383	5,402
1973..............................	12.5	19.6	23.1	24.0	6.6	4,559	5,165	5,469	5,319

¹Starting in 2003 respondents could identify more than one race. Except as noted, the race data in this table from 2003 onward represent those respondents who indicated only one race category.
r = Revised, controlled to 1990 census based population estimates; previous 1993 data controlled to 1980 census based population estimates.

Table A-11.   The Population 6 to 17 Years Old Enrolled Below Modal Grade, 1971–2008—*Continued*

(Numbers in thousands, percent.)

Year, sex, race, and Hispanic origin	Percent below modal grade				Dropout rate, 15 to 17 years old	Population in age group			
	6 to 8 years old	9 to 11 years old	12 to 14 years old	15 to 17 years old		6 to 8 years old	9 to 11 years old	12 to 14 years old	15 to 17 years old
1972	12.2	21.9	24.6	24.3	6.1	4,778	5,266	5,410	5,340
1971	12.6	21.6	23.9	24.4	4.6	5,106	5,461	5,455	5,185
Female									
2008	18.0	24.8	26.0	26.3	2.4	4,524	4,398	4,502	4,692
2007	18.2	23.9	25.7	24.6	2.7	4,447	4,401	4,582	4,812
2006	18.6	24.0	23.8	25.5	2.6	4,385	4,422	4,643	4,801
2005	18.3	20.1	24.8	25.8	2.5	4,353	4,479	4,685	5,015
2004	19.7	23.3	23.4	26.1	3.8	4,345	4,527	4,686	4,878
2003[1]	18.3	23.1	25.3	24.7	3.0	4,317	4,317	4,914	4,863
2002	14.4	21.7	21.9	24.3	3.0	4,493	4,717	4,788	4,645
2001	15.5	20.0	21.8	24.9	3.1	4,541	4,786	4,701	4,618
2000	16.1	19.7	22.9	25.2	4.5	4,587	4,843	4,570	4,588
1999	16.7	20.7	21.8	23.9	4.1	4,655	4,579	4,546	4,578
1998	16.9	20.5	21.2	24.4	3.2	4,629	4,589	4,444	4,355
1997	15.1	20.0	22.7	23.2	3.3	4,658	4,571	4,464	4,530
1996	15.3	19.2	22.7	23.2	5.3	4,609	4,583	4,477	4,441
1995	14.7	21.6	24.8	25.0	4.1	4,494	4,543	4,449	4,342
1994	16.7	23.5	25.7	23.6	3.4	4,427	4,504	4,443	4,212
1993[r]	15.9	22.6	24.8	24.4	4.3	4,393	4,366	4,252	3,982
1993	15.8	22.5	24.6	23.1	4.2	4,412	4,404	4,298	3,982
1992	17.3	22.9	23.2	23.6	4.3	4,354	4,389	4,161	3,916
1991	18.1	22.1	22.6	21.5	5.2	4,318	4,272	4,058	3,856
1990	19.0	22.2	23.2	21.8	4.5	4,305	4,270	3,954	3,855
1989	18.6	21.3	24.5	20.3	4.7	4,314	4,149	3,882	3,919
1988	17.1	22.2	21.9	18.8	5.6	4,265	4,051	3,867	4,072
1987	17.3	21.0	21.3	18.7	5.8	4,191	3,950	3,777	4,383
1986	15.0	21.1	20.2	19.3	4.8	4,088	3,892	3,929	4,413
1985	14.8	19.9	19.7	17.6	5.7	3,961	3,816	4,122	4,411
1984	14.3	18.3	20.5	17.0	5.4	3,854	3,787	4,326	4,311
1983	12.7	18.3	17.9	15.8	5.2	3,819	3,852	4,455	4,350
1982	13.4	17.2	17.8	15.8	6.0	3,773	4,034	4,444	4,473
1981	11.9	17.3	17.6	17.6	5.9	3,792	4,261	4,257	4,825
1980	11.7	16.0	16.5	14.7	6.6	3,728	4,306	4,340	5,066
1979	10.3	15.8	14.5	13.8	6.9	3,927	4,272	4,410	5,038
1978	10.0	14.7	13.7	15.2	6.4	4,132	4,245	4,679	5,071
1977	8.5	14.1	13.7	14.9	6.8	4,239	4,287	4,839	5,185
1976	8.4	14.1	15.1	14.5	6.9	4,210	4,434	4,987	5,224
1975	9.1	12.2	15.1	16.0	7.1	4,190	4,638	5,081	5,251
1974	8.2	13.4	15.5	15.0	6.7	4,234	4,846	5,125	5,276
1973	8.5	14.8	16.5	14.0	7.4	4,370	4,952	5,235	5,162
1972	8.3	14.2	15.4	15.5	7.2	4,581	5,047	5,196	5,166
1971	8.4	14.9	16.6	15.2	6.3	4,882	5,231	5,227	5,046
WHITE ALONE NON-HISPANIC									
Both Sexes									
2008	21.2	27.7	29.4	28.4	2.2	6,798	6,768	7,008	7,534
2007	21.3	25.3	26.5	26.8	2.1	6,763	6,783	7,182	7,784
2006	20.5	24.5	25.1	28.6	2.3	6,748	6,887	7,368	7,827
2005	22.4	23.2	26.3	29.0	2.1	6,728	7,052	7,584	8,150
2004	22.7	25.1	27.0	29.8	3.3	6,878	7,090	7,768	7,892
2003[1]	21.8	27.1	27.3	28.7	2.8	7,006	7,102	7,889	7,980
2002	18.9	24.9	25.8	28.1	2.5	7,118	7,627	7,913	7,803
2001	19.9	23.1	25.3	28.1	3.1	7,325	7,726	7,773	7,829
2000	19.4	23.7	26.1	28.8	3.5	7,418	8,045	7,727	7,852
1999	18.9	24.2	25.3	28.9	3.6	7,717	7,938	7,669	7,879
1998	20.5	23.7	26.0	28.9	3.0	7,755	7,794	7,697	7,859
1997	19.7	24.6	27.3	28.4	3.2	7,729	7,775	7,789	7,866
1996	18.8	22.7	26.2	28.6	4.2	7,803	7,792	7,731	7,716
1995	18.2	24.5	28.0	29.2	3.4	7,853	8,000	7,872	7,795
1994	19.8	25.6	30.0	28.0	3.1	7,779	7,864	7,845	7,490
1993	18.8	27.2	28.8	29.5	3.0	7,736	7,802	7,600	7,022
Male									
2008	24.4	29.9	33.2	31.8	2.4	3,485	3,459	3,599	3,862
2007	24.1	28.4	28.1	30.3	2.2	3,457	3,473	3,715	3,970
2006	23.1	26.0	27.6	32.4	2.9	3,449	3,537	3,775	3,984
2005	25.4	26.8	28.2	32.5	2.2	3,450	3,618	3,902	4,136

[1]Starting in 2003 respondents could identify more than one race. Except as noted, the race data in this table from 2003 onward represent those respondents who indicated only one race category.
r = Revised, controlled to 1990 census based population estimates; previous 1993 data controlled to 1980 census based population estimates.

Table A-11. The Population 6 to 17 Years Old Enrolled Below Modal Grade, 1971–2008—*Continued*

(Numbers in thousands, percent.)

Year, sex, race, and Hispanic origin	Percent below modal grade				Dropout rate, 15 to 17 years old	Population in age group			
	6 to 8 years old	9 to 11 years old	12 to 14 years old	15 to 17 years old		6 to 8 years old	9 to 11 years old	12 to 14 years old	15 to 17 years old
2004	25.0	27.9	30.6	35.0	3.4	3,548	3,605	4,054	3,994
2003[1]	24.6	31.7	30.7	33.4	2.9	3,668	3,725	3,960	4,101
2002	22.7	29.0	30.7	33.6	2.4	3,667	3,969	4,005	4,038
2001	23.1	26.2	28.5	31.6	3.7	3,808	3,971	3,920	4,020
2000	22.5	27.7	30.0	33.4	3.4	3,795	4,135	3,970	4,034
1999	20.3	27.7	29.7	35.1	3.5	3,955	4,076	3,913	4,058
1998	23.1	26.5	30.8	34.3	3.6	4,016	4,003	3,894	3,981
1997	24.1	29.0	32.5	35.3	3.8	3,977	3,971	3,996	4,020
1996	22.5	25.9	30.8	35.1	4.1	3,964	4,035	3,957	3,959
1995	22.1	27.3	31.9	34.9	3.1	4,038	4,094	4,017	4,010
1994	22.8	28.0	34.3	33.6	2.9	3,993	4,010	4,030	3,866
1993	22.0	31.5	33.2	35.6	2.4	3,952	4,021	3,889	3,578
Female									
2008	18.0	25.3	25.4	24.9	2.1	3,313	3,309	3,408	3,673
2007	18.4	22.0	24.7	23.1	2.0	3,306	3,310	3,467	3,814
2006	17.6	22.8	22.6	24.6	1.8	3,299	3,350	3,593	3,843
2005	19.2	19.4	24.2	25.3	2.0	3,277	3,434	3,682	4,014
2004	20.3	22.2	23.1	24.5	3.3	3,330	3,485	3,714	3,898
2003[1]	18.6	22.2	24.0	23.7	2.6	3,337	3,377	3,929	3,878
2002	14.8	20.4	20.9	22.2	2.6	3,451	3,658	3,908	3,765
2001	16.4	19.8	22.0	24.4	2.6	3,517	3,755	3,853	3,809
2000	16.2	19.6	21.9	23.9	3.7	3,623	3,910	3,757	3,818
1999	17.4	20.5	20.8	22.3	3.6	3,761	3,864	3,757	3,840
1998	17.6	20.8	21.2	23.5	2.5	3,740	3,791	3,803	3,878
1997	15.0	19.9	21.8	21.3	2.6	3,752	3,804	3,793	3,846
1996	15.0	19.3	21.3	21.7	4.3	3,839	3,757	3,773	3,757
1995	14.1	21.5	23.8	23.1	3.8	3,815	3,906	3,854	3,784
1994	16.6	23.1	25.5	22.1	3.2	3,786	3,854	3,814	3,624
1993	15.4	22.6	24.2	23.1	3.6	3,784	3,782	3,710	3,444
BLACK ALONE									
Both Sexes									
2008	18.6	27.3	40.9	37.8	3.1	1,781	1,797	1,851	1,994
2007	17.7	28.1	33.0	39.2	3.0	1,797	1,770	1,937	2,021
2006	19.1	29.9	35.7	35.7	3.1	1,813	1,811	1,960	2,059
2005	20.8	35.6	34.1	38.8	4.2	1,806	1,826	2,011	2,085
2004	19.8	27.4	34.1	40.1	2.3	1,775	1,906	2,034	1,992
2003[1]	22.7	34.2	33.9	37.4	3.7	1,760	2,043	2,110	1,950
2002	19.6	28.6	32.8	36.2	3.9	2,017	2,048	2,036	1,943
2001	17.3	29.7	31.1	35.6	4.0	1,937	2,144	1,998	1,823
2000	19.6	26.9	37.8	34.6	4.7	1,976	2,082	1,961	1,852
1999	16.1	30.2	31.7	34.8	3.5	1,948	2,108	1,912	1,911
1998	18.3	26.6	31.4	38.4	3.6	2,019	1,934	1,840	1,801
1997	18.4	26.1	33.5	40.0	3.8	2,061	1,908	1,845	1,938
1996	18.4	29.2	36.8	36.9	4.8	2,054	1,847	1,839	1,858
1995	16.8	31.1	38.3	41.3	4.1	1,909	1,890	1,822	1,851
1994	18.4	35.1	36.1	37.7	3.3	1,912	1,795	1,835	1,809
1993[r]	20.0	33.6	34.8	45.1	3.6	1,767	1,763	1,747	1,641
1993	19.9	33.4	38.8	43.3	3.6	1,709	1,710	1,695	1,642
1992	20.6	28.7	38.0	40.6	4.2	1,761	1,635	1,686	1,621
1991	21.0	34.3	40.7	43.4	5.3	1,674	1,701	1,643	1,574
1990	21.9	33.1	46.1	42.9	5.2	1,645	1,712	1,574	1,571
1989	19.6	34.0	41.3	39.3	3.9	1,642	1,682	1,554	1,618
1988	18.6	33.1	37.6	38.4	4.7	1,680	1,629	1,545	1,637
1987	19.8	33.1	35.6	35.3	5.1	1,679	1,554	1,552	1,654
1986	12.7	34.6	38.5	38.3	4.6	1,611	1,542	1,530	1,692
1985	18.0	33.9	37.9	37.7	4.6	1,568	1,498	1,635	1,627
1984	17.9	32.3	38.1	34.6	4.1	1,445	1,442	1,652	1,536
1983	15.3	34.9	34.4	35.8	4.7	1,429	1,450	1,601	1,617
1982	17.2	27.1	32.5	32.6	4.6	1,765	1,874	1,953	1,947
1981	13.9	26.2	33.7	36.1	6.3	1,437	1,594	1,615	1,679
1980	14.9	27.8	30.5	37.6	5.1	1,460	1,606	1,568	1,728
1979	12.5	29.5	29.2	34.3	6.4	1,515	1,576	1,636	1,722
1978	12.6	27.8	26.6	35.4	5.7	1,557	1,523	1,664	1,764
1977	11.3	24.9	26.3	32.2	5.4	1,552	1,558	1,698	1,754
1976	10.5	23.2	26.1	35.6	6.7	1,493	1,633	1,724	1,726
1975	11.9	26.1	29.2	34.9	8.0	1,489	1,656	1,720	1,760

[1]Starting in 2003 respondents could identify more than one race. Except as noted, the race data in this table from 2003 onward represent those respondents who indicated only one race category.

r = Revised, controlled to 1990 census based population estimates; previous 1993 data controlled to 1980 census based population estimates.

Table A-11.   The Population 6 to 17 Years Old Enrolled Below Modal Grade, 1971–2008—*Continued*

(Numbers in thousands, percent.)

Year, sex, race, and Hispanic origin	Percent below modal grade				Dropout rate, 15 to 17 years old	Population in age group			
	6 to 8 years old	9 to 11 years old	12 to 14 years old	15 to 17 years old		6 to 8 years old	9 to 11 years old	12 to 14 years old	15 to 17 years old
1974	11.6	26.2	33.2	34.4	8.2	1,509	1,684	1,750	1,682
1973	12.0	25.8	31.7	35.4	8.2	1,525	1,650	1,671	1,671
1972	13.2	30.5	33.1	37.3	6.6	1,585	1,638	1,691	1,636
1971	14.2	27.9	34.7	40.2	7.0	1,794	1,787	1,638	1,533
Male									
2008	19.4	26.2	46.3	41.3	3.4	917	908	934	992
2007	22.7	31.6	35.4	43.5	2.2	946	886	964	1027
2006	20.3	35.1	40.3	43.9	3.3	929	920	991	1,032
2005	22.6	37.9	35.8	43.0	5.2	912	913	1,011	1,041
2004	21.0	31.4	37.8	46.5	2.0	885	992	1,012	1,009
2003[1]	23.6	36.8	38.7	43.4	3.9	927	1,059	975	1,047
2002	17.5	32.5	37.0	44.7	5.0	1,044	1,036	1,012	973
2001	21.1	31.1	33.3	42.8	3.5	978	1,108	1,010	924
2000	20.8	27.5	43.3	37.0	6.4	1,003	1,057	994	941
1999	15.9	34.2	36.3	37.6	3.0	964	1,085	969	992
1998	20.9	29.3	33.3	41.9	3.0	1,027	973	926	928
1997	21.3	29.3	39.4	43.8	3.1	1,019	994	934	979
1996	21.3	30.4	45.1	43.2	4.5	1,054	925	931	943
1995	18.8	31.2	45.0	47.5	2.9	982	944	922	952
1994	19.4	30.3	39.9	39.8	3.2	951	928	928	898
1993[r]	21.8	36.5	44.3	53.0	2.5	903	884	891	832
1993	21.6	36.5	44.2	51.8	2.5	864	857	867	832
1992	24.5	28.7	44.5	47.0	2.8	864	862	860	813
1991	22.9	39.6	46.2	50.6	5.4	846	878	839	798
1990	23.2	37.3	52.7	49.1	4.3	828	877	791	795
1989	21.7	38.8	44.8	46.7	2.8	831	858	785	828
1988	18.9	37.2	43.7	41.4	4.1	851	828	780	828
1987	21.6	41.1	39.7	42.3	4.9	861	779	802	818
1986	15.0	39.0	45.2	45.9	4.0	806	792	770	855
1985	19.5	38.2	41.4	40.3	5.4	778	775	830	816
1984	24.1	38.1	42.5	42.8	4.2	729	727	832	769
1983	16.8	42.0	43.1	40.6	4.4	721	723	808	799
1982	18.8	27.5	36.2	36.9	4.8	898	937	975	977
1981	17.7	34.2	33.3	42.4	5.4	723	811	814	832
1980	16.8	31.8	36.2	43.3	4.9	736	807	770	876
1979	14.7	37.3	33.8	43.6	4.0	762	796	828	853
1978	15.4	33.0	30.3	43.1	4.1	774	767	847	870
1977	12.1	29.8	31.1	35.3	4.8	776	782	858	868
1976	11.5	26.1	30.9	43.3	5.7	755	816	870	855
1975	12.8	30.7	32.5	40.2	7.6	743	849	845	879
1974	13.5	31.0	40.9	41.1	7.2	747	858	861	849
1973	14.1	29.5	38.0	42.0	8.5	752	831	837	824
1972	14.5	36.8	41.3	43.8	6.6	787	828	836	818
1971	18.1	30.9	38.5	47.6	7.4	890	900	810	757
Female									
2008	17.7	28.4	35.5	34.2	2.9	864	889	917	1,003
2007	12.2	24.7	30.5	34.5	3.9	851	885	972	993
2006	17.7	24.7	31.0	27.5	2.8	884	891	968	1,027
2005	19.0	33.3	32.4	34.7	3.3	893	913	999	1,044
2004	18.6	23.1	30.5	33.4	2.6	890	914	1,022	983
2003[1]	21.7	31.5	39.8	30.3	3.4	833	983	1,135	903
2002	22.0	24.7	28.7	27.8	2.8	973	1,012	1,024	970
2001	13.3	28.2	29.0	27.9	4.5	959	1,036	988	900
2000	18.2	26.4	32.0	32.3	2.9	974	1,025	968	911
1999	16.3	25.8	27.0	31.6	4.0	984	1,022	944	919
1998	15.6	23.8	29.6	34.6	4.3	992	960	914	873
1997	15.9	22.8	27.4	36.0	4.5	1,041	915	911	959
1996	13.4	28.1	28.4	30.3	4.9	1,000	922	909	915
1995	14.8	23.6	30.9	34.6	5.3	928	946	901	898
1994	17.5	29.1	32.3	35.4	3.6	961	867	908	911
1993[r]	18.0	30.8	33.1	36.6	4.7	864	879	856	809
1993	18.1	30.3	33.2	34.6	4.7	844	854	828	809
1992	16.7	28.7	31.2	34.2	5.6	897	773	826	808
1991	19.0	28.6	35.0	36.0	5.2	828	823	804	776
1990	20.7	28.7	39.3	36.6	6.1	817	835	783	776
1989	17.5	29.0	37.7	31.5	5.1	811	824	769	790
1988	18.2	28.8	31.4	35.2	5.3	829	801	765	809

[1]Starting in 2003 respondents could identify more than one race. Except as noted, the race data in this table from 2003 onward represent those respondents who indicated only one race category.
r = Revised, controlled to 1990 census based population estimates; previous 1993 data controlled to 1980 census based population estimates.

Table A-11.   The Population 6 to 17 Years Old Enrolled Below Modal Grade, 1971–2008—*Continued*

(Numbers in thousands, percent.)

Year, sex, race, and Hispanic origin	Percent below modal grade				Dropout rate, 15 to 17 years old	Population in age group			
	6 to 8 years old	9 to 11 years old	12 to 14 years old	15 to 17 years old		6 to 8 years old	9 to 11 years old	12 to 14 years old	15 to 17 years old
1987...............................	18.0	25.2	31.3	28.5	5.3	818	775	750	836
1985...............................	16.6	29.3	34.2	35.1	3.8	790	723	805	811
1984...............................	11.5	26.4	33.5	26.3	4.0	716	715	820	767
1983...............................	13.8	27.8	25.5	31.2	5.0	708	727	793	818
1982...............................	15.5	26.7	28.7	28.1	4.3	867	937	978	970
1981...............................	10.1	17.9	34.2	29.9	7.1	714	783	801	847
1980...............................	12.8	23.8	25.1	31.7	5.3	724	799	798	852
1979...............................	10.4	21.5	24.5	25.2	8.7	753	780	808	869
1978...............................	9.8	22.6	22.6	27.9	7.2	783	756	817	894
1977...............................	10.6	20.0	21.3	29.1	6.0	776	776	840	886
1976...............................	9.5	20.3	21.2	28.1	7.7	738	817	854	871
1975...............................	11.0	21.3	25.9	29.6	8.3	746	807	875	881
1974...............................	9.7	21.3	25.8	27.5	9.2	762	826	889	833
1973...............................	10.0	22.1	25.4	28.9	7.9	773	819	834	847
1972...............................	11.9	24.1	25.1	30.9	6.6	798	810	855	818
1971...............................	10.4	24.9	31.0	33.1	6.7	904	887	828	776

ASIAN ALONE[2]

Both Sexes

2008...............................	17.2	22.7	26.7	18.8	4.4	491	517	482	507
2007...............................	11.3	21.9	17.0	24.2	3.7	545	534	497	463
2006...............................	15.2	19.7	20.9	23.0	3.2	425	472	490	476
2005...............................	12.8	12.2	16.3	19.1	1.2	502	429	486	457
2004...............................	12.1	11.4	20.9	23.6	1.7	417	468	490	491
2003[1]............................	7.5	13.6	19.7	24.5	1.6	486	453	459	458
2002...............................	11.1	12.3	20.4	18.6	2.7	602	490	530	553
2001...............................	11.9	17.9	20.3	21.0	2.8	503	565	523	565
2000...............................	10.7	15.5	17.5	22.2	0.6	524	490	490	475
1999...............................	7.5	16.5	17.9	25.5	3.2	533	496	560	555

Male

2008...............................	23.8	20.4	24.3	17.4	2.4	227	257	249	253
2007...............................	7.6	20.5	18.2	26.0	4.0	278	272	240	246
2006...............................	14.3	18.4	23.5	21.7	3.3	206	256	264	227
2005...............................	12.3	13.8	13.2	18.1	1.6	261	202	265	228
2004...............................	10.9	16.0	20.9	23.5	2.4	220	216	282	231
2003[1]............................	7.3	15.9	20.3	19.3	-	226	223	261	231
2002...............................	9.6	12.4	23.3	18.9	1.7	274	239	267	287
2001...............................	15.2	16.6	19.0	22.2	4.9	265	294	256	313
2000...............................	14.7	14.2	16.1	30.3	1.0	286	243	267	261
1999...............................	8.4	16.4	17.6	30.3	2.2	277	269	246	276

Female

2008...............................	11.5	25.0	29.3	20.3	6.5	264	260	233	254
2007...............................	15.2	23.5	15.8	22.2	3.4	268	263	257	217
2006...............................	16.1	21.2	17.9	24.2	3.1	218	216	226	249
2005...............................	13.4	10.8	20.0	20.1	0.9	241	227	221	229
2004...............................	13.5	7.3	20.8	23.7	1.1	196	253	208	260
2003[1]............................	7.6	11.3	18.8	29.9	3.2	259	230	198	227
2002...............................	12.4	12.2	17.5	18.2	3.7	327	251	263	266
2001...............................	8.3	19.3	21.4	19.6	0.2	238	270	268	252
2000...............................	5.9	16.7	19.2	12.3	0.1	239	247	224	215
1999...............................	6.6	16.7	18.5	20.6	4.0	256	227	314	278

HISPANIC[3]

Both Sexes

2008...............................	17.8	25.2	29.1	34.2	3.5	2,690	2,402	2,422	2,321
2007...............................	20.9	28.9	31.1	34.0	5.7	2,541	2,414	2,418	2,211
2006...............................	20.6	29.2	32.6	35.3	5.7	2,441	2,382	2,361	2,165
2005...............................	18.1	26.2	33.2	32.1	4.9	2,390	2,317	2,322	2,202
2004...............................	21.5	28.1	30.0	34.6	6.1	2,382	2,250	2,283	2,072
2003...............................	20.2	28.7	31.3	32.7	5.2	2,280	2,221	2,167	2,063
2002...............................	15.5	28.4	27.9	35.6	5.9	2,258	2,204	2,079	1,841
2001...............................	16.7	22.1	25.0	34.6	6.9	2,143	2,198	2,011	1,733
2000...............................	19.4	23.2	27.3	34.4	8.8	2,067	1,965	1,744	1,671
1999...............................	15.7	25.9	27.9	36.5	7.3	1,902	1,922	1,734	1,653
1998...............................	15.4	23.2	24.6	33.8	7.6	1,903	1,740	1,542	1,424

[1]Starting in 2003 respondents could identify more than one race. Except as noted, the race data in this table from 2003 onward represent those respondents who indicated only one race category.
[2]The data shown prior to 2003 consists of those identifying themselves as "Asian or Pacific Islanders."
[3]May be of any race.
- = Quantity zero or rounds to zero.

Table A-11.   The Population 6 to 17 Years Old Enrolled Below Modal Grade, 1971–2008—*Continued*

(Numbers in thousands, percent.)

Year, sex, race, and Hispanic origin	Percent below modal grade				Dropout rate, 15 to 17 years old	Population in age group			
	6 to 8 years old	9 to 11 years old	12 to 14 years old	15 to 17 years old		6 to 8 years old	9 to 11 years old	12 to 14 years old	15 to 17 years old
1997	15.2	21.5	31.0	41.4	5.5	1,909	1,666	1,444	1,575
1996	14.9	22.9	35.5	39.0	8.4	1,711	1,680	1,550	1,478
1995	14.4	26.1	38.5	43.6	7.4	1,597	1,628	1,496	1,373
1994	16.8	28.4	32.3	39.9	8.8	1,526	1,593	1,442	1,347
1993ʳ	18.9	29.2	33.2	42.2	8.2	1,390	1,255	1,204	1,225
1993	18.9	29.2	32.7	38.3	7.9	1,455	1,295	1,243	1,226
1992	16.2	25.3	34.3	39.9	8.1	1,272	1,371	1,141	1,110
1991	21.8	30.7	35.8	38.4	11.3	1,290	1,356	1,088	1,023
1990	21.5	34.8	37.7	39.8	9.0	1,270	1,230	1,095	1,062
1989	21.9	33.8	39.9	39.5	10.6	1,257	1,154	1,079	1,001
1988	23.2	37.0	45.0	36.8	13.7	1,248	1,107	1,052	953
1987	16.9	31.2	38.9	37.3	9.1	1,181	1,054	1,063	981
1986	19.1	33.3	42.5	35.5	11.0	1,067	1,119	1,025	1,018
1985	18.7	32.4	35.8	35.7	11.3	1,035	1,047	957	946
1984	20.2	32.7	34.7	38.5	10.7	901	829	806	816
1983	20.2	32.7	39.5	38.0	8.3	903	909	949	860
1982	21.9	32.6	37.3	37.0	10.9	923	875	924	883
1981	17.9	34.7	34.9	34.9	13.3	882	939	866	963
1980	20.8	26.1	34.8	35.8	12.6	881	949	863	889
1979	18.2	33.6	33.0	30.3	10.9	729	712	697	755
1978	19.8	29.1	33.6	37.8	12.3	723	684	666	751
1977	13.0	24.1	25.1	35.2	11.0	676	693	662	773
Male									
2008	17.8	26.6	30.9	36.3	3.7	1,377	1,218	1,233	1,198
2007	24.3	28.5	34.1	37.4	5.9	1,302	1,252	1,217	1,130
2006	20.0	31.0	37.7	40.6	4.9	1,251	1,214	1,208	1,111
2005	20.5	29.2	39.2	37.0	4.7	1,219	1,192	1,202	1,087
2004	25.2	28.8	34.3	36.6	6.4	1,247	1,142	1,202	1,001
2003	23.0	31.2	32.3	35.9	6.2	1,205	1,178	1,081	1,020
2002	17.4	31.6	28.7	38.5	7.4	1,140	1,090	1,137	911
2001	21.2	23.4	27.8	40.8	7.7	1,065	1,128	1,093	895
2000	23.1	26.7	27.7	36.9	9.0	1,048	993	875	872
1999	17.9	29.5	29.7	38.9	7.6	973	990	893	854
1998	16.8	26.6	26.9	44.9	8.1	933	887	841	792
1997	15.3	22.3	33.7	45.8	3.7	969	863	735	836
1996	13.5	25.8	40.5	45.1	6.8	914	808	798	764
1995	11.4	31.1	42.4	47.6	7.5	794	839	776	697
1994	16.4	27.5	36.3	45.1	11.4	778	845	721	676
1993ʳ	19.1	35.1	37.2	50.4	7.6	722	612	618	658
1993	19.1	34.3	36.9	46.0	7.3	778	637	648	658
1992	15.6	27.2	42.5	46.2	6.8	636	687	602	576
1991	22.7	31.5	43.9	42.6	10.7	651	691	544	521
1990	22.2	36.4	40.2	43.8	9.0	676	616	590	564
1989	23.7	36.1	40.0	45.2	7.8	642	584	560	511
1988	26.9	42.0	53.8	40.5	12.4	676	566	470	523
1987	19.8	31.7	44.8	38.7	6.4	600	524	569	517
1986	22.2	38.0	49.3	37.8	10.8	544	555	535	471
1985	16.7	36.8	38.4	43.4	7.8	521	527	502	449
1984	18.3	35.7	33.1	42.8	10.0	443	420	423	432
1983	22.2	38.8	45.7	41.8	8.2	445	479	479	428
1982	23.1	36.4	39.1	43.4	10.1	428	426	466	477
1981	19.9	39.8	38.0	40.0	14.3	438	480	439	495
1980	22.5	29.9	40.5	40.7	13.5	418	481	415	445
1979	19.0	34.6	36.4	31.3	8.8	368	358	349	386
1978	23.5	29.9	33.9	37.3	13.6	388	335	339	413
1977	11.5	31.4	23.3	38.4	6.7	365	325	330	406
Female									
2008	17.8	23.7	27.2	32.1	3.2	1,313	1,184	1,189	1,123
2007	17.3	29.4	28.2	30.5	5.4	1,239	1,162	1,202	1,080
2006	21.3	27.4	27.3	29.5	6.5	1,190	1,168	1,153	1,054
2005	15.6	23.0	26.7	27.3	5.1	1,171	1,126	1,119	1,115
2004	17.6	27.3	25.1	32.8	5.7	1,135	1,108	1,080	1,070
2003	17.1	25.7	30.3	29.7	4.3	1,075	1,043	1,086	1,042
2002	13.6	25.3	27.0	32.7	4.5	1,118	1,115	942	930
2001	12.2	20.8	21.6	28.0	6.0	1,078	1,070	918	838
2000	15.7	19.7	26.9	31.8	8.6	1,020	974	869	800
1999	13.5	22.0	26.1	33.8	6.9	930	932	841	800

r = Revised, controlled to 1990 census based population estimates; previous 1993 data controlled to 1980 census based population estimates.

Table A-11. The Population 6 to 17 Years Old Enrolled Below Modal Grade, 1971–2008—*Continued*

(Numbers in thousands, percent.)

Year, sex, race, and Hispanic origin	Percent below modal grade				Dropout rate, 15 to 17 years old	Population in age group			
	6 to 8 years old	9 to 11 years old	12 to 14 years old	15 to 17 years old		6 to 8 years old	9 to 11 years old	12 to 14 years old	15 to 17 years old
1998	14.1	19.7	21.8	31.1	7.0	970	853	701	632
1997	15.0	20.4	28.8	36.1	7.4	939	803	710	739
1996	16.6	20.3	30.4	32.4	10.4	798	871	753	712
1995	17.5	20.6	34.5	39.5	7.2	802	789	721	677
1994	17.2	29.2	28.5	34.9	6.1	748	747	722	671
1993ʳ	18.9	24.2	29.0	32.3	8.7	667	643	586	567
1993	18.7	24.3	28.3	29.3	8.6	678	658	597	567
1992	16.8	23.4	25.0	33.1	9.6	636	684	539	534
1991	20.8	29.8	27.6	34.1	12.0	639	665	544	502
1990	20.7	33.2	34.9	35.3	9.0	594	614	505	498
1989	20.0	31.4	39.7	33.5	13.5	615	570	519	490
1988	18.7	31.8	37.8	32.3	15.3	572	541	582	430
1987	13.8	30.8	32.2	35.8	12.1	581	530	494	464
1986	15.9	28.7	35.1	33.5	11.2	523	564	490	547
1985	20.8	27.9	33.0	28.8	14.5	514	520	455	497
1984	22.1	29.6	36.6	33.6	11.5	458	409	383	384
1983	18.1	25.8	33.2	34.3	8.3	458	430	470	432
1982	20.8	29.0	35.6	29.6	11.8	495	449	458	406
1981	16.0	29.4	31.6	29.5	12.2	444	459	427	468
1980	19.2	22.2	29.5	30.9	11.7	463	468	448	444
1979	17.5	32.5	29.6	29.3	13.0	361	354	348	369
1978	15.5	28.4	33.3	38.5	10.7	335	349	327	338
1977	14.8	17.7	26.8	31.6	15.8	311	368	332	367
WHITE ALONE OR IN COMBINATION									
Both Sexes									
2008	20.2	27.1	29.2	29.6	2.5	9,680	9,298	9,577	10,043
2007	21.1	26.1	27.4	28.5	2.8	9,502	9,326	9,734	10,169
2006	20.6	25.6	26.7	29.9	3.0	9,346	9,444	9,850	10,175
2005	21.1	23.9	27.9	29.4	2.6	9,314	9,588	10,026	10,479
2004	22.4	25.6	27.4	30.5	3.9	9,422	9,506	10,175	10,079
2003	21.7	27.4	28.1	29.4	3.2	9,447	9,446	10,194	10,151
Male									
2008	22.3	29.1	32.3	32.4	2.7	4,963	4,744	4,934	5,163
2007	24.0	28.2	29.1	32.0	2.9	4,857	4,770	4,997	5,203
2006	22.4	27.2	29.6	34.1	3.4	4,769	4,842	5,042	5,193
2005	23.9	27.3	30.9	33.1	2.7	4,751	4,925	5,151	5,268
2004	24.9	28.1	31.2	35.1	3.9	4,876	4,823	5,318	5,043
2003	24.5	31.6	31.0	33.8	3.4	4,965	4,946	5,108	5,172
Female									
2008	17.9	25.0	26.0	26.6	2.4	4,717	4,554	4,643	4,880
2007	18.1	23.9	25.5	24.7	2.7	4,646	4,555	4,737	4,966
2006	18.7	23.8	23.6	25.5	2.6	4,577	4,602	4,808	4,982
2005	18.2	20.2	24.7	25.7	2.6	4,563	4,663	4,875	5,211
2004	19.6	23.0	23.2	25.9	3.9	4,545	4,683	4,857	5,037
2003	18.6	22.7	25.2	24.8	3.0	4,482	4,500	5,086	4,979
BLACK ALONE OR IN COMBINATION									
Both Sexes									
2008	18.3	26.8	39.4	37.1	3.0	2,026	2,002	2,036	2,179
2007	17.6	27.3	32.1	38.8	2.8	1,998	1,950	2,071	2,146
2006	18.9	28.3	34.8	35.0	3.1	1,982	1,988	2,074	2,202
2005	20.3	34.8	33.4	37.9	4.4	1,970	1,982	2,137	2,194
2004	20.3	27.0	33.2	39.1	2.5	1,950	2,022	2,174	2,107
2003	23.2	33.5	33.4	36.8	3.8	1,921	2,183	2,220	2,034
Male									
2008	19.8	25.6	44.8	39.7	3.3	1,026	1,020	1,032	1,090
2007	21.7	29.9	34.4	42.6	2.1	1,053	983	1,034	1,086
2006	20.0	33.5	39.0	42.8	3.5	1,013	1,018	1,050	1,094
2005	22.1	37.0	35.5	41.8	5.0	981	999	1,061	1,082
2004	21.1	30.6	37.3	45.3	1.9	966	1,042	1,065	1,056
2003	24.2	36.6	38.5	42.9	4.0	1,014	1,116	1,033	1,083

r = Revised, controlled to 1990 census based population estimates; previous 1993 data controlled to 1980 census based population estimates.

Table A-11. The Population 6 to 17 Years Old Enrolled Below Modal Grade, 1971–2008—*Continued*

(Numbers in thousands, percent.)

Year, sex, race, and Hispanic origin	Percent below modal grade				Dropout rate, 15 to 17 years old	Population in age group			
	6 to 8 years old	9 to 11 years old	12 to 14 years old	15 to 17 years old		6 to 8 years old	9 to 11 years old	12 to 14 years old	15 to 17 years old
Female									
2008.......................................	16.8	28.1	34.0	34.5	2.7	1,000	982	1,004	1,089
2007.......................................	13.2	24.6	29.9	34.8	3.6	945	967	1,037	1,061
2006.......................................	17.8	23.0	30.6	27.3	2.7	969	969	1,024	1,108
2005.......................................	18.6	32.6	31.4	34.1	3.7	990	983	1,076	1,112
2004.......................................	17.8	23.0	30.6	27.3	2.7	969	969	1,024	1,108
2003.......................................	22.0	30.4	29.0	29.8	3.4	907	1,067	1,187	951
ASIAN ALONE OR IN COMBINATION									
Both Sexes									
2008.......................................	16.4	23.5	24.7	19.7	3.9	599	587	558	603
2007.......................................	11.4	20.6	15.6	25.3	3.6	650	613	600	548
2006.......................................	15.0	19.9	19.2	22.2	3.2	528	574	574	603
2005.......................................	13.0	12.3	16.5	18.4	1.2	600	531	576	581
2004.......................................	13.9	12.4	20.3	24.6	2.6	494	576	585	599
2003.......................................	8.8	14.9	18.4	23.5	2.4	579	548	552	543
Male									
2008.......................................	21.3	22.6	20.4	15.5	2.1	285	291	299	289
2007.......................................	8.4	20.2	16.7	28.4	4.3	316	307	287	289
2006.......................................	15.4	15.4	15.4	15.4	4.1	259	311	291	285
2005.......................................	12.5	13.2	14.5	16.5	1.6	318	254	307	286
2004.......................................	12.4	16.2	19.3	22.3	3.6	254	278	324	286
2003.......................................	9.3	19.8	19.4	19.2	1.8	263	268	299	277
Female									
2008.......................................	12	24.3	29.6	23.6	5.5	314	295	259	314
2007.......................................	14.3	21.1	14.6	21.8	2.9	334	306	314	259
2006.......................................	14.6	20.6	15.4	22.2	2.4	269	263	283	318
2005.......................................	13.7	11.5	18.8	20.2	0.9	282	276	269	295
2004.......................................	15.5	8.8	21.6	26.7	1.6	241	298	261	313
2003.......................................	8.4	10.3	17.2	28.0	3.1	316	280	253	266

Table A-12   Annual High School Dropout Rates of 15 to 24 Year Olds by Sex, Race, Grade, and Hispanic Origin, October 1967–2008

(Numbers in thousands, percent.)

Year, grade, race, and Hispanic origin	Total			Male			Female		
	Total students	Dropouts	Dropout rate	Total students	Dropouts	Dropout rate	Total students	Dropouts	Dropout rate
ALL RACES									
Grades 10–12									
2008	11,750	390	3.3	5,999	174	2.9	5,751	216	3.8
2007	11,584	383	3.3	5,879	206	3.5	5,705	177	3.1
2006	11,604	407	3.5	5,932	227	3.8	5,672	180	3.2
2005	11,494	414	3.6	5,843	233	4.0	5,651	181	3.2
2004	11,166	486	4.4	5,624	266	4.7	5,542	220	4.0
2003	11,378	429	3.8	5,705	225	4.0	5,674	203	3.6
2002	10,989	367	3.3	5,504	193	3.5	5,484	174	3.2
2001	10,777	507	4.7	5,534	293	5.3	5,243	214	4.1
2000	10,773	488	4.5	5,417	280	5.2	5,356	208	3.9
1999	11,067	520	4.7	5,659	243	4.3	5,411	277	5.1
1998	10,791	479	4.4	5,486	237	4.3	5,305	243	4.6
1997	10,645	454	4.3	5,330	251	4.7	5,313	203	3.8
1996	10,249	485	4.7	5,175	240	4.6	5,072	244	4.8
1995	10,106	544	5.4	5,161	297	5.8	4,946	247	5.0
1994	9,922	497	5.0	5,048	249	4.9	4,873	247	5.1
1993r	9,430	404	4.3	4,787	211	4.4	4,640	192	4.1
1993	9,021	382	4.2	4,570	199	4.4	4,452	183	4.1
1992	8,939	384	4.3	4,580	175	3.8	4,357	207	4.8
1991	8,612	348	4.0	4,380	167	3.8	4,231	180	4.3
1990	8,679	347	4.0	4,356	177	4.1	4,323	170	3.9
1989	8,974	404	4.5	4,519	203	4.5	4,453	199	4.5
1988	9,590	461	4.8	4,960	256	5.2	4,628	206	4.5
1987	9,802	403	4.1	4,921	215	4.4	4,879	187	3.8
1986	9,829	421	4.3	4,910	213	4.3	4,917	208	4.2
1985	9,704	504	5.2	4,831	259	5.4	4,874	245	5.0
1984	10,041	507	5.0	4,986	268	5.4	5,054	238	4.7
1983	10,331	535	5.2	5,130	294	5.7	5,200	241	4.6
1982	10,611	577	5.4	5,310	305	5.7	5,301	271	5.1
1981	10,868	639	5.9	5,379	322	6.0	5,487	316	5.8
1980	10,891	658	6.0	5,445	362	6.6	5,448	296	5.4
1979	11,136	744	6.7	5,479	369	6.7	5,658	377	6.7
1978	11,116	743	6.7	5,558	415	7.5	5,558	328	5.9
1977	11,300	734	6.5	5,657	392	6.9	5,643	342	6.1
1976	10,996	644	5.9	5,534	360	6.5	5,463	285	5.2
1975	11,033	639	5.8	5,485	296	5.4	5,548	343	6.2
1974	11,026	742	6.7	5,421	402	7.4	5,605	340	6.1
1973	10,851	683	6.3	5,407	370	6.8	5,444	313	5.7
1972	10,664	659	6.2	5,305	317	6.0	5,358	341	6.4
1971	10,451	562	5.4	5,193	297	5.7	5,258	266	5.1
1970	10,281	588	5.7	5,145	288	5.6	5,138	302	5.9
1969	10,212	551	5.4	5,069	273	5.4	5,142	278	5.4
1968	9,814	506	5.2	4,831	247	5.1	4,983	259	5.2
1967	9,350	486	5.2	4,605	237	5.1	4,745	249	5.2
Grade 10									
2008	4,154	56	1.4	2,104	25	1.2	2,050	31	1.5
2007	4,064	63	1.6	2,027	32	1.6	2,037	31	1.5
2006	4,179	31	0.7	2,053	19	0.9	2,126	12	0.5
2005	4,483	72	1.6	2,244	49	2.2	2,239	23	1.0
2004	4,028	99	2.5	2,096	56	2.7	1,931	42	2.2
2003	4,107	64	1.6	2,111	26	1.2	1,995	37	1.9
2002	3,896	55	1.4	1,963	36	1.8	1,934	19	1.0
2001	3,900	90	2.3	1,988	50	2.5	1,913	41	2.1
2000	3,957	77	1.9	2,036	48	2.4	1,920	28	1.5
1999	3,910	104	2.7	2,036	54	2.7	1,875	50	2.7
1998	3,883	90	2.3	1,971	36	1.8	1,911	54	2.8
1997	3,738	79	2.1	1,894	44	2.3	1,843	35	1.9
1996	3,691	94	2.5	1,906	50	2.6	1,784	43	2.4
1995	3,552	88	2.5	1,823	40	2.2	1,728	47	2.7
1994	3,474	76	2.2	1,793	45	2.5	1,681	31	1.8
1993r	3,265	86	2.6	1,696	52	3.1	1,567	33	2.1
1993	3,139	81	2.6	1,627	50	3.1	1,513	31	2.0
1992	3,197	81	2.5	1,657	37	2.2	1,539	43	2.8

r = Revised, controlled to 1990 census based population estimates; previous 1993 data controlled to 1980 census based population estimates.

Table A-12 Annual High School Dropout Rates of 15 to 24 Year Olds by Sex, Race, Grade, and Hispanic Origin, October 1967–2008—*Continued*

(Numbers in thousands, percent.)

Year, grade, race, and Hispanic origin	Total			Male			Female		
	Total students	Dropouts	Dropout rate	Total students	Dropouts	Dropout rate	Total students	Dropouts	Dropout rate
1991	3,132	105	3.4	1,571	46	2.9	1,561	59	3.8
1990	3,215	90	2.8	1,660	43	2.6	1,555	47	3.0
1989	3,071	99	3.2	1,567	56	3.6	1,504	43	2.9
1988	3,308	112	3.4	1,716	63	3.7	1,592	49	3.1
1987	3,492	106	3.0	1,818	45	2.5	1,674	61	3.6
1986	3,555	119	3.3	1,820	56	3.1	1,734	63	3.6
1985	3,491	143	4.1	1,797	74	4.1	1,695	69	4.1
1984	3,415	135	4.0	1,735	76	4.4	1,680	59	3.5
1983	3,468	129	3.7	1,755	70	4.0	1,713	59	3.4
1982	3,540	144	4.1	1,792	69	3.9	1,747	74	4.2
1981	3,735	144	3.9	1,816	65	3.6	1,918	78	4.1
1980	3,817	166	4.3	1,957	95	4.9	1,861	71	3.8
1979	3,920	217	5.5	1,985	102	5.1	1,934	114	5.9
1978	3,878	185	4.8	1,943	96	4.9	1,935	89	4.6
1977	3,970	177	4.5	2,021	96	4.8	1,949	81	4.2
1976	3,914	145	3.7	1,960	79	4.0	1,955	67	3.4
1975	3,983	183	4.6	2,017	87	4.3	1,967	97	4.9
1974	3,901	223	5.7	1,951	122	6.3	1,949	101	5.2
1973	3,899	210	5.4	1,930	112	5.8	1,969	98	5.0
1972	3,868	203	5.2	1,940	106	5.5	1,928	97	5.0
1971	3,762	174	4.6	1,925	95	4.9	1,838	79	4.3
1970	3,686	186	5.0	1,865	90	4.8	1,822	97	5.3
1969	3,485	159	4.6	1,756	84	4.8	1,729	75	4.3
1968	3,615	151	4.2	1,849	75	4.1	1,767	76	4.3
1967	3,370	129	3.8	1,726	64	3.7	1,644	65	4.0
Grade 11									
2008	4,186	96	2.3	2,113	60	2.9	2,073	36	1.7
2007	4,388	118	2.7	2,280	64	2.8	2,108	55	2.6
2006	4,324	112	2.6	2,209	62	2.7	2,053	50	2.4
2005	4,080	72	1.8	2,184	46	2.1	1,896	26	1.4
2004	4,010	141	3.5	2,012	76	3.8	1,998	65	3.3
2003	4,327	117	2.7	2,158	68	3.2	2,169	49	2.3
2002	4,137	99	2.4	2,111	54	2.6	2,026	45	2.2
2001	4,114	139	3.4	2,134	72	3.4	1,979	67	3.4
2000	3,833	170	4.4	1,933	78	4.0	1,901	93	4.9
1999	4,036	150	3.7	2,052	69	3.4	1,984	81	4.0
1998	3,735	110	2.9	1,902	55	2.9	1,833	55	3.0
1997	3,882	142	3.7	1,957	71	3.6	1,925	71	3.7
1996	3,606	138	3.8	1,828	76	4.2	1,778	62	3.5
1995	3,568	159	4.5	1,846	89	4.8	1,724	71	4.1
1994	3,587	132	3.7	1,864	61	3.3	1,722	70	4.1
1993ʳ	3,375	106	3.1	1,725	43	2.5	1,650	63	3.8
1993	3,218	100	3.1	1,643	40	2.4	1,575	60	3.8
1992	3,213	120	3.7	1,642	52	3.2	1,570	67	4.3
1991	3,083	101	3.3	1,598	42	2.6	1,484	58	3.9
1990	2,976	98	3.3	1,462	57	3.9	1,514	41	2.7
1989	3,302	125	3.8	1,683	67	4.0	1,618	57	3.5
1988	3,447	161	4.7	1,819	89	4.9	1,627	72	4.4
1987	3,566	122	3.4	1,766	71	4.0	1,800	51	2.8
1986	3,433	116	3.4	1,700	51	3.0	1,733	65	3.8
1985	3,274	139	4.2	1,618	70	4.3	1,656	69	4.2
1984	3,328	163	4.9	1,682	87	5.2	1,646	76	4.6
1983	3,601	162	4.5	1,825	87	4.8	1,775	75	4.2
1982	3,694	218	5.9	1,872	122	6.5	1,822	96	5.3
1981	3,787	262	6.9	1,937	144	7.4	1,850	118	6.4
1980	3,670	225	6.1	1,832	120	6.6	1,839	105	5.7
1979	3,718	229	6.2	1,840	102	5.5	1,879	128	6.8
1978	3,708	230	6.2	1,905	113	5.9	1,803	117	6.5
1977	3,832	244	6.4	1,964	133	6.8	1,867	110	5.9
1976	3,786	227	6.0	1,955	123	6.3	1,831	104	5.7
1975	3,596	230	6.4	1,828	103	5.6	1,767	126	7.1
1974	3,721	237	6.4	1,819	123	6.8	1,902	114	6.0
1973	3,631	237	6.5	1,877	126	6.7	1,754	111	6.3
1972	3,581	241	6.7	1,825	107	5.9	1,756	134	7.6
1971	3,585	185	5.2	1,772	82	4.6	1,811	103	5.7

r = Revised, controlled to 1990 census based population estimates; previous 1993 data controlled to 1980 census based population estimates.

Table A-12   Annual High School Dropout Rates of 15 to 24 Year Olds by Sex, Race, Grade, and Hispanic Origin, October 1967–2008—*Continued*

(Numbers in thousands, percent.)

Year, grade, race, and Hispanic origin	Total			Male			Female		
	Total students	Dropouts	Dropout rate	Total students	Dropouts	Dropout rate	Total students	Dropouts	Dropout rate
1970	3,456	198	5.7	1,750	96	5.5	1,706	102	6.0
1969	3,489	190	5.4	1,779	100	5.6	1,710	90	5.3
1968	3,255	179	5.5	1,640	91	5.5	1,614	88	5.5
1967	3,068	169	5.5	1,557	76	4.9	1,511	93	6.2
Grade 12									
2008	3,409	237	7.0	1,781	89	5.0	1,628	149	9.1
2007	3,133	202	6.4	1,572	111	7.0	1,561	91	5.8
2006	3,101	265	8.5	1,608	146	9.1	1,492	119	8.0
2005	2,931	270	9.2	1,415	138	9.7	1,516	132	8.7
2004	3,130	247	7.9	1,516	133	8.8	1,614	114	7.1
2003	2,945	248	8.4	1,435	131	9.1	1,510	117	7.7
2002	2,956	214	7.2	1,432	104	7.3	1,524	110	7.2
2001	2,762	277	10.0	1,411	171	12.1	1,351	106	7.8
2000	2,983	241	8.1	1,447	154	10.6	1,535	87	5.7
1999	3,121	266	8.5	1,571	120	7.6	1,552	146	9.4
1998	3,173	279	8.8	1,613	146	9.0	1,560	133	8.5
1997	3,025	233	7.7	1,479	136	9.2	1,545	97	6.3
1996	2,952	253	8.6	1,441	114	7.9	1,510	139	9.2
1995	2,986	297	9.9	1,492	168	11.3	1,494	129	8.6
1994	2,861	289	10.1	1,391	143	10.3	1,470	146	9.9
1993ʳ	2,790	212	7.6	1,366	116	8.5	1,423	96	6.7
1993	2,664	201	7.5	1,300	109	8.4	1,364	92	6.7
1992	2,529	183	7.2	1,281	86	6.7	1,248	97	7.8
1991	2,397	142	5.9	1,211	79	6.5	1,186	63	5.3
1990	2,488	159	6.4	1,234	77	6.2	1,254	82	6.5
1989	2,601	180	6.9	1,269	80	6.3	1,331	99	7.4
1988	2,835	188	6.6	1,425	104	7.3	1,409	85	6.0
1987	2,744	175	6.4	1,337	99	7.4	1,405	75	5.3
1986	2,841	186	6.5	1,390	106	7.6	1,450	80	5.5
1985	2,939	222	7.6	1,416	115	8.1	1,523	107	7.0
1984	3,298	209	6.3	1,569	105	6.7	1,728	103	6.0
1983	3,262	244	7.5	1,550	137	8.8	1,712	107	6.3
1982	3,377	215	6.4	1,646	114	6.9	1,732	101	5.8
1981	3,346	233	7.0	1,626	113	6.9	1,719	120	7.0
1980	3,404	267	7.8	1,656	147	8.9	1,748	120	6.9
1979	3,498	298	8.5	1,654	164	9.9	1,845	135	7.3
1978	3,530	328	9.3	1,710	206	12.0	1,820	122	6.7
1977	3,498	313	8.9	1,672	163	9.7	1,827	151	8.3
1976	3,296	272	8.3	1,619	158	9.8	1,677	114	6.8
1975	3,454	226	6.5	1,640	106	6.5	1,814	120	6.6
1974	3,404	282	8.3	1,651	157	9.5	1,754	125	7.1
1973	3,321	236	7.1	1,600	132	8.3	1,721	104	6.0
1972	3,215	215	6.7	1,540	104	6.8	1,674	110	6.6
1971	3,104	203	6.5	1,496	120	8.0	1,609	84	5.2
1970	3,139	204	6.5	1,530	102	6.7	1,610	103	6.4
1969	3,238	202	6.2	1,534	89	5.8	1,703	113	6.6
1968	2,944	176	6.0	1,342	81	6.0	1,602	95	5.9
1967	2,912	188	6.5	1,322	97	7.3	1,590	91	5.7
WHITE ALONE									
Grades 10–12									
2008	8,942	246	2.8	4,588	123	2.7	4,353	123	2.8
2007	8,927	246	2.8	4,518	126	2.8	4,409	120	2.7
2006	8,924	311	3.5	4,568	177	3.9	4,355	133	3.1
2005	8,855	271	3.1	4,472	151	3.4	4,382	120	2.7
2004	8,585	359	4.2	4,344	211	4.9	4,241	148	3.5
2003[1]	8,781	321	3.7	4,434	172	3.9	4,347	148	3.4
2002	8,636	259	3.0	4,371	133	3.0	4,265	126	3.0
2001	8,490	388	4.6	4,363	230	5.3	4,126	158	3.8
2000	8,540	371	4.3	4,368	204	4.7	4,172	167	4.0
1999	8,665	380	4.4	4,426	180	4.1	4,238	198	4.7
1998	8,487	371	4.4	4,306	188	4.4	4,181	183	4.4
1997	8,402	355	4.2	4,220	208	4.9	4,180	145	3.5
1996	8,005	361	4.5	4,077	198	4.8	3,928	163	4.1

[1]Starting in 2003 respondents could identify more than one race. Except as noted, the race data in this table from 2003 onward represent those respondents who indicated only one race category.

r = Revised, controlled to 1990 census based population estimates; previous 1993 data controlled to 1980 census based population estimates.

Table A-12   Annual High School Dropout Rates of 15 to 24 Year Olds by Sex, Race, Grade, and Hispanic Origin, October 1967–2008—Continued

(Numbers in thousands, percent.)

Year, grade, race, and Hispanic origin	Total			Male			Female		
	Total students	Dropouts	Dropout rate	Total students	Dropouts	Dropout rate	Total students	Dropouts	Dropout rate
1995	7,926	402	5.1	4,079	220	5.4	3,849	183	4.8
1994	7,862	371	4.7	4,014	184	4.6	3,848	188	4.9
1993ʳ	7,442	306	4.1	3,790	157	4.1	3,654	150	4.1
1993	7,152	290	4.1	3,623	147	4.1	3,530	143	4.1
1992	7,077	292	4.1	3,646	140	3.8	3,430	151	4.4
1991	6,856	254	3.7	3,514	127	3.6	3,343	128	3.8
1990	6,984	266	3.8	3,522	144	4.1	3,462	122	3.5
1989	7,243	286	3.9	3,653	149	4.1	3,589	136	3.8
1988	7,727	362	4.7	4,016	203	5.1	3,712	161	4.3
1987	7,979	299	3.7	4,023	163	4.1	3,953	135	3.4
1986	8,011	333	4.2	4,007	168	4.2	4,007	166	4.1
1985	7,967	384	4.8	3,963	195	4.9	4,003	188	4.7
1984	8,221	410	5.0	4,119	220	5.3	4,101	190	4.6
1983	8,531	410	4.8	4,264	232	5.4	4,264	177	4.2
1982	8,769	444	5.1	4,381	231	5.3	4,390	214	4.9
1981	9,067	478	5.3	4,532	254	5.6	4,536	224	4.9
1980	9,177	517	5.6	4,624	294	6.4	4,554	224	4.9
1979	9,437	588	6.2	4,694	311	6.6	4,742	277	5.8
1978	9,360	574	6.1	4,747	329	6.9	4,611	244	5.3
1977	9,536	594	6.2	4,766	327	6.9	4,770	267	5.6
1976	9,362	532	5.7	4,708	297	6.3	4,654	235	5.0
1975	9,440	507	5.4	4,709	234	5.0	4,732	274	5.8
1974	9,403	566	6.0	4,650	326	7.0	4,754	241	5.1
1973	9,359	537	5.7	4,708	288	6.1	4,649	248	5.3
1972	9,173	520	5.7	4,588	247	5.4	4,583	272	5.9
1971	9,140	470	5.1	4,577	244	5.3	4,562	226	5.0
1970	8,959	449	5.0	4,496	212	4.7	4,462	237	5.3
1969	8,878	429	4.8	4,438	208	4.7	4,439	221	5.0
1968	8,580	387	4.5	4,246	190	4.5	4,331	196	4.5
1967	8,186	379	4.6	4,060	189	4.7	4,126	190	4.6
WHITE ALONE NON-HISPANIC									
Grades 10–12									
2008	7,079	156	2.2	3,638	83	2.3	3,441	73	2.1
2007	7,274	155	2.1	3,684	82	2.2	3,590	73	2.0
2006	7,171	200	2.8	3,693	120	3.2	3,478	80	2.3
2005	7,227	196	2.7	3,652	103	2.8	3,575	93	2.6
2004	7,015	245	3.5	3,582	130	3.6	3,434	115	3.4
2003¹	7,139	214	3.0	3,665	116	3.2	3,474	98	2.8
2002	7,124	173	2.4	3,620	84	2.3	3,504	89	2.6
2001	7,070	272	3.8	3,647	173	4.7	3,423	98	2.9
2000	7,159	276	3.9	3,648	150	4.1	3,511	126	3.6
1999	7,265	274	3.8	3,744	130	3.5	3,523	145	4.1
1998	7,174	266	3.7	3,605	130	3.6	3,570	137	3.8
1997	7,090	242	3.4	3,533	140	4.0	3,558	103	2.9
1996	6,850	267	3.9	3,511	145	4.1	3,337	121	3.6
1995	6,905	296	4.3	3,564	164	4.6	3,341	131	3.9
1994	6,839	274	4.0	3,496	137	3.9	3,343	137	4.1
1993	6,277	237	3.8	3,229	128	4.0	3,047	108	3.5
BLACK									
Grades 10–12									
2008	1,868	114	6.1	925	42	4.6	943	72	7.6
2007	1,781	76	4.3	914	45	4.9	867	31	3.6
2006	1,767	65	3.7	902	29	3.2	864	37	4.3
2005	1,763	122	6.9	943	71	7.5	820	51	6.2
2004	1,716	90	5.2	833	40	4.8	883	50	5.7
2003¹	1,698	76	4.5	812	33	4.1	886	43	4.9
2002	1,664	73	4.4	782	40	5.1	882	33	3.8
2001	1,655	95	5.7	828	51	6.2	827	45	5.4
2000	1,706	96	5.6	819	62	7.6	888	34	3.8
1999	1,794	107	6.0	925	48	5.2	870	59	6.8
1998	1,759	88	5.0	918	42	4.6	841	46	5.5

¹Starting in 2003 respondents could identify more than one race. Except as noted, the race data in this table from 2003 onward represent those respondents who indicated only one race category.
r = Revised, controlled to 1990 census based population estimates; previous 1993 data controlled to 1980 census based population estimates.

Table A-12   Annual High School Dropout Rates of 15 to 24 Year Olds by Sex, Race, Grade, and Hispanic Origin, October 1967–2008—*Continued*

(Numbers in thousands, percent.)

Year, grade, race, and Hispanic origin	Total			Male			Female		
	Total students	Dropouts	Dropout rate	Total students	Dropouts	Dropout rate	Total students	Dropouts	Dropout rate
1997.............................	1,678	80	4.8	813	33	4.1	866	49	5.7
1996.............................	1,704	107	6.3	803	37	4.6	901	70	7.8
1995.............................	1,598	97	6.1	797	63	7.9	802	35	4.4
1994.............................	1,559	96	6.1	763	50	6.5	795	45	5.7
1993ʳ.............................	1,499	80	5.3	740	43	5.8	758	37	4.9
1993.............................	1,447	78	5.4	724	41	5.7	722	36	5.0
1992.............................	1,422	70	4.9	702	23	3.3	720	48	6.7
1991.............................	1,366	85	6.2	685	38	5.5	683	48	7.0
1990.............................	1,303	66	5.1	636	26	4.1	666	40	6.0
1989.............................	1,384	106	7.7	684	47	6.9	701	60	8.6
1988.............................	1,468	93	6.3	751	50	6.7	717	43	6.0
1987.............................	1,463	93	6.4	730	45	6.2	732	47	6.4
1986.............................	1,449	68	4.7	711	34	4.8	737	34	4.6
1985.............................	1,422	110	7.7	703	58	8.3	719	52	7.2
1984.............................	1,524	88	5.8	711	44	6.2	813	43	5.3
1983.............................	1,498	103	6.9	687	48	7.0	810	55	6.8
1982.............................	1,553	121	7.8	786	71	9.0	767	50	6.5
1981.............................	1,516	146	9.6	704	66	9.4	815	83	10.2
1980.............................	1,496	124	8.3	714	57	8.0	781	66	8.5
1979.............................	1,479	142	9.6	679	51	7.5	802	92	11.5
1978.............................	1,542	160	10.4	706	78	11.0	835	81	9.7
1977.............................	1,588	133	8.4	746	62	8.3	789	71	9.0
1976.............................	1,449	105	7.2	729	62	8.5	721	45	6.2
1975.............................	1,416	123	8.7	673	56	8.3	743	67	9.0
1974.............................	1,441	167	11.6	679	73	10.8	761	93	12.2
1973.............................	1,372	138	10.1	650	78	12.0	725	61	8.4
1972.............................	1,373	133	9.7	644	65	10.1	756	68	9.0
1971.............................	1,195	87	7.3	552	51	9.2	643	37	5.8
1970.............................	1,192	133	11.2	587	74	12.6	606	60	9.9
1969.............................	1,209	113	9.3	562	58	10.3	646	55	8.5
1968.............................	1,123	113	10.1	523	52	9.9	600	61	10.2
1967.............................	1,066	106	9.9	485	47	9.7	578	58	10.0
ASIAN²									
Grades 10–12									
2008.............................	429	17	3.9	219	0	0.2	210	16	7.8
2007.............................	404	30	7.5	202	13	6.6	202	17	8.3
2006.............................	445	19	4.2	237	11	4.5	208	8	3.7
2005.............................	425	6	1.5	219	5	2.4	206	1	0.5
2004.............................	452	4	0.9	233	-	-	219	4	1.9
2003¹.............................	457	11	2.4	237	3	1.4	221	7	3.4
2002.............................	515	12	2.3	266	8	3.0	249	4	1.6
2001.............................	470	10	2.1	274	9	3.3	197	1	0.5
2000.............................	399	13	3.3	178	12	6.7	221	1	0.5
1999.............................	523	25	4.8	269	13	4.8	253	12	4.7
HISPANIC³									
Grades 10–12									
2008.............................	2,062	101	4.9	1,052	44	4.2	1,011	57	5.6
2007.............................	1,785	99	5.5	904	49	5.5	882	49	5.6
2006.............................	1,923	124	6.4	958	61	6.3	965	63	6.6
2005.............................	1,814	86	4.7	910	51	5.6	904	35	3.9
2004.............................	1,723	138	8.0	842	97	11.5	881	40	4.6
2003.............................	1,792	116	6.5	846	65	7.7	945	51	5.4
2002.............................	1,614	86	5.3	801	50	6.2	814	36	4.4
2001.............................	1,487	121	8.1	755	57	7.5	732	64	8.7
2000.............................	1,465	100	6.8	761	54	7.1	704	46	6.5
1999.............................	1,482	105	7.1	729	50	6.9	751	55	7.3
1998.............................	1,368	115	8.4	731	63	8.6	637	52	8.2
1997.............................	1,377	119	8.6	710	74	10.4	668	45	6.7
1996.............................	1,195	100	8.4	588	54	9.2	608	46	7.6
1995.............................	1,251	145	11.6	644	70	10.9	608	76	12.5
1994.............................	1,179	109	9.2	607	51	8.4	572	58	10.1

²The data shown prior to 2003 consists of those identifying themselves as "Asian or Pacific Islanders."
³May be of any race.
r = Revised, controlled to 1990 census based population estimates; previous 1993 data controlled to 1980 census based population estimates.
- = Quantity zero or rounds to zero.

Table A-12   Annual High School Dropout Rates of 15 to 24 Year Olds by Sex, Race, Grade, and Hispanic Origin, October 1967–2008—*Continued*

(Numbers in thousands, percent.)

Year, grade, race, and Hispanic origin	Total			Male			Female		
	Total students	Dropouts	Dropout rate	Total students	Dropouts	Dropout rate	Total students	Dropouts	Dropout rate
1993r	1,061	69	6.5	488	25	5.1	573	44	7.5
1993	943	60	6.4	436	21	4.8	508	39	7.7
1992	917	72	7.9	468	27	5.8	441	38	8.6
1991	809	59	7.3	396	41	10.4	417	20	4.8
1990	811	65	8.0	379	33	8.7	428	31	7.2
1989	762	59	7.7	394	30	7.6	366	28	7.7
1988	730	77	10.5	398	49	12.3	333	28	8.4
1987	769	43	5.6	380	19	5.0	389	24	6.2
1986	764	91	11.9	376	44	11.7	388	48	12.4
1985	729	71	9.7	333	31	9.3	396	39	9.8
1984	706	77	10.9	311	38	12.2	396	40	10.1
1983	691	68	9.8	351	48	13.7	340	21	6.2
1982	692	65	9.4	370	35	9.5	321	29	9.0
1981	717	77	10.7	350	37	10.6	367	40	10.9
1980	646	74	11.5	295	50	16.9	350	24	6.9
1979	593	58	9.8	295	30	10.2	298	27	9.1
1978	567	70	12.3	295	46	15.6	271	23	8.5
1977	627	50	8.0	341	35	10.3	287	15	5.2
1976	638	46	7.2	300	22	7.3	336	23	6.8
1975	614	67	10.9	317	32	10.1	294	34	11.6
1974	547	53	9.7	271	34	12.5	278	20	7.2
1973	499	50	10.0	240	19	7.9	259	31	12.0
1972	498	55	11.0	253	28	11.1	247	27	10.9
WHITE ALONE OR IN COMBINATION									
Grades 10–12									
2008	9,277	257	2.8	4,766	129	2.7	4,511	128	2.8
2007	9,199	251	2.7	4,664	131	2.8	4,535	120	2.7
2006	9,212	320	3.5	4,695	185	3.9	4,517	136	3.0
2005	9,158	281	3.1	4,610	155	3.4	4,548	126	2.8
2004	8,821	382	4.3	4,464	222	5.0	4,357	160	3.7
2003	9,045	335	3.7	4,573	183	4.0	4,471	151	3.4
BLACK ALONE OR IN COMBINATION									
Grades 10–12									
2008	2,033	121	5.9	1,012	46	4.5	1,021	75	7.3
2007	1,900	78	4.1	977	47	4.8	923	31	3.4
2006	1,891	66	3.5	952	29	3.0	939	38	4.0
2005	1,870	129	6.9	979	71	7.3	890	58	6.5
2004	1,797	99	5.5	869	40	4.6	928	59	6.3
2003	1,808	79	4.4	853	36	4.2	955	43	4.5
ASIAN ALONE OR IN COMBINATION									
Grades 10–12									
2008	511	17	3.3	256	0	0.2	255	16	6.4
2007	483	30	6.2	233	13	5.8	250	17	6.7
2006	542	23	4.2	279	15	5.4	263	8	3.0
2005	525	8	1.5	270	6	2.3	255	2	0.6
2004	516	8	1.6	273	3	1.2	243	5	2.1
2003	533	17	3.1	278	8	3.0	254	8	3.3

r = Revised, controlled to 1990 census based population estimates; previous 1993 data controlled to 1980 census based population estimates.

Table A-13.   Population 14 to 24 Years Old by High School Graduate Status, College Enrollment, Attainment, Sex, Race, and Hispanic Origin, October 1967–2008

(Numbers in thousands, percent.)

Year, race, and Hispanic origin	Population 18 to 24 years old								High school graduates, 14 to 24 years old		
	Total	High school graduates		Percent			High school dropouts		All graduates	Percent	
		Total	Enrolled in college	High school graduates	Enrolled in college	High school graduate enrolled in college	Number	Percent		Enrolled in college	Enrolled or completed some college
ALL RACES											
Both Sexes											
2008	28,950	24,568	11,466	84.9	39.6	46.7	2,702	9.3	24,922	47.0	70.6
2007	28,778	24,146	11,161	83.9	38.8	46.2	2,937	10.2	24,491	46.3	69.7
2006	28,372	23,430	10,586	82.6	37.3	45.2	3,128	11.0	23,800	45.4	69.3
2005	27,855	23,103	10,834	82.9	38.9	49.3	3,154	11.3	23,445	47.0	69.8
2004	27,948	23,086	10,611	82.6	38.0	46.0	3,836	12.1	23,379	46.2	69.0
2003	27,404	22,603	10,364	82.5	37.8	45.9	3,228	11.8	22,898	45.9	68.8
2002	27,367	22,319	10,033	81.6	36.7	45.0	3,375	12.3	22,639	45.2	67.6
2001	26,965	21,836	9,629	81.0	35.7	44.1	3,519	13.0	22,136	44.1	66.7
2000	26,658	21,822	9,452	81.9	35.5	43.3	3,315	12.4	22,080	43.5	66.7
1999	26,041	21,127	9,259	81.1	35.6	43.8	3,413	13.1	21,390	44.0	67.2
1998	25,507	20,567	9,322	80.6	36.6	45.3	3,544	13.9	20,775	45.5	68.0
1997	24,973	20,338	9,204	81.4	36.9	45.2	3,236	13.0	20,577	45.6	67.3
1996	24,671	20,131	8,767	81.6	35.5	43.5	3,147	12.8	20,465	44.0	67.2
1995	24,900	20,125	8,539	80.8	34.3	42.4	3,471	13.9	20,359	42.7	67.1
1994	25,254	20,581	8,729	81.5	34.6	42.4	3,365	13.3	20,779	42.7	66.9
1993r	25,522	20,844	8,630	81.7	33.8	41.4	3,349	13.1	21,060	41.6	65.3
1993	24,100	19,772	8,193	82.0	34.0	41.4	3,070	12.7	19,979	41.6	65.4
1992	24,278	19,921	8,343	82.1	34.4	41.9	3,083	12.7	20,194	42.3	65.6
1991	24,572	19,883	8,172	80.9	33.3	41.1	3,486	14.2	20,065	41.4	60.7
1990	24,852	20,311	7,964	82.3	32.0	39.1	3,379	13.6	20,571	39.6	58.9
1989	25,261	20,461	7,804	81.0	30.9	38.1	3,644	14.4	20,749	38.5	57.9
1988	25,733	20,900	7,791	81.2	30.3	37.3	3,749	14.6	21,204	37.6	57.4
1987	25,950	21,118	7,693	81.4	29.6	36.4	3,751	14.5	21,477	36.9	56.2
1986	26,512	21,768	7,477	82.1	28.2	34.3	3,687	13.9	22,086	34.8	55.0
1985	27,122	22,349	7,537	82.4	27.8	33.7	3,687	13.9	22,722	34.3	54.3
1984	28,031	22,870	7,591	81.6	27.1	33.2	4,142	14.8	23,252	33.7	53.0
1983	28,580	22,988	7,477	80.4	26.2	32.5	4,410	15.4	23,359	33.1	52.8
1982	28,846	23,291	7,678	80.7	26.6	33.0	4,500	15.6	23,708	33.5	52.7
1981	28,965	23,343	7,575	80.6	26.2	32.5	4,520	15.6	23,705	32.9	51.7
1980	28,957	23,413	7,400	80.9	25.6	31.6	4,515	15.6	23,856	32.1	51.1
1979	27,974	22,421	6,991	80.1	25.0	31.2	4,560	16.3	22,911	31.9	51.6
1978	27,647	22,309	6,995	80.7	25.3	31.4	4,388	15.9	22,759	31.9	51.4
1977	27,331	22,008	7,142	80.5	26.1	32.5	4,313	15.8	22,499	33.0	52.0
1976	26,919	21,677	7,181	80.5	26.7	33.1	4,276	15.9	22,158	33.7	53.4
1975	26,387	21,326	6,935	80.8	26.3	32.5	4,110	15.6	21,824	33.1	52.5
1974	25,670	20,725	6,316	80.7	24.6	30.5	4,070	15.9	21,267	31.2	51.3
1973	25,237	20,377	6,055	80.7	24.0	29.7	3,973	15.7	20,895	30.4	50.7
1972	24,579	19,618	6,257	79.8	25.5	31.9	4,068	16.6	20,107	32.6	52.9
1971	23,668	18,691	6,210	79.0	26.2	33.2	4,025	17.0	19,130	33.9	53.1
1970	22,552	17,768	5,805	78.8	25.7	32.7	3,908	17.3	18,218	33.5	52.3
1969	21,362	16,703	5,840	78.2	27.3	35.0	3,769	17.6	17,152	35.7	52.5
1968	20,562	15,683	5,356	76.3	26.0	34.2	3,929	19.1	16,165	35.2	51.5
1967	20,009	15,114	5,100	75.5	25.5	33.7	3,967	19.8	15,642	34.9	50.5
Male											
2008	14,559	12,181	5,383	83.7	37.0	44.2	1,445	9.9	12,374	44.6	66.7
2007	14,515	11,825	5,156	81.5	35.5	43.6	1,680	11.6	11,972	43.7	66.0
2006	14,300	11,508	4,874	80.5	34.1	42.4	1,741	12.2	11,659	42.5	65.1
2005	14,077	11,182	4,973	79.4	35.3	43.2	1,852	13.2	11,330	44.4	65.9
2004	14,018	11,258	4,865	80.3	34.7	43.2	1,942	13.9	11,364	43.5	65.0
2003	13,681	10,919	4,697	79.8	34.3	43.0	1,875	13.7	11,040	43.1	65.0
2002	13,744	10,823	4,629	78.7	33.7	42.8	1,925	14.0	10,975	42.9	64.6
2001	13,434	10,461	4,437	77.9	33.0	42.4	2,028	15.1	10,587	42.4	63.9
2000	13,338	10,622	4,343	79.6	32.6	40.9	1,837	13.8	10,736	41.0	63.1
1999	12,905	10,201	4,396	79.1	34.0	43.1	1,818	14.9	10,331	43.3	64.5
1998	12,764	9,915	4,403	77.7	34.5	44.4	2,018	15.8	10,006	44.5	64.9

Note: The change in the educational attainment question and the college completion categories from "4 or more years of college," to "at least some college," in 1992 caused an increase in the proportion of 14-to-24-year-old high school graduates enrolled in college or completed some college, of approximately 5 percentage points. High school graduates are people who have completed 4 years of high school or more, for 1967 to 1991. Beginning in 1992, they were people whose highest degree was a high school diploma (including equivalency) or higher.
r = Revised, controlled to 1990 census based population estimates; previous 1993 data controlled to 1980 census based population estimates.

Table A-13. Population 14 to 24 Years Old by High School Graduate Status, College Enrollment, Attainment, Sex, Race, and Hispanic Origin, October 1967–2008—*Continued*

(Numbers in thousands, percent.)

Year, race, and Hispanic origin	Population 18 to 24 years old								High school graduates, 14 to 24 years old		
	Total	High school graduates		Percent			High school dropouts		All graduates	Percent	
		Total	Enrolled in college	High school graduates	Enrolled in college	High school graduate enrolled in college	Number	Percent		Enrolled in college	Enrolled or completed some college
1997	12,513	9,933	4,374	79.4	35.0	44.0	1,765	14.1	10,025	44.2	64.9
1996	12,285	9,815	4,187	80.0	34.1	42.6	1,628	13.2	9,960	43.0	65.6
1995	12,351	9,789	4,089	79.3	33.1	41.8	1,791	14.5	9,884	42.1	64.2
1994	12,557	9,970	4,152	79.4	33.1	41.6	1,804	14.4	10,051	41.9	64.9
1993ʳ	12,712	10,142	4,237	79.8	33.3	41.8	1,745	13.7	10,229	42.0	63.9
1993	11,898	9,541	3,994	80.2	33.6	41.9	1,575	13.2	9,625	42.0	64.1
1992	11,965	9,576	3,912	80.0	32.7	40.9	1,617	13.5	9,706	41.3	64.1
1991	12,036	9,493	3,954	78.9	32.9	41.7	1,810	15.0	9,564	41.9	59.2
1990	12,134	9,778	3,922	80.6	32.3	40.1	1,689	13.9	9,894	40.5	58.0
1989	12,325	9,700	3,717	78.7	30.2	38.3	1,941	15.7	9,810	38.6	57.2
1988	12,491	9,832	3,770	78.7	30.2	38.3	1,950	15.6	9,947	38.5	56.5
1987	12,626	10,030	3,867	79.4	30.6	38.6	1,948	15.4	10,207	39.0	56.0
1986	12,921	10,338	3,702	80.0	28.7	35.8	1,924	14.9	10,465	36.2	54.4
1985	13,199	10,614	3,749	80.4	28.4	35.3	2,015	15.3	10,784	36.0	54.6
1984	13,744	10,914	3,929	79.4	28.6	36.0	2,184	15.9	11,052	36.4	53.6
1983	14,003	10,906	3,820	77.9	27.3	35.0	2,379	17.0	10,959	35.5	52.7
1982	14,083	11,120	3,837	79.0	27.2	34.5	2,329	16.5	11,295	35.0	53.0
1981	14,127	11,052	3,833	78.2	27.1	34.7	2,424	17.2	11,203	35.1	52.1
1980	14,107	11,125	3,717	78.9	26.3	33.4	2,390	16.9	11,309	33.7	51.4
1979	13,571	10,657	3,508	78.5	25.8	32.9	2,320	17.1	10,838	33.6	52.4
1978	13,385	10,614	3,621	79.3	27.1	34.1	2,200	16.4	10,789	34.5	52.6
1977	13,218	10,440	3,712	79.0	28.1	35.6	2,170	16.4	10,626	36.0	54.2
1976	13,012	10,312	3,673	79.2	28.2	35.6	2,109	16.2	10,492	36.0	55.7
1975	12,724	10,214	3,693	80.3	29.0	36.2	1,928	15.2	10,415	36.7	56.1
1974	12,315	9,835	3,411	79.9	27.7	34.7	1,958	15.9	10,073	35.3	55.6
1973	12,111	9,716	3,360	80.2	27.7	34.6	1,853	15.3	9,908	35.1	55.4
1972	11,712	9,247	3,534	79.0	30.2	38.2	1,898	16.2	9,461	38.8	59.0
1971	11,092	8,669	3,599	78.2	32.4	41.5	1,865	16.8	8,855	42.1	60.1
1970	10,385	8,087	3,331	77.9	32.1	41.2	1,746	16.8	8,279	41.8	59.2
1969	9,649	7,445	3,392	77.2	35.2	45.6	1,640	17.0	7,609	46.2	61.2
1968	9,251	6,864	3,152	74.2	34.1	45.9	1,777	19.2	8,038	46.7	61.1
1967	8,999	6,678	2,982	74.2	33.1	44.7	1,804	20.0	6,829	45.1	58.8
Female											
2008	14,391	12,387	6,083	86.1	42.3	49.1	1,257	8.7	12,548	49.3	74.5
2007	14,263	12,321	6,005	86.4	42.1	48.7	1,256	8.8	12,519	48.8	73.3
2006	14,073	11,922	5,712	84.7	40.6	47.9	1,387	9.9	12,141	48.1	73.3
2005	13,778	11,921	5,861	86.5	42.5	55.8	1,302	9.5	12,115	49.4	73.4
2004	13,930	11,828	5,746	84.9	41.2	48.6	1,444	10.4	12,015	48.8	72.8
2003	13,724	11,684	5,667	85.1	41.3	48.5	1,354	9.9	11,858	48.5	72.2
2002	13,623	11,496	5,404	84.4	39.7	47.0	1,450	10.6	11,664	47.3	70.3
2001	13,531	11,375	5,192	84.1	38.4	45.7	1,491	11.0	11,549	45.7	69.4
2000	13,319	11,200	5,109	84.1	38.4	45.6	1,478	11.1	11,344	45.8	70.1
1999	13,136	10,926	4,863	83.2	37.0	44.5	1,594	12.1	11,058	44.6	69.8
1998	12,743	10,651	4,919	83.6	38.6	46.2	1,526	12.0	10,768	46.4	70.7
1997	12,460	10,403	4,829	83.5	38.8	46.4	1,471	11.8	10,549	46.8	69.6
1996	12,386	10,317	4,582	83.3	37.0	44.4	1,519	12.3	10,507	44.9	68.6
1995	12,548	10,338	4,452	82.4	35.5	43.1	1,679	13.4	10,477	43.4	69.8
1994	12,696	10,611	4,576	83.6	36.0	43.1	1,561	12.3	10,729	43.4	68.7
1993ʳ	12,810	10,702	4,393	83.5	34.3	41.0	1,604	12.5	10,831	41.3	66.6
1993	12,202	10,232	4,199	83.9	34.4	41.0	1,494	12.2	10,355	41.2	66.7
1992	12,313	10,344	4,429	84.0	36.0	42.8	1,466	11.9	10,486	43.3	66.9
1991	12,536	10,391	4,218	82.9	33.6	40.6	1,676	13.4	10,502	41.0	62.1
1990	12,718	10,533	4,042	82.8	31.8	38.4	1,690	13.3	10,676	38.7	59.8
1989	12,936	10,758	4,085	83.2	31.6	38.0	1,702	13.2	10,936	38.4	58.6
1988	13,242	11,068	4,021	83.6	30.4	36.3	1,799	13.5	11,257	36.8	58.2
1987	13,324	11,086	3,826	83.2	28.7	34.5	1,803	13.5	11,268	35.0	56.4
1986	13,591	11,430	3,775	84.1	27.8	33.0	1,751	12.9	11,623	33.5	55.5
1985	13,923	11,736	3,788	84.3	27.2	32.3	1,804	13.0	11,937	32.8	54.0

Note: The change in the educational attainment question and the college completion categories from "4 or more years of college," to "at least some college," in 1992 caused an increase in the proportion of 14-to-24-year-old high school graduates enrolled in college or completed some college, of approximately 5 percentage points. High school graduates are people who have completed 4 years of high school or more, for 1967 to 1991. Beginning in 1992, they were people whose highest degree was a high school diploma (including equivalency) or higher.

r = Revised, controlled to 1990 census based population estimates; previous 1993 data controlled to 1980 census based population estimates.

Table A-13. Population 14 to 24 Years Old by High School Graduate Status, College Enrollment, Attainment, Sex, Race, and Hispanic Origin, October 1967–2008—*Continued*

(Numbers in thousands, percent.)

| Year, race, and Hispanic origin | Total | Population 18 to 24 years old | | | | | | | | High school graduates, 14 to 24 years old | | |
| | | High school graduates | | Percent | | | High school dropouts | | | Percent | |
		Total	Enrolled in college	High school graduates	Enrolled in college	High school graduate enrolled in college	Number	Percent	All graduates	Enrolled in college	Enrolled or completed some college
1984	14,287	11,956	3,662	83.7	25.6	30.6	1,958	13.7	12,199	31.3	52.4
1983	14,577	12,082	3,657	82.9	25.1	30.3	2,031	13.9	12,294	31.0	52.8
1982	14,763	12,171	3,841	82.4	26.0	31.6	2,171	14.7	12,411	32.1	52.4
1981	14,838	12,290	3,741	82.8	25.2	30.4	2,097	14.1	12,503	31.0	51.3
1980	14,851	12,287	3,682	82.7	24.8	30.0	2,124	14.3	12,547	30.6	50.8
1979	14,403	11,763	3,482	81.7	24.2	29.6	2,240	15.6	12,074	30.4	50.8
1978	14,262	11,694	3,373	82.0	23.7	28.8	2,188	15.3	11,969	29.6	50.3
1977	14,113	11,569	3,431	82.0	24.3	29.7	2,143	15.2	11,875	30.3	50.0
1976	13,907	11,365	3,508	81.7	25.2	30.9	2,168	15.6	11,666	31.6	51.4
1975	13,663	11,113	3,243	81.3	23.7	29.2	2,181	16.0	11,407	29.9	49.2
1974	13,355	10,889	2,905	81.5	21.8	26.7	2,112	15.8	11,194	27.4	47.5
1973	13,126	10,663	2,696	81.2	20.5	25.3	2,119	16.1	10,986	26.1	46.5
1972	12,867	10,371	2,724	80.6	21.2	26.3	2,170	16.9	10,644	27.0	47.4
1971	12,576	10,020	2,610	79.7	20.8	26.0	2,159	17.2	10,272	26.9	47.1
1970	12,167	9,680	2,474	79.6	20.3	25.6	2,163	17.8	9,908	26.3	46.6
1969	11,713	9,259	2,448	79.0	20.9	26.4	2,128	18.2	9,499	27.1	45.7
1968	11,311	8,820	2,205	78.0	19.5	25.0	2,150	19.0	9,072	25.9	44.4
1967	11,011	8,436	2,117	76.6	19.2	25.1	2,162	19.6	8,694	26.0	44.7
WHITE ALONE											
Both Sexes											
2008	22,530	19,334	9,141	85.8	40.6	47.3	1,991	8.8	19,586	47.5	71.6
2007	22,392	18,913	8,780	84.5	39.2	46.4	2,248	10.0	19,170	46.5	70.3
2006	22,169	18,489	8,298	83.4	37.4	44.9	2,399	10.8	18,751	45.1	69.9
2005	21,777	18,130	8,498	83.3	39.0	50.4	2,466	11.3	18,352	46.9	70.0
2004	21,896	18,213	8,351	82.6	38.0	45.9	2,599	11.9	18,414	46.1	69.1
2003[1]	21,502	17,901	8,150	83.3	37.9	45.5	2,489	11.6	18,123	45.5	69.1
2002	21,704	17,793	7,921	82.0	36.5	44.5	2,641	12.2	17,995	44.6	67.5
2001	21,372	17,348	7,548	81.2	35.3	43.5	2,865	13.4	17,547	43.5	67.0
2000	21,257	17,512	7,566	82.4	35.6	43.2	2,598	12.2	17,714	43.4	66.9
1999	20,866	17,052	7,447	81.7	35.7	43.7	2,680	12.8	17,220	43.8	67.5
1998	20,465	16,701	7,541	81.6	36.9	45.2	2,810	13.7	16,855	45.3	68.3
1997	20,020	16,557	7,495	82.7	37.4	45.3	2,476	12.4	16,733	45.6	67.7
1996	19,676	16,199	7,123	82.3	36.2	44.0	2,458	12.5	16,436	44.3	68.4
1995	19,866	16,269	7,011	81.9	35.3	43.1	2,711	13.6	16,439	43.4	68.3
1994	20,171	16,670	7,118	82.6	35.3	42.7	2,553	12.7	16,814	42.9	67.6
1993r	20,493	16,989	7,074	82.9	34.5	41.6	2,595	12.7	17,161	41.8	66.5
1993	19,430	16,196	6,763	83.4	34.8	41.8	2,369	12.2	16,361	41.9	66.7
1992	19,671	16,379	6,916	83.3	35.2	42.2	2,398	12.2	16,586	42.7	67.0
1991	19,980	16,324	6,813	81.7	34.1	41.7	2,845	14.2	16,467	42.0	62.3
1990	20,393	16,823	6,635	82.5	32.5	39.4	2,751	13.5	17,022	39.8	60.1
1989	20,825	17,089	6,631	82.1	31.8	38.8	2,926	14.1	17,329	39.1	58.9
1988	21,261	17,491	6,659	82.3	31.3	38.1	3,012	14.2	17,720	38.4	58.5
1987	21,493	17,689	6,483	82.3	30.2	36.6	3,042	14.2	17,982	37.1	56.8
1986	22,020	18,291	6,307	83.1	28.6	34.5	2,961	13.4	18,554	34.9	55.5
1985	22,632	18,916	6,500	83.6	28.7	34.4	3,050	13.5	19,229	35.0	55.3
1984	23,347	19,373	6,256	83.0	28.0	33.7	3,281	14.1	19,686	34.2	53.8
1983	23,899	19,643	6,463	82.2	27.0	32.9	3,428	14.3	19,948	33.5	53.4
1982	24,206	19,944	6,694	82.4	27.2	33.1	3,523	14.6	20,292	33.6	53.1
1981	24,486	20,123	6,549	82.2	26.7	32.5	3,590	14.7	20,439	33.0	52.1
1980	24,482	20,214	6,423	82.6	26.2	31.8	3,525	14.4	20,583	32.3	51.4
1979	23,895	19,616	6,120	82.1	25.6	31.2	3,571	14.9	20,033	31.8	51.7
1978	23,650	19,526	6,077	82.6	25.7	31.1	3,464	14.6	19,911	31.7	51.3
1977	23,430	19,291	6,209	82.3	26.5	32.2	3,445	14.7	19,712	32.6	52.1
1976	23,119	19,045	6,276	82.4	27.1	33.0	3,407	14.7	19,462	33.5	53.5
1975	22,703	18,883	6,116	83.2	26.9	32.4	3,149	13.9	19,298	33.0	52.7
1974	22,141	18,318	5,589	82.7	25.2	30.5	3,212	14.5	18,794	31.2	51.7

Note: The change in the educational attainment question and the college completion categories from "4 or more years of college," to "at least some college," in 1992 caused an increase in the proportion of 14-to-24-year-old high school graduates enrolled in college or completed some college, of approximately 5 percentage points. High school graduates are people who have completed 4 years of high school or more, for 1967 to 1991. Beginning in 1992, they were people whose highest degree was a high school diploma (including equivalency) or higher.
[1]Starting in 2003 respondents could identify more than one race. Except as noted, the race data in this table from 2003 onward represent those respondents who indicated only one race category.
r = Revised, controlled to 1990 census based population estimates; previous 1993 data controlled to 1980 census based population estimates.

Table A-13.   Population 14 to 24 Years Old by High School Graduate Status, College Enrollment, Attainment, Sex, Race, and Hispanic Origin, October 1967–2008—*Continued*

(Numbers in thousands, percent.)

Year, race, and Hispanic origin	Population 18 to 24 years old								High school graduates, 14 to 24 years old		
	Total	High school graduates		Percent			High school dropouts		All graduates	Percent	
		Total	Enrolled in college	High school graduates	Enrolled in college	High school graduate enrolled in college	Number	Percent		Enrolled in college	Enrolled or completed some college
1973..............................	21,766	18,023	5,438	82.8	25.0	30.2	3,085	14.2	18,470	30.8	51.6
1972..............................	21,315	17,410	5,624	81.7	26.4	32.3	3,241	15.2	17,838	33.0	53.9
1971..............................	20,533	16,593	5,594	81.3	27.2	33.5	3,156	15.4	17,087	34.2	54.1
1970..............................	19,608	15,960	5,305	81.4	27.1	33.2	2,974	15.2	16,334	33.9	53.4
1969..............................	18,606	15,031	5,347	80.8	28.7	35.6	2,915	15.7	15,383	36.2	53.5
1968..............................	17,951	14,127	4,929	78.7	27.5	34.9	3,107	17.3	14,506	35.7	52.5
1967..............................	17,500	13,657	4,708	78.0	26.9	34.5	3,141	17.9	14,022	35.2	51.4
Male											
2008..............................	11,432	9,646	4,340	84.4	38.0	45.0	1,122	9.8	9,784	45.2	67.8
2007..............................	11,387	9,311	4,040	81.8	35.5	43.4	1,333	11.7	9,430	43.5	66.0
2006..............................	11,264	9,139	3,842	81.1	34.1	42.0	1,396	12.4	9,237	42.2	66.0
2005..............................	11,116	8,885	3,924	79.9	35.3	44.1	1,469	13.2	8,986	44.1	65.9
2004	11,107	9,001	3,855	81.0	34.7	42.8	1,524	13.7	9,067	43.1	64.4
2003[1]...........................	10,885	8,763	3,726	80.5	34.2	42.5	1,452	13.3	8,862	42.6	65.1
2002..............................	10,986	8,717	3,701	79.4	33.7	42.5	1,506	13.7	8,833	42.5	64.6
2001..............................	10,817	8,490	3,521	78.5	32.6	41.5	1,659	15.3	8,582	41.5	64.0
2000..............................	10,739	8,603	3,522	80.1	32.8	40.9	1,450	13.5	8,690	41.1	63.5
1999..............................	10,532	8,382	3,585	79.6	34.0	42.7	1,462	13.9	8,457	42.8	64.8
1998..............................	10,400	8,194	3,634	78.8	34.9	44.3	1,628	15.7	8,256	44.4	65.5
1997..............................	10,173	8,204	3,633	80.6	35.7	44.3	1,406	13.8	8,274	44.5	65.3
1996..............................	9,897	8,000	3,419	80.8	34.5	42.7	1,275	12.9	8,104	43.0	66.0
1995..............................	9,980	8,001	3,398	80.2	34.0	42.5	1,430	14.3	8,067	42.7	65.3
1994..............................	10,123	8,168	3,406	80.7	33.6	41.7	1,377	13.6	8,227	41.9	66.4
1993[1]...........................	10,294	8,338	3,498	81.0	34.0	42.0	1,388	13.5	8,411	42.1	65.1
1993..............................	9,641	7,857	3,313	81.5	34.4	42.2	1,379	12.9	7,926	42.3	65.4
1992..............................	9,744	7,911	3,291	81.2	33.8	41.6	1,300	13.3	8,016	42.1	65.8
1991..............................	9,896	7,843	3,270	79.3	33.0	41.7	1,520	15.4	7,899	41.9	59.9
1990..............................	10,053	8,157	3,292	81.1	32.7	40.3	1,430	14.2	8,246	40.7	58.8
1989..............................	10,240	8,177	3,223	79.9	31.5	39.4	1,572	15.4	8,271	39.7	58.5
1988..............................	10,380	8,268	3,260	79.7	31.4	39.4	1,594	15.4	8,365	39.6	57.8
1987..............................	10,549	8,498	3,289	80.6	31.2	38.7	1,593	15.1	8,647	39.2	56.4
1986..............................	10,814	8,780	3,168	81.2	29.3	36.1	1,575	14.6	8,886	36.4	55.1
1985..............................	11,108	9,077	3,254	81.7	29.3	35.8	1,637	14.7	9,229	36.6	55.5
1984..............................	11,521	9,348	3,406	81.1	29.6	36.4	1,744	15.1	9,459	36.8	54.2
1983..............................	11,787	9,411	3,335	79.8	28.3	35.4	1,865	15.8	9,534	35.9	53.5
1982..............................	11,874	9,611	3,308	80.9	27.9	34.4	1,810	15.2	9,761	34.9	53.2
1981..............................	12,040	9,619	3,340	79.9	27.7	34.7	1,960	16.3	9,754	35.1	52.8
1980..............................	12,011	9,686	3,275	80.6	27.3	33.8	1,883	15.7	9,838	34.1	51.8
1979..............................	11,721	9,457	3,104	80.7	26.5	32.8	1,830	15.6	9,615	33.4	52.7
1978..............................	11,572	9,438	3,195	81.6	27.6	33.9	1,722	14.9	9,582	34.3	52.5
1977..............................	11,445	9,263	3,286	80.9	28.7	35.5	1,779	15.5	9,422	35.8	54.5
1976..............................	11,279	9,186	3,250	81.4	28.8	35.4	1,691	15.0	9,340	35.7	55.9
1975..............................	11,050	9,139	3,326	82.7	30.1	36.4	1,490	13.5	9,310	36.9	56.6
1974..............................	10,722	8,768	3,035	81.8	28.3	34.6	1,579	14.7	8,980	35.2	55.9
1973..............................	10,511	8,637	3,032	82.2	28.8	35.1	1,453	13.8	8,817	35.6	56.5
1972..............................	10,212	8,278	3,195	81.1	31.3	38.6	1,506	14.7	8,462	39.2	60.1
1971..............................	9,653	7,807	3,284	80.9	34.0	42.1	1,429	14.8	7,978	42.6	61.4
1970..............................	9,053	7,324	3,096	80.9	34.2	42.3	1,297	14.3	7,496	42.9	60.9
1969..............................	8,420	6,740	3,146	80.0	37.4	46.7	1,248	14.8	6,882	47.3	62.8
1968..............................	8,084	6,221	2,949	77.0	36.5	47.4	1,401	17.3	6,372	48.1	62.7
1967..............................	7,864	6,073	2,761	77.2	35.1	45.5	1,391	17.7	6,210	45.9	60.0
Female											
2008..............................	11,098	9,688	4,801	87.3	43.3	49.6	869	7.8	9,802	49.9	75.4
2007..............................	11,005	9,603	4,741	87.3	43.1	49.4	915	8.3	9,741	49.5	74.4
2006..............................	10,905	9,350	4,456	85.7	40.9	47.7	1,003	9.2	9,513	47.9	73.7
2005..............................	10,661	9,245	4,574	86.7	42.9	57.3	997	9.4	9,366	49.7	73.9

Note: The change in the educational attainment question and the college completion categories from "4 or more years of college," to "at least some college," in 1992 caused an increase in the proportion of 14-to-24-year-old high school graduates enrolled in college or completed some college, of approximately 5 percentage points. High school graduates are people who have completed 4 years of high school or more, for 1967 to 1991. Beginning in 1992, they were people whose highest degree was a high school diploma (including equivalency) or higher.
[1]Starting in 2003 respondents could identify more than one race. Except as noted, the race data in this table from 2003 onward represent those respondents who indicated only one race category.
r = Revised, controlled to 1990 census based population estimates; previous 1993 data controlled to 1980 census based population estimates.

Table A-13. Population 14 to 24 Years Old by High School Graduate Status, College Enrollment, Attainment, Sex, Race, and Hispanic Origin, October 1967–2008—*Continued*

(Numbers in thousands, percent.)

Year, race, and Hispanic origin	Population 18 to 24 years old								High school graduates, 14 to 24 years old		
	Total	High school graduates		Percent			High school dropouts		All graduates	Percent	
		Total	Enrolled in college	High school graduates	Enrolled in college	High school graduate enrolled in college	Number	Percent		Enrolled in college	Enrolled or completed some college
2004	10,789	9,212	4,496	85.4	41.7	48.8	1,075	10.0	9,347	49.0	73.5
2003¹.............................	10,617	9,138	4,424	86.1	41.7	48.4	1,037	9.8	9,260	48.3	72.9
2002.............................	10,718	9,075	4,220	84.7	39.4	46.5	1,135	10.6	9,162	46.6	70.4
2001.............................	10,555	8,859	4,027	83.9	38.1	45.5	1,206	11.4	8,965	45.5	69.8
2000.............................	10,517	8,909	4,044	84.7	38.5	45.4	1,148	10.9	9,024	45.6	70.2
1999.............................	10,334	8,671	3,862	83.9	37.4	44.5	1,218	11.8	8,763	44.7	70.1
1998.............................	10,065	8,507	3,907	84.5	38.8	45.9	1,181	11.7	8,599	46.2	71.0
1997.............................	9,847	8,352	3,863	84.8	39.2	46.3	1,072	10.9	8,458	46.6	70.1
1996.............................	9,778	8,200	3,705	83.9	37.9	45.2	1,182	12.1	8,333	45.6	70.7
1995.............................	9,886	8,271	3,615	83.7	36.6	43.7	1,281	13.0	8,376	44.0	71.3
1994.............................	10,048	8,503	3,714	84.6	37.0	43.7	1,175	11.7	8,588	43.9	69.7
1993ʳ.............................	10,199	8,651	3,576	84.8	35.1	41.3	1,207	11.8	8,750	41.5	67.9
1993.............................	9,790	8,339	3,450	85.2	35.2	41.4	1,125	11.5	8,435	41.6	68.0
1992.............................	9,928	8,468	3,625	85.3	36.5	42.8	1,098	11.1	8,569	43.2	68.1
1991.............................	10,119	8,481	3,544	83.8	35.0	41.8	1,324	13.1	8,568	42.1	64.5
1990.............................	10,340	8,666	3,344	83.8	32.3	38.6	1,322	12.8	8,775	38.9	61.4
1989.............................	10,586	8,913	3,409	84.2	32.2	38.2	1,354	12.8	9,059	38.6	59.2
1988.............................	10,881	9,223	3,399	84.8	31.2	36.9	1,418	13.0	9,355	37.3	59.1
1987.............................	10,944	9,189	3,192	84.0	29.2	34.7	1,449	13.2	9,334	36.2	57.2
1986.............................	11,205	9,509	3,139	84.9	28.0	33.0	1,388	12.4	9,667	33.6	55.8
1985.............................	11,524	9,840	3,247	85.4	28.2	33.0	1,413	12.3	10,001	33.6	55.2
1984.............................	11,826	10,026	3,120	84.8	26.4	31.1	1,535	13.0	10,089	31.8	53.4
1983.............................	12,112	10,233	3,129	84.5	25.8	30.6	1,563	12.9	10,233	31.3	53.4
1982.............................	12,332	10,333	3,285	83.8	26.6	31.8	1,713	13.0	10,530	32.3	52.9
1981.............................	12,446	10,504	3,208	84.4	25.8	30.5	1,629	13.1	10,687	31.1	51.6
1980.............................	12,471	10,528	3,147	84.4	25.2	29.9	1,642	13.2	10,749	30.6	50.9
1979.............................	12,174	10,157	3,015	83.4	24.8	29.7	1,741	14.3	10,417	30.3	50.8
1978.............................	12,078	10,088	2,882	83.5	23.9	28.6	1,742	14.4	10,327	29.3	50.3
1977.............................	11,985	10,029	2,923	83.7	24.4	29.1	1,666	13.9	10,292	29.7	50.0
1976.............................	11,840	9,860	3,026	83.3	25.6	30.7	1,717	14.5	10,118	31.4	51.3
1975.............................	11,653	9,743	2,790	83.6	23.9	28.6	1,658	14.2	9,986	29.4	49.1
1974.............................	11,419	9,551	2,555	83.6	22.4	26.8	1,633	14.3	9,811	27.5	47.8
1973.............................	11,255	9,387	2,406	83.4	21.4	25.6	1,632	14.5	9,653	26.4	47.1
1972.............................	11,103	9,132	2,428	82.2	21.9	26.6	1,735	15.6	9,377	27.4	48.3
1971.............................	10,880	8,887	2,310	81.7	21.2	26.0	1,726	15.9	9,107	26.8	47.7
1970.............................	10,555	8,634	2,209	81.8	20.9	25.6	1,675	15.9	8,837	26.3	47.2
1969.............................	10,186	8,291	2,200	81.4	21.6	26.5	1,668	16.4	8,501	27.2	46.3
1968.............................	9,866	7,906	1,980	80.1	20.1	25.0	1,706	17.3	8,135	26.0	45.1
1967.............................	9,637	7,586	1,949	78.7	20.2	25.7	1,750	18.2	7,815	26.6	45.7
WHITE ALONE NON-HISPANIC											
Both Sexes											
2008.............................	17,839	16,038	7,894	89.9	44.2	49.2	960	5.4	16,224	49.4	74.2
2007.............................	17,669	15,727	7,533	89.0	42.6	47.9	1,064	6.0	15,921	48.0	72.9
2006.............................	17,565	15,452	7,200	88.0	41.0	46.6	1,189	6.8	15,642	46.8	72.5
2005.............................	17,293	15,187	7,393	87.8	42.8	54.9	1,216	7.0	15,368	48.7	72.6
2004.............................	17,326	15,224	7,228	87.9	41.7	47.5	1,313	7.6	15,382	47.7	71.8
2003¹.............................	17,158	15,070	7,129	87.8	41.6	47.3	1,267	7.4	15,255	47.3	71.5
2002.............................	17,131	14,910	7,004	87.0	40.9	47.0	1,289	7.5	15,089	47.1	70.4
2001.............................	16,721	14,480	6,565	86.6	39.3	45.3	1,390	8.3	14,646	45.3	69.7
2000.............................	17,327	15,187	6,709	87.7	38.7	44.2	1,316	7.6	15,344	44.3	69.0
1999.............................	17,080	14,812	6,735	86.7	39.4	45.5	1,404	8.2	14,952	45.6	70.2
1998.............................	16,634	14,402	6,757	86.6	40.6	46.9	1,491	9.0	14,542	47.0	70.6
1997.............................	16,575	14,414	6,728	87.0	40.6	46.7	1,432	8.6	14,527	46.9	70.0
1996.............................	16,339	14,288	6,447	87.5	39.5	45.1	1,303	8.0	14,501	45.5	70.7
1995.............................	16,867	14,523	6,393	86.1	37.9	44.0	1,647	9.8	14,672	44.3	70.2
1994.............................	17,114	14,916	6,521	87.2	38.1	43.7	1,505	8.8	15,049	44.0	69.2
1993.............................	16,895	14,665	6,221	86.8	36.8	42.4	1,524	9.0	14,801	42.6	68.1

Note: The change in the educational attainment question and the college completion categories from "4 or more years of college," to "at least some college," in 1992 caused an increase in the proportion of 14-to-24-year-old high school graduates enrolled in college or completed some college, of approximately 5 percentage points. High school graduates are people who have completed 4 years of high school or more, for 1967 to 1991. Beginning in 1992, they were people whose highest degree was a high school diploma (including equivalency) or higher.
¹Starting in 2003 respondents could identify more than one race. Except as noted, the race data in this table from 2003 onward represent those respondents who indicated only one race category.
r = Revised, controlled to 1990 census based population estimates; previous 1993 data controlled to 1980 census based population estimates.

Table A-13.   Population 14 to 24 Years Old by High School Graduate Status, College Enrollment, Attainment, Sex, Race, and Hispanic Origin, October 1967–2008—*Continued*

(Numbers in thousands, percent.)

Year, race, and Hispanic origin	Population 18 to 24 years old								High school graduates, 14 to 24 years old		
	Total	High school graduates		Percent			High school dropouts		All graduates	Percent	
		Total	Enrolled in college	High school graduates	Enrolled in college	High school graduate enrolled in college	Number	Percent		Enrolled in college	Enrolled or completed some college
Male											
2008...............................	9,032	8,028	3,766	88.9	41.7	46.9	546	6.0	8,126	47.1	70.4
2007...............................	8,940	7,786	3,541	87.1	39.6	45.5	622	7.0	7,883	45.5	68.8
2006...............................	8,842	7,660	3,354	86.6	37.9	43.8	647	7.3	7,734	43.9	68.4
2005...............................	8,700	7,443	3,429	85.5	39.4	48.7	685	7.9	7,526	46.0	68.6
2004...............................	8,644	7,527	3,322	87.1	38.4	44.1	691	8.0	7,576	44.4	66.7
2003[1]............................	8,538	7,325	3,291	85.8	38.5	44.9	721	8.4	7,401	45.0	68.5
2002...............................	8,453	7,244	3,287	85.7	38.9	45.4	668	7.9	7,352	45.5	67.9
2001...............................	8,343	7,112	3,094	85.3	37.1	43.4	741	8.9	7,191	43.4	67.1
2000...............................	8,670	7,493	3,136	86.4	36.2	41.9	677	7.8	7,556	42.0	65.4
1999...............................	8,580	7,301	3,284	85.1	38.3	45.0	753	8.8	7,369	45.0	67.7
1998...............................	8,380	7,094	3,300	84.7	39.4	46.5	826	9.9	7,151	46.6	68.2
1997...............................	8,326	7,112	3,276	85.4	39.3	46.1	797	9.6	7,154	46.3	68.1
1996...............................	8,168	7,050	3,130	86.3	38.3	44.4	651	8.0	7,143	44.7	68.6
1995...............................	8,399	7,089	3,105	84.4	37.0	43.8	883	10.5	7,147	44.0	67.3
1994...............................	8,457	7,261	3,126	85.9	37.0	43.1	777	9.2	7,317	43.3	67.0
1993...............................	8,403	7,138	3,071	84.9	36.6	43.0	811	9.7	7,191	43.2	67.1
Female											
2008...............................	8,808	8,010	4,127	90.9	46.9	51.5	414	4.7	8,099	51.7	78.0
2007...............................	8,728	7,941	3,992	91.0	45.7	50.3	442	5.1	8,039	50.4	76.9
2006...............................	8,724	7,791	3,846	89.3	44.1	49.4	542	6.2	7,908	49.5	76.4
2005...............................	8,593	7,744	3,964	90.1	46.1	61.4	531	6.2	7,842	51.4	76.4
2004...............................	8,628	7,697	3,906	89.2	45.3	50.7	622	7.2	7,805	50.9	76.8
2003[1]............................	8,620	7,745	3,838	89.9	44.5	49.6	546	6.3	7,854	49.5	74.4
2002...............................	8,678	7,666	3,717	88.3	42.8	48.5	621	7.2	7,736	48.6	72.8
2001...............................	8,378	7,368	3,471	87.9	41.4	47.2	648	7.7	7,455	47.2	72.3
2000...............................	8,657	7,693	3,573	88.9	41.3	46.4	638	7.4	7,789	46.6	72.5
1999...............................	8,500	7,510	3,451	88.4	40.6	46.0	651	7.7	7,583	46.2	72.5
1998...............................	8,254	7,308	3,457	88.5	41.9	47.3	665	8.1	7,391	47.5	73.0
1997...............................	8,249	7,302	3,452	88.5	41.9	47.3	636	7.7	7,373	47.5	71.9
1996...............................	8,171	7,238	3,317	88.6	40.6	45.8	652	8.0	7,358	46.3	72.8
1995...............................	8,467	7,433	3,288	87.8	38.8	44.2	764	9.0	7,525	44.6	73.1
1994...............................	8,657	7,655	3,395	88.4	39.2	44.4	728	8.4	7,732	44.6	71.3
1993...............................	8,492	7,527	3,150	88.6	37.1	41.9	714	8.4	7,610	42.0	69.1
BLACK ALONE											
Both Sexes											
2008...............................	4,265	3,387	1,349	79.4	31.6	40.0	548	12.1	3,445	40.2	60.7
2007...............................	4,182	3,423	1,396	81.8	33.4	40.8	425	10.2	3,483	40.9	61.4
2006...............................	4,085	3,156	1,321	77.3	32.3	41.9	532	13.0	3,224	41.9	60.8
2005...............................	3,964	3,137	1,297	79.1	32.7	40.0	512	12.9	3,212	41.3	63.5
2004...............................	3,940	3,050	1,238	77.4	31.4	40.6	596	15.1	3,112	41.1	63.2
2003[1]............................	3,837	2,948	1,225	76.8	31.9	41.6	545	14.2	2,997	41.8	62.5
2002...............................	3,924	3,040	1,226	77.5	31.3	40.3	571	14.5	3,117	41.1	61.2
2001...............................	3,916	3,016	1,206	77.0	30.8	40.0	540	13.8	3,095	40.0	59.0
2000...............................	4,013	3,090	1,216	77.0	30.3	39.4	615	15.3	3,129	39.5	61.0
1999...............................	3,827	2,911	1,145	76.1	29.9	39.4	613	16.0	2,985	39.9	60.4
1998...............................	3,745	2,747	1,116	73.4	29.8	40.6	642	17.1	2,790	40.8	61.8
1997...............................	3,650	2,725	1,085	74.7	29.7	39.8	611	16.7	2,762	40.2	60.0
1996...............................	3,637	2,738	983	75.3	27.0	35.9	581	16.0	2,805	36.6	54.6
1995...............................	3,625	2,788	988	76.9	27.3	35.4	522	14.4	2,828	35.8	58.0
1994...............................	3,661	2,818	1,001	77.0	27.3	35.5	568	15.5	2,859	36.3	59.2
1993[r]............................	3,666	2,747	897	74.9	24.5	32.7	600	16.4	2,771	32.8	54.0
1993...............................	3,516	2,629	861	74.8	24.5	32.8	578	16.4	2,653	32.9	53.9
1992...............................	3,521	2,625	886	74.6	25.2	33.8	575	16.3	2,668	34.3	53.3
1991...............................	3,504	2,630	828	75.1	23.6	31.5	545	15.6	2,658	31.8	46.0

Note: The change in the educational attainment question and the college completion categories from "4 or more years of college," to "at least some college," in 1992 caused an increase in the proportion of 14-to-24-year-old high school graduates enrolled in college or completed some college, of approximately 5 percentage points. High school graduates are people who have completed 4 years of high school or more, for 1967 to 1991. Beginning in 1992, they were people whose highest degree was a high school diploma (including equivalency) or higher.
[1]Starting in 2003 respondents could identify more than one race. Except as noted, the race data in this table from 2003 onward represent those respondents who indicated only one race category.
r = Revised, controlled to 1990 census based population estimates; previous 1993 data controlled to 1980 census based population estimates.

Table A-13.   Population 14 to 24 Years Old by High School Graduate Status, College Enrollment, Attainment, Sex, Race, and Hispanic Origin, October 1967–2008—*Continued*

(Numbers in thousands, percent.)

| Year, race, and Hispanic origin | Total | Population 18 to 24 years old | | | | | | | High school graduates, 14 to 24 years old | | |
| | | High school graduates | | Percent | | | High school dropouts | | All graduates | Percent | |
		Total	Enrolled in college	High school graduates	Enrolled in college	High school graduate enrolled in college	Number	Percent		Enrolled in college	Enrolled or completed some college
1990	3,520	2,710	894	77.0	25.4	33.0	530	15.1	2,759	33.7	48.0
1989	3,559	2,708	835	76.1	23.5	30.8	583	16.4	2,750	31.5	49.2
1988	3,568	2,680	752	75.1	21.1	28.1	631	17.7	2,741	28.6	46.3
1987	3,603	2,739	823	76.0	22.8	30.0	611	17.0	2,790	30.6	48.1
1986	3,653	2,795	812	76.5	22.2	29.1	617	16.8	2,837	29.3	47.8
1985	3,716	2,810	734	75.6	19.8	26.1	655	17.6	2,848	26.5	43.8
1984	3,862	2,885	786	74.7	20.4	27.2	712	18.4	2,950	28.0	45.2
1983	3,865	2,740	741	70.9	19.2	27.0	832	21.5	2,790	27.7	45.0
1982	3,872	2,744	767	70.9	19.8	28.0	851	22.0	2,793	28.2	45.5
1981	3,778	2,678	750	70.9	19.9	28.0	821	21.7	2,718	28.7	44.8
1980	3,721	2,592	715	69.7	19.2	27.6	876	23.5	2,656	28.1	45.9
1979	3,510	2,356	696	67.1	19.8	29.5	895	25.5	2,415	30.6	48.4
1978	3,452	2,340	694	67.8	20.1	29.7	850	24.6	2,396	30.6	47.8
1977	3,387	2,286	721	67.5	21.3	31.5	808	23.9	2,342	32.4	46.9
1976	3,315	2,239	749	67.5	22.6	33.5	803	24.2	2,291	34.2	50.4
1975	3,213	2,081	665	64.8	20.7	32.0	877	27.3	2,149	32.6	48.1
1974	3,105	2,083	555	67.1	17.9	26.6	780	25.1	2,145	27.5	44.8
1973	3,114	2,079	498	66.8	16.0	24.0	826	26.5	2,139	25.0	41.6
1972	2,986	1,992	540	66.7	18.1	27.1	782	26.2	2,044	28.0	42.0
1971	2,866	1,789	522	62.4	18.2	29.2	825	28.8	1,833	30.0	42.3
1970	2,692	1,602	416	59.5	15.5	26.0	897	33.3	1,635	26.7	39.4
1969	2,542	1,497	407	58.9	16.0	27.2	828	32.6	1,547	27.5	40.1
1968	2,421	1,399	352	57.8	14.5	25.2	799	33.0	1,432	26.0	38.1
1967	2,283	1,276	297	55.9	13.0	23.3	788	34.5	1,316	23.7	35.0
Male											
2008	2,045	1,641	595	80.2	29.1	36.3	210	10.2	1,668	36.9	54.8
2007	2,011	1,622	649	80.6	32.3	40.0	202	10.0	1,642	40.1	59.3
2006	1,959	1,488	541	76.0	27.6	36.4	219	11.2	1,519	36.3	53.4
2005	1,897	1,393	530	73.4	27.9	35.0	280	14.8	1,420	37.9	58.4
2004	1,852	1,341	479	72.4	25.9	35.7	331	17.9	1,363	36.1	60.9
2003¹	1,801	1,331	499	73.9	27.7	37.5	300	16.7	1,346	37.8	57.1
2002	1,843	1,354	475	73.5	25.8	35.1	311	16.9	1,372	35.6	56.1
2001	1,818	1,287	470	70.8	25.8	36.4	308	16.9	1,310	36.4	53.1
2000	1,885	1,389	470	73.7	24.9	33.8	329	17.4	1,409	34.1	53.5
1999	1,747	1,292	501	73.9	28.7	38.8	285	16.3	1,336	40.2	57.7
1998	1,724	1,163	445	67.5	25.8	38.2	354	20.5	1,186	38.5	57.5
1997	1,701	1,214	425	71.4	25.0	35.0	297	17.5	1,232	35.1	56.3
1996	1,682	1,199	422	71.3	25.1	35.2	292	17.4	1,225	35.8	53.7
1995	1,660	1,247	430	75.1	25.9	34.4	235	14.2	1,262	35.1	56.2
1994	1,733	1,277	440	73.7	25.4	34.5	303	17.5	1,293	35.3	57.9
1993¹	1,703	1,240	387	72.8	22.7	31.2	266	15.6	1,247	31.4	50.1
1993	1,659	1,207	379	72.8	22.8	31.4	258	15.6	1,214	31.5	50.0
1992	1,676	1,211	356	72.3	21.2	29.4	259	15.5	1,226	29.7	49.4
1991	1,635	1,174	378	71.8	23.1	32.2	252	15.4	1,188	32.4	47.0
1990	1,634	1,240	426	75.9	26.1	34.4	223	13.6	1,260	35.1	48.8
1989	1,654	1,195	324	72.2	19.6	27.1	307	18.6	1,207	27.5	45.8
1988	1,653	1,189	297	71.9	18.0	25.0	312	18.9	1,205	25.1	42.5
1987	1,666	1,188	377	71.3	22.6	31.7	312	18.7	1,209	32.3	48.0
1986	1,687	1,220	349	72.3	20.7	28.6	300	17.8	1,239	29.1	44.4
1985	1,720	1,244	345	72.3	20.1	27.7	323	18.8	1,258	28.2	43.6
1984	1,811	1,272	367	70.2	20.3	28.9	362	20.2	1,295	29.6	45.2
1983	1,807	1,202	331	66.5	18.3	27.5	435	24.1	1,228	27.9	43.6
1982	1,786	1,171	331	65.6	18.5	28.3	458	25.6	1,188	28.6	44.5
1981	1,730	1,154	325	66.7	18.8	28.2	419	24.2	1,165	28.5	42.3
1980	1,690	1,115	293	66.0	17.3	26.3	440	26.0	1,141	26.9	44.1
1979	1,577	973	304	61.7	19.3	31.2	457	29.0	988	32.0	46.7
1978	1,554	956	305	61.5	19.6	31.9	451	29.0	981	32.4	49.3

Note: The change in the educational attainment question and the college completion categories from "4 or more years of college," to "at least some college," in 1992 caused an increase in the proportion of 14-to-24-year-old high school graduates enrolled in college or completed some college, of approximately 5 percentage points. High school graduates are people who have completed 4 years of high school or more, for 1967 to 1991. Beginning in 1992, they were people whose highest degree was a high school diploma (including equivalency) or higher.
¹Starting in 2003 respondents could identify more than one race. Except as noted, the race data in this table from 2003 onward represent those respondents who indicated only one race category.
r = Revised, controlled to 1990 census based population estimates; previous 1993 data controlled to 1980 census based population estimates.

Table A-13. Population 14 to 24 Years Old by High School Graduate Status, College Enrollment, Attainment, Sex, Race, and Hispanic Origin, October 1967–2008—*Continued*

(Numbers in thousands, percent.)

Year, race, and Hispanic origin	Population 18 to 24 years old								High school graduates, 14 to 24 years old		
	Total	High school graduates		Percent			High school dropouts		All graduates	Percent	
		Total	Enrolled in college	High school graduates	Enrolled in college	High school graduate enrolled in college	Number	Percent		Enrolled in college	Enrolled or completed some college
1977.................................	1,528	970	309	63.5	20.2	31.9	369	24.1	991	33.0	47.6
1976.................................	1,503	936	331	62.3	22.0	35.4	393	26.1	952	35.9	50.3
1975.................................	1,451	897	294	61.8	20.3	32.8	404	27.8	923	33.4	50.5
1974.................................	1,396	919	280	65.8	20.1	30.5	346	24.8	941	31.1	47.3
1973.................................	1,434	952	266	66.4	18.5	27.9	371	25.9	962	28.4	44.2
1972.................................	1,373	870	287	63.4	20.9	33.0	373	27.2	897	34.0	47.4
1971.................................	1,318	769	262	58.3	19.9	34.1	416	31.6	783	34.9	45.8
1970.................................	1,220	668	192	54.8	15.7	28.7	436	35.7	684	29.5	41.4
1969.................................	1,141	631	202	55.3	17.7	32.0	383	33.6	653	32.5	44.6
1968.................................	1,087	582	170	53.5	15.6	29.2	370	34.0	600	30.3	43.2
1967.................................	1,032	525	167	50.9	16.2	31.8	397	38.5	539	32.3	41.6
Female											
2008.................................	2,220	1,746	754	78.7	34.0	43.2	304	13.7	1,777	43.3	66.2
2007.................................	2,171	1,801	747	82.9	34.4	41.5	223	10.3	1,841	41.5	63.3
2006.................................	2,126	1,668	780	78.5	36.7	46.7	313	14.7	1,705	46.9	67.3
2005.................................	2,067	1,745	767	84.4	37.1	44.9	232	11.2	1,793	44.0	67.5
2004.................................	2,088	1,709	759	81.8	36.3	44.4	266	12.7	1,749	44.9	65.0
2003[1]...............................	2,035	1,618	726	79.5	35.7	44.9	245	12.0	1,652	45.1	66.8
2002.................................	2,081	1,686	751	81.0	36.1	44.5	260	12.5	1,745	45.5	65.2
2001.................................	2,098	1,729	736	82.4	35.1	42.7	232	11.0	1,785	42.7	63.3
2000.................................	2,128	1,700	747	79.9	35.1	43.9	287	13.5	1,720	43.9	67.1
1999.................................	2,080	1,619	644	77.9	31.0	39.8	327	15.7	1,650	39.6	62.6
1998.................................	2,021	1,584	671	78.4	33.2	42.4	288	14.3	1,604	42.4	65.0
1997.................................	1,949	1,511	659	77.5	33.8	43.6	314	16.1	1,529	43.1	63.0
1996.................................	1,956	1,539	561	78.7	28.7	36.4	288	14.7	1,580	37.3	55.3
1995.................................	1,965	1,541	558	78.4	28.4	36.2	287	14.6	1,566	36.3	59.5
1994.................................	1,928	1,542	561	80.0	29.1	36.4	265	13.7	1,567	37.1	60.3
1993[r]..............................	1,965	1,508	511	76.7	26.0	33.9	337	17.2	1,526	34.1	57.2
1993.................................	1,857	1,425	484	76.7	26.1	34.0	319	17.2	1,441	34.1	57.1
1992.................................	1,845	1,417	531	76.8	28.8	37.5	315	17.1	1,446	38.2	56.6
1991.................................	1,869	1,455	450	77.8	24.1	30.9	296	15.8	1,468	31.4	45.2
1990.................................	1,886	1,468	467	77.8	24.8	31.8	306	16.2	1,498	32.4	47.3
1989.................................	1,905	1,511	511	79.3	26.8	33.8	277	14.5	1,541	34.7	51.8
1988.................................	1,915	1,492	455	77.9	23.8	30.5	318	16.6	1,538	31.3	49.2
1987.................................	1,937	1,550	445	80.0	23.0	28.7	298	15.4	1,579	29.4	48.9
1986.................................	1,966	1,574	462	80.1	23.5	29.4	306	15.6	1,598	29.3	50.4
1985.................................	1,996	1,565	389	78.4	19.5	24.9	332	16.6	1,592	25.1	44.0
1984.................................	2,052	1,613	419	78.6	20.4	26.0	349	17.0	1,655	26.8	45.1
1983.................................	2,058	1,539	411	74.8	20.0	26.7	398	19.3	1,561	27.5	46.3
1982.................................	2,086	1,572	436	75.4	20.9	27.7	393	18.8	1,604	27.9	46.3
1981.................................	2,049	1,526	424	74.5	20.7	27.8	402	19.6	1,554	28.8	46.6
1980.................................	2,031	1,475	422	72.6	20.8	28.6	436	21.5	1,511	29.1	47.4
1979.................................	1,934	1,383	392	71.5	20.3	28.3	439	22.7	1,426	29.7	49.8
1978.................................	1,897	1,384	390	73.0	20.6	28.2	398	21.0	1,415	29.3	46.7
1977.................................	1,859	1,317	413	70.8	22.2	31.4	439	23.6	1,354	31.9	46.2
1976.................................	1,813	1,302	417	71.8	23.0	32.0	410	22.6	1,338	32.9	50.3
1975.................................	1,761	1,182	372	67.1	21.1	31.5	473	26.9	1,224	32.0	46.4
1974.................................	1,709	1,167	277	68.3	16.2	23.7	434	25.4	1,207	24.8	42.9
1973.................................	1,681	1,125	231	66.9	13.7	20.5	456	27.1	1,177	22.2	39.4
1972.................................	1,613	1,123	253	69.6	15.7	22.5	408	25.3	1,150	23.2	37.9
1971.................................	1,547	1,019	259	65.9	16.7	25.4	409	26.4	1,049	26.4	39.8
1970.................................	1,471	935	225	63.6	15.3	24.1	461	31.3	955	24.7	39.3
1969.................................	1,402	867	206	61.8	14.7	23.8	444	31.7	896	24.0	38.6
1968.................................	1,334	819	183	61.4	13.7	22.3	430	32.2	834	22.9	35.9
1967.................................	1,249	751	130	60.1	10.4	17.3	391	31.3	778	17.9	33.2

Note: The change in the educational attainment question and the college completion categories from "4 or more years of college," to "at least some college," in 1992 caused an increase in the proportion of 14-to-24-year-old high school graduates enrolled in college or completed some college, of approximately 5 percentage points. High school graduates are people who have completed 4 years of high school or more, for 1967 to 1991. Beginning in 1992, they were people whose highest degree was a high school diploma (including equivalency) or higher.

[1]Starting in 2003 respondents could identify more than one race. Except as noted, the race data in this table from 2003 onward represent those respondents who indicated only one race category.

r = Revised, controlled to 1990 census based population estimates; previous 1993 data controlled to 1980 census based population estimates.

Table A-13. Population 14 to 24 Years Old by High School Graduate Status, College Enrollment, Attainment, Sex, Race, and Hispanic Origin, October 1967–2008—*Continued*

(Numbers in thousands, percent.)

Year, race, and Hispanic origin	Population 18 to 24 years old								High school graduates, 14 to 24 years old		
		High school graduates		Percent			High school dropouts			Percent	
	Total	Total	Enrolled in college	High school graduates	Enrolled in college	High school graduate enrolled in college	Number	Percent	All graduates	Enrolled in college	Enrolled or completed some college
ASIAN ALONE[2]											
Both Sexes											
2008	1,113	1,021	655	91.8	58.9	64.1	42	3.8	1,056	64.6	90.4
2007	1,165	1,010	658	86.7	56.4	65.1	86	7.4	1,026	65.1	91.6
2006	1,148	1,046	661	91.1	57.6	63.2	46	4.0	1,064	63.0	87.0
2005	1,145	1,072	693	93.6	60.5	74.9	34	3.0	1,098	65.1	87.0
2004	1,152	1,066	695	92.5	60.3	65.2	49	4.3	1,090	65.7	89.1
2003[1]	1,144	1,030	693	90.1	60.6	67.3	56	4.9	1,046	67.7	88.2
2002	1,339	1,230	803	91.8	60.0	65.3	57	4.2	1,265	65.7	86.9
2001	1,312	1,197	794	91.2	60.5	66.5	47	3.6	1,218	66.5	87.6
2000	1,143	1,038	639	90.8	55.9	61.6	52	4.6	1,053	61.8	83.9
1999	1,130	1,019	626	90.2	55.4	61.4	58	5.1	1,035	62.0	85.5
Male											
2008	547	487	295	89.1	53.9	60.5	21	3.9	510	62.0	89.9
2007	560	481	318	85.8	56.9	66.3	38	6.8	483	66.4	91.8
2006	591	525	338	88.8	57.2	64.4	34	5.8	536	64.0	84.0
2005	590	552	366	93.5	62.0	68.9	17	2.9	565	66.4	88.2
2004	586	549	373	93.7	63.6	67.9	15	2.5	561	68.4	88.2
2003[1]	543	483	337	88.9	62.0	69.8	43	7.8	486	69.9	90.0
2002	707	637	417	90.0	59.0	65.5	38	5.4	652	65.3	86.7
2001	661	583	417	88.1	63.1	72.0	35	5.3	594	72.0	88.9
2000	571	521	337	91.1	58.9	64.7	34	6.0	527	64.7	85.6
1999	505	443	284	87.8	56.2	64.0	39	7.7	454	64.9	82.5
Female											
2008	566	534	360	94.4	63.7	67.5	21	3.6	546	67.0	90.9
2007	605	529	339	87.4	56.0	64.1	48	7.9	543	63.9	91.5
2006	557	521	324	93.6	58.1	62.2	11	2.1	528	61.9	90.0
2005	555	521	327	93.8	58.9	81.4	17	3.0	533	63.7	85.8
2004	567	517	323	91.3	56.9	62.4	35	6.1	529	62.8	90.0
2003[1]	601	547	356	91.2	59.3	65.1	13	2.2	561	65.9	86.7
2002	632	593	386	93.8	61.0	65.1	19	2.9	613	66.1	87.2
2001	651	614	377	94.3	57.9	61.3	12	1.8	625	61.3	86.3
2000	572	517	302	90.4	52.9	58.5	18	3.1	526	58.9	82.3
1999	626	576	342	92.1	54.7	59.4	19	3.1	582	59.7	87.8
HISPANIC[3]											
Both Sexes											
2008	5,176	3,618	1,338	69.9	25.8	37.0	1,155	22.3	3,691	37.7	58.7
2007	5,175	3,487	1,375	67.4	26.6	39.4	1,310	25.3	3,553	39.9	58.0
2006	5,006	3,301	1,182	65.9	23.6	35.8	1,313	26.2	3,379	36.6	57.2
2005	4,898	3,230	1,215	66.0	24.8	32.4	1,335	27.3	3,280	38.0	57.3
2004	4,941	3,244	1,221	65.6	24.7	37.7	1,386	28.0	3,287	37.9	55.9
2003	4,754	3,096	1,115	65.1	23.5	36.0	1,353	28.4	3,135	36.0	56.5
2002	4,918	3,078	979	62.6	19.9	31.8	1,479	30.1	3,109	32.0	53.1
2001	4,892	3,031	1,035	62.0	21.1	34.2	1,548	31.7	3,068	34.2	52.8
2000	4,134	2,462	899	59.6	21.7	36.5	1,335	32.3	2,509	36.8	53.1
1999	3,953	2,325	739	58.8	18.7	31.8	1,340	33.9	2,359	31.7	49.6
1998	4,014	2,403	820	59.8	20.4	34.1	1,383	34.4	2,419	34.3	53.2
1997	3,606	2,236	806	62.0	22.4	36.0	1,103	30.6	2,302	37.1	54.3
1996	3,510	2,019	706	57.5	20.1	35.0	1,210	34.5	2,046	34.5	52.5
1995	3,603	2,112	745	58.6	20.7	35.3	1,250	34.7	2,142	35.7	55.8
1994	3,523	1,995	662	56.6	18.8	33.2	1,224	34.7	2,009	33.4	54.3
1993[1]	3,363	2,049	728	60.9	21.6	35.5	1,103	32.8	2,081	35.8	55.6
1993	2,772	1,682	602	60.7	21.7	35.8	907	32.7	1,712	36.0	55.8
1992	2,754	1,579	586	57.3	21.3	37.1	936	33.9	1,603	37.6	55.0

Note: The change in the educational attainment question and the college completion categories from "4 or more years of college," to "at least some college," in 1992 caused an increase in the proportion of 14-to-24-year-old high school graduates enrolled in college or completed some college, of approximately 5 percentage points. High school graduates are people who have completed 4 years of high school or more, for 1967 to 1991. Beginning in 1992, they were people whose highest degree was a high school diploma (including equivalency) or higher.
[1] Starting in 2003 respondents could identify more than one race. Except as noted, the race data in this table from 2003 onward represent those respondents who indicated only one race category.
[2] The data shown prior to 2003 consists of those identifying themselves as "Asian or Pacific Islanders."
[3] May be of any race.
r = Revised, controlled to 1990 census based population estimates; previous 1993 data controlled to 1980 census based population estimates.

Table A-13. Population 14 to 24 Years Old by High School Graduate Status, College Enrollment, Attainment, Sex, Race, and Hispanic Origin, October 1967–2008—*Continued*

(Numbers in thousands, percent.)

Year, race, and Hispanic origin	Population 18 to 24 years old								High school graduates, 14 to 24 years old		
	Total	High school graduates		Percent			High school dropouts		All graduates	Percent	
		Total	Enrolled in college	High school graduates	Enrolled in college	High school graduate enrolled in college	Number	Percent		Enrolled in college	Enrolled or completed some college
1991	2,874	1,498	516	52.1	18.0	34.4	1,139	39.6	1,519	34.6	47.6
1990	2,749	1,498	435	54.5	15.8	29.0	1,025	37.3	1,523	29.4	44.7
1989	2,818	1,576	453	55.9	16.1	28.7	1,062	37.7	1,600	29.4	43.6
1988	2,642	1,458	450	55.2	17.0	30.9	1,046	39.6	1,481	31.3	47.0
1987	2,592	1,597	455	61.6	17.6	28.5	849	32.8	1,612	28.7	44.0
1986	2,514	1,507	458	59.9	18.2	30.4	864	34.4	1,535	30.9	45.6
1985	2,221	1,396	375	62.9	16.9	26.9	700	31.5	1,419	27.6	46.7
1984	2,018	1,212	362	60.1	17.9	29.9	691	34.2	1,223	30.0	46.0
1983	2,025	1,110	349	54.8	17.2	31.4	759	37.5	1,134	32.3	48.4
1982	2,001	1,153	337	57.6	16.8	29.2	740	37.0	1,173	30.0	47.3
1981	2,052	1,144	342	55.8	16.7	29.9	790	38.5	1,166	30.5	45.8
1980	2,033	1,099	327	54.1	16.1	29.8	820	40.3	1,117	30.1	47.3
1979	1,754	968	292	55.2	16.6	30.2	687	39.2	1,001	31.2	45.7
1978	1,672	935	254	55.9	15.2	27.2	656	39.2	965	28.0	43.2
1977	1,609	880	277	54.7	17.2	31.5	622	38.7	900	32.4	43.8
1976	1,551	862	309	55.6	19.9	35.8	566	36.5	891	36.3	48.9
1975	1,446	832	295	57.5	20.4	35.5	505	34.9	849	36.5	50.8
1974	1,506	842	272	55.9	18.1	32.3	558	37.1	858	33.1	47.8
1973	1,285	709	206	55.2	16.0	29.1	500	38.9	732	30.3	43.0
1972	1,338	694	179	51.9	13.4	25.8	541	40.4	709	27.2	36.7
Male											
2008	2,675	1,797	615	67.2	23.0	34.2	649	24.3	1,841	35.1	54.4
2007	2,706	1,689	560	62.4	20.7	33.1	790	29.2	1,711	33.6	52.2
2006	2,618	1,600	523	61.1	20.0	32.7	812	31.0	1,628	33.2	53.2
2005	2,613	1,569	540	60.1	20.7	26.2	838	32.1	1,589	34.6	52.4
2004	2,648	1,597	574	60.3	21.7	36.0	888	33.5	1,614	35.9	53.0
2003	2,541	1,548	465	60.9	18.3	30.0	805	31.7	1,571	30.0	48.7
2002	2,707	1,562	439	57.7	16.2	28.1	914	33.8	1,572	28.1	48.4
2001	2,596	1,455	449	56.1	17.3	31.0	962	37.1	1,468	31.0	48.1
2000	2,171	1,172	401	54.0	18.5	34.2	800	36.8	1,197	34.5	50.8
1999	2,045	1,122	322	54.9	15.8	28.7	746	36.4	1,131	28.7	45.7
1998	2,109	1,146	346	54.3	16.4	30.2	838	39.7	1,153	30.0	47.2
1997	1,937	1,140	371	58.9	19.2	32.5	643	33.2	1,168	33.0	49.2
1996	1,815	994	300	54.8	16.5	30.2	657	36.2	1,005	30.6	48.8
1995	1,907	1,106	356	58.0	18.7	32.2	653	34.2	1,022	36.2	52.3
1994	1,896	1,021	312	53.8	16.5	30.6	685	36.1	1,026	30.7	52.7
1993ʳ	1,710	1,005	338	58.8	19.8	33.6	591	34.6	1,023	33.7	51.2
1993	1,354	786	266	58.1	19.6	33.8	470	34.7	803	33.9	51.1
1992	1,384	720	247	52.0	17.8	34.3	531	38.4	736	34.8	52.2
1991	1,503	719	211	47.8	14.0	29.3	668	44.4	728	29.7	42.2
1990	1,403	753	214	53.7	15.3	28.4	559	39.8	770	29.4	46.5
1989	1,439	756	211	52.5	14.7	27.9	580	40.3	767	28.2	42.7
1988	1,375	724	228	52.7	16.6	31.5	553	40.2	736	32.2	48.3
1987	1,337	795	247	59.5	18.5	31.1	461	34.5	803	31.1	45.1
1986	1,339	769	233	57.4	17.4	30.3	499	37.3	776	30.5	44.4
1985	1,132	659	168	58.2	14.8	25.5	405	35.8	675	26.4	44.9
1984	956	549	154	57.4	16.1	28.1	338	35.4	554	28.2	45.7
1983	968	476	152	49.2	15.7	31.9	396	40.9	489	33.1	47.4
1982	944	519	141	55.0	14.9	27.2	347	36.8	525	28.0	44.8
1981	988	498	164	50.4	16.6	32.9	428	43.3	506	33.6	48.6
1980	1,012	518	160	51.2	15.8	30.9	431	42.6	521	31.1	49.5
1979	837	454	153	54.2	18.3	33.7	328	39.2	469	34.3	49.5
1978	781	420	126	53.8	16.1	30.0	313	40.1	438	30.4	46.3
1977	754	396	139	52.5	18.4	35.1	295	39.1	404	35.9	46.5
1976	701	378	150	53.9	21.4	39.7	253	36.1	403	39.8	51.8
1975	678	383	145	56.5	21.4	37.9	221	32.6	390	37.9	55.4

Note: The change in the educational attainment question and the college completion categories from "4 or more years of college," to "at least some college," in 1992 caused an increase in the proportion of 14-to-24-year-old high school graduates enrolled in college or completed some college, of approximately 5 percentage points. High school graduates are people who have completed 4 years of high school or more, for 1967 to 1991. Beginning in 1992, they were people whose highest degree was a high school diploma (including equivalency) or higher.

r = Revised, controlled to 1990 census based population estimates; previous 1993 data controlled to 1980 census based population estimates.

Table A-13. Population 14 to 24 Years Old by High School Graduate Status, College Enrollment, Attainment, Sex, Race, and Hispanic Origin, October 1967–2008—*Continued*

(Numbers in thousands, percent.)

Year, race, and Hispanic origin	Population 18 to 24 years old								High school graduates, 14 to 24 years old		
	Total	High school graduates		Percent		High school graduate enrolled in college	High school dropouts		All graduates	Percent	
		Total	Enrolled in college	High school graduates	Enrolled in college		Number	Percent		Enrolled in college	Enrolled or completed some college
1974...................................	720	390	141	54.2	19.6	36.2	279	38.8	401	36.7	51.4
1973...................................	625	348	105	55.7	16.8	30.2	228	36.5	361	32.1	45.4
1972...................................	609	301	92	49.4	15.1	30.6	253	41.5	309	32.0	44.3
Female											
2008...................................	2,501	1,821	723	72.8	28.9	39.7	506	20.2	1,850	40.3	63.1
2007...................................	2,469	1,798	816	72.8	33.0	45.4	520	21.1	1,842	45.6	63.4
2006...................................	2,388	1,701	660	71.2	27.6	38.8	501	21.0	1,751	39.7	61.0
2005...................................	2,285	1,661	675	72.7	29.5	39.3	498	21.8	1,691	41.2	62.0
2004...................................	2,293	1,647	647	71.8	28.2	39.3	498	21.7	1,673	39.8	58.6
2003...................................	2,213	1,548	651	69.9	29.4	42.1	548	24.7	1,563	41.9	64.4
2002...................................	2,211	1,516	540	68.6	24.4	35.6	565	25.6	1,537	35.9	57.9
2001...................................	2,296	1,576	585	68.6	25.5	37.1	586	25.5	1,600	37.1	57.0
2000...................................	1,963	1,290	498	65.7	25.4	38.6	535	27.3	1,312	38.9	55.2
1999...................................	1,908	1,203	417	63.0	21.8	34.7	593	31.1	1,228	34.4	53.3
1998...................................	1,906	1,257	474	66.0	24.9	37.7	545	28.6	1,266	38.2	58.7
1997...................................	1,669	1,097	436	65.7	26.1	39.7	460	27.6	1,135	41.4	59.6
1996...................................	1,694	1,026	406	60.6	24.0	39.6	554	32.7	1,043	40.4	56.0
1995...................................	1,696	1,011	389	59.6	22.9	38.4	598	35.4	1,022	38.6	59.6
1994...................................	1,628	973	350	59.8	21.5	36.0	539	33.1	983	36.2	55.9
1993ʳ..................................	1,652	1,045	390	63.3	23.6	37.3	510	30.9	1,059	37.8	60.1
1993...................................	1,418	895	336	63.1	23.7	37.5	439	31.0	907	38.0	60.4
1992...................................	1,369	860	339	62.8	24.8	39.4	405	29.6	867	39.9	57.4
1991...................................	1,372	780	305	56.9	22.2	39.1	473	34.5	791	39.2	52.5
1990...................................	1,346	745	221	55.3	16.4	29.7	465	34.5	753	29.5	43.0
1989...................................	1,377	823	244	59.8	17.7	29.6	482	35.0	836	30.5	44.5
1988...................................	1,267	736	224	58.1	17.7	30.4	492	38.8	747	30.5	45.8
1987...................................	1,256	801	208	63.8	16.6	26.0	387	30.8	808	26.4	43.2
1986...................................	1,175	739	226	62.9	19.2	30.6	365	31.1	759	31.4	46.8
1985...................................	1,091	734	205	67.3	18.8	27.9	295	27.0	743	28.4	48.0
1984...................................	1,061	661	207	62.3	19.5	31.3	353	33.2	667	31.5	46.6
1983...................................	1,057	634	198	60.0	18.7	31.2	363	34.3	644	31.8	49.7
1982...................................	1,056	634	196	60.0	18.6	30.9	393	37.2	648	31.8	49.2
1981...................................	1,064	646	178	60.7	16.7	27.6	362	34.0	662	28.2	43.4
1980...................................	1,021	579	165	56.7	16.2	28.5	389	38.1	595	29.1	45.4
1979...................................	917	516	140	56.3	15.3	27.1	358	39.0	534	28.1	42.3
1978...................................	891	516	128	57.9	14.4	24.8	343	38.5	528	25.8	40.0
1977...................................	855	483	139	56.5	16.3	28.8	326	38.1	495	29.7	41.6
1976...................................	850	483	160	56.8	18.8	33.1	313	36.8	489	33.5	46.5
1975...................................	769	449	150	58.4	19.5	33.4	283	36.8	460	34.8	46.7
1974...................................	786	451	129	57.4	16.4	28.6	280	35.6	459	29.2	43.4
1973...................................	658	362	102	55.0	15.5	28.2	272	41.3	372	28.8	41.1
1972...................................	728	394	88	54.1	12.1	22.3	288	39.6	402	23.6	31.1
WHITE ALONE OR IN COMBINATION											
Both Sexes											
2008...................................	23,120	19,810	9,360	85.7	40.5	47.2	2,072	9.0	20,067	47.5	71.6
2007...................................	22,928	19,330	8,958	84.3	39.1	46.3	2,338	10.2	19,595	46.5	70.3
2006...................................	22,670	18,882	8,465	83.3	37.3	44.8	2,458	10.8	19,153	45.1	69.9
2005...................................	22,345	18,583	8,721	83.2	39.0	50.1	2,539	11.4	18,818	47.0	70.0
2004...................................	22,411	18,663	8,544	83.3	38.1	45.8	2,639	11.8	18,868	46.0	69.0
2003...................................	22,029	18,335	8,358	83.2	37.9	45.6	2,558	11.6	18,565	45.6	69.0

Note: The change in the educational attainment question and the college completion categories from "4 or more years of college," to "at least some college," in 1992 caused an increase in the proportion of 14-to-24-year-old high school graduates enrolled in college or completed some college, of approximately 5 percentage points. High school graduates are people who have completed 4 years of high school or more, for 1967 to 1991. Beginning in 1992, they were people whose highest degree was a high school diploma (including equivalency) or higher.
r = Revised, controlled to 1990 census based population estimates; previous 1993 data controlled to 1980 census based population estimates.

Table A-13. Population 14 to 24 Years Old by High School Graduate Status, College Enrollment, Attainment, Sex, Race, and Hispanic Origin, October 1967–2008—*Continued*

(Numbers in thousands, percent.)

| Year, race, and Hispanic origin | Population 18 to 24 years old | | | | | | | | High school graduates, 14 to 24 years old | | |
| | Total | High school graduates | | Percent | | | High school dropouts | | All graduates | Percent | |
		Total	Enrolled in college	High school graduates	Enrolled in college	High school graduate enrolled in college	Number	Percent		Enrolled in college	Enrolled or completed some college
Male											
2008..............................	11,738	9,891	4,444	84.3	37.9	44.9	1,165	9.9	10,031	45.2	67.8
2007..............................	11,670	9,511	4,116	81.5	35.3	43.3	1,397	12.0	9,634	43.4	66.0
2006..............................	11,502	9,331	3,923	81.1	34.1	42.0	1,427	12.4	9,435	42.2	66.1
2005..............................	11,394	9,086	4,018	79.7	35.3	43.5	1,519	13.3	9,193	44.2	60.0
2004..............................	11,371	9,227	3,956	81.1	34.8	42.9	1,548	13.6	9,296	43.1	64.4
2003..............................	11,147	8,967	3,815	80.4	34.2	42.5	1,493	13.4	9,070	42.6	65.1
Female											
2008..............................	11,381	9,919	4,916	87.2	43.2	49.6	908	8.0	10,036	49.9	75.4
2007..............................	11,258	9,820	4,842	87.2	43.0	49.3	941	8.4	9,960	49.4	74.4
2006..............................	11,168	9,551	4,542	85.5	40.7	47.6	1,032	9.2	9,718	47.8	73.6
2005..............................	10,952	9,497	4,702	86.7	42.9	57.1	1,020	9.3	9,625	49.7	73.9
2004..............................	11,040	9,436	4,588	85.5	41.6	48.6	1,091	9.9	9,572	48.8	73.5
2003..............................	10,882	9,367	4,543	86.1	41.7	48.5	1,065	9.8	9,495	48.5	72.7
BLACK ALONE OR IN COMBINATION											
Both Sexes											
2008..............................	4,531	3,588	1,435	79.2	31.7	40.0	548	12.1	3,646	40.3	60.9
2007..............................	4,425	3,603	1,468	81.4	33.2	40.7	477	10.8	3,671	40.9	61.8
2006..............................	4,264	3,287	1,387	77.1	32.5	42.2	560	13.1	3,359	42.2	61.1
2005..............................	4,158	3,303	1,371	79.4	33.0	31.7	530	12.7	3,378	41.5	63.5
2004..............................	4,115	3,190	1,318	77.5	32.0	41.3	620	15.1	3,253	41.8	63.5
2003..............................	4,016	3,091	1,285	77.0	32.0	41.6	563	14.0	3,141	41.9	62.0
Male											
2008..............................	2,190	1,743	633	79.6	28.9	36.3	235	10.7	1,770	36.9	54.9
2007..............................	2,132	1,703	686	79.9	32.2	40.3	234	11.0	1,728	40.4	59.6
2006..............................	2,032	1,545	577	76.0	28.4	37.3	225	11.0	1,576	37.2	54.5
2005..............................	1,988	1,466	557	73.7	28.0	42.5	290	14.6	1,492	37.9	58.2
2004..............................	1,951	1,418	521	72.7	26.7	36.7	347	17.8	1,442	37.0	61.3
2003..............................	1,868	1,382	525	74.0	28.1	38.0	311	16.6	1,397	38.3	57.4
Female											
2008..............................	2,341	1,845	802	78.8	34.2	43.5	313	13.4	1,876	43.5	66.5
2007..............................	2,293	1,900	782	82.9	34.1	41.2	243	10.6	1,942	41.3	63.7
2006..............................	2,232	1,742	810	78.1	36.3	46.5	335	15.0	1,783	46.5	66.8
2005..............................	2,170	1,837	814	84.7	37.5	21.2	240	11.1	1,885	44.3	67.7
2004..............................	2,164	1,772	797	81.9	36.8	45.0	272	12.6	1,811	45.5	65.3
2003..............................	2,148	1,708	760	79.5	35.4	44.5	252	11.7	1,744	44.7	65.7
ASIAN ALONE OR IN COMBINATION											
Both Sexes											
2008..............................	1,251	1,153	738	92.1	59.0	64.0	42	3.4	1,188	64.4	89.7
2007..............................	1,293	1,126	720	87.1	55.7	63.9	94	7.3	1,143	63.9	90.3
2006..............................	1,270	1,158	705	91.2	55.5	60.9	49	3.9	1,180	60.6	86.1
2005..............................	1,299	1,214	773	93.5	59.5	63.7	38	2.9	1,243	64.2	86.0
2004..............................	1,263	1,167	750	92.5	59.4	64.3	53	4.2	1,191	64.6	87.6
2003..............................	1,280	1,162	774	90.8	60.5	66.6	56	4.4	1,184	66.9	87.8

Note: The change in the educational attainment question and the college completion categories from "4 or more years of college," to "at least some college," in 1992 caused an increase in the proportion of 14-to-24-year-old high school graduates enrolled in college or completed some college, of approximately 5 percentage points. High school graduates are people who have completed 4 years of high school or more, for 1967 to 1991. Beginning in 1992, they were people whose highest degree was a high school diploma (including equivalency) or higher.

Table A-13. Population 14 to 24 Years Old by High School Graduate Status, College Enrollment, Attainment, Sex, Race, and Hispanic Origin, October 1967–2008—*Continued*

(Numbers in thousands, percent.)

Year, race, and Hispanic origin	Population 18 to 24 years old								High school graduates, 14 to 24 years old		
	Total	High school graduates		Percent			High school dropouts		All graduates	Percent	
		Total	Enrolled in college	High school graduates	Enrolled in college	High school graduate enrolled in college	Number	Percent		Enrolled in college	Enrolled or completed some college
Male											
2008...............................	626	560	340	89.4	54.4	60.8	22	3.4	582	62.2	89.2
2007...............................	560	481	318	85.8	56.9	66.3	38	6.8	483	66.4	91.8
2006...............................	649	578	362	89.1	55.8	62.7	34	5.3	591	62.3	83.8
2005...............................	653	603	392	92.4	59.9	65.0	20	3.1	621	65.1	86.3
2004...............................	634	588	398	92.8	62.7	67.7	18	2.9	601	68.0	87.8
2003...............................	609	545	370	89.5	60.8	67.9	43	7.1	551	67.7	88.7
Female											
2008...............................	625	593	397	94.9	63.6	67.0	21	3.3	605	66.5	90.3
2007...............................	605	529	339	87.4	56.0	64.1	48	7.9	543	63.9	91.5
2006...............................	621	580	343	93.4	55.3	59.2	14	2.3	589	58.8	88.5
2005...............................	645	610	381	94.6	59.1	62.5	17	2.7	622	63.3	85.8
2004...............................	628	579	352	92.1	56.0	60.8	35	5.5	591	61.2	87.5
2003...............................	671	617	404	92.0	60.2	65.5	13	1.9	633	66.3	87.0

Note: The change in the educational attainment question and the college completion categories from "4 or more years of college," to "at least some college," in 1992 caused an increase in the proportion of 14-to-24-year-old high school graduates enrolled in college or completed some college, of approximately 5 percentage points. High school graduates are people who have completed 4 years of high school or more, for 1967 to 1991. Beginning in 1992, they were people whose highest degree was a high school diploma (including equivalency) or higher.

Table A-14. Population 18 and 19 Years Old by School Enrollment Status, Sex, Race, and Hispanic Origin, October 1967–2008

(Numbers in thousands.)

Year, race, and Hispanic origin	Total	Population 18 and 19 years old							
		Still in high school	Percent	Dropped out	Percent	High school graduate only	Percent	In college	Percent
ALL RACES									
Both Sexes									
2008..	8,492	1,481	17.4	750	8.8	2,134	25.1	4,126	48.6
2007..	8,338	1,491	17.9	675	8.1	2,097	25.2	4,075	48.9
2006..	8,102	1,560	19.3	743	9.2	2,053	25.3	3,746	46.2
2005..	7,559	1,372	18.1	661	8.7	1,694	22.4	3,832	50.7
2004..	7,701	1,266	16.4	840	10.9	1,910	24.8	3,685	47.8
2003..	7,533	1,345	17.9	817	10.8	1,859	24.7	3,512	46.6
2002..	7,907	1,427	18.0	884	11.2	2,015	25.5	3,581	45.3
2001..	7,985	1,394	17.5	1,034	12.9	2,079	26.0	3,478	43.6
2000..	8,045	1,327	16.5	1,012	12.6	2,107	26.2	3,599	44.7
1999..	7,991	1,321	16.5	1,047	13.1	2,103	26.3	3,520	44.0
1998..	7,902	1,244	15.7	1,104	14.0	1,884	23.8	3,670	46.4
1997..	7,510	1,256	16.7	1,038	13.8	1,854	24.7	3,362	44.8
1996..	7,376	1,230	16.7	940	12.7	1,897	25.7	3,309	44.9
1995..	7,198	1,173	16.3	1,051	14.6	1,873	26.0	3,101	43.1
1994..	6,946	1,129	16.3	929	13.4	1,837	26.4	3,051	43.9
1993..	6,594	1,137	17.2	778	11.8	1,753	26.6	2,926	44.4
1992..	6,535	1,121	17.2	780	11.9	1,742	26.7	2,892	44.3
1991..	6,664	1,040	15.6	889	13.3	1,806	27.1	2,929	44.0
1990..	7,064	1,024	14.5	1,003	14.2	2,018	28.6	3,019	42.7
1989..	7,361	1,058	14.4	1,033	14.0	2,204	29.9	3,066	41.7
1988..	7,294	1,013	13.9	1,063	14.6	2,172	29.8	3,046	41.8
1987..	7,160	937	13.1	954	13.3	2,224	31.1	3,045	42.5
1986..	7,095	930	13.1	872	12.3	2,351	33.1	2,942	41.5
1985..	7,204	809	11.2	1,031	14.3	2,457	34.1	2,907	40.4
1984..	7,428	857	11.5	1,129	15.2	2,575	34.7	2,867	38.6
1983..	7,819	999	12.8	1,132	14.5	2,748	35.1	2,940	37.6
1982..	8,023	908	11.3	1,336	16.7	2,850	35.5	2,929	36.5
1981..	8,115	932	11.5	1,299	16.0	2,840	35.0	3,044	37.5
1980..	8,160	855	10.5	1,284	15.7	3,088	37.8	2,933	35.9
1979..	8,214	849	10.3	1,382	16.8	3,139	38.2	2,844	34.6
1978..	8,153	801	9.8	1,361	16.7	3,092	37.9	2,899	35.6
1977..	8,151	849	10.4	1,355	16.6	3,034	37.2	2,913	35.7
1976..	8,148	831	10.2	1,355	16.6	3,025	37.1	2,937	36.0
1975..	8,024	822	10.2	1,286	16.0	2,973	37.1	2,943	36.7
1974..	7,822	777	9.9	1,302	16.6	3,146	40.2	2,597	33.2
1973..	7,649	766	10.0	1,228	16.1	3,138	41.0	2,517	32.9
1972..	7,462	778	10.4	1,100	14.7	2,904	38.9	2,680	35.9
1971..	7,231	830	11.5	1,108	15.3	2,567	35.5	2,726	37.7
1970..	6,958	728	10.5	1,125	16.2	2,511	36.1	2,594	37.3
1969..	6,677	749	11.2	1,007	15.1	2,320	34.7	2,601	39.0
1968..	6,587	816	12.4	1,033	15.7	2,237	34.0	2,501	38.0
1967..	6,358	741	11.7	1,086	17.1	2,245	35.3	2,286	36.0
Male									
2008..	4,289	834	19.5	376	8.8	1,169	27.3	1,909	44.5
2007..	4,222	895	21.2	354	8.4	1,070	25.3	1,903	45.1
2006..	4,103	907	22.1	414	10.1	1,079	26.3	1,703	41.5
2005..	3,880	899	23.2	392	10.1	914	23.6	1,675	43.2
2004..	3,861	714	18.5	522	13.5	1,015	26.3	1,610	41.7
2003..	3,764	781	20.7	480	12.8	935	24.8	1,568	41.7
2002..	4,042	862	21.3	523	12.9	1,022	25.3	1,635	40.5
2001..	4,027	801	19.9	614	15.2	1,042	25.9	1,570	39.0
2000..	4,037	783	19.4	571	14.1	1,113	27.6	1,570	38.9
1999..	4,026	780	19.4	550	13.7	1,048	26.0	1,648	40.9
1998..	3,994	732	18.3	611	15.3	984	24.6	1,667	41.7
1997..	3,816	750	19.7	585	15.3	920	24.1	1,561	40.9
1996..	3,711	769	20.7	488	13.2	965	26.0	1,489	40.1
1995..	3,611	719	19.9	532	14.7	929	25.7	1,431	39.6
1994..	3,485	688	19.7	499	14.3	882	25.3	1,416	40.6
1993..	3,329	712	21.4	403	12.1	877	26.3	1,337	40.2
1992..	3,275	694	21.2	400	12.2	856	26.1	1,325	40.5

Note: High school graduates are people who have completed 4 years of high school or more, for 1967 to 1991. Beginning in 1992, they were people whose highest degree was a high school diploma (including equivalency) or higher.

Table A-14. Population 18 and 19 Years Old by School Enrollment Status, Sex, Race, and Hispanic Origin, October 1967–2008—*Continued*

(Numbers in thousands.)

Year, race, and Hispanic origin	Total	Population 18 and 19 years old							
		Still in high school	Percent	Dropped out	Percent	High school graduate only	Percent	In college	Percent
1991	3,307	650	19.7	453	13.7	878	26.5	1,326	40.1
1990	3,503	595	17.0	512	14.6	953	27.2	1,443	41.2
1989	3,640	640	17.6	531	14.6	1,047	28.8	1,422	39.1
1988	3,618	666	18.4	566	15.6	1,021	28.2	1,365	37.7
1987	3,537	564	15.9	493	13.9	997	28.2	1,483	41.9
1986	3,502	594	17.0	459	13.1	1,045	29.8	1,404	40.1
1985	3,550	503	14.2	580	16.3	1,118	31.5	1,349	38.0
1984	3,674	551	15.0	594	16.2	1,156	31.5	1,373	37.4
1983	3,877	616	15.9	630	16.2	1,291	33.3	1,340	34.6
1982	3,961	562	14.2	709	17.9	1,314	33.2	1,376	34.7
1981	3,996	567	14.2	706	17.7	1,273	31.9	1,450	36.3
1980	3,993	510	12.8	673	16.9	1,441	36.1	1,369	34.3
1979	4,023	533	13.2	739	18.4	1,410	35.0	1,341	33.3
1978	3,975	511	12.9	692	17.4	1,381	34.7	1,391	35.0
1977	3,961	522	13.2	702	17.7	1,341	33.9	1,396	35.2
1976	3,957	516	13.0	684	17.3	1,366	34.5	1,391	35.2
1975	3,891	514	13.2	603	15.5	1,348	34.6	1,426	36.6
1974	3,782	469	12.4	706	18.7	1,345	35.6	1,262	33.4
1973	3,720	490	13.2	589	15.8	1,348	36.2	1,293	34.8
1972	3,630	492	13.6	555	15.3	1,217	33.5	1,366	37.6
1971	3,503	496	14.2	551	15.7	1,012	28.9	1,444	41.2
1970	3,349	485	14.5	537	16.0	981	29.3	1,346	40.2
1969	3,173	489	15.4	473	14.9	814	25.7	1,397	44.0
1968	3,133	535	17.1	485	15.5	756	24.1	1,357	43.3
1967	2,908	438	15.1	500	17.2	772	26.5	1,198	41.2
Female									
2008	4,203	647	15.4	374	8.9	965	23.0	2,217	52.7
2007	4,116	595	14.5	321	7.8	1,027	25.0	2,172	52.8
2006	3,999	654	16.3	328	8.2	974	24.4	2,043	51.1
2005	3,679	472	12.8	269	7.3	886	24.1	2,052	55.8
2004	3,840	553	14.4	318	8.3	895	23.3	2,074	54.0
2003	3,769	565	15.0	337	8.9	923	24.5	1,944	51.6
2002	3,865	565	14.6	361	9.3	993	25.7	1,946	50.3
2001	3,958	594	15.0	420	10.6	1,037	26.2	1,907	48.2
2000	4,008	544	13.6	440	11.0	995	24.8	2,029	50.6
1999	3,965	540	13.6	497	12.5	1,056	26.6	1,872	47.2
1998	3,908	513	13.1	492	12.6	900	23.0	2,003	51.3
1997	3,694	506	13.7	453	12.3	934	25.3	1,801	48.8
1996	3,665	460	12.6	452	12.3	932	25.4	1,821	49.7
1995	3,587	453	12.6	519	14.5	944	26.3	1,671	46.6
1994	3,461	440	12.7	430	12.4	956	27.6	1,635	47.2
1993	3,265	425	13.0	375	11.5	877	26.9	1,588	48.6
1992	3,260	428	13.1	380	11.7	886	27.2	1,566	48.0
1991	3,357	389	11.6	436	13.0	929	27.7	1,603	47.8
1990	3,561	429	12.0	491	13.8	1,065	29.9	1,576	44.3
1989	3,721	421	11.3	501	13.5	1,156	31.1	1,643	44.2
1988	3,676	346	9.4	497	13.5	1,151	31.3	1,682	45.8
1987	3,623	374	10.3	461	12.7	1,226	33.8	1,562	43.1
1986	3,593	337	9.4	413	11.5	1,306	36.3	1,537	42.8
1985	3,654	304	8.3	451	12.3	1,340	36.7	1,559	42.7
1984	3,754	306	8.2	535	14.3	1,419	37.8	1,494	39.8
1983	3,942	383	9.7	502	12.7	1,457	37.0	1,600	40.6
1982	4,062	346	8.5	627	15.4	1,536	37.8	1,553	38.2
1981	4,119	364	8.8	594	14.4	1,567	38.0	1,594	38.7
1980	4,167	345	8.3	611	14.7	1,646	39.5	1,565	37.6
1979	4,191	317	7.6	643	15.3	1,728	41.2	1,503	35.9
1978	4,178	291	7.0	669	16.0	1,711	41.0	1,507	36.1
1977	4,190	326	7.8	654	15.6	1,693	40.4	1,517	36.2
1976	4,191	314	7.5	672	16.0	1,659	39.6	1,546	36.9
1975	4,133	308	7.5	683	16.5	1,625	39.3	1,517	36.7
1974	4,040	309	7.6	596	14.8	1,800	44.6	1,335	33.0
1973	3,929	276	7.0	638	16.2	1,791	45.6	1,224	31.2
1972	3,832	287	7.5	545	14.2	1,686	44.0	1,314	34.3

Note: High school graduates are people who have completed 4 years of high school or more, for 1967 to 1991. Beginning in 1992, they were people whose highest degree was a high school diploma (including equivalency) or higher.

Table A-14. Population 18 and 19 Years Old by School Enrollment Status, Sex, Race, and Hispanic Origin, October 1967–2008—*Continued*

(Numbers in thousands.)

Year, race, and Hispanic origin	Total	Population 18 and 19 years old							
		Still in high school	Percent	Dropped out	Percent	High school graduate only	Percent	In college	Percent
1971...	3,728	337	9.0	556	14.9	1,554	41.7	1,281	34.4
1970...	3,609	253	7.0	589	16.3	1,519	42.1	1,248	34.6
1969...	3,504	260	7.4	534	15.2	1,506	43.0	1,204	34.4
1968...	3,454	281	8.1	548	15.9	1,481	42.9	1,144	33.1
1967...	3,450	302	8.8	586	17.0	1,474	42.7	1,088	31.5
WHITE									
Both Sexes									
2008...	6,589	1,067	16.2	558	8.5	1,611	24.4	3,353	50.9
2007...	6,446	1,083	16.8	517	8.0	1,605	24.9	3,242	50.3
2006...	6,321	1,121	17.7	600	9.5	1,619	25.6	2,982	47.2
2005...	5,893	1,023	17.4	515	8.7	1,383	23.5	2,972	50.4
2004	6,043	963	15.9	634	10.5	1,500	24.8	2,946	48.8
2003[1]...	5,915	979	16.6	659	11.1	1,444	24.4	2,833	47.9
2002...	6,252	1,096	17.5	663	10.6	1,602	25.6	2,891	46.2
2001...	6,254	1,022	16.3	843	13.5	1,634	26.1	2,755	44.1
2000...	6,399	1,010	15.8	795	12.4	1,680	26.3	2,914	45.5
1999...	6,383	1,009	15.8	810	12.7	1,715	26.9	2,849	44.6
1998...	6,266	884	14.1	848	13.5	1,540	24.6	2,994	47.8
1997...	5,995	896	14.9	816	13.6	1,491	24.9	2,792	46.6
1996...	5,833	914	15.7	735	12.6	1,453	24.9	2,731	46.8
1995...	5,698	803	14.1	809	14.2	1,509	26.5	2,577	45.2
1994...	5,559	817	14.7	681	12.3	1,493	26.9	2,568	46.2
1993...	5,252	786	15.0	628	12.0	1,382	26.3	2,456	46.8
1992...	5,203	793	15.2	582	11.2	1,409	27.1	2,419	46.5
1991...	5,358	709	13.2	722	13.5	1,440	26.9	2,487	46.4
1990...	5,725	724	12.6	799	14.0	1,654	28.9	2,548	44.5
1989...	6,013	744	12.4	819	13.6	1,802	30.0	2,648	44.0
1988...	5,981	699	11.7	855	14.3	1,788	29.9	2,639	44.1
1987...	5,845	667	11.4	762	13.0	1,852	31.7	2,564	43.9
1986...	5,825	669	11.5	693	11.9	1,940	33.3	2,523	43.3
1985...	5,922	566	9.6	815	13.8	2,002	33.8	2,539	42.9
1984...	6,139	594	9.7	913	14.9	2,091	34.1	2,541	41.4
1983...	6,452	688	10.7	884	13.7	2,283	35.4	2,597	40.3
1982...	6,666	647	9.7	1,051	15.8	2,419	36.3	2,549	38.2
1981...	6,794	656	9.7	1,054	15.5	2,445	36.0	2,639	38.8
1980...	6,913	621	9.0	1,032	14.9	2,682	38.8	2,578	37.3
1979...	6,980	607	8.7	1,115	16.0	2,760	39.5	2,498	35.8
1978...	6,933	560	8.1	1,082	15.6	2,738	39.5	2,553	36.8
1977...	6,944	581	8.4	1,103	15.9	2,681	38.6	2,579	37.1
1976...	6,951	581	8.4	1,131	16.3	2,662	38.3	2,577	37.1
1975...	6,855	572	8.3	1,005	14.7	2,665	38.9	2,613	38.1
1974...	6,707	551	8.2	1,045	15.6	2,803	41.8	2,308	34.4
1973...	6,559	568	8.7	962	14.7	2,748	41.9	2,281	34.8
1972...	6,424	582	9.1	857	13.3	2,574	40.1	2,411	37.5
1971...	6,243	596	9.5	875	14.0	2,287	36.6	2,485	39.8
1970...	6,009	563	9.4	845	14.1	2,240	37.3	2,361	39.3
1969...	5,762	557	9.7	772	13.4	2,056	35.7	2,377	41.3
1968...	5,692	614	10.8	822	14.4	1,972	34.6	2,284	40.1
1967...	5,506	558	10.1	875	15.9	1,968	35.7	2,105	38.2
Male									
2008...	3,350	589	17.6	299	8.9	896	26.7	1,566	46.7
2007...	3,277	668	20.4	281	8.6	819	25.0	1,508	46.0
2006...	3,211	645	20.1	351	10.9	848	26.4	1,367	42.6
2005...	3,049	665	21.8	304	10.0	737	24.2	1,343	44.1
2004	3,062	524	17.1	406	13.3	824	26.9	1,308	42.7
2003[1]...	3,003	594	19.8	381	12.7	770	25.6	1,258	41.9
2002...	3,186	661	20.7	366	11.5	830	26.1	1,329	41.7
2001...	3,192	585	18.3	494	15.5	840	26.3	1,273	39.9
2000...	3,248	612	18.8	447	13.8	900	27.7	1,289	39.7
1999...	3,242	609	18.8	423	13.0	874	27.0	1,336	41.2

Note: High school graduates are people who have completed 4 years of high school or more, for 1967 to 1991. Beginning in 1992, they were people whose highest degree was a high school diploma (including equivalency) or higher.
[1]Starting in 2003 respondents could identify more than one race. Except as noted, the race data in this table from 2003 onward represent those respondents who indicated only one race category.

Table A-14. Population 18 and 19 Years Old by School Enrollment Status, Sex, Race, and Hispanic Origin, October 1967–2008—*Continued*

(Numbers in thousands.)

Year, race, and Hispanic origin	Total	Population 18 and 19 years old							
		Still in high school	Percent	Dropped out	Percent	High school graduate only	Percent	In college	Percent
1998	3,197	533	16.7	472	14.8	816	25.5	1,376	43.0
1997	3,060	523	17.1	473	15.5	750	24.5	1,314	42.9
1996	2,953	575	19.5	382	12.9	773	26.2	1,223	41.4
1995	2,886	519	18.0	408	14.1	764	26.5	1,195	41.4
1994	2,813	512	18.2	355	12.6	734	26.1	1,212	43.1
1993	2,641	497	18.8	338	12.8	703	26.6	1,103	41.8
1992	2,608	482	18.5	304	11.7	720	27.6	1,102	42.3
1991	2,677	451	16.8	381	14.2	733	27.4	1,112	41.5
1990	2,852	416	14.6	421	14.8	797	27.9	1,218	42.7
1989	2,997	463	15.4	433	14.4	848	28.3	1,253	41.8
1988	2,976	487	16.4	461	15.5	834	28.0	1,194	40.1
1987	2,906	404	13.9	400	13.8	842	29.0	1,260	43.4
1986	2,888	411	14.2	370	12.8	866	30.0	1,241	43.0
1985	2,937	349	11.9	478	16.3	934	31.8	1,176	40.0
1984	3,047	378	12.4	480	15.8	965	31.7	1,224	40.2
1983	3,216	434	13.5	500	15.5	1,085	33.7	1,197	37.2
1982	3,301	412	12.5	549	16.6	1,151	34.9	1,189	36.0
1981	3,356	394	11.7	599	17.8	1,104	32.9	1,259	37.5
1980	3,407	385	11.3	549	16.1	1,241	36.4	1,232	36.2
1979	3,445	395	11.5	610	17.7	1,248	36.2	1,192	34.6
1978	3,405	368	10.8	554	16.3	1,244	36.5	1,239	36.4
1977	3,396	348	10.2	577	17.0	1,199	35.3	1,272	37.5
1976	3,393	348	10.3	582	17.2	1,219	35.9	1,244	36.7
1975	3,343	374	11.2	458	13.7	1,228	36.7	1,283	38.4
1974	3,265	343	10.5	568	17.4	1,211	37.1	1,143	35.0
1973	3,208	375	11.7	454	14.2	1,202	37.5	1,177	36.7
1972	3,137	374	11.9	423	13.5	1,098	35.0	1,242	39.6
1971	3,035	367	12.1	432	14.2	908	29.9	1,328	43.8
1970	2,901	374	12.9	384	13.2	892	30.7	1,251	43.1
1969	2,745	374	13.6	345	12.6	728	26.5	1,298	47.3
1968	2,710	403	14.9	387	14.3	658	24.3	1,262	46.6
1967	2,511	340	13.5	386	15.4	688	27.4	1,097	43.7
Female									
2008	3,239	478	14.8	259	8.0	715	22.1	1,787	55.2
2007	3,169	414	13.1	235	7.4	785	24.8	1,734	54.7
2006	3,111	476	15.3	249	8.0	771	24.8	1,615	51.9
2005	2,844	358	12.6	210	7.4	647	22.7	1,629	57.3
2004	2,980	440	14.7	227	7.6	675	22.7	1,638	55.0
2003[1]	2,913	385	13.2	279	9.6	674	23.1	1,575	54.1
2002	3,066	435	14.2	297	9.7	772	25.2	1,562	50.9
2001	3,062	438	14.3	349	11.4	794	25.9	1,481	48.4
2000	3,151	397	12.6	348	11.0	781	24.8	1,625	51.6
1999	3,141	400	12.7	387	12.3	841	26.8	1,513	48.2
1998	3,069	351	11.4	376	12.3	724	23.6	1,618	52.7
1997	2,934	371	12.6	344	11.7	740	25.2	1,479	50.4
1996	2,879	338	11.7	353	12.3	680	23.6	1,508	52.4
1995	2,812	283	10.1	401	14.3	745	26.5	1,383	49.2
1994	2,746	305	11.1	325	11.8	759	27.6	1,357	49.4
1993	2,611	289	11.1	290	11.1	679	26.0	1,353	51.8
1992	2,595	311	12.0	278	10.7	689	26.6	1,317	50.8
1991	2,681	259	9.7	341	12.7	706	26.3	1,375	51.3
1990	2,873	307	10.7	378	13.2	857	29.8	1,331	46.3
1989	3,016	281	9.3	386	12.8	954	31.6	1,395	46.3
1988	3,005	212	7.1	394	13.1	954	31.7	1,445	48.1
1987	2,939	263	8.9	362	12.3	1,010	34.4	1,304	44.4
1986	2,937	257	8.8	323	11.0	1,074	36.6	1,283	43.7
1985	2,985	217	7.3	337	11.3	1,068	35.8	1,363	45.7
1984	3,092	216	7.0	432	14.0	1,127	36.4	1,317	42.6
1983	3,236	255	7.9	383	11.8	1,198	37.0	1,400	43.3
1982	3,365	234	7.0	502	14.9	1,269	37.7	1,360	40.4
1981	3,438	262	7.6	454	13.2	1,342	39.0	1,380	40.1
1980	3,506	237	6.8	483	13.8	1,440	41.1	1,346	38.4
1979	3,535	213	6.0	505	14.3	1,511	42.7	1,306	36.9

Note: High school graduates are people who have completed 4 years of high school or more, for 1967 to 1991. Beginning in 1992, they were people whose highest degree was a high school diploma (including equivalency) or higher.
[1]Starting in 2003 respondents could identify more than one race. Except as noted, the race data in this table from 2003 onward represent those respondents who indicated only one race category.

Table A-14. Population 18 and 19 Years Old by School Enrollment Status, Sex, Race, and Hispanic Origin, October 1967–2008—*Continued*

(Numbers in thousands.)

Year, race, and Hispanic origin	Total	Still in high school	Percent	Dropped out	Percent	High school graduate only	Percent	In college	Percent
1978	3,528	193	5.5	528	15.0	1,493	42.3	1,314	37.2
1977	3,548	232	6.5	526	14.8	1,483	41.8	1,307	36.8
1976	3,558	230	6.5	550	15.5	1,444	40.6	1,334	37.5
1975	3,512	199	5.7	547	15.6	1,436	40.9	1,330	37.9
1974	3,442	207	6.0	477	13.9	1,592	46.3	1,166	33.9
1973	3,351	192	5.7	508	15.2	1,547	46.2	1,104	32.9
1972	3,287	208	6.3	434	13.2	1,476	44.9	1,169	35.6
1971	3,208	229	7.1	442	13.8	1,380	43.0	1,157	36.1
1970	3,108	190	6.1	460	14.8	1,348	43.4	1,110	35.7
1969	3,017	183	6.1	427	14.2	1,328	44.0	1,079	35.8
1968	2,981	210	7.0	435	14.6	1,314	44.1	1,022	34.3
1967	2,996	218	7.3	489	16.3	1,280	42.7	1,009	33.7
WHITE NON-HISPANIC									
Both Sexes									
2008	5,185	780	15.0	296	5.7	1,258	24.3	2,850	55.0
2007	5,067	793	15.7	283	5.6	1,252	24.7	2,739	54.1
2006	5,018	843	16.8	361	7.2	1,251	24.9	2,564	51.1
2005	4,770	790	16.6	297	6.2	1,065	22.3	2,618	54.9
2004	4,885	731	15.0	363	7.4	1,195	24.5	2,596	53.1
2003[1]	4,780	758	15.9	379	7.9	1,157	24.2	2,486	52.0
2002	5,016	817	16.3	369	7.4	1,281	25.5	2,549	50.8
2001	4,928	780	15.8	467	9.5	1,298	26.3	2,383	48.4
2000	5,221	757	14.5	500	9.6	1,384	26.5	2,580	49.4
1999	5,228	779	14.9	491	9.4	1,384	26.5	2,574	49.2
1998	5,080	691	13.6	475	9.4	1,211	23.8	2,703	53.2
Male									
2008	2,649	423	16.0	170	6.4	709	26.8	1,346	50.8
2007	2,587	496	19.2	150	5.8	643	24.9	1,298	50.2
2006	2,553	501	19.6	204	8.0	679	26.6	1,168	45.7
2005	2,449	515	21.0	168	6.9	573	23.4	1,193	48.7
2004	2,443	408	16.7	204	8.4	681	27.9	1,150	47.1
2003[1]	2,407	460	19.1	230	9.6	602	25.0	1,115	46.3
2002	2,502	481	19.2	182	7.3	660	26.4	1,179	47.1
2001	2,526	453	17.9	257	10.2	685	27.1	1,131	44.8
2000	2,628	471	17.9	274	10.4	745	28.3	1,138	43.3
1999	2,648	473	17.9	255	9.6	706	26.7	1,214	45.8
1998	2,613	432	16.5	254	9.7	653	25.0	1,274	48.8
Female									
2008	2,536	357	14.1	126	5.0	549	21.7	1,504	59.3
2007	2,480	298	12.0	132	5.3	609	24.6	1,441	58.1
2006	2,466	341	13.8	157	6.4	571	23.2	1,396	56.6
2005	2,321	275	11.9	129	5.6	491	21.2	1,425	61.4
2004	2,441	323	13.2	159	6.5	513	21.0	1,446	59.2
2003[1]	2,373	298	12.6	149	6.3	555	23.4	1,371	57.8
2002	2,514	336	13.4	187	7.4	621	24.7	1,370	54.5
2001	2,402	328	13.7	209	8.7	613	25.5	1,252	52.1
2000	2,593	286	11.0	225	8.7	639	24.6	1,443	55.6
1999	2,580	307	11.9	236	9.1	677	26.2	1,360	52.7
1998	2,467	259	10.5	221	9.0	558	22.6	1,429	57.9
BLACK									
Both Sexes									
2008	1,335	311	23.3	145	10.8	400	30.0	479	35.9
2007	1,284	300	23.4	112	8.7	380	29.6	492	38.3
2006	1,230	332	27.0	103	8.3	332	27.0	464	37.7
2005	1,126	256	22.7	110	9.8	309	27.4	451	40.0
2004	1,112	218	19.6	162	14.5	292	26.3	440	39.6
2003[1]	1,052	277	26.3	128	12.2	273	26.0	374	35.6
2002	1,181	251	21.3	180	15.2	320	27.1	430	36.4

Note: High school graduates are people who have completed 4 years of high school or more, for 1967 to 1991. Beginning in 1992, they were people whose highest degree was a high school diploma (including equivalency) or higher.
[1]Starting in 2003 respondents could identify more than one race. Except as noted, the race data in this table from 2003 onward represent those respondents who indicated only one race category.

Table A-14.   Population 18 and 19 Years Old by School Enrollment Status, Sex, Race, and Hispanic Origin, October 1967–2008—*Continued*

(Numbers in thousands.)

Year, race, and Hispanic origin	Total	Population 18 and 19 years old							
		Still in high school	Percent	Dropped out	Percent	High school graduate only	Percent	In college	Percent
2001	1,246	299	24.0	152	12.2	351	28.2	444	35.6
2000	1,251	262	20.9	187	14.9	348	27.8	454	36.3
1999	1,199	259	21.6	190	15.8	320	26.7	430	35.9
1998	1,246	290	23.3	224	18.0	271	21.7	461	37.0
1997	1,133	278	24.5	172	15.2	302	26.7	381	33.6
1996	1,161	268	23.1	175	15.1	373	32.1	345	29.7
1995	1,099	287	26.1	177	16.1	291	26.5	344	31.3
1994	1,017	239	23.5	199	19.6	269	26.5	310	30.5
1993	1,040	290	27.9	133	12.8	306	29.4	311	29.9
1992	1,007	275	27.3	166	16.5	275	27.3	291	28.9
1991	1,041	276	26.5	146	14.0	316	30.4	303	29.1
1990	1,079	246	22.8	178	16.5	306	28.4	349	32.3
1989	1,078	239	22.2	194	18.0	343	31.8	302	28.0
1988	1,057	251	23.7	189	17.9	336	31.8	281	26.6
1987	1,043	213	20.4	166	15.9	323	31.0	341	32.7
1986	1,048	212	20.2	156	14.9	374	35.7	306	29.2
1985	1,072	213	19.9	186	17.4	414	38.6	259	24.2
1984	1,092	218	20.0	186	17.0	423	38.7	265	24.3
1983	1,134	265	23.4	199	17.5	412	36.3	258	22.8
1982	1,146	226	19.7	253	22.1	393	34.3	274	23.9
1981	1,128	238	21.1	218	19.3	366	32.4	306	27.1
1980	1,081	211	19.5	229	21.2	358	33.1	283	26.2
1979	1,072	221	20.6	246	22.9	326	30.4	279	26.0
1978	1,065	221	20.8	258	24.2	316	29.7	270	25.4
1977	1,072	249	23.2	235	21.9	319	29.8	269	25.1
1976	1,055	230	21.8	211	20.0	312	29.6	302	28.6
1975	1,030	225	21.8	262	25.4	283	27.5	260	25.2
1974	1,004	209	20.8	235	23.4	327	32.6	233	23.2
1973	997	182	18.3	252	25.3	369	37.0	194	19.5
1972	958	181	18.9	229	23.9	319	33.3	229	23.9
1971	908	219	24.1	219	24.1	266	29.3	204	22.5
1970	878	161	18.3	274	31.2	252	28.7	191	21.8
1969	837	179	21.4	227	27.1	238	28.4	193	23.1
1968	830	195	23.5	202	24.3	251	30.2	182	21.9
1967	780	175	22.4	203	26.0	261	33.5	141	18.1
Male									
2008	653	173	26.5	53	8.1	222	34.0	205	31.4
2007	628	161	25.7	54	8.6	186	29.6	227	36.2
2006	600	210	35.0	42	7.0	174	29.0	174	28.9
2005	552	178	32.2	60	10.9	121	21.9	193	35.0
2004	519	137	26.4	91	17.6	126	24.3	165	31.7
2003[1]	502	143	28.5	77	15.3	116	23.1	166	33.1
2002	608	155	25.5	123	20.2	151	24.8	179	29.4
2001	624	179	28.7	97	15.5	169	27.1	179	28.7
2000	593	148	25.0	105	17.7	177	29.8	163	27.5
1999	586	144	24.6	97	16.6	136	23.2	209	35.7
1998	613	163	26.6	128	20.9	128	20.9	194	31.6
1997	554	172	31.0	90	16.2	150	27.1	142	25.6
1996	564	167	29.6	90	16.0	162	28.7	145	25.7
1995	519	162	31.2	94	18.1	118	22.7	145	27.9
1994	497	134	27.0	116	23.3	115	23.1	132	26.6
1993	517	181	35.0	53	10.3	135	26.1	148	28.6
1992	499	180	36.1	82	16.4	114	22.8	123	24.6
1991	504	176	34.9	62	12.3	129	25.6	137	27.2
1990	520	152	29.2	80	15.4	124	23.8	164	31.5
1989	516	137	26.6	90	17.4	163	31.6	126	24.4
1988	510	145	28.4	92	18.0	165	32.4	108	21.2
1987	501	140	27.9	80	16.0	127	25.3	154	30.7
1986	506	149	29.4	74	14.6	165	32.6	118	23.3
1985	518	135	26.1	92	17.8	170	32.8	121	23.4
1984	524	143	27.3	103	19.7	166	31.7	112	21.4
1983	539	158	29.3	106	19.7	182	33.8	93	17.3
1982	549	132	24.0	145	26.4	148	27.0	124	22.6

Note: High school graduates are people who have completed 4 years of high school or more, for 1967 to 1991. Beginning in 1992, they were people whose highest degree was a high school diploma (including equivalency) or higher.
[1] Starting in 2003 respondents could identify more than one race. Except as noted, the race data in this table from 2003 onward represent those respondents who indicated only one race category.

Table A-14.   Population 18 and 19 Years Old by School Enrollment Status, Sex, Race, and Hispanic Origin, October 1967–2008—*Continued*

(Numbers in thousands.)

Year, race, and Hispanic origin	Total	Still in high school	Percent	Dropped out	Percent	High school graduate only	Percent	In college	Percent
					Population 18 and 19 years old				
1981	538	145	27.0	102	19.0	158	29.4	133	24.7
1980	503	118	23.5	114	22.7	173	34.4	98	19.5
1979	497	128	25.8	122	24.5	137	27.6	110	22.1
1978	493	135	27.4	127	25.8	117	23.7	114	23.1
1977	496	161	32.5	118	23.8	127	25.6	90	18.1
1976	499	153	30.7	96	19.2	129	25.9	121	24.2
1975	476	127	26.7	132	27.7	106	22.3	111	23.3
1974	474	116	24.5	128	27.0	128	27.0	102	21.5
1973	467	106	22.7	130	27.8	135	28.9	96	20.6
1972	445	110	24.7	121	27.2	112	25.2	102	22.9
1971	423	120	28.4	110	26.0	99	23.4	94	22.2
1970	414	98	23.7	151	36.5	92	22.2	73	17.6
1969	394	109	27.7	124	31.5	75	19.0	86	21.8
1968	390	124	31.8	93	23.8	90	23.1	83	21.3
1967	356	95	26.7	109	30.6	74	20.8	78	21.9
Female									
2008	681	138	20.3	92	13.5	178	26.1	274	40.2
2007	655	139	21.2	58	8.8	194	29.6	265	40.4
2006	631	122	19.3	60	9.6	158	25.0	291	46.1
2005	574	78	13.6	49	8.6	189	32.9	258	44.9
2004	593	81	13.7	70	11.9	167	28.2	275	46.5
2003[1]	550	133	24.2	51	9.3	157	28.5	209	38.0
2002	574	97	16.9	57	9.9	169	29.4	251	43.7
2001	623	122	19.6	54	8.7	182	29.2	265	42.5
2000	658	113	17.2	82	12.5	172	26.1	291	44.2
1999	613	114	18.6	94	15.3	184	30.0	221	36.1
1998	633	127	20.1	96	15.2	143	22.6	267	42.2
1997	579	107	18.5	82	14.2	152	26.3	238	41.1
1996	597	102	17.1	85	14.2	211	35.3	199	33.3
1995	581	126	21.7	83	14.3	173	29.8	199	34.3
1994	520	105	20.2	83	16.0	154	29.6	178	34.2
1993	523	108	20.7	80	15.3	172	32.9	163	31.2
1992	508	95	18.7	84	16.5	161	31.7	168	33.1
1991	537	99	18.4	85	15.8	187	34.8	166	30.9
1990	559	95	17.0	98	17.5	181	32.4	185	33.1
1989	562	102	18.1	104	18.5	180	32.0	176	31.3
1988	547	105	19.2	97	17.7	172	31.4	173	31.6
1987	542	75	13.8	85	15.7	196	36.2	186	34.3
1986	542	62	11.4	83	15.3	209	38.6	188	34.7
1985	554	78	14.1	94	17.0	244	44.0	138	24.9
1984	568	76	13.4	82	14.4	257	45.2	153	26.9
1983	595	108	18.2	93	15.6	230	38.7	164	27.6
1982	597	95	15.9	108	18.1	244	40.9	150	25.1
1981	590	93	15.8	116	19.7	209	35.4	172	29.2
1980	578	93	16.1	115	19.9	185	32.0	185	32.0
1979	576	93	16.1	125	21.7	189	32.8	169	29.3
1978	572	88	15.4	130	22.7	199	34.8	155	27.1
1977	576	88	15.3	117	20.3	192	33.3	179	31.1
1976	556	77	13.8	115	20.7	183	32.9	181	32.6
1975	553	97	17.5	130	23.5	176	31.8	150	27.1
1974	530	92	17.4	107	20.2	200	37.7	131	24.7
1973	530	77	14.5	122	23.0	234	44.2	97	18.3
1972	513	71	13.8	108	21.1	207	40.4	127	24.8
1971	485	100	20.6	109	22.5	167	34.4	109	22.5
1970	464	62	13.4	124	26.7	160	34.5	118	25.4
1969	443	70	15.8	102	23.0	163	36.8	108	24.4
1968	439	69	15.7	109	24.8	161	36.7	100	22.8
1967	424	81	19.1	93	21.9	187	44.1	63	14.9

Note: High school graduates are people who have completed 4 years of high school or more, for 1967 to 1991. Beginning in 1992, they were people whose highest degree was a high school diploma (including equivalency) or higher.
[1]Starting in 2003 respondents could identify more than one race. Except as noted, the race data in this table from 2003 onward represent those respondents who indicated only one race category.

Table A-14. Population 18 and 19 Years Old by School Enrollment Status, Sex, Race, and Hispanic Origin, October 1967–2008—*Continued*

(Numbers in thousands.)

Year, race, and Hispanic origin	Total	Population 18 and 19 years old							
		Still in high school	Percent	Dropped out	Percent	High school graduate only	Percent	In college	Percent
ASIAN ALONE[2]									
Both Sexes									
2008	259	49	19.0	7	2.7	31	12.0	172	66.4
2007	296	55	18.4	12	4.2	27	9.3	201	68.1
2006	297	43	14.4	9	3.0	41	14.0	204	68.6
2005	251	34	13.4	4	1.5	25	10.0	188	74.9
2004	257	31	11.9	10	3.8	34	13.2	182	70.7
2003[1]	286	41	14.3	3	1.0	33	11.5	209	73.1
2002	353	42	11.9	14	4.0	61	17.3	236	66.9
2001	353	50	14.2	18	5.1	38	10.8	247	70.0
2000	326	45	13.8	17	5.2	52	16.0	212	65.0
1999	339	43	12.7	22	6.5	51	15.0	223	65.8
Male									
2008	128	39	30.2	6	5.1	8	5.9	75	58.9
2007	150	33	22.1	2	1.1	11	7.1	104	69.7
2006	167	20	12.2	8	4.7	26	15.7	113	67.5
2005	131	21	16.3	3	2.0	17	13.0	90	68.9
2004	133	22	16.7	1	0.7	18	13.5	92	69.3
2003[1]	129	14	10.9	3	2.3	9	7.0	103	79.8
2002	179	22	12.3	10	5.6	26	14.5	121	67.6
2001	168	27	16.1	14	8.3	14	8.3	113	67.3
2000	162	14	8.6	14	8.6	26	16.0	108	66.7
1999	156	23	14.7	17	10.9	23	14.7	93	59.6
Female									
2008	132	11	8.0	0	0.4	24	17.9	97	73.7
2007	146	21	14.6	11	7.5	17	11.5	97	66.4
2006	130	23	17.3	1	0.9	15	11.8	91	70.0
2005	120	12	10.3	1	0.9	9	7.5	98	81.4
2004	124	8	6.8	9	7.1	18	14.5	89	72.2
2003[1]	157	26	16.6	-	-	24	15.3	107	68.2
2002	173	20	11.6	3	1.7	35	20.2	115	66.5
2001	185	23	12.4	4	2.2	24	13.0	134	72.4
2000	164	30	18.3	4	2.4	26	15.9	104	63.4
1999	183	20	10.9	5	2.7	28	15.3	130	71.0
HISPANIC[3]									
Both Sexes									
2008	1,539	320	20.8	296	19.3	395	25.7	528	34.3
2007	1,523	311	20.4	254	16.7	399	26.2	559	36.7
2006	1,406	307	21.8	253	18.0	402	28.6	444	31.6
2005	1,253	272	21.7	227	18.1	348	27.8	406	32.4
2004	1,270	244	19.2	296	23.3	346	27.2	384	30.2
2003	1,214	229	18.9	291	24.0	315	25.9	379	31.2
2002	1,309	303	23.1	310	23.7	336	25.7	360	27.5
2001	1,391	246	17.7	399	28.7	359	25.8	387	27.8
2000	1,248	268	21.5	311	24.9	320	25.6	349	28.0
1999	1,220	246	20.2	337	27.6	340	27.9	297	24.3
1998	1,209	199	16.5	402	33.3	320	26.5	288	23.8
1997	1,087	221	20.3	274	25.2	276	25.4	316	29.1
1996	1,000	229	22.9	295	29.5	236	23.6	240	24.0
1995	1,012	203	20.1	312	30.8	233	23.0	264	26.1
1994	925	250	27.0	237	25.6	213	23.0	225	24.3
1993	710	159	22.4	201	28.3	155	21.8	195	27.5
1992	778	188	24.2	197	25.3	163	21.0	230	29.6
1991	823	206	25.0	269	32.7	160	19.4	188	22.8
1990	746	181	24.3	255	34.2	162	21.7	148	19.8
1989	733	150	20.5	205	28.0	201	27.4	177	24.1
1988	734	121	16.5	229	31.2	181	24.7	203	27.7
1987	699	121	17.3	195	27.9	231	33.0	152	21.7
1986	614	114	18.6	164	26.7	171	27.9	165	26.9

Note: High school graduates are people who have completed 4 years of high school or more, for 1967 to 1991. Beginning in 1992, they were people whose highest degree was a high school diploma (including equivalency) or higher.
[1]Starting in 2003 respondents could identify more than one race. Except as noted, the race data in this table from 2003 onward represent those respondents who indicated only one race category.
[2]The data shown prior to 2003 consists of those identifying themselves as "Asian or Pacific Islanders."
[3]May be of any race.
- = Quantity zero or rounds to zero.

Table A-14. Population 18 and 19 Years Old by School Enrollment Status, Sex, Race, and Hispanic Origin, October 1967–2008—*Continued*

(Numbers in thousands.)

Year, race, and Hispanic origin	Total	Population 18 and 19 years old							
		Still in high school	Percent	Dropped out	Percent	High school graduate only	Percent	In college	Percent
1985........................	570	111	19.5	175	30.7	157	27.5	127	22.3
1984........................	561	88	15.7	146	26.0	191	34.0	136	24.2
1983........................	573	119	20.8	166	29.0	154	26.9	134	23.4
1982........................	600	92	15.3	198	33.0	167	27.8	143	23.8
1981........................	606	100	16.5	220	36.3	157	25.9	129	21.3
1980........................	597	89	14.9	233	39.0	138	23.1	137	22.9
1979........................	507	78	15.4	157	31.0	148	29.2	124	24.5
1978........................	478	61	12.8	183	38.3	125	26.2	109	22.8
1977........................	515	86	16.7	168	32.6	138	26.8	123	23.9
1976........................	534	98	18.4	164	30.7	129	24.2	143	26.8
1975........................	489	97	19.8	147	30.1	127	26.0	118	24.1
1974........................	467	99	21.2	139	29.8	117	25.1	112	24.0
1973........................	387	70	18.1	142	36.7	93	24.0	82	21.2
1972........................	381	88	23.1	117	30.7	106	27.8	70	18.4
Male									
2008........................	779	190	24.4	141	18.1	212	27.2	236	30.3
2007........................	780	185	23.7	145	18.5	205	26.3	246	31.5
2006........................	708	152	21.4	150	21.2	193	27.3	213	30.1
2005........................	663	166	25.1	144	21.7	180	27.1	173	26.2
2004........................	668	117	17.5	214	32.0	166	24.9	171	25.6
2003........................	635	142	22.4	161	25.4	179	28.2	153	24.1
2002........................	716	191	26.7	200	27.9	169	23.6	156	21.8
2001........................	701	131	18.7	254	36.2	167	23.8	149	21.3
2000........................	656	154	23.5	183	27.9	159	24.2	160	24.4
1999........................	642	148	23.1	180	28.0	171	26.6	143	22.3
1998........................	598	104	17.4	234	39.1	163	27.3	97	16.2
1997........................	579	130	22.5	162	28.0	154	26.6	133	23.0
1996........................	506	139	27.5	154	30.4	115	22.7	98	19.4
1995........................	535	132	24.7	145	27.1	137	25.6	121	22.6
1994........................	454	157	34.6	118	26.0	90	19.8	89	19.6
1993........................	325	86	26.5	105	32.3	65	20.0	69	21.2
1992........................	385	110	28.6	99	25.7	83	21.6	93	24.2
1991........................	416	107	25.7	161	38.7	80	19.2	68	16.3
1990........................	358	76	21.2	141	39.4	71	19.8	70	19.6
1989........................	371	89	24.0	96	25.9	111	29.9	75	20.2
1988........................	364	88	24.2	128	35.2	73	20.1	75	20.6
1987........................	333	66	19.8	105	31.5	86	25.8	76	22.8
1986........................	326	58	17.8	95	29.1	86	26.4	87	26.7
1985........................	275	62	22.5	116	42.2	53	19.3	44	16.0
1984........................	249	55	22.1	65	26.1	87	34.9	42	16.9
1983........................	266	66	24.8	87	32.7	72	27.1	41	15.4
1982........................	304	69	22.7	106	34.9	77	25.3	52	17.1
1981........................	288	47	16.3	127	44.1	57	19.8	57	19.8
1980........................	310	46	14.8	134	43.2	62	20.0	68	21.9
1979........................	256	42	16.4	89	34.8	58	22.7	67	26.2
1978........................	221	35	15.8	81	36.7	52	23.5	53	24.0
1977........................	238	49	20.6	80	33.6	55	23.1	54	22.7
1976........................	258	51	19.8	82	31.8	56	21.7	69	26.7
1975........................	229	66	28.8	60	26.2	50	21.8	53	23.1
1974........................	222	49	22.1	78	35.1	40	18.0	55	24.8
1973........................	190	48	25.3	62	32.6	41	21.6	39	20.5
1972........................	190	49	25.8	67	35.3	46	24.2	28	14.7
Female									
2008........................	760	130	17.1	156	20.5	183	24.0	292	38.4
2007........................	743	126	17.0	109	14.7	193	26.1	313	42.2
2006........................	698	156	22.3	102	14.7	209	30.0	231	33.1
2005........................	591	105	17.8	83	14.0	171	28.9	232	39.3
2004........................	602	127	21.1	82	13.6	180	29.9	213	35.4
2003........................	579	87	15.0	130	22.5	136	23.5	226	39.0
2002........................	593	112	18.9	110	18.5	167	28.2	204	34.4
2001........................	691	116	16.8	145	21.0	192	27.8	238	34.4
2000........................	591	114	19.3	128	21.7	161	27.2	188	31.8

Note: High school graduates are people who have completed 4 years of high school or more, for 1967 to 1991. Beginning in 1992, they were people whose highest degree was a high school diploma (including equivalency) or higher.
[1]Starting in 2003 respondents could identify more than one race. Except as noted, the race data in this table from 2003 onward represent those respondents who indicated only one race category.
[2]The data shown prior to 2003 consists of those identifying themselves as "Asian or Pacific Islanders."
[3]May be of any race.

Table A-14.   Population 18 and 19 Years Old by School Enrollment Status, Sex, Race, and Hispanic Origin, October 1967–2008—*Continued*

(Numbers in thousands.)

Year, race, and Hispanic origin	Total	Population 18 and 19 years old							
		Still in high school	Percent	Dropped out	Percent	High school graduate only	Percent	In college	Percent
1999	577	99	17.2	157	27.2	168	29.1	153	26.5
1998	611	95	15.5	169	27.7	156	25.5	191	31.3
1997	508	91	17.9	112	22.0	122	24.0	183	36.0
1996	494	91	18.4	140	28.3	121	24.5	142	28.7
1995	478	71	14.9	167	34.9	97	20.3	143	29.9
1994	471	93	19.7	119	25.3	123	26.1	136	28.9
1993	385	74	19.2	96	24.9	89	23.1	126	32.7
1992	393	78	19.8	98	24.9	80	20.4	137	34.9
1991	407	98	24.1	109	26.8	80	19.7	120	29.5
1990	388	105	27.1	114	29.4	91	23.5	78	20.1
1989	362	60	16.6	108	29.8	91	25.1	103	28.5
1988	370	32	8.6	101	27.3	108	29.2	129	34.9
1987	367	58	15.8	89	24.3	144	39.2	76	20.7
1986	288	54	18.8	69	24.0	86	29.9	79	27.4
1985	296	51	17.2	59	19.9	104	35.1	82	27.7
1984	311	33	10.6	81	26.0	103	33.1	94	30.2
1983	307	53	17.3	79	25.7	82	26.7	93	30.3
1982	296	23	7.8	92	31.1	90	30.4	91	30.7
1981	318	53	16.7	93	29.2	100	31.4	72	22.6
1980	287	44	15.3	99	34.5	76	26.5	68	23.7
1979	251	35	13.9	68	27.1	90	35.9	58	23.1
1978	257	26	10.1	102	39.7	73	28.4	56	21.8
1977	277	37	13.4	88	31.8	82	29.6	70	25.3
1976	276	49	17.8	81	29.3	72	26.1	74	26.8
1975	261	32	12.3	87	33.3	77	29.5	65	24.9
1974	245	50	20.4	62	25.3	77	31.4	56	22.9
1973	197	21	10.7	80	40.6	52	26.4	44	22.3
1972	191	37	19.4	50	26.2	61	31.9	43	22.5
WHITE ALONE OR IN COMBINATION									
Both Sexes									
2008	6,762	1,093	16.2	581	8.6	1,647	24.4	3,440	50.9
2007	6,595	1,108	16.8	525	8.0	1,644	24.9	3,318	50.3
2006	6,466	1,160	17.9	615	9.5	1,648	25.5	3,043	47.1
2005	6,078	1,064	17.5	537	8.8	1,442	23.7	3,035	49.9
2004	6,191	988	16.0	643	10.4	1,548	25.0	3,012	48.7
2003	6,093	994	16.3	675	11.1	1,519	24.9	2,905	47.7
Male									
2008	3,435	605	17.6	305	8.9	917	26.7	1,607	46.8
2007	3,350	684	20.4	284	8.5	842	25.1	1,540	46.0
2006	3,278	657	20.0	357	10.9	864	26.4	1,399	42.7
2005	3,149	692	22.0	321	10.2	358	11.4	1,778	56.5
2004	3,129	538	17.2	415	13.3	845	27.0	1,331	42.5
2003	3,078	604	19.6	390	12.7	801	26.0	1,283	41.7
Female									
2008	3,328	488	14.7	277	8.3	730	21.9	1,833	55.1
2007	3,245	424	13.1	241	7.4	801	24.7	1,779	54.8
2006	3,188	503	15.8	258	8.1	784	24.6	1,643	51.5
2005	2,929	372	12.7	216	7.4	669	22.8	1,672	57.1
2004	3,062	450	14.7	228	7.4	702	22.9	1,682	54.9
2003	3,015	390	12.9	284	9.4	719	23.8	1,622	53.8
BLACK ALONE OR IN COMBINATION									
Both Sexes									
2008	1,431	339	23.7	155	10.8	422	29.5	515	36.0
2007	1,347	306	22.7	116	8.6	395	29.3	530	39.3
2006	1,287	343	26.6	111	8.6	341	26.5	492	38.2
2005	1,195	266	22.3	112	9.4	336	28.1	481	40.2
2004	1,163	229	19.7	163	14.0	305	26.2	466	40.1
2003	1,129	288	25.5	131	11.6	310	27.5	400	35.4

Note: High school graduates are people who have completed 4 years of high school or more, for 1967 to 1991. Beginning in 1992, they were people whose highest degree was a high school diploma (including equivalency) or higher.

Table A-14.   Population 18 and 19 Years Old by School Enrollment Status, Sex, Race, and Hispanic Origin, October 1967–2008—*Continued*

(Numbers in thousands.)

Year, race, and Hispanic origin	Total	Population 18 and 19 years old							
		Still in high school	Percent	Dropped out	Percent	High school graduate only	Percent	In college	Percent
Male									
2008..	706	191	27.0	58	8.3	238	33.7	219	31.1
2007..	657	164	25.0	56	8.5	197	30.0	240	36.5
2006..	623	213	34.3	45	7.3	178	28.6	186	29.8
2005..	586	187	31.8	62	10.7	136	23.2	201	34.3
2004..	549	142	25.9	93	17.0	139	25.3	175	31.9
2003..	525	146	27.8	81	15.4	123	23.4	175	33.3
Female									
2008..	724	148	20.5	96	13.3	184	25.4	296	40.8
2007..	690	142	20.6	61	8.8	198	28.6	290	42.0
2006..	665	130	19.5	66	9.9	163	24.5	307	46.1
2005..	609	80	13.1	49	8.1	200	32.8	280	45.9
2004..	615	86	14.0	70	11.4	169	27.5	290	47.2
2003..	604	142	23.5	51	8.4	186	30.8	225	37.3
ASIAN ALONE OR IN COMBINATION									
Both Sexes									
2008..	309	52	16.8	7	2.3	37	11.8	214	69.1
2007..	336	58	17.2	12	3.7	34	10.0	232	69.1
2006..	318	47	14.8	9	2.8	47	14.9	215	67.5
2005..	286	42	14.7	4	1.3	36	12.6	204	71.5
2004..	299	36	12.0	14	4.5	46	15.4	203	67.9
2003..	320	43	13.4	3	1.1	38	11.9	236	73.8
Male									
2008..	150	41	27.6	6	4.3	9	6.0	93	62.1
2007..	161	33	20.7	2	1.0	14	8.4	113	69.9
2006..	179	22	12.4	8	4.3	31	17.5	118	65.8
2005..	152	30	19.5	3	1.7	22	14.5	97	64.1
2004..	149	27	18.1	5	3.2	20	13.4	97	65.1
2003..	144	17	11.8	3	2.3	12	8.3	112	77.8
Female									
2008..	159	11	6.6	-	0.3	28	17.3	121	75.8
2007..	174	24	13.9	11	6.3	20	11.5	119	68.3
2006..	139	25	18.0	1	0.8	16	11.4	97	69.7
2005..	134	12	9.2	1	0.9	14	10.4	107	80.0
2004..	150	8	5.3	9	5.9	27	18.0	106	70.7
2003..	176	25	14.2	-	-	27	15.3	124	70.5

Note: High school graduates are people who have completed 4 years of high school or more, for 1967 to 1991. Beginning in 1992, they were people whose highest degree was a high school diploma (including equivalency) or higher.
- = Quantity zero or rounds to zero.

Table A-15.   Age Distribution of College Students 14 Years Old and Over, by Sex, October 1947–2008

(Numbers in thousands.)

Year, sex, race, and Hispanic origin	All Students								Male							
	Total	14 to 17 years	18 and 19 years	20 and 21 years	22 to 24 years	25 to 29 years	30 to 34 years	35 years and over	Total	14 to 17 years	18 and 19 years	20 and 21 years	22 to 24 years	25 to 29 years	30 to 34 years	35 years and over
All Races																
2008	18,632	241	4,126	3,920	3,420	2,657	1,356	2,911	8,311	133	1,909	1,908	1,566	1,229	577	989
2007	17,956	186	4,075	3,794	3,292	2,496	1,342	2,772	7,826	76	1,903	1,729	1,524	1,029	596	968
2006	17,232	212	3,746	3,675	3,166	2,312	1,346	2,776	7,506	79	1,703	1,682	1,489	1,033	537	982
2005	17,472	181	3,727	3,945	3,162	2,291	1,309	2,857	7,539	62	1,675	1,878	1,420	923	562	1,019
2004	17,383	198	3,685	3,777	3,149	2,403	1,287	2,884	7,575	75	1,610	1,811	1,444	1,068	533	1,033
2003	16,638	150	3,512	3,533	3,320	2,164	1,330	2,630	7,318	61	1,568	1,551	1,578	982	607	970
2002	16,497	195	3,581	3,525	2,927	2,093	1,308	2,867	7,240	80	1,635	1,640	1,354	918	542	1,071
2001	15,873	138	3,478	3,421	2,731	2,084	1,337	2,685	6,875	54	1,570	1,579	1,287	917	559	908
2000	15,314	149	3,599	3,169	2,683	1,962	1,244	2,507	6,682	61	1,570	1,472	1,300	844	517	918
1999	15,203	151	3,520	3,120	2,620	1,940	1,155	2,697	6,956	78	1,648	1,525	1,224	911	547	1,023
1998	15,546	123	3,670	3,092	2,561	2,148	1,266	2,685	6,905	48	1,667	1,517	1,219	979	521	953
1997	15,436	171	3,362	3,143	2,699	2,154	1,116	2,791	6,843	59	1,561	1,521	1,292	1,052	457	899
1996	15,226	237	3,309	2,907	2,551	2,215	1,228	2,778	6,820	97	1,489	1,379	1,319	1,038	485	1,013
1995	14,715	158	3,101	2,940	2,498	2,143	1,206	2,669	6,703	68	1,431	1,423	1,235	1,008	553	985
1994[3]	15,022	150	3,051	3,028	2,650	2,026	1,393	2,725	6,764	65	1,416	1,414	1,322	972	617	958
1993[r]	14,394	130	3,070	2,892	2,668	1,914	1,226	2,493	6,599	55	1,407	1,405	1,425	892	534	880
1993	13,898	123	2,926	2,734	2,533	1,867	1,227	2,488	6,324	52	1,337	1,312	1,345	872	534	873
1992	14,035	205	2,892	2,938	2,512	1,829	1,296	2,364	6,192	97	1,325	1,344	1,243	845	547	789
1991	14,057	132	2,929	2,939	2,304	1,983	1,302	2,468	6,439	49	1,326	1,390	1,238	1,018	587	832
1990	13,621	178	3,019	2,767	2,178	1,927	1,235	2,319	6,192	86	1,443	1,364	1,115	910	502	772
1989	13,180	183	3,066	2,570	2,168	1,889	1,192	2,112	5,950	73	1,422	1,228	1,067	926	517	716
1988	13,116	182	3,046	2,681	2,064	1,735	1,228	2,179	5,950	58	1,365	1,295	1,110	835	560	727
1987	12,719	239	3,045	2,642	2,006	1,826	1,159	1,802	6,030	116	1,483	1,350	1,034	921	500	625
1986	12,651	201	2,967	2,374	2,136	1,860	1,245	1,867	5,957	82	1,421	1,161	1,120	968	577	628
1985	12,524	262	2,907	2,616	2,014	1,884	1,180	1,661	5,906	131	1,349	1,313	1,087	942	522	561
1984	12,304	253	2,867	2,597	2,127	1,857	1,158	1,445	5,989	91	1,373	1,337	1,219	965	527	476
1983	12,320	260	2,940	2,495	2,042	1,921	1,167	1,495	6,010	108	1,340	1,310	1,170	1,055	521	506
1982	12,308	254	2,929	2,689	2,060	1,859	1,129	1,389	5,899	112	1,376	1,346	1,115	968	492	490
1981	12,127	232	3,044	2,545	1,986	1,717	1,211	1,393	5,825	96	1,450	1,239	1,144	909	533	453
1980	11,387	249	2,933	2,423	1,870	1,641	1,062	1,207	5,430	96	1,369	1,246	989	853	472	405
1979	11,380	311	2,844	2,353	1,794	1,679	996	1,402	5,480	129	1,341	1,192	975	893	463	487
1978	11,141	274	2,899	2,298	1,798	1,619	950	1,303	5,580	106	1,391	1,202	1,028	922	474	457
1977	11,546	274	2,913	2,430	1,799	1,809	992	1,329	5,889	112	1,396	1,280	1,036	1,035	511	520
1976	11,139	281	2,937	2,398	1,846	1,686	803	1,189	5,785	105	1,391	1,209	1,073	1,067	451	489
1975	10,880	293	2,943	2,313	1,679	1,616	853	1,183	5,911	128	1,426	1,256	1,011	1,025	496	569
1974	9,852	309	2,597	2,192	1,527	1,482	720	1,025	5,402	145	1,262	1,206	943	951	420	476
1973	8,966	295	2,517	2,073	1,465	1,278	551	787	5,048	121	1,293	1,130	937	867	329	371
1972	9,096	295	2,680	2,116	1,461	1,229	531	783	5,218	141	1,366	1,170	998	848	330	365
1971	8,087	284	2,726	1,997	1,487	1,067	527	...	4,850	129	1,444	1,090	1,065	787	334	...
1970	7,413	260	2,594	1,857	1,354	939	410	...	4,401	130	1,346	902		684	256	...
1969	7,435	242	2,601	1,945	1,294	918	435	...	4,448	120	1,397	1,112	883	671	265	...
1968	6,801	281	2,501	1,826	1,029	790	373	...	4,124	134	1,357	1,093	702	603	236	...
1967	6,401	239	2,286	1,816	998	707	356	...	3,841	96	1,198	1,066	718	524	239	...
1966	6,085	254	2,440	1,472	987	679	254	...	3,749	105	1,355	899	722	494	174	...
1965	5,675	264	2,215	1,326	940	614	316	...	3,503	113	1,218	804	699	458	211	...
1964	4,643	291	1,616	1,287	670	523	256	...	2,888	165	866	769	510	396	182	...
1963	4,336	180	1,504	1,212	717	482	241	...	2,742	99	796	734	574	365	174	...
1962	4,208	233	1,612	996	630	486	251	...	2,742	125	891	617	508	406	195	...
1961	3,731	213	1,470	892	507	437	212	...	2,356	84	834	554	393	337	154	...
1960	3,570	222	1,299	790	509	491	259	...	2,339	99	734	503	411	399	193	...
1959	3,340	210	1,175	739	489	503	224	...	2,187	92	651	501	355	422	166	...
1958	3,242	167	1,114	-----1,221-----		534	206	...	2,129	73	621	-----850-----		439	146	...
1957	3,138	176	989	-----1,236-----		553	184	...	2,028	77	538	-----827-----		459	127	...
1956	2,883	167	934	-----1,105-----		494	183	...	1,932	77	512	-----781-----		429	133	...
1955	2,379	147	745	-----931-----		406	150	...	1,579	57	432	-----647-----		337	107	...
1950	2,175	180	733	-----939-----		324	...	...	1,474	74	395	-----692-----		314	...	...
1947	2,311	188	620	-----1,088-----		321	94	...	1,687	87	343	-----872-----		301	84	...
White Alone																
2008	14,405	171	3,353	3,119	2,669	1,952	907	2,234	6,570	85	1,566	1,524	1,250	938	413	794
2007	13,835	141	3,242	3,053	2,485	1,817	952	2,144	6,050	62	1,508	1,359	1,172	770	413	766
2006	13,273	161	2,982	2,958	2,358	1,740	985	2,090	5,829	57	1,367	1,344	1,131	799	396	734
2005	13,466	116	2,972	3,176	2,350	1,708	939	2,205	5,843	38	1,343	1,488	1,092	685	420	777
2004	13,381	134	2,946	3,016	2,389	1,776	974	2,146	5,944	49	1,308	1,437	1,110	837	421	782
2003[1]	12,870	100	2,833	2,796	2,521	1,585	960	2,075	5,714	48	1,258	1,236	1,232	723	435	783

[1]Starting in 2003 respondents could identify more than one race. Except as noted, the race data in this table from 2003 onward represent those respondents who indicated only one race category.
[3]Prior to 1972, total enrolled does not include the 35 and over population.
r = Revised, controlled to 1990 census based population estimates; previous 1993 data controlled to 1980 census based population estimates.
... = Not available.

Table A-15.   Age Distribution of College Students 14 Years Old and Over, by Sex, October 1947–2008—Continued

(Numbers in thousands.)

Year, sex, race, and Hispanic origin	Female							
	Total	14 to 17 years	18 and 19 years	20 and 21 years	22 to 24 years	25 to 29 years	30 to 34 years	35 years and over
All Races								
2008	10,321	108	2,217	2,013	1,854	1,428	779	1,922
2007	10,130	109	2,172	2,065	1,768	1,466	746	1,804
2006	9,726	133	2,043	1,993	1,677	1,278	809	1,793
2005	9,934	119	2,052	2,067	1,742	1,368	747	1,838
2004	9,808	123	2,074	1,966	1,705	1,335	753	1,850
2003	9,319	89	1,944	1,982	1,742	1,181	723	1,660
2002	9,258	116	1,946	1,885	1,573	1,175	766	1,797
2001	8,998	84	1,907	1,841	1,444	1,167	778	1,776
2000	8,631	88	2,029	1,697	1,383	1,118	728	1,589
1999	8,247	73	1,872	1,595	1,396	1,029	608	1,674
1998	8,641	74	2,003	1,574	1,342	1,170	745	1,732
1997	8,593	112	1,801	1,622	1,406	1,102	658	1,892
1996	8,406	140	1,821	1,528	1,233	1,177	743	1,765
1995	8,013	90	1,671	1,518	1,263	1,135	653	1,684
1994[3]	8,258	85	1,635	1,613	1,328	1,054	776	1,766
1993[r]	7,795	75	1,663	1,487	1,243	1,022	692	1,613
1993	7,574	71	1,588	1,422	1,189	995	693	1,616
1992	7,844	107	1,566	1,594	1,269	984	748	1,575
1991	7,618	83	1,603	1,549	1,066	965	715	1,636
1990	7,429	91	1,576	1,403	1,063	1,017	732	1,546
1989	7,231	110	1,643	1,342	1,100	964	675	1,396
1988	7,166	124	1,682	1,386	953	900	668	1,452
1987	6,689	123	1,562	1,292	972	905	659	1,176
1986	6,694	120	1,546	1,213	1,016	892	667	1,240
1985	6,618	129	1,559	1,303	926	941	658	1,100
1984	6,315	161	1,494	1,260	908	892	630	970
1983	6,310	153	1,600	1,185	872	865	645	989
1982	6,410	141	1,553	1,343	945	891	637	900
1981	6,303	136	1,594	1,305	842	808	677	940
1980	5,957	153	1,565	1,178	882	788	590	802
1979	5,900	183	1,503	1,161	818	786	533	914
1978	5,559	168	1,507	1,096	770	697	476	845
1977	5,657	162	1,517	1,151	763	774	481	809
1976	5,354	176	1,546	1,189	773	619	352	700
1975	4,969	164	1,517	1,058	668	590	357	614
1974	4,449	165	1,335	986	584	531	300	548
1973	3,918	174	1,224	944	528	411	222	416
1972	3,877	153	1,314	946	464	381	200	418
1971	3,236	154	1,281	906	423	280	192	...
1970	3,013	130	1,248	774	452	255	154	...
1969	2,987	122	1,204	833	411	247	171	...
1968	2,677	147	1,144	733	328	187	138	...
1967	2,560	143	1,088	749	280	183	117	...
1966	2,337	149	1,085	573	265	185	80	...
1965	2,172	151	997	522	241	156	105	...
1964	1,755	126	750	518	160	127	74	...
1963	1,594	81	708	478	143	117	67	...
1962	1,466	108	721	379	122	80	56	...
1961	1,375	129	636	338	114	100	58	...
1960	1,231	123	565	287	98	92	66	...
1959	1,153	118	524	238	134	81	58	...
1958	1,113	94	493	-----371-----		95	60	...
1957	1,110	99	451	-----409-----		94	57	...
1956	951	90	422	-----324-----		65	50	...
1955	800	90	313	-----285-----		69	43	...
1950	701	106	338	-----247-----		10	...	...
1947	624	101	277	-----216-----		20	10	...
White Alone								
2008	7,835	85	1,787	1,595	1,419	1,014	493	1,440
2007	7,785	80	1,734	1,694	1,313	1,047	539	1,378
2006	7,445	104	1,615	1,613	1,227	941	588	1,355
2005	7,624	79	1,629	1,688	1,258	1,024	519	1,428
2004	7,438	86	1,638	1,579	1,279	939	553	1,364
2003[1]	7,155	53	1,575	1,560	1,289	862	525	1,291

[1]Starting in 2003 respondents could identify more than one race. Except as noted, the race data in this table from 2003 onward represent those respondents who indicated only one race category.
[3]Prior to 1972, total enrolled does not include the 35 and over population.
r = Revised, controlled to 1990 census based population estimates; previous 1993 data controlled to 1980 census based population estimates.
... = Not available.

Table A-15. Age Distribution of College Students 14 Years Old and Over, by Sex, October 1947–2008—*Continued*

(Numbers in thousands.)

Year, sex, race, and Hispanic origin	All Students								Male							
	Total	14 to 17 years	18 and 19 years	20 and 21 years	22 to 24 years	25 to 29 years	30 to 34 years	35 years and over	Total	14 to 17 years	18 and 19 years	20 and 21 years	22 to 24 years	25 to 29 years	30 to 34 years	35 years and over
2002.........	12,781	109	2,891	2,810	2,220	1,582	933	2,236	5,719	57	1,329	1,306	1,066	712	394	855
2001.........	12,208	88	2,755	2,774	2,019	1,514	956	2,103	5,383	36	1,273	1,305	943	693	401	731
2000.........	11,999	117	2,914	2,590	2,062	1,433	906	1,978	5,311	47	1,289	1,225	1,008	662	367	713
1999.........	12,053	87	2,849	2,519	2,074	1,474	870	2,173	5,562	32	1,335	1,226	1,026	715	414	804
1998.........	12,401	93	2,994	2,537	2,010	1,604	964	2,199	5,602	30	1,376	1,256	1,002	746	396	795
1997.........	12,442	127	2,792	2,602	2,101	1,666	856	2,289	5,552	48	1,314	1,289	1,030	802	345	725
1996.........	12,189	167	2,731	2,362	2,030	1,704	940	2,254	5,453	70	1,223	1,117	1,079	797	357	811
1995.........	12,021	116	2,577	2,437	1,997	1,745	941	2,208	5,535	44	1,195	1,201	1,002	857	432	804
1994³.........	12,222	101	2,568	2,459	2,091	1,592	1,143	2,267	5,524	44	1,212	1,140	1,054	749	512	815
1993ʳ.........	11,735	103	2,566	2,356	2,152	1,507	1,003	2,049	5,403	44	1,157	1,196	1,145	705	451	705
1993.........	11,434	98	2,456	2,243	2,064	1,490	1,015	2,068	5,222	41	1,103	1,120	1,090	699	457	711
1992.........	11,710	158	2,419	2,466	2,031	1,512	1,070	2,053	5,210	82	1,102	1,162	1,027	689	471	678
1991.........	11,686	104	2,487	2,449	1,877	1,598	1,063	2,107	5,304	41	1,112	1,146	1,012	809	480	703
1990.........	11,488	132	2,548	2,341	1,746	1,638	1,060	2,023	5,235	63	1,218	1,151	923	782	434	665
1989.........	11,243	147	2,648	2,170	1,813	1,611	986	1,868	5,136	63	1,253	1,070	900	789	438	623
1988.........	11,140	137	2,639	2,270	1,750	1,425	1,023	1,896	5,078	50	1,194	1,114	952	685	470	613
1987.........	10,731	194	2,564	2,254	1,665	1,483	985	1,584	5,104	97	1,260	1,156	873	740	436	541
1986.........	10,707	173	2,549	2,015	1,743	1,580	1,037	1,609	5,074	69	1,254	982	932	835	475	528
1985.........	10,781	229	2,539	2,257	1,704	1,590	1,014	1,448	5,103	120	1,176	1,137	941	812	449	468
1984.........	10,520	209	2,541	2,206	1,779	1,566	967	1,252	5,111	73	1,224	1,143	1,039	796	434	402
1983.........	10,565	214	2,597	2,161	1,705	1,603	961	1,324	5,162	87	1,197	1,149	989	875	421	444
1982.........	10,551	216	2,549	2,348	1,697	1,581	938	1,222	5,077	95	1,189	1,188	931	831	415	428
1981.........	10,353	197	2,639	2,239	1,671	1,390	1,027	1,190	5,010	86	1,259	1,104	977	745	448	391
1980.........	9,925	212	2,578	2,131	1,625	1,413	915	1,051	4,804	79	1,232	1,114	878	735	400	366
1979.........	9,956	256	2,498	2,079	1,543	1,474	859	1,247	4,823	110	1,192	1,058	854	788	398	423
1978.........	9,661	229	2,553	1,993	1,531	1,399	808	1,148	4,913	90	1,239	1,056	900	810	413	405
1977.........	9,962	227	2,579	2,099	1,531	1,550	827	1,149	5,156	91	1,272	1,124	890	907	433	439
1976.........	9,679	237	2,577	2,108	1,591	1,458	673	1,035	5,084	89	1,244	1,073	933	936	382	427
1975.........	9,546	252	2,613	2,042	1,461	1,410	737	1,031	5,263	111	1,283	1,134	909	911	426	489
1974.........	8,689	271	2,308	1,940	1,341	1,308	613	908	4,782	128	1,143	1,067	825	855	350	414
1973.........	8,014	253	2,281	1,865	1,292	1,152	481	690	4,218	111	1,177	1,017	838	789	286	...
1972.........	7,458	259	2,411	1,917	1,296	1,119	456	...	4,395	120	1,242	1,062	891	784	296	...
1971.........	7,273	251	2,485	1,758	1,351	965	463	...	4,407	117	1,328	964	992	712	293	...
1970.........	6,759	230	2,361	1,684	1,260	853	371	...	4,066	117	1,251	995	850	622	231	...
1969.........	6,827	222	2,377	1,762	1,208	855	404	...	4,146	110	1,298	1,021	827	637	252	...
1968.........	6,255	251	2,284	1,691	954	741	333	...	3,843	117	1,262	1,021	666	564	213	...
1967.........	5,905	220	2,105	1,688	915	646	329	...	3,560	88	1,097	998	666	494	217	...
1966.........	5,708	233	2,293	----2,313----		----869------		...	3,536	93	1,281	----1,541----		------621----		...
1965.........	5,317	233	2,074	----2,139----		----871------		...	3,326	104	1,152	----1,441----		------629----		...
1964.........	4,337	257	1,519	----1,850----		----711------		...	2,720	147	823	----1,226----		------524----		...
1963.........	4,050	171	1,391	----1,817----		----671------		...	2,593	94	746	----1,246----		------507----		...
1962.........	3,934	217	1,509	----1,517----		----691------		...	2,586	120	836	----1,066----		------564----		...
1961.........	3,498	204	1,388	----1,296----		----610------		...	2,208	79	786	------883----		------460----		...
1960.........	3,342	214	1,211	----1,209----		----709------		...	2,214	97	691	------859----		------567----		...
1959.........	3,118	193	1,101	----1,134----		----690------		...	2,067	88	620	------798----		------561----		...
1958.........	3,030	155	1,044	----1,136----		----695------		...	1,999	68	577	------802----		------552----		...
1957.........	2,932	161	921	----1,165----		----685------		...	1,938	68	510	------797----		------563----		...
1956.........	2,687	152	869	----1,025----		----641------		...	1,808	68	474	------733----		------533----		...
1955.........	2,224	125	715	------880----		----504------		...	1,495	47	418	------621----		------409----		...
White Alone Non-Hispanic																
2008.........	12,324	121	2,850	2,734	2,309	1,625	779	1,906	5,602	58	1,346	1,322	1,098	766	347	664
2007.........	11,867	104	2,739	2,677	2,117	1,509	816	1,904	5,269	45	1,298	1,223	1,021	639	370	674
2006.........	11,485	114	2,564	2,606	2,030	1,494	830	1,848	5,085	41	1,168	1,208	979	702	347	640
2005.........	11,715	93	2,618	2,769	2,006	1,445	806	1,977	5,114	30	1,193	1,308	928	590	373	692
2004.........	11,571	111	2,596	2,618	2,014	1,513	814	1,905	5,146	44	1,150	1,242	930	710	372	698
2003¹.........	11,295	90	2,486	2,419	2,225	1,371	832	1,872	5,067	41	1,115	1,082	1,094	639	386	710
2002.........	11,236	97	2,549	2,525	1,931	1,317	812	2,007	5,060	57	1,179	1,162	947	596	350	770
2001.........	10,602	74	2,383	2,450	1,732	1,283	827	1,854	4,691	30	1,131	1,170	794	587	348	632
2000.........	10,636	92	2,580	2,333	1,796	1,275	770	1,790	4,716	35	1,138	1,109	890	603	296	646
1999.........	10,818	80	2,574	2,324	1,837	1,283	755	1,965	5,033	30	1,214	1,141	929	627	368	722
1998.........	11,109	84	2,715	2,281	1,760	1,408	840	2,020	5,084	30	1,280	1,123	897	668	348	738
1997.........	11,246	81	2,491	2,361	1,876	1,504	779	2,153	5,024	33	1,184	1,161	930	732	314	669
1996.........	11,034	147	2,504	2,156	1,788	1,514	834	2,091	4,961	61	1,136	1,039	955	727	303	740
1995.........	11,024	103	2,372	2,226	1,796	1,618	859	2,051	5,068	36	1,111	1,103	892	799	380	749
1994³.........	11,178	93	2,362	2,255	1,904	1,444	1,018	2,101	5,053	41	1,132	1,039	955	689	457	741
1993.........	10,554	83	2,270	2,026	1,924	1,367	923	1,960	4,838	36	1,038	1,016	1,017	663	399	670

¹Starting in 2003 respondents could identify more than one race. Except as noted, the race data in this table from 2003 onward represent those respondents who indicated only one race category.
³Prior to 1972, total enrolled does not include the 35 and over population.
r = Revised, controlled to 1990 census based population estimates; previous 1993 data controlled to 1980 census based population estimates.
... = Not available.

Table A-15. Age Distribution of College Students 14 Years Old and Over, by Sex, October 1947–2008—*Continued*

(Numbers in thousands.)

Year, sex, race, and Hispanic origin	Total	Female						
		14 to 17 years	18 and 19 years	20 and 21 years	22 to 24 years	25 to 29 years	30 to 34 years	35 years and over
2002	7,062	52	1,562	1,504	1,154	870	539	1,381
2001	6,826	52	1,481	1,468	1,077	820	555	1,372
2000	6,689	70	1,625	1,365	1,054	770	539	1,266
1999	6,491	55	1,513	1,296	1,053	760	455	1,358
1998	6,799	63	1,618	1,281	1,008	858	567	1,405
1997	6,890	79	1,479	1,313	1,071	864	511	1,573
1996	6,735	97	1,508	1,246	951	906	583	1,443
1995	6,486	72	1,383	1,237	995	887	508	1,404
1994[3]	6,698	57	1,357	1,320	1,037	844	631	1,453
1993[r]	6,331	59	1,409	1,160	1,007	802	552	1,344
1993	6,212	57	1,353	1,123	974	791	558	1,357
1992	6,499	76	1,317	1,303	1,005	823	599	1,376
1991	6,382	63	1,375	1,304	865	789	583	1,404
1990	6,253	69	1,331	1,190	823	856	627	1,358
1989	6,107	84	1,395	1,101	913	822	548	1,245
1988	6,063	87	1,445	1,156	798	740	554	1,283
1987	5,627	97	1,304	1,097	791	743	550	1,044
1986	5,632	105	1,295	1,033	811	745	562	1,081
1985	5,679	110	1,363	1,120	764	778	565	979
1984	5,410	136	1,317	1,063	740	770	533	851
1983	5,404	127	1,400	1,012	717	728	540	880
1982	5,472	120	1,360	1,159	766	749	523	795
1981	5,342	111	1,380	1,134	694	646	578	799
1980	5,121	133	1,346	1,017	747	678	514	686
1979	5,131	146	1,306	1,021	688	686	461	823
1978	4,748	139	1,314	937	631	590	395	742
1977	4,806	135	1,307	975	641	643	394	711
1976	4,593	147	1,334	1,034	658	521	291	608
1975	4,284	141	1,330	908	552	500	311	542
1974	3,907	143	1,166	873	516	453	263	493
1973	3,107	142	1,104	848	454	363	196	...
1972	3,061	138	1,169	855	404	334	160	...
1971	2,867	134	1,157	794	359	252	170	...
1970	2,693	113	1,110	689	410	231	140	...
1969	2,681	112	1,079	741	380	218	151	...
1968	2,412	134	1,022	670	288	177	120	...
1967	2,345	133	1,009	690	250	152	112	...
1966	2,172	140	1,012	-----772-----		-----248-----		...
1965	1,991	129	922	-----698-----		-----242-----		...
1964	1,617	110	696	-----624-----		-----187-----		...
1963	1,457	77	645	-----571-----		-----164-----		...
1962	1,348	97	673	-----451-----		-----127-----		...
1961	1,290	125	602	-----413-----		-----150-----		...
1960	1,128	117	520	-----350-----		-----142-----		...
1959	1,051	105	481	-----336-----		-----129-----		...
1958	1,031	87	467	-----334-----		-----143-----		...
1957	994	93	411	-----368-----		-----122-----		...
1956	879	84	395	-----292-----		-----108-----		...
1955	729	78	297	-----259-----		------95-----		...
White Alone Non-Hispanic								
2008	6,722	63	1,504	1,412	1,211	859	432	1,242
2007	6,598	59	1,441	1,455	1,096	870	447	1,230
2006	6,400	73	1,396	1,398	1,051	792	483	1,208
2005	6,601	63	1,425	1,461	1,078	855	433	1,285
2004	6,425	67	1,446	1,375	1,085	803	442	1,207
2003[1]	6,228	49	1,371	1,337	1,130	732	446	1,163
2002	6,177	40	1,370	1,364	984	721	462	1,237
2001	5,912	44	1,252	1,280	938	695	479	1,222
2000	5,921	57	1,443	1,224	906	672	474	1,145
1999	5,785	49	1,360	1,183	908	656	387	1,241
1998	6,025	54	1,435	1,158	863	740	493	1,282
1997	6,222	48	1,307	1,200	946	771	465	1,485
1996	6,073	86	1,367	1,117	833	787	531	1,352
1995	5,956	67	1,261	1,123	904	819	479	1,302
1994[3]	6,124	53	1,229	1,216	950	755	561	1,361
1993	5,715	48	1,232	1,010	907	704	524	1,290

[1]Starting in 2003 respondents could identify more than one race. Except as noted, the race data in this table from 2003 onward represent those respondents who indicated only one race category.
[3]Prior to 1972, total enrolled does not include the 35 and over population.
r = Revised, controlled to 1990 census based population estimates; previous 1993 data controlled to 1980 census based population estimates.
... = Not available.

Table A-15. Age Distribution of College Students 14 Years Old and Over, by Sex, October 1947–2008—*Continued*

(Numbers in thousands.)

Year, sex, race, and Hispanic origin[5]	All Students								Male							
	Total	14 to 17 years	18 and 19 years	20 and 21 years	22 to 24 years	25 to 29 years	30 to 34 years	35 years and over	Total	14 to 17 years	18 and 19 years	20 and 21 years	22 to 24 years	25 to 29 years	30 to 34 years	35 years and over
Black[4]																
2008..........	2,481	36	479	463	408	377	269	451	919	21	205	217	174	115	82	106
2007..........	2,501	27	492	436	468	400	229	449	1,016	10	227	213	209	126	102	130
2006..........	2,334	30	464	416	441	303	199	480	896	10	174	182	186	112	70	163
2005..........	2,217	28	431	393	435	282	217	430	832	6	182	178	153	99	64	150
2004..........	2,301	40	440	398	400	352	170	501	776	13	165	169	146	92	41	151
2003[1].......	2,144	28	374	415	435	289	214	388	798	10	166	153	180	100	84	105
2002..........	2,278	56	430	418	379	301	241	454	802	14	179	175	121	97	83	133
2001..........	2,230	33	444	383	379	283	279	429	781	7	179	137	153	88	90	126
2000..........	2,164	19	454	375	387	325	242	361	815	10	163	137	169	110	92	133
1999..........	1,998	45	430	389	325	254	199	354	833	34	210	193	98	93	79	123
1998..........	2,016	22	461	354	300	328	211	340	770	12	194	162	88	140	67	105
1997..........	1,903	24	381	321	383	258	165	372	723	7	142	137	146	110	65	117
1996..........	1,901	45	345	346	292	337	182	354	764	17	145	155	122	142	64	120
1995..........	1,772	24	344	339	305	233	193	334	710	13	145	142	143	65	80	122
1994..........	1,800	36	310	347	344	256	184	323	745	16	132	161	147	118	72	99
1993[r].......	1,599	13	322	311	264	253	143	293	652	4	151	109	127	118	36	107
1993..........	1,545	13	311	297	253	245	141	284	636	4	148	107	124	116	36	102
1992..........	1,424	28	291	316	279	170	132	208	527	8	123	114	119	73	37	54
1991..........	1,477	18	303	302	223	216	157	257	629	7	137	138	103	99	55	90
1990..........	1,393	35	349	287	258	150	108	207	587	16	164	151	111	52	26	65
1989..........	1,287	32	302	290	243	156	119	146	480	8	126	104	94	65	37	47
1988..........	1,321	33	281	273	198	188	142	206	494	6	108	90	99	75	48	68
1987..........	1,351	32	341	264	218	220	121	155	587	13	154	124	99	99	37	62
1986..........	1,359	19	308	242	262	187	143	198	580	12	120	111	118	81	64	74
1985..........	1,263	21	259	274	201	183	112	213	552	10	121	140	84	64	40	93
1984..........	1,332	40	265	274	247	182	131	193	618	16	112	129	126	99	62	74
1983..........	1,273	31	258	242	241	179	151	171	560	12	93	112	126	91	64	62
1982..........	1,294	22	274	242	251	196	142	167	544	9	124	92	115	91	51	62
1981..........	1,335	31	306	232	212	219	132	203	566	7	133	92	100	115	57	62
1980..........	1,163	30	283	225	180	176	113	156	476	14	98	101	79	92	53	39
1979..........	1,156	43	279	224	193	150	112	155	498	12	110	110	84	71	47	64
1978..........	1,175	38	270	238	186	167	121	155	504	13	114	106	85	82	52	52
1977..........	1,284	37	269	262	190	210	136	180	571	18	90	115	104	101	62	81
1976..........	1,217	34	302	252	195	171	109	154	551	11	121	113	97	90	57	62
1975..........	1,099	34	260	237	168	151	97	152	523	14	111	107	76	82	53	80
1974..........	930	34	233	190	132	136	88	117	485	13	102	100	78	70	60	62
1973..........	781	37	194	164	140	89	60	97	358	7	96	93	77	49	36	...
1972..........	727	32	229	168	143	87	68	...	384	18	102	91	94	49	30	...
1971..........	680	29	204	199	119	79	50	...	363	11	94	106	62	58	31	...
1970..........	522	21	191	152	73	54	31	...	253	10	73	81	38	33	19	...
1969..........	492	19	193	149	65	39	26	...	236	10	86	75	41	15	10	...
1968..........	434	20	182	112	58	33	29	...	221	12	83	61	26	27	13	...
1967..........	370	16	141	105	51	42	15	...	199	7	78	57	32	15	11	...
1966..........	282	17	112	-----112-----		-----41----		...	154	10	47	-----72-----		-----25-----		...
1965..........	274	30	111	-----99-----		-----34-----		...	126	8	52	-----47-----		-----19-----		...
1964..........	234	30	78	-----79-----		-----47-----		...	120	16	35	-----36-----		-----33-----		...
1963..........	286	9	113	-----112-----		-----52-----		...	149	5	50	-----62-----		-----32-----		...
1962..........	274	16	103	-----109-----		-----46-----		...	156	5	55	-----59-----		-----37-----		...
1961..........	233	9	82	-----103-----		-----39-----		...	148	5	48	-----64-----		-----31-----		...
1960..........	227	8	88	-----90-----		-----41-----		...	125	2	43	-----55-----		-----25-----		...
1959..........	222	17	74	-----94-----		-----37-----		...	120	4	31	-----58-----		-----27-----		...
1958..........	212	12	70	-----85-----		-----45-----		...	130	5	44	-----48-----		-----33-----		...
1957..........	206	15	68	-----71-----		-----52-----		...	90	9	28	-----30-----		-----23-----		...
1956..........	196	15	65	-----80-----		-----36-----		...	124	9	38	-----48-----		-----29-----		...
1955..........	155	21	31	-----51-----		-----52-----		...	84	9	15	-----25-----		-----35-----		...
Black Alone Non-Hispanic[5]																
2005..........	2,217	28	431	393	435	282	217	430	832	6	182	178	153	99	64	150
2004..........	2,231	40	430	392	379	344	163	483	760	13	161	166	143	92	38	147
2003[1].......	2,090	28	368	399	423	282	205	385	773	10	166	145	177	93	80	102
2002..........	2,217	56	428	410	358	293	233	439	782	14	177	174	113	95	83	126
2001..........	2,173	33	430	373	375	263	275	423	759	7	174	137	150	88	90	123
2000..........	2,119	19	439	373	370	321	242	355	798	10	154	137	164	110	92	130
1999..........	1,952	45	413	390	320	250	192	342	811	35	192	193	99	91	76	125

[1]Starting in 2003 respondents could identify more than one race. Except as noted, the race data in this table from 2003 onward represent those respondents who indicated only one race category.
[4]Data for 1955 to 1963 are for Black and other races.
[5]Series has been discontinued.
r = Revised, controlled to 1990 census based population estimates; previous 1993 data controlled to 1980 census based population estimates.
... = Not available.

Table A-15. Age Distribution of College Students 14 Years Old and Over, by Sex, October 1947–2008—*Continued*

(Numbers in thousands.)

Year, sex, race, and Hispanic origin	Total	Female						
		14 to 17 years	18 and 19 years	20 and 21 years	22 to 24 years	25 to 29 years	30 to 34 years	35 years and over
Black⁴								
2008	1,562	15	274	246	234	261	188	345
2007	1,485	18	265	223	259	274	127	320
2006	1,438	20	291	234	255	191	130	318
2005	1,385	22	249	215	282	183	153	281
2004	1,525	27	275	229	254	259	130	350
2003¹	1,346	19	209	262	255	188	130	283
2002	1,476	42	251	243	257	204	158	321
2001	1,449	26	265	245	226	195	190	302
2000	1,349	9	291	238	218	215	150	228
1999	1,164	10	221	196	227	161	120	229
1998	1,247	9	267	192	212	188	144	234
1997	1,180	17	238	184	237	149	100	255
1996	1,136	28	199	192	170	195	119	234
1995	1,062	11	199	197	162	168	113	212
1994	1,054	21	178	186	197	138	112	224
1993¹	947	9	172	202	137	135	107	186
1993	909	8	163	191	130	129	106	182
1992	897	21	168	202	161	97	95	154
1991	848	11	166	164	120	118	102	167
1990	807	19	185	136	146	98	82	141
1989	807	24	176	186	149	91	82	99
1988	827	27	173	183	99	113	94	138
1987	764	19	186	140	119	121	84	93
1986	779	7	187	131	144	106	79	124
1985	712	11	138	134	117	119	72	121
1984	714	24	153	145	121	83	69	119
1983	714	19	164	131	116	88	87	109
1982	750	12	150	150	136	105	92	105
1981	769	24	172	140	112	105	75	141
1980	686	16	185	124	101	84	60	116
1979	659	31	169	114	109	79	66	91
1978	671	25	155	133	102	85	68	103
1977	712	19	179	147	87	108	74	98
1976	665	23	181	139	97	81	52	92
1975	577	20	150	130	92	69	44	72
1974	448	22	131	91	55	66	28	55
1973	325	30	97	71	63	40	24	...
1972	343	14	127	77	49	38	38	...
1971	317	18	109	93	57	21	19	...
1970	269	11	118	71	36	22	11	...
1969	256	9	108	74	24	25	17	...
1968	213	8	100	51	32	7	15	...
1967	171	9	63	48	19	27	4	...
1966	128	7	65	-----40-----		-----16-----		...
1965	148	22	59	-----52-----		-----15-----		...
1964	114	14	43	-----43-----		-----14-----		...
1963	137	4	63	-----50-----		-----20-----		...
1962	118	11	48	-----50-----		------9-----		...
1961	85	4	34	-----39-----		------8-----		...
1960	102	6	45	-----35-----		-----16-----		...
1959	102	13	43	-----36-----		-----10-----		...
1958	82	7	26	-----37-----		-----12-----		...
1957	116	6	40	-----41-----		-----29-----		...
1956	72	6	27	-----32-----		------7-----		...
1955	71	12	16	-----26-----		-----17-----		...
Black Alone Non-Hispanic⁵								
2005	1,385	22	249	215	282	183	153	281
2004	1,471	27	268	227	237	251	125	336
2003¹	1,317	19	202	254	246	188	125	283
2002	1,435	42	251	237	244	198	150	313
2001	1,414	26	256	236	226	186	185	300
2000	1,321	9	285	235	206	211	150	225
1999	1,141	10	221	196	221	159	117	218

¹Starting in 2003 respondents could identify more than one race. Except as noted, the race data in this table from 2003 onward represent those respondents who indicated only one race category.
⁴Data for 1955 to 1963 are for Black and other races.
⁵Series has been discontinued.
r = Revised, controlled to 1990 census based population estimates; previous 1993 data controlled to 1980 census based population estimates.
... = Not available.

Table A-15. Age Distribution of College Students 14 Years Old and Over, by Sex, October 1947–2008—Continued

(Numbers in thousands.)

Year, sex, race, and Hispanic origin	All Students								Male							
	Total	14 to 17 years	18 and 19 years	20 and 21 years	22 to 24 years	25 to 29 years	30 to 34 years	35 years and over	Total	14 to 17 years	18 and 19 years	20 and 21 years	22 to 24 years	25 to 29 years	30 to 34 years	35 years and over
1998.........	1,971	22	453	351	282	322	211	331	752	12	194	159	83	134	67	102
1997.........	1,868	21	371	314	378	253	161	369	712	7	138	137	143	105	65	117
1996.........	1,863	41	342	342	281	329	176	350	750	17	142	155	122	134	64	117
1995.........	1,745	24	332	337	302	231	189	330	699	13	136	142	143	65	80	120
1994[3]........	1,783	36	308	347	342	253	182	314	734	16	131	161	145	116	72	93
1993.........	1,505	13	310	291	246	232	134	279	615	4	149	105	121	104	33	100
Asian[2]																
2008.........	1,220	27	172	247	236	245	137	156	567	22	75	123	96	132	61	58
2007.........	1,103	10	201	204	252	206	123	105	533	2	104	106	108	98	60	54
2006.........	1,084	8	204	215	242	187	103	125	535	5	113	121	104	80	51	61
2005.........	1,184	22	188	272	234	226	114	129	605	10	90	163	113	110	61	58
2004	1,191	20	182	245	269	217	113	146	636	11	92	135	145	116	65	71
2003[1]........	1,162	16	209	219	264	228	108	116	606	3	103	104	130	141	67	59
2002.........	1,258	28	236	269	299	182	105	140	649	8	121	137	160	101	56	67
2001.........	1,280	17	247	245	302	265	90	115	664	10	113	127	177	134	63	40
2000.........	1,049	12	212	200	227	188	81	130	517	4	108	109	120	66	51	60
1999.........	1,041	16	223	192	211	187	71	142	506	11	93	95	96	97	47	67
Hispanic[6]																
2008.........	2,227	53	528	407	402	359	141	337	1,042	31	236	210	169	186	76	135
2007.........	2,172	41	559	412	404	332	155	269	880	16	246	154	160	145	57	102
2006.........	1,968	54	444	386	353	271	190	271	808	19	213	146	164	109	64	94
2005.........	1,942	31	406	420	389	288	150	257	804	10	173	183	183	111	52	92
2004.........	1,975	23	384	431	407	280	179	271	852	5	171	212	191	131	53	89
2003.........	1,714	12	379	407	329	224	156	207	703	7	153	167	145	93	61	77
2002.........	1,656	15	360	303	316	274	140	249	705	3	156	151	132	118	49	97
2001.........	1,700	14	387	342	306	255	136	260	731	6	149	145	156	116	57	102
2000.........	1,426	24	349	268	282	167	142	194	619	12	160	118	123	61	75	70
1999.........	1,307	7	297	197	247	207	127	225	568	2	143	84	96	94	54	95
1998.........	1,363	9	288	263	269	206	130	198	550	...	97	139	110	86	54	64
1997.........	1,260	49	316	254	236	174	80	151	555	15	133	132	106	78	31	60
1996.........	1,223	22	240	213	253	198	112	184	529	8	98	78	124	79	54	90
1995.........	1,207	20	264	245	236	153	97	193	568	14	121	111	124	71	55	73
1994[3]........	1,187	9	225	230	207	180	132	205	529	3	89	115	108	73	55	86
1993[r]........	1,169	17	222	299	207	178	106	139	539	7	81	154	103	71	67	56
1993.........	995	15	195	241	166	149	100	129	442	6	69	118	79	57	63	51
1992.........	918	17	230	200	156	124	90	102	388	9	93	80	74	57	35	40
1991.........	830	10	188	203	125	124	72	109	347	5	68	79	64	64	30	37
1990.........	748	13	148	188	99	109	59	130	364	12	70	80	64	39	30	67
1989.........	754	17	177	134	142	112	58	114	353	5	75	66	70	63	31	42
1988.........	747	13	203	110	137	118	73	93	355	9	75	76	77	48	29	43
1987.........	739	8	152	155	148	137	67	73	390	3	76	100	71	77	42	21
1986.........	794	16	171	146	141	164	67	89	377	4	92	67	74	80	26	34
1985.........	580	16	127	128	120	111	78	...	279	10	44	53	71	72	29	...
1984.........	524	5	136	133	93	100	57	...	231	2	42	63	49	49	26	...
1983.........	521	17	134	124	91	114	41	...	253	10	41	61	50	74	17	...
1982.........	494	16	143	104	90	94	47	...	216	6	52	47	42	49	20	...
1981.........	510	15	129	123	90	103	50	...	258	6	57	68	39	55	33	...
1980.........	443	10	137	94	84	69	49	...	222	2	68	52	34	36	30	...
1979.........	439	18	124	95	73	73	56	...	225	8	67	43	43	39	25	...
1978.........	377	15	109	68	77	78	30	...	196	7	53	30	43	49	14	...
1977.........	417	14	123	95	59	81	45	...	224	6	54	45	40	56	23	...
1976.........	426	13	143	83	83	73	31	...	223	3	69	39	42	50	20	...
1975.........	411	13	118	101	76	68	35	...	218	3	53	52	40	45	25	...
1974.........	354	11	112	96	64	39	32	...	195	6	55	44	42	24	24	...
1973.........	289	15	82	69	55	45	23	...	168	11	39	37	29	32	20	...
1972.........	242	14	70	60	49	34	15	...	126	7	28	35	29	20	7	...
White Alone or in Combination																
2008.........	14,738	175	3,440	3,181	2,738	2,003	936	2,264	6,730	87	1,607	1,550	1,286	966	426	807
2007.........	14,114	147	3,318	3,111	2,529	1,857	978	2,174	6,169	64	1,540	1,390	1,186	789	425	774
2006.........	13,564	166	3,043	3,006	2,416	1,791	1,016	2,125	5,966	61	1,399	1,363	1,161	827	411	744
2005.........	13,791	125	3,043	3,244	2,433	1,740	954	2,251	5,978	43	1,371	1,519	1,128	696	424	796
2004.........	13,688	135	3,012	3,106	2,425	1,807	989	2,192	6,068	49	1,331	1,494	1,131	847	425	792
2003.........	13,164	106	2,905	2,868	2,584	1,613	989	2,099	5,837	48	1,283	1,274	1,257	730	446	798

[1]Starting in 2003 respondents could identify more than one race. Except as noted, the race data in this table from 2003 onward represent those respondents who indicated only one race category.
[2]The data shown prior to 2003 consists of those identifying themselves as "Asian or Pacific Islanders."
[3]Prior to 1972, total enrolled does not include the 35 and over population.
[6]May be of any race.
r = Revised, controlled to 1990 census based population estimates; previous 1993 data controlled to 1980 census based population estimates.
... = Not available.

Table A-15.   Age Distribution of College Students 14 Years Old and Over, by Sex, October 1947–2008—*Continued*

(Numbers in thousands.)

Year, sex, race, and Hispanic origin	Female							
	Total	14 to 17 years	18 and 19 years	20 and 21 years	22 to 24 years	25 to 29 years	30 to 34 years	35 years and over
1998.................................	1,219	9	259	192	199	188	144	229
1997.................................	1,156	14	233	177	235	149	96	252
1996.................................	1,113	25	199	188	160	195	113	234
1995.................................	1,046	11	196	195	159	167	109	210
1994³.................................	1,049	21	178	186	197	138	109	221
1993.................................	890	8	161	186	125	128	102	179
Asian²								
2008.................................	653	5	97	123	140	113	76	98
2007.................................	569	8	97	98	144	108	63	51
2006.................................	549	3	91	94	139	107	52	64
2005.................................	579	12	98	109	120	116	53	71
2004	556	9	89	110	124	101	48	75
2003¹.................................	556	13	107	115	134	88	42	57
2002.................................	609	19	115	132	139	82	49	73
2001.................................	616	6	134	118	125	131	27	75
2000.................................	532	8	104	91	107	122	30	69
1999.................................	534	5	130	97	115	89	24	74
Hispanic⁶								
2008.................................	1,185	23	292	197	233	173	65	202
2007.................................	1,292	25	313	258	244	187	98	167
2006.................................	1,161	36	231	240	189	162	126	177
2005.................................	1,137	21	232	237	206	178	98	165
2004	1,123	19	213	219	216	150	126	182
2003	1,011	5	226	240	185	131	95	130
2002.................................	951	12	204	152	184	156	92	152
2001.................................	969	8	238	197	150	139	80	157
2000.................................	807	13	188	150	160	106	67	124
1999.................................	739	5	154	113	151	113	73	130
1998.................................	814	9	191	124	159	120	77	134
1997.................................	704	34	183	123	130	96	49	91
1996.................................	693	15	142	136	128	119	59	95
1995.................................	639	6	143	134	112	82	42	120
1994³.................................	659	6	136	119	99	106	78	119
1993ʳ.................................	630	10	141	145	104	107	40	83
1993.................................	553	9	126	123	87	93	38	78
1992.................................	530	7	137	120	82	67	55	62
1991.................................	483	5	120	124	61	59	42	72
1990.................................	384	1	78	108	35	70	29	63
1989.................................	401	11	103	69	72	49	27	71
1988.................................	391	4	129	35	60	70	43	51
1987.................................	349	5	76	56	76	60	25	51
1986.................................	417	12	79	80	67	84	41	54
1985.................................	299	6	82	75	48	39	49	...
1984.................................	292	3	94	70	43	51	31	...
1983.................................	270	7	93	64	41	40	25	...
1982.................................	278	10	91	57	48	45	27	...
1981.................................	252	9	72	55	51	48	17	...
1980.................................	221	8	63	42	50	33	20	...
1979.................................	215	10	58	52	30	34	31	...
1978.................................	181	8	56	38	34	29	16	...
1977.................................	194	8	70	50	19	25	22	...
1976.................................	203	9	74	45	41	23	11	...
1975.................................	193	10	65	49	36	23	10	...
1974.................................	157	5	56	51	22	15	8	...
1973.................................	123	5	44	33	25	13	3	...
1972.................................	117	7	43	25	20	14	8	...
White Alone or in Combination								
2008.................................	8,008	88	1,833	1,631	1,452	1,037	510	1,457
2007.................................	7,945	82	1,779	1,721	1,343	1,068	553	1,400
2006.................................	7,598	105	1,643	1,643	1,255	964	605	1,382
2005.................................	7,813	82	1,672	1,725	1,305	1,044	530	1,454
2004.................................	7,600	86	1,682	1,612	1,295	960	564	1,401
2003.................................	7,328	57	1,622	1,594	1,327	883	543	1,302

¹Starting in 2003 respondents could identify more than one race. Except as noted, the race data in this table from 2003 onward represent those respondents who indicated only one race category.
²The data shown prior to 2003 consists of those identifying themselves as "Asian or Pacific Islanders."
³Prior to 1972, total enrolled does not include the 35 and over population.
⁶May be of any race.
r = Revised, controlled to 1990 census based population estimates; previous 1993 data controlled to 1980 census based population estimates.
... = Not available.

Table A-15. Age Distribution of College Students 14 Years Old and Over, by Sex, October 1947–2008—*Continued*

(Numbers in thousands.)

Year, sex, race, and Hispanic origin	All Students								Male							
	Total	14 to 17 years	18 and 19 years	20 and 21 years	22 to 24 years	25 to 29 years	30 to 34 years	35 years and over	Total	14 to 17 years	18 and 19 years	20 and 21 years	22 to 24 years	25 to 29 years	30 to 34 years	35 years and over
Black Alone or in Combination																
2008.........	2,619	36	515	490	429	400	278	470	983	21	219	229	184	127	85	116
2007.........	2,630	33	530	459	479	432	243	455	1,077	12	240	229	217	139	110	130
2006.........	2,444	30	492	423	471	318	217	493	951	10	186	186	206	120	74	170
2005.........	2,387	31	481	428	462	299	229	458	895	9	201	189	167	109	66	154
2004.........	2,412	40	466	436	416	371	170	512	827	13	175	187	159	100	41	153
2003.........	2,227	30	400	440	445	303	214	395	826	10	175	165	186	100	84	107
Asian Alone or in Combination																
2008.........	1,340	27	214	265	259	260	149	167	632	22	93	134	113	135	70	65
2007.........	1,204	11	232	220	268	232	126	116	592	2	113	116	123	113	61	64
2006.........	1,154	9	215	227	263	198	110	131	566	6	118	122	122	81	55	62
2005.........	1,297	25	204	292	277	240	122	137	640	13	97	170	124	113	63	60
2004.........	1,260	20	203	266	281	222	116	152	662	11	97	147	153	117	65	72
2003.........	1,262	19	236	248	290	232	117	121	649	3	112	115	143	142	72	61

Table A-15.   Age Distribution of College Students 14 Years Old and Over, by Sex, October 1947–2008—*Continued*

(Numbers in thousands.)

Year, sex, race, and Hispanic origin	Female							
	Total	14 to 17 years	18 and 19 years	20 and 21 years	22 to 24 years	25 to 29 years	30 to 34 years	35 years and over
Black Alone or in Combination								
2008...................................	1,636	15	296	261	245	272	193	354
2007...................................	1,553	20	290	230	263	292	133	325
2006...................................	1,493	20	307	238	265	198	143	323
2005...................................	1,493	22	280	239	295	190	164	303
2004...................................	1,584	27	290	249	258	271	130	359
2003...................................	1,401	20	225	275	260	203	130	288
Asian Alone or in Combination								
2008...................................	708	5	121	131	146	125	79	102
2007...................................	612	9	119	104	145	118	65	52
2006...................................	588	3	97	105	141	117	55	69
2005...................................	657	12	107	122	153	128	59	77
2004...................................	598	9	106	118	128	105	51	80
2003...................................	613	16	124	133	147	89	44	60

Table A-16. College Enrollment of Undergraduate Students 14 Years Old and Over, by Type of College, Attendance Status, Age, and Gender, October 1970–2008

(Numbers in thousands.)

Year and type of college	All students								Male			Female		
	Total	14 to 19 years	20 to 21 years	22 to 24 years	25 to 34 years	35 years and over	Public	Private	Total	Full-time	Part-time	Total	Full-time	Part-time
All Undergraduates														
2008.....................	14,955	4,347	3,862	2,600	2,430	1,716	12,340	2,616	6,737	5,220	1,517	8,218	6,158	2,060
2007.....................	14,365	4,237	3,732	2,513	2,277	1,605	11,811	2,554	6,405	5,053	1,353	7,959	5,813	2,146
2006.....................	13,854	3,940	3,591	2,437	2,178	1,709	11,269	2,585	6,135	4,686	1,450	7,719	5,695	2,024
2005.....................	14,169	3,901	3,847	2,588	2,142	1,690	11,292	2,876	6,189	4,799	1,391	7,979	5,852	2,127
2004.....................	14,004	3,863	3,700	2,431	2,257	1,753	11,384	2,620	6,156	4,714	1,442	7,848	5,704	3,102
2003.....................	13,370	3,633	3,449	2,687	2,094	1,506	10,980	2,389	5,902	4,476	1,425	7,468	5,391	2,077
2002.....................	13,426	3,743	3,457	2,355	2,106	1,764	10,830	2,595	5,929	4,462	1,467	7,497	5,273	2,223
2001.....................	12,552	3,568	3,329	2,136	1,979	1,540	10,188	2,364	5,522	4,057	1,464	7,030	4,949	2,082
2000.....................	12,401	3,710	3,093	2,113	1,988	1,498	10,044	2,357	5,520	4,059	1,461	6,881	4,832	2,049
1999.....................	12,046	3,625	3,043	2,000	1,885	1,493	9,689	2,357	5,554	4,143	1,411	6,492	4,548	1,945
1998.....................	12,509	3,749	3,019	2,025	2,101	1,616	10,100	2,410	5,621	4,051	1,570	6,888	4,765	2,123
1997.....................	12,409	3,504	3,080	2,137	1,970	1,718	10,074	2,335	5,539	4,165	1,375	6,870	4,752	2,118
1996.....................	12,305	3,526	2,856	2,017	2,226	1,680	10,121	2,183	5,533	4,032	1,502	6,772	4,502	2,269
1995.....................	11,966	3,251	2,881	2,033	2,151	1,651	9,570	2,396	5,413	3,911	1,501	6,554	4,433	2,121
1994.....................	12,410	3,192	3,006	2,099	2,281	1,832	9,983	2,427	5,526	3,969	1,557	6,883	4,480	2,404
1993ʳ....................	11,959	3,197	2,879	2,131	2,118	1,634	9,706	2,253	5,442	4,020	1,422	6,517	4,346	2,171
1993.....................	11,507	3,045	2,721	2,020	2,088	1,633	9,330	2,176	5,194	3,812	1,382	6,313	4,182	2,130
1992.....................	11,643	3,097	2,902	2,004	2,090	1,550	9,519	2,124	5,091	3,724	1,365	6,553	4,338	2,214
1991.....................	11,374	3,061	2,902	1,757	2,120	1,534	9,257	2,117	5,120	3,724	1,395	6,254	4,145	2,109
1990.....................	11,108	3,194	2,740	1,681	2,067	1,425	9,031	2,076	5,030	3,628	1,402	6,077	3,967	2,109
1989.....................	10,661	3,250	2,529	1,658	1,921	1,304	8,633	2,027	4,730	3,436	1,295	5,931	3,880	2,051
1988.....................	10,605	3,229	2,645	1,600	1,865	1,266	8,617	1,988	4,763	3,441	1,322	5,842	3,816	2,026
1987.....................	10,304	3,283	2,585	1,512	1,848	1,076	8,306	1,998	4,878	3,476	1,403	5,426	3,445	1,981
1986.....................	10,036	3,158	2,298	1,583	1,932	1,065	7,955	2,081	4,663	3,350	1,312	5,373	3,474	1,899
1985.....................	10,097	3,169	2,586	1,475	1,884	984	8,042	2,055	4,667	3,454	1,213	5,430	3,578	1,852
1984.....................	9,910	3,120	2,564	1,547	1,826	852	7,944	1,966	4,725	3,573	1,152	5,185	3,419	1,766
1983.....................	9,925	3,200	2,464	1,475	1,873	914	7,808	2,117	4,759	3,472	1,287	5,166	3,424	1,742
1982.....................	9,952	3,183	2,657	1,526	1,745	843	7,908	2,044	4,703	3,485	1,218	5,249	3,480	1,769
1981.....................	9,969	3,276	2,511	1,458	1,808	916	7,789	2,180	4,724	3,452	1,273	5,245	3,490	1,755
1980.....................	9,279	3,182	2,393	1,316	1,598	791	(NA)	(NA)	4,353	3,247	1,105	4,927	3,210	1,717
1979.....................	9,193	3,156	2,308	1,297	1,526	905	7,331	1,861	4,387	3,219	1,168	4,805	3,163	1,642
1978.....................	8,947	3,173	2,246	1,233	1,505	790	7,008	1,939	4,445	3,269	1,176	4,502	3,031	1,471
1977¹....................	8,408	3,184	2,376	1,206	1,640	...	6,683	1,724	4,372	3,304	1,068	4,027	3,002	1,025
1976.....................	8,988	3,216	2,358	1,224	1,472	718	7,196	1,787	4,569	3,353	1,213	4,419	3,166	1,253
1975.....................	8,108	3,237	2,255	1,072	1,546	...	6,598	1,510	4,393	3,394	999	3,715	2,902	813
1974.....................	7,338	2,906	2,131	1,028	1,272	...	5,843	1,494	4,030	3,128	902	3,307	2,561	746
1973.....................	6,794	2,812	2,031	924	1,028	...	5,279	1,516	3,791	3,035	756	3,004	2,423	581
1972.....................	6,992	2,974	2,065	944	1,011	...	5,460	1,532	3,982	3,231	751	3,010	2,445	565
1971.....................	6,895	3,008	1,936	1,019	931	...	5,472	1,423	4,017	3,240	777	2,878	2,348	530
1970.....................	6,274	2,854	1,803	866	750	...	4,910	1,363	3,627	3,045	582	2,646	2,164	482
Two-Year College Students														
2008.....................	5,345	1,731	1,001	726	1,095	792	5,006	339	2,331	1,487	844	3,014	1,910	1,104
2007.....................	4,814	1,496	856	774	963	725	4,418	396	2,061	1,322	739	2,753	1,666	1,087
2006.....................	4,294	1,367	788	573	836	731	3,878	416	1,788	1,169	620	2,506	1,531	975
2005.....................	4,327	1,259	833	603	882	751	3,890	437	1,866	1,197	669	2,462	1,436	1,026
2004.....................	4,340	1,243	802	568	898	829	3,939	401	1,756	1,141	615	2,584	1,461	1,123
2003.....................	4,384	1,178	746	843	834	784	3,999	385	1,782	1,055	726	2,603	1,507	1,095
2002.....................	4,378	1,227	777	656	880	838	3,948	431	1,884	1,102	783	2,494	1,363	1,131
2001.....................	4,159	1,200	776	605	832	746	3,749	410	1,802	1,057	745	2,357	1,252	1,105
2000.....................	3,881	1,232	710	525	673	741	3,590	291	1,655	969	686	2,226	1,224	1,002
1999.....................	3,794	1,187	715	460	683	749	3,482	312	1,637	949	688	2,157	1,157	1,000
1998.....................	4,234	1,301	701	619	839	774	3,865	369	1,845	1,049	796	2,389	1,287	1,103
1997.....................	4,078	1,178	760	528	806	807	3,780	298	1,663	983	680	2,415	1,307	1,108
1996.....................	4,174	1,223	669	515	922	845	3,890	284	1,752	974	778	2,423	1,235	1,187
1995.....................	3,882	1,028	608	593	892	761	3,553	330	1,626	898	728	2,256	1,124	1,132
1994.....................	4,208	1,063	623	621	1,011	890	3,846	362	1,704	937	766	2,504	1,234	1,270
1993ʳ....................	4,345	1,131	745	648	978	843	4,024	321	1,825	1,061	764	2,520	1,317	1,203
1993.....................	4,196	1,077	696	614	965	844	3,884	311	1,748	1,006	742	2,448	1,268	1,179
1992.....................	4,239	1,084	789	581	988	797	3,937	302	1,688	936	751	2,551	1,268	1,283
1991.....................	4,277	1,120	732	560	1,084	781	4,025	252	1,798	973	825	2,479	1,239	1,239
1990.....................	3,965	1,059	689	475	967	775	3,689	276	1,624	849	775	2,340	1,103	1,237
1989.....................	3,627	1,048	557	467	880	676	3,382	245	1,464	777	688	2,163	949	1,214
1988.....................	3,837	1,134	665	497	879	662	3,609	228	1,542	847	695	2,295	1,054	1,241

¹Data for 1970–1975 and 1977 do not include people ages 35 and over.
r = Revised, controlled to 1990 census based population estimates; previous 1993 data controlled to 1980 census based population estimates.

Table A-16. College Enrollment of Undergraduate Students 14 Years Old and Over, by Type of College, Attendance Status, Age, and Gender, October 1970–2008—*Continued*

(Numbers in thousands.)

Year and type of college	Full-Time						Part-Time					
	Total	14 to 19 years	20 to 21 years	22 to 24 years	25 to 34 years	35 years and over	Total	14 to 19 years	20 to 21 years	22 to 24 years	25 to 34 years	35 years and over
All Undergraduates												
2008...................	11,378	3,999	3,445	2,017	1,240	676	3,577	347	417	583	1,190	1,040
2007...................	10,866	3,879	3,282	1,858	1,285	562	3,499	358	450	656	992	1,043
2006...................	10,380	3,567	3,150	1,810	1,242	612	3,474	373	441	627	936	1,097
2005...................	10,651	3,540	3,369	1,977	1,139	625	3,518	360	479	611	1,003	1,065
2004...................	10,418	3,533	3,251	1,836	1,150	648	3,586	330	449	595	1,107	1,105
2003...................	9,868	3,299	2,992	1,948	1,081	547	3,502	334	457	739	1,013	959
2002...................	9,735	3,356	3,058	1,737	1,073	511	3,690	387	399	619	1,033	1,253
2001...................	9,006	3,190	2,840	1,524	976	476	3,546	378	489	612	1,003	1,064
2000...................	8,891	3,368	2,658	1,479	930	457	3,510	342	435	633	1,058	1,041
1999...................	8,691	3,280	2,625	1,485	888	412	3,355	345	418	514	997	1,081
1998...................	8,816	3,327	2,619	1,461	956	452	3,693	421	400	563	1,145	1,164
1997...................	8,917	3,144	2,704	1,576	960	532	3,492	360	376	560	1,010	1,186
1996...................	8,534	3,131	2,460	1,516	990	437	3,771	394	396	501	1,236	1,243
1995...................	8,344	2,902	2,462	1,444	1,004	533	3,622	349	419	589	1,147	1,118
1994...................	8,449	2,843	2,585	1,455	981	586	3,961	350	421	644	1,300	1,245
1993ʳ..................	8,366	2,866	2,513	1,513	941	533	3,593	332	366	619	1,176	1,102
1993...................	7,994	2,732	2,380	1,429	927	527	3,513	314	342	590	1,161	1,106
1992...................	8,063	2,838	2,506	1,427	834	458	3,580	259	396	578	1,255	1,092
1991...................	7,869	2,809	2,534	1,248	878	400	3,505	252	368	509	1,242	1,134
1990...................	7,597	2,912	2,333	1,165	824	363	3,511	282	408	515	1,244	1,062
1989...................	7,314	2,989	2,209	1,122	655	341	3,346	260	321	536	1,266	963
1988...................	7,257	2,925	2,275	1,079	691	285	3,348	303	371	521	1,173	981
1987...................	6,920	2,892	2,179	1,005	610	235	3,384	391	406	507	1,238	841
1986...................	6,825	2,880	1,973	1,055	680	237	3,212	278	324	528	1,254	828
1985...................	7,033	2,900	2,237	1,017	701	178	3,065	269	349	457	1,184	806
1984...................	6,992	2,846	2,221	1,067	689	170	2,918	274	344	480	1,139	683
1983...................	6,896	2,895	2,124	993	718	166	3,029	305	340	482	1,153	748
1982...................	6,965	2,880	2,286	979	662	159	2,987	302	372	547	1,083	684
1981...................	6,942	2,983	2,157	986	613	202	3,027	293	353	471	1,195	715
1980...................	6,457	2,897	2,107	810	500	142	2,822	283	287	505	1,098	649
1979...................	6,383	2,892	1,994	815	523	158	2,810	264	314	482	1,003	748
1978...................	6,300	2,872	1,918	820	559	132	2,647	302	328	412	947	658
1977ʳ..................	6,304	2,855	2,075	775	598	...	2,104	329	301	431	1,042	...
1976...................	6,519	2,963	2,033	821	563	138	2,466	253	325	403	909	577
1975...................	6,296	2,987	1,958	696	655	...	1,812	250	297	376	891	...
1974...................	5,689	2,661	1,842	697	488	...	1,649	245	289	331	784	...
1973...................	5,460	2,629	1,801	630	398	...	1,334	183	230	294	630	...
1972...................	5,678	2,797	1,845	624	412	...	1,314	177	220	320	599	...
1971...................	5,580	2,001	1,729	700	357	...	1,307	207	207	319	574	...
1970...................	5,208	2,685	1,628	591	301	...	1,066	169	175	275	449	...
Two-Year College Students												
2008...................	3,397	1,450	763	455	466	263	1,948	281	239	271	628	529
2007...................	2,988	1,276	627	425	443	219	1,826	221	230	349	520	506
2006...................	2,699	1,145	600	312	401	241	1,595	221	188	261	435	490
2005...................	2,632	1,031	605	373	393	231	1,695	228	228	230	489	520
2004...................	2,602	1,027	553	327	425	269	1,738	216	249	241	472	560
2003...................	2,563	973	516	386	429	258	1,822	205	230	457	404	526
2002...................	2,464	975	571	344	374	200	1,914	252	206	312	506	638
2001...................	2,310	951	529	301	307	222	1,850	250	247	304	524	525
2000...................	2,193	993	507	278	230	184	1,688	239	202	247	444	557
1999...................	2,105	955	498	261	230	161	1,688	231	217	199	453	588
1998...................	2,336	1,024	495	331	302	184	1,899	277	206	288	537	591
1997...................	2,290	947	522	283	327	212	1,788	231	238	245	479	595
1996...................	2,209	995	457	271	315	171	1,965	227	212	244	607	674
1995...................	2,022	810	397	298	321	195	1,860	218	211	295	571	565
1994...................	2,172	848	407	319	341	256	2,036	215	216	302	669	634
1993ʳ..................	2,378	891	515	348	365	259	1,967	240	230	300	613	585
1993...................	2,274	850	483	325	360	256	1,922	227	213	288	605	588
1992...................	2,205	897	528	287	304	188	2,034	187	261	294	683	609
1991...................	2,212	915	476	269	361	191	2,065	205	256	291	723	589
1990...................	1,953	847	408	227	310	160	2,012	212	281	247	657	615
1989...................	1,725	860	368	160	210	128	1,902	188	189	307	669	548
1988...................	1,901	926	410	209	227	128	1,936	207	256	288	651	534

ʳData for 1970–1975 and 1977 do not include people ages 35 and over.
r = Revised, controlled to 1990 census based population estimates; previous 1993 data controlled to 1980 census based population estimates.
- = Quantity zero or rounds to zero.
... = Not available.

Table A-16.   College Enrollment of Undergraduate Students 14 Years Old and Over, by Type of College, Attendance Status, Age, and Gender, October 1970–2008—*Continued*

(Numbers in thousands.)

Year and type of college	All students								Male			Female		
	Total	14 to 19 years	20 to 21 years	22 to 24 years	25 to 34 years	35 years and over	Public	Private	Total	Full-time	Part-time	Total	Full-time	Part-time
1987....................	3,648	1,111	624	457	851	605	3,405	243	1,522	780	742	2,127	937	1,190
1986....................	3,391	1,023	506	427	875	559	3,089	302	1,466	752	714	1,924	856	1,068
1985....................	3,289	959	558	403	851	518	3,009	281	1,336	702	634	1,954	914	1,040
1984....................	3,172	994	525	442	795	417	2,875	298	1,436	834	601	1,738	829	909
1983....................	3,416	1,050	595	405	882	485	3,136	280	1,498	807	691	1,919	897	1,022
1982....................	3,448	1,088	604	494	826	437	3,164	283	1,477	854	623	1,971	961	1,011
1981....................	3,347	1,144	566	414	768	455	3,091	255	1,475	837	638	1,872	909	963
1980....................	3,107	1,079	450	417	721	441	...	...	1,331	768	563	1,777	798	979
1979....................	2,897	933	403	407	664	490	2,710	187	1,251	684	567	1,646	725	921
1978....................	2,904	966	427	391	670	451	2,686	218	1,368	698	669	1,537	701	835
1977[1].................	2,510	933	455	380	741	...	2,362	148	1,253	681	572	1,256	691	565
1976....................	2,854	907	444	367	718	419	2,688	165	1,400	760	640	1,454	743	711
1975....................	2,561	1,024	431	354	752	...	2,437	123	1,412	850	562	1,148	717	431
1974....................	2,072	834	369	305	565	...	1,917	154	1,172	709	463	899	528	371
1973....................	1,797	816	278	254	449	...	1,669	128	1,012	629	383	785	471	314
1972....................	1,910	883	334	267	426	...	1,816	94	1,125	770	355	785	484	301
1971....................	1,830	928	307	263	331	...	1,726	105	1,087	726	361	743	473	270
1970....................	1,692	895	281	234	283	...	1,559	133	1,001	726	275	691	452	239
Graduate Students														
2008....................	3,676	20	58	819	1,583	1,195	2,399	1,277	1,574	880	694	2,103	987	1,116
2007....................	3,591	24	62	779	1,560	1,166	2,261	1,330	1,420	819	601	2,171	971	1,200
2006....................	3,378	18	84	729	1,480	1,067	2,197	1,181	1,371	692	678	2,007	998	1,009
2005....................	3,304	7	98	574	1,458	1,167	2,143	1,161	1,349	711	638	1,955	875	1,079
2004....................	3,378	20	77	718	1,433	1,131	2,267	1,111	1,419	726	693	1,959	845	1,114
2003....................	3,268	29	84	632	1,399	1,123	2,129	1,139	1,416	774	643	1,852	849	1,003
2002....................	3,072	33	68	572	1,296	1,104	2,003	1,068	1,311	632	679	1,761	774	987
2001....................	3,321	48	91	595	1,442	1,145	2,233	1,088	1,353	614	739	1,968	784	1,184
2000....................	2,913	38	77	571	1,218	1,009	1,965	948	1,162	546	616	1,750	722	1,028
1999....................	3,157	45	77	620	1,211	1,205	1,970	1,188	1,403	699	703	1,755	722	1,033
1998....................	3,037	45	73	536	1,313	1,070	1,884	1,153	1,284	614	669	1,753	758	995
1997....................	3,027	30	63	562	1,299	1,073	2,016	1,010	1,304	651	653	1,723	668	1,055
1996....................	2,922	21	52	534	1,217	1,098	1,893	1,029	1,288	650	638	1,634	655	979
1995....................	2,749	8	60	465	1,198	1,018	1,802	947	1,290	646	644	1,459	554	905
1994....................	2,613	9	21	551	1,138	893	1,710	902	1,238	619	619	1,375	505	870
1993[r].................	2,435	3	14	537	1,022	859	1,611	824	1,156	601	555	1,278	458	820
1993....................	2,391	3	13	514	1,006	856	1,580	812	1,130	579	551	1,261	446	815
1992....................	2,392	-	36	508	1,035	814	1,546	846	1,102	606	496	1,291	521	770
1991....................	2,683	-	37	547	1,165	934	1,824	859	1,320	688	631	1,364	491	872
1990....................	2,514	2	27	497	1,095	893	1,722	792	1,162	569	593	1,352	531	820
1989....................	2,520	-	40	509	1,161	809	1,662	857	1,219	626	594	1,300	515	786
1988....................	2,511	-	36	464	1,098	913	1,716	795	1,187	522	666	1,324	435	889
1987....................	2,415	1	57	494	1,137	725	1,655	760	1,152	579	573	1,263	462	801
1986....................	2,365	-	44	530	1,057	732	1,624	741	1,184	596	589	1,181	479	702
1985....................	2,427	-	31	540	1,179	678	1,652	775	1,239	607	632	1,188	395	793
1984....................	2,395	-	32	580	1,190	594	1,648	747	1,263	654	610	1,132	440	692
1983....................	2,442	-	32	568	1,214	629	1,614	829	1,279	665	614	1,163	438	725
1982....................	2,393	1	31	534	1,244	584	1,587	806	1,216	626	590	1,178	421	756
1981....................	2,205	-	34	528	1,120	523	1,478	726	1,127	546	581	1,078	347	731
1980....................	2,173	2	31	554	1,104	481	...	...	1,106	526	581	1,066	372	694
1979....................	2,214	-	45	497	1,149	523	1,537	678	1,105	503	602	1,109	355	754
1978....................	2,217	-	51	565	1,064	536	1,454	762	1,149	516	633	1,068	366	702
1977[1].................	1,810	2	53	593	1,161	...	1,241	568	995	548	447	813	338	475
1976....................	2,152	-	40	622	1,017	472	1,516	634	1,216	576	638	937	292	644
1975....................	1,590	-	59	607	923	...	1,105	484	949	542	407	640	267	373
1974....................	1,490	-	61	499	930	...	1,061	428	897	457	440	593	205	388
1973....................	1,385	-	42	541	801	...	945	439	887	467	420	498	163	335
1972....................	1,320	1	52	517	749	...	877	443	872	481	391	450	155	295
1971....................	1,192	1	60	468	663	...	799	393	833	480	353	359	136	223
1970....................	1,140	-	54	488	599	...	789	351	774	432	342	366	123	243

[1]Data for 1970–1975 and 1977 do not include people ages 35 and over.
r = Revised, controlled to 1990 census based population estimates; previous 1993 data controlled to 1980 census based population estimates.
- = Quantity zero or rounds to zero.
... = Not available.

Table A-16.   College Enrollment of Undergraduate Students 14 Years Old and Over, by Type of College, Attendance Status, Age, and Gender, October 1970–2008—*Continued*

(Numbers in thousands.)

Year and type of college	Full-Time						Part-Time					
	Total	14 to 19 years	20 to 21 years	22 to 24 years	25 to 34 years	35 years and over	Total	14 to 19 years	20 to 21 years	22 to 24 years	25 to 34 years	35 years and over
1987	1,716	839	368	192	212	105	1,932	272	256	264	639	500
1986	1,608	814	296	170	223	105	1,783	209	210	257	652	454
1985	1,615	779	341	174	244	78	1,674	180	217	229	607	440
1984	1,663	812	330	190	247	84	1,509	182	195	252	548	333
1983	1,703	855	374	159	250	65	1,713	195	221	245	631	420
1982	1,814	883	381	214	260	77	1,634	205	223	280	566	356
1981	1,745	927	357	170	188	102	1,601	217	209	243	579	353
1980	1,566	884	287	160	167	67	1,542	195	163	256	554	374
1979	1,408	749	251	156	185	68	1,489	184	152	251	480	423
1978	1,400	776	243	157	167	57	1,505	190	184	234	503	394
1977[1]	1,372	718	283	162	208	...	1,138	216	172	218	533	...
1976	1,503	764	261	177	228	74	1,351	143	183	190	490	346
1975	1,567	865	274	155	274	...	994	159	157	199	478	...
1974	1,237	702	233	151	152	...	835	132	136	154	413	...
1973	1,100	702	164	121	111	...	697	114	113	133	338	...
1972	1,255	772	223	134	126	...	655	111	111	133	300	...
1971	1,199	797	209	124	70	...	631	131	98	139	261	...
1970	1,177	786	197	114	80	...	515	109	84	120	203	...
Graduate Students												
2008	1,867	20	53	646	851	296	1,810	-	5	173	732	899
2007	1,790	23	59	569	815	324	1,801	1	4	210	745	842
2006	1,690	16	70	542	809	254	1,688	3	14	187	671	813
2005	1,587	4	98	423	767	294	1,717	3	-	150	691	873
2004	1,571	20	76	548	675	252	1,807	-	1	170	757	878
2003	1,622	26	76	479	738	304	1,646	3	8	153	662	820
2002	1,406	31	61	432	631	251	1,666	2	6	140	666	852
2001	1,398	38	77	455	630	197	1,923	10	14	139	812	947
2000	1,268	32	67	414	544	211	1,645	6	10	156	674	798
1999	1,421	38	71	487	539	287	1,736	8	6	133	672	918
1998	1,372	45	58	429	579	262	1,665	-	15	107	734	808
1997	1,319	26	57	401	605	229	1,708	3	6	160	694	844
1996	1,305	18	42	420	570	254	1,617	3	9	114	647	844
1995	1,199	8	43	352	571	225	1,550	-	17	112	627	793
1994	1,124	9	19	377	544	175	1,489	-	2	174	594	718
1993[1]	1,059	3	11	376	482	186	1,376	-	3	161	540	673
1993	1,025	3	10	358	469	184	1,366	-	3	156	536	672
1992	1,126	-	33	387	478	228	1,266	-	3	120	557	586
1991	1,180	-	29	423	539	188	1,504	-	8	124	626	746
1990	1,100	2	25	376	518	180	1,413	-	2	121	577	714
1989	1,140	-	33	375	525	208	1,380	-	7	135	637	601
1988	956	-	31	304	465	157	1,555	-	5	160	634	756
1987	1,041	1	52	343	477	167	1,374	-	5	151	660	558
1986	1,074	-	40	412	465	157	1,291	-	4	120	593	575
1985	1,002	-	27	385	449	141	1,424	-	4	155	728	537
1984	1,093	-	27	427	544	95	1,302	-	6	153	644	498
1983	1,103	-	32	420	530	121	1,339	-	-	148	685	507
1982	1,047	-	28	381	522	116	1,346	1	4	153	721	467
1981	893	-	28	355	447	64	1,312	-	6	173	673	459
1980	898	2	24	403	403	66	1,275	-	6	152	702	415
1979	858	-	32	358	397	72	1,356	-	14	140	752	451
1978	882	-	38	396	376	71	1,335	-	14	169	688	465
1977[1]	886	2	43	382	459	...	922	-	10	211	702	...
1976	869	-	35	405	355	73	1,282	-	5	217	662	398
1975	809	-	43	382	386	...	780	-	16	225	537	...
1974	662	-	41	289	330	...	828	-	20	210	600	...
1973	630	-	33	350	248	...	755	-	9	191	553	...
1972	636	1	44	332	262	...	686	-	8	185	487	...
1971	616	1	57	299	261	...	576	-	3	169	402	...
1970	555	-	42	304	212	...	585	-	12	184	387	...

[1]Data for 1970–1975 and 1977 do not include people ages 35 and over.
r = Revised, controlled to 1990 census based population estimates; previous 1993 data controlled to 1980 census based population estimates.
- = Quantity zero or rounds to zero.
... = Not available.

Table A-17. Educational Attainment of the Population 18 Years Old and Over, by Age, Sex, Race, and Hispanic Origin, 2009

(Numbers in thousands.)

Age, sex, race, and Hispanic origin	Total	None	1st to 4th grade	5th to 6th grade	7th to 8th grade	9th grade	10th grade	11th grade[1]	High school graduate
ALL RACES									
Both Sexes									
18 years old and over	226,973	903	1,999	3,732	4,766	4,269	5,374	10,946	70,044
18 to 24 years old	28,688	59	58	185	270	499	822	3,681	8,418
25 years old and over	198,285	844	1,941	3,547	4,496	3,770	4,551	7,265	61,626
25 to 29 years old	21,256	27	108	310	282	357	447	889	6,113
30 to 34 years old	19,264	68	119	369	265	432	356	721	5,239
35 to 39 years old	20,445	63	154	448	283	426	369	704	5,506
40 to 44 years old	20,877	63	159	329	329	335	379	776	6,336
45 to 49 years old	22,712	65	162	324	360	357	415	795	7,348
50 to 54 years old	21,654	85	158	339	305	304	421	766	6,930
55 to 59 years old	18,755	90	148	272	283	320	375	558	5,691
60 to 64 years old	15,534	67	175	224	351	229	324	390	4,681
65 to 69 years old	11,825	82	139	208	369	237	412	462	4,179
70 to 74 years old	8,579	76	158	181	384	211	302	394	3,241
75 years old and over	17,384	159	462	543	1,286	562	753	810	6,363
Male									
18 years old and over	110,026	417	1,024	1,934	2,383	2,140	2,662	5,736	34,710
18 to 24 years old	14,508	37	32	142	148	287	455	2,043	4,685
25 years old and over	95,518	380	992	1,792	2,235	1,854	2,207	3,693	30,025
25 to 29 years old	10,867	14	60	173	148	200	248	520	3,565
30 to 34 years old	9,574	42	69	219	155	227	206	405	2,931
35 to 39 years old	10,169	32	87	259	167	230	169	413	2,957
40 to 44 years old	10,322	29	89	167	183	179	200	446	3,355
45 to 49 years old	11,162	34	82	155	222	206	222	459	3,794
50 to 54 years old	10,611	54	93	170	136	143	210	400	3,539
55 to 59 years old	9,083	48	97	127	164	141	193	276	2,656
60 to 64 years old	7,423	20	94	132	176	116	141	166	2,013
65 to 69 years old	5,632	32	58	97	187	106	196	196	1,843
70 to 74 years old	3,769	22	80	76	188	78	116	154	1,209
75 years old and over	6,907	54	184	217	508	228	305	257	2,164
Female									
18 years old and over	116,947	486	975	1,797	2,383	2,128	2,712	5,209	35,334
18 to 24 years old	14,180	22	27	43	122	212	367	1,637	3,733
25 years old and over	102,767	464	949	1,755	2,262	1,916	2,344	3,572	31,601
25 to 29 years old	10,389	13	48	137	134	157	199	369	2,548
30 to 34 years old	9,691	26	50	150	110	205	150	315	2,308
35 to 39 years old	10,275	31	67	189	116	196	199	291	2,549
40 to 44 years old	10,556	34	70	162	146	156	178	329	2,981
45 to 49 years old	11,550	32	80	169	138	151	193	336	3,555
50 to 54 years old	11,043	31	65	168	169	161	211	366	3,391
55 to 59 years old	9,671	42	51	145	119	179	182	282	3,035
60 to 64 years old	8,112	47	81	92	174	113	182	224	2,668
65 to 69 years old	6,193	50	81	111	182	132	216	267	2,336
70 to 74 years old	4,810	53	77	105	196	133	186	240	2,031
75 years old and over	10,477	105	278	326	778	334	448	553	4,198
WHITE ALONE OR IN COMBINATION									
Both Sexes									
18 years old and over	187,041	635	1,611	3,206	4,027	3,559	4,175	8,287	57,777
18 to 24 years old	22,857	40	37	165	223	400	578	2,838	6,651
25 years old and over	164,183	595	1,574	3,041	3,804	3,159	3,597	5,448	51,126
25 to 29 years old	16,987	21	95	280	256	306	357	659	4,814
30 to 34 years old	15,324	61	105	340	238	362	287	557	4,095
35 to 39 years old	16,316	47	122	405	248	401	276	547	4,352
40 to 44 years old	16,923	49	143	306	281	301	296	572	5,071
45 to 49 years old	18,628	45	143	289	316	292	331	552	6,056
50 to 54 years old	17,968	56	136	290	261	254	324	563	5,703
55 to 59 years old	15,770	58	134	233	238	253	270	389	4,773

[1]12th grade, no diploma are included in this category.
[2]May be of any race.

Table A-17.   Educational Attainment of the Population 18 Years Old and Over, by Age, Sex, Race, and Hispanic Origin, 2009—*Continued*

(Numbers in thousands.)

Age, sex, race, and Hispanic origin	Educational attainment						
	Some college, no degree	Associate's degree, occupational	Associate's degree, academic	Bachelor's degree	Master's degree	Professional degree	Doctoral degree
ALL RACES							
Both Sexes							
18 years old and over	44,241	8,834	10,469	40,276	15,260	3,236	2,624
18 to 24 years old	10,409	642	823	2,640	142	30	10
25 years old and over	33,832	8,192	9,646	37,635	15,118	3,206	2,614
25 to 29 years old	4,361	817	1,039	4,927	1,258	204	117
30 to 34 years old	3,422	794	975	4,314	1,622	341	228
35 to 39 years old	3,472	936	1,150	4,487	1,754	403	290
40 to 44 years old	3,387	994	1,142	4,367	1,646	338	300
45 to 49 years old	3,824	1,170	1,250	4,350	1,615	346	330
50 to 54 years old	3,705	1,048	1,305	3,981	1,655	390	262
55 to 59 years old	3,413	866	957	3,466	1,722	301	292
60 to 64 years old	2,695	597	726	2,908	1,579	311	278
65 to 69 years old	1,904	371	410	1,711	893	250	195
70 to 74 years old	1,267	205	228	1,134	583	89	127
75 years old and over	2,382	392	465	1,990	792	233	193
Male							
18 years old and over	20,954	3,888	4,292	19,205	7,061	1,970	1,648
18 to 24 years old	4,861	277	362	1,104	53	17	5
25 years old and over	16,093	3,611	3,930	18,101	7,009	1,953	1,643
25 to 29 years old	2,196	374	482	2,228	516	93	52
30 to 34 years old	1,683	383	390	1,931	637	160	136
35 to 39 years old	1,753	406	477	2,100	754	206	157
40 to 44 years old	1,535	443	473	2,082	778	173	190
45 to 49 years old	1,811	513	475	2,020	767	204	199
50 to 54 years old	1,821	480	482	1,918	771	234	158
55 to 59 years old	1,657	395	403	1,756	779	214	177
60 to 64 years old	1,261	246	336	1,526	791	231	174
65 to 69 years old	825	175	169	943	466	193	146
70 to 74 years old	581	74	98	579	347	68	99
75 years old and over	971	122	144	1,017	402	177	156
Female							
18 years old and over	23,287	4,946	6,177	21,071	8,199	1,266	976
18 to 24 years old	5,548	366	461	1,536	89	13	5
25 years old and over	17,739	4,580	5,716	19,534	8,110	1,253	971
25 to 29 years old	2,165	443	557	2,699	743	111	65
30 to 34 years old	1,739	411	585	2,383	985	180	92
35 to 39 years old	1,719	530	672	2,387	1,000	197	133
40 to 44 years old	1,852	552	669	2,284	867	165	110
45 to 49 years old	2,013	657	774	2,330	848	142	132
50 to 54 years old	1,884	568	822	2,063	884	155	105
55 to 59 years old	1,756	472	554	1,710	943	87	115
60 to 64 years old	1,435	352	390	1,382	787	80	104
65 to 69 years old	1,080	196	241	768	427	57	49
70 to 74 years old	685	131	130	555	237	22	29
75 years old and over	1,411	270	320	973	390	56	37
WHITE ALONE OR IN COMBINATION							
Both Sexes							
18 years old and over	36,256	7,481	8,683	33,782	12,673	2,760	2,129
18 to 24 years old	8,370	541	673	2,210	98	22	10
25 years old and over	27,886	6,940	8,010	31,572	12,574	2,738	2,119
25 to 29 years old	3,393	670	846	4,076	962	175	79
30 to 34 years old	2,684	664	789	3,480	1,242	270	151
35 to 39 years old	2,712	785	903	3,621	1,339	330	228
40 to 44 years old	2,694	819	906	3,653	1,320	280	230
45 to 49 years old	3,079	987	1,056	3,621	1,338	285	240
50 to 54 years old	3,065	908	1,130	3,311	1,400	336	229
55 to 59 years old	2,879	756	813	2,946	1,510	263	256

Table A-17. Educational Attainment of the Population 18 Years Old and Over, by Age, Sex, Race, and Hispanic Origin, 2009—*Continued*

(Numbers in thousands.)

Age, sex, race, and Hispanic origin	Total	None	1st to 4th grade	5th to 6th grade	7th to 8th grade	9th grade	10th grade	11th grade[1]	High school graduate
60 to 64 years old	13,279	45	136	179	279	171	246	275	4,013
65 to 69 years old	10,211	52	112	173	296	182	316	351	3,658
70 to 74 years old	7,408	53	109	132	318	164	249	310	2,829
75 years old and over	15,371	108	340	414	1,073	473	646	675	5,763
Male									
18 years old and over	91,757	305	848	1,726	2,076	1,809	2,144	4,416	28,728
18 to 24 years old	11,644	23	23	129	123	226	331	1,584	3,737
25 years old and over	80,113	282	825	1,597	1,953	1,583	1,813	2,832	24,991
25 to 29 years old	8,835	9	55	157	137	169	211	407	2,831
30 to 34 years old	7,746	36	58	206	139	188	178	324	2,327
35 to 39 years old	8,265	24	72	242	155	219	124	348	2,368
40 to 44 years old	8,514	28	84	158	162	168	175	342	2,730
45 to 49 years old	9,297	22	68	145	197	174	183	334	3,193
50 to 54 years old	8,912	37	74	150	120	122	166	296	2,959
55 to 59 years old	7,731	35	90	114	142	117	142	189	2,259
60 to 64 years old	6,436	14	77	111	148	81	115	116	1,728
65 to 69 years old	4,918	24	46	83	153	91	151	154	1,600
70 to 74 years old	3,294	13	62	53	168	60	96	120	1,037
75 years old and over	6,167	39	137	177	432	192	272	203	1,957
Female									
18 years old and over	95,284	330	763	1,480	1,951	1,750	2,031	3,870	29,050
18 to 24 years old	11,214	17	14	36	100	174	247	1,254	2,914
25 years old and over	84,070	313	749	1,444	1,851	1,576	1,784	2,616	26,135
25 to 29 years old	8,152	12	40	122	119	137	146	252	1,983
30 to 34 years old	7,579	24	46	134	99	173	109	233	1,768
35 to 39 years old	8,051	23	50	164	94	182	152	199	1,983
40 to 44 years old	8,409	21	58	148	119	133	121	230	2,341
45 to 49 years old	9,331	23	75	144	119	118	148	218	2,863
50 to 54 years old	9,056	19	62	140	141	132	158	267	2,744
55 to 59 years old	8,039	23	43	119	96	135	128	200	2,514
60 to 64 years old	6,843	31	59	68	131	89	130	159	2,285
65 to 69 years old	5,293	28	66	90	143	92	165	197	2,058
70 to 74 years old	4,114	40	46	79	149	104	152	190	1,792
75 years old and over	9,204	69	203	237	641	281	373	472	3,806
BLACK ALONE OR IN COMBINATION									
Both Sexes									
18 years old and over	27,709	91	216	242	523	517	990	2,200	9,659
18 to 24 years old	4,428	21	11	6	34	84	208	703	1,482
25 years old and over	23,281	70	205	236	489	433	782	1,497	8,177
25 to 29 years old	3,012	4	6	7	23	36	81	180	1,056
30 to 34 years old	2,599	4	5	12	13	55	57	142	914
35 to 39 years old	2,647	2	13	15	17	12	78	124	905
40 to 44 years old	2,684	5	12	6	23	24	51	164	1,018
45 to 49 years old	2,841	6	14	6	36	38	75	202	1,022
50 to 54 years old	2,575	11	11	21	33	26	76	177	941
55 to 59 years old	2,065	7	8	11	26	54	92	131	705
60 to 64 years old	1,553	7	19	20	42	45	60	99	529
65 to 69 years old	1,079	2	13	23	52	38	70	98	381
70 to 74 years old	828	8	31	31	52	39	50	66	288
75 years old and over	1,397	16	74	85	171	67	92	116	416
Male									
18 years old and over	12,483	55	115	102	220	243	430	1,073	4,806
18 to 24 years old	2,145	16	8	3	21	48	101	379	796
25 years old and over	10,339	39	106	99	199	196	329	695	4,009
25 to 29 years old	1,420	4	-	4	8	24	34	90	615
30 to 34 years old	1,182	2	2	4	7	32	26	66	488
35 to 39 years old	1,169	-	6	8	4	5	35	47	479
40 to 44 years old	1,216	-	8	3	10	7	11	77	510

[1]12th grade, no diploma are included in this category.
- = Quantity zero or rounds to zero.

Table A-17.   Educational Attainment of the Population 18 Years Old and Over, by Age, Sex, Race, and Hispanic Origin, 2009—*Continued*

(Numbers in thousands.)

Age, sex, race, and Hispanic origin	Educational attainment						
	Some college, no degree	Associate's degree, occupational	Associate's degree, academic	Bachelor's degree	Master's degree	Professional degree	Doctoral degree
60 to 64 years old	2,311	501	615	2,548	1,434	276	252
65 to 69 years old	1,704	317	352	1,510	793	223	172
70 to 74 years old	1,157	169	187	1,004	538	81	109
75 years old and over	2,209	364	413	1,804	698	219	175
Male							
18 years old and over	17,403	3,333	3,589	16,404	5,911	1,725	1,340
18 to 24 years old	3,946	230	300	934	38	14	5
25 years old and over	13,456	3,103	3,289	15,470	5,873	1,711	1,335
25 to 29 years old	1,776	316	398	1,864	386	80	37
30 to 34 years old	1,344	326	320	1,587	485	136	89
35 to 39 years old	1,391	344	390	1,732	571	171	116
40 to 44 years old	1,240	374	378	1,756	623	154	142
45 to 49 years old	1,473	446	404	1,715	639	170	134
50 to 54 years old	1,536	414	411	1,622	663	205	137
55 to 59 years old	1,412	353	342	1,508	678	190	159
60 to 64 years old	1,090	205	285	1,380	723	206	158
65 to 69 years old	746	149	150	856	412	171	131
70 to 74 years old	542	63	80	521	326	63	87
75 years old and over	906	113	131	929	369	166	145
Female							
18 years old and over	18,853	4,148	5,094	17,379	6,761	1,035	789
18 to 24 years old	4,424	311	372	1,276	61	9	5
25 years old and over	14,429	3,837	4,721	16,102	6,701	1,027	784
25 to 29 years old	1,616	354	448	2,212	576	95	41
30 to 34 years old	1,340	338	469	1,892	757	134	62
35 to 39 years old	1,321	441	513	1,889	768	160	112
40 to 44 years old	1,455	445	528	1,898	697	127	88
45 to 49 years old	1,606	540	652	1,906	699	115	106
50 to 54 years old	1,529	494	719	1,689	738	131	92
55 to 59 years old	1,467	403	471	1,437	832	73	97
60 to 64 years old	1,221	296	330	1,168	711	69	94
65 to 69 years old	958	168	202	653	381	52	41
70 to 74 years old	615	106	107	483	213	18	22
75 years old and over	1,303	251	282	876	329	52	29
BLACK ALONE OR IN COMBINATION							
Both Sexes							
18 years old and over	6,221	987	1,274	3,238	1,246	171	133
18 to 24 years old	1,454	65	94	249	12	4	-
25 years old and over	4,767	923	1,179	2,989	1,234	167	133
25 to 29 years old	783	111	152	443	100	14	17
30 to 34 years old	573	102	132	416	143	16	14
35 to 39 years old	601	112	169	404	169	23	6
40 to 44 years old	548	133	175	349	142	18	17
45 to 49 years old	606	131	132	383	142	27	22
50 to 54 years old	535	106	135	333	150	13	7
55 to 59 years old	416	88	104	261	129	18	15
60 to 64 years old	309	58	81	161	93	17	12
65 to 69 years old	169	37	37	93	52	7	7
70 to 74 years old	98	27	30	55	37	5	11
75 years old and over	129	18	32	90	76	10	6
Male							
18 years old and over	2,664	365	477	1,301	485	82	65
18 to 24 years old	611	31	38	88	3	4	-
25 years old and over	2,053	335	440	1,214	483	78	65
25 to 29 years old	330	40	58	163	42	4	4
30 to 34 years old	251	45	42	164	44	4	7
35 to 39 years old	254	45	50	160	62	10	4
40 to 44 years old	232	49	72	150	76	5	6

- = Quantity zero or rounds to zero.

Table A-17. Educational Attainment of the Population 18 Years Old and Over, by Age, Sex, Race, and Hispanic Origin, 2009—*Continued*

(Numbers in thousands.)

Age, sex, race, and Hispanic origin	Total	None	*Educational attainment* 1st to 4th grade	5th to 6th grade	7th to 8th grade	9th grade	10th grade	11th grade[1]	High school graduate
45 to 49 years old	1,299	4	11	-	21	20	40	109	477
50 to 54 years old	1,169	8	9	9	16	11	34	90	452
55 to 59 years old	928	4	3	2	12	18	45	67	326
60 to 64 years old	664	4	12	13	15	30	26	42	213
65 to 69 years old	455	1	7	9	30	10	32	36	186
70 to 74 years old	343	5	17	18	15	13	19	28	127
75 years old and over	493	7	32	29	62	26	27	43	136
Female									
18 years old and over	15,226	36	101	140	304	274	560	1,127	4,854
18 to 24 years old	2,283	5	3	3	13	37	107	325	686
25 years old and over	12,943	32	99	137	290	237	453	802	4,168
25 to 29 years old	1,592	-	6	3	15	13	48	90	441
30 to 34 years old	1,418	2	3	8	6	24	31	76	427
35 to 39 years old	1,478	2	7	6	13	7	43	77	427
40 to 44 years old	1,468	5	4	4	13	17	39	87	508
45 to 49 years old	1,542	2	3	6	15	18	35	93	544
50 to 54 years old	1,405	3	2	12	18	15	42	87	489
55 to 59 years old	1,137	3	5	9	14	35	47	65	379
60 to 64 years old	889	4	7	7	27	15	34	57	317
65 to 69 years old	624	1	5	14	22	27	38	62	195
70 to 74 years old	486	3	14	12	37	26	31	37	162
75 years old and over	904	9	43	56	110	41	65	73	280
ASIAN ALONE OR IN COMBINATION									
Both Sexes									
18 years old and over	10,826	147	146	205	153	127	149	346	2,077
18 to 24 years old	1,309	1	5	2	7	11	15	122	226
25 years old and over	9,517	146	141	203	146	116	134	223	1,851
25 to 29 years old	1,130	-	3	7	2	7	7	29	184
30 to 34 years old	1,195	-	9	8	7	10	8	20	154
35 to 39 years old	1,326	14	13	20	10	4	9	26	204
40 to 44 years old	1,104	8	8	9	16	7	23	35	188
45 to 49 years old	1,080	9	6	18	7	15	13	20	217
50 to 54 years old	958	14	9	24	9	20	15	10	230
55 to 59 years old	809	24	7	24	17	15	8	31	167
60 to 64 years old	596	12	19	23	20	9	10	11	109
65 to 69 years old	475	26	10	11	17	12	24	11	118
70 to 74 years old	292	7	19	16	7	4	4	14	108
75 years old and over	551	32	38	43	32	14	12	16	172
Male									
18 years old and over	5,128	41	54	61	50	54	66	195	918
18 to 24 years old	696	1	-	-	4	8	11	80	129
25 years old and over	4,432	40	54	61	46	47	54	115	789
25 to 29 years old	548	-	2	-	-	5	4	13	86
30 to 34 years old	561	-	9	7	2	2	3	9	73
35 to 39 years old	655	8	7	6	5	4	6	16	85
40 to 44 years old	493	1	-	2	6	1	9	25	77
45 to 49 years old	508	4	4	3	3	6	4	7	102
50 to 54 years old	470	6	8	10	1	10	8	6	108
55 to 59 years old	377	9	5	5	10	7	3	14	57
60 to 64 years old	271	2	5	8	7	4	-	5	58
65 to 69 years old	224	6	2	5	2	3	10	6	42
70 to 74 years old	113	-	1	5	1	-	1	5	38
75 years old and over	212	6	11	10	9	7	5	9	63
Female									
18 years old and over	5,698	105	92	144	103	73	83	151	1,159
18 to 24 years old	613	-	5	2	4	3	4	43	97
25 years old and over	5,085	105	88	142	100	70	79	108	1,062
25 to 29 years old	582	-	1	7	2	2	3	16	98
30 to 34 years old	634	-	-	1	5	8	5	11	80

[1]12th grade, no diploma are included in this category.

- = Quantity zero or rounds to zero.

Table A-17. Educational Attainment of the Population 18 Years Old and Over, by Age, Sex, Race, and Hispanic Origin, 2009—*Continued*

(Numbers in thousands.)

Age, sex, race, and Hispanic origin	Educational attainment						
	Some college, no degree	Associate's degree, occupational	Associate's degree, academic	Bachelor's degree	Master's degree	Professional degree	Doctoral degree
45 to 49 years old	284	35	50	163	56	15	14
50 to 54 years old	233	49	56	139	55	5	4
55 to 59 years old	192	25	43	120	51	10	8
60 to 64 years old	131	21	38	63	38	10	6
65 to 69 years old	64	12	10	31	21	4	2
70 to 74 years old	36	7	15	22	12	3	4
75 years old and over	46	6	5	38	25	7	3
Female							
18 years old and over	3,557	622	796	1,937	761	89	68
18 to 24 years old	843	34	57	161	10	-	-
25 years old and over	2,714	588	739	1,775	751	89	68
25 to 29 years old	452	71	94	280	57	9	13
30 to 34 years old	322	57	90	253	99	12	7
35 to 39 years old	347	67	118	244	107	12	2
40 to 44 years old	316	84	102	198	66	14	11
45 to 49 years old	321	96	82	220	86	12	8
50 to 54 years old	302	57	80	194	95	7	3
55 to 59 years old	224	62	61	141	79	8	6
60 to 64 years old	178	37	43	98	55	7	6
65 to 69 years old	105	26	28	62	31	3	5
70 to 74 years old	63	20	15	33	25	2	7
75 years old and over	84	11	27	52	51	3	2
ASIAN ALONE OR IN COMBINATION							
Both Sexes							
18 years old and over	1,582	271	457	3,193	1,317	299	358
18 to 24 years old	601	28	55	200	32	5	-
25 years old and over	980	243	402	2,993	1,285	294	358
25 to 29 years old	161	28	46	422	196	17	22
30 to 34 years old	130	21	49	426	233	57	63
35 to 39 years old	134	24	65	459	244	45	53
40 to 44 years old	109	31	47	356	178	38	53
45 to 49 years old	121	38	61	320	132	31	71
50 to 54 years old	83	26	38	315	100	42	25
55 to 59 years old	97	18	32	243	84	21	20
60 to 64 years old	65	27	22	185	49	18	15
65 to 69 years old	30	13	19	105	45	17	16
70 to 74 years old	9	5	7	71	10	4	7
75 years old and over	42	11	16	92	15	5	13
Male							
18 years old and over	809	145	197	1,457	668	165	248
18 to 24 years old	322	12	23	95	12	1	-
25 years old and over	487	133	174	1,362	656	164	248
25 to 29 years old	87	15	26	202	90	9	10
30 to 34 years old	70	6	26	184	106	20	42
35 to 39 years old	84	12	32	201	127	26	36
40 to 44 years old	47	12	13	165	79	15	41
45 to 49 years old	47	30	24	129	74	19	52
50 to 54 years old	42	12	16	148	53	26	17
55 to 59 years old	45	12	14	121	49	14	12
60 to 64 years old	31	14	6	77	30	14	10
65 to 69 years old	12	13	9	53	33	17	13
70 to 74 years old	4	3	2	35	8	2	7
75 years old and over	18	3	6	47	8	3	8
Female							
18 years old and over	773	125	260	1,736	649	134	110
18 to 24 years old	280	15	32	105	19	4	-
25 years old and over	493	110	228	1,631	629	130	110
25 to 29 years old	75	13	19	220	105	8	12
30 to 34 years old	59	15	24	241	126	36	21

- = Quantity zero or rounds to zero.

Table A-17. Educational Attainment of the Population 18 Years Old and Over, by Age, Sex, Race, and Hispanic Origin, 2009—*Continued*

(Numbers in thousands.)

Age, sex, race, and Hispanic origin	Total	None	1st to 4th grade	5th to 6th grade	7th to 8th grade	9th grade	10th grade	11th grade[1]	High school graduate
35 to 39 years old	671	6	6	14	5	-	3	10	119
40 to 44 years old	612	8	8	7	10	6	13	9	111
45 to 49 years old	572	6	3	15	4	9	9	13	115
50 to 54 years old	488	8	1	13	8	10	7	4	122
55 to 59 years old	431	15	2	19	7	8	5	17	111
60 to 64 years old	325	10	13	15	13	5	10	6	51
65 to 69 years old	251	20	9	6	15	9	14	5	76
70 to 74 years old	179	7	18	11	6	4	2	9	70
75 years old and over	339	26	27	33	23	7	7	7	109
HISPANIC[2]									
Both Sexes									
18 years old and over	31,028	472	1,304	2,720	1,577	1,762	1,130	2,506	9,229
18 to 24 years old	5,072	23	34	162	121	224	224	792	1,618
25 years old and over	25,956	449	1,270	2,558	1,455	1,538	906	1,714	7,611
25 to 29 years old	4,260	14	96	296	184	218	171	344	1,468
30 to 34 years old	3,867	44	100	353	187	282	145	305	1,155
35 to 39 years old	3,768	26	124	400	167	318	106	259	1,056
40 to 44 years old	3,260	38	135	301	161	201	103	214	995
45 to 49 years old	2,835	41	134	279	156	151	92	181	862
50 to 54 years old	2,287	50	126	260	141	114	82	145	643
55 to 59 years old	1,757	37	111	192	108	81	61	78	439
60 to 64 years old	1,204	34	111	132	74	60	40	54	319
65 to 69 years old	950	39	87	116	95	29	40	56	258
70 to 74 years old	677	39	76	74	64	37	35	26	174
75 years old and over	1,090	86	168	157	119	47	30	49	244
Male									
18 years old and over	15,990	221	696	1,494	818	922	603	1,431	4,884
18 to 24 years old	2,635	17	23	123	65	127	122	440	884
25 years old and over	13,355	204	673	1,371	753	795	481	991	3,999
25 to 29 years old	2,415	5	56	172	115	129	105	235	858
30 to 34 years old	2,026	30	58	211	108	135	92	187	636
35 to 39 years old	2,009	14	70	238	95	179	45	150	567
40 to 44 years old	1,699	26	79	152	87	111	64	116	518
45 to 49 years old	1,442	19	59	145	94	81	45	104	441
50 to 54 years old	1,165	33	72	127	68	47	45	78	324
55 to 59 years old	848	17	71	99	53	36	23	43	206
60 to 64 years old	582	9	58	76	27	34	19	33	148
65 to 69 years old	436	15	37	55	37	8	15	22	131
70 to 74 years old	280	10	39	29	25	20	11	6	70
75 years old and over	453	27	74	67	44	15	16	16	101
Female									
18 years old and over	15,038	251	608	1,226	759	840	528	1,075	4,345
18 to 24 years old	2,437	6	11	39	57	96	102	352	733
25 years old and over	12,601	244	597	1,187	702	744	425	723	3,612
25 to 29 years old	1,845	9	41	124	69	89	66	110	610
30 to 34 years old	1,841	14	42	142	79	147	53	118	519
35 to 39 years old	1,759	12	54	162	72	139	61	109	489
40 to 44 years old	1,561	13	56	149	73	90	39	98	477
45 to 49 years old	1,394	22	75	135	63	71	47	77	420
50 to 54 years old	1,122	17	54	132	73	67	37	67	319
55 to 59 years old	908	21	40	92	55	46	38	36	233
60 to 64 years old	622	25	53	56	46	26	21	22	171
65 to 69 years old	514	24	50	61	58	21	25	33	127
70 to 74 years old	397	28	37	45	39	17	24	20	104
75 years old and over	638	59	95	90	76	31	14	33	143

[1] 12th grade, no diploma are included in this category.
[2] May be of any race.

Table A-17. Educational Attainment of the Population 18 Years Old and Over, by Age, Sex, Race, and Hispanic Origin, 2009—*Continued*

(Numbers in thousands.)

Age, sex, race, and Hispanic origin	Educational attainment						
	Some college, no degree	Associate's degree, occupational	Associate's degree, academic	Bachelor's degree	Master's degree	Professional degree	Doctoral degree
35 to 39 years old	50	12	33	257	118	20	18
40 to 44 years old	61	20	34	191	99	23	11
45 to 49 years old	73	8	36	191	59	12	18
50 to 54 years old	41	13	22	168	48	16	8
55 to 59 years old	52	5	18	122	35	7	9
60 to 64 years old	34	13	16	108	19	4	5
65 to 69 years old	18	1	11	52	12	-	4
70 to 74 years old	6	2	5	36	1	2	-
75 years old and over	23	8	11	45	7	2	5
HISPANIC[2]							
Both Sexes							
18 years old and over	4,852	809	997	2,719	671	186	94
18 to 24 years old	1,407	99	126	226	14	1	2
25 years old and over	3,445	710	872	2,493	658	185	92
25 to 29 years old	686	111	152	441	56	15	8
30 to 34 years old	519	125	125	393	92	37	5
35 to 39 years old	503	106	155	392	110	26	21
40 to 44 years old	419	96	121	342	102	18	14
45 to 49 years old	355	97	96	284	75	20	12
50 to 54 years old	333	60	64	184	62	17	8
55 to 59 years old	264	48	63	187	69	14	4
60 to 64 years old	154	22	40	104	49	7	4
65 to 69 years old	88	25	20	62	20	6	10
70 to 74 years old	57	10	11	48	15	7	4
75 years old and over	68	8	28	56	8	19	2
Male							
18 years old and over	2,356	354	456	1,276	324	105	51
18 to 24 years old	640	44	58	84	5	1	2
25 years old and over	1,715	310	398	1,191	319	103	49
25 to 29 years old	357	56	62	236	16	10	4
30 to 34 years old	262	57	45	157	34	10	5
35 to 39 years old	262	45	74	187	59	14	10
40 to 44 years old	210	41	67	161	52	10	6
45 to 49 years old	168	47	41	142	38	14	4
50 to 54 years old	176	26	30	92	35	8	4
55 to 59 years old	120	19	26	88	33	11	4
60 to 64 years old	72	7	17	45	28	7	1
65 to 69 years old	31	9	12	37	13	4	8
70 to 74 years old	25	2	8	17	9	5	3
75 years old and over	33	2	15	28	2	11	-
Female							
18 years old and over	2,496	454	541	1,443	347	82	43
18 to 24 years old	767	55	68	141	9	-	-
25 years old and over	1,729	399	474	1,302	338	82	43
25 to 29 years old	329	56	89	205	40	5	4
30 to 34 years old	257	69	80	236	58	27	-
35 to 39 years old	241	61	80	204	51	12	11
40 to 44 years old	209	55	54	181	49	8	8
45 to 49 years old	187	50	55	142	37	6	8
50 to 54 years old	157	34	34	92	27	8	4
55 to 59 years old	143	30	36	99	35	3	1
60 to 64 years old	83	16	22	59	20	-	3
65 to 69 years old	57	15	8	24	7	2	2
70 to 74 years old	32	8	3	31	6	2	1
75 years old and over	35	6	13	28	6	8	2

[2]May be of any race.
- = Quantity zero or rounds to zero.

Table A-18.   Percent of High School and College Graduates of the Population 18 Years Old and Over, by Age, Sex, Race, and Hispanic Origin, 2008

(Percent, except where noted.)

Age, sex, race, and Hispanic origin	Total population (thousands)	High school graduate status			Bachelor's degree status		
		Total	Not high school graduate	High school graduate or more	Total	Less than Bachelor's degree	Bachelor's degree or more
		Percent	Percent	Percent	Percent	Percent	Percent
ALL RACES							
Both Sexes							
18 years old and over	226,973	100.0	14.1	85.9	100.0	73.0	27.0
18 to 24 years old	28,688	100.0	19.4	80.6	100.0	90.2	9.8
25 years old and over	198,285	100.0	13.3	86.7	100.0	70.5	29.5
25 to 29 years old	21,256	100.0	11.4	88.6	100.0	69.4	30.6
30 to 34 years old	19,264	100.0	12.1	87.9	100.0	66.2	33.8
35 to 39 years old	20,445	100.0	12.0	88.0	100.0	66.1	33.9
40 to 44 years old	20,877	100.0	11.3	88.7	100.0	68.1	31.9
45 to 49 years old	22,712	100.0	10.9	89.1	100.0	70.8	29.2
50 to 54 years old	21,654	100.0	11.0	89.0	100.0	71.0	29.0
55 to 59 years old	18,755	100.0	10.9	89.1	100.0	69.2	30.8
60 to 64 years old	15,534	100.0	11.3	88.7	100.0	67.3	32.7
65 to 69 years old	11,825	100.0	16.2	83.8	100.0	74.2	25.8
70 to 74 years old	8,579	100.0	19.9	80.1	100.0	77.5	22.5
75 years old and over	17,384	100.0	26.3	73.7	100.0	81.5	18.5
Male							
18 years old and over	110,026	100.0	14.8	85.2	100.0	72.8	27.2
18 to 24 years old	14,508	100.0	21.7	78.3	100.0	91.9	8.1
25 years old and over	95,518	100.0	13.8	86.2	100.0	69.9	30.1
25 to 29 years old	10,867	100.0	12.5	87.5	100.0	73.4	26.6
30 to 34 years old	9,574	100.0	13.8	86.2	100.0	70.1	29.9
35 to 39 years old	10,169	100.0	13.4	86.6	100.0	68.4	31.6
40 to 44 years old	10,322	100.0	12.5	87.5	100.0	68.8	31.2
45 to 49 years old	11,162	100.0	12.4	87.6	100.0	71.4	28.6
50 to 54 years old	10,611	100.0	11.4	88.6	100.0	71.0	29.0
55 to 59 years old	9,083	100.0	11.5	88.5	100.0	67.8	32.2
60 to 64 years old	7,423	100.0	11.4	88.6	100.0	63.3	36.7
65 to 69 years old	5,632	100.0	15.5	84.5	100.0	69.0	31.0
70 to 74 years old	3,769	100.0	18.9	81.1	100.0	71.0	29.0
75 years old and over	6,907	100.0	25.4	74.6	100.0	74.6	25.4
Female							
18 years old and over	116,947	100.0	13.4	86.6	100.0	73.1	26.9
18 to 24 years old	14,180	100.0	17.1	82.9	100.0	88.4	11.6
25 years old and over	102,767	100.0	12.9	87.1	100.0	70.9	29.1
25 to 29 years old	10,389	100.0	10.2	89.8	100.0	65.2	34.8
30 to 34 years old	9,691	100.0	10.4	89.6	100.0	62.4	37.6
35 to 39 years old	10,275	100.0	10.6	89.4	100.0	63.8	36.2
40 to 44 years old	10,556	100.0	10.2	89.8	100.0	67.5	32.5
45 to 49 years old	11,550	100.0	9.5	90.5	100.0	70.1	29.9
50 to 54 years old	11,043	100.0	10.6	89.4	100.0	71.0	29.0
55 to 59 years old	9,671	100.0	10.3	89.7	100.0	70.5	29.5
60 to 64 years old	8,112	100.0	11.3	88.7	100.0	71.0	29.0
65 to 69 years old	6,193	100.0	16.8	83.2	100.0	79.0	21.0
70 to 74 years old	4,810	100.0	20.6	79.4	100.0	82.5	17.5
75 years old and over	10,477	100.0	26.9	73.1	100.0	86.1	13.9
WHITE ALONE OR IN COMBINATION							
Both Sexes							
18 years old and over	187,041	100.0	13.6	86.4	100.0	72.5	27.5
18 to 24 years old	22,857	100.0	18.7	81.3	100.0	89.8	10.2
25 years old and over	164,183	100.0	12.9	87.1	100.0	70.2	29.8
25 to 29 years old	16,987	100.0	11.6	88.4	100.0	68.8	31.2
30 to 34 years old	15,324	100.0	12.7	87.3	100.0	66.4	33.6
35 to 39 years old	16,316	100.0	12.5	87.5	100.0	66.2	33.8
40 to 44 years old	16,923	100.0	11.5	88.5	100.0	67.6	32.4
45 to 49 years old	18,628	100.0	10.6	89.4	100.0	70.6	29.4
50 to 54 years old	17,968	100.0	10.5	89.5	100.0	70.6	29.4
55 to 59 years old	15,770	100.0	10.0	90.0	100.0	68.5	31.5

Table A-18. Percent of High School and College Graduates of the Population 18 Years Old and Over, by Age, Sex, Race, and Hispanic Origin, 2008—*Continued*

(Percent, except where noted.)

Age, sex, race, and Hispanic origin	Total population (thousands)	High school graduate status			Bachelor's degree status		
		Total	Not high school graduate	High school graduate or more	Total	Less than Bachelor's degree	Bachelor's degree or more
		Percent	Percent	Percent	Percent	Percent	Percent
60 to 64 years old	13,279	100.0	10.0	90.0	100.0	66.0	34.0
65 to 69 years old	10,211	100.0	14.5	85.5	100.0	73.6	26.4
70 to 74 years old	7,408	100.0	18.0	82.0	100.0	76.6	23.4
75 years old and over	15,371	100.0	24.2	75.8	100.0	81.2	18.8
Male							
18 years old and over	91,757	100.0	14.5	85.5	100.0	72.3	27.7
18 to 24 years old	11,644	100.0	21.0	79.0	100.0	91.5	8.5
25 years old and over	80,113	100.0	13.6	86.4	100.0	69.6	30.4
25 to 29 years old	8,835	100.0	13.0	87.0	100.0	73.2	26.8
30 to 34 years old	7,746	100.0	14.6	85.4	100.0	70.3	29.7
35 to 39 years old	8,265	100.0	14.3	85.7	100.0	68.7	31.3
40 to 44 years old	8,514	100.0	13.1	86.9	100.0	68.6	31.4
45 to 49 years old	9,297	100.0	12.1	87.9	100.0	71.4	28.6
50 to 54 years old	8,912	100.0	10.8	89.2	100.0	70.5	29.5
55 to 59 years old	7,731	100.0	10.7	89.3	100.0	67.2	32.8
60 to 64 years old	6,436	100.0	10.3	89.7	100.0	61.7	38.3
65 to 69 years old	4,918	100.0	14.3	85.7	100.0	68.1	31.9
70 to 74 years old	3,294	100.0	17.5	82.5	100.0	69.7	30.3
75 years old and over	6,167	100.0	23.5	76.5	100.0	73.9	26.1
Female							
18 years old and over	95,284	100.0	12.8	87.2	100.0	72.8	27.2
18 to 24 years old	11,214	100.0	16.4	83.6	100.0	88.0	12.0
25 years old and over	84,070	100.0	12.3	87.7	100.0	70.7	29.3
25 to 29 years old	8,152	100.0	10.1	89.9	100.0	64.1	35.9
30 to 34 years old	7,579	100.0	10.8	89.2	100.0	62.5	37.5
35 to 39 years old	8,051	100.0	10.7	89.3	100.0	63.6	36.4
40 to 44 years old	8,409	100.0	9.9	90.1	100.0	66.6	33.4
45 to 49 years old	9,331	100.0	9.0	91.0	100.0	69.7	30.3
50 to 54 years old	9,056	100.0	10.2	89.8	100.0	70.7	29.3
55 to 59 years old	8,039	100.0	9.3	90.7	100.0	69.7	30.3
60 to 64 years old	6,843	100.0	9.8	90.2	100.0	70.2	29.8
65 to 69 years old	5,293	100.0	14.7	85.3	100.0	78.7	21.3
70 to 74 years old	4,114	100.0	18.4	81.6	100.0	82.1	17.9
75 years old and over	9,204	100.0	24.7	75.3	100.0	86.0	14.0
BLACK ALONE OR IN COMBINATION							
Both Sexes							
18 years old and over	27,709	100.0	17.3	82.7	100.0	82.7	17.3
18 to 24 years old	4,428	100.0	24.1	75.9	100.0	94.0	6.0
25 years old and over	23,281	100.0	15.9	84.1	100.0	80.6	19.4
25 to 29 years old	3,012	100.0	11.2	88.8	100.0	80.9	19.1
30 to 34 years old	2,599	100.0	11.1	88.9	100.0	77.3	22.7
35 to 39 years old	2,647	100.0	9.7	90.3	100.0	77.3	22.7
40 to 44 years old	2,684	100.0	10.6	89.4	100.0	80.4	19.6
45 to 49 years old	2,841	100.0	13.2	86.8	100.0	79.8	20.2
50 to 54 years old	2,575	100.0	13.8	86.2	100.0	80.5	19.5
55 to 59 years old	2,065	100.0	15.9	84.1	100.0	79.5	20.5
60 to 64 years old	1,553	100.0	18.9	81.1	100.0	81.8	18.2
65 to 69 years old	1,079	100.0	27.4	72.6	100.0	85.3	14.7
70 to 74 years old	828	100.0	33.5	66.5	100.0	87.0	13.0
75 years old and over	1,397	100.0	44.4	55.6	100.0	87.0	13.0
Male							
18 years old and over	12,483	100.0	17.9	82.1	100.0	84.5	15.5
18 to 24 years old	2,145	100.0	26.8	73.2	100.0	95.6	4.4
25 years old and over	10,339	100.0	16.1	83.9	100.0	82.2	17.8
25 to 29 years old	1,420	100.0	11.5	88.5	100.0	85.0	15.0
30 to 34 years old	1,182	100.0	11.6	88.4	100.0	81.5	18.5
35 to 39 years old	1,169	100.0	9.0	91.0	100.0	79.8	20.2
40 to 44 years old	1,216	100.0	9.5	90.5	100.0	80.5	19.5

Table A-18.   Percent of High School and College Graduates of the Population 18 Years Old and Over, by Age, Sex, Race, and Hispanic Origin, 2008—_Continued_

(Percent, except where noted.)

Age, sex, race, and Hispanic origin	Total population (thousands)	High school graduate status			Bachelor's degree status		
		Total	Not high school graduate	High school graduate or more	Total	Less than Bachelor's degree	Bachelor's degree or more
		Percent	Percent	Percent	Percent	Percent	Percent
45 to 49 years old	1,299	100.0	15.8	84.2	100.0	80.9	19.1
50 to 54 years old	1,169	100.0	15.1	84.9	100.0	82.6	17.4
55 to 59 years old	928	100.0	16.5	83.5	100.0	79.6	20.4
60 to 64 years old	664	100.0	21.7	78.3	100.0	82.4	17.6
65 to 69 years old	455	100.0	27.5	72.5	100.0	87.3	12.7
70 to 74 years old	343	100.0	34.1	65.9	100.0	88.0	12.0
75 years old and over	493	100.0	46.0	54.0	100.0	85.2	14.8
Female							
18 years old and over	15,226	100.0	16.7	83.3	100.0	81.2	18.8
18 to 24 years old	2,283	100.0	21.6	78.4	100.0	92.5	7.5
25 years old and over	12,943	100.0	15.8	84.2	100.0	79.3	20.7
25 to 29 years old	1,592	100.0	11.0	89.0	100.0	77.4	22.6
30 to 34 years old	1,418	100.0	10.6	89.4	100.0	73.8	26.2
35 to 39 years old	1,478	100.0	10.4	89.6	100.0	75.3	24.7
40 to 44 years old	1,468	100.0	11.5	88.5	100.0	80.3	19.7
45 to 49 years old	1,542	100.0	11.2	88.8	100.0	78.9	21.1
50 to 54 years old	1,405	100.0	12.7	87.3	100.0	78.7	21.3
55 to 59 years old	1,137	100.0	15.6	84.4	100.0	79.4	20.6
60 to 64 years old	889	100.0	16.6	83.4	100.0	81.3	18.7
65 to 69 years old	624	100.0	27.1	72.9	100.0	83.8	16.2
70 to 74 years old	486	100.0	32.7	67.3	100.0	86.2	13.8
75 years old and over	904	100.0	43.6	56.4	100.0	88.1	11.9
ASIAN ALONE OR IN COMBINATION							
Both Sexes							
18 years old and over	10,826	100.0	11.7	88.3	100.0	52.3	47.7
18 to 24 years old	1,309	100.0	12.4	87.6	100.0	81.9	18.1
25 years old and over	9,517	100.0	11.7	88.3	100.0	48.2	51.8
25 to 29 years old	1,130	100.0	4.8	95.2	100.0	41.9	58.1
30 to 34 years old	1,195	100.0	5.2	94.8	100.0	34.8	65.2
35 to 39 years old	1,326	100.0	7.4	92.6	100.0	39.6	60.4
40 to 44 years old	1,104	100.0	9.4	90.6	100.0	43.4	56.6
45 to 49 years old	1,080	100.0	8.2	91.8	100.0	48.7	51.3
50 to 54 years old	958	100.0	10.3	89.7	100.0	49.7	50.3
55 to 59 years old	809	100.0	15.7	84.3	100.0	54.5	45.5
60 to 64 years old	596	100.0	17.8	82.2	100.0	55.2	44.8
65 to 69 years old	475	100.0	23.6	76.4	100.0	61.5	38.5
70 to 74 years old	292	100.0	24.3	75.7	100.0	68.5	31.5
75 years old and over	551	100.0	33.6	66.4	100.0	77.3	22.7
Male							
18 years old and over	5,128	100.0	10.2	89.8	100.0	50.5	49.5
18 to 24 years old	696	100.0	14.7	85.3	100.0	84.5	15.5
25 years old and over	4,432	100.0	9.5	90.5	100.0	45.2	54.8
25 to 29 years old	548	100.0	4.2	95.8	100.0	43.2	56.8
30 to 34 years old	561	100.0	6.1	93.9	100.0	37.3	62.7
35 to 39 years old	655	100.0	7.9	92.1	100.0	40.5	59.5
40 to 44 years old	493	100.0	8.9	91.1	100.0	39.1	60.9
45 to 49 years old	508	100.0	6.1	93.9	100.0	46.1	53.9
50 to 54 years old	470	100.0	10.2	89.8	100.0	48.1	51.9
55 to 59 years old	377	100.0	14.1	85.9	100.0	48.0	52.0
60 to 64 years old	271	100.0	11.4	88.6	100.0	51.7	48.3
65 to 69 years old	224	100.0	14.3	85.7	100.0	48.2	51.8
70 to 74 years old	113	100.0	12.4	87.6	100.0	54.0	46.0
75 years old and over	212	100.0	26.4	73.6	100.0	68.9	31.1

Table A-18.   Percent of High School and College Graduates of the Population 18 Years Old and Over, by Age, Sex, Race, and Hispanic Origin, 2008—*Continued*

(Percent, except where noted.)

Age, sex, race, and Hispanic origin	Total population (thousands)	High school graduate status			Bachelor's degree status		
		Total	Not high school graduate	High school graduate or more	Total	Less than Bachelor's degree	Bachelor's degree or more
		Percent	Percent	Percent	Percent	Percent	Percent
Female							
18 years old and over	5,698	100.0	13.2	86.8	100.0	53.9	46.1
18 to 24 years old	613	100.0	10.0	90.0	100.0	79.1	20.9
25 years old and over	5,085	100.0	13.6	86.4	100.0	50.8	49.2
25 to 29 years old	582	100.0	5.5	94.5	100.0	40.7	59.3
30 to 34 years old	634	100.0	5.0	95.0	100.0	33.1	66.9
35 to 39 years old	671	100.0	6.6	93.4	100.0	38.5	61.5
40 to 44 years old	612	100.0	10.1	89.9	100.0	47.1	52.9
45 to 49 years old	572	100.0	10.5	89.5	100.0	51.0	49.0
50 to 54 years old	488	100.0	10.2	89.8	100.0	50.8	49.2
55 to 59 years old	431	100.0	16.7	83.3	100.0	59.9	40.1
60 to 64 years old	325	100.0	23.1	76.9	100.0	58.2	41.8
65 to 69 years old	251	100.0	30.7	69.3	100.0	72.9	27.1
70 to 74 years old	179	100.0	31.8	68.2	100.0	78.2	21.8
75 years old and over	339	100.0	38.1	61.9	100.0	82.6	17.4
HISPANIC[1]							
Both Sexes							
18 years old and over	31,028	100.0	37.0	63.0	100.0	88.2	11.8
18 to 24 years old	5,072	100.0	31.1	68.9	100.0	95.2	4.8
25 years old and over	25,956	100.0	38.1	61.9	100.0	86.8	13.2
25 to 29 years old	4,260	100.0	31.1	68.9	100.0	87.8	12.2
30 to 34 years old	3,867	100.0	36.6	63.4	100.0	86.4	13.6
35 to 39 years old	3,768	100.0	37.1	62.9	100.0	85.4	14.6
40 to 44 years old	3,260	100.0	35.4	64.6	100.0	85.4	14.6
45 to 49 years old	2,835	100.0	36.5	63.5	100.0	86.2	13.8
50 to 54 years old	2,287	100.0	40.1	59.9	100.0	88.2	11.8
55 to 59 years old	1,757	100.0	38.1	61.9	100.0	84.4	15.6
60 to 64 years old	1,204	100.0	41.9	58.1	100.0	86.4	13.6
65 to 69 years old	950	100.0	48.5	51.5	100.0	89.7	10.3
70 to 74 years old	677	100.0	51.8	48.2	100.0	89.1	10.9
75 years old and over	1,090	100.0	60.3	39.7	100.0	92.2	7.8
Male							
18 years old and over	15,990	100.0	38.7	61.3	100.0	89.0	11.0
18 to 24 years old	2,635	100.0	34.8	65.2	100.0	96.5	3.5
25 years old and over	13,355	100.0	39.5	60.5	100.0	87.6	12.4
25 to 29 years old	2,415	100.0	33.8	66.2	100.0	89.0	11.0
30 to 34 years old	2,026	100.0	40.5	59.5	100.0	89.8	10.2
35 to 39 years old	2,009	100.0	39.4	60.6	100.0	86.6	13.4
40 to 44 years old	1,699	100.0	37.3	62.7	100.0	86.5	13.5
45 to 49 years old	1,442	100.0	37.9	62.1	100.0	86.3	13.7
50 to 54 years old	1,165	100.0	40.3	59.7	100.0	88.1	11.9
55 to 59 years old	848	100.0	40.2	59.8	100.0	84.0	16.0
60 to 64 years old	582	100.0	44.2	55.8	100.0	86.1	13.9
65 to 69 years old	436	100.0	43.8	56.2	100.0	85.8	14.2
70 to 74 years old	280	100.0	50.4	49.6	100.0	87.9	12.1
75 years old and over	453	100.0	57.6	42.4	100.0	90.9	9.1
Female							
18 years old and over	15,038	100.0	35.2	64.8	100.0	87.3	12.7
18 to 24 years old	2,437	100.0	27.2	72.8	100.0	93.8	6.2
25 years old and over	12,601	100.0	36.7	63.3	100.0	86.0	14.0
25 to 29 years old	1,845	100.0	27.5	72.5	100.0	86.2	13.8
30 to 34 years old	1,841	100.0	32.3	67.7	100.0	82.6	17.4
35 to 39 years old	1,759	100.0	34.7	65.3	100.0	84.2	15.8
40 to 44 years old	1,561	100.0	33.3	66.7	100.0	84.2	15.8
45 to 49 years old	1,394	100.0	35.1	64.9	100.0	86.2	13.8
50 to 54 years old	1,122	100.0	39.8	60.2	100.0	88.3	11.7
55 to 59 years old	908	100.0	36.1	63.9	100.0	84.8	15.2
60 to 64 years old	622	100.0	39.9	60.1	100.0	86.8	13.2
65 to 69 years old	514	100.0	52.9	47.1	100.0	93.2	6.8
70 to 74 years old	397	100.0	52.9	47.1	100.0	89.9	10.1
75 years old and over	638	100.0	62.2	37.8	100.0	93.1	6.9

Table A-19.   Educational Attainment of the Population 25 Years Old and Over, by Marital Status and Sex, 2009

(Numbers in thousands.)

Sex and marital status	Total		None to 8th grade		9th to 11th grade		High school graduate		Some college, no degree		Associate degree		Bachelor's degree	
	Number	Percent	Number	Percent	Number	Percent	Number	Percent	Number	Percent	Number	Percent	Number	Percent
Both Sexes														
25 years old and over														
Total................................	198,285	100.0	10,828	100.0	15,587	100.0	61,626	100	33,832	100.0	17,838	100.0	37,635	100.0
Married spouse present	118,712	59.9	5,420	50.1	7,417	47.6	35,543	57.7	19,394	57.3	11,196	62.8	24,880	66.1
Married spouse absent,														
not separated	3,021	1.5	524	4.8	304	2.0	866	1.4	368	1.1	205	1.1	472	1.3
Separated	4,943	2.5	481	4.4	714	4.6	1,696	2.8	866	2.6	452	2.5	523	1.4
Widowed	14,217	7.2	1,900	17.5	1,964	12.6	5,414	8.8	2,085	6.2	887	5.0	1,265	3.4
Divorced............................	23,006	11.6	770	7.1	1,904	12.2	7,695	12.5	5,047	14.9	2,368	13.3	3,501	9.3
Never married	34,386	17.3	1,733	16.0	3,284	21.1	10,413	16.9	6,071	17.9	2,730	15.3	6,994	18.6
Male														
Total................................	95,518	100.0	5,399	100.0	7,754	100.0	30,025	100.0	16,093	100.0	7,541	100.0	18,101	100.0
Married spouse present	59,771	62.6	2,965	54.9	3,988	51.4	17,648	58.8	9,803	60.9	4,971	65.9	12,371	68.3
Married spouse absent,														
not separated	1,619	1.7	362	6.7	164	2.1	471	1.6	148	0.9	82	1.1	237	1.3
Separated	2,057	2.2	184	3.4	295	3.8	780	2.6	313	1.9	167	2.2	220	1.2
Widowed	2,803	2.9	378	7.0	411	5.3	956	3.2	400	2.5	172	2.3	286	1.6
Divorced............................	9,868	10.3	364	6.7	934	12.0	3,732	12.4	1,985	12.3	828	11.0	1,381	7.6
Never married	19,400	20.3	1,146	21.2	1,961	25.3	6,439	21.4	3,442	21.4	1,321	17.5	3,606	19.9
Female														
Total................................	102,767	100.0	5,429	100.0	7,833	100.0	31,601	100.0	17,739	100.0	10,297	100.0	19,534	100.0
Married spouse present	58,940	57.4	2,455	45.2	3,429	43.8	17,895	56.6	9,591	54.1	6,225	60.5	12,509	64.0
Married spouse absent,														
not separated	1,401	1.4	162	3.0	140	1.8	395	1.2	220	1.2	124	1.2	235	1.2
Separated	2,886	2.8	297	5.5	419	5.3	916	2.9	553	3.1	284	2.8	303	1.6
Widowed	11,415	11.1	1,522	28.0	1,553	19.8	4,458	14.1	1,685	9.5	715	6.9	978	5.0
Divorced............................	13,137	12.8	406	7.5	970	12.4	3,962	12.5	3,062	17.3	1,540	15.0	2,120	10.9
Never married	14,987	14.6	587	10.8	1,323	16.9	3,974	12.6	2,628	14.8	1,408	13.7	3,389	17.3

Table A-19. Educational Attainment of the Population 25 Years Old and Over, by Marital Status and Sex, 2009—*Continued*

(Numbers in thousands.)

Sex and marital status	Educational Attainment					
	Master's degree		Professional degree		Doctoral degree	
	Number	Percent	Number	Percent	Number	Percent
Both Sexes						
25 years old and over						
Total..	15,118	100.0	3,206	100.0	2,614	100.0
Married spouse present	10,611	70.2	2,362	73.7	1,889	72.3
Married spouse absent, not separated..........	181	1.2	47	1.5	52	2.0
Separated.......................................	162	1.1	23	0.7	27	1.0
Widowed...	519	3.4	105	3.3	79	3.0
Divorced...	1,311	8.7	211	6.6	199	7.6
Never married	2,334	15.4	458	14.3	369	14.1
Male						
Total..	7,009	100.0	1,953	100.0	1,643	100.0
Married spouse present	5,218	74.4	1,551	79.4	1,256	76.4
Married spouse absent, not separated..........	97	1.4	31	1.6	26	1.6
Separated.......................................	73	1.0	6	0.3	18	1.1
Widowed...	114	1.6	44	2.3	41	2.5
Divorced...	472	6.7	80	4.1	91	5.5
Never married	1,033	14.7	241	12.3	211	12.8
Female						
Total..	8,110	100.0	1,253	100.0	971	100.0
Married spouse present	5,393	66.5	811	64.7	633	65.2
Married spouse absent, not separated..........	84	1.0	16	1.3	26	2.7
Separated.......................................	89	1.1	16	1.3	9	0.9
Widowed...	405	5.0	60	4.8	38	3.9
Divorced...	838	10.3	131	10.5	108	11.1
Never married	1,301	16.0	218	17.4	157	16.2

Table A-20. Educational Attainment of the Population 25 Years Old and Over, by Household Relationship and Sex, 2009

(Numbers in thousands.)

Sex and Household Relationship	Educational Attainment											
	Total		None to 8th grade		9th to 11th grade		High school graduate		Some college, no degree		Associate degree	
	Number	Percent	Number	Percent	Number	Percent	Number	Percent	Number	Percent	Number	Percent
Both Sexes												
25 years old and over												
Total	198,285	100.0	10,828	100.0	15,587	100.0	61,626	100.0	33,832	100.0	17,838	100.0
Family householder												
Married spouse present	57,926	29.2	2,386	22.0	3,553	22.8	16,330	26.5	9,964	29.5	5,489	30.8
Other family householder	17,546	8.8	1,022	9.4	2,038	13.1	5,754	9.3	3,689	10.9	1,776	10.0
Nonfamily householder												
Living alone	30,153	15.2	1,786	16.5	2,690	17.3	8,973	14.6	5,549	16.4	2,518	14.1
Living with nonrelatives	5,254	2.6	157	1.4	373	2.4	1,376	2.2	1,045	3.1	464	2.6
Relative of householder												
Spouse	57,742	29.1	2,616	24.2	3,545	22.7	18,037	29.3	9,049	26.7	5,529	31.0
Other	19,704	9.9	2,150	19.9	2,430	15.6	7,610	12.3	2,975	8.8	1,357	7.6
Nonrelative	9,960	5.0	711	6.6	959	6.2	3,546	5.8	1,562	4.6	704	3.9
Male												
Total	95,518	48.2	5,399	49.9	7,754	49.7	30,025	48.7	16,093	47.6	7,541	42.3
Family householder												
Married spouse present	35,584	17.9	1,660	15.3	2,197	14.1	9,895	16.1	6,114	18.1	3,021	16.9
Other family householder	4,420	2.2	256	2.4	498	3.2	1,605	2.6	824	2.4	392	2.2
Nonfamily householder												
Living alone	12,900	6.5	654	6.0	1,119	7.2	3,781	6.1	2,404	7.1	994	5.6
Living with nonrelatives	3,215	1.6	108	1.0	256	1.6	908	1.5	644	1.9	265	1.5
Relative of householder												
Spouse	22,625	11.4	1,118	10.3	1,615	10.4	7,129	11.6	3,489	10.3	1,865	10.5
Other	10,970	5.5	1,101	10.2	1,481	9.5	4,498	7.3	1,696	5.0	665	3.7
Nonrelative	5,804	2.9	502	4.6	588	3.8	2,210	3.6	922	2.7	340	1.9
Female												
Total	102,767	51.8	5,429	50.1	7,833	50.3	31,601	51.3	17,739	52.4	10,297	57.7
Family householder												
Married spouse present	22,342	11.3	726	6.7	1,356	8.7	6,435	10.4	3,850	11.4	2,468	13.8
Other family householder	13,126	6.6	766	7.1	1,540	9.9	4,149	6.7	2,865	8.5	1,384	7.8
Nonfamily householder												
Living alone	17,253	8.7	1,132	10.5	1,571	10.1	5,193	8.4	3,145	9.3	1,525	8.5
Living with nonrelatives	2,040	1.0	48	0.4	117	0.8	468	0.8	401	1.2	199	1.1
Relative of householder												
Spouse	35,117	17.7	1,498	13.8	1,929	12.4	10,908	17.7	5,560	16.4	3,664	20.5
Other	8,734	4.4	1,049	9.7	949	6.1	3,113	5.1	1,279	3.8	692	3.9
Nonrelative	4,155	2.1	209	1.9	371	2.4	1,337	2.2	640	1.9	365	2.0

Table A-20.   Educational Attainment of the Population 25 Years Old and Over, by Household Relationship and Sex, 2009—_Continued_

(Numbers in thousands.)

Sex and Household Relationship	Educational Attainment									
	Associate degree		Bachelor's degree		Master's degree		Professional degree		Doctoral degree	
	Number	Percent	Number	Percent	Number	Percent	Number	Percent	Number	Percent
Both Sexes										
25 years old and over										
Total..	17,838	100.0	37,635	100.0	15,118	100.0	3,206	100.0	2,614	100.0
Family householder										
Married spouse present	5,489	30.8	12,476	33.1	5,478	36.2	1,221	38.1	1,028	39.3
Other family householder	1,776	10.0	2,298	6.1	717	4.7	151	4.7	101	3.9
Nonfamily householder										
Living alone.............................	2,518	14.1	5,397	14.3	2,388	15.8	396	12.4	456	17.4
Living with nonrelatives	464	2.6	1,243	3.3	455	3.0	73	2.3	69	2.6
Relative of householder										
Spouse	5,529	31.0	11,999	31.9	5,030	33.3	1,103	34.4	835	31.9
Other......................................	1,357	7.6	2,425	6.4	547	3.6	150	4.7	59	2.3
Nonrelative	704	3.9	1,798	4.8	502	3.3	113	3.5	65	2.5
Male										
Total..	7,541	42.3	18,101	48.1	7,009	46.4	1,953	60.9	1,643	62.9
Family householder										
Married spouse present	3,021	16.9	7,709	20.5	3,330	22.0	892	27.8	766	29.3
Other family householder	392	2.2	558	1.5	200	1.3	52	1.6	35	1.3
Nonfamily householder										
Living alone.............................	994	5.6	2,569	6.8	941	6.2	191	6.0	249	9.5
Living with nonrelatives	265	1.5	689	1.8	255	1.7	48	1.5	41	1.6
Relative of householder										
Spouse	1,865	10.5	4,456	11.8	1,843	12.2	632	19.7	477	18.2
Other......................................	665	3.7	1,188	3.2	228	1.5	80	2.5	34	1.3
Nonrelative	340	1.9	932	2.5	212	1.4	58	1.8	41	1.6
Female										
Total..	10,297	57.7	19,534	51.9	8,110	53.6	1,253	39.1	971	37.1
Family householder										
Married spouse present	2,468	13.8	4,768	12.7	2,148	14.2	329	10.3	262	10.0
Other family householder	1,384	7.8	1,739	4.6	518	3.4	98	3.1	66	2.5
Nonfamily householder										
Living alone.............................	1,525	8.5	2,827	7.5	1,447	9.6	205	6.4	208	8.0
Living with nonrelatives	199	1.1	554	1.5	200	1.3	25	0.8	28	1.1
Relative of householder										
Spouse	3,664	20.5	7,542	20.0	3,187	21.1	471	14.7	358	13.7
Other......................................	692	3.9	1,237	3.3	320	2.1	70	2.2	25	1.0
Nonrelative	365	2.0	866	2.3	290	1.9	54	1.7	23	0.9

Table A-21.   Educational Attainment of the Population 25 Years Old and Over, by Labor Force Status and Sex, 2009

(Numbers in thousands.)

Sex and Labor Force Status	Total	Educational attainment								
		None to 8th grade	9th to 11th grade	High school graduate	Some college, no degree	Associate's degree	Bachelor's degree	Master's degree	Professional degree	Doctoral degree
ALL RACES										
Both Sexes										
Total........................	198,285	10,828	15,587	61,626	33,832	17,838	37,635	15,118	3,206	2,614
Employed...................	121,526	3,901	6,359	34,175	21,128	12,602	27,503	11,233	2,581	2,044
Unemployed................	10,597	618	1,230	3,889	1,992	906	1,447	403	65	46
Unemployment Rate......	8.0	13.7	16.2	10.2	8.6	6.7	5.0	3.5	2.5	2.2
Not in Labor Force..........	66,161	6,309	7,997	23,562	10,712	4,330	8,685	3,482	560	524
Male										
Total........................	95,518	5,399	7,754	30,025	16,093	7,541	18,101	7,009	1,953	1,643
Employed...................	63,858	2,552	3,864	18,677	10,821	5,649	13,985	5,417	1,601	1,293
Unemployed................	6,595	394	839	2,597	1,175	486	810	227	36	30
Unemployment Rate......	9.4	13.4	17.8	12.2	9.8	7.9	5.5	4.0	2.2	2.3
Not in Labor Force..........	25,065	2,453	3,051	8,752	4,096	1,405	3,306	1,365	316	320
Female										
Total........................	102,767	5,429	7,833	31,601	17,739	10,297	19,534	8,110	1,253	971
Employed...................	57,668	1,349	2,496	15,498	10,307	6,952	13,518	5,816	980	752
Unemployed................	4,002	223	391	1,293	817	420	638	176	29	15
Unemployment Rate......	6.5	14.2	13.5	7.7	7.3	5.7	4.5	2.9	2.9	2.0
Not in Labor Force..........	41,096	3,856	4,946	14,810	6,616	2,925	5,379	2,117	244	204

Table A-22. Educational Attainment of Employed Civilians 25 Years Old and Over, by Occupation and Sex, 2009

(Numbers in thousands.)

Occupation and Sex	Total	Educational attainment								
		None to 8th grade	9th to 11th grade	High school graduate	Some college, no degree	Associate's degree	Bachelor's degree	Master's degree	Professional degree	Doctoral degree
Both Sexes										
Total Employed Civilians	121,526	3,901	6,359	34,175	21,128	12,602	27,503	11,233	2,581	2,044
Occupation										
Management, business, and financial occupations ..	20,772	129	331	3,633	3,240	1,832	7,567	3,418	293	329
Professional and related occupations..................	28,381	54	146	2,120	2,779	3,280	10,084	6,201	2,111	1,606
Service occupations	18,590	1,445	1,992	7,103	3,713	1,843	2,121	306	43	23
Sales and related occupations	12,347	190	525	3,669	2,658	1,172	3,420	638	48	27
Office and Administrative occupations	15,485	111	437	5,582	4,231	2,058	2,579	400	52	33
Farming, fishing, and forestry occupations	695	213	125	226	47	33	47	2	-	3
Construction and extraction occupations	6,375	638	851	2,967	977	510	371	47	5	8
Installation, maintenance, and repair occupations ...	4,545	120	362	1,956	940	777	322	54	9	5
Production occupations	7,000	570	779	3,240	1,187	650	478	81	9	6
Transportation and material moving occupations	7,338	430	811	3,678	1,357	446	514	86	12	3
Male										
Total Employed Civilians	63,858	2,552	3,864	18,677	10,821	5,649	13,985	5,417	1,601	1,293
Occupation										
Management, business, and financial occupations ..	11,892	90	224	2,058	1,752	936	4,344	2,091	200	196
Professional and related occupations..................	11,971	32	69	752	1,193	985	4,231	2,394	1,287	1,029
Service occupations	7,528	662	711	2,733	1,608	627	1,008	149	21	10
Sales and related occupations	6,567	75	206	1,653	1,381	591	2,201	403	42	16
Office and Administrative occupations	3,590	63	159	1,167	943	356	722	142	20	18
Farming, fishing, and forestry occupations	555	181	101	187	27	23	31	1	-	3
Construction and extraction occupations	6,228	638	839	2,896	937	503	355	46	5	8
Installation, maintenance, and repair occupations ...	4,372	120	345	1,892	909	749	295	48	9	5
Production occupations	4,986	344	534	2,291	923	500	322	61	6	5
Transportation and material moving occupations	6,170	346	677	3,048	1,146	379	476	82	12	3
Female										
Total Employed Civilians	57,668	1,349	2,496	15,498	10,307	6,952	13,518	5,816	980	752
Occupation										
Management, business, and financial occupations ..	8,880	38	107	1,575	1,488	896	3,223	1,326	93	134
Professional and related occupations..................	16,410	22	78	1,369	1,585	2,295	5,853	3,807	824	577
Service occupations	11,063	784	1,281	4,371	2,105	1,216	1,113	158	22	13
Sales and related occupations	5,780	115	319	2,016	1,277	582	1,219	234	6	11
Office and Administrative occupations	11,895	48	278	4,416	3,288	1,702	1,857	258	32	16
Farming, fishing, and forestry occupations	140	32	24	38	19	10	16	1	-	-
Construction and extraction occupations	148	-	12	71	40	7	16	1	-	-
Installation, maintenance, and repair occupations ...	173	-	17	64	31	28	27	6	-	-
Production occupations	2,014	226	245	949	263	150	156	20	3	1
Transportation and material moving occupations	1,167	83	135	630	211	67	37	5	-	-

- = Quantity zero or rounds to zero.

Table A-23. Educational Attainment of the Population 25 Years Old and Older, by Industry and Sex, 2009

(Numbers in thousands.)

Industry and sex	Total	Educational attainment								
		None to 8th grade	9th to 11th grade	High school graduate	Some college, no degree	Associate's degree	Bachelor's degree	Master's degree	Professional degree	Doctoral degree
Both Sexes										
Total Employed Civilians	121,526	3,901	6,359	34,175	21,128	12,602	27,503	11,233	2,581	2,044
Industry										
Agriculture, forestry, fishing, and Hunting	1,823	271	192	664	214	138	269	61	5	9
Mining	679	9	54	298	130	67	87	27	3	6
Construction	8,561	645	959	3,598	1,471	740	950	171	21	7
Manufacturing	13,116	643	880	4,593	2,139	1,240	2,466	953	76	127
Wholesale and retail trade	15,849	408	896	5,897	3,363	1,439	3,161	547	89	47
Transportation and utilities	6,751	139	396	2,714	1,512	722	984	226	35	23
Information	2,828	8	42	603	626	317	907	298	21	5
Financial activities	8,733	68	148	1,744	1,778	893	3,142	815	121	25
Professional and business services	13,617	431	559	2,536	2,072	1,112	4,142	1,594	765	407
Educational and health services	28,866	356	849	5,318	3,888	3,680	7,287	5,153	1,157	1,178
Leisure and hospitality	8,249	617	789	2,871	1,530	636	1,473	280	24	29
Other services	6,019	282	498	1,998	1,049	758	893	431	55	55
Public administration	6,435	26	98	1,341	1,357	859	1,744	677	208	127
Male										
Total Employed Civilians	63,858	2,552	3,864	18,677	10,821	5,649	13,985	5,417	1,601	1,293
Industry										
Agricultural, forestry, fishing, and Hunting	1,397	225	158	532	152	103	191	32	3	-
Mining	574	9	53	268	95	49	70	21	3	6
Construction	7,624	639	913	3,281	1,241	637	754	136	17	7
Manufacturing	9,360	422	607	3,246	1,547	896	1,781	730	41	90
Wholesale and retail trade	8,917	252	505	3,098	1,883	800	1,963	335	61	19
Transportation and utilities	5,157	125	303	2,101	1,144	528	750	160	32	14
Information	1,649	6	26	317	399	195	509	179	15	4
Financial activities	3,994	41	77	549	612	308	1,747	551	90	19
Professional and business services	7,749	303	363	1,282	1,060	509	2,397	1,043	493	299
Educational and health services	7,001	83	165	986	724	566	1,698	1,438	657	685
Leisure and hospitality	4,046	299	365	1,370	777	272	767	164	14	19
Other services	2,901	132	278	987	454	297	397	272	41	44
Public administration	3,489	16	52	658	735	490	961	356	134	87
Female										
Total Employed Civilians	57,668	1,349	2,496	15,498	10,307	6,952	13,518	5,816	980	752
Industry										
Agricultural, forestry, fishing, and Hunting	426	45	34	132	62	35	79	29	2	9
Mining	106	-	1	29	35	18	16	6	-	-
Construction	937	6	47	317	230	102	196	35	4	-
Manufacturing	3,756	221	273	1,347	592	345	684	222	35	36
Wholesale and retail trade	6,932	156	391	2,799	1,479	640	1,198	212	28	28
Transportation and utilities	1,593	14	93	612	368	194	234	66	4	10
Information	1,179	2	16	286	227	123	398	119	6	2
Financial activities	4,738	27	71	1,195	1,166	584	1,395	264	31	6
Professional and business services	5,868	127	196	1,253	1,012	603	1,744	552	272	108
Educational and health services	21,865	273	684	4,332	3,164	3,114	5,588	3,715	500	493
Leisure and hospitality	4,203	318	423	1,501	753	365	706	117	11	10
Other services	3,117	150	221	1,011	595	461	496	159	14	10
Public administration	2,947	9	46	682	622	369	783	321	74	40

- = Quantity zero or rounds to zero.

Table A–24. Educational Attainment of the Population 25 Years Old and Over, by Citizenship, Nativity, Period of Entry, and Sex, 2009

(Numbers in thousands.)

Citizenship, Nativity, Period of Entry, and Sex	Educational Attainment									
	Total		None to 8th grade		9th to 11th grade		High school graduate		Some college, no degree	
	Number	Percent	Number	Percent	Number	Percent	Number	Percent	Number	Percent
Both Sexes										
Total	198,285	100.0	10,828	100.0	15,587	100.0	61,626	100.0	33,832	100.0
Native..............................	167,129	84.3	4,700	43.4	12,121	77.8	53,944	87.5	30,615	90.5
Foreign-Born......................	31,152	15.7	6,128	56.6	3,466	22.2	7,682	12.5	3,217	9.5
Native										
Native Parentage[1]	152,257	76.8	4,002	37.0	11,018	70.7	49,670	80.6	28,035	82.9
Foreign or Mixed Parentage[2].....	14,872	7.5	698	6.4	1,103	7.1	4,274	6.9	2,580	7.6
Foreign Born										
Naturalized Citizen	14,282	7.2	1,755	16.2	994	6.4	3,648	5.9	1,885	5.6
Not a Citizen	16,870	8.5	4,373	40.4	2,472	15.9	4,033	6.5	1,332	3.9
Year of Entry										
2000 or later......................	7,911	4.0	1,571	14.5	932	6.0	1,771	2.9	630	1.9
1990-1999........................	8,663	4.4	1,688	15.6	1,143	7.3	2,284	3.7	784	2.3
1980-1989........................	7,004	3.5	1,386	12.8	818	5.2	1,666	2.7	786	2.3
1970-1979........................	4,029	2.0	835	7.7	350	2.2	969	1.6	519	1.5
Before 1970	3,544	1.8	648	6.0	222	1.4	991	1.6	498	1.5
Male										
Total.................................	95,518	48.2	5,399	49.9	7,754	49.7	30,025	48.7	16,093	47.6
Native..............................	80,140	40.4	2,329	21.5	5,931	38.1	26,353	42.8	14,547	43.0
Foreign-Born......................	15,374	7.8	3,070	28.4	1,823	11.7	3,672	6.0	1,546	4.6
Native										
Native Parentage[1]	72,757	36.7	2,014	18.6	5,368	34.4	24,334	39.5	13,224	39.1
Foreign or Mixed Parentage[2].....	7,383	3.7	315	2.9	563	3.6	2,019	3.3	1,323	3.9
Foreign Born										
Naturalized Citizen	6,595	3.3	748	6.9	454	2.9	1,587	2.6	892	2.6
Not a Citizen	8,780	4.4	2,322	21.4	1,368	8.8	2,084	3.4	655	1.9
Year of Entry										
2000 or later......................	4,085	2.1	877	8.1	521	3.3	921	1.5	309	0.9
1990-1999........................	4,261	2.1	794	7.3	612	3.9	1,166	1.9	392	1.2
1980-1989........................	3,522	1.8	691	6.4	424	2.7	798	1.3	383	1.1
1970-1979........................	1,945	1.0	415	3.8	170	1.1	434	0.7	264	0.8
Before 1970	1,561	0.8	294	2.7	95	0.6	353	0.6	198	0.6
Female										
Total.................................	102,767	51.8	5,429	50.1	7,833	50.3	31,601	51.3	17,739	52.4
Native..............................	86,989	43.9	2,371	21.9	6,190	39.7	27,591	44.8	16,068	47.5
Foreign-Born......................	15,777	8.0	3,058	28.2	1,643	10.5	4,010	6.5	1,671	4.9
Native										
Native Parentage[1]	79,500	40.1	1,988	18.4	5,649	36.2	25,336	41.1	14,811	43.8
Foreign or Mixed Parentage[2].....	7,489	3.8	383	3.5	540	3.5	2,255	3.7	1,258	3.7
Foreign Born										
Naturalized Citizen	7,687	3.9	1,007	9.3	540	3.5	2,061	3.3	994	2.9
Not a Citizen	8,090	4.1	2,051	18.9	1,103	7.1	1,949	3.2	677	2.0
Year of Entry										
2000 or later......................	3,825	1.9	694	6.4	411	2.6	849	1.4	321	0.9
1990-1999........................	4,402	2.2	894	8.3	532	3.4	1,119	1.8	392	1.2
1980-1989........................	3,482	1.8	695	6.4	394	2.5	868	1.4	403	1.2
1970-1979........................	2,085	1.1	420	3.9	180	1.2	535	0.9	254	0.8
Before 1970	1,983	1.0	355	3.3	127	0.8	638	1.0	301	0.9

[1]Native parentage: Both parents born in the United States
[2]Foreign or mixed parentage: One or both parents foreign born

Table A–24. Educational Attainment of the Population 25 Years Old and Over, by Citizenship, Nativity, Period of Entry, and Sex, 2009—*Continued*

(Numbers in thousands.)

Citizenship, Nativity, Period of Entry, and Sex	Educational Attainment									
	Associate degree		Bachelor's degree		Master's degree		Professional degree		Doctoral degree	
	Number	Percent	Number	Percent	Number	Percent	Number	Percent	Number	Percent
Both Sexes										
Total	17,838	100.0	37,635	100.0	15,118	100.0	3,206	100.0	2,614	100.0
Native	16,087	90.2	32,106	85.3	12,911	85.4	2,655	82.8	1,990	76.1
Foreign-Born	1,748	9.8	5,529	14.7	2,207	14.6	551	17.2	624	23.9
Native										
Native Parentage[1]	14,779	82.9	29,010	77.1	11,677	77.2	2,311	72.1	1,756	67.2
Foreign or Mixed Parentage[2]	1,308	7.3	3,096	8.2	1,234	8.2	344	10.7	234	9.0
Foreign Born										
Naturalized Citizen	1,072	6.0	3,129	8.3	1,088	7.2	368	11.5	342	13.1
Not a Citizen	676	3.8	2,399	6.4	1,120	7.4	184	5.7	282	10.8
Year of Entry										
2000 or later	342	1.9	1,639	4.4	754	5.0	125	3.9	147	5.6
1990-1999	451	2.5	1,374	3.7	617	4.1	139	4.3	184	7.0
1980-1989	397	2.2	1,316	3.5	396	2.6	102	3.2	137	5.2
1970-1979	293	1.6	676	1.8	226	1.5	95	3.0	66	2.5
Before 1970	265	1.5	523	1.4	215	1.4	92	2.9	90	3.4
Male										
Total	7,541	42.3	18,101	48.1	7,009	46.4	1,953	60.9	1,643	62.9
Native	6,807	38.2	15,488	41.2	5,817	38.5	1,629	50.8	1,240	47.4
Foreign-Born	732	4.1	2,613	6.9	1,192	7.9	324	10.1	403	15.4
Native										
Native Parentage[1]	6,190	34.7	13,907	37.0	5,222	34.5	1,422	44.4	1,076	41.2
Foreign or Mixed Parentage[2]	617	3.5	1,581	4.2	595	3.9	207	6.5	164	6.3
Foreign Born										
Naturalized Citizen	416	2.3	1,471	3.9	571	3.8	230	7.2	224	8.6
Not a Citizen	315	1.8	1,142	3.0	620	4.1	93	2.9	179	6.8
Year of Entry										
2000 or later	173	1.0	735	2.0	392	2.6	64	2.0	93	3.6
1990-1999	178	1.0	630	1.7	307	2.0	68	2.1	114	4.4
1980-1989	160	0.9	683	1.8	236	1.6	58	1.8	89	3.4
1970-1979	113	0.6	314	0.8	126	0.8	65	2.0	44	1.7
Before 1970	107	0.6	251	0.7	131	0.9	69	2.2	63	2.4
Female										
Total	10,297	57.7	19,534	51.9	8,110	53.6	1,253	39.1	971	37.1
Native	9,280	52.0	16,619	44.2	7,094	46.9	1,025	32.0	750	28.7
Foreign-Born	1,016	5.7	2,916	7.7	1,015	6.7	228	7.1	221	8.5
Native										
Native Parentage[1]	8,590	48.2	15,103	40.1	6,455	42.7	889	27.7	680	26.0
Foreign or Mixed Parentage[2]	691	3.9	1,516	4.0	639	4.2	137	4.3	70	2.7
Foreign Born										
Naturalized Citizen	656	3.7	1,658	4.4	516	3.4	137	4.3	118	4.5
Not a Citizen	360	2.0	1,257	3.3	499	3.3	90	2.8	103	3.9
Year of Entry										
2000 or later	169	0.9	905	2.4	362	2.4	61	1.9	54	2.1
1990-1999	273	1.5	744	2.0	309	2.0	70	2.2	69	2.6
1980-1989	237	1.3	633	1.7	160	1.1	44	1.4	48	1.8
1970-1979	180	1.0	362	1.0	101	0.7	30	0.9	22	0.8
Before 1970	157	0.9	272	0.7	83	0.5	23	0.7	27	1.0

[1]Native parentage: Both parents born in the United States
[2]Foreign or mixed parentage: One or both parents foreign born

Table A-25. Years of School Completed by People 25 Years Old and Over, by Age and Sex, Selected Years 1940–2009

(Numbers in thousands.)

Year, sex, and age	Total	Years of school completed						Median years
		Elementary		High school		College		
		0 to 4 years	5 to 8 years	1 to 3 years	4 years	1 to 3 years	4 years or more	

25 YEARS OLD AND OVER

Both Sexes

Year	Total	0 to 4	5 to 8	1 to 3	4	1 to 3	4+	Median
2009	198,285	2,785	8,043	15,587	61,626	51,670	58,574	...
2008	196,305	2,599	8,226	15,516	61,183	50,994	57,787	...
2007	194,318	2,830	8,462	16,451	61,490	49,243	55,842	...
2006	191,884	2,951	8,791	16,154	60,898	49,371	53,720	...
2005	189,367	2,983	8,935	16,099	60,893	48,076	52,381	...
2004	186,876	2,858	8,888	15,999	59,811	47,571	51,749	...
2003	185,183	2,915	9,361	16,323	59,292	46,910	50,383	...
2002	182,142	2,902	9,668	16,378	58,456	46,042	48,696	...
2001	180,389	2,810	9,518	16,279	58,272	46,281	47,228	...
2000	175,230	2,742	9,438	15,674	58,086	44,445	44,845	...
1999	173,754	2,742	9,655	15,674	57,935	43,176	43,803	...
1998	172,211	2,834	9,948	16,776	58,174	42,506	41,973	...
1997	170,581	2,840	10,472	17,211	57,586	41,774	40,697	...
1996	168,323	3,027	10,595	17,102	56,559	41,372	39,668	...
1995	166,438	3,074	10,873	16,566	56,450	41,249	38,226	...
1994	164,512	3,156	11,359	16,925	56,515	40,014	36,544	...
1993	162,826	3,380	11,747	17,067	57,589	37,451	35,590	...
1992	160,827	3,449	11,989	17,672	57,860	35,520	34,337	...
1991	158,694	3,803	13,046	17,379	61,272	29,170	34,026	12.7
1990	156,538	3,833	13,758	17,461	60,119	28,075	33,291	12.7
1989	154,155	3,861	14,061	17,719	59,336	26,614	32,565	12.7
1988	151,635	3,714	14,550	17,847	58,940	25,799	30,787	12.7
1987	149,144	3,640	15,301	17,417	57,669	25,479	29,637	12.7
1986	146,606	3,894	15,672	17,484	56,338	24,729	28,489	12.6
1985	143,524	3,873	16,020	17,553	54,866	23,405	27,808	12.6
1984	140,794	3,884	16,258	17,433	54,073	22,281	26,862	12.6
1983	138,020	4,119	16,714	17,681	52,060	21,531	25,915	12.6
1982	135,526	4,119	17,232	18,006	51,426	20,692	24,050	12.6
1981	132,899	4,358	17,868	18,041	49,915	20,042	22,674	12.5
1980	130,409	4,390	18,426	18,086	47,934	19,379	22,193	12.5
1979	125,295	4,324	18,504	17,579	45,915	18,393	20,579	12.5
1978	123,019	4,445	19,309	18,175	44,381	17,379	19,332	12.4
1977	120,870	4,509	19,567	18,318	43,602	16,247	18,627	12.4
1976	118,848	4,601	19,912	18,204	43,157	15,477	17,496	12.4
1975	116,897	4,912	20,633	18,237	42,353	14,518	16,244	12.3
1974	115,005	5,106	21,200	18,274	41,460	13,665	15,300	12.3
1973	112,866	5,100	21,838	18,420	40,448	12,831	14,228	12.3
1972	111,133	5,124	22,503	18,855	39,171	12,117	13,364	12.2
1971	110,627	5,574	24,029	18,601	38,029	11,782	12,612	12.2
1970	109,310	5,747	24,519	18,682	37,134	11,164	12,062	12.2
1969	107,750	6,014	24,976	18,527	36,133	10,564	11,535	12.1
1968	106,469	6,248	25,467	18,724	34,603	10,254	11,171	12.1
1967	104,864	6,400	26,178	18,647	33,173	9,914	10,550	12.0
1966	103,876	6,705	26,478	18,859	32,391	9,235	10,212	12.0
1965	103,245	6,982	27,063	18,617	31,703	9,139	9,742	11.8
1964	102,421	7,295	27,551	18,419	30,728	9,085	9,345	11.7
1962	100,664	7,826	28,438	17,751	28,477	9,170	9,002	11.4
1960	99,465	8,303	31,218	19,140	24,440	8,747	7,617	10.6
1959	97,478	7,816	28,490	17,520	26,219	7,888	7,734	11.0
1957	95,630	8,561	29,316	16,951	24,832	6,985	7,172	10.6
1952	88,358	8,004	30,274	15,228	21,074	6,714	6,118	10.1
1950	87,484	9,491	31,617	14,817	17,625	6,246	5,272	9.3
1947	82,578	8,611	32,308	13,487	16,926	5,533	4,424	9.0
1940	74,776	10,105	34,413	11,182	10,552	4,075	3,407	8.6

Male

Year	Total	0 to 4	5 to 8	1 to 3	4	1 to 3	4+	Median
2009	95,518	1,372	4,027	7,754	30,025	23,634	28,706	...
2008	94,470	1,310	4,136	7,853	29,491	23,247	28,433	...
2007	93,421	1,458	4,249	8,294	29,604	22,219	27,596	...
2006	92,233	1,472	4,395	7,940	29,380	22,136	26,910	...
2005	90,899	1,505	4,402	7,787	29,151	21,794	26,259	...
2004	89,558	1,496	4,308	7,766	27,889	21,763	26,336	...
2003	88,597	1,482	4,566	8,026	27,356	21,568	25,598	...
2002	86,996	1,457	4,743	7,894	26,947	21,127	24,828	...
2001	86,096	1,419	4,673	7,615	26,956	21,120	24,313	...
2000	83,611	1,341	4,577	7,298	26,651	20,493	23,252	...

... = Not available.

Table A-25. Years of School Completed by People 25 Years Old and Over, by Age and Sex, Selected Years 1940–2009—*Continued*

(Numbers in thousands.)

Year, sex, and age	Total	Years of school completed						Median years
		Elementary		High school		College		
		0 to 4 years	5 to 8 years	1 to 3 years	4 years	1 to 3 years	4 years or more	
1999	82,917	1,339	4,651	7,736	26,368	20,043	22,782	...
1998	82,376	1,431	4,727	8,017	26,575	19,792	21,832	...
1997	81,620	1,454	5,023	8,212	26,226	19,332	21,374	...
1996	80,339	1,537	5,067	7,930	25,649	19,301	20,854	...
1995	79,463	1,598	5,231	7,691	25,378	18,933	20,631	...
1994	78,539	1,669	5,427	7,789	25,404	18,544	19,705	...
1993	77,644	1,709	5,594	7,821	25,766	17,521	19,234	...
1992	76,579	1,737	5,726	8,085	25,774	16,631	18,627	...
1991	75,487	2,018	6,299	7,887	27,189	13,720	18,373	12.8
1990	74,421	2,004	6,557	8,000	26,426	13,271	18,164	12.8
1989	73,225	1,956	6,659	8,076	25,897	12,725	17,913	12.8
1988	71,911	1,852	6,849	8,247	25,638	12,057	17,268	12.7
1987	70,677	1,794	7,259	7,909	24,998	12,062	16,654	12.7
1986	69,503	1,978	7,446	7,872	24,260	11,856	16,091	12.7
1985	67,756	1,947	7,629	7,783	23,552	11,164	15,682	12.7
1984	66,350	1,945	7,688	7,837	22,990	10,678	15,211	12.7
1983	65,004	2,103	7,750	7,867	22,048	10,310	14,926	12.7
1982	63,764	2,074	7,987	7,960	21,749	10,020	13,974	12.6
1981	62,509	2,141	8,322	8,084	21,019	9,734	13,208	12.6
1980	61,389	2,212	8,627	8,046	20,080	9,593	12,832	12.6
1979	58,986	2,190	8,785	7,636	19,250	9,100	12,025	12.6
1978	57,922	2,230	9,195	7,821	18,620	8,657	11,398	12.5
1977	56,917	2,296	9,330	7,969	18,290	8,104	10,926	12.5
1976	55,902	2,371	9,463	7,923	18,048	7,699	10,397	12.5
1975	55,036	2,568	9,760	7,985	17,769	7,274	9,679	12.4
1974	54,167	2,637	10,186	7,966	17,488	6,756	9,135	12.4
1973	53,067	2,598	10,488	8,120	17,011	6,376	8,473	12.3
1972	52,351	2,634	10,854	8,413	16,424	5,972	8,055	12.3
1971	52,357	2,933	11,703	8,264	16,008	5,798	7,653	12.2
1970	51,784	3,031	11,925	8,355	15,571	5,580	7,321	12.2
1969	51,031	3,095	12,182	8,398	15,177	5,263	6,917	12.1
1968	50,510	3,261	12,407	8,564	14,613	4,945	6,721	12.1
1967	49,756	3,417	12,736	8,463	14,015	4,755	6,372	12.0
1966	49,410	3,614	12,992	8,611	13,672	4,342	6,180	11.8
1965	49,242	3,774	13,308	8,529	13,334	4,370	5,923	11.7
1964	48,975	3,959	13,467	8,537	12,902	4,394	5,714	11.5
1962	48,283	4,213	13,927	8,399	11,932	4,315	5,497	11.1
1960	47,997	4,522	15,562	8,988	10,175	4,127	4,626	10.3
1959	47,041	4,257	14,039	8,326	10,870	3,801	4,765	10.7
1957	46,208	4,610	14,634	8,003	10,230	3,347	4,359	10.3
1952	42,368	4,396	14,876	7,048	8,760	3,164	3,480	9.7
1950	42,627	5,074	15,852	6,974	7,511	2,888	3,008	9.0
1947	40,483	4,615	16,086	6,535	7,353	2,625	2,478	8.9
1940	37,463	5,550	17,639	5,333	4,507	1,824	2,021	8.6
Female								
2009	102,767	1,413	4,016	7,833	31,601	28,036	29,868	...
2008	101,835	1,289	4,090	7,663	31,692	27,747	29,354	...
2007	100,897	1,371	4,213	8,157	31,887	27,024	28,245	...
2006	99,651	1,479	4,395	8,215	31,518	27,234	26,810	...
2005	98,467	1,477	4,532	8,311	31,742	26,283	26,122	...
2004	97,319	1,363	4,580	8,233	31,921	25,808	25,413	...
2003	96,586	1,433	4,795	8,297	31,936	25,342	24,784	...
2002	95,146	1,445	4,926	8,484	31,509	24,915	23,868	...
2001	94,293	1,392	4,845	8,664	31,316	25,161	22,915	...
2000	91,620	1,400	4,861	8,378	31,435	23,953	21,594	...
1999	90,837	1,404	5,004	8,707	31,566	23,133	21,021	...
1998	89,835	1,403	5,220	8,758	31,599	22,714	20,142	...
1997	88,961	1,387	5,450	8,999	31,360	22,442	19,323	...
1996	87,984	1,491	5,528	9,171	30,911	22,071	18,813	...
1995	86,975	1,476	5,642	8,874	31,072	22,317	17,594	...
1994	85,973	1,487	5,932	9,135	31,111	21,470	16,838	...
1993	85,181	1,672	6,154	9,246	31,823	19,930	16,357	...
1992	84,248	1,712	6,263	9,587	32,086	18,889	15,709	...
1991	83,207	1,784	6,747	9,491	34,083	15,449	15,652	12.7
1990	82,116	1,829	7,200	9,462	33,693	14,806	15,126	12.7
1989	80,930	1,904	7,402	9,643	33,440	13,888	14,652	12.6
1988	79,724	1,862	7,700	9,599	33,303	13,741	13,519	12.6
1987	78,467	1,846	8,042	9,508	32,671	13,417	12,983	12.6

... = Not available.

Table A-25. Years of School Completed by People 25 Years Old and Over, by Age and Sex, Selected Years 1940–2009—*Continued*

(Numbers in thousands.)

Year, sex, and age	Total	Elementary		High school		College		Median years
		0 to 4 years	5 to 8 years	1 to 3 years	4 years	1 to 3 years	4 years or more	
1986	77,102	1,916	8,226	9,612	32,078	12,874	12,399	12.6
1985	75,768	1,926	8,390	9,770	31,314	12,242	12,126	12.6
1984	74,444	1,939	8,571	9,596	31,083	11,603	11,651	12.6
1983	73,016	2,015	8,964	9,814	30,012	11,220	10,990	12.5
1982	71,762	2,045	9,245	10,046	29,677	10,673	10,076	12.5
1981	70,390	2,217	9,545	9,957	28,896	10,309	9,466	12.5
1980	69,020	2,178	9,800	10,040	27,854	9,786	9,362	12.4
1979	66,309	2,133	9,720	9,945	26,665	9,293	8,554	12.4
1978	65,097	2,214	10,114	10,353	25,761	8,721	7,934	12.4
1977	63,953	2,213	10,236	10,349	25,312	8,142	7,701	12.4
1976	62,946	2,230	10,449	10,281	25,109	7,779	7,098	12.3
1975	61,861	2,344	10,871	10,252	24,584	7,243	6,565	12.3
1974	60,838	2,469	11,015	10,308	23,972	6,910	6,165	12.3
1973	59,799	2,502	11,350	10,300	23,437	6,454	5,755	12.2
1972	58,782	2,490	11,649	10,442	22,746	6,145	5,309	12.2
1971	58,270	2,641	12,327	10,339	22,021	5,984	4,959	12.2
1970	57,527	2,716	12,595	10,327	21,563	5,584	4,743	12.1
1969	56,719	2,919	12,796	10,131	20,955	5,301	4,619	12.1
1968	55,959	2,987	13,060	10,160	19,991	5,309	4,450	12.1
1967	55,107	2,985	13,439	10,185	19,157	5,162	4,178	12.0
1966	54,467	3,090	13,488	10,246	18,719	4,892	4,032	12.0
1965	54,004	3,207	13,753	10,085	18,369	4,767	3,820	12.0
1964	53,447	3,333	14,086	9,881	17,825	4,686	3,629	11.8
1962	52,381	3,613	14,511	9,352	16,545	4,855	3,505	11.6
1960	51,468	3,781	15,656	10,151	14,267	4,620	2,991	10.9
1959	50,437	3,559	14,451	9,194	15,349	4,087	2,969	11.2
1957	49,422	3,951	14,682	8,948	14,602	3,638	2,813	10.9
1952	45,990	3,608	15,398	8,180	12,314	3,550	2,638	10.4
1950	44,857	4,417	15,824	7,843	10,114	3,358	2,264	9.6
1947	42,095	3,996	16,222	6,952	9,573	2,908	1,946	8.9
1940	37,313	4,554	16,773	5,849	6,044	2,251	1,386	8.7
25 TO 34 YEARS OLD								
Both Sexes								
2009	40,520	321	1,226	3,202	11,351	11,409	13,010	...
2008	40,146	282	1,189	3,296	11,297	11,113	12,969	...
2007	39,868	380	1,283	3,462	11,408	10,961	12,375	...
2006	39,481	359	1,410	3,375	11,302	11,229	11,806	...
2005	39,310	414	1,375	3,422	11,269	10,865	11,965	...
2004	39,201	430	1,399	3,239	11,244	11,044	11,844	...
2003	39,242	370	1,370	3,336	11,392	10,986	11,791	...
2002	38,670	433	1,393	3,245	10,988	10,776	11,834	...
2001	38,865	380	1,317	3,202	11,294	11,146	11,526	...
2000	37,786	287	1,135	3,052	11,546	10,700	11,066	...
1999	38,474	280	1,142	3,296	11,826	10,893	11,040	...
1998	39,354	319	1,207	3,228	12,569	11,220	10,811	...
1997	40,256	334	1,163	3,624	12,710	11,524	10,892	...
1996	40,919	418	1,169	3,780	13,087	11,624	10,841	...
1995	41,388	394	1,264	3,667	14,061	11,659	10,342	...
1994	41,946	367	1,297	4,057	14,483	11,913	9,829	...
1993	41,864	382	1,223	3,894	15,036	11,361	9,968	...
1992	42,493	433	1,250	4,071	16,021	10,860	9,861	...
1991	42,905	465	1,322	4,178	17,503	9,283	10,153	12.9
1990	43,240	505	1,413	4,041	17,635	9,320	10,326	12.9
1989	43,240	446	1,352	4,013	17,901	9,072	10,454	12.9
1988	42,953	430	1,308	4,095	17,887	9,076	10,155	12.9
1987	42,635	390	1,360	3,995	17,539	9,157	10,196	12.9
1986	42,053	387	1,359	3,797	17,311	9,104	10,094	12.9
1985	40,858	362	1,328	3,703	16,748	8,980	9,737	12.9
1984	40,173	404	1,371	3,638	16,431	8,555	9,771	12.9
1983	39,342	376	1,324	3,664	15,804	8,567	9,605	12.9
1982	38,703	337	1,371	3,598	15,893	8,304	9,200	12.9
1981	37,828	337	1,428	3,665	15,419	8,198	8,782	12.9
1980	36,615	362	1,424	3,571	14,481	7,942	8,836	12.9
1979	34,053	370	1,381	3,452	13,338	7,415	8,096	12.9
1978	33,120	325	1,459	3,515	12,993	7,008	7,821	12.9
1977	32,284	269	1,383	3,715	12,845	6,398	7,676	12.8
1976	31,148	247	1,508	3,619	12,920	5,813	7,041	12.8

... = Not available.

Table A-25. Years of School Completed by People 25 Years Old and Over, by Age and Sex, Selected Years 1940–2009—*Continued*

(Numbers in thousands.)

Year, sex, and age	Total	Years of school completed						Median years
		Elementary		High school		College		
		0 to 4 years	5 to 8 years	1 to 3 years	4 years	1 to 3 years	4 years or more	
1975	30,092	313	1,644	3,743	12,544	5,403	6,443	12.7
1974	28,972	352	1,654	3,763	12,362	5,056	5,785	12.7
1973	27,793	333	1,850	3,915	12,194	4,454	5,047	12.6
1972	26,517	285	1,791	3,981	11,635	4,090	4,734	12.6
1971	25,545	327	2,011	3,986	11,232	3,822	4,169	12.6
1970	24,865	329	1,937	4,251	10,929	3,491	3,926	12.5
1969	24,072	359	2,086	4,140	10,592	3,202	3,693	12.5
1968	23,285	350	2,246	4,129	10,157	2,989	3,413	12.5
1967	22,388	319	2,293	4,017	9,645	2,946	3,169	12.5
1966	22,023	430	2,208	4,158	9,546	2,647	3,037	12.4
1965	21,980	543	2,437	4,058	9,500	2,561	2,880	12.4
1964	21,997	502	2,591	4,176	9,370	2,529	2,830	12.4
1962	22,130	597	2,936	4,371	8,815	2,552	2,859	12.4
1960	22,821	709	3,738	5,135	8,166	2,572	2,499	12.4
1959	22,922	761	3,348	4,741	8,979	2,398	2,480	12.3
1957	23,437	750	3,971	4,965	8,927	2,275	2,351	12.2
1952	23,138	844	4,362	4,898	8,620	2,220	2,052	12.2
1950	23,626	1,147	5,308	5,050	7,660	2,198	1,252	11.9
1947	22,627	1,015	5,523	4,997	7,630	1,908	1,378	11.9
1940	21,339	1,377	7,676	4,553	4,702	1,554	1,288	10.0
Male								
2009	20,440	184	695	1,806	6,495	5,508	5,752	...
2008	20,210	172	714	1,874	6,356	5,277	5,816	...
2007	20,024	246	757	1,930	6,361	5,137	5,593	...
2006	19,827	218	834	1,835	6,233	5,336	5,371	...
2005	19,677	241	769	1,827	6,216	5,198	5,426	...
2004	19,598	280	793	1,723	6,020	5,286	5,495	...
2003	19,564	216	771	1,831	6,028	5,252	5,466	...
2002	19,234	280	809	1,782	5,751	5,131	5,480	...
2001	19,330	233	748	1,677	6,099	5,161	5,411	...
2000	18,563	155	593	1,637	5,989	4,870	5,318	...
1999	18,294	157	616	1,724	6,114	5,052	5,260	...
1998	19,526	190	654	1,735	6,592	5,233	5,125	...
1997	20,039	193	629	2,007	6,482	5,477	5,249	...
1996	20,390	225	601	2,055	6,701	5,536	5,274	...
1995	20,589	229	708	1,930	7,176	5,373	5,174	...
1994	20,873	230	716	2,134	7,408	5,510	4,873	...
1993	20,856	237	679	1,986	7,604	5,308	5,041	...
1992	21,125	231	682	2,057	8,113	5,116	4,927	...
1991	21,319	270	694	2,095	8,810	4,441	5,009	12.9
1990	21,462	295	759	2,153	8,649	4,392	5,215	12.9
1989	21,461	251	698	2,129	8,659	4,391	5,335	12.9
1988	21,277	237	651	2,227	8,569	4,273	5,319	12.9
1987	21,142	223	698	2,030	8,544	4,384	5,263	12.9
1986	20,956	227	715	1,887	8,359	4,488	5,279	12.9
1985	20,184	194	700	1,823	7,955	4,433	5,080	12.9
1984	19,876	231	721	1,739	7,798	4,238	5,150	12.9
1983	19,438	213	659	1,724	7,351	4,284	5,207	13.0
1982	19,090	182	659	1,654	7,380	4,162	5,053	13.0
1981	18,625	176	733	1,679	6,991	4,185	4,863	13.0
1980	18,051	198	699	1,639	6,393	4,166	4,957	13.0
1979	16,719	197	695	1,476	5,852	3,862	4,637	13.0
1978	16,263	154	717	1,526	5,701	3,698	4,471	13.1
1977	15,863	134	672	1,625	5,634	3,403	4,396	13.0
1976	15,266	134	724	1,566	5,672	3,085	4,087	12.9
1975	14,776	177	815	1,605	5,508	2,915	3,757	12.9
1974	14,222	211	859	1,617	5,491	2,672	3,372	12.8
1973	13,638	204	966	1,760	5,363	2,416	2,927	12.7
1972	13,030	157	927	1,796	5,150	2,191	2,809	12.7
1971	12,596	170	1,092	1,771	5,049	2,005	2,506	12.6
1970	12,236	189	1,063	1,896	4,833	1,842	2,412	12.6
1969	11,788	204	1,121	1,849	4,652	1,719	2,241	12.6
1968	11,381	193	1,192	1,880	4,473	1,505	2,136	12.5
1967	10,876	170	1,209	1,814	4,187	1,522	1,973	12.5
1966	10,701	241	1,162	1,839	4,191	1,374	1,894	12.5
1965	10,693	325	1,240	1,802	4,188	1,316	1,822	12.5

... = Not available.

Table A-25.   Years of School Completed by People 25 Years Old and Over, by Age and Sex, Selected Years 1940–2009—*Continued*

(Numbers in thousands.)

Year, sex, and age	Total	Years of school completed						Median years
		Elementary		High school		College		
		0 to 4 years	5 to 8 years	1 to 3 years	4 years	1 to 3 years	4 years or more	
1964.................................	10,729	297	1,344	1,962	4,008	1,306	1,812	12.4
1962.................................	10,762	334	1,569	2,008	3,700	1,309	1,842	12.4
1960.................................	11,184	420	2,026	2,441	3,356	1,316	1,624	12.2
1959.................................	11,226	416	1,822	2,238	3,682	1,256	1,658	12.3
1957.................................	11,368	423	2,097	2,446	3,542	1,181	1,556	12.2
1952.................................	10,936	502	2,202	2,268	3,458	1,118	1,268	12.1
1950.................................	11,454	631	2,705	2,426	3,250	1,117	1,037	11.5
1947.................................	10,894	544	2,665	2,494	3,337	993	738	11.7
1940.................................	10,521	779	3,932	2,220	2,049	692	744	9.7
Female								
2009.................................	20,079	137	531	1,395	4,856	5,901	7,258	...
2008.................................	19,937	111	475	1,421	4,941	5,836	7,153	...
2007.................................	19,843	134	527	1,532	5,047	5,824	6,781	...
2006.................................	19,654	140	577	1,538	5,069	5,894	6,435	...
2005.................................	19,633	173	607	1,594	5,053	5,667	6,539	...
2004.................................	19,603	150	606	1,516	5,224	5,758	6,349	...
2003.................................	19,679	153	598	1,503	5,364	5,734	6,325	...
2002.................................	19,436	153	584	1,463	5,237	5,645	6,353	...
2001.................................	19,536	147	569	1,525	5,195	5,985	6,115	...
2000.................................	19,222	130	542	1,415	5,557	5,831	5,750	...
1999.................................	19,551	122	525	1,572	5,712	5,842	5,779	...
1998.................................	19,828	130	553	1,493	5,977	5,986	5,688	...
1997.................................	20,217	149	533	1,615	6,227	6,047	5,643	...
1996.................................	20,528	195	569	1,734	6,386	6,090	5,568	...
1995.................................	20,800	165	556	1,738	6,885	6,286	5,170	...
1994.................................	21,073	138	581	1,923	7,075	6,404	4,953	...
1993.................................	21,007	143	543	1,907	7,432	6,054	4,928	...
1992.................................	21,368	203	567	2,014	7,908	5,744	4,933	...
1991.................................	21,586	195	629	2,085	8,693	4,841	5,143	12.9
1990.................................	21,779	209	653	1,889	8,986	4,927	5,112	12.9
1989.................................	21,777	195	654	1,885	9,242	4,681	5,119	12.9
1988.................................	21,675	193	657	1,869	9,319	4,801	4,836	12.9
1987.................................	21,494	168	662	1,965	8,995	4,772	4,932	12.9
1986.................................	21,097	160	644	1,910	8,952	4,616	4,813	12.9
1985.................................	20,673	168	627	1,880	8,794	4,547	4,657	12.9
1984.................................	20,297	173	649	1,904	8,634	4,319	4,621	12.9
1983.................................	19,903	161	665	1,941	8,452	4,285	4,398	12.9
1982.................................	19,614	155	713	1,942	8,512	4,140	4,148	12.8
1981.................................	19,203	161	698	1,986	8,427	4,013	3,918	12.8
1980.................................	18,565	164	725	1,932	8,087	3,777	3,879	12.8
1979.................................	17,334	173	685	1,977	7,486	3,553	3,460	12.8
1978.................................	16,857	172	742	1,989	7,292	3,311	3,351	12.6
1977.................................	16,421	136	710	2,088	7,212	2,995	3,280	12.7
1976.................................	15,882	112	784	2,054	7,248	2,731	2,954	12.7
1975.................................	15,316	135	833	2,139	7,037	2,489	2,686	12.6
1974.................................	14,750	142	796	2,145	6,871	2,383	2,413	12.6
1973.................................	14,155	129	884	2,154	6,830	2,037	2,121	12.6
1972.................................	13,487	128	862	2,184	6,485	1,899	1,926	12.5
1971.................................	12,950	156	919	2,212	6,183	1,816	1,663	12.5
1970.................................	12,629	140	876	2,355	6,096	1,648	1,512	12.5
1969.................................	12,285	155	965	2,291	5,941	1,481	1,451	12.4
1968.................................	11,904	157	1,053	2,246	5,684	1,484	1,278	12.4
1967.................................	11,512	149	1,084	2,200	5,458	1,426	1,195	12.4
1966.................................	11,322	186	1,047	2,319	5,355	1,273	1,134	12.4
1965.................................	11,284	218	1,197	2,256	5,310	1,244	1,060	12.4
1964.................................	11,269	202	1,248	2,216	5,362	1,221	1,018	12.4
1962.................................	11,368	263	1,367	2,363	5,115	1,243	1,017	12.3
1960.................................	11,637	289	1,712	2,694	4,810	1,256	875	12.2
1959.................................	11,696	345	1,526	2,503	5,297	1,142	822	12.3
1957.................................	12,069	327	1,874	2,519	5,385	1,094	795	12.2
1952.................................	12,202	342	2,160	2,630	5,162	1,102	784	12.2
1950.................................	12,172	516	2,603	2,624	4,410	1,081	714	12.1
1947.................................	11,733	471	2,858	2,503	4,293	915	640	12.0
1940.................................	10,818	598	3,744	2,333	2,653	862	544	10.3

... = Not available.

Table A-25. Years of School Completed by People 25 Years Old and Over, by Age and Sex, Selected Years 1940–2009—*Continued*

(Numbers in thousands.)

Year, sex, and age	Total	Elementary		High school		College		Median years
		0 to 4 years	5 to 8 years	1 to 3 years	4 years	1 to 3 years	4 years or more	
35 TO 54 YEARS OLD								
Both Sexes								
2009	85,688	909	2,716	6,046	26,121	23,384	26,513	...
2008	86,067	905	2,742	5,882	26,108	23,504	26,926	...
2007	86,224	874	2,720	6,310	26,675	22,777	26,869	...
2006	85,918	965	2,769	6,274	26,636	23,317	25,958	...
2005	85,311	954	2,757	5,892	27,232	23,129	25,347	...
2004	84,642	963	2,582	5,938	26,649	23,093	25,417	...
2003	84,308	957	2,620	6,112	26,346	23,039	25,234	...
2002	83,829	941	2,636	5,874	26,740	23,148	24,489	...
2001	83,286	886	2,612	5,899	26,356	23,271	24,262	...
2000	81,435	932	2,521	5,702	26,481	22,618	23,183	...
1999	79,976	872	2,535	6,052	26,367	21,561	22,589	...
1998	78,520	890	2,613	6,164	26,079	21,267	21,506	...
1997	76,973	867	2,686	6,045	26,054	20,684	20,635	...
1996	74,661	968	2,710	5,803	24,924	20,105	20,152	...
1995	73,028	927	2,561	5,664	24,070	19,926	19,878	...
1994	71,049	987	2,680	5,415	23,804	19,210	18,956	...
1993	68,845	942	2,486	5,538	23,927	17,984	17,970	...
1992	66,594	899	2,608	5,845	23,442	16,658	17,144	...
1991	64,351	995	3,057	5,522	24,815	13,348	16,614	12.9
1990	62,499	980	3,104	5,529	24,434	12,553	15,899	12.9
1989	60,494	999	3,315	5,800	23,334	11,627	15,417	12.9
1988	58,555	958	3,272	5,889	23,049	11,017	14,369	12.8
1987	56,650	842	3,398	5,656	22,820	10,523	13,409	12.8
1986	55,170	896	3,614	5,769	22,151	10,110	12,629	12.8
1985	53,697	899	3,639	5,978	21,600	9,217	12,363	12.8
1984	52,297	893	3,754	6,158	21,290	8,702	11,500	12.7
1983	50,956	973	4,044	6,313	20,788	8,045	10,795	12.7
1982	49,722	963	4,320	6,657	20,445	7,580	9,756	12.6
1981	48,680	1,038	4,531	6,773	20,032	7,115	9,181	12.6
1980	48,124	1,034	4,676	7,063	19,584	6,943	8,822	12.6
1979	47,437	1,030	4,895	7,132	19,488	6,655	8,237	12.5
1978	46,921	1,107	5,262	7,590	19,012	6,286	7,667	12.5
1977	46,409	1,192	5,445	7,781	18,781	6,013	7,196	12.5
1976	46,271	1,245	5,729	7,671	18,893	5,957	6,776	12.5
1975	46,193	1,296	5,942	7,765	19,010	5,673	6,506	12.4
1974	46,217	1,293	6,244	7,896	19,038	5,375	6,372	12.4
1973	45,910	1,344	6,519	8,001	18,651	5,318	6,076	12.4
1972	45,956	1,367	7,004	8,521	18,400	5,074	5,589	12.3
1971	46,294	1,439	7,588	8,393	18,334	5,082	5,460	12.3
1970	46,319	1,461	7,935	8,555	18,200	4,875	5,294	12.3
1969	46,255	1,644	8,313	8,586	17,773	4,749	5,190	12.3
1968	46,396	1,654	8,698	8,838	17,362	4,642	5,200	12.2
1967	46,321	1,771	9,036	9,138	16,906	4,525	4,947	12.2
1966	46,313	1,837	9,528	9,309	16,605	4,230	4,805	12.1
1965	46,296	1,827	9,812	9,266	16,359	4,384	4,647	12.1
1964	46,089	1,905	10,259	9,289	15,760	4,397	4,482	12.1
1962	45,287	2,181	10,795	8,938	14,668	4,452	4,253	12.0
1960	44,742	2,424	12,536	9,502	12,517	4,123	3,639	11.3
1959	43,989	2,303	11,657	8,719	13,244	3,715	3,709	11.8
1957	42,645	2,658	12,349	8,384	12,041	3,248	3,360	11.3
1952	39,014	2,606	13,274	7,348	9,374	3,148	2,802	10.5
1950	38,432	3,404	14,420	6,976	7,262	2,878	2,516	9.7
1947	36,717	3,203	15,184	6,311	6,715	2,622	2,221	9.0
1940	33,845	4,549	16,270	4,972	4,217	1,836	1,540	8.6
Male								
2009	42,263	500	1,458	3,278	13,644	10,670	12,713	...
2008	42,419	507	1,490	3,228	13,625	10,711	12,858	...
2007	42,476	491	1,433	3,480	13,737	10,359	12,976	...
2006	42,344	549	1,472	3,356	13,660	10,608	12,701	...
2005	42,024	547	1,476	3,063	14,017	10,429	12,491	...
2004	41,612	577	1,323	3,157	13,238	10,636	12,682	...
2003	41,340	538	1,372	3,282	12,903	10,622	12,622	...
2002	41,154	513	1,333	3,063	13,133	10,739	12,373	...
2001	40,858	488	1,368	2,974	12,784	10,827	12,417	...
2000	40,024	479	1,288	2,845	12,845	10,716	11,854	...

... = Not available.

Table A-25.   Years of School Completed by People 25 Years Old and Over, by Age and Sex, Selected Years 1940–2009—*Continued*

(Numbers in thousands.)

Year, sex, and age	Total	Years of school completed						Median years
		Elementary		High school		College		
		0 to 4 years	5 to 8 years	1 to 3 years	4 years	1 to 3 years	4 years or more	
1999	39,300	470	1,290	3,101	12,544	10,233	11,664	...
1998	38,654	486	1,333	3,284	12,239	10,098	11,214	...
1997	37,912	486	1,370	3,143	12,326	9,713	10,870	...
1996	36,596	520	1,319	2,877	11,749	9,514	10,526	...
1995	35,994	529	1,368	2,781	11,223	9,305	10,784	...
1994	34,998	545	1,383	2,621	11,009	9,073	10,369	...
1993	33,751	478	1,316	2,660	10,983	8,624	9,687	...
1992	32,619	472	1,368	2,750	10,670	7,968	9,389	...
1991	31,460	530	1,624	2,612	11,092	6,430	9,169	13.0
1990	30,623	527	1,658	2,573	10,790	6,169	8,905	13.0
1989	29,597	504	1,762	2,628	10,235	5,719	8,749	13.0
1988	28,645	498	1,725	2,654	10,100	5,327	8,340	12.9
1987	27,680	412	1,801	2,617	9,781	5,173	7,895	12.9
1986	26,925	475	1,919	2,699	9,393	5,013	7,426	12.9
1985	26,181	501	1,928	2,726	9,210	4,502	7,314	12.9
1984	25,460	506	2,014	2,831	8,926	4,257	6,929	12.8
1983	24,796	548	2,108	2,862	8,795	3,884	6,601	12.8
1982	24,164	530	2,302	2,989	8,609	3,757	5,977	12.7
1981	23,646	572	2,425	3,112	8,431	3,519	5,588	12.7
1980	23,373	590	2,492	3,202	8,278	3,442	5,370	12.7
1979	22,976	545	2,612	3,194	8,232	3,306	5,090	12.6
1978	22,719	609	2,779	3,377	8,001	3,136	4,817	12.6
1977	22,445	661	2,889	3,554	7,822	3,000	4,520	12.5
1976	22,403	730	3,004	3,473	7,904	2,969	4,323	12.5
1975	22,358	763	3,100	3,510	7,952	2,879	4,153	12.5
1974	22,367	733	3,286	3,532	8,004	2,730	4,081	12.6
1973	22,166	716	3,413	3,586	7,836	2,714	3,901	12.4
1972	22,200	749	3,674	3,917	7,663	2,564	3,631	12.4
1971	22,474	849	3,985	3,823	7,674	2,578	3,567	12.3
1970	22,475	834	4,208	3,876	7,612	2,555	3,390	12.3
1969	22,420	889	4,359	4,012	7,427	2,456	3,277	12.3
1968	22,521	931	4,487	4,160	7,324	2,364	3,257	12.2
1967	22,482	1,000	4,700	4,270	7,143	2,244	3,128	12.2
1966	22,508	1,085	4,886	4,455	6,990	2,029	3,063	12.1
1965	22,534	1,081	5,076	4,462	6,815	2,161	2,937	12.1
1964	22,457	1,158	5,226	4,416	6,657	2,212	2,789	12.2
1962	22,081	1,235	5,545	4,359	6,202	2,142	2,598	11.9
1960	21,919	1,397	6,415	4,579	5,364	1,957	2,206	11.1
1959	21,511	1,350	5,781	4,329	5,604	1,827	2,250	11.5
1957	20,873	1,491	6,293	3,987	5,195	1,558	1,972	11.0
1952	18,888	1,466	6,512	3,462	4,040	1,518	1,576	10.3
1950	18,896	1,834	7,338	3,339	3,151	1,271	1,403	9.6
1947	18,165	1,678	7,765	3,102	2,907	1,168	1,258	8.6
1940	17,127	2,480	8,458	2,388	1,798	819	917	8.5
Female								
2009	43,424	409	1,258	2,768	12,476	12,713	13,800	...
2008	43,648	398	1,253	2,654	12,483	12,792	14,067	...
2007	43,748	382	1,288	2,830	12,938	12,419	13,892	...
2006	43,573	417	1,298	2,915	12,976	12,710	13,255	...
2005	43,287	407	1,280	2,829	13,215	12,700	12,856	...
2004	43,030	386	1,259	2,781	13,411	12,458	12,736	...
2003	42,968	419	1,248	2,830	13,443	12,417	12,611	...
2002	42,675	428	1,303	2,811	13,607	12,410	12,116	...
2001	42,428	398	1,244	2,926	13,572	12,444	11,844	...
2000	41,411	452	1,235	2,858	13,635	11,905	11,330	...
1999	40,676	402	1,248	2,950	13,825	11,326	10,925	...
1998	39,866	403	1,279	2,879	13,841	11,168	10,293	...
1997	39,061	381	1,319	2,902	13,726	10,969	9,766	...
1996	38,065	449	1,301	2,924	13,174	10,592	9,623	...
1995	37,034	396	1,192	2,881	12,846	10,623	9,096	...
1994	36,051	443	1,298	2,792	12,795	10,140	8,587	...
1993	35,093	462	1,169	2,877	12,944	9,358	8,283	...
1992	33,975	427	1,240	3,096	12,770	8,687	7,756	...
1991	32,891	464	1,431	2,910	13,723	6,919	7,443	12.8
1990	31,876	454	1,448	2,955	13,643	6,383	6,997	12.8
1989	30,898	498	1,552	3,171	13,099	5,908	6,669	12.8
1988	29,908	462	1,547	3,234	12,949	5,689	6,029	12.7
1987	28,969	430	1,598	3,039	13,038	5,349	5,513	12.7

... = Not available.

Table A-25. Years of School Completed by People 25 Years Old and Over, by Age and Sex, Selected Years 1940–2009—*Continued*

(Numbers in thousands.)

Year, sex, and age	Total	Elementary		High school		College		Median years
		0 to 4 years	5 to 8 years	1 to 3 years	4 years	1 to 3 years	4 years or more	
1986............................	28,244	420	1,694	3,071	12,759	5,098	5,202	12.7
1985............................	27,516	398	1,710	3,252	12,391	4,715	5,049	12.7
1984............................	26,838	389	1,740	3,331	12,364	4,444	4,570	12.6
1983............................	26,161	427	1,935	3,450	11,993	4,161	4,193	12.6
1982............................	25,555	433	2,017	3,666	11,833	3,827	3,778	12.6
1981............................	25,034	467	2,105	3,661	11,599	3,605	3,595	12.5
1980............................	24,751	444	2,186	3,862	11,307	3,501	3,452	12.5
1979............................	24,461	486	2,282	3,935	11,258	3,353	3,147	12.5
1978............................	24,202	497	2,483	4,212	11,012	3,149	2,849	12.5
1977............................	23,964	534	2,557	4,227	10,959	3,014	2,678	12.4
1976............................	23,868	517	2,721	4,198	10,989	2,988	2,455	12.4
1975............................	23,835	533	2,842	4,256	11,058	2,793	2,352	12.4
1974............................	23,850	559	2,956	4,364	11,033	2,647	2,290	12.4
1973............................	23,744	628	3,106	4,415	10,815	2,603	2,174	12.3
1972............................	23,756	618	3,330	4,604	10,736	2,509	1,958	12.3
1971............................	23,821	590	3,604	4,570	10,660	2,505	1,894	12.3
1970............................	23,845	629	3,728	4,679	10,588	2,318	1,903	12.3
1969............................	23,834	755	3,953	4,575	10,349	2,293	1,913	12.3
1968............................	23,874	725	4,212	4,676	10,038	2,281	1,943	12.2
1967............................	23,839	773	4,334	4,868	9,762	2,282	1,819	12.2
1966............................	23,806	752	4,644	4,853	9,615	2,200	1,741	12.2
1965............................	23,765	746	4,735	4,803	9,545	2,223	1,712	12.2
1964............................	23,632	748	5,033	4,871	9,103	2,183	1,691	12.1
1962............................	23,206	946	5,250	4,579	8,466	2,310	1,655	12.1
1960............................	22,823	1,027	6,121	4,923	7,153	2,166	1,433	11.6
1959............................	22,478	953	5,876	4,390	7,640	1,888	1,459	12.0
1957............................	21,772	1,167	6,056	4,397	6,846	1,690	1,388	11.5
1952............................	20,126	1,140	6,762	3,886	5,334	1,630	1,226	10.7
1950............................	19,536	1,570	7,082	3,637	4,111	1,607	1,113	9.7
1947............................	18,552	1,525	7,419	3,209	3,808	1,454	963	9.3
1940............................	16,718	2,070	7,812	2,584	2,419	1,017	623	8.7

55 YEARS OLD AND OVER

Both Sexes

Year, sex, and age	Total	0 to 4 years	5 to 8 years	1 to 3 years	4 years	1 to 3 years	4 years or more	Median years
2009............................	72,077	1,555	4,101	6,338	24,154	16,877	19,051	...
2008............................	70,092	1,411	4,294	6,338	23,779	16,378	17,892	...
2007............................	68,226	1,576	4,458	6,680	23,408	15,505	16,599	...
2006............................	66,485	1,628	4,610	6,508	22,961	14,824	15,956	...
2005............................	64,745	1,614	4,803	6,784	22,392	14,083	15,069	...
2004............................	63,034	1,465	4,907	6,821	21,918	13,434	14,488	...
2003............................	61,633	1,589	5,372	6,876	21,554	12,884	13,358	...
2002............................	59,644	1,528	5,639	7,258	20,728	12,117	12,374	...
2001............................	58,238	1,544	5,589	7,178	20,622	11,864	11,440	...
2000............................	56,008	1,524	5,780	6,921	20,059	11,126	10,598	...
1999............................	55,303	1,589	5,978	7,096	19,742	10,722	10,174	...
1998............................	54,337	1,624	6,126	7,385	19,526	10,022	9,654	...
1997............................	53,352	1,628	6,622	7,543	18,823	9,565	9,169	...
1996............................	52,742	1,642	6,716	7,520	18,549	9,642	8,677	...
1995............................	52,022	1,755	7,048	7,232	18,320	9,662	8,005	...
1994............................	51,516	1,802	7,382	7,454	18,228	8,890	7,761	...
1993............................	52,117	2,058	8,038	7,637	18,626	8,106	7,652	...
1992............................	51,740	2,118	8,133	7,756	18,397	8,005	7,332	...
1991............................	51,439	2,341	8,668	7,675	18,954	6,540	7,258	12.6
1990............................	50,798	2,349	9,239	7,893	18,050	6,202	7,064	12.3
1989............................	50,421	2,412	9,395	7,907	18,102	5,914	6,693	12.3
1988............................	50,128	2,325	9,969	7,860	18,004	5,705	6,263	12.3
1987............................	49,858	2,408	10,544	7,766	17,310	5,799	6,033	12.2
1986............................	49,383	2,611	10,699	7,917	16,876	5,515	5,767	12.2
1985............................	48,969	2,612	11,052	7,872	16,516	5,208	5,708	12.2
1984............................	48,324	2,584	11,131	7,636	16,353	5,026	5,593	12.2
1983............................	47,723	2,769	11,348	7,703	15,470	4,915	5,514	12.1
1982............................	47,102	2,818	11,541	7,751	15,091	4,807	5,095	12.1
1981............................	46,391	2,983	11,909	7,600	14,464	4,721	4,711	12.0
1980............................	45,670	2,994	12,326	7,451	13,869	4,494	4,535	12.0
1979............................	43,806	2,924	12,230	6,999	13,088	4,321	4,245	12.0
1978............................	42,977	3,013	12,593	7,069	12,376	4,086	3,843	11.6
1977............................	42,176	3,047	12,740	6,823	11,977	3,835	3,754	11.3
1976............................	41,429	3,107	12,674	6,915	11,346	3,709	3,677	11.1

... = Not available.

Table A-25. Years of School Completed by People 25 Years Old and Over, by Age and Sex, Selected Years 1940–2009—*Continued*

(Numbers in thousands.)

| Year, sex, and age | Total | Years of school completed ||||||| Median years |
| | | Elementary || High school || College || |
		0 to 4 years	5 to 8 years	1 to 3 years	4 years	1 to 3 years	4 years or more	
1975	40,613	3,303	13,045	6,730	10,798	3,442	3,295	10.8
1974	39,817	3,461	13,302	6,615	10,060	3,233	3,145	10.4
1973	39,163	3,424	13,467	6,504	9,604	3,060	3,105	10.2
1972	38,659	3,471	13,706	6,351	9,136	2,952	3,042	10.0
1971	38,787	3,808	14,430	6,225	8,463	2,878	2,982	9.6
1970	38,126	3,957	14,647	5,877	8,005	2,797	2,843	9.2
1969	37,424	4,012	14,576	5,801	7,768	2,615	2,653	9.1
1968	36,789	4,244	14,522	5,760	7,085	2,624	2,558	8.9
1967	36,155	4,310	14,849	5,495	6,622	2,443	2,434	8.7
1966	35,540	4,438	14,742	5,392	6,240	2,358	2,370	8.6
1965	34,969	4,612	14,814	5,293	5,844	2,194	2,215	8.5
1964	34,335	4,888	14,701	4,954	5,598	2,159	2,033	8.3
1962	33,247	5,048	14,707	4,442	4,994	2,166	1,890	8.1
1960	31,902	5,169	14,944	4,503	3,757	2,051	1,479	8.5
1959	30,567	4,752	13,485	4,060	3,996	1,775	1,545	8.1
1957	29,548	5,153	12,996	3,602	3,864	1,462	1,461	8.0
1952	26,206	4,554	12,638	2,982	3,080	1,346	1,264	7.7
1950	25,427	4,940	11,947	2,791	2,704	1,170	1,005	8.3
1947	23,234	4,393	11,601	2,179	2,581	1,003	825	7.5
1940	19,592	4,178	10,467	1,656	1,633	685	579	8.2
Male								
2009	32,814	689	1,874	2,669	9,886	7,456	10,241	...
2008	31,841	631	1,932	2,751	9,510	7,259	9,759	...
2007	30,920	721	2,060	2,884	9,505	6,723	9,026	...
2006	30,060	705	2,090	2,784	9,488	6,193	8,837	...
2005	29,198	717	2,157	2,896	8,918	6,167	8,341	...
2004	28,347	639	2,192	2,885	8,631	5,841	8,159	...
2003	27,694	729	2,423	2,912	8,425	5,694	7,510	...
2002	26,608	664	2,601	3,048	8,063	5,257	6,975	...
2001	25,908	697	2,558	2,964	8,073	5,131	6,485	...
2000	25,023	706	2,696	2,817	7,816	4,906	6,079	...
1999	24,694	712	2,746	2,911	7,712	4,756	5,856	...
1998	24,197	755	2,740	3,000	7,745	4,461	5,496	...
1997	23,668	773	3,026	3,060	7,417	4,139	5,255	...
1996	23,352	795	3,058	2,998	7,198	4,254	5,055	...
1995	22,881	839	3,153	2,980	6,980	4,254	4,675	...
1994	22,669	894	3,327	3,037	6,987	3,962	4,462	...
1993	23,038	992	3,595	3,174	7,178	3,587	4,508	...
1992	22,836	1,033	3,676	3,277	6,991	3,549	4,312	...
1991	22,708	1,217	3,980	3,183	7,287	2,850	4,193	12.4
1990	22,337	1,182	4,141	3,274	6,986	2,707	4,046	12.4
1989	22,167	1,202	4,198	3,317	7,003	2,616	3,829	12.3
1988	21,989	1,117	4,471	3,366	6,968	2,455	3,609	12.3
1987	21,855	1,160	4,762	3,261	6,673	2,504	3,496	12.3
1986	21,622	1,275	4,813	3,286	6,509	2,355	3,385	12.2
1985	21,391	1,252	5,001	3,234	6,387	2,229	3,289	12.2
1984	21,014	1,209	4,951	3,270	6,265	2,185	3,132	12.2
1983	20,769	1,343	4,986	3,282	5,906	2,141	3,117	12.1
1982	20,508	1,362	5,026	3,313	5,759	2,102	2,946	12.1
1981	20,237	1,394	5,165	3,292	5,597	2,032	2,758	12.0
1980	19,967	1,424	5,436	3,206	5,409	1,986	2,506	11.9
1979	19,292	1,446	5,479	2,964	5,167	1,935	2,301	11.8
1978	18,939	1,467	5,701	2,919	4,919	1,824	2,110	11.4
1977	18,608	1,502	5,770	2,787	4,835	1,700	2,011	11.2
1976	18,233	1,507	5,733	2,884	4,473	1,646	1,989	11.0
1975	17,903	1,628	5,845	2,871	4,308	1,480	1,768	10.5
1974	17,579	1,693	6,042	2,817	3,993	1,356	1,682	10.1
1973	17,263	1,678	6,111	2,774	3,811	1,245	1,645	9.9
1972	17,120	1,728	6,252	2,698	3,612	1,215	1,614	9.6
1971	17,288	1,913	6,629	2,668	3,285	1,214	1,579	9.1
1970	17,074	2,011	6,655	2,583	3,127	1,182	1,516	9.0
1969	16,822	2,003	6,701	2,536	3,099	1,086	1,397	8.8
1968	16,609	2,137	6,728	2,523	2,816	1,078	1,328	8.7
1967	16,398	2,247	6,827	2,379	2,685	989	1,271	8.5
1966	16,201	2,288	6,944	2,317	2,491	939	1,223	8.3
1965	16,015	2,368	6,992	2,265	2,331	893	1,164	8.2
1964	15,789	2,504	6,897	2,159	2,237	876	1,113	8.1
1962	15,440	2,644	6,813	2,032	2,030	864	1,057	8.0

... = Not available.

Table A-25.   Years of School Completed by People 25 Years Old and Over, by Age and Sex, Selected Years 1940–2009—*Continued*

(Numbers in thousands.)

Year, sex, and age	Total	Years of school completed						Median years
		Elementary		High school		College		
		0 to 4 years	5 to 8 years	1 to 3 years	4 years	1 to 3 years	4 years or more	
1960.................................	14,895	2,704	7,121	1,969	1,453	853	796	8.4
1959.................................	14,304	2,491	6,436	1,759	1,584	718	857	7.9
1957.................................	13,967	2,696	6,244	1,570	1,493	608	831	7.7
1952.................................	12,544	2,428	6,162	1,318	1,262	528	636	7.5
1950.................................	12,277	2,609	5,808	1,209	1,111	500	569	8.2
1947.................................	11,424	2,393	5,656	939	1,109	464	482	7.3
1940.................................	9,815	2,293	5,249	724	660	313	361	8.1
Female								
2009.................................	39,263	867	2,228	3,669	14,268	9,421	8,810	...
2008.................................	38,251	780	2,362	3,588	14,269	9,119	8,133	...
2007.................................	37,306	855	2,398	3,796	13,902	8,781	7,573	...
2006.................................	36,425	922	2,521	3,761	13,472	8,630	7,119	...
2005.................................	35,547	897	2,645	3,887	13,474	7,916	6,728	...
2004.................................	34,687	826	2,715	3,936	13,287	7,593	6,329	...
2003.................................	33,939	860	2,949	3,964	13,129	7,190	5,848	...
2002.................................	33,035	864	3,038	4,210	12,664	6,860	5,399	...
2001.................................	32,329	847	3,032	4,213	12,549	6,733	4,956	...
2000.................................	30,985	817	3,085	4,105	12,243	6,218	4,517	...
1999.................................	30,609	879	3,232	4,186	12,031	5,965	4,319	...
1998.................................	30,140	868	3,386	4,386	11,780	5,560	4,160	...
1997.................................	29,684	855	3,596	4,483	11,407	5,427	3,916	...
1996.................................	29,390	848	3,659	4,523	11,350	5,387	3,623	...
1995.................................	29,142	915	3,894	4,255	11,340	5,410	3,330	...
1994.................................	28,848	909	4,054	4,419	11,242	4,926	3,298	...
1993.................................	29,080	1,066	4,442	4,462	11,447	4,519	3,149	...
1992.................................	28,904	1,084	4,456	4,478	11,409	4,455	3,021	...
1991.................................	28,729	1,125	4,687	4,495	11,667	3,690	3,066	12.3
1990.................................	28,461	1,167	5,098	4,619	11,063	3,495	3,019	12.3
1989.................................	28,255	1,211	5,195	4,587	11,099	3,300	2,863	12.3
1988.................................	28,139	1,208	5,498	4,495	11,034	3,250	2,655	12.3
1987.................................	28,004	1,248	5,782	4,504	10,637	3,294	2,539	12.2
1986.................................	27,762	1,336	5,886	4,630	10,367	3,160	2,382	12.2
1985.................................	27,578	1,360	6,052	4,638	10,129	2,979	2,420	12.2
1984.................................	27,309	1,377	6,183	4,363	10,086	2,843	2,459	12.2
1983.................................	26,954	1,428	6,364	4,423	9,567	2,774	2,398	12.1
1982.................................	26,593	1,458	6,511	4,435	9,330	2,705	2,150	12.1
1981.................................	26,152	1,589	6,742	4,308	8,868	2,690	1,954	12.0
1980.................................	25,703	1,571	6,889	4,245	8,460	2,509	2,030	12.0
1979.................................	24,514	1,474	6,750	4,034	7,920	2,389	1,944	12.0
1978.................................	24,038	1,545	6,889	4,149	7,457	2,263	1,733	11.6
1977.................................	23,568	1,546	6,972	4,034	7,141	2,135	1,742	11.0
1976.................................	23,196	1,602	6,942	4,029	6,871	2,063	1,690	11.0
1975.................................	22,710	1,675	7,198	3,858	6,490	1,962	1,527	10.9
1974.................................	22,238	1,762	7,261	3,799	6,068	1,880	1,463	10.7
1973.................................	21,900	1,746	7,359	3,729	5,790	1,814	1,461	10.5
1972.................................	21,539	1,743	7,455	3,654	5,526	1,737	1,425	10.3
1971.................................	21,500	1,896	7,805	3,556	5,179	1,665	1,402	9.9
1970.................................	21,052	1,946	7,993	3,292	4,879	1,615	1,327	9.5
1969.................................	20,601	2,009	7,878	3,264	4,669	1,526	1,255	9.4
1968.................................	20,180	2,106	7,795	3,237	4,269	1,544	1,229	9.2
1967.................................	19,756	2,063	8,021	3,117	3,937	1,454	1,164	8.9
1966.................................	19,339	2,152	7,797	3,074	3,749	1,419	1,147	8.9
1965.................................	18,955	2,243	7,821	3,026	3,514	1,300	1,048	8.7
1964.................................	18,546	2,383	7,805	2,794	3,360	1,282	920	8.5
1962.................................	17,807	2,404	7,894	2,410	2,964	1,302	833	8.3
1960.................................	17,007	2,465	7,823	2,534	2,304	1,198	683	8.6
1959.................................	16,263	2,261	7,049	2,301	2,412	1,057	688	8.3
1957.................................	15,581	2,457	6,752	2,032	2,371	854	630	8.2
1952.................................	13,662	2,126	6,476	1,664	1,818	818	628	7.9
1950.................................	13,150	2,331	6,139	1,582	1,593	670	436	8.4
1947.................................	11,810	2,000	5,945	1,240	1,472	539	343	7.6
1940.................................	9,777	1,886	5,217	932	973	372	219	8.3

... = Not available.

Table A-26. Percent of People 25 Years Old and Over Who Have Completed High School or College, by Race, Hispanic Origin and Sex, Selected Years 1940–2009

(Noninstitutionalized population)

Age, educational attainment level, and year	All races			White			Non-Hispanic White			Black[1]			Asian		
	Both sexes	Male	Female	Both sexes	Male	Female	Both sexes	Male	Female	Both sexes	Male	Female	Both sexes	Male	Female
25 YEARS OLD AND OVER															
Completed 4 Years of High School or More															
2009	86.7	86.2	87.1	87.1	86.5	87.7	91.6	91.4	91.9	84.1	84.0	84.1	88.2	90.4	86.2
2008	86.6	85.9	87.2	87.1	86.3	87.8	91.5	91.1	91.8	83.0	81.8	84.0	88.7	90.8	86.9
2007	85.7	85.0	86.4	86.2	85.3	87.1	90.6	90.2	91.0	82.3	81.9	82.6	87.8	89.8	85.9
2006	85.5	85.0	85.9	86.1	85.5	86.7	90.5	90.2	90.8	80.7	80.1	81.2	87.4	89.6	85.5
2005	85.2	84.9	85.5	85.8	85.2	86.2	90.1	89.9	90.3	81.1	81.0	81.2	87.6	90.4	85.2
2004	85.2	84.8	85.4	85.8	85.3	86.3	90.0	89.9	90.1	80.6	80.4	80.8	86.8	88.7	85.0
2003[3]	84.6	84.1	85.0	85.1	84.5	85.7	89.4	89.0	89.7	80.0	79.6	80.3	87.6	89.5	86.0
2002	84.1	83.8	84.4	84.8	84.3	85.2	88.7	88.5	88.9	78.7	78.5	78.9	...	...	...
2001[4]	84.1	84.1	84.2	84.8	84.4	85.1	88.6	88.6	88.6	78.8	79.2	78.5	...	...	...
2000	84.1	84.2	84.0	84.9	84.8	85.0	88.4	88.5	88.4	78.5	78.7	78.3	...	...	...
1999	83.4	83.4	83.4	84.3	84.2	84.3	87.7	87.7	87.7	77.0	76.7	77.2	...	...	...
1998	82.8	82.8	82.9	83.7	83.6	83.8	87.1	87.1	87.1	76.0	75.2	76.7	...	...	...
1997	82.1	82.0	82.2	83.0	82.9	83.2	86.3	86.3	86.3	74.9	73.5	76.0	...	...	...
1996	81.7	81.9	81.6	82.8	82.7	82.8	86.0	86.1	85.9	74.3	74.3	74.2	...	...	...
1995	81.7	81.7	81.6	83.0	83.0	83.0	85.9	86.0	85.8	73.8	73.4	74.1	...	...	...
1994	80.9	81.0	80.7	82.0	82.1	81.9	84.9	85.1	84.7	72.9	71.7	73.8	...	...	...
1993	80.2	80.5	80.0	81.5	81.8	81.3	84.1	84.5	83.8	70.4	69.6	71.1	...	...	...
1992[5]	79.4	79.7	79.2	80.9	81.1	80.7	...	...	...	67.7	67.0	68.2	...	...	...
1991	78.4	78.5	78.3	79.9	79.8	79.9	...	...	...	66.7	66.7	66.7	...	...	...
1990	77.6	77.7	77.5	79.1	79.1	79.0	...	...	...	66.2	65.8	66.5	...	...	...
1989	76.9	77.2	76.6	78.4	78.6	78.2	...	...	...	64.6	64.2	65.0	...	...	...
1988	76.2	76.4	76.0	77.7	77.7	77.6	...	...	...	63.5	63.7	63.4	...	...	...
1987	75.6	76.0	75.3	77.0	77.3	76.7	...	...	...	63.4	63.0	63.7	...	...	...
1986	74.7	75.1	74.4	76.2	76.5	75.9	...	...	...	62.3	61.5	63.0	...	...	...
1985	73.9	74.4	73.5	75.5	76.0	75.1	...	...	...	59.8	58.4	60.8	...	...	...
1984	73.3	73.7	73.0	75.0	75.4	74.6	...	...	...	58.5	57.1	59.7	...	...	...
1983	72.1	72.7	71.5	73.8	74.4	73.3	...	...	...	56.8	56.5	57.1	...	...	...
1982	71.0	71.7	70.3	72.8	73.4	72.3	...	...	...	54.9	55.7	54.3	...	...	...
1981	69.7	70.3	69.1	71.6	72.1	71.2	...	...	...	52.9	53.2	52.6	...	...	...
1980	68.6	69.2	68.1	70.5	71.0	70.1	...	...	...	51.2	51.1	51.3	...	...	...
1979	67.7	68.4	67.1	69.7	70.3	69.2	...	...	...	49.4	49.2	49.5	...	...	...
1978	65.9	66.8	65.2	67.9	68.6	67.2	...	...	...	47.6	47.9	47.3	...	...	...
1977	64.9	65.6	64.4	67.0	67.5	66.5	...	...	...	45.5	45.6	45.4	...	...	...
1976	64.1	64.7	63.5	66.1	66.7	65.5	...	...	...	43.8	42.3	45.0	...	...	...
1975	62.5	63.1	62.1	64.5	65.0	64.1	...	...	...	42.5	41.6	43.3	...	...	...
1974	61.2	61.6	60.9	63.3	63.6	63.0	...	...	...	40.8	39.9	41.5	...	...	...
1973	59.8	60.0	59.6	61.9	62.1	61.7	...	...	...	39.2	38.2	40.1	...	...	...
1972	58.2	58.2	58.2	60.4	60.3	60.5	...	...	...	36.6	35.7	37.2	...	...	...
1971	56.4	56.3	56.6	58.6	58.4	58.8	...	...	...	34.7	33.8	35.4	...	...	...
1970	55.2	55.0	55.4	57.4	57.2	57.6	...	...	...	33.7	32.4	34.8	...	...	...
1969	54.0	53.6	54.4	56.3	55.7	56.7	...	...	...	32.3	31.9	32.6	...	...	...
1968	52.6	52.0	53.2	54.9	54.3	55.5	...	...	...	30.1	28.9	31.0	...	...	...
1967	51.1	50.5	51.7	53.4	52.8	53.8	...	...	...	29.5	27.1	31.5	...	...	...
1966	49.9	49.0	50.8	52.2	51.3	53.0	...	...	...	27.8	25.8	29.5	...	...	...
1965	49.0	48.0	49.9	51.3	50.2	52.2	...	...	...	27.2	25.8	28.4	...	...	...
1964	48.0	47.0	48.9	50.3	49.3	51.2	...	...	...	25.7	23.7	27.4	...	...	...
1962	46.3	45.0	47.5	48.7	47.4	49.9	...	...	...	24.8	23.2	26.2	...	...	...
1959	43.7	42.2	45.2	46.1	44.5	47.7	...	...	...	20.7	19.6	21.6	...	...	...
1957	41.6	39.7	43.3	43.2	41.1	45.1	...	...	...	18.4	16.9	19.7	...	...	...
1952	38.8	36.9	40.5	...	...	...	...	...	...	15.0	14.0	15.7	...	...	...
1950	34.3	32.6	36.0	...	...	...	...	...	...	13.7	12.5	14.7	...	...	...
1947	33.1	31.4	34.7	35.0	33.2	36.7	...	...	...	13.6	12.7	14.5	...	...	...
1940	24.5	22.7	26.3	26.1	24.2	28.1	...	...	...	7.7	6.9	8.4	...	...	...
Completed 4 Years of College or More															
2009	29.5	30.1	29.1	29.9	30.6	29.3	32.9	33.9	31.9	19.3	17.8	20.6	52.3	55.7	49.3
2008	29.4	30.1	28.8	29.8	30.5	29.1	32.6	33.8	31.5	19.6	18.7	20.4	52.6	55.8	49.8
2007	28.7	29.5	28.0	29.1	29.9	28.3	31.8	33.2	30.6	18.5	18.0	19.0	52.1	55.2	49.3

[1]Data in the column labeled "Black" include Black and other races from 1940 to 1962; from 1963 to 2003, data are for the Black population only.

[3]Starting in 2003, respondents could choose more than one race. The race data in this table from 2003 onward represent respondents who indicated only one race. Prior to 2003, Asians were grouped with Pacific Islanders.

[4]Starting in 2001, data are from the expanded Current Population Survey (CPS) sample and were calculated using population controls based on Census 2000.

[5]Beginning with data for 1992, a new question results in different categories than for earlier years. Data shown as "Completed 4 Years of High School or More" are now collected by the category "High School Graduate." Data shown as "Completed 4 Years of College or more," are now collected by the categories, Bachelor's degree; Master's degree; Doctorate degree; and Professional degree. Due to the change in question format, median years of schooling cannot be derived.

... = Not available.

Table A-26. Percent of People 25 Years Old and Over Who Have Completed High School or College, by Race, Hispanic Origin and Sex, Selected Years 1940–2009—*Continued*

(Noninstitutionalized population)

Age, educational attainment level, and year	Hispanic[2]			White alone or in combination			Non-Hispanic White alone or in combination			Black alone or in combination			Asian alone or in combination		
	Both sexes	Male	Female	Both sexes	Male	Female	Both sexes	Male	Female	Both sexes	Male	Female	Both sexes	Male	Female
25 YEARS OLD AND OVER															
Completed 4 Years of High School or More															
2009	61.9	60.6	63.3	87.1	86.4	87.7	91.6	91.4	91.8	84.1	83.9	84.2	88.3	90.6	86.4
2008	62.3	60.9	63.7	87.1	86.3	87.8	91.4	91.1	91.8	83.2	81.9	84.1	89.0	90.9	87.2
2007	60.3	58.2	62.5	86.2	85.3	87.0	90.6	90.2	91.0	82.4	82.0	82.6	87.8	89.2	86.5
2006	59.3	58.5	60.1	86.1	85.5	86.7	90.5	90.2	90.8	80.8	80.3	81.2	87.6	89.6	85.8
2005	58.5	57.9	59.1	85.7	85.2	86.2	90.1	89.9	90.3	81.3	81.2	81.3	87.9	90.5	85.6
2004	58.4	57.3	59.5	85.8	85.3	86.2	90.0	89.9	90.1	80.6	80.3	80.9	86.9	88.8	85.2
2003[3]	57.0	56.3	57.8	85.1	84.5	85.7	89.4	89.0	89.6	80.0	79.5	80.3	87.8	89.7	86.1
2002	57.0	56.1	57.9	...	...	...	...	...	...	...	...	...	...	...	...
2001[4]	56.8	55.5	58.0	...	...	...	...	...	...	...	...	...	...	...	...
2000	57.0	56.6	57.5	...	...	...	...	...	...	...	...	...	...	...	...
1999	56.1	56.0	56.3	...	...	...	...	...	...	...	...	...	...	...	...
1998	55.5	55.7	55.3	...	...	...	...	...	...	...	...	...	...	...	...
1997	54.7	54.9	54.6	...	...	...	...	...	...	...	...	...	...	...	...
1996	53.1	53.0	53.3	...	...	...	...	...	...	...	...	...	...	...	...
1995	53.4	52.9	53.8	...	...	...	...	...	...	...	...	...	...	...	...
1994	53.3	53.4	53.2	...	...	...	...	...	...	...	...	...	...	...	...
1993	53.1	52.9	53.2	...	...	...	...	...	...	...	...	...	...	...	...
1992[5]	52.6	53.7	51.5	...	...	...	...	...	...	...	...	...	...	...	...
1991	51.3	51.4	51.2	...	...	...	...	...	...	...	...	...	...	...	...
1990	50.8	50.3	51.3	...	...	...	...	...	...	...	...	...	...	...	...
1989	50.9	51.0	50.7	...	...	...	...	...	...	...	...	...	...	...	...
1988	51.0	52.0	50.0	...	...	...	...	...	...	...	...	...	...	...	...
1987	50.9	51.8	50.0	...	...	...	...	...	...	...	...	...	...	...	...
1986	48.5	49.2	47.8	...	...	...	...	...	...	...	...	...	...	...	...
1985	47.9	48.5	47.4	...	...	...	...	...	...	...	...	...	...	...	...
1984	47.1	48.6	45.7	...	...	...	...	...	...	...	...	...	...	...	...
1983	46.2	48.6	44.2	...	...	...	...	...	...	...	...	...	...	...	...
1982	45.9	48.1	44.1	...	...	...	...	...	...	...	...	...	...	...	...
1981	44.5	45.5	43.6	...	...	...	...	...	...	...	...	...	...	...	...
1980	45.3	46.4	44.1	...	...	...	...	...	...	...	...	...	...	...	...
1979	42.0	42.3	41.7	...	...	...	...	...	...	...	...	...	...	...	...
1978	40.8	42.2	39.6	...	...	...	...	...	...	...	...	...	...	...	...
1977	39.6	42.3	37.2	...	...	...	...	...	...	...	...	...	...	...	...
1976	39.3	41.4	37.3	...	...	...	...	...	...	...	...	...	...	...	...
1975	37.9	39.5	36.7	...	...	...	...	...	...	...	...	...	...	...	...
1974	36.5	38.3	34.9	...	...	...	...	...	...	...	...	...	...	...	...
1973	...	...	...	...	...	...	...	...	...	...	...	...	...	...	...
1972	...	...	...	...	...	...	...	...	...	...	...	...	...	...	...
1971	...	...	...	...	...	...	...	...	...	...	...	...	...	...	...
1970	...	...	...	...	...	...	...	...	...	...	...	...	...	...	...
1969	...	...	...	...	...	...	...	...	...	...	...	...	...	...	...
1968	...	...	...	...	...	...	...	...	...	...	...	...	...	...	...
1967	...	...	...	...	...	...	...	...	...	...	...	...	...	...	...
1966	...	...	...	...	...	...	...	...	...	...	...	...	...	...	...
1965	...	...	...	...	...	...	...	...	...	...	...	...	...	...	...
1964	...	...	...	...	...	...	...	...	...	...	...	...	...	...	...
1962	...	...	...	...	...	...	...	...	...	...	...	...	...	...	...
1959	...	...	...	...	...	...	...	...	...	...	...	...	...	...	...
1957	...	...	...	...	...	...	...	...	...	...	...	...	...	...	...
1952	...	...	...	...	...	...	...	...	...	...	...	...	...	...	...
1950	...	...	...	...	...	...	...	...	...	...	...	...	...	...	...
1947	...	...	...	...	...	...	...	...	...	...	...	...	...	...	...
1940	...	...	...	...	...	...	...	...	...	...	...	...	...	...	...
Completed 4 Years of College or More															
2009	13.2	12.5	14.0	29.8	30.4	29.3	32.8	33.8	31.8	19.4	17.8	20.7	51.8	54.8	49.2
2008	13.3	12.6	14.1	29.7	30.3	29.0	32.5	33.6	31.4	19.8	18.8	20.5	52.0	54.6	49.8
2007	12.7	11.8	13.7	29.0	29.8	28.3	31.7	33.0	30.5	18.7	18.2	19.1	47.1	49.1	45.4

[2]May be of any race.
[3]Starting in 2003, respondents could choose more than one race. The race data in this table from 2003 onward represent respondents who indicated only one race. Prior to 2003, Asians were grouped with Pacific Islanders.
[4]Starting in 2001, data are from the expanded Current Population Survey (CPS) sample and were calculated using population controls based on Census 2000.
[5]Beginning with data for 1992, a new question results in different categories than for earlier years. Data shown as "Completed 4 Years of High School or More" are now collected by the category "High School Graduate." Data shown as "Completed 4 Years of College or more," are now collected by the categories, Bachelor's degree; Master's degree; Doctorate degree; and Professional degree. Due to the change in question format, median years of schooling cannot be derived.
... = Not available.

Table A-26. Percent of People 25 Years Old and Over Who Have Completed High School or College, by Race, Hispanic Origin and Sex, Selected Years 1940–2009—*Continued*

(Noninstitutionalized population)

Age, educational attainment level, and year	All races Both sexes	All races Male	All races Female	White Both sexes	White Male	White Female	Non-Hispanic White Both sexes	Non-Hispanic White Male	Non-Hispanic White Female	Black[1] Both sexes	Black[1] Male	Black[1] Female	Asian Both sexes	Asian Male	Asian Female
2006	28.0	29.2	26.9	28.4	29.7	27.1	31.0	32.8	29.3	18.5	17.2	19.4	49.7	52.5	47.1
2005	27.7	28.9	26.5	28.1	29.4	26.8	30.6	32.4	28.9	17.6	16.0	18.8	50.2	54.0	46.8
2004	27.7	29.4	26.1	28.2	30.0	26.4	30.6	32.9	28.4	17.6	16.6	18.5	49.4	53.7	45.6
2003[3]	27.2	28.9	25.7	27.6	29.4	25.9	30.0	32.3	27.9	17.3	16.7	17.8	49.8	53.9	46.1
2002	26.7	28.5	25.1	27.2	29.1	25.4	29.4	31.7	27.3	17.0	16.4	17.5	...	...	...
2001[4]	26.2	28.2	24.3	26.6	28.7	24.6	28.7	31.3	26.3	15.7	15.3	16.1	...	...	...
2000	25.6	27.8	23.6	26.1	28.5	23.9	28.1	30.8	25.5	16.5	16.3	16.7	...	...	...
1999	25.2	27.5	23.1	25.9	28.5	23.5	27.7	30.6	25.0	15.4	14.2	16.4	...	...	...
1998	24.4	26.5	22.4	25.0	27.3	22.8	26.6	29.3	24.1	14.7	13.9	15.4	...	...	...
1997	23.9	26.2	21.7	24.6	27.0	22.3	26.2	29.0	23.7	13.3	12.5	13.9	...	...	...
1996	23.6	26.0	21.4	24.3	26.9	21.8	25.9	28.8	23.2	13.6	12.4	14.6	...	...	...
1995	23.0	26.0	20.2	24.0	27.2	21.0	25.4	28.9	22.1	13.2	13.6	12.9	...	...	...
1994	22.2	25.1	19.6	22.9	26.1	20.0	24.3	27.8	21.1	12.9	12.8	13.0	...	...	...
1993	21.9	24.8	19.2	22.6	25.7	19.7	23.8	27.2	20.7	12.2	11.9	12.4	...	...	...
1992[5]	21.4	24.3	18.6	22.1	25.2	19.1	...	...	...	11.9	11.9	12.0	...	...	...
1991	21.4	24.3	18.8	22.2	25.4	19.3	...	...	...	11.5	11.4	11.6	...	...	...
1990	21.3	24.4	18.4	22.0	25.3	19.0	...	...	...	11.3	11.9	10.8	...	...	...
1989	21.1	24.5	18.1	21.8	25.4	18.5	...	...	...	11.8	11.7	11.9	...	...	...
1988	20.3	24.0	17.0	20.9	25.0	17.3	...	...	...	11.2	11.1	11.4	...	...	...
1987	19.9	23.6	16.5	20.5	24.5	16.9	...	...	...	10.7	11.0	10.4	...	...	...
1986	19.4	23.2	16.1	20.1	24.1	16.4	...	...	...	10.9	11.2	10.7	...	...	...
1985	19.4	23.1	16.0	20.0	24.0	16.3	...	...	...	11.1	11.2	11.0	...	...	...
1984	19.1	22.9	15.7	19.8	23.9	16.0	...	...	...	10.4	10.4	10.4	...	...	...
1983	18.8	23.0	15.1	19.5	24.0	15.4	...	...	...	9.5	10.0	9.2	...	...	...
1982	17.7	21.9	14.0	18.5	23.0	14.4	...	...	...	8.8	9.1	8.5	...	...	...
1981	17.1	21.1	13.4	17.8	22.2	13.8	...	...	...	8.2	8.2	8.2	...	...	...
1980	17.0	20.9	13.6	17.8	22.1	14.0	...	...	...	7.9	7.7	8.1	...	...	...
1979	16.4	20.4	12.9	17.2	21.4	13.3	...	...	...	7.9	8.3	7.5	...	...	...
1978	15.7	19.7	12.2	16.4	20.7	12.6	...	...	...	7.2	7.3	7.1	...	...	...
1977	15.4	19.2	12.0	16.1	20.2	12.4	...	...	...	7.2	7.0	7.4	...	...	...
1976	14.7	18.6	11.3	15.4	19.6	11.6	...	...	...	6.6	6.3	6.8	...	...	...
1975	13.9	17.6	10.6	14.5	18.4	11.0	...	...	...	6.4	6.7	6.2	...	...	...
1974	13.3	16.9	10.1	14.0	17.7	10.6	...	...	...	5.5	5.7	5.3	...	...	...
1973	12.6	16.0	9.6	13.1	16.8	9.9	...	...	...	6.0	5.9	6.0	...	...	...
1972	12.0	15.4	9.0	12.6	16.2	9.4	...	...	...	5.1	5.5	4.8	...	...	...
1971	11.4	14.6	8.5	12.0	15.5	8.9	...	...	...	4.5	4.7	4.3	...	...	...
1970	11.0	14.1	8.2	11.6	15.0	8.6	...	...	...	4.5	4.6	4.4	...	...	...
1969	10.7	13.6	8.1	11.2	14.3	8.5	...	...	...	4.6	4.8	4.5	...	...	...
1968	10.5	13.3	8.0	11.0	14.1	8.3	...	...	...	4.3	3.7	4.8	...	...	...
1967	10.1	12.8	7.6	10.6	13.6	7.9	...	...	...	4.0	3.4	4.4	...	...	...
1966	9.8	12.5	7.4	10.4	13.3	7.7	...	...	...	3.8	3.9	3.7	...	...	...
1965	9.4	12.0	7.1	9.9	12.7	7.3	...	...	...	4.7	4.9	4.5	...	...	...
1964	9.1	11.7	6.8	9.6	12.3	7.1	...	...	...	3.9	4.5	3.4	...	...	...
1962	8.9	11.4	6.7	9.5	12.2	7.0	...	...	...	4.0	3.9	4.0	...	...	...
1959	8.1	10.3	6.0	8.6	11.0	6.2	...	...	...	3.3	3.8	2.9	...	...	...
1957	7.6	9.6	5.8	8.0	10.1	6.0	...	...	...	2.9	2.7	3.0	...	...	...
1952	7.0	8.3	5.8	...	...	...	...	...	...	2.4	2.0	2.7	...	...	...
1950	6.2	7.3	5.2	...	...	...	...	...	...	2.3	2.1	2.4	...	...	...
1947	5.4	6.2	4.7	5.7	6.6	4.9	...	...	...	2.5	2.4	2.6	...	...	...
1940	4.6	5.5	3.8	4.9	5.9	4.0	...	...	...	1.3	1.4	1.2	...	...	...
25 TO 29 YEARS OLD															
Completed 4 Years of High School or More															
2009	88.6	87.5	89.8	88.4	87.0	89.9	94.6	94.4	94.8	88.9	88.6	89.1	95.2	95.6	94.9
2008	87.8	85.8	89.9	87.6	85.5	89.8	93.7	92.6	94.7	87.4	85.4	89.2	95.6	95.4	95.7
2007	87.0	84.9	89.1	86.5	84.2	89.0	93.5	92.7	94.2	87.4	87.0	87.8	97.2	95.8	98.5
2006	86.4	84.4	88.5	86.1	84.1	88.3	93.4	92.3	94.6	85.6	83.1	87.8	96.6	97.2	96.0
2005	86.2	85.0	87.4	85.7	84.3	87.1	92.8	91.8	93.8	86.5	86.4	86.6	95.5	96.7	94.5
2004	86.6	85.2	88.0	85.9	83.7	88.1	93.3	92.1	94.5	87.9	90.1	86.1	96.2	96.9	95.4
2003[3]	86.5	84.9	88.2	85.7	83.8	87.6	93.7	92.8	94.5	87.6	86.4	88.5	97.1	97.4	96.8
2002	86.4	84.7	88.1	85.9	84.1	87.7	93.0	92.1	93.8	86.6	85.0	88.0	...	...	...

[1]Data in the column labeled "Black" include Black and other races from 1940 to 1962; from 1963 to 2003, data are for the Black population only.
[3]Starting in 2003, respondents could choose more than one race. The race data in this table from 2003 onward represent respondents who indicated only one race. Prior to 2003, Asians were grouped with Pacific Islanders.
[4]Starting in 2001, data are from the expanded Current Population Survey (CPS) sample and were calculated using population controls based on Census 2000.
[5]Beginning with data for 1992, a new question results in different categories than for earlier years. Data shown as "Completed 4 Years of High School or More" are now collected by the category "High School Graduate." Data shown as "Completed 4 Years of College or more," are now collected by the categories, Bachelor's degree; Master's degree; Doctorate degree; and Professional degree. Due to the change in question format, median years of schooling cannot be derived.
... = Not available.

Table A-26. Percent of People 25 Years Old and Over Who Have Completed High School or College, by Race, Hispanic Origin and Sex, Selected Years 1940–2009—*Continued*

(Noninstitutionalized population)

Age, educational attainment level, and year	Hispanic[2]			White alone or in combination			Non-Hispanic White alone or in combination			Black alone or in combination			Asian alone or in combination		
	Both sexes	Male	Female	Both sexes	Male	Female	Both sexes	Male	Female	Both sexes	Male	Female	Both sexes	Male	Female
2006	12.4	11.9	12.9	28.3	29.6	27.0	30.9	32.7	29.2	18.7	17.4	19.7	49.0	51.4	46.8
2005	12.0	11.8	12.1	28.0	29.3	26.7	30.5	32.3	28.9	17.6	16.0	18.9	49.8	53.3	46.6
2004	12.1	11.8	12.3	28.0	29.9	26.3	30.5	32.8	28.3	17.7	16.5	18.6	48.9	52.8	45.4
2003[3]	11.4	11.2	11.6	27.5	29.3	25.8	29.9	32.2	27.9	17.5	16.8	18.0	49.2	52.7	46.0
2002	11.1	11.0	11.2	...	...	...	...	...	...	...	...	...	...	...	...
2001[4]	11.1	10.8	11.4	...	...	...	...	...	...	...	...	...	...	...	...
2000	10.6	10.7	10.6	...	...	...	...	...	...	...	...	...	...	...	...
1999	10.9	10.7	11.0	...	...	...	...	...	...	...	...	...	...	...	...
1998	11.0	11.1	10.9	...	...	...	...	...	...	...	...	...	...	...	...
1997	10.3	10.6	10.1	...	...	...	...	...	...	...	...	...	...	...	...
1996	9.3	10.3	8.3	...	...	...	...	...	...	...	...	...	...	...	...
1995	9.3	10.1	8.4	...	...	...	...	...	...	...	...	...	...	...	...
1994	9.1	9.6	8.6	...	...	...	...	...	...	...	...	...	...	...	...
1993	9.0	9.5	8.5	...	...	...	...	...	...	...	...	...	...	...	...
1992[5]	9.3	10.2	8.5	...	...	...	...	...	...	...	...	...	...	...	...
1991	9.7	10.0	9.4	...	...	...	...	...	...	...	...	...	...	...	...
1990	9.2	9.8	8.7	...	...	...	...	...	...	...	...	...	...	...	...
1989	9.9	11.0	8.8	...	...	...	...	...	...	...	...	...	...	...	...
1988	10.1	12.3	8.1	...	...	...	...	...	...	...	...	...	...	...	...
1987	8.6	9.7	7.5	...	...	...	...	...	...	...	...	...	...	...	...
1986	8.4	9.5	7.4	...	...	...	...	...	...	...	...	...	...	...	...
1985	8.5	9.7	7.3	...	...	...	...	...	...	...	...	...	...	...	...
1984	8.2	9.5	7.0	...	...	...	...	...	...	...	...	...	...	...	...
1983	7.9	9.2	6.8	...	...	...	...	...	...	...	...	...	...	...	...
1982	7.8	9.6	6.2	...	...	...	...	...	...	...	...	...	...	...	...
1981	7.7	9.7	5.9	...	...	...	...	...	...	...	...	...	...	...	...
1980	7.9	9.7	6.2	...	...	...	...	...	...	...	...	...	...	...	...
1979	6.7	8.2	5.3	...	...	...	...	...	...	...	...	...	...	...	...
1978	7.0	8.6	5.7	...	...	...	...	...	...	...	...	...	...	...	...
1977	6.2	8.1	4.4	...	...	...	...	...	...	...	...	...	...	...	...
1976	6.1	8.6	4.0	...	...	...	...	...	...	...	...	...	...	...	...
1975	6.3	8.3	4.6	...	...	...	...	...	...	...	...	...	...	...	...
1974	5.5	7.1	4.0	...	...	...	...	...	...	...	...	...	...	...	...
1973	...	...	...	...	...	...	...	...	...	...	...	...	...	...	...
1972	...	...	...	...	...	...	...	...	...	...	...	...	...	...	...
1971	...	...	...	...	...	...	...	...	...	...	...	...	...	...	...
1970	...	...	...	...	...	...	...	...	...	...	...	...	...	...	...
1969	...	...	...	...	...	...	...	...	...	...	...	...	...	...	...
1968	...	...	...	...	...	...	...	...	...	...	...	...	...	...	...
1967	...	...	...	...	...	...	...	...	...	...	...	...	...	...	...
1966	...	...	...	...	...	...	...	...	...	...	...	...	...	...	...
1965	...	...	...	...	...	...	...	...	...	...	...	...	...	...	...
1964	...	...	...	...	...	...	...	...	...	...	...	...	...	...	...
1962	...	...	...	...	...	...	...	...	...	...	...	...	...	...	...
1959	...	...	...	...	...	...	...	...	...	...	...	...	...	...	...
1957	...	...	...	...	...	...	...	...	...	...	...	...	...	...	...
1952	...	...	...	...	...	...	...	...	...	...	...	...	...	...	...
1950	...	...	...	...	...	...	...	...	...	...	...	...	...	...	...
1947	...	...	...	...	...	...	...	...	...	...	...	...	...	...	...
1940	...	...	...	...	...	...	...	...	...	...	...	...	...	...	...

25 TO 29 YEARS OLD

Completed 4 Years of High School or More

	Both sexes	Male	Female	Both sexes	Male	Female	Both sexes	Male	Female	Both sexes	Male	Female	Both sexes	Male	Female
2009	68.9	66.2	72.5	88.4	87.0	89.9	94.5	94.4	94.6	88.8	88.5	89.1	95.1	95.7	94.6
2008	68.3	65.6	71.9	87.6	85.5	89.8	93.7	92.6	94.8	87.7	85.6	89.4	95.7	95.5	95.9
2007	65.0	60.5	70.7	86.5	84.2	88.8	93.4	92.7	94.1	87.4	87.0	87.8	96.3	95.8	96.8
2006	63.3	60.6	66.7	86.0	83.9	88.2	93.3	92.2	94.5	85.6	83.2	87.7	96.0	96.4	95.7
2005	63.3	63.2	63.4	85.6	84.2	87.0	92.8	91.7	93.8	86.6	86.4	86.7	95.5	96.7	94.4
2004	62.4	60.1	65.2	85.9	83.9	87.9	93.2	92.1	94.4	87.8	89.9	86.2	95.7	97.0	94.5
2003[3]	61.7	59.6	64.2	85.7	83.9	87.6	93.6	92.8	94.4	87.4	86.4	88.5	97.2	97.5	97.0
2002	62.4	60.2	65.0	...	...	...	...	...	...	...	...	...	...	...	...

[2]May be of any race.
[3]Starting in 2003, respondents could choose more than one race. The race data in this table from 2003 onward represent respondents who indicated only one race. Prior to 2003, Asians were grouped with Pacific Islanders.
[4]Starting in 2001, data are from the expanded Current Population Survey (CPS) sample and were calculated using population controls based on Census 2000.
[5]Beginning with data for 1992, a new question results in different categories than for earlier years. Data shown as "Completed 4 Years of High School or More" are now collected by the category "High School Graduate." Data shown as "Completed 4 Years of College or more," are now collected by the categories, Bachelor's degree; Master's degree; Doctorate degree; and Professional degree. Due to the change in question format, median years of schooling cannot be derived.
... = Not available.

Table A-26. Percent of People 25 Years Old and Over Who Have Completed High School or College, by Race, Hispanic Origin and Sex, Selected Years 1940–2009—*Continued*

(Noninstitutionalized population)

Age, educational attainment level, and year	All races			White			Non-Hispanic White			Black[1]			Asian		
	Both sexes	Male	Female	Both sexes	Male	Female	Both sexes	Male	Female	Both sexes	Male	Female	Both sexes	Male	Female
2001[4]	86.8	85.3	88.3	86.4	84.6	88.3	93.4	93.1	93.7	86.3	85.4	87.0	...	...	...
2000	88.1	86.7	89.4	88.3	86.6	90.0	94.0	92.9	95.2	85.9	86.6	85.3	...	...	...
1999	87.8	86.1	89.5	87.6	85.8	89.3	93.0	91.9	94.1	88.2	87.7	88.6	...	...	...
1998	88.1	86.6	89.6	88.1	86.3	90.0	93.6	92.5	94.6	87.6	87.6	87.6	...	...	...
1997	87.4	85.8	88.9	87.6	85.8	89.4	92.9	91.7	94.0	86.2	85.2	87.1	...	...	...
1996	87.3	86.5	88.1	87.5	86.3	88.8	92.6	92.0	93.1	85.6	87.2	84.2	...	...	...
1995	86.8	86.3	87.4	87.4	86.6	88.2	92.5	92.0	93.0	86.5	88.1	85.1	...	...	...
1994	86.1	84.5	87.6	86.5	84.7	88.3	91.1	90.0	92.3	84.1	82.9	85.0	...	...	...
1993	86.7	86.0	87.4	87.3	86.1	88.5	91.2	90.6	91.8	82.8	85.0	80.9	...	...	...
1992[5]	86.3	86.1	86.5	87.0	86.5	87.6	...	...	...	80.9	82.5	79.5	...	...	...
1991	85.4	84.9	85.8	85.8	85.1	86.6	...	...	...	81.7	83.5	80.1	...	...	...
1990	85.7	84.4	87.0	86.3	84.6	88.1	...	...	...	81.7	81.5	81.8	...	...	...
1989	85.5	84.4	86.5	86.0	84.8	87.1	...	...	...	82.2	80.6	83.6	...	...	...
1988	85.7	84.4	87.0	86.5	84.8	88.2	...	...	...	80.7	80.6	80.7	...	...	...
1987	86.0	85.5	86.4	86.3	85.6	87.0	...	...	...	83.3	84.8	82.1	...	...	...
1986	86.1	85.9	86.4	86.5	85.6	87.4	...	...	...	83.4	86.5	80.6	...	...	...
1985	86.1	85.6	86.4	86.8	86.4	87.3	...	...	...	80.6	80.8	80.4	...	...	...
1984	85.9	85.6	86.3	86.9	86.8	87.0	...	...	...	78.9	75.9	81.5	...	...	...
1983	86.0	86.0	86.0	86.9	86.9	86.9	...	...	...	79.4	78.9	79.8	...	...	...
1982	86.2	86.3	86.1	86.9	87.0	86.8	...	...	...	80.9	80.5	81.3	...	...	...
1981	86.3	86.5	86.1	87.6	87.6	87.6	...	...	...	77.3	78.4	76.4	...	...	...
1980	85.4	85.4	85.5	86.9	86.8	87.0	...	...	...	76.6	74.8	78.1	...	...	...
1979	85.6	86.3	84.9	87.0	87.7	86.4	...	...	...	74.8	73.9	75.4	...	...	...
1978	85.3	86.0	84.6	86.3	86.8	85.8	...	...	...	77.3	78.5	76.3	...	...	...
1977	85.4	86.6	84.2	86.8	87.6	86.0	...	...	...	74.4	77.5	72.0	...	...	...
1976	84.7	86.0	83.5	85.9	87.3	84.6	...	...	...	73.8	72.5	74.9	...	...	...
1975	83.1	84.5	81.8	84.4	85.7	83.2	...	...	...	71.0	72.2	70.1	...	...	...
1974	81.9	83.1	80.8	83.4	84.1	82.7	...	...	...	68.2	71.1	66.0	...	...	...
1973	80.2	80.6	79.8	82.0	82.4	81.6	...	...	...	64.2	63.1	64.9	...	...	...
1972	79.8	80.5	79.2	81.5	82.3	80.8	...	...	...	64.1	61.8	66.2	...	...	...
1971	77.2	78.1	76.4	79.5	80.8	78.3	...	...	...	57.5	54.1	60.7	...	...	...
1970	75.4	76.6	74.2	77.8	79.2	76.4	...	...	...	56.2	54.5	57.9	...	...	...
1969	74.7	75.6	73.8	77.0	77.5	76.6	...	...	...	55.8	59.8	52.3	...	...	...
1968	73.2	73.7	72.7	75.3	75.5	75.0	...	...	...	55.8	58.1	53.6	...	...	...
1967	72.5	72.1	72.9	74.8	74.3	75.3	...	...	...	53.4	51.7	55.0	...	...	...
1966	71.0	70.9	71.2	73.8	73.2	74.4	...	...	...	47.9	48.9	47.0	...	...	...
1965	70.3	70.5	70.1	72.8	72.7	72.8	...	...	...	50.3	50.3	50.4	...	...	...
1964	69.2	68.8	69.5	72.1	71.8	72.4	...	...	...	45.0	41.6	47.9	...	...	...
1962	65.9	65.8	66.1	69.2	69.2	69.3	...	...	...	41.6	38.9	43.8	...	...	...
1959	63.9	63.9	64.0	67.2	66.9	67.4	...	...	...	39.5	40.6	38.6	...	...	...
1957	60.2	57.9	62.4	63.3	60.7	65.7	...	...	...	31.6	27.4	35.2	...	...	...
1952	57.1	55.3	58.7	...	...	...	...	...	...	28.1	27.9	28.3	...	...	...
1950	52.8	50.6	55.0	...	...	...	...	...	...	23.6	21.3	25.5	...	...	...
1947	51.4	49.4	53.3	54.9	52.9	56.8	...	...	...	22.3	19.6	24.7	...	...	...
1940	38.1	36.0	40.1	41.2	38.9	43.4	...	...	...	12.3	10.6	13.6	...	...	...
Completed 4 Years of College or More															
2009	30.6	26.6	34.8	31.3	27.0	36.0	37.2	32.6	42.0	19.0	15.2	22.4	59.3	58.0	60.6
2008	30.8	26.8	34.9	31.1	26.7	35.9	37.1	32.6	41.7	20.6	18.7	22.3	59.4	55.1	63.5
2007	29.6	26.3	33.0	29.8	25.8	34.0	35.5	31.9	39.2	18.9	17.9	19.9	60.9	59.8	62.0
2006	28.4	25.3	31.6	28.3	25.0	31.7	34.3	31.4	37.2	18.6	14.9	21.6	60.9	59.8	61.9
2005	28.8	25.5	32.2	28.9	25.3	32.7	34.5	30.7	38.2	17.4	14.1	20.1	61.6	60.5	62.5
2004	28.7	26.1	31.4	28.9	25.8	32.1	34.5	31.4	37.5	16.9	13.4	19.7	61.4	62.0	60.9
2003[3]	28.4	26.0	30.9	28.3	25.3	31.5	34.2	31.4	37.1	17.2	17.5	17.0	61.6	60.9	62.3
2002	29.3	26.9	31.8	29.7	26.5	33.1	35.9	32.6	39.2	17.5	17.4	17.7	...	...	...
2001[4]	28.4	25.5	31.3	28.5	25.1	32.1	33.7	30.4	36.9	16.8	15.6	17.9	...	...	...
2000	29.1	27.9	30.1	29.6	27.8	31.3	34.0	32.3	35.8	17.5	18.1	17.0	...	...	...
1999	28.2	26.8	29.5	29.3	27.6	30.9	33.6	32.0	35.1	15.0	13.1	16.5	...	...	...
1998	27.3	25.6	29.0	28.4	26.5	30.4	32.3	30.5	34.2	15.8	14.2	17.0	...	...	...
1997	27.8	26.3	29.3	28.9	27.2	30.7	32.6	31.2	34.1	14.4	12.1	16.4	...	...	...
1996	27.1	26.1	28.2	28.1	27.2	29.1	31.6	30.9	32.3	14.6	12.4	16.4	...	...	...
1995	24.7	24.5	24.9	26.0	25.4	26.6	28.8	28.4	29.2	15.3	17.2	13.6	...	...	...

[1]Data in the column labeled "Black" include Black and other races from 1940 to 1962; from 1963 to 2003, data are for the Black population only.
[3]Starting in 2003, respondents could choose more than one race. The race data in this table from 2003 onward represent respondents who indicated only one race. Prior to 2003, Asians were grouped with Pacific Islanders.
[4]Starting in 2001, data are from the expanded Current Population Survey (CPS) sample and were calculated using population controls based on Census 2000.
[5]Beginning with data for 1992, a new question results in different categories than for earlier years. Data shown as "Completed 4 Years of High School or More" are now collected by the category "High School Graduate." Data shown as "Completed 4 Years of College or more," are now collected by the categories, Bachelor's degree; Master's degree; Doctorate degree; and Professional degree. Due to the change in question format, median years of schooling cannot be derived.
... = Not available.

Table A-26. Percent of People 25 Years Old and Over Who Have Completed High School or College, by Race, Hispanic Origin and Sex, Selected Years 1940–2009—*Continued*

(Noninstitutionalized population)

Age, educational attainment level, and year	Hispanic[2]			White alone or in combination			Non-Hispanic White alone or in combination			Black alone or in combination			Asian alone or in combination		
	Both sexes	Male	Female	Both sexes	Male	Female	Both sexes	Male	Female	Both sexes	Male	Female	Both sexes	Male	Female
2001[4]	62.4	58.3	67.3	...	...	...	...	...	...	...	...	...	...	...	...
2000	62.8	59.2	66.4	...	...	...	...	...	...	...	...	...	...	...	...
1999	61.6	57.4	66.0	...	...	...	...	...	...	...	...	...	...	...	...
1998	62.8	59.9	66.3	...	...	...	...	...	...	...	...	...	...	...	...
1997	61.8	59.2	64.9	...	...	...	...	...	...	...	...	...	...	...	...
1996	61.1	59.7	62.9	...	...	...	...	...	...	...	...	...	...	...	...
1995	57.1	55.7	58.7	...	...	...	...	...	...	...	...	...	...	...	...
1994	60.3	58.0	63.0	...	...	...	...	...	...	...	...	...	...	...	...
1993	60.9	58.3	64.0	...	...	...	...	...	...	...	...	...	...	...	...
1992[5]	60.9	61.1	60.6	...	...	...	...	...	...	...	...	...	...	...	...
1991	56.7	56.4	57.1	...	...	...	...	...	...	...	...	...	...	...	...
1990	58.2	56.6	59.9	...	...	...	...	...	...	...	...	...	...	...	...
1989	61.0	61.0	61.0	...	...	...	...	...	...	...	...	...	...	...	...
1988	62.0	59.4	65.0	...	...	...	...	...	...	...	...	...	...	...	...
1987	59.8	58.6	61.0	...	...	...	...	...	...	...	...	...	...	...	...
1986	59.1	58.2	60.0	...	...	...	...	...	...	...	...	...	...	...	...
1985	60.9	58.6	63.1	...	...	...	...	...	...	...	...	...	...	...	...
1984	58.6	56.8	60.2	...	...	...	...	...	...	...	...	...	...	...	...
1983	58.3	57.8	58.9	...	...	...	...	...	...	...	...	...	...	...	...
1982	60.9	60.7	61.2	...	...	...	...	...	...	...	...	...	...	...	...
1981	59.8	59.1	60.4	...	...	...	...	...	...	...	...	...	...	...	...
1980	58.6	58.3	58.8	...	...	...	...	...	...	...	...	...	...	...	...
1979	57.0	55.5	58.5	...	...	...	...	...	...	...	...	...	...	...	...
1978	56.6	58.5	54.7	...	...	...	...	...	...	...	...	...	...	...	...
1977	58.1	62.1	54.8	...	...	...	...	...	...	...	...	...	...	...	...
1976	58.1	57.6	58.4	...	...	...	...	...	...	...	...	...	...	...	...
1975	51.7	51.1	52.1	...	...	...	...	...	...	...	...	...	...	...	...
1974	52.5	55.1	49.9	...	...	...	...	...	...	...	...	...	...	...	...
1973	...	...	...	...	...	...	...	...	...	...	...	...	...	...	...
1972	...	...	...	...	...	...	...	...	...	...	...	...	...	...	...
1971	...	...	...	...	...	...	...	...	...	...	...	...	...	...	...
1970	...	...	...	...	...	...	...	...	...	...	...	...	...	...	...
1969	...	...	...	...	...	...	...	...	...	...	...	...	...	...	...
1968	...	...	...	...	...	...	...	...	...	...	...	...	...	...	...
1967	...	...	...	...	...	...	...	...	...	...	...	...	...	...	...
1966	...	...	...	...	...	...	...	...	...	...	...	...	...	...	...
1965	...	...	...	...	...	...	...	...	...	...	...	...	...	...	...
1964	...	...	...	...	...	...	...	...	...	...	...	...	...	...	...
1962	...	...	...	...	...	...	...	...	...	...	...	...	...	...	...
1959	...	...	...	...	...	...	...	...	...	...	...	...	...	...	...
1957	...	...	...	...	...	...	...	...	...	...	...	...	...	...	...
1952	...	...	...	...	...	...	...	...	...	...	...	...	...	...	...
1950	...	...	...	...	...	...	...	...	...	...	...	...	...	...	...
1947	...	...	...	...	...	...	...	...	...	...	...	...	...	...	...
1940	...	...	...	...	...	...	...	...	...	...	...	...	...	...	...
Completed 4 Years of College or More															
2009	12.2	11.0	13.8	31.1	26.8	35.9	37.1	32.4	41.9	19.0	15.0	22.6	58.0	56.7	59.3
2008	12.4	10.0	15.5	31.0	26.6	35.8	36.9	32.4	41.5	20.9	19.3	22.3	57.4	52.9	61.8
2007	11.6	8.6	15.4	29.7	25.7	33.8	35.3	31.7	39.0	19.1	18.1	19.9	59.0	57.8	60.1
2006	9.5	6.9	12.8	28.1	24.8	31.6	34.1	31.2	37.0	18.9	15.0	22.3	59.4	58.4	60.5
2005	11.2	10.2	12.4	28.8	25.3	32.5	34.3	30.6	38.1	17.6	14.6	20.3	60.3	59.0	61.5
2004	10.9	9.6	12.4	28.7	25.7	31.8	34.2	31.2	37.2	16.8	13.4	19.5	59.9	61.1	58.9
2003[3]	10.0	8.4	12.0	28.2	25.2	31.4	34.0	31.2	36.9	17.3	17.4	17.3	60.3	58.8	61.7
2002	8.9	8.3	9.7	...	...	...	...	...	...	...	...	...	...	...	...
2001[4]	10.5	8.2	13.3	...	...	...	...	...	...	...	...	...	...	...	...
2000	9.7	8.3	11.0	...	...	...	...	...	...	...	...	...	...	...	...
1999	8.9	7.5	10.4	...	...	...	...	...	...	...	...	...	...	...	...
1998	10.4	9.5	11.3	...	...	...	...	...	...	...	...	...	...	...	...
1997	11.0	9.6	10.1	...	...	...	...	...	...	...	...	...	...	...	...
1996	10.0	10.2	9.8	...	...	...	...	...	...	...	...	...	...	...	...
1995	8.9	7.8	10.1	...	...	...	...	...	...	...	...	...	...	...	...

[2]May be of any race.
[3]Starting in 2003, respondents could choose more than one race. The race data in this table from 2003 onward represent respondents who indicated only one race. Prior to 2003, Asians were grouped with Pacific Islanders.
[4]Starting in 2001, data are from the expanded Current Population Survey (CPS) sample and were calculated using population controls based on Census 2000.
[5]Beginning with data for 1992, a new question results in different categories than for earlier years. Data shown as "Completed 4 Years of High School or More" are now collected by the category "High School Graduate." Data shown as "Completed 4 Years of College or more," are now collected by the categories, Bachelor's degree; Master's degree; Doctorate degree; and Professional degree. Due to the change in question format, median years of schooling cannot be derived.
... = Not available.

Table A-26.   Percent of People 25 Years Old and Over Who Have Completed High School or College, by Race, Hispanic Origin and Sex, Selected Years 1940–2009—*Continued*

(Noninstitutionalized population)

Age, educational attainment level, and year	All races			White			Non-Hispanic White			Black[1]			Asian		
	Both sexes	Male	Female	Both sexes	Male	Female	Both sexes	Male	Female	Both sexes	Male	Female	Both sexes	Male	Female
1994	23.3	22.5	24.0	24.2	23.6	24.8	27.1	26.8	27.4	13.7	11.7	15.4	...	...	...
1993	23.7	23.4	23.9	24.7	24.4	25.1	27.2	27.2	27.1	13.2	12.6	13.8	...	...	...
1992[5]	23.6	23.2	24.0	25.0	24.2	25.7	...	...	...	11.3	12.0	10.6	...	...	...
1991	23.2	23.0	23.4	24.6	24.1	25.0	...	...	...	11.0	11.5	10.6	...	...	...
1990	23.2	23.7	22.8	24.2	24.2	24.3	...	...	...	13.4	15.1	11.9	...	...	...
1989	23.4	23.9	22.9	24.4	24.8	24.0	...	...	...	12.7	12.0	13.3	...	...	...
1988	22.5	23.2	21.9	23.5	24.0	22.9	...	...	...	12.2	12.6	11.9	...	...	...
1987	22.0	22.3	21.7	23.0	23.3	22.8	...	...	...	11.4	11.6	11.1	...	...	...
1986	22.4	22.9	21.9	23.5	24.1	22.9	...	...	...	11.8	10.1	13.3	...	...	...
1985	22.2	23.1	21.3	23.2	24.2	22.2	...	...	...	11.5	10.3	12.6	...	...	...
1984	21.9	23.2	20.7	23.1	24.3	21.9	...	...	...	11.6	12.9	10.5	...	...	...
1983	22.5	23.9	21.1	23.4	25.0	21.8	...	...	...	12.9	13.1	12.8	...	...	...
1982	21.7	23.3	20.2	22.7	24.5	20.9	...	...	...	12.6	11.8	13.2	...	...	...
1981	21.3	23.1	19.6	22.4	24.3	20.5	...	...	...	11.6	12.1	11.1	...	...	...
1980	22.5	24.0	21.0	23.7	25.5	22.0	...	...	...	11.6	10.5	12.5	...	...	...
1979	23.1	25.6	20.5	24.3	27.1	21.5	...	...	...	12.4	13.3	11.7	...	...	...
1978	23.3	26.0	20.6	24.5	27.6	21.4	...	...	...	11.8	10.7	12.6	...	...	...
1977	24.0	27.0	21.1	25.3	28.5	22.1	...	...	...	12.6	12.8	12.4	...	...	...
1976	23.7	27.5	20.1	24.6	28.7	20.6	...	...	...	13.0	12.0	13.6	...	...	...
1975	21.9	25.1	18.7	22.8	26.3	19.4	...	...	...	10.7	11.4	10.1	...	...	...
1974	20.7	23.9	17.6	22.0	25.3	18.8	...	...	...	7.9	8.8	7.2	...	...	...
1973	19.0	21.6	16.4	19.9	22.8	17.0	...	...	...	8.1	7.1	8.8	...	...	...
1972	19.0	22.0	16.0	19.9	23.1	16.7	...	...	...	8.3	7.1	9.4	...	...	...
1971	16.9	20.1	13.8	17.9	21.3	14.6	...	...	...	6.4	6.4	6.5	...	...	...
1970	16.4	20.0	12.9	17.3	21.3	13.3	...	...	...	7.3	6.7	8.0	...	...	...
1969	16.0	19.4	12.8	17.0	20.6	13.4	...	...	...	6.7	8.1	5.5	...	...	...
1968	14.7	18.0	11.6	15.6	19.1	12.3	...	...	...	5.3	5.3	5.3	...	...	...
1967	14.6	17.2	12.1	15.5	18.3	12.7	...	...	...	5.4	4.2	6.3	...	...	...
1966	14.0	16.8	11.3	14.7	17.9	11.8	...	...	...	5.9	5.4	6.4	...	...	...
1965	12.4	15.6	9.5	13.0	16.4	9.8	...	...	...	6.8	7.3	6.8	...	...	...
1964	12.8	16.6	9.2	13.6	17.5	9.9	...	...	...	5.5	7.5	3.9	...	...	...
1962	13.1	17.2	9.2	14.3	18.7	10.0	...	...	...	4.2	5.7	3.0	...	...	...
1959	11.1	14.8	7.6	11.9	15.9	8.1	...	...	...	4.6	5.6	3.7	...	...	...
1957	10.4	13.5	7.5	11.1	14.5	7.8	...	...	...	4.1	3.3	5.0	...	...	...
1952	10.1	13.8	6.7	...	...	...	...	...	...	4.6	3.2	5.8	...	...	...
1950	7.7	9.6	5.9	...	...	...	...	...	...	2.9	2.4	3.2	...	...	...
1947	5.6	5.8	5.4	5.9	6.2	5.7	...	...	...	2.8	2.6	2.9	...	...	...
1940	5.9	6.9	4.9	6.4	7.5	5.3	...	...	...	1.6	1.5	1.7	...	...	...

[1]Data in the column labeled "Black" include Black and other races from 1940 to 1962; from 1963 to 2003, data are for the Black population only.
[5]Beginning with data for 1992, a new question results in different categories than for earlier years. Data shown as "Completed 4 Years of High School or More" are now collected by the category "High School Graduate." Data shown as "Completed 4 Years of College or more," are now collected by the categories, Bachelor's degree; Master's degree; Doctorate degree; and Professional degree. Due to the change in question format, median years of schooling cannot be derived.
... = Not available.

Table A-26.   Percent of People 25 Years Old and Over Who Have Completed High School or College, by Race, Hispanic Origin and Sex, Selected Years 1940–2009—*Continued*

(Noninstitutionalized population)

Age, educational attainment level, and year	Hispanic[2]			White alone or in combination			Non-Hispanic White alone or in combination			Black alone or in combination			Asian alone or in combination		
	Both sexes	Male	Female	Both sexes	Male	Female	Both sexes	Male	Female	Both sexes	Male	Female	Both sexes	Male	Female
1994................................	8.0	6.6	9.8	...	...	...	...	...	...	...	...	...	...	...	...
1993................................	8.3	7.1	9.8	...	...	...	...	...	...	...	...	...	...	...	...
1992[5]............................	9.5	8.8	10.3	...	...	...	...	...	...	...	...	...	...	...	...
1991................................	9.2	8.1	10.4	...	...	...	...	...	...	...	...	...	...	...	...
1990................................	8.1	7.3	9.1	...	...	...	...	...	...	...	...	...	...	...	...
1989................................	10.1	9.6	10.6	...	...	...	...	...	...	...	...	...	...	...	...
1988................................	11.4	12.1	10.6	...	...	...	...	...	...	...	...	...	...	...	...
1987................................	8.7	9.2	8.2	...	...	...	...	...	...	...	...	...	...	...	...
1986................................	9.0	8.9	9.1	...	...	...	...	...	...	...	...	...	...	...	...
1985................................	11.1	10.9	11.2	...	...	...	...	...	...	...	...	...	...	...	...
1984................................	10.6	9.6	11.6	...	...	...	...	...	...	...	...	...	...	...	...
1983................................	10.4	9.6	11.1	...	...	...	...	...	...	...	...	...	...	...	...
1982................................	9.7	10.7	8.7	...	...	...	...	...	...	...	...	...	...	...	...
1981................................	7.5	8.6	6.5	...	...	...	...	...	...	...	...	...	...	...	...
1980................................	7.7	8.4	6.9	...	...	...	...	...	...	...	...	...	...	...	...
1979................................	7.3	7.9	6.8	...	...	...	...	...	...	...	...	...	...	...	...
1978................................	9.6	9.6	9.7	...	...	...	...	...	...	...	...	...	...	...	...
1977................................	6.7	7.2	6.4	...	...	...	...	...	...	...	...	...	...	...	...
1976................................	7.4	10.3	4.8	...	...	...	...	...	...	...	...	...	...	...	...
1975................................	8.8	10.0	7.3	...	...	...	...	...	...	...	...	...	...	...	...
1974................................	5.7	7.2	4.6	...	...	...	...	...	...	...	...	...	...	...	...
1973................................	...	...	...	...	...	...	...	...	...	...	...	...	...	...	...
1972................................	...	...	...	...	...	...	...	...	...	...	...	...	...	...	...
1971................................	...	...	...	...	...	...	...	...	...	...	...	...	...	...	...
1970................................	...	...	...	...	...	...	...	...	...	...	...	...	...	...	...
1969................................	...	...	...	...	...	...	...	...	...	...	...	...	...	...	...
1968................................	...	...	...	...	...	...	...	...	...	...	...	...	...	...	...
1907................................	...	...	...	...	...	...	...	...	...	...	...	...	...	...	...
1966................................	...	...	...	...	...	...	...	...	...	...	...	...	...	...	...
1965................................	...	...	...	...	...	...	...	...	...	...	...	...	...	...	...
1964................................	...	...	...	...	...	...	...	...	...	...	...	...	...	...	...
1962................................	...	...	...	...	...	...	...	...	...	...	...	...	...	...	...
1959................................	...	...	...	...	...	...	...	...	...	...	...	...	...	...	...
1957................................	...	...	...	...	...	...	...	...	...	...	...	...	...	...	...
1952................................	...	...	...	...	...	...	...	...	...	...	...	...	...	...	...
1950................................	...	...	...	...	...	...	...	...	...	...	...	...	...	...	...
1947................................	...	...	...	...	...	...	...	...	...	...	...	...	...	...	...
1940................................	...	...	...	...	...	...	...	...	...	...	...	...	...	...	...

[5]Beginning with data for 1992, a new question results in different categories than for earlier years. Data shown as "Completed 4 Years of High School or More" are now collected by the category "High School Graduate." Data shown as "Completed 4 Years of College or more," are now collected by the categories, Bachelor's degree; Master's degree; Doctorate degree; and Professional degree. Due to the change in question format, median years of schooling cannot be derived.
... = Not available.

Table A-27. Mean Earnings of Workers 18 Years Old and Over, by Educational Attainment, Race, Hispanic Origin, and Sex, 1975–2008

(Dollars, numbers in thousands.)

Sex, race, Hispanic origin, and year	Total			Not a high school graduate			High school graduate		
	Mean	Number with earnings	Standard error	Mean	Number with earnings	Standard error	Mean	Number with earnings	Standard error
ALL RACES									
Both Sexes									
2008	$42,588	155,989	$161	$21,023	15,217	$303	$31,283	45,182	$200
2007	$42,064	155,738	$155	$21,484	15,330	$269	$31,286	45,393	$197
2006	$41,412	154,438	$170	$20,873	16,652	$223	$31,071	45,936	$235
2005	$39,579	152,215	$162	$19,915	16,317	$184	$29,448	45,652	$185
2004	$37,899	150,095	$155	$19,182	16,372	$252	$28,631	45,571	$193
2003	$37,046	148,660	$144	$18,734	16,282	$183	$27,915	45,064	$159
2002	$36,308	148,492	$148	$18,826	16,931	$265	$27,280	45,407	$177
2001	$35,805	147,829	$155	$18,793	17,293	$308	$26,795	45,641	$186
2000	$34,514	147,966	$148	$17,738	17,425	$269	$25,692	45,977	$142
1999	$32,356	144,640	$183	$16,121	16,737	$299	$24,572	46,082	$186
1998	$30,928	142,053	$183	$16,053	16,742	$306	$23,594	45,987	$203
1997	$29,514	140,367	$183	$16,124	16,962	$346	$22,895	45,976	$206
1996	$28,106	138,703	$176	$15,011	17,075	$286	$22,154	45,908	$209
1995	$26,792	136,221	$164	$14,013	16,990	$201	$21,431	44,546	$225
1994	$25,852	135,096	$153	$13,697	16,479	$288	$20,248	44,614	$170
1993	$24,674	133,119	$148	$12,820	16,575	$237	$19,422	44,779	$162
1992	$23,227	130,860	$99	$12,809	16,612	$152	$18,737	45,340	$110
1991	$22,332	130,371	$93	$12,613	17,553	$153	$18,261	46,508	$104
1990	$21,793	130,080	$91	$12,582	18,698	$115	$17,820	51,977	$95
1989	$21,414	129,094	$92	$12,242	19,137	$112	$17,594	51,846	$100
1988	$20,060	127,564	$88	$11,889	19,635	$118	$16,750	51,297	$98
1987	$19,016	124,874	$83	$11,824	19,748	$133	$15,939	50,815	$91
1986	$18,149	122,757	$72	$11,203	19,665	$149	$15,120	50,104	$77
1985	$17,181	120,651	$67	$10,726	19,692	$133	$14,457	49,674	$74
1984	$16,083	118,183	$57	$10,384	20,206	$130	$13,893	48,452	$68
1983	$15,137	115,095	...	$9,853	20,020	...	$13,044	47,560	...
1982	$14,351	113,451	$52	$9,387	20,789	$101	$12,560	46,584	$64
1981	$13,624	113,301	$48	$9,357	22,296	$110	$12,109	47,332	$59
1980	$12,665	111,919	$45	$8,845	23,028	$95	$11,314	46,795	$54
1979	$11,795	110,826	$43	$8,420	23,783	$75	$10,624	45,497	$50
1978	$10,812	106,436	$41	$7,759	23,787	$71	$9,834	43,510	$49
1977	$9,887	103,119	$35	$7,066	24,854	$60	$9,013	41,696	$41
1976	$9,180	100,510	$32	$6,720	25,035	$57	$8,393	40,570	$39
1975	$8,552	97,881	$31	$6,198	24,916	$53	$7,843	39,827	$38
Male									
2008	$51,148	82,727	$264	$24,831	9,596	$460	$36,753	25,290	$308
2007	$50,110	82,932	$249	$24,985	9,780	$387	$36,839	25,396	$299
2006	$49,647	82,310	$275	$24,072	10,541	$285	$37,356	25,489	$388
2005	$48,034	81,258	$273	$23,222	10,273	$261	$35,248	25,348	$303
2004	$46,008	79,765	$257	$22,537	10,188	$386	$34,050	25,209	$301
2003	$44,726	78,869	$235	$21,447	10,173	$245	$33,266	24,292	$245
2002	$44,310	78,757	$244	$22,091	10,526	$398	$32,673	24,174	$276
2001	$43,648	78,342	$251	$21,508	10,572	$347	$32,363	24,239	$277
2000	$42,772	78,319	$250	$21,007	10,535	$372	$31,446	24,439	$223
1999	$40,257	76,233	$308	$18,855	9,917	$277	$30,414	24,235	$294
1998	$38,134	75,213	$301	$19,155	10,085	$426	$28,742	24,155	$312
1997	$36,556	74,596	$307	$19,575	10,348	$493	$28,307	24,152	$348
1996	$34,705	73,955	$291	$17,826	10,583	$440	$27,642	23,966	$364
1995	$33,251	72,634	$275	$16,748	10,312	$296	$26,333	23,473	$349
1994	$32,087	72,246	$251	$16,633	9,981	$457	$25,038	23,418	$286
1993	$30,568	71,183	$244	$14,946	10,151	$233	$23,973	23,388	$259
1992	$28,448	70,409	$158	$14,934	10,335	$212	$22,978	23,610	$173
1991	$27,494	70,145	$148	$15,056	10,679	$187	$22,663	24,110	$163
1990	$27,164	70,218	$151	$14,991	11,412	$155	$22,378	26,753	$158
1989	$27,025	69,798	$155	$14,727	11,774	$150	$22,508	26,469	$172
1988	$25,344	69,006	$146	$14,551	11,993	$163	$21,481	26,080	$166
1987	$24,015	67,951	$138	$14,544	12,117	$188	$20,364	25,981	$150
1986	$23,057	67,189	$120	$13,703	12,208	$217	$19,453	25,562	$131
1985	$21,823	66,439	$111	$13,124	12,137	$185	$18,575	25,496	$125
1984	$20,452	65,005	$92	$12,775	12,325	$170	$18,016	24,827	$116
1983	$19,175	63,816	$89	$12,052	12,376	$160	$16,728	24,449	$108
1982	$18,244	63,489	$85	$11,513	12,868	$144	$16,160	24,059	$107
1981	$17,542	63,547	$79	$11,668	13,701	$146	$15,900	24,435	$101
1980	$16,382	62,825	$73	$11,042	14,273	$129	$15,002	24,023	$92

Table A-27. Mean Earnings of Workers 18 Years Old and Over, by Educational Attainment, Race, Hispanic Origin, and Sex, 1975–2008—*Continued*

(Dollars, numbers in thousands.)

Sex, race, Hispanic origin, and year	Some college/associate's degree[1]			Bachelor's degree[1]			Advanced degree[1]		
	Mean	Number with earnings	Standard error	Mean	Number with earnings	Standard error	Mean	Number with earnings	Standard error
ALL RACES									
Both Sexes									
2008	$34,808	46,663	$202	$58,613	31,890	$444	$83,144	17,035	$785
2007	$35,138	46,577	$209	$57,181	31,832	$404	$80,977	16,604	$783
2006	$34,650	45,073	$227	$56,788	31,006	$460	$82,320	15,769	$889
2005	$33,496	45,434	$221	$54,689	29,658	$457	$79,946	15,152	$905
2004	$32,010	44,387	$190	$51,568	29,004	$396	$78,224	14,713	$952
2003	$31,498	44,048	$193	$51,206	28,672	$420	$74,602	14,592	$803
2002	$31,046	43,776	$206	$51,194	28,257	$435	$72,824	14,119	$785
2001	$30,782	43,214	$203	$50,623	27,980	$452	$72,869	13,700	$880
2000	$29,939	43,874	$194	$49,595	27,488	$451	$71,194	13,200	$924
1999	$28,403	42,860	$262	$45,678	26,215	$531	$67,697	12,749	$1,122
1998	$27,566	41,412	$302	$43,782	25,818	$533	$63,473	12,095	$1,018
1997	$26,235	40,802	$289	$40,478	25,035	$489	$63,229	11,591	$1,162
1996	$25,181	40,410	$279	$38,112	24,028	$436	$61,317	11,281	$1,204
1995	$23,862	40,142	$245	$36,980	23,285	$463	$56,667	11,258	$490
1994	$22,226	40,135	$193	$37,224	22,712	$491	$56,105	11,155	$961
1993	$21,539	39,429	$173	$35,121	21,815	$425	$55,789	10,521	$1,140
1992	$20,867	37,339	$109	$32,629	21,091	$288	$48,652	10,479	$571
1991	$20,551	35,732	$116	$31,323	20,475	$275	$46,039	10,103	$571
1990	$20,694	28,993	$165	$31,112	18,128	$300	$41,458	12,285	$488
1989	$20,255	28,078	$161	$30,736	17,767	$304	$41,019	12,265	$506
1988	$19,066	27,217	$171	$28,344	17,308	$286	$37,724	12,109	$458
1987	$18,054	26,404	$156	$26,919	16,497	$289	$35,968	11,411	$447
1986	$17,073	26,113	$135	$26,511	15,788	$251	$34,787	11,087	$393
1985	$16,349	25,402	$127	$24,877	15,373	$238	$32,909	10,510	$367
1984	$14,936	24,463	$107	$23,072	14,653	$191	$30,192	10,410	$281
1983	$14,245	23,208	...	$21,532	13,929	...	$28,333	10,377	...
1982	$13,503	22,602	$105	$20,272	13,425	$181	$26,915	10,051	$272
1981	$13,176	21,759	$101	$19,006	12,579	$173	$25,281	9,336	$266
1980	$12,409	21,384	$97	$18,075	12,175	$171	$23,308	8,535	$254
1979	$11,377	21,174	$90	$16,514	11,751	$163	$21,874	8,621	$251
1978	$10,357	20,121	$85	$15,291	11,001	$159	$20,173	8,017	$248
1977	$9,607	18,905	$76	$14,207	10,357	$136	$19,077	7,309	$222
1976	$8,813	17,786	$76	$13,033	10,132	$120	$17,911	6,985	$218
1975	$8,388	16,917	$70	$12,332	9,764	$121	$16,725	6,457	$206
Male									
2008	$42,221	22,830	$341	$72,868	16,100	$745	$103,980	8,909	$1,315
2007	$41,709	22,916	$300	$70,898	16,109	$686	$100,550	8,730	$1,324
2006	$41,521	21,952	$357	$69,818	15,769	$757	$101,441	8,556	$1,436
2005	$40,995	22,173	$393	$67,980	15,217	$782	$100,379	8,245	$1,526
2004	$39,509	21,473	$333	$63,753	14,860	$656	$97,855	8,032	$1,550
2003	$38,451	21,534	$332	$63,084	14,849	$702	$91,831	8,019	$1,262
2002	$38,377	21,599	$371	$63,503	14,667	$710	$90,761	7,788	$1,269
2001	$37,429	21,390	$321	$63,354	14,507	$772	$90,130	7,631	$1,411
2000	$37,372	21,526	$349	$62,609	14,375	$779	$88,077	7,442	$1,468
1999	$35,326	21,173	$471	$57,706	13,683	$888	$84,051	7,225	$1,836
1998	$34,179	20,545	$531	$55,057	13,486	$901	$77,217	6,942	$1,543
1997	$32,641	20,359	$499	$50,056	13,008	$818	$78,032	6,728	$1,865
1996	$31,426	20,208	$488	$46,702	12,562	$720	$74,406	6,636	$1,792
1995	$29,851	19,918	$433	$46,111	12,251	$802	$69,588	6,679	$1,570
1994	$27,636	19,859	$324	$46,278	12,324	$796	$67,032	6,663	$1,422
1993	$26,614	19,532	$301	$43,499	11,810	$669	$68,221	6,302	$1,756
1992	$25,660	18,768	$169	$40,039	11,353	$456	$58,324	6,344	$837
1991	$25,345	18,076	$183	$38,484	11,126	$432	$54,449	6,154	$837
1990	$26,120	14,844	$288	$38,901	9,807	$505	$49,768	7,402	$751
1989	$25,555	14,384	$278	$38,692	9,737	$510	$50,144	7,434	$777
1988	$23,827	14,019	$285	$35,906	9,466	$479	$45,677	7,449	$689
1987	$22,781	13,433	$268	$33,677	9,286	$472	$43,140	7,134	$663
1986	$21,784	13,502	$229	$33,376	8,908	$406	$41,836	7,009	$583
1985	$20,698	13,385	$208	$31,433	8,794	$386	$39,768	6,627	$548
1984	$18,863	12,818	$178	$29,203	8,387	$301	$35,804	6,648	$403
1983	$18,052	12,261	$187	$27,239	8,010	$295	$33,635	6,719	$388
1982	$17,108	12,103	$172	$25,758	7,865	$285	$32,109	6,594	$390
1981	$16,870	11,784	$168	$24,353	7,393	$273	$30,072	6,235	$376
1980	$15,871	11,663	$158	$23,340	7,132	$272	$27,846	5,733	$360

[1]For data prior to 1991, "Some college/Associate degree" equals 1 to 3 years of college completed; "Bachelor's degree" equals 4 years of college; "Advanced degree" equals 5 or more years of college completed.
... = Not available.

Table A-27.   Mean Earnings of Workers 18 Years Old and Over, by Educational Attainment, Race, Hispanic Origin, and Sex, 1975–2008—*Continued*

(Dollars, numbers in thousands.)

Sex, race, Hispanic origin, and year	Total			Not a high school graduate			High school graduate		
	Mean	Number with earnings	Standard error	Mean	Number with earnings	Standard error	Mean	Number with earnings	Standard error
1979............................	$15,430	62,464	$70	$10,628	14,711	$102	$14,317	23,318	$87
1978............................	$14,154	60,586	$67	$9,894	14,550	$93	$13,188	22,650	$85
1977............................	$12,888	59,441	$56	$8,939	15,369	$81	$12,092	21,846	$70
1976............................	$11,923	58,419	$52	$8,522	15,634	$79	$11,189	21,499	$65
1975............................	$11,091	57,297	$49	$7,843	15,613	$71	$10,475	21,347	$64
Female									
2008............................	$32,922	73,262	$162	$14,521	5,621	$210	$24,329	19,892	$218
2007............................	$32,899	72,805	$164	$15,315	5,550	$277	$24,234	19,997	$224
2006............................	$32,015	72,128	$178	$15,352	6,110	$345	$23,236	20,447	$194
2005............................	$29,897	70,956	$141	$14,294	6,044	$200	$22,208	20,304	$156
2004............................	$28,691	70,285	$149	$13,655	6,183	$182	$21,923	20,361	$205
2003............................	$28,367	69,790	$147	$14,214	6,108	$255	$21,659	20,772	$182
2002............................	$27,271	69,735	$143	$13,459	6,404	$230	$21,141	21,233	$200
2001............................	$26,962	69,487	$162	$14,524	6,720	$569	$20,489	21,402	$232
2000............................	$25,228	69,647	$131	$12,739	6,890	$360	$19,162	21,538	$152
1999............................	$23,551	68,409	$165	$12,145	6,819	$604	$18,092	21,847	$196
1998............................	$22,818	66,840	$180	$11,353	6,657	$401	$17,898	21,832	$237
1997............................	$21,528	65,771	$163	$10,725	6,614	$415	$16,906	21,824	$179
1996............................	$20,570	64,748	$165	$10,421	6,492	$193	$16,161	21,942	$160
1995............................	$19,414	63,587	$144	$9,790	6,678	$208	$15,970	21,073	$263
1994............................	$18,684	62,850	$143	$9,189	6,498	$165	$14,955	21,195	$149
1993............................	$17,900	61,937	$141	$9,462	6,425	$482	$14,446	21,391	$174
1992............................	$17,145	60,451	$96	$9,311	6,277	$178	$14,128	21,730	$117
1991............................	$16,320	60,226	$91	$8,818	6,875	$161	$13,523	22,398	$109
1990............................	$15,493	59,862	$86	$8,808	7,286	$169	$12,986	25,224	$103
1989............................	$14,809	59,296	$84	$8,268	7,363	$167	$12,468	25,377	$98
1988............................	$13,833	58,558	$84	$7,711	7,642	$165	$11,857	25,217	$100
1987............................	$13,049	56,923	$80	$7,504	7,631	$171	$11,309	24,834	$100
1986............................	$12,214	55,568	$67	$7,109	7,457	$169	$10,606	24,542	$78
1985............................	$11,493	54,212	$63	$6,874	7,555	$179	$10,115	24,178	$76
1984............................	$10,742	53,178	$56	$6,644	7,881	$203	$9,561	23,625	$69
1983............................	$10,111	51,279	...	$6,292	7,644	...	$9,147	23,111	...
1982............................	$9,403	49,962	$50	$5,932	7,921	$123	$8,715	22,525	$66
1981............................	$8,619	49,754	$44	$5,673	8,595	$165	$8,063	22,897	$57
1980............................	$7,909	49,094	$42	$5,263	8,755	$134	$7,423	22,772	$53
1979............................	$7,099	48,362	$38	$4,840	9,072	$106	$6,741	22,179	$48
1978............................	$6,396	45,850	$35	$4,397	9,237	$111	$6,192	20,860	$46
1977............................	$5,804	43,678	$30	$4,032	9,485	$86	$5,624	19,850	$39
1976............................	$5,373	42,091	$28	$3,723	9,401	$76	$5,240	19,071	$37
1975............................	$4,968	40,584	$26	$3,438	9,303	$75	$4,802	18,480	$34
WHITE									
Both Sexes									
2008............................	$43,666	127,552	$183	$21,590	12,379	$326	$32,126	36,819	$222
2007............................	$43,139	127,413	$176	$22,289	12,363	$325	$32,223	37,058	$223
2006............................	$42,395	126,570	$190	$21,464	13,582	$263	$32,083	37,362	$270
2005............................	$40,717	124,870	$186	$20,264	13,157	$206	$30,569	37,122	$219
2004............................	$38,946	123,452	$176	$19,367	13,289	$259	$29,605	37,114	$227
2003............................	$38,053	122,599	$164	$19,110	13,094	$199	$28,708	36,951	$182
2002............................	$37,376	122,699	$168	$19,264	13,740	$289	$28,145	37,380	$205
2001............................	$36,844	122,930	$174	$19,120	14,012	$337	$27,700	37,969	$218
2000............................	$35,527	123,039	$169	$18,285	14,172	$322	$26,444	38,133	$162
1999............................	$33,326	120,916	$210	$16,623	13,585	$359	$25,270	38,428	$211
1998............................	$32,057	119,201	$211	$16,474	13,531	$362	$24,409	38,397	$236
1997............................	$30,515	117,985	$210	$16,596	13,780	$409	$23,618	38,409	$240
1996............................	$28,844	117,230	$192	$15,358	13,972	$340	$22,782	38,463	$235
1995............................	$27,556	115,636	$181	$14,234	13,869	$234	$22,154	37,802	$261
1994............................	$26,696	114,586	$173	$13,941	13,119	$350	$20,911	37,562	$196
1993............................	$25,440	113,342	$165	$13,171	13,480	$283	$19,918	37,826	$166
1992............................	$23,932	112,120	$106	$13,193	13,494	$174	$19,265	38,692	$123
1991............................	$22,998	111,830	$103	$12,914	14,041	$178	$18,766	39,764	$115
1990............................	$22,401	111,972	$101	$12,773	15,191	$126	$18,257	44,635	$105
1989............................	$22,035	111,243	$102	$12,654	15,628	$124	$18,011	44,726	$111
1988............................	$20,616	110,159	$97	$12,236	16,042	$129	$17,183	44,399	$107
1987............................	$19,599	108,407	$93	$12,502	16,165	$145	$16,339	44,235	$99
1986............................	$18,698	106,384	$79	$11,605	16,094	$134	$15,514	43,593	$84
1985............................	$17,709	104,818	$75	$11,115	16,149	$118	$14,815	43,347	$81

... = Not available.

Table A-27.   Mean Earnings of Workers 18 Years Old and Over, by Educational Attainment, Race, Hispanic Origin, and Sex, 1975–2008—Continued

(Dollars, numbers in thousands.)

Sex, race, Hispanic origin, and year	Some college/associate's degree[1]			Bachelor's degree[1]			Advanced degree[1]		
	Mean	Number with earnings	Standard error	Mean	Number with earnings	Standard error	Mean	Number with earnings	Standard error
1979	$14,716	11,781	$145	$21,482	6,889	$260	$26,411	5,765	$358
1978	$13,382	11,352	$137	$19,861	6,611	$250	$24,274	5,422	$351
1977	$12,393	10,848	$122	$18,187	6,341	$210	$22,786	5,038	$311
1976	$11,376	10,282	$122	$16,714	6,135	$186	$21,202	4,868	$301
1975	$10,805	9,851	$112	$15,758	5,960	$188	$19,672	4,526	$283
Female									
2008	$27,708	23,833	$213	$44,078	15,789	$441	$60,301	8,126	$690
2007	$28,773	23,660	$284	$43,127	15,722	$381	$59,273	7,873	$655
2006	$28,126	23,121	$275	$43,302	15,237	$482	$59,636	7,213	$843
2005	$26,348	23,260	$202	$40,684	14,440	$412	$55,553	6,906	$655
2004	$24,983	22,914	$179	$38,776	14,143	$396	$54,623	6,680	$894
2003	$24,848	22,514	$193	$38,447	13,823	$405	$53,579	6,572	$808
2002	$23,905	22,176	$172	$37,909	13,589	$448	$50,756	6,330	$675
2001	$24,268	21,824	$241	$36,913	13,472	$396	$51,160	6,068	$790
2000	$22,779	22,348	$161	$35,328	13,113	$357	$49,368	5,757	$842
1999	$21,644	22,687	$215	$32,546	12,533	$477	$46,307	5,523	$802
1998	$21,056	20,867	$273	$31,452	12,332	$467	$44,954	5,153	$1,018
1997	$19,856	20,442	$277	$30,119	12,027	$460	$42,744	4,863	$863
1996	$18,933	20,202	$406	$28,701	11,466	$421	$42,625	4,646	$1,333
1995	$17,962	20,224	$213	$26,841	11,034	$341	$37,813	4,578	$702
1994	$16,928	20,276	$199	$26,483	10,388	$463	$39,905	4,493	$1,040
1993	$16,555	19,897	$155	$25,232	10,005	$441	$37,212	4,218	$986
1992	$16,023	18,571	$138	$23,991	9,738	$272	$33,814	4,135	$594
1991	$15,643	17,657	$141	$22,802	9,348	$258	$32,929	3,948	$594
1990	$15,002	14,149	$154	$21,933	8,321	$270	$28,862	4,883	$459
1989	$14,688	13,694	$155	$21,089	8,030	$264	$26,977	4,831	$469
1988	$14,009	13,198	$179	$19,216	7,842	$253	$25,010	4,660	$451
1987	$13,158	12,971	$155	$18,217	7,211	$261	$24,004	4,277	$447
1986	$12,029	12,611	$133	$17,623	6,880	$233	$22,672	4,078	$367
1985	$11,504	12,017	$134	$16,114	6,579	$207	$21,202	3,883	$334
1984	$10,614	11,645	$110	$14,865	6,266	$193	$20,275	3,762	$313
1983	$9,981	10,947	…	$13,808	5,919	…	$18,593	3,658	…
1982	$9,348	10,499	$108	$12,511	5,560	$167	$17,000	3,457	$272
1981	$8,811	9,975	$98	$11,384	5,186	$156	$15,647	3,101	$264
1980	$8,256	9,721	$99	$10,628	5,043	$152	$14,022	2,802	$241
1979	$7,190	9,393	$89	$9,474	4,862	$137	$12,717	2,856	$231
1978	$6,441	8,769	$79	$8,408	4,390	$128	$11,603	2,595	$222
1977	$5,856	8,057	$69	$7,923	4,016	$115	$10,848	2,271	$191
1976	$5,301	7,504	$70	$7,383	3,997	$102	$10,345	2,117	$199
1975	$5,019	7,066	$62	$6,963	3,804	$98	$9,818	1,931	$187
WHITE									
Both Sexes									
2008	$35,622	37,891	$228	$59,866	26,487	$507	$84,739	13,973	$887
2007	$35,685	37,988	$218	$58,652	26,310	$466	$82,384	13,692	$895
2006	$35,338	36,878	$253	$57,932	25,763	$506	$83,185	12,983	$979
2005	$34,326	37,409	$254	$55,785	24,652	$515	$81,697	12,527	$1,045
2004	$32,751	36,547	$210	$52,877	24,061	$447	$79,071	12,397	$1,070
2003	$32,346	36,318	$221	$52,259	24,010	$475	$75,638	12,226	$901
2002	$31,878	36,023	$235	$52,479	23,638	$494	$73,870	11,916	$869
2001	$31,482	35,722	$224	$51,631	23,531	$492	$74,398	11,694	$990
2000	$30,638	36,334	$224	$50,969	23,110	$517	$71,983	11,288	$1,006
1999	$29,105	35,634	$305	$46,894	22,322	$609	$68,910	10,949	$1,236
1998	$28,318	34,540	$342	$44,852	22,266	$604	$65,379	10,467	$1,147
1997	$26,906	34,274	$337	$41,439	21,528	$556	$65,058	9,994	$1,279
1996	$25,511	34,087	$293	$38,936	20,846	$489	$61,779	9,861	$1,230
1995	$24,349	33,850	$264	$37,711	20,203	$503	$57,054	9,914	$1,040
1994	$22,648	34,006	$218	$37,996	19,917	$551	$56,475	9,981	$1,020
1993	$21,924	33,728	$193	$35,846	18,922	$469	$56,964	9,386	$1,241
1992	$21,357	32,014	$120	$33,092	18,555	$312	$49,347	9,363	$611
1991	$21,013	30,973	$127	$31,837	18,033	$301	$46,498	9,019	$611
1990	$21,095	25,105	$182	$31,626	15,993	$328	$41,908	11,049	$522
1989	$20,678	24,212	$177	$31,266	15,723	$331	$41,610	10,952	$546
1988	$19,384	23,643	$187	$28,886	15,221	$314	$38,129	10,854	$489
1987	$18,265	23,083	$171	$27,741	14,624	$317	$36,175	10,300	$477
1986	$17,371	22,653	$146	$27,061	14,055	$271	$35,265	9,987	$422
1985	$16,701	22,131	$138	$25,376	13,670	$261	$33,401	9,522	$391

[1]For data prior to 1991, "Some college/Associate degree" equals 1 to 3 years of college completed; "Bachelor's degree" equals 4 years of college; "Advanced degree" equals 5 or more years of college completed.
… = Not available.

Table A-27. Mean Earnings of Workers 18 Years Old and Over, by Educational Attainment, Race, Hispanic Origin, and Sex, 1975–2008—*Continued*

(Dollars, numbers in thousands.)

Sex, race, Hispanic origin, and year	Total			Not a high school graduate			High school graduate		
	Mean	Number with earnings	Standard error	Mean	Number with earnings	Standard error	Mean	Number with earnings	Standard error
1984	$16,546	103,022	$62	$10,732	16,559	$113	$14,274	42,547	$74
1983	$15,556	101,035	...	$10,239	16,568	...	$13,357	42,007	...
1982	$14,767	99,488	$57	$9,719	17,132	$95	$12,854	41,157	$70
1981	$14,027	99,510	$53	$9,737	18,298	$105	$12,355	42,080	$64
1980	$13,040	98,358	$49	$9,743	18,925	$86	$11,524	41,600	$58
1979	$12,155	97,544	$47	$8,827	19,504	$80	$10,431	40,458	$54
1978	$11,135	94,002	$44	$8,135	19,516	$83	$10,020	38,915	$53
1977	$10,191	91,254	$37	$7,415	20,492	$65	$9,173	37,521	$44
1976	$9,469	89,099	$35	$7,018	20,625	$62	$8,559	36,523	$41
1975	$8,815	86,894	$33	$6,438	20,696	$57	$8,005	35,799	$41
Male									
2008	$52,672	68,816	$295	$25,386	8,113	$477	$37,852	20,899	$333
2007	$51,781	69,099	$285	$25,886	8,170	$453	$38,214	21,129	$350
2006	$51,013	68,752	$305	$24,579	8,932	$324	$38,833	21,090	$449
2005	$49,611	67,874	$309	$23,556	8,582	$285	$36,753	20,914	$355
2004	$47,404	66,677	$288	$22,598	8,591	$380	$35,360	20,781	$350
2003	$46,114	66,199	$266	$21,791	8,500	$251	$34,224	20,238	$276
2002	$45,793	66,202	$273	$22,539	8,841	$416	$33,920	20,156	$321
2001	$45,071	66,216	$279	$22,006	8,833	$400	$33,545	20,465	$319
2000	$44,181	66,222	$282	$21,561	8,859	$431	$32,528	20,553	$253
1999	$41,598	64,856	$349	$19,320	8,286	$313	$31,279	20,526	$326
1998	$39,638	64,181	$341	$19,632	8,430	$490	$29,782	20,388	$359
1997	$37,933	63,738	$347	$20,071	8,670	$563	$29,298	20,426	$402
1996	$35,821	63,532	$320	$18,246	8,899	$514	$28,591	20,329	$405
1995	$34,276	62,520	$298	$17,032	8,660	$338	$27,467	19,982	$403
1994	$33,292	62,029	$283	$16,835	8,133	$547	$26,125	19,833	$330
1993	$31,719	61,356	$270	$15,295	8,430	$265	$24,781	19,835	$264
1992	$29,515	60,919	$174	$15,414	8,487	$241	$23,844	20,259	$192
1991	$28,516	60,770	$163	$15,499	8,720	$211	$23,475	20,765	$179
1990	$28,105	60,676	$167	$15,319	9,476	$168	$23,135	23,088	$174
1989	$28,013	60,877	$171	$15,217	9,805	$165	$23,291	23,029	$191
1988	$26,184	60,221	$160	$14,943	10,008	$175	$22,216	22,707	$181
1987	$24,898	59,468	$152	$15,303	10,132	$202	$21,012	22,682	$162
1986	$23,892	58,932	$131	$14,168	10,239	$183	$20,128	22,392	$143
1985	$22,604	58,385	$122	$13,579	10,163	$158	$19,203	22,357	$136
1984	$21,174	57,362	$100	$13,248	10,280	$148	$18,681	21,989	$125
1983	$19,812	56,641	$96	$12,573	10,387	$140	$17,281	21,733	$117
1982	$18,859	56,364	$92	$11,952	10,816	$129	$16,662	21,436	$116
1981	$18,141	56,397	$86	$12,094	11,523	$142	$16,352	21,809	$109
1980	$16,945	55,772	$79	$11,539	11,937	$114	$15,382	21,453	$99
1979	$15,971	55,556	$76	$11,127	12,291	$109	$13,916	20,834	$94
1978	$14,627	54,113	$72	$10,358	12,141	$103	$13,534	20,328	$91
1977	$13,329	53,174	$60	$9,366	12,903	$86	$12,377	19,773	$74
1976	$12,342	52,312	$56	$8,867	13,117	$85	$11,497	19,446	$69
1975	$11,448	51,510	$53	$8,110	13,191	$77	$10,726	19,361	$69
Female									
2008	$33,115	58,735	$185	$14,370	4,265	$227	$24,610	15,919	$255
2007	$32,899	58,313	$172	$15,278	4,192	$343	$24,276	15,929	$214
2006	$32,148	57,818	$195	$15,483	4,650	$437	$23,334	16,272	$186
2005	$30,125	56,995	$165	$14,086	4,575	$228	$22,590	16,208	$183
2004	$28,966	56,705	$171	$13,459	4,703	$195	$22,260	16,358	$247
2003	$28,591	56,400	$162	$14,149	4,593	$310	$22,028	16,712	$211
2002	$27,512	56,496	$165	$13,354	4,898	$286	$21,388	17,224	$226
2001	$27,240	56,714	$181	$14,197	5,178	$596	$20,866	17,503	$278
2000	$25,441	56,816	$148	$12,823	5,313	$458	$19,330	17,579	$173
1999	$23,756	56,061	$189	$12,405	5,299	$770	$18,381	17,902	$230
1998	$23,213	55,020	$211	$11,255	5,102	$498	$18,327	18,009	$280
1997	$21,779	54,247	$189	$10,700	5,111	$527	$17,166	17,983	$207
1996	$20,590	53,697	$161	$10,290	5,073	$210	$16,270	18,134	$178
1995	$19,647	53,117	$164	$9,582	5,208	$239	$16,196	17,820	$304
1994	$18,912	52,557	$163	$9,220	4,987	$192	$15,078	17,729	$168
1993	$18,028	51,986	$154	$9,624	5,050	$606	$14,557	17,991	$174
1992	$17,289	51,200	$106	$9,428	5,007	$207	$14,233	18,434	$129
1991	$16,431	51,060	$98	$8,677	5,321	$174	$13,621	18,999	$118
1990	$15,559	50,905	$94	$8,725	5,715	$186	$13,031	21,547	$113
1989	$14,810	50,366	$91	$8,338	5,823	$182	$12,406	21,697	$107
1988	$13,902	49,938	$93	$7,747	6,034	$184	$11,915	21,692	$110

... = Not available.

Table A-27.   Mean Earnings of Workers 18 Years Old and Over, by Educational Attainment, Race, Hispanic Origin, and Sex, 1975–2008—*Continued*

(Dollars, numbers in thousands.)

Sex, race, Hispanic origin, and year	Some college/associate's degree[1]			Bachelor's degree[1]			Advanced degree[1]		
	Mean	Number with earnings	Standard error	Mean	Number with earnings	Standard error	Mean	Number with earnings	Standard error
1984	$15,197	21,451	$117	$23,472	13,056	$207	$30,515	9,409	$298
1983	$14,486	20,452	...	$21,914	12,577	...	$28,532	9,430	...
1982	$13,799	19,967	$114	$20,760	12,103	$195	$27,040	9,127	$286
1981	$13,424	19,102	$112	$19,389	11,450	$185	$25,564	8,582	$280
1980	$12,677	18,888	$106	$18,434	11,067	$183	$23,466	7,876	$267
1979	$11,574	18,835	$98	$16,758	10,807	$172	$22,085	7,940	$266
1978	$10,504	18,022	$91	$15,463	10,171	$168	$20,531	7,376	$265
1977	$9,771	16,968	$82	$14,462	9,534	$144	$19,337	6,739	$235
1976	$8,958	16,127	$82	$13,279	9,325	$127	$18,153	6,498	$230
1975	$8,525	15,423	$75	$12,597	8,955	$129	$16,920	6,021	$217
Male									
2008	$43,463	18,849	$374	$75,053	13,596	$835	$107,099	7,356	$1,491
2007	$42,903	18,995	$332	$73,477	13,577	$790	$103,293	7,227	$1,514
2006	$42,684	18,340	$403	$71,735	13,326	$831	$103,340	7,063	$1,555
2005	$42,206	18,583	$444	$69,852	12,900	$857	$103,144	6,893	$1,747
2004	$40,639	17,990	$358	$65,652	12,555	$722	$100,084	6,758	$1,767
2003	$39,594	18,060	$375	$65,264	12,665	$800	$94,017	6,734	$1,418
2002	$39,605	18,068	$414	$65,439	12,512	$787	$92,733	6,623	$1,390
2001	$38,501	17,957	$344	$65,046	12,396	$838	$92,304	6,562	$1,577
2000	$38,476	18,179	$398	$64,831	12,271	$880	$89,812	6,359	$1,617
1999	$36,518	17,928	$544	$59,606	11,851	$1,004	$85,345	6,265	$2,016
1998	$35,277	17,407	$588	$56,620	11,874	$1,001	$79,734	6,083	$1,716
1997	$33,691	17,423	$571	$51,678	11,340	$920	$80,322	5,879	$2,023
1996	$32,238	17,418	$534	$48,014	11,065	$800	$75,481	5,821	$1,871
1995	$30,529	17,136	$451	$47,016	10,851	$852	$70,155	5,891	$1,634
1994	$28,240	17,091	$361	$47,575	10,992	$880	$67,629	5,979	$1,504
1993	$27,297	16,959	$334	$44,505	10,452	$722	$70,000	5,680	$1,914
1992	$26,387	16,335	$187	$40,893	10,118	$488	$59,329	5,720	$890
1991	$26,090	15,873	$198	$39,547	9,893	$468	$55,257	5,519	$890
1990	$26,841	13,003	$317	$39,780	8,770	$546	$50,385	6,731	$798
1989	$26,260	12,582	$303	$39,654	8,750	$553	$51,031	6,710	$831
1988	$24,462	12,277	$310	$36,637	8,467	$521	$46,181	6,762	$728
1987	$23,310	11,771	$295	$34,865	8,384	$510	$43,440	6,499	$702
1986	$22,303	11,846	$248	$34,273	8,041	$437	$42,480	6,413	$618
1985	$21,240	11,831	$224	$32,165	7,970	$416	$40,358	6,064	$580
1984	$19,344	11,387	$193	$29,781	7,624	$321	$36,219	6,081	$423
1983	$18,388	10,974	$202	$27,726	7,379	$309	$33,981	6,168	$409
1982	$17,571	10,822	$186	$26,404	7,242	$302	$32,266	6,047	$406
1981	$17,303	10,448	$184	$24,943	6,824	$289	$30,396	5,794	$393
1980	$16,313	10,400	$171	$23,803	6,618	$286	$27,991	5,363	$373
1979	$15,043	10,572	$157	$21,785	6,464	$271	$26,645	5,395	$374
1978	$13,589	10,350	$146	$20,085	6,205	$263	$24,635	5,088	$369
1977	$12,657	9,853	$131	$18,521	5,941	$219	$23,093	4,704	$325
1976	$11,616	9,394	$130	$16,995	5,765	$194	$21,490	4,589	$314
1975	$11,028	9,096	$119	$16,079	5,587	$197	$19,858	4,275	$295
Female									
2008	$27,859	19,041	$248	$43,848	12,891	$512	$59,877	6,616	$736
2007	$28,466	18,993	$271	$42,846	12,733	$414	$59,006	6,464	$726
2006	$28,069	18,537	$296	$43,142	12,437	$512	$59,141	5,920	$974
2005	$26,547	18,825	$234	$40,344	11,751	$484	$55,461	5,634	$744
2004	$25,104	18,556	$208	$38,898	11,445	$467	$53,895	5,641	$894
2003	$25,177	18,258	$222	$37,739	11,344	$410	$53,102	5,492	$889
2002	$24,101	17,954	$200	$37,903	11,126	$526	$50,270	5,293	$754
2001	$24,387	17,764	$276	$36,698	11,135	$407	$51,499	5,131	$895
2000	$22,790	18,155	$184	$35,273	10,838	$413	$48,982	4,929	$849
1999	$21,598	17,705	$242	$32,507	10,471	$550	$45,741	4,684	$832
1998	$21,246	17,132	$321	$31,406	10,393	$536	$45,462	4,384	$1,249
1997	$19,892	16,852	$325	$30,041	10,188	$523	$43,236	4,114	$967
1996	$18,482	16,669	$185	$28,667	9,781	$467	$42,049	4,041	$1,202
1995	$18,011	16,714	$246	$26,916	9,352	$383	$37,864	4,022	$709
1994	$16,998	16,915	$225	$26,198	8,925	$525	$39,816	4,002	$1,113
1993	$16,490	16,769	$168	$25,161	8,470	$501	$36,988	3,705	$967
1992	$16,116	15,679	$149	$23,738	8,437	$295	$33,675	3,643	$635
1991	$15,677	15,100	$155	$22,471	8,140	$276	$32,687	3,500	$635
1990	$14,922	12,102	$165	$21,725	7,223	$294	$28,694	4,318	$486
1989	$14,640	11,630	$170	$20,741	6,973	$272	$26,709	4,242	$510
1988	$13,898	11,366	$198	$19,169	6,754	$274	$24,824	4,092	$488

[1]For data prior to 1991, "Some college/Associate degree" equals 1 to 3 years of college completed; "Bachelor's degree" equals 4 years of college; "Advanced degree" equals 5 or more years of college completed.
... = Not available.

Table A-27. Mean Earnings of Workers 18 Years Old and Over, by Educational Attainment, Race, Hispanic Origin, and Sex, 1975–2008—*Continued*

(Dollars, numbers in thousands.)

Sex, race, Hispanic origin, and year	Total			Not a high school graduate			High school graduate		
	Mean	Number with earnings	Standard error	Mean	Number with earnings	Standard error	Mean	Number with earnings	Standard error
1987	$13,161	48,939	$89	$7,798	6,033	$190	$11,421	21,553	$110
1986	$12,247	47,452	$72	$7,123	5,855	$181	$10,641	21,201	$84
1985	$11,555	46,433	$70	$6,931	5,986	$172	$10,142	20,990	$82
1984	$10,732	45,660	$61	$6,614	6,279	$175	$9,561	20,558	$74
1983	$10,126	44,394	...	$6,317	6,181	...	$9,150	20,274	...
1982	$9,419	43,124	$55	$5,896	6,316	$135	$8,714	19,721	$72
1981	$8,646	43,113	$48	$5,727	6,775	$148	$8,054	20,271	$61
1980	$7,926	42,586	$45	$6,675	6,988	$127	$7,415	20,147	$57
1979	$7,105	41,988	$41	$4,909	7,213	$110	$6,731	19,624	$51
1978	$6,398	39,889	$38	$4,476	7,375	$138	$6,176	18,587	$49
1977	$5,808	38,080	$32	$4,097	7,589	$95	$5,604	17,748	$41
1976	$5,383	36,787	$31	$3,788	7,508	$86	$5,214	17,077	$40
1975	$4,982	35,384	$28	$3,500	7,505	$80	$4,800	16,438	$36
NON-HISPANIC WHITE									
Both Sexes									
2008	$46,179	107,294	$208	$21,765	5,798	$461	$33,159	30,598	$258
2007	$45,542	107,434	$200	$23,015	5,908	$524	$33,094	30,855	$249
2006	$44,813	106,828	$216	$22,206	6,876	$348	$32,931	31,345	$295
2005	$42,963	106,337	$213	$21,134	6,603	$347	$31,445	31,484	$248
2004	$40,943	105,505	$198	$19,742	6,754	$421	$30,197	31,793	$244
2003	$40,094	105,214	$185	$19,769	6,768	$303	$29,571	31,831	$206
2002	$39,220	105,706	$199	$19,423	7,380	$353	$28,756	32,365	$240
2001	$38,711	106,384	$195	$19,659	7,812	$466	$28,426	33,050	$241
2000	$37,346	106,709	$187	$19,147	7,957	$468	$27,122	33,231	$180
1999	$34,838	106,573	$232	$16,957	8,219	$447	$25,847	34,121	$231
1998	$33,336	105,523	$229	$16,837	8,488	$379	$24,801	34,344	$249
Male									
2008	$56,538	56,822	$339	$26,479	3,654	$691	$39,405	17,206	$390
2007	$55,662	57,080	$331	$27,874	3,716	$784	$39,764	17,309	$397
2006	$54,843	56,843	$352	$26,100	4,289	$450	$40,180	17,470	$494
2005	$53,263	56,675	$359	$25,511	4,127	$503	$38,134	17,507	$406
2004	$50,597	55,930	$328	$23,590	4,203	$644	$36,324	17,568	$373
2003	$49,386	55,774	$305	$22,957	4,224	$401	$35,589	17,225	$315
2002	$48,817	55,994	$329	$23,250	4,580	$529	$34,909	17,218	$375
2001	$47,973	56,528	$316	$23,096	4,749	$549	$34,627	17,672	$352
2000	$47,084	56,675	$318	$23,296	4,763	$706	$33,669	17,733	$281
1999	$44,032	56,575	$390	$20,256	4,842	$471	$32,321	18,047	$362
1998	$41,612	56,246	$372	$20,781	5,152	$584	$30,429	18,048	$374
Female									
2008	$34,517	50,471	$209	$13,730	2,144	$336	$25,133	13,391	$294
2007	$34,069	50,353	$190	$14,779	2,192	$412	$24,570	13,546	$229
2006	$33,407	49,984	$218	$15,751	2,857	$518	$23,805	13,875	$210
2005	$31,208	49,661	$184	$13,837	2,476	$336	$23,004	13,977	$203
2004	$30,051	49,575	$190	$13,401	2,550	$295	$22,631	14,224	$278
2003	$29,613	49,439	$178	$14,475	2,543	$431	$22,473	14,605	$236
2002	$28,410	49,712	$191	$13,163	2,800	$287	$21,762	15,146	$271
2001	$28,210	49,856	$197	$14,328	3,062	$816	$21,301	15,378	$313
2000	$26,315	50,034	$158	$12,962	3,194	$474	$19,631	15,498	$192
1999	$24,436	49,998	$199	$12,227	3,378	$838	$18,579	16,074	$247
1998	$23,891	49,277	$226	$10,746	3,336	$268	$18,568	16,295	$305
BLACK									
Both Sexes									
2008	$32,874	17,509	$362	$18,123	1,748	$1,293	$27,265	6,060	$565
2007	$33,333	17,453	$389	$17,439	1,854	$417	$27,179	5,996	$564
2006	$32,443	17,234	$404	$17,823	1,943	$457	$26,368	6,159	$588
2005	$30,472	17,000	$327	$17,216	2,025	$445	$23,904	6,101	$325
2004	$29,096	16,631	$305	$17,827	2,044	$1,131	$23,498	6,138	$256
2003	$28,838	16,389	$334	$16,201	2,095	$391	$23,777	5,941	$337
2002	$28,179	16,352	$329	$16,516	2,148	$711	$22,823	5,822	$380
2001	$27,031	16,683	$300	$17,248	2,382	$1,062	$21,743	5,729	$260
2000	$26,204	16,756	$260	$15,201	2,434	$419	$21,789	6,020	$325
1999	$24,979	16,936	$313	$13,569	2,393	$426	$20,991	6,112	$432

... = Not available.

Table A-27. Mean Earnings of Workers 18 Years Old and Over, by Educational Attainment, Race, Hispanic Origin, and Sex, 1975–2008—*Continued*

(Dollars, numbers in thousands.)

Sex, race, Hispanic origin, and year	Some college/associate's degree[1]			Bachelor's degree[1]			Advanced degree[1]		
	Mean	Number with earnings	Standard error	Mean	Number with earnings	Standard error	Mean	Number with earnings	Standard error
1987	$13,015	11,312	$167	$18,170	6,240	$289	$23,753	3,801	$482
1986	$11,964	10,807	$140	$17,418	6,014	$245	$22,320	3,574	$397
1985	$11,488	10,300	$148	$15,883	5,700	$229	$21,202	3,458	$357
1984	$10,504	10,064	$119	$14,617	5,432	$209	$20,092	3,328	$332
1983	$9,969	9,478	...	$13,664	5,198	...	$18,230	3,262	...
1982	$9,336	9,145	$117	$12,352	4,861	$181	$16,779	3,080	$287
1981	$8,740	8,654	$107	$11,196	4,626	$167	$15,523	2,788	$279
1980	$8,221	8,488	$108	$10,447	4,449	$159	$13,809	2,513	$253
1979	$7,135	8,263	$96	$9,275	4,343	$145	$12,420	2,545	$243
1978	$6,342	7,672	$85	$8,231	3,966	$131	$11,404	2,288	$235
1977	$5,774	7,115	$73	$7,750	3,593	$123	$10,655	2,035	$203
1976	$5,250	6,733	$74	$7,262	3,560	$109	$10,131	1,909	$207
1975	$4,926	6,327	$65	$6,822	3,368	$105	$9,728	1,746	$199
NON-HISPANIC WHITE									
Both Sexes									
2008	$36,158	33,221	$247	$60,866	24,445	$532	$85,017	13,230	$912
2007	$36,290	33,431	$238	$59,727	24,366	$497	$82,900	12,871	$930
2006	$35,872	32,403	$274	$58,917	23,855	$540	$83,785	12,347	$1,015
2005	$34,866	33,355	$279	$56,462	23,013	$545	$82,205	11,879	$1,081
2004	$33,192	33,200	$234	$53,411	22,544	$466	$79,166	11,961	$1,082
2003	$32,825	32,460	$234	$52,856	22,474	$495	$76,200	11,680	$931
2002	$32,318	32,344	$250	$53,185	22,221	$551	$74,122	11,395	$882
2001	$31,905	32,118	$240	$52,300	22,204	$514	$74,932	11,198	$1,017
2000	$31,217	32,836	$243	$51,351	21,824	$528	$72,356	10,859	$1,027
1999	$29,557	32,454	$328	$47,401	21,272	$630	$68,910	10,507	$1,237
1998	$23,897	31,459	$364	$45,342	21,175	$630	$65,461	10,059	$1,153
Male									
2008	$44,237	16,439	$400	$76,613	12,562	$872	$107,498	6,960	$1,532
2007	$43,835	16,684	$364	$75,214	12,597	$842	$104,317	6,772	$1,576
2006	$43,589	16,024	$438	$73,376	12,321	$888	$104,031	6,738	$1,606
2005	$43,137	16,456	$491	$70,932	12,048	$906	$104,107	6,535	$1,806
2004	$41,490	16,259	$406	$66,527	11,739	$755	$100,220	6,527	$1,781
2003	$40,316	16,048	$394	$66,390	11,849	$838	$95,029	6,427	$1,465
2002	$40,368	16,121	$440	$66,638	11,764	$878	$93,686	6,309	$1,429
2001	$39,133	16,114	$370	$66,196	11,692	$881	$92,954	6,299	$1,613
2000	$39,379	16,435	$431	$65,459	11,594	$899	$90,150	6,149	$1,641
1999	$37,224	16,343	$585	$60,384	11,307	$1,036	$85,918	6,036	$2,057
1998	$29,555	15,849	$625	$57,346	11,335	$1,042	$79,524	5,862	$1,709
Female									
2008	$28,244	16,781	$274	$44,220	11,883	$542	$60,063	6,270	$759
2007	$28,772	16,746	$294	$43,150	11,769	$439	$59,121	6,099	$757
2006	$28,322	16,379	$319	$43,473	11,534	$544	$59,458	5,608	$1,015
2005	$26,812	16,899	$255	$40,562	10,964	$513	$55,422	5,344	$769
2004	$25,228	16,940	$223	$39,161	10,805	$478	$53,875	5,433	$910
2003	$25,499	16,411	$241	$37,761	10,624	$415	$53,164	5,253	$919
2002	$24,318	16,222	$216	$38,049	10,457	$579	$49,845	5,085	$712
2001	$24,628	16,004	$294	$36,844	10,512	$404	$51,756	4,898	$930
2000	$23,038	16,401	$199	$35,362	10,230	$414	$49,126	4,710	$876
1999	$21,779	16,112	$258	$32,667	9,964	$573	$45,943	4,470	$859
1998	$18,198	15,610	$347	$31,516	9,840	$554	$45,805	4,196	$1,294
BLACK									
Both Sexes									
2008	$30,248	5,933	$370	$46,527	2,550	$957	$66,198	1,216	$2,491
2007	$32,787	5,813	$820	$46,502	2,682	$759	$64,247	1,107	$1,813
2006	$31,234	5,581	$674	$47,903	2,503	$1,366	$64,834	1,045	$2,254
2005	$28,848	5,390	$464	$47,101	2,412	$1,378	$63,664	1,071	$2,145
2004	$27,779	5,191	$2,348	$42,342	2,348	$863	$65,538	909	$2,474
2003	$27,187	5,119	$422	$42,968	2,321	$1,249	$64,164	911	$3,341
2002	$27,626	5,255	$505	$42,285	2,275	$901	$59,944	851	$3,302
2001	$26,907	5,481	$448	$40,165	2,212	$911	$55,771	877	$2,320
2000	$26,324	5,431	$351	$41,513	2,060	$1,198	$52,373	809	$1,921
1999	$25,176	5,417	$447	$37,422	2,140	$986	$52,437	873	$2,705

[1]For data prior to 1991, "Some college/Associate degree" equals 1 to 3 years of college completed; "Bachelor's degree" equals 4 years of college; "Advanced degree" equals 5 or more years of college completed.
... = Not available.

Table A-27. Mean Earnings of Workers 18 Years Old and Over, by Educational Attainment, Race, Hispanic Origin, and Sex, 1975–2008—*Continued*

(Dollars, numbers in thousands.)

Sex, race, Hispanic origin, and year	Total			Not a high school graduate			High school graduate		
	Mean	Number with earnings	Standard error	Mean	Number with earnings	Standard error	Mean	Number with earnings	Standard error
1998	$22,829	16,201	$264	$13,672	2,402	$508	$19,236	6,053	$307
1997	$21,909	15,873	$254	$13,185	2,437	$401	$18,980	5,964	$322
1996	$21,978	15,255	$485	$13,110	2,383	$434	$18,722	5,844	$554
1995	$20,537	14,847	$374	$12,956	2,389	$437	$17,072	5,453	$315
1994	$19,772	14,754	$274	$12,705	2,290	$463	$16,446	5,596	$276
1993	$18,614	14,315	$316	$11,065	2,352	$370	$16,122	5,521	$584
1992	$17,416	13,836	$210	$11,077	2,451	$345	$15,260	5,379	$249
1991	$16,809	13,865	$197	$11,248	2,860	$335	$15,060	5,512	$264
1990	$16,627	13,731	$186	$11,184	2,853	$298	$14,794	6,049	$213
1989	$16,072	13,600	$177	$10,066	2,883	$266	$14,613	5,894	$206
1988	$15,318	13,356	$191	$10,202	2,970	$343	$13,835	5,760	$236
1987	$14,136	13,023	$171	$9,976	3,015	$264	$12,862	5,699	$224
1986	$13,494	12,729	$167	$9,365	3,028	$282	$12,276	5,470	$190
1985	$12,926	12,427	$153	$9,116	3,009	$275	$11,791	5,223	$192
1984	$12,002	11,948	$131	$8,725	3,127	$292	$10,882	4,927	$170
1983	$11,299	11,296	...	$7,867	3,035	...	$10,557	4,692	...
1982	$10,612	11,081	$124	$7,799	3,188	$227	$10,287	4,591	$161
1981	$10,117	11,088	$109	$7,520	3,514	$208	$9,994	4,388	$159
1980	$11,085	5,576	$170	$8,421	2,054	$291	$11,563	2,119	$260
1979	$8,720	10,856	$97	$6,424	3,776	$187	$8,723	4,267	$135
1978	$7,981	10,420	$91	$5,918	3,841	$160	$8,152	3,944	$133
1977	$7,271	10,014	$70	$5,406	3,946	$126	$7,553	3,604	$116
1976	$6,716	9,744	$66	$5,304	4,008	$127	$6,805	3,515	$95
1975	$6,190	9,368	$57	$4,989	3,922	$116	$6,281	3,495	$83
Male									
2008	$36,057	8,116	$640	$22,344	866	$2,544	$30,985	3,166	$1,003
2007	$35,668	8,088	$412	$19,705	985	$611	$29,640	2,994	$501
2006	$36,045	7,932	$621	$21,294	982	$715	$30,122	3,067	$889
2005	$34,165	7,836	$609	$19,890	1,056	$711	$27,360	3,050	$551
2004	$33,020	7,668	$563	$22,796	1,029	$2,194	$26,608	3,119	$403
2003	$32,545	7,469	$519	$17,915	1,039	$539	$28,102	2,910	$543
2002	$31,790	7,483	$600	$19,294	1,072	$1,364	$25,582	2,832	$487
2001	$30,502	7,727	$487	$18,543	1,210	$656	$25,037	2,759	$430
2000	$30,109	7,700	$478	$17,992	1,235	$717	$25,219	2,942	$504
1999	$28,821	7,806	$509	$16,391	1,199	$686	$25,849	2,934	$791
1998	$26,090	7,488	$444	$16,013	1,190	$744	$22,698	2,974	$480
1997	$25,080	7,370	$428	$15,423	1,304	$647	$22,440	2,862	$517
1996	$25,067	7,125	$785	$15,461	1,290	$648	$22,267	2,836	$1,034
1995	$23,876	7,090	$718	$14,877	1,280	$652	$19,514	2,812	$443
1994	$22,614	7,009	$445	$15,984	1,191	$770	$18,527	2,818	$413
1993	$21,108	6,833	$518	$13,074	1,305	$574	$18,668	2,775	$903
1992	$19,278	6,822	$342	$12,661	1,457	$510	$16,978	2,683	$382
1991	$18,607	6,830	$284	$15,714	1,624	$423	$17,352	2,731	$382
1990	$18,859	6,781	$300	$13,031	1,563	$430	$17,046	3,013	$332
1989	$18,108	6,654	$283	$11,827	1,614	$355	$16,658	2,848	$328
1988	$17,782	6,593	$326	$12,439	1,671	$529	$16,345	2,795	$404
1987	$16,171	6,505	$283	$11,899	1,711	$375	$14,800	2,769	$374
1986	$15,441	6,326	$256	$11,248	1,691	$409	$14,214	2,666	$294
1985	$14,932	6,237	$254	$10,802	1,716	$396	$13,721	2,572	$308
1984	$13,560	5,899	$212	$10,216	1,780	$374	$12,382	2,339	$280
1983	$12,789	5,707	$205	$9,094	1,768	$339	$11,956	2,312	$265
1982	$12,203	5,535	$203	$9,153	1,798	$340	$11,952	2,213	$268
1981	$11,937	5,651	$174	$9,266	1,925	$318	$11,905	2,191	$261
1980	$11,085	5,576	$170	$8,421	2,054	$291	$11,563	2,119	$260
1979	$10,403	5,581	$157	$7,938	2,138	$278	$10,662	2,087	$225
1978	$9,651	5,350	$147	$7,423	2,156	$233	$9,869	1,982	$219
1977	$8,710	5,220	$110	$6,648	2,230	$187	$9,332	1,770	$184
1976	$7,991	5,156	$105	$6,670	2,289	$187	$8,056	1,766	$155
1975	$7,541	4,864	$89	$6,364	2,247	$173	$7,847	1,684	$138
Female									
2008	$29,734	9,392	$384	$13,976	881	$521	$23,195	2,893	$428
2007	$31,317	9,365	$631	$14,869	868	$540	$24,724	3,001	$1,008
2006	$29,371	9,302	$527	$14,277	961	$531	$22,643	3,092	$762
2005	$27,314	9,163	$304	$14,300	968	$488	$20,449	3,051	$331
2004	$25,738	8,962	$290	$12,785	1,014	$408	$20,284	3,019	$298
2003	$25,735	8,919	$430	$14,513	1,056	$558	$19,623	3,030	$384
2002	$25,131	8,868	$328	$13,748	1,075	$385	$20,209	2,989	$573

... = Not available.

Table A-27.   Mean Earnings of Workers 18 Years Old and Over, by Educational Attainment, Race, Hispanic Origin, and Sex, 1975–2008—*Continued*

(Dollars, numbers in thousands.)

Sex, race, Hispanic origin, and year	Some college/associate's degree[1]			Bachelor's degree[1]			Advanced degree[1]		
	Mean	Number with earnings	Standard error	Mean	Number with earnings	Standard error	Mean	Number with earnings	Standard error
1998	$23,927	4,559	$413	$36,373	1,897	$1,005	$44,760	764	$2,020
1997	$22,899	4,902	$456	$32,062	1,846	$773	$42,791	724	$2,139
1996	$23,628	4,783	$1,084	$31,955	1,655	$1,080	$48,731	590	$5,269
1995	$21,824	4,727	$885	$29,666	1,684	$876	$46,654	595	$3,603
1994	$19,631	4,610	$573	$30,938	1,679	$907	$48,653	579	$3,282
1993	$18,867	4,279	$413	$29,953	1,638	$1,015	$41,221	525	$2,456
1992	$18,719	4,054	$338	$27,457	1,429	$819	$41,439	523	$1,885
1991	$17,850	3,581	$327	$25,630	1,383	$709	$38,002	528	$1,885
1990	$18,209	3,004	$411	$26,448	1,217	$745	$32,962	607	$1,461
1989	$17,385	3,008	$340	$25,357	1,121	$779	$32,740	694	$1,422
1988	$16,760	2,802	$443	$23,689	1,204	$702	$30,802	621	$1,346
1987	$15,491	2,617	$363	$20,805	1,097	$608	$29,163	596	$1,411
1986	$14,743	2,662	$423	$21,403	1,004	$810	$27,503	564	$1,130
1985	$13,805	2,615	$348	$20,533	1,046	$579	$26,246	535	$1,254
1984	$12,890	2,396	$277	$19,330	937	$551	$24,072	561	$884
1983	$12,426	2,206	…	$17,207	828	…	$23,506	535	…
1982	$11,119	2,067	$271	$15,152	747	$494	$22,959	488	$1,162
1981	$11,456	2,078	$255	$14,587	708	$457	$19,463	398	$788
1980	$12,393	964	$417	$15,616	283	$739	$19,960	353	$1,026
1979	$9,895	1,826	$237	$13,473	622	$534	$18,182	366	$872
1978	$9,026	1,689	$230	$12,870	557	$544	$15,076	389	$573
1977	$8,321	1,578	$182	$11,088	532	$342	$14,749	354	$494
1976	$7,331	1,370	$184	$10,331	547	$314	$15,013	305	$696
1975	$7,212	1,193	$170	$9,473	517	$280	$12,333	241	$433
Male									
2008	$34,209	2,505	$676	$51,691	1,059	$1,668	$73,948	518	$3,989
2007	$34,035	2,492	$617	$53,029	1,155	$1,179	$74,351	459	$3,275
2006	$34,750	2,334	$1,037	$52,569	1,086	$1,910	$74,507	460	$4,518
2005	$33,544	2,273	$915	$52,070	1,011	$2,998	$77,210	444	$4,358
2004	$32,367	2,176	$935	$47,746	956	$1,570	$79,168	386	$5,014
2003	$31,556	2,156	$732	$45,635	966	$1,138	$76,871	397	$6,553
2002	$32,764	2,283	$1,034	$47,018	974	$1,589	$75,050	321	$7,972
2001	$31,084	2,457	$887	$46,511	943	$1,767	$67,007	356	$5,050
2000	$30,966	2,291	$686	$49,270	880	$2,526	$60,207	349	$3,911
1999	$28,442	2,338	$712	$42,530	971	$1,635	$59,587	365	$4,070
1998	$26,586	2,215	$707	$42,539	792	$1,889	$51,198	318	$4,289
1997	$27,215	2,108	$847	$35,792	818	$1,243	$49,940	278	$4,564
1996	$26,365	2,047	$1,442	$35,558	700	$1,664	$65,981	253	$11,509
1995	$26,846	2,047	$1,948	$36,026	659	$1,815	$57,186	293	$6,801
1994	$23,748	1,959	$844	$34,073	758	$1,628	$52,829	281	$5,010
1993	$21,734	1,804	$691	$35,147	721	$1,811	$47,372	228	$4,974
1992	$22,697	1,796	$527	$30,989	643	$1,489	$48,968	244	$3,719
1991	$20,548	1,570	$542	$26,075	650	$966	$43,927	255	$3,719
1990	$21,152	1,372	$708	$29,471	564	$1,291	$39,104	269	$2,888
1989	$20,253	1,352	$566	$27,493	515	$1,201	$38,166	326	$2,655
1988	$19,265	1,311	$818	$28,506	533	$1,220	$36,452	283	$2,650
1987	$18,081	1,250	$612	$23,345	482	$1,091	$34,073	294	$2,645
1986	$17,419	1,226	$693	$23,412	480	$1,161	$31,054	263	$2,035
1985	$16,415	1,230	$628	$23,818	477	$1,072	$31,947	243	$2,484
1984	$14,960	1,106	$471	$21,986	424	$961	$27,893	250	$1,670
1983	$15,113	996	$500	$20,370	363	$1,033	$25,466	268	$1,470
1982	$12,926	953	$458	$17,658	319	$861	$26,452	253	$2,006
1981	$13,740	1,002	$432	$16,624	327	$776	$21,082	205	$1,197
1980	$12,393	964	$417	$15,616	283	$739	$23,346	156	$1,986
1979	$11,971	931	$384	$16,161	259	$1,071	$21,092	166	$1,673
1978	$11,197	770	$409	$16,009	260	$944	$18,083	181	$1,031
1977	$10,023	799	$300	$12,978	234	$641	$16,385	188	$808
1976	$8,688	726	$300	$12,246	233	$597	$17,859	143	$1,388
1975	$8,505	599	$267	$11,318	213	$572	$13,720	121	$702
Female									
2008	$27,354	3,428	$397	$42,858	1,491	$1,115	$60,430	697	$3,147
2007	$31,850	3,320	$1,359	$41,560	1,526	$963	$57,076	647	$1,982
2006	$28,706	3,246	$883	$44,326	1,417	$1,911	$57,206	584	$1,798
2005	$25,422	3,116	$431	$43,516	1,401	$959	$54,044	626	$1,837
2004	$24,468	3,015	$411	$38,626	1,391	$960	$55,436	522	$2,021
2003	$24,007	2,963	$487	$41,066	1,355	$1,977	$54,346	514	$2,972
2002	$23,679	2,972	$388	$38,741	1,301	$1,019	$50,766	529	$2,027

… = Not available.

Table A-27.   Mean Earnings of Workers 18 Years Old and Over, by Educational Attainment, Race, Hispanic Origin, and Sex, 1975–2008—*Continued*

(Dollars, numbers in thousands.)

Sex, race, Hispanic origin, and year	Total			Not a high school graduate			High school graduate		
	Mean	Number with earnings	Standard error	Mean	Number with earnings	Standard error	Mean	Number with earnings	Standard error
2001	$24,036	8,956	$363	$15,912	1,172	$2,049	$18,683	2,970	$289
2000	$22,884	9,056	$252	$12,321	1,198	$401	$18,510	3,078	$403
1999	$21,694	9,130	$375	$10,734	1,194	$465	$16,506	3,178	$345
1998	$20,026	8,713	$299	$11,372	1,212	$675	$15,892	3,078	$357
1997	$19,161	8,503	$286	$10,607	1,132	$399	$15,789	3,102	$371
1996	$19,271	8,129	$592	$10,337	1,094	$526	$15,379	3,008	$433
1995	$17,485	7,757	$277	$10,739	1,108	$544	$14,473	2,641	$433
1994	$17,200	7,745	$326	$9,150	1,099	$423	$14,333	2,777	$356
1993	$16,336	7,481	$371	$8,562	1,048	$388	$13,550	2,746	$730
1992	$15,605	7,014	$241	$8,756	995	$376	$13,550	2,696	$312
1991	$15,065	7,034	$231	$9,151	1,237	$524	$12,810	2,781	$301
1990	$14,449	6,950	$221	$8,946	1,290	$402	$12,560	3,036	$269
1989	$14,122	6,946	$215	$7,827	1,269	$403	$12,701	3,046	$255
1988	$12,916	6,763	$203	$7,325	1,299	$391	$11,469	2,965	$255
1987	$12,106	6,518	$193	$7,452	1,304	$360	$11,030	2,930	$256
1986	$11,571	6,403	$215	$6,984	1,337	$375	$10,434	2,804	$244
1985	$10,904	6,190	$170	$6,879	1,293	$366	$9,918	2,651	$233
1984	$10,482	6,049	$157	$6,754	1,347	$464	$9,527	2,588	$201
1983	$9,778	5,589	...	$6,154	1,267	...	$9,197	2,380	...
1982	$9,024	5,546	$141	$6,047	1,390	$279	$8,737	2,378	$186
1981	$8,225	5,437	$129	$5,404	1,589	$252	$8,088	2,197	$183
1980	$7,684	...	$121	$4,685	...	$242	$7,508	...	$164
1979	$6,940	5,275	$112	$4,448	1,638	$232	$6,866	2,180	$154
ASIAN									
Both Sexes									
2008	$51,063	7,118	$904	$21,200	540	$1,178	$29,390	1,213	$1,510
2007	$49,571	7,137	$869	$21,305	512	$764	$28,773	1,241	$730
2006	$50,940	7,073	$1,177	$20,573	599	$719	$29,426	1,301	$1,239
2005	$45,751	6,684	$807	$22,909	598	$1,509	$27,082	1,304	$699
2004	$44,361	6,369	$901	$19,684	497	$914	$28,289	1,192	$1,039
2003	$42,163	6,190	$731	$19,558	539	$1,908	$25,704	1,162	$816
2002	$40,793	6,086	$801	$16,746	536	$621	$24,900	1,138	$778
Male									
2008	$60,007	3,776	$1,491	$23,814	279	$1,473	$34,904	606	$2,879
2007	$57,890	3,731	$1,347	$24,213	244	$1,216	$33,607	630	$1,103
2006	$60,516	3,757	$1,911	$23,311	298	$1,164	$32,528	710	$1,244
2005	$54,257	3,564	$1,351	$28,150	307	$2,650	$30,547	721	$1,019
2004	$52,544	3,440	$1,391	$20,691	235	$1,198	$31,710	676	$1,563
2003	$48,890	3,333	$1,058	$23,745	291	$3,439	$28,522	582	$1,192
2002	$48,934	3,272	$1,338	$17,659	298	$866	$29,547	578	$1,260
Female									
2008	$40,954	3,341	$887	$18,395	260	$1,841	$23,886	607	$842
2007	$40,455	3,405	$1,036	$18,643	267	$908	$23,785	611	$889
2006	$40,089	3,315	$1,233	$17,855	300	$806	$25,696	590	$2,269
2005	$36,033	3,119	$726	$17,383	291	$1,231	$22,789	582	$880
2004	$34,748	2,928	$1,043	$18,780	262	$1,358	$23,802	515	$1,211
2003	$34,315	2,857	$963	$14,614	247	$758	$22,876	580	$1,096
2002	$31,328	2,814	$704	$15,595	237	$873	$20,094	559	$831
HISPANIC[4]									
Both Sexes									
2008	$30,291	21,853	$331	$21,310	6,972	$469	$27,020	6,702	$332
2007	$29,910	21,561	$292	$21,303	6,888	$401	$27,604	6,682	$492
2006	$29,155	21,209	$331	$20,581	7,134	$401	$27,508	6,495	$667
2005	$27,760	20,025	$269	$19,294	6,995	$228	$25,659	6,080	$420
2004	$27,263	19,343	$336	$19,025	6,935	$305	$25,823	5,740	$610
2003	$25,810	18,786	$287	$18,349	6,767	$260	$23,472	5,517	$336
2002	$25,824	18,409	$352	$18,981	6,748	$500	$24,163	5,499	$481
2001	$24,786	17,575	$327	$18,334	6,533	$495	$22,866	5,265	$443
2000	$23,855	17,161	$348	$17,156	6,428	$441	$22,009	5,145	$340
1999	$22,096	15,122	$397	$16,106	5,601	$615	$20,704	4,539	$418
1998	$22,117	14,372	$508	$15,832	5,281	$752	$20,978	4,219	$759
1997	$20,766	13,972	$421	$15,069	5,238	$600	$19,558	4,082	$605
1996	$19,439	13,365	$458	$13,287	5,062	$263	$18,528	3,783	$444

[4]May be of any race.
... = Not available.

Table A-27. Mean Earnings of Workers 18 Years Old and Over, by Educational Attainment, Race, Hispanic Origin, and Sex, 1975–2008—*Continued*

(Dollars, numbers in thousands.)

Sex, race, Hispanic origin, and year	Some college/associate's degree[1]			Bachelor's degree[1]			Advanced degree[1]		
	Mean	Number with earnings	Standard error	Mean	Number with earnings	Standard error	Mean	Number with earnings	Standard error
2001	$23,511	3,023	$360	$35,448	1,269	$860	$48,080	521	$1,713
2000	$22,937	3,140	$324	$35,719	1,179	$851	$46,416	459	$1,532
1999	$22,699	3,080	$560	$33,184	1,170	$1,149	$47,358	509	$3,569
1998	$20,371	2,870	$470	$31,952	1,105	$1,012	$40,214	448	$1,496
1997	$19,643	2,794	$452	$29,091	1,027	$946	$38,392	448	$1,902
1996	$21,581	2,736	$1,555	$29,311	954	$1,402	$35,785	337	$1,542
1995	$17,985	2,679	$429	$25,577	1,025	$768	$36,585	304	$1,616
1994	$16,589	2,651	$472	$28,356	921	$946	$44,618	297	$4,220
1993	$16,778	2,475	$495	$25,865	917	$1,073	$36,485	296	$1,862
1992	$15,553	2,256	$440	$24,572	786	$821	$34,902	281	$1,272
1991	$15,743	2,010	$400	$25,235	733	$912	$32,467	273	$1,272
1990	$15,734	1,632	$466	$23,837	653	$827	$28,074	338	$1,265
1989	$15,044	1,656	$411	$23,541	606	$1,017	$27,933	368	$1,290
1988	$14,557	1,491	$419	$19,862	671	$804	$26,072	338	$1,094
1987	$13,123	1,367	$412	$18,815	615	$668	$24,383	302	$1,062
1986	$12,459	1,436	$516	$19,562	524	$1,129	$24,400	301	$1,149
1985	$11,488	1,385	$347	$17,779	569	$569	$21,502	292	$1,003
1984	$11,115	1,290	$318	$17,134	513	$618	$21,000	311	$860
1983	$10,215	1,210	...	$14,738	465	...	$21,539	267	...
1982	$9,574	1,114	$315	$13,284	428	$576	$19,198	235	$1,077
1981	$9,329	1,076	$285	$12,839	381	$527	$17,743	193	$1,011
1980	$8,544	...	$266	$12,389	...	$568	$17,278	...	$951
1979	$7,735	895	$273	$11,555	363	$504	$15,766	200	$785

ASIAN

Both Sexes

Sex, race, Hispanic origin, and year	Mean	Number with earnings	Standard error	Mean	Number with earnings	Standard error	Mean	Number with earnings	Standard error
2008	$32,671	1,466	$1,214	$58,524	2,298	$1,619	$83,721	1,600	$2,486
2007	$34,423	1,456	$1,666	$54,451	2,354	$1,458	$81,943	1,572	$2,513
2006	$33,238	1,350	$1,526	$56,197	2,268	$2,223	$88,408	1,553	$3,608
2005	$31,460	1,337	$1,187	$51,064	2,108	$1,394	$80,145	1,335	$2,646
2004	$29,524	1,364	$1,060	$47,912	2,118	$1,445	$81,259	1,196	$3,354
2003	$27,209	1,355	$857	$48,333	1,878	$1,282	$74,046	1,254	$2,278
2002	$27,340	1,325	$1,388	$46,628	1,911	$1,407	$72,852	1,174	$2,587

Male

Sex, race, Hispanic origin, and year	Mean	Number with earnings	Standard error	Mean	Number with earnings	Standard error	Mean	Number with earnings	Standard error
2008	$37,283	773	$2,008	$67,088	1,186	$2,790	$97,068	931	$3,655
2007	$41,876	773	$2,971	$60,356	1,156	$1,884	$93,604	926	$3,705
2006	$37,263	658	$1,565	$67,144	1,150	$3,622	$101,676	939	$5,632
2005	$35,401	675	$2,055	$60,739	1,048	$2,504	$92,552	811	$3,936
2004	$33,798	679	$1,857	$56,998	1,078	$2,623	$90,870	770	$3,975
2003	$31,775	673	$1,447	$52,508	992	$1,475	$83,098	793	$2,989
2002	$32,750	664	$2,608	$55,198	971	$2,453	$82,170	758	$3,647

Female

Sex, race, Hispanic origin, and year	Mean	Number with earnings	Standard error	Mean	Number with earnings	Standard error	Mean	Number with earnings	Standard error
2008	$27,528	693	$1,216	$49,380	1,111	$1,455	$65,148	669	$2,865
2007	$25,992	683	$1,016	$48,748	1,197	$2,196	$65,206	645	$2,850
2006	$29,415	692	$2,567	$44,932	1,118	$2,477	$68,084	613	$2,730
2005	$27,439	662	$1,137	$41,494	1,059	$1,145	$60,934	524	$2,581
2004	$25,280	684	$992	$38,488	1,040	$1,012	$63,894	426	$5,957
2003	$22,703	682	$880	$43,655	885	$2,143	$58,489	461	$3,283
2002	$21,912	661	$871	$37,766	939	$1,232	$55,851	415	$2,755

HISPANIC[4]

Both Sexes

Sex, race, Hispanic origin, and year	Mean	Number with earnings	Standard error	Mean	Number with earnings	Standard error	Mean	Number with earnings	Standard error
2008	$31,644	5,149	$622	$48,081	2,225	$1,605	$77,630	802	$3,815
2007	$31,040	5,000	$496	$44,696	2,114	$916	$73,111	874	$3,168
2006	$31,380	4,863	$633	$45,371	2,038	$1,026	$70,432	678	$3,385
2005	$29,836	4,467	$485	$45,933	1,775	$1,185	$70,916	705	$3,870
2004	$29,260	4,369	$561	$45,166	1,669	$1,754	$69,839	629	$4,460
2003	$28,494	4,235	$716	$43,676	1,663	$1,632	$62,794	603	$3,093
2002	$27,757	4,024	$676	$40,949	1,568	$1,640	$67,679	569	$4,744
2001	$27,523	3,842	$600	$40,586	1,416	$1,570	$62,194	517	$4,311
2000	$25,276	3,737	$459	$44,661	1,395	$2,676	$63,908	455	$5,138
1999	$24,577	3,392	$713	$36,212	1,117	$2,063	$55,352	472	$5,416
1998	$23,091	3,289	$925	$35,014	1,156	$1,650	$62,583	425	$7,812
1997	$22,001	3,075	$546	$33,465	1,140	$1,685	$58,571	437	$6,897
1996	$22,209	3,096	$1,185	$32,955	1,027	$2,746	$49,873	398	$7,497

[1]For data prior to 1991, "Some college/Associate degree" equals 1 to 3 years of college completed; "Bachelor's degree" equals 4 years of college; "Advanced degree" equals 5 or more years of college completed.
[4]May be of any race.
... = Not available.

Table A-27. Mean Earnings of Workers 18 Years Old and Over, by Educational Attainment, Race, Hispanic Origin, and Sex, 1975–2008—*Continued*

(Dollars, numbers in thousands.)

Sex, race, Hispanic origin, and year	Total			Not a high school graduate			High school graduate		
	Mean	Number with earnings	Standard error	Mean	Number with earnings	Standard error	Mean	Number with earnings	Standard error
1995........................	$18,262	12,434	$428	$13,068	4,784	$305	$18,333	3,594	$1,070
1994........................	$18,568	12,035	$478	$13,733	4,686	$944	$17,323	3,444	$401
1993........................	$17,102	11,644	$344	$11,852	4,425	$263	$16,591	3,367	$419
1992........................	$16,824	10,171	$252	$11,836	3,962	$273	$16,714	2,991	$425
1991........................	$16,300	10,006	$237	$11,335	3,906	$230	$16,142	3,045	$344
1990........................	$15,943	9,729	$222	$10,368	3,929	$210	$15,417	3,282	$297
1989........................	$15,714	9,570	$234	$11,500	3,985	$222	$14,901	3,188	$296
1988........................	$15,007	9,226	$245	$11,045	3,824	$240	$14,667	2,953	$315
1987........................	$14,695	8,817	$250	$10,961	3,457	$272	$13,958	2,982	$342
1986........................	$13,558	8,393	$205	$9,896	3,379	$237	$13,389	2,835	$300
1985........................	$13,120	7,840	$195	$9,956	3,223	$257	$13,044	2,661	$297
1984........................	$12,583	7,349	$228	$9,671	3,129	$293	$12,858	2,457	$343
1983........................	$11,901	6,222	...	$9,473	2,674	...	$12,077	2,030	...
1982........................	$11,307	5,914	$221	$8,498	2,583	$283	$11,539	1,967	$317
1981........................	$10,872	5,930	$194	$8,645	2,648	$255	$11,046	1,966	$304
1980........................	$10,062	5,723	$197	$8,119	2,649	$284	$10,182	1,824	$309
1979........................	$9,248	5,545	$175	$7,683	2,533	$272	$9,338	1,812	$272
1978........................	$8,460	4,898	$169	$7,138	2,345	$305	$8,512	1,554	$258
1977........................	$7,761	4,752	$130	$6,547	2,306	$205	$8,079	1,461	$226
1976........................	$7,081	4,303	$128	$5,984	2,107	$199	$7,580	1,309	$215
1975........................	$6,567	4,078	$124	$5,462	2,028	$198	$6,759	1,293	$183
Male									
2008........................	$34,240	12,857	$509	$24,340	4,720	$670	$30,618	3,990	$476
2007........................	$33,040	12,885	$421	$23,923	4,726	$519	$30,932	4,111	$698
2006........................	$32,532	12,711	$488	$23,060	4,920	$470	$32,148	3,884	$1,080
2005........................	$31,008	12,015	$401	$21,623	4,744	$294	$29,471	3,667	$638
2004........................	$30,828	11,562	$513	$21,606	4,633	$426	$29,694	3,439	$978
2003........................	$28,806	11,195	$419	$20,637	4,556	$310	$26,652	3,234	$502
2002........................	$29,084	10,979	$516	$21,611	4,506	$689	$27,992	3,205	$782
2001........................	$27,964	10,258	$456	$20,614	4,289	$598	$26,745	2,985	$727
2000........................	$27,253	9,996	$516	$19,501	4,236	$460	$25,629	2,940	$532
1999........................	$24,970	8,713	$527	$18,020	3,592	$378	$23,736	2,597	$560
1998........................	$25,534	8,288	$775	$17,756	3,428	$883	$24,739	2,413	$1,248
1997........................	$23,520	8,261	$595	$17,447	3,444	$712	$22,253	2,391	$918
1996........................	$21,870	7,975	$657	$14,986	3,382	$347	$21,593	2,116	$628
1995........................	$20,312	7,337	$544	$14,774	3,140	$347	$20,882	2,039	$1,467
1994........................	$21,288	7,117	$754	$16,355	3,111	$1,409	$19,667	1,937	$557
1993........................	$19,460	6,957	$526	$13,572	2,928	$357	$18,765	1,954	$566
1992........................	$18,842	6,034	$365	$13,313	2,633	$366	$19,357	1,665	$662
1991........................	$18,516	5,932	$316	$13,133	2,548	$263	$18,582	1,705	$471
1990........................	$18,320	5,745	$332	$13,182	2,562	$276	$18,100	1,812	$455
1989........................	$18,087	5,641	$352	$13,167	2,632	$265	$17,579	1,711	$452
1988........................	$17,357	5,477	$361	$12,836	2,517	$316	$17,446	1,621	$475
1987........................	$17,048	5,248	$372	$12,823	2,281	$369	$16,774	1,616	$523
1986........................	$15,624	5,037	$305	$11,262	2,262	$313	$15,948	1,546	$476
1985........................	$15,293	4,702	$285	$11,671	2,111	$342	$15,602	1,491	$464
1984........................	$14,957	4,344	$344	$11,441	2,022	$385	$15,763	1,319	$549
1983........................	$14,265	3,577	$324	$11,353	1,678	$400	$14,584	1,074	$549
1982........................	$13,484	3,480	$339	$10,108	1,622	$392	$13,883	1,083	$488
1981........................	$13,052	3,504	$292	$10,447	1,686	$342	$13,513	1,037	$489
1980........................	$12,310	3,401	$303	$9,825	1,707	$394	$13,108	961	$526
1979........................	$11,332	3,269	$268	$9,393	1,615	$378	$11,714	952	$448
1978........................	$10,473	2,915	$258	$8,836	1,498	$427	$10,940	815	$426
1977........................	$9,655	2,833	$198	$8,192	1,460	$281	$10,386	776	$372
1976........................	$8,787	2,571	$195	$7,440	1,321	$272	$9,640	712	$345
1975........................	$8,162	2,456	$189	$6,745	1,287	$268	$8,546	691	$289
Female									
2008........................	$24,646	8,995	$334	$14,960	2,552	$318	$21,725	2,712	$399
2007........................	$25,262	8,676	$362	$15,574	2,162	$559	$22,283	2,570	$602
2006........................	$24,104	8,497	$378	$15,072	2,214	$743	$20,608	2,611	$359
2005........................	$22,887	8,009	$290	$14,365	2,250	$308	$19,864	2,413	$383
2004........................	$21,967	7,781	$327	$13,830	2,302	$286	$20,037	2,300	$378
2003........................	$21,391	7,591	$342	$13,632	2,210	$451	$18,967	2,283	$363
2002........................	$21,008	7,430	$418	$13,694	2,241	$568	$18,810	2,293	$324
2001........................	$20,330	7,316	$450	$13,976	2,243	$867	$17,786	2,279	$336
2000........................	$19,115	7,164	$415	$12,622	2,191	$930	$17,180	2,204	$314
1999........................	$18,187	6,409	$594	$12,684	2,010	$1,567	$16,653	1,943	$593

... = Not available.

Table A-27. Mean Earnings of Workers 18 Years Old and Over, by Educational Attainment, Race, Hispanic Origin, and Sex, 1975–2008—*Continued*

(Dollars, numbers in thousands.)

Sex, race, Hispanic origin, and year	Some college/associate's degree[1]			Bachelor's degree[1]			Advanced degree[1]		
	Mean	Number with earnings	Standard error	Mean	Number with earnings	Standard error	Mean	Number with earnings	Standard error
1995	$19,923	2,856	$904	$30,602	866	$1,678	$45,612	334	$3,004
1994	$21,041	2,723	$693	$29,165	844	$1,337	$51,898	337	$6,534
1993	$19,043	2,728	$548	$30,359	799	$3,355	$45,034	325	$4,169
1992	$19,778	2,242	$446	$28,260	702	$1,272	$46,736	274	$2,871
1991	$19,123	2,080	$456	$26,623	665	$1,249	$40,154	311	$2,871
1990	$19,206	1,534	$540	$25,703	601	$1,208	$38,075	382	$2,477
1989	$18,707	1,513	$608	$28,157	535	$1,519	$39,273	349	$2,861
1988	$18,101	1,511	$716	$23,745	596	$1,134	$33,843	340	$3,064
1987	$16,899	1,400	$524	$23,105	644	$1,139	$34,413	335	$3,055
1986	$16,523	1,411	$584	$22,707	471	$1,248	$28,316	295	$1,822
1985	$15,318	1,226	$513	$20,878	458	$1,104	$28,357	273	$1,843
1984	$14,359	1,116	$622	$19,924	381	$1,226	$26,327	265	$2,222
1983	$13,371	976	…	$17,972	320	…	$24,352	222	…
1982	$13,108	873	$546	$18,186	303	$1,463	$28,167	186	$2,784
1981	$12,971	834	$516	$16,114	320	$1,174	$24,082	161	$2,557
1980	$11,891	808	$558	$15,676	283	$1,267	$21,910	157	$2,623
1979	$10,181	768	$458	$14,940	240	$1,315	$18,273	190	$1,780
1978	$9,575	661	$446	$13,985	213	$1,195	$17,333	125	$1,903
1977	$8,172	656	$333	$12,572	210	$864	$16,660	118	$1,753
1976	$7,252	592	$333	$11,242	177	$887	$14,000	118	$1,667
1975	$7,154	474	$351	$10,573	173	$796	$15,756	111	$1,994
Male									
2008	$37,864	2,615	$1,044	$56,980	1,109	$2,868	$96,976	422	$6,556
2007	$35,861	2,510	$724	$50,805	1,057	$1,436	$87,195	478	$5,348
2006	$36,217	2,500	$981	$51,336	1,066	$1,565	$87,835	340	$5,886
2005	$34,754	2,326	$770	$54,700	896	$2,021	$84,033	380	$6,680
2004	$34,447	2,241	$975	$53,567	915	$2,750	$84,152	331	$7,566
2003	$34,157	2,193	$1,296	$49,298	867	$2,485	$71,446	344	$4,795
2002	$32,935	2,112	$1,210	$46,115	815	$2,412	$73,836	338	$5,926
2001	$32,595	1,962	$882	$45,445	748	$1,713	$75,746	272	$7,676
2000	$30,155	1,873	$797	$55,050	722	$4,651	$81,447	223	$9,696
1999	$29,387	1,698	$1,211	$42,733	577	$3,697	$66,745	250	$9,708
1998	$26,483	1,652	$1,677	$40,889	569	$2,451	$83,754	226	$13,919
1997	$25,923	1,598	$852	$37,963	557	$2,021	$68,097	272	$10,265
1996	$26,682	1,687	$2,101	$38,130	531	$5,090	$49,307	259	$6,300
1995	$22,171	1,475	$978	$35,109	466	$2,695	$50,802	215	$4,151
1994	$24,517	1,410	$855	$33,797	450	$2,185	$60,858	210	$10,036
1993	$22,417	1,444	$859	$37,554	438	$5,974	$52,441	194	$6,150
1992	$23,033	1,193	$596	$33,430	380	$1,957	$53,645	164	$4,216
1991	$21,974	1,131	$693	$31,699	356	$1,729	$45,873	193	$4,216
1990	$22,376	852	$831	$31,485	314	$1,966	$47,479	205	$4,339
1989	$22,374	810	$996	$32,767	292	$2,536	$49,088	196	$4,778
1988	$21,631	811	$1,205	$26,935	333	$1,807	$40,916	194	$4,602
1987	$19,414	758	$773	$26,581	383	$1,782	$39,014	211	$4,410
1986	$19,675	778	$962	$27,427	274	$1,975	$32,538	176	$2,705
1985	$18,168	678	$771	$24,723	267	$1,723	$32,831	155	$2,792
1984	$17,261	611	$1,014	$23,835	223	$1,878	$30,727	168	$3,231
1983	$16,626	514	$864	$21,911	170	$2,111	$28,680	141	$2,681
1982	$15,560	495	$845	$22,565	153	$2,632	$34,474	125	$3,995
1981	$15,432	489	$785	$19,201	177	$1,928	$27,619	114	$3,427
1980	$14,331	451	$890	$19,224	167	$1,986	$24,642	114	$3,439
1979	$12,489	441	$714	$18,923	142	$2,113	$21,299	118	$2,619
1978	$11,545	393	$665	$16,898	127	$1,861	$20,702	82	$2,730
1977	$9,924	391	$501	$15,189	120	$1,420	$19,025	85	$2,291
1976	$8,843	342	$508	$13,650	114	$1,299	$16,184	81	$2,339
1975	$8,807	279	$536	$12,881	113	$1,142	$17,991	86	$2,535
Female									
2008	$25,226	2,534	$626	$39,231	1,115	$1,382	$56,175	380	$2,930
2007	$26,179	2,489	$659	$38,584	1,057	$1,094	$56,129	396	$2,312
2006	$26,260	2,362	$770	$38,825	971	$1,248	$52,896	337	$2,901
2005	$24,493	2,141	$536	$37,003	879	$1,110	$55,554	324	$2,732
2004	$23,796	2,127	$484	$34,949	753	$1,886	$53,887	297	$3,939
2003	$22,411	2,042	$466	$37,550	795	$2,042	$51,294	258	$3,160
2002	$22,035	1,911	$437	$35,357	753	$2,175	$58,623	230	$7,783
2001	$22,229	1,879	$783	$35,142	668	$2,699	$47,176	245	$2,786
2000	$20,372	1,864	$413	$33,489	672	$2,303	$47,057	232	$3,340
1999	$19,754	1,694	$694	$29,249	540	$1,459	$42,503	222	$2,979

[1]For data prior to 1991, "Some college/Associate degree" equals 1 to 3 years of college completed; "Bachelor's degree" equals 4 years of college; "Advanced degree" equals 5 or more years of college completed.
… = Not available.

Table A-27.   Mean Earnings of Workers 18 Years Old and Over, by Educational Attainment, Race, Hispanic Origin, and Sex, 1975–2008—*Continued*

(Dollars, numbers in thousands.)

Sex, race, Hispanic origin, and year	Total			Not a high school graduate			High school graduate		
	Mean	Number with earnings	Standard error	Mean	Number with earnings	Standard error	Mean	Number with earnings	Standard error
1998	$17,461	6,804	$557	$12,273	1,854	$1,377	$15,952	1,806	$539
1997	$16,781	5,711	$554	$10,503	1,794	$1,072	$15,747	1,691	$637
1996	$15,841	5,390	$578	$9,867	1,680	$332	$14,635	1,667	$577
1995	$15,310	5,096	$685	$9,809	1,644	$565	$14,989	1,555	$1,541
1994	$14,631	4,918	$404	$8,559	1,576	$304	$14,313	1,508	$546
1993	$13,602	4,687	$329	$8,489	1,498	$297	$13,584	1,413	$595
1992	$13,880	4,137	$304	$8,913	1,330	$334	$13,396	1,326	$435
1991	$13,069	4,072	$273	$4,809	1,358	$307	$13,043	1,339	$380
1990	$12,516	3,984	$254	$5,093	1,367	$309	$12,109	1,470	$354
1989	$12,307	3,929	$266	$8,256	1,353	$401	$11,799	1,477	$365
1988	$11,573	3,749	$290	$7,597	1,307	$349	$11,284	1,332	$392
1987	$11,234	3,569	$286	$7,350	1,176	$354	$10,627	1,366	$417
1986	$10,457	3,356	$231	$7,130	1,117	$338	$10,319	1,289	$332
1985	$9,865	3,138	$236	$6,699	1,112	$367	$9,784	1,170	$327
1984	$9,150	3,005	$252	$6,438	1,107	$436	$9,492	1,138	$380
1983	$8,704	2,645	...	$6,305	996	...	$9,261	956	...
1982	$8,195	2,434	$233	$5,781	961	$373	$8,668	884	$374
1981	$7,723	2,426	$215	$5,486	962	$364	$8,292	929	$342
1980	$6,770	2,322	$199	$5,028	942	$358	$6,923	863	$287
1979	$6,255	2,276	$184	$4,675	918	$347	$6,708	860	$286
1978	$5,501	1,983	$173	$4,135	847	$377	$5,834	739	$273
1977	$4,964	1,919	$137	$3,707	846	$276	$5,466	685	$236
1976	$4,548	1,732	$132	$3,537	786	$273	$5,124	597	$229
1975	$4,152	1,622	$122	$3,233	741	$277	$4,708	602	$209
WHITE ALONE OR IN COMBINATION									
Both Sexes									
2008	$43,550	129,419	$181	$21,483	12,630	$321	$32,072	37,299	$220
2007	$43,000	129,203	$174	$22,245	12,568	$321	$32,126	37,570	$221
2006	$42,249	128,366	$188	$21,389	13,800	$260	$31,998	37,915	$266
2005	$40,592	126,882	$184	$20,225	13,424	$204	$30,494	37,723	$216
2004	$38,855	125,387	$175	$19,365	13,539	$256	$29,595	37,639	$227
2003	$37,958	124,456	$144	$18,734	16,282	$183	$27,915	45,064	$159
2002	$37,290	124,337	$167	$19,278	13,957	$303	$28,107	37,863	$203
Male									
2008	$52,502	69,829	$292	$25,254	8,263	$469	$37,740	21,192	$329
2007	$51,599	70,073	$282	$25,848	8,305	$447	$38,072	21,436	$345
2006	$50,826	69,702	$302	$24,524	9,055	$321	$38,699	21,401	$444
2005	$49,437	68,987	$306	$23,526	8,740	$281	$36,608	21,289	$350
2004	$47,275	67,758	$285	$22,576	8,751	$374	$35,348	21,073	$351
2003	$45,989	67,198	$264	$21,787	8,682	$247	$34,225	20,534	$278
2002	$45,682	67,082	$272	$22,601	8,977	$439	$33,846	20,430	$317
Female									
2008	$33,060	59,590	$184	$14,345	4,366	$223	$24,615	16,107	$256
2007	$32,810	59,130	$170	$15,226	4,263	$338	$24,226	16,134	$213
2006	$32,059	58,663	$193	$15,408	4,745	$429	$23,313	16,514	$185
2005	$30,053	57,895	$163	$14,066	4,684	$225	$22,574	16,434	$181
2004	$28,954	57,629	$169	$13,498	4,788	$202	$22,277	16,565	$244
2003	$28,532	57,257	$161	$14,086	4,684	$306	$22,029	16,926	$210
2002	$27,457	57,254	$163	$13,286	4,979	$282	$21,381	17,433	$224
NON-HISPANIC WHITE ALONE OR IN COMBINATION									
Both Sexes									
2008	$46,050	108,823	$206	$21,579	5,959	$451	$33,105	30,982	$257
2007	$45,393	108,929	$198	$22,945	6,040	$516	$32,992	31,288	$246
2006	$44,652	108,297	$214	$22,094	6,995	$345	$32,844	31,802	$291
2005	$42,839	107,945	$211	$21,088	6,744	$342	$31,367	31,951	$245
2004	$40,847	107,086	$197	$19,667	6,892	$414	$30,195	32,216	$245
2003	$39,989	106,658	$184	$19,764	6,906	$300	$29,561	32,225	$205
2002	$39,135	107,050	$185	$19,491	7,516	$375	$28,714	32,758	$222

[1]For data prior to 1991, "Some college/Associate degree" equals 1 to 3 years of college completed; "Bachelor's degree" equals 4 years of college; "Advanced degree" equals 5 or more years of college completed.
[2]Starting in 2003, respondents could choose more than one race. The race data in this table from 2003 onward represent respondents who indicated only one race.
[3]Beginning in 2000, earnings data are from the expanded Current Population Survey (CPS) sample and were calculated using population controls based on Census 2000.
[4]May be of any race.
... = Not available.

Table A-27.   Mean Earnings of Workers 18 Years Old and Over, by Educational Attainment, Race, Hispanic Origin, and Sex, 1975–2008—*Continued*

(Dollars, numbers in thousands.)

Sex, race, Hispanic origin, and year	Some college/associate's degree[1]			Bachelor's degree[1]			Advanced degree[1]		
	Mean	Number with earnings	Standard error	Mean	Number with earnings	Standard error	Mean	Number with earnings	Standard error
1998	$20,460	1,639	$689	$29,317	587	$2,144	$38,422	200	$3,471
1997	$17,759	1,477	$611	$29,173	584	$2,635	$43,051	165	$6,178
1996	$16,856	1,409	$581	$27,407	495	$1,503	$50,960	139	$17,662
1995	$17,521	1,380	$1,542	$25,338	399	$1,722	$36,255	118	$3,079
1994	$17,309	1,313	$1,081	$23,867	393	$1,272	$37,269	127	$4,428
1993	$15,250	1,284	$609	$21,627	361	$1,258	$34,001	131	$4,391
1992	$16,076	1,049	$669	$22,160	322	$1,343	$34,551	110	$3,141
1991	$15,721	948	$564	$20,791	309	$1,377	$30,721	117	$3,141
1990	$15,245	682	$629	$19,378	287	$1,331	$27,184	177	$1,824
1989	$14,482	703	$629	$22,617	243	$1,379	$26,700	153	$2,265
1988	$14,012	700	$662	$19,707	263	$1,171	$24,444	146	$3,675
1987	$13,929	642	$688	$18,003	261	$1,033	$26,584	124	$3,436
1986	$12,648	633	$547	$16,142	197	$1,165	$22,071	119	$2,096
1985	$11,791	548	$639	$15,503	191	$1,098	$22,480	118	$2,173
1984	$10,848	505	$619	$14,404	158	$1,310	$18,706	97	$2,355
1983	$9,750	462	...	$13,507	150	...	$16,817	81	...
1982	$9,896	378	$605	$13,719	150	$1,235	$15,244	61	$2,247
1981	$9,483	345	$563	$12,292	143	$1,101	$15,503	47	$2,767
1980	$8,808	357	$576	$10,568	116	$1,177	$14,668	43	$2,935
1979	$7,069	327	$482	$9,168	98	$1,001	$13,313	72	$1,905
1978	$6,686	268	$507	$9,684	86	$1,098	$10,908	43	$1,872
1977	$5,588	265	$367	$9,082	90	$691	$10,569	33	$2,119
1976	$5,075	250	$373	$6,884	63	$826	$9,218	37	$1,425
1975	$4,790	195	$376	$6,226	60	$805	$8,067	25	$1,536
WHITE ALONE OR IN COMBINATION									
Both Sexes									
2008	$35,528	38,593	$226	$59,824	26,784	$503	$84,687	14,111	$886
2007	$35,565	38,664	$215	$58,565	26,583	$462	$82,309	13,816	$888
2006	$35,276	37,530	$249	$57,807	26,035	$501	$83,002	13,084	$974
2005	$34,279	38,149	$252	$55,758	24,919	$514	$81,437	12,665	$1,036
2004	$32,736	37,287	$213	$52,790	24,361	$444	$78,747	12,560	$1,051
2003	$31,498	44,048	$193	$51,206	28,672	$420	$74,601	14,592	$803
2002	$31,767	36,639	$231	$52,509	23,865	$497	$73,773	12,011	$863
Male									
2008	$43,307	19,210	$369	$75,024	13,734	$828	$107,065	7,428	$1,491
2007	$42,760	19,343	$327	$73,390	13,697	$784	$103,214	7,291	$1,503
2006	$42,605	18,686	$397	$71,602	13,443	$825	$103,097	7,116	$1,546
2005	$42,139	18,954	$439	$69,821	13,045	$855	$102,904	6,957	$1,734
2004	$40,627	18,361	$367	$65,498	12,728	$717	$99,534	6,842	$1,733
2003	$39,555	18,421	$374	$65,237	12,774	$801	$93,792	6,785	$1,408
2002	$39,439	18,377	$408	$65,548	12,621	$795	$92,575	6,675	$1,381
Female									
2008	$27,819	19,383	$250	$43,826	13,050	$507	$59,814	6,683	$731
2007	$28,362	19,321	$267	$42,807	12,886	$410	$58,951	6,525	$721
2006	$28,008	18,844	$292	$43,078	12,591	$507	$59,042	5,968	$968
2005	$25,518	19,194	$233	$40,306	11,873	$480	$55,273	5,707	$736
2004	$25,079	18,925	$205	$38,886	11,632	$460	$53,859	5,717	$886
2003	$25,093	18,616	$218	$37,750	11,476	$407	$53,021	5,552	$882
2002	$24,046	18,261	$198	$37,872	11,243	$521	$50,255	5,336	$749
NON-HISPANIC WHITE ALONE OR IN COMBINATION									
Both Sexes									
2008	$36,042	33,806	$243	$60,818	24,717	$528	$84,996	13,358	$911
2007	$36,176	33,994	$235	$59,637	24,622	$493	$82,840	12,983	$924
2006	$35,795	32,962	$270	$58,785	24,103	$535	$83,629	12,433	$1,010
2005	$34,824	33,991	$276	$56,441	23,253	$544	$81,944	12,003	$1,072
2004	$33,192	33,200	$234	$53,335	22,814	$463	$79,166	11,961	$1,082
2003	$32,732	33,062	$231	$52,823	22,686	$494	$76,029	11,777	$924
2002	$32,210	32,876	$246	$53,244	22,415	$518	$74,011	11,482	$877

[1]For data prior to 1991, "Some college/Associate degree" equals 1 to 3 years of college completed; "Bachelor's degree" equals 4 years of college; "Advanced degree" equals 5 or more years of college completed.
... = Not available.

Table A-27. Mean Earnings of Workers 18 Years Old and Over, by Educational Attainment, Race, Hispanic Origin, and Sex, 1975–2008—*Continued*

(Dollars, numbers in thousands.)

Sex, race, Hispanic origin, and year	Total			Not a high school graduate			High school graduate		
	Mean	Number with earnings	Standard error	Mean	Number with earnings	Standard error	Mean	Number with earnings	Standard error
Male									
2008..........................	$56,357	57,636	$336	$26,226	3,743	$676	$39,288	17,435	$386
2007..........................	$55,457	57,886	$327	$27,810	3,800	$771	$39,602	17,567	$392
2006..........................	$54,624	57,615	$348	$25,996	4,358	$448	$40,034	17,723	$488
2005..........................	$53,084	57,553	$356	$25,469	4,213	$496	$38,034	17,787	$401
2004..........................	$50,488	56,761	$327	$23,520	4,287	$633	$36,323	17,817	$375
2003..........................	$49,227	56,549	$302	$22,947	4,313	$397	$35,550	17,549	$314
2002..........................	$48,700	56,714	$307	$23,426	4,663	$573	$34,830	17,446	$346
Female									
2008..........................	$34,445	51,187	$207	$13,726	2,215	$329	$25,148	13,547	$296
2007..........................	$33,979	51,043	$188	$14,690	2,239	$406	$24,530	13,721	$227
2006..........................	$33,316	50,682	$215	$15,642	2,636	$509	$23,794	14,079	$208
2005..........................	$31,139	50,391	$182	$13,793	2,530	$331	$22,994	14,163	$201
2004..........................	$29,972	50,324	$187	$13,325	2,605	$290	$22,613	14,399	$275
2003..........................	$29,564	50,108	$177	$14,469	2,592	$427	$22,479	14,765	$235
2002..........................	$28,359	50,335	$176	$13,060	2,853	$265	$21,745	15,312	$251
BLACK ALONE OR IN COMBINATION									
Both Sexes									
2008..........................	$32,878	18,157	$358	$18,049	1,826	$1,243	$27,123	6,220	$553
2007..........................	$33,318	18,023	$380	$17,555	1,903	$430	$27,096	6,149	$552
2006..........................	$32,384	17,721	$395	$17,842	1,995	$463	$26,290	6,305	$576
2005..........................	$30,521	17,540	$333	$17,264	2,097	$437	$23,810	6,246	$320
2004..........................	$29,031	17,109	$298	$17,821	2,085	$1,110	$23,458	6,298	$253
2003..........................	$28,854	16,871	$332	$16,238	2,177	$388	$23,956	6,082	$368
2002..........................	$28,255	16,833	$334	$17,114	2,217	$974	$22,762	5,940	$374
Male									
2008..........................	$36,386	8,442	$621	$21,894	913	$2,417	$30,690	3,263	$976
2007..........................	$35,669	8,405	$405	$19,932	1,019	$644	$29,508	3,083	$493
2006..........................	$36,026	8,170	$608	$21,361	1,006	$738	$29,973	3,146	$869
2005..........................	$34,258	8,127	$626	$19,996	1,093	$701	$27,189	3,142	$539
2004..........................	$32,919	7,884	$550	$22,755	1,049	$2,153	$26,575	3,202	$397
2003..........................	$32,574	7,689	$520	$17,982	1,088	$530	$28,323	2,981	$607
2002..........................	$31,967	7,734	$617	$20,537	1,114	$1,893	$25,510	2,902	$479
Female									
2008..........................	$29,829	9,715	$392	$14,204	913	$540	$23,187	2,957	$423
2007..........................	$31,263	9,618	$616	$14,816	884	$533	$24,669	3,065	$989
2006..........................	$29,268	9,551	$515	$14,257	988	$520	$22,622	3,159	$748
2005..........................	$27,295	9,413	$300	$14,289	1,003	$478	$20,389	3,104	$327
2004..........................	$25,707	9,224	$285	$12,818	1,035	$406	$20,236	3,096	$294
2003..........................	$25,739	9,182	$423	$14,495	1,089	$560	$19,765	3,100	$405
2002..........................	$25,099	9,098	$323	$13,656	1,103	$378	$20,137	3,038	$565
ASIAN ALONE OR IN COMBINATION									
Both Sexes									
2008..........................	$50,622	7,553	$892	$21,195	569	$1,157	$29,163	1,300	$1,425
2007..........................	$48,865	7,563	$829	$21,399	530	$760	$28,524	1,331	$709
2006..........................	$50,094	7,501	$1,117	$20,142	631	$702	$29,502	1,413	$1,162
2005..........................	$45,269	7,131	$806	$22,330	629	$1,445	$27,059	1,413	$667
2004..........................	$43,856	6,771	$871	$19,536	524	$894	$27,946	1,292	$975
2003..........................	$41,563	6,560	$699	$19,548	564	$1,838	$25,554	1,256	$778
2002..........................	$40,323	6,424	$767	$16,969	559	$646	$25,038	1,221	$759

... = Not available.

Table A-27. **Mean Earnings of Workers 18 Years Old and Over, by Educational Attainment, Race, Hispanic Origin, and Sex, 1975–2008—***Continued*

(Dollars, numbers in thousands.)

Sex, race, Hispanic origin, and year	Some college/associate's degree[1]			Bachelor's degree[1]			Advanced degree[1]		
	Mean	Number with earnings	Standard error	Mean	Number with earnings	Standard error	Mean	Number with earnings	Standard error
Male									
2008	$44,075	16,739	$395	$76,560	12,692	$864	$107,540	7,025	$1,533
2007	$43,707	16,973	$359	$75,109	12,715	$836	$104,236	6,830	$1,565
2006	$43,491	16,320	$432	$73,244	12,424	$882	$103,794	6,787	$1,597
2005	$43,083	16,769	$486	$70,891	12,187	$905	$103,850	6,593	$1,794
2004	$41,490	16,259	$406	$66,467	11,869	$752	$100,220	6,527	$1,781
2003	$40,196	16,358	$389	$66,368	11,946	$839	$94,830	6,471	$1,456
2002	$40,195	16,390	$434	$66,776	11,859	$830	$100,412	6,510	$1,799
Female									
2008	$28,163	17,067	$271	$44,203	12,025	$537	$59,983	6,332	$754
2007	$28,665	17,020	$290	$43,115	11,907	$435	$59,092	6,153	$752
2006	$28,248	16,641	$315	$43,402	11,678	$538	$59,389	5,646	$1,010
2005	$26,782	17,222	$253	$40,527	11,065	$509	$55,242	5,409	$762
2004	$25,228	16,940	$223	$39,092	10,945	$473	$53,875	5,433	$910
2003	$25,422	16,704	$238	$37,757	10,739	$411	$53,102	5,306	$912
2002	$24,271	16,485	$214	$38,042	10,556	$536	$49,827	5,127	$708
BLACK ALONE OR IN COMBINATION									
Both Sexes									
2008	$30,266	6,207	$399	$46,983	2,654	$941	$66,247	1,248	$2,438
2007	$32,580	6,056	$790	$46,555	2,761	$747	$64,714	1,152	$1,767
2006	$31,175	5,759	$656	$47,740	2,580	$1,330	$64,563	1,080	$2,206
2005	$28,817	5,576	$453	$47,641	2,501	$1,490	$63,065	1,118	$2,079
2004	$27,801	5,369	$453	$42,131	2,414	$848	$64,545	941	$2,401
2003	$27,095	5,296	$414	$42,991	2,374	$1,226	$63,966	940	$3,245
2002	$27,582	5,441	$493	$42,099	2,340	$004	$60,458	884	$3,202
Male									
2008	$34,159	2,631	$657	$52,773	1,103	$1,645	$73,362	530	$3,922
2007	$33,845	2,621	$601	$52,951	1,200	$1,155	$75,355	480	$3,182
2006	$34,784	2,417	$1,008	$52,382	1,124	$1,854	$74,769	475	$4,415
2005	$33,449	2,380	$884	$53,556	1,049	$3,296	$76,407	462	$4,227
2004	$32,400	2,250	$915	$47,448	976	$1,548	$77,648	398	$4,900
2003	$31,591	2,233	$721	$45,705	982	$1,122	$76,954	402	$6,481
2002	$32,696	2,375	$1,003	$46,942	1,009	$1,558	$76,003	332	$7,767
Female									
2008	$27,399	3,575	$488	$42,861	1,550	$1,091	$60,996	718	$3,075
2007	$31,614	3,435	$1,316	$41,636	1,561	$953	$57,105	672	$1,926
2006	$28,565	3,342	$860	$44,157	1,456	$1,864	$56,541	605	$1,770
2005	$25,366	3,195	$424	$43,369	1,452	$937	$53,669	656	$1,796
2004	$24,415	3,111	$402	$38,522	1,438	$945	$54,931	543	$1,959
2003	$23,816	3,063	$475	$41,073	1,391	$1,935	$54,265	538	$2,852
2002	$23,621	3,066	$380	$38,447	1,339	$996	$51,101	552	$1,964
ASIAN ALONE OR IN COMBINATION									
Both Sexes									
2008	$32,577	1,630	$1,159	$58,179	2,403	$1,570	$84,523	1,649	$2,608
2007	$33,846	1,630	$1,505	$54,204	2,454	$1,413	$81,694	1,615	$2,457
2006	$33,050	1,495	$1,405	$55,827	2,375	$2,131	$87,887	1,585	$3,553
2005	$31,332	1,504	$1,141	$51,750	2,204	$1,561	$79,229	1,379	$2,570
2004	$29,377	1,490	$1,183	$47,711	2,226	$1,386	$81,310	1,237	$3,279
2003	$27,083	1,495	$798	$47,945	1,948	$1,246	$73,812	1,295	$2,234
2002	$27,146	1,456	$1,280	$46,218	1,984	$1,364	$72,943	1,202	$2,546

... = Not available.

Table A-27.　Mean Earnings of Workers 18 Years Old and Over, by Educational Attainment, Race, Hispanic Origin, and Sex, 1975–2008—*Continued*

(Dollars, numbers in thousands.)

Sex, race, Hispanic origin, and year	Total			Not a high school graduate			High school graduate		
	Mean	Number with earnings	Standard error	Mean	Number with earnings	Standard error	Mean	Number with earnings	Standard error
Male									
2008............................	$59,565	4,007	$1,483	$23,204	297	$1,419	$34,568	655	$2,680
2007............................	$56,990	3,945	$1,288	$24,261	254	$1,202	$33,105	685	$1,054
2006............................	$59,328	3,980	$1,815	$22,631	318	$1,134	$32,716	783	$1,177
2005............................	$53,761	3,797	$1,363	$27,107	328	$2,502	$30,490	790	$965
2004............................	$52,032	3,633	$1,361	$20,799	251	$1,190	$31,194	730	$1,468
2003............................	$48,062	3,522	$1,015	$23,122	308	$3,258	$28,514	635	$1,137
2002............................	$48,128	3,469	$1,274	$18,101	312	$933	$29,493	633	$1,216
Female									
2008............................	$40,518	3,546	$851	$18,999	272	$1,848	$23,665	644	$837
2007............................	$40,002	3,617	$986	$18,753	275	$910	$23,660	645	$884
2006............................	$39,652	3,520	$1,172	$17,610	313	$788	$25,508	630	$2,143
2005............................	$35,593	3,333	$697	$17,122	301	$1,199	$22,703	622	$847
2004............................	$34,387	3,137	$985	$18,375	273	$1,316	$23,721	561	$1,143
2003............................	$34,031	3,038	$921	$15,233	255	$896	$22,530	621	$1,041
2002............................	$31,157	2,954	$685	$15,536	247	$851	$20,242	588	$814

... = Not available.

Table A-27. Mean Earnings of Workers 18 Years Old and Over, by Educational Attainment, Race, Hispanic Origin, and Sex, 1975–2008—_Continued_

(Dollars, numbers in thousands.)

Sex, race, Hispanic origin, and year	Some college/associate's degree[1]			Bachelor's degree[1]			Advanced degree[1]		
	Mean	Number with earnings	Standard error	Mean	Number with earnings	Standard error	Mean	Number with earnings	Standard error
Male									
2008............................	$37,228	865	$1,912	$66,880	1,228	$2,733	$98,718	959	$3,915
2007............................	$40,965	875	$2,650	$60,606	1,187	$1,866	$93,566	942	$3,651
2006............................	$37,104	736	$1,462	$66,740	1,191	$3,505	$101,474	950	$5,586
2005............................	$35,583	758	$1,972	$62,247	1,097	$2,874	$92,170	823	$3,884
2004............................	$34,237	736	$2,177	$56,581	1,126	$2,526	$91,406	788	$3,940
2003............................	$31,430	746	$1,341	$52,179	1,024	$1,452	$83,131	807	$2,948
2002............................	$32,427	744	$2,350	$54,683	1,006	$2,384	$82,134	772	$3,596
Female									
2008............................	$27,315	764	$1,153	$49,076	1,174	$1,399	$64,802	690	$2,804
2007............................	$25,597	755	$947	$48,200	1,266	$2,087	$65,098	673	$2,766
2006............................	$29,116	759	$2,364	$44,846	1,183	$2,356	$67,514	634	$2,676
2005............................	$27,007	745	$1,097	$41,350	1,107	$1,129	$60,077	556	$2,452
2004............................	$24,634	754	$931	$38,618	1,099	$984	$63,553	448	$5,677
2003............................	$22,750	748	$826	$43,252	924	$2,062	$58,391	487	$3,204
2002............................	$21,615	711	$831	$37,507	978	$1,192	$56,417	429	$2,743

[1]For data prior to 1991, "Some college/Associate degree" equals 1 to 3 years of college completed; "Bachelor's degree" equals 4 years of college; "Advanced degree" equals 5 or more years of college completed.
… = Not available.

Table A-28. Educational Attainment of Persons 25 Years Old and Over, by Median Income and Sex, 1991–2009

(Dollars, numbers in thousands.)

Educational attainment and year	Male			Female		
	Number with income	Median income		Number with income	Median income	
		Current dollars	2009 dollars		Current dollars	2009 dollars
Total						
2009	91,745	36,801	36,801	93,426	23,159	23,159
2008	91,653	37,463	37,321	93,143	22,944	22,857
2007	90,647	37,828	39,132	92,075	23,052	23,847
2006	89,816	36,847	39,199	91,315	21,900	23,298
2005	88,804	35,758	39,288	90,762	20,806	22,860
2004	87,570	34,823	39,543	89,794	20,147	22,878
2003	86,532	33,517	39,089	89,118	19,679	22,950
2002	85,668	32,471	38,714	88,903	18,965	22,612
2001	84,389	32,494	39,368	88,075	18,549	22,473
2000	83,860	32,155	40,051	87,619	18,032	22,460
1999	82,795	31,545	40,608	87,229	17,022	21,912
1998	80,869	30,654	40,284	84,819	16,258	21,365
1997	80,263	28,919	38,534	83,821	15,573	20,751
1996	79,423	27,248	37,092	83,056	14,682	19,986
1995	78,264	26,346	36,819	82,457	13,821	19,315
1994	77,546	25,465	36,445	81,829	12,766	18,270
1993	76,419	24,605	35,966	80,898	12,234	17,883
1992	75,872	23,894	35,790	79,854	11,922	17,857
1991	75,137	23,686	36,378	79,383	11,580	17,785
Less than 9th grade						
2009	4,736	16,473	16,473	4,036	10,516	10,516
2008	4,973	17,043	16,978	4,201	10,625	10,585
2007	5,036	16,625	17,198	4,070	10,539	10,902
2006	5,283	17,169	18,265	4,257	10,451	11,118
2005	5,475	16,321	17,932	4,579	9,496	10,433
2004	5,520	16,171	18,363	4,742	9,576	10,874
2003	5,405	15,461	18,031	4,734	9,296	10,841
2002	5,705	15,130	18,039	5,015	8,965	10,689
2001	5,809	14,594	17,681	5,196	8,846	10,717
2000	5,724	14,131	17,601	5,195	8,546	10,644
1999	5,728	13,529	17,416	5,397	8,261	10,634
1998	5,641	12,571	16,520	5,419	7,914	10,400
1997	5,839	12,157	16,199	5,647	7,505	10,000
1996	6,139	12,174	16,572	5,775	7,276	9,905
1995	6,277	11,723	16,383	6,020	7,096	9,917
1994	6,507	11,324	16,207	6,183	6,865	9,825
1993	6,734	10,895	15,925	6,423	6,480	9,472
1992	7,000	10,374	15,539	6,921	6,337	9,492
1991	7,143	10,319	15,848	7,065	6,268	9,627
9th to 12th grade (no diploma)						
2009	6,948	19,720	19,720	6,175	12,278	12,278
2008	7,158	20,845	20,766	6,413	11,904	11,859
2007	7,200	20,643	21,355	6,286	11,982	12,395
2006	7,684	21,184	22,536	6,750	11,914	12,674
2005	7,276	20,934	23,000	6,812	11,136	12,235
2004	7,254	19,593	22,249	6,982	10,751	12,208
2003	7,245	18,990	22,147	6,965	10,786	12,579
2002	7,488	19,802	23,610	7,103	10,613	12,654
2001	7,421	19,434	23,545	7,376	10,330	12,515
2000	7,226	18,915	23,560	7,565	10,063	12,534
1999	7,085	17,653	22,725	7,525	9,632	12,399
1998	7,366	17,462	22,948	7,559	9,582	12,592
1997	7,601	16,818	22,410	7,661	8,861	11,807
1996	7,671	16,058	21,859	7,929	8,544	11,631
1995	7,490	15,791	22,068	8,122	8,057	11,260
1994	7,286	14,584	20,872	7,943	7,618	10,903
1993	7,377	14,550	21,268	8,152	7,187	10,505
1992	7,524	14,218	21,297	8,248	7,293	10,924
1991	7,759	14,736	22,632	8,561	7,055	10,835

Table A-28. Educational Attainment of Persons 25 Years Old and Over, by Median Income and Sex, 1991–2009—*Continued*

(Dollars, numbers in thousands.)

Educational attainment and year	Male			Female		
	Number with income	Median income		Number with income	Median income	
		Current dollars	2009 dollars		Current dollars	2009 dollars
High School Graduate (includes equivalency)						
2009	28,946	30,303	30,303	28,154	18,340	18,340
2008	28,450	30,879	30,762	28,217	18,293	18,224
2007	27,988	31,337	32,418	28,134	18,162	18,788
2006	28,253	31,009	32,988	28,538	17,546	18,666
2005	28,077	30,134	33,109	28,409	16,695	18,343
2004	27,799	29,332	33,308	28,561	16,165	18,356
2003	26,800	28,763	33,544	28,976	15,962	18,615
2002	26,298	27,526	32,819	29,161	15,972	19,043
2001	25,954	28,343	34,339	28,945	15,665	18,979
2000	26,175	27,480	34,228	28,968	15,153	18,874
1999	26,278	27,188	34,999	29,798	14,652	18,861
1998	25,636	26,542	34,880	29,330	13,786	18,117
1997	25,777	25,453	33,916	29,332	13,407	17,865
1996	25,510	24,814	33,779	29,212	12,702	17,291
1995	24,909	23,365	32,653	28,785	12,046	16,834
1994	24,704	22,387	32,040	29,110	11,390	16,301
1993	24,682	21,782	31,839	29,171	11,089	16,209
1992	25,143	21,645	32,421	29,596	10,901	16,328
1991	25,297	21,546	33,091	30,149	10,818	16,615
Some College, No Degree						
2009	15,184	36,693	36,693	16,208	23,107	23,107
2008	15,523	37,297	37,155	16,329	23,252	23,164
2007	15,321	37,447	38,738	16,600	23,532	24,343
2006	14,526	37,271	39,650	16,099	22,709	24,159
2005	14,505	36,930	40,575	16,402	21,545	23,672
2004	14,405	36,162	41,064	15,791	21,159	24,027
2003	14,586	35,073	40,903	15,691	21,007	24,499
2002	14,747	35,023	41,757	15,616	20,602	24,563
2001	14,340	33,777	40,922	15,420	20,101	24,353
2000	14,433	33,319	41,501	15,825	20,166	25,118
1999	14,440	32,575	41,933	15,693	19,599	25,230
1998	13,935	31,627	41,562	15,173	18,445	24,239
1997	13,892	30,536	40,689	14,677	17,153	22,856
1996	13,756	29,160	39,695	14,528	16,255	22,128
1995	13,715	28,004	39,136	14,619	15,552	21,734
1994	13,573	26,768	38,309	14,911	14,585	20,874
1993	13,247	26,323	38,477	14,390	14,489	21,179
1992	12,728	26,318	39,421	13,615	14,401	21,571
1991	12,366	26,591	40,839	13,013	13,963	21,445
Associate Degree						
2009	7,399	42,163	42,163	9,936	27,027	27,027
2008	7,375	42,608	42,446	9,662	27,715	27,610
2007	7,244	43,006	44,489	9,166	27,668	28,622
2006	6,973	41,807	44,476	9,043	26,295	27,973
2005	7,000	41,903	46,039	9,070	26,074	28,648
2004	6,782	39,765	45,155	8,861	25,199	28,615
2003	6,618	39,015	45,501	8,523	24,808	28,932
2002	6,274	37,970	45,271	8,323	23,766	28,336
2001	6,352	38,870	47,093	8,177	22,638	27,427
2000	6,272	38,026	47,363	8,108	23,124	28,802
1999	5,939	36,558	47,061	7,482	21,916	28,212
1998	5,766	35,962	47,259	6,931	21,290	27,978
1997	5,591	32,930	43,879	6,914	21,073	28,080
1996	5,210	33,065	45,011	6,839	20,460	27,852
1995	5,230	31,027	43,361	6,642	19,450	27,182
1994	5,046	30,643	43,855	6,573	17,954	25,695
1993	4,901	29,736	43,466	6,282	18,346	26,817
1992	4,540	28,791	43,125	5,539	17,331	25,959
1991	4,083	29,358	45,089	5,236	17,364	26,668

Table A-28. Educational Attainment of Persons 25 Years Old and Over, by Median Income and Sex, 1991–2009—*Continued*

(Dollars, numbers in thousands.)

Educational attainment and year	Male			Female		
	Number with income	Median income		Number with income	Median income	
		Current dollars	2009 dollars		Current dollars	2009 dollars
Bachelor's Degree or More						
2009	28,532	61,280	61,280	28,917	40,766	40,766
2008	28,174	63,277	63,037	28,321	40,801	40,646
2007	27,857	62,421	64,573	27,820	40,712	42,116
2006	27,097	61,168	65,072	26,626	39,450	41,968
2005	26,470	58,114	63,850	25,490	37,055	40,713
2004	25,810	56,434	64,083	24,857	35,726	40,568
2003	25,879	55,751	65,019	24,229	35,125	40,964
2002	25,155	55,188	65,799	23,686	34,292	40,886
2001	24,512	54,069	65,507	22,961	33,842	41,001
2000	24,028	53,488	66,622	21,958	33,148	41,288
1999	23,325	52,246	67,256	21,334	31,604	40,684
1998	22,525	50,272	66,065	20,409	30,692	40,334
1997	21,563	47,126	62,795	19,590	29,781	39,683
1996	21,136	44,161	60,115	18,775	27,556	37,511
1995	20,644	43,322	60,543	18,269	26,843	37,514
1994	20,429	42,027	60,148	17,109	26,237	37,550
1993	19,479	41,649	60,879	16,480	25,246	36,903
1992	18,937	40,557	60,749	15,933	25,093	37,586
1991	18,490	39,803	61,131	15,359	23,627	36,287
Bachelor's Degree						
2009	18,205	54,091	54,091	18,844	35,972	35,972
2008	17,726	57,278	57,061	18,381	36,294	36,156
2007	17,654	56,826	58,786	18,347	36,167	37,414
2006	17,129	54,403	57,876	17,931	35,094	37,334
2005	16,764	51,700	56,803	17,090	32,668	35,893
2004	16,302	51,081	58,005	16,668	31,585	35,866
2003	16,295	50,916	59,380	16,198	31,309	36,514
2002	16,057	50,600	60,329	16,003	30,788	36,708
2001	15,723	49,985	60,559	15,660	30,973	37,525
2000	15,452	49,080	61,132	15,102	30,418	37,887
1999	14,922	47,289	60,875	14,690	28,520	36,714
1998	14,614	45,749	60,121	14,218	27,415	36,027
1997	13,900	41,949	55,897	13,787	26,401	35,179
1996	13,510	39,624	53,939	13,247	25,192	34,293
1995	13,065	39,040	54,559	12,875	24,065	33,631
1994	12,997	38,701	55,388	11,773	23,405	33,496
1993	12,360	37,474	54,776	11,447	22,452	32,818
1992	11,938	36,745	55,039	11,133	22,383	33,527
1991	11,657	36,067	55,393	10,721	20,967	32,202
Master's Degree						
2009	6,728	69,825	69,825	7,945	50,576	50,576
2008	6,896	70,973	70,704	7,801	48,000	47,818
2007	6,759	71,097	73,549	7,590	48,077	49,735
2006	6,350	67,425	71,729	6,876	46,250	49,202
2005	6,137	64,468	70,832	6,560	44,385	48,766
2004	6,059	63,260	71,835	6,464	42,243	47,969
2003	6,076	61,698	71,954	6,268	41,334	48,205
2002	5,768	60,830	72,526	6,073	40,939	48,811
2001	5,522	61,960	75,067	5,749	40,744	49,363
2000	5,346	59,732	74,399	5,421	40,619	50,593
1999	5,178	59,189	76,193	5,220	39,712	51,121
1998	4,772	55,784	73,308	4,837	36,888	48,476
1997	4,583	52,530	69,996	4,488	35,882	47,812
1996	4,709	50,003	68,068	4,285	33,302	45,333
1995	4,774	49,076	68,584	4,205	33,509	46,829
1994	4,558	46,635	66,743	4,166	32,069	45,896
1993	4,320	45,597	66,650	4,003	31,389	45,882
1992	4,308	44,293	66,345	3,873	30,169	45,189
1991	4,356	43,125	66,233	3,745	29,747	45,687

[1]For data prior to 1991, "Some college/Associate degree" equals 1 to 3 years of college completed; "Bachelor's degree" equals 4 years of college; "Advance degree" equals 5 or more years of college completed.

Table A-28. Educational Attainment of Persons 25 Years Old and Over, by Median Income and Sex, 1991–2009—*Continued*

(Dollars, numbers in thousands.)

Educational attainment and year	Male			Female		
	Number with income	Median income		Number with income	Median income	
		Current dollars	2009 dollars		Current dollars	2009 dollars
Professional Degree						
2009	1,844	102,398	102,398	1,142	60,259	60,259
2008	1,930	100,000	(X)	1,197	58,364	58,143
2007	1,843	100,000	(X)	1,060	61,875	64,009
2006	1,969	96,926	103,113	1,037	60,463	64,322
2005	1,912	90,878	99,849	1,090	59,934	65,850
2004	1,876	90,210	102,437	991	50,311	57,130
2003	1,901	88,530	103,247	990	48,536	56,604
2002	1,816	88,216	105,178	946	44,748	53,352
2001	1,779	81,602	98,864	899	46,635	56,500
2000	1,711	83,701	104,254	852	46,084	57,400
1999	1,774	81,545	104,972	824	45,432	58,484
1998	1,695	76,362	100,351	788	43,490	57,152
1997	1,741	72,274	96,304	807	45,199	60,227
1996	1,702	71,869	97,834	715	42,059	57,254
1995	1,657	66,257	92,595	732	38,588	53,927
1994	1,691	61,739	88,359	709	35,806	51,244
1993	1,650	69,678	101,850	583	32,742	47,860
1992	1,639	68,429	102,497	569	36,640	54,882
1991	1,547	63,741	97,896	556	34,064	52,317
Doctorate Degree						
2009	1,755	89,845	09,845	987	65,587	65,587
2008	1,622	90,575	90,231	942	60,619	60,389
2007	1,601	86,171	89,142	823	61,554	63,677
2006	1,649	90,511	96,288	782	61,091	64,990
2005	1,656	76,937	84,531	749	56,820	62,429
2004	1,573	80,033	90,881	734	55,996	63,586
2003	1,606	73,853	86,130	773	53,003	61,814
2002	1,514	76,147	90,788	663	52,336	62,399
2001	1,488	72,642	88,009	653	52,181	63,219
2000	1,520	71,271	88,772	584	51,460	64,096
1999	1,451	70,461	90,704	600	46,511	59,873
1998	1,443	65,319	85,838	567	46,275	60,812
1997	1,338	68,643	91,466	508	46,545	62,021
1996	1,215	62,255	84,746	527	42,431	57,760
1995	1,149	57,356	80,156	457	39,821	55,650
1994	1,183	57,478	82,261	462	40,793	58,382
1993	1,149	55,751	81,492	447	42,737	62,469
1992	1,053	51,681	77,411	358	39,322	58,899
1991	929	51,845	79,625	337	37,242	57,198

Table A-29. Total Fall Enrollment in Degree-granting Institutions, by Attendance Status, Sex of Student, and Control of Institution: Selected Years, 1947–2008

(Numbers in thousands.)

Year	Total enrolled	Attendance status			Sex of student			Control of institution			
		Full-time	Part-time	Percent part-time	Male	Female	Percent Female	Public	Private		
									Total	Not-for-profit	For-profit
2008	19,103	11,748	7,355	38.5	8,189	10,914	57.1	13,972	5,131	3,662	1,469
2007	18,248	11,270	6,978	38.2	7,816	10,432	57.2	13,491	4,757	3,571	1,186
2006	17,759	10,957	6,802	38.3	7,575	10,184	57.3	13,180	4,579	3,513	1,066
2005	17,487	10,797	6,690	38.3	7,456	10,032	57.4	13,022	4,466	3,455	1,011
2004	17,272	10,610	6,662	38.6	7,387	9,885	57.2	12,980	4,292	3,412	880
2003	16,911	10,326	6,585	38.9	7,260	9,651	57.1	12,859	4,053	3,341	712
2002	16,612	9,946	6,665	40.1	7,202	9,410	56.6	12,752	3,860	3,265	594
2001	15,928	9,448	6,480	40.7	6,961	8,967	56.3	12,233	3,695	3,167	528
2000	15,312	9,010	6,303	41.2	6,722	8,591	56.1	11,753	3,560	3,109	450
1999	14,791	8,786	6,005	40.6	6,491	8,301	56.1	11,309	3,482	3,052	430
1998	14,507	8,563	5,944	41.0	6,369	8,138	56.1	11,138	3,369	3,005	364
1997	14,502	8,438	6,064	41.8	6,396	8,106	55.9	11,196	3,306	2,978	329
1996	14,368	8,303	6,065	42.2	6,353	8,015	55.8	11,120	3,247	2,943	304
1995	14,262	8,129	6,133	43.0	6,343	7,919	55.5	11,092	3,169	2,929	240
1994	14,279	8,138	6,141	43.0	6,372	7,907	55.4	11,134	3,145	2,910	235
1993	14,305	8,128	6,177	43.2	6,427	7,877	55.1	11,189	3,116	2,889	227
1992	14,487	8,162	6,325	43.7	6,524	7,963	55.0	11,385	3,103	2,873	230
1991	14,359	8,115	6,244	43.5	6,502	7,857	54.7	11,310	3,049	2,819	230
1990	13,819	7,821	5,998	43.4	6,284	7,535	54.5	10,845	2,974	2,760	214
1989	13,539	7,661	5,878	43.4	6,190	7,349	54.3	10,578	2,961	2,731	229
1988	13,055	7,437	5,619	43.0	6,002	7,053	54.0	10,161	2,894	2,674	220
1987	12,767	7,231	5,536	43.4	5,932	6,835	53.5	9,973	2,793	2,602	191 [4]
1986	12,504	7,120	5,384	43.1	5,885	6,619	52.9	9,714	2,790	2,572	217 [4]
1985	12,247	7,075	5,172	42.2	5,818	6,429	52.5	9,479	2,768	2,572	196
1984	12,242	7,098	5,144	42.0	5,864	6,378	52.1	9,477	2,765	2,574	190
1983	12,465	7,261	5,204	41.7	6,024	6,441	51.7	9,683	2,782	2,589	193
1982	12,426	7,221	5,205	41.9	6,031	6,394	51.5	9,696	2,730	2,553	177 [3]
1981	12,372	7,181	5,190	42.0	5,975	6,397	51.7	9,647	2,725	2,572	152 [3]
1980	12,097	7,098	4,999	41.3	5,874	6,223	51.4	9,457	2,640	2,528	112 [3]
1979	11,570	6,794	4,776	41.3	5,683	5,887	50.9	9,037	2,533	2,462	71
1978	11,260	6,668	4,592	40.8	5,641	5,619	49.9	8,786	2,474	2,408	66
1977	11,286	6,793	4,493	39.8	5,789	5,497	48.7	8,847	2,439	2,387	52
1976	11,012	6,717	4,295	39.0	5,811	5,201	47.2	8,653	2,359	2,314	44
1975	11,185	6,841	4,344	38.8	6,149	5,036	45.0	8,835	2,350	2,311	39
1974	10,224	6,370	3,853	37.7	5,622	4,601	45.0	7,989	2,235	2,201	34
1973	9,602	6,189	3,413	35.5	5,371	4,231	44.1	7,420	2,183	2,149	34
1972	9,215	6,072	3,142	34.1	5,239	3,976	43.1	7,071	2,144	2,123	21
1971	8,949	6,077	2,871	32.1	5,207	3,742	41.8	6,804	2,144	2,122	22
1970	8,581	5,816	2,765	32.2	5,044	3,537	41.2	6,428	2,153	2,134	18
1969	8,005	5,499	2,506	31.3	4,746	3,258	40.7	5,897	2,108	2,088	20
1968	7,513	5,210	2,303	30.7	4,478	3,035	40.4	5,431	2,082	2,061	21
1967	6,912	4,793	2119 [2]	30.7	4,133	2,779	40.2	4,816	2,096	2,074	22
1966	6,390	4,439	1951 [2]	30.5	3,856	2,534	39.7	4,349	2,041	...	...
1965	5,921	4,096	1825 [2]	30.8	3,630	2,291	38.7	3,970	1,951	...	...
1964	5,280	3,573	1707 [2]	32.3	3,249	2,031	38.5	3,468	1,812	...	...
1963	4,780	3,184	1596 [2]	33.4	2,962	1,818	38.0	3,081	1,698	...	...
1961	4,145	2,785	1360 [2]	32.8	2,586	1,559	37.6	2,561	1,584	...	...
1959	3,640	2,421	1219 [2]	33.5	2,333	1,307	35.9	2,181	1,459	...	...
1957	3,324	...	...	...	2,171	1,153	34.7	1,973	1,351	...	...
1956 [1]	2,918	...	...	...	1,911	1,007	34.5	1,656	1,262	...	...
1955 [1]	2,653	...	...	...	1,733	920	34.7	1,476	1,177	...	...
1954 [1]	2,447	...	...	...	1,563	883	36.1	1,354	1,093	...	...
1953 [1]	2,231	...	...	...	1,423	808	36.2	1,186	1,045	...	...
1952 [1]	2,134	...	...	...	1,380	754	35.3	1,101	1,033	...	...
1951 [1]	2,102	...	...	...	1,391	711	33.8	1,038	1,064	...	...
1950 [1]	2,281	...	...	...	1,560	721	31.6	1,140	1,142	...	...
1949 [1]	2,445	...	...	...	1,722	723	29.6	1,207	1,238	...	...
1948 [1]	2,403	...	...	...	1,709	694	28.9	1,186	1,218	...	...
1947 [1]	2,338	...	...	...	1,659	679	29.0	1,152	1,186	...	...

... = Not available.
[1] Degree-credit enrollment only.
[2] Includes part-time resident students and all extension students (students attending courses at sites separate from the primary reporting campus).
[3] Large increases are due to the addition of schools accredited by the Accrediting Commission of Career Schools and Colleges of Technology.
[4] Because of imputation techniques, data are not consistent with figures for other years.

Table A-30.   Total Fall Enrollment in Degree-Granting Institutions, by Control and Type of Institution: 1963–2008

(Numbers in thousands).

Year	All institutions					Public institutions				
	Total	4-year			2-year	Total	4-year			2-year
		Total	University	Other 4-year			Total	University	Other 4-year	
2008.............	19,103	12,131	3,412	8,719	6,971	13,972	7,332	2,545	4,787	6,640
2007.............	18,248	11,630	3,349	8,281	6,618	13,491	7,167	2,491	4,676	6,324
2006.............	17,759	11,240	3,307	7,933	6,519	13,180	6,955	2,460	4,495	6,225
2005.............	17,487	10,999	3,272	7,728	6,488	13,022	6,838	2,444	4,394	6,184
2004.............	17,272	10,726	3,259	7,467	6,546	12,980	6,737	2,426	4,310	6,244
2003.............	16,911	10,417	3,243	7,175	6,494	12,859	6,649	2,420	4,230	6,209
2002.............	16,612	10,082	3,210	6,872	6,529	12,752	6,482	2,403	4,078	6,270
2001.............	15,928	9,677	3,127	6,551	6,251	12,233	6,236	2,337	3,900	5,997
2000.............	15,312	9,364	3,062	6,302	5,948	11,753	6,055	2,280	3,775	5,697
1999	14,791	9,199	3,044	6,154	5,593	11,309	5,970	2,266	3,703	5,339
1998	14,507	9,018	3,021	5,997	5,489	11,138	5,892	2,250	3,642	5,246
1997	14,502	8,897	2,996	5,901	5,606	11,196	5,835	2,231	3,604	5,361
1996	14,368	8,804	2,985	5,819	5,563	11,120	5,806	2,227	3,580	5,314
1995	14,262	8,769	3,000	5,770	5,493	11,092	5,815	2,236	3,579	5,278
1994	14,279	8,749	3,009	5,740	5,530	11,134	5,825	2,245	3,581	5,308
1993	14,305	8,739	3,023	5,716	5,566	11,189	5,852	2,260	3,592	5,337
1992	14,487	8,765	3,050	5,715	5,722	11,385	5,900	2,284	3,616	5,485
1991	14,359	8,707	3,065	5,642	5,652	11,310	5,905	2,301	3,604	5,405
1990	13,819	8,579	3,045	5,534	5,240	10,845	5,848	2,290	3,558	4,996
1989	13,539	8,388	3,019	5,369	5,151	10,578	5,694	2,266	3,428	4,884
1988	13,055	8,180	2,979	5,202	4,875	10,161	5,546	2,230	3,316	4,615
1987	12,767	7,990	2,929	5,061	4,776	9,973	5,432	2,188	3,244	4,541
1986	12,504	7,824	2,897	4,927	4,680	9,714	5,300	2,161	3,140	4,414
1985	12,247	7,716	2,871	4,845	4,531	9,479	5,210	2,141	3,068	4,270
1984	12,242	7,711	2,870	4,841	4,531	9,477	5,198	2,139	3,060	4,279
1983	12,465	7,741	2,889	4,852	4,723	9,683	5,223	2,155	3,069	4,459
1982	12,426	7,654	2,884	4,770	4,772	9,696	5,176	2,153	3,024	4,520
1981	12,372	7,655	2,901	4,754	4,716	9,647	5,166	2,152	3,014	4,481
1980	12,097	7,571	2,902	4,669	4,526	9,457	5,129	2,154	2,974	4,329
1979	11,570	7,353	2,840	4,514	4,217	9,037	4,980	2,100	2,880	4,057
1978	11,260	7,232	2,781	4,451	4,028	8,786	4,912	2,062	2,850	3,874
1977	11,286	7,243	2,793	4,449	4,043	8,847	4,945	2,070	2,875	3,902
1976	11,012	7,129	2,780	4,349	3,883	8,653	4,902	2,080	2,822	3,752
1975	11,185	7,215	2,838	4,376	3,970	8,835	4,998	2,124	2,874	3,836
1974	10,224	6,820	2,702	4,117	3,404	7,989	4,703	2,007	2,696	3,285
1973	9,602	6,590	2,630	3,960	3,012	7,420	4,530	1,951	2,579	2,890
1972	9,215	6,459	2,621	3,838	2,756	7,071	4,430	1,941	2,489	2,641
1971	8,949	6,369	2,594	3,775	2,579	6,804	4,347	1,914	2,433	2,457
1970	8,581	6,262	2,534	3,727	2,319	6,428	4,233	1,833	2,400	2,195
1969	8,005	5,937	2,420	3,517	2,068	5,897	3,963	1,738	2,224	1,934
1968	7,513	5,720	2,266	3,454	1,793	5,431	3,784	1,593	2,191	1,647
1967	6,912	5,399	2,186	3,213	1,513	4,816	3,444	1,510	1,934	1,372
1966[1].............	6,390	5,064	...	...	1,326	4,349	3,160	...	...	1,189
1965[1].............	5,921	4,748	...	...	1,173	3,970	2,928	...	...	1,041
1964[1].............	5,280	4,291	...	...	989	3,468	2,593	...	...	875
1963[1].............	4,780	3,929	...	...	850	3,081	2,341	...	...	740

... = Not available
[1] Data for 2-year branch campuses of 4-year institutions are included with the 4-year institutions.

Table A-30.   Total Fall Enrollment in Degree-Granting Institutions, by Control and Type of Institution: 1963–2008—*Continued*

(Numbers in thousands).

Year	Private institutions				
	Total	4-year			2-year
		Total	University	Other 4-year	
2008..............................	5,131	4,800	868	3,932	331
2007..............................	4,757	4,464	859	3,605	294
2006..............................	4,579	4,285	847	3,438	293
2005..............................	4,466	4,162	828	3,334	304
2004..............................	4,292	3,990	832	3,157	302
2003..............................	4,053	3,768	823	2,945	285
2002..............................	3,860	3,601	807	2,794	259
2001..............................	3,695	3,441	790	2,651	254
2000..............................	3,560	3,308	782	2,527	251
1999..............................	3,482	3,229	778	2,451	253
1998..............................	3,369	3,126	771	2,355	243
1997..............................	3,306	3,061	765	2,297	245
1996..............................	3,247	2,998	758	2,240	249
1995..............................	3,169	2,955	764	2,191	215
1994..............................	3,145	2,924	764	2,159	221
1993..............................	3,116	2,887	763	2,124	229
1992..............................	3,103	2,865	767	2,098	238
1991..............................	3,049	2,802	764	2,038	247
1990..............................	2,974	2,730	754	1,976	244
1989..............................	2,961	2,693	753	1,940	267
1988..............................	2,894	2,634	749	1,886	260
1987..............................	2,793	2,558	741	1,817	235
1986..............................	2,790	2,524	737	1,787	266 [2]
1985..............................	2,768	2,506	730	1,777	261 [2]
1984..............................	2,765	2,513	732	1,781	252
1983..............................	2,782	2,518	734	1,784	264
1982..............................	2,730	2,478	731	1,746	252 [3]
1981..............................	2,725	2,489	749	1,740	236 [3]
1980..............................	2,640	2,442	748	1,694	198 [3]
1979..............................	2,533	2,373	740	1,633	160
1978..............................	2,474	2,319	718	1,601	155
1977..............................	2,439	2,298	723	1,574	141
1976..............................	2,359	2,227	700	1,527	132
1975..............................	2,350	2,217	714	1,503	134
1974..............................	2,235	2,117	696	1,421	119
1973..............................	2,183	2,060	679	1,381	122
1972..............................	2,144	2,029	680	1,349	115
1971..............................	2,144	2,022	681	1,342	122
1970..............................	2,153	2,029	702	1,327	124
1969..............................	2,108	1,975	682	1,293	133
1968..............................	2,082	1,937	673	1,263	146
1967..............................	2,096	1,955	676	1,279	141
1966 [1]..............................	2,041	1,904	...	...	137
1965 [1]..............................	1,951	1,820	...	...	132
1964 [1]..............................	1,812	1,698	...	...	114
1963 [1]..............................	1,698	1,588	...	...	111

... = Not available

[1] Data for 2-year branch campuses of 4-year institutions are included with the 4-year institutions.

[2] Large increases are due to the addition of schools accredited by the Accrediting Commission of Career Schools and Colleges of Technology.

[3] Because of imputation techniques, data are not consistent with figures for other years.

Table A-31.   Total Fall Enrollment in Degree-Granting Institutions, by Level of Enrollment, Sex, Age, and Attendance Status of Student, 2007

Age of student and attendance status	All levels						Undergraduate					
	Total		Males		Females		Total		Males		Females	
	Number	Percent	Number	Percent	Number	Percent	Number	Percent	Number	Percent	Number	Percent
All students	18,248,128	100.0	7,815,914	100.0	10,432,214	100.0	15,603,771	100.0	6,727,600	100.0	8,876,171	100.0
Under 18	668,426	3.7	277,582	3.6	390,844	3.7	668,193	4.3	277,489	4.1	390,704	4.4
18 and 19	3,963,371	21.7	1,794,001	23.0	2,169,370	20.8	3,961,149	25.4	1,793,284	26.7	2,167,865	24.4
20 and 21	3,642,872	20.0	1,647,492	21.1	1,995,380	19.1	3,612,195	23.1	1,635,396	24.3	1,976,799	22.3
22 to 24	3,009,713	16.5	1,381,504	17.7	1,628,209	15.6	2,474,561	15.9	1,168,612	17.4	1,305,949	14.7
25 to 29	2,550,482	14.0	1,091,510	14.0	1,458,972	14.0	1,710,195	11.0	728,331	10.8	981,864	11.1
30 to 34	1,365,912	7.5	551,208	7.1	814,704	7.8	944,123	6.1	357,944	5.3	586,179	6.6
35 to 39	980,818	5.4	368,814	4.7	612,004	5.9	709,012	4.5	251,299	3.7	457,713	5.2
40 to 49	1,266,171	6.9	423,603	5.4	842,568	8.1	935,783	6.0	304,967	4.5	630,816	7.1
50 to 64	627,603	3.4	208,067	2.7	419,536	4.0	445,568	2.9	150,103	2.2	295,465	3.3
65 and over	77,379	0.4	31,040	0.4	46,339	0.4	70,608	0.5	27,847	0.4	42,761	0.5
Age unknown	95,381	0.5	41,093	0.5	54,288	0.5	72,384	0.5	32,328	0.5	40,056	0.5
Full-time	11,269,892	100.0	5,029,444	100.0	6,240,448	100.0	9,840,978	100.0	4,396,868	100.0	5,444,110	100.0
Under 18	171,784	1.5	69,033	1.4	102,751	1.6	171,705	1.7	69,000	1.6	102,705	1.9
18 and 19	3,383,318	30.0	1,522,297	30.3	1,861,021	29.8	3,381,502	34.4	1,521,669	34.6	1,859,833	34.2
20 and 21	2,964,697	26.3	1,346,897	26.8	1,617,800	25.9	2,937,292	29.8	1,335,936	30.4	1,601,356	29.4
22 to 24	1,986,776	17.6	949,700	18.9	1,037,076	16.6	1,572,230	16.0	778,160	17.7	794,070	14.6
25 to 29	1,284,698	11.4	584,798	11.6	699,900	11.2	776,416	7.9	346,671	7.9	429,745	7.9
30 to 34	565,710	5.0	235,321	4.7	330,389	5.3	365,008	3.7	135,611	3.1	229,397	4.2
35 to 39	347,864	3.1	130,397	2.6	217,467	3.5	241,500	2.5	81,381	1.9	160,119	2.9
40 to 49	380,043	3.4	125,982	2.5	254,061	4.1	270,137	2.7	84,186	1.9	185,951	3.4
50 to 64	145,757	1.3	47,812	1.0	97,945	1.6	93,913	1.0	30,478	0.7	63,435	1.2
65 and over	4,868	-	2,260	-	2,608	-	3,185	-	1,471	-	1,714	-
Age unknown	34,377	0.3	14,947	0.3	19,430	0.3	28,090	0.3	12,305	0.3	15,785	0.3
Part-time	6,978,236	100.0	2,786,470	100.0	4,191,766	100.0	5,762,793	100.0	2,330,732	100.0	3,432,061	100.0
Under 18	496,642	7.1	208,549	7.5	288,093	6.9	496,488	8.6	208,489	8.9	287,999	8.4
18 and 19	580,053	8.3	271,704	9.8	308,349	7.4	579,647	10.1	271,615	11.7	308,032	9.0
20 and 21	678,175	9.7	300,595	10.8	377,580	9.0	674,903	11.7	299,460	12.8	375,443	10.9
22 to 24	1,022,937	14.7	431,804	15.5	591,133	14.1	902,331	15.7	390,452	16.8	511,879	14.9
25 to 29	1,265,784	18.1	506,712	18.2	759,072	18.1	933,779	16.2	381,660	16.4	552,119	16.1
30 to 34	800,202	11.5	315,887	11.3	484,315	11.6	579,115	10.0	222,333	9.5	356,782	10.4
35 to 39	632,954	9.1	238,417	8.6	394,537	9.4	467,512	8.1	169,918	7.3	297,594	8.7
40 to 49	886,128	12.7	297,621	10.7	588,507	14.0	665,646	11.6	220,781	9.5	444,865	13.0
50 to 64	481,846	6.9	160,255	5.8	321,591	7.7	351,655	6.1	119,625	5.1	232,030	6.8
65 and over	72,511	1.0	28,780	1.0	43,731	1.0	67,423	1.2	26,376	1.1	41,047	1.2
Age unknown	61,004	0.9	26,146	0.9	34,858	0.8	44,294	0.8	20,023	0.9	24,271	0.7

- =Quantity zero or equals zero

Table A-31. Total Fall Enrollment in Degree-Granting Institutions, by Level of Enrollment, Sex, Age, and Attendance Status of Student, 2007—*Continued*

Age of student and attendance status	Professional						Graduate					
	Total		Males		Females		Total		Males		Females	
	Number	Percent	Number	Percent	Number	Percent	Number	Percent	Number	Percent	Number	Percent
All students	350,764	100.0	177,988	100.0	172,776	100.0	2,293,593	100.0	910,326	100.0	1,383,267	100.0
Under 18	18	-	5	-	13	-	215	-	88	-	127	-
18 and 19	1,291	0.4	464	0.3	827	0.5	931	-	253	-	678	-
20 and 21	11,926	3.4	4,454	2.5	7,472	4.3	18,751	0.8	7,642	0.8	11,109	0.8
22 to 24	133,563	38.1	61,463	34.5	72,100	41.7	401,589	17.5	151,429	16.6	250,160	18.1
25 to 29	138,825	39.6	74,285	41.7	64,540	37.4	701,462	30.6	288,894	31.7	412,568	29.8
30 to 34	31,764	9.1	19,067	10.7	12,697	7.3	390,025	17.0	174,197	19.1	215,828	15.6
35 to 39	13,326	3.8	7,895	4.4	5,431	3.1	258,480	11.3	109,620	12.0	148,860	10.8
40 to 49	12,314	3.5	6,613	3.7	5,701	3.3	318,074	13.9	112,023	12.3	206,051	14.9
50 to 64	6,197	1.8	2,902	1.6	3,295	1.9	175,838	7.7	55,062	6.0	120,776	8.7
65 and over	288	0.1	132	0.1	156	0.1	6,483	0.3	3,061	0.3	3,422	0.2
Age unknown	1,252	0.4	708	0.4	544	0.3	21,745	0.9	8,057	0.9	13,688	1.0
Full-time	316,549	100.0	159,328	100.0	157,221	100.0	1,112,365	100.0	473,248	100.0	639,117	100.0
Under 18	15	-	4	-	11	-	64	-	29	-	35	-
18 and 19	1,286	0.4	461	0.3	825	0.5	530	-	167	-	363	-
20 and 21	11,695	3.7	4,354	2.7	7,341	4.7	15,710	1.4	6,607	1.4	9,103	1.4
22 to 24	128,394	40.6	58,966	37.0	69,428	44.2	286,152	25.7	112,574	23.8	173,578	27.2
25 to 29	127,726	40.3	68,108	42.7	59,618	37.9	380,556	34.2	170,019	35.9	210,537	32.9
30 to 34	26,135	8.3	15,665	9.8	10,470	6.7	174,567	15.7	84,045	17.8	90,522	14.2
35 to 39	9,555	3.0	5,666	3.6	3,889	2.5	96,809	8.7	43,350	9.2	53,459	8.4
40 to 49	7,527	2.4	4,056	2.5	3,471	2.2	102,379	9.2	37,740	8.0	64,639	10.1
50 to 64	3,153	1.0	1,449	0.9	1,704	1.1	48,691	4.4	15,885	3.4	32,806	5.1
65 and over	149	-	68	-	81	0.1	1,534	0.1	721	0.2	813	0.1
Age unknown	914	0.3	531	0.3	383	0.2	5,373	0.5	2,111	0.4	3,262	0.5
Part-time	34,215	100.0	18,660	100.0	15,555	100.0	1,181,228	100.0	437,078	100.0	744,150	100.0
Under 18	3	-	1	-	2	-	151	-	59	-	92	-
18 and 19	5	-	3	-	2	-	401	-	86	-	315	-
20 and 21	231	0.7	100	0.5	131	0.8	3,041	0.3	1,035	0.2	2,006	0.3
22 to 24	5,169	15.1	2,497	13.4	2,672	17.2	115,437	9.8	38,855	8.9	76,582	10.3
25 to 29	11,099	32.4	6,177	33.1	4,922	31.6	320,906	27.2	118,875	27.2	202,031	27.1
30 to 34	5,629	16.5	3,402	18.2	2,227	14.3	215,458	18.2	90,152	20.6	125,306	16.8
35 to 39	3,771	11.0	2,229	11.9	1,542	9.9	161,671	13.7	66,270	15.2	95,401	12.8
40 to 49	4,787	14.0	2,557	13.7	2,230	14.3	215,695	18.3	74,283	17.0	141,412	19.0
50 to 64	3,044	8.9	1,453	7.8	1,591	10.2	127,147	10.8	39,177	9.0	87,970	11.8
65 and over	139	0.4	64	0.3	75	0.5	4,949	0.4	2,340	0.5	2,609	0.4
Age unknown	338	1.0	177	0.9	161	1.0	16,372	1.4	5,946	1.4	10,426	1.4

- =Quantity zero or equals zero

Table A-32. Total Fall Enrollment in Degree-Granting Institutions, by Control and Type of Institution, Age, and Attendance Status of Student, 2007

Age of student and attendance status	All institutions						Public institutions					
	Total		4-year		2-year		Total		4-year		2-year	
	Number	Percent	Number	Percent	Number	Percent	Number	Percent	Number	Percent	Number	Percent
All students	18,248,128	100.0	11,630,198	100.0	6,617,930	100.0	13,490,780	100.0	7,166,661	100.0	6,324,119	100.0
Under 18	668,426	3.7	226,437	1.9	441,989	6.7	603,430	4.5	164,703	2.3	438,727	6.9
18 and 19	3,963,371	21.7	2,496,501	21.5	1,466,870	22.2	3,087,771	22.9	1,667,313	23.3	1,420,458	22.5
20 and 21	3,642,872	20.0	2,540,470	21.8	1,102,402	16.7	2,749,406	20.4	1,698,286	23.7	1,051,120	16.6
22 to 24	3,009,713	16.5	2,108,489	18.1	901,224	13.6	2,286,919	17.0	1,437,269	20.1	849,650	13.4
25 to 29	2,550,482	14.0	1,690,509	14.5	859,973	13.0	1,765,751	13.1	962,096	13.4	803,655	12.7
30 to 34	1,365,912	7.5	855,514	7.4	510,398	7.7	919,828	6.8	440,675	6.1	479,153	7.6
35 to 39	980,818	5.4	584,732	5.0	396,086	6.0	654,855	4.9	279,752	3.9	375,103	5.9
40 to 49	1,266,171	6.9	718,209	6.2	547,962	8.3	858,630	6.4	332,290	4.6	526,340	8.3
50 to 64	627,603	3.4	332,951	2.9	294,652	4.5	447,534	3.3	160,410	2.2	287,124	4.5
65 and over	77,379	0.4	17,459	0.2	59,920	0.9	70,649	0.5	10,981	0.2	59,668	0.9
Age unknown	95,381	0.5	58,927	0.5	36,454	0.6	46,007	0.3	12,886	0.2	33,121	0.5
Full-time	11,269,892	100.0	8,577,299	100.0	2,692,593	100.0	7,686,981	100.0	5,244,841	100.0	2,442,140	100.0
Under 18	171,784	1.5	100,932	1.2	70,852	2.6	137,294	1.8	68,699	1.3	68,595	2.8
18 and 19	3,383,318	30.0	2,379,998	27.7	1,003,320	37.3	2,534,326	33.0	1,574,654	30.0	959,672	39.3
20 and 21	2,964,697	26.3	2,355,947	27.5	608,750	22.6	2,116,672	27.5	1,553,773	29.6	562,899	23.0
22 to 24	1,986,776	17.6	1,642,119	19.1	344,657	12.8	1,404,007	18.3	1,103,749	21.0	300,258	12.3
25 to 29	1,284,698	11.4	1,011,469	11.8	273,229	10.1	763,452	9.9	537,312	10.2	226,140	9.3
30 to 34	565,710	5.0	425,187	5.0	140,523	5.2	303,239	3.9	188,066	3.6	115,173	4.7
35 to 39	347,864	3.1	254,514	3.0	93,350	3.5	170,684	2.2	94,094	1.8	76,590	3.1
40 to 49	380,043	3.4	275,167	3.2	104,876	3.9	176,521	2.3	88,159	1.7	88,362	3.6
50 to 64	145,757	1.3	105,578	1.2	40,179	1.5	66,065	0.9	31,490	0.6	34,575	1.4
65 and over	4,868	-	2,990	-	1,878	0.1	2,608	-	894	-	1,714	0.1
Age unknown	34,377	0.3	23,398	0.3	10,979	0.4	12,113	0.2	3,951	0.1	8,162	0.3
Part-time	6,978,236	100.0	3,052,899	100.0	3,925,337	100.0	5,803,799	100.0	1,921,820	100.0	3,881,979	100.0
Under 18	496,642	7.1	125,505	4.1	371,137	9.5	466,136	8.0	96,004	5.0	370,132	9.5
18 and 19	580,053	8.3	116,503	3.8	463,550	11.8	553,445	9.5	92,659	4.8	460,786	11.9
20 and 21	678,175	9.7	184,523	6.0	493,652	12.6	632,734	10.9	144,513	7.5	488,221	12.6
22 to 24	1,022,937	14.7	466,370	15.3	556,567	14.2	882,912	15.2	333,520	17.4	549,392	14.2
25 to 29	1,265,784	18.1	679,040	22.2	586,744	14.9	1,002,299	17.3	424,784	22.1	577,515	14.9
30 to 34	800,202	11.5	430,327	14.1	369,875	9.4	616,589	10.6	252,609	13.1	363,980	9.4
35 to 39	632,954	9.1	330,218	10.8	302,736	7.7	484,171	8.3	185,658	9.7	298,513	7.7
40 to 49	886,128	12.7	443,042	14.5	443,086	11.3	682,109	11.8	244,131	12.7	437,978	11.3
50 to 64	481,846	6.9	227,373	7.4	254,473	6.5	381,469	6.6	128,920	6.7	252,549	6.5
65 and over	72,511	1.0	14,469	0.5	58,042	1.5	68,041	1.2	10,087	0.5	57,954	1.5
Age unknown	61,004	0.9	35,529	1.2	25,475	0.6	33,894	0.6	8,935	0.5	24,959	0.6

- =Quantity zero or equals zero

Table A-32. Total Fall Enrollment in Degree-Granting Institutions, by Control and Type of Institution, Age, and Attendance Status of Student, 2007—*Continued*

Age of student and attendance status	Private (not-for-profit and for-profit) institutions						Private not-for-profit institutions only					
	Total		4-year		2-year		Total		4-year		2-year	
	Number	Percent	Number	Percent	Number	Percent	Number	Percent	Number	Percent	Number	Percent
All students	4,757,348	100.0	4,463,537	100.0	293,811	100.0	3,571,150	100.0	3,537,664	100.0	33,486	100.0
Under 18	64,996	1.4	61,734	1.4	3,262	1.1	60,050	1.7	58,797	1.7	1,253	3.7
18 and 19	875,600	18.4	829,188	18.6	46,412	15.8	784,185	22.0	776,105	21.9	8,080	24.1
20 and 21	893,466	18.8	842,184	18.9	51,282	17.5	768,560	21.5	763,235	21.6	5,325	15.9
22 to 24	722,794	15.2	671,220	15.0	51,574	17.6	557,120	15.6	552,583	15.6	4,537	13.5
25 to 29	784,731	16.5	728,413	16.3	56,318	19.2	529,744	14.8	525,022	14.8	4,722	14.1
30 to 34	446,084	9.4	414,839	9.3	31,245	10.6	269,966	7.6	267,016	7.5	2,950	8.8
35 to 39	325,963	6.9	304,980	6.8	20,983	7.1	192,261	5.4	189,966	5.4	2,295	6.9
40 to 49	407,541	8.6	385,919	8.6	21,622	7.4	249,823	7.0	246,893	7.0	2,930	8.7
50 to 64	180,069	3.8	172,541	3.9	7,528	2.6	118,491	3.3	117,375	3.3	1,116	3.3
65 and over	6,730	0.1	6,478	0.1	252	0.1	5,268	0.1	5,206	0.1	62	0.2
Age unknown	49,374	1.0	46,041	1.0	3,333	1.1	35,682	1.0	35,466	1.0	216	0.6
Full-time	3,582,911	100.0	3,332,458	100.0	250,453	100.0	2,664,502	100.0	2,643,207	100.0	21,295	100.0
Under 18	34,490	1.0	32,233	1.0	2,257	0.9	30,484	1.1	30,135	1.1	349	1.6
18 and 19	848,992	23.7	805,344	24.2	43,648	17.4	767,454	28.8	760,108	28.8	7,346	34.5
20 and 21	848,025	23.7	802,174	24.1	45,851	18.3	741,692	27.8	737,467	27.9	4,225	19.8
22 to 24	582,769	16.3	538,370	16.2	44,399	17.7	449,656	16.9	446,735	16.9	2,921	13.7
25 to 29	521,246	14.5	474,157	14.2	47,089	18.8	325,658	12.2	323,127	12.2	2,531	11.9
30 to 34	262,471	7.3	237,121	7.1	25,350	10.1	130,701	4.9	129,371	4.9	1,330	6.2
35 to 39	177,180	4.9	160,420	4.8	16,760	6.7	79,146	3.0	78,154	3.0	992	4.7
40 to 49	203,522	5.7	187,008	5.6	16,514	6.6	89,721	3.4	88,639	3.4	1,082	5.1
50 to 64	79,692	2.2	74,088	2.2	5,604	2.2	36,587	1.4	36,195	1.4	392	1.8
65 and over	2,260	0.1	2,096	0.1	164	0.2	1,364	0.1	1,347	0.1	17	0.2
Age unknown	22,264	0.6	19,447	0.6	2,817	1.1	12,039	0.5	11,929	0.5	110	0.5
Part-time	1,174,437	100.0	1,131,079	100.0	43,358	100.0	906,648	100.0	894,457	100.0	12,191	100.0
Under 18	30,506	2.6	29,501	2.6	1,005	2.3	29,566	3.3	28,662	3.2	904	7.4
18 and 19	26,608	2.3	23,844	2.1	2,764	6.4	16,731	1.8	15,997	1.8	734	6.0
20 and 21	45,441	3.9	40,010	3.5	5,431	12.5	26,868	3.0	25,768	2.9	1,100	9.0
22 to 24	140,025	11.9	132,850	11.7	7,175	16.5	107,464	11.9	105,848	11.8	1,616	13.3
25 to 29	263,485	22.4	254,256	22.5	9,229	21.3	204,086	22.5	201,895	22.6	2,191	18.0
30 to 34	183,613	15.6	177,718	15.7	5,895	13.6	139,265	15.4	137,645	15.4	1,620	13.3
35 to 39	148,783	12.7	144,560	12.8	4,223	9.7	113,115	12.5	111,812	12.5	1,303	10.7
40 to 49	204,019	17.4	198,911	17.6	5,108	11.8	160,102	17.7	158,254	17.7	1,848	15.2
50 to 64	100,377	8.5	98,453	8.7	1,924	4.4	81,904	9.0	81,180	9.1	724	5.9
65 and over	4,470	0.4	4,382	0.4	88	0.2	3,904	0.4	3,859	0.4	45	0.4
Age unknown	27,110	2.3	26,594	2.4	516	1.2	23,643	2.6	23,537	2.6	106	0.9

- =Quantity zero or equals zero

Table A-33.   Total Undergraduate Fall Enrollment in Degree-Granting Institutions, by Attendance Status, Sex of Student, and Control of Institution, 1967–2008

(Numbers in thousands.)

Year	Total	Full-time	Part-time	Males	Females	Males Full-time	Males Part-time	Females Full-time	Females Part-time	Males Public	Males Private	Females Public	Females Private
2008	16,366	10,255	6,111	7,067	9,299	4,577	2,489	5,677	3,622	5,532	1,535	7,059	2,240
2007	15,604	9,841	5,763	6,728	8,876	4,397	2,331	5,444	3,432	5,301	1,427	6,837	2,039
2006	15,184	9,571	5,613	6,514	8,671	4,265	2,249	5,306	3,364	5,134	1,380	6,714	1,957
2005	14,964	9,446	5,518	6,409	8,555	4,201	2,208	5,246	3,310	5,046	1,363	6,652	1,903
2004	14,781	9,284	5,496	6,340	8,441	4,141	2,199	5,144	3,297	5,009	1,331	6,641	1,799
2003	14,480	9,045	5,435	6,227	8,253	4,049	2,179	4,997	3,256	4,956	1,271	6,567	1,686
2002	14,257	8,734	5,523	6,192	8,065	3,934	2,258	4,800	3,265	4,960	1,232	6,473	1,592
2001	13,716	8,328	5,388	6,004	7,711	3,769	2,236	4,559	3,152	4,804	1,200	6,182	1,529
2000	13,155	7,923	5,232	5,778	7,377	3,588	2,190	4,335	3,042	4,622	1,156	5,917	1,460
1999	12,681	7,735	4,946	5,559	7,122	3,516	2,044	4,219	2,903	4,431	1,128	5,679	1,443
1998	12,437	7,539	4,898	5,446	6,991	3,428	2,018	4,111	2,880	4,361	1,085	5,589	1,402
1997	12,451	7,419	5,032	5,469	6,982	3,380	2,089	4,039	2,943	4,408	1,060	5,599	1,383
1996	12,327	7,299	5,028	5,421	6,906	3,339	2,082	3,960	2,947	4,383	1,038	5,553	1,354
1995	12,232	7,145	5,086	5,401	6,831	3,297	2,105	3,849	2,982	4,380	1,021	5,524	1,307
1994	12,263	7,169	5,094	5,422	6,840	3,342	2,081	3,827	3,013	4,394	1,028	5,551	1,290
1993	12,324	7,179	5,144	5,484	6,840	3,382	2,102	3,797	3,043	4,447	1,036	5,565	1,276
1992	12,538	7,244	5,293	5,583	6,955	3,425	2,158	3,820	3,135	4,537	1,046	5,679	1,275
1991	12,439	7,221	5,218	5,571	6,868	3,436	2,135	3,786	3,082	4,531	1,040	5,617	1,251
1990	11,959	6,976	4,983	5,380	6,579	3,337	2,043	3,639	2,940	4,353	1,027	5,357	1,223
1989	11,743	6,841	4,902	5,311	6,432	3,279	2,032	3,562	2,869	4,272	1,039	5,216	1,216
1988	11,317	6,642	4,674	5,138	6,179	3,206	1,931	3,436	2,743	4,113	1,024	4,990	1,189
1987	11,046	6,463	4,584	5,068	5,978	3,164	1,905	3,299	2,679	4,076	992	4,842	1,136
1986	10,798	6,352	4,446	5,018	5,780	3,146	1,871	3,206	2,575	4,002	1,015	4,658	1,122
1985	10,597	6,320	4,277	4,962	5,635	3,156	1,806	3,163	2,471	3,953	1,010	4,525	1,110
1984	10,618	6,348	4,270	5,007	5,611	3,195	1,812	3,153	2,459	3,990	1,017	4,504	1,107
1983	10,846	6,514	4,332	5,158	5,688	3,304	1,854	3,210	2,478	4,117	1,042	4,580	1,107
1982	10,825	6,484	4,341	5,170	5,655	3,299	1,871	3,184	2,470	4,140	1,031	4,573	1,081
1981	10,755	6,449	4,305	5,108	5,646	3,260	1,848	3,189	2,458	4,090	1,018	4,558	1,088
1980	10,475	6,362	4,113	5,000	5,475	3,227	1,773	3,135	2,340	4,015	985	4,427	1,048
1979	9,998	6,079	3,919	4,820	5,178	3,087	1,733	2,993	2,185	3,865	955	4,182	996
1978	9,684	5,963	3,722	4,761	4,923	3,069	1,692	2,894	2,029	3,812	949	3,975	948
1977	9,717	6,094	3,623	4,897	4,820	3,188	1,709	2,906	1,914	3,937	960	3,906	914
1976	9,435	6,033	3,401	4,906	4,528	3,244	1,662	2,789	1,739	3,951	955	3,669	859
1975	9,679	6,168	3,511	5,257	4,422	3,459	1,798	2,709	1,713	4,245	1,012	3,581	841
1974	8,799	5,726	3,072	4,766	4,033	3,192	1,574	2,535	1,499	3,800	966	3,232	801
1973	8,260	5,579	2,681	4,538	3,722	3,134	1,403	2,444	1,278	3,580	958	2,943	779
1972	7,942	5,489	2,453	4,429	3,514	3,121	1,308	2,368	1,146	3,466	963	2,757	757
1971	7,744	5,513	2,231	4,418	3,326	3,201	1,217	2,312	1,015	3,427	991	2,581	746
1970	7,369	5,280	2,089	4,250	3,119	3,096	1,153	2,184	935	3,236	1,014	2,384	735
1969	6,884	4,992	1,892	4,008	2,877	2,952	1,055	2,040	837	2,996	1,012	2,162	715
1968	6,476	4,740	1,735	3,781	2,695	2,810	971	1,930	764	2,787	994	1,995	700
1967	6,016	4,345	1,671	3,502	2,514	2,569	933	1,775	738	2,492	1,010	1,802	712

Table A-34.   Total Postbaccalaureate Fall Enrollment in Degree-Granting Institutions, by Attendance Status, Sex of Student, and Control of Institution, 1967–2008

Year	Total	Full- time	Part- time	Males	Females	Males Full-time	Males Part-time	Females Full-time	Females Part-time	Males Public	Males Private	Females Public	Females Private
2008	2,737	1,493	1,244	1,122	1,615	657	465	836	779	569	554	812	802
2007	2,644	1,429	1,215	1,088	1,556	633	456	796	760	557	532	796	760
2006	2,575	1,386	1,188	1,061	1,514	615	446	772	742	546	516	787	726
2005	2,524	1,351	1,173	1,047	1,476	603	445	748	728	543	504	781	696
2004	2,491	1,326	1,166	1,047	1,444	599	448	727	717	550	497	779	665
2003	2,431	1,281	1,150	1,033	1,398	589	444	692	707	556	477	780	619
2002	2,355	1,212	1,143	1,010	1,345	567	443	645	700	552	458	767	577
2001	2,212	1,120	1,093	956	1,256	531	425	589	667	524	433	724	532
2000	2,157	1,087	1,070	944	1,213	523	421	564	650	510	433	703	510
1999	2,110	1,051	1,059	931	1,179	510	421	542	637	510	421	689	490
1998	2,070	1,025	1,045	923	1,147	505	418	519	628	508	415	680	467
1997	2,052	1,019	1,032	927	1,124	511	417	509	616	516	412	673	451
1996	2,041	1,004	1,036	932	1,108	512	420	492	616	520	412	666	443
1995	2,030	984	1,047	941	1,089	511	431	473	616	528	414	661	428
1994	2,016	969	1,047	950	1,066	514	436	455	611	536	414	653	414
1993	1,981	948	1,033	944	1,037	509	435	440	598	537	407	640	397
1992	1,950	918	1,032	941	1,009	502	439	416	593	537	404	631	378
1991	1,920	894	1,026	931	989	494	437	400	589	535	395	626	363
1990	1,860	845	1,015	904	955	471	433	374	582	522	382	613	342
1989	1,796	820	976	879	917	462	417	359	558	505	374	586	331
1988	1,739	794	944	864	875	455	409	339	536	495	369	563	312
1987	1,720	769	952	864	857	447	416	321	535	497	366	558	299
1986	1,706	767	938	867	839	453	414	315	524	503	364	550	288
1985	1,650	756	895	856	794	451	405	304	490	485	371	517	277
1984	1,624	751	873	857	767	453	404	298	469	485	372	499	268
1983	1,619	747	872	865	753	456	410	291	462	493	372	492	261
1982	1,601	737	864	861	740	454	407	283	457	493	368	490	250
1981	1,617	732	885	867	750	452	414	280	471	497	370	502	249
1980	1,622	736	886	874	748	462	412	274	474	508	367	508	240
1979	1,572	715	857	863	709	456	407	258	451	504	359	486	223
1978	1,576	705	871	880	696	459	421	246	450	519	361	479	216
1977	1,569	699	870	892	677	462	430	237	440	536	356	468	209
1976	1,578	684	894	905	673	459	445	225	448	556	349	477	196
1975	1,505	673	832	892	613	467	425	206	408	560	332	448	165
1974	1,425	644	781	857	568	455	402	189	379	539	318	418	150
1973	1,342	611	732	833	509	444	389	167	342	523	310	374	135
1972	1,272	583	689	810	462	437	374	147	315	507	303	341	121
1971	1,204	564	640	789	415	428	361	136	279	514	276	306	110
1970	1,212	536	676	794	418	408	386	129	290	497	297	311	107
1969	1,120	507	613	739	382	384	355	123	258	457	282	281	100
1968	1,037	470	568	697	341	359	338	111	230	411	286	238	103
1967	896	448	448	631	265	355	276	94	172	352	279	171	95

Table A-35. Total Fall Enrollment in Degree-Granting Institutions, by Race/Ethnicity, Sex, Attendance Status, and Level of Student: Selected Years, 1980–2008

(Numbers in thousands.)

Race/ethnicity, sex, attendance status, and level of student	1980 Number	1980 Percent	1990 Number	1990 Percent	2000 Number	2000 Percent	2008 Number	2008 Percent
All students, total	12,087	100.0	13,819	100.0	15,312	100.0	19,103	100.0
White	9,833	81.3	10,722	77.5	10,462	68.3	12,089	63.2
Total, selected races/ethnicities	1,949	16.1	2,705	19.5	4,321	28.2	6,353	33.2
Black	1,107	9.1	1,247	9.0	1,730	11.3	2,584	13.5
Hispanic	472	3.9	782	5.6	1,462	9.5	2,273	11.9
Asian/Pacific Islander	286	2.3	572	4.1	978	6.3	1,303	6.8
American Indian/Alaska Native	84	0.6	103	0.7	151	0.9	193	1.0
Nonresident alien	305	2.5	391	2.8	529	3.4	661	3.4
Male	5,868	100.0	6,284	100.0	6,722	100.0	8,189	100.0
White	4,773	81.3	4,861	77.3	4,635	68.9	5,303	64.7
Total, selected races/ethnicities	884	15.0	1,177	18.7	1,790	26.6	2,533	30.9
Black	464	7.9	485	7.7	635	9.4	912	11.1
Hispanic	232	3.9	354	5.6	627	9.3	947	11.5
Asian/Pacific Islander	151	2.5	295	4.6	466	6.9	597	7.2
American Indian/Alaska Native	38	0.6	43	0.6	61	0.9	77	0.9
Nonresident alien	211	3.5	246	3.9	297	4.4	353	4.3
Female	6,219	100.0	7,535	100.0	8,591	100.0	10,914	100.0
White	5,060	81.3	5,861	77.7	5,827	67.8	6,786	62.1
Total, selected races/ethnicities	1,064	17.1	1,528	20.2	2,532	29.4	3,821	35.0
Black	643	10.3	762	10.1	1,095	12.7	1,673	15.3
Hispanic	240	3.8	429	5.6	835	9.7	1,326	12.1
Asian/Pacific Islander	135	2.1	278	3.6	512	5.9	705	6.4
American Indian/Alaska Native	46	0.7	60	0.7	90	1.0	116	1.0
Nonresident alien	94	1.5	145	1.9	231	2.6	307	2.8
Full-time	7,089	100.0	7,821	100.0	9,010	100.0	11,748	100.0
White	5,717	80.6	6,016	76.9	6,231	69.1	7,594	64.6
Total, selected races/ethnicities	1,138	16.0	1,515	19.3	2,368	26.2	3,632	30.9
Black	686	9.6	718	9.1	983	10.9	1,531	13.0
Hispanic	247	3.4	395	5.0	710	7.8	1,177	10.0
Asian/Pacific Islander	162	2.2	347	4.4	591	6.5	809	6.8
American Indian/Alaska Native	43	0.6	54	0.7	84	0.9	115	0.9
Nonresident alien	234	3.3	290	3.7	410	4.5	522	4.4
Part-time	4,998	100.0	5,998	100.0	6,303	100.0	7,355	100.0
White	4,116	82.3	4,706	78.4	4,231	67.1	4,495	61.1
Total, selected races/ethnicities	811	16.2	1,190	19.8	1,953	30.9	2,722	37.0
Black	421	8.4	529	8.8	748	11.8	1,054	14.3
Hispanic	225	4.5	388	6.4	751	11.9	1,096	14.9
Asian/Pacific Islander	124	2.4	225	3.7	387	6.1	494	6.7
American Indian/Alaska Native	41	0.8	48	0.8	67	1.0	78	1.0
Nonresident alien	71	1.4	102	1.7	119	1.8	138	1.8
Undergraduate, total	10,469	100.0	11,959	100.0	13,155	100.0	16,366	100.0
White	8,481	81.0	9,273	77.5	8,983	68.2	10,339	63.1
Total, selected races/ethnicities	1,779	16.9	2,468	20.6	3,884	29.5	5,666	34.6
Black	1,019	9.7	1,147	9.5	1,549	11.7	2,269	13.8
Hispanic	433	4.1	725	6.0	1,351	10.2	2,104	12.8
Asian/Pacific Islander	249	2.3	500	4.1	846	6.4	1,118	6.8
American Indian/Alaska Native	78	0.7	95	0.8	139	1.0	176	1.0
Nonresident alien	210	2.0	219	1.8	288	2.1	360	2.2

Table A-35. Total Fall Enrollment in Degree-Granting Institutions, by Race/Ethnicity, Sex, Attendance Status, and Level of Student: Selected Years, 1980–2008—*Continued*

(Numbers in thousands.)

Race/ethnicity, sex, attendance status, and level of student	1980 Number	1980 Percent	1990 Number	1990 Percent	2000 Number	2000 Percent	2008 Number	2008 Percent
Male	4,997	100.0	5,380	100.0	5,778	100.0	7,067	100.0
White	4,055	81.1	4,184	77.7	4,010	69.4	4,599	65.0
Total, selected races/ethnicities	803	16.0	1,069	19.8	1,618	28.0	2,290	32.4
Black	428	8.5	448	8.3	577	9.9	821	11.6
Hispanic	211	4.2	327	6.0	583	10.0	884	12.5
Asian/Pacific Islander	129	2.5	254	4.7	402	6.9	515	7.2
American Indian/Alaska Native	35	0.7	40	0.7	56	0.9	70	1.0
Nonresident alien	140	2.8	126	2.3	150	2.6	178	2.5
Female	5,472	100.0	6,579	100.0	7,377	100.0	9,299	100.0
White	4,426	80.8	5,088	77.3	4,973	67.4	5,741	61.7
Total, selected races/ethnicities	976	17.8	1,398	21.2	2,266	30.7	3,376	36.3
Black	591	10.7	699	10.6	972	13.1	1,448	15.5
Hispanic	222	4.0	398	6.0	768	10.4	1,219	13.1
Asian/Pacific Islander	120	2.2	246	3.7	444	6.0	603	6.4
American Indian/Alaska Native	43	0.7	56	0.8	82	1.1	105	1.1
Nonresident alien	70	1.2	93	1.4	138	1.8	183	1.9
Postbaccalaureate, total	1,618	100.0	1,860	100.0	2,157	100.0	2,737	100.0
White	1,352	83.6	1,450	77.9	1,479	68.5	1,750	63.9
Total, selected races/ethnicities	170	10.5	237	12.7	438	20.2	687	25.1
Black	88	5.4	100	5.3	181	8.4	315	11.5
Hispanic	39	2.3	58	3.1	111	5.1	169	6.1
Asian/Pacific Islander	38	2.3	72	3.8	133	6.1	185	6.7
American Indian/Alaska Native	6	0.3	7	0.3	13	0.5	18	0.6
Nonresident alien	95	5.8	173	9.2	241	11.1	300	10.9
Male	871	100.0	904	100.0	944	100.0	1,122	100.0
White	718	82.4	677	74.8	625	66.1	704	62.7
Total, selected races/ethnicities	82	9.3	107	11.8	172	18.2	242	21.6
Black	36	4.0	37	4.0	58	6.1	90	8.0
Hispanic	20	2.3	27	2.9	45	4.7	63	5.5
Asian/Pacific Islander	23	2.6	40	4.4	64	6.7	83	7.3
American Indian/Alaska Native	3	0.3	3	0.3	5	0.5	7	0.5
Nonresident alien	71	8.1	120	13.2	147	15.5	176	15.6
Female	747	100.0	955	100.0	1,213	100.0	1,615	100.0
White	634	84.9	773	80.9	854	70.3	1,045	64.7
Total, selected races/ethnicities	89	11.8	130	13.5	266	21.9	445	27.5
Black	52	7.0	63	6.6	123	10.1	225	13.9
Hispanic	18	2.4	31	3.2	66	5.4	107	6.6
Asian/Pacific Islander	15	2.0	32	3.3	69	5.6	102	6.3
American Indian/Alaska Native	3	0.4	4	0.4	8	0.6	11	0.6
Nonresident alien	24	3.2	53	5.5	94	7.7	125	7.7

Table A-36. Total Fall Enrollment in Degree-Granting Institutions, by Race/Ethnicity of Student and Type and Control of Institution: Selected Years, 1980–2008

(Numbers in thousands.)

Race/ethnicity of student and type and control of institution	1980 Number	1980 Percent	1990 Number	1990 Percent	2000 Number	2000 Percent	2008 Number	2008 Percent
All students, total	12,087	100.0	13,819	100.0	15,312	100.0	19,103	100.0
White	9,833	81.3	10,722	77.5	10,462	68.3	12,089	63.2
Total, selected races/ethnicities	1,949	16.1	2,705	19.5	4,321	28.2	6,353	33.2
Black	1,107	9.1	1,247	9.0	1,730	11.3	2,584	13.5
Hispanic	472	3.9	782	5.6	1,462	9.5	2,273	11.9
Asian/Pacific Islander	286	2.3	572	4.1	978	6.3	1,303	6.8
American Indian/Alaska Native	84	0.6	103	0.7	151	0.9	193	1.0
Nonresident alien	305	2.5	391	2.8	529	3.4	661	3.4
Public	9,456	100.0	10,845	100.0	11,753	100.0	13,972	100.0
White	7,656	80.9	8,385	77.3	7,963	67.7	8,818	63.1
Total, selected races/ethnicities	1,596	16.8	2,199	20.2	3,446	29.3	4,728	33.8
Black	876	9.2	976	9.0	1,319	11.2	1,759	12.5
Hispanic	406	4.2	671	6.1	1,229	10.4	1,832	13.1
Asian/Pacific Islander	240	2.5	461	4.2	771	6.5	983	7.0
American Indian/Alaska Native	74	0.7	90	0.8	127	1.0	153	1.1
Nonresident alien	204	2.1	260	2.4	343	2.9	427	3.0
Private	2,630	100.0	2,974	100.0	3,560	100.0	5,131	100.0
White	2,177	82.7	2,337	78.5	2,499	70.2	3,271	63.7
Total, selected races/ethnicities	353	13.4	505	17.0	875	24.5	1,626	31.6
Black	231	8.7	271	9.1	411	11.5	825	16.0
Hispanic	66	2.4	111	3.7	233	6.5	440	8.5
Asian/Pacific Islander	47	1.7	111	3.7	208	5.8	320	6.2
American Indian/Alaska Native	10	0.3	12	0.4	24	0.6	40	0.7
Nonresident alien	101	3.8	131	4.4	186	5.2	234	4.5
4-year, total	7,565	100.0	8,579	100.0	9,364	100.0	12,131	100.0
White	6,275	82.9	6,768	78.9	6,658	71.1	7,987	65.8
Total, selected races/ethnicities	1,050	13.8	1,486	17.3	2,266	24.2	3,588	29.5
Black	634	8.3	723	8.4	995	10.6	1,565	12.9
Hispanic	217	2.8	358	4.1	618	6.6	1,092	9.0
Asian/Pacific Islander	162	2.1	357	4.1	576	6.1	823	6.7
American Indian/Alaska Native	37	0.4	48	0.5	76	0.8	108	0.8
Nonresident alien	241	3.1	324	3.7	440	4.7	556	4.5
Public	5,128	100.0	5,848	100.0	6,055	100.0	7,332	100.0
White	4,243	82.7	4,606	78.7	4,311	71.2	4,879	66.5
Total, selected races/ethnicities	741	14.4	1,046	17.8	1,486	24.	2,128	29.0
Black	438	8.5	495	8.4	628	10.3	827	11.2
Hispanic	156	3.0	263	4.4	420	6.9	710	9.6
Asian/Pacific Islander	117	2.2	251	4.2	381	6.3	518	7.0
American Indian/Alaska Native	29	0.5	38	0.6	57	0.9	73	0.9
Nonresident alien	144	2.8	196	3.3	258	4.2	324	4.4
Private	2,438	100.0	2,730	100.0	3,308	100.0	4,800	100.0
White	2,032	83.3	2,163	79.2	2,347	70.9	3,108	64.7
Total, selected races/ethnicities	309	12.6	440	16.1	780	23.5	1,460	30.4
Black	196	8.0	228	8.3	368	11.1	738	15.3
Hispanic	60	2.4	96	3.5	198	5.9	382	7.9
Asian/Pacific Islander	45	1.8	107	3.9	195	5.8	305	6.3
American Indian/Alaska Native	8	0.3	10	0.3	19	0.5	35	0.7
Nonresident alien	97	3.9	128	4.6	182	5.5	231	4.8
2-year, total	4,521	100.0	5,240	100.0	5,948	100.0	6,971	100.0
White	3,558	78.7	3,954	75.4	3,804	63.9	4,102	58.8
Total, selected races/ethnicities	899	19.8	1,219	23.2	2,055	34.5	2,765	39.6
Black	472	10.4	524	10.0	735	12.3	1,020	14.6

Table A-36.   Total Fall Enrollment in Degree-Granting Institutions, by Race/Ethnicity of Student and Type and Control of Institution: Selected Years, 1980–2008 —*Continued*

(Numbers in thousands.)

Race/ethnicity of student and type and control of institution	1980		1990		2000		2008	
	Number	Percent	Number	Percent	Number	Percent	Number	Percent
Hispanic	255	5.6	424	8.1	844	14.1	1,181	16.9
Asian/Pacific Islander	124	2.7	215	4.1	402	6.7	479	6.8
American Indian/Alaska Native	47	1.0	55	1.0	75	1.2	85	1.2
Nonresident alien	64	1.4	67	1.2	89	1.5	105	1.5
Public	4,329	100.0	4,996	100.0	5,697	100.0	6,640	100.0
White	3,413	78.8	3,780	75.6	3,652	64.1	3,938	59.3
Total, selected races/ethnicities	855	19.7	1,153	23.0	1,960	34.4	2,599	39.1
Black	438	10.1	481	9.6	691	12.1	932	14.0
Hispanic	250	5.7	409	8.1	809	14.2	1,122	16.9
Asian/Pacific Islander	123	2.8	210	4.2	389	6.8	465	7.0
American Indian/Alaska Native	45	1.0	52	1.0	70	1.2	80	1.2
Nonresident alien	60	1.3	64	1.2	85	1.5	103	1.5
Private	193	100.0	244	100.0	251	100.0	331	100.0
White	145	75.4	174	71.6	152	60.4	163	49.3
Total, selected races/ethnicities	44	22.5	66	26.9	95	38.0	166	50.0
Black	35	17.9	43	17.6	44	17.3	88	26.4
Hispanic	5	2.7	15	6.2	35	13.8	58	17.5
Asian/Pacific Islander	2	0.9	5	2.0	13	5.0	15	4.4
American Indian/Alaska Native	2	0.9	3	1.0	5	1.8	5	1.5
Nonresident alien	4	1.9	3	1.4	4	1.5	2	0.6

Table A-37.   Tuition and Required Fees for Full-Time Students, by Student Level, Sector, and Residency, 2000–2010

Student level, sector, and residency	Academic year				Percent Change 2000-01 to 2009-10
	2000-2001	2003-2004	2006-2007	2009-2010	
Average tuition and required fees [1]					
Undergraduate					
Public 4-year					
In-state..	$4,376	$5,292	$5,848	$6,393	46.1
Out-of-state...	$11,223	$13,137	$13,974	$15,078	34.3
Public 2-year					
In-state..	$2,230	$2,612	$2,814	$2,970	33.2
Out-of-state...	$5,387	$5,936	$6,114	$6,187	14.8
Public less-than-2-year					
In-state..	$5,020	$5,703	$5,998	$5,106	1.7
Out-of-state...	$5,518	$6,395	$6,387	$5,584	1.2
Private not-for-profit 4-year	$16,094	$17,629	$19,094	$21,050	30.8
Private not-for-profit 2-year	$8,264	$9,010	$9,644	$10,266	24.2
Private not-for-profit less-than-2-year	$8,177	$10,358	$8,863	$8,982	9.8
Private for-profit 4-year.............................	$13,100	$14,027	$15,176	$15,715	20.0
Private for-profit 2-year.............................	$11,291	$12,720	$12,728	$14,280	26.5
Private for-profit less-than-2-year............	$9,780	$11,287	$11,945	$12,807	31.0
Graduate [2]					
Public 4-year					
In-state..	$4,943	$6,203	$7,012	$7,943	60.7
Out-of-state...	$11,317	$13,409	$14,487	$15,762	39.3
Private not-for-profit 4-year	$12,531	$13,218	$14,065	$14,984	19.6
Private for-profit 4-year.............................	$15,016	$14,145	$14,711	$14,687	-2.2
Median tuition and required fees [1]					
Undergraduate					
Public 4-year					
In-state..	$4,055	$4,876	$5,514	$6,033	48.8
Out-of-state...	$11,075	$12,647	$12,781	$14,648	32.3
Public 2-year					
In-state..	$1,900	$2,434	$2,630	$2,834	49.2
Out-of-state...	$5,062	$5,703	$5,784	$5,850	15.6
Public less-than-2-year					
In-state..	$4,119	$4,917	$5,214	$4,760	15.6
Out-of-state...	$4,361	$5,646	$5,321	$4,760	9.1
Private not-for-profit 4-year	$15,970	$17,613	$19,002	$21,120	32.2
Private not-for-profit 2-year	$8,411	$8,967	$9,507	$9,158	8.9
Private not-for-profit less-than-2-year	$7,080	$9,681	$8,306	$8,710	23.0
Private for-profit 4-year.............................	$12,912	$12,740	$14,185	$14,800	14.6
Private for-profit 2-year.............................	$10,396	$11,537	$11,861	$13,200	27.0
Private for-profit less-than-2-year............	$9,205	$10,710	$11,955	$13,259	44.0
Graduate [2]					
Public 4-year					
In-state..	$4,503	$5,562	$6,404	$7,238	60.7
Out-of-state...	$10,728	$12,567	$14,084	$15,430	43.8
Private not-for-profit 4-year	$10,684	$11,226	$11,938	$12,625	18.2
Private for-profit 4-year.............................	$16,039	$11,333	$13,281	$12,990	-19

NOTE: Tuition and required fees are average institutional charges for all full-time students at the institution as reported by the institution, not average amounts paid by students (i.e., charges are not weighted by enrollment). The time points displayed in this table were chosen to demonstrate the range of data available from IPEDS for trend analysis, not to emphasize any particular period of change. Data for years included in the range of this table, but not specifically displayed in the table, are available via the IPEDS Data Center. These figures for undergraduates differ from the pricing data in table 5 that apply only to full-time, first-time degree/certificate-seeking undergraduates. Institutions with academic calendars that differ by program or allow continuous enrollment (2,269 in fall 2009, 2,141 in fall 2006, 1,929 in fall 2003, and 1,836 in fall 2000) are not included. U.S. service academies are not included. All amounts from prior years were converted to 2009-10 dollars using the average Consumer Price Index values for the 12-month period ending in October of the academic year the data represent (e.g., October 2000) and the CPI value for the 12-month period ending in October 2009. Medians were calculated using SAS, Version 9, Proc Univariate.
SOURCE: U.S. Department of Education, National Center for Education Statistics, Integrated Postsecondary Education Data System (IPEDS), Fall 2000, Fall2003, Fall2006, and Fall 2009, Institutional Characteristics component.
[1]Out-of-state average and median tuition and required fees were used for private institutions that reported varying tuitions by residency.
[2]Tuition and fee charges for graduate students do not include charges for programs designated as doctor's degrees—professional practice.

Table A-37.   Tuition and Required Fees for Full-Time Students, by Student Level, Sector, and Residency, 2000–2010—*Continued*

Student level, sector, and residency	Academic year				Percent Change 2000-01 to 2009-10
	2000-2001	2003-2004	2006-2007	2009-2010	
Number of institutions reporting tuition and required fees					
Undergraduate					
Public 4-year					
In-state	$595	$608	$619	$652	9.6
Out-of-state	$595	$608	$619	$652	9.6
Public 2-year					
In-state	$1,112	$1,105	$1,063	$1,006	-9.5
Out-of-state	$1,113	$1,106	$1,063	$1,006	-9.5
Public less-than-2-year					
In-state	$89	$88	$49	$44	-50.6
Out-of-state	$89	$87	$49	$44	-50.6
Private not-for-profit 4-year	$1,258	$1,300	$1,294	$1,297	3.1
Private not-for-profit 2-year	$214	$204	$179	$140	-34.6
Private not-for-profit less-than-2-year	$20	$28	$12	$15	-25.0
Private for-profit 4-year	$161	$310	$413	$513	218.6
Private for-profit 2-year	$363	$401	$382	$436	20.1
Private for-profit less-than-2-year	$101	$133	$88	$69	-32.7
Graduate [2]					
Public 4-year					
In-state	$516	$543	$554	$561	8.7
Out-of-state	$516	$544	$554	$561	8.7
Private not-for-profit 4-year	$933	$1,011	$1,058	$1,116	19.6
Private for-profit 4-year	$97	$162	$188	$218	124.7

NOTE: Tuition and required fees are average institutional charges for all full-time students at the institution as reported by the institution, not average amounts paid by students (i.e., charges are not weighted by enrollment). The time points displayed in this table were chosen to demonstrate the range of data available from IPEDS for trend analysis, not to emphasize any particular period of change. Data for years included in the range of this table, but not specifically displayed in the table, are available via the IPEDS Data Center. These figures for undergraduates differ from the pricing data in table 5 that apply only to full-time, first-time degree/certificate-seeking undergraduates. Institutions with academic calendars that differ by program or allow continuous enrollment (2,269 in fall 2009, 2,141 in fall 2006, 1,929 in fall 2003, and 1,836 in fall 2000) are not included. U.S. service academies are not included. All amounts from prior years were converted to 2009-10 dollars using the average Consumer Price Index values for the 12-month period ending in October of the academic year the data represent (e.g., October 2000) and the CPI value for the 12-month period ending in October 2009. Medians were calculated using SAS, Version 9, Proc Univariate.
SOURCE: U.S. Department of Education, National Center for Education Statistics, Integrated Postsecondary Education Data System (IPEDS), Fall 2000, Fall2003, Fall2006, and Fall 2009, Institutional Characteristics component.
[2]Tuition and fee charges for graduate students do not include charges for programs designated as doctor's degrees—professional practice.

Table A-38.   Price of Undergraduate College Attendance by Level and Control of Institution, Student Housing, and Residency, 2007–2008 and 2009–2010

Control in institution, student housing, and residency	4-year			2-year			Less-than-2-year		
	2007-2008	2009-2010	Percent change	2007-2008	2009-2010	Percent Change	2007-2008	2009-2010	Percent Change
Public									
On campus[1]									
In-district[2]	17,183	18,598	8.2	10,945	11,880	8.5	...	...	...
In-state	17,185	18,599	8.2	11,171	12,115	8.5	...	...	...
Out-of-state	25,694	27,687	7.8	13,639	14,436	5.8	...	...	...
Off campus (not with family)[3]									
In-district[2]	18,608	19,902	7.0	13,849	14,652	5.8	15,478	15,964	3.1
In-state	18,612	19,906	7.0	14,276	15,109	5.8	15,503	15,988	3.1
Out-of-state	26,798	28,620	6.8	17,552	18,337	4.5	15,984	16,478	3.1
Off campus (with family)[3]									
In-district[2]	10,541	11,353	7.7	6,977	7,450	6.8	9,156	9,525	4.0
In-state	10,545	11,357	7.7	7,404	7,906	6.8	9,181	9,548	4.0
Out-of-state	18,731	20,071	7.2	10,680	11,134	4.3	9,662	10,038	3.9
Private not-for-profit									
On campus[1]	32,159	34,160	6.2	22,207	23,834	7.3	20,068	20,597	2.6
Off campus (not with family)[3]	29,987	31,708	5.7	23,550	24,859	5.6	21,429	22,460	4.8
Off campus (with family)[3]	22,238	23,636	6.3	15,267	16,316	6.9	14,351	15,168	5.7
Private for-profit									
On campus[1]	34,548	36,665	6.1	27,648	29,544	6.9	31,962	38,250	19.7
Off campus (not with family)[3]	29,992	31,322	4.4	25,964	27,488	5.9	23,437	25,309	8.0
Off campus (with family)[3]	21,572	22,761	5.5	18,407	19,801	7.6	15,665	17,110	9.2

NOTE: Price of attendance includes tuition and required fees, books and supplies, room and board charges, and other expenses. Amounts are institutional averages as reported by the institution, not average amounts paid by students (i.e., charges are not weighted by enrollment). The time period of the percentage change was chosen to reflect the same period as the College Affordability Index. The College Affordability Index, which is calculated over a three year period, is the ratio of the percentage change in tuition and required fees for full-time, first-time undergraduate students to the percentage change in the Consumer Price Index (CPI). Out-of-state average tuition and required fees were used for private institutions that reported varying tuitions by residency. The average components of academic year price of attendance in table 5 may not sum to the corresponding average price of attendance in this table because not all institutions report all components of academic year price of attendance separately (e.g., an institution may report a comprehensive fee in lieu of the individual components). The 2,226 institutions with academic calendars that differ by program or allow continuous enrollment are not included. U.S. service academies are not included. All amounts from 2007-08 were converted to 2009-10 dollars using the average Consumer Price Index values for the 12-month periods ending in October 2007 and October 2009.
SOURCE: U.S. Department of Education, National Center for Education Statistics, Integrated Postsecondary Education Data System (IPEDS), Fall 2009, Institutional Characteristics component.
...= Not Applicable
[1]On-campus average price is based on those institutions that offer on-campus housing and/or meal service.
[2]For public institutions, "in district" refers to the charges paid by a student who lives in the locality surrounding the institution, such as county.
[3]Off-campus average price is based on those institutions that do not require full-time, first-time students to live on campus.

NOTES AND DEFINITIONS: NATIONAL SCHOOL ENROLLMENT, EDUCATIONAL ATTAINMENT, AND POSTSECONDARY EDUCATION

ENROLLMENT TABLES A-1 THROUGH A-16

Source: U.S. Census Bureau. School Enrollment in the United States. *Current Population Survey (CPS) Report.* <http://www.census.gov/population/www/socdemo/school.html>.

ATTAINMENT TABLES A-17 THROUGH A-28

Source: U.S. Census Bureau. Educational Attainment in the United States: 2008. *Annual Social and Economic Supplement to the Current Population Survey.* http://www.census.gov/population/www/socdemo/education/cps2008.html and Historical Income Tables (Table P-16). http://www.census.gov/hhes/www/income/data/historical/people/index.html

POSTSECONDARY EDUCATION TABLES A-29 THROUGH A-38

U.S. Department of Education, National Center for Education Statistics, Institute of Education Sciences, *Digest of Education Statistics 2009* (NCES 2010-013). < http://www.nces.ed.gov/pubsearch/pubsinfo.asp?pubid=2010013> and *Postsecondary Institutions and Price of Attendance in the United States: Fall 2009, Degrees and Other Awards Conferred: 2008–09, and 12-Month Enrollment: 2008–09* (NCES 2010-161). http://www.nces.ed.gov/pubsearch/pubsinfo.asp?pubid=2010161

SCHOOL ENROLLMENT AND EDUCATIONAL ATTAINMENT TABLES

The School Enrollment and Educational Attainment tables in Part A are derived from the Current Population Survey (CPS). The Census Bureau disseminated comparable tables in the P-20 series of *Current Population Reports* (CPR) for most years between 1947 and 1994. Since then, these tables have not been available in printed form. However, they can be found on the Census Bureau Web site at <http://www.census.gov>. In the historical series, data prior to 1992 are not strictly comparable to data after 1992. Before 1992, the CPS did not ask questions about degrees received; educational attainment was gauged only by years of school completed. For information about the availability of earlier reports, or for answers to data questions not addressed in this section, contact the Education and Social Stratification Branch, Population Division, Census Bureau at (301) 763-2464.

Age. Age classification is based on the age of the person at his or her last birthday.

Citizenship status. There are five categories of citizenship status: 1) born in the United States; 2) born in Puerto Rico or another outlying area of the United States; 3) born abroad to U.S. citizen parents; 4) naturalized citizens; and 5) non-citizens. Place of birth was asked for every household member and for the parents of every household member in the CPS sample. People born in the United States or its outlying areas, or whose parents were born in the United States or its outlying areas, were not asked citizenship questions. Citizenship statuses (1), (2), and (3) were assigned during the editing phase of data preparation, based on the place of birth of the household member or the place of birth of his or her parents. People born outside the United States and its outlying areas, whose parents were born outside the United States and its outlying areas, were asked, "Are you a citizen of the United States?" 'Yes' answers were assigned to the "naturalized citizen" category (4), and 'No' answers were assigned to the "not a citizen" category (5) during the editing process. People for whom no birthplace was provided were also assigned a citizenship status during the editing process; for example, the citizenship status of a child might have been assigned based on the citizenship status of his or her mother.

Dropouts. See School, dropout rate, annual high school.

Earnings. See Income.

Educational attainment. Data on educational attainment are derived from a single question that asks, "What is the highest grade of school ... completed, or the highest degree ... received?"

The single educational attainment question now in use was introduced into the CPS in January 1992. It is similar to the question used in the 1990 Decennial Census of Population and Housing. Consequently, data on educational attainment from the 1992 CPS are not directly comparable to CPS data from earlier years. The new question replaces the previous two-part question used in the CPS, which asked respondents to report the highest grade they attended and whether or not they completed that grade.

The question concerning educational attainment applies only to progress in "regular" schools. Such schools include graded public, private, and parochial elementary and high schools (both junior and senior high schools), colleges, universities, and professional schools, and both day schools and night schools. Thus, regular schooling is that which may advance a person toward an elementary school certificate, a high school diploma, or a college, university, or professional school degree. Non-regular schooling was counted only if the credits obtained were regarded as transferable to a school within the regular school system.

Family. A family is a group of two people or more residing together (including the householder) related by birth, marriage, or adoption; all such people (including related subfamily members) are considered members of one family. Beginning with the 1980 Current Population Survey, unrelated subfamilies (formerly referred to as secondary families)

are no longer included in the count of families, nor are members of unrelated subfamilies included in the count of family members. The number of families is equal to the number of family households; however, the count of family members differs from the count of family household members, as family household members include any non-relatives living in the household.

Family household. A family household is a household maintained by a householder within a family (as defined above). It includes any unrelated people (unrelated subfamily members and/or secondary individuals) residing in the household. The number of family households is equal to the number of families; however, the count of family household members differs from the count of family members. Family household members include all people living in the household, whereas family members include only the householder and his or her relatives. (See Family for more information.)

Hispanic origin. People of Hispanic origin were identified by a question that asked respondents to self-identify their origin or descent. Respondents were asked to select their origin (and the origin of other household members) from a "flash card" listing different ethnicities. People of Hispanic origin were those who indicated that their descent was of Mexican, Puerto Rican, Cuban, Central or South American, or some other Hispanic origin. It should be noted that people of Hispanic origin may be of any race.

People who were of non-Hispanic White origin were identified by crossing the responses to two self-identification questions: (1) origin or descent; and (2) race. Respondents were asked to select their race (and the race of other household members) from a "flash card" listing racial groups. Since March 1989, the population has been divided into five groups on the basis of race: White; Black; American Indian, Eskimo, or Aleut; Asian or Pacific Islander; and Other races. The last category includes any race other than the four indicated races. Respondents who identified their race as White and did not select one of the Hispanic origin subgroups (Mexican, Puerto Rican, Cuban, Central or South American) were classified as non-Hispanic White.

Household. A household consists of all the people who occupy a housing unit. A house, apartment, group of rooms, or single room is regarded as a housing unit when it is occupied or intended for occupancy as separate living quarters (meaning that occupants do not live and eat with any other persons in the structure and have direct access to their dwelling from outside or through a common hall). A household includes related family members and all unrelated people—such as lodgers, foster children, wards, or employees—who share the housing unit. A person living alone in a housing unit, or a group of unrelated people sharing a dwelling (such as partners or roomers), are also counted as a household. The count of households excludes group quarters. There are two major categories of households: "family" and "nonfamily." (See Family household and Nonfamily household for more information.)

Householder. The householder is the person (or one of the people) in whose name the housing unit is owned or rented (maintained). If there is no such person, any adult member of the household—excluding roomers, boarders, and paid employees—can be counted as the householder. If a married couple jointly owns or rents the housing unit, the householder may be either the husband or the wife. The person designated as the householder is the "reference person" to whom the relationship of all other household members, if any, is recorded.

The number of householders is equal to the number of households. The number of family householders is also equal to the number of families.

Head versus householder. The Census Bureau discontinued the use of the terms "head of household" and "head of family" beginning with the 1980 CPS. Instead, the terms "householder" and "family householder" are used. Recent social changes have resulted in a greater sharing of household responsibilities among the adult members. This has made the term "head" increasingly inappropriate in the analysis of household and family data. Specifically, beginning in 1980, the Census Bureau discontinued its longtime practice of always classifying the husband as the reference person (head of household) when he was living with his wife.

INCOME. Definitions of income and the types of income are found below.

Income, Official definition of. For each person age 15 years and over in the sample, the CPS asks questions about the amount of money income received during the preceding calendar year from each of the following sources: earnings; unemployment compensation; workers' compensation; Social Security; Supplemental Security Income; public assistance or welfare payments; veterans' payments; survivor benefits; disability benefits; pension or retirement income; interest, dividends, rents, royalties, and estates and trusts; educational assistance; child support; alimony; financial assistance from outside the household; and other income.

Although the income statistics refer to receipts during the preceding calendar year, demographic characteristics such as age, labor force status, and family or household composition are as of the survey date. The income of the family/household does not include amounts received by members who were members of the family/household during all or part of the income year if these people no longer resided in the family/household at the time of interview. However, the CPS collects income data for people who are current residents, but who did not reside in the household during the income year.

Data on consumer income collected in the CPS by the Census Bureau cover money income (exclusive of certain money receipts, such as capital gains) received before payments for personal income taxes, Social Security, union dues, Medicare deductions, etc. Therefore, money income does not reflect the fact that some families receive part of their income in the form of noncash benefits, such as food stamps, health benefits, rent-free housing, and goods produced and consumed on the farm. Money income also does not reflect the fact that noncash benefits are also received by some nonfarm residents. These benefits often take the form of the use of business transportation and facilities, full or partial payments by business for retirement programs, medical and educational expenses, etc. Data users should consider these elements when comparing income levels. Moreover, readers should be aware that respondents in household surveys tend to underreport their income for many different reasons. Based on an analysis of independently derived income estimates, the Census Bureau determined that respondents report income earned from wages or salaries much more accurately than income earned from other sources of income, and that the reported wage and salary income is nearly equal to independent estimates of aggregate income.

The Census Bureau collects data for the following income sources:

Alimony. Alimony includes all periodic payments received from ex-spouses. It excludes one-time property settlements.

Child support. Child support includes all periodic payments received from an absent parent for the support of his or her children, even if these payments are made through a state or local government office.

Disability benefits. Disability benefits include payments people received due to a health problem or disability (other than those received from Social Security). Respondents can report payments from 10 sources, including workers' compensation, companies or unions, federal government (civil service), military, state or local governments, railroad retirement, accident or disability insurance, Black Lung payments, state temporary sickness, or other disability payments.

Dividends. Dividends include income received from stock holdings and mutual fund shares. The CPS does not include capital gains from the sale of stock holdings as income.

Earnings. The Census Bureau classifies earnings from respondents' longest job (or self-employment) and other employment earnings into three types:

- Money wage, or salary income, is the total income people receive for work performed as an employee during the income year. This category includes wages, salary, armed forces pay, commissions, tips, piece-rate payments, and cash bonuses earned, before deductions are made for items such as taxes, bonds, pensions, and union dues.

- Net income from nonfarm self-employment is the net money income (gross receipts minus expenses) from a respondent's own business, professional enterprise, or partnership. Gross receipts include the value of all goods sold and all services rendered. Expenses include items such as the costs of goods purchased; rent, heat, power, and depreciation charges; wages and salaries paid; and business taxes (but not personal income taxes). In general, the Census Bureau considers inventory changes in determining net income from nonfarm self-employment; replies based on income tax returns or other official records reflect inventory changes. However, when respondents do not report values of inventory changes, interviewers will accept net income figures exclusive of inventory changes. The Census Bureau does not include the value of saleable merchandise consumed by the proprietors of retail stores as part of net income.

- Net income from farm self-employment is the net money income (gross receipts minus operating expenses) from the operation of a farm by a person acting on their own account as owner, renter, or sharecropper. Gross receipts include the value of all products sold, payments from government farm programs, money received from renting farm equipment to others, rent received from farm property if payment is based on the percentage of crops produced, and incidental receipts from the sale of items such as wood, sand, and gravel.

Operating expenses include items such as the cost of feed, fertilizer, seed, and other farming supplies; cash wages paid to farmhands; depreciation charges; cash rent; interest on farm mortgages; farm building repairs; and farm taxes (not state and federal personal income taxes). The Census Bureau does not include the value of fuel, food, or other farm products used for family living as part of net income, and only considers inventory changes in determining net income when they are accounted for in income tax returns or other official records. Otherwise, the Census Bureau does not take inventory changes into account.

Educational assistance. Educational assistance includes Pell Grants, other govern-

ment educational assistance, scholarships or grants, and any financial assistance received from employers, friends, or relatives not residing in the student's household.

Financial assistance from outside the household. Financial assistance from outside the household includes periodic payments received from nonhousehold members. This type of assistance excludes gifts and sporadic assistance.

Government transfers. Government transfers include payments received from the following sources: unemployment compensation, state workers' compensation, Social Security, Supplemental Security Income (SSI), public assistance, veterans' payments, government survivor benefits, government disability benefits, government pensions, and government educational assistance.

Interest income. Interest income includes payments received or credited to accounts from bonds, treasury notes, individual retirement accounts (IRAs), certificates of deposit, interest-bearing savings and checking accounts, and all other interest-paying investments.

Other income. Other income includes any other unclassified payments received regularly. Some examples are state programs such as foster child payments, military family allotments, and income received from foreign government pensions.

Pension or retirement income. Pension or retirement income includes payments received from eight sources, including companies or unions; federal government (civil service); military; state or local governments; railroad retirement; annuities or paid-up insurance policies; IRAs, Keogh, or 401(k) payments; or other retirement income.

Public assistance or welfare payments. Public assistance or welfare payments include cash payments to low-income persons, including payments given under programs such as Aid to Families with Dependent Children (AFDC, ADC) and Temporary Assistance to Needy Families (TANF), emergency assistance, and other general assistance.

Rents, royalties, and estates and trusts. Rents, royalties, and estates and trusts include net income received from the rental of a house, a store, or other property; receipts from boarders or lodgers; net royalty income; and periodic payments from estate or trust funds.

Social Security. Social Security includes pensions, survivors' benefits, and permanent disability insurance payments made by the Social Security Administration prior to medical insurance deductions. The Census Bureau does not include Medicare reimbursements for health services as Social Security benefits.

Supplemental Security Income. Supplemental Security Income includes federal, state, and local welfare agency payments to low-income people age 65 years and over and to blind or disabled people of any age.

Survivor benefits. Survivor benefits include payments received from survivors' or widows' pensions, estates, trusts, annuities, or any other types of survivors' benefits. Respondents can report payments from 10 different sources, including private companies or unions, federal government (civil service), military, state or local governments, railroad retirement, workers' compensation, Black Lung payments, estates and trusts, annuities or paid-up insurance policies, and other survivor payments.

Unemployment compensation. Unemployment compensation includes payments made to the respondent from government unemployment agencies or private companies during periods of unemployment. It also accounts for any strike benefits the respondent received from union funds.

Veterans' payments. Veterans' payments include periodic payments from the Department of Veterans Affairs to disabled members of the armed forces or survivors of deceased veterans for education and on-the-job training. These payments also include means-tested assistance to veterans.

Workers' compensation. Workers' compensation includes periodic payments from public or private insurance companies for work-related injuries.

The Census Bureau does not count the following receipts as income: (1) capital gains (or losses) from the sale of property, including stocks, bonds, houses, or cars (unless the person was engaged in the business of selling such property, in which case the CPS counts the net proceeds as income from self-employment); (2) withdrawals of bank deposits; (3) money borrowed; (4) tax refunds; (5) gifts; and (6) lump-sum inheritances or insurance payments.

The Census Bureau combines all sources of income into two major types:

Total money earnings. Total money earnings is the algebraic sum of money wages, salary, and net income from farm and nonfarm self-employment.

Income other than earnings. Income other than earnings is the algebraic sum of all sources of money income, except wages and salaries and income from self-employment.

Mean (average) income. Mean (average) income is the amount obtained by dividing the total aggregate income of a group by the number of units in that group. The means for households, families, and unrelated individuals are based respectively on all households, all families, and all unrelated individuals. The means (averages) for people are based on people age 15 years and over with income.

Median income. Median income is the amount that divides the income distribution into two equal groups. Half of all people have incomes above the median, and half of all people have incomes below the median. The medians for households, families, and unrelated individuals are respectively based on all households, all families, and all unrelated individuals. The medians for people are based on people age 15 years and over with income.

LABOR FORCE STATUS. Definitions of labor force characteristics are found below:

Current job (basic data). A worker's current job is the job held during the reference week (the week before the survey). A person holding two or more jobs is classified as being in the job at which he or she spent the most hours during the reference week. The unemployed are classified according to their most recent full-time job of two weeks or more, or by the job (either the full-time or part-time job) from which they were laid off. The occupation/industry classification system for the 1990 Decennial Census of Population was first used to code CPS data for the January 1992 file. The occupation/industry classification system for the 2000 Decennial Census of Population was first used to code CPS data for the January 2003 file.

Employed. Employed persons include all civilians who, during the survey week, did any work at all as paid employees or in their own business or profession, or on their own farm, or who worked 15 hours or more as unpaid workers on a farm or a business operated by a member of the family; and all people who had jobs but were not working due to illness, bad weather, vacation, labor-management dispute, or personal reasons, whether or not they were seeking other jobs. Each employed person is counted only once. People who held two or more jobs are counted as working in the job at which they worked the greatest number of hours during the survey

week. If a person worked an equal number of hours at two or more jobs, he or she is counted as working at the job that they have held the longest.

Labor force. Workers are classified as being in the labor force if they are employed, unemployed, or in the armed forces during the survey week. The "civilian labor force" includes all civilians classified as employed or unemployed. The file includes labor force data for civilians age 15 years and over. However, the official definition of the civilian labor force consists of workers age 16 years and over.

Not in labor force. All civilians age 15 years and over who are not classified as employed or unemployed are considered not to be in the labor force. These people are further classified as being engaged in a major activity such as keeping house, going to school, unable to work because of long-term physical or mental illness, and "other," which is mostly composed of retired persons. Those who report doing unpaid work on a family-owned farm or in a family-owned business for less than 15 hours are also classified as not in the labor force.

For persons not in the labor force, questions about previous work experience, intentions to seek work again, current desire for a job, and reasons for not seeking work are only asked of households in the fourth and eighth months of the sample. These are the "outgoing" groups—those that were in the sample for three previous months and would not be in it for the subsequent month.

Finally, it should be noted that the unemployment rate represents the number of unemployed persons as a percentage of the civilian labor force age 16 years and over. This measure can be computed for groups within the labor force by sex, age, marital status, race, etc. The job loser, job leaver, reentrant, and new entrant rates are each calculated as a percentage of the civilian labor force age 16 years and over; the sum of the rates for the four groups thus equals the total unemployment rate.

Unemployed. Unemployed persons are civilians who, during the survey week, had no employment but were available for work and had engaged in any specific job-seeking activity within the past four previous weeks, such as registering at a public or private employment office, meeting with prospective employers, checking with friends or relatives, placing and answering advertisements, writing letters of application, or being on a union or professional register. Others in this category were waiting to be called back to a job from which they had been laid off or were within 30 days of starting a new wage or salary job. This category consists of job leavers, job losers, new job entrants, and job reentrants.

Work experience. A person with work experience is one who did any work for pay or profit or worked without pay on a family-operated farm or business at any time during the preceding calendar year, on a part time or full time basis. A full-time worker is a worker who worked 35 hours or more per week during a majority of the weeks in the preceding calendar year. A year-round worker is a worker who worked for 50 weeks or more during the preceding calendar year. A full-time, year-round worker is a person who worked full time (35 or more hours per week) for 50 or more weeks during the previous calendar year.

Level of school completed. The statistics on level of school completed indicate the number of persons enrolled at each of five levels: nursery school, kindergarten, elementary school (first to eighth grades), high school (ninth to twelfth grades), and college or professional school. The last group includes graduate students at colleges and universities. Those enrolled in elementary school,

middle school, intermediate school, or junior high through eighth grade are classified as being in elementary school. All persons enrolled in ninth through twelfth grade are classified as being in high school.

Modal grade. See School, Modal grade.

Nativity. There are two major categories of nativity, native born and foreign born. A person who is native is a citizen at birth. All people with the following citizenship status are native born: (1) born in the United States; (2) born in Puerto Rico or an outlying area of the U.S.; and (3) born abroad of American parents. (See Citizenship status for more information.) All other people are classified as foreign born.

Nonfamily household. A nonfamily household consists of a householder living alone (a one-person household) or a household shared exclusively by unrelated people.

Population coverage. The sample for the CPS includes the civilian noninstitutional population of the United States, along with members of the armed forces in the United States living off post or with their families on post. It excludes all other members of the armed forces. The information on the Hispanic population from the CPS was collected in the 50 states and the District of Columbia and does not include residents of outlying areas or of U.S. territories such as Guam, Puerto Rico, and the U.S. Virgin Islands.

Race. The race of individuals was identified through a question requiring self-identification of the person's race. Respondents were asked to select their race from a "flash card" listing racial groups. Since March 1989, the population has been divided into five groups on the basis of race: White; Black; American Indian, Eskimo, or Aleut; Asian or Pacific Islander; and Other races. The last category includes any other race except the four mentioned. In most of the published tables, Other races are included in the total population data line but are not shown individually.

Reference person. The reference person serves as the central point for determining relationships within the household. The household reference person is the person listed as the householder. (See Householder for more information.) The subfamily reference person is either the single parent or the husband or wife in a married-couple situation.

Rounding. Percentages are rounded to the nearest 10th of a percent; therefore, the percentages in a distribution do not always sum to exactly 100 percent.

School, Dropout rate, annual high school. The annual high school dropout rate is an estimate of the proportion of students who drop out of school in a single year. This section briefly explains how the annual dropout rate is calculated; for further explanation and details of its derivation, see *Current Population Report (Series P-20, No. 413): "School Enrollment—Social and Economic Characteristics of Students: October 1983."*

Annual dropout rates for a single grade (X) are estimated as the ratio between the number of people enrolled in grade (X) in the year preceding the survey who did not complete grade (X) and are not currently enrolled to the number enrolled in grade (X) at the start of the year preceding this survey. People reported as enrolled last year but not currently enrolled are presented by the highest grade completed in Table 8 of the *Current Population Report* on school enrollment. They are presumed to have dropped out of the succeeding grade (except for those who graduated this year). Thus, individuals counted as 10th grade dropouts are those whose highest grade completed is the 9th grade, but who are not currently enrolled in school. (The dropout classification also includes those people who finished the 9th grade in the spring preceding the survey and

were not enrolled on the survey date.) These estimates form the numerator of the annual grade-specific dropout rate.

People currently enrolled in high school are presumed to have been enrolled in and have successfully completed the preceding grade during the preceding year. For example, those who have successfully completed the 10th grade would be enrolled in the 11th grade. Along with the people who dropped out of that grade, they comprise the denominator of the estimate of the annual grade-specific dropout rate:

$$\text{Dropout from Grade } n = \frac{\text{Not enrolled and highest grade completed} = n\text{-}1}{(\text{Enrolled in } n\text{+}1 + \text{Not enrolled and highest grade completed} = n\text{-}1)}$$

It cannot be presumed that all 12th grade graduates will enroll in college. The estimate of the number of people enrolled in the 12th grade one year prior to the survey is constructed as the sum of the number of people reported to have graduated from high school "this year" (whether or not they are currently enrolled in college) and those not currently enrolled who were enrolled last year and whose highest grade completed is the 11th grade (dropouts). The annual dropout rate for all grades during one year can be obtained by summing the components of the rates for the individual grades—the sum of all people previously enrolled in the 10th, 11th, or 12th grade last year, but who are not currently enrolled and do not have a high school diploma.

In addition to the annual rate, two other estimates of dropouts are frequently used. The annual dropout rate is different from a "pool" (or status) measure, such as the proportion of high school dropouts within an age group. A third measure of dropouts is the "cohort measure," most commonly from a longitudinal study, in which the proportion of a specific group of people enrolled in a specific year is calculated. These people did not receive diplomas (and are no longer in school) some years later. For example, the proportion of a cohort enrolled in 9th grade in year X, who were not enrolled and had not received a diploma by year X equals 4.

School enrollment. The school enrollment statistics from the CPS are based on replies to inquiries concerning current regular school enrollment. Those counted as enrolled had attended a public, parochial, or other private school in the regular school system at any time during the current or previous school year. Such schools include nursery schools, kindergartens, elementary schools, high schools, colleges, universities, and professional schools. Attendance could have been on either a full-time or part-time basis during the day or night. Regular schooling is that which advances a person toward an elementary or high school diploma or toward a college, university, or professional school degree. Children enrolled in nursery schools and kindergarten are included in the enrollment figures for regular schools and are shown separately.

Enrollment in schools not in the regular school system, such as trade schools, business colleges, and schools for the mentally handicapped is not included, as these schools do not advance students toward regular school degrees.

People enrolled in classes not requiring their physical presence in school, such as correspondence courses or other courses of independent study, and those enrolled in training courses given directly on the job, are also excluded from the count of those enrolled in school, unless such courses are being counted for credit at a regular school.

School enrollment in the year preceding current survey. All respondents were asked to state their school enrollment status as of October of the preceding year. Before 1988, this

question was only asked of people not currently attending regular school and people who were enrolled in college. In the tabulations of previous year's secondary school enrollment, those currently enrolled in high school were assumed to have been enrolled the previous year.

Comparability of enrollment data in previous years. Changes in the edit and tabulation packages used to process the October CPS school enrollment supplement caused some minor revisions to the estimates. The current edit and tabulation package began with 1987 data. The 1986 data published in the *Current Population Report (Series P-20 No. 429)* were reprocessed with the rewritten programs in order to clarify comparability. Time series tables usually show only the revised estimates for 1986. The previous edit and tabulation package was used from 1967 to 1986.

Major changes in the data caused by to the 1987 edit revisions were: (1) Among 14- and 15-year-olds, an edit improvement allowed people with unreported enrollment data, who were previously imputed as "not enrolled," to be enrolled; (2) Revisions in the tabulation of enrollment in the previous year simplified the calculation of an annual high school dropout rate; (3) Edit improvements caused increases in college enrollment estimates, most notably above the age of 24. This age group was largely ignored in earlier edits; (4) Type of college is fully allocated (discussed earlier in the section); (5) Tabulations of type of college (2-year and 4-year colleges) were made available by race; (6) Dependent family members became consistently defined; (7) New tabulations of employment status, vocational course enrollment, college retention and re-entry, and families with children enrolled in public and private school became available beginning in 1987.

In the series of reports on school enrollment for 1987 to 1992, race and Hispanic origin were erroneously tabulated for a small percentage of children age 3 to 14 years. Race and Hispanic origin of an adult in the household were attributed to the child, rather than using the child's reported characteristics. In the vast majority of cases, these characteristics were the same for family members, but for a small percentage of children, they were different. The correction made the following proportional changes in the numbers of children in each group: White (-0.5 percent), Black (+3.1 percent), and Hispanic (-4.6 percent).

Published data on enrollment from the October CPS for 1981 to 1993 used population controls based on the 1980 census. Beginning in 1994, estimates used 1990 census–based population controls, including adjustment for undercount. Time series tables show two sets of data for 1993; the data labeled "1993r" were processed using population controls based on the 1990 census with adjustments for undercount. The change in 1994 from a paper-and-pencil survey to a computer-assisted survey had some affect on the data. Most notably, the enrollment question for children age 3 to 5 years was different from the question for older children—it included a reference to nursery school. In 1994, reported nursery school enrollment was significantly higher than in earlier years.

Attendance, full time and part time. College students are classified according to their attendance status. A student is categorized as attending college full time if he or she was taking 12 or more hours of classes during the average school week, and part time if he or she was taking less than 12 hours of classes per average school week.

College enrollment. The college enrollment statistics are based on reports of school enrollment, including the grade in which the respondent was enrolled. Students enrolled in college at any time during the current term or school year were counted as enrolled, ex-

cept those who had left for the remainder of the term. Thus, regular college enrollment includes those attending two-year or four-year colleges, universities, or professional schools (such as medical or law schools) in courses that advance students toward a recognized college or university degree (such as a B.A. or an M.A.). Attendance may be full time or part time during the day or night. The college student need not be working toward a degree, but he or she must be enrolled in a class for which credit would be applied toward a degree. (See school enrollment for more information.) Students are classified by year of college, based on the academic year (not calendar year). The undergraduate years are the first through fourth year, or freshman through senior years. Graduate or professional school years include the fifth year and higher.

Two-year and four-year colleges. College students were asked if their school was a two-year college (junior or community college) or a four-year college or university. Students enrolled in the first four years of college (undergraduates) were classified by the type of school that they attended. Graduate students are shown as a separate group.

Vocational school enrollment. Vocational school enrollment includes enrollment in business, vocational, technical, secretarial, trade, or correspondence courses that are not counted as regular school enrollment. This category excludes recreation or adult education classes. Courses that counted as college enrollment are also excluded.

School, Modal grade. Enrolled people are classified according to their relative progress in school and whether the grade or year in which they were enrolled was below, at, or above the modal (or typical) grade for students of their age at the time of the survey. The modal grade is the year of school in which the largest proportion of students of a given age were enrolled.

School, Nursery. A nursery school is defined as a group or class that has been organized to provide educational experiences for children during the year or years preceding kindergarten. It includes instruction as an important and integral phase of its childcare program. Private homes, in which essentially custodial care is provided, are not considered nursery schools. Children attending nursery school are classified as attending for part of the day or for the full day. Part-day attendance refers to those who attend either in the morning or in the afternoon. Full-day attendance refers to those who attend in the morning and in the afternoon. Children enrolled in Head Start programs or similar local agency-sponsored programs that provide preschool education to young children are counted as being enrolled in nursery school.

School, Public or private. A public school is defined as any educational institution operated by publicly elected or appointed school officials and supported by public funds. Private schools include educational institutions established and operated by religious bodies, as well as those that are under other private controls. In cases in which a school or college was both publicly and privately controlled or supported, enrollment was counted according to whether the school was primarily public or private.

Undocumented immigrants or illegal aliens. Since all residents of the United States living in households are represented in the sample of households interviewed by the CPS, undocumented immigrants or illegal aliens are probably included in CPS data. Because the CPS makes no attempt to ascertain the legal status of any person interviewed, these individuals cannot be identified from CPS data.

POSTSECONDARY EDUCATION TABLES

Tables A-29 through A-38 were adapted from published tables in two publications from the National Center for Education Statistics: the *Digest of Education Statistics 2009* (NCES 2010-013). (http://www.nces.ed.gov/pubsearch/pubsinfo.asp?pubid=2010013) and *Postsecondary Institutions and Price of Attendance in the United States: Fall 2009, Degrees and Other Awards Conferred: 2008–09, and 12-Month Enrollment: 2008–09* (NCES 2010-161). (http://www.nces.ed.gov/pubsearch/pubsinfo.asp?pubid=2010161). The data in these tables come primarily from the Integrated Postsecondary Education Data System (IPEDS) fall 2009 data collection, which included three survey components: Institutional Characteristics for the 2009-10 academic year, Completions covering the period July 1, 2008, through June 30, 2009, and 12-Month Enrollment covering academic year 2008-09. Enrollment data for 1967 through 1985 are from Higher Education General Information Survey (HEGIS), "Fall Enrollment in Colleges and Universities" surveys,

Control of institution describes whether an institution is operated by publicly elected or appointed officials (public control) or by privately elected or appointed officials and derives its major source of funds from private sources (private control). There are nine institutional categories resulting from dividing the universe according to control and level. Control categories are public, private not-for-profit, and private for-profit. Level categories are 4-year and higher (4 year), 2-but-less-than 4-year (2 year), and less than 2-year. For example: Public, 4-year is one of the institution sectors.

Fall enrollment. IPEDS collects data on the number of students enrolled in the fall at postsecondary institutions. Students reported are those enrolled in courses creditable toward a degree or other formal award; students enrolled in courses that are part of a vocational or occupational program, including those enrolled in off-campus or extension centers; and high school students taking regular college courses for credit. Institutions report annually the number of full- and part-time students, by gender, race/ethnicity, and level (undergraduate, graduate, first-professional); the total number of undergraduate entering students (first-time, full-and part-time students, transfer-ins, and non-degree students); and retention rates. In even-numbered years, data are collected for state of residence of first-time students and for the number of those students who graduated from high school or received high school equivalent certificates in the past 12 months. Also in even-numbered years, 4-year institutions are required to provide enrollment data by gender, race/ethnicity, and level for selected fields of study. In odd-numbered years, data are collected for enrollment by age category by student level and gender.

Data through 1995 are for institutions of higher education, while later data are for degree-granting institutions. Degree-granting institutions grant associate's or higher degrees and participate in Title IV federal financial aid programs. The degree-granting classification is very similar to the earlier higher education classification, but it includes more 2-year colleges and excludes a few higher education institutions that did not grant degrees.

A **nonresident alien** is a person who is not a citizen or national of the United States and who is in this country on a visa or temporary basis and does not have the right to remain indefinitely.

A **Postbaccalaureate student** is a student with a bachelor's degree who is enrolled in graduate-level or first-professional courses.

Price of attendance includes tuition and required fees, books and supplies, room and board charges, and other expenses. Amounts are institutional averages as reported by the institution, not average amounts paid by students (i.e., charges are not weighted by enrollment). Out-of-state average tuition and required fees were used for private institu-

tions that reported varying tuitions by residency. The 2,226 institutions with academic calendars that differ by program or allow continuous enrollment are not included. U.S. service academies are not included. All amounts from 2007-08 were converted to 2009-10 dollars using the average Consumer Price Index values for the 12-month periods ending in October 2007 and October 2009. On-campus average price is based on those institutions that offer on-campus housing and/or meal service. Off-campus average price is based on those institutions that do not require full-time, first-time students to live on campus. For public institutions, "in district" refers to the charges paid by a student who lives in the locality surrounding the institution, such as a county.

Race/ethnicity categories were developed in 1997 by the Office of Management and Budget (OMB) and are used to describe groups to which individuals belong, identify with, or belong in the eyes of the community. The categories do not denote scientific definitions of anthropological origins. The designations are used to categorize U.S. citizens, resident aliens, and other eligible non-citizens. Individuals are asked to first designate ethnicity as Hispanic/Latino or not Hispanic/Latino. Hispanic/Latino refers to a person of Cuban, Mexican, Puerto Rican, South or Central American, or other Spanish culture or origin, regardless of race. Second, individuals are asked to indicate all races that apply among the following:

American Indian or Alaska Native (A person having origins in any of the original peoples of North and South America (including Central America) who maintains cultural identification through tribal affiliation or community attachment.

Asian (A person having origins in any of the original peoples of the Far East, Southeast Asia, or the Indian Subcontinent, including, for example, Cambodia, China, India, Japan, Korea, Malaysia, Pakistan, the Philippine Islands, Thailand, and Vietnam).

Black or African American (A person having origins in any of the black racial groups of Africa)

Native Hawaiian or Other Pacific Islander (A person having origins in any of the original peoples of Hawaii, Guam, Samoa, or other Pacific Islands.

White (A person having origins in any of the original peoples of Europe, the Middle East, or North Africa.)

Prior to 1997, slightly different race/ethnicity categories were used and persons could identify with only one racial category.

Tuition and required fees is the amount of tuition and required fees covering a full academic year most frequently charged to students. These values represent what a typical student would be charged and may not be the same for all students at an institution. If tuition is charged on a per-credit-hour basis, the average full-time credit hour load for an entire academic year is used to estimate average tuition. Required fees include all fixed sum charges that are required of such a large proportion of all students that the student who does not pay the charges is an exception.

PART B
REGION AND STATE EDUCATION STATISTICS

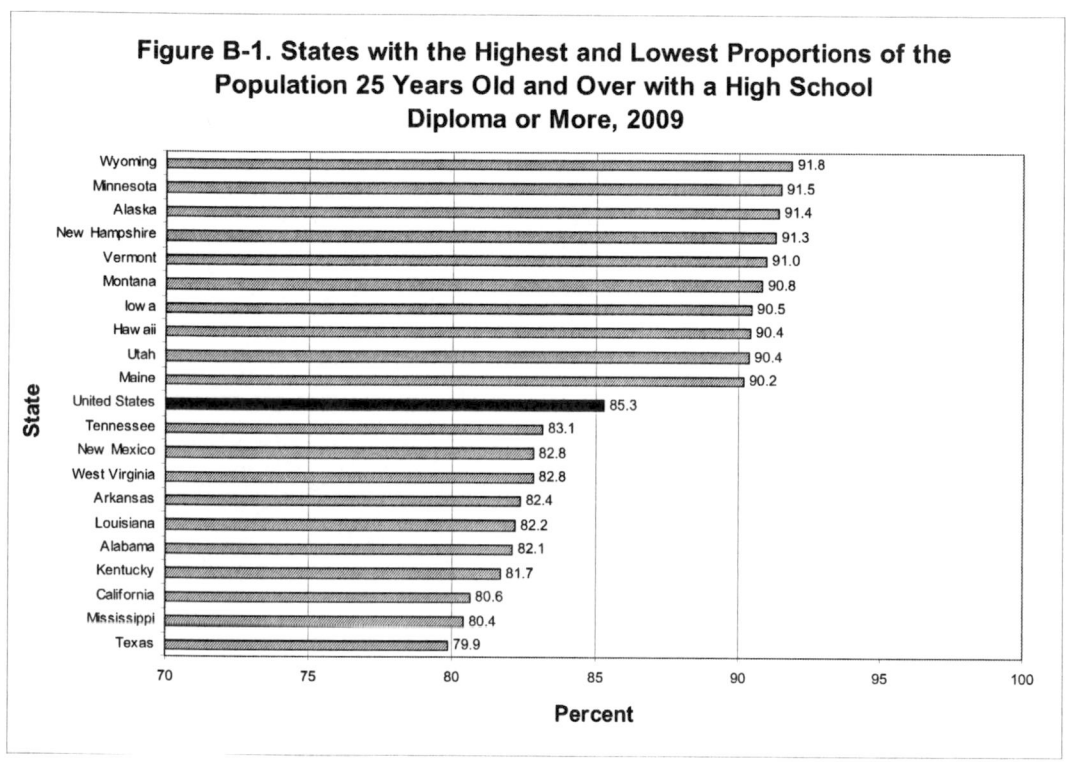

Figure B-1. States with the Highest and Lowest Proportions of the Population 25 Years Old and Over with a High School Diploma or More, 2009

In 2009, 85.3 percent of the U.S. population 25 years old and over had graduated from high school. Eleven states had high school attainment levels of 90 percent or more, and only one state had high school attainment levels below 80 percent. In 1975, less than two-thirds of people over 25 years of age had graduated from high school. The high school graduation rate for women 25 years old and over (85.9 percent) continued to exceed that of men (84.5 percent).

Among the four regions of the United States, the Midwest had the highest proportion of high school graduates (88.1 percent), followed by the Northeast (87.0 percent), the West (84.1 percent), and the South (83.4 percent).

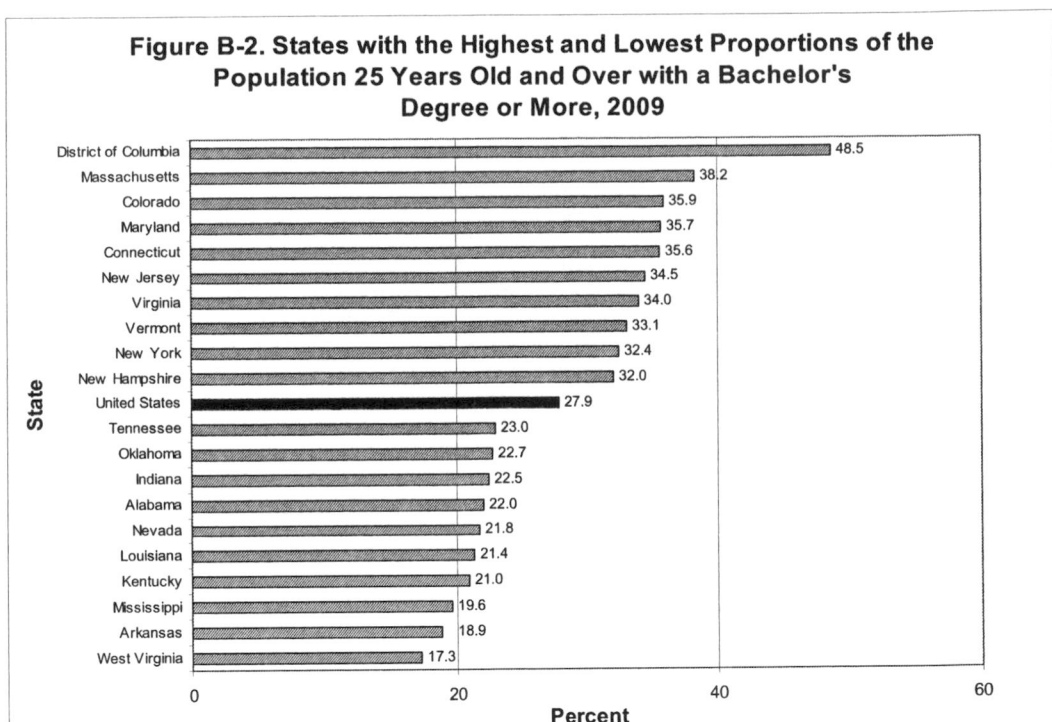

Figure B-2. States with the Highest and Lowest Proportions of the Population 25 Years Old and Over with a Bachelor's Degree or More, 2009

The proportion of the U.S. population with a bachelor's degree has increased slightly since 2006, from 27.0 percent to 27.9 percent in 2009. In the District of Columbia, 48.5 percent of residents held a bachelor's degree or more, by far the highest rate in the nation. Among the states, five had proportions of college graduates exceeding 35 percent. Only three states had college attainment levels of less than 20 percent, with West Virginia at 17.3 percent, Arkansas at 18.9 percent, and Mississippi at 19.6. In 2009, more men 25 years old and over held a bachelor's degree or more (28.4 percent) than women (27.4 percent), but the proportion of women holding degrees is higher than men in the age groups under 45 in all four regions of the country.

The Northeast region had the highest college attainment rate, with 32.1 percent, followed by the West region with 29.3 percent. The South region had the lowest proportion of its residents holding a bachelor's degree (25.8 percent).

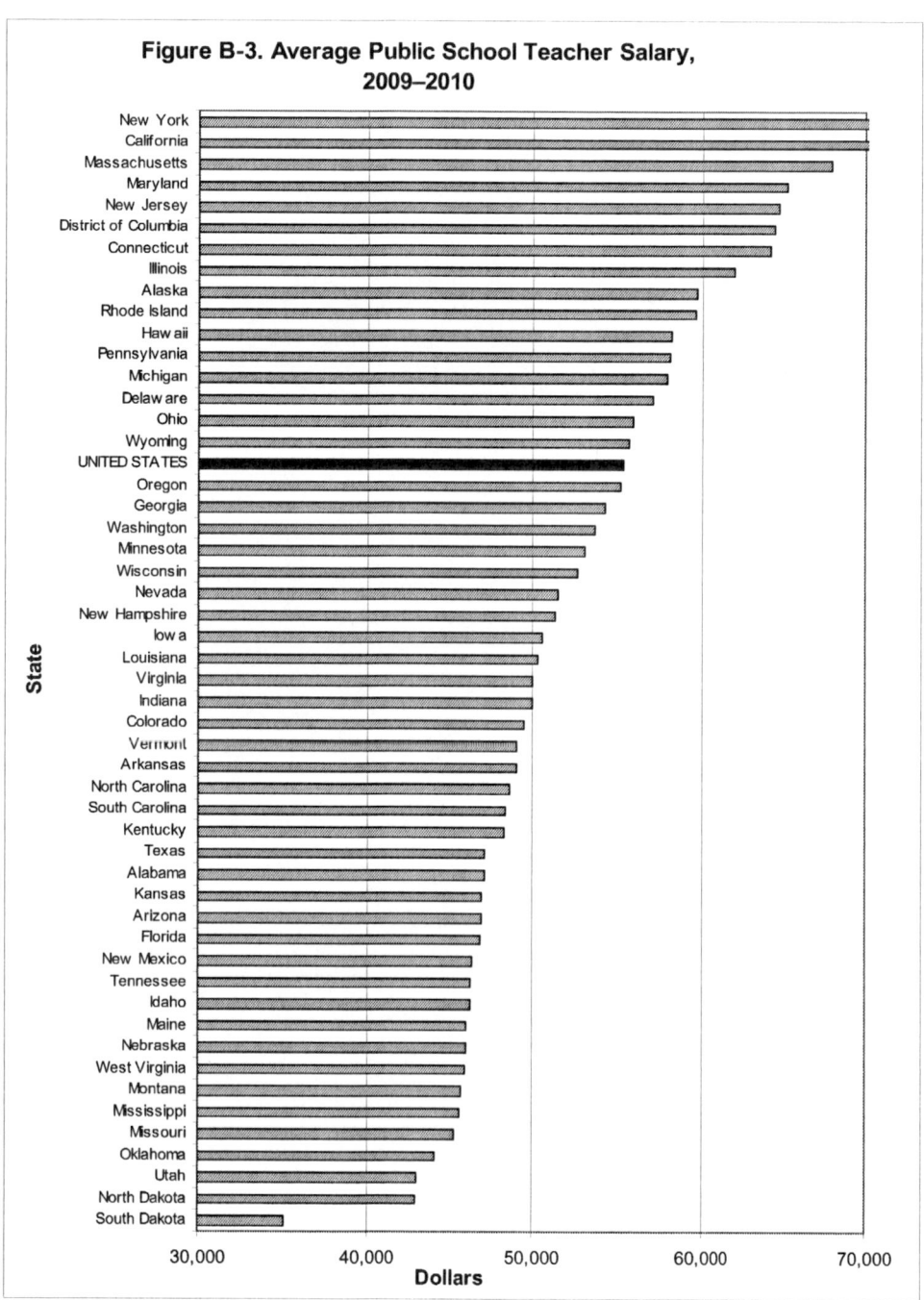

Figure B-3. Average Public School Teacher Salary, 2009–2010

For the 2009–2010 school year, the average public school teacher's salary was $55,350, an increase of 8.9 percent from the 2006–2007 school year. Salaries ranged from $35,136 in South Dakota to $71,470 in New York. Teacher salaries were typically higher in the New England states; three of these six states ranked in the top ten nationally. Four of the seven states in the West North Central division had among the ten lowest teacher salaries in the nation.

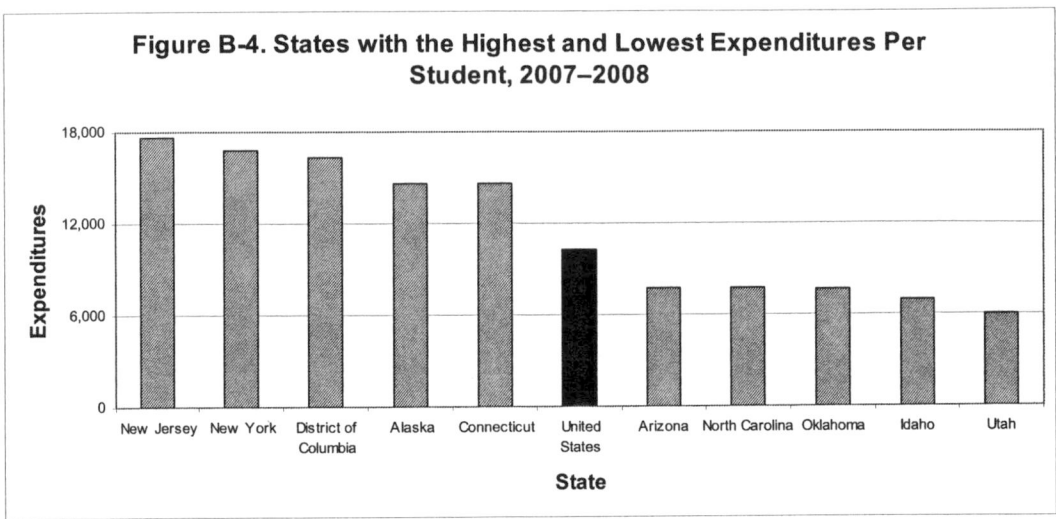

Nationally, the average expenditure per student was $10,282 for the 2007–2008 school year. New Jersey had the highest expenditure per student at $17,620, followed by New York at $16,794 and the District of Columbia at $16,353. Utah had the lowest expenditure per student at $5,978 and was the only state with a per student expenditure of less than $6,000. Utah also had the highest proportion of population age 5 to 17 years old. The District of Columbia had the lowest proportion of school-age population, with just 12.8 percent. Nationally, 17.3 percent of the population was 5 to 17 years old.

Teacher salaries were also significantly below average in Utah. Ten states had per student expenditures of over $13,000, and 7 states spent less than $8,000 per student. All 6 states in the New England division ranked among the highest 15 per student expenditures in the nation. Four New England states (Connecticut, Massachusetts, New Hampshire, and Rhode Island) had among the 10 highest median household incomes for a family of four in 2009. The East South Central states (Alabama, Kentucky, Mississippi, and Tennessee) all ranked among the 10 lowest per student expenditures. Mississippi, Alabama, and Kentucky had among the 10 lowest median household incomes.

Nationally, instruction accounted for 65.8 percent of all expenses, with support services at 35.2 percent and non-instructional expenses at 4 percent. New York had the highest proportion of instruction and instruction-related expenditures, at 71.7 percent. The District of Columbia had the lowest at 59.1 percent.

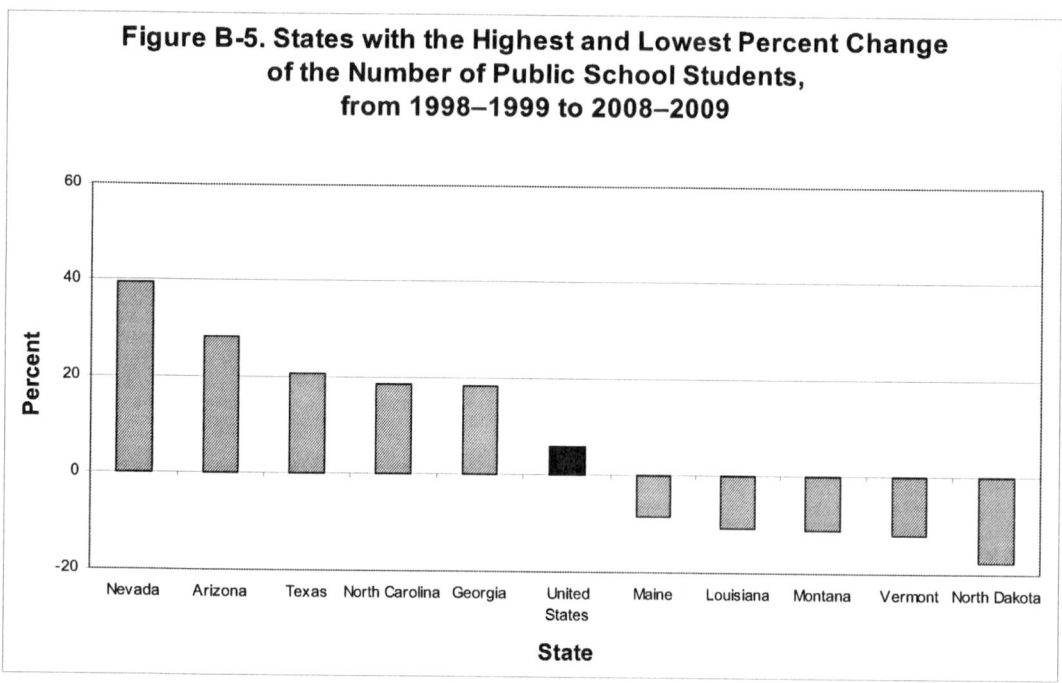

Figure B-5. States with the Highest and Lowest Percent Change of the Number of Public School Students, from 1998–1999 to 2008–2009

There was a huge variation by state in the percent change in the number of students from the 1998–1999 school year to the 2008–2009 school year. In the past 10 years, the number of students in the United States increased by 5.9 percent. However, in Nevada, the number of students increased substantially, rising 39.3 percent. Arizona had the next-highest increase at 28.2 percent. North Dakota saw the biggest decrease at 17.8 percent.

Nationally, the student-teacher ratio was 15.3 during the 2008–2009 school year. Utah and California exceeded 20 students per teacher. These states ranked among the top 10 for the proportion of school-age population. Vermont, North Dakota, and Connecticut had the three lowest student-teacher ratios in the nation. Similarly, Vermont and North Dakota ranked among the 10 states with the lowest proportion of population age 5 to 17 years old.

During the 2007–2008 school year, 9.3 percent of students attended private elementary and secondary schools. The District of Columbia, Delaware, Hawaii, and Louisiana had the highest proportion of students attending private schools. Wyoming, Utah, and Alaska had the lowest proportion of students enrolled in private schools.

Table B-1. Educational Attainment of the Population 18 Years and Over, by Region, Age, Sex, 2008

Region, age, sex	Total		High school				College			
			Less than High School		High school graduate, GED or alternative		Some college or associate's degree		Bachelor's degree or higher	
	Number	Percent	Number	Percent	Number	Percent	Number	Percent	Number	Percent
ALL RACES										
Northeast										
Both sexes										
18 years and over	42,540,007	100.0	5,724,549	13.5	12,831,713	30.2	11,460,953	26.9	12,522,792	29.4
18 to 24 years..............	5,395,405	100.0	743,665	13.8	1,564,630	29.0	2,385,336	44.2	701,774	13.0
25 to 34 years..............	6,758,297	100.0	686,845	10.2	1,644,545	24.3	1,849,951	27.4	2,576,956	38.1
35 to 44 years..............	7,897,780	100.0	796,828	10.1	2,160,259	27.4	2,085,607	26.4	2,855,086	36.2
45 to 64 years..............	14,873,033	100.0	1,637,569	11.0	4,553,519	30.6	3,856,434	25.9	4,825,511	32.4
65 years and over	7,615,492	100.0	1,859,642	24.4	2,908,760	38.2	1,283,625	16.9	1,563,465	20.5
Male										
18 years and over	20,395,119	100.0	2,856,809	14.0	6,214,499	30.5	5,270,914	25.8	6,052,897	29.7
18 to 24 years..............	2,732,594	100.0	428,327	15.7	873,355	32.0	1,134,080	41.5	296,832	10.9
25 to 34 years..............	3,400,060	100.0	402,593	11.8	950,588	28.0	894,374	26.3	1,152,505	33.9
35 to 44 years..............	3,907,213	100.0	450,888	11.5	1,164,094	29.8	948,840	24.3	1,343,391	34.4
45 to 64 years..............	7,220,855	100.0	840,121	11.6	2,206,554	30.6	1,753,335	24.3	2,420,845	33.5
65 years and over	3,134,397	100.0	734,880	23.4	1,019,908	32.5	540,285	17.2	839,324	26.8
Female										
18 years and over	22,144,888	100.0	2,867,740	12.9	6,617,214	29.9	6,190,039	28.0	6,469,895	29.2
18 to 24 years..............	2,662,811	100.0	315,338	11.8	691,275	26.0	1,251,256	47.0	404,942	15.2
25 to 34 years..............	3,358,237	100.0	284,252	8.5	693,957	20.7	955,577	28.5	1,424,451	42.4
35 to 44 years..............	3,990,567	100.0	345,940	8.7	996,165	25.0	1,136,767	28.5	1,511,695	37.9
45 to 64 years..............	7,652,178	100.0	797,448	10.4	2,346,965	30.7	2,103,099	27.5	2,404,666	31.4
65 years and over	4,481,095	100.0	1,124,762	25.1	1,888,852	42.2	743,340	16.6	724,141	16.2
Midwest										
Both sexes										
18 years and over	50,493,733	100.0	6,314,870	12.5	15,793,231	31.3	16,185,516	32.1	12,200,116	24.2
18 to 24 years..............	6,621,694	100.0	1,018,819	15.4	1,987,329	30.0	2,972,247	44.9	643,299	9.7
25 to 34 years..............	8,589,087	100.0	896,428	10.4	2,169,774	25.3	2,925,401	34.1	2,597,484	30.2
35 to 44 years..............	9,053,185	100.0	833,616	9.2	2,485,519	27.5	2,940,693	32.5	2,793,357	30.9
45 to 64 years..............	17,510,580	100.0	1,626,518	9.3	5,661,958	32.3	5,533,094	31.6	4,689,010	26.8
65 years and over	8,719,187	100.0	1,939,489	22.2	3,488,651	40.0	1,814,081	20.8	1,476,966	16.9
Male										
18 years and over	24,554,155	100.0	3,278,604	13.4	7,814,739	31.8	7,498,242	30.5	5,962,570	24.3
18 to 24 years..............	3,381,478	100.0	596,209	17.6	1,108,878	32.8	1,410,470	41.7	265,921	7.9
25 to 34 years..............	4,364,713	100.0	520,105	11.9	1,277,658	29.3	1,400,350	32.1	1,166,600	26.7
35 to 44 years..............	4,540,564	100.0	477,887	10.5	1,370,523	30.2	1,362,222	30.0	1,329,932	29.3
45 to 64 years..............	8,616,533	100.0	870,533	10.1	2,773,114	32.2	2,565,860	29.8	2,407,026	27.9
65 years and over	3,650,867	100.0	813,870	22.3	1,284,566	35.2	759,340	20.8	793,091	21.7
Female										
18 years and over	25,939,578	100.0	3,036,266	11.7	7,978,492	30.8	8,687,274	33.5	6,237,546	24.0
18 to 24 years..............	3,240,216	100.0	422,610	13.0	878,451	27.1	1,561,777	48.2	377,378	11.6
25 to 34 years..............	4,224,374	100.0	376,323	8.9	892,116	21.1	1,525,051	36.1	1,430,884	33.9
35 to 44 years..............	4,512,621	100.0	355,729	7.9	1,114,996	24.7	1,578,471	35.0	1,463,425	32.4
45 to 64 years..............	8,894,047	100.0	755,985	8.5	2,888,844	32.5	2,967,234	33.4	2,281,984	25.7
65 years and over	5,068,320	100.0	1,125,619	22.2	2,204,085	43.5	1,054,741	20.8	683,875	13.5
South										
Both sexes										
18 years and over	84,186,087	100.0	14,401,918	17.1	24,928,847	29.6	25,266,053	30.0	19,589,269	23.3
18 to 24 years..............	10,922,751	100.0	2,030,899	18.6	3,508,319	32.1	4,525,212	41.4	858,321	7.9
25 to 34 years..............	14,904,615	100.0	2,273,623	15.3	4,021,737	27.0	4,692,245	31.5	3,917,010	26.3
35 to 44 years..............	15,768,760	100.0	2,145,748	13.6	4,422,241	28.0	4,769,971	30.2	4,430,800	28.1
45 to 64 years..............	28,315,961	100.0	4,041,868	14.3	8,373,985	29.6	8,270,323	29.2	7,629,785	26.9
65 years and over	14,274,000	100.0	3,909,780	27.4	4,602,565	32.2	3,008,302	21.1	2,753,353	19.3

Table B-1. Educational Attainment of the Population 18 Years and Over, by Region, Age, Sex, 2008—*Continued*

| Region, age, sex | Total | | High school | | | | College | | | |
| | | | Less than High School | | High school graduate, GED or alternative | | Some college or associate's degree | | Bachelor's degree or higher | |
	Number	Percent	Number	Percent	Number	Percent	Number	Percent	Number	Percent
Male										
18 years and over	40,760,167	100.0	7,491,097	18.4	12,213,855	30.0	11,493,296	28.2	9,561,919	23.5
18 to 24 years..............	5,641,409	100.0	1,214,602	21.5	1,951,048	34.6	2,122,269	37.6	353,490	6.3
25 to 34 years..............	7,523,914	100.0	1,339,282	17.8	2,272,048	30.2	2,195,511	29.2	1,717,073	22.8
35 to 44 years..............	7,851,659	100.0	1,238,707	15.8	2,377,510	30.3	2,168,988	27.6	2,066,454	26.3
45 to 64 years..............	13,693,624	100.0	2,141,090	15.6	3,948,434	28.8	3,729,226	27.2	3,874,874	28.3
65 years and over	6,049,561	100.0	1,557,416	25.7	1,664,815	27.5	1,277,302	21.1	1,550,028	25.6
Female										
18 years and over	43,425,920	100.0	6,910,821	15.9	12,714,992	29.3	13,772,757	31.7	10,027,350	23.1
18 to 24 years..............	5,281,342	100.0	816,297	15.5	1,557,271	29.5	2,402,943	45.5	504,831	9.6
25 to 34 years..............	7,380,701	100.0	934,341	12.7	1,749,689	23.7	2,496,734	33.8	2,199,937	29.8
35 to 44 years..............	7,917,101	100.0	907,041	11.5	2,044,731	25.8	2,600,983	32.9	2,364,346	29.9
45 to 64 years..............	14,622,337	100.0	1,900,778	13.0	4,425,551	30.3	4,541,097	31.1	3,754,911	25.7
65 years and over	8,224,439	100.0	2,352,364	28.6	2,937,750	35.7	1,731,000	21.0	1,203,325	14.6
West										
Both sexes										
18 years and over	52,918,005	100.0	8,732,332	16.5	12,700,759	24.0	17,662,122	33.4	13,822,792	26.1
18 to 24 years..............	7,167,964	100.0	1,311,521	18.3	2,162,058	30.2	3,119,992	43.5	574,393	8.0
25 to 34 years..............	10,067,447	100.0	1,626,787	16.2	2,310,409	22.9	3,338,405	33.2	2,791,846	27.7
35 to 44 years..............	10,024,867	100.0	1,653,979	16.5	2,197,421	21.9	3,095,582	30.9	3,077,885	30.7
45 to 64 years..............	17,454,153	100.0	2,402,279	13.8	3,734,762	21.4	5,907,376	33.8	5,409,736	31.0
65 years and over	8,203,574	100.0	1,737,766	21.2	2,296,109	28.0	2,200,767	26.8	1,968,932	24.0
Male										
18 years and over	26,300,520	100.0	4,572,949	17.4	6,415,171	24.4	8,360,120	31.8	6,952,280	26.4
18 to 24 years..............	3,734,094	100.0	778,080	20.8	1,209,742	32.4	1,509,779	40.4	236,493	6.3
25 to 34 years..............	5,242,792	100.0	958,046	18.3	1,326,326	25.3	1,674,210	31.9	1,284,210	24.5
35 to 44 years..............	5,126,873	100.0	935,045	18.2	1,202,276	23.5	1,470,576	28.7	1,518,976	29.6
45 to 64 years..............	8,609,775	100.0	1,205,792	14.0	1,829,418	21.2	2,782,247	32.3	2,792,318	32.4
65 years and over	3,586,986	100.0	695,986	19.4	847,409	23.6	923,308	25.7	1,120,283	31.2
Female										
18 years and over	26,617,485	100.0	4,159,383	15.6	6,285,588	23.6	9,302,002	34.9	6,870,512	25.8
18 to 24 years..............	3,433,870	100.0	533,441	15.5	952,316	27.7	1,610,213	46.9	337,900	9.8
25 to 34 years..............	4,824,655	100.0	668,741	13.9	984,083	20.4	1,664,195	34.5	1,507,636	31.2
35 to 44 years..............	4,897,994	100.0	718,934	14.7	995,145	20.3	1,625,006	33.2	1,558,909	31.8
45 to 64 years..............	8,844,378	100.0	1,196,487	13.5	1,905,344	21.5	3,125,129	35.3	2,617,418	29.6
65 years and over	4,616,588	100.0	1,041,780	22.6	1,448,700	31.4	1,277,459	27.7	848,649	18.4

Table B-2.   Educational Attainment of the Population 25 Years Old and Over by Sex, Race, Hispanic Origin, and Region or State, 2009

Region/State	Total, age 25 years and over			Male, age 25 years and over			Female, age 25 years and over		
	Population	High School Graduate or higher (percent)	Bachelor's degree or higher (percent)	Population	High School Graduate or higher (percent)	Bachelor's degree or higher (percent)	Population	High School Graduate or higher (percent)	Bachelor's degree or higher (percent)
United States	201,952,383	85.3	27.9	97,482,149	84.5	28.4	104,470,234	85.9	27.4
Northeast Region	37,541,068	87.0	32.1	17,881,717	86.6	32.5	19,659,351	87.3	31.7
Midwest Region	44,089,929	88.1	26.5	21,281,752	87.5	26.8	22,808,177	88.6	26.1
South Region	74,090,779	83.4	25.8	35,508,213	82.3	26.3	38,582,566	84.4	25.3
West Region	46,230,607	84.1	29.3	22,810,467	83.6	29.9	23,420,140	84.6	28.7
Alabama	3,115,982	82.1	22.0	1,470,221	81.7	22.1	1,645,761	82.5	22.0
Alaska	431,178	91.4	26.6	221,191	91.3	24.5	209,987	91.5	28.8
Arizona	4,248,231	84.2	25.6	2,095,513	83.3	26.4	2,152,718	85.0	24.7
Arkansas	1,903,914	82.4	18.9	906,422	81.0	18.7	997,492	83.6	19.0
California	23,782,109	80.6	29.9	11,719,302	80.2	30.4	12,062,807	81.1	29.4
Colorado	3,293,368	89.3	35.9	1,636,840	89.0	36.3	1,656,528	89.6	35.5
Connecticut	2,370,028	88.6	35.6	1,127,786	88.1	36.8	1,242,242	89.0	34.5
Delaware	595,133	87.4	28.7	280,845	86.6	29.6	314,288	88.1	28.0
District of Columbia	413,396	87.1	48.5	191,593	87.8	49.8	221,803	86.5	47.3
Florida	12,800,944	85.3	25.3	6,159,578	84.4	26.5	6,641,366	86.1	24.1
Georgia	6,230,326	83.9	27.5	2,972,993	82.6	27.8	3,257,333	85.1	27.3
Hawaii	882,883	90.4	29.6	437,293	91.0	28.4	445,590	89.8	30.7
Idaho	963,730	88.4	23.9	476,503	87.6	25.3	487,227	89.1	22.6
Illinois	8,437,673	86.4	30.6	4,072,084	85.8	31.1	4,365,589	87.0	30.2
Indiana	4,193,210	86.6	22.5	2,021,195	86.3	23.1	2,172,015	86.9	22.0
Iowa	1,980,897	90.5	25.1	956,973	89.8	25.0	1,023,924	91.2	25.1
Kansas	1,809,054	89.7	29.5	881,241	89.1	29.8	927,813	90.3	29.2
Kentucky	2,877,333	81.7	21.0	1,375,669	80.4	20.9	1,501,664	82.9	21.1
Louisiana	2,896,932	82.2	21.4	1,368,743	80.7	20.8	1,528,189	83.5	22.0
Maine	924,973	90.2	26.9	440,535	89.0	25.7	484,438	91.3	28.1
Maryland	3,797,739	88.2	35.7	1,793,173	87.4	36.6	2,004,566	89.0	34.9
Massachusetts	4,490,445	89.0	38.2	2,137,459	88.4	38.3	2,352,986	89.5	38.1
Michigan	6,624,875	87.9	24.6	3,193,116	87.3	25.2	3,431,759	88.4	24.0
Minnesota	3,486,153	91.5	31.5	1,709,230	91.0	31.3	1,776,923	92.0	31.7
Mississippi	1,865,862	80.4	19.6	873,311	79.0	18.9	992,551	81.6	20.2
Missouri	3,961,562	86.8	25.2	1,892,612	86.4	25.6	2,068,950	87.1	24.9
Montana	648,828	90.8	27.4	317,621	90.2	27.5	331,207	91.5	27.3
Nebraska	1,153,230	89.8	27.4	562,303	88.9	27.1	590,927	90.6	27.6
Nevada	1,728,239	83.9	21.8	874,164	83.0	22.1	854,075	84.8	21.5
New Hampshire	902,747	91.3	32.0	438,835	90.4	31.9	463,912	92.1	32.1
New Jersey	5,905,302	87.4	34.5	2,831,385	87.1	35.8	3,073,917	87.7	33.3
New Mexico	1,290,920	82.8	25.3	626,071	82.0	25.0	664,849	83.6	25.7
New York	13,197,392	84.7	32.4	6,263,140	84.2	32.3	6,934,252	85.0	32.5
North Carolina	6,150,247	84.3	26.5	2,916,650	82.5	26.3	3,233,597	86.0	26.7
North Dakota	419,435	90.1	25.8	205,902	89.3	24.4	213,533	90.8	27.1
Ohio	7,738,348	87.6	24.1	3,689,403	87.3	24.9	4,048,945	88.0	23.4
Oklahoma	2,376,783	85.6	22.7	1,143,366	84.8	22.9	1,233,417	86.2	22.6
Oregon	2,586,798	89.1	29.2	1,261,589	88.0	29.8	1,325,209	90.1	28.6
Pennsylvania	8,609,133	87.9	26.4	4,098,547	87.7	27.3	4,510,586	88.1	25.6
Rhode Island	715,565	84.7	30.5	338,798	84.0	32.0	376,767	85.4	29.1
South Carolina	3,019,333	83.6	24.3	1,423,802	82.4	25.0	1,595,531	84.7	23.8
South Dakota	523,836	89.9	25.1	254,475	88.4	24.2	269,361	91.3	25.9
Tennessee	4,213,368	83.1	23.0	2,002,966	82.1	23.6	2,210,402	84.0	22.5
Texas	15,361,557	79.9	25.5	7,531,016	78.9	26.3	7,830,541	80.8	24.7
Utah	1,573,179	90.4	28.5	780,062	89.8	31.6	793,117	91.0	25.4
Vermont	425,483	91.0	33.1	205,232	89.9	31.4	220,251	92.0	34.6
Virginia	5,207,987	86.6	34.0	2,492,370	85.6	34.8	2,715,617	87.5	33.3
Washington	4,445,351	89.7	31.0	2,185,981	89.2	32.0	2,259,370	90.1	30.1
West Virginia	1,263,943	82.8	17.3	605,495	82.0	17.3	658,448	83.6	17.2
Wisconsin	3,761,656	89.8	25.7	1,843,218	89.0	25.4	1,918,438	90.5	25.9
Wyoming	355,793	91.8	23.8	178,337	91.4	24.8	177,456	92.2	22.8

Table B-2. Educational Attainment of the Population 25 Years Old and Over by Sex, Race, Hispanic Origin, and Region or State, 2009—*Continued*

Region/State	White alone, not Hispanic or Latino age 25 years and over[1]			Black or African Amerian alone, age 25 years and over[1]		
	Population	High School Graduate or higher (percent)	Bachelor's degree or higher (percent)	Population	High School Graduate or higher (percent)	Bachelor's degree or higher (percent)
United States....................	139,962,199	90.4	31.1	22,975,410	81.4	17.6
Northeast Region..............	27,580,901	91.0	34.7	3,967,373	81.6	19.3
Midwest Region................	36,221,701	90.6	27.8	4,022,822	81.4	15.8
South Region....................	48,676,944	88.2	29.3	12,942,058	80.3	17.0
West Region.....................	27,482,653	93.3	35.0	2,043,157	87.5	21.3
Alabama..........................	2,227,745	84.3	24.5	740,939	78.2	14.2
Alaska............................	303,541	94.7	31.5	13,838	90.9	18.1
Arizona...........................	2,760,906	92.5	31.4	144,222	88.2	22.5
Arkansas.........................	1,509,150	85.2	20.4	259,727	76.9	12.0
California.........................	11,250,383	93.4	38.9	1,406,765	87.4	21.4
Colorado.........................	2,487,371	95.0	41.3	117,813	88.9	21.2
Connecticut......................	1,821,786	92.3	39.3	207,780	80.9	17.0
Delaware.........................	426,060	90.0	31.2	112,743	84.9	17.7
District of Columbia	149,499	98.8	86.5	212,139	82.3	21.4
Florida............................	8,189,165	90.4	28.0	1,704,707	77.2	15.8
Georgia	3,820,803	87.8	31.9	1,756,140	82.2	19.0
Hawaii............................	235,896	95.7	42.3	18,246	97.5	28.7
Idaho.............................	851,343	91.7	25.3	4,361	78.7	27.6
Illinois............................	5,819,567	91.8	34.3	1,130,967	82.1	18.2
Indiana...........................	3,583,790	88.3	23.4	336,661	82.5	13.7
Iowa..............................	1,829,253	91.9	25.4	42,140	81.3	16.9
Kansas...........................	1,509,828	92.7	31.6	91,325	87.2	19.6
Kentucky.........................	2,575,694	82.0	21.3	194,889	82.9	14.0
Louisiana	1,892,035	85.9	25.1	835,547	75.1	12.8
Maine.............................	889,128	90.5	27.2	6,855	73.1	13.6
Maryland..........................	2,266,510	91.6	40.1	1,053,569	86.8	24.8
Massachusetts...................	3,664,663	92.0	40.3	247,276	81.7	21.1
Michigan..........................	5,326,380	89.9	25.6	838,381	81.3	14.8
Minnesota........................	3,077,193	93.8	32.5	126,564	78.5	18.7
Mississippi.......................	1,171,752	84.9	23.5	620,733	73.2	12.3
Missouri..........................	3,348,212	88.1	26.2	399,082	80.9	15.2
Montana..........................	589,919	91.9	28.4	...	...	...
Nebraska.........................	1,004,428	93.1	28.9	42,092	84.5	16.6
Nevada...........................	1,073,199	92.3	25.3	121,566	86.5	17.3
New Hampshire..................	852,935	91.8	32.0	8,788	83.0	20.6
New Jersey	3,801,782	91.7	37.5	744,723	83.5	20.4
New Mexico	611,128	94.2	37.6	23,438	88.5	23.4
New York.........................	8,318,542	91.2	37.5	1,922,703	80.6	20.9
North Carolina...................	4,362,790	88.2	29.9	1,208,179	80.3	17.4
North Dakota.....................	383,916	90.7	26.4	...	...	...
Ohio..............................	6,557,203	88.9	24.9	824,532	80.6	14.6
Oklahoma.........................	1,799,610	88.4	24.8	154,092	84.3	16.8
Oregon...........................	2,172,693	92.5	30.5	39,234	85.3	23.0
Pennsylvania.....................	7,234,900	89.7	27.6	792,792	82.7	14.5
Rhode Island.....................	587,847	87.8	33.1	34,449	74.8	19.6
South Carolina	2,078,098	87.5	28.6	777,718	76.8	13.3
South Dakota....................	468,789	91.5	26.0	3,760	75.8	34.3
Tennessee.......................	3,370,549	84.7	24.2	618,374	79.8	16.2
Texas.............................	8,026,049	91.7	33.9	1,705,709	85.0	18.1
Utah..............................	1,324,963	94.1	30.9	12,172	81.4	20.8
Vermont..........................	409,318	91.2	33.1	...	...	...
Virginia...........................	3,616,964	89.5	37.4	951,816	80.1	18.2
Washington.......................	3,506,856	93.3	32.1	137,327	87.1	20.3
West Virginia.....................	1,194,471	82.7	17.1	35,037	86.5	12.9
Wisconsin.........................	3,313,142	92.0	26.8	184,361	78.1	12.4
Wyoming	314,455	93.6	25.2	2,773	84.3	30.1

...= Not available
[1]Race categories do not include persons of Hispanic origin

Table B-2. Educational Attainment of the Population 25 Years Old and Over by Sex, Race, Hispanic Origin, and Region or State, 2009—*Continued*

Region/State	Asian alone, age 25 years and over[1]			Hispanic or Latino, age 25 years and over[2]		
	Population	High School Graduate or higher (percent)	Bachelor's degree or higher (percent)	Population	High School Graduate or higher (percent)	Bachelor's degree or higher (percent)
United States..................................	9,404,493	85.3	49.7	26,106,587	60.9	12.6
Northeast Region.............................	1,944,954	82.2	52.6	3,774,754	65.0	15.1
Midwest Region................................	1,025,211	87.3	56.5	2,228,093	60.6	12.1
South Region....................................	1,966,756	86.0	52.0	9,435,874	61.9	14.2
West Region.....................................	4,467,572	85.9	45.8	10,667,866	58.6	10.4
Alabama...	33,035	85.3	50.7	70,526	53.9	13.0
Alaska..	23,448	83.3	24.3	20,875	80.4	17.4
Arizona..	113,658	87.4	52.7	1,043,446	62.5	10.2
Arkansas..	19,336	77.3	36.4	80,013	47.8	7.1
California..	3,263,368	85.8	47.7	7,312,489	56.7	9.9
Colorado	86,852	86.6	47.8	535,911	63.2	12.8
Connecticut......................................	80,944	87.8	62.1	236,735	66.4	13.8
Delaware..	18,490	90.5	67.9	32,175	57.2	12.0
District of Columbia..........................	13,205	94.3	79.7	33,040	59.0	34.6
Florida..	303,890	84.9	46.2	2,513,758	73.9	20.0
Georgia	187,805	85.6	50.9	404,624	53.2	13.0
Hawaii..	380,050	87.0	29.7	57,823	89.6	19.3
Idaho...	11,694	86.1	39.6	75,848	52.0	7.0
Illinois..	376,701	90.2	61.1	1,044,047	59.2	12.0
Indiana...	54,949	85.6	54.9	174,387	60.9	11.3
Iowa...	28,814	80.3	47.8	63,442	58.6	11.4
Kansas...	38,389	83.8	46.7	130,809	58.3	9.7
Kentucky..	26,837	85.9	56.2	51,358	59.7	12.6
Louisiana	42,772	78.8	36.4	93,636	71.8	17.6
Maine...	6,796	87.7	38.7	8,281	88.4	25.6
Maryland..	202,840	88.8	58.4	227,037	59.9	21.1
Massachusetts..................................	214,913	81.6	54.8	312,750	64.3	15.8
Michigan..	151,426	88.7	62.0	213,922	65.3	13.3
Minnesota..	110,644	80.2	42.4	107,578	56.9	13.0
Mississippi.......................................	15,687	75.8	41.6	35,558	59.2	12.0
Missouri...	56,031	89.4	60.0	97,675	67.4	15.6
Montana...	3,453	80.5	26.6	13,248	78.7	21.0
Nebraska..	17,193	86.6	54.1	70,355	47.1	7.3
Nevada...	125,916	87.8	37.7	359,116	55.9	7.4
New Hampshire.................................	14,797	89.3	59.7	17,723	71.9	16.0
New Jersey.......................................	461,716	92.2	67.7	859,854	68.4	15.1
New Mexico......................................	18,043	89.7	44.7	529,049	70.0	13.2
New York..	945,032	77.3	44.8	1,944,276	63.3	15.4
North Carolina..................................	115,204	83.9	49.4	342,456	51.8	11.7
North Dakota....................................	2,947	80.6	42.3	7,462	84.2	16.9
Ohio	118,210	89.6	60.2	161,571	69.6	14.7
Oklahoma...	38,084	84.2	40.4	143,397	55.0	9.7
Oregon...	91,909	84.9	46.2	207,271	56.1	11.6
Pennsylvania....................................	198,577	80.6	49.6	324,574	65.4	13.7
Rhode Island....................................	19,188	75.9	40.3	65,831	62.0	11.5
South Carolina	37,329	82.2	48.5	99,143	58.3	12.2
South Dakota	4,209	71.6	32.6	9,164	71.7	14.1
Tennessee	57,515	85.5	49.8	122,110	56.1	13.2
Texas...	580,159	85.8	53.2	4,876,517	57.5	10.9
Utah...	34,967	83.5	37.5	161,900	63.0	10.7
Vermont..	2,991	73.6	29.0	4,730	90.6	40.6
Virginia..	266,676	89.2	56.8	300,398	69.0	21.8
Washington.......................................	311,661	85.2	48.0	326,511	56.8	12.7
West Virginia....................................	7,892	91.3	67.9	10,128	77.2	19.0
Wisconsin	65,698	81.9	44.6	147,681	58.9	11.4
Wyoming	2,553	85.1	30.0	24,379	74.0	9.5

[1] Race categories do not include persons of Hispanic origin
[2] May be of any race

Table B-3.   Population, School, and Student Characteristics by State

FIPS code	State	Population, 2009		Median income for a family of four, 2009 (dollars)	Children under 18 years old in poverty, 2009 (percent)	Poverty and health insurance, 2009		
		Total	5 to 17 years old (percent)			Total children under 19 years old (thousands)	Low-income children under 19 years old (percent)	Low-income children with no health insurance (percent)
		1	2	3	4	5	6	7
00	**UNITED STATES**	307,006,550	17.3	$73,714	20.7	78,857	42.0	6.6
01	Alabama	4,708,708	17.3	$62,983	25.8	1,165	55.7	6.2
02	Alaska..............................	698,473	18.5	$84,577	15.3	194	34.0	5.0
04	Arizona.............................	6,595,778	18.4	$66,030	31.3	1,811	50.7	10.6
05	Arkansas...........................	2,889,450	17.5	$53,523	25.7	742	50.2	7.2
06	California	36,961,664	18.1	$77,596	21.0	9,964	44.1	6.7
08	Colorado...........................	5,024,748	17.2	$82,621	18.2	1,312	36.4	6.7
09	Connecticut........................	3,518,288	17.0	$101,647	10.0	852	23.0	3.8
10	Delaware...........................	885,122	16.6	$83,928	19.0	223	35.7	5.7
11	District of Columbia	599,657	12.8	$70,862	31.3	119	53.3	6.1
12	Florida..............................	18,537,969	15.6	$64,084	21.0	4,197	45.1	12.4
13	Georgia	9,829,211	18.6	$68,122	23.3	2,717	44.8	8.0
15	Hawaii..............................	1,295,178	15.5	$85,190	18.9	312	41.2	1.7
16	Idaho...............................	1,545,801	19.0	$60,488	19.7	441	44.7	7.1
17	Illinois..............................	12,910,409	17.7	$79,788	19.5	3,384	42.0	6.4
18	Indiana.............................	6,423,113	17.8	$68,109	26.3	1,723	44.1	5.5
19	Iowa................................	3,007,856	16.9	$74,349	14.7	754	37.4	4.1
20	Kansas	2,818,747	17.7	$68,154	18.0	743	40.6	5.5
21	Kentucky...........................	4,314,113	16.8	$62,739	22.4	1,066	43.5	5.0
22	Louisiana	4,492,076	17.9	$66,154	19.5	1,225	43.9	5.8
23	Maine	1,318,301	15.2	$67,361	17.1	287	37.1	1.8
24	Maryland	5,699,478	17.0	$101,693	12.3	1,409	29.5	4.5
25	Massachusetts....................	6,593,587	15.9	$100,462	16.7	1,545	33.3	1.9
26	Michigan	9,969,727	17.4	$70,600	20.7	2,503	39.0	3.3
27	Minnesota	5,266,214	17.0	$83,772	17.4	1,306	34.3	3.5
28	Mississippi	2,951,996	18.5	$54,812	31.9	825	57.8	6.5
29	Missouri	5,987,580	17.2	$68,705	23.8	1,517	42.7	6.8
30	Montana	974,989	16.1	$66,825	21.0	229	44.4	7.0
31	Nebraska...........................	1,796,619	17.6	$69,950	13.6	477	35.2	4.4
32	Nevada.............................	2,643,085	18.1	$69,371	17.9	706	43.4	8.8
33	New Hampshire...................	1,324,575	16.2	$88,538	10.5	303	22.9	1.2
34	New Jersey	8,707,739	17.1	$99,474	12.8	2,191	29.1	5.0
35	New Mexico	2,009,671	17.8	$52,842	29.2	545	53.1	11.0
36	New York	19,541,453	16.4	$82,587	25.0	4,700	44.4	4.9
37	North Carolina	9,380,884	17.2	$66,487	24.5	2,425	43.9	9.3
38	North Dakota......................	646,844	15.5	$78,352	14.4	153	33.1	2.7
39	Ohio................................	11,542,645	17.1	$71,453	18.7	2,843	41.0	6.2
40	Oklahoma..........................	3,687,050	17.5	$63,004	20.3	976	44.2	6.4
41	Oregon.............................	3,825,657	16.3	$71,593	18.3	906	42.6	7.3
42	Pennsylvania	12,604,767	16.1	$78,626	14.5	2,990	36.0	4.0
44	Rhode Island	1,053,209	15.8	$87,163	22.2	240	41.5	4.5
45	South Carolina	4,561,242	16.9	$62,056	17.6	1,154	40.2	6.9
46	South Dakota......................	812,383	17.2	$66,918	18.4	209	43.1	6.2
47	Tennessee	6,296,254	17.0	$62,197	23.1	1,565	45.3	5.5
48	Texas...............................	24,782,302	19.5	$64,420	25.6	7,293	50.4	11.0
49	Utah................................	2,784,572	21.4	$68,707	13.9	921	33.1	7.4
50	Vermont	621,760	15.1	$77,127	12.0	130	35.6	3.9
51	Virginia.............................	7,882,590	16.7	$85,586	14.8	2,016	33.0	4.2
53	Washington	6,664,195	16.8	$81,269	18.0	1,629	36.8	2.7
54	West Virginia......................	1,819,777	15.4	$59,307	21.2	410	40.9	3.2
55	Wisconsin	5,654,774	16.7	$76,188	15.5	1,369	32.7	2.6
56	Wyoming	544,270	16.8	$75,129	10.5	143	34.9	4.9

Table B-3. Population, School, and Student Characteristics by State—*Continued*

FIPS code	State	Educational attainment, 2009			Public schools and school districts, 2008–2009					
		Population 25 years old and over (thousands)	High school graduate or more (percent)	Bachelor's degree or more (percent)	Number of school districts	Type of school				
						Total schools	Regular schools	Special education schools	Vocational schools	Alternative schools
		8	9	10	11	12	13	14	15	16
00	**UNITED STATES**	201,952	85.3	27.9	17,735	98,706	88,801	2,289	1,409	6,207
01	Alabama	3,116	82.1	22.0	171	1,605	1,375	41	73	116
02	Alaska	431	91.4	26.6	54	507	451	2	3	51
04	Arizona	4,248	84.2	25.6	619	2,186	1,908	20	172	86
05	Arkansas	1,904	82.4	18.9	295	1,129	1,089	4	24	12
06	California	23,782	80.6	29.9	1,122	10,029	8,451	145	76	1,357
08	Colorado	3,293	89.3	35.9	262	1,779	1,672	10	5	92
09	Connecticut	2,370	88.6	35.6	200	1,150	1,037	48	17	48
10	Delaware	595	87.4	28.7	40	240	182	19	6	33
11	District of Columbia	413	87.1	48.5	62	230	206	10	1	13
12	Florida	12,801	85.3	25.3	77	3,985	3,328	173	53	431
13	Georgia	6,230	83.9	27.5	207	2,472	2,230	73	1	168
15	Hawaii	883	90.4	29.6	1	290	286	3	0	1
16	Idaho	964	88.4	23.9	135	735	629	11	11	84
17	Illinois	8,438	86.4	30.6	1,078	4,402	4,010	150	53	189
18	Indiana	4,193	86.6	22.5	379	1,973	1,885	37	29	22
19	Iowa	1,981	90.5	25.1	372	1,490	1,423	8	0	59
20	Kansas	1,809	89.7	29.5	330	1,428	1,416	10	1	1
21	Kentucky	2,877	81.7	21.0	194	1,531	1,235	11	126	159
22	Louisiana	2,897	82.2	21.4	114	1,643	1,262	202	6	173
23	Maine	925	90.2	26.9	299	663	633	1	27	2
24	Maryland	3,798	88.2	35.7	24	1,457	1,328	39	24	66
25	Massachusetts	4,490	89.0	38.2	500	1,855	1,771	26	39	19
26	Michigan	6,625	87.9	24.6	846	4,078	3,365	317	62	334
27	Minnesota	3,486	91.5	31.5	559	2,263	1,654	271	12	326
28	Mississippi	1,866	80.4	19.6	164	1,077	921	4	90	62
29	Missouri	3,962	86.8	25.2	560	2,423	2,193	66	63	101
30	Montana	649	90.8	27.4	506	830	823	2	0	5
31	Nebraska	1,153	89.8	27.4	296	1,122	1,081	36	0	5
32	Nevada	1,728	83.9	21.8	18	617	579	7	1	30
33	New Hampshire	903	91.3	32.0	276	492	492	0	0	0
34	New Jersey	5,905	87.4	34.5	682	2,588	2,351	74	55	108
35	New Mexico	1,291	82.8	25.3	99	853	808	6	1	38
36	New York	13,197	84.7	32.4	854	4,690	4,587	47	28	28
37	North Carolina	6,150	84.3	26.5	233	2,548	2,417	33	10	88
38	North Dakota	419	90.1	25.8	228	525	484	34	7	0
39	Ohio	7,738	87.6	24.1	1,051	3,852	3,710	61	72	9
40	Oklahoma	2,377	85.6	22.7	583	1,796	1,787	4	0	5
41	Oregon	2,587	89.1	29.2	221	1,304	1,261	3	0	40
42	Pennsylvania	8,609	87.9	26.4	790	3,248	3,136	12	87	13
44	Rhode Island	716	84.7	30.5	50	327	299	3	10	15
45	South Carolina	3,019	83.6	24.3	103	1,211	1,139	10	39	23
46	South Dakota	524	89.9	25.1	169	721	687	7	0	27
47	Tennessee	4,213	83.1	23.0	140	1,755	1,689	19	21	26
48	Texas	15,362	79.9	25.5	1,272	8,530	7,434	20	0	1,076
49	Utah	1,573	90.4	28.5	112	1,029	849	81	6	93
50	Vermont	425	91.0	33.1	362	328	312	0	15	1
51	Virginia	5,208	86.6	34.0	139	2,009	1,865	5	32	107
53	Washington	4,445	89.7	31.0	309	2,321	1,883	106	12	320
54	West Virginia	1,264	82.8	17.3	57	762	697	6	31	28
55	Wisconsin	3,762	89.8	25.7	461	2,268	2,159	9	8	92
56	Wyoming	356	91.8	23.8	60	360	332	3	0	25

Table B-3. Population, School, and Student Characteristics by State—*Continued*

FIPS code	State	Public schools and students, 2008–2009									
		Total schools	Charter schools	Magnet schools	Title I status			Number of students	Primary schools (percent)	Middle schools (percent)	High schools (percent)
					Title I eligible schools	Title I school-wide schools	Students in Title I school-wide schools (percent)				
		17	18	19	20	21	22	23	24	25	26
00	**UNITED STATES**	98,706	4,694	3,021	62,305	40,984	41.4	49,265,044	39.7	29.6	30.2
01	Alabama	1,605	...	27	855	768	46.7	745,668	39.8	31.0	29.2
02	Alaska	507	24	13	358	312	41.5	130,662	39.0	29.3	31.7
04	Arizona	2,186	477	...	1,188	774	41.0	1,087,817	40.7	30.2	29.1
05	Arkansas	1,129	32	39	818	692	54.3	478,965	41.5	29.7	28.6
06	California	10,029	751	438	6,032	4,556	46.4	6,322,528	38.0	30.1	31.8
08	Colorado	1,779	148	24	615	372	17.9	818,443	42.0	28.9	29.1
09	Connecticut	1,150	18	56	529	158	13.2	567,198	39.1	30.1	30.8
10	Delaware	240	18	3	111	101	42.6	125,430	39.0	30.3	30.8
11	District of Columbia	230	90	4	216	206	93.5	68,681	47.2	26.7	26.0
12	Florida	3,985	399	357	2,538	2,323	59.8	2,631,020	40.0	30.3	29.7
13	Georgia	2,472	63	...	1,320	1,166	44.1	1,655,792	41.6	30.0	28.4
15	Hawaii	290	31	...	182	172	53.5	179,478	40.7	29.4	29.8
16	Idaho	735	31	...	508	415	55.0	275,154	40.3	30.1	29.6
17	Illinois	4,402	39	337	3,037	1,275	33.4	2,119,707	40.4	29.4	30.2
18	Indiana	1,973	51	26	1,353	889	42.4	1,046,147	39.2	30.6	30.2
19	Iowa	1,490	9	...	940	482	31.2	487,559	40.1	28.7	31.2
20	Kansas	1,428	35	33	1,180	712	47.5	471,060	40.8	29.0	29.5
21	Kentucky	1,531	...	41	1,062	964	71.9	670,030	41.0	29.4	29.5
22	Louisiana	1,643	88	81	1,222	1,123	74.5	684,873	44.1	29.5	26.4
23	Maine	663	...	1	...	...	...	192,935	37.0	30.0	33.0
24	Maryland	1,457	34	87	359	315	15.7	843,861	38.9	29.4	31.7
25	Massachusetts	1,855	61	...	1,019	479	22.9	958,910	39.4	30.0	30.5
26	Michigan	4,078	283	479	3,514	1,426	35.1	1,659,921	37.6	29.1	32.3
27	Minnesota	2,263	174	75	868	277	10.7	836,048	37.9	29.1	33.0
28	Mississippi	1,077	1	6	709	682	67.0	491,962	40.3	30.3	27.8
29	Missouri	2,423	41	37	1,133	523	18.6	917,871	39.7	29.5	30.8
30	Montana	830	...	...	662	370	38.1	141,899	38.1	30.2	31.7
31	Nebraska	1,122	...	...	485	262	22.3	292,590	41.0	28.3	30.6
32	Nevada	617	30	1	319	270	41.6	433,371	39.8	31.3	28.9
33	New Hampshire	492	15	...	238	37	5.4	197,934	36.2	31.0	32.8
34	New Jersey	2,588	62	...	1,367	379	14.8	1,381,420	37.7	28.9	29.6
35	New Mexico	853	67	2	713	678	75.2	330,245	40.7	29.4	29.9
36	New York	4,690	115	318	4,410	2,197	44.7	2,740,805	36.8	28.5	30.6
37	North Carolina	2,548	96	127	1,135	982	30.0	1,488,645	41.3	29.9	28.9
38	North Dakota	525	...	...	310	77	14.0	94,728	37.3	30.2	32.5
39	Ohio	3,852	326	...	2,837	1,830	41.4	1,817,163	38.6	29.6	31.8
40	Oklahoma	1,796	16	...	1,123	926	46.7	645,108	44.0	28.4	27.4
41	Oregon	1,304	87	...	579	399	26.9	575,393	38.8	29.9	31.3
42	Pennsylvania	3,248	127	57	2,425	704	21.3	1,775,029	37.0	30.2	32.6
44	Rhode Island	327	11	...	231	121	37.3	145,342	36.7	30.7	32.6
45	South Carolina	1,211	36	57	928	869	67.4	718,113	41.1	29.6	29.3
46	South Dakota	721	...	...	621	331	32.9	126,764	39.7	29.5	30.8
47	Tennessee	1,755	14	34	1,355	1,275	67.5	971,950	40.7	29.7	29.6
48	Texas	8,530	499	...	6,411	6,044	70.4	4,752,148	43.4	29.1	27.5
49	Utah	1,029	67	20	245	193	15.8	559,778	42.6	29.7	27.7
50	Vermont	328	...	...	223	142	36.7	92,446	38.9	28.6	32.5
51	Virginia	2,009	4	158	713	378	13.4	1,235,795	39.6	29.5	30.8
53	Washington	2,321	...	...	1,249	547	22.0	1,037,018	38.0	30.0	32.0
54	West Virginia	762	...	...	357	351	35.3	282,729	41.3	29.3	29.4
55	Wisconsin	2,268	221	5	1,517	380	16.9	873,750	39.5	28.0	32.5
56	Wyoming	360	3	...	186	80	20.1	87,161	39.5	30.1	30.4

... = Not available or not applicable.

Table B-3. Population, School, and Student Characteristics by State—*Continued*

		Characteristics of public school students, 2008–2009 (percent)								
FIPS code	State	Students in charter schools	Students eligible for free or reduced-price lunch	Students with IEP[1]	English language learners	Race and hispanic origin of students				
						Non-Hispanic White	Non-Hispanic Black	Hispanic or Latino[2]	Asian and Pacific Islander	American Indian, Alaska Native
		27	28	29	30	31	32	33	34	35
00	**UNITED STATES**	1.6	43.8	12.7	8.9	54.9	17.0	21.5	5.0	1.2
01	Alabama	0.0	52.4	0.9	2.6	58.8	35.3	3.9	1.2	0.8
02	Alaska	0.0	34.1	13.5	9.2	53.3	3.5	5.8	7.2	23.1
04	Arizona	9.6	47.5	11.4	11.5	44.4	5.8	41.4	3.0	5.5
05	Arkansas	0.9	57.1	13.5	5.8	66.6	22.4	8.6	1.6	0.7
06	California	0.1	52.4	10.6	24.2	27.9	7.3	49.0	11.7	0.7
08	Colorado	0.7	35.4	10.2	10.9	60.9	6.0	28.4	3.6	1.2
09	Connecticut	0.7	30.2	12.2	5.2	64.5	13.9	17.1	4.2	0.4
10	Delaware	6.9	39.5	15.1	5.7	52.1	33.2	10.9	3.4	0.4
11	District of Columbia	35.4	67.1	15.5	8.5	6.0	81.5	10.8	1.6	0.1
12	Florida	0.0	49.6	14.6	8.6	47.0	24.0	26.1	2.6	0.3
13	Georgia	0.3	53.0	10.9	5.0	47.2	39.0	10.4	3.3	0.2
15	Hawaii	0.0	41.7	11.2	10.3	19.5	2.3	4.6	72.9	0.6
16	Idaho	2.6	39.7	10.2	6.4	81.2	1.3	14.1	1.7	1.7
17	Illinois	0.0	39.3	15.0	9.7	54.3	20.0	21.3	4.2	0.2
18	Indiana	1.6	41.8	16.8	4.4	78.3	12.8	7.1	1.5	0.3
19	Iowa	0.0	34.4	13.8	4.2	84.5	5.8	7.0	2.2	0.6
20	Kansas	0.0	42.9	14.0	7.2	72.8	8.8	14.0	2.8	1.6
21	Kentucky	0.0	51.6	16.1	2.2	84.7	11.0	3.0	1.1	0.1
22	Louisiana	2.6	64.9	12.6	1.8	48.8	46.1	2.9	1.4	0.8
23	Maine	0.0	38.1	15.9	0.0	93.7	2.7	1.2	1.6	0.8
24	Maryland	0.0	34.7	12.2	0.0	46.2	38.0	9.5	5.9	0.4
25	Massachusetts	2.8	30.7	17.6	5.1	69.9	8.2	14.3	5.2	0.3
26	Michigan	6.3	41.8	14.0	3.7	71.4	20.2	4.8	2.7	0.9
27	Minnesota	3.9	32.7	14.4	7.4	75.6	9.6	6.4	6.2	2.2
28	Mississippi	0.0	68.3	0.0	1.3	46.3	50.5	2.1	0.9	0.2
29	Missouri	1.9	38.7	14.5	1.8	76.0	17.8	3.9	1.9	0.4
30	Montana	0.0	36.7	12.4	3.2	83.7	1.0	2.6	1.2	11.4
31	Nebraska	0.0	38.4	15.1	6.3	74.6	8.1	13.5	2.1	1.7
32	Nevada	0.6	39.0	11.1	17.5	42.3	11.2	36.9	8.1	1.5
33	New Hampshire	0.0	20.5	15.2	1.8	91.9	2.1	3.3	2.4	0.3
34	New Jersey	1.4	30.0	16.6	3.9	54.0	17.1	19.9	8.5	0.2
35	New Mexico	0.3	61.7	13.9	0.0	28.9	2.6	56.1	1.4	11.0
36	New York	1.3	44.7	16.2	6.7	51.1	19.3	21.4	7.7	0.5
37	North Carolina	2.5	33.9	12.6	7.6	54.3	31.2	10.6	2.5	1.4
38	North Dakota	0.0	31.6	14.0	3.7	85.3	2.2	2.2	1.1	9.2
39	Ohio	4.8	36.4	14.6	2.0	78.4	16.9	2.8	1.7	0.1
40	Oklahoma	0.0	56.1	0.0	0.0	57.3	10.9	10.5	2.1	19.2
41	Oregon	0.1	46.0	14.1	11.2	71.7	3.1	18.1	5.0	2.1
42	Pennsylvania	4.1	33.4	16.7	2.6	73.6	15.8	7.5	2.9	0.2
44	Rhode Island	1.4	39.8	19.0	0.0	68.6	9.0	18.5	3.2	0.7
45	South Carolina	0.3	52.5	14.1	4.4	53.8	38.8	5.5	1.6	0.4
46	South Dakota	0.0	34.7	14.0	2.8	81.3	2.5	2.7	1.3	12.2
47	Tennessee	0.0	50.0	12.2	2.8	68.3	24.6	5.2	1.6	0.2
48	Texas	2.2	48.8	9.5	15.1	34.0	14.2	47.9	3.6	0.4
49	Utah	4.8	31.2	11.6	7.9	79.4	1.4	14.5	3.3	1.4
50	Vermont	0.0	30.1	14.2	1.6	93.7	1.7	1.1	1.7	0.2
51	Virginia	0.0	33.1	13.5	7.0	58.2	26.4	9.2	5.9	0.3
53	Washington	0.0	38.2	12.1	8.0	67.1	5.7	15.8	8.9	2.6
54	West Virginia	0.0	50.0	16.5	0.6	92.8	5.4	0.9	0.7	0.1
55	Wisconsin	0.6	33.5	14.3	5.5	76.3	10.5	8.0	3.7	1.5
56	Wyoming	0.0	31.0	16.9	2.6	83.3	1.6	10.4	1.1	3.5

[1]IEP = Individual Education Program. See notes and definitions for more information.
[2]May be of any race.
0.0 = Rounds to zero.

Table B-3. Population, School, and Student Characteristics by State—*Continued*

FIPS code	State	Public school outcomes					Private schools		
		Dropouts, grades 9–12, 2007–2008 (percent)	9th grade membership, 2004–2005	12th grade membership, 2007–2008	High school graduates (regular diplomas), 2007–2008	Averaged freshman graduation rates, 2007–2008	Number of schools, 2007–2008	Enrollment, 2007–2008	High school graduates, 2006–2007
		36	37	38	39	40	41	42	43
00	**UNITED STATES**	4.1	4,281,345	3,374,786	2,965,286	74.9	33,740	5,072,451	306,605
01	Alabama	2.2	64,569	46,474	41,346	69.0	423	72,037	4,576
02	Alaska	7.3	11,934	10,092	7,855	69.1	63	4,173	198
04	Arizona	6.7	91,860	76,275	61,667	70.7	361	51,590	2,593
05	Arkansas	4.7	38,279	30,708	28,725	76.4	305	34,850	1,379
06	California	5.0	549,463	468,281	374,561	71.2	4,013	607,141	34,878
08	Colorado	6.4	64,446	55,334	46,082	75.4	415	48,945	2,524
09	Connecticut	2.8	49,177	40,927	38,419	82.2	423	76,520	7,993
10	Delaware	6.0	11,249	7,681	7,388	72.1	214	26,403	1,797
11	District of Columbia	5.5	6,285	4,002	3,352	56.0	92	17,985	1,665
12	Florida	3.3	250,263	169,832	149,046	66.9	1,938	329,646	18,583
13	Georgia	4.3	142,079	95,443	83,505	65.4	910	136,987	7,574
15	Hawaii	5.4	16,971	11,234	11,613	76.0	136	33,441	2,385
16	Idaho	2.0	21,344	18,598	16,567	80.1	190	20,878	908
17	Illinois	5.2	178,240	144,342	135,143	80.4	1,924	264,012	15,105
18	Indiana	1.7	87,829	71,755	61,901	74.1	807	104,062	4,788
19	Iowa	2.9	41,196	39,114	34,573	86.4	242	41,796	2,261
20	Kansas	2.5	39,293	33,149	30,737	79.1	246	43,413	2,378
21	Kentucky	2.8	56,919	41,958	39,339	74.4	404	67,376	4,028
22	Louisiana	7.5	59,182	37,806	34,401	63.5	393	123,476	7,531
23	Maine	4.4	16,766	16,322	14,350	79.1	200	19,553	2,618
24	Maryland	3.6	81,270	61,767	59,171	80.4	823	143,661	9,454
25	Massachusetts	3.4	84,628	68,757	65,197	81.5	947	127,967	10,435
26	Michigan	6.2	158,797	126,380	115,183	76.3	908	139,314	8,522
27	Minnesota	2.8	70,751	74,749	60,409	86.4	585	90,973	4,930
28	Mississippi	4.6	40,195	27,688	24,795	63.9	219	47,955	3,355
29	Missouri	4.9	78,748	65,443	61,717	82.4	690	112,368	7,330
30	Montana	5.2	13,200	11,057	10,396	82.0	141	13,778	1,703
31	Nebraska	2.5	25,214	22,400	20,035	83.8	223	35,872	2,156
32	Nevada	5.1	36,056	21,828	17,149	51.3	161	22,310	695
33	New Hampshire	3.0	18,584	15,959	14,982	83.4	312	23,200	2,294
34	New Jersey	1.7	111,479	97,078	94,994	84.6	1,441	204,486	13,344
35	New Mexico	5.2	30,134	19,594	18,264	66.8	212	23,582	1,495
36	New York	3.9	262,635	185,680	176,310	70.8	2,130	458,231	29,891
37	North Carolina	5.2	126,414	85,893	83,307	72.8	656	108,810	5,594
38	North Dakota	2.4	8,547	7,662	6,999	83.8	50	6,345	**
39	Ohio	4.3	165,656	134,417	120,758	79.0	1,189	215,592	13,057
40	Oklahoma	3.1	50,035	39,321	37,630	78.0	300	34,354	2,033
41	Oregon	3.8	46,700	45,559	34,949	76.7	564	53,243	2,814
42	Pennsylvania	2.6	163,848	139,930	130,298	82.7	2,503	281,958	17,477
44	Rhode Island	5.3	14,591	10,848	10,347	76.4	226	23,951	1,582
45	South Carolina	3.9	65,564	39,459	...	...	409	56,492	3,211
46	South Dakota	2.3	10,377	8,901	8,582	84.4	80	10,692	556
47	Tennessee	3.9	80,890	62,040	57,486	74.9	557	106,097	5,889
48	Texas	4.0	386,182	273,867	252,121	73.1	1,651	235,241	11,923
49	Utah	4.2	38,069	40,375	28,167	74.3	146	17,551	1,351
50	Vermont	...	8,533	7,714	7,392	89.3	150	11,713	1,759
51	Virginia	2.7	109,375	85,413	77,369	77.0	872	116,934	6,913
53	Washington	5.7	89,802	78,429	61,625	71.9	730	86,811	4,565
54	West Virginia	4.4	24,199	18,625	17,489	77.3	139	13,400	605
55	Wisconsin	2.3	76,173	72,380	65,183	89.6	990	123,174	5,426
56	Wyoming	5.0	7,355	6,246	5,494	76.0	38	2,113	**

... = Not available.
** = Reporting standards not met.

Table B-3. Population, School, and Student Characteristics by State—*Continued*

		Public and private school characteristics, 2007–2008							Average public school teacher salary, 2009–2010[3]
		Public schools					Private schools 2007–2008		
		Student membership		Teachers		Student-teacher ratio 2008–2009	Total enrollment	Total teachers	Student-teacher ratio
FIPS code	State	Total students 2008–2009	Percent change from 1998–1999 to 2008–2009	Total teachers 2008–2009	Percent change from 1998–1999 to 2008–2009				
		44	45	46	47	48	49	50	51	52
00	UNITED STATES	49,265,044	5.9	3,221,917	13.8	15.3	5,072,451	456,266	11.1	55,350
01	Alabama	745,668	-0.3	47,819	0.1	15.6	72,037	6,405	11.2	47,156
02	Alaska	130,662	-3.5	7,927	-2.4	16.5	4,173	464	9.0	59,729
04	Arizona	1,087,817	28.2	54,696	29.1	19.9	51,590	4,222	12.2	46,952
05	Arkansas	478,965	5.9	37,162	32.9	12.9	34,850	3,147	11.1	49,051
06	California	6,322,528	6.7	303,647	7.8	20.8	607,141	50,152	12.1	70,458
08	Colorado	818,443	17.1	48,692	23.5	16.8	48,945	4,825	10.1	49,505
09	Connecticut	567,198	4.1	48,463	25.0	11.7	76,520	8,237	9.3	64,350
10	Delaware	125,430	10.7	8,322	17.6	15.1	26,403	2,438	10.8	57,080
11	District of Columbia	68,681	-4.5	5,321	2.6	12.9	17,985	2,189	8.2	64,548
12	Florida	2,631,020	12.6	186,361	47.0	14.1	329,646	29,783	11.1	46,912
13	Georgia	1,655,792	18.2	118,839	34.0	13.9	136,987	14,007	9.8	54,274
15	Hawaii	179,478	-4.6	11,295	6.2	15.9	33,441	2,880	11.6	58,168
16	Idaho	275,154	12.4	15,148	12.8	18.2	20,878	1,677	12.4	46,283
17	Illinois	2,119,707	5.4	135,704	11.5	15.6	264,012	20,751	12.7	62,077
18	Indiana	1,046,147	5.8	62,668	7.9	16.7	104,062	8,104	12.8	49,986
19	Iowa	487,559	-2.1	35,961	9.6	13.6	41,796	3,408	12.3	50,547
20	Kansas	471,060	-0.3	35,883	12.1	13.1	43,413	3,498	12.4	46,957
21	Kentucky	670,030	2.2	43,451	6.5	15.4	67,376	5,644	11.9	48,354
22	Louisiana	684,873	-10.9	49,377	0.5	13.9	123,476	9,085	13.6	50,349
23	Maine	192,935	-8.6	15,912	0.1	12.1	19,553	2,137	9.1	46,106
24	Maryland	843,861	0.3	58,940	18.3	14.3	143,661	14,286	10.1	65,333
25	Massachusetts	958,910	-0.4	70,398	0.9	13.6	127,967	15,042	8.5	68,000
26	Michigan	1,659,921	-3.5	94,754	1.6	17.5	139,314	10,871	12.8	57,958
27	Minnesota	836,048	-2.4	53,083	-2.5	15.7	90,973	7,178	12.7	53,069
28	Mississippi	491,962	-2.1	33,358	7.1	14.7	47,955	4,148	11.6	45,644
29	Missouri	917,871	0.5	67,737	8.5	13.6	112,368	9,724	11.6	45,317
30	Montana	141,899	-11.3	10,467	2.4	13.6	13,778	1,195	11.5	45,759
31	Nebraska	292,590	0.5	22,057	8.6	13.3	35,872	2,819	12.7	46,080
32	Nevada	433,371	39.3	21,993	34.0	19.7	22,310	1,550	14.4	51,524
33	New Hampshire	197,934	-3.3	15,661	17.8	12.6	23,200	2,969	7.8	51,365
34	New Jersey	1,381,420	8.9	114,713	24.3	12.0	204,486	19,522	10.5	64,809
35	New Mexico	330,245	0.5	22,825	14.2	14.5	23,582	2,171	10.9	46,401
36	New York	2,740,805	-4.7	217,944	10.5	12.6	458,231	42,845	10.7	71,470
37	North Carolina	1,488,645	18.6	109,634	37.9	13.6	108,810	10,846	10.0	48,648
38	North Dakota	94,728	-17.6	8,181	2.6	11.6	6,345	556	11.4	42,964
39	Ohio	1,817,163	-1.4	112,845	-1.0	16.1	215,592	16,369	13.2	55,931
40	Oklahoma	645,108	2.6	46,571	13.9	13.9	34,354	3,899	8.8	44,143
41	Oregon	575,393	6.0	30,152	11.0	19.1	53,243	4,744	11.2	55,224
42	Pennsylvania	1,775,029	-2.3	129,708	16.8	13.7	281,958	24,645	11.4	58,124
44	Rhode Island	145,342	-6.1	11,356	2.1	12.8	23,951	2,535	9.4	59,636
45	South Carolina	718,113	8.1	49,941	14.3	14.4	56,492	5,550	10.2	48,417
46	South Dakota	126,764	-4.3	9,244	-0.3	13.7	10,692	925	11.6	35,136
47	Tennessee	971,950	7.3	64,926	9.6	15.0	106,097	10,111	10.5	46,290
48	Texas	4,752,148	20.4	327,905	26.2	14.5	235,241	23,623	10.0	47,157
49	Utah	559,778	16.3	23,657	10.0	23.7	17,551	1,715	10.2	43,068
50	Vermont	92,446	-12.1	8,766	6.6	10.5	11,713	1,553	7.5	49,053
51	Virginia	1,235,795	9.9	71,415	-10.0	17.3	116,934	12,919	9.1	49,999
53	Washington	1,037,018	3.9	54,428	9.6	19.1	86,811	7,464	11.6	53,653
54	West Virginia	282,729	-5.0	20,209	-3.7	14.0	13,400	1,261	10.6	45,959
55	Wisconsin	873,750	-0.7	59,401	-2.9	14.7	123,174	9,915	12.4	52,644
56	Wyoming	87,161	-8.5	7,000	4.3	12.5	2,113	261	8.1	55,694

[3]National Education Association. Highlights Table 2: Summary of Selected Estimates Data for 2009–10. *Rankings & Estimates: Rankings of the States 2009 and Estimates of School Statistics, 2010,* page 67. Reprinted with permission of the National Education Association © 2010. All rights reserved. <http://www.nea.org>.

Table B-3. Population, School, and Student Characteristics by State—*Continued*

FIPS code	State	Staff employed by public elementary and secondary school systems and percent of total staff, 2008–2009								
		Total staff	Teachers		Instructional aides		Instructional coordinators		Guidance couselors	
			Number	Percent	Number	Percent	Number	Percent	Number	Percent
		53	54	55	56	57	58	59	60	61
00	**UNITED STATES**	6,328,318	3,221,917	50.9	727,615	11.5	80,553	1.3	107,802	1.7
01	Alabama	97,614	47,819	49.0	698	0.7	8,013	8.2	1,873	1.9
02	Alaska.................................	17,160	7,927	46.2	2,190	12.8	190	1.1	280	1.6
04	Arizona...............................	105,548	54,696	51.8	15,621	14.8	133	0.1	1,465	1.4
05	Arkansas.............................	71,270	37,162	52.1	7,794	10.9	837	1.2	1,440	2.0
06	California	590,016	303,647	51.5	68,652	11.6	7,129	1.2	7,768	1.3
08	Colorado.............................	102,566	48,692	47.5	15,010	14.6	2,201	2.1	2,117	2.1
09	Connecticut.........................	92,474	48,463	52.4	13,752	14.9	2,000	2.2	1,119	1.2
10	Delaware.............................	14,821	8,322	56.2	1,550	10.5	296	2.0	285	1.9
11	District of Columbia	12,131	5,321	43.9	1,252	10.3	405	3.3	250	2.1
12	Florida.................................	340,713	186,361	54.7	28,622	8.4	686	0.2	6,058	1.8
13	Georgia	239,139	118,839	49.7	27,950	11.7	2,042	0.9	3,691	1.5
15	Hawaii.................................	21,610	11,295	52.3	2,231	10.3	616	2.9	661	3.1
16	Idaho..................................	27,261	15,148	55.6	2,909	10.7	264	1.0	634	2.3
17	Illinois.................................	221,005	135,704	61.4	30,148	13.6	3,168	1.4	3,155	1.4
18	Indiana...............................	141,979	62,668	44.1	23,120	16.3	1,983	1.4	1,939	1.4
19	Iowa...................................	72,350	35,961	49.7	10,805	14.9	459	0.6	1,377	1.9
20	Kansas...............................	55,355	35,883	64.8	9,204	16.6	96	0.2	1,125	2.0
21	Kentucky.............................	100,217	43,451	43.4	14,076	14.0	942	0.9	1,461	1.5
22	Louisiana	100,873	49,377	48.9	11,380	11.3	1,864	1.8	2,878	2.9
23	Maine	36,459	15,912	43.6	5,900	16.2	293	0.8	606	1.7
24	Maryland	116,856	58,940	50.4	11,256	9.6	1,888	1.6	2,428	2.1
25	Massachusetts.....................	123,636	70,398	56.9	22,832	18.5	493	0.4	2,222	1.8
26	Michigan.............................	208,058	94,754	45.5	22,396	10.8	3,573	1.7	2,602	1.3
27	Minnesota	109,222	53,083	48.6	16,128	14.8	1,783	1.6	1,101	1.0
28	Mississippi	72,050	33,358	46.3	8,978	12.5	712	1.0	2,099	2.9
29	Missouri	132,347	67,737	51.2	13,017	9.8	951	0.7	2,462	1.9
30	Montana	19,212	10,467	54.5	2,184	11.4	159	0.8	459	2.4
31	Nebraska.............................	45,243	22,057	48.8	6,024	13.3	883	2.0	799	1.8
32	Nevada................................	33,548	21,993	65.6	4,143	12.3	1,368	4.1	848	2.5
33	New Hampshire.....................	32,849	15,661	47.7	7,095	21.6	282	0.9	851	2.6
34	New Jersey..........................	205,672	114,713	55.8	25,891	12.6	2,803	1.4	2,252	1.1
35	New Mexico	47,850	22,825	47.7	6,347	13.3	807	1.7	844	1.8
36	New York	428,139	217,944	50.9	39,748	9.3	2,556	0.6	6,673	1.6
37	North Carolina	207,859	109,634	52.7	29,008	14.0	2,366	1.1	3,984	1.9
38	North Dakota.......................	15,636	8,181	52.3	2,062	13.2	124	0.8	283	1.8
39	Ohio...................................	244730	112845	46.1	19053	7.8	1600	0.7	3,642	1.5
40	Oklahoma............................	87,478	46,571	53.2	8,039	9.2	381	0.4	1,693	1.9
41	Oregon...............................	65,106	30152	46.3	10,401	16.0	367	0.6	1,103	1.7
42	Pennsylvania	251,928	129,708	51.5	28,839	11.4	1,689	0.7	4,597	1.8
44	Rhode Island	18,290	11356	62.1	1,991	10.9	80	0.4	409	2.2
45	South Carolina	69,790	49941	71.6	8,521	12.2	520	0.7	1,873	2.7
46	South Dakota.......................	18,391	9244	50.3	2,520	13.7	102	0.6	317	1.7
47	Tennessee	126,841	64,926	51.2	15,790	12.4	839	0.7	2,756	2.2
48	Texas.................................	649,381	327905	50.5	62,746	9.7	3,531	0.5	10,936	1.7
49	Utah...................................	49,057	23657	48.2	7,933	16.2	1,526	3.1	764	1.6
50	Vermont	19,370	8766	45.3	4,467	23.1	256	1.3	447	2.3
51	Virginia...............................	203,567	71,415	35.1	20,204	9.9	12,599	6.2	4,009	2.0
53	Washington	104,617	54428	52.0	10,436	10.0	542	0.5	2,111	2.0
54	West Virginia.......................	38,596	20,209	52.4	3,514	9.1	252	0.7	730	1.9
55	Wisconsin	106,597	59,401	55.7	10,978	10.3	1,469	1.4	1,884	1.8
56	Wyoming	15,841	7,000	44.2	2,210	14.0	435	2.7	442	2.8

Table B-3. Population, School, and Student Characteristics by State—*Continued*

FIPS code	State	Staff employed by public elementary and secondary school systems and percent of total staff, 2008–2009									
		Librarians		Student/other support staff		School administrators		School district administrators		School and school district administrative support staff	
		Number	Percent	Number	Percent	Number	Percent	Number	Percent	Number	Percent
		62	63	64	65	66	67	68	69	70	71
00	**UNITED STATES**	53,802	0.9	1,478,856	23.4	159,877	2.5	62,150	1.0	435,746	6.9
01	Alabama	1,426	1.5	29,099	29.8	2,711	2.8	882	0.9	5,093	5.2
02	Alaska	170	1.0	3,227	18.8	758	4.4	523	3.0	1,895	11.0
04	Arizona	733	0.7	23,696	22.5	2,610	2.5	439	0.4	6,155	5.8
05	Arkansas	1,007	1.4	15,129	21.2	1,703	2.4	713	1.0	5,485	7.7
06	California	1,159	0.2	126,822	21.5	14,556	2.5	3,959	0.7	56,324	9.5
08	Colorado	840	0.8	20,379	19.9	2,816	2.7	1,199	1.2	9,312	9.1
09	Connecticut	817	0.9	20,433	22.1	340	0.4	725	0.8	4,825	5.2
10	Delaware	137	0.9	2,743	18.5	402	2.7	340	2.3	746	5.0
11	District of Columbia	127	1.0	2,780	22.9	368	3.0	226	1.9	1,402	11.6
12	Florida	2,834	0.8	76,343	22.4	7,819	2.3	2,046	0.6	29,944	8.8
13	Georgia	2,300	1.0	63,924	26.7	6,546	2.7	2,352	1.0	11,495	4.8
15	Hawaii	249	1.2	4,260	19.7	519	2.4	228	1.1	1,551	7.2
16	Idaho	140	0.5	5,810	21.3	751	2.8	137	0.5	1,468	5.4
17	Illinois	2,057	0.9	32,685	14.8	7,478	3.4	2,369	1.1	4,241	1.9
18	Indiana	951	0.7	38,666	27.2	3,199	2.3	1,145	0.8	8,308	5.9
19	Iowa	590	0.8	16,447	22.7	1,655	2.3	977	1.4	4,079	5.6
20	Kansas	895	1.6	3,493	6.3	1,868	3.4	479	0.9	2,312	4.2
21	Kentucky	1,120	1.1	26,883	26.8	3,048	3.0	932	0.9	8,304	8.3
22	Louisiana	1,195	1.2	24,753	24.5	2,852	2.8	350	0.3	6,224	6.2
23	Maine	247	0.7	8,784	24.1	1,194	3.3	676	1.9	2,847	7.8
24	Maryland	1,235	1.1	25,516	21.8	3,646	3.1	3,400	2.9	8,547	7.3
25	Massachusetts	667	0.7	10,734	8.7	4,414	3.6	2,264	1.8	9,412	7.6
26	Michigan	1,037	0.5	61,306	29.5	5,006	2.4	3,292	1.6	14,092	6.8
27	Minnesota	813	0.7	25,710	23.5	2,118	1.9	2,069	1.9	6,417	5.9
28	Mississippi	973	1.4	18,361	25.5	1,967	2.7	1,008	1.4	4,594	6.4
29	Missouri	1,396	1.1	33,349	25.2	2,979	2.3	1,329	1.0	9,127	6.9
30	Montana	381	2.0	4,317	22.5	544	2.8	169	0.9	532	2.8
31	Nebraska	568	1.3	10,722	23.7	1,038	2.3	624	1.4	2,528	5.6
32	Nevada	367	1.1	1,433	4.3	1,049	3.1	25	0.1	2,322	6.9
33	New Hampshire	324	1.0	6,104	18.6	492	1.5	677	2.1	1,363	4.1
34	New Jersey	1,777	0.9	40,681	19.8	1,377	0.7	1,458	0.7	14,720	7.2
35	New Mexico	295	0.6	10,655	22.3	1,335	2.8	842	1.8	3,900	8.2
36	New York	3,128	0.7	115,082	26.9	9,507	2.2	3,114	0.7	30,387	7.1
37	North Carolina	2,352	1.1	41,279	19.9	5,016	2.4	1,676	0.8	12,544	6.0
38	North Dakota	193	1.2	3,453	22.1	409	2.6	468	3.0	463	3.0
39	Ohio	1,355	0.6	72,763	29.7	5,121	2.1	2,109	0.9	26,242	10.7
40	Oklahoma	1,116	1.3	20,260	23.2	2,209	2.5	609	0.7	6,600	7.5
41	Oregon	377	0.6	13,172	20.2	1,671	2.6	464	0.7	7,399	11.4
42	Pennsylvania	2,197	0.9	59,153	23.5	5,846	2.3	2,693	1.1	17,206	6.8
44	Rhode Island	308	1.7	2,532	13.8	468	2.6	72	0.4	1,074	5.9
45	South Carolina	1,135	1.6	3,445	4.9	2,522	3.6	643	0.9	1,190	1.7
46	South Dakota	141	0.8	4,167	22.7	415	2.3	624	3.4	861	4.7
47	Tennessee	1,907	1.5	31,801	25.1	3,336	2.6	166	0.1	5,320	4.2
48	Texas	5,084	0.8	166,791	25.7	20,934	3.2	6,075	0.9	45,379	7.0
49	Utah	262	0.5	10,196	20.8	1,223	2.5	382	0.8	3,114	6.3
50	Vermont	225	1.2	3,413	17.6	520	2.7	147	0.8	1,129	5.8
51	Virginia	2,041	1.0	74,911	36.8	4,697	2.3	1,735	0.9	11,956	5.9
53	Washington	1,238	1.2	25,620	24.5	2,878	2.8	1,189	1.1	6,175	5.9
54	West Virginia	364	0.9	10,086	26.1	1,104	2.9	744	1.9	1,593	4.1
55	Wisconsin	1,182	1.1	21,648	20.3	2,495	2.3	1,027	1.0	6,513	6.1
56	Wyoming	170	1.1	3,840	24.2	348	2.2	359	2.3	1037	6.5

Table B-3. Population, School, and Student Characteristics by State—*Continued*

FIPS code	State	Highest degree earned and years of experience for teachers in public elementary and secondary schools, 2007–2008								
		Number of teachers	Highest degree earned (percent)				Years of experience (percent distribution)			
			Bachelor's degree	Master's degree or higher	Education specialist	Doctor's	Under 3 years	3–9 years	10–20 years	20 years or more
		72	73	74	75	76	77	78	79	80
00	**UNITED STATES**	3,404,519	47.4	44.5	6.4	0.9	13.4	33.6	29.3	23.7
01	Alabama	53,241	44.3	46.9	6.9	0.6	14.4	31.3	36.1	18.2
02	Alaska	8,117	56.3	36.3	5.4	0.7	12.0	27.5	39.7	20.7
04	Arizona	66,517	49.1	41.6	7.1	0.7	21.0	34.6	26.1	18.4
05	Arkansas	35,807	58.6	34.1	5.3	0.2	10.7	25.7	32.1	31.6
06	California	310,004	52.7	34.3	10.2	1.9	13.5	35.9	30.3	20.3
08	Colorado	50,091	42.9	48.4	6.9	1.4	17.2	37.9	28.1	16.8
09	Connecticut	50,128	19.2	64.3	15.0	0.9	12.2	29.7	31.1	27.1
10	Delaware	8,283	38.2	53.0	6.2	1.2	10.6	43.3	27.9	18.2
11	District of Columbia	4,394	41.3	45.3	7.1	5.9	20.0	29.9	24.6	25.5
12	Florida	177,203	60.9	34.1	3.1	1.1	14.8	35.0	27.4	22.8
13	Georgia	121,896	38.8	43.4	15.0	2.3	10.3	32.4	35.9	21.4
15	Hawaii	12,775	46.9	32.6	17.7	1.4	18.6	34.3	28.6	18.6
16	Idaho	16,214	66.1	29.7	2.7	0.8	12.5	31.0	33.6	22.8
17	Illinois	145,010	45.5	49.8	4.0	0.3	13.4	35.6	29.3	21.6
18	Indiana	68,446	37.4	57.0	4.9	0.4	9.2	32.3	29.1	29.4
19	Iowa	39,635	59.8	37.9	1.4	...	11.4	30.5	29.9	28.2
20	Kansas	37,671	53.0	41.8	4.7	0.2	13.0	30.2	27.2	29.6
21	Kentucky	44,438	20.9	57.5	18.9	0.7	10.2	35.5	30.1	24.2
22	Louisiana	48,117	71.9	23.5	3.7	0.4	12.7	33.3	27.6	26.3
23	Maine	17,802	54.4	37.9	5.1	0.6	12.3	27.0	31.5	29.1
24	Maryland	59,878	42.6	47.0	8.2	1.5	12.0	37.1	26.2	24.8
25	Massachusetts	80,402	30.6	62.0	5.6	0.7	11.1	39.9	27.2	21.8
26	Michigan	98,299	37.2	57.6	4.4	0.3	9.4	32.5	36.3	21.8
27	Minnesota	63,984	41.6	51.4	6.1	0.8	12.7	28.5	35.3	23.6
28	Mississippi	35,470	56.6	37.2	4.2	0.7	17.1	31.8	26.1	25.1
29	Missouri	73,254	47.2	47.5	3.9	0.6	13.3	34.2	31.6	20.8
30	Montana	12,701	62.8	33.4	3.5	...	11.0	26.9	28.8	33.3
31	Nebraska	23,176	53.1	44.2	2.0	...	11.4	24.2	30.2	34.2
32	Nevada	23,653	41.5	49.5	7.5	1.0	15.6	37.3	27.8	19.4
33	New Hampshire	17,437	49.4	45.4	4.5	...	13.3	31.7	29.1	26.0
34	New Jersey	124,538	55.8	36.5	6.3	1.4	12.3	40.8	22.8	24.1
35	New Mexico	22,691	53.0	39.5	5.4	1.5	13.3	35.6	29.6	21.5
36	New York	228,142	11.8	77.6	8.9	1.1	12.8	38.0	28.5	20.6
37	North Carolina	96,047	64.6	28.0	5.4	0.4	15.6	37.3	25.0	22.0
38	North Dakota	8,921	68.2	28.1	2.8	...	12.0	23.3	30.0	34.7
39	Ohio	134,252	31.9	62.3	3.7	0.7	12.1	29.9	31.6	26.3
40	Oklahoma	46,464	66.5	28.9	2.9	0.7	10.9	31.4	30.7	27.0
41	Oregon	31,699	37.0	52.3	9.0	1.2	18.0	31.5	29.5	21.0
42	Pennsylvania	136,852	45.3	45.2	8.0	...	12.5	33.6	26.7	27.2
44	Rhode Island	13,234	44.7	48.7	5.7	...	7.7	37.0	32.2	23.1
45	South Carolina	49,009	40.9	52.1	5.1	0.5	12.8	31.5	27.3	28.5
46	South Dakota	10,591	66.8	30.9	1.1	0.8	11.4	23.7	32.5	32.4
47	Tennessee	67,104	44.9	43.0	9.3	0.9	13.6	28.8	30.8	26.8
48	Texas	340,429	70.1	26.3	2.5	0.6	17.1	31.2	27.7	24.0
49	Utah	27,220	61.1	30.3	6.1	0.5	19.9	32.9	26.0	21.2
50	Vermont	10,237	42.6	50.0	5.9	0.5	11.7	30.5	30.5	27.3
51	Virginia	94,044	57.4	36.1	4.5	1.0	14.1	32.8	26.6	26.5
53	Washington	58,108	31.4	60.7	6.4	0.6	14.1	27.8	32.6	25.5
54	West Virginia	22,894	39.5	51.6	6.7	0.5	13.1	26.4	23.1	37.4
55	Wisconsin	70,060	44.8	49.3	5.5	0.3	9.8	32.4	31.4	26.4
56	Wyoming	7,939	56.0	37.6	5.3	0.6	10.3	27.3	32.5	29.9

... = Not available.

Table B-3. Population, School, and Student Characteristics by State—*Continued*

FIPS code	State	National Assessment of Educational Progress: percent of public school students at or above the proficient level					ACT, 2010[4]	
		Math, 2009		Reading, 2009		Writing, 2007	Average score	Percent of graduates taking ACT
		Grade 4	Grade 8	Grade 4	Grade 8	Grade 8		
		81	82	83	84	85	86	87
00	**UNITED STATES**	38	33	32	30	31	21.0	47
01	Alabama	24	20	28	24	24	20.3	78
02	Alaska................................	38	33	27	27	...	21.1	28
04	Arizona..............................	28	29	25	27	23	20.0	28
05	Arkansas............................	36	27	29	27	27	20.3	81
06	California	30	23	24	22	25	22.2	22
08	Colorado	45	40	40	32	38	20.6	100
09	Connecticut........................	46	40	42	43	53	23.7	24
10	Delaware............................	36	32	35	31	34	23.0	13
11	District of Columbia	17	11	17	14	...	19.8	29
12	Florida...............................	34	29	36	32	36	19.5	65
13	Georgia	34	27	29	27	29	20.7	44
15	Hawaii...............................	37	25	26	22	20	21.6	22
16	Idaho................................	41	38	32	33	29	21.8	60
17	Illinois...............................	38	33	32	33	37	20.7	100
18	Indiana..............................	42	36	34	32	30	22.3	26
19	Iowa.................................	41	34	34	32	32	22.2	60
20	Kansas	46	39	35	33	33	22.0	75
21	Kentucky............................	37	27	36	33	26	19.4	100
22	Louisiana	23	20	18	20	17	20.1	98
23	Maine	45	35	35	35	38	23.2	10
24	Maryland	44	40	37	36	...	22.3	18
25	Massachusetts.....................	57	52	47	43	46	24.0	21
26	Michigan............................	35	31	30	31	27	19.7	100
27	Minnesota	54	47	37	38	32	22.9	70
28	Mississippi	22	15	22	19	15	18.8	96
29	Missouri	41	35	36	34	26	21.6	69
30	Montana	45	44	35	38	33	22.0	58
31	Nebraska............................	38	35	35	35	...	22.1	73
32	Nevada..............................	32	25	24	22	21	21.5	30
33	New Hampshire....................	56	43	41	39	39	23.7	17
34	New Jersey	49	44	40	42	56	23.2	17
35	New Mexico	26	20	20	22	17	20.1	66
36	New York	40	34	36	33	31	23.3	27
37	North Carolina	43	36	32	29	29	21.9	16
38	North Dakota	45	43	35	34	27	21.5	81
39	Ohio.................................	45	36	36	37	32	21.8	66
40	Oklahoma...........................	33	24	28	26	26	20.7	73
41	Oregon	37	37	31	33	...	21.5	34
42	Pennsylvania	46	40	37	40	36	21.9	17
44	Rhode Island	39	28	36	28	32	22.8	11
45	South Carolina	34	30	28	24	23	20.0	52
46	South Dakota.......................	42	42	33	37	...	21.8	79
47	Tennessee	28	25	28	28	30	19.6	100
48	Texas................................	38	36	28	27	26	20.8	33
49	Utah	41	35	31	33	31	21.8	71
50	Vermont	51	43	41	41	40	23.2	26
51	Virginia..............................	43	36	38	32	31	22.3	22
53	Washington	43	39	33	36	35	22.7	19
54	West Virginia.......................	28	19	26	22	22	20.7	64
55	Wisconsin	45	39	33	34	36	22.1	69
56	Wyoming	40	35	33	34	34	20.0	100

[4]2010 *ACT Composite Averages by State.* © 2010 by ACT, Inc. Reprinted with permission. All rights reserved. <http://www.act.org>.
... = Not available.

Table B-3. Population, School, and Student Characteristics by State—*Continued*

FIPS code	State	Preliminary SAT (PSAT) National Merit Scholarship Qualifying Test (NMSQT) scores, 2009–2010[5]				SAT Reasoning Test average scores, 2010[6]			
		Number of high school juniors taking the PSAT/NMSQT	Percent of test-takers achieving scores of 65 and above			Critical reading	Math	Writing	Percent of graduates taking SAT
			Critical reading	Math	Writing skills				
		88	89	90	91	92	93	94	95
00	UNITED STATES	1,545,856	6.8	8.5	5.7	501	516	492	47
01	Alabama	14,381	6.2	6.0	6.8	556	550	544	7
02	Alaska	2,209	11.2	9.7	6.7	518	515	491	48
04	Arizona	17,583	8.3	9.4	5.9	519	525	500	25
05	Arkansas	6,398	6.3	7.3	6.5	566	566	552	4
06	California	175,882	7.6	10.2	6.7	501	516	500	50
08	Colorado	20,219	8.8	9.8	6.8	568	572	555	18
09	Connecticut	32,846	7.7	9.0	6.0	509	514	513	84
10	Delaware	5,883	5.7	7.0	5.0	493	495	481	71
11	District of Columbia	4,261	10.8	9.1	9.6	474	464	466	76
12	Florida	65,776	6.6	7.5	5.5	496	498	479	59
13	Georgia	37,689	7.1	8.5	7.0	488	490	475	74
15	Hawaii	7,487	5.1	7.9	3.8	483	505	470	58
16	Idaho	5,617	7.7	7.4	4.9	543	541	517	19
17	Illinois	46,058	8.8	13.1	7.1	585	600	577	6
18	Indiana	37,374	5.2	6.8	4.6	494	505	477	64
19	Iowa	8,498	9.8	13.1	7.3	603	613	582	3
20	Kansas	9,781	9.0	10.3	7.6	590	595	567	6
21	Kentucky	11,081	7.9	8.5	7.5	575	575	563	6
22	Louisiana	12,622	6.2	6.2	6.4	555	550	547	7
23	Maine	14,199	4.5	4.5	3.6	468	467	454	92
24	Maryland	44,564	7.4	9.0	6.6	501	506	495	70
25	Massachusetts	51,940	9.2	11.0	7.1	512	526	509	86
26	Michigan	33,775	7.1	9.5	5.4	585	605	576	5
27	Minnesota	22,901	9.1	12.0	6.7	594	607	580	7
28	Mississippi	6,111	6.2	4.6	8.1	566	548	552	3
29	Missouri	13,467	11.2	12.0	9.6	593	595	580	4
30	Montana	4,345	5.8	6.9	5.0	538	538	517	24
31	Nebraska	6,279	8.3	9.9	6.0	585	593	568	4
32	Nevada	7,106	5.6	6.8	4.2	496	501	473	43
33	New Hampshire	9,008	10.4	10.3	7.2	520	524	510	77
34	New Jersey	71,081	7.1	9.8	6.2	495	514	497	76
35	New Mexico	6,176	6.1	5.5	4.7	553	549	534	11
36	New York	154,941	5.1	6.5	3.8	484	499	478	85
37	North Carolina	44,095	5.8	7.5	5.2	497	511	477	63
38	North Dakota	1,995	5.5	8.7	4.3	580	594	559	4
39	Ohio	52,080	7.0	8.9	6.0	538	548	522	21
40	Oklahoma	7,507	9.4	9.2	8.6	569	568	547	5
41	Oregon	16,258	8.8	8.2	5.8	523	524	499	54
42	Pennsylvania	78,193	6.5	7.3	5.4	492	501	480	71
44	Rhode Island	6,379	6.8	6.0	4.9	494	495	488	67
45	South Carolina	17,441	5.5	6.1	5.0	484	495	468	66
46	South Dakota	2,654	6.2	8.5	6.0	592	603	571	3
47	Tennessee	14,464	10.2	10.4	9.8	576	571	565	10
48	Texas	185,502	4.4	6.1	3.9	484	505	473	53
49	Utah	5,250	10.5	10.2	7.4	568	559	547	6
50	Vermont	4,551	7.7	8.2	5.2	519	521	506	66
51	Virginia	53,610	7.5	7.3	5.8	512	512	497	67
53	Washington	32,010	9.4	9.7	6.6	524	532	508	54
54	West Virginia	4,018	5.7	5.7	5.0	515	507	500	16
55	Wisconsin	20,552	7.2	10.5	6.2	595	604	579	4
56	Wyoming	1,624	6.1	6.7	4.0	570	567	546	5

[5]"PSAT/NMSQT 2009–2010 College-Bound High School Juniors Summary Report." Copyright © 2010. The College Board. www.collegeboard.com. Reproduced with permission.
[6]"2010 College-Bound Seniors." Copyright © 2010. The College Board. www.collegeboard.com. Reproduced with permission.

Table B-3. Population, School, and Student Characteristics by State—*Continued*

FIPS code	State	Revenues for public elementary and secondary schools by source, 2007–2008 school year				Current expenditures for public elementary and secondary schools, by function, 2007–2008				
		Total revenue (thousands of dollars)	Percent from:			Total current expenditures (thousands of dollars)	Percent for:			Per student expenditures (dollars)
			Federal government	State government	Local government		Instruction and instruction-related	Support services	Non-instruction	
		96	97	98	99	100	101	102	103	104
00	**UNITED STATES**	584,728,896	8.2	48.3	43.3	506,827,246	65.8	35.2	4.0	10,282
01	Alabama	7,693,742	9.7	60.6	29.5	6,832,439	63.5	34.8	6.5	9,197
02	Alaska	2,289,219	13.4	66.3	20.4	1,918,375	63.5	38.7	3.0	14,641
04	Arizona	10,283,842	10.6	51.7	37.6	8,403,221	59.2	38.5	5.0	7,727
05	Arkansas	4,674,053	10.8	56.7	32.4	4,156,368	66.0	36.0	5.6	8,677
06	California	71,224,024	9.4	61.3	29.3	61,570,555	67.0	36.2	3.8	9,706
08	Colorado	8,113,611	6.9	42.2	50.7	7,338,766	63.3	38.5	3.6	9,152
09	Connecticut	9,459,433	4.4	39.6	56.0	8,336,789	65.9	33.9	3.4	14,610
10	Delaware	1,690,557	7.9	62.0	30.1	1,489,594	61.5	35.6	4.2	12,153
11	District of Columbia	1,364,048	11.4	0.0	88.6	1,282,437	59.1	41.7	4.6	16,353
12	Florida	29,321,189	8.6	38.8	52.5	24,224,114	67.0	35.4	4.3	9,084
13	Georgia	18,671,345	8.0	45.4	46.6	16,030,039	68.3	31.7	5.1	9,718
15	Hawaii	2,541,703	12.2	84.8	3.0	2,122,779	64.0	35.0	4.6	11,800
16	Idaho	2,167,455	9.9	67.1	23.1	1,891,505	65.1	34.2	4.8	6,951
17	Illinois	25,426,959	7.9	31.2	60.9	21,874,484	63.4	38.1	3.2	10,353
18	Indiana	12,295,901	7.1	53.5	39.3	9,281,709	64.9	41.6	4.1	8,867
19	Iowa	5,297,527	7.6	46.5	45.8	4,499,236	65.1	34.8	4.6	9,275
20	Kansas	5,528,071	7.9	57.5	32.8	4,627,994	64.8	35.4	4.5	9,883
21	Kentucky	6,561,268	10.8	57.3	31.9	5,822,550	64.7	34.8	5.9	8,740
22	Louisiana	7,861,130	16.8	44.8	38.4	6,814,455	64.0	35.7	5.5	10,006
23	Maine	2,601,563	9.0	44.9	46.0	2,308,071	68.3	32.6	3.3	11,761
24	Maryland	13,060,333	5.5	42.1	52.4	11,192,623	66.7	34.6	4.2	13,235
25	Massachusetts	14,632,845	5.1	41.9	53.0	13,160,383	69.7	32.1	2.8	13,667
26	Michigan	19,620,055	7.8	57.5	34.6	17,053,521	61.4	40.1	3.2	10,075
27	Minnesota	10,293,655	5.9	65.9	26.7	8,415,969	69.2	31.0	4.6	10,048
28	Mississippi	4,388,016	16.1	54.5	29.4	3,898,401	63.6	35.2	5.9	7,890
29	Missouri	9,876,930	8.1	33.3	58.1	8,526,641	64.6	35.6	4.5	9,297
30	Montana	1,559,091	12.1	49.7	30.3	1,392,449	64.1	35.5	4.3	9,749
31	Nebraska	3,286,862	9.1	33.1	57.1	2,970,323	67.6	29.0	6.7	10,199
32	Nevada	4,364,266	6.6	30.8	62.6	3,515,004	64.6	36.9	3.6	8,187
33	New Hampshire	2,613,798	5.2	38.6	56.2	2,399,330	67.6	32.7	2.8	11,951
34	New Jersey	24,892,358	4.0	42.1	54.0	24,357,079	62.7	37.7	2.9	17,620
35	New Mexico	3,655,607	13.6	70.8	15.6	3,057,061	60.9	38.3	4.1	9,291
36	New York	52,766,249	6.0	44.8	48.7	46,443,426	71.7	29.0	2.1	16,794
37	North Carolina	12,426,731	10.0	65.7	24.3	11,482,912	65.7	30.6	5.8	7,709
38	North Dakota	1,056,726	13.8	36.3	48.4	886,317	61.3	33.7	8.2	9,324
39	Ohio	22,796,037	7.3	45.6	46.7	18,892,374	63.5	39.5	3.3	10,340
40	Oklahoma	5,482,414	11.8	54.2	31.9	4,932,913	61.3	35.7	6.6	7,683
41	Oregon	6,118,492	9.1	52.3	37.3	5,409,630	62.5	38.1	3.5	9,565
42	Pennsylvania	24,973,392	7.2	36.5	56.3	21,157,430	64.6	35.4	3.9	11,741
44	Rhode Island	2,223,575	7.8	39.9	52.3	2,134,609	65.3	37.2	2.5	14,459
45	South Carolina	7,773,773	9.2	50.8	40.0	6,453,817	63.9	37.5	5.4	9,060
46	South Dakota	1,206,955	15.3	33.9	49.7	1,037,875	62.3	36.2	5.7	8,535
47	Tennessee	8,230,341	10.5	45.6	43.9	7,540,306	68.9	31.9	5.0	7,820
48	Texas	45,574,722	10.0	44.8	45.0	39,033,235	65.2	35.0	5.2	8,350
49	Utah	4,396,364	7.8	56.7	35.6	3,444,936	69.3	29.4	5.5	5,978
50	Vermont	1,504,572	6.3	85.9	7.9	1,356,165	66.8	34.4	2.7	14,421
51	Virginia	14,527,472	6.2	41.0	52.9	13,125,666	67.6	35.4	3.6	10,664
53	Washington	11,107,344	8.1	62.5	29.4	9,331,539	64.0	35.7	4.7	9,058
54	West Virginia	3,166,494	10.9	59.1	29.8	2,841,962	63.3	35.1	5.7	10,059
55	Wisconsin	10,485,161	6.4	50.0	43.6	9,366,134	65.7	35.7	3.5	10,709
56	Wyoming	1,601,628	6.4	52.8	31.2	1,191,736	65.5	37.8	3.1	13,790

Table B-3. Population, School, and Student Characteristics by State—*Continued*

FIPS code	State	Enrollment in degree-granting institutions of higher education, fall 2007									
		Total	Attendance status		Level of enrollment				Control of institution		
			Full-time	Part-time	Undergraduate		First Pro-fessional	Graduate	Public	Private, not-for-profit	Private, for-profit
					Four-year	Two-year					
		105	106	107	108	109	110	111	112	113	114
00	**UNITED STATES**	18,248,128	11,269,892	6,978,236	8,986,150	6,617,621	350,764	2,293,593	13,490,780	3,571,150	1,186,198
01	Alabama	268,183	177,308	90,875	149,384	80,047	4,571	34,181	237,632	22,527	8,024
02	Alaska	30,616	12,780	17,836	26,873	1,348	0	2,395	29,381	719	516
04	Arizona	624,147	420,015	204,132	319,911	210,163	3,370	90,703	332,154	7,789	284,204
05	Arkansas	152,168	97,017	55,151	84,545	51,930	1,988	13,705	135,525	14,766	1,877
06	California	2,529,522	1,277,393	1,252,129	736,470	1,525,072	33,222	234,758	2,136,087	277,554	115,881
08	Colorado	310,637	194,619	116,018	174,660	87,741	4,260	43,976	227,984	31,948	50,705
09	Connecticut	179,005	116,712	62,293	93,750	51,281	3,320	30,654	114,072	61,646	3,287
10	Delaware	52,343	33,947	18,396	28,084	15,205	934	8,120	39,092	13,251	0
11	District of Columbia	115,153	64,458	50,695	68,124	0	9,755	37,274	5,608	73,460	36,085
12	Florida	913,793	524,133	389,660	535,571	263,381	17,511	97,330	683,328	150,807	79,658
13	Georgia	453,711	302,958	150,753	251,672	142,254	9,340	50,445	359,883	65,720	28,108
15	Hawaii	66,601	39,050	27,551	33,418	23,891	737	8,555	50,454	13,119	3,028
16	Idaho	78,846	52,719	26,127	58,351	13,130	572	6,793	60,526	16,672	1,648
17	Illinois	837,018	498,168	338,850	335,500	355,593	18,006	127,919	550,940	220,491	65,587
18	Indiana	380,477	264,903	115,574	252,939	76,142	6,768	44,628	278,951	83,110	18,416
19	Iowa	256,259	160,346	95,913	141,470	87,028	7,224	20,537	154,644	56,170	45,445
20	Kansas	194,102	114,403	79,699	93,408	74,460	2,872	23,362	170,054	22,452	1,596
21	Kentucky	258,213	156,484	101,729	130,204	97,810	4,799	25,400	211,234	31,913	15,066
22	Louisiana	224,754	160,313	64,441	137,793	57,325	6,195	23,441	193,316	24,204	7,234
23	Maine	67,173	42,434	24,739	43,834	15,415	826	7,098	48,357	17,308	1,508
24	Maryland	327,597	177,095	150,502	137,376	125,075	4,485	60,661	269,719	52,673	5,205
25	Massachusetts	463,366	319,066	144,300	251,303	91,746	16,746	103,571	198,700	260,400	4,266
26	Michigan	643,279	376,154	267,125	322,084	230,078	14,149	76,968	519,449	116,000	7,830
27	Minnesota	392,393	238,168	154,225	176,746	121,768	8,082	85,797	250,397	71,851	70,145
28	Mississippi	155,232	119,330	35,902	66,633	71,464	2,141	14,994	139,931	13,461	1,840
29	Missouri	384,366	233,734	150,632	212,499	98,772	11,327	61,768	223,155	143,481	17,730
30	Montana	47,371	35,074	12,297	33,075	9,753	609	3,934	42,857	4,514	0
31	Nebraska	127,378	82,537	44,841	65,242	42,238	3,690	16,208	96,680	28,177	2,521
32	Nevada	116,276	54,501	61,775	88,674	15,814	1,532	10,256	104,797	1,504	9,975
33	New Hampshire	70,724	49,513	21,211	44,641	13,829	792	11,462	41,982	24,629	4,113
34	New Jersey	398,136	243,154	154,982	178,326	159,548	6,193	54,069	318,296	73,822	6,018
35	New Mexico	134,375	69,382	64,993	51,730	68,590	1,008	13,047	124,773	2,932	6,670
36	New York	1,172,811	835,336	337,475	630,062	310,488	32,853	199,408	652,428	474,411	45,972
37	North Carolina	502,330	317,411	184,919	237,155	203,748	8,262	53,165	410,746	85,809	5,775
38	North Dakota	49,945	36,665	13,280	34,329	9,928	837	4,851	43,016	5,723	1,206
39	Ohio	630,497	432,158	198,339	343,976	199,658	13,554	73,309	460,240	138,712	31,545
40	Oklahoma	206,382	133,108	73,274	118,406	63,567	4,395	20,014	177,643	21,490	7,249
41	Oregon	202,928	122,217	80,711	92,740	83,594	4,724	21,870	165,260	29,602	8,066
42	Pennsylvania	725,397	523,296	202,101	433,623	165,605	20,804	105,365	396,774	280,713	47,910
44	Rhode Island	82,900	61,012	21,888	54,765	17,450	1,529	9,156	41,503	40,758	639
45	South Carolina	217,755	148,345	69,410	107,793	85,543	3,325	21,094	180,479	33,875	3,401
46	South Dakota	49,747	32,427	17,320	37,664	5,729	710	5,644	38,917	7,702	3,128
47	Tennessee	297,785	215,380	82,405	167,931	88,366	6,313	35,175	208,524	69,572	19,689
48	Texas	1,269,098	706,073	563,025	544,347	572,964	21,269	130,518	1,109,666	126,003	33,429
49	Utah	203,679	125,973	77,706	141,506	42,635	1,434	18,104	147,982	47,173	8,524
50	Vermont	42,191	31,437	10,754	29,755	6,089	974	5,373	24,829	16,725	637
51	Virginia	478,268	289,994	188,274	228,811	175,463	10,721	63,273	370,486	77,753	30,029
53	Washington	352,075	215,863	136,212	154,750	164,102	4,875	28,348	301,793	41,726	8,556
54	West Virginia	116,846	77,314	39,534	77,266	21,676	2,214	15,692	87,838	11,965	17,045
55	Wisconsin	343,747	223,815	119,932	202,179	100,800	4,505	36,263	273,708	62,368	7,671
56	Wyoming	35,246	18,926	16,320	9,528	22,325	442	2,951	33,705	0	1,541

Table B-3. Population, School, and Student Characteristics by State—*Continued*

FIPS code	State	Race and ethnicity of students enrolled in institutions of higher education, fall 2008							Migration patterns of college freshmen, fall 2008	
		Total	Non-Hispanic White (percent)	Non-Hispanic Black (percent)	Hispanic or Latino[2] (percent)	Asian and Pacific Islander (percent)	American Indian, Alaska Native (percent)	Nonresident alien (percent)	Percent of out-of-state students enrolled	Percent of students enrolled in out-of-state institutions
		115	116	117	118	119	120	121	122	123
00	UNITED STATES	19,102,814	63.3	13.5	11.9	6.8	1.0	3.5	27.1	25.2
01	Alabama	310,941	64.3	29.1	2.3	1.7	0.8	1.9	33.6	10.5
02	Alaska	30,717	69.6	3.4	4.2	6.0	14.1	2.7	9.9	61.2
04	Arizona	704,245	61.0	14.4	15.2	3.6	2.8	3.0	38.3	14.6
05	Arkansas	158,374	72.5	18.9	3.3	1.8	1.1	2.3	26.9	10.9
06	California	2,652,241	40.2	8.2	28.8	18.5	0.9	3.3	11.6	18.9
08	Colorado	325,232	73.7	6.9	11.7	4.0	1.5	2.2	28.4	27.3
09	Connecticut	184,178	69.8	11.2	9.6	4.7	0.3	4.4	46.5	71.4
10	Delaware	53,088	67.9	20.2	4.3	4.0	0.3	3.2	60.6	38.8
11	District of Columbia	126,110	44.0	39.0	5.3	6.4	0.5	4.7	93.5	20.6
12	Florida	972,699	54.2	18.4	20.3	3.6	0.4	3.1	18.7	15.2
13	Georgia	476,581	56.9	32.2	3.3	4.2	0.3	3.0	16.0	22.1
15	Hawaii	70,104	24.5	2.2	3.2	62.2	0.5	7.3	31.9	70.8
16	Idaho	80,456	87.0	1.1	5.7	2.3	1.3	2.6	39.3	25.8
17	Illinois	859,242	63.3	14.9	12.3	5.9	0.3	3.2	25.2	44.9
18	Indiana	401,956	80.6	9.6	3.4	2.3	0.4	3.8	29.2	10.5
19	Iowa	286,891	76.1	6.5	3.7	10.3	0.6	2.9	42.2	16.6
20	Kansas	198,991	78.6	6.5	5.3	2.6	1.7	5.3	26.6	20.7
21	Kentucky	257,583	85.8	9.5	1.4	1.3	0.3	1.6	25.8	12.2
22	Louisiana	236,375	61.3	30.2	2.7	2.4	0.7	2.8	20.9	9.2
23	Maine	67,796	91.1	2.1	1.5	1.9	1.4	1.8	40.7	40.4
24	Maryland	338,914	55.6	28.3	4.4	7.1	0.4	4.2	35.7	79.0
25	Massachusetts	477,056	70.2	8.4	7.2	7.5	0.4	6.4	48.9	35.3
26	Michigan	652,799	75.0	14.0	2.9	3.4	0.8	3.8	12.9	15.0
27	Minnesota	411,055	78.8	10.0	2.5	4.6	1.2	3.0	28.4	44.9
28	Mississippi	160,441	56.9	39.3	1.0	1.0	0.4	1.3	34.4	15.4
29	Missouri	396,409	77.6	13.0	3.1	2.7	0.6	3.0	28.3	21.5
30	Montana	47,840	84.3	0.7	2.0	1.4	9.3	2.4	32.3	22.6
31	Nebraska	130,458	84.7	4.9	4.3	2.6	0.8	2.8	24.9	19.3
32	Nevada	120,490	58.5	8.5	17.2	12.1	1.4	2.3	14.8	29.3
33	New Hampshire	71,739	88.8	2.2	2.9	2.7	0.7	2.7	60.0	54.3
34	New Jersey	410,160	57.6	14.2	14.8	8.7	0.3	4.3	15.9	120.2
35	New Mexico	142,413	41.6	3.1	41.3	2.0	9.1	3.0	20.8	21.1
36	New York	1,234,858	58.8	14.0	12.0	8.4	0.4	6.4	27.9	26.7
37	North Carolina	528,977	66.0	24.3	3.3	2.8	1.2	2.4	26.7	12.5
38	North Dakota	51,327	84.6	1.9	1.2	1.1	6.1	5.0	51.7	14.7
39	Ohio	653,585	79.4	12.7	2.3	2.3	0.4	2.9	18.4	19.3
40	Oklahoma	206,757	69.1	9.4	4.3	2.7	10.2	4.4	26.9	11.6
41	Oregon	220,474	79.3	2.7	6.6	6.7	1.8	3.0	37.4	27.2
42	Pennsylvania	740,288	76.9	10.9	3.8	4.5	0.3	3.6	35.0	18.5
44	Rhode Island	83,893	76.8	6.2	7.9	4.7	0.5	4.0	73.3	23.3
45	South Carolina	230,695	66.8	27.6	2.0	1.7	0.4	1.5	35.5	10.9
46	South Dakota	50,444	86.6	1.7	1.2	1.1	7.1	2.4	34.6	23.0
47	Tennessee	307,610	73.6	19.9	2.1	2.1	0.4	1.9	25.0	18.5
48	Texas	1,327,148	48.8	12.8	28.4	5.5	0.5	3.9	7.6	20.9
49	Utah	217,224	85.1	1.7	5.8	3.6	1.1	2.8	33.9	6.5
50	Vermont	42,946	90.4	2.2	2.4	2.5	0.6	2.0	73.3	36.2
51	Virginia	500,796	65.4	20.6	4.6	6.2	0.5	2.7	31.2	23.9
53	Washington	362,535	73.3	4.6	7.3	9.6	1.7	3.4	24.8	29.7
54	West Virginia	125,333	85.5	7.3	2.9	1.7	0.5	2.1	39.8	7.7
55	Wisconsin	352,875	84.1	5.9	3.4	3.2	1.1	2.2	25.9	21.4
56	Wyoming	35,936	88.4	1.1	5.2	1.2	1.8	2.2	46.1	43.6

Table B-3. Population, School, and Student Characteristics by State—*Continued*

FIPS code	State	Degrees conferred by institutions of higher education, 2007–2008							
		Total degrees	Associate degrees	Bachelor's degrees			Master's degrees	First Professional degrees	Doctoral degrees
				Total	Public	Private			
		124	125	126	127	128	129	130	131
00	**UNITED STATES**	3,093,277	750,164	1,563,069	996,435	566,634	625,023	91,309	63,712
01	Alabama	45,136	9,171	23,448	18,926	4,522	10,619	1,120	778
02	Alaska	3,250	1,031	1,498	1,408	90	692	0	29
04	Arizona	102,693	33,325	39,016	19,198	19,818	28,042	968	1,342
05	Arkansas	21,403	5,567	11,574	9,306	2,268	3,509	517	236
06	California	331,844	97,010	158,652	116,177	42,475	59,652	9,006	7,524
08	Colorado	54,371	11,219	29,185	20,915	8,270	11,841	1,059	1,067
09	Connecticut	34,067	5,056	18,715	9,850	8,865	8,586	944	766
10	Delaware	9,617	1,475	5,322	3,955	1,367	2,291	266	263
11	District of Columbia	25,322	1,047	10,736	318	10,418	10,066	2,837	636
12	Florida	178,383	65,948	77,460	50,359	27,101	26,576	4,942	3,457
13	Georgia	69,849	13,684	39,035	28,208	10,827	13,131	2,299	1,700
15	Hawaii	11,333	3,128	5,853	3,698	2,155	1,959	154	239
16	Idaho	12,733	2,924	7,912	5,054	2,858	1,576	165	156
17	Illinois	150,955	34,013	69,621	33,729	35,892	39,339	4,958	3,024
18	Indiana	69,240	14,598	38,991	24,986	14,005	12,292	1,808	1,551
19	Iowa	45,726	13,537	24,265	11,113	13,152	5,251	1,746	927
20	Kansas	32,865	8,175	17,048	13,414	3,634	6,268	834	540
21	Kentucky	38,608	10,148	19,639	15,036	4,603	7,113	1,116	592
22	Louisiana	34,321	4,997	21,163	17,631	3,532	5,962	1,630	569
23	Maine	11,716	2,679	7,109	4,338	2,771	1,661	198	69
24	Maryland	54,275	10,964	26,085	19,954	6,131	14,653	1,112	1,461
25	Massachusetts	97,484	10,926	49,526	14,763	34,763	29,370	4,526	3,136
26	Michigan	106,793	26,443	54,010	41,260	12,750	20,858	3,502	1,980
27	Minnesota	68,868	16,592	30,378	18,697	11,681	17,991	1,843	2,064
28	Mississippi	26,081	8,822	12,186	10,190	1,996	3,987	613	473
29	Missouri	72,288	14,445	35,736	17,637	18,099	17,534	2,819	1,754
30	Montana	8,191	1,601	5,198	4,604	594	1,114	141	137
31	Nebraska	22,674	4,836	12,360	7,401	4,959	4,148	865	465
32	Nevada	13,387	3,415	6,860	6,058	802	2,568	371	173
33	New Hampshire	15,197	3,179	8,460	4,555	3,905	3,185	177	196
34	New Jersey	66,875	16,904	33,645	24,267	9,378	13,219	1,785	1,322
35	New Mexico	16,666	5,053	7,791	6,538	1,253	3,300	269	253
36	New York	253,700	57,807	118,387	49,875	68,512	63,720	8,849	4,937
37	North Carolina	80,189	19,622	43,452	30,084	13,368	13,450	2,052	1,613
38	North Dakota	9,570	2,211	5,531	4,740	791	1,326	233	269
39	Ohio	113,131	26,830	59,385	38,126	21,259	20,991	3,521	2,404
40	Oklahoma	35,647	9,457	19,218	15,576	3,642	5,435	1,128	409
41	Oregon	33,606	8,023	17,920	12,860	5,060	5,924	1,091	648
42	Pennsylvania	147,207	26,575	82,132	40,505	41,627	29,867	4,835	3,798
44	Rhode Island	16,882	3,692	10,265	3,447	6,818	2,240	363	322
45	South Carolina	34,983	7,943	20,257	14,719	5,538	5,180	1,000	603
46	South Dakota	8,613	2,045	4,992	3,636	1,356	1,243	224	109
47	Tennessee	48,930	9,712	27,649	17,135	10,514	9,104	1,471	994
48	Texas	187,273	45,867	98,205	77,475	20,730	33,929	5,439	3,833
49	Utah	36,913	9,904	20,959	12,159	8,800	5,056	430	564
50	Vermont	9,224	1,264	5,315	2,796	2,519	2,302	254	89
51	Virginia	78,425	17,675	41,236	30,080	11,156	14,975	2,748	1,791
53	Washington	61,804	21,194	29,524	21,641	7,883	8,796	1,338	952
54	West Virginia	19,972	3,844	11,488	8,529	2,959	3,897	492	251
55	Wisconsin	56,190	11,884	33,187	24,035	9,152	8,812	1,134	1,173
56	Wyoming	5,119	2,703	1,802	1,786	16	423	117	74

Table B-3. Population, School, and Student Characteristics by State—*Continued*

FIPS code	State	Enrollment, 2009								Total population 16–19 years old	High school dropouts (percent)
		Total enrollment		K–12 enrollment		College and graduate school enrollment					
		Number	Percent public	Number	Percent public	Number	Percent public	Percent female	Percent 25 years old and over		
		132	133	134	135	136	137	138	139	140	141
00	UNITED STATES	81,173,053	82.9	53,774,626	89.3	22,255,504	73.9	56.3	42.1	17,630,099	6.0
01	Alabama	1,210,355	84.7	821,296	88.5	316,106	81.9	58.0	38.8	267,398	7.2
02	Alaska	193,502	89.0	133,781	92.6	50,924	84.0	54.4	53.7	46,432	5.5
04	Arizona	1,751,398	88.7	1,216,290	93.0	447,870	82.7	54.7	50.5	358,833	7.5
05	Arkansas	733,029	88.5	501,289	92.5	178,035	83.2	57.8	44.1	159,761	7.0
06	California	10,430,379	85.8	6,833,824	91.1	2,985,196	79.9	55.2	44.0	2,191,896	5.2
08	Colorado	1,326,513	85.9	861,454	91.8	370,465	80.4	54.4	45.6	267,244	7.5
09	Connecticut	940,736	77.8	607,755	89.3	268,289	58.9	55.7	38.1	206,082	4.4
10	Delaware	229,640	76.5	148,088	81.4	66,623	73.5	56.7	42.4	50,509	5.8
11	District of Columbia	151,647	59.8	79,388	83.0	63,004	29.6	57.2	42.9	38,311	7.4
12	Florida	4,423,764	82.3	2,927,709	88.5	1,216,543	74.9	56.1	43.9	945,810	7.1
13	Georgia	2,765,555	83.4	1,858,310	89.3	714,575	75.2	59.7	44.5	601,318	7.5
15	Hawaii	315,773	74.5	204,317	79.3	90,889	72.1	56.7	51.5	64,156	7.4
16	Idaho	419,556	84.9	291,616	91.3	105,249	75.3	52.9	45.8	98,011	6.2
17	Illinois	3,541,594	80.7	2,297,461	89.0	992,581	66.6	55.5	41.7	749,484	5.9
18	Indiana	1,700,399	82.8	1,147,777	88.1	450,322	76.7	56.2	40.9	364,693	7.3
19	Iowa	794,086	83.2	506,247	90.3	233,223	72.5	55.2	36.0	175,874	5.1
20	Kansas	772,985	85.5	494,841	89.3	225,561	83.4	55.3	38.9	162,132	5.1
21	Kentucky	1,060,210	85.2	726,057	89.3	268,940	79.1	58.8	41.2	241,104	7.0
22	Louisiana	1,184,998	80.3	815,180	81.7	279,284	82.5	58.6	37.2	263,145	7.8
23	Maine	302,669	81.0	201,889	88.9	84,409	69.1	60.1	39.0	75,588	3.9
24	Maryland	1,525,619	78.7	967,920	85.2	463,022	71.7	57.3	47.6	334,600	4.7
25	Massachusetts	1,729,862	71.7	1,055,237	87.8	554,736	46.8	56.8	37.1	379,907	4.2
26	Michigan	2,714,290	86.4	1,748,443	89.9	809,811	82.6	56.4	42.2	599,835	5.7
27	Minnesota	1,373,953	82.7	897,649	89.3	379,445	72.9	57.0	39.9	297,414	3.7
28	Mississippi	802,241	86.3	552,229	89.1	199,458	83.5	61.1	36.5	189,222	7.4
29	Missouri	1,543,258	79.7	1,029,095	86.2	413,151	68.6	56.8	43.4	335,763	7.2
30	Montana	245,580	88.0	160,999	91.4	69,846	87.7	50.4	37.3	59,305	8.6
31	Nebraska	486,397	82.1	312,456	87.8	139,184	76.9	54.8	39.4	103,093	5.2
32	Nevada	660,101	88.9	482,778	94.2	147,855	77.5	57.8	54.3	142,958	11.0
33	New Hampshire	333,252	77.6	221,015	88.7	90,577	60.8	59.1	37.9	80,654	2.6
34	New Jersey	2,245,888	80.0	1,508,974	88.3	555,245	68.1	55.9	39.3	464,110	3.4
35	New Mexico	547,834	88.9	371,623	91.5	145,826	85.9	54.0	50.9	121,051	9.1
36	New York	5,040,594	75.1	3,250,005	85.4	1,484,334	57.3	56.0	36.6	1,116,159	5.5
37	North Carolina	2,480,531	84.6	1,640,670	90.4	688,757	78.7	58.9	44.2	534,250	7.3
38	North Dakota	161,531	88.0	96,813	91.2	57,624	85.7	50.8	29.2	41,453	4.7
39	Ohio	3,010,651	81.4	1,995,872	86.4	823,568	74.8	57.6	43.6	661,569	5.0
40	Oklahoma	967,673	88.0	653,585	91.2	252,062	82.2	55.2	41.2	210,275	8.3
41	Oregon	952,008	84.8	627,650	90.1	269,990	80.6	54.8	47.2	205,933	5.9
42	Pennsylvania	3,112,656	74.6	2,026,327	85.0	886,642	57.2	57.7	36.6	734,633	5.1
44	Rhode Island	275,220	75.2	167,541	87.7	91,202	58.3	57.3	33.4	64,186	6.7
45	South Carolina	1,167,469	84.6	790,965	90.4	306,094	76.8	59.8	43.1	268,614	6.6
46	South Dakota	209,414	87.4	139,438	91.8	55,714	82.2	54.0	35.2	51,558	5.5
47	Tennessee	1,545,457	82.3	1,076,263	87.6	382,188	73.3	57.8	44.0	349,389	5.1
48	Texas	6,934,432	88.6	4,849,364	93.4	1,615,115	81.9	55.0	42.4	1,447,533	7.3
49	Utah	915,426	84.6	594,538	95.0	263,261	70.0	48.0	41.2	175,128	4.8
50	Vermont	151,196	80.6	95,166	91.4	47,466	63.9	56.3	30.9	38,358	4.5
51	Virginia	2,094,831	82.5	1,326,954	89.6	634,885	76.2	57.0	43.1	465,274	3.6
53	Washington	1,674,498	84.7	1,130,002	90.1	443,258	79.3	55.9	47.5	367,759	6.1
54	West Virginia	406,265	89.1	272,254	92.9	109,934	83.7	56.2	36.7	96,646	8.8
55	Wisconsin	1,476,430	82.9	970,923	87.0	424,959	77.9	57.1	39.0	333,948	3.9
56	Wyoming	139,708	90.1	87,309	95.5	42,207	89.0	56.6	41.3	31,741	7.8

NOTES AND DEFINITIONS: REGION AND STATE EDUCATION STATISTICS

This section provides details about each items source and relevant definitions. Internet references are provided when available. In some cases, the Internet reference will lead to a general Web page instead of to the precise data included in this volume. Additional data sources, such as the U.S. Census Bureau's online FERRET (Federal Electronic Research and Review Extraction Tool) and online databases from the National Center for Education Statistics (NCES), were often used.

TABLE B-1

Source: U.S. Census Bureau. *American Community Survey, 2008.* Table C15001. Educational attainment of the population 18 years and over by region, sex, and age, 2008. http://factfinder.census.gov/servlet/DatasetMainPageServlet?_program=ACS&_submenuId=&_lang=en&_ds_name=ACS_2009_1YR_G00_&ts=

TABLE B-2

Source: U.S. Census Bureau. *American Community Survey, 2009.* Tables C15002, C15002A–C15002H. Educational attainment of the population 25 years and over by region, sex, race, and Hispanic origin, 2009. http://factfinder.census.gov/servlet/DatasetMainPageServlet?_lang=en&_ts=306759109989&_ds_name=ACS_2008_1YR_G00_&_program=

Tables B-1 and B-2 are from the American Community Survey (ACS), the sample survey that has replaced the long form of the decennial census. The sample data are estimates of the actual figures that would have been obtained from a complete count. Estimates derived from a sample are expected to be different from the 100-percent figures because they are subject to sampling and nonsampling errors. Sampling error in data arises from the selection of people and housing units included in the sample. Nonsampling error affects both sample and 100-percent data. It is introduced as a result of errors that may occur during the data collection and processing phases of the census. Conclusions should not be based on small numbers or small differences and users should consult the ACS web site to determine the appropriate margins of error. The ACS is ongoing and data are released on an annual basis for all regions and states.

For additional information about the American Community Survey, see <http://www.census.gov/acs/www/>.

Educational Attainment. In the ACS, respondents are classified according to the highest degree or the highest level of school completed. The question includes instructions for people currently enrolled in school to report the level of the previous grade attended or the highest degree received.

High school graduate or more. This category includes persons who have received a high school diploma or its equivalent (for example, GED), and those who reported any level higher than a high school diploma.

Bachelor's degree or more. This category includes persons who have received bachelor's degrees, master's degrees, professional school degrees (such as law school or medical school degrees), and doctoral degrees.

Geographic Definitions

Data are presented for the four major regions and nine divisions of the United States. These groups of states are as follows:

Northeast: Connecticut, Maine, Massachusetts, New Hampshire, New Jersey, New York, Pennsylvania, Rhode Island, and Vermont

New England—Connecticut, Maine, Massachusetts, New Hampshire, Rhode Island, and Vermont
Middle Atlantic—New Jersey, New York, and Pennsylvania

Midwest: Illinois, Indiana, Iowa, Kansas, Michigan, Minnesota, Missouri, Nebraska, North Dakota, Ohio, South Dakota, and Wisconsin

East North Central—Illinois, Indiana, Michigan, Ohio, and Wisconsin
West North Central—Iowa, Kansas, Minnesota, Missouri, Nebraska, North Dakota, and South Dakota

South: Alabama, Arkansas, Delaware, District of Columbia, Florida, Georgia, Kentucky, Louisiana, Maryland, Mississippi, North Carolina, Oklahoma, South Carolina, Tennessee, Texas, Virginia, and West Virginia

East South Central—Alabama, Kentucky, Mississippi, and Tennessee
South Atlantic—Delaware, District of Columbia, Florida, Georgia, Maryland, North Carolina, South Carolina, Virginia, and West Virginia
West South Central—Arkansas, Louisiana, Oklahoma, and Texas

West: Alaska, Arizona, California, Colorado, Hawaii, Idaho, Montana, Nevada, New Mexico, Oregon, Utah, Washington, and Wyoming

Mountain—Arizona, Colorado, Idaho, Montana, Nevada, New Mexico, Utah, and Wyoming
Pacific—Alaska, California, Hawaii, Oregon, and Washington

TABLE B-3

POPULATION, ITEMS 1–2
Source: U.S. Census Bureau. *Population Estimates Program.* <http://www.census.gov/popest/states/>.

The population data for 2009 are U.S. Census Bureau estimates of the resident population as of July 1, 2009.

INCOME, POVERTY, AND HEALTH INSURANCE, Items 3–7
Source: U.S. Census Bureau. September 2010. *Income, Poverty, and Health Insurance Coverage in the United States: 2009* (Current Population Reports, P60-238). <http://www.census.gov/prod/2010pubs/p60-238.pdf >.

Additional Internet sources:
• <http://www.census.gov/acs/www/>
• <http://www.census.gov/hhes/www/cpstables/032010/pov/new46_000.htm>
• <http://www.census.gov/hhes/www/cpstables/032010/health/h10_000.htm>

The Census Bureau reports income from several major household surveys and programs. Each of these surveys differs from the others in some way, such as the length and detail of its questionnaire, the number of households included (sample size), and the methodology used to collect and process the data. The Current Population Survey Annual Social and Economic Supplement (CPS ASEC) is the preferred source for national analysis. It provides the most timely and most accurate cross-section data for the nation on income and poverty and is the official source of national poverty estimates. The American Community Survey (ACS) is preferred for subnational data on income and poverty by detailed demographic characteristics, because of its large sample size. The Census Bureau recommends using the ACS for single-year estimates of income and poverty at the state level, but still produces some state-level estimates from the CPS ASEC.

The median income for a family of four is from ACS table B19119 on American FactFinder. "Total income" is the sum of the amounts reported separately for wages, salary, commissions, bonuses, or tips; self-employment income from own nonfarm or farm businesses, including proprietorships and partnerships; interest, dividends, net rental income, royalty income, or income from estates and trusts; Social Security or Railroad Retirement income; Supplemental Security Income (SSI); any public assistance or welfare payments from the state or local welfare office; retirement, survivor, or disability pensions; and any other sources of income received regularly such as Veterans' (VA) payments, unemployment compensation, child support, or alimony. Receipts not counted as income include various "lump sum" payments, such as capital gains or inheritances. The total represents the amount of income received before deductions for personal income taxes, Social Security, bond purchases, union dues, Medicare deductions, and the like.

Family income includes the income of all family members 15 years old and over. Median family income is usually higher than median household income, because many households consist of only one person. The median divides the income distribution into two equal parts—one part consisting of families with incomes above the median and the other part consisting of families with incomes below the median.

The poverty and health insurance estimates are from the CPS ASEC. Poverty status is based on the definition prescribed by the U.S. Office of Management and Budget as the standard to be used by federal agencies for statistical purposes. A family is classified as below the poverty level (or "in poverty") if its total family income was less than the poverty threshold specified for the applicable family size, age of householder, and number of related children under 18 years old present in the family. The poverty threshold for a four-person family with two children under 18 years old was $21,756 in 2009. A child is defined as low income if his or her family's income was less than 200 percent of the poverty threshold.

Persons lacking health insurance coverage include those not covered by a private health plan or by Medicaid, Medicare, or a military health plan.

EDUCATIONAL ATTAINMENT,
Items 8–10
Source: U.S. Census Bureau. September 2010, American Community Survey, <http://www.census.gov/acs/www/>, Table C15002 on American FactFinder.

Statistics for educational attainment only include persons 25 years old and over. Respondents are classified according to the highest degree or the highest level of school completed. The question includes instructions for people currently enrolled in school to report the level of the previous grade attended or the highest degree received.

High school graduate or more. This category includes persons who have received a high school diploma or its equivalent, and those who reported any level higher than a high school diploma.

Bachelor's degree or more. This category includes persons who have received bachelor's degrees, master's degrees, professional school degrees (such as law school or medical school degrees), and doctoral degrees.

SCHOOL DISTRICTS, Item 11
Source: U.S. Department of Education. National Center for Education Statistics. *Common Core of Data, 2008-2009* (Local Education Agency Universe, 2008–2009, version 1a). <http://nces.ed.gov/ccd/>, as published in *Numbers and Types of Public Elementary and Secondary Education Agencies From the Common Core of Data: School Year 2008–09* (NCES 2010-346).

A school district or Local Education Agency (LEA) is a local-level education agency that exists primarily to operate public schools or to contract for public school services. A public school is controlled and operated by publicly elected or appointed officials, and it derives its primary support from public funds.

The state numbers are aggregated from the Common Core of Data (CCD) Local Education Agency universe, which includes nearly 18,000 school districts. These school districts include regular local school districts, local school district components of supervisory unions, supervisory union administrative centers, regional education service agencies, state-operated institutions, federally operated institutions, and other agencies. The CCD data now include charter schools. Since charter schools are typically managed independently from the local school district, each one is considered a single district.

NUMBER AND TYPE OF SCHOOLS, Items 12–22

Sources: U.S. Department of Education. National Center for Education Statistics. *Common Core of Data, 2008–2009.* <http://nces. ed.gov/ccd; as published in *Numbers and Types of Public Elementary and Secondary Schools From the Common Core of Data: School Year 2008–2009: First Look* (NCES 2010-345) and *Numbers and Types of Public Elementary and Secondary Local Education Agencies From the Common Core of Data: School Year 2008–09: First Look* (NCES 2010-346).

The state data are from the CCD school universe. There are almost 99,000 schools represented, including all those that were operating in 2008-2009.

Regular schools do not focus primarily on special, vocational, or alternative education, though they may offer these programs in addition to the regular curriculum. Special education schools focus primarily on special education, with materials and instructional

approaches adapted to meet students' needs. Vocational education schools focus on vocational, technical, or career education. They provide education or training in at least one semi-skilled or technical occupation. Alternative education schools address students' needs that typically cannot be met in a regular school setting. These schools provide nontraditional educational experiences.

A charter school is a school that provides free public elementary and/or secondary education to eligible students under a specific charter granted by the state legislature or other appropriate authority; the school must have also been designated as a charter school by these authorities. Charter schools can be administered by regular school districts, State Education Agencies (SEAs), or chartering organizations.

A magnet school or program is a special school or program designed to attract students of different racial and ethnic backgrounds for the purpose of reducing, preventing, or eliminating racial isolation and/or to provide an academic or social focus on a particular theme.

A Title I eligible school is a school designated under appropriate state and federal regulations as being high poverty and eligible for participation in programs authorized by Title I of P.L. 107–110. A Title I school is one in which the percentage of children from low-income families is at least as high as the percentage of children from low-income families served by the LEA as a whole, or a school designated by the LEA as Title I eligible because 35 percent or more of the children are from low-income families. A Title I school wide school is a school in which all the students are designated under appropriate state and federal regulations as eligible for participation in Title I programs authorized by Title I of P.L. 107–110.

NUMBER AND GRADE LEVEL OF STUDENTS, Items 23–26

Source: U.S. Department of Education. National Center for Education Statistics. *Common Core of Data State Nonfiscal Survey of Public Elementary/Secondary Education: School Year 2008–2009* v.1a. <http://nces.ed.gov/ccd/stnfis.asp, as published in *Public Elementary and Secondary School Student Enrollment and Staff From the Common Core of Data: School Year 2008–09*, <http://nces.ed.gov/pubsearch/pubsinfo.asp?pubid=2010347>.

The primary grades include pre-kindergarten through grade 4. Middle school grades included grades 5–8. High school grades include grades 9–12. Ungraded students are included in the total but are not separately listed. Some states have no ungraded students.

STUDENTS IN CHARTER SCHOOLS, Item 27

Source: U.S. Department of Education, National Center for Education Statistics, *Common Core of Data (CCD), Local Education Agency Universe Survey, 2008–09, v.1a.*

A charter school is a school providing free public elementary and/or secondary education to eligible students under a specific charter granted by the state legislature or other appropriate authority, and designated by such authority to be a charter school.

STUDENTS WHO ARE ELIGIBLE FOR FREE OR REDUCED-PRICE LUNCH, Item 28

Sources: U.S. Department of Education. National Center for Education Statistics. *Common Core of Data, Public Elementary/Secondary School Universe Survey, 2008–09 v.1b.* <http://nces.ed.gov/ccd/pubschuniv.asp>.

The Free and Reduced-Price Lunch Program is a program under the National School Lunch Act that provides cash subsidies for free or reduced-price meals to students based on family size and income criteria. Participation in the Free and Reduced-Price Lunch Program depends on income, and eligibility is often used to estimate student needs.

STUDENTS WITH INDIVIDUAL EDUCATION PROGRAMS, Item 29

Sources: U.S. Department of Education. National Center for Education Statistics. *Common Core of Data, Local Education Agency Universe Survey, 2008–09 v.1a.* <http://nces.ed.gov/ccd/pubagency.asp>.

An Individualized Education Program (IEP) is a written instructional plan for students with disabilities who are designated as special education students under IDEA (Individuals with Disabilities Education Act). An IEP includes a statement of present levels of educational performance of a child; a statement of annual goals, including short-term instructional objectives; a statement of specific educational services to be provided and the extent to which the child will be able to participate in regular educational programs; a projected date for initiation and the anticipated duration of services; appropriate objectives, criteria, and evaluation procedures; and schedules for determining, on at least an annual basis, whether instructional objectives are being achieved.

STUDENTS WHO ARE ENGLISH-LANGUAGE LEARNERS, Item 30

Sources: U.S. Department of Education. National Center for Education Statistics. *Local Education Agency Universe Survey, 2008–09 v.1a.* < http://nces.ed.gov/ccd/pubagency.asp>.

This category includes the number of students who are served in appropriate programs of language assistance (e.g., English as a Second Language, High Intensity Language Training, and bilingual education). This designation changed from Limited-English Proficient

(LEP) to English-Language Learners (ELL) in the 2001–2002 school year.

RACE AND HISPANIC ORIGIN, Items 31–35

Sources: U.S. Department of Education. National Center for Education Statistics. *Common Core of Data State Nonfiscal Survey of Public Elementary/Secondary Education: School Year 2008-2009 v.1a.* <http://nces. ed.gov/ccd/stnfis.asp, as published in *Public Elementary and Secondary School Student Enrollment and Staff From the Common Core of Data: School Year 2008–09*, <http://nces.ed.gov/ pubsearch/pubsinfo.asp?pubid=2010347>.

The racial and ethnic categories used in the CCD are those approved by the U.S. Office of Management and Budget at the time these data were collected. These categories are mutually exclusive. Because some students do not report their race or ethnicity, the percentages do not always add to 100 percent.

DROPOUTS, Item 36

Sources: U.S. Department of Education. National Center for Education Statistics. *Common Core of Data, 2007–2008, Public School Graduates and Dropouts From the Common Core of Data: School Year 2007– 08: First Look* (NCES Report 2010-341) <http://nces.ed.gov/pubsearch/pubsinfo. asp?pubid=2010341/>.

A dropout is a student who was enrolled in school at some time during the previous school year, who was not enrolled at the beginning of the current school year and who had not graduated from high school or completed a state or district-approved educational program and who did not meet any of the following exclusionary conditions: transferal to another public school district, private school, or state- or district-approved educational program; temporary absence due to suspension or school-approved illness; or death. The school year is the 12-month period of time from the first day of school

(operationally set as October 1), with dropouts from the previous summer reported for the year and grade in which they fail to enroll. Individuals who are not accounted for on October 1 are considered dropouts.

Most of the states that reported on dropouts used an October through September cycle; however, some states used a different cycle, and there is variation among the states in definitions and record-keeping methods concerning graduates and dropouts.

MEMBERSHIP AND GRADUATES, Items 37–39

Sources: U.S. Department of Education. National Center for Education Statistics. *Common Core of Data, State Nonfiscal Survey of Public Elementary/Secondary Education, 2004–2005 and 2007–2008.* http://nces.ed.gov/ ccd/ and *Public School Graduates and Dropouts From the Common Core of Data: School Year 2007–08: First Look* <http://nces.ed.gov/ pubsearch/pubsinfo.asp?pubid=2010341>.

Column 37 shows the number of 9th graders enrolled in 2004–2005, while column 38 shows the number of 12th graders enrolled, according to the State Nonfiscal Survey of Public Elementary/Secondary Education from the appropriate year, accessed through the Build-a-Table data tool.

The number of graduates includes individuals who received a regular diploma, but does not include individuals who received a diploma from a program different than the regular school program, and individuals who received a certificate of attendance or other certificate of completion in lieu of a diploma during the previous school year and subsequent summer school session. Recipients of high school equivalency certificates are also not included.

AVERAGED FRESHMAN GRADUATION RATE, Item 40

Sources: U.S. Department of Education. National Center for Education Statistics.

Common Core of Data, Public School Graduates and Dropouts From the Common Core of Data: School Year 2007–08: First Look (NCES Report 2010-341) <http://nces.ed.gov/pubsearch/pubsinfo.asp?pubid=2010341.

The averaged freshman graduation rate provides an estimate of the percentage of high school students who graduate on time. The rate uses aggregate student enrollment data (to estimate the size of an incoming freshman class) and aggregate counts of the number of diplomas awarded 4 years later. The incoming freshman class size is estimated by summing the enrollment in 8th grade in one year, 9th grade in the next year, and 10th grade in the year after that, and then dividing by three. The averaging is intended to account for prior-year retentions in the 9th grade.

PRIVATE SCHOOLS, Items 41–43
Sources: U.S. Department of Education. National Center for Education Statistics. *Characteristics of Private Schools in the United States: Results from the 2007–08 Private School Universe Survey* (NCES Report 2009-313). <http://nces.ed.gov/pubsearch/pubsinfo.asp?pubid=2009313>.

Since 1989, the Census Bureau has conducted the biennial Private School Universe Survey (PSS) for NCES. The PSS is designed to generate biennial data on the total number of private schools, students, and teachers and to build a universe of private schools in all of the states and the District of Columbia to serve as a sampling frame of private schools for NCES sample surveys. The target population for the PSS is every school in all of the states and the District of Columbia that are not primarily supported by public funds, provide instruction for one or more grades between kindergarten and grade 12 (or comparable ungraded levels), and have one or more teachers. Organizations or institutions that provide support for home schooling, but do not provide classroom instruction, are not

included. Although the PSS has begun to collect limited data on the many private schools for which kindergarten is the highest grade, the data in this volume are for (traditional) schools that include at least one grade between grades 1 and 12.

A private school is controlled by an individual or agency other than a state, a subdivision of a state, or the federal government; is usually supported primarily by nonpublic funds; and the operation of its program does not rest with publicly elected or appointed officials. Private schools include both nonprofit and proprietary institutions.

Data for private schools in Arkansas, Delaware, Idaho, Montana, and Oklahoma, for students in Arkansas, Idaho, and Montana, and for private high school graduates in Idaho and Montana should be interpreted with caution. The coefficient of variation for these estimates is larger than 25 percent. Reporting standards were not met for private high school graduates in North Dakota and Wyoming.

PUBLIC AND PRIVATE SCHOOL CHARACTERISTICS, Items 44–51
Sources: U.S. Department of Education. National Center for Education Statistics. *Common Core of Data, 1998–1999* and *2008–2009* <http://nces.ed.gov/ccd/>; *State Nonfiscal Survey of Public Elementary/Secondary Education*; *Private School Universe Survey, 2007–2008*. <http://nces.ed.gov/surveys/pss/>; *Characteristics of Private Schools in the United States: Results from the 2007–2008 Private School Universe Survey: First Look* (NCES Report 2009-313).

The public school numbers are from the CCD state universe. Teacher counts measure the number of full-time equivalent teachers, including teachers who are employed by agencies and not assigned to specific schools. The student-teacher ratio is calculated by dividing the number of students in all schools by the number of full-time equivalent teachers employed by all schools and agencies.

The private school numbers are derived from the Private School Survey Universe (PSS). These estimates measured full-time equivalent teachers. The student-teacher ratio is calculated by dividing the number of students enrolled in all schools by the number of full-time equivalent teachers employed by all schools.

TEACHER SALARIES, Item 52
Source: National Education Association. Rankings & estimates database. *Rankings & Estimates: Rankings of the States 2009 and Estimates of School Statistics, 2010.* (Washington, D.C.: NEA, 2009.) < http://www.nea.org/assets/docs/010rankings.pdf >. Reprinted with permission of the National Education Association © 2009. All rights reserved.

The National Education Association (NEA) publishes average teacher salaries by state in its annual *Estimates of School Statistics*. The information is compiled from surveys conducted by the state departments of education. If a state does not provide a salary amount, the NEA develops an estimate. The states then have the option of replacing this estimate with one of their own. At the time of this publication, about half of the states used NEA estimates.

The average salary for public school teachers is defined as the arithmetic mean of the salaries of the group described. This figure is the average gross salary before deductions for Social Security, retirement, health insurance, and the like.

PUBLIC SCHOOL STAFF, Items 53–71
Sources: U.S. Department of Education. National Center for Education Statistics. *Common Core of Data, 2008–2009.* <http://nces.ed.gov/ccd/>. State Nonfiscal survey of Public Elementary/Secondary Education,

2008–2009, as published in Public Elementary and Secondary School Student Enrollment and Staff Counts From the Common Core of Data: School Year 2008–09: First Look (NCES Report 2010-347).

The number of teachers represents full-time equivalent teachers employed within the state. Instructional aides directly assist teachers in providing instruction. Instructional coordinators help teachers through curriculum development and in-service training. Support staff includes those involved with food, health, library, maintenance, transportation, security, and other services in public schools. School administrators are principals and assistant principals. School district administrators include the Local Education Agency (LEA) superintendents, deputies, assistant superintendents, and other persons with district-wide responsibilities.

CHARACTERISTICS OF TEACHERS, Items 72–80
Source: U.S. Department of Education. National Center for Education Statistics. Schools and staffing survey, Public Teacher Questionnaire, 2007-2008. Table 67, *Digest of Education Statistics, 2009.* <http://nces.ed.gov/programs/digest/d09/tables/dt09_067.asp?referrer=list>.

The highest degree earned and years of experience are from the Schools and Staffing Survey (SASS), "Public Teacher Questionnaire," 2007–2008, as published in the *Digest of Education Statistics, 2009.* Data are based on a head count of all teachers and exclude prekindergarten teachers. Detail may not sum to totals because of rounding, cell suppression, and omitted categories (less than bachelor's). Elementary teachers are those who taught self-contained classes at the elementary level, and secondary teachers are those who taught departmentalized classes (e.g., science, art, social science, or other course subjects) at the secondary level. Teachers were classified as elementary or secondary on the basis of the grades they taught, rather than on the level of the school in which they taught. Education specialist includes certificate of advanced graduate studies.

NATIONAL ASSESSMENT OF EDUCATIONAL PROGRESS,
Items 81–85
Source: U.S. Department of Education. Institute of Education Sciences, National Center for Education Statistics. *National Assessment of Educational Progress, 2009 and 2007.* <http://nces.ed.gov/nationsreportcard/>.

The National Assessment of Educational Progress (NAEP) is a congressionally mandated project of the National Center for Education Statistics (NCES) that has, for more than a quarter of a century, continually collected and reported information on what American students know and what they can do. It is the nation's only ongoing, comparable, and representative assessment of student achievement. Its assessments are based on a national probability sample of public and nonpublic school students enrolled in grades 4, 8, or 12. Results are only provided for group performance, as NAEP is forbidden by law to report results at an individual or school level. The assessment questions are written around a framework prepared for each content area—reading, writing, mathematics, science, and other; this framework represents the consensus of groups of curriculum experts, educators, and members of the general public on what such a test should cover.

In response to legislation passed by Congress in 1988, the NAEP program includes voluntary state-by-state assessments. To help ensure valid state-by-state results, NCES applies minimum school and student participation rate standards for its reporting activities. Results are not reported for jurisdictions that failed to meet these standards.

This volume includes the proportion of students in specific grades whose NAEP mathematics, reading, and writing assessment

results were designated as "proficient," or better for their grades. The achievement level results describe what students participating in the NAEP assessment should know and what they should be able to do. The National Assessment Governing Board (NAGB) adopted three achievement levels: basic, proficient, and advanced. The basic level denotes partial mastery of fundamental knowledge and skills, the proficient level shows solid academic performance and competency in challenging subject matter, and the advanced level signifies superior performance. Achievement levels are based on collective judgments gathered from a broadly representative panel of teachers, education specialists, and members of the general public about what students should know and be able to do relative to the body of content reflected in the NAEP assessment framework.

ACT ASSESSMENT COMPOSITE SCORES, Items 86–87
Source: ACT, Inc. *2010 ACT Composite Averages by State.* <http://www.act.org/news/data/10/states.html>. © 2010 by ACT, Inc.

Totals for graduating seniors were obtained from: ACT, Inc. *Knocking at the College Door—March 2009, Projections of High School Graduates by State and Race/Ethnicity, 1992–2022.* (Boulder, CO: Western Interstate Commission for Higher Education, 2008).

In Spring 2009, all public high school eleventh graders in the states of Colorado, Illinois, Kentucky, Michigan, and Wyoming were tested with the ACT as required by each state. Colorado, Illinois, Kentucky, Michigan, and Wyoming students who met ACT's 2010 graduating class criteria are included in the 2010 graduating class average score results. Consistent with ACT's reporting policies, graduating class test results are reported only for students tested under standard time conditions.

Founded in 1959 as the American College Testing Program, ACT, Inc., is an independent, not-for-profit organization that provides over 100 assessment, research, information, and program management services in the broad areas of educational planning, career planning, and workforce development. The ACT Assessment is designed to assess high school students' general educational development and their ability to complete college-level work. The test covers four skill areas: English, mathematics, reading, and science reasoning. Data in this volume are based on all high school graduates in the class of 2010 who took the ACT Assessment during their sophomore, junior, or senior year. For students who took the test more than once, only their most recent scores are used. Students who tested on campus, used extended time testing, or failed to list a valid high school code are not included.

College-bound students who take the ACT Assessment are not representative of college-bound students nationally. Students residing in the Midwest, the Mountain West, the Plains, and the South are overrepresented among ACT-tested students, compared with college-bound students nationally. ACT-tested students also tend to enroll in public college and universities more frequently than college-bound students nationally.

Caution should be used in comparing state and national norms. State norms may differ from national norms for non-educational reasons, such as the representativeness of the ACT-tested population and the demographic makeup of a state.

PSAT/NMSQT® (PRELIMINARY SAT/ NATIONAL MERIT SCHOLARSHIP QUALIFYING TEST), Items 88–91

Source: The College Entrance Examination Board. *PSAT/NMSQT® 2009-2010 College-Bound High School Juniors State Summary Reports.* <http://professionals.collegeboard. com/data-reports-research/psat/cb-jr-soph/ juniors>. Reproduced with permission. All rights reserved.

The PSAT/NMSQT (Preliminary SAT/National Merit Scholarship Qualifying Test) is a program co-sponsored by the College Board and the National Merit Scholarship Corporation. The test serves several functions: it helps assess skills necessary for college-level work, prepares students for the SAT, enters students in competitions for national scholarships (including the National Merit Scholarship Corporation scholarship programs), and helps students receive access to information and applications for educational and financial aid information from colleges, universities, and scholarship programs.

Verbal, math, and writing skills scores are each reported on a 20 to 80 scale. The average scores of juniors in each section are between 47 and 49. Unless students earn scores that are much lower than average, the PSAT/NMSQT shows that they are likely developing the kinds of critical reading, math problem-solving, and writing skills needed for academic success in college.

The sum of the verbal, math, and writing skills scores makes up the Selection Index, which is used by National Merit Scholarship Corporation to designate those who will be honored in its scholarship programs. The qualifying score varies from state to state, depending on the scores and the proportion of test takers in each state. Scores between 65 and 80 on each skill mark the approximate level of the achievement needed to qualify. In states with higher percentages of scores in this range, a student must achieve a higher Selection Index to be a designated a National Merit semifinalist.

SAT REASONING TEST SCORES, Items 92–95

Source: The College Board. *SAT Trends 2010.* (New York: The College Board, 2010.) <http://professionals.collegeboard.com/ data-reports-research/sat/cb-seniors-2010/ tables>. Reprinted with permission. All rights reserved.

The percentage of high school graduates is based on the recently revised projection of high school graduates in 2010 by the Western Interstate Commission for Higher Education (*Knocking at the College Door: Projections of High School Graduates by State and Race/Ethnicity, 1992–2022*, Western Interstate Commission for Higher Education, March 2008), and the number of students in the class of 2010 who took the SAT in each state through March 2010. Senior test-takers in May and June are not included in the analysis.

The SAT is an examination administered by the Educational Testing Service that is used to predict the facility with which an individual will progress in college-level academic classes.

SAT Trends: Background on the SAT Takers in the Class of 2010 presents data for high school graduates who participated in the SAT program during their high school years. Students are counted once no matter how often they tested, and only their most recent scores are included in the data. The class of 2006 was the first to take the new SAT, which includes writing as well as critical reading and math. Each test is scored on a scale of 200 to 800.

The College Board cautions that relationships between test scores and other factors such as educational background, gender, race/ethnic background, parental education, and household income are complex and interdependent. These factors do not directly affect test performance; rather, they are associated with educational experiences both on tests such as the SAT and in school work. Moreover, not all students in a high school, school district, or state take the SAT. Since the population of test takers is self-selected, using aggregate SAT scores to compare or evaluate teachers, schools, districts, states, or other educational units is not valid, and the College Board strongly discourages such uses.

Interpreting SAT scores for states requires unique considerations. The most significant factor to consider in interpreting SAT scores for any group or subgroup of test takers is the proportion of students taking the test. For example, it is important to recognize that some states have lower participation rates. Typically, test takers in these low-participation states have strong academic backgrounds and apply to the nation's most selective colleges and scholarship programs. For these states, it is expected that the SAT mean scores reported for students will be higher than the national average.

REVENUES, Items 96–99

Source: U.S. Department of Education. National Center for Education Statistics. *Common Core of Data,* "National Public Education Financial Survey (State Fiscal)" 2007–2008 (FY 2008) v.1a. <http://nces.ed.gov/ccd/>. *Revenues and Expenditures for Public Elementary and Secondary Education: School Year 2007–08 (Fiscal Year 2008)* (NCES 2010-326)

The state data include adjustments made by NCES. Values that were missing and not reported elsewhere in the survey were imputed based on corresponding proportions in reporting states. Other adjustments were made when a single value was reported that included two or more categories. NCES distributed portions of the single reported value to the missing items. In addition to these adjustments, the NPEFS may also include state-run education programs. Consequently, these numbers may differ from the state totals in Table C, which are derived from a different survey.

Charter school systems' reporting requirements vary from state to state and data are not currently reported uniformly to the State Education Agencies (SEAs). Note that some charter school data may be missing from this volume, since some charter schools were not required to submit finance data to their SEAs. Only those charter schools that submit data to the SEAs, and whose SEAs maintain the data, are included in the CCD fiscal files.

Revenues from federal sources include direct grants-in-aid from the federal government, federal grants-in-aid through the state or an intermediate agency, and other revenue in lieu of taxes to compensate a school district for nontaxable federal institutions within a district's boundaries.

State revenues include revenues that can be used without restriction, revenues for categorical purposes, and revenues in lieu of taxation. Also included are revenues from payments made by a state for the benefit of the Local Education Agency (LEA) or contributions of equipment or supplies. Such revenues include the payment of a pension fund by the state on behalf of an LEA employee for services rendered and contributions of fixed assets (property, plant, or equipment), such as school buses and textbooks.

Revenues from local sources include local property and non-property tax revenues, taxes levied or assessed by an LEA, revenues from a local government to the LEA, tuition received, transportation fees, earnings on investments from LEA holdings, net revenues from food services (gross receipts less gross expenditures), net revenues from student activities (gross receipts less gross expenditures), and other revenues (textbook sales, donations, and property rentals). Intermediate revenues were included in local revenue totals. Intermediate revenues are derived from sources other than Local or State Education Agencies; these sources operate at an intermediate level between Local and State Education Agencies and possess independent fundraising capabilities (such as county or municipal agencies).

EXPENDITURES, Items 100–104
Source: U.S. Department of Education. National Center for Education Statistics.

"National Public Education Financial Survey (State Fiscal)" 2007–2008 (FY 2008) v.1a. <http://nces.ed.gov/ccd/>. *Revenues and Expenditures for Public Elementary and Secondary Education: School Year 2007–08 (Fiscal Year 2008)* (NCES 2010-326).

The state data include adjustments made by NCES. Values that were missing and not reported elsewhere in the survey were imputed based on proportions in reporting states. Other adjustments were made when a single value was reported that included two or more categories. NCES distributed portions of the single reported value to the missing items. In addition to these adjustments, the NPEFS may include state-run education programs. Consequently, these numbers may differ from the state totals in Table C, which come from a different survey.

Current expenditures consist of expenditures for the categories of instruction, support services, and non-instructional services for salaries; employee benefits; purchased services and supplies; and payments by the state made for or on behalf of school systems. These expenditures do not include expenditures for debt service, capital outlay, and property (e.g., equipment), or direct costs (e.g., Head Start, adult education, community colleges, etc.) and community services expenditures.

Instructional and instruction-related expenses comprise current expenditures for activities that deal directly with the interaction between students and teachers. These expenditures include teacher salaries and benefits, supplies (such as textbooks), instructional staff support (i.e., salaries for librarians and instructional specialists), and purchased instructional services.

Support services expenditures consist of current expenditures for activities supporting instruction. These services include operation and maintenance of buildings, school administration, student support services (e.g., nurses, therapists, and guidance counselors), student transportation, school district administration, business services, research, and data processing.

Noninstructional expenditures are mostly for food service, but also consist of expenditures for enterprise operations, such as bookstores and interscholastic athletics.

Current expenditures per student are derived by dividing total current expenditures by the fall student membership count from the CCD. Student membership consists of the count of students enrolled on or about October 1 and is comparable across all states.

HIGHER EDUCATION, Items 105–131
Sources: U.S. Department of Education. National Center for Education Statistics. Integrated Postsecondary Education Data System (IPEDS). *Digest of Education Statistics, 2009.* <http://nces.ed.gov/programs/digest/d09/tables_3.asp/>.

The Integrated Postsecondary Education Data System (IPEDS) surveys approximately 10,000 postsecondary institutions, including universities, colleges, and institutions offering technical and vocational education beyond the high school level. This survey, which began in 1986, replaced the Higher Education General Information Survey (HEGIS). IPEDS is made up of eight integrated components that obtain information on who provides postsecondary education (institutions), who participates in it and completes it (students), what programs are offered and which ones are completed, and the specific human and financial resources involved in the provision of institutionally based postsecondary education. These components are organized into the following categories: Institutional Characteristics, including instructional activity; Fall Enrollment, including age and residence; Enrollment in Occupationally Specific Programs; Completions; Finance;

Staff; Salaries of Full-Time Instructional Faculty; and Academic Libraries.

Institutions of higher education include those with courses leading to an associate's degree or higher, or those with courses accepted for credit toward such degrees. A public institution is controlled and operated by publicly elected or appointed officials and derives its primary support from public funds. A private institution is controlled by an individual or agency other than a state, a subdivision of a state, or the federal government; it is usually primarily supported by nonpublic funds, and the operation of its program does not rest with publicly elected or appointed officials. Private institutions comprise both not-for-profit and proprietary institutions.

Full-time students include undergraduate students enrolled for 12 or more semester credits, 12 or more quarter credits, or 24 or more contact hours a week each term; graduate students enrolled for 9 or more semester credits or 9 or more quarter credits, or students involved in thesis or dissertation preparation who are considered full time students by the institution; and first-professional students (as defined by the institution).

Types of institutions include the following:

- Degree-granting institutions, which offer associate's, bachelor's, master's, doctoral and/or first-professional degrees.

- Level categories include four-year and higher (four-year) institutions, at least two but less than four-year (two-year) institutions, and less than two-year institutions.

A four-year institution is a postsecondary institution that offers programs of at least four years' duration or programs at or above the baccalaureate level. This category includes schools that only offer post-baccalaureate certificates and those that only offer graduate programs. Also included are freestanding medical, law, and other first-professional schools.

A two-year institution is a postsecondary institution that offers programs of at least two years' duration but less than four years' duration. This category includes occupational and vocational schools with programs of at least 1,800 hours and academic institutions with programs of less than four years' duration. It does not include bachelor's degree–granting institutions where the baccalaureate program can be completed in three years.

Control categories are public, private not-for-profit, and private for-profit.

Race/ethnicity categories are categories used to describe groups to which individuals belong, identify with, or belong to in the eyes of the community. A person may be counted in only one group. Classification is based on self-identification. Race categories exclude persons of Hispanic ethnicity.

A nonresident alien is a person who is not a citizen or national of the United States, and who is in this country on a visa or temporary basis; a nonresident alien does not have the right to remain in the United States indefinitely.

Migration refers to the movement of students from their home state of residence to another state to attend a postsecondary institution. The percentages in columns 122 and 123 refer to freshmen who had graduated from high school within the previous 12 months and who were enrolled in 4-year degree granting institutions in Fall 2008.

An associate's degree is a degree granted for the successful completion of a sub-baccalaureate program of studies, and usually requires at least two years (or the equivalent) of full-time college-level study. This category

also includes degrees granted in a cooperative or work-study program.

A bachelor's degree is a degree granted for the successful completion of a baccalaureate program of studies, and usually requires at least four years (or the equivalent) of full-time college-level study. This category includes degrees granted in a cooperative or work-study program.

A master's degree is awarded for successful completion of a program generally requiring 1 or 2 years of full-time, college-level study beyond the bachelor's degree. One type of master's degree, including the master of arts degree (M.A.), and the master of science degree (M.S.), is awarded in the liberal arts and sciences for advanced scholarship in a subject field or discipline and demonstrated ability to perform scholarly research. A second type of master's degree is awarded for the completion of a professionally oriented program. These include master's degrees in education (M.Ed.), business administration (M.B.A.), fine arts (M.F.A.), music (M.M.), social work (M.S.W.), and public administration (M.P.W.) A third type of master's degree is awarded in professional fields for study beyond the first-professional degree, such as the master of laws (LL.M.) and the masters of science in various medical specializations.

A first-professional degree requires the completion of a program that meets all of the following criteria: (1) completion of the academic requirements to begin practice in the profession, (2) at least 2 years of college work prior to entering the program, and (3) a total of at least 6 academic years of college work to complete the degree program, including prior required college work plus the length of the professional program itself. First-professional degrees are awarded in the following 10 fields: chiropractic (D.C. or D.C.M.), dentistry (D.D.S. or D.M.D.), law (L.L.B. or J.D.), medicine (M.D.), optometry (O.D.), osteopathic medicine (D.O.), pharmacy (Pharm.D.), podiatry (D.P.M., D.P., or Pod.D.), theology (M.Div., M.H.L., B.D., or Ordination), and veterinary medicine (D.V.M.).

A doctoral degree carries the title of doctor. The doctor of philosophy degree (Ph.D.) is the highest academic degree and requires mastery within a field of knowledge and a demonstrated ability to perform scholarly research. Other doctoral degrees are awarded for fulfilling specialized requirements in a professional field, such as education (Ed.D.), musical arts (D.M.A.), business administration (D.B.A.), and engineering (D.Eng. or D.E.S.). Many doctoral degrees in academic and professional fields require a master's degree as a prerequisite. First-professional degrees, such as M.D. and D.D.S. degrees, are not included under this heading.

SCHOOL ENROLLMENT AND TYPE OF SCHOOL, Items 132–139
Source: U.S. Census Bureau. *2009 American Community Survey.* <http://www.census.gov/acs/www/>; Tables C14002 and B14004 from American FactFinder.

School enrollment is enrollment in a regular school, either public or private, including nursery schools, kindergarten, and elementary schools, as well as schooling that leads to a high school diploma or college degree. Schools supported and controlled primarily by the federal, state, or local government are defined as public schools (including tribal schools). Schools primarily supported and controlled by religious organizations or other private groups are considered private schools.

DROPOUTS, Items 140-141
Source: U.S. Census Bureau. *2009 American Community Survey.* <http://www.census.gov/acs/www/>; Table B14005 from American FactFinder.

The "high school dropout" category includes people of compulsory school attendance age or older who were not enrolled in school and were not high school graduates. However, there is no criterion regarding when they dropped out of school, thus, some may have never attended high school. This column includes only persons 16 to 19 years old.

PART C
COUNTY EDUCATION STATISTICS

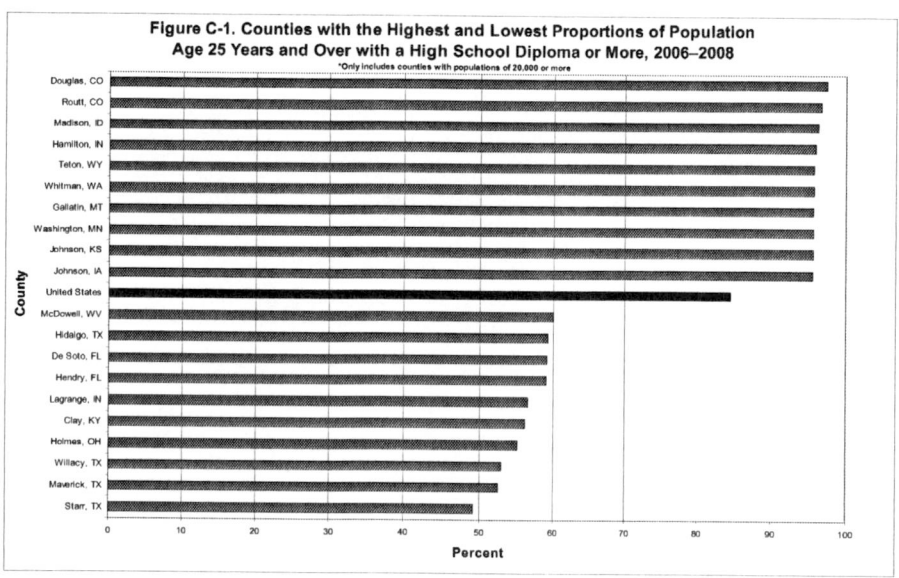

Figure C-1. Counties with the Highest and Lowest Proportions of Population Age 25 Years and Over with a High School Diploma or More, 2006–2008
*Only includes counties with populations of 20,000 or more

Among counties with populations of 20,000 or more, there were twelve counties where more than 95 percent of the population age 25 years old and over had graduated from high school. Only 9 counties had high school attainment levels of less than 60 percent; 4 of these counties were in Texas. In the 2006-2008 time period, 22 counties had college attainment levels that exceeded 50 percent. Just three counties, in Tennessee, Kentucky, and Missouri, had college attainment levels of less than 6 percent.

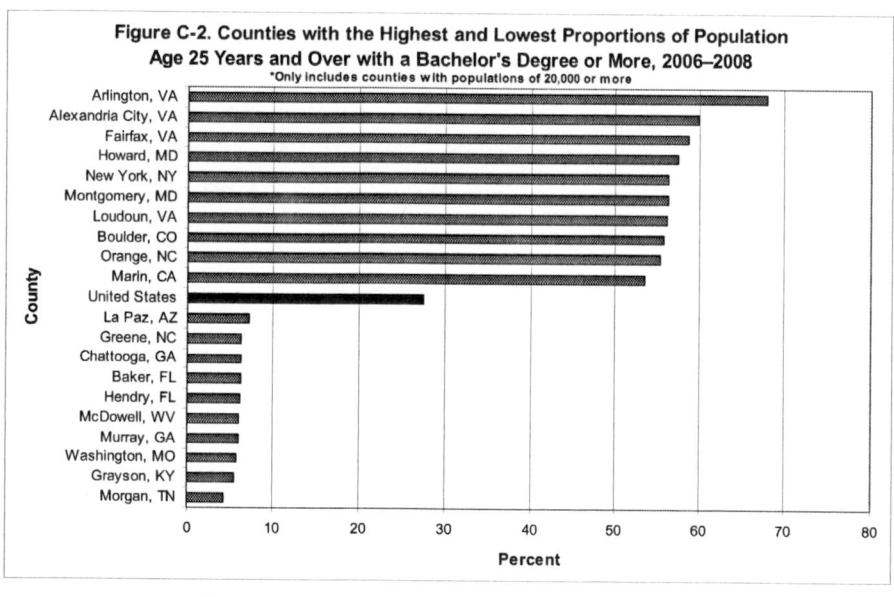

Figure C-2. Counties with the Highest and Lowest Proportions of Population Age 25 Years and Over with a Bachelor's Degree or More, 2006–2008
*Only includes counties with populations of 20,000 or more

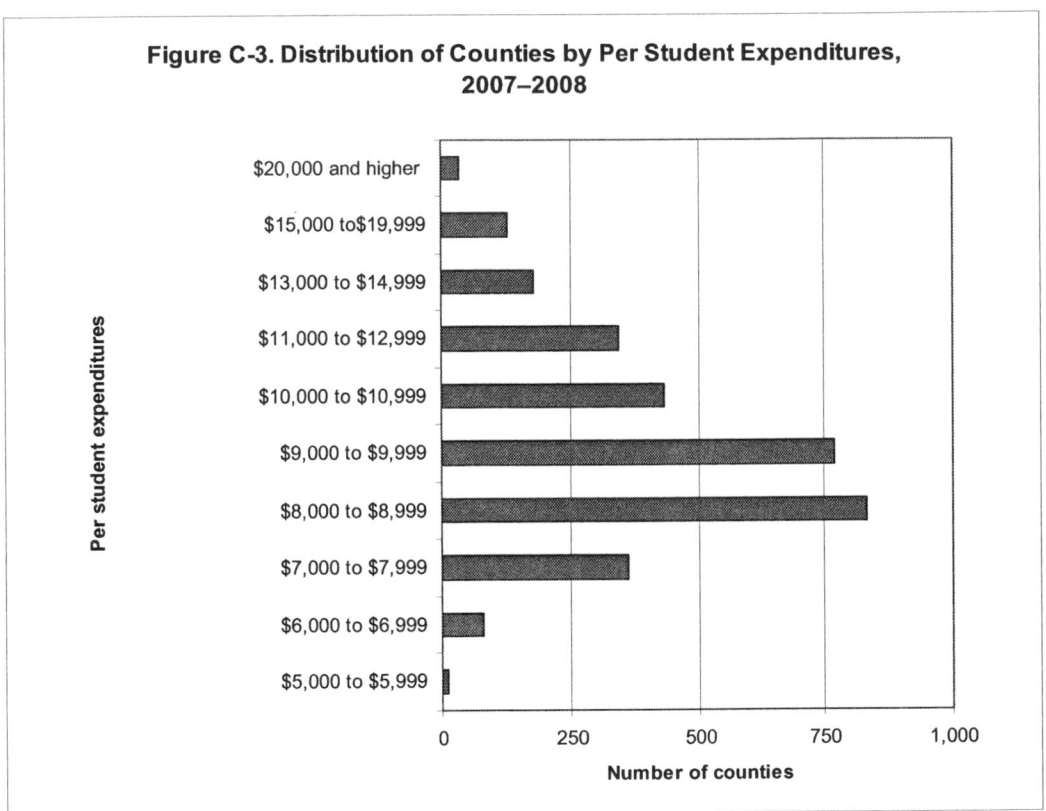

Figure C-3. Distribution of Counties by Per Student Expenditures, 2007–2008

Expenditures per student range from almost $44,667 in remote Keweenaw County, Michigan, to less than $5,500 in Utah, Morgan, and Tooele Counties in Utah, fast-growing counties with high proportions of children. With the highest proportion of student-age population of all the states, Utah has many counties with low expenditures per student. At the other extreme, the 7 counties with expenditures above $30,000 per student have small student populations. The median per student expenditure was $9,344 (with half of the counties spending more and half spending less). Los Angeles County had the largest enrollment (1,920,037 students), but New York City had the highest educational expenditures with $18.5 billion spent in fiscal year 2007–2008, followed closely by Los Angeles with $17 billion. Slope County, North Dakota, and Keweenaw County, Michigan, all spent less than $1 million.

In the United States, there were approximately 3,200 counties (including county equivalents), about 18,000 Local Education Agencies (school districts), over 100,000 public schools, and 49.2 million public school students. Some counties—even large counties, such as Miami-Dade County in Florida—had only one school district, while others had many. For example, Arizona's Maricopa County had 285 school districts and Cook County in Illinois had 169.

Student-teacher ratios varied greatly from county to county, ranging from a handful of counties that exceeded 24 students per teacher to a low of 3.5 students per teacher in Logan, Kansas, and Billings, North Dakota. Yukon-Koyukuk, Alaska, had the highest student-teacher ration at 38.5 percent. The median student-teacher ratio was 15.4.

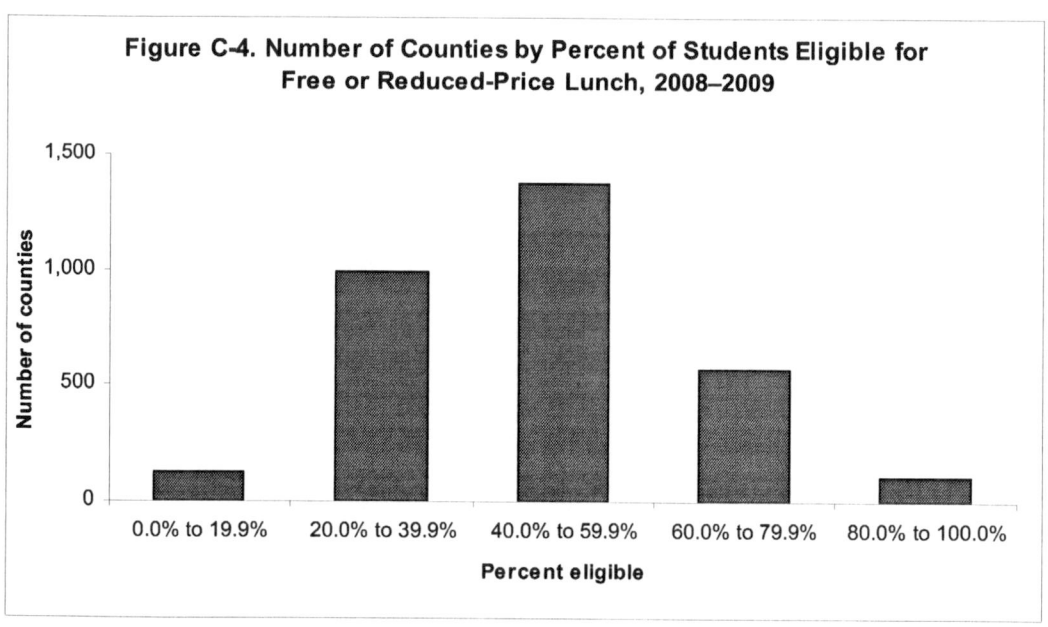

Figure C-4. Number of Counties by Percent of Students Eligible for Free or Reduced-Price Lunch, 2008–2009

There were 49 counties (most located in the South), in which 90 percent or more of students were eligible for free or reduced-price lunches in the 2008–2009 school year. Among the 12 counties with proportions exceeding 98 percent, half were in Mississippi. Only 19 counties had less than 10 percent of students who were poor enough to qualify for these federal programs.

California and Texas were home to 46 of the 111 counties with proportions of English-language learners of 20 percent or more. In many of these counties, the students' native language was Spanish. In many others, the students spoke Native American languages at home.

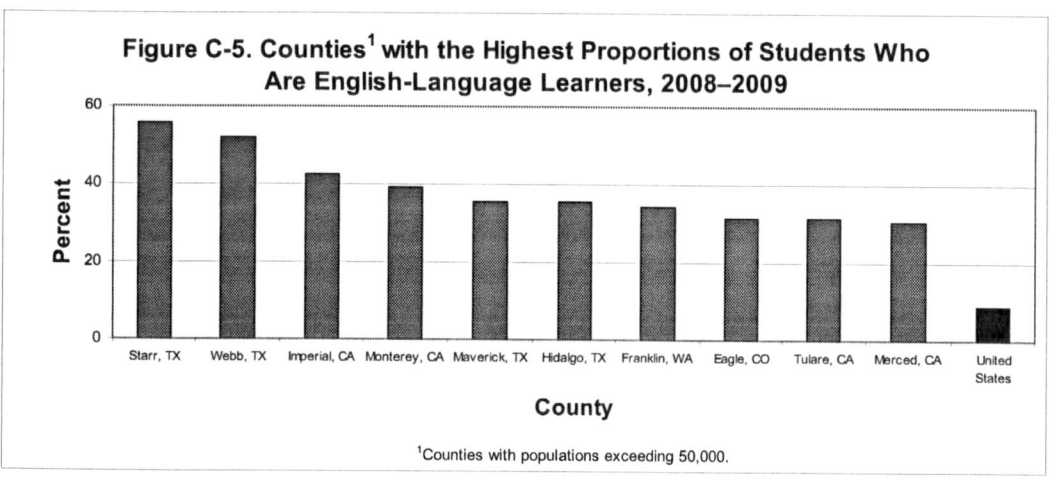

Figure C-5. Counties[1] with the Highest Proportions of Students Who Are English-Language Learners, 2008–2009

[1]Counties with populations exceeding 50,000.

Table C-1. Population, School, and Student Characteristics by County

County	State/County Code	County Type[1]	Population, 2009		Percent of related children 5-17 years in poverty, 2008	Percent of children under 19 years with no health insurance, 2007	Number of Schools and Students, 2008-2009			Resident enrollment, 2006-2008 K-12 enrollment	
			Total	Percent 5-17 years			School Districts	Schools	Students	Number	Percent public
			1	2	3	4	5	6	7	8	9
UNITED STATES	00000	X	307,006,550	17.3	16.5	11.2	17,885	101,979	4,917,6431	53,451,983	89.1
ALABAMA	01000	X	4,708,708	17.3	19.8	8.4	171	1,639	745,668	813,432	88.6
Autauga, AL	01001	2	50,756	20.8	12.9	9.6	1	14	9,923	9,962	91.5
Baldwin, AL	01003	4	179,878	16.7	13.7	11.9	1	47	27,120	29,298	86.4
Barbour, AL	01005	6	29,737	16.1	28.8	7.0	2	10	3,964	5,309	91.0
Bibb, AL	01007	1	21,587	17.4	21.8	8.6	3	12	3,565	3,607	85.3
Blount, AL	01009	1	58,345	17.9	15.5	11.6	2	19	9,806	9,852	91.5
Bullock, AL	01011	6	10,985	16.6	35.2	7.0	1	5	1,616	...	...
Butler, AL	01013	6	19,964	17.7	28.1	7.5	1	9	3,347	3,777	88.2
Calhoun, AL	01015	3	114,081	16.7	20.1	6.9	5	40	18,539	18,384	90.1
Chambers, AL	01017	6	34,320	16.5	23.4	7.0	2	14	5,030	6,325	85.9
Cherokee, AL	01019	8	24,448	15.7	23.0	9.4	1	9	4,084	3,686	98.2
Chilton, AL	01021	1	42,971	17.9	21.7	10.2	1	13	7,617	7,219	95.6
Choctaw, AL	01023	9	13,990	17.4	25.6	8.1	1	5	1,886	...	...
Clarke, AL	01025	7	26,042	19.4	26.1	10.2	2	11	5,013	5,260	91.7
Clay, AL	01027	9	13,640	16.0	21.5	9.2	1	4	2,130	...	...
Cleburne, AL	01029	8	14,759	16.8	20.2	8.6	1	8	2,657	...	...
Coffee, AL	01031	6	48,635	17.3	19.9	9.4	4	19	9,127	8,082	96.9
Colbert, AL	01033	3	54,639	16.3	18.6	7.6	4	27	8,468	9,271	95.7
Conecuh, AL	01035	9	12,931	16.9	33.3	6.9	2	8	1,662	...	...
Coosa, AL	01037	8	10,556	15.3	21.4	7.9	1	4	1,349	...	...
Covington, AL	01039	7	36,678	16.3	23.8	8.0	3	15	6,165	5,829	95.5
Crenshaw, AL	01041	8	13,781	18.0	24.2	10.0	1	4	2,487	...	...
Cullman, AL	01043	6	81,778	17.0	17.9	9.1	2	36	12,805	13,235	91.2
Dale, AL	01045	4	48,147	17.3	20.4	9.4	3	17	6,585	8,755	91.3
Dallas, AL	01047	4	41,925	19.2	40.6	6.1	2	28	8,198	8,913	89.8
De Kalb, AL	01049	6	69,380	18.1	22.0	9.4	2	19	11,929	11,522	96.5
Elmore, AL	01051	2	79,233	17.7	13.7	11.5	3	24	12,835	14,313	81.9
Escambia, AL	01053	6	37,434	16.6	27.6	7.4	3	18	5,874	6,456	92.3
Etowah, AL	01055	3	103,645	17.1	20.9	7.5	7	47	16,285	17,123	90.2
Fayette, AL	01057	6	17,371	17.0	22.5	7.0	1	6	2,512	...	...
Franklin, AL	01059	6	31,091	17.4	25.5	9.6	2	13	5,745	5,127	98.9
Geneva, AL	01061	3	25,961	15.8	26.5	7.6	2	12	3,962	4,219	96.6
Greene, AL	01063	3	8,829	19.0	36.8	6.1	1	5	1,427	...	...
Hale, AL	01065	3	17,975	18.9	26.4	7.1	1	10	3,011	...	...
Henry, AL	01067	3	16,647	17.5	24.2	10.7	1	9	2,765	...	...
Houston, AL	01069	3	100,085	17.6	20.5	8.2	3	33	15,445	17,176	85.1
Jackson, AL	01071	6	52,838	16.9	20.0	7.6	3	26	8,651	8,896	92.8
Jefferson, AL	01073	1	665,027	16.8	17.6	6.6	21	227	104,953	114,667	89.1
Lamar, AL	01075	9	14,200	15.6	24.0	8.3	1	5	2,346	...	...
Lauderdale, AL	01077	3	89,599	15.5	19.6	8.0	2	22	13,180	13,523	89.4
Lawrence, AL	01079	3	34,106	16.8	19.2	8.1	2	17	5,419	5,936	95.0
Lee, AL	01081	3	135,883	15.7	12.6	10.2	4	32	19,907	21,159	91.9
Limestone, AL	01083	2	78,572	17.3	13.7	9.5	2	20	11,773	13,037	89.5
Lowndes, AL	01085	2	12,293	18.6	33.6	12.2	1	9	1,953	...	...
Macon, AL	01087	6	21,789	14.8	34.5	6.5	2	8	2,925	3,982	89.1
Madison, AL	01089	2	327,744	17.5	12.9	10.0	6	94	51,456	55,576	86.5
Marengo, AL	01091	7	20,943	18.8	27.5	7.5	3	13	4,530	4,247	89.9
Marion, AL	01093	8	29,116	15.7	23.3	8.0	2	14	5,070	4,401	95.6
Marshall, AL	01095	4	90,399	18.0	24.0	10.0	5	35	16,245	14,997	93.8
Mobile, AL	01097	2	411,721	18.6	25.4	8.1	6	122	64,066	77,768	81.5
Monroe, AL	01099	7	22,389	18.9	24.8	8.4	1	12	4,214	4,554	83.4
Montgomery, AL	01101	2	224,119	17.7	24.3	7.5	5	71	31,307	41,268	79.9
Morgan, AL	01103	3	117,293	17.8	17.0	8.6	3	45	19,781	20,361	92.8
Perry, AL	01105	8	10,623	19.5	41.7	9.2	1	5	1,956	...	...
Pickens, AL	01107	8	19,218	17.4	35.4	10.3	1	10	3,032	...	...
Pike, AL	01109	6	30,461	15.4	24.7	7.3	2	10	4,428	4,975	86.7
Randolph, AL	01111	6	22,557	16.9	23.0	8.0	2	10	3,856	3,846	91.7
Russell, AL	01113	2	50,846	17.8	31.0	8.3	2	19	9,467	9,111	92.1
St. Clair, AL	01115	1	81,895	16.7	15.7	10.0	2	26	12,510	13,438	87.3
Shelby, AL	01117	1	192,503	18.8	6.9	9.4	2	40	27,194	34,569	83.1
Sumter, AL	01119	8	12,853	17.5	37.7	7.1	1	7	2,332	...	...
Talladega, AL	01121	4	80,242	17.0	22.2	6.0	4	35	12,777	13,341	93.2
Tallapoosa, AL	01123	6	41,008	16.0	24.6	7.6	2	12	6,481	6,926	94.8
Tuscaloosa, AL	01125	3	184,035	16.0	16.9	8.1	4	61	27,809	28,662	90.1
Walker, AL	01127	1	68,742	16.4	22.4	7.0	2	29	11,071	11,344	96.3
Washington, AL	01129	8	17,069	18.2	20.8	10.4	1	8	3,487	...	...
Wilcox, AL	01131	8	12,384	21.5	40.4	12.9	1	7	2,163	...	...
Winston, AL	01133	6	23,997	16.4	24.2	6.7	2	14	4,396	...	...

[1]County type codes are from the Economic Research Service of the United States Department of Agriculture. See notes and definitions for more information.
... Not available

Table C-1. Population, School, and Student Characteristics by County—*Continued*

County	State/ County Code	Characteristics of students, 2008-2009				Number of graduates, 2006-2007	Staff and students, 2008-2009			
		Percent with IEP[2]	Percent eligible for free or reduced lunch	Percent minority	Percent English Language Learners		Total staff	Number of teachers	Student/ teacher ratio	Central admin. Staff
		10	11	12	13	14	15	16	17	18
UNITED STATES	00000	12.7	43.8	44.7	8.9	2,917,733	6,201,006	3,202,881	15.4	241,108
ALABAMA	01000	0.9	52.4	41.2	2.6	41,220	97,605	47,817	15.6	2,626
Autauga, AL...............................	01001	0.7	37.3	29.2	1.1	575	1,083	563	17.6	18
Baldwin, AL...............................	01003	1.0	37.3	20.1	2.6	1,380	4,098	1,888	14.4	90
Barbour, AL...............................	01005	1.3	71.0	69.6	2.7	206	543	273	14.5	18
Bibb, AL....................................	01007	1.2	60.8	26.3	...	181	475	210	17.0	10
Blount, AL.................................	01009	0.8	48.0	14.0	5.7	555	1,170	623	15.7	18
Bullock, AL................................	01011	0.7	92.1	99.8	3.9	98	223	106	15.2	8
Butler, AL..................................	01013	0.6	74.8	62.0	0.3	215	430	202	16.6	18
Calhoun, AL...............................	01015	0.9	54.0	30.9	2.1	966	2,324	1,094	16.9	60
Chambers, AL.............................	01017	1.1	68.3	56.9	0.5	285	651	318	15.8	16
Cherokee, AL.............................	01019	0.7	53.8	8.3	0.4	242	557	272	15.0	14
Chilton, AL................................	01021	1.1	51.8	20.2	5.2	419	930	503	15.1	21
Choctaw, AL..............................	01023	1.1	75.8	69.5	0.3	128	264	106	17.8	14
Clarke, AL.................................	01025	0.8	65.3	59.6	0.1	279	668	318	15.8	19
Clay, AL	01027	0.6	60.8	25.4	2.1	113	264	121	17.6	9
Cleburne, AL..............................	01029	1.0	58.1	6.3	0.9	149	362	160	16.6	9
Coffee, AL.................................	01031	0.8	45.7	30.9	2.0	513	1,074	535	17.1	34
Colbert, AL................................	01033	0.9	49.3	24.1	0.8	478	1,094	538	15.7	39
Conecuh, AL..............................	01035	1.0	87.4	84.1	0.1	108	273	122	13.6	7
Coosa, AL.................................	01037	0.4	70.7	50.3	0.4	72	192	85	15.9	5
Covington, AL............................	01039	1.9	54.0	20.1	0.2	360	807	432	14.3	24
Crenshaw, AL	01041	1.0	56.8	35.8	1.4	155	297	155	16.0	10
Cullman, AL...............................	01043	1.3	48.4	7.0	3.2	709	1,673	850	15.1	33
Dale, AL....................................	01045	0.8	56.5	37.4	0.7	433	846	399	16.5	35
Dallas, AL.................................	01047	1.0	81.9	88.0	0.2	459	1,099	485	16.9	37
De Kalb, AL...............................	01049	0.9	60.8	33.2	15.9	591	1,500	797	15.0	40
Elmore, AL................................	01051	1.3	44.9	29.3	1.3	696	1,550	754	17.0	32
Escambia, Al	01053	1.0	66.0	47.0	0.1	334	783	376	15.6	24
Etowah, AL................................	01055	0.8	54.8	26.2	3.2	945	2,114	1,097	14.8	43
Fayette, AL................................	01057	1.0	49.8	17.0	1.0	151	337	157	16.0	14
Franklin, AL..............................	01059	1.1	61.9	22.5	11.7	316	758	415	13.8	18
Geneva, AL	01061	1.2	54.5	18.7	1.2	223	527	256	15.5	17
Greene, AL................................	01063	1.1	92.7	99.9	...	57	203	88	16.2	11
Hale, AL....................................	01065	1.3	72.9	76.3	0.2	178	396	191	15.8	9
Henry, AL..................................	01067	1.0	63.7	41.5	0.4	129	347	157	17.6	7
Houston, AL...............................	01069	1.1	56.5	42.4	1.1	857	1,902	873	17.7	38
Jackson, AL...............................	01071	0.9	55.0	13.9	1.8	508	1,270	594	14.6	38
Jefferson, AL.............................	01073	0.7	48.1	58.2	2.4	6,536	13,442	6,797	15.4	450
Lamar, AL..................................	01075	1.4	52.2	18.4	0.4	144	307	148	15.9	9
Lauderdale, AL...........................	01077	1.1	42.3	17.3	1.2	767	1,605	810	16.3	32
Lawrence, AL.............................	01079	0.9	52.1	33.4	1.0	390	737	347	15.6	18
Lee, AL.....................................	01081	1.0	43.2	38.3	1.4	1,063	2,613	1,326	15.0	72
Limestone, AL............................	01083	0.7	40.5	22.6	4.6	653	1,546	735	16.0	35
Lowndes, AL..............................	01085	3.0	93.4	99.3	...	114	290	113	17.3	12
Macon, AL.................................	01087	0.9	98.1	98.5	0.1	204	359	160	18.3	13
Madison, AL..............................	01089	0.9	33.4	38.9	2.8	2,963	6,628	3,473	14.8	147
Marengo, AL..............................	01091	1.3	67.7	66.0	2.6	260	612	328	13.8	20
Marion, AL................................	01093	1.1	50.2	6.5	1.1	272	611	334	15.2	17
Marshall, AL..............................	01095	0.9	52.5	17.6	9.0	870	2,051	1,078	15.1	60
Mobile, AL.................................	01097	1.0	64.9	54.9	1.8	3,170	8,611	3,857	16.6	174
Monroe, AL	01099	0.5	64.3	54.9	...	240	559	277	15.2	12
Montgomery, AL	01101	0.7	70.2	84.1	2.9	1,171	4,251	1,936	16.2	177
Morgan, AL	01103	1.0	43.8	27.6	6.3	1,080	2,921	1,495	13.2	54
Perry, AL...................................	01105	2.0	98.5	99.1	0.2	115	248	114	17.2	13
Pickens, AL...............................	01107	1.7	70.4	62.5	0.3	207	386	179	16.9	11
Pike, AL	01109	1.4	66.4	57.8	1.0	252	598	294	15.1	22
Randolph, AL.............................	01111	0.9	57.8	29.6	1.6	223	479	238	16.2	17
Russell, AL................................	01113	0.7	69.4	57.7	0.1	457	1,252	574	16.5	34
St. Clair, AL..............................	01115	1.0	41.4	13.5	1.2	678	1,435	748	16.7	34
Shelby, AL.................................	01117	0.8	24.3	23.8	6.3	1,467	3,743	1,862	14.6	65
Sumter, AL................................	01119	1.8	86.6	99.7	...	180	268	78	29.9	18
Talladega, AL.............................	01121	0.8	66.0	43.3	0.4	692	1,737	854	15.0	50
Tallapoosa, AL............................	01123	0.9	56.3	39.3	1.2	359	862	458	14.2	27
Tuscaloosa, AL...........................	01125	1.6	51.9	48.2	1.5	1,361	3,485	1,703	16.3	86
Walker, AL	01127	1.3	52.7	11.3	0.7	628	1,457	699	15.8	51
Washington, AL	01129	0.7	55.2	40.9	0.2	220	502	261	13.4	10
Wilcox, AL.................................	01131	1.1	96.3	99.6	...	148	291	123	17.6	11
Winston, AL...............................	01133	1.2	56.2	4.0	1.6	273	643	312	14.1	21

[2]IEP= Individual Education Program. See notes and definitions for more information
... Not available

Table C-1. Population, School, and Student Characteristics by County—*Continued*

County	State/County Code	Revenues, 2007-2008				Current expenditures, 2007-2008			Resident population 16 to 19 years, 2006-2008			
		Total revenue ($1,000's)	Percentage of revenue from			Amount ($1,000's)	Amount per student	Percent for instruction	Total population 16 to 19 years	Percent enrolled in school	Percent high school graduates, not enrolled in school	Percent not enrolled, not grads, not employed or not in labor force
			Federal gov't	State gov't	Local gov't							
		19	20	21	22	23	24	25	26	27	28	29
UNITED STATES	00000	597,065,811	8.0	46.9	45.1	505,304,237	10,325	60.8	17,364,134	83.7	9.8	4.1
ALABAMA	01000	7,726,213	9.2	60.2	30.6	6,765,565	9,107	58.3	263,629	80.7	10.6	5.9
Autauga, AL	01001	83,791	7.1	70.1	22.9	74,704	7,583	61.3	2,944	83.4	9.9	4.4
Baldwin, AL	01003	287,620	6.1	47.5	46.4	266,775	10,062	58.8	8,480	77.4	14.4	5.9
Barbour, AL	01005	39,350	14.1	62.5	23.4	37,051	9,416	58.0	...	...	...	...
Bibb, AL	01007	38,554	9.7	73.0	17.3	31,361	8,837	56.4	...	...	...	...
Blount, AL	01009	92,672	6.9	72.0	21.1	75,277	7,689	60.6	...	...	...	...
Bullock, AL	01011	17,023	17.0	68.3	14.7	15,875	9,461	49.0	...	...	...	...
Butler, AL	01013	36,076	14.5	66.9	18.6	31,359	9,281	57.7	...	...	...	...
Calhoun, AL	01015	179,663	9.1	68.2	22.7	160,135	8,690	57.7	6,373	83.6	7.7	5.9
Chambers, AL	01017	47,075	11.3	68.6	20.2	42,931	8,377	56.4	...	...	...	...
Cherokee, AL	01019	41,630	8.6	67.5	23.9	37,801	9,078	58.7	...	...	...	...
Chilton, AL	01021	71,593	9.2	73.7	17.0	60,341	7,906	59.6	...	...	...	...
Choctaw, AL	01023	24,436	11.9	54.2	33.8	18,312	9,253	50.9	...	...	...	...
Clarke, AL	01025	49,257	11.8	65.9	22.2	44,283	8,928	57.7	...	...	...	...
Clay, AL	01027	20,307	8.8	74.2	17.0	17,957	8,434	62.4	...	...	...	...
Cleburne, AL	01029	29,642	7.7	74.2	18.0	22,836	8,683	59.2	...	...	...	...
Coffee, AL	01031	98,411	13.7	59.1	27.1	78,081	8,638	60.6	2,406	79.1	12.1	2.2
Colbert, AL	01033	92,389	7.6	59.3	33.1	82,237	9,812	56.8	...	...	...	...
Conecuh, AL	01035	21,919	13.8	61.3	24.9	18,779	11,306	55.1	...	...	...	...
Coosa, AL	01037	15,011	13.9	69.8	16.4	13,070	9,717	53.3	...	...	...	...
Covington, AL	01039	66,535	9.2	64.6	26.2	54,858	8,857	59.4	...	...	...	...
Crenshaw, AL	01041	23,330	13.2	68.7	18.1	20,938	8,797	59.2	...	...	...	...
Cullman, AL	01043	131,420	8.4	61.8	29.8	112,828	8,802	60.1	3,953	80.9	13.1	4.3
Dale, AL	01045	66,341	11.0	68.2	20.8	60,598	9,130	58.1	...	...	...	...
Dallas, AL	01047	83,656	15.7	69.6	14.7	75,397	8,980	55.4	...	...	...	...
De Kalb, AL	01049	118,994	9.9	69.8	20.3	102,424	8,786	61.8	...	...	...	...
Elmore, AL	01051	121,778	8.8	68.1	23.0	103,361	8,020	61.9	4,259	70.4	19.1	8.2
Escambia, AL	01053	62,898	10.4	62.6	27.0	53,676	9,065	57.8	...	...	...	...
Etowah, AL	01055	154,567	10.9	68.2	20.9	139,702	8,553	59.2	5,293	75.9	11.9	8.3
Fayette, AL	01057	24,803	9.1	69.6	21.3	22,920	9,077	56.5	...	...	...	...
Franklin, AL	01059	59,976	9.7	67.7	22.7	50,580	9,084	59.4	...	...	...	...
Geneva, AL	01061	39,313	9.8	73.2	17.0	32,867	8,264	58.8	...	...	...	...
Greene, AL	01063	18,376	16.7	60.4	22.8	15,014	10,234	50.0	...	...	...	...
Hale, AL	01065	30,768	14.2	70.8	14.9	28,391	8,878	59.2	...	...	...	...
Henry, AL	01067	25,990	11.2	70.5	18.3	23,395	8,573	56.3	...	...	...	...
Houston, AL	01069	145,982	11.4	61.3	27.2	136,010	8,868	60.8	5,042	79.6	10.1	7.8
Jackson, AL	01071	97,984	7.9	64.9	27.1	81,674	9,472	55.1	...	...	...	...
Jefferson, AL	01073	1,218,202	7.9	50.1	42.0	1,024,877	9,739	57.3	36,615	81.0	10.5	6.2
Lamar, AL	01075	23,012	8.8	71.7	19.5	20,215	8,628	56.7	...	...	...	...
Lauderdale, AL	01077	132,766	8.8	61.3	29.9	121,131	9,349	62.2	...	...	...	...
Lawrence, AL	01079	54,458	9.9	67.6	22.5	49,148	9,040	58.5	...	...	...	...
Lee, AL	01081	210,388	6.5	56.4	37.0	182,709	9,202	61.6	11,029	91.4	5.1	2.0
Limestone, AL	01083	120,013	6.1	60.5	33.4	108,020	9,360	63.4	...	...	...	...
Lowndes, AL	01085	28,891	21.6	64.4	14.0	23,762	11,729	55.2	...	...	...	...
Macon, AL	01087	31,860	17.3	65.1	17.5	28,328	9,352	52.2	...	...	...	...
Madison, AL	01089	524,593	6.5	57.7	35.9	464,771	9,250	59.8	18,302	85.3	8.1	4.3
Marengo, AL	01091	46,297	12.4	67.8	19.7	40,192	8,930	59.5	...	...	...	...
Marion, AL	01093	49,874	8.3	70.1	21.6	42,135	8,355	61.6	...	...	...	...
Marshall, AL	01095	163,551	9.5	65.6	24.8	142,311	8,901	58.8	...	...	...	...
Mobile, AL	01097	623,910	12.1	60.5	27.5	585,200	9,090	55.3	23,622	80.4	10.6	7.8
Monroe, AL	01099	38,997	11.5	71.6	16.9	36,789	8,556	59.7	...	...	...	...
Montgomery, AL	01101	310,018	12.3	61.6	26.1	278,471	8,807	56.1	14,098	80.4	7.6	6.6
Morgan, AL	01103	224,143	6.4	56.9	36.6	187,629	9,467	60.2	5,755	82.7	4.0	6.3
Perry, AL	01105	22,867	16.8	72.5	10.7	19,028	9,519	57.9	...	...	...	...
Pickens, AL	01107	29,701	12.1	72.6	15.3	27,444	8,726	57.5	...	...	...	...
Pike, AL	01109	45,902	12.0	61.2	26.8	42,374	9,412	57.2	...	...	...	...
Randolph, AL	01111	36,092	10.3	67.9	21.8	32,149	8,507	60.8	...	...	...	...
Russell, AL	01113	93,904	11.8	65.2	23.0	84,544	9,195	57.5	2,618	62.3	14.7	15.5
St. Clair, AL	01115	121,894	7.3	68.0	24.7	99,987	8,023	62.0	3,907	79.5	12.0	2.6
Shelby, AL	01117	285,107	4.7	52.6	42.7	239,192	9,095	58.6	9,708	88.3	8.8	1.0
Sumter, AL	01119	24,491	18.4	63.1	18.5	23,585	10,331	52.4	...	...	...	...
Talladega, AL	01121	126,110	10.6	62.6	26.8	116,625	9,068	54.8	4,577	78.3	9.4	9.9
Tallapoosa, AL	01123	66,821	9.4	60.7	29.9	60,493	9,106	62.2	...	...	...	...
Tuscaloosa, AL	01125	292,062	8.2	55.1	36.7	242,776	8,873	57.6	12,662	81.2	10.1	5.4
Walker, AL	01127	115,420	9.5	62.9	27.6	105,831	9,535	59.3	3,340	79.7	10.2	9.3
Washington, AL	01129	34,743	10.5	63.7	25.8	30,937	8,637	60.2	...	...	...	...
Wilcox, AL	01131	23,528	16.4	65.7	17.9	20,786	9,601	53.0	...	...	...	...
Winston, AL	01133	47,468	8.6	65.5	25.8	40,328	9,122	57.4	...	...	...	...

... Not available

Table C-1. Population, School, and Student Characteristics by County—*Continued*

County	State/County Code	High school graduates, 2006-2008			College enrollment, 2006-2008		College graduates, 2006-2008 (percent)						
		Population 25 years and over	High school diploma or less (percent)	High school diploma or more (percent)	Number	Percent public	Bachelor's degree or more	+/- U.S. percent with Bachelor's degree or more	Non-Hispanic White	Black or African American	American Indian and Alaska Native	Asian, Hawaiian, and Pacific Islander	Hispanic or Latino[3]
		30	31	32	33	34	35	36	37	38	39	40	41
UNITED STATES	00000	197,794,576	45.0	84.5	20,841,033	73.8	27.4	...	30.4	17.2	12.7	48.5	12.6
ALABAMA	01000	3,052,298	51.3	80.9	283,571	84.4	21.5	-5.9	23.9	14.2	12.9	50.3	12.6
Autauga, AL..........................	01001	32,049	51.8	84.3	2,302	78.8	21.3	-6.1	23.4	10.9	...	...	23.8
Baldwin, AL..........................	01003	117,651	42.7	87.7	7,203	86.9	27.2	-0.2	29.3	9.8	...	...	21.2
Barbour, AL..........................	01005	19,551	66.0	72.5	1,272	93.7	13.1	-14.3	20.1	5.6	...	...	...
Bibb, AL...............................	01007	14,549	68.1	73.6	596	90.3	12.1	-15.3	14.1	4.3	...	...	...
Blount, AL............................	01009	38,163	63.0	73.0	2,497	88.9	11.6	-15.8	12.2	...	...	...	0.2
Bullock, AL...........................	01011	...	...	...	...	...	...	...	...	...	...	...	...
Butler, AL.............................	01013	13,275	64.3	74.6	794	99.0	10.6	-16.8	14.8	4.2	...	...	...
Calhoun, AL..........................	01015	75,244	56.3	78.9	7,550	91.9	16.3	-11.1	16.8	12.0	...	...	13.9
Chambers, AL........................	01017	23,896	61.9	71.5	1,445	93.2	11.0	-16.4	14.9	4.3	...	...	...
Cherokee, AL........................	01019	17,595	66.2	70.0	985	96.1	9.2	-18.2	9.8	...	...	...	...
Chilton, AL...........................	01021	28,342	65.1	74.2	707	80.6	11.4	-16.0	12.1	8.1	...	...	...
Choctaw, AL.........................	01023	...	...	...	...	...	...	...	...	...	...	...	...
Clarke, AL	01025	17,179	65.7	74.1	1,589	88.2	16.1	-11.3	21.8	7.5	...	...	...
Clay, AL...............................	01027	...	...	...	...	...	...	...	...	...	...	...	...
Cleburne, AL.........................	01029	...	...	...	...	...	...	...	...	...	...	...	...
Coffee, AL............................	01031	31,559	51.0	77.8	1,823	90.0	21.0	-6.4	23.4	9.6	...	...	15.1
Colbert, AL...........................	01033	37,839	53.9	80.4	2,073	90.1	16.8	-10.6	17.3	14.3	...	...	2.0
Conecuh, AL.........................	01035	...	...	...	...	...	...	...	...	...	...	...	...
Coosa, AL............................	01037	...	...	...	...	...	...	...	...	...	...	...	...
Covington, AL.......................	01039	25,641	60.9	78.6	1,370	88.1	15.1	-12.3	16.9	3.6	...	...	...
Crenshaw, AL........................	01041	...	...	...	...	...	...	...	...	...	...	...	...
Cullman, AL..........................	01043	55,380	58.7	76.0	3,918	89.3	13.1	-14.3	13.6	...	...	...	3.2
Dale, AL...............................	01045	31,059	48.0	82.9	2,191	87.4	16.8	-10.6	18.6	8.7	...	24.9	20.6
Dallas, AL.............................	01047	27,280	62.0	76.1	2,233	76.0	14.2	-13.2	18.5	11.3	...	...	...
De Kalb, AL..........................	01049	45,801	66.6	69.1	2,564	94.6	10.7	-16.7	11.3	1.4	15.2	...	...
Elmore, AL...........................	01051	50,173	55.5	82.2	3,491	78.8	18.4	-9.0	21.5	6.6	...	...	15.8
Escambia, AL........................	01053	25,485	60.7	75.3	1,105	86.6	11.3	-16.1	13.3	6.9	2.8	...	...
Etowah, AL...........................	01055	70,651	52.9	80.3	4,280	91.4	16.1	-11.3	16.8	12.5	...	32.4	...
Fayette, AL...........................	01057	...	...	...	...	...	...	...	...	...	...	...	...
Franklin, AL	01059	20,614	64.8	67.4	973	90.4	11.6	-15.8	12.3	3.3	...	...	7.7
Geneva, AL...........................	01061	18,001	64.6	70.6	658	95.4	9.4	-18.0	10.4	0.7	...	...	...
Greene, AL...........................	01063	...	...	...	...	...	...	...	...	...	...	...	...
Hale, AL...............................	01065	...	...	...	...	...	...	...	...	...	...	...	...
Henry, AL.............................	01067	...	...	...	...	...	...	...	...	...	...	...	...
Houston, AL..........................	01069	64,767	51.9	81.1	3,829	85.6	19.3	-8.1	22.3	8.8	10.4	27.2	21.4
Jackson, AL..........................	01071	37,035	63.2	74.0	1,726	95.8	11.5	-15.9	11.7	2.2	...	...	...
Jefferson, AL........................	01073	438,356	42.3	86.3	40,856	72.4	28.1	0.7	35.1	16.7	13.2	69.3	21.1
Lamar, AL	01075	...	...	...	...	...	...	...	...	...	...	...	...
Lauderdale, AL......................	01077	59,825	52.0	82.4	6,320	93.9	21.5	-5.9	22.8	7.1	...	...	...
Lawrence, AL........................	01079	23,487	65.3	75.6	963	94.9	9.4	-18.0	8.6	11.2	22.5	...	...
Lee, AL.................................	01081	73,095	41.3	85.1	26,016	95.2	31.9	4.5	35.7	16.9	...	62.9	29.5
Limestone, AL.......................	01083	49,696	54.8	79.2	3,886	88.0	18.1	-9.3	18.5	16.1	...	...	6.4
Lowndes, AL.........................	01085	...	...	...	...	...	...	...	...	...	...	...	...
Macon, AL............................	01087	13,204	50.4	77.7	4,036	36.1	22.8	-4.6	17.4	23.5	...	...	...
Madison, AL..........................	01089	205,086	35.3	87.5	26,930	81.9	37.6	10.2	39.7	30.8	23.6	57.1	19.4
Marengo, AL.........................	01091	13,719	61.4	78.5	645	100.0	15.2	-12.2	21.6	8.5	...	...	...
Marion, AL............................	01093	20,778	66.0	68.2	1,376	95.5	8.3	-19.1	8.5	2.1	...	...	...
Marshall, AL..........................	01095	58,562	58.5	72.7	2,872	88.7	15.3	-12.1	16.0	...	...	...	3.7
Mobile, AL............................	01097	259,479	53.5	82.1	23,175	79.5	19.6	-7.8	22.8	12.7	9.4	29.0	17.4
Monroe, AL	01099	14,845	64.3	77.3	748	92.1	13.2	-14.2	19.0	2.0	...	...	...
Montgomery, AL	01101	141,038	42.9	84.0	17,952	79.2	30.0	2.6	40.1	19.2	...	49.0	18.5
Morgan, AL...........................	01103	78,255	50.1	82.1	4,913	89.4	19.6	-7.8	21.0	10.9	14.2	...	8.1
Perry, AL..............................	01105	...	...	...	...	...	...	...	...	...	...	...	...
Pickens, AL...........................	01107	...	...	...	...	...	...	...	...	...	...	...	...
Pike, AL................................	01109	18,238	57.9	76.2	4,494	97.5	22.1	-5.3	29.7	8.9	...	...	...
Randolph, AL........................	01111	15,283	64.1	72.8	993	92.2	13.5	-13.9	14.7	9.8	...	...	...
Russell, AL...........................	01113	33,525	60.1	75.5	2,179	88.9	10.8	-16.6	10.9	10.0	...	...	20.4
St. Clair, AL..........................	01115	52,039	60.1	76.9	2,405	87.3	12.9	-14.5	13.2	11.0	...	...	...
Shelby, AL............................	01117	118,267	30.2	91.9	10,972	85.6	39.8	12.4	41.3	31.3	25.1	55.7	12.5
Sumter, AL............................	01119	...	...	...	...	...	...	...	...	...	...	...	...
Talladega, AL........................	01121	54,526	62.8	74.5	4,477	65.2	11.9	-15.5	14.6	5.6	...	...	...
Tallapoosa, AL......................	01123	28,403	58.1	73.4	1,342	87.7	15.9	-11.5	19.4	5.5	...	...	...
Tuscaloosa, AL......................	01125	108,975	47.7	83.6	23,020	93.9	26.3	-1.1	29.6	17.4	...	...	7.4
Walker, AL............................	01127	48,135	60.2	75.7	2,346	89.1	9.2	-18.2	9.4	4.7	...	...	11.4
Washington, AL	01129	...	...	...	...	...	...	...	...	...	...	...	...
Wilcox, AL............................	01131	...	...	...	...	...	...	...	...	...	...	...	...
Winston, AL..........................	01133	16,961	63.0	67.1	...	...	10.3	-17.1	10.7	...	...	...	...

[3]May be of any race
... Not available

Table C-1. Population, School, and Student Characteristics by County—*Continued*

County	State/ County Code	County Type[1]	Population, 2009 Total	Population, 2009 Percent 5–17 years	Percent of related children 5-17 years in poverty, 2008	Percent of children under 19 years with no health insurance, 2007	Number of Schools and Students, 2008-2009 School Districts	Schools	Students	Resident enrollment, 2006-2008 K–12 enrollment Number	Percent public
			1	2	3	4	5	6	7	8	9
ALASKA	02000	X	698,473	18.5	10.5	12.8	54	516	130,662	131,578	92.3
Aleutians East Borough, AK	02013	9	2,744	8.5	9.2	15.3	1	7	275	...	...
Aleutians West Census Area, AK	02016	7	4,659	11.9	6.9	10.6	2	4	519	...	...
Anchorage, AK	02020	2	286,174	18.0	7.9	11.2	3	105	49,122	51,928	93.4
Bethel, AK	02050	7	17,352	24.1	26.7	11.1	3	41	4,791	...	...
Bristol Bay, AK	02060	9	881	15.1	9.8	17.4	2	17	566	...	...
Denali Borough	02068	8	1,851	17.0	6.3	15.6	1	4	425	...	...
Dillingham, AK	02070	9	4,957	22.8	22.9	15.5	2	11	1,138	...	...
Fairbanks North Star, AK	02090	3	98,660	17.6	7.5	13.3	2	44	15,741	18,122	87.5
Haines, AK	02100	9	2,399	14.5	13.8	16.6	1	4	312	...	...
Hoonah-Angoon, AK	02105		2,127	14.9	19.3	...	3	8	298	...	...
Juneau, AK	02110	5	30,796	16.6	6.8	10.9	1	14	5,036	5,464	93.6
Kenai Peninsula, AK	02122	7	54,665	17.5	11.2	12.6	1	44	9,487	10,228	92.2
Ketchikan Gateway, AK	02130	7	13,005	17.5	9.2	12.0	1	10	2,164	...	...
Kodiak Island, AK	02150	7	13,346	20.6	7.7	16.0	1	16	2,618	...	...
Lake and Peninsula Borough, AK	02164	9	1,485	20.7	22.2	20.7	...	...	...	...	...
Matanuska-Susitna, AK	02170	2	88,379	20.0	10.5	16.9	1	42	16,468	17,574	88.2
Nome, AK	02180	7	9,391	21.4	24.1	12.5	2	20	2,354	...	...
North Slope, AK	02185	7	6,752	22.0	10.0	10.1	1	11	1,820	...	...
Northwest Arctic Borough, AK	02188	7	7,444	24.0	15.8	8.9	1	12	2,011	...	...
Petersburg, AK	02195		3,773	16.7	...	...	2	4	622	...	...
Prince of Wales-Hyder, AK	02198		5,560	18.0	...	...	5	21	1,376	...	...
Prince of Wales-Outer Ketchikan, AK	02201	9	...	...	17.6	15.7	...	...	...	...	...
Sitka, AK	02220	7	8,747	16.0	7.4	12.7	2	7	1,761	...	...
Skagway Municipality, AK	02230		920	12.9	5.1	...	1	1	100	...	...
Skagway-Hoonah-Angoon, AK	02232	9	...	...	...	15.4	...	...	...	...	...
Southeast Fairbanks, AK	02240	8	6,892	21.5	16.0	22.1	2	15	1,632	...	...
Valdez-Cordova, AK	02261	9	9,324	18.2	8.7	16.2	3	13	1,581	...	...
Wade Hampton, AK	02270	9	7,731	26.7	35.1	13.8	3	13	2,571	...	...
Wrangell City and Borough, AK	02275		2,147	16.6	...	...	1	3	325	...	...
Wrangell-Petersburg, AK	02280	7	...	...	10.6	13.2	...	...	...	...	...
Yakutat Borough	02282	9	685	18.2	12.9	19.2	1	1	124	...	...
Yukon-Koyukuk, AK	02290	8	5,627	19.3	27.8	13.7	5	24	5,425	...	...
ARIZONA	04000	X	6,595,778	18.4	19.2	15.0	649	2,234	1,087,631	1,162,745	93.2
Apache, AZ	04001	6	70,591	23.4	36.1	7.8	14	44	13,357	16,424	96.2
Cochise, AZ	04003	4	129,518	16.9	22.6	14.2	30	73	20,670	22,059	92.3
Coconino, AZ	04005	3	129,849	18.1	20.6	14.0	21	64	20,613	22,611	96.4
Gila, AZ	04007	4	52,199	16.3	26.4	9.8	14	36	8,304	8,620	91.9
Graham, AZ	04009	6	37,045	19.2	22.1	10.6	15	34	6,442	6,636	94.2
Greenlee, AZ	04011	7	8,041	23.1	11.7	8.8	8	9	1,908	...	...
La Paz, AZ	04012	6	20,012	13.1	35.7	10.5	7	13	2,635	2,484	97.6
Maricopa, AZ	04013	1	4,023,132	19.0	17.1	15.6	285	1,141	690,411	724,025	93.3
Mohave, AZ	04015	4	194,825	15.6	23.6	11.1	24	62	26,909	30,384	93.0
Navajo, AZ	04017	4	112,975	21.8	30.6	11.5	23	82	20,310	25,448	97.2
Pima, AZ	04019	2	1,020,200	16.6	20.5	13.8	87	382	149,742	169,735	91.4
Pinal, AZ	04021	1	340,962	18.5	17.4	13.8	33	109	50,829	53,666	91.9
Santa Cruz, AZ	04023	4	43,771	22.4	29.1	17.6	13	27	10,631	12,026	98.4
Yavapai, AZ	04025	3	215,686	14.1	17.9	17.5	55	90	26,388	29,613	91.1
Yuma, AZ	04027	3	196,972	20.4	31.9	19.6	17	64	37,802	37,283	96.2
ARKANSAS	05000	X	2,889,450	17.5	22.4	11.7	295	1,151	478,965	494,409	92.1
Arkansas, AR	05001	6	18,971	18.1	23.6	9.6	4	12	3,362	...	...
Ashley, AR	05003	7	21,941	18.3	25.2	9.7	2	11	4,102	4,159	96.2
Baxter, AR	05005	7	42,157	13.4	26.6	13.2	3	10	5,114	6,016	97.1
Benton, AR	05007	2	225,504	19.4	13.7	13.5	9	57	36,407	37,716	92.0
Boone, AR	05009	7	36,821	17.1	21.3	11.4	8	20	6,374	5,822	96.1
Bradley, AR	05011	6	11,790	16.3	31.3	12.6	2	8	2,046	...	...
Calhoun, AR	05013	9	5,196	16.3	21.3	14.4	1	2	651	...	...
Carroll, AR	05015	6	27,938	16.1	24.0	21.8	3	10	3,821	4,332	94.0
Chicot, AR	05017	7	11,823	17.5	41.9	6.0	2	7	1,835	...	...
Clark, AR	05019	7	23,835	14.6	24.4	12.2	4	11	4,003	3,314	100.0
Clay, AR	05021	7	15,585	16.1	25.0	7.8	3	7	2,822	...	...
Cleburne, AR	05023	6	25,600	14.8	21.8	12.9	4	10	3,372	3,526	89.1
Cleveland, AR	05025	3	8,436	17.5	25.1	13.5	2	5	1,435	...	...
Columbia, AR	05027	7	23,854	16.8	27.1	9.2	2	9	3,689	3,971	90.7
Conway, AR	05029	6	20,799	17.6	23.0	10.7	4	11	3,355	3,663	96.4
Craighead, AR	05031	3	95,457	17.2	21.0	11.5	8	37	16,340	15,825	92.3
Crawford, AR	05033	2	60,102	19.4	20.3	11.2	5	25	11,393	11,786	91.3
Crittenden, AR	05035	1	53,022	20.8	27.3	9.2	5	24	11,131	11,582	95.5
Cross, AR	05037	6	18,544	18.7	25.5	12.0	2	7	3,689	...	...

[1]County type codes are from the Economic Research Service of the United States Department of Agriculture. See notes and definitions for more information.
... Not available

Table C-1. Population, School, and Student Characteristics by County—*Continued*

County	State/County Code	Characteristics of students, 2008-2009				Number of graduates, 2006-2007	Staff and students, 2008-2009			
		Percent with IEP[2]	Percent eligible for free or reduced lunch	Percent minority	Percent English Language Learners		Total staff	Number of teachers	Student/ teacher ratio	Central admin. Staff
		10	11	12	13	14	15	16	17	18
ALASKA	02000	13.5	34.1	46.7	9.2	7,939	16,962	7,925	16.5	1,277
Aleutians East Borough, AK	02013	11.3	41.8	90.2	...	15	60	34	8.1	4
Aleutians West Census Area, AK	02016	9.8	13.1	72.8	21.6	34	89	42	12.4	7
Anchorage, AK	02020	14.0	32.6	50.7	8.7	2,946	5,930	2,856	17.2	414
Bethel, AK	02050	14.2	70.0	96.3	68.1	194	887	364	13.2	103
Bristol Bay, AK	02060	11.1	46.0	66.5	0.2	39	154	60	9.4	17
Denali Borough	02068	9.2	...	23.1	...	22	58	26	16.3	8
Dillingham, AK	02070	16.0	71.4	94.7	27.7	86	271	99	11.5	28
Fairbanks North Star, AK	02090	14.0	20.1	31.0	2.6	979	1,944	849	18.5	131
Haines, AK	02100	14.4	32.6	25.9	0.3	16	54	22	14.2	2
Hoonah-Angoon, AK	02105	14.1	36.9	75.5	26.2	...	76	30	9.9	9
Juneau, AK	02110	14.9	18.5	43.4	7.6	354	703	333	15.1	48
Kenai Peninsula, AK	02122	14.0	29.8	20.1	2.1	672	1,106	570	16.6	60
Ketchikan Gateway, AK	02130	12.1	32.0	46.2	2.4	142	334	152	14.2	24
Kodiak Island, AK	02150	14.0	41.3	55.6	11.7	200	382	177	14.8	34
Lake and Peninsula Borough, AK	02164	...	66.2	86.9	...	...	...	...	...	...
Matanuska-Susitna, AK	02170	14.1	29.7	19.7	2.5	895	1,734	949	17.4	118
Nome, AK	02180	13.1	80.0	95.3	41.2	113	532	221	10.7	26
North Slope, AK	02185	11.3	44.0	95.1	29.0	133	382	135	13.5	34
Northwest Arctic Borough, AK	02188	12.3	74.4	96.8	...	99	347	143	14.1	28
Petersburg, AK	02195	19.1	52.1	39.7	2.1	...	106	50	12.4	9
Prince of Wales-Hyder, AK	02198	14.7	46.0	53.1	0.1	...	226	101	13.6	20
Prince of Wales-Outer Ketchikan, AK	02201	...	...	...	...	76	...	...	...	...
Sitka, AK	02220	12.2	31.3	59.7	7.2	155	240	125	14.1	19
Skagway Municipality, AK	02230	17.0	8.0	15.0	...	...	21	12	8.3	3
Skagway-Hoonah-Angoon, AK	02232	...	...	...	...	34	...	...	...	...
Southeast Fairbanks, AK	02240	10.5	35.9	36.4	14.7	100	190	92	17.7	18
Valdez-Cordova, AK	02261	14.7	30.4	37.9	2.2	126	274	110	14.4	19
Wade Hampton, AK	02270	10.5	85.9	98.8	5.0	131	436	194	13.3	41
Wrangell City and Borough, AK	02275	10.5	...	36.6	...	...	52	24	13.5	6
Wrangell-Petersburg, AK	02280	...	...	...	...	83	...	...	...	...
Yakutat Borough	02282	12.1	66.9	79.0	...	11	25	13	9.5	4
Yukon-Koyukuk, AK	02290	7.1	17.6	64.7	3.8	284	353	141	38.5	42
ARIZONA	04000	11.4	47.5	55.6	11.5	55,939	105,507	54,692	19.9	1,169
Apache, AZ	04001	13.7	71.3	83.5	12.5	801	2,021	838	15.9	39
Cochise, AZ	04003	11.3	50.1	57.5	11.6	1,280	2,302	1,078	19.2	58
Coconino, AZ	04005	14.7	44.0	56.9	8.2	1,522	2,634	1,218	16.9	39
Gila, AZ	04007	13.9	57.8	46.2	3.0	492	1,023	484	17.2	29
Graham, AZ	04009	12.6	47.5	47.3	0.2	336	741	382	16.9	19
Greenlee, AZ	04011	9.6	31.3	57.8	0.1	56	217	107	17.8	8
La Paz, AZ	04012	15.6	71.8	66.0	8.2	173	382	157	16.8	15
Maricopa, AZ	04013	10.8	44.6	54.0	12.1	35,096	63,103	33,806	20.4	540
Mohave, AZ	04015	12.2	52.1	28.9	4.0	1,412	2,473	1,285	20.9	31
Navajo, AZ	04017	13.4	62.1	58.8	11.4	974	2,470	1,210	16.8	51
Pima, AZ	04019	12.7	46.5	61.1	10.2	8,506	15,335	7,870	19.0	148
Pinal, AZ	04021	12.7	51.3	54.2	6.2	1,321	5,422	2,606	19.5	85
Santa Cruz, AZ	04023	8.7	75.0	95.7	26.4	590	1,079	557	19.1	11
Yavapai, AZ	04025	10.5	39.9	28.3	5.2	1,442	2,604	1,312	20.1	50
Yuma, AZ	04027	10.3	74.2	82.6	23.7	1,938	3,703	1,783	21.2	47
ARKANSAS	05000	13.5	57.1	33.4	5.8	27,166	71,270	37,162	12.9	3,000
Arkansas, AR	05001	11.3	60.6	36.6	1.2	242	572	314	10.7	29
Ashley, AR	05003	9.2	76.4	39.1	4.8	240	620	313	13.1	24
Baxter, AR	05005	8.8	53.1	2.7	0.3	85	677	385	13.3	34
Benton, AR	05007	9.8	43.9	28.9	16.8	1,671	5,041	2,484	14.7	171
Boone, AR	05009	16.7	52.6	3.1	0.1	372	1,016	534	11.9	40
Bradley, AR	05011	9.3	70.9	51.0	9.0	139	392	185	11.1	16
Calhoun, AR	05013	8.8	56.8	32.4	1.7	60	94	52	12.5	4
Carroll, AR	05015	9.9	60.4	24.4	15.1	254	648	330	11.6	32
Chicot, AR	05017	9.2	93.7	86.4	4.3	122	345	158	11.6	25
Clark, AR	05019	27.7	56.6	36.2	3.9	245	640	322	12.4	27
Clay, AR	05021	15.1	58.4	1.6	0.2	158	459	240	11.8	14
Cleburne, AR	05023	12.1	51.5	3.3	0.7	262	528	291	11.6	27
Cleveland, AR	05025	10.2	45.5	18.5	...	101	236	128	11.2	10
Columbia, AR	05027	9.6	60.4	53.6	0.8	228	561	315	11.7	22
Conway, AR	05029	37.9	59.8	23.8	2.0	193	509	270	12.4	20
Craighead, AR	05031	11.8	52.0	26.6	2.2	912	2,151	1,212	13.5	87
Crawford, AR	05033	10.8	52.8	14.1	4.2	717	1,586	829	13.7	67
Crittenden, AR	05035	12.0	81.7	69.0	0.3	623	1,516	791	14.1	64
Cross, AR	05037	12.3	64.3	29.7	0.1	290	512	285	12.9	23

[2]IEP= Individual Education Program. See notes and definitions for more information
... Not available

Table C-1. Population, School, and Student Characteristics by County—*Continued*

County	State/County Code	Revenues, 2007-2008				Current expenditures, 2007-2008			Resident population 16 to 19 years, 2006-2008			
		Total revenue ($1,000's)	Percentage of revenue from			Amount ($1,000's)	Amount per student	Percent for instruction	Total population 16 to 19 years	Percent enrolled in school	Percent high school graduates, not enrolled in school	Percent not enrolled, not grads, not employed or not in labor force
			Federal gov't	State gov't	Local gov't							
		19	20	21	22	23	24	25	26	27	28	29
ALASKA	02000	2,188,587	13.9	64.9	21.3	1,911,066	14,630	58.3	44,805	77.3	15.1	4.5
Aleutians East Borough, AK	02013	8,215	19.5	66.6	13.9	7,903	27,926	58.1	...	...	...	...
Aleutians West Census Area, AK	02016	12,012	11.0	51.4	37.6	10,720	21,355	57.9	...	...	...	...
Anchorage, AK	02020	658,541	9.8	60.6	29.6	618,472	12,587	59.6	16,164	79.8	11.7	4.3
Bethel, AK	02050	154,947	29.8	67.4	2.7	111,293	22,961	54.7	...	...	...	...
Bristol Bay, AK	02060	23,064	17.1	57.1	25.8	18,126	30,567	49.4	...	...	...	...
Denali Borough	02068	7,808	2.7	75.4	21.9	7,573	11,687	54.9	...	...	...	...
Dillingham, AK	02070	43,605	21.2	71.8	7.0	29,911	25,370	51.2	...	...	...	...
Fairbanks North Star, AK	02090	225,488	13.5	65.2	21.3	221,005	14,186	59.6	6,297	71.3	20.0	5.5
Haines, AK	02100	5,956	10.1	59.8	30.1	5,304	16,627	59.7	...	...	...	...
Hoonah-Angoon, AK	02105	11,323	23.2	70.0	6.8	8,919	27,613	56.5	...	...	...	...
Juneau, AK	02110	76,123	7.5	59.8	32.7	70,238	13,748	60.5	...	...	...	...
Kenai Peninsula, AK	02122	138,313	6.1	64.3	29.5	128,416	13,537	59.6	...	...	...	...
Ketchikan Gateway, AK	02130	33,624	10.0	65.6	24.4	33,133	14,570	61.4	...	...	...	...
Kodiak Island, AK	02150	45,485	10.4	68.1	21.5	44,427	16,522	56.2	...	...	...	...
Lake and Peninsula Borough, AK	02164	...	...	...	...	...	...	...	...	...	...	...
Matanuska-Susitna, AK	02170	212,855	6.8	70.7	22.5	201,739	12,485	59.0	7,660	78.7	15.4	3.4
Nome, AK	02180	102,093	21.0	73.6	5.4	60,717	25,437	61.1	...	...	...	...
North Slope, AK	02185	56,786	19.3	35.7	44.9	54,418	29,194	52.1	...	...	...	...
Northwest Arctic Borough, AK	02188	79,567	16.7	73.1	10.2	48,936	25,199	52.5	...	...	...	...
Petersburg, AK	02195	...	...	...	...	...	...	...	...	...	...	...
Prince of Wales-Hyder, AK	02198	...	...	...	...	...	...	...	...	...	...	...
Prince of Wales-Outer Ketchikan, AK	02201	30,558	32.6	61.3	6.0	26,889	19,043	57.7	...	...	...	...
Sitka, AK	02220	23,287	10.4	61.2	28.4	21,508	15,363	67.3	...	...	...	...
Skagway Municipality, AK	02230	3,529	26.3	36.9	36.8	2,980	27,091	68.2	...	...	...	...
Skagway-Hoonah-Angoon, AK	02232	12,632	30.2	52.5	17.3	10,384	20,851	65.0	...	...	...	...
Southeast Fairbanks, AK	02240	26,643	13.5	84.3	2.2	23,791	14,263	55.7	...	...	...	...
Valdez-Cordova, AK	02261	40,581	5.7	71.4	22.9	30,167	18,010	57.0	...	...	...	...
Wade Hampton, AK	02270	86,245	36.3	61.1	2.6	55,439	21,631	54.8	...	...	...	...
Wrangell City and Borough, AK	02275	...	...	...	...	...	...	...	...	...	...	...
Wrangell-Petersburg, AK	02280	18,266	11.3	69.0	19.7	17,129	16,959	58.8	...	...	...	...
Yakutat Borough	02282	2,919	16.2	60.0	23.8	2,811	23,041	63.7	...	...	...	...
Yukon-Koyukuk, AK	02290	60,754	11.9	83.6	4.5	49,102	9,188	52.4	...	...	...	...
ARIZONA	04000	10,066,505	10.5	51.1	38.5	8,145,365	7,504	56.3	345,169	78.8	11.9	5.5
Apache, AZ	04001	181,723	42.9	42.0	15.1	147,371	10,962	48.5	5,929	70.3	20.4	8.0
Cochise, AZ	04003	192,623	15.3	55.6	29.0	167,493	8,085	56.4	7,669	74.3	15.3	8.8
Coconino, AZ	04005	222,627	19.2	40.2	40.6	188,273	8,956	54.7	9,486	84.9	7.0	6.5
Gila, AZ	04007	78,321	21.3	47.4	31.4	71,414	8,495	55.1	...	...	...	...
Graham, AZ	04009	53,072	15.9	63.5	20.7	49,509	7,910	58.1	...	...	...	...
Greenlee, AZ	04011	14,857	5.2	25.7	69.1	13,002	7,300	55.3	...	...	...	...
La Paz, AZ	04012	27,927	32.0	41.2	26.8	25,744	9,585	51.0	...	...	...	...
Maricopa, AZ	04013	6,268,005	7.9	49.7	42.4	5,026,184	7,278	57.6	201,321	78.9	12.1	5.0
Mohave, AZ	04015	215,216	12.2	49.1	38.7	186,176	6,760	57.2	8,629	66.6	14.7	10.4
Navajo, AZ	04017	236,003	30.7	48.9	20.4	197,916	9,545	52.6	8,158	78.8	10.6	5.4
Pima, AZ	04019	1,377,855	10.5	53.0	36.5	1,159,494	7,835	54.6	57,495	83.9	8.8	4.3
Pinal, AZ	04021	550,263	7.9	64.6	27.5	358,419	7,448	53.2	14,942	74.2	12.3	10.5
Santa Cruz, AZ	04023	102,468	12.2	58.1	29.7	81,111	7,519	54.0	...	...	...	...
Yavapai, AZ	04025	214,841	8.7	50.6	40.7	191,150	7,147	57.5	9,882	71.8	13.5	6.4
Yuma, AZ	04027	325,671	16.6	58.6	24.8	276,755	7,298	52.0	11,072	76.5	15.6	4.9
ARKANSAS	05000	4,615,619	10.6	56.3	33.1	4,076,607	8,545	58.7	161,891	80.2	12.5	5.2
Arkansas, AR	05001	29,870	11.5	55.5	33.0	28,457	8,497	59.5	...	...	...	...
Ashley, AR	05003	39,720	12.0	54.7	33.3	35,428	8,419	58.1	...	...	...	...
Baxter, AR	05005	43,220	10.2	46.9	42.9	41,402	8,074	60.8	...	...	...	...
Benton, AR	05007	330,309	6.4	46.1	47.5	281,192	8,007	61.4	10,904	79.8	14.7	5.0
Boone, AR	05009	64,720	8.7	61.7	29.6	55,497	8,612	60.1	...	...	...	...
Bradley, AR	05011	21,691	13.4	63.7	22.9	19,334	9,094	56.3	...	...	...	...
Calhoun, AR	05013	6,085	9.7	52.0	38.3	5,763	8,364	54.6	...	...	...	...
Carroll, AR	05015	37,417	9.2	55.1	35.7	30,528	8,004	59.7	...	...	...	...
Chicot, AR	05017	23,315	19.4	52.9	27.7	18,267	9,863	53.5	...	...	...	...
Clark, AR	05019	50,561	15.3	58.0	26.7	44,667	10,988	48.4	...	...	...	...
Clay, AR	05021	23,313	10.9	58.6	30.5	22,565	7,813	63.2	...	...	...	...
Cleburne, AR	05023	31,581	10.8	46.2	43.0	27,510	7,838	60.2	...	...	...	...
Cleveland, AR	05025	13,840	12.9	61.3	25.8	12,122	8,406	58.0	...	...	...	...
Columbia, AR	05027	34,593	10.9	57.2	32.0	30,235	8,141	56.7	...	...	...	...
Conway, AR	05029	44,666	8.4	57.9	33.7	35,443	10,391	49.0	...	...	...	...
Craighead, AR	05031	140,513	10.1	57.0	32.9	122,675	7,666	60.4	...	...	...	...
Crawford, AR	05033	102,400	9.6	62.6	27.8	90,566	7,873	59.1	...	...	...	...
Crittenden, AR	05035	108,550	14.5	62.5	23.0	94,826	8,389	59.4	...	...	...	...
Cross, AR	05037	34,110	11.9	63.8	24.3	29,327	7,909	60.4	...	...	...	...

... Not available

Table C-1. Population, School, and Student Characteristics by County—*Continued*

County	State/ County Code	High school graduates, 2006-2008			College enrollment, 2006-2008		College graduates, 2006-2008 (percent)						
		Population 25 years and over	High school diploma or less (percent)	High school diploma or more (percent)	Number	Percent public	Bachelor's degree or more	+/- U.S. percent with Bachelor's degree or more	Non-Hispanic White	Black or African American	American Indian and Alaska Native	Asian, Hawaiian, and Pacific Islander	Hispanic or Latino[3]
		30	31	32	33	34	35	36	37	38	39	40	41
ALASKA	02000	422,721	37.9	90.6	46,927	83.6	26.5	-0.9	31.8	17.0	5.4	23.2	16.9
Aleutians East Borough, AK	02013	...	...	...	...	...	...	...	...	...	...	...	...
Aleutians West Census Area, AK	02016	...	...	...	...	...	...	...	...	...	...	...	...
Anchorage, AK	02020	175,812	31.9	91.8	21,642	80.2	32.4	5.0	37.7	18.8	9.1	24.2	19.9
Bethel, AK	02050	...	...	...	...	...	...	...	...	...	...	...	...
Bristol Bay, AK	02060	...	...	...	...	...	...	...	...	...	...	...	...
Denali Borough	02068	...	...	...	...	...	...	...	...	...	...	...	...
Dillingham, AK	02070	...	...	...	...	...	...	...	...	...	...	...	...
Fairbanks North Star, AK	02090	56,997	34.5	93.2	9,554	90.9	25.4	-2.0	28.6	14.5	5.2	33.0	15.9
Haines, AK	02100	...	...	...	...	...	...	...	...	...	...	...	...
Hoonah-Angoon, AK	02105	...	...	...	...	...	...	...	...	...	...	...	...
Juneau, AK	02110	20,161	27.7	95.1	2,133	88.3	36.8	9.4	41.7	...	13.0	33.3	...
Kenai Peninsula, AK	02122	34,776	45.1	91.8	3,005	86.0	21.0	-6.4	22.1	...	3.6	...	12.3
Ketchikan Gateway, AK	02130	...	...	...	...	...	...	...	...	...	...	...	...
Kodiak Island, AK	02150	...	...	...	...	...	...	...	...	...	...	...	...
Lake and Peninsula Borough, AK	02164	...	...	...	...	...	...	...	...	...	...	...	...
Matanuska-Susitna, AK	02170	48,763	43.1	89.6	4,808	87.0	19.7	-7.7	21.2	...	5.6	23.6	9.2
Nome, AK	02180	...	...	...	...	...	...	...	...	...	...	...	...
North Slope, AK	02185	...	...	...	...	...	...	...	...	...	...	...	...
Northwest Arctic Borough, AK	02188	...	...	...	...	...	...	...	...	...	...	...	...
Petersburg, AK	02195	...	...	...	...	...	...	...	...	...	...	...	...
Prince of Wales-Hyder, AK	02198	...	...	...	...	...	...	...	...	...	...	...	...
Prince of Wales-Outer Ketchikan, AK	02201	...	...	...	...	...	...	...	...	...	...	...	...
Sitka, AK	02220	...	...	...	...	...	...	...	...	...	...	...	...
Skagway Municipality, AK	02230	...	...	...	...	...	...	...	...	...	...	...	...
Skagway-Hoonah-Angoon, AK	02232	...	...	...	...	...	...	...	...	...	...	...	...
Southeast Fairbanks, AK	02240	...	...	...	...	...	...	...	...	...	...	...	...
Valdez-Cordova, AK	02261	...	...	...	...	...	...	...	...	...	...	...	...
Wade Hampton, AK	02270	...	...	...	...	...	...	...	...	...	...	...	...
Wrangell City and Borough, AK	02275	...	...	...	...	...	...	...	...	...	...	...	...
Wrangell-Petersburg, AK	02280	...	...	...	...	...	...	...	...	...	...	...	...
Yakutat Borough	02282	...	...	...	...	...	...	...	...	...	...	...	...
Yukon-Koyukuk, AK	02290	...	...	...	...	...	...	...	...	...	...	...	...
ARIZONA	04000	4,082,038	42.4	83.7	403,438	82.7	25.3	-2.1	31.0	23.2	8.8	48.2	9.5
Apache, AZ	04001	39,124	61.7	70.1	2,872	92.0	9.9	-17.5	20.8	...	6.4	...	5.5
Cochise, AZ	04003	84,024	40.5	84.4	7,675	86.8	21.5	-5.9	25.9	18.6	15.1	32.2	9.4
Coconino, AZ	04005	75,832	35.7	87.9	16,610	95.6	32.5	5.1	43.3	...	11.3	47.9	16.6
Gila, AZ	04007	35,640	52.3	83.1	2,040	88.9	13.0	-14.4	15.2	...	3.3	...	8.6
Graham, AZ	04009	20,912	52.6	81.5	2,624	96.9	14.1	-13.3	19.5	...	6.1	...	5.1
Greenlee, AZ	04011	...	...	...	...	...	...	...	...	...	...	...	...
La Paz, AZ	04012	14,976	61.9	76.2	315	79.7	7.2	-20.2	7.2	...	...	...	3.5
Maricopa, AZ	04013	2,462,070	41.0	83.9	238,262	81.2	27.5	0.1	33.4	24.4	11.3	51.1	9.3
Mohave, AZ	04015	138,410	54.7	81.3	5,906	85.2	11.0	-16.4	11.4	13.8	5.2	23.8	7.5
Navajo, AZ	04017	64,810	52.0	80.2	5,232	85.7	13.1	-14.3	20.1	15.4	6.2	...	5.6
Pima, AZ	04019	654,944	38.4	86.7	82,626	86.5	28.9	1.5	36.1	22.3	10.3	43.5	12.1
Pinal, AZ	04021	193,112	47.6	82.8	15,143	75.0	18.0	-9.4	22.3	17.7	5.7	43.1	7.2
Santa Cruz, AZ	04023	24,471	63.7	66.8	1,944	75.9	15.9	-11.5	39.7	...	...	...	10.8
Yavapai, AZ	04025	151,834	41.2	87.5	13,077	67.5	23.0	-4.4	24.3	...	18.7	53.2	7.9
Yuma, AZ	04027	116,945	56.0	72.1	8,819	85.6	12.6	-14.8	18.0	13.7	16.5	35.1	5.7
ARKANSAS	05000	1,863,115	54.6	81.2	162,128	83.2	18.8	-8.6	20.3	12.1	15.5	38.4	8.5
Arkansas, AR	05001	...	...	...	...	...	...	...	...	...	...	...	...
Ashley, AR	05003	15,107	64.7	80.3	673	93.9	14.1	-13.3	18.0	5.2	...	...	...
Baxter, AR	05005	31,104	59.0	80.9	1,500	91.6	11.7	-15.7	11.9	...	...	...	...
Benton, AR	05007	129,040	48.5	83.4	8,728	69.5	24.7	-2.7	26.5	36.5	21.6	33.4	9.2
Boone, AR	05009	25,472	57.1	83.2	1,240	87.7	14.4	-13.0	14.3	...	...	...	...
Bradley, AR	05011	...	...	...	...	...	...	...	...	...	...	...	...
Calhoun, AR	05013	...	...	...	...	...	...	...	...	...	...	...	...
Carroll, AR	05015	18,971	61.2	75.9	830	85.2	14.0	-13.4	14.5	...	...	...	2.4
Chicot, AR	05017	...	...	...	...	...	...	...	...	...	...	...	...
Clark, AR	05019	13,833	53.5	80.3	3,964	59.4	24.1	-3.3	29.2	7.9	...	...	...
Clay, AR	05021	...	...	...	...	...	...	...	...	...	...	...	...
Cleburne, AR	05023	18,394	57.9	78.1	826	87.3	14.3	-13.1	14.1	...	...	...	...
Cleveland, AR	05025	...	...	...	...	...	...	...	...	...	...	...	...
Columbia, AR	05027	15,454	55.6	83.7	2,737	97.2	21.7	-5.7	27.5	9.7	...	...	...
Conway, AR	05029	13,930	64.3	77.8	886	92.8	12.9	-14.5	13.0	11.6	...	...	...
Craighead, AR	05031	57,583	51.3	84.5	7,896	92.1	23.2	-4.2	23.6	15.4	...	...	17.3
Crawford, AR	05033	38,412	58.1	76.3	2,160	93.7	11.4	-16.0	11.6	...	...	...	5.8
Crittenden, AR	05035	31,767	59.3	76.3	3,459	89.7	14.7	-12.7	18.8	9.3	...	...	...
Cross, AR	05037	...	...	...	...	...	...	...	...	...	...	...	...

[3]May be of any race
... Not available

Table C-1. Population, School, and Student Characteristics by County—*Continued*

County	State/County Code	County Type[1]	Population, 2009 Total	Population, 2009 Percent 5–17 years	Percent of related children 5-17 years in poverty, 2008	Percent of children under 19 years with no health insurance, 2007	Number of Schools and Students, 2008-2009 School Districts	Number of Schools and Students, 2008-2009 Schools	Number of Schools and Students, 2008-2009 Students	Resident enrollment, 2006-2008 K–12 enrollment Number	Resident enrollment, 2006-2008 K–12 enrollment Percent public
			1	2	3	4	5	6	7	8	9
Dallas, AR	05039	6	7,991	18.0	26.8	9.5	1	3	1,044	...	...
Desha, AR	05041	6	13,358	18.4	35.4	9.3	2	8	2,852	...	...
Drew, AR	05043	7	18,624	17.4	25.8	10.4	3	8	3,194	...	...
Faulkner, AR	05045	2	109,386	17.2	16.5	11.8	6	38	17,426	17,566	89.5
Franklin, AR	05047	2	18,016	17.9	21.0	10.9	3	7	2,799	...	...
Fulton, AR	05049	9	11,585	15.5	26.9	9.7	3	6	1,579	...	...
Garland, AR	05051	3	98,479	15.1	24.0	12.2	8	28	14,195	14,794	92.6
Grant, AR	05053	2	17,760	17.7	14.6	13.5	2	9	4,826	...	...
Greene, AR	05055	6	40,996	18.0	19.3	9.5	3	13	7,173	7,127	95.8
Hempstead, AR	05057	6	23,027	18.2	28.7	12.2	4	11	3,829	3,843	92.2
Hot Spring, AR	05059	6	31,787	16.6	20.3	10.4	6	15	5,426	5,770	95.6
Howard, AR	05061	7	14,291	18.6	29.6	12.8	3	10	3,141	...	...
Independence, AR	05063	7	34,634	16.8	20.4	10.0	5	18	6,028	5,243	96.9
Izard, AR	05065	9	13,038	14.5	28.6	12.6	4	9	1,851	...	...
Jackson, AR	05067	6	16,658	15.0	30.7	8.0	3	9	3,100	...	...
Jefferson, AR	05069	3	78,705	17.4	25.5	9.7	7	32	13,213	13,693	94.2
Johnson, AR	05071	6	24,994	18.2	24.4	12.1	3	10	4,301	4,234	96.2
Lafayette, AR	05073	8	7,504	15.9	30.8	9.9	2	4	1,162	...	...
Lawrence, AR	05075	6	16,882	16.6	32.7	7.2	6	13	3,297	...	...
Lee, AR	05077	6	10,319	15.2	38.7	6.8	1	4	1,264	...	...
Lincoln, AR	05079	3	13,553	14.2	27.5	12.7	1	3	1,751	...	...
Little River, AR	05081	6	12,952	16.5	22.3	9.8	2	7	2,074	...	...
Logan, AR	05083	6	22,342	17.9	22.9	9.1	5	12	4,194	3,983	97.7
Lonoke, AR	05085	2	66,677	20.0	13.7	12.6	4	23	13,249	11,865	93.5
Madison, AR	05087	2	15,875	17.3	25.2	15.1	1	6	2,424	...	...
Marion, AR	05089	9	16,594	13.4	27.8	11.3	2	6	1,833	...	...
Miller, AR	05091	3	43,522	16.8	26.9	12.2	3	15	6,587	8,428	92.3
Mississippi, AR	05093	4	46,605	20.1	32.0	8.0	8	29	9,115	9,686	98.5
Monroe, AR	05095	7	8,171	16.5	34.0	8.7	2	6	1,396	...	...
Montgomery, AR	05097	8	9,009	15.4	28.1	16.1	2	4	1,156	...	...
Nevada, AR	05099	7	9,164	17.1	28.2	7.8	2	5	1,461	...	...
Newton, AR	05101	9	8,191	15.3	32.4	12.6	2	10	1,338	...	...
Ouachita, AR	05103	7	25,432	16.5	27.2	9.1	6	16	4,661	4,392	89.7
Perry, AR	05105	2	10,312	17.5	22.2	15.4	2	4	1,724	...	...
Phillips, AR	05107	7	20,921	21.0	46.6	7.5	5	13	4,495	4,736	91.6
Pike, AR	05109	9	10,627	17.2	23.0	15.6	3	6	1,333	...	...
Poinsett, AR	05111	3	24,682	18.5	33.3	7.7	6	13	4,620	4,572	97.0
Polk, AR	05113	7	20,259	17.3	29.0	12.4	4	16	3,846	3,640	93.7
Pope, AR	05115	5	60,214	16.7	19.1	11.6	5	24	9,953	10,083	93.7
Prairie, AR	05117	8	8,582	15.1	23.6	12.6	2	5	1,308	...	...
Pulaski, AR	05119	2	381,904	17.2	22.7	9.7	16	125	56,878	66,880	80.9
Randolph, AR	05121	7	17,952	17.1	25.6	7.8	3	10	2,787	...	...
St. Francis, AR	05123	6	26,255	18.3	37.3	10.9	4	11	4,808	4,385	89.6
Saline, AR	05125	2	99,449	18.0	11.8	12.0	5	23	14,479	16,848	92.8
Scott, AR	05127	6	11,123	18.6	27.7	9.9	2	6	2,757	...	...
Searcy, AR	05129	9	7,944	14.6	39.0	8.3	2	10	1,660	...	...
Sebastian, AR	05131	2	123,597	18.2	21.7	13.5	6	39	19,511	22,411	92.4
Sevier, AR	05133	7	16,904	20.7	30.7	17.0	3	10	3,432	...	...
Sharp, AR	05135	7	17,664	15.5	30.7	10.1	2	8	2,978	...	...
Stone, AR	05137	9	11,991	14.4	32.3	14.2	1	7	1,713	...	...
Union, AR	05139	5	42,782	17.6	25.4	10.2	7	21	7,944	7,306	95.1
Van Buren, AR	05141	8	16,418	15.4	27.0	14.4	3	8	2,393	...	...
Washington, AR	05143	2	200,181	17.3	17.6	15.9	11	66	34,855	33,017	92.3
White, AR	05145	4	76,338	17.3	19.8	11.8	10	28	12,610	11,955	91.7
Woodruff, AR	05147	9	7,359	17.1	34.8	11.4	1	3	566	...	...
Yell, AR	05149	6	22,496	18.9	23.5	15.7	4	15	4,435	...	...
CALIFORNIA	06000	X	36,961,664	18.1	17.3	12.4	1,126	10,233	6,252,031	6,856,169	90.8
Alameda, CA	06001	1	1,491,482	16.1	12.1	7.7	27	408	215,062	247,376	88.6
Alpine, CA	06003	8	1,041	15.1	25.0	20.1	2	7	129	...	...
Amador, CA	06005	6	37,876	13.0	11.6	10.8	4	17	4,944	5,532	92.8
Butte, CA	06007	3	220,577	15.2	24.5	9.1	16	97	32,069	34,824	94.0
Calaveras, CA	06009	6	46,731	15.0	14.3	12.0	6	30	6,500	6,886	93.4
Colusa, CA	06011	6	21,321	21.7	18.9	19.2	6	27	4,743	4,690	97.1
Contra Costa, CA	06013	1	1,041,274	18.3	11.5	9.4	20	272	166,958	187,531	89.2
Del Norte, CA	06015	7	29,114	16.0	28.5	8.6	3	21	4,575	4,906	88.9
El Dorado, CA	06017	1	178,447	17.8	8.9	11.3	17	73	28,900	29,645	91.4
Fresno, CA	06019	2	915,267	21.0	28.6	10.2	37	340	193,838	193,940	96.1

[1]County type codes are from the Economic Research Service of the United States Department of Agriculture. See notes and definitions for more information.
... Not available

Table C-1. Population, School, and Student Characteristics by County—*Continued*

County	State/County Code	Characteristics of students, 2008-2009				Number of graduates, 2006-2007	Staff and students, 2008-2009			
		Percent with IEP[2]	Percent eligible for free or reduced lunch	Percent minority	Percent English Language Learners		Total staff	Number of teachers	Student/teacher ratio	Central admin. Staff
		10	11	12	13	14	15	16	17	18
Dallas, AR	05039	19.3	59.6	49.1	0.6	109	176	103	10.1	6
Desha, AR	05041	10.8	77.7	63.3	2.7	182	472	237	12.0	23
Drew, AR	05043	32.8	59.8	35.7	1.5	205	522	275	11.6	18
Faulkner, AR	05045	12.2	39.5	20.4	1.9	1,002	2,283	1,268	13.7	82
Franklin, AR	05047	22.7	44.6	6.0	0.5	198	367	206	13.6	16
Fulton, AR	05049	13.3	58.8	2.7	...	127	275	161	9.8	14
Garland, AR	05051	11.3	54.4	23.8	3.2	754	1,937	1,070	13.3	80
Grant, AR	05053	9.7	47.0	14.7	2.0	301	654	339	14.2	34
Greene, AR	05055	14.4	52.5	4.0	1.1	408	1,046	544	13.2	44
Hempstead, AR	05057	20.8	72.8	57.4	8.0	233	645	316	12.1	25
Hot Spring, AR	05059	11.4	57.5	18.1	1.5	330	851	454	12.0	31
Howard, AR	05061	10.1	65.1	39.2	6.7	209	493	282	11.1	17
Independence, AR	05063	19.3	54.8	11.4	3.9	387	1,023	518	11.6	44
Izard, AR	05065	32.0	57.3	2.9	...	132	362	174	10.6	15
Jackson, AR	05067	14.1	68.2	25.7	1.2	197	538	274	11.3	21
Jefferson, AR	05069	14.1	66.2	71.8	0.1	783	2,080	1,005	13.1	93
Johnson, AR	05071	10.1	65.9	19.4	11.3	246	632	322	13.4	20
Lafayette, AR	05073	10.8	77.6	57.2	0.1	84	218	114	10.2	12
Lawrence, AR	05075	22.9	64.5	1.5	...	208	533	311	10.6	28
Lee, AR	05077	14.4	99.1	92.7	0.1	78	251	112	11.3	15
Lincoln, AR	05079	9.0	59.3	29.6	1.2	112	264	133	13.2	14
Little River, AR	05081	10.3	52.4	31.6	...	160	375	186	11.2	19
Logan, AR	05083	10.7	55.8	8.2	1.5	263	678	381	11.0	27
Lonoke, AR	05085	12.0	39.0	12.0	0.9	674	1,755	931	14.2	72
Madison, AR	05087	7.9	55.2	8.7	5.4	155	341	180	13.5	8
Marion, AR	05089	12.9	58.8	2.5	...	110	302	177	10.4	16
Miller, AR	05091	10.6	61.9	37.4	0.1	331	1,043	504	13.1	48
Mississippi, AR	05093	12.2	80.8	50.7	1.2	439	1,512	740	12.3	63
Monroe, AR	05095	12.8	88.9	60.5	0.9	88	250	144	9.7	13
Montgomery, AR	05097	12.2	69.9	9.1	0.1	83	209	112	10.3	6
Nevada, AR	05099	13.1	72.8	45.7	0.6	91	262	133	11.0	13
Newton, AR	05101	15.4	66.3	5.4	0.3	124	327	180	7.4	13
Ouachita, AR	05103	16.7	70.0	57.3	0.4	373	824	406	11.5	39
Perry, AR	05105	14.2	48.4	4.9	...	106	251	136	12.7	8
Phillips, AR	05107	23.7	92.1	84.1	0.2	248	729	355	12.7	42
Pike, AR	05109	11.3	61.0	15.5	0.5	101	219	133	10.0	14
Poinsett, AR	05111	24.9	70.7	13.6	0.9	291	769	416	11.1	30
Polk, AR	05113	10.2	67.3	10.2	4.5	277	675	362	10.6	30
Pope, AR	05115	9.9	52.7	15.8	4.7	629	1,490	799	12.5	61
Prairie, AR	05117	9.6	63.3	23.5	...	87	234	120	10.9	10
Pulaski, AR	05119	17.1	59.9	65.1	3.7	2,626	8,765	4,392	13.0	386
Randolph, AR	05121	16.4	63.1	3.7	0.2	198	425	240	11.6	15
St. Francis, AR	05123	11.7	97.2	74.5	0.1	273	763	364	13.2	38
Saline, AR	05125	11.1	33.8	11.4	2.4	785	1,721	982	14.7	67
Scott, AR	05127	10.1	56.5	15.9	5.4	164	419	212	13.0	13
Searcy, AR	05129	17.3	72.1	2.9	0.1	112	413	198	8.4	16
Sebastian, AR	05131	13.1	56.9	37.3	15.4	1,155	2,646	1,343	14.5	124
Sevier, AR	05133	18.6	69.5	52.1	26.4	162	540	286	12.0	19
Sharp, AR	05135	11.0	63.6	3.1	...	167	454	248	12.0	12
Stone, AR	05137	11.6	61.0	2.9	0.1	99	273	163	10.5	13
Union, AR	05139	8.4	56.1	46.1	2.0	527	1,192	651	12.2	67
Van Buren, AR	05141	14.2	62.5	5.3	1.2	150	384	209	11.4	20
Washington, AR	05143	11.6	49.4	35.8	22.5	1,874	4,613	2,394	14.6	188
White, AR	05145	14.6	50.2	10.8	1.3	752	1,817	978	12.9	68
Woodruff, AR	05147	17.7	98.4	62.5	1.4	50	125	64	8.8	5
Yell, AR	05149	13.8	69.9	31.5	19.3	243	750	387	11.5	29
CALIFORNIA	06000	10.6	52.4	72.2	24.2	342,366	586,110	299,892	20.8	27,429
Alameda, CA	06001	10.4	38.8	76.5	22.2	12,932	20,030	11,035	19.5	1,065
Alpine, CA	06003	22.5	...	54.7	...	3	38	17	7.6	5
Amador, CA	06005	11.7	27.6	30.5	2.4	427	523	273	18.1	24
Butte, CA	06007	12.3	54.3	36.5	11.2	2,219	3,378	1,638	19.6	183
Calaveras, CA	06009	11.0	33.5	21.9	2.6	507	692	336	19.3	38
Colusa, CA	06011	3.7	66.6	73.4	33.6	272	524	277	17.1	31
Contra Costa, CA	06013	11.5	34.8	59.9	17.1	9,912	14,333	8,078	20.7	469
Del Norte, CA	06015	11.2	57.9	39.6	9.7	280	521	239	19.1	24
El Dorado, CA	06017	11.6	22.9	25.2	5.8	2,023	2,826	1,471	19.6	173
Fresno, CA	06019	9.3	65.5	78.0	25.2	9,568	18,812	9,730	19.9	805

[2]IEP= Individual Education Program. See notes and definitions for more information
... Not available

Table C-1. Population, School, and Student Characteristics by County—*Continued*

County	State/County Code	Total revenue ($1,000's)	Percentage of revenue from — Federal gov't	State gov't	Local gov't	Current expenditures, 2007-2008 Amount ($1,000's)	Amount per student	Percent for instruction	Resident population 16 to 19 years, 2006-2008 Total population 16 to 19 years	Percent enrolled in school	Percent high school graduates, not enrolled in school	Percent not enrolled, not grads, not employed or not in labor force
		19	20	21	22	23	24	25	26	27	28	29
Dallas, AR	05039	11,043	10.3	72.0	17.7	10,487	9,737	67.3	...	...	...	...
Desha, AR	05041	28,521	15.0	57.5	27.5	27,474	9,461	58.0	...	...	...	...
Drew, AR	05043	43,627	20.6	53.4	26.0	37,411	11,518	55.1	...	...	...	...
Faulkner, AR	05045	156,522	7.8	59.5	32.7	133,137	7,789	60.7	...	...	...	...
Franklin, AR	05047	29,646	20.5	53.0	26.5	25,488	8,865	50.9	...	...	...	...
Fulton, AR	05049	13,805	11.7	64.1	24.3	13,466	8,112	62.6	...	...	...	...
Garland, AR	05051	135,030	9.6	44.8	45.5	117,319	8,406	57.8	...	...	...	...
Grant, AR	05053	37,897	7.4	68.1	24.5	34,190	6,965	61.1	...	...	...	...
Greene, AR	05055	61,555	10.5	61.8	27.7	55,717	7,820	59.7	...	...	...	...
Hempstead, AR	05057	40,869	12.8	62.8	24.4	38,299	9,748	58.5	...	...	...	...
Hot Spring, AR	05059	51,630	9.6	55.7	34.7	44,237	8,026	59.1	...	...	...	...
Howard, AR	05061	26,930	11.8	59.4	28.8	24,969	8,039	63.2	...	...	...	...
Independence, AR	05063	60,408	10.5	56.6	32.9	51,167	8,403	58.8	...	...	...	...
Izard, AR	05065	23,906	9.7	60.4	29.8	19,220	10,566	51.8	...	...	...	...
Jackson, AR	05067	28,365	12.5	59.4	28.1	26,920	8,439	58.7	...	...	...	...
Jefferson, AR	05069	140,662	10.6	65.4	24.0	119,572	8,791	58.6	5376	73.5	16.6	8.5
Johnson, AR	05071	38,652	11.8	63.1	25.1	33,655	7,751	61.4	...	...	...	...
Lafayette, AR	05073	12,541	14.2	57.5	28.4	11,393	8,845	57.8	...	...	...	...
Lawrence, AR	05075	35,638	11.3	65.7	23.0	30,595	9,160	58.0	...	...	...	...
Lee, AR	05077	14,333	21.2	62.8	16.0	13,799	10,014	56.0	...	...	...	...
Lincoln, AR	05079	15,426	10.8	65.0	24.2	13,538	7,623	58.3	...	...	...	...
Little River, AR	05081	21,275	10.1	38.5	51.4	18,825	9,007	54.4	...	...	...	...
Logan, AR	05083	40,694	10.8	58.0	31.1	34,179	8,061	58.6	...	...	...	...
Lonoke, AR	05085	110,416	8.0	65.2	26.8	96,133	7,376	61.0	3268	78.2	7.9	10.7
Madison, AR	05087	21,305	11.9	63.8	24.3	20,379	8,119	59.0	...	...	...	...
Marion, AR	05089	17,217	10.9	57.2	31.8	15,705	8,314	61.6	...	...	...	...
Miller, AR	05091	65,652	13.3	59.7	26.9	58,253	8,832	59.0	...	...	...	...
Mississippi, AR	05093	84,255	13.3	64.1	22.7	78,891	8,763	57.2	...	...	...	...
Monroe, AR	05095	18,024	14.1	49.3	36.5	13,877	9,357	58.0	...	...	...	...
Montgomery, AR	05097	11,564	17.8	55.7	26.5	10,109	8,552	60.2	...	...	...	...
Nevada, AR	05099	13,388	11.9	60.3	27.8	12,569	8,385	54.3	...	...	...	...
Newton, AR	05101	15,736	17.6	63.1	19.3	13,737	10,391	57.9	...	...	...	...
Ouachita, AR	05103	52,421	15.1	63.2	21.7	49,249	10,150	55.2	...	...	...	...
Perry, AR	05105	14,270	11.1	67.9	21.1	13,304	7,542	59.6	...	...	...	...
Phillips, AR	05107	56,141	19.7	63.7	16.5	50,637	11,321	52.8	...	...	...	...
Pike, AR	05109	11,472	10.5	59.6	29.8	10,886	8,154	62.5	...	...	...	...
Poinsett, AR	05111	50,691	14.6	64.1	21.3	43,136	9,307	56.9	...	...	...	...
Polk, AR	05113	35,923	13.5	64.6	21.9	34,138	8,610	59.7	...	...	...	...
Pope, AR	05115	93,859	10.4	51.4	38.1	79,757	8,045	59.6	...	...	...	...
Prairie, AR	05117	12,069	10.2	58.2	31.7	11,324	8,376	57.6	...	...	...	...
Pulaski, AR	05119	617,418	9.0	48.9	42.1	553,255	9,999	56.3	18605	78.4	13.6	5.7
Randolph, AR	05121	25,761	11.5	66.1	22.3	22,858	7,998	62.5	...	...	...	...
St. Francis, AR	05123	46,902	15.5	66.0	18.5	45,229	9,089	56.5	...	...	...	...
Saline, AR	05125	112,646	6.8	62.2	31.0	99,752	7,134	63.2	4792	80.0	16.6	3.0
Scott, AR	05127	25,587	14.6	63.6	21.7	22,644	8,061	60.8	...	...	...	...
Searcy, AR	05129	18,226	13.1	63.7	23.3	17,133	9,955	57.5	...	...	...	...
Sebastian, AR	05131	177,029	11.7	52.6	35.7	159,744	8,170	57.9	6501	82.0	15.0	2.3
Sevier, AR	05133	37,682	12.1	69.7	18.2	33,690	9,953	58.1	...	...	...	...
Sharp, AR	05135	25,650	12.3	59.8	27.8	22,638	7,625	59.7	...	...	...	...
Stone, AR	05137	15,253	11.5	63.9	24.5	13,524	7,890	65.1	...	...	...	...
Union, AR	05139	68,030	10.4	56.9	32.7	64,760	8,047	60.4	...	...	...	...
Van Buren, AR	05141	22,338	11.9	54.6	33.4	18,813	7,858	60.5	...	...	...	...
Washington, AR	05143	319,570	8.3	51.9	39.8	285,323	8,358	60.6	11950	85.5	9.3	2.9
White, AR	05145	122,382	9.8	59.4	30.8	100,419	7,968	58.7	...	...	...	...
Woodruff, AR	05147	6,750	19.5	58.4	22.1	6,602	10,841	57.6	...	...	...	...
Yell, AR	05149	40,543	15.1	63.3	21.6	37,278	8,505	59.0	...	...	...	...
CALIFORNIA	06000	7,4507,354	9.7	57.9	32.4	60,964,266	9,742	59.9	2201500	83.5	10.1	3.9
Alameda, CA	06001	2,479,695	7.8	54.8	37.4	2,022,473	9,548	60.9	79417	87.0	7.3	3.8
Alpine, CA	06003	5,936	22.5	29.9	47.7	4,282	33,984	45.6	...	...	...	...
Amador, CA	06005	51,387	6.0	35.3	58.7	41,030	8,864	60.6	1810	72.7	22.7	3.5
Butte, CA	06007	399,071	15.9	54.7	29.4	331,043	10,167	58.4	15152	88.2	9.0	1.8
Calaveras, CA	06009	79,765	6.3	30.7	63.1	70,428	10,425	58.3	...	...	...	...
Colusa, CA	06011	64,395	11.8	61.7	26.5	53,336	11,210	60.3	...	...	...	...
Contra Costa, CA	06013	1,930,912	5.9	49.0	45.1	1,518,882	9,108	61.8	57709	86.5	8.9	2.8
Del Norte, CA	06015	49,710	17.0	61.9	21.1	46,982	10,390	62.6	...	...	...	...
El Dorado, CA	06017	336,921	7.7	50.8	41.5	276,091	9,424	59.9	...	...	...	...
Fresno, CA	06019	2,232,075	11.6	66.7	21.7	1,897,046	9,835	58.8	60660	81.4	10.1	6.0

... Not available

Table C-1. Population, School, and Student Characteristics by County—*Continued*

County	State/County Code	High school graduates, 2006-2008			College enrollment, 2006-2008		College graduates, 2006-2008 (percent)						
		Population 25 years and over	High school diploma or less (percent)	High school diploma or more (percent)	Number	Percent public	Bachelor's degree or more	+/- U.S. percent with Bachelor's degree or more	Non-Hispanic White	Black or African American	American Indian and Alaska Native	Asian, Hawaiian, and Pacific Islander	Hispanic or Latino[3]
		30	31	32	33	34	35	36	37	38	39	40	41
Dallas, AR	05039	...	...	...	...	...	...	...	...	...	...	...	...
Desha, AR	05041	...	...	...	...	...	...	...	...	...	...	...	...
Drew, AR	05043	...	...	...	...	...	...	...	...	...	...	...	...
Faulkner, AR	05045	62,361	45.6	87.9	12,973	83.2	26.1	-1.3	27.4	14.9	...	...	10.5
Franklin, AR	05047	...	...	...	...	...	...	...	...	...	...	...	...
Fulton, AR	05049	...	...	...	...	...	...	...	...	...	...	...	...
Garland, AR	05051	68,608	48.3	85.2	3,966	79.2	18.8	-8.6	19.6	12.7	...	...	5.3
Grant, AR	05053	...	...	...	...	...	...	...	...	...	...	...	...
Greene, AR	05055	27,291	64.1	78.0	1,775	85.3	12.4	-15.0	12.1	...	...	...	...
Hempstead, AR	05057	15,166	60.4	76.7	1,048	98.4	12.8	-14.6	16.8	8.4	...	...	2.0
Hot Spring, AR	05059	22,055	58.1	80.8	1,773	91.9	12.9	-14.5	13.5	10.4	...	...	...
Howard, AR	05061	...	...	...	...	...	...	...	...	...	...	...	...
Independence, AR	05063	23,650	58.5	80.8	1,903	59.4	13.2	-14.2	13.3	4.7	...	...	...
Izard, AR	05065	...	...	...	...	...	...	...	...	...	...	...	...
Jackson, AR	05067	...	...	...	...	...	...	...	...	...	...	...	...
Jefferson, AR	05069	51,208	58.3	80.1	6,485	90.5	16.4	-11.0	15.7	17.6	...	26.8	...
Johnson, AR	05071	16,046	64.3	74.7	1,250	46.7	15.6	-11.8	16.3	...	...	...	5.7
Lafayette, AR	05073	...	...	...	...	...	...	...	...	...	...	...	...
Lawrence, AR	05075	...	...	...	...	...	...	...	...	...	...	...	...
Lee, AR	05077	...	...	...	...	...	...	...	...	...	...	...	...
Lincoln, AR	05079	...	...	...	...	...	...	...	...	...	...	...	...
Little River, AR	05081	...	...	...	...	...	...	...	...	...	...	...	...
Logan, AR	05083	15,396	68.4	74.9	780	73.2	11.1	-16.3	11.2	...	...	...	...
Lonoke, AR	05085	41,158	51.8	84.6	3,254	89.5	16.6	-10.8	17.2	12.9	...	...	6.6
Madison, AR	05087	...	...	...	...	...	...	...	...	...	...	...	...
Marion, AR	05089	...	...	...	...	...	...	...	...	...	...	...	...
Miller, AR	05091	28,253	58.7	80.4	1,393	90.0	13.9	-13.5	14.7	11.1	...	...	...
Mississippi, AR	05093	29,536	62.9	74.2	1,351	97.4	10.2	-17.2	11.0	7.8	...	...	...
Monroe, AR	05095	...	...	...	...	...	...	...	...	...	...	...	...
Montgomery, AR	05097	...	...	...	...	...	...	...	...	...	...	...	...
Nevada, AR	05099	...	...	...	...	...	...	...	...	...	...	...	...
Newton, AR	05101	...	...	...	...	...	...	...	...	...	...	...	...
Ouachita, AR	05103	17,733	60.9	81.1	1,037	90.5	11.2	-16.2	14.7	5.0	...	...	...
Perry, AR	05105	...	...	...	...	...	...	...	...	...	...	...	...
Phillips, AR	05107	13,411	59.7	67.8	756	95.6	11.2	-16.2	14.6	8.3	...	...	...
Pike, AR	05109	...	...	...	...	...	...	...	...	...	...	...	...
Poinsett, AR	05111	16,662	72.7	73.7	750	80.5	8.3	-19.1	8.4	10.4	...	...	...
Polk, AR	05113	13,893	57.7	76.9	1,140	83.4	9.8	-17.6	9.8	...	...	...	...
Pope, AR	05115	37,473	54.9	81.6	4,684	95.1	19.8	-7.6	20.2	...	...	...	18.2
Prairie, AR	05117	...	...	...	...	...	...	...	...	...	...	...	...
Pulaski, AR	05119	246,711	39.8	88.8	22,335	83.0	31.3	3.9	38.2	16.5	30.9	54.1	15.5
Randolph, AR	05121	...	...	...	...	...	...	...	...	...	...	...	...
St. Francis, AR	05123	17,452	65.2	73.7	736	80.7	11.2	-16.2	13.0	8.8	...	...	...
Saline, AR	05125	65,324	50.2	84.9	4,421	84.2	21.1	-6.3	21.5	11.4	...	...	21.7
Scott, AR	05127	...	...	...	...	...	...	...	...	...	...	...	...
Searcy, AR	05129	...	...	...	...	...	...	...	...	...	...	...	...
Sebastian, AR	05131	79,451	51.6	81.1	4,322	89.1	17.4	-10.0	19.4	6.4	16.1	18.9	4.5
Sevier, AR	05133	...	...	...	...	...	...	...	...	...	...	...	...
Sharp, AR	05135	...	...	...	...	...	...	...	...	...	...	...	...
Stone, AR	05137	...	...	...	...	...	...	...	...	...	...	...	...
Union, AR	05139	29,613	56.6	80.8	1,486	83.5	16.2	-11.2	19.6	8.6	...	...	...
Van Buren, AR	05141	...	...	...	...	...	...	...	...	...	...	...	...
Washington, AR	05143	117,042	46.7	82.0	19,450	92.5	27.5	0.1	30.1	19.7	23.7	43.6	7.4
White, AR	05145	47,114	58.9	80.5	7,299	36.5	17.0	-10.4	17.5	12.4	...	...	9.2
Woodruff, AR	05147	...	...	...	...	...	...	...	...	...	...	...	...
Yell, AR	05149	13,704	70.6	67.5	...	...	9.6	-17.8	10.3	...	...	...	5.9
CALIFORNIA	06000	23,237,728	42.1	80.3	2,851,004	79.9	29.4	2.0	37.9	21.0	13.3	46.5	9.9
Alameda, CA	06001	973,384	35.4	85.7	127,074	83.7	39.4	12.0	48.4	22.0	16.5	51.2	14.5
Alpine, CA	06003	...	...	...	...	...	...	...	...	...	...	...	...
Amador, CA	06005	28,969	48.0	86.5	1,415	63.2	17.4	-10.0	19.2	...	...	...	5.1
Butte, CA	06007	137,724	39.1	84.1	32,425	95.7	24.0	-3.4	26.0	8.3	8.4	29.1	11.6
Calaveras, CA	06009	33,755	42.2	88.7	1,869	77.4	20.3	-7.1	21.4	...	...	...	5.7
Colusa, CA	06011	12,793	57.6	67.5	378	55.0	11.8	-15.6	20.6	...	...	...	1.5
Contra Costa, CA	06013	672,840	31.9	88.1	68,937	78.4	37.7	10.3	44.5	21.4	15.5	52.2	13.7
Del Norte, CA	06015	19,711	51.8	79.8	1,355	91.7	14.2	-13.2	17.5	...	4.3	...	5.2
El Dorado, CA	06017	119,815	31.9	92.0	12,998	86.1	30.6	3.2	31.2	...	27.5	50.4	17.4
Fresno, CA	06019	523,099	51.2	72.9	67,056	86.4	18.8	-8.6	28.9	12.6	9.0	28.5	7.3

[3]May be of any race
... Not available

Table C-1. Population, School, and Student Characteristics by County—*Continued*

County	State/County Code	County Type[1]	Population, 2009		Percent of related children 5-17 years in poverty, 2008	Percent of children under 19 years with no health insurance, 2007	Number of Schools and Students, 2008-2009			Resident enrollment, 2006-2008	
			Total	Percent 5–17 years			School Districts	Schools	Students	K–12 enrollment	
										Number	Percent public
	1		1	2	3	4	5	6	7	8	9
Glenn, CA	06021	6	28,299	20.7	22.7	15.4	10	33	5,554	5,369	98.2
Humboldt, CA	06023	5	129,623	14.1	23.5	10.0	33	90	17,475	18,779	95.0
Imperial, CA	06025	3	166,874	21.1	28.4	11.5	18	66	36,268	34,198	97.2
Inyo, CA	06027	7	17,293	15.6	16.2	13.6	9	31	3,059	...	...
Kern, CA	06029	2	807,407	21.8	24.6	10.2	53	274	174,132	169,420	94.5
Kings, CA	06031	3	148,764	18.8	21.0	13.2	16	69	28,354	28,561	94.0
Lake, CA	06033	4	65,279	16.4	22.1	8.7	9	46	9,663	11,137	97.9
Lassen, CA	06035	6	34,473	14.0	17.6	8.8	12	38	5,022	4,834	90.1
Los Angeles, CA	06037	1	9,848,011	18.0	20.9	11.6	103	2093	1,631,988	1,920,037	90.3
Madera, CA	06039	3	148,632	20.8	25.4	15.1	10	84	29,409	29,673	97.1
Marin, CA	06041	1	250,750	14.8	7.3	10.2	21	78	29,615	35,005	80.2
Mariposa, CA	06043	8	17,792	13.8	18.4	11.0	2	17	2,255	...	...
Mendocino, CA	06045	4	86,040	15.8	23.9	13.6	15	78	13,305	13,857	91.2
Merced, CA	06047	3	245,321	22.7	27.1	11.6	22	104	56,153	56,205	97.1
Modoc, CA	06049	6	9,107	15.4	26.1	8.9	4	19	1,277	...	...
Mono, CA	06051	7	12,927	12.7	13.1	22.2	4	22	1,709	...	...
Monterey, CA	06053	2	410,370	18.5	17.3	16.3	27	131	70,552	77,818	92.2
Napa, CA	06055	3	134,650	16.9	10.7	14.7	7	52	20,370	21,538	88.5
Nevada, CA	06057	4	97,751	14.5	11.5	12.7	12	64	17,562	14,069	89.9
Orange, CA	06059	1	3,026,786	17.8	12.4	14.9	32	610	504,136	560,283	89.1
Placer, CA	06061	1	348,552	17.9	6.9	9.4	19	114	63,854	54,281	90.7
Plumas, CA	06063	7	20,122	13.6	17.6	11.8	3	16	2,529	2,842	91.5
Riverside, CA	06065	1	2,125,440	21.0	15.6	18.5	26	485	420,159	422,795	92.8
Sacramento, CA	06067	1	1,400,949	18.2	17.2	9.2	14	386	235,497	265,484	91.0
San Benito, CA	06069	1	55,058	21.0	12.9	12.5	11	23	11,354	11,928	86.8
San Bernardino, CA	06071	1	2,017,673	21.5	19.1	16.7	36	555	420,220	439,340	94.1
San Diego, CA	06073	1	3,053,793	16.7	15.4	14.3	45	763	496,702	528,704	91.6
San Francisco, CA	06075	1	815,358	9.3	13.8	8.9	4	120	56,454	76,281	74.1
San Joaquin, CA	06077	2	674,860	21.5	21.0	10.8	17	225	135,508	141,854	92.8
San Luis Obispo, CA	06079	3	266,971	13.4	11.8	11.2	12	84	34,707	36,471	89.9
San Mateo, CA	06081	1	718,989	15.5	7.1	12.9	26	179	89,971	113,279	79.7
Santa Barbara, CA	06083	2	407,057	16.2	15.0	15.6	25	129	65,920	68,494	89.8
Santa Clara, CA	06085	1	1,784,642	16.9	8.8	9.3	34	403	261,540	296,483	87.2
Santa Cruz, CA	06087	2	256,218	15.0	16.2	12.4	15	81	38,684	38,891	90.0
Shasta, CA	06089	3	181,099	16.9	21.7	9.3	27	112	28,348	29,958	90.5
Sierra, CA	06091	8	3,174	14.4	16.6	12.0	3	10	473	...	...
Siskiyou, CA	06093	7	44,634	15.2	25.0	9.6	28	72	6,718	6,437	95.2
Solano, CA	06095	2	407,234	18.2	10.4	9.6	9	120	69,342	78,855	91.7
Sonoma, CA	06097	2	472,102	15.9	11.1	13.4	44	184	71,049	76,863	90.5
Stanislaus, CA	06099	2	510,385	20.9	18.1	10.7	29	192	105,678	107,257	95.4
Sutter, CA	06101	3	92,614	19.6	20.8	13.6	14	48	20,020	1,7407	96.1
Tehama, CA	06103	4	61,138	18.3	22.3	9.5	20	53	11,017	1,1265	92.9
Trinity, CA	06105	8	14,165	13.0	27.5	10.7	11	24	1,785	...	...
Tulare, CA	06107	2	429,668	23.0	28.4	10.3	48	193	96,376	96,063	95.7
Tuolumne, CA	06109	4	55,175	12.9	16.1	10.2	13	46	6,977	7,859	90.6
Ventura, CA	06111	2	802,983	18.5	10.6	11.2	23	217	141,641	153,200	89.5
Yolo, CA	06113	1	199,407	16.5	13.0	10.8	7	65	29,591	31,899	93.4
Yuba, CA	06115	3	72,925	20.2	22.3	9.6	6	43	14,341	14,522	92.5
COLORADO	08000	X	5,024,748	17.2	12.8	12.7	262	1837	818,443	833,980	91.2
Adams, CO	08001	1	440,994	19.2	15.5	13.7	13	139	79,284	79,589	92.6
Alamosa, CO	08003	7	15,424	17.4	27.2	13.4	4	8	2,436	...	...
Arapahoe, CO	08005	1	565,360	18.2	10.0	12.3	12	157	108,224	96,357	91.2
Archuleta, CO	08007	7	12,430	15.4	17.8	18.7	1	5	1,525	...	...
Baca, CO	08009	9	3,723	16.2	23.2	10.5	5	15	1,072	...	...
Bent, CO	08011	7	6,560	11.8	29.7	10.1	2	7	874	...	...
Boulder, CO	08013	2	303,482	15.3	7.6	13.7	5[4]	104[4]	54,761[4]	43,340	91.2
Broomfield, CO	08014	1	55,990	19.3	5.0	8.3	([4])	([4])	([4])	10,188	87.0
Chaffee, CO	08015	7	17,156	12.3	15.2	15.1	2	8	2,022	...	...
Cheyenne, CO	08017	9	1,746	17.8	14.9	15.6	2	5	304	...	...
Clear Creek, CO	08019	1	8,706	14.9	9.2	14.3	3	5	994	...	...
Conejos, CO	08021	9	7,844	20.3	28.8	11.0	3	10	1,689	...	...
Costilla, CO	08023	9	3,148	14.6	35.0	8.3	2	6	457	...	...
Crowley, CO	08025	8	6,403	8.5	30.1	7.8	1	4	486	...	...
Custer, CO	08027	8	4,000	13.9	19.6	23.3	1	3	514	...	...
Delta, CO	08029	6	31,322	16.3	15.0	15.3	2	20	5,510	4,873	96.1
Denver, CO	08031	1	610,345	14.5	25.4	14.5	9	177	80,264	88,532	87.3
Dolores, CO	08033	9	1,940	14.8	13.6	18.5	1	3	293	...	...
Douglas, CO	08035	1	288,225	21.5	2.6	7.7	2	79	58,723	56,290	90.1
Eagle, CO	08037	5	53,653	15.5	8.0	23.1	1	21	6,007	7,593	86.8

[1]County type codes are from the Economic Research Service of the United States Department of Agriculture. See notes and definitions for more information.
[4]Broomfield county is included with Boulder county
... Not available

Table C-1. Population, School, and Student Characteristics by County—*Continued*

County	State/County Code	Characteristics of students, 2008-2009				Number of graduates, 2006-2007	Staff and students, 2008-2009			
		Percent with IEP[2]	Percent eligible for free or reduced lunch	Percent minority	Percent English Language Learners		Total staff	Number of teachers	Student/teacher ratio	Central admin. Staff
		10	11	12	13	14	15	16	17	18
Glenn, CA	06021	9.0	65.0	57.3	20.5	346	704	304	18.3	43
Humboldt, CA	06023	14.6	53.1	33.8	5.8	940	2,175	937	18.6	99
Imperial, CA	06025	8.4	69.5	92.0	42.4	2,067	3,709	1,743	20.8	196
Inyo, CA	06027	11.3	42.5	51.4	11.7	226	394	183	16.7	40
Kern, CA	06029	9.2	62.7	71.5	22.0	8,723	17,188	8,416	20.7	862
Kings, CA	06031	8.1	59.4	72.7	23.0	1,189	2,872	1,424	19.9	177
Lake, CA	06033	11.8	66.8	37.3	10.7	612	1,029	495	19.5	61
Lassen, CA	06035	7.1	36.9	25.3	3.5	361	562	269	18.7	28
Los Angeles, CA	06037	11.1	62.6	85.1	27.2	81,756	158,891	78,197	20.9	7,035
Madera, CA	06039	8.7	66.2	72.4	30.1	1,487	2,895	1423	20.7	169
Marin, CA	06041	11.4	22.0	37.2	14.4	1,994	3,104	1,629	18.2	176
Mariposa, CA	06043	18.8	45.5	25.7	2.0	191	249	124	18.2	11
Mendocino, CA	06045	11.3	60.3	47.0	19.0	832	1,814	801	16.6	95
Merced, CA	06047	9.5	71.2	77.9	30.6	3,239	5,835	2,736	20.5	267
Modoc, CA	06049	4.9	57.9	31.1	4.9	142	192	96	13.3	9
Mono, CA	06051	11.3	50.1	52.7	32.6	87	292	130	13.1	24
Monterey, CA	06053	9.2	56.8	82.6	39.2	3,454	6,944	3,433	20.6	281
Napa, CA	06055	12.3	39.5	64.0	23.0	1,105	2,041	1,072	19.0	75
Nevada, CA	06057	9.6	27.1	16.8	6.7	1,526	1,782	949	18.5	72
Orange, CA	06059	10.2	42.0	67.2	27.9	29,485	41,297	21,754	23.2	1,579
Placer, CA	06061	9.9	19.7	29.9	6.0	3,961	5,731	3,091	20.7	296
Plumas, CA	06063	10.4	37.4	24.9	3.5	221	295	124	20.4	17
Riverside, CA	06065	10.4	53.7	73.0	22.7	21,737	36,309	19,218	21.9	1,526
Sacramento, CA	06067	9.4	51.1	62.7	18.2	13,499	22,203	11,304	20.8	945
San Benito, CA	06069	9.5	51.1	70.2	24.4	646	1,002	524	21.7	58
San Bernardino, CA	06071	10.3	60.3	76.9	21.8	21,795	36,311	19,084	22.0	1,615
San Diego, CA	06073	11.6	46.6	66.3	24.8	29,124	46,166	23,863	20.8	2,005
San Francisco, CA	06075	10.4	55.6	89.3	30.3	3,412	5,875	3,274	17.2	392
San Joaquin, CA	06077	9.9	55.4	74.7	23.3	6,564	12,867	6,751	20.1	780
San Luis Obispo, CA	06079	11.4	27.3	38.7	14.8	2,700	3,688	1,794	19.3	199
San Mateo, CA	06081	11.5	33.3	68.1	24.7	5,334	8,419	4,635	19.4	457
Santa Barbara, CA	06083	10.2	46.3	69.5	30.0	3,672	6,266	3,126	21.1	319
Santa Clara, CA	06085	10.1	35.0	75.9	26.0	14,540	22,686	12,733	20.5	1,330
Santa Cruz, CA	06087	12.4	44.6	58.7	28.3	2,538	3,834	1,753	22.1	271
Shasta, CA	06089	10.4	43.0	24.6	2.9	1,927	3,056	1,452	19.5	188
Sierra, CA	06091	9.3	41.6	19.5	5.9	45	68	34	13.9	5
Siskiyou, CA	06093	10.6	61.7	30.7	6.6	397	944	422	15.9	54
Solano, CA	06095	11.5	42.0	68.5	15.0	4,096	6,714	3,455	20.1	279
Sonoma, CA	06097	12.9	37.4	47.9	23.4	4,384	6,716	3,591	19.8	370
Stanislaus, CA	06099	11.7	57.5	64.5	24.9	5,776	10,074	5,039	21.0	639
Sutter, CA	06101	10.4	54.2	56.6	17.2	1,167	2,019	1,024	19.6	96
Tehama, CA	06103	8.0	63.3	39.0	14.9	682	1,298	586	18.8	99
Trinity, CA	06105	6.9	57.7	21.8	0.5	139	344	126	14.2	22
Tulare, CA	06107	7.0	67.7	77.7	31.4	4,462	9,124	4,612	20.9	396
Tuolumne, CA	06109	11.3	39.6	19.2	1.4	563	785	379	18.4	37
Ventura, CA	06111	10.7	41.4	60.7	23.2	8,685	13,188	6,479	21.9	712
Yolo, CA	06113	10.1	44.2	58.6	22.5	1,801	2,868	1,460	20.3	131
Yuba, CA	06115	12.9	62.3	53.3	18.4	594	1,615	750	19.1	82
COLORADO	08000	10.2	35.4	39.1	10.9	48,432	102,558	48,690	16.8	6,201
Adams, CO	08001	9.4	44.2	54.8	17.6	3,693	8,660	4,155	19.1	458
Alamosa, CO	08003	28.5	64.9	58.5	9.6	172	428	175	13.9	30
Arapahoe, CO	08005	10.7	34.1	46.6	15.9	6,611	13,138	6,078	17.8	713
Archuleta, CO	08007	...	46.2	29.2	7.0	150	196	101	15.1	13
Baca, CO	08009	...	51.5	21.5	1.5	224	202	102	10.5	17
Bent, CO	08011	...	61.2	45.8	1.5	49	137	66	13.2	8
Boulder, CO	08013	9.2[4]	23.0	29.3	9.6[4]	3,505[4]	6,796[4]	3,125[4]	17.5[4]	403[4]
Broomfield, CO	08014	(4)	18.1	23.5	(4)	(4)	(4)	(4)	(4)	(4)
Chaffee, CO	08015	...	33.7	11.8	1.2	146	321	151	13.4	15
Cheyenne, CO	08017	...	35.2	14.1	2.3	33	76	38	8.0	3
Clear Creek, CO	08019	32.8	20.9	12.3	0.7	75	166	64	15.5	8
Conejos, CO	08021	...	69.4	59.0	1.1	150	230	128	13.2	13
Costilla, CO	08023	...	77.2	86.7	27.4	46	91	48	9.5	10
Crowley, CO	08025	...	68.3	33.5	1.0	33	76	35	13.9	3
Custer, CO	08027	...	30.5	7.0	...	40	74	39	13.2	5
Delta, CO	08029	11.3	42.0	20.7	4.2	363	670	294	18.7	24
Denver, CO	08031	12.0	65.9	77.7	26.2	3,343	9,807	4,701	17.1	564
Dolores, CO	08033	...	35.2	11.9	...	25	52	26	11.3	5
Douglas, CO	08035	8.5	5.0	14.7	2.7	2,855	6,757	3,133	18.7	304
Eagle, CO	08037	...	31.5	50.9	31.4	321	793	450	13.3	40

[2]IEP= Individual Education Program. See notes and definitions for more information
[4]Broomfield county is included with Boulder county
... Not available

Table C-1. Population, School, and Student Characteristics by County—*Continued*

County	State/County Code	Revenues, 2007-2008				Current expenditures, 2007-2008			Resident population 16 to 19 years, 2006-2008			
		Total revenue ($1,000's)	Percentage of revenue from			Amount ($1,000's)	Amount per student	Percent for instruction	Total population 16 to 19 years	Percent enrolled in school	Percent high school graduates, not enrolled in school	Percent not enrolled, not grads, not employed or not in labor force
			Federal gov't	State gov't	Local gov't							
	19	19	20	21	22	23	24	25	26	27	28	29
Glenn, CA	06021	76,994	19.2	56.6	24.2	63,744	11,846	57.2	...	...	...	...
Humboldt, CA	06023	231,928	10.3	63.0	26.7	185,597	10,359	59.8	7,819	77.1	16.5	2.7
Imperial, CA	06025	458,027	14.8	65.9	19.3	379,696	10,448	55.6	11,259	85.5	9.5	4.4
Inyo, CA	06027	49,138	11.9	38.5	49.5	38,517	13,137	54.9	...	...	...	...
Kern, CA	06029	2,206,547	11.6	63.4	25.0	1,685,823	9,690	57.3	50,144	78.0	13.6	6.3
Kings, CA	06031	321,812	11.8	72.4	15.8	266,316	9,418	57.6	9,123	76.3	15.1	7.0
Lake, CA	06033	124,124	12.7	54.9	32.4	104,309	10,639	53.9	...	...	...	...
Lassen, CA	06035	63,029	11.2	64.0	24.8	52,372	11,892	56.3	...	...	...	...
Los Angeles, CA	06037	20,574,587	11.5	67.8	20.7	17,036,273	10,351	59.7	609,836	83.8	9.2	4.3
Madera, CA	06039	360,552	10.5	64.3	25.2	280,888	9,556	56.9	8,323	71.2	15.7	8.0
Marin, CA	06041	425,883	5.0	26.2	68.8	346,977	11,924	59.0	11,085	88.2	8.7	1.7
Mariposa, CA	06043	26,747	9.3	34.8	55.8	25,649	11,089	55.9	...	...	...	...
Mendocino, CA	06045	196,584	11.2	52.9	35.9	158,507	11,638	57.7	4,801	77.2	15.3	3.6
Merced, CA	06047	635,449	13.1	67.6	19.3	564,609	9,884	58.4	17,315	80.3	12.5	4.0
Modoc, CA	06049	24,007	24.0	53.0	23.1	18,124	10,944	54.9	...	...	...	...
Mono, CA	06051	39,669	5.3	27.2	67.5	26,502	13,732	54.1	...	...	...	...
Monterey, CA	06053	894,662	10.5	49.3	40.2	732,594	10,487	58.6	25,967	78.7	13.0	4.2
Napa, CA	06055	258,662	10.4	25.3	64.3	214,488	10,776	58.7	7,472	80.8	9.7	2.7
Nevada, CA	06057	204,436	5.2	37.6	57.3	173,504	10,607	60.9	...	...	...	...
Orange, CA	06059	5,374,443	7.7	49.3	43.0	4,602,973	9,147	62.3	173,570	87.2	7.4	2.7
Placer, CA	06061	709,789	5.3	37.2	57.5	508,053	8,126	60.5	17,043	85.9	11.5	1.7
Plumas, CA	06063	37,986	19.6	23.8	56.7	27,744	10,505	52.3	...	...	...	...
Riverside, CA	06065	4,650,038	8.5	59.2	32.2	3,715,155	8,820	60.7	125,112	80.9	12.5	3.8
Sacramento, CA	06067	2,639,010	9.4	62.9	27.7	2,255,124	9,537	59.5	80,115	82.9	11.3	3.7
San Benito, CA	06069	121,883	7.5	51.1	41.4	108,553	9,490	62.7	...	...	...	...
San Bernardino, CA	06071	4,905,240	9.1	71.5	19.4	3,764,735	8,828	60.0	136,842	78.7	13.4	5.1
San Diego, CA	06073	5,820,882	8.0	47.4	44.6	4,818,205	9,806	58.5	180,629	82.4	12.3	3.4
San Francisco, CA	06075	779,310	10.6	41.2	48.1	667,829	11,979	54.5	25,527	89.3	6.8	1.5
San Joaquin, CA	06077	1,494,691	8.9	66.1	24.9	1,251,258	9,190	60.7	44,289	83.0	9.3	4.3
San Luis Obispo, CA	06079	397,266	8.9	32.3	58.8	336,193	9,580	60.2	18,531	91.3	6.2	0.7
San Mateo, CA	06081	1,206,661	5.9	26.1	68.0	919,202	10,331	60.8	34,254	87.4	8.1	2.7
Santa Barbara, CA	06083	752,079	8.9	45.9	45.2	652,574	9,854	59.6	29,710	88.1	6.5	2.5
Santa Clara, CA	06085	3,173,827	7.4	32.9	59.6	2,574,315	9,950	61.6	90,474	87.8	7.5	2.9
Santa Cruz, CA	06087	464,698	12.6	46.8	40.5	401,660	10,424	56.2	17,119	86.4	8.7	2.1
Shasta, CA	06089	381,232	12.1	55.7	32.2	296,967	10,443	59.5	11,380	77.7	13.6	5.9
Sierra, CA	06091	9,856	23.9	41.5	34.7	7,833	15,888	48.9	...	...	...	...
Siskiyou, CA	06093	110,654	15.2	49.5	35.3	91,282	13,574	54.4	...	...	...	...
Solano, CA	06095	745,903	7.7	62.5	29.8	625,342	8,873	60.3	25,270	82.2	9.5	5.5
Sonoma, CA	06097	856,562	6.9	42.2	51.0	695,476	9,857	63.3	27,631	85.5	9.8	2.0
Stanislaus, CA	06099	1,293,380	9.6	59.3	31.2	1,021,660	9,482	62.1	33,727	81.5	12.5	4.5
Sutter, CA	06101	204,598	10.4	60.3	29.3	172,545	8,924	57.3	5,484	81.3	12.7	5.2
Tehama, CA	06103	142,639	13.2	59.5	27.3	118,643	10,937	57.5	3,689	70.4	21.1	8.4
Trinity, CA	06105	38,175	25.9	51.9	22.2	28,911	15,773	51.6	...	...	...	...
Tulare, CA	06107	1,193,548	13.8	67.8	18.4	918,861	9,641	60.8	29,049	77.5	14.3	5.9
Tuolumne, CA	06109	89,762	8.8	49.5	41.7	75,190	10,601	57.5	...	...	...	...
Ventura, CA	06111	1,593,455	8.1	55.7	36.2	1,274,144	9,030	61.8	51,580	85.3	8.3	2.9
Yolo, CA	06113	348,568	9.0	56.6	34.4	274,850	9,419	57.0	17,574	91.0	7.0	1.3
Yuba, CA	06115	168,515	12.2	58.3	29.4	142,907	10,276	55.7	4,258	74.6	16.6	5.5
COLORADO	08000	8,108,464	6.8	42.2	51.0	7,274,824	9,079	58.2	261,031	82.1	10.2	4.4
Adams, CO	08001	739,828	6.2	51.2	42.6	626,331	8,266	58.3	20,956	73.4	13.8	7.8
Alamosa, CO	08003	30,340	24.0	51.3	24.7	25,978	10,488	52.2	...	...	...	...
Arapahoe, CO	08005	1,030,018	6.1	46.5	47.5	913,173	8,634	60.8	28,314	82.7	10.7	3.4
Archuleta, CO	08007	14,935	6.4	23.7	69.9	12,751	8,253	60.8	...	...	...	...
Baca, CO	08009	29,074	2.3	86.1	11.6	27,695	6,340	31.2	...	...	...	...
Bent, CO	08011	10,097	9.5	66.1	24.4	7,278	8,985	61.6	...	...	...	...
Boulder, CO	08013	519,934[4]	4.6[4]	30.8[4]	64.6[4]	436,224[4]	8,211[4]	61.2[4]	19,136	92.4	5.4	0.9
Broomfield, CO	08014	(4)	(4)	(4)	(4)	(4)	(4)	(4)	...	...	...	...
Chaffee, CO	08015	20,998	6.7	38.4	54.8	18,257	8,850	56.8	...	...	...	...
Cheyenne, CO	08017	6,324	1.4	39.2	59.4	4,558	14,244	53.5	...	...	...	...
Clear Creek, CO	08019	14,055	5.1	17.3	77.6	10,014	9,592	53.3	...	...	...	...
Conejos, CO	08021	17,984	7.7	77.4	14.9	15,054	8,539	57.8	...	...	...	...
Costilla, CO	08023	7,162	11.5	37.0	51.5	6,463	13,839	47.1	...	...	...	...
Crowley, CO	08025	6,182	6.6	71.3	22.1	4,642	9,229	49.1	...	...	...	...
Custer, CO	08027	5,023	6.0	28.7	65.3	4,436	8,547	60.6	...	...	...	...
Delta, CO	08029	50,098	8.0	56.3	35.6	40,692	7,483	62.5	...	...	...	...
Denver, CO	08031	903,217	10.8	29.5	59.7	1,185,258	15,299	56.1	24,208	74.1	10.7	9.3
Dolores, CO	08033	3,987	3.2	40.6	56.1	3,022	10,314	55.8	...	...	...	...
Douglas, CO	08035	515,086	2.2	39.5	58.3	446,001	8,418	60.3	12,507	88.8	7.9	2.1
Eagle, CO	08037	75,552	3.9	2.2	93.9	54,615	9,617	60.2	...	...	...	...

[4]Broomfield county is included with Boulder county
... Not available

Table C-1. Population, School, and Student Characteristics by County—*Continued*

County	State/ County Code	Population 25 years and over	High school diploma or less (percent)	High school diploma or more (percent)	Number	Percent public	Bachelor's degree or more	+/- U.S. percent with Bachelor's degree or more	Non-Hispanic White	Black or African American	American Indian and Alaska Native	Asian, Hawaiian, and Pacific Islander	Hispanic or Latino[3]
					College enrollment, 2006-2008		College graduates, 2006-2008 (percent)						
		30	31	32	33	34	35	36	37	38	39	40	41
Glenn, CA	06021	17,282	53.0	73.3	1,348	81.2	13.5	-13.9	15.8	...	...	...	7.0
Humboldt, CA	06023	85,068	37.2	89.3	13,730	96.2	26.4	-1.0	27.4	14.6	15.7	33.5	23.8
Imperial, CA	06025	92,832	61.8	63.0	12,044	94.4	11.2	-16.2	20.9	8.9	7.9	20.4	8.0
Inyo, CA	06027	...	...	...	...	...	...	...	...	...	...	...	...
Kern, CA	06029	462,717	56.5	70.9	48,429	83.5	14.3	-13.1	20.3	11.2	7.6	31.9	5.2
Kings, CA	06031	88,449	59.6	70.4	9,123	81.2	11.7	-15.7	19.1	5.5	6.1	31.0	3.9
Lake, CA	06033	45,467	50.7	85.9	2,475	93.2	15.2	-12.2	16.8	...	9.1	...	6.3
Lassen, CA	06035	24,500	49.0	80.8	2,029	81.3	11.2	-16.2	14.5	...	3.1	...	3.8
Los Angeles, CA	06037	6,229,170	47.0	75.3	771,746	75.2	28.1	0.7	43.3	22.2	15.8	47.5	9.4
Madera, CA	06039	89,625	59.0	68.1	6,841	83.6	12.6	-14.8	19.2	9.7	12.3	31.3	4.4
Marin, CA	06041	180,781	21.7	91.8	15,556	72.2	53.6	26.2	59.4	17.3	...	62.6	20.3
Mariposa, CA	06043	...	...	...	...	...	...	...	...	...	...	...	...
Mendocino, CA	06045	58,798	44.0	81.8	3,736	90.7	23.0	-4.4	27.4	...	7.7	37.3	3.0
Merced, CA	06047	138,718	60.0	66.1	16,430	81.0	12.5	-14.9	18.3	6.1	4.3	31.3	4.9
Modoc, CA	06049	...	...	...	...	...	...	...	...	...	...	...	...
Mono, CA	06051	...	...	...	...	...	...	...	...	...	...	...	...
Monterey, CA	06053	249,053	50.8	70.2	29,799	83.5	23.3	-4.1	39.6	12.1	12.0	36.6	5.8
Napa, CA	06055	89,008	40.4	80.8	8,497	68.0	29.3	1.9	36.2	22.9	...	46.8	6.0
Nevada, CA	06057	70,310	30.1	93.3	5,665	81.6	31.1	3.7	32.2	...	18.3	39.0	15.0
Orange, CA	06059	1,926,651	36.5	82.5	247,921	80.9	35.2	7.8	42.8	34.2	15.5	49.3	11.5
Placer, CA	06061	228,209	29.6	92.4	23,911	84.1	33.0	5.6	33.8	45.6	20.8	50.5	15.9
Plumas, CA	06063	15,463	36.9	91.5	865	87.3	19.2	-8.2	20.1	...	...	...	...
Riverside, CA	06065	1,264,116	49.1	78.6	130,765	79.1	19.7	-7.7	25.7	21.5	12.1	40.4	7.8
Sacramento, CA	06067	887,190	38.6	85.1	105,846	86.0	27.6	0.2	31.7	18.2	16.8	33.5	12.7
San Benito, CA	06069	32,956	50.3	72.1	3,531	81.1	19.6	-7.8	29.5	...	...	33.5	8.7
San Bernardino, CA	06071	1,177,835	50.4	77.3	148,019	76.7	17.9	-9.5	22.3	18.9	9.0	47.0	8.0
San Diego, CA	06073	1,881,397	35.2	85.1	258,194	80.8	33.8	6.4	41.4	21.1	16.6	43.7	13.9
San Francisco, CA	06075	622,591	30.2	84.5	71,522	72.8	50.3	22.9	68.9	24.5	26.1	35.5	25.7
San Joaquin, CA	06077	403,403	52.4	76.4	41,004	74.8	16.3	-11.1	20.3	13.5	8.4	27.2	5.3
San Luis Obispo, CA	06079	172,220	34.2	87.8	35,465	94.5	30.4	3.0	35.0	5.4	5.3	42.9	10.5
San Mateo, CA	06081	486,771	30.0	88.8	51,294	77.7	43.6	16.2	51.2	22.0	29.2	52.0	16.1
Santa Barbara, CA	06083	248,333	37.7	80.7	48,142	88.0	31.7	4.3	43.3	24.9	8.4	47.2	8.7
Santa Clara, CA	06085	1,155,655	31.5	85.8	146,143	74.0	44.2	16.8	51.1	28.5	18.2	57.6	12.7
Santa Cruz, CA	06087	163,854	31.7	85.0	29,434	92.7	38.9	11.5	47.1	36.2	7.0	51.7	12.0
Shasta, CA	06089	120,669	40.3	88.3	12,294	83.0	18.0	-9.4	18.9	...	5.9	23.7	9.4
Sierra, CA	06091	...	...	...	...	...	...	...	...	...	...	...	...
Siskiyou, CA	06093	31,378	40.9	87.6	3,034	90.7	19.5	-7.9	21.1	...	2.6	...	8.3
Solano, CA	06095	262,223	40.0	85.3	29,610	80.7	23.2	-4.2	26.9	17.3	13.0	34.4	10.3
Sonoma, CA	06097	312,402	36.3	86.3	36,733	89.8	30.8	3.4	35.6	21.7	13.4	43.9	8.3
Stanislaus, CA	06099	308,183	53.5	74.9	33,291	85.1	15.7	-11.7	19.8	14.7	11.0	28.7	6.3
Sutter, CA	06101	57,814	47.0	78.3	5,985	87.4	18.1	-9.3	20.6	21.9	18.1	23.8	7.9
Tehama, CA	06103	40,333	52.8	78.6	2,883	79.0	12.3	-15.1	13.7	...	13.0	...	5.4
Trinity, CA	06105	...	...	...	...	...	...	...	...	...	...	...	...
Tulare, CA	06107	238,310	58.4	67.4	22,650	83.3	12.7	-14.7	20.0	11.2	11.2	27.9	5.0
Tuolumne, CA	06109	41,017	42.8	87.4	2,561	86.2	17.0	-10.4	18.2	...	5.7	...	9.6
Ventura, CA	06111	504,199	38.6	82.1	56,118	78.2	30.4	3.0	38.2	32.9	10.3	54.8	10.1
Yolo, CA	06113	113,129	36.3	84.6	35,616	93.7	39.5	12.1	46.9	34.6	15.7	63.2	13.6
Yuba, CA	06115	42,575	52.1	77.5	4,177	90.7	12.2	-15.2	13.4	...	14.0	17.8	6.8
COLORADO	08000	3,189,198	35.5	88.6	335,192	79.7	35.0	7.6	40.3	22.2	16.2	46.3	11.6
Adams, CO	08001	264,448	49.7	80.7	17,222	72.5	20.2	-7.2	25.4	16.5	11.5	32.9	8.3
Alamosa, CO	08003	...	...	...	...	...	...	...	...	...	...	...	...
Arapahoe, CO	08005	359,225	32.3	89.8	33,101	72.9	37.6	10.2	43.7	23.5	13.3	44.8	12.9
Archuleta, CO	08007	...	...	...	...	...	...	...	...	...	...	...	...
Baca, CO	08009	...	...	...	...	...	...	...	...	...	...	...	...
Bent, CO	08011	...	...	...	...	...	...	...	...	...	...	...	...
Boulder, CO	08013	188,999	21.5	93.2	38,258	88.1	55.9	28.5	60.4	41.5	32.9	72.7	16.1
Broomfield, CO	08014	34,330	27.5	94.5	3,685	68.3	42.9	15.5	44.5	...	...	46.0	24.7
Chaffee, CO	08015	...	...	...	...	...	...	...	...	...	...	...	...
Cheyenne, CO	08017	...	...	...	...	...	...	...	...	...	...	...	...
Clear Creek, CO	08019	...	...	...	...	...	...	...	...	...	...	...	...
Conejos, CO	08021	...	...	...	...	...	...	...	...	...	...	...	...
Costilla, CO	08023	...	...	...	...	...	...	...	...	...	...	...	...
Crowley, CO	08025	...	...	...	...	...	...	...	...	...	...	...	...
Custer, CO	08027	...	...	...	...	...	...	...	...	...	...	...	...
Delta, CO	08029	21,498	52.8	83.5	892	82.0	18.2	-9.2	20.6	...	...	...	1.0
Denver, CO	08031	395,644	39.5	82.5	36,000	61.2	38.0	10.6	53.2	20.2	18.7	50.4	9.7
Dolores, CO	08033	...	...	...	...	...	...	...	...	...	...	...	...
Douglas, CO	08035	171,745	16.7	97.5	15,567	74.9	52.9	25.5	53.4	53.1	...	64.9	38.8
Eagle, CO	08037	34,844	32.5	87.2	1,727	66.0	46.0	18.6	55.8	...	...	...	13.0

[3] May be of any race
... Not available

Table C-1. Population, School, and Student Characteristics by County—*Continued*

County	State/ County Code	County Type[1]	Population, 2009		Percent of related children 5-17 years in poverty, 2008	Percent of children under 19 years with no health insurance, 2007	Number of Schools and Students, 2008-2009			Resident enrollment, 2006-2008	
			Total	Percent 5–17 years			School Districts	Schools	Students	K–12 enrollment	
										Number	Percent public
			1	2	3	4	5	6	7	8	9
Elbert, CO	08039	1	23,287	19.6	5.8	15.4	5	18	3,828	4,297	94.2
El Paso, CO	08041	2	604,542	18.5	12.1	12.1	27	218	105,897	109,037	92.2
Fremont, CO	08043	4	47,815	12.8	17.5	9.6	4	17	5,676	5,907	86.6
Garfield, CO	08045	5	56,298	19.3	8.8	20.4	4	28	11,578	9,892	93.2
Gilpin, CO	08047	1	5,604	12.9	4.7	8.0	1	2	357	...	...
Grand, CO	08049	8	13,911	14.8	8.8	22.0	2	9	1,921	...	...
Gunnison, CO	08051	7	15,350	12.2	10.9	18.1	2	7	1,839	...	...
Hinsdale, CO	08053	9	821	13.9	11.1	31.1	1	1	103	...	...
Huerfano, CO	08055	6	7,558	12.6	27.6	8.1	2	7	948	...	...
Jackson, CO	08057	9	1,369	16.5	21.1	22.6	1	2	232	...	...
Jefferson, CO	08059	1	536,922	16.4	8.2	10.5	2	165	85,946	89,661	90.9
Kiowa, CO	08061	9	1,238	18.1	14.2	13.7	2	5	281	...	...
Kit Carson, CO	08063	7	8,402	15.2	17.3	15.7	5	13	1,440	...	...
Lake, CO	08065	7	8,046	18.2	16.4	21.1	2	9	1,410	...	...
La Plata, CO	08067	6	51,464	14.1	10.8	16.7	5	22	7,016	6,828	91.3
Larimer, CO	08069	2	298,382	15.1	9.2	10.9	7	90	42,478	44,599	92.7
Las Animas, CO	08071	7	16,020	15.2	19.0	11.3	6	17	2,799	...	...
Lincoln, CO	08073	8	5,169	14.0	18.3	15.0	5	8	933	...	...
Logan, CO	08075	7	20,772	15.8	14.7	13.6	5	14	3,136	3,158	89.0
Mesa, CO	08077	3	146,093	16.7	12.0	13.0	5	52	22,845	22,701	91.2
Mineral, CO	08079	9	912	14.7	14.8	25.1	1	2	115	...	...
Moffat, CO	08081	7	13,980	18.7	10.1	15.0	2	8	2,386	...	...
Montezuma, CO	08083	6	25,368	17.2	21.6	15.5	5	18	4,188	4,394	93.8
Montrose, CO	08085	7	41,412	18.3	16.3	17.8	3	17	6,857	6,585	86.8
Morgan, CO	08087	6	27,850	20.4	15.3	17.2	5	18	5,537	5,572	96.6
Otero, CO	08089	6	18,670	18.4	28.1	10.6	8	19	3,372	...	...
Ouray, CO	08091	9	4,602	13.4	10.2	26.5	4	6	632	...	...
Park, CO	08093	1	16,762	15.0	9.1	18.9	2	8	1,899	...	...
Phillips, CO	08095	9	4,472	19.8	14.5	24.1	4	5	899	...	...
Pitkin, CO	08097	7	16,043	10.9	4.7	15.7	1	5	1,656	...	...
Prowers, CO	08099	7	12,982	20.3	24.4	15.6	6	14	2,491	...	...
Pueblo, CO	08101	3	157,224	17.9	21.0	7.7	7	66	27,425	26,661	93.9
Rio Blanco, CO	08103	9	6,534	17.6	9.7	20.5	4	6	1,242	...	...
Rio Grande, CO	08105	7	11,581	17.4	25.2	13.5	3	13	2,197	...	...
Routt, CO	08107	7	23,469	13.6	6.1	14.1	5	13	3,060	3,241	83.6
Saguache, CO	08109	9	7,097	18.0	34.4	17.7	3	11	913	...	...
San Juan, CO	08111	9	555	14.2	18.2	20.5	1	3	64	...	...
San Miguel, CO	08113	9	7,558	11.9	10.2	24.1	2	5	1,010	...	...
Sedgwick, CO	08115	9	2,326	15.9	15.6	17.3	2	5	919	...	...
Summit, CO	08117	7	27,239	12.0	8.2	21.0	1	8	3,067	3,040	81.5
Teller, CO	08119	2	21,685	16.2	10.8	12.7	4	7	3,342	3,594	92.1
Washington, CO	08121	9	4,420	16.4	15.9	19.6	5	11	905	...	...
Weld, CO	08123	3	254,759	19.2	12.9	14.7	16	78	36,384	44,177	92.3
Yuma, CO	08125	7	9,734	18.8	16.0	19.3	4	11	1,781	...	...
CONNECTICUT	09000	X	3,518,288	17.0	10.5	6.6	200	1,163	567,198	616,391	89.5
Fairfield, CT	09001	2	901,208	18.3	8.7	5.7	33	245	146,832	165,784	86.3
Hartford, CT	09003	1	879,835	16.9	12.7	7.6	39	314	145,469	154,683	91.8
Litchfield, CT	09005	4	188,728	16.6	5.5	8.7	24	78	27,178	31,367	87.3
Middlesex, CT	09007	1	165,760	15.9	5.0	5.8	15	72	33,879	27,333	89.3
New Haven, CT	09009	2	848,006	16.6	13.7	5.9	31	263	131,181	147,580	89.6
New London, CT	09011	2	266,830	16.0	7.6	7.8	24	99	42,033	46,974	91.8
Tolland, CT	09013	1	150,461	15.4	4.7	6.9	16	47	22,717	23,101	92.1
Windham, CT	09015	4	117,518	16.5	12.9	6.0	18	45	17,909	19,569	92.0
DELAWARE	10000	X	885,122	16.6	12.8	8.2	43	244	125,430	145,272	82.1
Kent, DE	10001	3	157,741	18.0	14.8	9.9	11	52	24,764	26,950	87.7
New Castle, DE	10003	1	534,634	17.0	10.3	6.6	23	141	73,305	90,546	77.8
Sussex, DE	10005	4	192,747	14.5	18.7	11.7	9	51	27,361	27,776	90.5
DISTRICT OF COLUMBIA	11000	X	599,657	12.8	24.8	6.9	62	265	68,681	80,094	79.3
District of Columbia	11001	1	599,657	12.8	24.8	6.9	62	265	68,681	80,094	79.3

[1]County type codes are from the Economic Research Service of the United States Department of Agriculture. See notes and definitions for more information.
... Not available

Table C-1. Population, School, and Student Characteristics by County—*Continued*

County	State/County Code	Characteristics of students, 2008-2009				Number of graduates, 2006-2007	Staff and students, 2008-2009			
		Percent with IEP[2]	Percent eligible for free or reduced lunch	Percent minority	Percent English Language Learners		Total staff	Number of teachers	Student/teacher ratio	Central admin. Staff
		10	11	12	13	14	15	16	17	18
Elbert, CO	08039	...	13.5	10.6	1.0	281	542	268	14.3	25
El Paso, CO	08041	9.8	31.5	33.8	4.5	6,687	13,665	6,624	16.0	739
Fremont, CO	08043	10.4	41.5	12.5	0.7	463	817	380	14.9	48
Garfield, CO	08045	20.3	34.7	45.7	19.0	551	1,424	745	15.5	64
Gilpin, CO	08047	...	18.8	9.5	0.6	30	62	31	11.5	6
Grand, CO	08049	...	19.3	14.2	8.4	40	285	149	12.9	14
Gunnison, CO	08051	6.8	15.3	15.8	6.5	111	242	136	13.5	13
Hinsdale, CO	08053	...	22.3	9.7	4.9	1	25	10	10.3	4
Huerfano, CO	08055	...	61.8	55.0	...	65	147	75	12.6	12
Jackson, CO	08057	...	43.1	17.2	7.8	20	32	23	10.1	3
Jefferson, CO	08059	9.5	24.4	26.3	5.7	5,913	10,778	4,959	17.3	1,047
Kiowa, CO	08061	...	45.6	13.2	1.4	23	60	32	8.8	4
Kit Carson, CO	08063	...	51.3	26.5	11.0	104	245	122	11.8	16
Lake, CO	08065	...	57.9	67.8	26.2	98	337	99	14.2	36
La Plata, CO	08067	11.3	27.6	25.2	2.3	477	979	483	14.5	79
Larimer, CO	08069	10.6	26.3	21.2	5.3	3,146	5,422	2,514	16.9	358
Las Animas, CO	08071	...	48.4	51.7	1.5	238	360	192	14.6	37
Lincoln, CO	08073	111.4	35.8	14.1	1.8	80	199	78	12.0	23
Logan, CO	08075	11.3	39.6	19.3	3.3	212	510	218	14.4	34
Mesa, CO	08077	11.3	36.7	22.9	4.1	1,468	2,822	1,329	17.2	168
Mineral, CO	08079	...	27.8	9.6	...	11	29	18	6.4	3
Moffat, CO	08081	9.9	30.6	20.5	8.0	147	351	140	17.0	17
Montezuma, CO	08083	12.5	49.8	38.7	8.2	260	616	285	14.7	47
Montrose, CO	08085	8.5	54.3	33.6	12.7	388	804	419	16.4	39
Morgan, CO	08087	5.5	57.7	51.0	16.7	335	802	378	14.6	46
Otero, CO	08089	12.5	61.5	52.1	4.4	240	528	267	12.6	34
Ouray, CO	08091	30.9	23.9	14.4	4.6	41	130	66	9.6	13
Park, CO	08093	...	24.4	10.5	...	130	289	127	15.0	21
Phillips, CO	08095	60.3	37.5	25.6	12.5	58	182	76	11.8	17
Pitkin, CO	08097	...	13.8	27.1	5.7	129	234	137	12.1	12
Prowers, CO	08099	14.4	58.9	50.4	5.6	155	408	197	12.6	31
Pueblo, CO	08101	14.0	56.4	54.7	3.3	1,584	3,461	1,614	17.0	173
Rio Blanco, CO	08103	11.7	17.1	18.0	5.7	80	187	82	15.1	15
Rio Grande, CO	08105	...	59.6	54.9	7.6	193	317	166	13.2	19
Routt, CO	08107	20.3	13.5	11.2	5.0	211	442	226	13.5	27
Saguache, CO	08109	...	78.2	68.8	13.8	68	177	83	11.0	17
San Juan, CO	08111	...	57.8	28.1	14.1	2	16	8	8.0	4
San Miguel, CO	08113	...	20.9	14.8	8.0	50	163	87	11.6	12
Sedgwick, CO	08115	...	24.2	25.2	0.7	18	75	37	24.8	4
Summit, CO	08117	...	28.5	29.5	21.5	191	428	205	15.0	20
Teller, CO	08119	14.6	27.3	9.4	0.2	287	466	230	14.5	23
Washington, CO	08121	...	39.4	13.0	0.9	71	181	93	9.7	8
Weld, CO	08123	11.4	40.4	42.4	15.2	1,833	4,358	2,230	16.3	212
Yuma, CO	08125	...	45.6	31.9	16.5	108	293	148	12.0	23
CONNECTICUT	09000	12.2	30.2	35.6	5.2	37,002	92,436	48,451	11.7	3,809
Fairfield, CT	09001	11.0	27.1	37.1	6.7	9,591	22,921	12,317	11.9	935
Hartford, CT	09003	13.0	35.1	43.4	5.6	8,686	23,632	12,463	11.7	1,021
Litchfield, CT	09005	13.9	16.1	10.4	2.2	1,986	4,667	2,300	11.8	203
Middlesex, CT	09007	10.6	14.9	16.4	1.9	3,561	5,656	3,216	10.5	244
New Haven, CT	09009	12.4	38.2	43.0	5.9	7,776	21,016	11,008	11.9	783
New London, CT	09011	12.7	24.9	27.1	3.8	2,708	7,167	3,611	11.6	308
Tolland, CT	09013	11.7	11.8	11.5	0.8	1,673	3,799	1,952	11.6	159
Windham, CT	09015	13.8	34.9	20.0	4.9	1,021	3,578	1,584	11.3	156
DELAWARE	10000	15.1	39.5	47.8	5.7	7,205	14,724	8,261	15.2	662
Kent, DE	10001	17.3	36.2	41.2	2.1	1,396	2,918	1,653	15.0	159
New Castle, DE	10003	13.9	38.3	53.6	6.7	4,277	8,428	4,735	15.5	369
Sussex, DE	10005	16.3	46.3	37.9	6.5	1,532	3,379	1,873	14.6	135
DISTRICT OF COLUMBIA	11000	15.5	67.1	93.5	8.5	2,944	12,131	5,321	12.9	1,002
District of Columbia	11001	15.5	67.2	93.5	8.5	2,944	12,131	5,321	12.9	1,002

[2]IEP= Individual Education Program. See notes and definitions for more information
... Not available

Table C-1. Population, School, and Student Characteristics by County—*Continued*

County	State/County Code	Revenues, 2007-2008				Current expenditures, 2007-2008			Resident population 16 to 19 years, 2006-2008			
		Total revenue ($1,000's)	Percentage of revenue from			Amount ($1,000's)	Amount per student	Percent for instruction	Total population 16 to 19 years	Percent enrolled in school	Percent high school graduates, not enrolled in school	Percent not enrolled, not grads, not employed or not in labor force
			Federal gov't	State gov't	Local gov't							
	19		20	21	22	23	24	25	26	27	28	29
Elbert, CO	08039	36,875	1.9	58.3	39.9	30,059	7,532	58.4	...	...	...	...
El Paso, CO	08041	1,010,160	7.6	49.9	42.5	870,610	8,282	58.4	32,071	84.2	9.2	3.7
Fremont, CO	08043	53,365	8.2	55.4	36.4	45,415	7,865	58.0	...	...	...	...
Garfield, CO	08045	135,635	6.2	30.9	62.9	95,760	8,818	56.5	...	...	...	...
Gilpin, CO	08047	6,494	2.0	25.4	72.5	4,154	11,319	52.6	...	...	...	...
Grand, CO	08049	24,839	1.4	11.6	87.0	17,474	9,221	58.9	...	...	...	...
Gunnison, CO	08051	16,769	4.7	1.9	93.4	14,266	8,110	61.9	...	...	...	...
Hinsdale, CO	08053	1,408	3.6	19.2	77.2	1,254	13,063	53.6	...	...	...	...
Huerfano, CO	08055	12,916	7.3	58.1	34.6	8,709	8,788	53.0	...	...	...	...
Jackson, CO	08057	3,369	1.1	52.8	46.1	2,528	11,596	56.1	...	...	...	...
Jefferson, CO	08059	858,375	4.7	40.4	54.9	714,118	8,288	59.0	29,305	82.1	10.0	4.6
Kiowa, CO	08061	3,404	4.1	56.8	39.1	3,037	12,004	57.3	...	...	...	...
Kit Carson, CO	08063	16,171	3.4	55.8	40.8	13,151	9,261	58.7	...	...	...	...
Lake, CO	08065	12,484	14.1	48.5	37.4	10,053	8,254	56.7	...	...	...	...
La Plata, CO	08067	82,902	7.8	33.2	59.0	64,106	9,172	55.7	...	...	...	...
Larimer, CO	08069	403,453	5.8	39.2	55.0	351,006	8,336	55.7	17,883	89.9	6.8	1.9
Las Animas, CO	08071	29,732	6.9	57.9	35.2	23,902	8,149	54.8	...	...	...	...
Lincoln, CO	08073	17,665	24.0	43.0	33.0	12,768	13,626	47.2	...	...	...	...
Logan, CO	08075	33,762	5.8	56.4	37.8	27,803	8,732	58.8	...	...	...	...
Mesa, CO	08077	196,386	7.0	47.0	46.0	169,725	7,745	61.9	6,990	79.0	15.1	2.8
Mineral, CO	08079	2,077	4.0	47.2	48.7	1,886	15,333	65.6	...	...	...	...
Moffat, CO	08081	24,049	5.1	17.1	77.9	19,677	8,151	62.4	...	...	...	...
Montezuma, CO	08083	40,493	11.8	48.6	39.5	34,687	8,326	56.2	...	...	...	...
Montrose, CO	08085	58,235	11.1	51.7	37.2	51,212	7,640	59.1	...	...	...	...
Morgan, CO	08087	55,151	9.5	50.3	40.2	46,067	8,406	58.4	...	...	...	...
Otero, CO	08089	40,101	9.6	67.2	23.2	33,423	9,816	56.0	...	...	...	...
Ouray, CO	08091	9,275	6.4	33.1	60.5	7,750	12,500	56.5	...	...	...	...
Park, CO	08093	19,119	3.1	34.8	62.1	16,743	8,766	56.6	...	...	...	...
Phillips, CO	08095	13,738	16.5	43.6	39.9	10,887	12,528	52.1	...	...	...	...
Pitkin, CO	08097	28,289	0.4	4.0	95.6	19,900	12,186	68.5	...	...	...	...
Prowers, CO	08099	28,580	14.3	57.8	27.9	23,688	9,381	59.3	...	...	...	...
Pueblo, CO	08101	238,567	11.3	59.8	28.9	209,960	7,751	54.8	8,662	86.4	6.7	4.9
Rio Blanco, CO	08103	13,983	5.3	31.4	63.2	11,951	10,085	57.6	...	...	...	...
Rio Grande, CO	08105	21,394	9.5	59.0	31.4	18,539	8,196	56.6	...	...	...	...
Routt, CO	08107	48,353	4.7	10.8	84.6	38,312	12,913	57.1	...	...	...	...
Saguache, CO	08109	12,058	10.6	63.0	26.3	9,885	10,340	55.2	...	...	...	...
San Juan, CO	08111	1,088	4.1	20.6	75.3	1,169	18,266	57.1	...	...	...	...
San Miguel, CO	08113	17,406	1.5	20.0	78.5	11,592	11,466	60.0	...	...	...	...
Sedgwick, CO	08115	5,075	2.1	57.7	40.2	4,216	10,810	58.5	...	...	...	...
Summit, CO	08117	43,852	2.2	5.3	92.5	32,607	10,656	57.4	...	...	...	...
Teller, CO	08119	45,272	4.1	33.2	62.7	28,949	8,266	62.2	...	...	...	...
Washington, CO	08121	14,254	2.1	60.2	37.7	10,264	11,292	58.1	...	...	...	...
Weld, CO	08123	350,128	8.5	47.5	44.0	293,042	8,223	56.5	14,759	80.8	9.6	5.7
Yuma, CO	08125	21,869	5.0	39.5	55.4	16,078	9,135	58.8	...	...	...	...
CONNECTICUT	09000	9,365,658	4.2	38.0	57.9	7,881,406	14,266	62.4	199,961	88.1	7.6	3.0
Fairfield, CT	09001	2,587,906	3.5	27.3	69.2	2,197,697	15,046	62.7	48,523	90.4	5.8	2.7
Hartford, CT	09003	2,348,449	4.7	42.0	53.3	2,022,015	14,218	62.2	48,712	87.4	7.4	3.1
Litchfield, CT	09005	439,398	2.4	33.8	63.9	385,914	13,867	62.3	9,867	91.6	6.2	1.7
Middlesex, CT	09007	414,977	2.5	29.8	67.7	330,951	14,041	62.5	8,422	88.3	9.7	1.6
New Haven, CT	09009	2,195,351	5.0	44.4	50.7	1,830,652	14,049	61.8	49,463	88.0	7.9	3.3
New London, CT	09011	713,348	3.7	41.9	54.4	566,274	13,658	62.5	15,234	80.9	13.8	3.6
Tolland, CT	09013	351,321	2.4	41.8	55.8	303,447	13,256	63.3	12,242	94.0	3.8	1.6
Windham, CT	09015	314,908	7.5	53.7	38.9	244,456	13,498	64.4	7,498	79.4	13.2	5.8
DELAWARE	10000	1,782,490	6.1	61.4	32.4	1,483,558	12,103	60.4	49,103	84.6	7.9	4.6
Kent, DE	10001	336,639	7.1	71.5	21.3	280,576	11,650	61.2	9,013	83.3	10.7	4.2
New Castle, DE	10003	1,035,678	5.6	56.5	37.9	877,580	12,255	60.0	32,021	86.6	6.9	4.4
Sussex, DE	10005	410,173	6.6	65.6	27.8	325,402	12,106	60.9	8,069	78.0	8.8	6.1
DISTRICT OF COLUMBIA	11000	1,591,604	9.1	...	90.9	1,327,098	17,078	54.5	33,933	82.7	9.8	6.1
District of Columbia	11001	1,591,604	9.1	...	90.9	1,327,098	17,078	54.5	33,933	82.7	9.8	6.1

... Not available

Table C-1. Population, School, and Student Characteristics by County—*Continued*

County	State/County Code	Population 25 years and over	High school diploma or less (percent)	High school diploma or more (percent)	College enrollment, 2006-2008 Number	College enrollment, 2006-2008 Percent public	Bachelor's degree or more	+/- U.S. percent with Bachelor's degree or more	Non-Hispanic White	Black or African American	American Indian and Alaska Native	Asian, Hawaiian, and Pacific Islander	Hispanic or Latino[3]
		30	31	32	33	34	35	36	37	38	39	40	41
Elbert, CO	08039	15,400	39.2	94.0	1,024	76.2	25.7	-1.7	26.3	...	...	...	28.8
El Paso, CO	08041	376,399	31.4	91.9	44,593	76.6	34.6	7.2	38.2	22.0	19.6	37.7	15.0
Fremont, CO	08043	35,927	55.8	79.0	1,748	88.5	15.0	-12.4	16.8	...	...	...	9.5
Garfield, CO	08045	34,605	46.7	85.0	1,644	86.8	23.3	-4.1	28.1	...	...	...	3.6
Gilpin, CO	08047	...	...	...	...	...	...	...	...	...	...	...	...
Grand, CO	08049	...	...	...	...	...	...	...	...	...	...	...	...
Gunnison, CO	08051	...	...	...	...	...	...	...	...	...	...	...	...
Hinsdale, CO	08053	...	...	...	...	...	...	...	...	...	...	...	...
Huerfano, CO	08055	...	...	...	...	...	...	...	...	...	...	...	...
Jackson, CO	08057	...	...	...	...	...	...	...	...	...	...	...	...
Jefferson, CO	08059	360,719	31.0	92.3	31,893	74.5	38.1	10.7	41.3	26.0	19.0	37.3	16.9
Kiowa, CO	08061	...	...	...	...	...	...	...	...	...	...	...	...
Kit Carson, CO	08063	...	...	...	...	...	...	...	...	...	...	...	...
Lake, CO	08065	...	...	...	...	...	...	...	...	...	...	...	...
La Plata, CO	08067	32,948	27.5	93.3	5,244	93.2	42.3	14.9	46.2	...	14.1	...	21.0
Larimer, CO	08069	185,554	27.9	93.1	36,296	91.8	41.6	14.2	43.7	...	24.3	64.2	16.1
Las Animas, CO	08071	...	...	...	...	...	...	...	...	...	...	...	...
Lincoln, CO	08073	...	...	...	...	...	...	...	...	...	...	...	...
Logan, CO	08075	13,923	46.0	86.0	1,515	92.2	17.6	-9.8	20.1	...	...	...	1.7
Mesa, CO	08077	93,536	43.4	89.0	7,905	87.8	23.5	-3.9	24.9	...	7.8	...	11.8
Mineral, CO	08079	...	...	...	...	...	...	...	...	...	...	...	...
Moffat, CO	08081	...	...	...	...	...	...	...	...	...	...	...	...
Montezuma, CO	08083	16,780	43.6	88.4	721	74.8	24.3	-3.1	26.8	...	4.6	...	10.0
Montrose, CO	08085	26,764	47.2	85.7	1,258	76.9	21.2	-6.2	23.6	...	...	...	2.6
Morgan, CO	08087	17,512	58.6	77.0	750	92.9	14.3	-13.1	18.4	...	...	...	3.3
Otero, CO	08089	...	...	...	...	...	...	...	...	...	...	...	...
Ouray, CO	08091	...	...	...	...	...	...	...	...	...	...	...	...
Park, CO	08093	...	...	...	...	...	...	...	...	...	...	...	...
Phillips, CO	08095	...	...	...	...	...	...	...	...	...	...	...	...
Pitkin, CO	08097	...	...	...	...	...	...	...	...	...	...	...	...
Prowers, CO	08099	...	...	...	...	...	...	...	...	...	...	...	...
Pueblo, CO	08101	102,038	45.5	85.1	11,482	86.8	20.0	-7.4	25.3	19.6	13.2	52.6	9.5
Rio Blanco, CO	08103	...	...	...	...	...	...	...	...	...	...	...	...
Rio Grande, CO	08105	...	...	...	...	...	...	...	...	...	...	...	...
Routt, CO	08107	15,996	24.3	96.7	1,188	97.7	44.5	17.1	45.8	...	...	...	...
Saguache, CO	08109	...	...	...	...	...	...	...	...	...	...	...	...
San Juan, CO	08111	...	...	...	...	...	...	...	...	...	...	...	...
San Miguel, CO	08113	...	...	...	...	...	...	...	...	...	...	...	...
Sedgwick, CO	08115	...	...	...	...	...	...	...	...	...	...	...	...
Summit, CO	08117	19,606	27.6	94.9	867	95.3	47.8	20.4	52.1	...	...	...	14.1
Teller, CO	08119	15,671	33.1	93.5	801	87.5	29.1	1.7	29.1	...	...	...	...
Washington, CO	08121	...	...	...	...	...	...	...	...	...	...	...	...
Weld, CO	08123	147,635	44.5	83.4	23,579	90.2	25.2	-2.2	30.2	...	25.0	38.5	7.2
Yuma, CO	08125	...	...	...	...	...	...	...	...	...	...	...	...
CONNECTICUT	09000	2,352,649	40.7	88.2	254,204	58.2	34.8	7.4	38.0	17.7	13.9	62.5	14.5
Fairfield, CT	09001	594,147	35.9	88.2	56,207	49.4	43.4	16.0	50.0	19.0	20.4	67.5	16.5
Hartford, CT	09003	592,924	42.3	86.8	62,676	62.2	32.8	5.4	37.1	16.5	12.3	59.1	10.4
Litchfield, CT	09005	132,507	40.9	91.1	11,271	64.7	31.5	4.1	31.5	29.0	...	57.3	22.1
Middlesex, CT	09007	114,178	36.7	91.3	11,877	47.3	36.9	9.5	37.6	17.7	...	66.5	25.8
New Haven, CT	09009	565,905	43.5	87.8	66,052	49.3	31.3	3.9	33.9	18.0	16.2	65.1	14.9
New London, CT	09011	180,620	42.5	90.3	15,640	57.8	30.1	2.7	31.4	14.0	6.3	46.8	16.9
Tolland, CT	09013	93,683	34.8	92.2	21,590	88.8	37.2	9.8	37.3	16.8	...	68.7	23.3
Windham, CT	09015	78,685	52.5	84.1	8,891	83.7	21.2	-6.2	22.0	24.9	...	42.0	8.3
DELAWARE	10000	573,425	46.1	86.7	63,117	77.4	26.8	-0.6	28.5	18.4	10.9	62.7	12.0
Kent, DE	10001	97,639	50.7	84.8	11,770	82.4	19.0	-8.4	19.7	15.8	...	33.3	10.7
New Castle, DE	10003	345,253	41.8	88.3	43,811	76.3	31.6	4.2	34.2	20.8	16.5	70.1	13.2
Sussex, DE	10005	130,533	54.1	83.8	7,536	75.8	20.0	-7.4	22.0	9.6	12.0	35.9	8.6
DISTRICT OF COLUMBIA	11000	401,222	35.4	85.3	60,442	36.3	47.2	19.8	86.4	21.4	43.5	72.0	32.8
District of Columbia	11001	401,222	35.4	85.3	60,442	36.3	47.2	19.8	86.4	21.4	43.5	72.0	32.8

[3]May be of any race
... Not available

Table C-1. Population, School, and Student Characteristics by County—*Continued*

County	State/County Code	County Type[1]	Population, 2009 Total	Population, 2009 Percent 5–17 years	Percent of related children 5-17 years in poverty, 2008	Percent of children under 19 years with no health insurance, 2007	Number of Schools and Students, 2008-2009 School Districts	Number of Schools and Students, 2008-2009 Schools	Number of Schools and Students, 2008-2009 Students	Resident enrollment, 2006-2008 K–12 enrollment Number	Resident enrollment, 2006-2008 K–12 enrollment Percent public
			1	2	3	4	5	6	7	8	9
FLORIDA	12000	X	18,537,969	15.6	16.7	17.7	77	4,491	2,631,020	2,893,717	87.8
Alachua, FL	12001	3	243,574	12.5	16.7	15.6	2	72	28,698	30,247	87.0
Baker, FL	12003	1	26,336	18.1	19.3	14.2	1	11	5,065	4,294	92.5
Bay, FL	12005	3	164,767	15.7	18.0	13.4	1	51	25,958	26,323	93.5
Bradford, FL	12007	6	29,235	14.0	21.9	15.3	1	14	3,403	4,300	85.8
Brevard, FL	12009	2	536,357	14.8	13.4	13.2	1	130	73,098	81,466	87.0
Broward, FL	12011	1	1,766,476	16.6	14.2	20.0	1	325	256,351	304,320	86.7
Calhoun, FL	12013	6	13,821	14.8	23.3	15.2	1	9	2,246	...	...
Charlotte, FL	12015	3	156,952	10.9	15.1	21.6	1	26	17,370	19,001	93.1
Citrus, FL	12017	4	140,357	12.1	20.3	16.1	1	28	16,030	17,157	90.9
Clay, FL	12019	1	186,756	19.9	10.3	18.2	1	46	35,949	32,930	92.3
Collier, FL	12021	2	318,537	14.0	16.4	25.7	1	79	42,534	44,407	90.4
Columbia, FL	12023	6	69,264	16.3	22.6	15.7	1	20	9,989	11,003	90.8
De Soto, FL	12027	6	35,297	15.0	30.4	24.7	1	18	4,952	5,432	91.6
Dixie, FL	12029	6	14,824	14.1	32.8	10.9	1	8	2,119	...	...
Duval, FL	12031	1	857,040	16.9	15.4	13.7	2	189	123,162	153,619	82.3
Escambia, FL	12033	2	303,343	15.1	20.8	13.0	1	80	40,924	48,084	87.7
Flagler, FL	12035	4	91,622	14.4	15.5	20.2	1	20	12,890	11,933	88.7
Franklin, FL	12037	6	11,280	11.4	28.3	19.2	1	10	1,281	...	...
Gadsden, FL	12039	2	47,474	16.1	29.6	15.5	1	26	6,417	7,853	83.9
Gilchrist, FL	12041	3	17,116	16.7	20.4	20.0	1	9	2,750	...	...
Glades, FL	12043	6	10,950	13.3	21.2	19.8	1	11	1,388	...	...
Gulf, FL	12045	6	15,755	11.8	22.3	15.0	1	10	2,049	...	...
Hamilton, FL	12047	6	14,592	14.8	31.7	12.6	1	11	1,948	...	...
Hardee, FL	12049	6	29,415	18.7	28.4	23.5	1	14	5,108	5,227	98.0
Hendry, FL	12051	4	39,594	19.4	29.3	24.1	1	20	7,038	7,944	97.2
Hernando, FL	12053	1	171,233	14.7	15.7	14.6	1	33	22,728	24,292	90.2
Highlands, FL	12055	4	98,704	13.3	22.8	19.2	1	23	12,249	13,641	94.3
Hillsborough, FL	12057	1	1,195,317	17.3	17.0	14.9	1	313	192,007	203,988	89.2
Holmes, FL	12059	6	19,099	15.8	27.5	12.4	1	11	3,371	...	...
Indian River, FL	12061	3	135,167	13.9	16.3	18.5	1	33	17,606	17,697	86.1
Jackson, FL	12063	6	50,930	14.5	20.8	13.3	1	24	7,319	7,822	94.4
Jefferson, FL	12065	2	14,010	13.3	21.3	17.6	1	11	1,106	...	...
Lafayette, FL	12067	8	7,949	13.6	27.6	28.2	1	7	1,119	...	...
Lake, FL	12069	1	312,119	13.8	15.5	16.4	1	60	40,960	41,918	88.2
Lee, FL	12071	2	586,908	14.3	15.1	22.3	1	126	79,434	85,385	90.3
Leon, FL	12073	2	265,714	13.7	15.9	14.3	4	72	35,231	38,215	84.8
Levy, FL	12075	8	39,147	15.4	25.6	17.9	1	21	6,024	6,163	86.1
Liberty, FL	12077	8	7,983	15.6	23.4	19.9	1	12	1,484	...	...
Madison, FL	12079	6	18,901	15.6	28.6	12.2	1	12	2,707	...	...
Manatee, FL	12081	2	318,361	14.6	17.2	18.7	1	83	42,580	47,496	88.6
Marion, FL	12083	2	328,547	14.5	22.2	20.9	1	67	42,625	45,785	85.3
Martin, FL	12085	2	139,794	13.6	14.1	19.2	1	41	18,067	19,047	87.6
Miami-Dade, FL	12086	1	2,500,625	16.2	20.4	19.6	1	557	345,525	397,338	85.7
Monroe, FL	12087	4	73,165	10.9	14.0	20.4	1	26	8,278	8,419	89.6
Nassau, FL	12089	1	70,576	16.5	12.2	17.6	1	23	10,982	11,121	89.5
Okaloosa, FL	12091	3	178,473	15.9	12.3	19.3	1	65	29,126	29,366	93.8
Okeechobee, FL	12093	4	40,241	17.7	25.3	22.6	1	19	7,004	6,812	97.6
Orange, FL	12095	1	1,086,480	17.1	16.6	16.9	3	269	172,774	185,879	85.6
Osceola, FL	12097	1	270,618	19.7	17.5	20.3	1	70	51,941	46,921	91.8
Palm Beach, FL	12099	1	1,279,950	15.0	14.3	20.3	2	270	172,775	192,483	85.2
Pasco, FL	12101	1	471,709	15.4	15.3	16.1	1	111	66,784	68,863	92.1
Pinellas, FL	12103	1	909,013	13.3	14.6	12.5	1	180	106,061	127,745	86.6
Polk, FL	12105	2	583,403	17.1	20.4	18.0	1	175	94,657	95,070	92.2
Putnam, FL	12107	4	72,893	16.4	32.0	12.4	1	26	11,493	12,492	92.4
St. Johns, FL	12109	1	187,436	16.8	8.9	16.2	2	60	29,664	27,404	88.4
St. Lucie, FL	12111	2	266,502	16.1	17.5	18.4	1	56	38,839	41,977	90.0
Santa Rosa, FL	12113	2	151,759	17.5	13.0	15.7	1	42	25,397	25,056	94.1
Sarasota, FL	12115	2	369,765	11.9	13.4	20.1	1	67	41,070	45,269	89.0
Seminole, FL	12117	1	413,204	17.3	9.9	16.6	1	81	64,927	70,280	87.1
Sumter, FL	12119	4	77,681	10.0	22.5	20.2	1	18	7,650	8,117	93.5
Suwannee, FL	12121	6	40,149	16.2	25.3	15.7	1	13	5,970	6,611	91.5
Taylor, FL	12123	6	21,400	14.6	27.8	13.1	1	11	3,298	5,714	88.7
Union, FL	12125	6	14,584	13.7	18.9	14.5	1	9	2,315	...	...
Volusia, FL	12127	2	495,890	14.1	16.9	17.4	1	104	63,018	70,863	91.3
Wakulla, FL	12129	2	32,815	16.2	15.8	21.5	1	16	5,264	4,889	90.1
Walton, FL	12131	6	55,105	14.2	22.9	21.4	1	21	6,991	7,829	94.5
Washington, FL	12133	6	23,916	15.7	28.0	13.6	2	16	3,883	...	...

[1]County type codes are from the Economic Research Service of the United States Department of Agriculture. See notes and definitions for more information.
... Not available

Table C-1. Population, School, and Student Characteristics by County—*Continued*

County	State/ County Code	Characteristics of students, 2008-2009				Number of graduates, 2006-2007	Staff and students, 2008-2009			
		Percent with IEP[2]	Percent eligible for free or reduced lunch	Percent minority	Percent English Language Learners		Total staff	Number of teachers	Student/ teacher ratio	Central admin. Staff
		10	11	12	13	14	15	16	17	18
FLORIDA	12000	14.6	49.6	50.9	8.6	151,939	340,711	186,359	14.1	16,609
Alachua, FL	12001	17.5	44.8	45.9	1.6	1,942	4,646	2,314	12.4	365
Baker, FL	12003	11.1	45.8	14.4	0.2	260	589	317	16.0	45
Bay, FL	12005	17.3	47.6	21.5	1.4	1,646	3,518	2,012	12.9	187
Bradford, FL	12007	23.4	53.4	26.2	0.3	214	541	278	12.2	22
Brevard, FL	12009	18.4	34.6	25.4	2.4	4,858	9,296	5,290	13.8	330
Broward, FL	12011	12.1	47.7	67.5	10.0	15,292	31,048	18,729	13.7	1,052
Calhoun, FL	12013	23.6	55.1	18.3	0.5	117	316	192	11.7	14
Charlotte, FL	12015	18.3	50.4	18.9	1.1	1,341	2,586	1,279	13.6	152
Citrus, FL	12017	16.1	46.9	11.5	0.9	897	2,485	1,263	12.7	132
Clay, FL	12019	18.7	29.7	22.5	1.3	2,323	5,001	2,772	13.0	299
Collier, FL	12021	14.3	50.7	55.2	14.8	2,603	5,733	3,055	13.9	281
Columbia, FL	12023	18.1	57.8	26.8	0.7	588	1,476	726	13.8	86
De Soto, FL	12027	17.0	67.6	51.3	10.5	237	728	375	13.2	59
Dixie, FL	12029	25.0	69.6	9.6	...	126	296	140	15.1	28
Duval, FL	12031	14.2	45.6	55.2	2.8	6,443	12,830	7,991	15.4	1,288
Escambia, FL	12033	17.3	58.8	43.2	0.9	2,265	6,192	3,550	11.5	335
Flagler, FL	12035	13.7	47.8	28.2	2.6	662	1,892	983	13.1	112
Franklin, FL	12037	16.9	69.3	14.5	0.8	69	190	80	16.0	18
Gadsden, FL	12039	14.0	89.2	94.6	7.5	200	1,013	473	13.6	47
Gilchrist, FL	12041	25.7	53.3	7.8	1.6	35	380	186	14.8	39
Glades, FL	12043	14.8	54.1	55.6	3.8	44	235	110	12.6	14
Gulf, FL	12045	19.7	45.6	17.2	0.3	156	296	150	13.7	20
Hamilton, FL	12047	14.8	66.0	53.9	4.5	85	293	123	15.8	32
Hardee, FL	12049	16.8	69.4	62.8	6.7	256	708	357	14.3	70
Hendry, FL	12051	16.3	69.8	68.9	5.7	465	927	406	17.3	61
Hernando, FL	12053	14.7	50.6	21.9	2.9	1,270	3,205	1,735	13.1	90
Highlands, FL	12055	14.4	63.8	46.5	5.2	696	1,745	916	13.4	130
Hillsborough, FL	12057	15.0	51.3	52.8	11.5	10,331	25,893	13,986	13.7	1,075
Holmes, FL	12059	15.0	59.3	5.3	0.1	198	496	252	13.4	23
Indian River, FL	12061	13.4	45.3	34.9	5.7	1,033	2,196	1,210	14.6	71
Jackson, FL	12063	16.2	57.2	35.0	0.7	432	1,127	556	13.2	69
Jefferson, FL	12065	24.0	75.0	76.4	2.0	58	203	95	11.6	18
Lafayette, FL	12067	13.3	53.3	24.3	4.3	50	170	80	14.0	13
Lake, FL	12069	14.2	44.8	35.2	5.1	2,266	5,814	2,885	14.2	357
Lee, FL	12071	14.7	52.2	44.8	8.4	4,086	9,469	5,034	15.8	357
Leon, FL	12073	16.3	38.8	48.2	1.4	2,011	5,137	2,672	13.2	201
Levy, FL	12075	25.4	63.1	23.9	2.3	314	946	432	13.9	59
Liberty, FL	12077	20.5	53.0	19.1	0.3	84	244	142	10.5	13
Madison, FL	12079	21.9	75.6	60.8	0.2	187	390	178	15.2	30
Manatee, FL	12081	19.0	46.8	40.5	9.7	2,348	5,503	2,646	16.1	353
Marion, FL	12083	16.3	54.9	36.5	4.6	2,472	6,363	3,006	14.2	266
Martin, FL	12085	16.4	33.4	28.6	11.9	1,149	2,249	1,210	14.9	135
Miami-Dade, FL	12086	11.3	63.4	89.5	15.2	19,874	38,954	22,384	15.4	1,412
Monroe, FL	12087	18.2	35.9	39.6	5.8	554	1,397	681	12.2	91
Nassau, FL	12089	15.0	35.9	11.6	0.7	708	1,493	766	14.3	65
Okaloosa, FL	12091	15.6	32.6	20.9	2.1	2,157	2,952	1,924	15.1	103
Okeechobee, FL	12093	21.3	59.7	42.0	7.4	386	941	486	14.4	47
Orange, FL	12095	14.1	48.6	63.2	19.5	10,071	22,626	11,545	15.0	1,938
Osceola, FL	12097	14.2	65.2	64.1	19.1	3,015	6,672	3,117	16.7	372
Palm Beach, FL	12099	15.6	44.1	55.9	10.2	10,292	22,328	13,348	12.9	906
Pasco, FL	12101	16.9	46.3	22.1	4.0	3,242	9,709	5,082	13.1	494
Pinellas, FL	12103	14.9	43.5	33.0	3.6	6,490	14,692	7,878	13.5	641
Polk, FL	12105	12.2	57.6	45.9	8.9	4,629	13,993	7,548	12.5	466
Putnam, FL	12107	18.6	69.9	38.4	5.7	629	1,743	720	16.0	67
St. Johns, FL	12109	16.3	20.2	16.4	0.8	1,673	4,002	1,874	15.8	238
St. Lucie, FL	12111	12.7	57.5	53.5	7.4	1,856	5,325	2,826	13.7	297
Santa Rosa, FL	12113	15.0	35.0	10.7	0.5	1,613	2,708	1,770	14.3	45
Sarasota, FL	12115	15.6	40.8	24.1	5.5	2,722	5,408	2,683	15.3	189
Seminole, FL	12117	13.5	34.4	35.6	3.8	4,189	7,695	4,519	14.4	213
Sumter, FL	12119	14.2	54.4	27.5	4.9	396	1,058	526	14.5	52
Suwannee, FL	12121	13.3	60.4	24.2	3.4	315	700	365	16.4	47
Taylor, FL	12123	17.6	61.8	27.0	...	202	509	231	14.3	25
Union, FL	12125	16.7	53.4	18.9	0.1	120	384	199	11.6	32
Volusia, FL	12127	16.7	46.7	32.2	4.6	3,825	8,537	4,445	14.2	342
Wakulla, FL	12129	21.2	41.2	12.9	0.1	277	702	358	14.7	42
Walton, FL	12131	12.2	46.6	14.5	2.5	356	1,171	591	11.8	54
Washington, FL	12133	18.3	58.4	21.4	0.7	239	665	325	11.9	83

[2]IEP= Individual Education Program. See notes and definitions for more information
... Not available

Table C-1. Population, School, and Student Characteristics by County—*Continued*

County	State/ County Code	Revenues, 2007-2008				Current expenditures, 2007-2008			Resident population 16 to 19 years, 2006-2008			
		Total revenue ($1,000's)	Percentage of revenue from			Amount ($1,000's)	Amount per student	Percent for instruction	Total population 16 to 19 years	Percent enrolled in school	Percent high school graduates, not enrolled in school	Percent not enrolled, not grads, not employed or not in labor force
			Federal gov't	State gov't	Local gov't							
		19	20	21	22	23	24	25	26	27	28	29
FLORIDA	12000	30,001,821	8.3	39.4	52.3	23,903,255	9,035	60.2	931,116	80.8	11.6	4.9
Alachua, FL	12001	298,689	10.2	48.4	41.3	254,424	8,966	55.2	20,295	90.2	5.7	3.4
Baker, FL	12003	44,853	8.2	71.0	20.8	41,478	8,364	55.2	...	...	...	...
Bay, FL	12005	267,771	8.3	37.0	54.8	222,563	8,483	60.1	7,666	72.7	17.0	3.4
Bradford, FL	12007	36,905	10.3	62.6	27.1	33,117	9,261	58.1	...	...	...	...
Brevard, FL	12009	747,371	7.0	44.2	48.8	627,018	8,431	62.6	26,639	84.8	10.2	3.2
Broward, FL	12011	2,874,695	8.1	39.4	52.5	2,339,595	9,037	60.5	89,175	83.3	10.6	4.3
Calhoun, FL	12013	21,344	9.5	71.3	19.2	20,168	9,048	58.2	...	...	...	...
Charlotte, FL	12015	217,239	7.4	21.0	71.5	163,149	9,168	56.6	5,666	81.2	14.3	1.9
Citrus, FL	12017	178,729	7.4	35.6	57.0	139,622	8,635	56.6	...	...	...	...
Clay, FL	12019	368,132	4.7	67.1	28.2	291,313	8,071	64.4	9,718	80.2	12.7	4.2
Collier, FL	12021	621,216	6.7	16.7	76.6	440,921	10,320	58.7	11,709	77.5	12.4	4.5
Columbia, FL	12023	94,708	10.6	63.1	26.3	85,356	8,493	58.6	4,024	69.5	19.1	8.7
De Soto, FL	12027	52,120	14.4	56.3	29.4	48,849	9,758	57.2	...	...	...	...
Dixie, FL	12029	22,427	12.3	61.6	26.1	19,746	9,016	54.1	...	...	...	...
Duval, FL	12031	1,238,175	8.6	46.7	44.8	1,079,389	8,653	60.5	46,303	77.2	14.1	5.7
Escambia, FL	12033	417,944	10.5	51.5	38.0	358,866	8,574	57.9	21,638	67.9	24.2	4.9
Flagler, FL	12035	181,456	4.2	36.5	59.3	108,157	8,467	59.7	...	...	...	...
Franklin, FL	12037	21,793	7.4	15.9	76.7	13,260	10,642	61.7	...	...	...	...
Gadsden, FL	12039	66,361	18.5	61.0	20.6	60,441	9,276	50.9	...	...	...	...
Gilchrist, FL	12041	29,103	8.3	67.5	24.2	26,620	9,214	56.6	...	...	...	...
Glades, FL	12043	14,915	11.0	48.2	40.9	13,436	9,843	54.6	...	...	...	...
Gulf, FL	12045	22,141	7.5	24.9	67.6	20,154	9,296	55.2	...	...	...	...
Hamilton, FL	12047	21,603	15.0	54.9	30.0	19,088	9,459	51.2	...	...	...	...
Hardee, FL	12049	50,980	13.4	56.5	30.1	46,095	9,193	55.9	...	...	...	...
Hendry, FL	12051	74,219	13.1	54.5	32.4	68,361	9,354	58.1	...	...	...	...
Hernando, FL	12053	253,140	6.6	48.1	45.3	177,713	7,782	59.7	6,902	76.8	15.6	5.8
Highlands, FL	12055	134,894	10.7	43.1	46.2	112,455	9,068	54.5	4,319	75.6	11.1	7.2
Hillsborough, FL	12057	2,068,665	11.9	50.0	38.1	1,613,384	8,352	61.1	62,796	79.3	12.1	5.3
Holmes, FL	12059	31,647	12.3	74.6	13.1	30,164	8,911	57.2	...	...	...	...
Indian River, FL	12061	198,399	6.2	18.8	75.0	153,977	8,726	57.4	5,599	77.4	14.8	4.9
Jackson, FL	12063	74,303	13.1	66.1	20.7	65,713	8,925	56.1	...	...	...	...
Jefferson, FL	12065	14,689	15.5	50.9	33.6	12,994	11,260	48.9	...	...	...	...
Lafayette, FL	12067	12,489	18.8	62.3	18.9	10,528	9,668	51.4	...	...	...	...
Lake, FL	12069	473,899	6.7	49.2	44.1	332,093	8,166	61.6	11,624	79.9	12.2	5.3
Lee, FL	12071	980,391	6.8	22.5	70.7	701,153	8,706	57.0	23,490	80.7	10.4	4.2
Leon, FL	12073	367,517	7.9	47.8	44.3	281,883	8,681	55.5	21,296	90.3	7.4	1.7
Levy, FL	12075	60,532	10.8	54.7	34.5	54,271	8,714	56.1	...	...	...	...
Liberty, FL	12077	18,080	12.1	71.0	16.9	14,685	9,706	57.7	...	...	...	...
Madison, FL	12079	26,968	14.8	65.7	19.5	26,011	9,370	49.5	...	...	...	...
Manatee, FL	12081	517,955	7.5	31.7	60.8	392,530	9,231	59.6	12,956	77.6	13.9	5.1
Marion, FL	12083	463,326	9.1	42.5	48.5	365,998	8,596	56.7	14,622	73.7	18.4	6.4
Martin, FL	12085	225,340	5.7	22.3	72.0	164,794	9,100	59.3	6,197	83.0	6.0	5.3
Miami-Dade, FL	12086	3,959,408	10.8	36.1	53.1	3,457,902	9,933	61.0	133,913	84.4	9.4	4.4
Monroe, FL	12087	137,417	6.9	16.9	76.2	104,003	12,438	59.1	...	...	...	...
Nassau, FL	12089	117,465	5.8	37.4	56.8	93,681	8,456	53.2	...	...	...	...
Okaloosa, FL	12091	296,801	8.2	38.9	52.9	249,844	8,450	63.8	9,184	75.9	20.7	2.6
Okeechobee, FL	12093	67,710	10.4	56.8	32.8	58,312	8,286	58.4	...	...	...	...
Orange, FL	12095	1,974,283	7.9	36.8	55.3	1,524,737	8,756	58.5	61,442	81.8	9.9	5.4
Osceola, FL	12097	628,244	7.0	51.0	42.0	450,830	8,548	57.2	13,410	80.8	12.9	4.9
Palm Beach, FL	12099	2,183,132	6.3	22.6	71.0	1,605,194	9,394	61.9	58,562	81.6	8.7	5.9
Pasco, FL	12101	713,902	7.7	53.0	39.3	557,214	8,403	57.4	20,563	80.2	9.9	7.0
Pinellas, FL	12103	1,211,026	7.8	37.5	54.7	966,587	8,959	60.1	39,964	81.8	11.9	3.5
Polk, FL	12105	1,250,657	6.6	48.9	44.5	1,017,453	10,826	70.2	28,865	76.1	12.7	6.7
Putnam, FL	12107	115,776	11.9	57.3	30.7	107,591	9,110	57.1	4,529	71.2	21.9	6.6
St. Johns, FL	12109	335,431	4.0	34.6	61.4	235,915	8,467	56.6	8,695	81.4	11.7	3.4
St. Lucie, FL	12111	487,180	7.5	44.8	47.7	349,362	8,659	55.0	12,264	78.6	12.0	5.1
Santa Rosa, FL	12113	242,133	7.5	55.2	37.3	206,113	8,017	60.5	8,394	83.3	10.8	4.8
Sarasota, FL	12115	626,334	4.7	18.2	77.1	455,337	10,838	60.1	13,512	82.8	11.1	3.7
Seminole, FL	12117	633,500	6.3	47.0	46.6	529,379	8,097	62.9	21,939	87.4	7.1	3.3
Sumter, FL	12119	76,323	8.5	29.9	61.5	66,901	8,895	63.4	...	...	...	...
Suwannee, FL	12121	55,360	12.7	57.8	29.6	49,204	8,217	59.0	...	...	...	...
Taylor, FL	12123	34,453	15.4	48.8	35.8	31,509	9,300	54.5	...	...	...	...
Union, FL	12125	23,265	11.3	72.4	16.3	20,076	8,744	57.2	...	...	...	...
Volusia, FL	12127	713,726	7.2	36.5	56.3	564,674	8,756	60.3	26,320	85.7	7.8	4.3
Wakulla, FL	12129	67,066	5.3	71.8	22.9	41,540	8,021	57.1	...	...	...	...
Walton, FL	12131	94,620	5.9	17.6	76.5	70,328	10,102	57.8	...	...	...	...
Washington, FL	12133	49,486	11.2	63.8	25.0	38,037	10,607	56.6	...	...	...	...

... Not available

Table C-1. Population, School, and Student Characteristics by County—*Continued*

County	State/ County Code	High school graduates, 2006-2008			College enrollment, 2006-2008		College graduates, 2006-2008 (percent)					
		Population 25 years and over	High school diploma or less (percent)	High school diploma or more (percent)	Number	Percent public	Bachelor's degree or more	+/- U.S. percent with Bachelor's degree or more	Non-His-panic White	Black or African Ameri-can	Ameri-can Indian and Alaska Native	Asian, Hawai-ian, and Pacific Islander	His-panic or Latino[3]
		30	31	32	33	34	35	36	37	38	39	40	41
FLORIDA	12000	12,566,850	45.9	84.9	1,099,721	74.8	25.7	-1.7	28.2	15.9	16.9	44.8	21.4
Alachua, FL	12001	139,753	31.4	90.0	55,611	96.6	41.9	14.5	46.4	15.4	...	81.8	42.1
Baker, FL	12003	16,605	74.1	75.4	756	81.7	6.3	-21.1	6.4	1.5	...	...	...
Bay, FL	12005	113,219	45.1	86.3	7,527	86.4	20.9	-6.5	22.5	10.6	...	21.0	16.1
Bradford, FL	12007	19,113	63.0	79.1	1,549	84.5	8.3	-19.1	8.5	6.7	...	...	...
Brevard, FL	12009	382,446	40.3	90.2	33,754	70.1	26.0	-1.4	27.0	15.1	10.9	44.6	21.3
Broward, FL	12011	1,203,495	42.8	86.8	107,673	67.3	29.3	1.9	32.8	19.5	21.5	46.1	27.6
Calhoun, FL	12013	...	...	...	...	...	...	...	...	...	...	...	...
Charlotte, FL	12015	118,466	47.9	88.4	4,325	81.8	20.8	-6.6	21.2	16.0	...	30.8	14.2
Citrus, FL	12017	107,659	55.3	83.3	4,185	77.9	15.9	-11.5	15.4	22.2	...	58.9	13.8
Clay, FL	12019	119,582	42.9	89.8	10,886	79.6	22.5	-4.9	22.2	22.9	...	33.2	21.2
Collier, FL	12021	228,790	43.9	84.2	10,431	69.6	30.5	3.1	36.4	13.9	...	50.1	10.4
Columbia, FL	12023	45,364	57.6	80.7	2,997	89.0	14.7	-12.7	14.5	14.0	...	...	8.8
De Soto, FL	12027	23,203	70.9	59.2	472	75.6	11.5	-15.9	15.6	11.9	...	...	1.8
Dixie, FL	12029	...	...	...	...	...	...	...	...	...	...	...	...
Duval, FL	12031	552,995	44.5	87.1	50,307	75.5	24.3	-3.1	27.2	15.0	21.1	42.8	22.7
Escambia, FL	12033	199,067	43.9	86.0	21,000	71.1	23.5	-3.9	27.0	12.4	11.6	25.4	18.6
Flagler, FL	12035	63,135	46.3	89.4	4,499	84.2	20.0	-7.4	20.3	17.0	...	42.9	13.5
Franklin, FL	12037	...	...	...	...	...	...	...	...	...	...	...	...
Gadsden, FL	12039	31,068	63.9	77.2	1,906	83.2	10.6	-16.8	16.8	5.5	...	...	4.8
Gilchrist, FL	12041	...	...	...	...	...	...	...	...	...	...	...	...
Glades, FL	12043	...	...	...	...	...	...	...	...	...	...	...	...
Gulf, FL	12045	...	...	...	...	...	...	...	...	...	...	...	...
Hamilton, FL	12047	...	...	...	...	...	...	...	...	...	...	...	...
Hardee, FL	12049	17,689	72.5	61.5	589	48.0	7.9	-19.5	10.9	...	...	...	3.6
Hendry, FL	12051	22,715	77.4	59.1	1,266	81.8	6.2	-21.2	9.7	3.8	...	...	2.8
Hernando, FL	12053	123,740	53.2	84.8	7,785	77.4	15.1	-12.3	15.3	12.1	...	32.2	12.6
Highlands, FL	12055	73,235	59.7	76.1	2,945	82.4	13.7	-13.7	14.2	6.1	...	55.5	10.2
Hillsborough, FL	12057	772,255	43.0	85.6	79,880	77.4	28.8	1.4	32.9	20.1	16.3	54.4	18.0
Holmes, FL	12059	...	...	...	...	...	...	...	...	...	...	...	...
Indian River, FL	12061	96,455	42.7	86.7	4,916	79.1	26.6	-0.8	28.8	12.9	...	48.1	10.9
Jackson, FL	12063	34,321	59.6	76.7	2,259	82.6	11.8	-15.6	14.2	4.6	...	...	11.3
Jefferson, FL	12065	...	...	...	...	...	...	...	...	...	...	...	...
Lafayette, FL	12067	...	...	...	...	...	...	...	...	...	...	...	...
Lake, FL	12069	220,094	49.1	85.4	10,994	73.5	19.8	-7.6	20.2	16.8	11.6	37.5	16.3
Lee, FL	12071	421,175	45.7	86.6	23,785	79.6	25.0	-2.4	27.4	11.7	21.5	46.2	13.8
Leon, FL	12073	155,271	30.4	90.7	51,889	94.4	40.9	13.5	46.3	26.0	...	69.2	37.1
Levy, FL	12075	27,054	61.3	79.9	1,378	86.9	10.5	-16.9	11.7	2.7	...	...	5.8
Liberty, FL	12077	...	...	...	...	...	...	...	...	...	...	...	...
Madison, FL	12079	...	...	...	...	...	...	...	...	...	...	...	...
Manatee, FL	12081	225,490	46.0	86.1	12,916	75.7	25.5	-1.9	28.1	14.2	...	24.5	11.5
Marion, FL	12083	232,857	54.6	84.3	11,836	76.5	16.5	-10.9	17.2	9.6	16.6	39.8	14.0
Martin, FL	12085	103,624	41.8	88.7	6,410	83.6	29.3	1.9	31.3	10.3	...	...	12.5
Miami-Dade, FL	12086	1,607,310	50.6	76.8	177,320	69.6	26.8	-0.6	44.8	14.5	19.7	49.5	24.2
Monroe, FL	12087	57,486	37.4	90.4	2,652	75.0	30.0	2.6	33.7	1.4	...	...	20.5
Nassau, FL	12089	47,751	52.6	84.8	2,927	83.6	20.4	-7.0	20.6	11.3	...	...	...
Okaloosa, FL	12091	122,771	36.6	91.0	10,445	88.8	27.9	0.5	29.8	14.7	15.1	27.2	21.3
Okeechobee, FL	12093	26,180	69.0	70.8	1,033	90.9	10.0	-17.4	12.0	2.2	...	...	2.8
Orange, FL	12095	688,510	41.1	86.7	78,942	72.1	30.1	2.7	36.7	18.4	20.9	42.8	21.1
Osceola, FL	12097	165,858	51.0	84.5	11,807	65.1	18.5	-8.9	21.5	17.6	...	26.3	13.9
Palm Beach, FL	12099	902,450	40.9	86.5	63,913	72.4	31.5	4.1	36.0	16.5	22.2	49.9	19.5
Pasco, FL	12101	328,357	51.2	85.5	19,175	71.4	18.9	-8.5	18.4	21.3	...	41.5	17.9
Pinellas, FL	12103	678,290	43.0	87.8	44,025	76.0	26.8	-0.6	28.1	15.3	15.7	36.1	20.9
Polk, FL	12105	384,148	55.9	81.5	23,212	61.1	17.8	-9.6	19.7	11.5	13.3	40.7	10.2
Putnam, FL	12107	49,694	64.9	76.6	2,299	79.6	12.7	-14.7	14.3	6.8	...	...	5.4
St. Johns, FL	12109	122,356	32.4	92.0	11,003	66.8	36.8	9.4	37.6	15.3	...	60.5	36.2
St. Lucie, FL	12111	179,487	52.7	81.6	11,386	80.5	17.4	-10.0	18.6	13.0	...	43.8	11.8
Santa Rosa, FL	12113	100,289	42.8	87.9	9,042	80.1	23.7	-3.7	24.3	10.8	4.2	33.2	24.3
Sarasota, FL	12115	287,594	41.8	89.9	13,578	70.3	28.4	1.0	29.4	12.5	...	45.4	17.5
Seminole, FL	12117	278,516	35.9	90.0	30,681	78.7	32.3	4.9	34.1	20.9	...	53.6	24.9
Sumter, FL	12119	56,562	61.2	78.6	1,562	73.8	11.1	-16.3	12.4	6.5	...	...	6.1
Suwannee, FL	12121	27,676	65.5	77.5	1,332	78.0	8.8	-18.6	9.6	4.6	...	...	5.5
Taylor, FL	12123	16,218	60.9	76.9	1,062	89.8	11.9	-15.5	13.5	2.7	...	...	...
Union, FL	12125	...	...	...	...	...	...	...	...	...	...	...	...
Volusia, FL	12127	354,767	47.2	87.6	36,816	58.8	20.8	-6.6	21.5	16.2	22.2	50.2	14.1
Wakulla, FL	12129	21,552	55.9	83.0	1,501	61.2	14.7	-12.7	14.0	16.7	...	...	17.5
Walton, FL	12131	38,153	46.1	83.0	1,587	77.4	25.6	-1.8	27.1	12.3	...	...	4.7
Washington, FL	12133	15,840	66.5	75.2	...	...	11.0	-16.4	12.0	3.9	...	...	...

[3]May be of any race
... Not available

Table C-1. Population, School, and Student Characteristics by County—*Continued*

County	State/ County Code	County Type[1]	Population, 2009 Total	Percent 5–17 years	Percent of related children 5-17 years in poverty, 2008	Percent of children under 19 years with no health insurance, 2007	School Districts	Schools	Students	Resident enrollment, 2006-2008 K–12 enrollment Number	Percent public
			1	2	3	4	5	6	7	8	9
GEORGIA	13000	X	9,829,211	18.6	18.3	12.6	207	2,600	1,655,792	1,787,048	90.0
Appling, GA	13001	7	18,011	19.1	28.6	12.8	1	10	3,540	...	...
Atkinson, GA	13003	9	8,230	21.9	31.6	17.3	1	3	1,733	...	...
Bacon, GA	13005	7	10,601	18.0	26.1	11.1	1	4	1,851	...	...
Baker, GA	13007	3	3,637	18.1	28.6	9.5	1	1	433	...	...
Baldwin, GA	13009	4	46,337	13.9	25.0	10.5	1	10	5,806	6,580	81.3
Banks, GA	13011	8	16,799	18.4	18.7	16.1	1	4	2,915	...	...
Barrow, GA	13013	1	72,158	19.5	14.6	17.5	1	16	12,421	13,341	94.2
Bartow, GA	13015	1	96,217	19.7	16.1	13.5	2	27	18,687	18,271	90.4
Ben Hill, GA	13017	7	17,567	19.2	32.5	9.9	1	5	3,365	...	...
Berrien, GA	13019	6	17,044	17.9	30.9	9.8	1	5	3,113	...	...
Bibb, GA	13021	3	156,060	18.8	29.6	7.9	1	52	24,968	29,677	83.6
Bleckley, GA	13023	6	12,855	18.3	24.1	9.7	1	6	2,482	...	...
Brantley, GA	13025	3	15,643	19.4	23.0	15.9	1	6	3,621	...	...
Brooks, GA	13027	3	16,354	16.8	31.5	9.2	1	5	2,378	...	...
Bryan, GA	13029	2	32,559	21.9	13.4	12.6	1	12	7,054	6,367	93.6
Bulloch, GA	13031	4	69,213	14.6	22.1	13.5	3	21	9,506	10,264	94.1
Burke, GA	13033	2	22,797	21.5	41.9	11.1	1	6	4,728	5,501	91.1
Butts, GA	13035	1	24,392	16.6	20.3	12.4	1	8	3,545	4,585	85.5
Calhoun, GA	13037	8	6,306	13.5	37.9	10.4	1	2	657	...	...
Camden, GA	13039	4	48,277	19.4	14.3	15.9	1	13	9,701	10,532	97.3
Candler, GA	13043	7	10,680	17.8	33.3	15.1	1	5	1,992	...	...
Carroll, GA	13045	1	114,778	18.3	16.3	11.1	3	33	19,401	20,544	93.8
Catoosa, GA	13047	2	64,035	18.5	14.3	8.7	1	18	10,658	11,105	93.0
Charlton, GA	13049	6	10,725	16.4	26.0	10.2	1	5	1,801	...	...
Chatham, GA	13051	2	256,992	15.9	20.3	12.6	1	60	33,994	44,031	79.5
Chattahoochee, GA	13053	2	14,402	14.3	13.9	13.2	1	3	919	...	...
Chattooga, GA	13055	6	26,619	16.7	20.3	8.8	2	13	4,283	...	...
Cherokee, GA	13057	1	215,084	19.9	7.5	15.8	1	42	37,275	41,220	87.4
Clarke, GA	13059	3	116,342	11.6	25.1	16.9	2	22	12,262	13,502	86.8
Clay, GA	13061	9	3,113	17.2	47.2	8.1	1	2	330	...	...
Clayton, GA	13063	1	275,772	21.2	19.1	12.3	2	66	49,602	57,141	94.4
Clinch, GA	13065	6	6,988	20.3	29.0	8.4	1	7	1,444	...	...
Cobb, GA	13067	1	714,692	18.5	9.7	12.3	3	139	114,616	125,984	88.1
Coffee, GA	13069	7	40,868	19.0	26.6	13.8	1	12	8,016	7,820	97.4
Colquitt, GA	13071	6	45,596	19.4	27.5	13.7	1	16	8,933	8,303	97.8
Columbia, GA	13073	2	112,958	21.0	7.4	12.9	1	30	22,767	21,815	92.4
Cook, GA	13075	6	16,603	19.2	28.9	12.4	2	5	3,267	...	...
Coweta, GA	13077	1	127,111	19.9	11.6	12.7	3	33	26,746	23,979	91.3
Crawford, GA	13079	3	12,240	17.2	21.9	15.4	1	5	1,879	...	...
Crisp, GA	13081	6	22,210	19.5	37.3	9.2	1	7	4,374	4,328	92.1
Dade, GA	13083	2	16,127	16.6	14.9	9.8	1	5	2,545	...	...
Dawson, GA	13085	1	22,555	16.8	14.1	19.4	1	7	3,470	3,865	91.4
Decatur, GA	13087	6	28,838	18.9	33.8	10.3	1	10	5,664	5,537	94.2
De Kalb, GA	13089	1	747,274	16.5	24.4	10.6	4	196	103,022	124,519	87.8
Dodge, GA	13091	7	19,749	18.2	27.1	11.3	2	7	3,386	2,851	97.1
Dooly, GA	13093	6	11,819	15.2	31.5	9.3	1	3	1,463	...	...
Dougherty, GA	13095	3	95,859	18.5	33.2	8.7	1	30	16,222	18,234	88.5
Douglas, GA	13097	1	129,703	21.6	13.5	14.1	1	37	24,800	26,615	91.8
Early, GA	13099	6	11,560	19.6	35.0	8.8	1	5	2,454	...	...
Echols, GA	13101	3	4,213	18.1	33.1	24.3	1	1	741	...	...
Effingham, GA	13103	2	53,541	21.5	11.9	13.2	1	21	11,359	10,753	93.0
Elbert, GA	13105	6	20,372	17.2	24.1	13.9	1	8	3,441	3,620	91.1
Emanuel, GA	13107	7	23,075	18.0	35.6	14.6	1	10	4,424	3,915	90.4
Evans, GA	13109	6	11,695	17.9	33.6	16.2	1	4	1,860	...	...
Fannin, GA	13111	8	22,945	14.8	23.0	16.8	1	5	3,159	3,044	92.0
Fayette, GA	13113	1	106,788	21.6	5.4	12.7	1	32	22,118	20,625	89.6
Floyd, GA	13115	3	96,250	17.6	23.2	11.4	3	34	16,199	16,398	89.6
Forsyth, GA	13117	1	174,520	21.7	5.4	14.7	1	31	32,374	31,944	89.0
Franklin, GA	13119	8	21,748	16.9	25.0	11.9	2	14	7,933	3,516	99.0
Fulton, GA	13121	1	1,033,756	17.2	17.9	8.4	5	219	137,331	173,627	84.8
Gilmer, GA	13123	6	29,021	16.8	22.6	17.6	2	8	4,226	5,263	95.4
Glascock, GA	13125	9	2,801	19.6	17.5	10.2	1	1	653	...	...
Glynn, GA	13127	3	76,820	17.7	26.4	14.2	1	26	12,759	13,372	92.6
Gordon, GA	13129	6	53,292	19.2	16.6	16.1	2	16	10,332	9,673	95.5
Grady, GA	13131	6	25,187	19.1	31.2	13.9	1	8	4,446	4,711	96.5
Greene, GA	13133	6	15,743	15.2	28.1	13.5	1	6	1,945	...	...
Gwinnett, GA	13135	1	808,167	21.4	11.0	15.2	3	124	160,360	155,682	91.7
Habersham, GA	13137	6	43,613	17.1	16.9	19.6	1	13	6,969	7,337	92.1
Hall, GA	13139	3	187,743	19.8	17.2	20.5	2	43	31,984	34,047	94.0
Hancock, GA	13141	7	9,219	14.7	36.6	8.0	1	4	1,297	...	...

[1]County type codes are from the Economic Research Service of the United States Department of Agriculture. See notes and definitions for more information.
... Not available

Table C-1. Population, School, and Student Characteristics by County—*Continued*

County	State/County Code	Characteristics of students, 2008-2009				Number of graduates, 2006-2007	Staff and students, 2008-2009			
		Percent with IEP[2]	Percent eligible for free or reduced lunch	Percent minority	Percent English Language Learners		Total staff	Number of teachers	Student/teacher ratio	Central admin. Staff
		10	11	12	13	14	15	16	17	18
GEORGIA	13000	10.9	53.0	51.1	5.0	85,862	239,130	118,837	13.9	5,040
Appling, GA	13001	15.3	60.9	34.0	3.5	170	541	260	13.6	12
Atkinson, GA	13003	11.7	80.7	50.5	6.1	65	260	117	14.8	6
Bacon, GA	13005	13.2	58.0	25.3	3.8	100	294	131	14.1	10
Baker, GA	13007	15.9	91.9	83.6	4.6	...	78	39	11.1	2
Baldwin, GA	13009	12.5	64.8	68.1	0.8	246	867	458	12.7	16
Banks, GA	13011	14.4	59.5	15.9	3.2	121	427	210	13.9	13
Barrow, GA	13013	11.8	51.4	30.1	6.9	538	1,636	880	14.1	27
Bartow, GA	13015	11.6	51.2	21.5	5.3	911	2,580	1,322	14.1	38
Ben Hill, GA	13017	11.2	72.4	52.5	4.4	175	477	232	14.5	14
Berrien, GA	13019	11.3	62.5	19.1	1.8	205	439	212	14.7	16
Bibb, GA	13021	11.6	74.9	76.4	1.3	1,076	3,769	1,645	15.2	103
Bleckley, GA	13023	14.7	54.0	30.5	1.1	140	387	180	13.8	10
Brantley, GA	13025	10.7	59.4	4.8	0.6	165	533	242	15.0	11
Brooks, GA	13027	10.6	76.7	61.6	1.9	119	385	177	13.4	12
Bryan, GA	13029	6.7	31.7	21.9	...	410	936	470	15.0	17
Bulloch, GA	13031	12.5	55.2	40.1	2.0	551	1,603	718	13.2	50
Burke, GA	13033	9.9	83.7	67.7	0.3	225	860	343	13.8	18
Butts, GA	13035	13.3	55.6	33.5	0.5	205	551	243	14.6	18
Calhoun, GA	13037	12.2	99.1	97.9	1.4	41	131	46	14.3	5
Camden, GA	13039	10.2	40.4	29.7	0.6	528	1,454	683	14.2	27
Candler, GA	13043	11.6	65.5	46.6	3.8	68	307	139	14.3	12
Carroll, GA	13045	11.0	55.8	29.9	2.7	990	2,798	1,304	14.9	43
Catoosa, GA	13047	14.0	42.9	6.5	0.7	576	1,620	744	14.3	32
Charlton, GA	13049	8.9	64.7	32.6	0.4	119	252	121	14.9	8
Chatham, GA	13051	11.0	61.8	71.3	1.8	1,530	5,001	2,715	12.5	109
Chattahoochee, GA	13053	12.1	63.4	43.0	3.5	...	178	64	14.4	8
Chattooga, GA	13055	12.7	59.6	13.7	2.1	226	631	308	13.9	21
Cherokee, GA	13057	11.3	24.2	19.7	3.3	1,779	4,902	2,604	14.3	86
Clarke, GA	13059	12.8	73.7	76.7	10.4	494	2,361	1,056	11.6	46
Clay, GA	13061	14.2	95.8	97.9	...	...	82	29	11.4	3
Clayton, GA	13063	9.4	76.8	91.8	7.2	2,431	7,994	3,730	13.3	179
Clinch, GA	13065	15.5	65.7	38.1	1.0	77	219	104	13.9	6
Cobb, GA	13067	11.2	39.5	51.6	8.3	7,123	16,050	8,870	12.9	318
Coffee, GA	13069	8.9	70.4	45.1	4.2	374	1,166	573	14.0	28
Colquitt, GA	13071	12.2	67.3	47.1	7.7	417	1,327	610	14.6	24
Columbia, GA	13073	7.8	26.7	24.1	1.1	1,391	3,132	1,492	15.3	46
Cook, GA	13075	12.5	65.8	42.0	3.1	170	536	220	14.9	22
Coweta, GA	13077	10.4	38.6	28.8	1.8	1,162	3,459	1,629	16.4	72
Crawford, GA	13079	17.9	72.2	29.2	0.1	122	278	133	14.1	8
Crisp, GA	13081	11.6	74.1	60.1	1.1	218	708	331	13.2	19
Dade, GA	13083	14.6	47.1	1.6	0.3	168	361	164	15.5	9
Dawson, GA	13085	11.7	35.2	4.9	2.0	209	541	266	13.0	15
Decatur, GA	13087	10.2	68.0	58.3	3.2	343	873	392	14.4	20
De Kalb, GA	13089	9.9	65.4	85.6	7.3	5,713	14,839	7,126	14.5	255
Dodge, GA	13091	12.4	65.2	38.3	1.2	214	597	253	13.4	26
Dooly, GA	13093	9.8	91.6	88.9	3.4	52	252	108	13.5	7
Dougherty, GA	13095	9.6	79.1	89.3	0.7	725	2,509	1,115	14.5	54
Douglas, GA	13097	10.8	52.1	58.4	3.5	1,364	3,467	1,777	14.0	51
Early, GA	13099	11.4	73.0	65.3	1.0	175	395	201	12.2	11
Echols, GA	13101	8.9	63.6	33.5	5.0	40	120	55	13.5	6
Effingham, GA	13103	12.7	35.9	18.8	0.7	592	1,746	814	14.0	34
Elbert, GA	13105	9.8	66.3	42.7	2.7	204	603	274	12.6	13
Emanuel, GA	13107	14.9	72.0	47.9	1.8	243	659	309	14.3	19
Evans, GA	13109	13.7	79.0	58.4	8.7	98	288	135	13.8	11
Fannin, GA	13111	14.0	57.8	10.7	0.9	200	473	209	15.1	10
Fayette, GA	13113	8.3	17.4	34.5	2.1	1,750	3,251	1,573	14.1	59
Floyd, GA	13115	14.1	56.9	31.0	4.7	857	2,441	1,244	13.0	56
Forsyth, GA	13117	11.1	15.8	16.7	4.6	1,392	4,140	2,215	14.6	62
Franklin, GA	13119	12.0	49.2	15.5	1.6	206	1,270	581	13.7	24
Fulton, GA	13121	9.9	52.0	70.6	4.3	6,677	19,385	10,294	13.3	589
Gilmer, GA	13123	10.0	64.0	16.4	7.4	208	770	343	12.3	24
Glascock, GA	13125	12.7	50.5	7.5	...	29	102	43	15.2	5
Glynn, GA	13127	10.3	48.8	45.2	3.8	627	1,934	906	14.1	42
Gordon, GA	13129	10.3	57.9	23.4	6.6	503	1,461	720	14.4	39
Grady, GA	13131	8.9	62.9	53.2	4.9	214	664	318	14.0	13
Greene, GA	13133	12.6	78.4	76.2	5.0	12	340	166	11.7	12
Gwinnett, GA	13135	11.1	45.7	60.5	13.0	8,152	20,507	11,212	14.3	267
Habersham, GA	13137	14.3	49.2	23.4	6.8	310	1,046	525	13.3	15
Hall, GA	13139	10.1	57.8	48.4	19.6	1,450	4,252	2,329	13.7	52
Hancock, GA	13141	12.8	74.6	98.1	0.3	91	257	116	11.2	12

[2]IEP= Individual Education Program. See notes and definitions for more information
... Not available

Table C-1. Population, School, and Student Characteristics by County—*Continued*

County	State/ County Code	Revenues, 2007-2008				Current expenditures, 2007-2008			Resident population 16 to 19 years, 2006-2008			
		Total revenue ($1,000's)	Percentage of revenue from			Amount ($1,000's)	Amount per student	Percent for instruc- tion	Total population 16 to 19 years	Percent en- rolled in school	Percent high school graduates, not enrolled in school	Percent not enrolled, not grads, not employed or not in labor force
			Federal gov't	State gov't	Local gov't							
		19	20	21	22	23	24	25	26	27	28	29
GEORGIA	13000	18,688,674	7.8	45.1	47.1	16,182,888	9,828	63.6	558,713	80.7	10.3	6.1
Appling, GA	13001	37,681	9.7	53.5	36.7	35,303	10,032	63.9	...	...	...	...
Atkinson, GA	13003	17,499	12.5	69.3	18.2	15,845	8,957	64.3	...	...	...	...
Bacon, GA	13005	18,985	10.7	64.7	24.6	18,230	9,640	63.5	...	...	...	...
Baker, GA	13007	6,328	20.2	45.8	34.0	6,509	13,938	56.0	...	...	...	...
Baldwin, GA	13009	64,010	12.0	59.2	28.8	56,725	9,728	64.6	...	...	...	...
Banks, GA	13011	28,709	8.8	50.4	40.8	26,276	9,425	65.3	...	...	...	...
Barrow, GA	13013	126,016	5.9	53.5	40.6	107,990	8,878	64.8	...	...	...	...
Bartow, GA	13015	202,068	6.2	50.3	43.4	171,651	9,211	64.9	4,195	82.9	9.4	4.2
Ben Hill, GA	13017	34,355	11.1	60.5	28.4	32,166	9,517	66.2	...	...	...	...
Berrien, GA	13019	33,773	9.8	67.8	22.3	25,850	8,293	66.9	...	...	...	...
Bibb, GA	13021	267,929	11.7	45.7	42.7	235,055	9,391	60.2	9,283	80.5	7.0	9.7
Bleckley, GA	13023	23,446	9.7	69.5	20.8	22,635	8,943	66.3	...	...	...	...
Brantley, GA	13025	33,459	8.8	68.8	22.5	30,284	8,514	66.1	...	...	...	...
Brooks, GA	13027	31,004	13.3	60.8	25.9	24,292	9,984	59.6	...	...	...	...
Bryan, GA	13029	64,202	5.8	55.3	39.0	54,158	8,059	66.6	...	...	...	...
Bulloch, GA	13031	121,599	8.8	54.2	37.0	97,967	10,768	60.8	...	...	...	...
Burke, GA	13033	49,091	13.1	40.6	46.4	51,684	10,913	58.7	...	...	...	...
Butts, GA	13035	39,441	7.7	45.8	46.5	31,913	9,089	60.0	...	...	...	...
Calhoun, GA	13037	8,925	16.5	53.2	30.3	8,195	11,774	56.0	...	...	...	...
Camden, GA	13039	98,832	12.9	59.5	27.5	91,086	9,347	63.1	...	...	...	...
Candler, GA	13043	19,998	11.7	61.7	26.6	18,384	9,605	63.6	...	...	...	...
Carroll, GA	13045	204,635	7.3	53.1	39.6	179,190	9,275	62.8	7,016	80.9	12.3	2.5
Catoosa, GA	13047	113,033	6.1	55.1	38.9	101,225	9,454	66.8	...	...	...	...
Charlton, GA	13049	19,538	10.5	58.5	31.0	18,210	9,696	62.3	...	...	...	...
Chatham, GA	13051	403,159	9.5	34.1	56.4	339,417	9,966	64.0	15,543	80.1	9.7	7.5
Chattahoochee, GA	13053	9,907	16.2	64.0	19.8	9,505	10,309	56.0	...	...	...	...
Chattooga, GA	13055	45,752	8.0	62.7	29.4	42,138	9,651	62.4	...	...	...	...
Cherokee, GA	13057	406,706	3.6	42.4	54.0	338,282	9,305	70.6	10,598	81.4	11.1	4.0
Clarke, GA	13059	184,039	10.2	34.4	55.5	156,676	12,876	60.4	...	...	...	...
Clay, GA	13061	5,237	20.0	46.9	33.2	4,912	14,238	51.6	...	...	...	...
Clayton, GA	13063	567,961	9.8	46.6	43.7	487,680	9,251	60.6	16,908	76.2	14.2	6.5
Clinch, GA	13065	16,022	11.7	54.1	34.3	14,368	9,978	62.6	...	...	...	...
Cobb, GA	13067	1,276,616	6.2	38.6	55.2	1,130,318	9,804	68.6	36,650	85.2	8.5	3.7
Coffee, GA	13069	79,236	10.6	62.1	27.2	76,546	9,445	63.6	...	...	...	...
Colquitt, GA	13071	93,135	10.6	65.1	24.3	85,399	9,580	63.5	2,872	67.5	16.7	11.8
Columbia, GA	13073	223,610	4.2	53.9	41.9	192,848	8,585	66.5	...	...	...	...
Cook, GA	13075	45,481	12.6	57.8	29.6	32,618	10,080	56.2	...	...	...	...
Coweta, GA	13077	222,745	6.0	46.2	47.8	196,460	9,016	64.7	5,747	79.8	12.8	6.2
Crawford, GA	13079	18,731	15.0	58.1	26.9	19,689	10,303	62.9	...	...	...	...
Crisp, GA	13081	48,638	13.0	57.1	29.9	45,355	10,227	64.5	...	...	...	...
Dade, GA	13083	25,490	7.6	56.8	35.7	22,682	8,881	63.2	...	...	...	...
Dawson, GA	13085	49,044	3.6	30.9	65.5	41,273	12,251	55.5	...	...	...	...
Decatur, GA	13087	66,766	12.9	59.7	27.5	54,418	9,500	64.9	...	...	...	...
De Kalb, GA	13089	1,286,435	6.6	35.8	57.6	1,095,509	10,649	60.6	39,196	81.9	10.9	4.2
Dodge, GA	13091	39,988	16.7	59.8	23.5	38,405	11,122	57.7	...	...	...	...
Dooly, GA	13093	18,088	18.2	47.9	33.8	15,400	10,343	61.3	...	...	...	...
Dougherty, GA	13095	182,288	12.9	50.6	36.5	165,825	10,089	62.4	6,740	74.8	10.1	7.7
Douglas, GA	13097	266,731	6.8	45.5	47.7	226,736	9,168	65.8	7,223	82.3	11.3	4.8
Early, GA	13099	28,059	18.2	50.5	31.3	26,200	10,650	65.5	...	...	...	...
Echols, GA	13101	7,344	14.8	57.3	27.9	7,364	9,925	60.1	...	...	...	...
Effingham, GA	13103	113,506	5.1	57.9	37.0	98,697	8,934	65.5	...	...	...	...
Elbert, GA	13105	39,037	9.4	58.6	32.0	36,410	10,350	66.0	...	...	...	...
Emanuel, GA	13107	43,292	14.2	63.5	22.3	39,986	8,943	65.6	...	...	...	...
Evans, GA	13109	18,767	13.0	59.8	27.1	17,411	9,427	61.3	...	...	...	...
Fannin, GA	13111	38,590	6.6	43.7	49.7	32,991	10,252	62.7	...	...	...	...
Fayette, GA	13113	232,377	3.0	43.8	53.2	213,138	9,591	67.0	...	...	...	...
Floyd, GA	13115	188,437	8.9	51.3	39.8	174,979	10,814	62.6	5,674	83.3	7.4	6.8
Forsyth, GA	13117	332,290	3.0	37.7	59.3	280,773	9,159	68.5	7,069	83.6	7.8	6.7
Franklin, GA	13119	38,772	7.7	52.8	39.6	34,337	8,903	63.7	...	...	...	...
Fulton, GA	13121	1,938,049	6.9	24.4	68.7	1,597,528	11,728	58.4	53,791	86.3	7.2	4.5
Gilmer, GA	13123	55,225	9.9	43.9	46.2	52,627	12,299	64.0	...	...	...	...
Glascock, GA	13125	6,721	12.3	62.6	25.1	6,079	9,695	53.2	...	...	...	...
Glynn, GA	13127	162,534	6.7	30.3	62.9	131,602	10,420	64.5	...	...	...	...
Gordon, GA	13129	107,769	7.5	53.1	39.4	95,149	9,181	63.6	2,754	71.7	18.1	4.6
Grady, GA	13131	41,456	10.8	63.1	26.1	37,894	8,508	64.5	...	...	...	...
Greene, GA	13133	29,863	10.8	24.0	65.3	24,282	11,475	57.4	...	...	...	...
Gwinnett, GA	13135	1,802,041	5.4	44.5	50.0	1,525,502	9,627	64.8	40,571	85.5	7.4	4.4
Habersham, GA	13137	76,963	6.3	48.4	45.3	64,429	9,397	66.3	...	...	...	...
Hall, GA	13139	332,783	8.2	50.0	41.8	297,172	9,367	64.8	9,483	76.6	9.7	10.0
Hancock, GA	13141	17,665	18.2	44.7	37.1	16,077	11,813	51.7	...	...	...	...

... Not available

Table C-1. Population, School, and Student Characteristics by County—*Continued*

County	State/County Code	High school graduates, 2006-2008			College enrollment, 2006-2008		College graduates, 2006-2008 (percent)						
		Population 25 years and over	High school diploma or less (percent)	High school diploma or more (percent)	Number	Percent public	Bachelor's degree or more	+/- U.S. percent with Bachelor's degree or more	Non-Hispanic White	Black or African American	American Indian and Alaska Native	Asian, Hawaiian, and Pacific Islander	Hispanic or Latino[3]
		30	31	32	33	34	35	36	37	38	39	40	41
GEORGIA	13000	6,069,802	47.0	82.9	608,350	75.1	27.0	-0.4	30.9	19.0	19.0	49.0	13.2
Appling, GA	13001	...	...	...	...	...	...	...	...	...	...	...	...
Atkinson, GA	13003	...	...	...	...	...	...	...	...	...	...	...	...
Bacon, GA	13005	...	...	...	...	...	...	...	...	...	...	...	...
Baker, GA	13007	...	...	...	...	...	...	...	...	...	...	...	...
Baldwin, GA	13009	29,195	61.9	77.4	5,885	93.7	16.8	-10.6	23.2	7.9	...	...	...
Banks, GA	13011	...	...	...	...	...	...	...	...	...	...	...	...
Barrow, GA	13013	41,367	59.2	74.7	2,209	81.8	12.3	-15.1	13.2	8.8	...	15.0	6.2
Bartow, GA	13015	59,221	58.4	78.8	3,087	77.9	17.1	-10.3	17.6	20.0	...	...	5.5
Ben Hill, GA	13017	...	...	...	...	...	...	...	...	...	...	...	...
Berrien, GA	13019	...	...	...	...	...	...	...	...	...	...	...	...
Bibb, GA	13021	97,739	50.7	79.9	11,990	58.5	24.0	-3.4	33.0	13.7	...	35.0	8.1
Bleckley, GA	13023	...	...	...	...	...	...	...	...	...	...	...	...
Brantley, GA	13025	...	...	...	...	...	...	...	...	...	...	...	...
Brooks, GA	13027	...	...	...	...	...	...	...	...	...	...	...	...
Bryan, GA	13029	18,561	42.2	88.4	1,643	80.9	25.7	-1.7	24.6	30.6	...	...	...
Bulloch, GA	13031	34,942	46.6	84.3	15,141	98.5	24.4	-3.0	29.9	9.5	...	...	...
Burke, GA	13033	13,472	68.4	73.2	1,262	91.0	9.5	-17.9	14.2	4.1	...	...	...
Butts, GA	13035	15,587	70.4	75.2	711	41.5	9.7	-17.7	10.6	3.8	...	...	...
Calhoun, GA	13037	...	...	...	...	...	...	...	...	...	...	...	...
Camden, GA	13039	27,906	46.2	88.4	2,644	85.6	19.3	-8.1	20.0	15.1	...	...	...
Candler, GA	13043	...	...	...	...	...	...	...	...	...	...	...	...
Carroll, GA	13045	69,406	56.6	79.5	8,794	88.6	18.1	-9.3	19.1	12.8	...	...	16.0
Catoosa, GA	13047	41,424	48.9	83.0	3,068	83.1	15.6	-11.8	15.5	...	...	...	...
Charlton, GA	13049	...	...	...	...	...	...	...	...	...	...	...	...
Chatham, GA	13051	157,262	43.2	87.1	19,143	61.5	29.3	1.9	39.4	12.1	...	43.7	25.8
Chattahoochee, GA	13053	...	...	...	...	...	...	...	...	...	...	...	...
Chattooga, GA	13055	18,282	71.8	69.3	...	...	6.3	-21.1	6.9	0.3	...	...	...
Cherokee, GA	13057	127,532	36.5	89.1	10,939	70.7	33.2	5.8	34.1	38.1	...	39.3	19.2
Clarke, GA	13059	59,727	37.6	84.7	31,399	96.7	41.5	14.1	56.4	11.5	...	...	18.0
Clay, GA	13061	...	...	...	...	...	...	...	...	...	...	...	...
Clayton, GA	13063	165,797	51.9	83.2	14,335	67.6	17.8	-9.6	14.6	21.1	...	14.1	8.0
Clinch, GA	13065	...	...	...	...	...	...	...	...	...	...	...	...
Cobb, GA	13067	446,659	31.8	90.1	50,269	73.9	42.2	14.8	47.1	34.5	26.8	57.4	18.1
Coffee, GA	13069	25,191	64.5	71.6	1,906	90.8	11.6	-15.8	14.8	4.5	...	...	7.1
Colquitt, GA	13071	28,175	68.1	71.3	1,764	98.0	10.0	-17.4	13.3	0.8	...	...	6.5
Columbia, GA	13073	67,962	37.5	89.9	7,602	84.7	34.2	6.8	33.6	30.2	...	58.9	31.6
Cook, GA	13075	...	...	...	...	...	...	...	...	...	...	...	...
Coweta, GA	13077	75,970	47.0	86.6	5,097	72.6	23.8	-3.6	26.3	14.0	...	35.9	13.7
Crawford, GA	13079	...	...	...	...	...	...	...	...	...	...	...	...
Crisp, GA	13081	13,840	65.1	70.1	861	94.3	11.2	-16.2	15.6	4.6	...	...	...
Dade, GA	13083	...	...	...	...	...	...	...	...	...	...	...	...
Dawson, GA	13085	14,476	60.2	81.4	877	72.1	15.8	-11.6	16.3	...	...	...	...
Decatur, GA	13087	18,256	62.8	74.3	2,083	93.1	12.9	-14.5	18.5	4.1	...	...	...
De Kalb, GA	13089	487,921	36.8	86.7	51,721	56.9	37.7	10.3	61.8	23.6	23.1	50.0	14.6
Dodge, GA	13091	13,108	67.1	76.8	860	79.8	12.5	-14.9	15.9	1.0	...	...	...
Dooly, GA	13093	...	...	...	...	...	...	...	...	...	...	...	...
Dougherty, GA	13095	58,342	48.2	80.7	8,818	94.4	21.2	-6.2	28.8	15.2	...	...	...
Douglas, GA	13097	76,952	47.4	85.3	7,334	65.4	23.8	-3.6	20.5	30.5	...	59.1	11.4
Early, GA	13099	...	...	...	...	...	...	...	...	...	...	...	...
Echols, GA	13101	...	...	...	...	...	...	...	...	...	...	...	...
Effingham, GA	13103	31,427	62.1	82.4	1,847	86.6	13.9	-13.5	14.9	7.2	...	...	...
Elbert, GA	13105	13,815	68.1	71.9	559	86.6	9.2	-18.2	11.5	3.2	...	...	...
Emanuel, GA	13107	14,515	70.4	65.9	633	100.0	7.7	-19.7	10.1	3.7	...	...	...
Evans, GA	13109	...	...	...	...	...	...	...	...	...	...	...	...
Fannin, GA	13111	16,316	61.8	77.1	577	42.8	16.2	-11.2	16.6	...	...	...	...
Fayette, GA	13113	70,106	29.6	93.8	7,227	72.2	40.7	13.3	40.4	43.5	...	49.9	24.2
Floyd, GA	13115	62,185	55.1	77.0	7,449	42.9	17.8	-9.6	20.1	7.5	...	35.2	3.9
Forsyth, GA	13117	100,267	30.2	90.5	7,101	71.0	43.7	16.3	43.9	66.1	...	66.0	19.5
Franklin, GA	13119	14,745	65.0	79.3	1,040	67.7	12.7	-14.7	13.9	1.4	...	...	...
Fulton, GA	13121	651,593	32.6	88.4	70,518	66.4	46.3	18.9	66.1	25.0	32.0	67.9	18.0
Gilmer, GA	13123	18,672	65.0	72.6	441	79.4	10.5	-16.9	11.0	...	...	...	...
Glascock, GA	13125	...	...	...	...	...	...	...	...	...	...	...	...
Glynn, GA	13127	49,451	45.5	85.9	3,770	81.0	27.3	-0.1	32.1	10.9	...	...	19.9
Gordon, GA	13129	33,432	66.1	72.6	1,633	81.1	11.0	-16.4	11.7	6.4	...	...	5.5
Grady, GA	13131	15,858	65.5	76.0	1,164	93.2	10.0	-17.4	12.6	4.0	...	...	...
Greene, GA	13133	...	...	...	...	...	...	...	...	...	...	...	...
Gwinnett, GA	13135	481,532	35.9	87.4	44,803	71.9	35.5	8.1	39.4	33.2	22.5	48.7	14.5
Habersham, GA	13137	27,737	58.8	74.4	2,234	66.4	19.0	-8.4	20.5	16.0	...	...	4.2
Hall, GA	13139	111,967	56.8	73.8	7,777	77.8	19.3	-8.1	24.1	11.5	...	26.9	4.4
Hancock, GA	13141	...	...	...	...	...	...	...	...	...	...	...	...

[3]May be of any race
... Not available

Table C-1. Population, School, and Student Characteristics by County—*Continued*

County	State/County Code	County Type[1]	Population, 2009 Total	Population, 2009 Percent 5–17 years	Percent of related children 5-17 years in poverty, 2008	Percent of children under 19 years with no health insurance, 2007	Number of Schools and Students, 2008-2009 School Districts	Number of Schools and Students, 2008-2009 Schools	Number of Schools and Students, 2008-2009 Students	Resident enrollment, 2006-2008 K–12 enrollment Number	Resident enrollment, 2006-2008 K–12 enrollment Percent public
			1	2	3	4	5	6	7	8	9
Haralson, GA	13143	1	28,890	18.9	24.3	11.2	2	12	5,854	5,637	97.1
Harris, GA	13145	2	30,138	18.5	10.8	16.2	1	8	4,905	5,498	90.3
Hart, GA	13147	6	24,067	16.7	20.6	12.5	1	6	3,535	3,985	91.3
Heard, GA	13149	1	11,528	19.7	20.2	13.5	1	5	2,161	...	...
Henry, GA	13151	1	195,370	22.8	10.2	13.3	1	47	39,956	41,372	87.5
Houston, GA	13153	3	135,715	19.3	15.2	14.3	1	39	26,285	26,349	94.2
Irwin, GA	13155	7	10,086	19.8	28.9	10.0	1	4	1,748	...	...
Jackson, GA	13157	6	63,544	18.8	14.4	15.3	3	23	11,326	11,415	94.3
Jasper, GA	13159	1	13,953	18.7	21.9	15.6	1	5	2,189	...	...
Jeff Davis, GA	13161	7	13,659	19.7	28.4	12.6	1	5	2,903	...	...
Jefferson, GA	13163	6	16,478	18.9	31.7	11.2	1	7	3,120	...	...
Jenkins, GA	13165	6	8,450	18.6	35.9	8.0	1	4	1,531	...	...
Johnson, GA	13167	9	9,300	14.9	30.3	13.3	1	4	1,246	...	...
Jones, GA	13169	3	27,740	18.9	14.5	12.5	1	10	5,669	4,868	89.3
Lamar, GA	13171	1	17,550	16.0	19.6	9.9	1	4	2,498	...	...
Lanier, GA	13173	3	8,423	18.8	29.2	11.5	1	4	1,739	...	...
Laurens, GA	13175	6	48,295	19.1	28.4	10.7	2	17	9,467	8,761	92.9
Lee, GA	13177	3	34,410	21.0	10.3	11.3	1	8	6,186	6,931	89.9
Liberty, GA	13179	3	62,186	19.6	18.6	12.9	1	18	10,971	14,402	93.2
Lincoln, GA	13181	8	7,913	16.5	25.7	17.7	1	3	1,323	...	...
Long, GA	13183	3	12,234	20.9	27.6	18.5	1	3	2,520	...	...
Lowndes, GA	13185	3	106,814	16.7	23.1	13.4	2	26	17,273	17,528	92.0
Lumpkin, GA	13187	6	27,528	16.2	18.1	18.4	1	6	3,836	4,418	94.4
McDuffie, GA	13189	2	21,862	19.0	26.0	10.8	2	10	4,208	4,339	90.2
McIntosh, GA	13191	3	11,378	17.6	27.9	13.6	1	4	1,877	...	...
Macon, GA	13193	6	13,336	17.2	32.0	10.6	1	4	1,890	...	...
Madison, GA	13195	3	28,232	18.3	18.5	16.0	1	8	4,772	5,181	86.2
Marion, GA	13197	2	6,995	18.9	34.3	13.5	1	3	1,427	...	...
Meriwether, GA	13199	1	22,783	17.3	26.5	11.6	1	10	3,449	4,313	87.1
Miller, GA	13201	8	6,228	16.5	42.1	13.1	1	4	1,134	...	...
Mitchell, GA	13205	6	23,800	17.7	30.8	9.3	3	10	4,060	4,568	89.1
Monroe, GA	13207	3	25,425	17.3	15.8	12.4	1	6	3,989	4,710	85.5
Montgomery, GA	13209	9	8,930	17.9	27.4	17.5	1	4	1,098	...	...
Morgan, GA	13211	6	18,761	19.5	17.1	13.5	1	5	3,307	...	...
Murray, GA	13213	3	40,621	19.6	17.7	11.7	1	10	7,828	8,098	97.5
Muscogee, GA	13215	2	190,414	18.1	24.0	9.5	1	66	32,585	36,219	91.6
Newton, GA	13217	1	99,944	21.1	16.5	14.7	1	25	19,315	19,486	88.0
Oconee, GA	13219	3	33,320	21.8	6.7	14.3	1	9	6,462	6,368	88.0
Oglethorpe, GA	13221	3	14,328	18.0	16.8	18.1	1	5	2,469	...	...
Paulding, GA	13223	1	136,655	22.3	8.0	14.0	1	33	27,908	27,032	91.7
Peach, GA	13225	6	27,247	15.7	26.1	13.0	2	7	4,077	5,094	88.9
Pickens, GA	13227	1	31,264	16.1	17.2	14.9	1	7	4,527	5,077	93.3
Pierce, GA	13229	6	18,580	18.7	26.1	13.8	1	4	3,563	...	...
Pike, GA	13231	1	17,721	20.8	13.0	16.8	1	4	3,473	...	...
Polk, GA	13233	6	42,298	18.6	23.4	12.3	1	13	7,454	7,640	96.5
Pulaski, GA	13235	6	9,897	15.8	23.0	10.4	1	5	1,593	...	...
Putnam, GA	13237	6	20,495	14.3	24.6	15.7	1	4	2,765	3,415	80.1
Quitman, GA	13239	9	2,659	16.7	32.2	12.3	1	1	283	...	...
Rabun, GA	13241	9	16,611	15.6	23.1	22.6	1	6	2,244	...	...
Randolph, GA	13243	6	7,180	18.1	36.6	8.0	1	4	1,402	...	...
Richmond, GA	13245	2	199,768	17.5	32.9	10.0	1	62	32,716	36,366	88.8
Rockdale, GA	13247	1	84,569	20.8	16.2	14.2	1	22	15,705	16,229	89.1
Schley, GA	13249	8	4,325	23.0	21.9	11.3	2	2	1,388	...	...
Screven, GA	13251	6	15,054	18.5	27.1	10.0	1	5	2,704	...	...
Seminole, GA	13253	6	9,094	17.4	33.7	10.0	1	3	1,665	...	...
Spalding, GA	13255	1	64,708	18.8	24.3	10.6	2	21	10,823	11,991	89.2
Stephens, GA	13257	7	25,700	16.2	21.9	11.0	...	...	...	4,475	94.3
Stewart, GA	13259	8	4,558	15.3	36.9	11.2	1	3	609	...	...
Sumter, GA	13261	6	32,084	18.4	38.0	10.0	1	11	5,211	6,694	85.8
Talbot, GA	13263	8	6,355	16.4	28.2	13.2	1	1	656	...	...
Taliaferro, GA	13265	8	1,812	13.6	37.1	10.7	1	2	231	...	...
Tattnall, GA	13267	6	24,493	15.6	30.8	17.2	1	8	3,482	3,703	90.2
Taylor, GA	13269	8	8,587	19.0	30.8	13.0	1	5	1,590	...	...
Telfair, GA	13271	7	12,792	13.8	32.4	6.5	1	4	1,751	...	...
Terrell, GA	13273	3	10,320	17.6	33.9	9.7	1	4	1,515	...	...
Thomas, GA	13275	4	46,188	18.2	24.6	10.3	2	17	8,536	8,197	91.2
Tift, GA	13277	4	42,959	18.8	26.8	13.8	1	14	7,551	8,230	94.9
Toombs, GA	13279	7	27,959	18.7	31.4	13.0	2	13	5,549	5,128	93.3
Towns, GA	13281	9	11,010	11.7	20.4	18.3	1	3	1,167	...	...
Treutlen, GA	13283	7	7,058	16.8	33.8	10.5	1	2	1,228	...	...

[1]County type codes are from the Economic Research Service of the United States Department of Agriculture. See notes and definitions for more information.
... Not available

Table C-1. Population, School, and Student Characteristics by County—*Continued*

County	State/County Code	Characteristics of students, 2008-2009				Number of graduates, 2006-2007	Staff and students, 2008-2009			
		Percent with IEP[2]	Percent eligible for free or reduced lunch	Percent minority	Percent English Language Learners		Total staff	Number of teachers	Student/teacher ratio	Central admin. Staff
		10	11	12	13	14	15	16	17	18
Haralson, GA	13143	14.8	43.2	6.0	0.4	336	859	404	14.5	20
Harris, GA	13145	7.0	33.9	23.0	0.3	301	708	327	15.0	14
Hart, GA	13147	9.3	55.1	29.4	2.3	200	539	258	13.7	6
Heard, GA	13149	9.4	58.7	11.4	...	120	308	153	14.1	9
Henry, GA	13151	12.0	41.6	52.6	2.3	1,999	5,031	2,675	14.9	22
Houston, GA	13153	11.2	48.5	42.8	2.7	1,484	3,903	1,911	13.8	84
Irwin, GA	13155	15.7	67.2	37.0	0.7	94	273	127	13.8	12
Jackson, GA	13157	12.3	44.3	17.6	3.7	538	1,770	849	13.3	34
Jasper, GA	13159	11.9	63.2	33.9	1.8	89	373	147	14.9	9
Jeff Davis, GA	13161	16.1	62.0	28.8	7.2	157	408	192	15.1	14
Jefferson, GA	13163	11.3	83.8	73.4	1.0	189	479	230	13.6	12
Jenkins, GA	13165	13.7	76.7	60.3	1.9	110	234	108	14.2	9
Johnson, GA	13167	14.6	72.2	49.4	0.2	64	202	84	14.8	8
Jones, GA	13169	10.6	41.3	28.7	0.1	295	795	394	14.4	13
Lamar, GA	13171	11.3	66.3	39.7	0.4	139	377	159	15.7	10
Lanier, GA	13173	10.9	67.2	32.3	1.3	80	252	117	14.9	11
Laurens, GA	13175	9.5	63.3	48.9	0.6	524	1,277	662	14.3	25
Lee, GA	13177	8.2	36.9	22.0	1.2	326	809	393	15.7	14
Liberty, GA	13179	9.7	59.2	61.4	0.7	518	1,615	702	15.6	33
Lincoln, GA	13181	13.9	60.2	39.9	0.2	103	222	102	13.0	7
Long, GA	13183	7.9	67.4	40.0	3.0	103	331	153	16.5	8
Lowndes, GA	13185	12.3	53.2	49.6	1.8	896	2,529	1,260	13.7	57
Lumpkin, GA	13187	13.2	45.8	8.3	1.9	169	570	270	14.2	13
McDuffie, GA	13189	12.7	64.2	51.7	1.0	243	738	319	13.2	28
McIntosh, GA	13191	9.8	76.1	46.8	0.7	118	306	131	14.3	9
Macon, GA	13193	11.3	82.3	87.4	1.6	93	327	131	14.4	8
Madison, GA	13195	14.7	53.0	14.9	1.5	261	776	344	13.9	16
Marion, GA	13197	10.9	67.3	45.5	2.8	91	238	94	15.2	7
Meriwether, GA	13199	17.9	81.0	60.6	0.9	241	629	259	13.3	12
Miller, GA	13201	8.3	63.7	38.1	0.8	72	180	79	14.4	4
Mitchell, GA	13205	10.9	71.8	58.1	1.2	202	739	321	12.6	28
Monroe, GA	13207	12.8	53.2	32.8	0.5	219	587	262	15.2	11
Montgomery, GA	13209	10.4	72.8	44.3	2.3	69	197	86	12.8	8
Morgan, GA	13211	10.9	43.8	34.5	1.1	214	493	250	13.2	12
Murray, GA	13213	8.3	67.0	20.2	6.3	340	1,093	538	14.6	14
Muscogee, GA	13215	11.2	59.2	63.9	1.6	1,819	5,396	2,363	13.8	151
Newton, GA	13217	12.7	55.8	54.5	2.3	764	2,738	1,330	14.5	32
Oconee, GA	13219	9.6	19.7	12.3	2.2	485	932	450	14.4	22
Oglethorpe, GA	13221	14.3	50.1	22.5	3.0	142	382	176	14.0	12
Paulding, GA	13223	9.4	32.3	26.7	1.4	1,146	3,662	1,975	14.1	58
Peach, GA	13225	10.3	67.7	59.6	3.9	214	618	285	14.3	25
Pickens, GA	13227	10.6	45.1	5.1	1.2	248	745	338	13.4	16
Pierce, GA	13229	9.8	53.2	14.1	2.9	174	493	250	14.3	16
Pike, GA	13231	7.0	38.5	15.7	...	162	492	236	14.7	16
Polk, GA	13233	14.5	58.3	30.7	5.8	358	1,017	531	14.0	17
Pulaski, GA	13235	14.3	60.1	44.8	1.3	105	259	124	12.8	10
Putnam, GA	13237	13.8	71.5	53.2	2.6	141	511	238	11.6	15
Quitman, GA	13239	11.3	98.9	74.6	...	...	70	22	12.9	5
Rabun, GA	13241	10.2	60.7	12.4	5.8	134	399	169	13.3	11
Randolph, GA	13243	11.6	89.3	89.6	0.1	87	293	116	12.1	9
Richmond, GA	13245	9.7	70.2	76.6	0.5	1,612	4,747	2,345	14.0	69
Rockdale, GA	13247	8.3	54.6	68.5	3.7	881	2,273	1,179	13.3	34
Schley, GA	13249	8.2	49.1	21.3	0.2	62	212	90	15.4	11
Screven, GA	13251	17.3	78.1	54.0	...	213	401	198	13.7	11
Seminole, GA	13253	10.2	72.9	51.2	0.3	87	247	119	14.0	5
Spalding, GA	13255	11.1	66.6	49.9	1.0	519	1,720	772	14.0	60
Stephens, GA	13257	...	53.2	17.6	...	231	...	...	...	...
Stewart, GA	13259	14.0	93.4	95.6	...	33	130	51	11.9	6
Sumter, GA	13261	10.5	83.6	80.6	3.0	244	933	418	12.5	17
Talbot, GA	13263	12.3	89.9	97.0	...	41	140	56	11.7	7
Taliaferro, GA	13265	12.6	93.5	81.4	...	14	52	24	9.6	4
Tattnall, GA	13267	11.7	72.0	43.0	4.7	173	536	236	14.8	12
Taylor, GA	13269	11.4	70.9	47.5	...	68	276	121	13.1	8
Telfair, GA	13271	11.1	76.0	47.8	1.6	85	271	126	13.9	8
Terrell, GA	13273	12.6	71.4	96.6	0.4	67	259	109	13.9	6
Thomas, GA	13275	12.3	61.4	48.3	0.7	457	1,268	597	14.3	30
Tift, GA	13277	11.2	64.9	49.3	6.3	404	1,065	552	13.7	18
Toombs, GA	13279	10.4	68.3	45.0	4.2	301	813	399	13.9	20
Towns, GA	13281	9.7	48.6	1.8	1.0	222	216	95	12.3	9
Treutlen, GA	13283	14.0	72.4	39.3	0.1	69	179	87	14.1	6

[2]IEP= Individual Education Program. See notes and definitions for more information
... Not available

Table C-1. Population, School, and Student Characteristics by County—*Continued*

County	State/ County Code	Revenues, 2007-2008				Current expenditures, 2007-2008			Resident population 16 to 19 years, 2006-2008			
		Total revenue ($1,000's)	Percentage of revenue from			Amount ($1,000's)	Amount per student	Percent for instruction	Total population 16 to 19 years	Percent enrolled in school	Percent high school graduates, not enrolled in school	Percent not enrolled, not grads, not employed or not in labor force
			Federal gov't	State gov't	Local gov't							
		19	20	21	22	23	24	25	26	27	28	29
Haralson, GA	13143	59,334	9.2	58.6	32.2	53,898	9,315	66.5	...	...	...	...
Harris, GA	13145	54,358	4.5	51.3	44.3	46,003	9,288	63.5	...	...	...	...
Hart, GA	13147	37,283	7.0	46.3	46.7	34,128	9,485	67.1	...	...	...	...
Heard, GA	13149	29,136	6.7	41.2	52.1	20,573	9,322	67.0	...	...	...	...
Henry, GA	13151	409,143	4.4	44.6	51.0	340,447	8,729	68.2	10308	84.5	10.1	4.3
Houston, GA	13153	274,811	7.2	54.2	38.6	246,068	9,493	65.0	...	...	...	...
Irwin, GA	13155	18,784	10.0	62.7	27.3	16,879	9,684	62.7	...	...	...	...
Jackson, GA	13157	131,092	5.8	44.8	49.4	112,674	10,197	62.4	...	...	...	...
Jasper, GA	13159	21,692	12.1	45.7	42.3	19,578	8,807	60.9	...	...	...	...
Jeff Davis, GA	13161	28,132	13.2	64.4	22.4	26,050	9,077	65.4	...	...	...	...
Jefferson, GA	13163	34,021	11.8	60.1	28.1	29,245	9,199	63.0	...	...	...	...
Jenkins, GA	13165	16,548	15.0	63.4	21.7	15,815	9,738	64.0	...	...	...	...
Johnson, GA	13167	12,882	18.1	60.8	21.2	12,573	10,297	60.6	...	...	...	...
Jones, GA	13169	53,599	7.4	60.8	31.7	47,989	8,512	64.8	...	...	...	...
Lamar, GA	13171	25,608	11.0	48.3	40.6	23,466	9,386	58.8	...	...	...	...
Lanier, GA	13173	17,650	9.7	68.0	22.4	15,457	9,162	62.4	...	...	...	...
Laurens, GA	13175	104,031	8.6	61.4	30.0	86,173	9,196	66.7	...	...	...	...
Lee, GA	13177	54,454	5.6	59.7	34.7	48,759	7,959	66.0	...	...	...	...
Liberty, GA	13179	114,306	16.6	59.4	24.0	97,599	8,994	62.6	4155	76.7	17.5	4.9
Lincoln, GA	13181	16,300	10.3	55.1	34.6	14,729	11,008	64.4	...	...	...	...
Long, GA	13183	20,166	13.4	67.8	18.8	18,877	8,102	61.6	...	...	...	...
Lowndes, GA	13185	183,788	9.7	49.3	41.1	161,221	9,460	65.0	7008	82.5	10.8	4.0
Lumpkin, GA	13187	39,483	6.8	44.1	49.1	36,342	9,442	62.7	...	...	...	...
McDuffie, GA	13189	48,082	11.6	57.6	30.8	44,551	10,382	61.8	...	...	...	...
McIntosh, GA	13191	20,224	10.0	42.9	47.1	18,026	9,141	57.8	...	...	...	...
Macon, GA	13193	22,571	15.8	49.2	35.0	20,218	10,119	60.6	...	...	...	...
Madison, GA	13195	49,753	7.6	57.3	35.2	46,230	9,788	64.8	...	...	...	...
Marion, GA	13197	15,615	10.1	56.5	33.4	14,487	9,822	57.0	...	...	...	...
Meriwether, GA	13199	43,900	12.0	59.8	28.2	39,621	11,089	62.2	...	...	...	...
Miller, GA	13201	21,481	6.8	76.4	16.8	11,427	10,360	61.9	...	...	...	...
Mitchell, GA	13205	47,997	14.8	56.1	29.0	45,322	10,987	60.1	...	...	...	...
Monroe, GA	13207	42,756	7.5	38.7	53.8	38,942	9,977	60.2	...	...	...	...
Montgomery, GA	13209	14,908	11.6	60.7	27.8	13,877	11,984	62.5	...	...	...	...
Morgan, GA	13211	35,907	6.7	44.4	48.9	33,846	10,170	71.9	...	...	...	...
Murray, GA	13213	73,782	9.4	62.0	28.7	70,742	8,885	66.4	...	...	...	...
Muscogee, GA	13215	383,045	9.4	53.6	36.9	32,7428	9,994	62.2	13961	71.6	23.3	3.7
Newton, GA	13217	204,512	6.2	56.2	37.7	17,2543	9,028	65.2	5461	80.0	13.3	5.5
Oconee, GA	13219	72,317	3.6	44.8	51.6	60,315	9,404	64.6	...	...	...	...
Oglethorpe, GA	13221	25,398	7.2	56.0	36.8	22,976	9,279	61.4	...	...	...	...
Paulding, GA	13223	285,118	4.2	55.4	40.4	233,890	8,709	68.6	6332	76.2	11.0	10.0
Peach, GA	13225	43,490	12.7	54.9	32.5	40,948	9,687	57.9	...	...	...	...
Pickens, GA	13227	51,602	6.7	39.4	53.9	45,818	10,535	63.7	...	...	...	...
Pierce, GA	13229	34,014	8.7	63.5	27.8	31,848	9,146	67.0	...	...	...	...
Pike, GA	13231	30,040	5.2	60.3	34.5	28,264	8,318	64.2	...	...	...	...
Polk, GA	13233	76,984	7.8	58.4	33.8	67,369	9,110	66.5	...	...	...	...
Pulaski, GA	13235	16,857	11.5	59.3	29.2	16,047	10,017	64.1	...	...	...	...
Putnam, GA	13237	37,261	11.1	30.5	58.4	31,976	11,387	64.3	...	...	...	...
Quitman, GA	13239	4,677	25.8	47.4	26.8	4,568	16,856	52.2	...	...	...	...
Rabun, GA	13241	36,638	7.6	23.4	69.0	29,455	12,539	66.9	...	...	...	...
Randolph, GA	13243	17,575	23.2	50.4	26.5	17,290	11,965	56.1	...	...	...	...
Richmond, GA	13245	355,388	11.9	50.9	37.2	313,338	9,522	63.7	13115	68.2	19.1	8.4
Rockdale, GA	13247	163,316	6.5	43.4	50.1	152,278	9,753	61.4	5683	83.0	6.8	4.2
Schley, GA	13249	15,673	10.1	62.9	27.0	14,078	10,224	55.1	...	...	...	...
Screven, GA	13251	26,970	12.3	62.3	25.4	26,117	9,291	61.6	...	...	...	...
Seminole, GA	13253	17,817	14.0	60.3	25.6	16,421	9,682	65.1	...	...	...	...
Spalding, GA	13255	119,129	10.0	52.2	37.8	106,483	9,722	60.8	3773	77.8	3.7	11.3
Stephens, GA	13257	48,475	8.8	51.7	39.5	43,722	10,344	67.2	...	...	...	...
Stewart, GA	13259	8,336	17.6	52.6	29.8	7,557	11,520	55.2	...	...	...	...
Sumter, GA	13261	60,802	16.0	50.9	33.1	55,372	10,138	62.3	...	...	...	...
Talbot, GA	13263	10,789	26.9	35.2	37.8	10,333	15,129	53.2	...	...	...	...
Taliaferro, GA	13265	3,377	13.4	54.2	32.5	3,432	14,481	59.8	...	...	...	...
Tattnall, GA	13267	33,601	12.9	63.5	23.5	31,483	9,203	63.1	...	...	...	...
Taylor, GA	13269	17,944	14.2	61.2	24.6	17,208	10,701	62.7	...	...	...	...
Telfair, GA	13271	18,430	12.4	59.0	28.6	17,055	9,718	65.0	...	...	...	...
Terrell, GA	13273	17,592	16.8	54.6	28.6	15,821	9,833	59.2	...	...	...	...
Thomas, GA	13275	90,796	10.1	55.3	34.6	84,094	9,787	62.4	...	...	...	...
Tift, GA	13277	76,035	10.6	55.7	33.7	71,676	9,371	70.1	...	...	...	...
Toombs, GA	13279	55,777	13.0	60.6	26.4	50,672	9,063	65.2	...	...	...	...
Towns, GA	13281	14,331	8.3	28.3	63.4	14,561	12,298	63.0	...	...	...	...
Treutlen, GA	13283	11,988	15.8	64.3	19.9	11,405	9,465	62.1	...	...	...	...

... Not available

Table C-1. Population, School, and Student Characteristics by County—*Continued*

County	State/County Code	High school graduates, 2006-2008			College enrollment, 2006-2008		College graduates, 2006-2008 (percent)						
		Population 25 years and over	High school diploma or less (percent)	High school diploma or more (percent)	Number	Percent public	Bachelor's degree or more	+/- U.S. percent with Bachelor's degree or more	Non-Hispanic White	Black or African American	American Indian and Alaska Native	Asian, Hawaiian, and Pacific Islander	Hispanic or Latino[3]
		30	31	32	33	34	35	36	37	38	39	40	41
Haralson, GA	13143	18,978	68.1	69.6	1,022	91.3	10.2	-17.2	10.4	...	...	...	...
Harris, GA	13145	19,276	40.9	88.3	1,528	82.3	27.1	-0.3	30.3	14.1	...	...	11.4
Hart, GA	13147	16,792	66.1	74.2	759	82.1	13.1	-14.3	15.1	5.7	...	...	...
Heard, GA	13149	...	...	...	...	...	...	...	...	...	...	...	...
Henry, GA	13151	113,761	44.2	89.4	10,817	67.3	23.6	-3.8	21.7	27.3	...	40.7	16.5
Houston, GA	13153	82,465	42.8	87.5	9,668	86.3	23.9	-3.5	26.8	17.5	...	27.4	12.8
Irwin, GA	13155	...	...	...	...	...	...	...	...	...	...	...	...
Jackson, GA	13157	38,343	62.7	76.4	2,121	76.0	12.9	-14.5	13.8	3.5	...	...	6.5
Jasper, GA	13159	...	...	...	...	...	...	...	...	...	...	...	...
Jeff Davis, GA	13161	...	...	...	...	...	...	...	...	...	...	...	...
Jefferson, GA	13163	...	...	...	...	...	...	...	...	...	...	...	...
Jenkins, GA	13165	...	...	...	...	...	...	...	...	...	...	...	...
Johnson, GA	13167	...	...	...	...	...	...	...	...	...	...	...	...
Jones, GA	13169	18,414	54.0	79.2	1,465	84.8	18.9	-8.5	22.8	7.4	...	...	...
Lamar, GA	13171	...	...	...	...	...	...	...	...	...	...	...	...
Lanier, GA	13173	...	...	...	...	...	...	...	...	...	...	...	...
Laurens, GA	13175	31,161	62.5	80.2	2,454	87.2	15.3	-12.1	19.4	6.2	...	33.3	...
Lee, GA	13177	20,413	48.5	85.1	2,510	96.9	17.0	-10.4	17.7	12.4	...	...	...
Liberty, GA	13179	32,131	45.6	86.4	4,167	77.7	14.3	-13.1	17.0	10.3	...	16.5	16.2
Lincoln, GA	13181	...	...	...	...	...	...	...	...	...	...	...	...
Long, GA	13183	...	...	...	...	...	...	...	...	...	...	...	...
Lowndes, GA	13185	60,365	47.1	84.5	13,029	93.9	23.1	-4.3	28.0	13.6	...	13.8	14.5
Lumpkin, GA	13187	16,346	55.2	78.3	3,372	83.6	18.7	-8.7	18.8	...	...	...	...
McDuffie, GA	13189	14,040	67.2	70.5	771	83.1	11.0	-16.4	15.4	3.8	...	...	...
McIntosh, GA	13191	...	...	...	...	...	...	...	...	...	...	...	...
Macon, GA	13193	...	...	...	...	...	...	...	...	...	...	...	...
Madison, GA	13195	18,647	69.0	72.6	1,185	58.6	12.5	-14.9	12.5	15.0	...	...	...
Marion, GA	13197	...	...	...	...	...	...	...	...	...	...	...	...
Meriwether, GA	13199	15,113	74.3	70.8	558	76.5	8.5	-18.9	11.2	4.4	...	...	...
Miller, GA	13201	...	...	...	...	...	...	...	...	...	...	...	...
Mitchell, GA	13205	15,436	68.2	66.8	787	100.0	10.4	-17.0	15.4	3.9	...	...	...
Monroe, GA	13207	16,337	56.9	79.6	1,209	58.6	19.4	-8.0	22.3	11.6	...	...	...
Montgomery, GA	13209	...	...	...	...	...	...	...	...	...	...	...	...
Morgan, GA	13211	...	...	...	...	...	...	...	...	...	...	...	...
Murray, GA	13213	26,128	76.7	66.5	1,229	94.7	6.1	-21.3	6.5	...	...	...	1.4
Muscogee, GA	13215	113,882	46.4	83.3	14,319	89.4	21.9	-5.5	28.7	13.8	...	44.8	18.3
Newton, GA	13217	58,460	52.8	81.8	4,542	72.7	19.1	-8.3	19.0	19.8	...	...	6.7
Oconee, GA	13219	19,917	33.0	89.0	2,662	83.9	43.8	16.4	46.2	21.0	...	...	...
Oglethorpe, GA	13221	...	...	...	...	...	...	...	...	...	...	...	...
Paulding, GA	13223	79,049	54.9	84.8	4,602	79.5	18.5	-8.9	18.3	22.0	...	...	13.6
Peach, GA	13225	15,380	56.4	80.1	3,262	88.7	17.5	-9.9	20.2	14.1	...	...	4.8
Pickens, GA	13227	21,171	53.6	79.9	1,096	81.3	21.2	-6.2	21.9	...	...	...	...
Pierce, GA	13229	...	...	...	...	...	...	...	...	...	...	...	...
Pike, GA	13231	...	...	...	...	...	...	...	...	...	...	...	...
Polk, GA	13233	26,836	68.6	70.6	1,280	80.0	9.8	-17.6	10.8	7.1	...	...	...
Pulaski, GA	13235	...	...	...	...	...	...	...	...	...	...	...	...
Putnam, GA	13237	13,810	53.5	80.1	1,172	71.5	17.9	-9.5	21.8	5.8	...	...	...
Quitman, GA	13239	...	...	...	...	...	...	...	...	...	...	...	...
Rabun, GA	13241	...	...	...	...	...	...	...	...	...	...	...	...
Randolph, GA	13243	...	...	...	...	...	...	...	...	...	...	...	...
Richmond, GA	13245	123,289	51.4	80.8	13,670	75.9	19.4	-8.0	26.5	11.9	...	39.6	20.3
Rockdale, GA	13247	51,391	47.0	84.5	5,407	67.9	22.3	-5.1	22.1	23.1	...	...	10.5
Schley, GA	13249	...	...	...	...	...	...	...	...	...	...	...	...
Screven, GA	13251	...	...	...	...	...	...	...	...	...	...	...	...
Seminole, GA	13253	...	...	...	...	...	...	...	...	...	...	...	...
Spalding, GA	13255	40,780	63.9	72.8	2,982	78.2	12.7	-14.7	13.9	10.0	...	...	4.1
Stephens, GA	13257	16,937	62.1	73.9	2,039	44.2	14.3	-13.1	15.7	4.0	...	...	...
Stewart, GA	13259	...	...	...	...	...	...	...	...	...	...	...	...
Sumter, GA	13261	19,771	58.4	74.3	1,953	83.0	19.1	-8.3	27.8	8.9	...	...	...
Talbot, GA	13263	...	...	...	...	...	...	...	...	...	...	...	...
Taliaferro, GA	13265	...	...	...	...	...	...	...	...	...	...	...	...
Tattnall, GA	13267	15,107	74.0	70.8	935	82.9	10.1	-17.3	13.5	2.7	...	...	...
Taylor, GA	13269	...	...	...	...	...	...	...	...	...	...	...	...
Telfair, GA	13271	...	...	...	...	...	...	...	...	...	...	...	...
Terrell, GA	13273	...	...	...	...	...	...	...	...	...	...	...	...
Thomas, GA	13275	29,803	55.5	79.9	1,731	74.4	21.2	-6.2	26.4	12.1	...	...	...
Tift, GA	13277	25,791	54.4	77.6	2,369	92.1	15.4	-12.0	20.2	5.1	...	...	1.7
Toombs, GA	13279	16,834	61.6	76.0	873	86.6	15.0	-12.4	18.8	4.1	...	...	2.6
Towns, GA	13281	...	...	...	...	...	...	...	...	...	...	...	...
Treutlen, GA	13283	...	...	...	...	...	...	...	...	...	...	...	...

[3]May be of any race
... Not available

Table C-1. Population, School, and Student Characteristics by County—*Continued*

County	State/County Code	County Type[1]	Population, 2009 Total	Population, 2009 Percent 5–17 years	Percent of related children 5-17 years in poverty, 2008	Percent of children under 19 years with no health insurance, 2007	Number of Schools and Students, 2008-2009 School Districts	Number of Schools and Students, 2008-2009 Schools	Number of Schools and Students, 2008-2009 Students	Resident enrollment, 2006-2008 K–12 enrollment Number	Resident enrollment, 2006-2008 K–12 enrollment Percent public
			1	2	3	4	5	6	7	8	9
Troup, GA	13285	4	64,653	19.0	23.9	9.9	1	25	12,544	12,179	93.0
Turner, GA	13287	6	9,254	18.8	38.4	11.7	1	6	1,715	...	...
Twiggs, GA	13289	3	10,111	16.8	27.1	11.2	1	4	1,038	...	...
Union, GA	13291	9	21,252	13.5	19.8	17.9	2	8	3,344	2,905	88.2
Upson, GA	13293	6	27,551	18.0	23.2	9.0	1	6	4,793	4,951	97.0
Walker, GA	13295	2	64,983	17.5	18.6	7.5	2	21	10,724	11,385	88.9
Walton, GA	13297	1	87,311	19.5	14.1	13.0	2	21	14,642	15,580	87.8
Ware, GA	13299	4	35,914	17.1	29.4	11.5	2	16	6,008	6,666	97.0
Warren, GA	13301	8	5,755	16.5	32.9	11.8	1	3	780	...	...
Washington, GA	13303	7	20,879	17.2	28.0	10.0	2	8	3,329	3,702	91.0
Wayne, GA	13305	6	29,407	18.1	26.5	10.5	1	10	5,424	5,435	99.7
Webster, GA	13307	8	2,192	18.4	25.6	15.2	1	2	489	...	...
Wheeler, GA	13309	9	7,010	14.0	33.5	14.6	1	3	1,029	...	...
White, GA	13311	8	25,294	16.7	19.2	20.9	2	9	3,852	4,147	91.8
Whitfield, GA	13313	3	93,698	20.2	18.8	18.6	2	32	20,146	18,833	94.0
Wilcox, GA	13315	9	8,895	13.8	33.9	11.5	1	3	1,316	...	...
Wilkes, GA	13317	6	10,268	15.9	29.6	9.5	1	5	1,744	...	...
Wilkinson, GA	13319	8	10,076	18.5	25.5	15.9	1	4	1,673	...	...
Worth, GA	13321	3	21,214	18.3	28.6	10.8	1	6	3,726	4,119	83.0
HAWAII	15000	X	1,295,178	15.5	9.3	5.4	1	290	179,478	204,505	81.1
Hawaii, HI	15001	5	177,835	16.3	14.0	6.4	(5)	(5)	(5)	28,636	82.9
Honolulu, HI	15003	2	907,574	15.3	8.4	5.2	1[5]	290[5]	179,478[5]	142,460	79.9
Kalawao, HI	15005	9	83	...	...	...	(5)	(5)	(5)	...	...
Kauai, HI	15007	5	64,529	16.3	9.6	5.6	(5)	(5)	(5)	10,330	84.3
Maui, HI	15009	5	145,157	16.1	9.0	5.9	(5)	(5)	(5)	23,079	85.3
IDAHO	16000	X	1,545,801	19.0	13.3	11.1	135	764	275,154	283,127	92.1
Ada, ID	16001	2	384,656	18.4	8.9	9.5	10	129	69,036	69,377	91.0
Adams, ID	16003	8	3,520	13.2	18.6	15.8	2	3	483	...	...
Bannock, ID	16005	3	82,539	18.2	14.1	7.6	4	39	13,899	15,280	95.3
Bear Lake, ID	16007	7	5,774	20.2	14.0	9.1	1	6	1,128	...	...
Benewah, ID	16009	6	9,258	18.2	18.7	8.1	2	8	1,556	...	...
Bingham, ID	16011	6	44,668	23.5	14.6	11.7	5	33	9,952	9,678	95.3
Blaine, ID	16013	7	22,328	16.0	8.1	18.3	1	9	3,290	3,539	89.6
Boise, ID	16015	2	7,445	17.1	14.1	17.3	3	7	994	...	...
Bonner, ID	16017	6	41,403	15.8	19.2	11.2	2	19	5,370	6,708	83.1
Bonneville, ID	16019	3	101,329	21.4	12.0	9.5	5	43	20,730	19,116	95.2
Boundary, ID	16021	7	10,951	18.9	19.4	12.5	1	7	1,591	...	...
Butte, ID	16023	8	2,764	19.7	17.9	14.5	1	4	465	...	...
Camas, ID	16025	9	1,109	14.6	9.4	20.8	1	2	162	...	...
Canyon, ID	16027	2	186,615	21.8	15.2	12.7	13	82	35,427	37,640	90.6
Caribou, ID	16029	6	6,914	20.6	13.0	9.6	3	10	1,507	...	...
Cassia, ID	16031	7	21,698	23.6	18.5	12.6	1	17	5,161	5,045	95.3
Clark, ID	16033	8	952	21.0	24.8	20.7	1	2	210	...	...
Clearwater, ID	16035	6	8,043	13.7	19.8	7.4	1	8	1,221	...	...
Custer, ID	16037	9	4,240	15.2	16.4	12.1	2	7	648	...	...
Elmore, ID	16039	4	28,820	16.8	16.4	15.8	4	15	4,926	5,672	98.5
Franklin, ID	16041	3	12,676	24.9	10.8	13.0	2	8	3,087	...	...
Fremont, ID	16043	6	12,691	22.1	17.7	18.5	1	11	2,467	...	...
Gem, ID	16045	2	16,437	17.8	17.3	12.0	1	10	2,641	...	...
Gooding, ID	16047	7	14,430	21.0	18.3	14.7	6	12	3,075	...	...
Idaho, ID	16049	6	15,461	15.8	22.4	9.5	3	12	1,724	...	...
Jefferson, ID	16051	3	24,802	24.7	12.5	16.2	3	15	5,956	4,944	97.8
Jerome, ID	16053	7	21,262	21.6	17.2	16.2	2	9	4,253	4,343	94.8
Kootenai, ID	16055	3	139,390	17.8	10.8	9.4	4	43	21,053	24,341	85.8
Latah, ID	16057	4	38,046	12.3	11.7	10.3	6	20	5,048	4,893	84.8
Lemhi, ID	16059	7	7,908	15.7	21.7	9.3	2	8	1,070	...	...
Lewis, ID	16061	8	3,735	15.2	21.1	8.8	3	5	902	...	...
Lincoln, ID	16063	9	4,645	23.1	15.6	21.5	3	5	1,027	...	...
Madison, ID	16065	6	38,440	16.4	15.9	11.7	2	18	6,095	6,534	97.6
Minidoka, ID	16067	7	19,226	21.5	16.4	13.2	1	11	4,097	...	...
Nez Perce, ID	16069	3	39,211	15.8	13.1	7.4	3	19	5,645	6,184	89.8
Oneida, ID	16071	8	4,221	21.5	15.1	12.4	1	5	891	...	...
Owyhee, ID	16073	2	11,223	20.9	22.4	13.3	3	13	2,648	...	...
Payette, ID	16075	6	23,099	20.4	16.5	9.7	3	15	4,412	4,875	95.7
Power, ID	16077	3	7,734	21.5	20.3	12.3	3	7	1,666	...	...
Shoshone, ID	16079	6	12,660	15.3	20.5	7.2	4	11	2,046	...	...
Teton, ID	16081	9	9,337	19.9	11.3	28.2	1	7	1,589	...	...
Twin Falls, ID	16083	5	75,296	18.9	16.0	11.6	9	32	12,789	12,904	91.3
Valley, ID	16085	8	8,726	15.4	13.8	17.4	2	8	1,317	...	...
Washington, ID	16087	6	10,119	18.9	20.5	9.5	3	9	1,887	...	...

[1]County type codes are from the Economic Research Service of the United States Department of Agriculture. See notes and definitions for more information.
[5]Hawaii, Kalawao, Kauai, and Maui counties are included with Honolulu county
... Not available

Table C-1. Population, School, and Student Characteristics by County—*Continued*

County	State/ County Code	Characteristics of students, 2008-2009				Number of graduates, 2006-2007	Staff and students, 2008-2009			
		Percent with IEP[2]	Percent eligible for free or reduced lunch	Percent minority	Percent English Language Learners		Total staff	Number of teachers	Student/ teacher ratio	Central admin. Staff
		10	11	12	13	14	15	16	17	18
Troup, GA	13285	7.9	59.7	43.2	1.1	623	1,803	871	14.4	32
Turner, GA	13287	14.0	73.8	60.7	0.8	94	304	138	12.4	12
Twiggs, GA	13289	15.5	69.7	48.7	...	76	190	74	14.0	5
Union, GA	13291	13.9	40.6	5.2	2.8	169	500	254	13.2	16
Upson, GA	13293	11.6	62.6	39.6	0.7	282	706	315	15.2	12
Walker, GA	13295	14.0	58.3	6.5	0.3	523	1,608	762	14.1	34
Walton, GA	13297	9.8	43.3	28.2	1.0	676	1,874	1,003	14.6	48
Ware, GA	13299	12.1	62.6	40.5	1.1	302	1,107	461	13.0	28
Warren, GA	13301	10.1	88.2	95.9	...	44	141	60	13.0	6
Washington, GA	13303	9.0	67.5	68.9	0.8	230	512	232	14.3	22
Wayne, GA	13305	12.0	60.6	28.0	1.6	287	842	384	14.1	15
Webster, GA	13307	5.1	66.1	57.3	...	...	82	35	14.0	4
Wheeler, GA	13309	13.4	74.0	40.7	2.8	58	161	76	13.5	4
White, GA	13311	12.1	47.6	5.9	1.2	203	716	312	12.3	37
Whitfield, GA	13313	8.3	65.3	49.2	15.2	1,004	2,642	1,423	14.2	49
Wilcox, GA	13315	11.2	70.7	43.7	0.2	60	194	94	14.0	11
Wilkes, GA	13317	10.7	70.9	56.9	1.6	89	277	123	14.2	8
Wilkinson, GA	13319	12.6	79.9	58.4	1.2	99	274	127	13.2	7
Worth, GA	13321	6.8	65.0	39.7	0.4	208	545	263	14.2	17
HAWAII	15000	11.2	41.7	80.5	10.3	11,239	21,604	11,294	15.9	588
Hawaii, HI	15001	...[5]	53.4	78.8	(5)	(5)	(5)	(5)	(5)	(5)
Honolulu, HI	15003	11.2[5]	40.2	81.2	10.3[5]	11,239[5]	21,604[5]	11,294[5]	15.9[5]	588[5]
Kalawao, HI	15005	(5)	...	...	(5)	(5)	(5)	(5)	(5)	(5)
Kauai, HI	15007	...[5]	37.8	79.6	(5)	(5)	(5)	(5)	(5)	(5)
Maui, HI	15009	...[5]	37.5	79.4	(5)	(5)	(5)	(5)	(5)	(5)
IDAHO	16000	10.2	39.7	18.8	6.4	16,319	27,253	15,146	18.2	761
Ada, ID	16001	10.2	26.2	13.0	4.9	3,660	6,402	3,610	19.1	162
Adams, ID	16003	13.5	44.5	7.0	0.6	48	62	40	12.1	3
Bannock, ID	16005	10.7	38.3	16.5	0.5	885	1,288	705	19.7	41
Bear Lake, ID	16007	9.7	38.4	4.5	0.1	112	126	66	17.1	4
Benewah, ID	16009	13.3	57.5	15.8	...	88	211	105	14.8	8
Bingham, ID	16011	10.2	47.2	26.0	14.6	676	1,002	538	18.5	29
Blaine, ID	16013	10.4	29.0	33.4	20.7	179	446	256	12.9	17
Boise, ID	16015	11.0	45.5	5.1	0.3	69	137	72	13.8	6
Bonner, ID	16017	11.1	44.7	5.3	0.3	444	588	323	16.6	19
Bonneville, ID	16019	9.4	35.6	15.7	4.5	1,287	1,877	1,037	20.0	41
Boundary, ID	16021	11.6	52.3	9.6	3.7	105	179	101	15.8	6
Butte, ID	16023	15.7	46.7	4.9	0.4	31	66	33	14.1	3
Camas, ID	16025	6.2	38.3	4.9	...	17	26	17	9.5	2
Canyon, ID	16027	10.3	53.7	34.5	12.0	1,435	3,250	1,851	19.1	92
Caribou, ID	16029	10.6	34.6	6.1	0.7	117	183	96	15.7	7
Cassia, ID	16031	9.0	51.8	31.9	13.8	289	539	282	18.3	9
Clark, ID	16033	6.7	62.9	45.2	22.9	19	34	20	10.5	2
Clearwater, ID	16035	11.6	51.6	11.5	0.1	107	157	82	14.9	5
Custer, ID	16037	14.8	32.3	8.9	1.7	59	98	52	12.5	5
Elmore, ID	16039	12.7	37.8	27.5	8.0	318	490	283	17.4	16
Franklin, ID	16041	8.7	42.9	9.1	3.4	249	281	160	19.3	7
Fremont, ID	16043	10.2	43.9	20.3	8.7	130	257	140	17.6	5
Gem, ID	16045	11.8	45.9	13.3	3.7	202	279	147	18.0	5
Gooding, ID	16047	11.8	55.8	32.2	16.7	196	331	195	15.8	13
Idaho, ID	16049	12.1	49.2	6.4	...	120	233	127	13.6	7
Jefferson, ID	16051	7.6	40.8	14.3	5.5	380	561	321	18.6	16
Jerome, ID	16053	8.8	57.8	41.7	17.2	201	388	230	18.5	7
Kootenai, ID	16055	8.8	38.2	7.0	0.2	1,448	1,950	1,083	19.4	33
Latah, ID	16057	10.8	24.4	8.1	0.2	319	580	314	16.1	39
Lemhi, ID	16059	10.7	46.1	2.9	...	83	133	71	15.1	8
Lewis, ID	16061	13.2	53.2	19.3	...	65	122	68	13.3	6
Lincoln, ID	16063	9.1	64.3	35.6	23.1	59	126	71	14.5	7
Madison, ID	16065	9.1	38.2	8.4	4.7	450	581	315	19.3	8
Minidoka, ID	16067	10.6	56.5	42.4	13.7	213	442	244	16.8	9
Nez Perce, ID	16069	13.1	37.2	17.1	0.3	420	660	344	16.4	24
Oneida, ID	16071	10.9	38.7	8.5	2.6	84	90	54	16.5	3
Owyhee, ID	16073	9.4	63.5	38.7	15.5	156	311	159	16.7	11
Payette, ID	16075	10.3	45.0	21.9	10.0	279	439	239	18.5	10
Power, ID	16077	10.5	47.0	32.9	26.8	120	211	108	15.4	7
Shoshone, ID	16079	11.9	39.2	6.3	...	137	277	136	15.0	11
Teton, ID	16081	11.3	36.1	24.9	13.2	91	156	88	18.1	3
Twin Falls, ID	16083	10.0	48.1	20.9	5.5	726	1,280	743	17.2	35
Valley, ID	16085	11.5	27.1	7.1	2.1	91	178	103	12.8	6
Washington, ID	16087	8.7	51.0	24.2	11.7	155	224	119	15.9	7

[2]IEP= Individual Education Program. See notes and definitions for more information
... Not available

Table C-1. Population, School, and Student Characteristics by County—*Continued*

County	State/County Code	Revenues, 2007-2008					Current expenditures, 2007-2008			Resident population 16 to 19 years, 2006-2008			
		Total revenue ($1,000's)	Percentage of revenue from			Amount ($1,000's)	Amount per student	Percent for instruc-tion	Total population 16 to 19 years	Percent en-rolled in school	Percent high school graduates, not enrolled in school	Percent not enrolled, not grads, not employed or not in labor force
			Federal gov't	State gov't	Local gov't							
		19	20	21	22	23	24	25	26	27	28	29
Troup, GA.......................	13285	130,780	8.7	51.6	39.7	119,931	9,640	60.4	...	...	...	...
Turner, GA......................	13287	20,014	22.1	57.8	20.0	20,157	11,331	58.7	...	...	...	...
Twiggs, GA......................	13289	14,252	25.4	47.7	26.9	12,317	10,978	56.6	...	...	...	...
Union, GA.......................	13291	37,600	7.9	49.7	42.4	33,586	10,341	64.0	...	...	...	...
Upson, GA.......................	13293	47,261	10.9	57.9	31.2	44,393	9,017	64.4	...	...	...	...
Walker, GA......................	13295	107,076	7.5	57.7	34.8	97,466	9,173	65.2	...	...	...	...
Walton, GA......................	13297	159,063	5.5	46.7	47.8	131,299	9,036	65.5	3642	73.8	11.7	11.2
Ware, GA.........................	13299	94,000	8.5	47.8	43.7	67,660	10,934	62.5	...	...	...	...
Warren, GA......................	13301	10,368	19.2	43.9	36.9	9,851	11,984	50.0	...	...	...	...
Washington, GA	13303	54,684	8.9	43.0	48.1	37,500	10,848	56.0	...	...	...	...
Wayne, GA	13305	47,467	10.5	63.4	26.0	47,718	8,893	64.0	...	...	...	...
Webster, GA....................	13307	5,753	15.9	51.9	32.3	4,963	10,696	63.1	...	...	...	...
Wheeler, GA....................	13309	12,104	23.0	53.5	23.5	12,114	11,682	54.0	...	...	...	...
White, GA........................	13311	56,670	10.1	49.0	41.0	49,096	12,274	55.6	...	...	...	...
Whitfield, GA...................	13313	218,449	7.9	51.3	40.8	191,568	9,492	64.8	4783	73.6	9.1	13.4
Wilcox, GA	13315	14,221	10.7	67.5	21.8	12,573	9,065	62.6	...	...	...	...
Wilkes, GA	13317	25,023	9.5	60.9	29.6	17,246	10,027	60.2	...	...	...	...
Wilkinson, GA..................	13319	19,987	14.4	42.0	43.6	19,194	11,364	61.6	...	...	...	...
Worth, GA	13321	36,330	12.6	62.1	25.3	34,674	9,084	61.4	...	...	...	...
HAWAII...........................	15000	2,541,703	12.2	84.8	3.0	2,122,779	11,800	60.4	65729	78.3	15.9	3.6
Hawaii, HI	15001	(5)	(5)	(5)	(5)	(5)	(5)	(5)	9240	82.4	11.2	2.2
Honolulu, HI	15003	2,541,703[5]	12.2[5]	84.8[5]	3.0[5]	2,122,779[5]	11,800[5]	60.4[5]	46662	78.2	16.4	3.6
Kalawao, HI	15005	(5)	(5)	(5)	(5)	(5)	(5)	(5)	...	...	...	...
Kauai, HI	15007	(5)	(5)	(5)	(5)	(5)	(5)	(5)	3653	73.3	17.2	6.6
Maui, HI...........................	15009	(5)	(5)	(5)	(5)	(5)	(5)	(5)	6174	75.6	18.1	3.3
IDAHO	16000	2,187,936	9.5	65.9	24.6	1,875,748	6,895	61.2	89338	80.5	12.4	3.6
Ada, ID	16001	545,932	6.3	61.1	32.6	456,149	6,784	62.2	19160	84.0	10.0	2.4
Adams, ID	16003	5,717	11.2	65.8	23.0	5,162	10,799	54.8	...	...	...	...
Bannock, ID	16005	98,394	12.0	70.7	17.3	92,015	6,804	61.9	4737	76.6	16.6	5.0
Bear Lake, ID	16007	9,065	8.6	76.1	15.3	8,082	6,955	58.7	...	...	...	...
Benewah, ID	16009	14,793	19.3	67.0	13.7	14,228	8,750	52.0	...	...	...	...
Bingham, ID	16011	71,685	12.5	74.4	13.1	65,425	6,592	60.3	...	...	...	...
Blaine, ID	16013	61,186	2.3	29.5	68.2	46,604	14,406	64.0	...	...	...	...
Boise, ID	16015	10,660	13.0	67.0	20.0	9,112	8,881	49.9	...	...	...	...
Bonner, ID	16017	43,024	10.5	70.8	18.7	40,885	7,351	59.1	...	...	...	...
Bonneville, ID	16019	140,779	8.2	71.3	20.5	122,618	6,044	62.0	5378	73.6	16.8	4.9
Boundary, ID	16021	13,825	14.3	66.4	19.3	12,069	7,386	61.5	...	...	...	...
Butte, ID	16023	4,796	9.6	70.6	19.9	4,112	8,549	51.2	...	...	...	...
Camas, ID	16025	2,269	6.2	62.9	30.9	1,825	9,973	55.5	...	...	...	...
Canyon, ID	16027	281,229	9.5	63.3	27.2	221,419	6,369	60.8	9996	70.4	16.0	8.7
Caribou, ID	16029	13,944	8.6	76.3	15.1	12,769	8,238	61.7	...	...	...	...
Cassia, ID	16031	38,209	12.0	72.5	15.5	32,602	6,488	60.4	...	...	...	...
Clark, ID	16033	2,597	10.9	73.2	15.8	2,264	10,937	55.6	...	...	...	...
Clearwater, ID	16035	11,877	15.1	67.1	17.8	10,877	8,598	59.2	...	...	...	...
Custer, ID	16037	6,469	8.5	78.8	12.7	6,046	8,891	57.1	...	...	...	...
Elmore, ID.......................	16039	38,712	22.2	67.7	10.1	35,067	6,876	60.7	...	...	...	...
Franklin, ID.....................	16041	20,097	11.5	78.2	10.3	17,358	5,632	61.8	...	...	...	...
Fremont, ID.....................	16043	18,545	12.4	72.3	15.3	16,358	6,943	63.8	...	...	...	...
Gem, ID	16045	19,465	10.9	80.6	8.6	17,791	6,293	62.6	...	...	...	...
Gooding, ID	16047	23,816	12.8	74.5	12.7	21,236	7,145	60.8	...	...	...	...
Idaho, ID.........................	16049	19,508	17.7	61.9	20.4	17,203	9,944	58.1	...	...	...	...
Jefferson, ID....................	16051	42,118	9.5	72.7	17.8	35,254	6,062	60.2	...	...	...	...
Jerome, ID.......................	16053	30,026	10.9	73.9	15.2	25,936	6,329	60.9	...	...	...	...
Kootenai, ID	16055	147,884	9.0	70.8	20.2	132,307	6,311	64.0	7359	84.5	11.9	2.1
Latah, ID	16057	46,919	6.2	63.5	30.3	42,516	8,197	57.9	...	...	...	...
Lemhi, ID	16059	9,162	11.8	79.9	8.3	8,679	7,883	62.9	...	...	...	...
Lewis, ID.........................	16061	9,753	13.1	72.0	14.9	8,838	9,352	58.9	...	...	...	...
Lincoln, ID.......................	16063	9,313	10.3	75.9	13.8	8,208	7,765	61.0	...	...	...	...
Madison, ID.....................	16065	45,093	11.7	70.0	18.2	36,178	6,018	61.0	...	...	...	...
Minidoka, ID....................	16067	33,502	13.5	74.9	11.6	29,073	7,029	62.4	...	...	...	...
Nez Perce, ID..................	16069	50,939	12.8	59.8	27.4	48,833	8,613	60.8	...	...	...	...
Oneida, ID	16071	6,737	11.0	78.3	10.6	5,997	6,799	62.1	...	...	...	...
Owyhee, ID......................	16073	21,298	14.1	71.3	14.6	19,259	7,517	60.6	...	...	...	...
Payette, ID	16075	32,622	11.7	74.2	14.1	28,996	6,534	62.4	...	...	...	...
Power, ID.........................	16077	16,523	12.1	66.3	21.5	14,782	8,747	57.6	...	...	...	...
Shoshone, ID....................	16079	23,146	14.0	55.8	30.2	19,871	9,693	56.8	...	...	...	...
Teton, ID	16081	13,911	7.2	57.4	35.5	10,495	6,754	60.0	...	...	...	...
Twin Falls, ID	16083	96,928	10.6	70.8	18.6	82,562	6,504	59.2	...	...	...	...
Valley, ID.........................	16085	19,690	7.8	43.6	48.7	13,916	10,187	59.4	...	...	...	...
Washington, ID	16087	15,529	11.5	78.0	10.4	14,552	7,667	62.7	...	...	...	...

[5]Hawaii, Kalawao, Kauai, and Maui counties are included with Honolulu county
... Not available

Table C-1. Population, School, and Student Characteristics by County—*Continued*

County	State/County Code	High school graduates, 2006-2008			College enrollment, 2006-2008		College graduates, 2006-2008 (percent)						
		Population 25 years and over	High school diploma or less (percent)	High school diploma or more (percent)	Number	Percent public	Bachelor's degree or more	+/- U.S. percent with Bachelor's degree or more	Non-Hispanic White	Black or African American	American Indian and Alaska Native	Asian, Hawaiian, and Pacific Islander	Hispanic or Latino[3]
		30	31	32	33	34	35	36	37	38	39	40	41
Troup, GA	13285	40,302	55.3	80.1	3,877	57.3	20.7	-6.7	27.0	6.5	...	...	...
Turner, GA	13287	...	...	...	...	...	...	...	...	...	...	...	...
Twiggs, GA	13289	...	...	...	...	...	...	...	...	...	...	...	...
Union, GA	13291	15,299	47.9	80.3	683	80.7	20.8	-6.6	19.9	...	...	...	...
Upson, GA	13293	18,492	67.3	72.6	1,117	82.3	10.6	-16.8	12.7	4.8	...	...	...
Walker, GA	13295	43,945	60.4	73.2	2,027	79.2	11.8	-15.6	11.7	13.8	...	...	...
Walton, GA	13297	53,827	61.7	77.4	2,144	75.8	16.0	-11.4	16.5	11.5	...	...	...
Ware, GA	13299	23,471	62.3	79.5	1,783	95.9	11.2	-16.2	12.4	7.8	...	...	...
Warren, GA	13301	...	...	...	...	...	...	...	...	...	...	...	...
Washington, GA	13303	13,616	65.3	75.4	587	95.9	11.7	-15.7	21.1	2.9	...	...	...
Wayne, GA	13305	19,168	61.5	77.7	1,403	90.6	12.3	-15.1	13.8	6.3	...	...	...
Webster, GA	13307	...	...	...	...	...	...	...	...	...	...	...	...
Wheeler, GA	13309	...	...	...	...	...	...	...	...	...	...	...	...
White, GA	13311	17,032	52.3	80.4	1,085	62.7	19.7	-7.7	19.6	...	...	...	...
Whitfield, GA	13313	57,754	62.8	67.2	3,544	82.5	15.0	-12.4	17.4	6.2	...	...	5.7
Wilcox, GA	13315	...	...	...	...	...	...	...	...	...	...	...	...
Wilkes, GA	13317	...	...	...	...	...	...	...	...	...	...	...	...
Wilkinson, GA	13319	...	...	...	...	...	...	...	...	...	...	...	...
Worth, GA	13321	13,963	68.1	75.8	974	93.7	8.7	-18.7	11.2	1.8	...	...	...
HAWAII	15000	868,474	40.0	89.5	84,447	72.9	29.2	1.8	42.0	27.3	26.7	26.6	16.6
Hawaii, HI	15001	116,861	41.5	89.9	10,030	90.9	26.8	-0.6	36.1	34.3	20.8	23.6	10.3
Honolulu, HI	15003	609,523	38.8	89.7	67,287	69.5	30.7	3.3	46.0	27.2	29.7	28.2	18.9
Kalawao, HI	15005	...	...	...	...	...	...	...	...	...	...	...	...
Kauai, HI	15007	43,394	43.1	88.6	2,183	86.6	23.6	-3.8	35.0	...	...	18.8	19.7
Maui, HI	15009	98,616	43.9	88.3	4,947	76.9	25.3	-2.1	38.0	...	...	19.4	12.1
IDAHO	16000	939,967	41.3	87.9	93,824	76.4	24.0	-3.4	25.2	25.4	9.9	38.6	8.0
Ada, ID	16001	240,935	31.0	92.7	25,925	84.4	34.7	7.3	35.7	24.2	11.3	49.1	18.6
Adams, ID	16003	...	...	...	...	...	...	...	...	...	...	...	...
Bannock, ID	16005	47,102	34.5	89.8	7,125	94.2	27.9	0.5	28.6	...	12.1	...	17.5
Bear Lake, ID	16007	...	...	...	...	...	...	...	...	...	...	...	...
Benewah, ID	16009	...	...	...	...	...	...	...	...	...	...	...	...
Bingham, ID	16011	25,137	47.7	83.6	2,080	81.3	15.6	-11.8	18.3	...	1.3	...	3.5
Blaine, ID	16013	15,089	28.0	90.8	882	83.6	44.4	17.0	48.2	...	...	...	15.5
Boise, ID	16015	...	...	...	...	...	...	...	...	...	...	...	...
Bonner, ID	16017	28,955	42.7	91.4	1,021	80.2	22.7	-4.7	23.1	...	...	...	...
Bonneville, ID	16019	58,445	38.7	90.7	4,297	78.6	26.2	-1.2	27.3	...	...	38.3	9.4
Boundary, ID	16021	...	...	...	...	...	...	...	...	...	...	...	...
Butte, ID	16023	...	...	...	...	...	...	...	...	...	...	...	...
Camas, ID	16025	...	...	...	...	...	...	...	...	...	...	...	...
Canyon, ID	16027	106,781	50.9	81.5	8,216	63.4	16.9	-10.5	19.3	...	5.5	36.1	4.8
Caribou, ID	16029	...	...	...	...	...	...	...	...	...	...	...	...
Cassia, ID	16031	12,284	43.7	81.0	783	89.8	16.8	-10.6	19.5	...	...	...	2.9
Clark, ID	16033	...	...	...	...	...	...	...	...	...	...	...	...
Clearwater, ID	16035	...	...	...	...	...	...	...	...	...	...	...	...
Custer, ID	16037	...	...	...	...	...	...	...	...	...	...	...	...
Elmore, ID	16039	17,378	42.7	85.5	1,733	82.2	14.3	-13.1	15.7	...	...	...	...
Franklin, ID	16041	...	...	...	...	...	...	...	...	...	...	...	...
Fremont, ID	16043	...	...	...	...	...	...	...	...	...	...	...	...
Gem, ID	16045	...	...	...	...	...	...	...	...	...	...	...	...
Gooding, ID	16047	...	...	...	...	...	...	...	...	...	...	...	...
Idaho, ID	16049	...	...	...	...	...	...	...	...	...	...	...	...
Jefferson, ID	16051	13,086	45.6	83.9	1,096	61.4	16.4	-11.0	17.6	...	...	...	...
Jerome, ID	16053	11,820	58.7	72.2	768	92.4	11.0	-16.4	12.6	...	...	...	...
Kootenai, ID	16055	89,205	39.2	90.9	6,354	86.4	21.3	-6.1	21.1	...	30.0	...	19.8
Latah, ID	16057	20,127	31.4	93.2	9,392	97.7	42.4	15.0	41.5	...	...	...	...
Lemhi, ID	16059	...	...	...	...	...	...	...	...	...	...	...	...
Lewis, ID	16061	...	...	...	...	...	...	...	...	...	...	...	...
Lincoln, ID	16063	...	...	...	...	...	...	...	...	...	...	...	...
Madison, ID	16065	14,755	25.3	96.3	11,041	16.3	26.8	-0.6	27.3	...	...	...	...
Minidoka, ID	16067	...	...	...	...	...	...	...	...	...	...	...	...
Nez Perce, ID	16069	26,435	46.4	90.7	2,569	89.5	17.2	-10.2	17.5	...	8.7	...	...
Oneida, ID	16071	...	...	...	...	...	...	...	...	...	...	...	...
Owyhee, ID	16073	...	...	...	...	...	...	...	...	...	...	...	...
Payette, ID	16075	14,319	56.6	80.7	576	81.3	12.8	-14.6	13.8	...	...	...	1.2
Power, ID	16077	...	...	...	...	...	...	...	...	...	...	...	...
Shoshone, ID	16079	...	...	...	...	...	...	...	...	...	...	...	...
Teton, ID	16081	...	...	...	...	...	...	...	...	...	...	...	...
Twin Falls, ID	16083	46,285	46.9	82.7	3,665	85.4	16.7	-10.7	18.2	...	...	...	1.8
Valley, ID	16085	...	...	...	...	...	...	...	...	...	...	...	...
Washington, ID	16087	...	...	...	...	...	...	...	...	...	...	...	...

[3]May be of any race
... Not available

Table C-1. Population, School, and Student Characteristics by County—*Continued*

County	State/ County Code	County Type[1]	Population, 2009		Percent of related children 5-17 years in poverty, 2008	Percent of children under 19 years with no health insurance, 2007	Number of Schools and Students, 2008-2009			Resident enrollment, 2006-2008	
			Total	Percent 5–17 years			School Districts	Schools	Students	K–12 enrollment	
										Number	Percent public
			1	2	3	4	5	6	7	8	9
ILLINOIS	17000	X	12,910,409	17.7	15.4	9.0	1,078	4,450	2,119,707	2,314,680	87.9
Adams, IL	17001	5	67,054	16.4	15.3	7.3	9	29	9,097	11,396	85.6
Alexander, IL	17003	7	7,914	16.8	42.8	5.5	5	17	1,217	...	...
Bond, IL	17005	1	18,103	14.8	13.5	8.9	2	8	2,459	...	...
Boone, IL	17007	2	54,020	21.9	9.3	11.8	3	18	10,710	11,140	89.8
Brown, IL	17009	7	6,591	12.1	13.1	7.5	1	3	809	...	...
Bureau, IL	17011	6	34,699	17.7	13.1	10.4	15	26	5,789	5,687	88.5
Calhoun, IL	17013	1	5,019	15.5	12.0	11.0	2	4	716	...	...
Carroll, IL	17015	7	15,749	15.8	16.0	10.3	3	11	2,711	...	...
Cass, IL	17017	6	13,559	18.3	16.0	11.4	4	11	2,433	...	...
Champaign, IL	17019	3	195,671	13.4	15.4	9.4	18	65	23,479	26,512	90.7
Christian, IL	17021	6	34,253	16.7	16.9	7.7	7	27	6,505	5,952	92.1
Clark, IL	17023	6	16,657	17.1	17.1	9.1	3	10	2,950	...	...
Clay, IL	17025	7	13,538	16.6	16.8	9.8	5	14	2,894	...	...
Clinton, IL	17027	1	36,368	16.6	8.4	10.8	13	24	5,523	6,171	86.2
Coles, IL	17029	5	52,065	12.7	17.7	7.5	6	27	6,585	6,585	90.5
Cook, IL	17031	1	5,287,037	17.1	20.2	9.4	169	1,330	807,119	949,980	85.7
Crawford, IL	17033	6	19,433	15.3	17.0	9.0	5	12	3,146	...	...
Cumberland, IL	17035	9	10,716	16.8	15.1	13.9	2	7	1,824	...	...
De Kalb, IL	17037	1	107,333	15.5	8.4	10.5	14	45	17,574	16,484	92.2
De Witt, IL	17039	6	16,034	17.8	14.2	8.1	2	10	3,045	...	...
Douglas, IL	17041	6	19,169	18.9	11.6	14.3	4	11	2,879	...	...
Du Page, IL	17043	1	932,541	18.3	6.5	7.3	49	251	160,915	171,714	86.1
Edgar, IL	17045	6	18,471	15.8	17.0	7.4	5	15	3,238	...	...
Edwards, IL	17047	9	6,444	15.9	13.6	13.5	1	3	988	...	...
Effingham, IL	17049	7	34,424	18.1	12.5	10.5	4	16	5,404	6,119	85.8
Fayette, IL	17051	6	20,935	16.5	19.9	10.3	8	20	3,632	3,412	89.7
Ford, IL	17053	3	13,911	18.5	12.4	9.4	4	11	3,231	...	...
Franklin, IL	17055	5	39,312	16.4	26.3	8.7	11	21	6,632	6,251	97.6
Fulton, IL	17057	6	36,652	15.4	19.3	9.2	9	27	6,933	5,602	94.8
Gallatin, IL	17059	8	5,705	15.1	25.5	10.2	1	3	802	...	...
Greene, IL	17061	6	13,567	17.6	20.1	8.7	3	8	2,202	...	...
Grundy, IL	17063	1	48,421	19.4	7.6	8.9	15	31	12,483	8,481	94.2
Hamilton, IL	17065	7	8,096	16.4	19.9	8.5	3	8	2,024	...	...
Hancock, IL	17067	7	18,359	16.3	14.3	10.2	8	16	3,126	...	...
Hardin, IL	17069	9	4,358	14.2	26.7	6.9	1	3	643	...	...
Henderson, IL	17071	9	7,354	15.4	16.8	12.4	1	4	1,037	...	...
Henry, IL	17073	2	49,314	17.3	11.3	8.6	10	30	8,861	8,325	95.4
Iroquois, IL	17075	6	29,690	18.1	15.2	11.0	10	27	4,988	5,072	96.7
Jackson, IL	17077	5	58,103	12.2	27.2	12.0	10	24	7,269	7,170	84.5
Jasper, IL	17079	7	9,530	16.5	15.9	12.3	2	6	1,424	...	...
Jefferson, IL	17081	7	39,944	15.8	21.1	8.0	20	25	6,262	6,389	89.1
Jersey, IL	17083	1	22,549	17.0	11.2	8.5	3	14	4,655	3,533	84.7
Jo Daviess, IL	17085	6	21,990	15.3	10.9	11.2	9	22	3,340	3,183	94.7
Johnson, IL	17087	7	13,730	13.5	16.6	11.4	7	8	2,063	...	...
Kane, IL	17089	1	511,892	21.1	10.6	11.7	15	171	121,404	104,126	88.9
Kankakee, IL	17091	3	113,215	18.2	17.7	8.1	16	46	19,705	20,505	89.1
Kendall, IL	17093	1	104,821	21.6	4.7	9.6	7	38	23,467	18,680	91.6
Knox, IL	17095	4	51,648	15.1	20.3	7.3	8	27	7,779	8,021	94.5
Lake, IL	17097	1	712,567	20.4	9.1	8.7	51	221	141,195	147,785	90.2
La Salle, IL	17099	4	112,498	17.2	13.2	9.3	30	51	17,426	19,074	88.1
Lawrence, IL	17101	7	16,408	13.8	20.9	9.1	2	7	2,447	...	...
Lee, IL	17103	4	34,919	16.2	11.5	7.6	6	14	4,892	5,612	87.5
Livingston, IL	17105	4	37,777	17.5	12.0	9.0	14	25	6,692	6,267	94.1
Logan, IL	17107	6	29,776	14.5	14.0	8.7	10	16	3,509	4,579	89.2
McDonough, IL	17109	5	32,770	10.7	19.9	9.8	6	20	3,446	3,062	95.2
McHenry, IL	17111	1	320,961	20.1	5.3	9.7	21	81	54,176	63,582	90.7
McLean, IL	17113	3	167,699	16.0	9.5	7.1	15	54	24,390	25,541	86.2
Macon, IL	17115	3	108,204	16.3	19.0	6.8	11	51	16,971	18,337	88.8
Macoupin, IL	17117	1	47,774	16.3	16.0	8.9	9	29	7,422	7,967	95.2
Madison, IL	17119	1	268,457	16.6	15.5	7.0	19	89	43,053	44,911	88.6
Marion, IL	17121	4	39,008	17.1	21.1	7.4	16	32	7,268	6,776	92.4
Marshall, IL	17123	2	12,702	17.3	11.4	9.4	3	7	1,729	...	...
Mason, IL	17125	6	14,785	17.2	19.4	8.9	3	10	3,137	...	...
Massac, IL	17127	7	14,970	16.4	21.2	6.5	2	10	2,638	...	...
Menard, IL	17129	3	12,466	17.8	13.0	11.3	3	11	2,673	...	...
Mercer, IL	17131	2	16,276	17.0	10.4	10.1	3	12	3,124	...	...
Monroe, IL	17133	1	33,236	18.3	3.6	8.5	6	13	5,327	5,744	77.0
Montgomery, IL	17135	6	29,500	15.6	21.6	9.4	6	19	4,796	4,770	91.0
Morgan, IL	17137	4	34,897	15.4	16.1	7.7	7	25	5,222	5,467	92.7

[1]County type codes are from the Economic Research Service of the United States Department of Agriculture. See notes and definitions for more information.
... Not available

Table C-1. Population, School, and Student Characteristics by County—*Continued*

County	State/County Code	Characteristics of students, 2008-2009				Number of graduates, 2006-2007	Staff and students, 2008-2009			
		Percent with IEP[2]	Percent eligible for free or reduced lunch	Percent minority	Percent English Language Learners		Total staff	Number of teachers	Student/teacher ratio	Central admin. Staff
		10	11	12	13	14	15	16	17	18
ILLINOIS	17000	15.0	39.3	44.5	9.7	130,213	163,215	135,665	15.6	2364
Adams, IL	17001	20.2	44.7	7.1	...	695	810	686	13.3	14
Alexander, IL	17003	19.4	72.4	51.1	...	83	155	121	10.1	6
Bond, IL	17005	18.6	33.6	6.5	...	144	168	150	16.4	4
Boone, IL	17007	14.3	40.1	32.2	11.9	520	783	674	15.9	9
Brown, IL	17009	18.7	34.7	2.7	...	54	62	55	14.7	1
Bureau, IL	17011	18.3	33.7	12.8	5.3	375	515	429	13.5	13
Calhoun, IL	17013	24.2	44.4	0.4	...	60	70	58	12.3	2
Carroll, IL	17015	17.3	39.9	4.2	...	186	225	198	13.7	3
Cass, IL	17017	17.1	52.8	25.0	19.1	133	200	176	13.8	4
Champaign, IL	17019	16.7	41.1	36.3	5.8	1,506	2,192	1,814	12.9	42
Christian, IL	17021	17.6	40.0	2.0	...	477	632	531	12.3	12
Clark, IL	17023	19.0	36.9	2.3	...	210	235	200	14.8	3
Clay, IL	17025	18.2	40.7	2.4	...	154	258	219	13.2	5
Clinton, IL	17027	19.2	26.3	5.8	...	330	442	394	14.0	16
Coles, IL	17029	20.3	38.3	6.0	0.3	503	696	563	11.7	14
Cook, IL	17031	13.5	53.7	71.7	15.0	45,129	57,507	47,568	17.0	630
Crawford, IL	17033	18.9	39.3	3.0	...	245	266	231	13.6	7
Cumberland, IL	17035	20.5	30.4	0.2	...	141	148	127	14.4	2
De Kalb, IL	17037	12.7	23.3	18.3	5.3	1,086	1,415	1,172	15.0	25
De Witt, IL	17039	18.4	35.1	4.1	...	177	235	207	14.7	2
Douglas, IL	17041	21.5	30.5	11.8	1.9	197	264	230	12.5	4
Du Page, IL	17043	13.9	13.3	33.6	9.8	12,093	13,004	10,485	15.3	185
Edgar, IL	17045	21.8	36.3	4.0	...	221	297	260	12.5	5
Edwards, IL	17047	21.7	33.2	2.5	...	67	83	73	13.5	1
Effingham, IL	17049	16.8	25.8	2.2	0.7	416	415	355	15.2	8
Fayette, IL	17051	18.0	46.2	1.4	...	240	295	259	14.0	8
Ford, IL	17053	15.5	30.1	3.7	...	207	280	240	13.5	3
Franklin, IL	17055	19.9	47.9	1.6	...	407	530	445	14.9	10
Fulton, IL	17057	17.0	40.7	2.0	0.2	387	562	497	13.9	15
Gallatin, IL	17059	23.6	47.5	2.0	...	69	62	56	14.3	1
Greene, IL	17061	20.7	41.8	1.8	...	166	189	167	13.2	3
Grundy, IL	17063	15.2	13.8	13.7	1.7	830	988	830	15.0	21
Hamilton, IL	17065	23.1	46.8	1.4	...	84	161	139	14.6	5
Hancock, IL	17067	21.8	41.7	1.6	...	252	303	265	11.8	8
Hardin, IL	17069	20.4	58.3	2.0	...	48	51	45	14.3	1
Henderson, IL	17071	16.3	45.2	2.1	...	63	92	82	12.6	1
Henry, IL	17073	14.6	31.3	8.7	2.0	610	655	573	15.5	13
Iroquois, IL	17075	17.1	34.0	9.9	1.8	344	460	389	12.8	10
Jackson, IL	17077	18.4	50.8	26.5	3.5	539	686	549	13.2	12
Jasper, IL	17079	15.4	39.0	0.8	...	125	176	128	11.1	2
Jefferson, IL	17081	22.5	46.5	14.6	0.2	412	548	475	13.2	19
Jersey, IL	17083	16.6	36.2	1.4	...	243	329	277	16.8	6
Jo Daviess, IL	17085	16.3	29.8	3.9	1.0	295	341	289	11.6	8
Johnson, IL	17087	17.6	42.8	2.3	0.2	108	158	138	14.9	6
Kane, IL	17089	14.0	35.7	46.1	18.8	7,191	8,553	7,199	16.9	88
Kankakee, IL	17091	15.8	44.6	36.9	1.8	1,207	1,516	1,275	15.5	29
Kendall, IL	17093	14.6	12.7	28.9	6.1	1,073	1,773	1,452	16.2	19
Knox, IL	17095	15.0	46.1	12.6	...	484	683	584	13.3	12
Lake, IL	17097	15.2	21.8	39.6	12.6	9,257	11,760	9,621	14.7	191
La Salle, IL	17099	17.1	30.7	13.7	2.2	1,297	1,468	1,245	14.0	33
Lawrence, IL	17101	14.8	41.5	2.1	0.4	147	201	171	14.3	3
Lee, IL	17103	14.5	31.7	7.4	...	361	388	332	14.7	7
Livingston, IL	17105	18.5	31.0	5.0	...	514	617	525	12.7	12
Logan, IL	17107	17.2	35.8	4.5	...	261	338	297	11.8	10
McDonough, IL	17109	22.3	42.5	7.5	1.2	323	380	304	11.3	8
McHenry, IL	17111	15.3	14.4	17.4	6.4	3,643	4,078	3,346	16.2	76
McLean, IL	17113	16.2	25.6	20.9	3.0	1,551	2,067	1,728	14.1	31
Macon, IL	17115	15.5	9.1	29.1	0.5	1,048	1,443	1,204	14.1	28
Macoupin, IL	17117	18.4	36.4	2.0	...	628	544	470	15.8	10
Madison, IL	17119	18.0	37.5	16.5	1.0	2,896	3,280	2,726	15.8	46
Marion, IL	17121	25.3	54.2	7.3	...	506	654	535	13.6	18
Marshall, IL	17123	17.5	33.1	3.7	...	123	158	141	12.3	3
Mason, IL	17125	22.3	43.4	1.1	...	237	269	235	13.3	3
Massac, IL	17127	13.8	48.0	8.5	...	160	197	172	15.3	4
Menard, IL	17129	15.6	22.8	1.5	...	189	190	167	16.0	3
Mercer, IL	17131	15.9	29.8	2.3	...	220	276	242	12.9	3
Monroe, IL	17133	13.0	12.8	2.4	0.1	428	392	334	15.9	7
Montgomery, IL	17135	15.6	39.6	2.1	...	364	326	283	16.9	7
Morgan, IL	17137	21.0	43.5	7.9	0.4	410	515	422	12.4	9

[2]IEP= Individual Education Program. See notes and definitions for more information
... Not available

Table C-1. Population, School, and Student Characteristics by County—*Continued*

County	State/County Code	Total revenue ($1,000's)	Percentage of revenue from — Federal gov't	State gov't	Local gov't	Current expenditures, 2007-2008 Amount ($1,000's)	Amount per student	Percent for instruc-tion	Resident population 16 to 19 years, 2006-2008 Total population 16 to 19 years	Percent en-rolled in school	Percent high school graduates, not enrolled in school	Percent not enrolled, not grads, not employed or not in labor force
		19	20	21	22	23	24	25	26	27	28	29
ILLINOIS	17000	25,435,685	7.9	29.7	62.5	21,569,167	10,274	58.8	762,216	85.7	8.8	3.6
Adams, IL	17001	91,454	10.3	39.2	50.5	83,787	8,804	57.7	...	...	...	...
Alexander, IL	17003	19,457	21.2	51.3	27.5	17,538	13,897	52.0	...	...	...	...
Bond, IL	17005	20,040	5.4	56.1	38.4	17,856	7,315	61.4	...	...	...	...
Boone, IL	17007	109,915	4.6	35.2	60.1	93,602	8,667	62.1	...	...	...	...
Brown, IL	17009	7,148	4.2	47.0	48.8	6,407	8,183	56.0	...	...	...	...
Bureau, IL	17011	61,264	6.8	38.8	54.4	52,819	8,883	56.6	...	...	...	...
Calhoun, IL	17013	6,726	10.1	47.4	42.6	7,080	10,085	58.8	...	...	...	...
Carroll, IL	17015	28,935	5.2	37.1	57.7	26,643	9,643	57.3	...	...	...	...
Cass, IL	17017	22,138	11.4	56.2	32.4	18,337	7,593	62.3	...	...	...	...
Champaign, IL	17019	250,335	7.9	31.7	60.4	225,754	9,737	58.5	21,564	94.6	3.5	1.1
Christian, IL	17021	71,483	8.3	44.4	47.3	61,074	9,105	62.2	...	...	...	...
Clark, IL	17023	25,368	5.8	61.5	32.7	22,315	7,637	54.8	...	...	...	...
Clay, IL	17025	21,786	7.1	60.9	32.0	19,474	7,697	59.3	...	...	...	...
Clinton, IL	17027	46,548	4.3	47.8	47.9	40,843	7,367	64.2	...	...	...	...
Coles, IL	17029	80,274	15.2	38.3	46.5	76,412	11,579	56.9	...	...	...	...
Cook, IL	17031	10,529,117	10.3	29.0	60.7	8,913,308	11,286	58.8	303,939	84.6	8.8	4.5
Crawford, IL	17033	31,104	6.4	46.3	47.3	26,913	8,382	54.5	...	...	...	...
Cumberland, IL	17035	16,484	4.6	62.6	32.8	13,831	7,692	59.0	...	...	...	...
De Kalb, IL	17037	208,654	4.6	29.2	66.2	180,495	10,283	58.1	10,406	94.6	3.9	0.8
De Witt, IL	17039	30,025	5.9	24.4	69.7	24,171	7,928	61.9	...	...	...	...
Douglas, IL	17041	26,654	3.7	37.6	58.8	24,608	8,445	61.2	...	...	...	...
Du Page, IL	17043	2,134,693	3.2	14.9	81.9	1,801,044	11,211	61.7	53,500	89.9	6.6	1.7
Edgar, IL	17045	32,048	7.5	47.7	44.8	27,294	8,271	62.7	...	...	...	...
Edwards, IL	17047	8,282	5.2	61.3	33.4	8,030	8,111	64.0	...	...	...	...
Effingham, IL	17049	48,167	6.3	49.4	44.3	43,960	8,015	59.1	...	...	...	...
Fayette, IL	17051	35,993	5.8	54.7	39.5	27,575	7,459	56.0	...	...	...	...
Ford, IL	17053	31,449	5.7	40.3	54.1	28,789	8,952	56.7	...	...	...	...
Franklin, IL	17055	65,260	15.4	57.4	27.2	59,470	9,016	60.2	1,933	76.0	12.7	8.9
Fulton, IL	17057	59,175	5.7	40.2	54.1	47,475	8,834	57.8	...	...	...	...
Gallatin, IL	17059	8,173	11.9	57.2	30.9	7,314	8,780	59.3	...	...	...	...
Greene, IL	17061	18,966	6.6	59.6	33.8	17,522	7,622	61.3	...	...	...	...
Grundy, IL	17063	151,975	2.5	16.6	80.9	109,525	8,905	59.2	...	...	...	...
Hamilton, IL	17065	11,429	5.9	62.4	31.7	10,791	8,564	56.0	...	...	...	...
Hancock, IL	17067	32,194	5.5	52.2	42.4	29,681	8,492	58.4	...	...	...	...
Hardin, IL	17069	5,668	8.9	69.1	21.9	5,497	8,576	56.6	...	...	...	...
Henderson, IL	17071	10,566	5.6	49.9	44.5	8,816	8,568	57.5	...	...	...	...
Henry, IL	17073	85,463	6.8	45.1	48.1	73,539	8,299	58.7	...	...	...	...
Iroquois, IL	17075	55,990	7.7	42.4	49.9	46,738	9,270	56.0	...	...	...	...
Jackson, IL	17077	85,383	13.4	39.3	47.2	77,243	10,687	58.9	...	...	...	...
Jasper, IL	17079	19,920	18.8	25.8	55.4	20,012	13,688	49.4	...	...	...	...
Jefferson, IL	17081	58,979	11.6	52.9	35.5	55,270	8,835	58.9	2,135	76.5	10.2	6.8
Jersey, IL	17083	26,133	7.4	49.3	43.4	24,892	8,765	60.5	...	...	...	...
Jo Daviess, IL	17085	39,679	5.3	22.7	72.0	34,197	10,223	61.7	...	...	...	...
Johnson, IL	17087	17,971	7.1	57.6	35.3	15,630	7,681	58.8	...	...	...	...
Kane, IL	17089	1,292,241	5.0	26.3	68.7	1,112,422	9,280	58.0	27,754	84.9	9.5	3.4
Kankakee, IL	17091	204,947	10.3	41.3	48.4	178,634	9,078	58.0	7,141	84.9	7.5	6.9
Kendall, IL	17093	262,925	2.3	26.7	71.0	196,712	8,846	56.5	4,862	81.9	9.2	2.9
Knox, IL	17095	86,244	8.1	39.8	52.1	68,776	8,995	62.4	...	...	...	...
Lake, IL	17097	1,970,560	4.5	19.8	75.7	1,613,642	11,524	57.4	44,611	81.3	14.2	2.5
La Salle, IL	17099	198,527	6.2	30.2	63.6	172,542	9,938	58.4	5,819	80.1	14.9	4.4
Lawrence, IL	17101	20,174	7.1	65.6	27.3	18,514	7,743	58.1	...	...	...	...
Lee, IL	17103	52,891	6.3	34.2	59.5	45,744	9,334	60.9	...	...	...	...
Livingston, IL	17105	74,379	6.4	37.2	56.4	67,766	10,056	59.6	...	...	...	...
Logan, IL	17107	37,790	6.2	36.6	57.2	34,083	9,623	61.5	...	...	...	...
McDonough, IL	17109	43,816	12.7	35.7	51.6	39,936	11,774	57.0	...	...	...	...
McHenry, IL	17111	625,921	3.5	21.9	74.6	506,093	9,437	58.8	18,272	88.5	8.7	1.8
McLean, IL	17113	225,305	5.9	28.7	65.4	220,418	9,230	59.8	12,931	93.5	3.9	2.0
Macon, IL	17115	186,008	9.1	40.4	50.5	162,231	9,371	54.8	6,580	76.8	15.6	5.0
Macoupin, IL	17117	78,950	7.2	56.6	36.2	67,763	7,289	59.8	...	...	...	...
Madison, IL	17119	428,563	8.6	38.8	52.7	385,830	8,955	56.6	15,130	90.8	5.8	2.7
Marion, IL	17121	79,709	12.2	53.6	34.3	68,130	9,319	58.5	2,319	84.5	9.7	4.1
Marshall, IL	17123	15,232	3.3	34.5	62.2	13,343	9,285	60.5	...	...	...	...
Mason, IL	17125	30,958	7.7	48.1	44.2	26,368	7,964	60.8	...	...	...	...
Massac, IL	17127	22,798	10.0	50.5	39.5	20,460	7,660	56.5	...	...	...	...
Menard, IL	17129	24,565	4.4	42.1	53.5	20,035	7,549	55.6	...	...	...	...
Mercer, IL	17131	28,547	5.3	50.0	44.7	26,092	8,187	59.2	...	...	...	...
Monroe, IL	17133	48,569	3.6	28.9	67.5	39,603	7,679	60.4	...	...	...	...
Montgomery, IL	17135	44,012	6.9	46.9	46.3	37,451	7,759	58.5	...	...	...	...
Morgan, IL	17137	55,999	12.2	35.4	52.3	52,106	10,209	57.1	...	...	...	...

... Not available

Table C-1. Population, School, and Student Characteristics by County—*Continued*

County	State/County Code	High school graduates, 2006-2008			College enrollment, 2006-2008		College graduates, 2006-2008 (percent)						
		Population 25 years and over	High school diploma or less (percent)	High school diploma or more (percent)	Number	Percent public	Bachelor's degree or more	+/- U.S. percent with Bachelor's degree or more	Non-Hispanic White	Black or African American	American Indian and Alaska Native	Asian, Hawaiian, and Pacific Islander	Hispanic or Latino[3]
		30	31	32	33	34	35	36	37	38	39	40	41
ILLINOIS	17000	8,336,919	42.8	85.6	961,052	67.1	29.5	2.1	32.9	18.4	19.0	61.3	11.2
Adams, IL	17001	45,175	51.1	88.8	4,298	54.9	21.0	-6.4	20.9	14.4	...	...	...
Alexander, IL	17003	...	...	...	...	...	...	...	...	...	...	...	...
Bond, IL	17005	...	...	...	...	...	...	...	...	...	...	...	...
Boone, IL	17007	32,920	55.2	86.0	2,443	67.7	19.2	-8.2	21.2	...	...	...	3.8
Brown, IL	17009	...	...	...	...	...	...	...	...	...	...	...	...
Bureau, IL	17011	24,106	54.6	87.8	1,303	90.8	15.0	-12.4	15.7	...	...	...	2.1
Calhoun, IL	17013	...	...	...	...	...	...	...	...	...	...	...	...
Carroll, IL	17015	...	...	...	...	...	...	...	...	...	...	...	...
Cass, IL	17017	...	...	...	...	...	...	...	...	...	...	...	...
Champaign, IL	17019	106,714	31.1	92.1	49,838	97.7	43.0	15.6	42.2	22.1	...	80.7	36.7
Christian, IL	17021	24,014	57.8	82.8	1,449	79.0	12.1	-15.3	12.1	...	...	...	...
Clark, IL	17023	...	...	...	...	...	...	...	...	...	...	...	...
Clay, IL	17025	...	...	...	...	...	...	...	...	...	...	...	...
Clinton, IL	17027	24,815	46.2	83.5	2,260	78.3	17.6	-9.8	17.7	...	...	...	...
Coles, IL	17029	29,945	47.0	89.5	12,276	99.7	22.4	-5.0	21.3	...	...	...	...
Cook, IL	17031	3,442,826	43.3	82.3	376,528	54.8	31.8	4.4	42.6	18.6	21.2	57.6	11.1
Crawford, IL	17033	...	...	...	...	...	...	...	...	...	...	...	...
Cumberland, IL	17035	...	...	...	...	...	...	...	...	...	...	...	...
De Kalb, IL	17037	58,130	39.3	90.4	23,501	95.4	27.7	0.3	27.9	34.9	...	...	12.8
De Witt, IL	17039	...	...	...	...	...	...	...	...	...	...	...	...
Douglas, IL	17041	...	...	...	...	...	...	...	...	...	...	...	...
Du Page, IL	17043	609,231	28.8	92.1	73,745	58.3	44.6	17.2	45.6	37.1	16.7	68.6	16.1
Edgar, IL	17045	...	...	...	...	...	...	...	...	...	...	...	...
Edwards, IL	17047	...	...	...	...	...	...	...	...	...	...	...	...
Effingham, IL	17049	22,411	48.7	87.8	1,850	94.8	21.1	-6.3	21.2	...	...	...	...
Fayette, IL	17051	14,406	61.1	79.9	964	86.6	12.8	-14.6	12.8	...	...	...	...
Ford, IL	17053	...	...	...	...	...	...	...	...	...	...	...	...
Franklin, IL	17055	27,609	53.0	81.0	1,643	96.5	12.7	-14.7	12.1	...	...	...	...
Fulton, IL	17057	26,271	55.6	83.8	1,957	86.2	12.8	-14.6	13.1	...	...	...	...
Gallatin, IL	17059	...	...	...	...	...	...	...	...	...	...	...	...
Greene, IL	17061	...	...	...	...	...	...	...	...	...	...	...	...
Grundy, IL	17063	30,738	46.7	90.0	2,537	83.2	17.2	-10.2	17.2	...	...	...	11.3
Hamilton, IL	17065	...	...	...	...	...	...	...	...	...	...	...	...
Hancock, IL	17067	...	...	...	...	...	...	...	...	...	...	...	...
Hardin, IL	17069	...	...	...	...	...	...	...	...	...	...	...	...
Henderson, IL	17071	...	...	...	...	...	...	...	...	...	...	...	...
Henry, IL	17073	34,159	48.2	87.1	2,433	69.2	19.6	-7.8	20.0	...	...	...	9.8
Iroquois, IL	17075	20,859	56.6	85.6	1,112	81.3	12.8	-14.6	12.4	...	...	...	9.0
Jackson, IL	17077	32,416	35.2	89.4	16,915	97.3	36.2	8.8	34.9	32.9	...	...	...
Jasper, IL	17079	...	...	...	...	...	...	...	...	...	...	...	...
Jefferson, IL	17081	27,695	53.6	82.7	1,626	85.5	13.8	-13.6	14.1	4.1	...	...	...
Jersey, IL	17083	15,003	51.1	87.7	1,247	60.8	15.6	-11.8	14.7	...	...	...	...
Jo Daviess, IL	17085	16,332	48.7	88.6	641	59.8	22.5	-4.9	22.4	...	...	...	...
Johnson, IL	17087	...	...	...	...	...	...	...	...	...	...	...	...
Kane, IL	17089	305,977	42.3	83.0	28,567	67.4	31.8	4.4	39.7	17.1	...	59.1	7.8
Kankakee, IL	17091	71,186	49.4	85.7	7,753	61.8	17.5	-9.9	18.8	10.2	...	...	7.4
Kendall, IL	17093	59,071	35.7	91.1	6,854	69.1	30.7	3.3	32.1	42.2	...	56.8	14.7
Knox, IL	17095	36,030	52.7	84.6	3,761	62.6	15.0	-12.4	15.5	3.1	...	...	12.6
Lake, IL	17097	442,651	33.3	87.9	44,797	65.2	41.1	13.7	47.7	21.1	33.7	65.0	9.7
La Salle, IL	17099	76,094	52.6	87.0	4,680	88.0	15.5	-11.9	15.5	...	...	...	9.5
Lawrence, IL	17101	...	...	...	...	...	...	...	...	...	...	...	...
Lee, IL	17103	24,272	52.2	85.2	2,095	85.5	14.6	-12.8	14.9	...	...	...	7.4
Livingston, IL	17105	25,872	59.8	83.9	1,392	95.5	13.3	-14.1	13.6	1.0	...	...	8.4
Logan, IL	17107	19,362	54.5	84.8	4,507	20.2	18.6	-8.8	20.5	2.6	...	...	...
McDonough, IL	17109	17,316	37.4	92.8	11,431	98.2	36.5	9.1	33.7	...	...	...	...
McHenry, IL	17111	200,941	37.5	91.1	18,404	73.7	31.3	3.9	32.1	45.4	...	63.3	13.7
McLean, IL	17113	96,761	33.6	93.8	28,542	84.7	39.9	12.5	39.7	27.9	...	84.2	20.7
Macon, IL	17115	72,815	50.0	86.7	6,741	59.2	20.2	-7.2	21.5	5.4	...	...	31.9
Macoupin, IL	17117	32,886	52.5	87.0	3,304	52.3	15.7	-11.7	15.8	...	...	...	...
Madison, IL	17119	177,759	44.8	89.1	22,781	89.4	23.2	-4.2	23.7	12.9	...	62.4	17.2
Marion, IL	17121	27,053	53.8	81.6	2,117	87.5	13.2	-14.2	13.4	12.0	...	...	...
Marshall, IL	17123	...	...	...	...	...	...	...	...	...	...	...	...
Mason, IL	17125	...	...	...	...	...	...	...	...	...	...	...	...
Massac, IL	17127	...	...	...	...	...	...	...	...	...	...	...	...
Menard, IL	17129	...	...	...	...	...	...	...	...	...	...	...	...
Mercer, IL	17131	...	...	...	...	...	...	...	...	...	...	...	...
Monroe, IL	17133	21,795	40.5	91.1	2,223	74.3	25.5	-1.9	25.5	...	...	...	...
Montgomery, IL	17135	20,968	59.1	82.8	1,412	89.2	14.8	-12.6	14.6	...	...	...	...
Morgan, IL	17137	23,859	52.9	85.9	3,329	37.2	20.7	-6.7	21.0	17.4	...	...	...

[3]May be of any race
... Not available

Table C-1. Population, School, and Student Characteristics by County—*Continued*

County	State/ County Code	County Type[1]	Population, 2009		Percent of related children 5-17 years in poverty, 2008	Percent of children under 19 years with no health insurance, 2007	Number of Schools and Students, 2008-2009			Resident enrollment, 2006-2008	
			Total	Percent 5–17 years			School Districts	Schools	Students	K–12 enrollment	
										Number	Percent public
	1	2	3	4	5	6	7	8	9		
Moultrie, IL	17139	6	14,392	18.2	12.8	10.8	3	9	1,995	...	...
Ogle, IL	17141	4	55,336	18.7	9.6	9.8	12	28	10,258	10,504	95.4
Peoria, IL	17143	2	185,816	17.2	20.1	6.9	21	84	27,826	31,220	85.5
Perry, IL	17145	7	22,424	15.4	18.6	9.1	6	8	2,986	3,780	95.1
Piatt, IL	17147	3	16,550	18.0	7.0	10.5	5	16	3,382	...	...
Pike, IL	17149	7	16,273	16.4	17.7	9.3	4	13	2,782	...	...
Pope, IL	17151	9	3,991	13.5	27.3	8.8	1	2	539	...	...
Pulaski, IL	17153	9	6,218	17.5	35.2	9.6	3	12	1,155	...	...
Putnam, IL	17155	8	6,009	16.8	10.8	13.1	1	3	924	...	...
Randolph, IL	17157	6	32,686	15.2	16.5	9.5	8	16	4,316	4,655	77.7
Richland, IL	17159	7	15,523	16.3	17.9	9.3	2	10	2136	...	...
Rock Island, IL	17161	2	146,826	15.7	17.6	9.9	13	58	21,486	24,402	88.6
St. Clair, IL	17163	1	263,617	18.1	21.7	8.1	35	110	44,408	49,025	88.4
Saline, IL	17165	7	25,738	17.5	27.4	6.0	5	15	4,328	4,507	96.2
Sangamon, IL	17167	3	195,716	17.1	14.4	8.0	16	114	30,238	32,999	85.0
Schuyler, IL	17169	7	6,730	16.2	15.7	10.2	1	5	1,279	...	...
Scott, IL	17171	9	5,193	16.8	12.2	13.1	2	5	956	...	...
Shelby, IL	17173	6	21,803	16.6	12.9	11.3	4	11	2,553	3,540	97.1
Stark, IL	17175	2	6,019	18.3	14.0	14.1	3	5	956	...	...
Stephenson, IL	17177	4	46,537	16.8	16.3	7.9	7	24	7,172	8,074	91.1
Tazewell, IL	17179	2	132,466	16.7	10.1	7.1	22	54	19,996	22,216	91.2
Union, IL	17181	7	18,005	15.8	22.8	8.6	6	15	3,160	...	...
Vermilion, IL	17183	3	80,067	17.5	20.5	6.9	15	42	13,844	13,963	94.0
Wabash, IL	17185	6	11,997	15.7	16.8	8.7	2	5	1,927	...	...
Warren, IL	17187	7	17,409	15.3	16.0	8.6	4	14	2,836	...	...
Washington, IL	17189	6	14,560	16.7	9.8	10.2	7	8	2,010	...	...
Wayne, IL	17191	7	16,294	16.3	18.1	9.4	7	14	2,658	...	...
White, IL	17193	6	14,661	15.3	20.1	9.0	3	10	1,698	...	...
Whiteside, IL	17195	4	58,961	17.2	14.3	8.7	15	32	9,901	10,130	90.9
Will, IL	17197	1	685,251	21.3	7.3	9.0	36	182	118,516	137,038	91.0
Williamson, IL	17199	5	65,169	15.8	21.8	7.1	8	24	10,261	10,281	92.8
Winnebago, IL	17201	2	299,702	18.2	18.4	9.2	14	95	47,461	54,361	83.8
Woodford, IL	17203	2	38,862	18.8	6.9	10.3	12	26	8,279	6,772	92.9
INDIANA	18000	X	6,423,113	17.8	15.9	7.6	379	1995	1,046,147	1,137,278	88.3
Adams, IN	18001	6	34,256	21.2	23.3	8.4	3	11	4,724	6,474	72.3
Allen, IN	18003	2	353,888	19.0	14.7	8.3	7	95	56,031	67,089	82.5
Bartholomew, IN	18005	3	76,063	17.9	12.8	9.0	2	20	12,174	13,685	83.7
Benton, IN	18007	3	8,613	19.2	12.6	12.1	1	4	1,836	...	...
Blackford, IN	18009	6	13,051	17.2	17.9	6.7	1	5	2,133	...	...
Boone, IN	18011	1	56,287	20.5	6.3	9.0	3	17	10,795	9,938	87.4
Brown, IN	18013	1	14,548	15.5	13.2	12.1	1	6	2,197	...	...
Carroll, IN	18015	3	19,752	18.5	10.5	10.4	2	5	2,783	...	...
Cass, IN	18017	4	39,065	18.8	15.2	8.8	3	14	6,882	7,129	91.6
Clark, IN	18019	1	108,634	16.8	13.2	6.7	4	31	16,366	17,891	88.0
Clay, IN	18021	3	26,533	18.1	15.8	8.1	1	10	4,573	4,810	94.6
Clinton, IN	18023	6	34,367	18.9	16.1	9.9	4	16	6,254	6,083	97.5
Crawford, IN	18025	8	10,540	16.5	23.5	8.3	1	6	1,682	...	...
Daviess, IN	18027	7	30,620	19.5	21.4	12.0	4	11	4,294	5,398	90.2
Dearborn, IN	18029	1	50,502	18.3	10.2	7.2	3	17	9,053	9,151	87.3
Decatur, IN	18031	6	25,079	18.9	16.5	8.8	2	7	4,502	4,588	91.5
De Kalb, IN	18033	4	42,060	19.1	11.4	7.7	4	16	7,872	8,144	88.2
Delaware, IN	18035	3	115,192	14.6	19.3	6.2	10	39	16,476	17,173	94.2
Dubois, IN	18037	7	41,419	18.7	6.8	11.5	5	18	7,443	7,396	87.5
Elkhart, IN	18039	3	200,502	19.9	16.2	10.6	7	57	35,882	38,699	88.8
Fayette, IN	18041	7	24,101	17.1	19.1	6.0	2	12	4,239	4,097	93.0
Floyd, IN	18043	1	74,426	17.6	13.6	6.4	2	20	12,269	13,007	86.4
Fountain, IN	18045	6	16,852	18.1	13.0	7.7	3	7	3,206	...	...
Franklin, IN	18047	1	23,148	19.4	12.3	8.6	2	9	5,044	4,390	84.5
Fulton, IN	18049	7	20,265	18.0	15.8	8.8	2	6	2,700	3,588	96.2
Gibson, IN	18051	2	32,750	17.7	12.5	6.9	3	13	5,115	5,490	94.6
Grant, IN	18053	4	68,796	15.6	23.2	6.9	6	35	12,050	11,071	94.0
Greene, IN	18055	3	32,463	17.0	18.0	7.7	6	14	5,519	5,607	95.3
Hamilton, IN	18057	1	279,287	21.2	4.2	7.2	8	63	50,779	57,142	86.5
Hancock, IN	18059	1	68,334	19.3	6.1	8.2	5	23	12,862	11,862	90.6
Harrison, IN	18061	1	37,562	17.4	13.0	8.3	3	15	6,132	6,216	91.4
Hendricks, IN	18063	1	140,606	19.6	5.5	6.8	6	38	26,257	26,352	89.2
Henry, IN	18065	4	47,827	16.6	14.1	7.1	6	23	8,229	8,032	97.8
Howard, IN	18067	3	82,895	17.7	16.1	6.0	5	31	13,737	15,063	93.1
Huntington, IN	18069	6	37,777	17.2	13.5	8.2	1	11	6,049	6,392	94.4
Jackson, IN	18071	4	42,362	17.9	13.4	8.6	4	16	6,741	7,175	86.0

[1]County type codes are from the Economic Research Service of the United States Department of Agriculture. See notes and definitions for more information.
... Not available

Table C-1. Population, School, and Student Characteristics by County—*Continued*

County	State/ County Code	Characteristics of students, 2008-2009				Number of graduates, 2006-2007	Staff and students, 2008-2009			
		Percent with IEP[2]	Percent eligible for free or reduced lunch	Percent minority	Percent English Language Learners		Total staff	Number of teachers	Student/ teacher ratio	Central admin. Staff
		10	11	12	13	14	15	16	17	18
Moultrie, IL	17139	19.2	34.5	1.3	...	123	170	147	13.6	3
Ogle, IL	17141	14.4	19.7	13.3	5.1	814	860	721	14.2	18
Peoria, IL	17143	19.5	41.2	42.0	2.4	1,713	2,291	1,954	14.2	36
Perry, IL	17145	19.2	37.9	5.2	...	205	220	196	15.2	6
Piatt, IL	17147	15.1	24.8	2.4	...	241	270	237	14.3	5
Pike, IL	17149	21.4	39.8	1.3	...	163	253	216	12.9	5
Pope, IL	17151	22.1	48.6	2.4	...	46	48	42	12.8	1
Pulaski, IL	17153	16.5	73.5	45.0	...	78	117	94	12.3	4
Putnam, IL	17155	15.6	29.5	6.5	...	68	83	72	12.8	1
Randolph, IL	17157	16.5	39.4	7.5	...	293	388	330	13.1	9
Richland, IL	17159	13.8	42.0	2.2	...	208	191	161	13.3	4
Rock Island, IL	17161	16.5	44.1	30.8	6.0	1,383	1,700	1,408	15.3	29
St. Clair, IL	17163	18.1	44.2	45.1	0.2	2,932	3,418	2,898	15.3	59
Saline, IL	17165	19.2	48.7	9.9	...	278	335	289	15.0	8
Sangamon, IL	17167	19.1	37.5	21.6	0.2	1,731	2,970	2,482	12.2	38
Schuyler, IL	17169	23.8	31.1	2.8	1.0	93	104	87	14.7	2
Scott, IL	17171	18.0	31.2	1.3	...	56	92	78	12.3	2
Shelby, IL	17173	17.5	32.5	1.5	...	174	227	196	13.0	4
Stark, IL	17175	18.3	34.1	2.3	...	57	143	110	8.7	2
Stephenson, IL	17177	13.2	40.1	18.3	1.0	543	635	537	13.4	12
Tazewell, IL	17179	17.8	29.0	3.4	...	1,379	1,598	1,342	14.9	35
Union, IL	17181	19.2	49.9	8.4	2.1	216	256	223	14.2	6
Vermilion, IL	17183	18.1	53.3	24.4	1.1	761	1,134	953	14.5	18
Wabash, IL	17185	18.6	34.9	2.0	...	136	148	126	15.3	2
Warren, IL	17187	13.9	39.9	16.5	5.5	196	235	197	14.4	7
Washington, IL	17189	20.1	24.9	2.8	...	153	165	145	13.9	7
Wayne, IL	17191	18.0	41.8	1.3	...	178	223	195	13.6	7
White, IL	17193	23.0	38.4	1.5	...	205	221	162	10.5	9
Whiteside, IL	17195	16.6	38.7	13.4	1.7	684	812	697	14.2	17
Will, IL	17197	14.4	22.4	36.7	6.8	6,080	8,791	7,220	16.4	124
Williamson, IL	17199	18.3	41.2	7.9	...	694	788	676	15.2	13
Winnebago, IL	17201	14.3	54.4	37.9	7.3	2,588	3,660	3,085	15.4	36
Woodford, IL	17203	15.0	18.3	2.3	...	595	665	566	14.6	15
INDIANA	18000	16.8	41.8	20.8	4.4	59,887	141,923	62,655	16.7	1923
Adams, IN	18001	13.7	34.2	6.5	3.0	350	618	289	16.3	10
Allen, IN	18003	16.3	46.3	31.0	5.4	3,282	6,707	3,259	17.2	137
Bartholomew, IN	18005	15.5	36.1	10.2	6.2	688	1,562	675	18.0	16
Benton, IN	18007	27.3	38.7	7.3	2.9	136	288	130	14.1	6
Blackford, IN	18009	20.4	45.8	1.3	0.4	131	317	135	15.8	6
Boone, IN	18011	17.2	19.3	5.1	0.7	633	1,468	628	17.2	18
Brown, IN	18013	21.3	39.8	1.4	...	152	301	145	15.2	7
Carroll, IN	18015	13.9	34.6	5.1	3.8	162	362	153	18.2	5
Cass, IN	18017	14.0	42.7	19.7	13.7	429	1,239	486	14.2	13
Clark, IN	18019	17.5	43.5	15.3	3.4	870	2,121	968	16.9	26
Clay, IN	18021	21.5	45.9	1.3	0.3	286	649	272	16.8	6
Clinton, IN	18023	15.4	45.7	18.2	13.6	395	844	415	15.1	13
Crawford, IN	18025	18.0	52.5	1.4	...	110	280	99	17.0	4
Daviess, IN	18027	20.1	41.4	5.9	5.4	254	599	283	15.2	11
Dearborn, IN	18029	18.4	25.3	1.4	0.3	610	1,067	509	17.8	14
Decatur, IN	18031	16.1	38.7	1.9	1.0	278	601	269	16.7	11
De Kalb, IN	18033	15.2	36.5	3.2	0.9	513	1,172	487	16.2	15
Delaware, IN	18035	20.7	43.7	11.5	0.6	1,095	2,252	1,087	15.2	51
Dubois, IN	18037	12.1	23.4	7.8	5.2	556	961	406	18.3	17
Elkhart, IN	18039	16.0	50.0	28.4	15.7	1,942	4,735	2,143	16.7	44
Fayette, IN	18041	15.7	55.3	2.2	0.1	209	632	260	16.3	5
Floyd, IN	18043	18.3	36.4	10.7	1.6	730	1,657	696	17.6	11
Fountain, IN	18045	14.7	36.9	2.1	1.1	190	441	211	15.2	8
Franklin, IN	18047	15.6	32.5	1.6	1.0	340	659	272	18.5	11
Fulton, IN	18049	14.6	39.0	4.4	0.7	173	381	145	18.6	9
Gibson, IN	18051	22.2	31.6	2.3	0.1	308	605	291	17.6	11
Grant, IN	18053	18.1	49.0	13.5	1.3	706	1,604	692	17.4	21
Greene, IN	18055	17.5	41.1	1.1	...	341	803	361	15.3	14
Hamilton, IN	18057	14.2	12.5	12.2	2.6	2,624	6,451	2,728	18.6	59
Hancock, IN	18059	17.8	20.6	4.7	0.5	761	1,771	772	16.7	19
Harrison, IN	18061	18.2	36.3	2.5	0.5	417	793	347	17.7	10
Hendricks, IN	18063	13.5	18.6	10.3	2.3	1,540	3,450	1,426	18.4	34
Henry, IN	18065	22.3	40.2	1.7	0.1	549	1,236	548	15.0	19
Howard, IN	18067	21.6	40.1	12.9	1.1	813	2,084	899	15.3	23
Huntington, IN	18069	16.3	36.0	2.1	0.3	383	789	375	16.1	8
Jackson, IN	18071	18.2	38.7	6.9	4.7	418	834	386	17.5	24

[2]IEP= Individual Education Program. See notes and definitions for more information
... Not available

Table C-1. Population, School, and Student Characteristics by County—*Continued*

County	State/County Code	Revenues, 2007-2008				Current expenditures, 2007-2008			Resident population 16 to 19 years, 2006-2008			
		Total revenue ($1,000's)	Percentage of revenue from			Amount ($1,000's)	Amount per student	Percent for instruction	Total population 16 to 19 years	Percent enrolled in school	Percent high school graduates, not enrolled in school	Percent not enrolled, not grads, not employed or not in labor force
			Federal gov't	State gov't	Local gov't							
	19		20	21	22	23	24	25	26	27	28	29
Moultrie, IL	17139	18,123	4.6	46.3	49.1	15,403	7,576	55.9	...	...	...	...
Ogle, IL	17141	120,011	4.2	30.6	65.2	93,615	9,143	62.5	...	...	...	...
Peoria, IL	17143	313,493	8.7	36.6	54.7	277,644	9,503	58.1	11292	84.2	8.1	5.5
Perry, IL	17145	27,019	7.0	57.0	36.0	22,918	8,087	63.1	...	...	...	...
Piatt, IL	17147	32,295	3.2	24.2	72.6	26,794	7,916	54.8	...	...	...	...
Pike, IL	17149	26,088	6.7	54.9	38.3	23,655	8,370	59.1	...	...	...	...
Pope, IL	17151	5,074	14.7	55.3	30.0	4,521	8,205	52.5	...	...	...	...
Pulaski, IL	17153	11,329	11.6	69.5	18.9	11,819	10,171	59.4	...	...	...	...
Putnam, IL	17155	11,691	3.3	25.5	71.2	8,336	8,489	61.0	...	...	...	...
Randolph, IL	17157	48,504	13.0	40.6	46.4	41,714	9,767	55.9	...	...	...	...
Richland, IL	17159	22,679	8.7	52.5	38.8	20,314	8,026	56.4	...	...	...	...
Rock Island, IL	17161	240,489	9.5	33.0	57.6	200,277	9,183	61.8	8227	87.4	7.0	3.1
St. Clair, IL	17163	511,331	11.5	47.5	40.9	443,457	9,776	56.6	15848	87.5	7.0	4.2
Saline, IL	17165	36,437	9.0	62.8	28.1	33,142	7,598	61.4	...	...	...	...
Sangamon, IL	17167	33,3042	8.5	33.4	58.0	276,014	9,234	56.6	9283	84.2	9.6	3.9
Schuyler, IL	17169	12,484	5.2	59.4	35.4	11,637	8,652	54.7	...	...	...	...
Scott, IL	17171	8,420	6.0	56.9	37.0	7,952	8,478	62.6	...	...	...	...
Shelby, IL	17173	22,189	4.9	57.2	37.9	20,445	7,968	59.4	...	...	...	...
Stark, IL	17175	11,833	3.5	36.9	59.6	9,045	7,927	62.3	...	...	...	...
Stephenson, IL	17177	80,525	6.9	42.4	50.7	69,887	9,768	55.6	...	...	...	...
Tazewell, IL	17179	211,891	7.5	32.9	59.7	174,473	8,565	58.7	6620	86.9	9.3	2.2
Union, IL	17181	28,964	8.4	56.7	34.9	25,688	7,931	59.5	...	...	...	...
Vermilion, IL	17183	139,301	10.2	50.1	39.7	124,081	8,774	59.4	4337	78.1	10.4	8.5
Wabash, IL	17185	16,233	6.6	54.9	38.6	14,077	7,168	60.9	...	...	...	...
Warren, IL	17187	24,038	6.1	52.9	41.0	21,630	7,891	59.4	...	...	...	...
Washington, IL	17189	18,691	4.4	45.6	50.0	16,809	8,120	60.5	...	...	...	...
Wayne, IL	17191	24,057	7.3	62.9	29.7	21,664	8,015	63.4	...	...	...	...
White, IL	17193	32,248	18.3	47.7	34.1	30,631	11,882	56.6	...	...	...	...
Whiteside, IL	17195	106,406	6.5	37.7	55.8	88,201	8,989	61.9	3420	83.2	9.8	3.6
Will, IL	17197	1,333,603	4.7	27.5	67.9	1,101,367	9,404	58.5	39100	85.9	10.4	2.0
Williamson, IL	17199	102,242	8.7	46.0	45.3	84,789	8,544	58.8	...	...	...	...
Winnebago, IL	17201	535,220	8.9	35.3	55.8	450,696	9,276	59.5	15654	81.3	9.4	5.6
Woodford, IL	17203	81,640	5.3	37.4	57.4	68,207	8,249	60.1	...	...	...	...
INDIANA	18000	11,388,165	7.1	47.3	45.5	9,374,267	9,031	58.9	365435	85.0	7.8	4.6
Adams, IN	18001	39,363	7.7	58.7	33.7	39,366	8,363	58.3	...	...	...	...
Allen, IN	18003	604,799	7.7	46.2	46.1	513,249	9,338	62.7	19441	84.5	8.3	4.8
Bartholomew, IN	18005	133,999	8.0	43.6	48.4	114,368	9,358	57.8	...	...	...	...
Benton, IN	18007	22,185	2.0	47.6	50.4	19,212	9,949	59.7	...	...	...	...
Blackford, IN	18009	23,708	7.0	55.3	37.7	20,070	9,086	59.3	...	...	...	...
Boone, IN	18011	116,244	2.0	43.5	54.5	91,985	8,604	57.2	...	...	...	...
Brown, IN	18013	28,242	4.5	37.4	58.2	21,012	9,368	58.0	...	...	...	...
Carroll, IN	18015	28,244	3.8	49.7	46.5	21,604	7,768	54.4	...	...	...	...
Cass, IN	18017	82,644	9.3	48.6	42.1	66,737	9,583	61.8	...	...	...	...
Clark, IN	18019	167,134	7.2	50.1	42.7	142,856	8,818	62.9	4965	73.3	14.5	7.8
Clay, IN	18021	45,259	7.2	56.1	36.7	37,841	8,119	64.0	...	...	...	...
Clinton, IN	18023	65,276	10.4	51.7	37.9	53,557	8,445	58.7	1852	74.8	10.2	13.0
Crawford, IN	18025	18,109	9.2	57.9	32.9	15,951	9,104	62.5	...	...	...	...
Daviess, IN	18027	44,729	10.1	51.2	38.7	40,735	9,390	64.3	...	...	...	...
Dearborn, IN	18029	95,740	5.8	44.3	49.8	77,801	8,663	60.3	...	...	...	...
Decatur, IN	18031	41,405	5.4	51.5	43.1	35,137	7,884	60.7	...	...	...	...
De Kalb, IN	18033	98,756	10.4	41.0	48.6	81,855	10,292	58.2	...	...	...	...
Delaware, IN	18035	199,416	9.0	46.5	44.5	151,982	9,508	62.5	...	...	...	...
Dubois, IN	18037	68,994	8.5	47.0	44.4	69,222	9,233	58.4	...	...	...	...
Elkhart, IN	18039	427,009	7.0	46.1	46.9	333,826	9,213	59.4	10445	76.7	6.6	7.7
Fayette, IN	18041	46,802	12.9	50.6	36.5	38,226	9,106	59.3	...	...	...	...
Floyd, IN	18043	169,085	5.3	36.8	57.9	103,941	8,385	59.4	...	...	...	...
Fountain, IN	18045	26,773	7.2	60.6	32.1	26,157	8,019	59.0	...	...	...	...
Franklin, IN	18047	44,575	3.7	52.0	44.3	37,941	7,466	59.7	...	...	...	...
Fulton, IN	18049	27,355	4.5	49.3	46.2	20,739	7,710	55.9	...	...	...	...
Gibson, IN	18051	51,612	3.0	46.9	50.0	44,031	8,622	61.2	...	...	...	...
Grant, IN	18053	135,373	10.0	52.3	37.7	115,228	9,400	58.8	...	...	...	...
Greene, IN	18055	58,094	8.5	57.1	34.5	49,925	8,906	61.8	...	...	...	...
Hamilton, IN	18057	518,414	3.0	35.6	61.3	398,225	8,127	59.0	13378	93.7	4.1	1.5
Hancock, IN	18059	132,096	4.3	43.3	52.4	102,739	8,129	58.5	...	...	...	...
Harrison, IN	18061	65,805	5.4	46.3	48.3	50,740	8,244	58.3	...	...	...	...
Hendricks, IN	18063	239,257	3.5	47.2	49.3	202,383	7,925	55.5	6777	87.4	7.2	3.5
Henry, IN	18065	98,745	6.2	48.4	45.4	78,441	9,273	60.4	...	...	...	...
Howard, IN	18067	137,129	9.4	49.1	41.5	131,522	9,504	57.8	...	...	...	...
Huntington, IN	18069	50,706	8.7	57.8	33.5	49,728	8,147	60.2	...	...	...	...
Jackson, IN	18071	69,037	5.4	46.7	48.0	54,981	8,189	64.0	...	...	...	...

... Not available

Table C-1. Population, School, and Student Characteristics by County—*Continued*

County	State/ County Code	High school graduates, 2006-2008			College enrollment, 2006-2008		College graduates, 2006-2008 (percent)						
		Population 25 years and over	High school diploma or less (percent)	High school diploma or more (percent)	Number	Percent public	Bachelor's degree or more	+/- U.S. percent with Bachelor's degree or more	Non-Hispanic White	Black or African American	American Indian and Alaska Native	Asian, Hawaiian, and Pacific Islander	Hispanic or Latino[3]
		30	31	32	33	34	35	36	37	38	39	40	41
Moultrie, IL	17139	...	...	...	...	...	...	...	...	...	...	...	...
Ogle, IL	17141	36,602	50.7	86.8	2,570	82.4	17.1	-10.3	17.3	...	...	...	11.8
Peoria, IL	17143	117,934	41.5	87.8	14,763	47.4	27.1	-0.3	28.6	12.6	...	68.2	24.8
Perry, IL	17145	15,416	55.9	82.3	1,282	96.9	12.9	-14.5	13.5	...	...	...	...
Piatt, IL	17147	...	...	...	...	...	...	...	...	...	...	...	...
Pike, IL	17149	...	...	...	...	...	...	...	...	...	...	...	...
Pope, IL	17151	...	...	...	...	...	...	...	...	...	...	...	...
Pulaski, IL	17153	...	...	...	...	...	...	...	...	...	...	...	...
Putnam, IL	17155	...	...	...	...	...	...	...	...	...	...	...	...
Randolph, IL	17157	23,464	60.7	79.2	1,321	86.8	12.1	-15.3	13.5	1.7	...	...	...
Richland, IL	17159	...	...	...	...	...	...	...	...	...	...	...	...
Rock Island, IL	17161	99,233	47.2	86.3	10,485	62.4	20.3	-7.1	21.4	12.2	...	37.1	8.9
St. Clair, IL	17163	168,317	42.3	87.2	20,816	76.9	23.7	-3.7	26.2	16.4	...	44.7	18.5
Saline, IL	17165	17,864	49.0	81.9	1,378	88.0	14.0	-13.4	14.4	5.3	...	...	...
Sangamon, IL	17167	132,035	40.2	90.3	11,924	79.2	29.7	2.3	30.4	17.4	...	68.4	28.5
Schuyler, IL	17169	...	...	...	...	...	...	...	...	...	...	...	...
Scott, IL	17171	...	...	...	...	...	...	...	...	...	...	...	...
Shelby, IL	17173	15,014	54.8	86.9	887	94.4	14.8	-12.6	14.9	...	...	...	...
Stark, IL	17175	...	...	...	...	...	...	...	...	...	...	...	...
Stephenson, IL	17177	32,063	47.9	87.6	2,147	77.6	16.6	-10.8	17.5	6.9	...	...	...
Tazewell, IL	17179	90,014	42.6	90.1	6,788	73.1	23.9	-3.5	24.1	4.7	...	...	20.8
Union, IL	17181	...	...	...	...	...	...	...	...	...	...	...	...
Vermilion, IL	17183	54,814	56.1	84.5	2,680	93.0	13.3	-14.1	13.9	5.9	...	...	3.7
Wabash, IL	17185	...	...	...	...	...	...	...	...	...	...	...	...
Warren, IL	17187	...	...	...	...	...	...	...	...	...	...	...	...
Washington, IL	17189	...	...	...	...	...	...	...	...	...	...	...	...
Wayne, IL	17191	...	...	...	...	...	...	...	...	...	...	...	...
White, IL	17193	...	...	...	...	...	...	...	...	...	...	...	...
Whiteside, IL	17195	40,314	55.3	84.6	2,657	72.9	14.5	-12.9	15.2	...	...	...	5.4
Will, IL	17197	417,216	39.2	89.4	44,828	65.2	29.9	2.5	32.1	21.0	...	70.7	9.3
Williamson, IL	17199	44,381	46.7	87.9	4,638	93.0	19.4	-8.0	19.9	5.1	...	...	...
Winnebago, IL	17201	196,856	51.1	83.1	16,275	70.3	20.2	-7.2	22.1	8.0	15.4	47.0	8.4
Woodford, IL	17203	24,919	40.2	92.3	2,524	61.6	25.7	-1.7	26.0	...	...	...	...
INDIANA	18000	4,145,875	50.6	85.7	421,309	76.7	22.3	-5.1	22.9	14.9	16.5	60.4	11.3
Adams, IN	18001	20,801	60.9	82.0	1,353	79.2	11.9	-15.5	11.6	...	...	...	14.6
Allen, IN	18003	223,480	44.0	88.1	21,040	79.5	25.7	-1.7	27.5	13.2	11.7	45.9	12.4
Bartholomew, IN	18005	50,077	47.5	89.0	3,322	85.5	27.6	0.2	25.7	54.5	...	...	11.8
Benton, IN	18007	...	...	...	...	...	...	...	...	...	...	...	...
Blackford, IN	18009	...	...	...	...	...	...	...	...	...	...	...	...
Boone, IN	18011	35,451	37.7	92.0	2,926	80.1	37.2	9.8	36.7	...	...	...	...
Brown, IN	18013	...	...	...	...	...	...	...	...	...	...	...	...
Carroll, IN	18015	...	...	...	...	...	...	...	...	...	...	...	...
Cass, IN	18017	26,461	62.7	80.6	1,269	84.4	13.7	-13.7	14.2	...	...	...	7.1
Clark, IN	18019	71,431	51.7	84.5	5,279	84.0	17.3	-10.1	17.5	14.0	...	...	8.6
Clay, IN	18021	18,024	57.3	86.5	1,531	83.1	15.3	-12.1	15.5	...	...	...	...
Clinton, IN	18023	22,241	63.6	79.8	903	90.1	13.3	-14.1	14.5	...	...	...	2.4
Crawford, IN	18025	...	...	...	...	...	...	...	...	...	...	...	...
Daviess, IN	18027	19,348	64.6	71.7	689	68.1	11.4	-16.0	11.5	...	...	...	...
Dearborn, IN	18029	33,139	55.8	87.5	2,647	86.9	17.7	-9.7	16.7	...	...	...	...
Decatur, IN	18031	16,833	61.4	84.6	969	86.6	14.5	-12.9	13.1	...	...	...	...
De Kalb, IN	18033	27,496	56.0	87.7	1,767	77.1	17.8	-9.6	18.1	...	...	...	8.1
Delaware, IN	18035	71,706	51.9	84.5	17,180	96.7	22.4	-5.0	22.8	9.4	...	...	25.0
Dubois, IN	18037	27,691	58.7	82.7	1,404	82.0	20.3	-7.1	20.9	...	...	...	...
Elkhart, IN	18039	126,065	58.2	77.9	7,320	69.7	17.4	-10.0	19.4	5.4	...	45.0	5.8
Fayette, IN	18041	17,078	66.0	76.9	1,329	85.4	9.0	-18.4	8.9	...	...	...	...
Floyd, IN	18043	49,147	48.1	87.1	3,760	78.0	21.8	-5.6	22.2	8.8	...	...	17.6
Fountain, IN	18045	...	...	...	...	...	...	...	...	...	...	...	...
Franklin, IN	18047	15,621	56.9	85.9	1,103	69.1	16.7	-10.7	17.0	...	...	...	...
Fulton, IN	18049	14,072	62.8	86.4	513	68.2	14.3	-13.1	14.0	...	...	...	...
Gibson, IN	18051	22,454	54.7	87.6	1,696	61.0	14.5	-12.9	15.0	...	...	...	...
Grant, IN	18053	45,735	57.8	83.8	6,237	28.1	17.3	-10.1	17.7	10.9	...	...	7.4
Greene, IN	18055	22,617	62.4	83.5	1,365	90.2	11.6	-15.8	11.7	...	...	...	...
Hamilton, IN	18057	162,713	21.4	96.0	15,341	77.4	53.4	26.0	53.4	43.9	...	77.8	30.5
Hancock, IN	18059	43,809	44.6	90.7	3,103	78.1	25.6	-1.8	25.5	25.1	...	...	15.8
Harrison, IN	18061	25,203	56.6	87.3	1,890	81.5	14.0	-13.4	13.7	...	...	...	...
Hendricks, IN	18063	87,530	38.0	93.5	7,140	75.2	31.2	3.8	31.0	27.3	...	57.3	22.7
Henry, IN	18065	33,309	60.1	82.6	2,337	81.9	14.2	-13.2	14.6	...	...	...	...
Howard, IN	18067	57,384	52.7	84.0	3,490	89.0	19.2	-8.2	19.6	7.4	...	57.3	11.7
Huntington, IN	18069	25,310	58.3	87.3	2,362	53.7	15.3	-12.1	15.4	...	...	...	...
Jackson, IN	18071	28,442	60.3	83.1	1,171	78.5	13.9	-13.5	14.2	...	...	...	7.5

[3]May be of any race
... Not available

Table C-1. Population, School, and Student Characteristics by County—*Continued*

County	State/County Code	County Type[1]	Population, 2009 Total	Population, 2009 Percent 5–17 years	Percent of related children 5-17 years in poverty, 2008	Percent of children under 19 years with no health insurance, 2007	Number of Schools and Students, 2008-2009 School Districts	Number of Schools and Students, 2008-2009 Schools	Number of Schools and Students, 2008-2009 Students	Resident enrollment, 2006-2008 K–12 enrollment Number	Resident enrollment, 2006-2008 K–12 enrollment Percent public
			1	2	3	4	5	6	7	8	9
Jasper, IN	18073	1	32,816	18.8	11.4	9.6	2	9	5,421	5,720	92.0
Jay, IN	18075	6	21,117	19.0	21.4	8.4	1	10	3,671	3,861	97.5
Jefferson, IN	18077	6	33,010	16.6	15.9	8.0	3	11	4,791	5,808	86.6
Jennings, IN	18079	6	28,043	19.0	15.9	7.9	1	10	5,195	5,422	94.4
Johnson, IN	18081	1	141,501	18.7	8.7	6.8	8	39	24,773	25,467	90.2
Knox, IN	18083	4	37,907	14.9	21.6	6.9	4	14	5,211	5,718	89.8
Kosciusko, IN	18085	4	76,499	18.8	11.0	10.3	4	23	14,359	14,138	91.1
Lagrange, IN	18087	6	37,204	22.5	15.1	14.2	3	14	6,108	6,896	69.0
Lake, IN	18089	1	494,211	19.3	22.0	6.8	27	147	87,994	95,013	88.5
La Porte, IN	18091	3	111,063	16.9	16.3	7.6	10	38	18,395	19,517	88.2
Lawrence, IN	18093	4	45,842	17.2	18.6	7.9	2	20	7,362	7,654	89.6
Madison, IN	18095	3	131,417	16.6	18.9	6.4	6	37	19,709	21,743	92.3
Marion, IN	18097	1	890,879	17.4	22.0	5.7	38	242	140,775	159,850	84.8
Marshall, IN	18099	6	46,903	19.7	11.3	10.3	6	17	7,777	8,578	84.3
Martin, IN	18101	6	9,946	17.2	15.5	7.5	2	5	1,723	...	...
Miami, IN	18103	6	36,001	16.5	18.3	7.4	3	11	5,708	6,846	93.1
Monroe, IN	18105	3	130,738	11.5	16.6	8.3	2	28	13,873	15,185	90.8
Montgomery, IN	18107	6	37,862	17.6	15.1	8.2	3	17	6,447	6,825	98.2
Morgan, IN	18109	1	70,876	18.3	12.9	8.6	4	23	11,984	13,140	91.1
Newton, IN	18111	1	13,736	17.6	11.9	10.4	2	7	2,446	...	...
Noble, IN	18113	6	48,028	19.5	13.0	11.5	3	16	7,824	9,291	86.9
Ohio, IN	18115	1	5,909	15.9	11.3	9.9	1	2	927	...	...
Orange, IN	18117	6	19,559	18.1	22.0	6.9	5	8	3,401	...	...
Owen, IN	18119	3	22,397	16.8	19.0	10.5	1	6	2,976	3,935	95.1
Parke, IN	18121	6	16,896	15.6	23.1	8.7	3	7	2,443	...	...
Perry, IN	18123	6	18,812	15.1	14.4	7.0	3	6	3,025	...	...
Pike, IN	18125	6	12,259	16.2	12.2	7.2	2	6	2,045	...	...
Porter, IN	18127	1	163,598	18.0	9.4	8.4	8	50	27,551	28,934	92.3
Posey, IN	18129	2	26,004	18.0	10.1	7.8	3	11	3,971	4,416	88.0
Pulaski, IN	18131	6	13,614	17.8	16.8	9.5	2	6	2,171	...	...
Putnam, IN	18133	1	36,837	15.8	12.8	8.1	7	17	6,613	6,353	93.3
Randolph, IN	18135	6	25,696	17.8	19.2	7.8	6	14	4,813	4,579	92.8
Ripley, IN	18137	6	27,421	19.3	12.2	8.5	4	8	3,508	5,224	91.6
Rush, IN	18139	6	17,175	18.5	13.8	8.1	1	6	2,696	...	...
St. Joseph, IN	18141	2	267,613	17.7	17.6	8.6	7	71	40,648	48,624	80.4
Scott, IN	18143	6	23,624	17.8	22.1	5.9	2	9	4,268	4,120	98.6
Shelby, IN	18145	1	44,503	18.0	13.0	7.5	6	17	7,772	7,999	94.3
Spencer, IN	18147	8	20,039	17.7	11.6	9.9	2	10	3,545	3,447	85.4
Starke, IN	18149	6	23,530	17.4	22.2	7.4	3	8	4,093	4,114	97.3
Steuben, IN	18151	7	33,579	17.4	13.0	9.3	2	9	4,311	5,729	89.2
Sullivan, IN	18153	3	21,153	16.1	16.7	8.5	3	11	3,377	3,427	90.6
Switzerland, IN	18155	8	9,675	17.3	23.9	9.8	1	4	1,499	...	...
Tippecanoe, IN	18157	3	167,964	14.3	14.8	9.2	6	35	21,237	23,782	89.7
Tipton, IN	18159	3	15,892	17.9	9.1	7.7	2	5	2,847	...	...
Union, IN	18161	8	7,040	17.7	17.0	10.7	1	4	1,617	...	...
Vanderburgh, IN	18163	2	175,434	15.3	21.2	5.5	3	44	22,792	28,057	82.4
Vermillion, IN	18165	3	16,172	17.3	14.6	7.3	2	7	2,811	...	...
Vigo, IN	18167	3	105,967	15.3	24.2	6.7	2	30	15,971	16,570	94.0
Wabash, IN	18169	6	32,558	16.4	13.6	6.5	4	16	5,440	5,102	96.7
Warren, IN	18171	8	8,491	17.6	9.9	10.6	1	4	1,276	...	...
Warrick, IN	18173	2	58,521	18.8	8.5	7.1	1	15	9,647	10,291	87.3
Washington, IN	18175	1	27,729	18.0	19.5	8.1	3	9	4,737	5,302	89.4
Wayne, IN	18177	5	67,552	16.4	23.7	6.1	6	27	10,916	11,004	93.2
Wells, IN	18179	2	27,566	17.8	10.8	9.3	4	9	4,741	5,038	92.1
White, IN	18181	6	23,452	17.7	15.9	9.8	4	16	5,172	4,137	98.6
Whitley, IN	18183	2	32,861	18.1	8.7	9.0	3	9	4,864	5,692	91.6
IOWA	19000	X	3,007,856	16.9	12.0	6.1	372	1525	487,559	514,141	91.0
Adair, IA	19001	8	7,350	15.2	11.5	8.1	2	6	949	...	...
Adams, IA	19003	9	3,930	16.7	14.9	7.6	2	4	540	...	...
Allamakee, IA	19005	6	14,407	16.9	17.4	9.5	3	11	2,283	...	...
Appanoose, IA	19007	7	12,698	15.8	20.6	4.7	3	15	2,190	...	...
Audubon, IA	19009	8	6,032	17.1	11.6	11.6	2	4	889	...	...
Benton, IA	19011	3	26,734	18.5	8.0	6.5	3	14	3,975	4,785	94.4
Black Hawk, IA	19013	3	129,276	15.0	15.5	5.0	6	41	17,650	20,084	88.9
Boone, IA	19015	6	26,072	16.9	9.4	6.1	4	16	3,815	4,671	97.4
Bremer, IA	19017	3	23,460	16.6	6.2	7.3	6	25	4,766	3,914	92.5
Buchanan, IA	19019	6	20,910	19.8	14.6	7.6	3	15	2,853	3,887	87.5
Buena Vista, IA	19021	7	19,601	18.9	15.2	10.9	5	21	3,910	...	...
Butler, IA	19023	8	14,341	16.3	10.7	9.5	4	10	1,869	...	...
Calhoun, IA	19025	9	9,671	15.3	15.1	8.5	4	10	1,955	...	...

[1]County type codes are from the Economic Research Service of the United States Department of Agriculture. See notes and definitions for more information.
... Not available

Table C-1. Population, School, and Student Characteristics by County—*Continued*

County	State/County Code	Characteristics of students, 2008-2009					Staff and students, 2008-2009			
		Percent with IEP[2]	Percent eligible for free or reduced lunch	Percent minority	Percent English Language Learners	Number of graduates, 2006-2007	Total staff	Number of teachers	Student/teacher ratio	Central admin. Staff
		10	11	12	13	14	15	16	17	18
Jasper, IN	18073	17.4	32.6	6.6	3.1	366	773	303	17.9	8
Jay, IN	18075	21.7	45.1	3.8	2.8	225	521	244	15.0	4
Jefferson, IN	18077	22.4	48.8	2.6	0.5	285	829	329	14.6	17
Jennings, IN	18079	23.8	50.4	2.7	1.1	254	662	314	16.5	5
Johnson, IN	18081	14.7	29.1	6.3	2.4	1,371	3,245	1,376	18.0	44
Knox, IN	18083	16.0	45.3	2.4	0.3	354	814	361	14.4	12
Kosciusko, IN	18085	15.5	41.5	12.8	6.6	811	1,826	826	17.4	25
Lagrange, IN	18087	13.9	45.2	6.3	13.9	317	827	376	16.2	16
Lake, IN	18089	13.8	49.0	52.2	5.5	4,613	11,891	4,866	18.1	117
La Porte, IN	18091	15.6	46.3	19.6	2.5	1,045	2,723	1,101	16.7	44
Lawrence, IN	18093	19.2	37.3	1.9	0.2	404	1,113	444	16.6	10
Madison, IN	18095	19.1	47.7	14.0	2.0	1,094	2,590	1,170	16.8	44
Marion, IN	18097	16.5	58.8	50.7	8.7	6,424	19,174	8,667	16.2	274
Marshall, IN	18099	13.5	42.8	12.5	8.2	504	1,313	550	14.1	17
Martin, IN	18101	20.3	36.7	1.0	...	117	233	104	16.6	8
Miami, IN	18103	16.6	44.8	4.5	0.7	361	724	337	16.9	14
Monroe, IN	18105	16.8	32.0	9.7	2.8	883	2,090	861	16.1	27
Montgomery, IN	18107	17.7	37.4	5.4	2.8	437	1,047	408	15.8	17
Morgan, IN	18109	14.9	33.9	1.6	0.3	644	1,488	689	17.4	19
Newton, IN	18111	18.0	37.6	6.7	3.2	141	370	160	15.3	6
Noble, IN	18113	15.4	46.6	16.1	11.7	458	1,060	458	17.1	14
Ohio, IN	18115	18.8	29.4	1.2	0.3	64	125	57	16.3	3
Orange, IN	18117	19.3	45.0	2.0	0.2	221	664	272	12.5	10
Owen, IN	18119	20.5	40.6	1.5	0.2	166	417	189	15.7	4
Parke, IN	18121	21.4	47.9	0.8	...	174	380	172	14.2	8
Perry, IN	18123	12.8	36.5	1.6	0.3	189	381	166	18.2	7
Pike, IN	18125	22.2	35.5	1.1	0.4	149	647	209	9.8	10
Porter, IN	18127	15.0	28.4	12.7	1.4	1,781	3,365	1,534	18.0	38
Posey, IN	18129	24.2	25.4	2.5	0.5	313	620	271	14.7	8
Pulaski, IN	18131	19.4	38.3	2.8	0.7	157	333	145	15.0	4
Putnam, IN	18133	19.8	38.6	2.0	0.3	405	1,003	429	15.4	14
Randolph, IN	18135	20.9	46.1	3.3	1.6	306	738	327	14.7	21
Ripley, IN	18137	17.3	34.9	0.8	0.1	211	502	236	14.9	8
Rush, IN	18139	11.6	43.1	3.0	0.7	171	379	163	16.5	4
St. Joseph, IN	18141	18.9	51.3	31.9	6.8	2,195	5,648	2,366	17.2	53
Scott, IN	18143	17.8	51.9	1.4	0.2	249	591	252	16.9	10
Shelby, IN	18145	16.9	34.9	5.8	3.1	488	1,062	463	16.8	14
Spencer, IN	18147	15.2	30.5	4.5	1.9	271	502	219	16.2	8
Starke, IN	18149	14.4	50.5	4.2	1.0	265	538	230	17.8	10
Steuben, IN	18151	13.4	39.9	4.8	2.6	255	543	251	17.2	8
Sullivan, IN	18153	17.8	45.9	1.2	0.1	216	499	222	15.2	10
Switzerland, IN	18155	18.9	45.0	1.5	0.4	105	188	85	17.6	5
Tippecanoe, IN	18157	17.3	38.0	20.6	8.6	1,224	2,683	1,291	16.5	18
Tipton, IN	18159	18.2	27.7	3.2	1.0	189	382	176	16.2	11
Union, IN	18161	17.0	37.7	1.0	0.2	96	241	120	13.5	3
Vanderburgh, IN	18163	20.9	52.6	18.0	1.3	1,365	2,963	1,513	15.1	57
Vermillion, IN	18165	17.4	43.9	0.9	...	189	393	173	16.2	6
Vigo, IN	18167	23.7	48.9	8.0	1.0	886	2,122	1,045	15.3	10
Wabash, IN	18169	15.6	40.4	2.7	0.8	395	887	385	14.1	10
Warren, IN	18171	21.1	26.6	0.4	...	111	184	84	15.2	3
Warrick, IN	18173	21.9	24.6	4.8	1.2	645	990	499	19.3	18
Washington, IN	18175	17.1	42.8	1.5	0.3	274	607	258	18.4	13
Wayne, IN	18177	19.5	49.7	8.2	1.3	662	1,483	697	15.7	26
Wells, IN	18179	16.3	27.8	3.3	1.4	363	806	352	13.5	11
White, IN	18181	17.8	41.1	10.0	6.3	312	741	321	16.1	12
Whitley, IN	18183	13.4	25.9	2.3	0.2	343	670	292	16.7	10
IOWA	19000	13.8	34.4	15.5	4.2	34,385	72,343	35,959	13.6	2567
Adair, IA	19001	15.6	32.7	3.3	0.6	97	164	82	11.6	11
Adams, IA	19003	17.4	40.0	4.3	0.4	50	105	53	10.2	6
Allamakee, IA	19005	13.1	43.0	12.5	4.9	218	334	174	13.1	11
Appanoose, IA	19007	15.2	46.9	3.0	0.1	172	344	178	12.3	11
Audubon, IA	19009	10.1	33.5	2.5	0.1	85	140	69	12.9	7
Benton, IA	19011	14.9	26.3	3.0	0.2	330	561	297	13.4	18
Black Hawk, IA	19013	17.3	40.8	27.5	4.8	1,153	3,254	1,461	12.1	127
Boone, IA	19015	13.2	33.8	6.9	1.7	319	507	243	15.7	19
Bremer, IA	19017	14.2	18.5	2.7	1.7	418	602	337	14.1	22
Buchanan, IA	19019	17.4	26.8	3.7	2.4	214	435	224	12.7	16
Buena Vista, IA	19021	10.5	50.1	46.1	33.2	286	580	285	13.7	28
Butler, IA	19023	15.0	28.1	4.7	0.7	141	244	133	14.1	17
Calhoun, IA	19025	10.8	30.9	3.5	0.2	174	331	181	10.8	10

[2]IEP= Individual Education Program. See notes and definitions for more information
... Not available

Table C-1. Population, School, and Student Characteristics by County—*Continued*

County	State/County Code	Revenues, 2007-2008				Current expenditures, 2007-2008			Resident population 16 to 19 years, 2006-2008			
		Total revenue ($1,000's)	Percentage of revenue from			Amount ($1,000's)	Amount per student	Percent for instruction	Total population 16 to 19 years	Percent enrolled in school	Percent high school graduates, not enrolled in school	Percent not enrolled, not grads, not employed or not in labor force
			Federal gov't	State gov't	Local gov't							
	19		20	21	22	23	24	25	26	27	28	29
Jasper, IN	18073	50,190	3.6	45.8	50.6	40,912	7,670	61.0	...	...	...	...
Jay, IN	18075	34,801	8.4	62.6	29.0	36,221	9,626	62.2	...	...	...	...
Jefferson, IN	18077	62,917	10.9	43.1	46.0	52,977	10,823	61.2	...	...	...	...
Jennings, IN	18079	54,442	7.1	57.1	35.8	44,391	8,398	61.0	...	...	...	...
Johnson, IN	18081	289,427	4.1	40.9	55.1	203,735	8,265	56.1	8222	79.3	10.1	6.2
Knox, IN	18083	58,062	9.1	52.0	38.8	49,370	9,180	62.0	...	...	...	...
Kosciusko, IN	18085	145,717	7.1	44.8	48.1	118,758	8,263	58.1	4031	78.3	12.6	4.3
Lagrange, IN	18087	67,845	3.7	44.9	51.4	53,625	8,637	59.7	...	...	...	...
Lake, IN	18089	1,010,692	7.0	49.9	43.0	804,015	9,362	57.4	28394	85.2	8.6	4.5
La Porte, IN	18091	196,603	7.7	45.1	47.2	161,008	8,679	57.8	5731	81.7	5.8	10.4
Lawrence, IN	18093	74,728	8.0	54.3	37.7	64,196	8,597	60.9	...	...	...	...
Madison, IN	18095	227,317	7.1	51.0	42.0	179,212	9,091	60.0	7360	76.3	11.1	8.6
Marion, IN	18097	1,611,952	9.2	49.2	41.5	1,352,702	10,024	55.9	46292	82.8	8.0	7.0
Marshall, IN	18099	88,409	8.5	44.4	47.0	75,406	9,572	60.1	2510	80.0	10.5	3.5
Martin, IN	18101	14,921	6.9	64.3	28.9	15,283	8,922	60.9	...	...	...	...
Miami, IN	18103	57,988	4.7	59.4	35.9	50,810	8,779	57.5	...	...	...	...
Monroe, IN	18105	136,457	7.3	39.8	52.9	122,430	8,762	57.1	14155	94.4	4.3	1.0
Montgomery, IN	18107	86,041	9.0	40.4	50.7	61,015	9,357	54.8	2194	77.6	7.8	8.6
Morgan, IN	18109	113,175	5.8	51.6	42.6	96,303	7,971	59.5	...	...	...	...
Newton, IN	18111	21,591	4.1	56.4	39.5	22,765	9,073	57.8	...	...	...	...
Noble, IN	18113	82,797	5.1	50.2	44.7	67,591	8,603	59.2	2623	79.8	10.8	7.1
Ohio, IN	18115	8,573	2.9	50.4	46.7	7,604	8,030	64.6	...	...	...	...
Orange, IN	18117	44,210	10.0	46.7	43.3	35,170	10,086	65.0	...	...	...	...
Owen, IN	18119	27,646	6.4	63.8	29.9	27,649	9,006	60.8	...	...	...	...
Parke, IN	18121	25,474	6.0	54.2	39.8	21,824	8,966	58.2	...	...	...	...
Perry, IN	18123	29,766	4.1	54.4	41.6	25,804	8,452	63.5	...	...	...	...
Pike, IN	18125	32,891	13.2	31.8	55.1	30,404	14,437	50.1	...	...	...	...
Porter, IN	18127	302,625	4.4	41.9	53.8	230,399	8,355	57.8	...	...	...	...
Posey, IN	18129	37,533	7.1	44.6	48.3	40,958	9,841	58.5	...	...	...	...
Pulaski, IN	18131	26,965	14.7	45.4	39.9	22,603	10,041	56.5	...	...	...	...
Putnam, IN	18133	75,154	3.6	50.4	46.0	57,558	8,672	54.9	...	...	...	...
Randolph, IN	18135	48,322	9.1	55.9	34.9	41,942	8,798	61.1	...	...	...	...
Ripley, IN	18137	40,181	6.0	52.7	41.3	32,816	9,166	57.3	...	...	...	...
Rush, IN	18139	24,456	5.6	52.0	42.4	21,768	8,236	58.8	...	...	...	...
St. Joseph, IN	18141	510,446	8.8	45.8	45.4	410,215	9,975	61.6	17475	90.8	5.8	2.7
Scott, IN	18143	42,683	6.1	62.1	31.9	37,074	8,582	58.0	...	...	...	...
Shelby, IN	18145	81,708	6.5	46.9	46.6	68,911	8,781	62.0	...	...	...	...
Spencer, IN	18147	32,794	3.9	46.8	49.3	30,039	8,298	61.9	...	...	...	...
Starke, IN	18149	38,501	6.3	61.1	32.6	31,336	7,457	59.7	...	...	...	...
Steuben, IN	18151	47,148	4.7	36.8	58.4	36,144	8,519	61.6	...	...	...	...
Sullivan, IN	18153	35,203	5.1	52.0	42.9	30,494	9,277	61.0	...	...	...	...
Switzerland, IN	18155	12,812	6.1	60.7	33.2	13,128	8,569	56.0	...	...	...	...
Tippecanoe, IN	18157	184,664	7.9	49.1	42.9	181,927	8,642	60.4	16875	93.0	3.8	0.9
Tipton, IN	18159	23,879	3.0	54.0	43.0	21,353	7,396	59.0	...	...	...	...
Union, IN	18161	20,077	9.9	43.5	46.5	15,295	9,459	59.3	...	...	...	...
Vanderburgh, IN	18163	251,132	11.0	45.2	43.9	213,254	9,451	59.1	10305	86.6	9.3	2.8
Vermillion, IN	18165	29,820	6.0	49.8	44.2	24,267	8,667	58.7	...	...	...	...
Vigo, IN	18167	166,891	9.7	51.0	39.3	141,473	8,731	62.0	7263	86.5	8.3	2.8
Wabash, IN	18169	55,389	8.0	52.2	39.8	52,392	9,476	59.0	...	...	...	...
Warren, IN	18171	13,076	9.1	50.4	40.5	11,828	9,098	58.2	...	...	...	...
Warrick, IN	18173	89,494	2.7	45.7	51.6	68,533	7,098	62.9	...	...	...	...
Washington, IN	18175	46,736	4.3	59.6	36.1	38,791	8,098	58.9	...	...	...	...
Wayne, IN	18177	114,060	6.9	54.2	38.9	95,546	8,858	60.4	3813	82.2	9.9	3.4
Wells, IN	18179	53,835	7.4	46.0	46.6	44,587	9,199	61.5	...	...	...	...
White, IN	18181	55,499	5.1	44.1	50.9	44,003	8,370	57.7	...	...	...	...
Whitley, IN	18183	50,337	2.8	46.9	50.3	41,140	8,465	56.8	...	...	...	...
IOWA	19000	5,496,908	7.1	44.8	48.0	4,495,682	9,267	60.9	174658	87.9	8.3	2.2
Adair, IA	19001	10,850	4.4	45.7	49.9	8,893	9,302	62.2	...	...	...	...
Adams, IA	19003	7,634	6.6	40.7	52.8	5,829	9,747	62.4	...	...	...	...
Allamakee, IA	19005	26,347	9.6	46.0	44.4	20,843	8,945	61.3	...	...	...	...
Appanoose, IA	19007	22,169	6.9	53.2	40.0	18,487	8,324	65.0	...	...	...	...
Audubon, IA	19009	9,417	4.5	48.2	47.2	8,073	8,728	63.3	...	...	...	...
Benton, IA	19011	41,260	3.7	51.8	44.5	32,615	8,105	65.6	...	...	...	...
Black Hawk, IA	19013	216,483	13.0	44.6	42.4	184,757	10,432	52.7	8414	92.6	4.6	1.4
Boone, IA	19015	44,137	3.4	45.2	51.4	34,739	9,087	65.2	...	...	...	...
Bremer, IA	19017	47,755	3.2	47.0	49.7	36,010	7,591	63.4	...	...	...	...
Buchanan, IA	19019	29,558	4.2	49.2	46.6	23,962	8,367	65.6	...	...	...	...
Buena Vista, IA	19021	44,241	8.4	45.3	46.3	35,883	9,345	64.9	...	...	...	...
Butler, IA	19023	21,791	3.5	40.3	56.2	14,495	7,735	60.9	...	...	...	...
Calhoun, IA	19025	22,980	4.5	38.8	56.7	20,069	10,329	65.3	...	...	...	...

... Not available

Table C-1. Population, School, and Student Characteristics by County—*Continued*

County	State/County Code	High school graduates, 2006-2008			College enrollment, 2006-2008		College graduates, 2006-2008 (percent)						
		Population 25 years and over	High school diploma or less (percent)	High school diploma or more (percent)	Number	Percent public	Bachelor's degree or more	+/- U.S. percent with Bachelor's degree or more	Non-Hispanic White	Black or African American	American Indian and Alaska Native	Asian, Hawaiian, and Pacific Islander	Hispanic or Latino[3]
		30	31	32	33	34	35	36	37	38	39	40	41
Jasper, IN	18073	20,844	59.2	86.6	1,865	50.0	15.2	-12.2	15.4	...	...	...	...
Jay, IN	18075	14,424	64.8	82.8	873	72.2	11.1	-16.3	11.5	...	...	...	...
Jefferson, IN	18077	21,579	55.5	83.9	2,167	35.3	18.3	-9.1	17.8	...	...	...	...
Jennings, IN	18079	18,793	66.2	80.8	854	78.8	8.1	-19.3	8.3	...	...	...	...
Johnson, IN	18081	88,637	45.3	89.5	7,217	71.3	25.9	-1.5	25.6	...	...	43.3	26.5
Knox, IN	18083	24,734	50.6	85.9	3,364	91.4	15.2	-12.2	14.9	...	...	...	...
Kosciusko, IN	18085	50,202	55.3	82.6	2,840	77.3	19.6	-7.8	20.2	...	...	...	8.5
Lagrange, IN	18087	22,299	73.7	56.5	427	94.6	9.5	-17.9	9.2	...	...	...	13.3
Lake, IN	18089	319,928	52.0	85.7	26,771	74.7	18.9	-8.5	21.5	14.3	11.8	63.1	10.0
La Porte, IN	18091	75,657	54.8	85.6	5,037	83.5	16.3	-11.1	17.2	8.9	...	...	12.9
Lawrence, IN	18093	32,466	66.2	80.6	1,459	80.3	11.9	-15.5	11.9	...	...	...	...
Madison, IN	18095	89,950	57.2	85.7	6,609	62.5	16.5	-10.9	16.9	12.3	...	...	9.2
Marion, IN	18097	570,424	46.4	84.3	50,720	69.3	27.5	0.1	32.1	15.7	23.7	52.7	10.8
Marshall, IN	18099	30,642	59.7	82.7	1,448	76.4	17.6	-9.8	18.9	...	...	...	3.6
Martin, IN	18101	...	...	...	...	...	...	...	...	...	...	...	...
Miami, IN	18103	24,911	59.2	83.9	1,873	91.9	11.3	-16.1	11.4	...	...	...	...
Monroe, IN	18105	71,946	33.1	91.9	37,146	97.2	41.7	14.3	40.0	37.1	...	84.0	43.5
Montgomery, IN	18107	25,483	59.2	85.2	1,696	61.6	16.9	-10.5	16.5	...	...	...	...
Morgan, IN	18109	47,156	56.4	83.7	3,551	75.3	13.7	-13.7	13.6	...	...	...	...
Newton, IN	18111	...	...	...	...	...	...	...	...	...	...	...	...
Noble, IN	18113	30,965	60.7	79.7	1,676	78.5	13.6	-13.8	15.0	...	...	...	2.4
Ohio, IN	18115	...	...	...	...	...	...	...	...	...	...	...	...
Orange, IN	18117	...	...	...	...	...	...	...	...	...	...	...	...
Owen, IN	18119	15,559	67.0	80.9	876	83.9	7.5	-19.9	7.5	...	...	...	...
Parke, IN	18121	...	...	...	...	...	...	...	...	...	...	...	...
Perry, IN	18123	...	...	...	...	...	...	...	...	...	...	...	...
Pike, IN	18125	...	...	...	...	...	...	...	...	...	...	...	...
Porter, IN	18127	105,859	44.8	91.6	12,807	59.2	24.5	-2.9	25.2	20.9	...	32.3	11.0
Posey, IN	18129	17,865	55.6	87.7	1,187	82.1	16.7	-10.7	16.5	...	...	...	...
Pulaski, IN	18131	...	...	...	...	...	...	...	...	...	...	...	...
Putnam, IN	18133	23,999	55.4	84.8	3,054	61.1	16.2	-11.2	16.5	...	...	...	...
Randolph, IN	18135	18,032	64.2	83.5	826	80.4	9.2	-18.2	9.2	...	...	...	...
Ripley, IN	18137	18,268	59.7	84.5	1,219	81.7	15.1	-12.3	15.4	...	...	...	...
Rush, IN	18139	...	...	...	...	...	...	...	...	...	...	...	...
St. Joseph, IN	18141	167,630	47.6	85.3	26,038	42.0	26.4	-1.0	28.5	10.2	...	58.8	13.0
Scott, IN	18143	16,162	69.1	74.5	555	88.5	11.2	-16.2	10.4	...	...	...	...
Shelby, IN	18145	29,798	56.7	86.9	2,275	78.2	15.0	-12.4	14.6	...	...	...	16.2
Spencer, IN	18147	13,979	54.4	87.0	927	80.6	17.3	-10.1	17.1	...	...	...	...
Starke, IN	18149	15,964	67.9	77.2	708	78.8	9.6	-17.8	9.9	...	...	...	...
Steuben, IN	18151	22,141	53.5	90.2	2,360	40.1	17.5	-9.9	17.4	...	...	...	...
Sullivan, IN	18153	14,861	57.4	87.6	985	88.6	15.6	-11.8	15.6	...	...	...	...
Switzerland, IN	18155	...	...	...	...	...	...	...	...	...	...	...	...
Tippecanoe, IN	18157	89,392	39.6	89.4	38,968	95.9	35.7	8.3	34.1	33.4	...	90.6	16.5
Tipton, IN	18159	...	...	...	...	...	...	...	...	...	...	...	...
Union, IN	18161	...	...	...	...	...	...	...	...	...	...	...	...
Vanderburgh, IN	18163	114,699	47.8	86.8	14,490	82.6	21.5	-5.9	22.3	9.8	...	54.7	6.8
Vermillion, IN	18165	...	...	...	...	...	...	...	...	...	...	...	...
Vigo, IN	18167	67,586	49.4	84.2	12,375	77.7	21.8	-5.6	22.0	7.5	...	...	17.4
Wabash, IN	18169	22,401	58.7	84.8	1,852	42.5	17.7	-9.7	18.0	...	...	...	...
Warren, IN	18171	...	...	...	...	...	...	...	...	...	...	...	...
Warrick, IN	18173	38,429	42.8	91.2	2,373	87.1	24.8	-2.6	23.8	...	...	...	...
Washington, IN	18175	18,852	68.1	79.8	907	79.1	9.9	-17.5	9.8	...	...	...	...
Wayne, IN	18177	46,525	57.7	82.8	3,581	78.7	15.2	-12.2	15.1	10.2	...	...	...
Wells, IN	18179	18,853	55.4	88.9	1,151	79.9	14.6	-12.8	14.7	...	...	...	...
White, IN	18181	16,506	61.8	84.8	588	88.9	11.9	-15.5	12.4	...	...	...	...
Whitley, IN	18183	21,926	49.4	88.9	1,504	76.9	17.0	-10.4	16.8	...	...	...	...
IOWA	19000	1,965,813	45.4	89.6	216,473	71.4	24.2	-3.2	24.4	16.7	16.6	49.6	11.2
Adair, IA	19001	...	...	...	...	...	...	...	...	...	...	...	...
Adams, IA	19003	...	...	...	...	...	...	...	...	...	...	...	...
Allamakee, IA	19005	...	...	...	...	...	...	...	...	...	...	...	...
Appanoose, IA	19007	...	...	...	...	...	...	...	...	...	...	...	...
Audubon, IA	19009	...	...	...	...	...	...	...	...	...	...	...	...
Benton, IA	19011	17,902	48.4	92.1	1,339	73.6	17.3	-10.1	17.1	...	...	...	...
Black Hawk, IA	19013	79,714	45.5	88.5	16,735	91.3	24.9	-2.5	25.6	11.6	...	60.6	21.5
Boone, IA	19015	18,186	46.2	91.8	1,209	91.8	18.2	-9.2	18.5	...	...	...	...
Bremer, IA	19017	15,233	45.1	93.7	2,370	24.7	24.6	-2.8	24.4	...	...	...	...
Buchanan, IA	19019	13,737	49.9	90.6	1,092	85.8	20.8	-6.6	20.3	...	...	...	...
Buena Vista, IA	19021	...	...	...	...	...	...	...	...	...	...	...	...
Butler, IA	19023	...	...	...	...	...	...	...	...	...	...	...	...
Calhoun, IA	19025	...	...	...	...	...	...	...	...	...	...	...	...

[3]May be of any race
... Not available

Table C-1. Population, School, and Student Characteristics by County—*Continued*

County	State/ County Code	County Type[1]	Population, 2009		Percent of related children 5-17 years in poverty, 2008	Percent of children under 19 years with no health insurance, 2007	Number of Schools and Students, 2008-2009			Resident enrollment, 2006-2008	
			Total	Percent 5–17 years			School Districts	Schools	Students	K–12 enrollment	
										Number	Percent public
			1	2	3	4	5	6	7	8	9
Carroll, IA	19027	7	20,674	17.8	9.0	6.9	4	11	3,146	3,664	70.2
Cass, IA	19029	6	13,758	16.3	17.9	6.6	4	13	2,579	...	...
Cedar, IA	19031	6	18,006	17.4	7.6	7.1	5	14	3,401	...	...
Cerro Gordo, IA	19033	5	43,609	15.5	13.6	5.0	4	20	6,249	6,762	95.2
Cherokee, IA	19035	6	11,409	16.8	11.7	6.4	3	11	1,788	...	...
Chickasaw, IA	19037	6	12,017	17.6	12.0	8.3	3	9	2,175	...	...
Clarke, IA	19039	6	9,086	17.4	14.9	6.5	2	7	1,720	...	...
Clay, IA	19041	7	16,617	16.5	12.4	6.9	3	9	2,460	...	...
Clayton, IA	19043	8	17,463	16.7	13.5	7.3	4	9	2,147	...	...
Clinton, IA	19045	4	48,934	17.3	14.4	5.0	6	21	8,292	8,671	94.0
Crawford, IA	19047	6	16,416	19.1	14.5	8.6	5	16	3,246	...	...
Dallas, IA	19049	2	61,950	19.0	5.9	6.3	6	29	12,822	10,530	93.6
Davis, IA	19051	9	8,562	19.2	21.9	11.3	1	4	1,236	...	...
Decatur, IA	19053	9	8,231	15.4	22.3	7.4	2	6	1,148	...	...
Delaware, IA	19055	6	17,205	18.6	10.3	7.3	3	11	2,995	...	...
Des Moines, IA	19057	5	41,058	16.4	19.4	5.1	4	17	6,481	7,124	95.6
Dickinson, IA	19059	7	16,623	14.0	7.5	7.2	4	10	2,645	...	...
Dubuque, IA	19061	3	93,072	17.2	10.6	5.7	2	29	14,113	16,256	79.8
Emmet, IA	19063	7	10,241	17.2	14.5	6.8	2	6	1,718	...	...
Fayette, IA	19065	6	20,164	16.4	14.6	6.6	5	19	3,865	3,368	96.0
Floyd, IA	19067	7	15,910	17.5	14.7	6.5	3	9	2,624	...	...
Franklin, IA	19069	7	10,540	17.4	13.2	8.9	3	11	1,867	...	...
Fremont, IA	19071	8	7,345	17.0	13.2	7.0	3	6	939	...	...
Greene, IA	19073	6	9,251	17.1	12.7	6.5	3	10	1,634	...	...
Grundy, IA	19075	3	12,177	16.8	6.7	9.4	4	15	2,758	...	...
Guthrie, IA	19077	2	10,833	17.6	11.2	10.2	4	13	2,710	...	...
Hamilton, IA	19079	6	15,238	17.2	9.9	5.8	4	12	2,854	...	...
Hancock, IA	19081	7	11,046	17.1	10.1	7.3	4	10	1,802	...	...
Hardin, IA	19083	6	17,144	17.5	12.2	7.5	5	13	2,853	...	...
Harrison, IA	19085	2	15,328	17.4	11.3	6.0	5	11	3,029	...	...
Henry, IA	19087	7	19,929	16.3	12.9	4.1	5	16	4,644	3,351	96.8
Howard, IA	19089	7	9,410	16.7	14.1	6.5	1	8	1,411	...	...
Humboldt, IA	19091	7	9,473	16.7	12.7	6.8	3	8	1,504	...	...
Ida, IA	19093	8	6,762	16.5	11.7	9.0	2	8	1,239	...	...
Iowa, IA	19095	8	15,811	17.8	6.4	7.8	5	10	2,689	...	...
Jackson, IA	19097	6	19,728	17.4	14.3	6.9	5	15	3,285	3,524	88.1
Jasper, IA	19099	6	36,257	17.1	9.6	6.2	5	20	6,006	6,127	94.3
Jefferson, IA	19101	7	15,472	14.4	16.5	6.9	2	10	2,540	...	...
Johnson, IA	19103	3	131,005	13.1	9.4	5.6	4	34	14,735	17,408	90.6
Jones, IA	19105	3	20,364	15.9	11.0	7.5	4	12	3,149	3,321	94.2
Keokuk, IA	19107	8	10,562	17.6	15.0	9.1	3	10	1,346	...	...
Kossuth, IA	19109	7	15,154	17.0	11.3	8.0	5	14	1,994	...	...
Lee, IA	19111	5	35,447	16.1	17.8	5.6	2	13	4,348	6,143	81.8
Linn, IA	19113	3	209,226	17.3	9.1	4.8	12	78	35,058	36,922	88.2
Louisa, IA	19115	8	11,245	19.2	13.8	10.7	4	10	2,761	...	...
Lucas, IA	19117	6	9,179	18.0	21.1	5.3	1	5	1,537	...	...
Lyon, IA	19119	8	11,172	19.3	8.6	12.8	3	10	1,836	...	...
Madison, IA	19121	2	15,409	19.9	7.7	6.6	3	12	3,287	...	...
Mahaska, IA	19123	7	22,000	17.2	13.6	5.2	4	13	4,068	3,938	92.7
Marion, IA	19125	6	32,682	17.4	9.1	5.6	5	19	5,929	5,618	85.3
Marshall, IA	19127	4	39,259	18.0	16.2	6.1	3	16	6,754	6,602	92.4
Mills, IA	19129	2	15,002	19.0	10.4	5.0	4	13	3,244	...	...
Mitchell, IA	19131	7	10,781	18.4	12.0	8.1	3	9	1,964	...	...
Monona, IA	19133	6	8,882	16.0	15.4	5.6	3	8	1,397	...	...
Monroe, IA	19135	7	7,549	17.4	16.4	5.5	1	6	1,175	...	...
Montgomery, IA	19137	6	10,796	17.4	20.6	5.5	3	10	1,848	...	...
Muscatine, IA	19139	4	42,934	18.8	12.8	5.6	3	18	7,596	7,932	97.7
O'Brien, IA	19141	7	13,928	16.7	9.5	8.0	3	9	2,379	...	...
Osceola, IA	19143	7	6,344	17.1	10.7	8.0	1	4	869	...	...
Page, IA	19145	7	15,260	16.1	16.9	5.1	4	13	2,740	...	...
Palo Alto, IA	19147	7	9,279	15.8	11.1	6.9	4	11	1,576	...	...
Plymouth, IA	19149	6	24,210	19.0	7.7	5.8	5	20	4,308	4,546	87.1
Pocahontas, IA	19151	9	7,346	15.8	13.5	9.4	2	7	970	...	...
Polk, IA	19153	2	429,439	17.4	10.5	5.2	10	124	67,472	76,661	91.2
Pottawattamie, IA	19155	2	90,224	16.9	13.7	4.8	9	40	16,090	16,129	91.6
Poweshiek, IA	19157	7	18,423	15.4	11.2	6.2	3	10	2,958	...	...
Ringgold, IA	19159	9	4,944	15.7	23.8	7.7	2	4	786	...	...
Sac, IA	19161	9	10,059	16.4	12.2	10.6	4	10	1,732	...	...
Scott, IA	19163	2	166,650	17.7	14.3	5.9	5	56	27,813	29,625	89.6
Shelby, IA	19165	6	11,957	17.5	9.3	7.3	2	7	1,967	...	...

[1]County type codes are from the Economic Research Service of the United States Department of Agriculture. See notes and definitions for more information.
... Not available

Table C-1. Population, School, and Student Characteristics by County—*Continued*

County	State/County Code	Characteristics of students, 2008-2009				Number of graduates, 2006-2007	Staff and students, 2008-2009			
		Percent with IEP[2]	Percent eligible for free or reduced lunch	Percent minority	Percent English Language Learners		Total staff	Number of teachers	Student/ teacher ratio	Central admin. Staff
		10	11	12	13	14	15	16	17	18
Carroll, IA	19027	13.5	30.9	4.5	1.1	236	479	245	12.8	16
Cass, IA	19029	16.8	38.0	2.6	0.8	205	398	193	13.4	13
Cedar, IA	19031	13.2	21.9	4.0	0.2	271	484	250	13.6	15
Cerro Gordo, IA	19033	17.2	35.1	11.7	0.8	424	828	447	14.0	24
Cherokee, IA	19035	15.8	35.5	7.1	1.3	163	259	143	12.5	11
Chickasaw, IA	19037	13.3	24.9	2.9	1.1	152	301	161	13.5	9
Clarke, IA	19039	15.1	42.6	12.6	8.1	95	250	135	12.7	9
Clay, IA	19041	14.4	34.0	8.4	1.0	188	368	177	13.9	13
Clayton, IA	19043	14.7	33.6	2.4	0.3	262	584	189	11.4	28
Clinton, IA	19045	16.3	38.2	11.0	0.6	577	1,197	641	12.9	34
Crawford, IA	19047	11.9	51.3	36.2	27.2	294	502	239	13.6	24
Dallas, IA	19049	9.4	19.9	13.0	4.0	653	1,687	900	14.2	59
Davis, IA	19051	11.7	33.5	3.2	...	77	262	184	6.7	4
Decatur, IA	19053	18.1	49.0	4.5	0.9	95	199	93	12.3	10
Delaware, IA	19055	11.5	27.5	1.9	0.1	229	437	238	12.6	16
Des Moines, IA	19057	17.1	42.5	17.2	0.4	416	903	473	13.7	31
Dickinson, IA	19059	11.4	26.6	4.4	0.1	186	423	200	13.2	18
Dubuque, IA	19061	15.7	34.0	9.0	1.2	1,008	1,991	1,010	14.0	51
Emmet, IA	19063	14.6	41.2	16.5	4.5	132	268	123	14.0	11
Fayette, IA	19065	16.5	35.2	3.5	0.3	342	585	286	13.5	23
Floyd, IA	19067	15.4	38.8	8.2	1.5	199	381	198	13.3	14
Franklin, IA	19069	17.4	39.5	17.4	7.1	145	297	157	11.9	11
Fremont, IA	19071	15.1	41.8	4.8	2.7	106	175	93	10.1	6
Greene, IA	19073	13.7	41.0	6.6	1.2	120	254	127	12.9	11
Grundy, IA	19075	13.9	22.6	4.3	0.2	250	337	193	14.3	12
Guthrie, IA	19077	12.8	30.9	4.9	0.7	196	408	220	12.3	11
Hamilton, IA	19079	11.0	30.4	9.9	4.1	199	436	226	12.6	19
Hancock, IA	19081	11.5	31.2	7.0	1.1	166	267	150	12.0	11
Hardin, IA	19083	18.2	33.9	7.2	1.5	237	474	242	11.8	14
Harrison, IA	19085	14.3	32.2	3.6	0.5	229	482	239	12.7	19
Henry, IA	19087	13.3	36.4	9.9	2.2	275	695	356	13.0	21
Howard, IA	19089	16.0	32.6	2.7	0.2	152	208	117	12.1	7
Humboldt, IA	19091	9.0	31.7	7.0	1.7	135	234	124	12.1	8
Ida, IA	19093	12.2	29.6	3.9	1.0	112	183	98	12.6	9
Iowa, IA	19095	12.8	22.8	6.2	2.6	212	380	209	12.9	13
Jackson, IA	19097	16.5	36.2	4.2	0.1	296	504	270	12.2	22
Jasper, IA	19099	14.0	32.6	3.5	0.2	452	852	451	13.3	24
Jefferson, IA	19101	13.5	32.6	6.0	1.4	215	418	220	11.5	16
Johnson, IA	19103	13.3	26.1	26.1	3.2	1,037	1,929	955	15.4	57
Jones, IA	19105	14.4	29.2	3.4	0.2	248	501	253	12.4	15
Keokuk, IA	19107	12.8	28.4	2.0	...	123	216	116	11.6	7
Kossuth, IA	19109	16.2	34.1	5.1	0.3	168	317	149	13.4	17
Lee, IA	19111	20.3	51.3	12.6	0.2	358	670	312	13.9	17
Linn, IA	19113	13.6	29.1	14.8	1.3	2,272	5,421	2,464	14.2	167
Louisa, IA	19115	13.9	50.5	30.0	9.3	206	443	229	12.1	15
Lucas, IA	19117	14.6	44.5	0.7	6.6	129	166	82	18.7	5
Lyon, IA	19119	12.9	26.2	3.3	0.9	156	260	143	12.8	7
Madison, IA	19121	12.1	23.9	3.2	0.4	246	493	247	13.3	15
Mahaska, IA	19123	12.4	39.1	5.1	1.0	296	602	302	13.5	16
Marion, IA	19125	12.8	26.0	4.8	0.9	461	832	411	14.4	21
Marshall, IA	19127	14.8	51.0	33.3	21.5	465	1,038	460	14.7	27
Mills, IA	19129	15.5	34.0	4.0	0.2	197	549	225	14.4	20
Mitchell, IA	19131	12.3	23.1	1.6	0.3	141	291	162	12.1	8
Monona, IA	19133	14.3	41.2	3.8	0.2	145	216	110	12.7	10
Monroe, IA	19135	10.9	32.3	4.2	0.8	88	157	86	13.7	5
Montgomery, IA	19137	16.7	43.3	5.5	1.7	133	292	157	11.8	12
Muscatine, IA	19139	13.0	41.5	29.9	8.7	496	1139	551	13.8	42
O'Brien, IA	19141	14.0	29.7	7.2	1.9	200	358	182	13.1	10
Osceola, IA	19143	11.0	26.4	12.1	3.9	81	125	65	13.4	4
Page, IA	19145	11.4	39.9	11.3	1.1	205	389	216	12.7	10
Palo Alto, IA	19147	14.0	35.5	2.4	0.1	155	262	136	11.6	13
Plymouth, IA	19149	9.9	20.9	7.2	2.1	334	571	337	12.8	21
Pocahontas, IA	19151	10.5	35.6	4.3	0.4	113	171	90	10.8	9
Polk, IA	19153	13.6	34.6	25.7	8.4	3,930	9,875	4,785	14.1	339
Pottawattamie, IA	19155	14.5	44.6	12.6	4.9	950	2,257	1,078	14.9	86
Poweshiek, IA	19157	14.4	27.8	5.9	0.9	243	388	208	14.2	16
Ringgold, IA	19159	16.5	42.2	3.1	0.8	70	144	73	10.8	5
Sac, IA	19161	9.4	37.3	5.3	1.6	138	238	126	13.7	13
Scott, IA	19163	11.3	39.0	25.1	1.8	1,862	3,759	1,879	14.8	121
Shelby, IA	19165	10.6	29.7	3.8	0.8	185	279	152	12.9	6

[2]IEP= Individual Education Program. See notes and definitions for more information
... Not available

Table C-1. Population, School, and Student Characteristics by County—*Continued*

County	State/ County Code	Total revenue ($1,000's)	Percentage of revenue from			Amount ($1,000's)	Amount per student	Percent for instruction	Total population 16 to 19 years	Percent enrolled in school	Percent high school graduates, not enrolled in school	Percent not enrolled, not grads, not employed or not in labor force
			Federal gov't	State gov't	Local gov't							
		19	20	21	22	23	24	25	26	27	28	29
Carroll, IA	19027	31,753	4.5	47.1	48.4	25,938	8,597	64.2	...	...	...	...
Cass, IA	19029	28,144	4.5	45.5	49.9	24,013	9,380	63.7	...	...	...	...
Cedar, IA	19031	36,820	2.9	43.1	54.0	27,269	8,025	63.2	...	...	...	...
Cerro Gordo, IA	19033	68,191	3.8	42.8	53.4	52,999	8,581	65.1	...	...	...	...
Cherokee, IA	19035	19,125	4.0	46.8	49.1	15,659	8,609	65.0	...	...	...	...
Chickasaw, IA	19037	22,449	3.9	44.2	51.9	17,879	8,316	66.0	...	...	...	...
Clarke, IA	19039	16,809	5.8	52.7	41.5	14,164	8,538	64.1	...	...	...	...
Clay, IA	19041	27,131	4.1	44.6	51.3	22,467	8,972	66.4	...	...	...	...
Clayton, IA	19043	33,410	27.9	34.8	37.3	37,389	17,182	33.3	...	...	...	...
Clinton, IA	19045	87,870	5.1	50.7	44.1	70,587	8,714	62.6	...	...	...	...
Crawford, IA	19047	34,656	7.3	51.2	41.6	28,043	8,897	63.2	...	...	...	...
Dallas, IA	19049	134,485	3.2	40.0	56.9	97,428	8,065	62.4	...	...	...	...
Davis, IA	19051	11,338	7.8	52.2	40.0	10,279	8,371	64.1	...	...	...	...
Decatur, IA	19053	12,202	7.4	52.4	40.2	9,716	8,996	64.7	...	...	...	...
Delaware, IA	19055	32,036	4.4	45.0	50.7	25,188	8,484	63.4	...	...	...	...
Des Moines, IA	19057	70,162	5.3	49.8	44.9	55,053	8,491	66.9	...	...	...	...
Dickinson, IA	19059	32,662	2.9	23.9	73.2	22,652	8,484	64.8	...	...	...	...
Dubuque, IA	19061	151,104	4.6	46.4	49.0	124,275	9,179	64.9	...	...	...	...
Emmet, IA	19063	20,612	5.5	43.8	50.7	16,135	9,142	65.4	...	...	...	...
Fayette, IA	19065	42,541	5.1	49.6	45.4	34,678	8,977	65.8	...	...	...	...
Floyd, IA	19067	27,912	5.4	48.9	45.7	22,875	8,675	64.2	...	...	...	...
Franklin, IA	19069	21,836	4.2	44.9	50.9	17,038	8,671	65.6	...	...	...	...
Fremont, IA	19071	11,032	6.1	45.4	48.4	8,747	8,907	61.2	...	...	...	...
Greene, IA	19073	18,610	5.2	44.5	50.2	15,032	9,194	62.3	...	...	...	...
Grundy, IA	19075	29,673	3.7	45.2	51.1	21,875	7,799	60.5	...	...	...	...
Guthrie, IA	19077	28,016	4.5	45.0	50.4	21,632	8,142	62.5	...	...	...	...
Hamilton, IA	19079	30,682	4.0	45.4	50.6	24,956	8,671	63.9	...	...	...	...
Hancock, IA	19081	19,646	3.8	41.4	54.8	15,334	8,240	64.1	...	...	...	...
Hardin, IA	19083	39,000	3.7	39.3	57.1	29,259	10,110	66.1	...	...	...	...
Harrison, IA	19085	33,249	4.8	46.8	48.4	26,654	8,654	62.0	...	...	...	...
Henry, IA	19087	37,645	4.7	49.2	46.0	30,646	8,240	65.9	...	...	...	...
Howard, IA	19089	20,690	7.0	40.2	52.8	16,024	9,482	60.2	...	...	...	...
Humboldt, IA	19091	17,056	4.6	41.3	54.1	13,859	8,783	65.2	...	...	...	...
Ida, IA	19093	12,212	4.7	44.9	50.4	10,079	8,096	63.9	...	...	...	...
Iowa, IA	19095	30,232	3.3	45.2	51.6	23,997	8,835	64.4	...	...	...	...
Jackson, IA	19097	35,551	4.5	49.8	45.6	29,162	8,829	65.4	...	...	...	...
Jasper, IA	19099	60,793	3.9	51.4	44.7	49,622	8,226	64.2	...	...	...	...
Jefferson, IA	19101	28,085	4.5	46.4	49.0	23,614	9,195	61.9	...	...	...	...
Johnson, IA	19103	169,873	3.8	37.8	58.4	128,041	8,651	64.0	...	...	...	...
Jones, IA	19105	35,516	5.4	47.0	47.6	27,425	8,520	61.8	...	...	...	...
Keokuk, IA	19107	14,590	6.3	43.6	50.1	11,430	8,289	63.2	...	...	...	...
Kossuth, IA	19109	25,050	5.6	36.4	58.0	20,805	10,492	66.3	...	...	...	...
Lee, IA	19111	58,532	6.3	53.0	40.7	48,468	9,007	66.4	...	...	...	...
Linn, IA	19113	420,187	7.5	42.3	50.2	341,960	9,864	57.6	11,609	89.2	7.1	2.2
Louisa, IA	19115	32,672	5.0	47.8	47.2	25,668	8,827	67.0	...	...	...	...
Lucas, IA	19117	16,092	5.6	56.7	37.8	12,801	7,772	66.4	...	...	...	...
Lyon, IA	19119	20,061	4.8	46.5	48.7	15,413	8,372	65.1	...	...	...	...
Madison, IA	19121	32,694	4.6	51.6	43.7	26,021	7,842	64.9	...	...	...	...
Mahaska, IA	19123	43,172	4.1	44.9	51.0	35,191	8,844	62.3	...	...	...	...
Marion, IA	19125	57,142	3.7	52.3	44.0	46,383	7,801	64.7	...	...	...	...
Marshall, IA	19127	71,479	6.5	52.7	40.8	56,836	8,326	64.4	...	...	...	...
Mills, IA	19129	35,940	4.3	45.8	49.9	26,939	8,390	63.4	...	...	...	...
Mitchell, IA	19131	17,433	3.2	45.4	51.4	13,894	8,197	66.1	...	...	...	...
Monona, IA	19133	16,899	5.4	43.9	50.7	12,548	9,047	63.9	...	...	...	...
Monroe, IA	19135	11,861	4.9	55.2	40.0	9,846	8,918	62.7	...	...	...	...
Montgomery, IA	19137	19,879	5.5	50.1	44.5	16,791	8,884	62.9	...	...	...	...
Muscatine, IA	19139	75,068	5.1	53.6	41.2	62,923	8,390	65.9	2,765	77.0	14.2	5.9
O'Brien, IA	19141	23,886	4.3	47.2	48.5	19,804	8,424	66.2	...	...	...	...
Osceola, IA	19143	8,770	4.2	50.5	45.3	7,296	8,319	62.7	...	...	...	...
Page, IA	19145	27,724	6.0	46.7	47.3	22,504	8,249	64.5	...	...	...	...
Palo Alto, IA	19147	19,139	3.7	35.3	60.9	15,532	10,105	64.5	...	...	...	...
Plymouth, IA	19149	42,323	3.6	47.2	49.1	35,480	8,217	65.8	...	...	...	...
Pocahontas, IA	19151	11,744	3.8	42.2	53.9	9,106	8,893	65.2	...	...	...	...
Polk, IA	19153	822,588	9.2	41.7	49.1	677,316	10,089	58.7	20,683	87.5	8.6	1.7
Pottawattamie, IA	19155	184,141	9.7	45.6	44.8	154,317	9,538	58.1	5,203	84.6	9.3	3.7
Poweshiek, IA	19157	31,497	3.5	43.8	52.8	24,434	8,478	62.3	...	...	...	...
Ringgold, IA	19159	10,663	10.6	38.3	51.1	8,498	10,853	66.6	...	...	...	...
Sac, IA	19161	18,289	4.9	44.1	51.0	16,732	9,426	67.4	...	...	...	...
Scott, IA	19163	309,098	9.2	43.8	47.0	261,301	9,566	59.4	9,390	80.1	13.6	4.7
Shelby, IA	19165	19,300	4.3	49.1	46.6	16,273	8,260	64.8	...	...	...	...

... Not available

Table C-1. Population, School, and Student Characteristics by County—*Continued*

County	State/County Code	High school graduates, 2006-2008			College enrollment, 2006-2008		College graduates, 2006-2008 (percent)						
		Population 25 years and over	High school diploma or less (percent)	High school diploma or more (percent)	Number	Percent public	Bachelor's degree or more	+/- U.S. percent with Bachelor's degree or more	Non-Hispanic White	Black or African American	American Indian and Alaska Native	Asian, Hawaiian, and Pacific Islander	Hispanic or Latino[3]
		30	31	32	33	34	35	36	37	38	39	40	41
Carroll, IA	19027	14,124	51.5	88.9	758	88.3	17.7	-9.7	17.7	...	...	...	...
Cass, IA	19029	...	...	...	...	...	...	...	...	...	...	...	...
Cedar, IA	19031	...	...	...	...	...	...	...	...	...	...	...	...
Cerro Gordo, IA	19033	30,743	39.8	92.4	2,561	84.1	22.3	-5.1	22.8	...	...	...	...
Cherokee, IA	19035	...	...	...	...	...	...	...	...	...	...	...	...
Chickasaw, IA	19037	...	...	...	...	...	...	...	...	...	...	...	...
Clarke, IA	19039	...	...	...	...	...	...	...	...	...	...	...	...
Clay, IA	19041	...	...	...	...	...	...	...	...	...	...	...	...
Clayton, IA	19043	...	...	...	...	...	...	...	...	...	...	...	...
Clinton, IA	19045	33,312	51.5	88.4	2,324	63.0	16.5	-10.9	16.8	...	...	...	...
Crawford, IA	19047	...	...	...	...	...	...	...	...	...	...	...	...
Dallas, IA	19049	37,019	34.1	92.2	2,932	58.6	35.8	8.4	36.3	...	...	...	16.0
Davis, IA	19051	...	...	...	...	...	...	...	...	...	...	...	...
Decatur, IA	19053	...	...	...	...	...	...	...	...	...	...	...	...
Delaware, IA	19055	...	...	...	...	...	...	...	...	...	...	...	...
Des Moines, IA	19057	27,587	47.1	89.0	1,832	90.8	16.6	-10.8	16.4	...	...	...	...
Dickinson, IA	19059	...	...	...	...	...	...	...	...	...	...	...	...
Dubuque, IA	19061	60,085	48.2	89.3	6,336	38.7	25.5	-1.9	25.1	11.9	...	...	...
Emmet, IA	19063	...	...	...	...	...	...	...	...	...	...	...	...
Fayette, IA	19065	14,112	56.2	87.9	1,105	40.2	16.3	-11.1	16.4	...	...	...	...
Floyd, IA	19067	...	...	...	...	...	...	...	...	...	...	...	...
Franklin, IA	19069	...	...	...	...	...	...	...	...	...	...	...	...
Fremont, IA	19071	...	...	...	...	...	...	...	...	...	...	...	...
Greene, IA	19073	...	...	...	...	...	...	...	...	...	...	...	...
Grundy, IA	19075	...	...	...	...	...	...	...	...	...	...	...	...
Guthrie, IA	19077	...	...	...	...	...	...	...	...	...	...	...	...
Hamilton, IA	19079	...	...	...	...	...	...	...	...	...	...	...	...
Hancock, IA	19081	...	...	...	...	...	...	...	...	...	...	...	...
Hardin, IA	19083	...	...	...	...	...	...	...	...	...	...	...	...
Harrison, IA	19085	...	...	...	...	...	...	...	...	...	...	...	...
Henry, IA	19087	13,649	48.4	89.3	1,408	61.9	19.2	-8.2	19.7	...	...	...	...
Howard, IA	19089	...	...	...	...	...	...	...	...	...	...	...	...
Humboldt, IA	19091	...	...	...	...	...	...	...	...	...	...	...	...
Ida, IA	19093	...	...	...	...	...	...	...	...	...	...	...	...
Iowa, IA	19095	...	...	...	...	...	...	...	...	...	...	...	...
Jackson, IA	19097	13,947	57.8	86.2	752	67.7	14.1	-13.3	14.0	...	...	...	...
Jasper, IA	19099	25,683	55.1	89.1	1,306	61.0	16.4	-11.0	16.5	...	...	...	...
Jefferson, IA	19101	...	...	...	...	...	...	...	...	...	...	...	...
Johnson, IA	19103	72,953	22.1	95.6	28,989	97.1	51.9	24.5	51.7	28.0	...	77.8	34.1
Jones, IA	19105	14,166	57.5	89.5	662	66.9	14.3	-13.1	14.2	...	...	...	...
Keokuk, IA	19107	...	...	...	...	...	...	...	...	...	...	...	...
Kossuth, IA	19109	...	...	...	...	...	...	...	...	...	...	...	...
Lee, IA	19111	24,756	55.3	85.9	1,475	84.7	14.5	-12.9	14.4	...	...	...	...
Linn, IA	19113	135,409	36.8	92.9	14,398	67.2	29.0	1.6	29.1	15.7	...	52.4	16.0
Louisa, IA	19115	...	...	...	...	...	...	...	...	...	...	...	...
Lucas, IA	19117	...	...	...	...	...	...	...	...	...	...	...	...
Lyon, IA	19119	...	...	...	...	...	...	...	...	...	...	...	...
Madison, IA	19121	...	...	...	...	...	...	...	...	...	...	...	...
Mahaska, IA	19123	14,693	57.2	87.1	1,393	26.6	16.5	-10.9	16.3	...	...	...	...
Marion, IA	19125	21,265	47.9	89.6	2,725	28.0	25.4	-2.0	25.0	...	...	...	...
Marshall, IA	19127	26,243	52.5	84.6	1,859	86.6	18.0	-9.4	19.6	...	...	...	5.6
Mills, IA	19129	...	...	...	...	...	...	...	...	...	...	...	...
Mitchell, IA	19131	...	...	...	...	...	...	...	...	...	...	...	...
Monona, IA	19133	...	...	...	...	...	...	...	...	...	...	...	...
Monroe, IA	19135	...	...	...	...	...	...	...	...	...	...	...	...
Montgomery, IA	19137	...	...	...	...	...	...	...	...	...	...	...	...
Muscatine, IA	19139	27,681	48.0	86.1	1,811	79.5	22.4	-5.0	23.8	...	...	...	6.9
O'Brien, IA	19141	...	...	...	...	...	...	...	...	...	...	...	...
Osceola, IA	19143	...	...	...	...	...	...	...	...	...	...	...	...
Page, IA	19145	...	...	...	...	...	...	...	...	...	...	...	...
Palo Alto, IA	19147	...	...	...	...	...	...	...	...	...	...	...	...
Plymouth, IA	19149	16,101	49.1	90.8	848	79.4	19.3	-8.1	19.3	...	...	...	...
Pocahontas, IA	19151	...	...	...	...	...	...	...	...	...	...	...	...
Polk, IA	19153	272,489	37.1	90.8	24,352	51.3	32.8	5.4	34.7	15.7	18.0	43.4	10.0
Pottawattamie, IA	19155	59,687	49.8	88.2	4,662	77.6	17.2	-10.2	17.6	...	...	...	10.4
Poweshiek, IA	19157	...	...	...	...	...	...	...	...	...	...	...	...
Ringgold, IA	19159	...	...	...	...	...	...	...	...	...	...	...	...
Sac, IA	19161	...	...	...	...	...	...	...	...	...	...	...	...
Scott, IA	19163	105,727	39.6	89.9	11,313	63.2	29.4	2.0	30.7	14.1	...	37.8	15.9
Shelby, IA	19165	...	...	...	...	...	...	...	...	...	...	...	...

[3]May be of any race
... Not available

Table C-1. Population, School, and Student Characteristics by County—*Continued*

County	State/County Code	County Type[1]	Population, 2009		Percent of related children 5-17 years in poverty, 2008	Percent of children under 19 years with no health insurance, 2007	Number of Schools and Students, 2008-2009			Resident enrollment, 2006-2008 K–12 enrollment	
			Total	Percent 5–17 years			School Districts	Schools	Students	Number	Percent public
			1	2	3	4	5	6	7	8	9
Sioux, IA	19167	6	32,244	18.5	7.5	10.4	5	15	4,480	5,894	65.5
Story, IA	19169	3	87,214	12.0	7.4	6.5	7	27	10,872	10,615	94.1
Tama, IA	19171	6	17,377	19.7	11.7	7.9	3	8	2,643	...	...
Taylor, IA	19173	9	6,344	17.0	14.9	8.2	3	5	991	...	...
Union, IA	19175	6	12,241	15.8	17.1	5.4	3	8	2,012	...	...
Van Buren, IA	19177	9	7,679	17.2	18.8	8.5	2	7	1,165	...	...
Wapello, IA	19179	5	35,334	16.3	17.4	4.9	3	13	5,463	5,850	95.3
Warren, IA	19181	2	45,275	18.5	6.4	5.7	5	20	8,771	7,719	95.1
Washington, IA	19183	3	21,258	18.7	10.8	7.6	3	15	3,802	3,792	86.3
Wayne, IA	19185	9	6,283	16.5	24.7	7.0	4	9	1,194	...	...
Webster, IA	19187	5	38,346	16.2	15.6	5.0	4	18	5,311	6,976	87.7
Winnebago, IA	19189	7	10,602	16.5	11.4	6.2	3	11	2,491	...	...
Winneshiek, IA	19191	7	20,629	14.8	8.7	6.5	4	12	2,865	2,983	87.2
Woodbury, IA	19193	3	102,831	19.0	16.4	6.8	8	46	17,950	19,824	90.7
Worth, IA	19195	9	7,541	16.8	9.7	9.2	2	4	941	...	...
Wright, IA	19197	7	12,716	16.9	12.3	7.2	4	14	2,664	...	...
KANSAS	20000	X	2,818,747	17.7	12.3	8.8	330	1,447	471,060	499,934	89.3
Allen, KS	20001	7	13,203	16.5	19.9	8.0	4	11	2,299	...	...
Anderson, KS	20003	6	7,872	18.8	17.3	9.7	2	8	1,382	...	...
Atchison, KS	20005	6	16,411	18.4	15.4	7.8	3	10	2,396	...	...
Barber, KS	20007	9	4,593	16.2	15.5	11.6	2	5	780	...	...
Barton, KS	20009	7	27,464	17.4	14.5	11.5	4	16	4,333	4,870	93.4
Bourbon, KS	20011	6	14,884	17.7	22.2	6.8	2	6	2,518	...	...
Brown, KS	20013	6	9,927	18.1	19.0	8.3	3	6	1,559	...	...
Butler, KS	20015	2	64,084	19.7	8.7	7.7	9	46	14,614	11,836	93.8
Chase, KS	20017	8	2,798	18.6	13.8	10.7	1	3	432	...	...
Chautauqua, KS	20019	9	3,745	14.1	18.7	11.1	2	4	532	...	...
Cherokee, KS	20021	6	21,064	18.3	20.5	6.3	4	17	3,875	...	...
Cheyenne, KS	20023	9	2,700	15.5	15.7	13.3	2	4	443	...	...
Clark, KS	20025	9	2,081	17.8	15.2	17.3	2	5	514	...	...
Clay, KS	20027	7	8,704	17.4	15.4	11.9	2	10	1,742	...	...
Cloud, KS	20029	7	9,263	15.0	14.5	7.7	2	8	1,419	...	...
Coffey, KS	20031	6	8,436	18.0	10.7	8.4	3	11	1,700	...	...
Comanche, KS	20033	9	1,873	17.0	9.9	19.8	1	3	331	...	...
Cowley, KS	20035	4	33,634	18.3	17.6	8.3	7	24	6,402	6,247	96.0
Crawford, KS	20037	4	38,869	15.3	18.8	7.6	7	19	5,988	5,972	83.8
Decatur, KS	20039	9	2,855	13.9	17.0	14.1	1	2	383	...	...
Dickinson, KS	20041	7	19,015	18.1	11.5	10.6	5	20	3,982	...	...
Doniphan, KS	20043	3	7,624	16.4	12.9	11.4	6	10	1,384	...	...
Douglas, KS	20045	3	116,383	12.5	10.6	9.3	4	32	13,744	15,187	86.1
Edwards, KS	20047	9	3,071	18.3	15.4	15.9	2	3	415	...	...
Elk, KS	20049	8	3,001	14.9	26.5	11.6	2	5	584	...	...
Ellis, KS	20051	5	27,739	13.6	10.4	9.9	3	12	3,561	3,653	82.3
Ellsworth, KS	20053	7	6,179	14.3	11.3	9.4	2	7	1,014	...	...
Finney, KS	20055	5	42,074	22.2	15.7	16.1	2	21	8,162	10,050	93.3
Ford, KS	20057	5	33,692	21.6	15.7	16.0	3	16	6,826	7,186	95.4
Franklin, KS	20059	1	26,441	18.3	11.8	8.0	4	16	4,736	5,145	93.1
Geary, KS	20061	5	31,751	15.5	12.4	8.8	1	19	7,016	6,263	96.3
Gove, KS	20063	9	2,480	16.4	15.8	13.5	3	6	428	...	...
Graham, KS	20065	9	2,435	13.9	11.8	14.4	1	3	394	...	...
Grant, KS	20067	7	7,353	22.4	12.9	13.8	2	5	1,733	...	...
Gray, KS	20069	9	6,005	22.7	11.4	23.0	5	8	1,211	...	...
Greeley, KS	20071	9	1,234	18.2	13.7	20.1	1	2	228	...	...
Greenwood, KS	20073	6	6,666	16.5	18.6	9.4	3	6	1,010	...	...
Hamilton, KS	20075	9	2,625	19.6	16.6	23.7	1	2	503	...	...
Harper, KS	20077	8	5,667	16.9	17.6	12.3	2	5	1,006	...	...
Harvey, KS	20079	2	34,247	18.4	10.2	8.9	5	20	6,139	6,065	88.3
Haskell, KS	20081	9	4,006	23.0	14.1	22.1	2	5	878	...	...
Hodgeman, KS	20083	9	1,906	17.9	9.7	12.3	2	3	286	...	...
Jackson, KS	20085	3	13,412	19.9	11.0	9.9	3	9	2,360	...	...
Jefferson, KS	20087	3	18,207	17.4	8.4	12.4	6	18	3,981	...	...
Jewell, KS	20089	9	3,059	13.4	15.4	14.8	2	6	379	...	...
Johnson, KS	20091	1	542,737	18.1	4.4	6.0	7	157	88,735	97,287	84.4
Kearny, KS	20093	9	4,169	23.3	14.3	21.9	2	6	975	...	...
Kingman, KS	20095	6	7,571	17.9	12.2	11.1	2	8	1,290	...	...
Kiowa, KS	20097	9	2,322	16.6	15.6	15.6	3	8	678	...	...
Labette, KS	20099	7	21,776	17.1	18.3	6.7	5	23	4,085	3,833	86.4
Lane, KS	20101	9	1,742	16.7	9.1	19.9	2	4	370	...	...
Leavenworth, KS	20103	1	75,227	18.3	9.3	7.7	8	33	12,981	13,562	88.2
Lincoln, KS	20105	9	3,123	16.8	13.4	15.5	2	3	519	...	...

[1]County type codes are from the Economic Research Service of the United States Department of Agriculture. See notes and definitions for more information.
... Not available

Table C-1. Population, School, and Student Characteristics by County—*Continued*

County	State/County Code	Characteristics of students, 2008-2009				Number of graduates, 2006-2007	Staff and students, 2008-2009			
		Percent with IEP[2]	Percent eligible for free or reduced lunch	Percent minority	Percent English Language Learners		Total staff	Number of teachers	Student/teacher ratio	Central admin. Staff
		10	11	12	13	14	15	16	17	18
Sioux, IA	19167	12.2	28.7	18.4	10.2	318	614	325	13.8	20
Story, IA	19169	10.3	20.8	13.4	2.3	836	1,342	774	14.0	44
Tama, IA	19171	15.3	32.2	22.6	5.9	213	406	208	12.7	13
Taylor, IA	19173	17.1	43.4	11.8	3.2	56	167	86	11.5	7
Union, IA	19175	14.4	40.7	5.7	1.9	157	397	159	12.7	21
Van Buren, IA	19177	14.8	36.0	3.1	0.4	97	202	87	13.4	10
Wapello, IA	19179	13.5	47.4	19.9	8.4	379	950	401	13.6	61
Warren, IA	19181	11.8	19.9	4.5	0.4	555	1,211	623	14.1	33
Washington, IA	19183	14.5	31.3	11.9	2.5	277	531	281	13.5	15
Wayne, IA	19185	14.5	47.8	1.2	0.5	111	217	119	10.0	11
Webster, IA	19187	17.5	46.4	15.3	0.9	374	1,030	435	12.2	60
Winnebago, IA	19189	14.1	29.4	5.2	0.7	184	386	200	12.5	15
Winneshiek, IA	19191	13.5	21.4	4.4	1.0	285	428	219	13.1	23
Woodbury, IA	19193	13.5	44.0	32.5	13.9	1,104	2,579	1289	13.9	110
Worth, IA	19195	15.8	26.7	3.6	0.1	67	154	82	11.5	8
Wright, IA	19197	13.9	39.4	14.5	5.8	183	393	196	13.6	17
KANSAS	20000	14.0	42.9	26.7	7.2	30,136	55,308	35,871	13.1	600
Allen, KS	20001	17.5	55.0	8.7	...	151	383	263	8.7	7
Anderson, KS	20003	15.1	48.3	4.0	...	112	155	116	11.9	4
Atchison, KS	20005	19.6	56.3	15.4	0.1	157	277	182	13.2	5
Barber, KS	20007	18.2	35.5	5.9	...	68	100	71	11.0	2
Barton, KS	20009	14.7	51.4	24.4	12.4	353	582	373	11.6	7
Bourbon, KS	20011	9.7	57.8	7.7	0.6	164	268	199	12.7	3
Brown, KS	20013	19.0	54.9	19.7	5.3	95	198	149	10.5	4
Butler, KS	20015	13.2	25.9	8.5	0.8	978	1,811	1,064	13.7	19
Chase, KS	20017	15.0	39.4	4.4	...	31	57	41	10.5	1
Chautauqua, KS	20019	18.2	50.0	10.5	...	54	74	51	10.4	1
Cherokee, KS	20021	12.0	55.5	12.2	0.6	231	423	285	13.6	5
Cheyenne, KS	20023	17.4	43.1	9.7	5.4	49	71	52	8.5	2
Clark, KS	20025	14.2	41.8	16.1	4.7	32	62	41	12.5	2
Clay, KS	20027	17.2	35.6	4.6	0.3	110	300	172	10.1	5
Cloud, KS	20029	17.7	52.2	6.2	1.9	97	259	153	9.3	4
Coffey, KS	20031	19.4	38.9	5.8	0.2	138	279	161	10.6	4
Comanche, KS	20033	21.1	40.8	6.6	...	21	39	29	11.4	...
Cowley, KS	20035	17.5	51.3	24.1	5.8	434	847	496	12.9	9
Crawford, KS	20037	13.2	55.5	13.4	2.9	372	859	667	9.0	15
Decatur, KS	20039	16.2	42.8	4.2	...	48	50	35	10.9	1
Dickinson, KS	20041	16.5	40.8	8.6	0.6	282	422	289	13.8	5
Doniphan, KS	20043	18.1	39.7	8.1	...	120	194	139	10.0	3
Douglas, KS	20045	13.5	31.1	21.6	3.8	986	1,677	1,029	13.4	9
Edwards, KS	20047	12.3	46.5	25.8	16.4	29	68	43	9.7	3
Elk, KS	20049	27.9	55.7	10.4	...	49	142	63	9.3	2
Ellis, KS	20051	18.4	34.3	11.8	3.3	215	519	325	11.0	7
Ellsworth, KS	20053	16.5	42.3	8.1	...	92	137	95	10.7	3
Finney, KS	20055	11.4	63.3	67.4	31.0	389	934	627	13.0	10
Ford, KS	20057	12.5	73.1	71.3	38.4	384	686	419	16.3	5
Franklin, KS	20059	15.2	44.9	7.2	0.8	253	573	359	13.2	9
Geary, KS	20061	15.9	52.9	46.5	7.3	279	860	534	13.1	7
Gove, KS	20063	18.7	28.5	3.9	0.5	29	101	65	6.6	2
Graham, KS	20065	25.1	36.8	5.3	...	34	55	35	11.3	1
Grant, KS	20067	13.7	54.7	59.2	25.0	81	200	122	14.2	2
Gray, KS	20069	9.7	42.3	21.1	22.3	72	183	114	10.6	3
Greeley, KS	20071	14.0	45.6	19.7	15.4	18	32	25	9.1	1
Greenwood, KS	20073	17.4	52.1	3.9	...	89	143	93	10.9	2
Hamilton, KS	20075	10.9	57.5	44.9	37.6	32	71	41	12.3	1
Harper, KS	20077	18.7	56.9	10.6	4.2	68	118	85	11.8	2
Harvey, KS	20079	15.3	42.1	20.3	5.1	368	706	449	13.7	12
Haskell, KS	20081	9.1	57.5	42.6	37.7	42	127	80	11.0	3
Hodgeman, KS	20083	21.0	39.9	11.5	5.9	22	50	27	10.6	1
Jackson, KS	20085	14.7	36.2	17.8	0.3	172	390	218	10.8	6
Jefferson, KS	20087	14.6	31.6	4.4	0.1	261	427	292	13.6	8
Jewell, KS	20089	12.1	39.3	3.4	...	46	75	47	8.1	1
Johnson, KS	20091	10.8	18.7	18.8	3.9	5,688	9,439	6,211	14.3	44
Kearny, KS	20093	12.2	59.0	42.9	29.6	73	128	83	11.7	3
Kingman, KS	20095	21.9	41.0	4.4	0.2	88	153	115	11.2	2
Kiowa, KS	20097	12.4	38.8	20.9	...	93	79	54	12.6	2
Labette, KS	20099	14.7	58.2	17.2	0.1	306	448	289	14.1	7
Lane, KS	20101	19.5	44.6	4.6	2.2	31	70	40	9.3	1
Leavenworth, KS	20103	15.9	28.0	19.0	1.5	902	1,427	923	14.1	15
Lincoln, KS	20105	16.0	42.2	5.6	...	44	66	47	11.0	2

[2]IEP= Individual Education Program. See notes and definitions for more information
... Not available

Table C-1. Population, School, and Student Characteristics by County—*Continued*

County	State/ County Code	Revenues, 2007-2008				Current expenditures, 2007-2008			Resident population 16 to 19 years, 2006-2008			
		Total revenue ($1,000's)	Percentage of revenue from			Amount ($1,000's)	Amount per student	Percent for instruc-tion	Total population 16 to 19 years	Percent en-rolled in school	Percent high school graduates, not enrolled in school	Percent not enrolled, not grads, not employed or not in labor force
			Federal gov't	State gov't	Local gov't							
	19		20	21	22	23	24	25	26	27	28	29
Sioux, IA	19167	45,199	5.3	47.0	47.7	36,793	8,328	66.6	...	...	...	...
Story, IA	19169	120,456	2.9	39.0	58.1	93,247	8,639	66.7	...	...	...	...
Tama, IA	19171	26,879	7.2	49.9	42.9	21,588	8,271	64.0	...	...	...	...
Taylor, IA	19173	12,879	6.5	47.1	46.5	10,285	10,224	64.5	...	...	...	...
Union, IA	19175	25,398	17.7	44.0	38.3	23,637	12,735	47.3	...	...	...	...
Van Buren, IA	19177	14,515	13.2	45.9	40.9	11,448	9,580	58.4	...	...	...	...
Wapello, IA	19179	64,104	22.6	50.4	27.0	65,190	12,165	44.9	...	...	...	...
Warren, IA	19181	87,361	2.7	52.7	44.6	67,520	7,715	62.6	...	...	...	...
Washington, IA	19183	39,789	7.6	47.4	45.0	31,521	8,374	65.3	...	...	...	...
Wayne, IA	19185	15,199	12.4	44.5	43.0	11,899	9,999	63.4	...	...	...	...
Webster, IA	19187	70,384	19.0	43.3	37.7	71,008	13,624	45.0	...	...	...	...
Winnebago, IA	19189	26,569	3.1	47.0	49.9	22,066	8,657	64.6	...	...	...	...
Winneshiek, IA	19191	34,287	3.2	40.4	56.4	26,112	9,111	65.0	...	...	...	...
Woodbury, IA	19193	208,312	10.5	48.6	40.9	185,769	10,385	59.3	6,067	82.1	10.2	4.6
Worth, IA	19195	12,031	3.6	43.1	53.3	9,118	9,371	63.8	...	...	...	...
Wright, IA	19197	30,202	5.6	43.2	51.3	23,634	8,962	63.9	...	...	...	...
KANSAS	20000	5,378,095	6.4	58.4	35.2	4,520,267	9,664	61.3	160,994	86.1	9.8	2.2
Allen, KS	20001	26,961	6.7	72.7	20.7	24,660	10,436	63.5	...	...	...	...
Anderson, KS	20003	15,324	4.7	70.0	25.3	14,046	10,120	63.1	...	...	...	...
Atchison, KS	20005	27,327	7.1	66.7	26.2	22,728	9,530	58.4	...	...	...	...
Barber, KS	20007	10,094	3.7	51.6	44.7	9,201	11,416	59.6	...	...	...	...
Barton, KS	20009	52,402	7.1	63.7	29.2	41,479	9,531	64.4	...	...	...	...
Bourbon, KS	20011	24,915	7.6	71.9	20.5	21,601	8,640	65.7	...	...	...	...
Brown, KS	20013	20,001	5.6	70.5	23.8	17,290	10,874	64.4	...	...	...	...
Butler, KS	20015	152,488	2.6	64.4	32.9	122,852	8,416	62.3	...	...	...	...
Chase, KS	20017	5,735	3.6	55.0	41.3	5,124	11,237	61.0	...	...	...	...
Chautauqua, KS	20019	6,668	4.6	74.1	21.3	6,188	11,251	66.1	...	...	...	...
Cherokee, KS	20021	43,281	5.7	73.7	20.6	39,601	10,337	62.2	...	...	...	...
Cheyenne, KS	20023	5,618	4.4	61.0	34.6	5,157	11,090	63.2	...	...	...	...
Clark, KS	20025	6,887	3.5	55.4	41.1	6,263	12,305	58.7	...	...	...	...
Clay, KS	20027	13,938	4.7	70.8	24.5	12,290	8,594	62.1	...	...	...	...
Cloud, KS	20029	15,575	4.7	71.1	24.2	14,008	9,991	63.1	...	...	...	...
Coffey, KS	20031	23,359	4.1	37.6	58.4	18,794	10,914	62.8	...	...	...	...
Comanche, KS	20033	4,326	3.5	42.4	54.1	3,804	11,090	56.7	...	...	...	...
Cowley, KS	20035	67,414	6.1	75.8	18.1	61,022	9,493	62.9	...	...	...	...
Crawford, KS	20037	64,489	6.6	70.5	22.9	57,356	9,664	62.5	...	...	...	...
Decatur, KS	20039	5,166	4.3	59.5	36.2	4,475	10,941	61.4	...	...	...	...
Dickinson, KS	20041	41,629	4.7	70.1	25.2	36,386	8,905	62.7	...	...	...	...
Doniphan, KS	20043	17,817	4.2	76.2	19.5	17,065	11,900	66.4	...	...	...	...
Douglas, KS	20045	155,926	6.0	45.9	48.1	123,550	9,204	61.5	...	...	...	...
Edwards, KS	20047	6,045	8.1	61.0	30.9	5,559	12,663	63.6	...	...	...	...
Elk, KS	20049	7,700	5.0	73.8	21.2	6,909	12,058	66.3	...	...	...	...
Ellis, KS	20051	40,993	7.5	51.6	40.8	36,932	9,878	65.5	...	...	...	...
Ellsworth, KS	20053	12,823	3.6	59.7	36.7	11,437	11,414	61.1	...	...	...	...
Finney, KS	20055	89,756	10.2	59.0	30.8	77,148	9,523	58.2	...	...	...	...
Ford, KS	20057	78,011	10.0	70.9	19.1	64,591	9,586	61.0	...	...	...	...
Franklin, KS	20059	53,267	4.4	68.5	27.1	45,961	9,650	63.3	...	...	...	...
Geary, KS	20061	77,067	22.9	59.7	17.5	66,950	9,682	56.7	...	...	...	...
Gove, KS	20063	7,634	3.3	67.2	29.5	7,231	14,757	65.3	...	...	...	...
Graham, KS	20065	4,857	4.1	53.7	42.2	4,466	12,136	67.5	...	...	...	...
Grant, KS	20067	18,874	9.0	23.9	67.1	15,696	8,954	63.8	...	...	...	...
Gray, KS	20069	15,834	3.9	69.1	27.1	14,237	10,977	61.2	...	...	...	...
Greeley, KS	20071	3,166	5.3	50.9	43.8	3,055	12,028	56.7	...	...	...	...
Greenwood, KS	20073	12,953	6.0	69.7	24.2	11,151	10,986	58.1	...	...	...	...
Hamilton, KS	20075	6,277	5.8	41.9	52.3	5,036	10,236	62.2	...	...	...	...
Harper, KS	20077	12,589	5.7	61.6	32.7	11,071	10,615	59.5	...	...	...	...
Harvey, KS	20079	64,206	4.4	70.3	25.3	54,078	8,783	61.8	...	...	...	...
Haskell, KS	20081	13,083	4.5	21.1	74.3	10,242	11,243	64.5	...	...	...	...
Hodgeman, KS	20083	5,302	3.5	54.8	41.8	4,509	14,687	56.5	...	...	...	...
Jackson, KS	20085	27,651	6.3	76.8	16.9	24,726	10,105	65.3	...	...	...	...
Jefferson, KS	20087	46,131	3.2	73.1	23.6	40,821	10,142	63.6	...	...	...	...
Jewell, KS	20089	6,786	2.9	65.1	31.9	6,082	14,834	56.8	...	...	...	...
Johnson, KS	20091	1,021,716	3.4	41.8	54.8	807,599	9,268	63.2	25,997	87.1	10.1	1.4
Kearny, KS	20093	13,709	6.4	18.5	75.1	10,516	10,830	63.1	...	...	...	...
Kingman, KS	20095	15,031	4.3	56.1	39.6	13,233	9,965	62.0	...	...	...	...
Kiowa, KS	20097	26,569	1.9	17.4	80.6	7,636	12,416	60.7	...	...	...	...
Labette, KS	20099	47,726	7.0	73.5	19.6	41,089	10,024	64.4	...	...	...	...
Lane, KS	20101	5,183	3.6	52.1	44.3	4,563	12,675	60.4	...	...	...	...
Leavenworth, KS	20103	133,087	10.5	62.4	27.1	110,063	8,666	60.8	...	...	...	...
Lincoln, KS	20105	6,619	3.4	65.3	31.2	5,772	11,590	62.6	...	...	...	...

... Not available

Table C-1. Population, School, and Student Characteristics by County—*Continued*

County	State/County Code	High school graduates, 2006-2008			College enrollment, 2006-2008		College graduates, 2006-2008 (percent)						
		Population 25 years and over	High school diploma or less (percent)	High school diploma or more (percent)	Number	Percent public	Bachelor's degree or more	+/- U.S. percent with Bachelor's degree or more	Non-Hispanic White	Black or African American	American Indian and Alaska Native	Asian, Hawaiian, and Pacific Islander	Hispanic or Latino[3]
		30	31	32	33	34	35	36	37	38	39	40	41
Sioux, IA	19167	19,044	47.4	86.0	3,661	17.5	22.9	-4.5	23.6	...	...	...	...
Story, IA	19169	45,827	25.4	94.8	24,360	97.6	46.9	19.5	44.5	48.2	...	80.2	50.3
Tama, IA	19171	...	...	...	...	...	...	...	...	...	...	...	...
Taylor, IA	19173	...	...	...	...	...	...	...	...	...	...	...	...
Union, IA	19175	...	...	...	...	...	...	...	...	...	...	...	...
Van Buren, IA	19177	...	...	...	...	...	...	...	...	...	...	...	...
Wapello, IA	19179	24,124	57.7	83.8	1,401	78.9	13.5	-13.9	14.1	...	...	...	1.3
Warren, IA	19181	28,916	41.3	93.7	3,514	33.5	26.2	-1.2	26.4	...	...	...	...
Washington, IA	19183	14,361	50.4	88.7	479	74.5	18.6	-8.8	18.7	...	...	...	14.1
Wayne, IA	19185	...	...	...	...	...	...	...	...	...	...	...	...
Webster, IA...........................	19187	25,274	50.8	90.0	2,447	86.9	17.0	-10.4	16.7	...	...	...	...
Winnebago, IA	19189	...	...	...	...	...	...	...	...	...	...	...	...
Winneshiek, IA......................	19191	13,000	47.9	89.1	2,934	24.8	24.9	-2.5	25.0	...	...	...	...
Woodbury, IA........................	19193	64,620	50.5	86.1	6,750	50.8	20.9	-6.5	22.6	20.2	4.9	18.9	6.1
Worth, IA	19195	...	...	...	...	...	...	...	...	...	...	...	...
Wright, IA	19197	...	...	...	...	...	...	...	...	...	...	...	...
KANSAS..............................	20000	1,792,057	40.5	89.0	208,775	83.1	29.0	1.6	30.8	18.2	20.1	46.8	11.6
Allen, KS	20001	...	...	...	...	...	...	...	...	...	...	...	...
Anderson, KS........................	20003	...	...	...	...	...	...	...	...	...	...	...	...
Atchison, KS.........................	20005	...	...	...	...	...	...	...	...	...	...	...	...
Barber, KS	20007	...	...	...	...	...	...	...	...	...	...	...	...
Barton, KS	20009	18,476	45.7	85.2	1,598	91.2	19.7	-7.7	21.3	...	...	...	5.5
Bourbon, KS	20011	...	...	...	...	...	...	...	...	...	...	...	...
Brown, KS	20013	...	...	...	...	...	...	...	...	...	...	...	...
Butler, KS	20015	40,837	36.1	91.5	4,465	82.1	24.9	-2.5	25.2	...	...	...	15.6
Chase, KS	20017	...	...	...	...	...	...	...	...	...	...	...	...
Chautauqua, KS	20019	...	...	...	...	...	...	...	...	...	...	...	...
Cherokee, KS	20021	14,276	55.4	86.9	...	...	12.6	-14.8	13.0	...	...	...	...
Cheyenne, KS	20023	...	...	...	...	...	...	...	...	...	...	...	...
Clark, KS	20025	...	...	...	...	...	...	...	...	...	...	...	...
Clay, KS	20027	...	...	...	...	...	...	...	...	...	...	...	...
Cloud, KS	20029	...	...	...	...	...	...	...	...	...	...	...	...
Coffey, KS	20031	...	...	...	...	...	...	...	...	...	...	...	...
Comanche, KS	20033	...	...	...	...	...	...	...	...	...	...	...	...
Cowley, KS	20035	22,275	43.8	87.3	2,236	65.5	20.3	-7.1	20.9	...	...	...	10.1
Crawford, KS	20037	23,494	42.4	87.5	6,250	95.5	26.9	-0.5	27.0	...	...	...	...
Decatur, KS	20039	...	...	...	...	...	...	...	...	...	...	...	...
Dickinson, KS	20041	...	...	...	...	...	...	...	...	...	...	...	...
Doniphan, KS........................	20043	...	...	...	...	...	...	...	...	...	...	...	...
Douglas, KS	20045	64,816	25.2	94.7	27,923	90.0	47.3	19.9	46.3	45.8	53.6	68.2	41.2
Edwards, KS	20047	...	...	...	...	...	...	...	...	...	...	...	...
Elk, KS	20049	...	...	...	...	...	...	...	...	...	...	...	...
Ellis, KS	20051	16,722	33.9	90.8	4,740	96.1	32.4	5.0	32.4	...	...	...	...
Ellsworth, KS	20053	...	...	...	...	...	...	...	...	...	...	...	...
Finney, KS	20055	22,829	54.5	69.9	2,377	87.8	19.6	-7.8	28.3	...	...	...	6.3
Ford, KS	20057	19,674	57.7	67.1	1,500	81.1	16.2	-11.2	25.6	...	...	...	2.3
Franklin, KS..........................	20059	17,247	52.6	89.8	1,184	76.4	16.8	-10.6	17.5	...	...	...	...
Geary, KS	20061	17,694	41.1	91.2	1,588	87.5	19.4	-8.0	20.7	11.5	...	27.6	15.1
Gove, KS	20063	...	...	...	...	...	...	...	...	...	...	...	...
Graham, KS	20065	...	...	...	...	...	...	...	...	...	...	...	...
Grant, KS.............................	20067	...	...	...	...	...	...	...	...	...	...	...	...
Gray, KS..............................	20069	...	...	...	...	...	...	...	...	...	...	...	...
Greeley, KS	20071	...	...	...	...	...	...	...	...	...	...	...	...
Greenwood, KS	20073	...	...	...	...	...	...	...	...	...	...	...	...
Hamilton, KS	20075	...	...	...	...	...	...	...	...	...	...	...	...
Harper, KS	20077	...	...	...	...	...	...	...	...	...	...	...	...
Harvey, KS	20079	22,093	42.6	90.3	2,225	54.3	26.4	-1.0	28.2	...	...	...	5.6
Haskell, KS	20081	...	...	...	...	...	...	...	...	...	...	...	...
Hodgeman, KS.......................	20083	...	...	...	...	...	...	...	...	...	...	...	...
Jackson, KS	20085	...	...	...	...	...	...	...	...	...	...	...	...
Jefferson, KS	20087	...	...	...	...	...	...	...	...	...	...	...	...
Jewell, KS	20089	...	...	...	...	...	...	...	...	...	...	...	...
Johnson, KS..........................	20091	343,069	21.4	95.7	35,666	78.3	50.6	23.2	52.3	35.4	28.5	59.6	26.9
Kearny, KS	20093	...	...	...	...	...	...	...	...	...	...	...	...
Kingman, KS	20095	...	...	...	...	...	...	...	...	...	...	...	...
Kiowa, KS	20097	...	...	...	...	...	...	...	...	...	...	...	...
Labette, KS...........................	20099	14,618	48.4	85.4	1,082	88.7	16.1	-11.3	17.2	12.9	...	...	...
Lane, KS	20101	...	...	...	...	...	...	...	...	...	...	...	...
Leavenworth, KS....................	20103	48,490	43.9	90.8	4,965	76.9	27.9	0.5	29.1	16.4	16.0	53.9	13.3
Lincoln, KS...........................	20105	...	...	...	...	...	...	...	...	...	...	...	...

[3]May be of any race
... Not available

Table C-1. Population, School, and Student Characteristics by County—*Continued*

County	State/ County Code	County Type[1]	Population, 2009 Total	Population, 2009 Percent 5–17 years	Percent of related children 5-17 years in poverty, 2008	Percent of children under 19 years with no health insurance, 2007	Number of Schools and Students, 2008-2009 School Districts	Number of Schools and Students, 2008-2009 Schools	Number of Schools and Students, 2008-2009 Students	Resident enrollment, 2006-2008 K–12 enrollment Number	Resident enrollment, 2006-2008 K–12 enrollment Percent public
			1	2	3	4	5	6	7	8	9
Linn, KS	20107	1	9,335	17.2	15.2	10.5	3	10	1,942	...	...
Logan, KS	20109	9	2,549	16.8	12.7	14.5	4	5	558	...	...
Lyon, KS	20111	5	33,601	15.8	15.1	11.3	3	19	5,775	5,765	97.0
McPherson, KS	20113	6	28,866	16.8	7.4	8.9	4	16	3,676	4,629	84.4
Marion, KS	20115	6	11,982	16.9	10.3	11.5	6	12	2,150	...	...
Marshall, KS	20117	7	10,123	16.7	12.1	11.8	4	13	2,081	...	...
Meade, KS	20119	9	4,407	21.2	11.0	19.5	2	4	670	...	...
Miami, KS	20121	1	30,969	19.5	8.0	8.2	3	14	4,945	5,232	92.9
Mitchell, KS	20123	7	6,344	16.2	12.7	12.4	3	8	1,118	...	...
Montgomery, KS	20125	5	34,254	16.8	17.0	6.6	5	13	5,705	5,552	89.4
Morris, KS	20127	9	5,994	16.5	13.7	13.0	1	4	811	...	...
Morton, KS	20129	9	3,031	22.4	14.3	16.9	2	6	992	...	...
Nemaha, KS	20131	8	9,968	19.4	10.1	15.6	3	9	1,637	...	...
Neosho, KS	20133	7	16,046	17.0	18.4	8.7	2	10	2,490	...	...
Ness, KS	20135	9	2,835	16.4	11.6	16.3	2	5	465	...	...
Norton, KS	20137	7	5,330	15.4	11.5	10.7	3	7	926	...	...
Osage, KS	20139	3	16,104	18.7	12.2	9.5	6	14	2,931	...	...
Osborne, KS	20141	9	3,849	14.8	14.3	14.3	2	4	486	...	...
Ottawa, KS	20143	9	5,974	19.1	9.4	13.3	2	6	1,283	...	...
Pawnee, KS	20145	7	6,206	17.9	12.4	8.5	3	9	1,130	...	...
Phillips, KS	20147	7	5,272	16.0	13.4	10.1	3	5	867	...	...
Pottawatomie, KS	20149	6	19,994	19.6	10.2	12.3	5	15	3,825	...	...
Pratt, KS	20151	7	9,304	16.4	12.4	9.3	3	7	1,404	...	...
Rawlins, KS	20153	9	2,425	14.6	18.2	13.7	1	2	327	...	...
Reno, KS	20155	4	63,357	16.6	14.3	8.0	8	38	9,799	10,343	91.0
Republic, KS	20157	9	4,808	13.3	16.3	14.1	2	7	772	...	...
Rice, KS	20159	7	10,079	17.1	13.7	11.1	4	15	1,779	...	...
Riley, KS	20161	5	71,341	12.3	13.2	10.2	3	17	7,071	9,384	94.4
Rooks, KS	20163	9	4,984	16.7	13.3	16.0	3	7	957	...	...
Rush, KS	20165	9	3,143	14.4	16.1	13.6	2	6	485	...	...
Russell, KS	20167	7	6,596	15.2	15.5	9.6	1	6	962	...	...
Saline, KS	20169	5	54,364	17.1	14.1	9.1	5	21	9,178	9,309	91.4
Scott, KS	20171	7	4,560	18.4	11.6	10.6	1	3	888	...	...
Sedgwick, KS	20173	2	490,864	18.9	13.3	8.7	11	153	77,093	93,251	86.5
Seward, KS	20175	7	23,013	22.1	16.1	17.1	2	15	5,422	4,831	97.5
Shawnee, KS	20177	3	176,255	17.2	14.5	6.9	7	65	27,393	30,367	88.9
Sheridan, KS	20179	9	2,435	15.9	15.8	15.0	2	5	560	...	...
Sherman, KS	20181	7	5,860	14.9	18.9	9.0	1	5	940	...	...
Smith, KS	20183	9	3,753	14.1	16.0	12.7	2	5	711	...	...
Stafford, KS	20185	9	4,342	16.1	16.7	15.5	3	6	964	...	...
Stanton, KS	20187	9	2,107	20.7	14.3	24.2	1	3	454	...	...
Stevens, KS	20189	7	5,129	21.6	11.5	15.3	2	5	1,286	...	...
Sumner, KS	20191	2	23,488	19.2	11.9	9.0	9	25	6,061	4,597	94.7
Thomas, KS	20193	7	7,343	16.7	8.0	9.6	2	6	1,038	...	...
Trego, KS	20195	9	2,920	15.3	14.1	11.8	1	2	451	...	...
Wabaunsee, KS	20197	3	6,846	17.9	9.6	13.8	2	7	974	...	...
Wallace, KS	20199	9	1,408	19.4	19.3	14.6	2	4	311	...	...
Washington, KS	20201	9	5,683	16.7	11.5	17.3	2	6	856	...	...
Wichita, KS	20203	9	2,109	19.9	17.3	23.5	1	3	468	...	...
Wilson, KS	20205	7	9,474	16.9	17.9	9.0	3	8	1,755	...	...
Woodson, KS	20207	9	3,240	12.8	25.1	11.7	1	2	435	...	...
Wyandotte, KS	20209	1	155,085	19.0	24.9	7.9	6	66	28,568	31,236	89.7
KENTUCKY	21000	X	4,314,113	16.8	20.9	9.9	194	1,560	670,030	727,473	88.4
Adair, KY	21001	7	18,029	16.1	29.2	11.1	1	6	2,547	...	...
Allen, KY	21003	6	18,982	17.2	23.7	9.7	1	5	3,037	...	...
Anderson, KY	21005	6	21,790	18.4	11.1	12.2	1	7	4,009	3,990	97.0
Ballard, KY	21007	9	8,161	16.5	20.1	12.2	1	4	1,420	...	...
Barren, KY	21009	6	41,747	17.2	23.1	10.1	3	23	7,418	6,553	93.7
Bath, KY	21011	8	11,618	16.9	34.7	9.1	1	6	2,030	...	...
Bell, KY	21013	7	28,972	16.4	37.1	5.3	3	21	5,244	4,653	92.7
Boone, KY	21015	1	118,576	19.5	7.1	10.2	2	25	20,003	22,288	86.4
Bourbon, KY	21017	2	19,729	17.5	19.3	9.8	2	10	3,582	...	...
Boyd, KY	21019	2	48,527	15.5	21.7	8.3	5	24	7,464	7,448	88.2
Boyle, KY	21021	7	29,263	16.0	17.8	10.1	3	14	4,647	4,899	92.3
Bracken, KY	21023	1	8,653	18.1	17.8	12.7	2	4	1,582	...	...
Breathitt, KY	21025	7	15,575	16.6	40.4	5.2	2	11	2,708	...	...
Breckinridge, KY	21027	8	19,057	17.8	25.7	13.6	2	10	2,987	...	...
Bullitt, KY	21029	1	75,653	18.2	11.2	11.4	1	25	12,741	13,650	88.8
Butler, KY	21031	8	13,329	16.3	24.2	12.2	1	7	2,155	...	...
Caldwell, KY	21033	6	12,870	15.8	21.4	8.8	1	5	2,022	...	...

[1]County type codes are from the Economic Research Service of the United States Department of Agriculture. See notes and definitions for more information.
... Not available

Table C-1.   Population, School, and Student Characteristics by County—*Continued*

County	State/ County Code	Characteristics of students, 2008-2009					Staff and students, 2008-2009			
		Percent with IEP[2]	Percent eligible for free or reduced lunch	Percent minority	Percent English Language Learners	Number of graduates, 2006-2007	Total staff	Number of teachers	Student/ teacher ratio	Central admin. Staff
		10	11	12	13	14	15	16	17	18
Linn, KS	20107	15.2	47.6	3.5	0.6	155	209	150	12.9	4
Logan, KS	20109	19.0	43.0	2.9	...	37	212	160	3.5	8
Lyon, KS	20111	12.3	60.1	42.0	24.5	370	850	517	11.2	11
McPherson, KS	20113	16.7	30.9	8.2	1.4	344	597	303	12.1	6
Marion, KS	20115	18.8	37.9	5.5	0.2	200	290	212	10.1	5
Marshall, KS	20117	17.8	36.6	5.1	0.4	220	307	189	11.0	5
Meade, KS	20119	17.5	48.8	23.7	4.6	41	88	62	10.8	2
Miami, KS	20121	14.8	30.4	5.5	0.2	328	762	392	12.6	6
Mitchell, KS	20123	17.6	39.4	4.3	0.4	95	192	112	10.0	4
Montgomery, KS	20125	11.9	55.5	27.2	1.7	417	664	459	12.4	10
Morris, KS	20127	14.1	42.9	7.4	2.1	155	99	75	10.8	2
Morton, KS	20129	8.0	46.4	27.3	18.4	72	112	77	12.9	2
Nemaha, KS	20131	15.0	28.9	3.8	0.1	149	242	155	10.6	5
Neosho, KS	20133	16.5	54.1	8.0	0.7	142	253	176	14.1	4
Ness, KS	20135	18.1	32.7	11.8	5.4	38	69	45	10.3	2
Norton, KS	20137	20.8	45.9	3.7	...	69	107	82	11.3	3
Osage, KS	20139	19.3	38.7	6.1	0.1	238	374	281	10.4	7
Osborne, KS	20141	19.1	46.9	4.8	...	45	72	50	9.7	2
Ottawa, KS	20143	16.3	34.6	5.0	...	75	132	96	13.4	2
Pawnee, KS	20145	24.2	49.5	16.5	0.1	105	252	120	9.4	3
Phillips, KS	20147	16.0	39.8	5.6	...	88	160	131	6.6	4
Pottawatomie, KS	20149	16.4	30.8	6.2	0.1	299	533	330	11.6	7
Pratt, KS	20151	17.0	38.7	8.8	3.6	96	255	207	6.8	6
Rawlins, KS	20153	17.4	50.5	4.6	...	32	50	30	10.9	1
Reno, KS	20155	15.7	50.3	18.1	3.0	619	1,154	785	12.5	16
Republic, KS	20157	23.3	46.2	3.8	...	57	96	64	12.1	2
Rice, KS	20159	17.2	54.0	18.4	8.7	127	282	182	9.8	4
Riley, KS	20161	16.3	34.4	22.9	3.6	468	819	537	13.2	10
Rooks, KS	20163	18.1	42.0	4.6	...	77	120	90	10.6	2
Rush, KS	20165	19.8	41.2	3.7	...	22	66	50	9.7	1
Russell, KS	20167	20.7	46.4	6.9	...	66	143	93	10.3	3
Saline, KS	20169	15.9	50.8	24.5	5.1	505	1,422	789	11.6	12
Scott, KS	20171	13.7	50.9	21.2	19.4	74	94	76	11.7	1
Sedgwick, KS	20173	13.5	52.3	36.4	9.6	4,237	7,383	4,845	15.9	58
Seward, KS	20175	8.7	71.5	75.1	41.1	235	613	373	14.5	6
Shawnee, KS	20177	15.5	47.1	31.5	3.5	1,775	3,277	2,177	12.6	41
Sheridan, KS	20179	18.9	37.7	7.5	4.6	54	78	50	11.2	1
Sherman, KS	20181	20.1	46.4	21.9	8.8	67	138	76	12.4	1
Smith, KS	20183	17.6	41.0	4.9	...	49	93	70	10.2	2
Stafford, KS	20185	17.4	51.9	20.6	8.5	84	128	88	11.0	3
Stanton, KS	20187	12.1	59.5	48.2	38.8	25	55	36	12.6	1
Stevens, KS	20189	8.4	52.8	43.6	23.1	61	152	103	12.5	2
Sumner, KS	20191	17.0	41.1	7.8	0.2	476	841	495	12.2	12
Thomas, KS	20193	18.7	40.3	6.9	0.7	82	155	94	11.0	2
Trego, KS	20195	22.0	32.4	2.4	...	31	67	43	10.5	1
Wabaunsee, KS	20197	19.6	33.8	4.4	0.2	68	144	90	10.8	3
Wallace, KS	20199	15.4	39.9	8.4	2.9	17	53	39	8.0	2
Washington, KS	20201	15.8	36.0	4.1	0.9	106	104	80	10.7	3
Wichita, KS	20203	13.5	48.7	33.1	25.9	33	64	39	12.0	1
Wilson, KS	20205	14.6	49.8	5.1	...	126	195	142	12.4	4
Woodson, KS	20207	16.8	48.3	6.9	...	38	54	36	12.1	1
Wyandotte, KS	20209	12.6	71.7	69.8	20.9	1,415	2,849	1,947	14.7	19
KENTUCKY	21000	16.1	51.6	14.9	2.2	39,412	100,209	43,448	15.4	3,457
Adair, KY	21001	16.2	58.0	6.2	0.7	167	402	174	14.6	17
Allen, KY	21003	10.7	59.2	2.6	0.6	204	428	184	16.5	18
Anderson, KY	21005	19.9	38.7	4.2	0.4	255	532	244	16.4	13
Ballard, KY	21007	19.4	50.3	3.9	...	83	242	100	14.2	6
Barren, KY	21009	16.6	53.3	7.8	1.4	399	1,133	484	15.3	47
Bath, KY	21011	12.6	66.2	3.0	0.3	96	307	135	15.0	15
Bell, KY	21013	17.9	75.4	2.2	0.1	328	851	388	13.5	32
Boone, KY	21015	13.4	27.7	8.6	3.9	1,118	2,626	1,238	16.2	55
Bourbon, KY	21017	13.6	51.9	17.1	3.4	235	562	235	15.2	19
Boyd, KY	21019	17.0	46.0	4.0	0.1	535	1,204	504	14.8	58
Boyle, KY	21021	23.2	45.8	11.9	0.9	324	758	328	14.2	28
Bracken, KY	21023	15.2	49.5	1.5	...	98	235	100	15.8	15
Breathitt, KY	21025	23.3	75.4	1.7	...	154	502	200	13.5	25
Breckinridge, KY	21027	18.0	56.6	3.4	0.3	211	477	178	16.8	26
Bullitt, KY	21029	12.5	41.6	2.6	0.3	671	1,549	757	16.8	41
Butler, KY	21031	16.3	46.4	3.5	1.0	144	310	135	16.0	9
Caldwell, KY	21033	14.0	54.2	7.7	0.2	128	323	133	15.2	17

[2]IEP= Individual Education Program. See notes and definitions for more information
... Not available

Table C-1. Population, School, and Student Characteristics by County—*Continued*

County	State/ County Code	Revenues, 2007-2008				Current expenditures, 2007-2008			Resident population 16 to 19 years, 2006-2008			
		Total revenue ($1,000's)	Percentage of revenue from			Amount ($1,000's)	Amount per student	Percent for instruc-tion	Total population 16 to 19 years	Percent en-rolled in school	Percent high school graduates, not enrolled in school	Percent not enrolled, not grads, not employed or not in labor force
			Federal gov't	State gov't	Local gov't							
		19	20	21	22	23	24	25	26	27	28	29
Linn, KS	20107	24,055	3.9	56.8	39.3	20,959	10,607	59.5	...	...	...	...
Logan, KS	20109	6,339	3.6	59.3	37.1	5,830	11,190	66.2	...	...	...	...
Lyon, KS	20111	66,403	7.3	69.5	23.2	56,131	9,834	62.3	...	...	...	...
McPherson, KS	20113	53,474	5.0	57.9	37.1	44,992	9,288	64.2	...	...	...	...
Marion, KS	20115	27,482	3.3	71.8	24.9	23,258	10,758	61.7	...	...	...	...
Marshall, KS	20117	24,560	3.6	70.2	26.2	22,560	10,702	61.4	...	...	...	...
Meade, KS	20119	8,614	3.7	52.8	43.5	7,380	10,513	61.0	...	...	...	...
Miami, KS	20121	57,545	3.4	56.4	40.2	45,291	9,084	61.6	...	...	...	...
Mitchell, KS	20123	14,560	3.6	63.3	33.1	12,301	10,944	63.1	...	...	...	...
Montgomery, KS	20125	58,298	5.7	67.3	27.0	50,159	8,713	63.5	...	...	...	...
Morris, KS	20127	8,944	4.2	68.8	27.0	8,492	10,207	66.2	...	...	...	...
Morton, KS	20129	12,873	8.8	30.4	60.8	10,206	10,393	68.2	...	...	...	...
Nemaha, KS	20131	23,006	3.7	57.8	38.5	16,146	9,809	60.8	...	...	...	...
Neosho, KS	20133	29,787	6.6	70.6	22.8	24,819	9,841	65.7	...	...	...	...
Ness, KS	20135	5,978	3.2	55.7	41.2	5,368	11,544	59.3	...	...	...	...
Norton, KS	20137	10,903	3.7	75.3	21.1	10,186	11,120	62.7	...	...	...	...
Osage, KS	20139	32,850	4.7	76.1	19.1	29,203	9,770	63.5	...	...	...	...
Osborne, KS	20141	6,698	3.7	62.5	33.9	6,113	12,251	64.8	...	...	...	...
Ottawa, KS	20143	15,274	3.0	67.7	29.3	12,768	9,913	60.5	...	...	...	...
Pawnee, KS	20145	14,454	3.6	65.3	31.0	12,759	12,304	59.9	...	...	...	...
Phillips, KS	20147	10,242	3.4	71.6	24.9	9,089	10,756	63.9	...	...	...	...
Pottawatomie, KS	20149	42,830	3.5	56.0	40.5	35,913	9,396	62.0	...	...	...	...
Pratt, KS	20151	17,633	5.6	64.4	30.0	15,900	10,700	65.3	...	...	...	...
Rawlins, KS	20153	4,088	4.4	61.4	34.2	3,846	12,094	64.8	...	...	...	...
Reno, KS	20155	111,990	8.1	63.2	28.7	93,555	9,540	61.0	...	...	...	...
Republic, KS	20157	9,794	4.1	72.0	23.9	8,955	11,437	62.2	...	...	...	...
Rice, KS	20159	23,543	5.1	68.9	26.0	21,280	11,776	64.9	...	...	...	...
Riley, KS	20161	72,925	9.7	49.5	40.8	66,067	9,910	62.2	...	...	...	...
Rooks, KS	20163	12,115	3.5	50.7	45.8	10,426	10,883	62.4	...	...	...	...
Rush, KS	20165	6,677	4.3	64.1	31.6	6,155	12,188	61.5	...	...	...	...
Russell, KS	20167	10,739	7.1	60.7	32.2	9,492	9,686	63.1	...	...	...	...
Saline, KS	20169	102,000	9.8	56.4	33.8	83,171	10,106	60.6	...	...	...	...
Scott, KS	20171	10,641	3.5	50.9	45.5	8,709	9,818	64.6	...	...	...	...
Sedgwick, KS	20173	856,342	8.0	63.4	28.7	737,493	9,672	57.6	25,511	84.9	9.1	3.7
Seward, KS	20175	53,484	9.1	66.4	24.4	45,973	8,547	64.9	...	...	...	...
Shawnee, KS	20177	295,990	9.3	60.4	30.3	254,627	9,544	61.3	8,748	86.6	9.7	2.4
Sheridan, KS	20179	6,471	3.9	62.0	34.1	5,638	10,421	60.6	...	...	...	...
Sherman, KS	20181	10,461	4.6	65.1	30.3	9,230	9,457	65.1	...	...	...	...
Smith, KS	20183	10,383	5.1	69.2	25.7	9,169	11,740	64.9	...	...	...	...
Stafford, KS	20185	12,951	6.4	59.7	33.9	11,513	11,832	62.7	...	...	...	...
Stanton, KS	20187	5,857	5.6	29.8	64.6	5,063	10,818	58.4	...	...	...	...
Stevens, KS	20189	16,326	7.6	12.5	79.9	13,584	10,252	64.8	...	...	...	...
Sumner, KS	20191	67,420	4.9	74.1	21.1	56,750	9,250	63.4	...	...	...	...
Thomas, KS	20193	12,457	3.3	65.9	30.8	11,126	10,437	59.2	...	...	...	...
Trego, KS	20195	5,521	10.3	53.6	36.0	4,809	11,158	65.2	...	...	...	...
Wabaunsee, KS	20197	13,442	4.2	63.0	32.8	10,785	10,481	58.5	...	...	...	...
Wallace, KS	20199	4,737	3.9	61.4	34.7	4,230	12,857	61.6	...	...	...	...
Washington, KS	20201	14,937	3.4	68.5	28.0	12,916	10,918	65.3	...	...	...	...
Wichita, KS	20203	5,785	5.4	62.3	32.3	5,196	10,939	57.4	...	...	...	...
Wilson, KS	20205	20,541	4.9	74.1	21.0	18,446	10,069	60.5	...	...	...	...
Woodson, KS	20207	5,170	5.6	73.2	21.2	5,049	10,812	59.7	...	...	...	...
Wyandotte, KS	20209	334,521	7.8	62.3	29.9	287,892	10,314	58.0	8,580	76.1	14.0	5.8
KENTUCKY	21000	6,637,062	10.5	57.9	31.6	5,784,936	8,686	59.2	231,145	82.1	10.5	5.2
Adair, KY	21001	26,235	13.2	70.5	16.3	23,506	8,840	63.5	...	...	...	...
Allen, KY	21003	27,827	10.9	70.2	19.0	23,568	7,627	61.3	...	...	...	...
Anderson, KY	21005	35,594	7.1	62.8	30.1	30,839	7,679	65.5	...	...	...	...
Ballard, KY	21007	15,443	8.8	67.6	23.6	12,698	8,769	57.8	...	...	...	...
Barren, KY	21009	72,782	11.4	62.0	26.5	63,572	8,638	62.7	...	...	...	...
Bath, KY	21011	19,102	13.7	70.4	15.9	16,357	7,860	59.9	...	...	...	...
Bell, KY	21013	53,518	15.8	70.4	13.8	49,644	9,269	59.2	...	...	...	...
Boone, KY	21015	183,982	4.9	43.0	52.0	147,566	7,595	59.6	...	...	...	...
Bourbon, KY	21017	34,835	13.8	61.0	25.2	31,075	8,561	60.4	...	...	...	...
Boyd, KY	21019	70,127	13.9	62.4	23.6	64,605	8,732	63.3	...	...	...	...
Boyle, KY	21021	47,047	8.9	60.3	30.8	43,175	9,527	57.7	...	...	...	...
Bracken, KY	21023	14,119	11.1	71.9	16.9	12,180	7,873	60.5	...	...	...	...
Breathitt, KY	21025	29,212	16.3	72.1	11.6	27,272	9,896	60.6	...	...	...	...
Breckinridge, KY	21027	30,601	15.7	62.2	22.1	26,634	8,810	57.3	...	...	...	...
Bullitt, KY	21029	109,119	8.2	60.1	31.6	94,952	7,495	62.7	3,911	79.3	16.5	3.5
Butler, KY	21031	22,820	11.4	75.2	13.3	18,418	8,696	61.9	...	...	...	...
Caldwell, KY	21033	19,194	11.0	70.3	18.7	17,185	8,457	60.7	...	...	...	...

... Not available

Table C-1. Population, School, and Student Characteristics by County—*Continued*

County	State/ County Code	High school graduates, 2006-2008			College enrollment, 2006-2008		College graduates, 2006-2008 (percent)						
		Population 25 years and over	High school diploma or less (percent)	High school diploma or more (percent)	Number	Percent public	Bachelor's degree or more	+/- U.S. percent with Bachelor's degree or more	Non-Hispanic White	Black or African American	American Indian and Alaska Native	Asian, Hawaiian, and Pacific Islander	Hispanic or Latino[3]
		30	31	32	33	34	35	36	37	38	39	40	41
Linn, KS	20107	...	...	...	...	...	...	...	...	...	...	...	...
Logan, KS	20109	...	...	...	...	...	...	...	...	...	...	...	...
Lyon, KS	20111	21,088	49.5	81.7	4,984	96.6	23.5	-3.9	27.6	...	...	...	3.9
McPherson, KS	20113	19,497	45.8	88.9	2,138	31.4	23.5	-3.9	23.4	...	...	...	...
Marion, KS	20115	...	...	...	...	...	...	...	...	...	...	...	...
Marshall, KS	20117	...	...	...	...	...	...	...	...	...	...	...	...
Meade, KS	20119	...	...	...	...	...	...	...	...	...	...	...	...
Miami, KS	20121	20,229	45.1	92.1	1,151	77.9	20.8	-6.6	20.7	...	...	...	...
Mitchell, KS	20123	...	...	...	...	...	...	...	...	...	...	...	...
Montgomery, KS	20125	23,359	45.8	86.8	1,917	92.7	18.4	-9.0	19.7	4.7	15.2	...	5.5
Morris, KS	20127	...	...	...	...	...	...	...	...	...	...	...	...
Morton, KS	20129	...	...	...	...	...	...	...	...	...	...	...	...
Nemaha, KS	20131	...	...	...	...	...	...	...	...	...	...	...	...
Neosho, KS	20133	...	...	...	...	...	...	...	...	...	...	...	...
Ness, KS	20135	...	...	...	...	...	...	...	...	...	...	...	...
Norton, KS	20137	...	...	...	...	...	...	...	...	...	...	...	...
Osage, KS	20139	...	...	...	...	...	...	...	...	...	...	...	...
Osborne, KS	20141	...	...	...	...	...	...	...	...	...	...	...	...
Ottawa, KS	20143	...	...	...	...	...	...	...	...	...	...	...	...
Pawnee, KS	20145	...	...	...	...	...	...	...	...	...	...	...	...
Phillips, KS	20147	...	...	...	...	...	...	...	...	...	...	...	...
Pottawatomie, KS	20149	...	...	...	...	...	...	...	...	...	...	...	...
Pratt, KS	20151	...	...	...	...	...	...	...	...	...	...	...	...
Rawlins, KS	20153	...	...	...	...	...	...	...	...	...	...	...	...
Reno, KS	20155	43,146	46.5	87.0	3,138	88.7	17.9	-9.5	18.8	6.4	...	...	10.6
Republic, KS	20157	...	...	...	...	...	...	...	...	...	...	...	...
Rice, KS	20159	...	...	...	...	...	...	...	...	...	...	...	...
Riley, KS	20161	34,841	27.7	94.0	20,595	96.9	41.8	14.4	41.0	42.7	...	73.3	28.0
Rooks, KS	20163	...	...	...	...	...	...	...	...	...	...	...	...
Rush, KS	20165	...	...	...	...	...	...	...	...	...	...	...	...
Russell, KS	20167	...	...	...	...	...	...	...	...	...	...	...	...
Saline, KS	20169	36,340	45.3	87.4	2,744	67.2	22.4	-5.0	23.5	4.0	...	...	21.9
Scott, KS	20171	...	...	...	...	...	...	...	...	...	...	...	...
Sedgwick, KS	20173	300,280	41.7	87.8	30,805	79.9	27.2	-0.2	30.0	14.9	19.8	35.8	11.2
Seward, KS	20175	13,200	61.9	70.7	606	79.5	15.9	-11.5	23.7	...	...	...	8.3
Shawnee, KS	20177	115,669	41.6	89.8	11,272	72.3	29.7	2.3	32.0	19.4	20.0	55.6	11.1
Sheridan, KS	20179	...	...	...	...	...	...	...	...	...	...	...	...
Sherman, KS	20181	...	...	...	...	...	...	...	...	...	...	...	...
Smith, KS	20183	...	...	...	...	...	...	...	...	...	...	...	...
Stafford, KS	20185	...	...	...	...	...	...	...	...	...	...	...	...
Stanton, KS	20187	...	...	...	...	...	...	...	...	...	...	...	...
Stevens, KS	20189	...	...	...	...	...	...	...	...	...	...	...	...
Sumner, KS	20191	15,751	44.9	91.2	1,069	80.4	18.5	-8.9	18.7	...	...	...	3.2
Thomas, KS	20193	...	...	...	...	...	...	...	...	...	...	...	...
Trego, KS	20195	...	...	...	...	...	...	...	...	...	...	...	...
Wabaunsee, KS	20197	...	...	...	...	...	...	...	...	...	...	...	...
Wallace, KS	20199	...	...	...	...	...	...	...	...	...	...	...	...
Washington, KS	20201	...	...	...	...	...	...	...	...	...	...	...	...
Wichita, KS	20203	...	...	...	...	...	...	...	...	...	...	...	...
Wilson, KS	20205	...	...	...	...	...	...	...	...	...	...	...	...
Woodson, KS	20207	...	...	...	...	...	...	...	...	...	...	...	...
Wyandotte, KS	20209	95,962	59.9	78.3	6,330	75.8	14.2	-13.2	18.1	12.3	5.3	26.1	4.4
KENTUCKY	21000	2,840,521	54.4	80.4	25,5998	80.0	20.0	-7.4	20.2	13.4	12.3	53.9	14.9
Adair, KY	21001	...	...	...	...	...	...	...	...	...	...	...	...
Allen, KY	21003	...	...	...	...	...	...	...	...	...	...	...	...
Anderson, KY	21005	14,342	53.4	87.5	1,096	87.7	17.0	-10.4	17.4	...	...	...	...
Ballard, KY	21007	...	...	...	...	...	...	...	...	...	...	...	...
Barren, KY	21009	28,790	65.8	76.5	1,600	81.9	14.4	-13.0	14.4	...	...	...	...
Bath, KY	21011	...	...	...	...	...	...	...	...	...	...	...	...
Bell, KY	21013	20,139	67.4	65.4	1,516	70.2	12.5	-14.9	12.1	24.1	...	...	...
Boone, KY	21015	71,881	41.8	90.3	6,209	78.1	26.9	-0.5	26.4	38.8	...	51.9	17.9
Bourbon, KY	21017	...	...	...	...	...	...	...	...	...	...	...	...
Boyd, KY	21019	34,417	54.7	82.8	2,513	91.0	16.2	-11.2	16.4	10.8	...	...	...
Boyle, KY	21021	19,254	53.7	83.7	2,292	36.1	24.5	-2.9	26.3	10.6	...	...	...
Bracken, KY	21023	...	...	...	...	...	...	...	...	...	...	...	...
Breathitt, KY	21025	...	...	...	...	...	...	...	...	...	...	...	...
Breckinridge, KY	21027	...	...	...	...	...	...	...	...	...	...	...	...
Bullitt, KY	21029	50,023	58.9	82.5	4,049	73.1	11.4	-16.0	11.4	...	...	...	...
Butler, KY	21031	...	...	...	...	...	...	...	...	...	...	...	...
Caldwell, KY	21033	...	...	...	...	...	...	...	...	...	...	...	...

[3]May be of any race
... Not available

Table C-1. Population, School, and Student Characteristics by County—*Continued*

County	State/ County Code	County Type[1]	Population, 2009		Percent of related children 5-17 years in poverty, 2008	Percent of children under 19 years with no health insurance, 2007	Number of Schools and Students, 2008-2009			Resident enrollment, 2006-2008	
			Total	Percent 5–17 years			School Districts	Schools	Students	K–12 enrollment	
										Number	Percent public
			1	2	3	4	5	6	7	8	9
Calloway, KY	21035	7	36,348	12.5	18.2	12.7	4	11	4,815	4,989	87.2
Campbell, KY	21037	1	88,423	16.2	13.6	8.6	8	30	11,448	15,042	76.9
Carlisle, KY	21039	9	5,209	16.2	20.5	16.6	1	3	816	...	...
Carroll, KY	21041	6	10,703	17.9	20.8	9.0	1	6	1,986	...	...
Carter, KY	21043	6	26,771	17.4	27.7	8.6	1	11	5,000	4,866	92.8
Casey, KY	21045	9	16,498	17.9	33.1	10.6	2	6	2,433	...	...
Christian, KY	21047	3	80,938	19.8	25.0	15.0	1	20	9,144	17,558	87.9
Clark, KY	21049	2	36,159	17.1	19.2	9.0	1	14	5,568	5,899	93.1
Clay, KY	21051	7	23,629	16.8	45.7	6.0	1	11	3,680	...	...
Clinton, KY	21053	9	9,403	16.4	35.5	8.7	1	6	1,764	...	...
Crittenden, KY	21055	6	9,110	15.9	28.4	12.6	1	4	1,350	...	...
Cumberland, KY	21057	9	6,706	15.4	33.0	11.6	1	3	1,014	...	...
Daviess, KY	21059	3	95,394	17.7	16.0	9.3	3	36	15,421	16,281	88.7
Edmonson, KY	21061	3	11,926	16.1	25.1	13.2	1	5	2,068	...	...
Elliott, KY	21063	9	9,083	12.6	33.8	8.6	1	4	1,142	...	...
Estill, KY	21065	6	14,859	16.8	32.8	7.6	1	5	2,504	...	...
Fayette, KY	21067	2	296,545	14.6	17.4	11.4	3	71	36,110	40,487	84.2
Fleming, KY	21069	7	14,667	18.0	25.7	10.1	1	6	2,353	...	...
Floyd, KY	21071	7	41,899	15.9	38.1	6.2	1	17	6,446	6,462	93.2
Franklin, KY	21073	4	48,968	15.4	16.2	9.5	2	17	6,897	7,503	89.4
Fulton, KY	21075	7	6,814	15.5	38.7	6.9	2	4	1,061	...	...
Gallatin, KY	21077	1	8,202	18.6	22.2	13.4	1	5	1,593	...	...
Garrard, KY	21079	6	17,085	16.6	20.0	11.8	1	6	2,650	...	...
Grant, KY	21081	1	25,542	20.1	19.5	12.6	2	9	4,717	4,755	97.7
Graves, KY	21083	7	37,719	17.6	25.0	11.9	2	18	6,304	6,674	93.5
Grayson, KY	21085	6	25,581	16.8	24.7	8.6	1	7	4,274	4,253	92.3
Green, KY	21087	8	11,510	16.4	26.9	11.7	1	6	1,707	...	...
Greenup, KY	21089	2	38,020	16.1	19.8	9.4	3	18	6,466	6,055	94.9
Hancock, KY	21091	3	8,635	19.5	14.9	11.4	1	4	1,725	...	...
Hardin, KY	21093	3	99,770	18.0	16.9	13.3	3	30	16,335	18,279	92.9
Harlan, KY	21095	7	30,956	16.8	38.2	5.0	2	17	5,220	5,411	98.3
Harrison, KY	21097	6	18,794	17.4	19.3	9.1	1	8	3,208	...	...
Hart, KY	21099	8	18,396	17.9	30.1	10.5	1	6	2,395	...	...
Henderson, KY	21101	2	45,496	16.7	18.2	8.9	1	13	6,932	7,853	88.3
Henry, KY	21103	1	16,060	18.0	18.4	15.0	2	8	2,958	...	...
Hickman, KY	21105	9	4,851	15.9	23.6	13.2	1	2	809	...	...
Hopkins, KY	21107	4	46,167	16.5	25.0	10.1	3	19	7,861	7,924	93.2
Jackson, KY	21109	9	13,243	17.1	34.2	8.5	1	7	2,287	...	...
Jefferson, KY	21111	1	721,594	16.5	18.8	8.1	4	176	99,217	123,187	78.3
Jessamine, KY	21113	2	47,589	18.1	15.9	12.5	1	12	7,668	8,276	86.9
Johnson, KY	21115	7	23,827	17.2	31.6	7.0	2	15	4,566	3,698	96.0
Kenton, KY	21117	1	158,729	17.3	13.1	7.8	5	48	22,264	28,946	78.7
Knott, KY	21119	9	17,126	15.3	35.1	6.5	1	10	2,512	...	...
Knox, KY	21121	7	32,710	17.5	42.6	6.0	2	16	5,493	5,815	99.6
Larue, KY	21123	3	13,663	16.8	21.8	12.9	1	5	2,435	...	...
Laurel, KY	21125	7	57,749	17.8	24.4	7.6	2	21	9,815	9,954	90.8
Lawrence, KY	21127	6	16,573	16.5	31.6	6.6	1	7	2,457	...	...
Lee, KY	21129	9	7,339	14.7	43.1	5.4	1	6	1,140	...	...
Leslie, KY	21131	9	11,503	15.6	34.3	5.9	1	7	1,891	...	...
Letcher, KY	21133	9	23,633	15.4	37.3	6.6	2	12	3,836	3,810	96.2
Lewis, KY	21135	8	13,752	16.9	37.0	7.8	1	7	2,441	...	...
Lincoln, KY	21137	7	25,172	17.9	26.0	9.9	1	11	4,075	4,311	95.5
Livingston, KY	21139	9	9,598	14.4	17.2	12.0	1	4	1,302	...	...
Logan, KY	21141	6	27,174	17.9	20.1	10.5	2	12	4,752	4,611	93.9
Lyon, KY	21143	8	8,291	10.1	17.0	15.5	1	5	939	...	...
McCracken, KY	21145	5	65,880	16.1	20.9	10.0	2	22	10,206	10,702	88.3
McCreary, KY	21147	9	17,795	17.2	48.0	8.1	1	8	3,260	...	...
McLean, KY	21149	3	9,607	17.3	21.2	14.9	1	5	1,679	...	...
Madison, KY	21151	4	83,258	15.0	15.6	9.9	3	24	11,879	11,939	84.7
Magoffin, KY	21153	9	13,166	17.8	45.7	6.5	1	10	2,348	...	...
Marion, KY	21155	6	19,486	17.5	19.6	10.6	1	8	3,226	...	...
Marshall, KY	21157	7	31,200	15.0	14.9	10.5	1	12	4,838	4,709	97.3
Martin, KY	21159	8	13,070	16.0	41.0	6.0	1	8	2,235	...	...
Mason, KY	21161	6	17,378	16.8	23.5	8.4	1	5	2,819	...	...
Meade, KY	21163	1	26,501	19.9	14.1	15.0	1	12	4,979	5,310	97.1
Menifee, KY	21165	9	6,593	16.2	39.9	8.3	1	5	1,126	...	...
Mercer, KY	21167	6	21,920	17.9	16.9	10.8	2	10	3,693	3,801	98.3
Metcalfe, KY	21169	9	10,063	16.8	32.0	11.3	1	6	1,771	...	...
Monroe, KY	21171	9	11,569	17.2	31.1	10.4	1	6	2,025	...	...
Montgomery, KY	21173	6	25,835	17.7	21.2	8.9	1	10	4,687	4,342	92.7

[1]County type codes are from the Economic Research Service of the United States Department of Agriculture. See notes and definitions for more information.
... Not available

Table C-1. Population, School, and Student Characteristics by County—*Continued*

County	State/County Code	Characteristics of students, 2008-2009				Number of graduates, 2006-2007	Staff and students, 2008-2009			
		Percent with IEP[2]	Percent eligible for free or reduced lunch	Percent minority	Percent English Language Learners		Total staff	Number of teachers	Student/teacher ratio	Central admin. Staff
		10	11	12	13	14	15	16	17	18
Calloway, KY	21035	16.7	37.9	8.4	1.2	344	770	311	15.5	33
Campbell, KY	21037	18.3	42.6	5.0	0.7	761	1,657	760	15.1	83
Carlisle, KY	21039	18.8	54.5	3.1	...	52	143	62	13.2	4
Carroll, KY	21041	13.5	48.0	9.3	3.0	116	336	119	16.7	17
Carter, KY	21043	17.7	58.7	1.0	0.4	277	859	344	14.5	14
Casey, KY	21045	20.1	67.3	3.2	1.5	157	412	167	14.6	15
Christian, KY	21047	15.1	65.5	37.9	1.2	498	1,372	602	15.2	35
Clark, KY	21049	13.8	49.7	9.2	0.7	357	797	367	15.2	22
Clay, KY	21051	20.4	65.7	1.5	0.4	219	732	290	12.7	19
Clinton, KY	21053	18.8	67.6	3.5	1.9	97	320	117	15.1	18
Crittenden, KY	21055	17.6	46.5	2.4	0.1	75	193	81	16.7	11
Cumberland, KY	21057	21.5	69.7	3.1	0.1	74	180	76	13.3	6
Daviess, KY	21059	19.8	49.6	10.2	1.0	977	2,482	1,033	14.9	87
Edmonson, KY	21061	18.9	53.1	3.0	0.2	144	348	136	15.2	9
Elliott, KY	21063	15.0	70.7	1.3	0.1	69	191	85	13.4	6
Estill, KY	21065	14.6	66.2	1.1	...	149	363	163	15.4	11
Fayette, KY	21067	10.8	44.7	36.6	7.0	1,981	5,270	2,648	13.6	136
Fleming, KY	21069	15.9	58.4	3.7	0.7	153	373	154	15.3	15
Floyd, KY	21071	20.4	67.8	1.1	...	385	996	418	15.4	28
Franklin, KY	21073	14.3	44.6	14.7	1.4	424	1,023	453	15.2	33
Fulton, KY	21075	25.0	84.1	37.2	...	91	193	85	12.5	11
Gallatin, KY	21077	19.0	65.2	6.2	2.7	72	260	104	15.3	12
Garrard, KY	21079	16.8	45.6	5.5	0.5	143	406	182	14.6	13
Grant, KY	21081	13.7	52.2	2.7	0.9	264	677	277	17.0	28
Graves, KY	21083	14.5	53.4	14.6	4.9	406	941	402	15.7	28
Grayson, KY	21085	15.1	61.0	1.7	0.1	241	627	281	15.2	13
Green, KY	21087	16.2	61.6	2.5	0.1	123	282	116	14.7	8
Greenup, KY	21089	14.2	46.4	2.1	0.1	423	952	397	16.3	39
Hancock, KY	21091	15.5	43.4	3.4	0.1	95	269	108	16.0	13
Hardin, KY	21093	17.5	48.4	23.0	1.5	1,097	2,396	1,033	15.8	70
Harlan, KY	21095	19.9	71.3	3.4	0.1	304	814	338	15.4	36
Harrison, KY	21097	15.8	47.5	4.7	1.2	217	448	192	16.7	11
Hart, KY	21099	18.6	62.0	6.0	0.2	158	411	176	13.6	13
Henderson, KY	21101	16.2	53.0	12.2	0.8	438	1,104	445	15.6	32
Henry, KY	21103	13.4	49.8	9.6	1.2	147	414	178	16.6	26
Hickman, KY	21105	22.7	43.3	12.1	...	36	132	57	14.2	5
Hopkins, KY	21107	23.3	51.1	11.9	0.3	467	1,210	537	14.6	43
Jackson, KY	21109	25.9	88.8	0.6	...	132	418	160	14.3	14
Jefferson, KY	21111	14.1	55.6	43.5	5.0	5,057	14.223	6,180	16.1	502
Jessamine, KY	21113	16.1	47.5	7.6	2.2	384	1,177	507	15.1	33
Johnson, KY	21115	17.2	70.0	0.5	0.1	273	750	339	13.5	20
Kenton, KY	21117	17.7	43.5	11.3	1.7	1,282	3,037	1,364	16.3	84
Knott, KY	21119	18.1	72.2	1.3	...	145	422	169	14.9	7
Knox, KY	21121	18.8	63.7	1.9	0.2	289	862	375	14.6	24
Larue, KY	21123	18.9	55.9	7.1	1.6	157	358	152	16.0	9
Laurel, KY	21125	17.1	57.7	2.5	0.1	499	1,399	572	17.2	40
Lawrence, KY	21127	17.2	65.3	0.7	...	163	378	170	14.5	13
Lee, KY	21129	18.4	75.9	1.0	0.1	75	190	75	15.2	11
Leslie, KY	21131	22.0	65.5	0.7	0.1	113	323	121	15.6	9
Letcher, KY	21133	24.2	65.4	0.9	...	243	661	270	14.2	29
Lewis, KY	21135	14.4	68.0	0.7	...	141	413	166	14.7	11
Lincoln, KY	21137	20.3	60.9	4.3	0.5	283	772	306	13.3	24
Livingston, KY	21139	16.4	49.5	2.2	1.1	96	236	93	14.0	8
Logan, KY	21141	17.6	51.3	10.6	1.2	297	731	312	15.2	26
Lyon, KY	21143	13.1	37.0	7.0	0.7	72	146	62	15.1	4
McCracken, KY	21145	13.8	50.0	21.7	0.6	582	1,350	626	16.3	47
McCreary, KY	21147	19.9	84.4	3.6	...	315	537	214	15.2	14
McLean, KY	21149	18.6	58.0	2.3	0.8	111	265	115	14.6	5
Madison, KY	21151	18.3	45.8	8.2	0.9	631	1,595	757	15.7	37
Magoffin, KY	21153	19.0	83.6	0.7	0.2	125	408	173	13.6	17
Marion, KY	21155	19.2	55.1	10.6	1.7	176	476	212	15.2	14
Marshall, KY	21157	13.7	39.8	1.1	0.3	326	700	316	15.3	34
Martin, KY	21159	20.5	67.3	0.3	...	124	403	145	15.4	16
Mason, KY	21161	18.2	56.6	10.7	1.0	193	411	199	14.2	15
Meade, KY	21163	15.5	45.0	4.1	0.3	312	681	290	17.2	13
Menifee, KY	21165	22.5	75.8	5.1	...	68	197	79	14.3	11
Mercer, KY	21167	17.5	45.1	6.7	1.1	232	558	250	14.8	25
Metcalfe, KY	21169	17.4	70.1	2.4	0.3	103	253	108	16.4	13
Monroe, KY	21171	15.0	66.1	5.4	1.1	113	373	133	15.2	13
Montgomery, KY	21173	14.0	55.5	5.5	1.7	233	643	289	16.2	40

[2]IEP= Individual Education Program. See notes and definitions for more information
... Not available

Table C-1. Population, School, and Student Characteristics by County—*Continued*

County	State/County Code	Revenues, 2007-2008				Current expenditures, 2007-2008			Resident population 16 to 19 years, 2006-2008			
		Total revenue ($1,000's)	Percentage of revenue from			Amount ($1,000's)	Amount per student	Percent for instruction	Total population 16 to 19 years	Percent enrolled in school	Percent high school graduates, not enrolled in school	Percent not enrolled, not grads, not employed or not in labor force
			Federal gov't	State gov't	Local gov't							
	19		20	21	22	23	24	25	26	27	28	29
Calloway, KY	21035	46,403	12.5	60.0	27.6	39,333	8,424	61.2	...	...	...	...
Campbell, KY	21037	119,910	9.0	50.8	40.2	108,409	9,429	57.6	...	...	...	...
Carlisle, KY	21039	8,131	7.9	73.7	18.4	7,241	8,798	58.3	...	...	...	...
Carroll, KY	21041	21,898	10.9	50.9	38.1	18,095	9,265	57.3	...	...	...	...
Carter, KY	21043	47,165	11.1	76.3	12.5	42,319	8,319	62.0	...	...	...	...
Casey, KY	21045	27,101	12.3	72.4	15.3	21,294	8,639	64.1	...	...	...	...
Christian, KY	21047	87,148	13.6	64.7	21.7	78,441	8,434	60.7	4342	66.7	21.6	7.0
Clark, KY	21049	47,110	8.9	60.0	31.1	41,872	7,436	63.6	...	...	...	...
Clay, KY	21051	39,514	15.9	72.3	11.8	36,648	9,815	59.6	...	...	...	...
Clinton, KY	21053	19,624	19.2	62.5	18.3	17,631	10,402	63.7	...	...	...	...
Crittenden, KY	21055	12,107	11.4	68.5	20.0	11,127	8,230	51.6	...	...	...	...
Cumberland, KY	21057	11,623	13.5	68.6	17.9	10,155	9,544	59.6	...	...	...	...
Daviess, KY	21059	155,011	9.2	60.5	30.3	140,315	9,075	59.3	5280	81.9	13.7	3.4
Edmonson, KY	21061	20,261	10.0	73.7	16.3	18,137	8,682	60.9	...	...	...	...
Elliott, KY	21063	12,413	13.9	74.0	12.1	11,045	9,546	58.6	...	...	...	...
Estill, KY	21065	24,511	13.2	72.5	14.3	21,182	8,356	57.3	...	...	...	...
Fayette, KY	21067	392,707	7.8	37.2	55.0	326,008	9,205	60.0	15428	86.6	7.1	4.2
Fleming, KY	21069	22,184	12.2	71.8	16.0	20,203	8,390	58.8	...	...	...	...
Floyd, KY	21071	65,509	14.1	67.8	18.1	57,130	8,715	56.1	...	...	...	...
Franklin, KY	21073	67,235	7.4	57.6	35.1	56,973	8,293	59.0	...	...	...	...
Fulton, KY	21075	14,001	14.2	67.4	18.4	10,990	10,037	61.4	...	...	...	...
Gallatin, KY	21077	16,755	8.7	62.7	28.6	13,527	8,391	54.1	...	...	...	...
Garrard, KY	21079	25,767	8.9	66.9	24.2	21,823	8,050	61.6	...	...	...	...
Grant, KY	21081	45,252	10.0	68.5	21.5	38,523	8,047	58.9	...	...	...	...
Graves, KY	21083	58,179	11.3	68.3	20.4	52,481	8,270	61.5	...	...	...	...
Grayson, KY	21085	39,240	11.0	71.2	17.9	33,298	7,778	60.8	...	...	...	...
Green, KY	21087	16,512	10.8	72.3	17.0	14,387	8,625	58.1	...	...	...	...
Greenup, KY	21089	59,619	9.3	68.7	22.0	52,468	8,179	59.4	...	...	...	...
Hancock, KY	21091	16,470	6.9	59.9	33.2	14,280	8,566	57.1	...	...	...	...
Hardin, KY	21093	155,648	9.4	62.4	28.3	133,804	8,186	58.8	5972	76.6	17.8	4.9
Harlan, KY	21095	53,072	16.1	69.7	14.2	45,035	8,388	57.4	...	...	...	...
Harrison, KY	21097	27,288	9.4	68.7	21.9	25,086	7,747	58.7	...	...	...	...
Hart, KY	21099	25,519	12.3	70.9	16.8	22,388	9,267	53.9	...	...	...	...
Henderson, KY	21101	65,729	9.3	62.3	28.4	59,386	8,418	59.6	...	...	...	...
Henry, KY	21103	27,046	10.1	65.4	24.5	23,297	8,011	60.2	...	...	...	...
Hickman, KY	21105	8,545	12.4	65.2	22.4	7,327	9,382	57.3	...	...	...	...
Hopkins, KY	21107	77,340	10.6	68.6	20.9	66,473	8,340	62.3	...	...	...	...
Jackson, KY	21109	25,261	19.4	72.1	8.5	22,316	9,549	59.8	...	...	...	...
Jefferson, KY	21111	109,4455	10.4	41.8	47.8	961,086	9,984	53.7	35258	83.7	9.2	4.9
Jessamine, KY	21113	72,025	9.2	54.4	36.4	62,306	8,296	60.8	...	...	...	...
Johnson, KY	21115	46,483	11.4	70.3	18.3	41,610	9,179	65.9	...	...	...	...
Kenton, KY	21117	215,633	9.1	51.1	39.8	192,732	8,760	60.3	8228	85.9	7.1	4.1
Knott, KY	21119	25,021	15.4	60.6	24.0	23,229	9,207	57.5	...	...	...	...
Knox, KY	21121	55,012	13.9	72.7	13.4	48,691	8,921	61.2	...	...	...	...
Larue, KY	21123	20,783	10.7	68.1	21.3	16,424	6,655	60.3	...	...	...	...
Laurel, KY	21125	89,123	11.6	67.0	21.3	77,099	7,801	58.4	2665	73.7	14.0	10.2
Lawrence, KY	21127	23,993	12.7	71.8	15.5	22,542	8,788	60.7	...	...	...	...
Lee, KY	21129	11,691	19.3	68.9	11.8	11,113	10,021	52.6	...	...	...	...
Leslie, KY	21131	21,357	14.3	67.1	18.6	19,151	9,811	55.1	...	...	...	...
Letcher, KY	21133	41,575	15.3	67.5	17.2	36,827	9,504	58.0	...	...	...	...
Lewis, KY	21135	24,255	15.0	73.2	11.8	21,887	8,682	60.0	...	...	...	...
Lincoln, KY	21137	42,624	17.0	68.9	14.1	40,010	9,264	63.8	...	...	...	...
Livingston, KY	21139	11,368	11.0	55.4	33.6	10,688	8,006	60.2	...	...	...	...
Logan, KY	21141	45,893	10.9	67.8	21.2	40,222	8,475	61.3	...	...	...	...
Lyon, KY	21143	9,062	8.6	51.2	40.2	8,260	8,194	57.9	...	...	...	...
McCracken, KY	21145	97,976	11.3	53.9	34.8	85,777	8,700	60.5	3002	81.3	10.7	5.8
McCreary, KY	21147	32,947	15.8	74.5	9.6	29,715	9,152	60.1	...	...	...	...
McLean, KY	21149	17,405	8.9	72.3	18.7	13,119	7,932	56.6	...	...	...	...
Madison, KY	21151	109,457	9.7	62.1	28.2	93,745	7,920	63.0	...	...	...	...
Magoffin, KY	21153	27,271	13.5	69.6	17.0	22,136	9,189	56.1	...	...	...	...
Marion, KY	21155	31,007	9.5	66.8	23.7	27,823	8,725	65.9	...	...	...	...
Marshall, KY	21157	43,327	8.3	59.1	32.6	39,241	7,982	63.7	...	...	...	...
Martin, KY	21159	23,151	14.4	67.1	18.4	20,840	9,613	55.4	...	...	...	...
Mason, KY	21161	27,068	9.3	61.5	29.2	23,308	8,384	63.5	...	...	...	...
Meade, KY	21163	44,852	7.6	72.2	20.1	37,486	7,500	60.2	...	...	...	...
Menifee, KY	21165	11,599	12.7	75.2	12.2	10,322	9,282	58.2	...	...	...	...
Mercer, KY	21167	39,361	7.9	65.8	26.3	31,781	8,514	62.8	...	...	...	...
Metcalfe, KY	21169	17,228	14.0	68.7	17.3	14,324	8,043	56.5	...	...	...	...
Monroe, KY	21171	21,756	13.2	71.7	15.2	19,873	9,838	57.2	...	...	...	...
Montgomery, KY	21173	42,596	10.9	66.2	22.9	35,518	7,769	62.7	...	...	...	...

... Not available

Table C-1. Population, School, and Student Characteristics by County—*Continued*

County	State/County Code	High school graduates, 2006-2008			College enrollment, 2006-2008		College graduates, 2006-2008 (percent)						
		Population 25 years and over	High school diploma or less (percent)	High school diploma or more (percent)	Number	Percent public	Bachelor's degree or more	+/- U.S. percent with Bachelor's degree or more	Non-Hispanic White	Black or African American	American Indian and Alaska Native	Asian, Hawaiian, and Pacific Islander	Hispanic or Latino[3]
		30	31	32	33	34	35	36	37	38	39	40	41
Calloway, KY	21035	21,942	48.0	85.8	6,904	96.4	28.0	0.6	27.3	...	...	...	...
Campbell, KY	21037	57,264	47.1	87.9	7,545	90.4	26.2	-1.2	26.1	11.8	...	...	...
Carlisle, KY	21039	...	...	...	...	...	...	...	...	...	...	...	...
Carroll, KY	21041	...	...	...	...	...	...	...	...	...	...	...	...
Carter, KY	21043	18,504	67.3	73.5	1,628	53.1	11.6	-15.8	11.7	...	...	...	...
Casey, KY	21045	...	...	...	...	...	...	...	...	...	...	...	...
Christian, KY	21047	44,905	53.8	82.2	3,729	80.0	14.2	-13.2	15.4	9.7	...	...	6.7
Clark, KY	21049	24,538	54.8	82.1	1,493	92.0	18.4	-9.0	19.1	4.3	...	...	...
Clay, KY	21051	15,213	82.8	56.2	...	...	7.7	-19.7	7.2	...	...	...	...
Clinton, KY	21053	...	...	...	...	...	...	...	...	...	...	...	...
Crittenden, KY	21055	...	...	...	...	...	...	...	...	...	...	...	...
Cumberland, KY	21057	...	...	...	...	...	...	...	...	...	...	...	...
Daviess, KY	21059	62,465	51.2	85.9	4,857	76.5	18.5	-8.9	19.0	5.7	...	...	...
Edmonson, KY	21061	...	...	...	...	...	...	...	...	...	...	...	...
Elliott, KY	21063	...	...	...	...	...	...	...	...	...	...	...	...
Estill, KY	21065	...	...	...	...	...	...	...	...	...	...	...	...
Fayette, KY	21067	182,250	32.7	88.3	33,155	85.6	39.4	12.0	42.8	17.0	...	76.2	18.3
Fleming, KY	21069	...	...	...	...	...	...	...	...	...	...	...	...
Floyd, KY	21071	29,401	68.6	66.2	1,357	80.9	11.5	-15.9	11.5	...	...	...	...
Franklin, KY	21073	33,389	47.9	85.3	2,490	91.0	25.2	-2.2	24.1	28.6	...	46.0	...
Fulton, KY	21075	...	...	...	...	...	...	...	...	...	...	...	...
Gallatin, KY	21077	...	...	...	...	...	...	...	...	...	...	...	...
Garrard, KY	21079	...	...	...	...	...	...	...	...	...	...	...	...
Grant, KY	21081	16,433	65.8	76.2	989	73.2	11.1	-16.3	11.2	...	...	...	...
Graves, KY	21083	25,750	60.7	78.2	1,850	84.4	13.1	-14.3	13.8	1.0	...	...	...
Grayson, KY	21085	17,619	73.0	71.1	884	89.6	5.6	-21.8	5.5	...	...	...	...
Green, KY	21087	...	...	...	...	...	...	...	...	...	...	...	...
Greenup, KY	21089	26,402	58.3	80.5	1,391	89.4	14.6	-12.8	14.4	...	...	...	...
Hancock, KY	21091	...	...	...	...	...	...	...	...	...	...	...	...
Hardin, KY	21093	62,633	47.2	86.9	4,989	88.5	18.4	-9.0	19.0	12.8	...	29.7	14.3
Harlan, KY	21095	21,288	68.9	67.0	1,212	73.3	11.4	-16.0	11.7	3.0	...	...	...
Harrison, KY	21097	...	...	...	...	...	...	...	...	...	...	...	...
Hart, KY	21099	...	...	...	...	...	...	...	...	...	...	...	...
Henderson, KY	21101	31,258	55.6	83.3	1,569	86.6	16.2	-11.2	16.7	7.8	...	...	...
Henry, KY	21103	...	...	...	...	...	...	...	...	...	...	...	...
Hickman, KY	21105	...	...	...	...	...	...	...	...	...	...	...	...
Hopkins, KY	21107	32,256	59.5	76.8	1,878	92.8	13.4	-14.0	13.7	6.1	...	...	...
Jackson, KY	21109	...	...	...	...	...	...	...	...	...	...	...	...
Jefferson, KY	21111	479,026	43.6	86.7	41,710	74.9	27.9	0.5	30.7	14.0	5.1	57.5	17.9
Jessamine, KY	21113	29,481	47.4	84.9	3,669	48.4	27.6	0.2	28.0	13.3	...	...	...
Johnson, KY	21115	16,596	68.4	68.2	895	100.0	11.0	-16.4	11.0	...	...	...	...
Kenton, KY	21117	102,925	43.4	87.1	9,539	76.7	27.8	0.4	28.4	15.6	...	41.7	23.2
Knott, KY	21119	...	...	...	...	...	...	...	...	...	...	...	...
Knox, KY	21121	21,557	78.8	63.7	1,522	48.6	8.7	-18.7	8.6	...	...	...	...
Larue, KY	21123	...	...	...	...	...	...	...	...	...	...	...	...
Laurel, KY	21125	38,686	64.1	71.7	2,632	80.4	14.4	-13.0	14.4	...	...	...	...
Lawrence, KY	21127	...	...	...	...	...	...	...	...	...	...	...	...
Lee, KY	21129	...	...	...	...	...	...	...	...	...	...	...	...
Leslie, KY	21131	...	...	...	...	...	...	...	...	...	...	...	...
Letcher, KY	21133	17,020	66.4	69.7	1,023	82.4	11.4	-16.0	11.4	...	...	...	...
Lewis, KY	21135	...	...	...	...	...	...	...	...	...	...	...	...
Lincoln, KY	21137	17,224	66.7	72.1	904	91.9	11.8	-15.6	12.0	...	...	...	...
Livingston, KY	21139	...	...	...	...	...	...	...	...	...	...	...	...
Logan, KY	21141	18,837	69.8	74.0	822	85.8	10.5	-16.9	10.4	...	...	...	...
Lyon, KY	21143	...	...	...	...	...	...	...	...	...	...	...	...
McCracken, KY	21145	45,214	45.3	85.1	3,209	81.1	19.9	-7.5	21.5	5.6	...	...	...
McCreary, KY	21147	...	...	...	...	...	...	...	...	...	...	...	...
McLean, KY	21149	...	...	...	...	...	...	...	...	...	...	...	...
Madison, KY	21151	50,039	46.2	83.3	12,490	84.2	28.2	0.8	28.2	29.2	...	...	...
Magoffin, KY	21153	...	...	...	...	...	...	...	...	...	...	...	...
Marion, KY	21155	...	...	...	...	...	...	...	...	...	...	...	...
Marshall, KY	21157	22,261	58.9	82.5	1,298	89.5	13.5	-13.9	13.3	...	...	...	...
Martin, KY	21159	...	...	...	...	...	...	...	...	...	...	...	...
Mason, KY	21161	...	...	...	...	...	...	...	...	...	...	...	...
Meade, KY	21163	18,151	57.7	83.7	1,616	88.3	12.4	-15.0	12.4	...	...	...	...
Menifee, KY	21165	...	...	...	...	...	...	...	...	...	...	...	...
Mercer, KY	21167	15,295	58.8	82.3	684	59.9	16.1	-11.3	17.3	...	...	...	...
Metcalfe, KY	21169	...	...	...	...	...	...	...	...	...	...	...	...
Monroe, KY	21171	...	...	...	...	...	...	...	...	...	...	...	...
Montgomery, KY	21173	17,175	62.6	75.2	850	74.6	14.1	-13.3	14.0	...	...	...	...

[3]May be of any race
... Not available

Table C-1.   Population, School, and Student Characteristics by County—*Continued*

County	State/ County Code	County Type[1]	Population, 2009		Percent of related children 5-17 years in poverty, 2008	Percent of children under 19 years with no health insurance, 2007	Number of Schools and Students, 2008-2009			Resident enrollment, 2006-2008 K-12 enrollment	
			Total	Percent 5-17 years			School Districts	Schools	Students	Number	Percent public
	1	2		3	4	5	6	7	8	9	
Morgan, KY	21175	7	14,092	14.8	31.6	8.3	1	9	2,146	...	...
Muhlenberg, KY	21177	6	31,274	16.4	26.8	10.1	1	13	5,179	5,100	94.4
Nelson, KY	21179	1	43,550	18.7	14.9	12.4	3	22	10,106	7,716	85.3
Nicholas, KY	21181	8	6,874	17.2	22.6	10.9	1	2	1,253	...	...
Ohio, KY	21183	6	23,534	17.0	25.8	9.6	1	9	4,039	3,963	92.5
Oldham, KY	21185	1	58,095	21.0	4.9	11.6	1	26	11,806	10,750	86.5
Owen, KY	21187	8	11,380	17.6	20.0	14.1	1	4	1,907	...	...
Owsley, KY	21189	9	4,619	16.2	50.3	5.2	1	2	789	...	...
Pendleton, KY	21191	1	14,887	18.6	17.4	13.9	1	4	2,729	...	...
Perry, KY	21193	7	29,136	16.9	35.2	6.1	3	18	5,314	5,153	98.7
Pike, KY	21195	7	65,446	16.2	28.5	7.1	2	30	11,239	10,469	96.4
Powell, KY	21197	6	13,566	16.6	34.2	10.2	1	5	2,478	...	...
Pulaski, KY	21199	5	60,853	16.1	30.4	9.9	3	22	10,161	9,993	93.7
Robertson, KY	21201	8	2,237	15.8	27.9	11.5	1	2	403	...	...
Rockcastle, KY	21203	7	16,504	16.4	33.6	7.8	1	7	3,048	...	...
Rowan, KY	21205	7	22,872	13.5	25.2	10.2	1	11	3,270	3,405	88.5
Russell, KY	21207	9	17,377	16.1	30.6	10.0	1	7	3,009	...	...
Scott, KY	21209	2	45,841	18.9	12.3	10.1	1	13	8,059	8,208	92.0
Shelby, KY	21211	1	42,078	17.7	13.9	14.4	3	12	6,496	7,260	84.7
Simpson, KY	21213	6	17,019	17.7	17.8	9.7	1	6	2,964	...	...
Spencer, KY	21215	1	17,737	18.6	9.2	16.2	...	...	...	...	...
Taylor, KY	21217	7	24,420	15.7	23.9	8.2	2	7	3,759	3,670	97.2
Todd, KY	21219	8	12,253	19.3	25.1	16.0	1	6	2,162	...	...
Trigg, KY	21221	3	13,290	15.3	17.9	11.7	1	4	2,127	...	...
Trimble, KY	21223	1	8,958	17.8	18.2	11.5	1	4	1,513	...	...
Union, KY	21225	6	14,990	18.4	19.1	12.1	1	10	2,410	...	...
Warren, KY	21227	3	108,669	16.1	18.9	12.9	4	40	16,977	16,170	91.0
Washington, KY	21229	8	11,257	18.1	19.8	12.9	1	5	1,743	...	...
Wayne, KY	21231	7	20,748	17.1	33.2	7.4	2	12	3,478	3,846	96.7
Webster, KY	21233	2	13,706	16.4	20.8	12.6	1	8	2,283	...	...
Whitley, KY	21235	7	38,813	17.7	32.6	6.7	4	22	8,226	6,952	96.0
Wolfe, KY	21237	9	7,099	17.6	52.1	7.2	1	5	1,252	...	...
Woodford, KY	21239	2	24,986	18.0	10.9	14.2	1	8	4,074	4,231	85.0
LOUISIANA	22000	X	4,492,076	17.9	22.9	14.7	114	1,660	684,873	821,012	82.9
Acadia, LA	22001	4	60,095	19.8	24.8	13.2	1	29	9,334	12,185	80.1
Allen, LA	22003	6	25,636	16.8	22.0	12.9	1	14	4,196	4,568	93.4
Ascension, LA	22005	2	104,822	20.6	12.6	14.4	1	27	19,104	20,935	87.3
Assumption, LA	22007	6	22,874	18.0	23.5	12.1	1	11	4,006	4,381	81.3
Avoyelles, LA	22009	6	42,511	18.3	28.4	13.3	2	17	6,890	8,146	89.3
Beauregard, LA	22011	6	35,419	19.2	18.4	17.9	1	15	5,959	6,849	92.4
Bienville, LA	22013	6	14,729	17.0	27.0	13.3	1	11	2,207	...	...
Bossier, LA	22015	2	111,492	18.2	16.8	19.7	1	38	19,707	20,998	94.9
Caddo, LA	22017	2	253,623	17.9	25.3	18.8	1	78	42,610	47,185	90.4
Calcasieu, LA	22019	3	187,554	18.4	18.7	13.9	2	68	33,996	34,861	88.2
Caldwell, LA	22021	8	10,439	17.0	25.5	16.9	1	8	1,715	...	...
Cameron, LA	22023	3	6,584	18.0	15.2	23.0	...	...	...	...	...
Catahoula, LA	22025	9	10,460	17.3	32.8	16.5	1	12	1,674	...	...
Claiborne, LA	22027	7	16,118	15.6	38.0	14.5	1	11	2,349	...	...
Concordia, LA	22029	7	18,989	18.8	32.7	10.8	1	13	3,906	...	...
De Soto, LA	22031	2	26,401	18.2	24.4	15.6	1	17	4,841	5,023	93.2
East Baton Rouge, LA	22033	2	434,633	17.3	23.0	13.7	13	158	58,618	78,783	73.2
East Carroll, LA	22035	7	8,102	18.6	54.2	10.6	1	7	1,410	...	...
East Feliciana, LA	22037	2	20,970	15.6	23.0	20.5	1	10	2,228	3,659	69.4
Evangeline, LA	22039	6	35,330	20.1	28.6	10.5	1	14	5,997	7,450	83.4
Franklin, LA	22041	7	19,807	17.9	36.7	12.3	1	10	3,313	3,640	86.7
Grant, LA	22043	3	20,164	19.4	20.5	20.8	1	11	3,457	...	...
Iberia, LA	22045	4	75,101	20.2	25.5	14.7	1	36	13,797	14,866	86.3
Iberville, LA	22047	2	32,505	16.4	26.6	12.9	1	11	4,265	6,146	76.6
Jackson, LA	22049	6	15,063	16.4	24.0	15.7	1	7	2,242	...	...
Jefferson, LA	22051	1	443,342	16.5	18.8	14.0	3	94	44,368	74,262	66.5
Jefferson Davis, LA	22053	6	31,097	20.1	20.2	13.3	1	15	5,839	6,124	90.4
Lafayette, LA	22055	3	210,954	17.8	17.9	15.8	1	48	29,653	37,674	76.1
Lafourche, LA	22057	3	93,682	18.0	19.9	13.0	2	40	15,005	16,621	81.6
La Salle, LA	22059	6	13,964	18.7	21.0	15.1	1	11	2,607	...	...
Lincoln, LA	22061	4	43,286	14.8	25.6	16.5	3	21	6,703	6,357	90.4
Livingston, LA	22063	2	123,326	20.0	13.8	15.5	1	43	24,131	23,478	93.2
Madison, LA	22065	7	11,385	19.1	45.2	12.8	1	7	2,058	...	...
Morehouse, LA	22067	6	28,223	18.0	35.3	12.2	1	16	4,746	5,438	93.8
Natchitoches, LA	22069	6	39,255	17.3	34.3	15.0	2	19	7,098	6,947	88.0
Orleans, LA	22071	1	354,850	14.2	34.9	11.9	24	110	35,101	55,858	80.7

[1]County type codes are from the Economic Research Service of the United States Department of Agriculture. See notes and definitions for more information.
... Not available

Table C-1. Population, School, and Student Characteristics by County—*Continued*

County	State/County Code	Characteristics of students, 2008-2009				Number of graduates, 2006-2007	Staff and students, 2008-2009			
		Percent with IEP[2]	Percent eligible for free or reduced lunch	Percent minority	Percent English Language Learners		Total staff	Number of teachers	Student/teacher ratio	Central admin. Staff
		10	11	12	13	14	15	16	17	18
Morgan, KY	21175	21.1	70.8	1.2	...	146	373	152	14.1	18
Muhlenberg, KY	21177	15.9	52.3	5.8	0.2	359	833	368	14.1	22
Nelson, KY	21179	16.2	41.9	9.8	0.7	422	1,362	580	17.4	48
Nicholas, KY	21181	14.8	35.6	1.0	...	81	181	83	15.1	13
Ohio, KY	21183	15.5	59.3	4.3	2.9	258	665	250	16.2	19
Oldham, KY	21185	15.3	17.1	7.7	2.1	748	1,648	710	16.6	83
Owen, KY	21187	13.9	51.5	3.7	1.4	118	272	121	15.8	5
Owsley, KY	21189	19.3	87.7	0.8	...	47	181	82	9.6	8
Pendleton, KY	21191	17.7	47.5	1.9	0.1	207	427	179	15.2	19
Perry, KY	21193	19.3	60.1	3.2	...	324	901	366	14.5	26
Pike, KY	21195	14.9	62.8	1.5	0.1	718	1,790	711	15.8	103
Powell, KY	21197	18.7	69.2	1.0	0.1	157	392	170	14.6	15
Pulaski, KY	21199	14.8	54.5	4.5	0.7	595	1,540	652	15.6	50
Robertson, KY	21201	17.4	55.6	0.7	...	23	67	31	13.0	3
Rockcastle, KY	21203	19.9	61.5	0.8	...	204	494	195	15.6	18
Rowan, KY	21205	18.6	58.0	3.7	0.8	182	499	215	15.2	16
Russell, KY	21207	19.0	68.1	3.2	1.0	180	508	214	14.1	22
Scott, KY	21209	16.3	1.8	10.0	2.0	405	1,041	484	16.7	31
Shelby, KY	21211	16.7	40.9	23.5	8.6	335	872	413	15.7	34
Simpson, KY	21213	12.4	51.5	14.3	1.1	222	450	180	16.5	19
Spencer, KY	21215	...	42.0	3.8	...	163	...	...		26
Taylor, KY	21217	16.6	55.0	7.4	0.9	229	576	247	15.2	26
Todd, KY	21219	19.0	59.4	15.0	2.3	120	343	136	15.9	8
Trigg, KY	21221	13.4	52.8	12.7	0.2	127	318	132	16.1	17
Trimble, KY	21223	14.5	49.1	3.0	0.7	111	231	96	15.8	7
Union, KY	21225	21.1	53.2	15.5	...	169	403	154	15.6	17
Warren, KY	21227	13.6	45.5	20.1	7.8	966	2,384	1,068	15.9	66
Washington, KY	21229	20.9	58.8	15.7	2.6	125	279	123	14.2	11
Wayne, KY	21231	17.1	74.4	5.8	2.0	197	600	208	16.7	32
Webster, KY	21233	16.6	50.5	9.2	3.8	141	379	144	15.9	9
Whitley, KY	21235	16.7	60.2	1.1	0.1	474	1,293	557	14.8	50
Wolfe, KY	21237	26.3	78.7	0.8	...	66	240	92	13.6	10
Woodford, KY	21239	13.1	30.9	13.6	4.9	267	534	241	16.9	11
LOUISIANA	22000	12.6	64.9	51.2	1.8	36,241	100,867	49,375	13.9	3,139
Acadia, LA	22001	13.0	62.7	30.3	0.4	483	1,414	632	14.8	41
Allen, LA	22003	10.5	61.6	28.5	0.4	219	684	347	12.1	13
Ascension, LA	22005	12.5	43.8	36.3	1.2	908	2,604	1,333	14.3	53
Assumption, LA	22007	13.7	65.9	44.7	0.8	236	636	294	13.6	19
Avoyelles, LA	22009	9.0	81.3	46.1	0.1	312	806	439	15.7	19
Beauregard, LA	22011	15.4	51.3	20.7	0.2	349	869	426	14.0	20
Bienville, LA	22013	10.7	72.5	59.1	0.7	127	396	197	11.2	13
Bossier, LA	22015	11.0	43.0	37.2	2.8	1,063	2,729	1,311	15.0	59
Caddo, LA	22017	10.9	63.1	67.2	0.9	2,292	6,659	2,913	14.6	193
Calcasieu, LA	22019	15.6	58.1	38.8	0.9	1,762	5,310	2,618	13.0	155
Caldwell, LA	22021	15.1	64.8	19.2	0.2	100	300	139	12.3	8
Cameron, LA	22023	...	60.9	6.1	...	123	...	...		...
Catahoula, LA	22025	9.9	72.1	42.8	...	95	274	123	13.6	10
Claiborne, LA	22027	16.7	76.7	70.1	0.5	142	402	188	12.5	12
Concordia, LA	22029	10.1	73.4	52.4	0.4	181	601	274	14.3	27
De Soto, LA	22031	12.2	65.9	53.2	1.4	254	794	358	13.5	23
East Baton Rouge, LA	22033	12.1	75.1	79.0	2.3	2,621	8,573	4,292	13.7	289
East Carroll, LA	22035	12.0	91.5	96.6	...	93	269	104	13.6	11
East Feliciana, LA	22037	14.1	85.2	76.0	...	133	374	159	14.0	16
Evangeline, LA	22039	15.1	76.5	42.1	0.1	236	895	436	13.8	26
Franklin, LA	22041	11.0	81.2	52.5	...	144	511	227	14.6	19
Grant, LA	22043	15.6	62.5	14.6	...	216	456	229	15.1	13
Iberia, LA	22045	13.4	67.0	53.1	1.5	732	1,925	1,036	13.3	57
Iberville, LA	22047	12.3	83.6	76.1	0.6	209	730	364	11.7	20
Jackson, LA	22049	9.6	58.3	38.3	...	137	335	159	14.1	12
Jefferson, LA	22051	12.1	74.8	68.3	9.6	2,165	6,799	3,178	14.0	253
Jefferson Davis, LA	22053	15.4	52.9	25.3	0.2	341	866	396	14.7	24
Lafayette, LA	22055	10.3	60.3	48.3	2.6	1,736	4,270	2,212	13.4	130
Lafourche, LA	22057	10.7	60.7	30.5	1.3	869	2,415	1,094	13.7	49
La Salle, LA	22059	9.1	48.9	12.1	...	139	405	192	13.6	11
Lincoln, LA	22061	11.8	58.4	53.0	1.1	418	965	535	12.5	18
Livingston, LA	22063	13.0	50.8	8.9	0.9	1,178	3,201	1,612	15.0	51
Madison, LA	22065	11.4	90.2	93.4	...	83	301	119	17.3	12
Morehouse, LA	22067	16.2	76.9	65.3	0.4	192	700	344	13.8	20
Natchitoches, LA	22069	11.8	67.1	60.6	0.1	443	913	502	14.1	26
Orleans, LA	22071	8.7	83.4	94.8	2.0	1,615	4,266	2,456	14.3	211

[2]IEP= Individual Education Program. See notes and definitions for more information
... Not available

Table C-1. Population, School, and Student Characteristics by County—*Continued*

County	State/County Code	Revenues, 2007-2008				Current expenditures, 2007-2008			Resident population 16 to 19 years, 2006-2008			
		Total revenue ($1,000's)	Percentage of revenue from			Amount ($1,000's)	Amount per student	Percent for instruction	Total population 16 to 19 years	Percent enrolled in school	Percent high school graduates, not enrolled in school	Percent not enrolled, not grads, not employed or not in labor force
			Federal gov't	State gov't	Local gov't							
	19	20	21	22	23	24	25	26	27	28	29	
Morgan, KY	21175	22,591	13.7	71.5	14.8	20,068	9,193	56.2	...	...	...	...
Muhlenberg, KY	21177	54,333	8.5	62.1	29.4	47,305	9,067	62.6	...	...	...	...
Nelson, KY	21179	67,726	7.9	60.9	31.3	59,817	8,121	57.0	...	...	...	...
Nicholas, KY	21181	10,673	10.6	71.7	17.6	9,458	7,683	58.9	...	...	...	...
Ohio, KY	21183	38,934	10.9	70.2	18.9	34,610	8,539	58.3	...	...	...	...
Oldham, KY	21185	93,603	4.8	45.3	49.9	72,506	6,170	59.5	...	...	...	...
Owen, KY	21187	19,082	12.6	65.8	21.6	16,984	8,750	61.3	...	...	...	...
Owsley, KY	21189	10,701	30.7	58.3	11.0	9,858	12,216	59.5	...	...	...	...
Pendleton, KY	21191	27,596	8.1	71.1	20.8	25,117	9,285	53.6	...	...	...	...
Perry, KY	21193	53,548	12.0	69.1	18.9	47,487	8,962	60.3	...	...	...	...
Pike, KY	21195	112,266	13.0	62.1	24.9	99,818	8,840	58.7	...	...	...	...
Powell, KY	21197	23,234	14.7	73.4	11.9	21,661	8,572	62.7	...	...	...	...
Pulaski, KY	21199	93,389	11.7	63.6	24.7	85,850	8,465	63.2	...	...	...	...
Robertson, KY	21201	4,264	15.2	70.3	14.5	3,763	9,551	58.9	...	...	...	...
Rockcastle, KY	21203	30,120	11.3	76.7	12.0	26,570	8,778	63.2	...	...	...	...
Rowan, KY	21205	29,880	10.1	64.1	25.8	26,435	8,045	62.1	...	...	...	...
Russell, KY	21207	32,506	11.2	67.4	21.4	28,084	9,424	59.1	...	...	...	...
Scott, KY	21209	72,154	6.1	54.2	39.8	61,076	7,868	60.5	...	...	...	...
Shelby, KY	21211	63,523	6.8	54.3	38.9	53,247	8,364	60.8	...	...	...	...
Simpson, KY	21213	26,908	8.9	63.8	27.3	24,428	8,175	60.2	...	...	...	...
Spencer, KY	21215	24,176	6.7	61.7	31.6	20,516	7,579	57.8	...	...	...	...
Taylor, KY	21217	35,694	11.2	66.6	22.3	33,208	8,675	61.9	...	...	...	...
Todd, KY	21219	21,187	11.2	71.4	17.4	18,496	8,496	54.5	...	...	...	...
Trigg, KY	21221	19,502	8.4	61.4	30.1	17,732	8,380	57.0	...	...	...	...
Trimble, KY	21223	14,921	12.3	62.7	25.0	12,089	7,435	61.3	...	...	...	...
Union, KY	21225	24,620	10.1	64.7	25.2	21,505	8,968	56.8	...	...	...	...
Warren, KY	21227	154,697	9.9	56.9	33.2	128,483	7,739	64.7	...	...	...	...
Washington, KY	21229	19,028	11.1	64.4	24.4	16,067	8,996	60.5	...	...	...	...
Wayne, KY	21231	36,035	13.4	72.1	14.5	31,332	8,848	58.8	...	...	...	...
Webster, KY	21233	20,181	11.9	66.5	21.6	18,465	8,351	51.8	...	...	...	...
Whitley, KY	21235	77,676	14.2	72.0	13.8	68,132	8,373	63.3	...	...	...	...
Wolfe, KY	21237	14,879	16.0	73.7	10.2	12,680	9,992	60.8	...	...	...	...
Woodford, KY	21239	33,716	6.7	51.8	41.5	29,511	7,285	62.6	...	...	...	...
LOUISIANA	22000	7,927,710	16.8	43.5	39.7	6,748,942	9,948	58.7	276,549	79.2	10.5	6.9
Acadia, LA	22001	85,836	15.5	59.7	24.8	79,513	8,427	59.0	...	...	...	...
Allen, LA	22003	46,431	8.7	60.2	31.0	43,152	10,156	58.5	...	...	...	...
Ascension, LA	22005	196,643	7.3	45.2	47.4	166,255	8,941	61.1	6,170	85.6	6.2	1.7
Assumption, LA	22007	45,869	14.3	58.3	27.4	43,855	10,593	60.5	...	...	...	...
Avoyelles, LA	22009	57,681	18.4	64.5	17.1	51,404	7,562	60.3	...	...	...	...
Beauregard, LA	22011	57,238	6.7	59.5	33.8	51,341	8,489	57.9	1,773	72.7	18.4	5.6
Bienville, LA	22013	36,337	10.8	30.5	58.8	29,212	12,657	59.6	...	...	...	...
Bossier, LA	22015	191,025	9.0	48.4	42.6	172,676	8,843	58.4	6,461	68.4	16.7	8.4
Caddo, LA	22017	447,996	12.2	48.3	39.5	406,440	9,482	59.0	14,913	79.7	8.6	8.8
Calcasieu, LA	22019	373,566	12.1	43.6	44.2	331,028	9,721	56.8	10,344	85.1	9.8	3.2
Caldwell, LA	22021	17,816	11.9	67.0	21.2	17,425	9,940	59.7	...	...	...	...
Cameron, LA	22023	...	...	...	...	...	...	...	...	...	...	...
Catahoula, LA	22025	16,930	15.8	64.6	19.6	16,035	9,394	54.9	...	...	...	...
Claiborne, LA	22027	26,956	11.9	59.5	28.6	24,207	9,714	58.8	...	...	...	...
Concordia, LA	22029	41,905	16.9	56.2	27.0	35,464	8,767	59.4	...	...	...	...
De Soto, LA	22031	66,672	10.7	40.8	48.5	55,339	11,431	58.1	...	...	...	...
East Baton Rouge, LA	22033	672,424	12.6	37.7	49.7	581,789	10,240	58.3	29,922	84.1	7.9	5.2
East Carroll, LA	22035	17,364	20.9	59.1	20.0	15,832	11,134	58.3	...	...	...	...
East Feliciana, LA	22037	23,217	14.4	62.4	23.2	24,180	10,508	57.7	...	...	...	...
Evangeline, LA	22039	59,096	14.5	61.8	23.7	57,279	9,429	61.0	...	...	...	...
Franklin, LA	22041	32,272	24.7	55.4	19.9	30,081	8,816	55.7	...	...	...	...
Grant, LA	22043	29,256	13.4	71.3	15.4	26,653	7,818	56.1	...	...	...	...
Iberia, LA	22045	145,662	14.0	53.0	32.9	127,717	9,189	61.3	4,497	76.2	13.5	6.5
Iberville, LA	22047	63,046	13.8	28.4	57.9	56,452	13,518	46.4	...	...	...	...
Jackson, LA	22049	25,809	9.0	39.3	51.7	22,668	10,004	57.4	...	...	...	...
Jefferson, LA	22051	552,956	20.2	28.7	51.1	503,964	11,393	57.5	23,438	77.8	10.3	7.3
Jefferson Davis, LA	22053	62,000	10.0	58.5	31.6	56,471	9,622	57.8	...	...	...	...
Lafayette, LA	22055	312,317	11.9	40.1	48.1	271,055	9,107	62.5	12,607	80.4	11.4	4.0
Lafourche, LA	22057	153,794	11.0	50.8	38.3	137,920	9,409	58.4	5,995	73.2	17.5	4.6
La Salle, LA	22059	27,051	10.5	60.1	29.5	25,120	9,447	60.0	...	...	...	...
Lincoln, LA	22061	74,652	8.7	44.1	47.1	60,260	10,322	58.2	...	...	...	...
Livingston, LA	22063	205,192	7.4	66.1	26.5	191,112	8,215	64.1	6,522	79.8	8.9	6.5
Madison, LA	22065	26,063	23.4	51.5	25.0	21,446	9,998	58.5	...	...	...	...
Morehouse, LA	22067	50,470	16.9	57.8	25.3	46,022	9,556	58.7	...	...	...	...
Natchitoches, LA	22069	69,594	13.3	55.8	30.9	61,001	8,868	62.9	3,340	74.1	16.6	8.4
Orleans, LA	22071	817,023	41.3	18.1	40.6	490,045	15,687	50.6	24,802	80.1	11.5	6.3

[3]May be of any race
... Not available

Table C-1. Population, School, and Student Characteristics by County—*Continued*

County	State/County Code	High school graduates, 2006-2008			College enrollment, 2006-2008		College graduates, 2006-2008 (percent)						
		Population 25 years and over	High school diploma or less (percent)	High school diploma or more (percent)	Number	Percent public	Bachelor's degree or more	+/- U.S. percent with Bachelor's degree or more	Non-Hispanic White	Black or African American	American Indian and Alaska Native	Asian, Hawaiian, and Pacific Islander	Hispanic or Latino[3]
		30	31	32	33	34	35	36	37	38	39	40	41
Morgan, KY	21175	...	...	...	...	...	...	...	...	...	...	...	...
Muhlenberg, KY	21177	22,115	66.8	73.6	1,455	90.0	7.7	-19.7	8.1	...	...	...	...
Nelson, KY	21179	28,144	58.7	82.9	1,618	67.4	13.3	-14.1	13.7	2.6	...	...	...
Nicholas, KY	21181	...	...	...	...	...	...	...	...	...	...	...	...
Ohio, KY	21183	16,169	64.3	74.8	855	88.8	11.4	-16.0	11.4	...	...	...	...
Oldham, KY	21185	37,181	35.2	89.6	3,274	79.1	34.6	7.2	35.2	17.9	...	...	38.0
Owen, KY	21187	...	...	...	...	...	...	...	...	...	...	...	...
Owsley, KY	21189	...	...	...	...	...	...	...	...	...	...	...	...
Pendleton, KY	21191	...	...	...	...	...	...	...	...	...	...	...	...
Perry, KY	21193	19,744	67.9	69.6	1,256	89.3	11.6	-15.8	11.2	...	...	...	...
Pike, KY	21195	46,321	66.1	72.3	2,626	51.6	13.5	-13.9	13.0	...	...	...	...
Powell, KY	21197	...	...	...	...	...	...	...	...	...	...	...	...
Pulaski, KY	21199	42,165	61.4	76.3	3,056	90.5	14.3	-13.1	14.3	...	...	...	...
Robertson, KY	21201	...	...	...	...	...	...	...	...	...	...	...	...
Rockcastle, KY	21203	...	...	...	...	...	...	...	...	...	...	...	...
Rowan, KY	21205	12,987	57.5	77.1	3,686	97.4	25.0	-2.4	25.8	...	...	...	...
Russell, KY	21207	...	...	...	...	...	...	...	...	...	...	...	...
Scott, KY	21209	27,208	45.3	85.4	3,316	50.2	24.3	-3.1	25.2	13.2	...	...	...
Shelby, KY	21211	26,382	53.1	82.5	2,393	67.6	23.1	-4.3	24.5	19.4	...	...	3.6
Simpson, KY	21213	...	...	...	...	...	...	...	...	...	...	...	...
Spencer, KY	21215	...	...	...	...	...	...	...	...	...	...	...	...
Taylor, KY	21217	16,101	66.9	69.4	1,608	45.9	13.3	-14.1	13.3	...	...	...	...
Todd, KY	21219	...	...	...	...	...	...	...	...	...	...	...	...
Trigg, KY	21221	...	...	...	...	...	...	...	...	...	...	...	...
Trimble, KY	21223	...	...	...	...	...	...	...	...	...	...	...	...
Union, KY	21225	...	...	...	...	...	...	...	...	...	...	...	...
Warren, KY	21227	65,068	46.5	84.8	12,762	94.6	25.9	-1.5	27.0	17.1	...	64.9	8.7
Washington, KY	21229	...	...	...	...	...	...	...	...	...	...	...	...
Wayne, KY	21231	14,047	71.3	69.2	785	97.1	10.6	-16.8	10.8	...	...	...	...
Webster, KY	21233	...	...	...	...	...	...	...	...	...	...	...	...
Whitley, KY	21235	25,548	66.9	67.8	2,395	42.3	13.8	-13.6	13.4	...	...	...	...
Wolfe, KY	21237	...	...	...	...	...	...	...	...	...	...	...	...
Woodford, KY	21239	16,145	41.9	87.7	1,176	71.7	34.7	7.3	35.7	28.7	...	...	...
LOUISIANA	22000	2,750,274	55.0	80.2	265,368	81.8	20.4	-7.0	23.7	11.8	11.3	39.9	18.5
Acadia, LA	22001	37,028	71.7	67.5	2,343	91.2	10.9	-16.5	11.3	7.0	...	...	...
Allen, LA	22003	16,856	68.6	72.4	964	94.7	9.5	-17.9	11.9	3.3	...	...	...
Ascension, LA	22005	60,603	54.4	84.6	4,472	77.3	20.3	-7.1	22.0	14.5	...	...	6.9
Assumption, LA	22007	14,802	74.9	68.5	864	78.7	8.5	-18.9	9.6	5.6	...	...	...
Avoyelles, LA	22009	27,519	71.3	68.8	859	80.4	9.4	-18.0	10.8	3.7	...	...	...
Beauregard, LA	22011	22,758	58.9	83.5	1,190	86.6	14.8	-12.6	15.3	12.2	...	...	10.6
Bienville, LA	22013	...	...	...	...	...	...	...	...	...	...	...	...
Bossier, LA	22015	68,282	45.8	86.9	5,196	87.0	21.3	-6.1	23.6	12.1	...	37.8	12.5
Caddo, LA	22017	162,986	52.2	82.9	15,712	85.7	21.6	-5.8	29.1	11.5	...	55.0	23.1
Calcasieu, LA	22019	118,632	54.9	81.1	9,908	91.4	18.9	-8.5	21.1	11.6	...	46.4	9.2
Caldwell, LA	22021	...	...	...	...	...	...	...	...	...	...	...	...
Cameron, LA	22023	...	...	...	...	...	...	...	...	...	...	...	...
Catahoula, LA	22025	...	...	...	...	...	...	...	...	...	...	...	...
Claiborne, LA	22027	...	...	...	...	...	...	...	...	...	...	...	...
Concordia, LA	22029	...	...	...	...	...	...	...	...	...	...	...	...
De Soto, LA	22031	16,870	62.3	79.3	1,253	84.0	13.5	-13.9	17.0	8.6	...	...	...
East Baton Rouge, LA	22033	261,101	40.0	87.2	46,882	90.4	32.5	5.1	42.1	18.6	...	53.0	26.4
East Carroll, LA	22035	...	...	...	...	...	...	...	...	...	...	...	...
East Feliciana, LA	22037	14,188	60.8	78.9	1,222	80.7	11.8	-15.6	17.0	5.7	...	...	...
Evangeline, LA	22039	22,308	71.4	64.4	892	96.0	11.4	-16.0	13.0	7.2	...	...	...
Franklin, LA	22041	13,204	72.3	67.4	705	91.9	10.5	-16.9	12.5	4.1	...	...	...
Grant, LA	22043	...	...	...	...	...	...	...	...	...	...	...	...
Iberia, LA	22045	47,608	68.5	74.4	1,948	90.8	14.4	-13.0	14.9	13.8	...	13.0	6.8
Iberville, LA	22047	21,399	71.1	71.7	1,542	77.2	11.2	-16.2	15.9	5.3	...	...	...
Jackson, LA	22049	...	...	...	...	...	...	...	...	...	...	...	...
Jefferson, LA	22051	291,287	50.8	81.5	24,154	71.7	22.4	-5.0	25.6	12.9	19.7	33.2	17.3
Jefferson Davis, LA	22053	20,108	68.0	74.7	868	95.0	12.9	-14.5	13.4	8.7	...	...	...
Lafayette, LA	22055	128,379	46.3	83.5	16,366	92.1	27.6	0.2	32.5	10.6	10.2	58.6	20.6
Lafourche, LA	22057	60,306	68.5	70.1	4,484	85.9	13.6	-13.8	15.0	5.1	3.0	...	11.5
La Salle, LA	22059	...	...	...	...	...	...	...	...	...	...	...	...
Lincoln, LA	22061	22,192	44.4	84.2	10,650	94.7	29.5	2.1	34.7	19.6	...	...	...
Livingston, LA	22063	73,457	57.6	83.0	4,739	84.7	16.0	-11.4	16.0	12.7	...	...	19.5
Madison, LA	22065	...	...	...	...	...	...	...	...	...	...	...	...
Morehouse, LA	22067	19,172	68.1	72.5	1,162	81.5	10.6	-16.8	14.1	5.3	...	...	...
Natchitoches, LA	22069	23,076	57.5	78.7	4,274	94.3	20.0	-7.4	27.1	8.6	12.1	...	15.0
Orleans, LA	22071	157,170	46.2	82.4	27,144	49.1	30.5	3.1	51.8	11.6	...	35.1	31.4

[3]May be of any race
... Not available

Table C-1. Population, School, and Student Characteristics by County—*Continued*

County	State/County Code	County Type¹	Population, 2009 Total	Population, 2009 Percent 5–17 years	Percent of related children 5-17 years in poverty, 2008	Percent of children under 19 years with no health insurance, 2007	Number of Schools and Students, 2008-2009 School Districts	Schools	Students	Resident enrollment, 2006-2008 K–12 enrollment Number	Percent public
			1	2	3	4	5	6	7	8	9
Ouachita, LA	22073	3	151,502	18.9	28.7	14.8	3	61	28,233	28,706	90.1
Plaquemines, LA	22075	1	20,942	20.2	17.6	18.4	2	11	4,472	4,258	78.4
Pointe Coupee, LA	22077	2	22,447	17.4	26.3	12.0	1	7	2,634	3,991	63.5
Rapides, LA	22079	3	133,937	18.8	24.9	14.3	2	55	23,621	24,630	89.2
Red River, LA	22081	6	9,003	19.3	31.6	18.0	1	7	1,512	...	...
Richland, LA	22083	6	20,422	18.6	34.8	13.8	2	15	3,932	3,738	91.9
Sabine, LA	22085	6	23,733	18.5	27.2	17.1	1	14	4,253	4,282	96.1
St. Bernard, LA	22087	1	40,655	17.7	31.4	7.9	1	10	4,645	7,980	85.8
St. Charles, LA	22089	1	51,611	20.1	13.4	12.4	1	22	9,535	10,450	83.8
St. Helena, LA	22091	2	10,551	19.0	28.3	20.3	1	5	1,208	...	...
St. James, LA	22093	6	21,054	19.4	20.7	15.2	1	12	4,085	4,310	78.4
St. John the Baptist, LA	22095	1	47,086	20.2	19.0	13.3	1	14	6,355	9,923	71.7
St. Landry, LA	22097	4	92,326	20.0	32.0	12.5	1	41	15,095	17,874	81.9
St. Martin, LA	22099	3	52,217	19.3	24.6	16.9	1	19	8,404	10,171	81.3
St. Mary, LA	22101	4	50,815	19.4	23.4	12.8	2	30	9,902	9,819	89.3
St. Tammany, LA	22103	1	231,495	19.1	12.3	13.7	1	55	35,490	43,363	78.8
Tangipahoa, LA	22105	4	118,688	17.9	27.8	15.2	1	40	19,402	21,286	86.2
Tensas, LA	22107	9	5,609	17.7	44.0	14.9	1	5	745	...	...
Terrebonne, LA	22109	3	109,291	19.0	21.4	12.9	2	44	19,004	20,999	84.1
Union, LA	22111	3	22,584	16.5	25.7	16.5	1	10	2,826	4,222	87.0
Vermilion, LA	22113	4	56,141	19.1	23.5	15.6	1	20	8,937	10,081	89.9
Vernon, LA	22115	4	46,616	18.4	20.0	25.2	1	22	9,603	9,680	93.6
Washington, LA	22117	6	45,669	18.7	30.0	12.6	2	24	7,599	8,425	85.1
Webster, LA	22119	6	40,544	17.6	24.5	13.1	1	23	7,227	6,870	95.0
West Baton Rouge, LA	22121	2	22,638	18.0	20.0	16.2	1	12	3,789	4,093	84.4
West Carroll, LA	22123	9	11,329	17.5	30.0	15.2	1	8	2,257	...	...
West Feliciana, LA	22125	2	15,055	13.1	16.0	21.1	1	7	2,309	...	...
Winn, LA	22127	6	15,331	16.0	28.2	14.0	1	10	2,669	...	...
MAINE	23000	X	1,318,301	15.2	13.8	6.1	323	675	192,563	208,597	91.2
Androscoggin, ME	23001	3	106,539	15.7	15.6	4.4	15	42	16,508	17,643	94.1
Aroostook, ME	23003	7	71,488	15.2	17.0	6.1	27	50	10,755	10,814	95.5
Cumberland, ME	23005	2	278,559	15.3	10.4	5.9	22	92	37,564	45,211	91.2
Franklin, ME	23007	6	29,735	14.4	19.2	5.1	10	18	4,004	4,432	94.1
Hancock, ME	23009	6	53,447	13.6	13.7	10.3	35	37	6,880	7,843	90.2
Kennebec, ME	23011	4	121,090	15.5	12.8	5.0	28	57	17,781	18,786	89.1
Knox, ME	23013	7	40,801	14.0	14.8	8.0	14	29	6,287	6,084	95.2
Lincoln, ME	23015	8	34,576	14.3	14.8	10.5	19	16	3,730	5,096	82.6
Oxford, ME	23017	6	56,244	15.9	18.0	5.1	13	40	9,762	9,056	89.1
Penobscot, ME	23019	3	149,419	14.4	15.2	6.4	49	90	22,871	21,912	90.7
Piscataquis, ME	23021	8	16,795	14.8	23.3	6.3	9	14	2,644	...	...
Sagadahoc, ME	23023	2	36,391	15.5	11.7	6.1	3	19	5,543	5,932	93.9
Somerset, ME	23025	6	50,947	16.2	20.6	6.7	12	39	8,670	8,237	92.4
Waldo, ME	23027	6	38,287	15.3	17.1	6.3	6	23	4,187	6,272	94.8
Washington, ME	23029	7	32,107	14.7	24.9	7.3	44	39	4,541	4,933	88.1
York, ME	23031	2	201,876	15.8	9.7	5.8	17	70	30,836	33,922	89.5
MARYLAND	24000	X	5,699,478	17.0	9.1	9.5	24	1,470	843,781	979,602	83.2
Allegany, MD	24001	3	72,532	13.5	16.5	6.7	1	28	9,232	9,962	89.8
Anne Arundel, MD	24003	1	521,209	16.6	5.9	9.3	1	124	73,653	88,944	82.0
Baltimore, MD	24005	1	789,814	15.7	8.4	8.3	1	173	103,180	127,177	78.7
Calvert, MD	24009	1	89,212	20.0	5.5	8.5	1	28	17,052	17,282	90.3
Caroline, MD	24011	6	33,367	17.4	13.8	10.7	1	10	5,513	5,887	85.7
Carroll, MD	24013	1	170,089	18.8	4.7	8.3	1	47	27,964	29,973	88.0
Cecil, MD	24015	1	100,796	18.2	9.3	8.3	1	29	16,209	18,029	82.9
Charles, MD	24017	1	142,226	20.0	7.0	8.4	1	37	26,727	27,713	85.6
Dorchester, MD	24019	6	32,043	15.1	20.5	7.9	1	13	4,560	4,724	90.2
Frederick, MD	24021	1	227,980	18.8	5.3	7.8	1	64	40,070	41,027	92.8
Garrett, MD	24023	6	29,555	16.4	18.6	12.2	1	16	4,425	4,950	88.4
Harford, MD	24025	1	242,514	18.4	6.0	7.6	1	54	38,610	44,321	84.1
Howard, MD	24027	1	281,884	19.4	4.1	8.7	1	73	49,905	52,625	86.9
Kent, MD	24029	6	20,247	12.9	14.5	12.0	1	8	2,219	2,550	85.4
Montgomery, MD	24031	1	971,600	17.3	6.1	10.8	1	205	139,282	164,933	81.6
Prince George's, MD	24033	1	834,560	17.5	7.3	13.0	1	215	127,977	148,277	81.4
Queen Anne's, MD	24035	1	47,958	17.7	6.4	9.9	1	14	7,859	8,012	83.9
St. Mary's, MD	24037	4	102,999	18.3	8.7	9.7	1	27	16,752	17,357	86.1
Somerset, MD	24039	3	25,959	13.0	25.3	8.6	1	9	2,912	3,352	84.0
Talbot, MD	24041	6	36,262	14.4	11.1	11.2	1	8	4,419	5,160	79.3
Washington, MD	24043	3	145,910	16.5	11.3	8.4	1	45	21,734	24,041	89.7
Wicomico, MD	24045	3	94,222	16.4	16.1	10.7	1	25	14,590	15,391	84.7
Worcester, MD	24047	4	49,122	13.8	16.1	11.5	1	14	6,671	6,787	87.4
Baltimore city, MD	24510	1	637,418	15.3	23.2	6.8	1	204	82,266	111,128	82.3

¹County type codes are from the Economic Research Service of the United States Department of Agriculture. See notes and definitions for more information.
... Not available

Table C-1. Population, School, and Student Characteristics by County—*Continued*

County	State/ County Code	Characteristics of students, 2008-2009				Number of graduates, 2006-2007	Staff and students, 2008-2009			
		Percent with IEP[2]	Percent eligible for free or reduced lunch	Percent minority	Percent English Language Learners		Total staff	Number of teachers	Student/ teacher ratio	Central admin. Staff
		10	11	12	13	14	15	16	17	18
Ouachita, LA	22073	13.2	60.5	51.3	0.6	1,414	4,470	1,981	14.3	144
Plaquemines, LA	22075	11.0	62.3	44.8	2.4	239	841	355	12.6	47
Pointe Coupee, LA	22077	17.8	75.7	66.5	0.9	153	393	179	14.7	18
Rapides, LA	22079	12.7	66.2	47.4	1.5	1,306	3,592	1,690	14.0	178
Red River, LA	22081	11.4	84.9	66.5	...	68	260	112	13.5	9
Richland, LA	22083	11.9	71.4	47.4	0.1	186	594	279	14.1	19
Sabine, LA	22085	12.6	66.5	47.3	0.7	253	685	325	13.1	18
St. Bernard, LA	22087	9.5	68.7	30.7	0.9	278	709	358	13.0	27
St. Charles, LA	22089	11.3	47.8	41.2	1.1	564	1,634	815	11.7	60
St. Helena, LA	22091	16.8	91.5	94.6	...	70	185	86	14.0	9
St. James, LA	22093	12.1	71.6	67.9	0.6	248	651	336	12.2	25
St. John the Baptist, LA	22095	14.8	85.4	83.6	1.4	317	1,014	537	11.8	30
St. Landry, LA	22097	13.7	74.4	58.7	0.8	820	2,208	1,096	13.8	48
St. Martin, LA	22099	12.7	67.1	49.3	1.0	536	1,140	553	15.2	31
St. Mary, LA	22101	15.0	72.0	50.8	3.5	600	1,582	760	13.0	37
St. Tammany, LA	22103	16.9	43.4	24.3	1.4	2,168	5,274	2,606	13.6	176
Tangipahoa, LA	22105	12.3	73.9	50.0	1.4	1,044	2,586	1,211	16.0	71
Tensas, LA	22107	18.3	93.6	93.2	1.5	36	163	65	11.5	8
Terrebonne, LA	22109	12.8	59.8	41.5	1.3	1,104	2,768	1,444	13.2	55
Union, LA	22111	13.3	79.1	56.7	4.4	159	429	195	14.5	16
Vermilion, LA	22113	14.1	59.6	25.6	1.9	488	1,249	671	13.3	35
Vernon, LA	22115	13.5	57.4	28.6	0.4	466	943	653	14.7	29
Washington, LA	22117	18.0	87.2	46.0	0.8	336	1,191	524	14.5	46
Webster, LA	22119	12.1	62.3	45.4	...	453	958	475	15.2	23
West Baton Rouge, LA	22121	11.2	65.6	54.7	0.6	201	597	294	12.9	11
West Carroll, LA	22123	11.6	75.5	20.9	0.5	119	309	162	13.9	10
West Feliciana, LA	22125	12.2	46.6	43.8	0.3	141	395	196	11.8	18
Winn, LA	22127	11.5	68.3	37.2	...	128	402	180	14.8	12
MAINE	23000	15.9	38.1	6.4	...	13,263	36,450	15,910	12.1	1845
Androscoggin, ME	23001	16.8	45.2	12.1	...	1,024	2,961	1,341	12.3	124
Aroostook, ME	23003	16.8	48.5	5.3	...	825	2,212	915	11.8	120
Cumberland, ME	23005	14.1	26.3	10.3	...	2,747	7,270	3,151	11.9	366
Franklin, ME	23007	14.6	50.1	3.7	...	347	876	376	10.6	43
Hancock, ME	23009	16.0	33.7	4.3	...	500	1,452	656	10.5	73
Kennebec, ME	23011	15.8	40.0	3.8	...	1,079	3,037	1,347	13.2	146
Knox, ME	23013	18.1	34.7	3.0	...	528	1,360	611	10.3	73
Lincoln, ME	23015	16.5	41.2	2.9	...	125	645	266	14.0	31
Oxford, ME	23017	15.0	51.1	3.1	...	670	1,923	833	11.7	103
Penobscot, ME	23019	16.1	40.5	5.7	...	1,614	4,152	1,908	12.0	207
Piscataquis, ME	23021	15.4	54.9	2.8	...	135	508	197	13.4	31
Sagadahoc, ME	23023	17.1	30.2	5.6	...	444	1,078	490	11.3	57
Somerset, ME	23025	17.5	53.2	2.9	...	566	1,669	692	12.5	79
Waldo, ME	23027	20.2	51.8	3.0	...	321	910	390	10.7	37
Washington, ME	23029	16.4	60.3	11.4	...	296	1,052	430	10.6	81
York, ME	23031	16.1	28.8	4.3	...	2,042	5,345	2,309	13.4	272
MARYLAND	24000	12.2	34.7	53.8	...	58,167	116,812	58,930	14.3	5686
Allegany, MD	24001	14.5	46.2	7.7	...	703	1,392	703	13.1	77
Anne Arundel, MD	24003	...	...	95.8	...	5,123	9,235	4,939	14.9	455
Baltimore, MD	24005	12.9	36.5	51.1	...	7,473	14,187	7,339	14.1	600
Calvert, MD	24009	11.0	15.2	21.5	...	1,348	2,253	1,117	15.3	137
Caroline, MD	24011	10.0	46.9	26.2	...	438	781	402	13.7	47
Carroll, MD	24013	11.7	12.6	8.8	...	2,384	3,580	1,938	14.4	184
Cecil, MD	24015	13.3	30.6	15.1	...	970	2,254	1,172	13.8	98
Charles, MD	24017	8.7	25.1	61.0	...	1,976	3,323	1,727	15.5	137
Dorchester, MD	24019	10.7	53.0	45.0	...	336	695	376	12.1	42
Frederick, MD	24021	11.6	18.4	25.7	...	2,842	5,398	2,718	14.7	252
Garrett, MD	24023	13.1	43.9	1.2	...	331	636	348	12.7	33
Harford, MD	24025	13.9	22.8	27.5	...	2,821	5,302	2,742	14.1	218
Howard, MD	24027	9.0	12.9	42.7	...	3,576	7,506	3,887	12.8	304
Kent, MD	24029	15.5	41.5	30.1	...	176	353	175	12.7	29
Montgomery, MD	24031	11.8	27.0	60.9	...	10,186	19,870	9,401	14.8	1139
Prince George's, MD	24033	11.4	47.3	95.3	...	8,247	18,292	8,870	14.4	717
Queen Anne's, MD	24035	11.6	17.8	14.5	...	569	951	522	15.1	62
St. Mary's, MD	24037	12.8	24.9	27.8	...	1,036	1,984	1,021	16.4	120
Somerset, MD	24039	13.4	57.8	52.0	...	169	465	236	12.3	25
Talbot, MD	24041	8.3	31.1	29.7	...	309	606	300	14.7	39
Washington, MD	24043	12.0	40.3	20.1	...	1,471	2,851	1,488	14.6	146
Wicomico, MD	24045	11.8	49.9	45.5	...	908	2,257	1,095	13.3	131
Worcester, MD	24047	10.0	35.4	29.6	...	573	1,125	577	11.6	46
Baltimore city, MD	24510	16.9	73.0	92.3	...	4,202	11,517	5,839	14.1	649

[2]IEP= Individual Education Program. See notes and definitions for more information
... Not available

Table C-1. Population, School, and Student Characteristics by County—*Continued*

County	State/County Code	Revenues, 2007-2008				Current expenditures, 2007-2008			Resident population 16 to 19 years, 2006-2008			
		Total revenue ($1,000's)	Percentage of revenue from			Amount ($1,000's)	Amount per student	Percent for instruction	Total population 16 to 19 years	Percent enrolled in school	Percent high school graduates, not enrolled in school	Percent not enrolled, not grads, not employed or not in labor force
			Federal gov't	State gov't	Local gov't							
		19	20	21	22	23	24	25	26	27	28	29
Ouachita, LA	22073	299,158	12.2	52.3	35.5	266,756	9,435	59.0	9,503	81.5	8.6	7.3
Plaquemines, LA	22075	73,887	21.1	31.1	47.8	66,895	15,053	54.4	...	...	...	...
Pointe Coupee, LA	22077	34,146	18.3	42.3	39.3	32,408	10,272	54.7	...	...	...	...
Rapides, LA	22079	217,919	12.9	55.1	32.0	206,087	8,813	61.6	7,524	76.1	11.3	9.1
Red River, LA	22081	19,377	14.5	56.6	28.8	16,891	11,253	57.3	...	...	...	...
Richland, LA	22083	39,414	13.5	62.7	23.9	35,417	9,140	57.8	...	...	...	...
Sabine, LA	22085	43,101	16.0	57.2	26.7	38,262	9,138	60.9	...	...	...	...
St. Bernard, LA	22087	159,030	52.7	14.9	32.3	54,784	13,125	60.3	...	...	...	...
St. Charles, LA	22089	151,551	7.8	22.6	69.6	124,385	12,987	58.2	...	...	...	...
St. Helena, LA	22091	13,620	22.8	59.6	17.6	12,825	10,067	51.8	...	...	...	...
St. James, LA	22093	55,248	11.4	33.8	54.8	45,457	11,082	56.9	...	...	...	...
St. John the Baptist, LA	22095	83,194	12.9	43.0	44.2	74,797	11,482	64.6	...	...	...	...
St. Landry, LA	22097	137,679	15.6	60.0	24.4	134,342	8,820	61.8	5,562	73.1	15.7	7.5
St. Martin, LA	22099	80,038	13.2	60.4	26.4	71,712	8,462	58.6	...	...	...	...
St. Mary, LA	22101	105,015	11.5	51.6	36.8	94,615	9,302	58.4	...	...	...	...
St. Tammany, LA	22103	429,450	11.5	43.4	45.1	361,543	10,280	61.3	12,866	80.0	8.8	6.4
Tangipahoa, LA	22105	176,389	14.7	59.7	25.6	160,787	8,213	61.3	...	...	...	...
Tensas, LA	22107	10,205	25.7	51.2	23.1	9,673	12,778	53.8	...	...	...	...
Terrebonne, LA	22109	182,616	12.1	52.8	35.0	171,291	8,948	63.0	6,683	83.7	7.5	5.8
Union, LA	22111	28,142	12.3	62.2	25.5	26,875	9,163	60.4	...	...	...	...
Vermilion, LA	22113	89,092	16.5	48.4	35.1	78,987	8,754	61.3	...	...	...	...
Vernon, LA	22115	90,392	19.8	61.2	19.0	83,878	8,806	58.5	2,567	60.4	28.7	6.9
Washington, LA	22117	84,899	17.2	60.0	22.8	77,323	10,183	57.4	...	...	...	...
Webster, LA	22119	75,581	10.4	55.1	34.5	64,425	8,733	60.7	...	...	...	...
West Baton Rouge, LA	22121	44,027	9.2	36.5	54.2	37,400	10,300	60.6	...	...	...	...
West Carroll, LA	22123	20,750	13.0	67.2	19.8	18,988	8,321	60.4	...	...	...	...
West Feliciana, LA	22125	28,468	10.1	45.8	44.0	26,388	10,990	53.9	...	...	...	...
Winn, LA	22127	27,143	12.4	59.2	28.4	25,338	9,501	55.7	...	...	...	...
MAINE	23000	259,4335	7.5	43.2	49.2	2,314,164	11,987	58.8	71,408	85.9	8.7	3.6
Androscoggin, ME	23001	205,823	8.4	55.9	35.7	182,933	10,960	59.2	5,771	87.3	4.9	6.3
Aroostook, ME	23003	140,937	10.5	58.2	31.3	127,510	11,938	55.7	3,877	82.5	11.0	4.6
Cumberland, ME	23005	514,507	5.0	32.1	62.9	461,279	12,092	60.1	15,187	89.5	7.3	1.5
Franklin, ME	23007	56,020	6.1	44.0	49.8	52,742	13,195	55.4	...	...	...	...
Hancock, ME	23009	113,518	6.1	24.4	69.5	99,080	14,464	58.2	...	...	...	...
Kennebec, ME	23011	217,524	8.3	53.1	38.6	196,771	11,629	57.8	6,951	86.8	9.1	3.4
Knox, ME	23013	98,341	6.2	29.7	64.1	84,136	13,109	57.7	...	...	...	...
Lincoln, ME	23015	57,132	4.7	29.4	65.8	47,600	13,420	61.4	...	...	...	...
Oxford, ME	23017	136,208	8.8	45.6	45.5	118,873	11,942	56.0	2,648	86.7	9.3	4.0
Penobscot, ME	23019	289,484	8.3	51.9	39.9	252,339	11,118	59.9	9,430	88.7	6.1	3.0
Piscataquis, ME	23021	34,369	10.9	52.6	36.5	31,312	11,337	60.9	...	...	...	...
Sagadahoc, ME	23023	85,863	5.6	42.8	51.6	77,336	13,313	56.5	...	...	...	...
Somerset, ME	23025	113,326	9.3	55.4	35.4	103,370	11,533	61.9	...	...	...	...
Waldo, ME	23027	62,647	9.6	44.6	45.8	55,272	13,042	55.7	2,132	79.8	11.9	5.2
Washington, ME	23029	76,200	19.6	41.6	38.8	68,696	16,168	58.1	1,610	81.5	15.1	2.6
York, ME	23031	392,436	6.1	39.8	54.1	354,915	11,400	59.3	10,075	83.9	11.3	4.0
MARYLAND	24000	1,309,8112	5.4	42.0	52.7	10,965,435	12,966	60.3	331,305	82.7	11.0	4.1
Allegany, MD	24001	142,922	7.7	62.4	29.9	120,753	12,797	62.2	...	...	...	...
Anne Arundel, MD	24003	1,003,238	4.6	32.2	63.2	877,288	11,952	61.8	28,208	76.8	17.7	3.5
Baltimore, MD	24005	1,518,801	5.4	42.5	52.2	1,263,668	12,118	61.1	46,990	82.1	12.7	3.1
Calvert, MD	24009	240,110	3.3	44.8	51.9	205,426	11,810	61.7	5,753	83.6	11.1	2.9
Caroline, MD	24011	70,209	7.8	66.0	26.2	62,135	10,982	60.5	...	...	...	...
Carroll, MD	24013	407,110	3.0	40.4	56.6	323,110	11,409	59.6	10,356	84.5	12.4	1.9
Cecil, MD	24015	215,964	4.6	51.2	44.2	183,438	11,261	60.1	5,688	69.2	17.0	4.9
Charles, MD	24017	365,859	4.0	45.8	50.3	318,873	11,954	57.3	8,136	82.3	12.3	4.5
Dorchester, MD	24019	68,487	9.4	57.6	33.0	58,788	12,632	58.8	...	...	...	...
Frederick, MD	24021	568,284	3.1	42.2	54.8	455,881	11,260	61.5	13,653	83.3	11.4	2.6
Garrett, MD	24023	60,471	8.3	47.3	44.4	56,674	12,566	59.2	...	...	...	...
Harford, MD	24025	586,552	3.6	43.1	53.3	455,028	11,616	60.5	13,548	82.5	11.3	3.4
Howard, MD	24027	805,247	2.5	29.1	68.4	688,449	13,896	63.2	14,814	91.6	5.9	1.7
Kent, MD	24029	34,812	8.2	37.4	54.4	31,295	13,762	53.4	...	...	...	...
Montgomery, MD	24031	2,604,887	3.6	21.7	74.7	2,066,022	15,002	63.7	48,792	89.2	6.7	2.4
Prince George's, MD	24033	1,926,633	6.1	54.0	39.9	1,757,026	13,541	55.7	54,074	84.1	9.7	4.0
Queen Anne's, MD	24035	108,979	4.4	35.4	60.3	85,002	10,887	60.3	...	...	...	...
St. Mary's, MD	24037	225,345	5.7	47.6	46.7	188,031	11,133	57.7	6,054	76.1	14.3	6.8
Somerset, MD	24039	48,746	12.1	59.4	28.5	40,955	14,074	55.2	...	...	...	...
Talbot, MD	24041	65,038	5.0	23.3	71.7	48,826	11,107	59.4	...	...	...	...
Washington, MD	24043	309,316	5.5	52.5	42.0	246,832	11,373	59.1	7,023	77.3	16.1	4.8
Wicomico, MD	24045	193,205	7.3	59.1	33.6	178,170	12,374	58.7	5,757	85.5	6.0	5.2
Worcester, MD	24047	129,914	6.1	22.9	71.0	99,481	14,749	62.6	...	...	...	...
Baltimore city, MD	24510	1,397,983	11.6	67.1	21.3	1,154,284	14,201	58.8	41,863	78.3	10.7	8.7

[3]May be of any race

Table C-1. Population, School, and Student Characteristics by County—*Continued*

County	State/ County Code	High school graduates, 2006-2008			College enrollment, 2006-2008		College graduates, 2006-2008 (percent)						
		Population 25 years and over	High school diploma or less (percent)	High school diploma or more (percent)	Number	Percent public	Bachelor's degree or more	+/- U.S. percent with Bachelor's degree or more	Non-Hispanic White	Black or African American	American Indian and Alaska Native	Asian, Hawaiian, and Pacific Islander	Hispanic or Latino[3]
		30	31	32	33	34	35	36	37	38	39	40	41
Ouachita, LA	22073	93,273	50.3	82.5	11,412	93.5	23.5	-3.9	27.4	14.4	...	63.6	9.1
Plaquemines, LA	22075	13,742	53.9	80.1	968	67.5	18.2	-9.2	21.0	6.6	...	...	...
Pointe Coupee, LA	22077	14,803	65.8	72.9	614	68.1	14.9	-12.5	18.8	8.3	...	...	...
Rapides, LA	22079	86,187	54.5	81.7	6,157	74.2	19.0	-8.4	22.7	9.6	22.7	40.3	19.4
Red River, LA	22081	...	...	...	...	...	...	...	...	...	...	...	...
Richland, LA	22083	13,531	65.0	73.8	452	47.3	12.4	-15.0	15.8	5.5	...	...	...
Sabine, LA	22085	15,662	67.3	80.8	937	89.9	11.9	-15.5	13.5	3.6	9.3	...	2.2
St. Bernard, LA	22087	14,460	69.5	76.5	2,611	28.7	8.5	-18.9	7.3	20.5	...	...	9.9
St. Charles, LA	22089	32,740	53.6	84.3	3,326	71.2	19.2	-8.2	21.3	12.4	...	...	13.6
St. Helena, LA	22091	...	...	...	...	...	...	...	...	...	...	...	...
St. James, LA	22093	13,421	65.3	82.1	858	97.9	14.1	-13.3	16.0	12.2	...	...	...
St. John the Baptist, LA	22095	28,687	55.6	81.8	2,326	83.2	16.8	-10.6	19.3	13.3	...	...	17.5
St. Landry, LA	22097	57,603	69.3	71.5	2,709	87.4	12.3	-15.1	14.1	9.4	...	...	...
St. Martin, LA	22099	33,024	71.0	72.6	1,674	91.2	10.3	-17.1	10.3	9.0	...	49.0	...
St. Mary, LA	22101	33,177	70.9	66.9	1,441	84.7	9.1	-18.3	10.8	6.3	5.8	8.4	1.7
St. Tammany, LA	22103	146,411	39.2	87.7	11,720	82.0	29.9	2.5	31.2	18.8	...	51.9	25.2
Tangipahoa, LA	22105	70,613	58.0	79.6	8,055	88.6	19.4	-8.0	23.0	9.1	...	...	15.6
Tensas, LA	22107	...	...	...	...	...	...	...	...	...	...	...	...
Terrebonne, LA	22109	68,786	66.9	72.1	3,844	90.2	13.1	-14.3	13.5	12.0	4.4	39.0	20.6
Union, LA	22111	15,197	64.3	80.3	731	88.1	13.7	-13.7	16.4	6.1	...	...	...
Vermilion, LA	22113	36,317	71.1	75.0	1,787	84.6	11.0	-16.4	11.8	4.0	...	6.2	...
Vernon, LA	22115	26,928	55.2	84.9	2,067	80.1	15.0	-12.4	15.3	12.3	2.5	36.3	11.8
Washington, LA	22117	29,041	67.1	76.0	1,888	89.5	13.2	-14.2	14.8	8.3	...	...	...
Webster, LA	22119	27,425	63.5	75.3	1,392	96.6	12.8	-14.6	14.1	10.1	...	...	...
West Baton Rouge, LA	22121	14,334	61.6	80.3	1,275	87.1	15.9	-11.5	16.5	12.9	...	...	...
West Carroll, LA	22123	...	...	...	...	...	...	...	...	...	...	...	...
West Feliciana, LA	22125	...	...	...	...	...	...	...	...	...	...	...	...
Winn, LA	22127	...	...	...	...	...	...	...	...	...	...	...	...
MAINE	23000	922,980	46.7	89.3	80,706	69.7	25.9	-1.5	26.1	22.3	8.3	41.8	20.5
Androscoggin, ME	23001	73,353	55.2	84.3	6,823	49.2	17.6	-9.8	18.3	17.1	...	...	...
Aroostook, ME	23003	51,425	56.0	84.2	4,157	86.1	15.7	-11.7	15.5	...	10.7	...	...
Cumberland, ME	23005	191,510	33.9	93.0	20,383	67.4	38.8	11.4	39.3	21.4	...	43.2	24.7
Franklin, ME	23007	20,392	49.8	86.5	1,801	94.8	24.5	-2.9	25.0	...	...	...	...
Hancock, ME	23009	38,160	44.3	90.9	3,239	75.7	29.5	2.1	29.2	...	...	...	...
Kennebec, ME	23011	84,655	49.4	90.0	7,249	54.4	23.8	-3.6	23.7	...	...	37.7	...
Knox, ME	23013	29,860	49.1	88.6	1,639	79.7	26.5	-0.9	26.5	...	...	...	...
Lincoln, ME	23015	25,657	39.1	92.3	1,103	66.2	31.4	4.0	31.5	...	...	...	...
Oxford, ME	23017	40,835	56.6	87.3	2,486	68.6	16.4	-11.0	16.6	...	...	...	...
Penobscot, ME	23019	100,462	48.8	89.1	15,317	82.8	22.4	-5.0	21.9	...	14.6	...	...
Piscataquis, ME	23021	...	...	...	...	...	...	...	...	...	...	...	...
Sagadahoc, ME	23023	25,484	43.2	92.6	1,656	76.0	29.1	1.7	29.2	...	...	...	...
Somerset, ME	23025	36,558	59.4	86.2	2,170	62.6	14.1	-13.3	14.3	...	...	...	...
Waldo, ME	23027	27,054	51.0	90.1	1,569	68.6	22.8	-4.6	22.8	...	...	...	...
Washington, ME	23029	23,442	55.2	85.7	1,199	85.6	18.2	-9.2	18.5	...	8.3	...	...
York, ME	23031	141,564	45.8	89.2	9,345	63.4	26.4	-1.0	26.8	...	12.7	18.0	17.6
MARYLAND	24000	3,724,359	39.4	87.5	442,167	73.3	35.1	7.7	39.2	24.1	20.0	60.3	20.5
Allegany, MD	24001	49,845	58.2	84.9	6,120	92.4	14.7	-12.7	15.1	4.2	...	...	18.3
Anne Arundel, MD	24003	340,709	36.9	90.2	34,845	75.8	35.3	7.9	37.3	22.7	23.3	51.0	29.7
Baltimore, MD	24005	532,395	39.5	88.6	67,207	77.2	34.4	7.0	35.9	26.4	9.5	59.0	25.9
Calvert, MD	24009	57,542	43.2	91.1	6,098	78.8	27.8	0.4	28.3	18.6	...	...	39.3
Caroline, MD	24011	21,841	58.9	80.3	1,186	71.5	16.0	-11.4	15.3	13.7	...	...	...
Carroll, MD	24013	111,594	43.4	88.8	12,671	57.7	29.5	2.1	29.3	20.8	...	68.1	24.2
Cecil, MD	24015	66,219	52.3	86.0	5,065	69.9	20.7	-6.7	20.4	19.6	...	49.9	...
Charles, MD	24017	90,195	41.0	90.6	10,228	76.9	26.1	-1.3	27.0	23.4	...	47.9	29.5
Dorchester, MD	24019	22,446	60.1	79.0	1,633	86.0	16.3	-11.1	18.9	5.2	...	...	...
Frederick, MD	24021	146,243	37.3	91.5	16,355	57.7	34.6	7.2	35.2	25.8	...	62.3	18.9
Garrett, MD	24023	20,635	58.1	82.9	932	84.7	15.8	-11.6	15.9	...	...	...	...
Harford, MD	24025	158,498	38.1	90.8	15,350	76.6	29.3	1.9	30.3	19.6	...	49.9	24.0
Howard, MD	24027	179,899	20.4	94.4	20,814	76.1	57.5	30.1	59.4	45.6	...	67.9	42.9
Kent, MD	24029	13,780	49.3	85.2	2,168	37.2	30.2	2.8	34.3	10.2	...	...	...
Montgomery, MD	24031	635,345	23.6	91.1	72,351	68.5	56.4	29.0	66.2	39.8	24.7	63.4	23.3
Prince George's, MD	24033	529,037	41.9	86.2	80,202	77.5	30.1	2.7	40.1	28.5	26.9	55.0	9.9
Queen Anne's, MD	24035	31,537	42.8	87.8	2,410	83.8	27.8	0.4	29.4	11.7	...	...	...
St. Mary's, MD	24037	63,913	46.0	88.7	7,441	78.6	25.9	-1.5	27.9	12.7	...	36.9	19.6
Somerset, MD	24039	16,870	64.9	81.4	4,376	96.3	13.7	-13.7	17.4	7.1	...	...	...
Talbot, MD	24041	26,539	40.0	88.3	1,527	68.4	32.8	5.4	36.5	10.8	...	...	...
Washington, MD	24043	99,468	55.1	82.6	7,510	77.1	18.3	-9.1	18.6	9.7	...	52.0	23.5
Wicomico, MD	24045	60,024	51.4	83.5	9,160	91.3	23.5	-3.9	26.0	14.2	...	48.8	15.0
Worcester, MD	24047	36,699	46.0	87.2	2,141	75.7	26.6	-0.8	30.0	5.0	...	...	...
Baltimore city, MD	24510	413,086	53.8	75.8	54,377	65.0	24.2	-3.2	43.1	12.8	16.1	63.3	18.9

[3] May be of any race
... Not available

Table C-1. Population, School, and Student Characteristics by County—*Continued*

County	State/County Code	County Type[1]	Population, 2009 Total	Population, 2009 Percent 5–17 years	Percent of related children 5-17 years in poverty, 2008	Percent of children under 19 years with no health insurance, 2007	Number of Schools and Students, 2008-2009 School Districts	Number of Schools and Students, 2008-2009 Schools	Number of Schools and Students, 2008-2009 Students	Resident enrollment, 2006-2008 K–12 enrollment Number	Resident enrollment, 2006-2008 K–12 enrollment Percent public
			1	2	3	4	5	6	7	8	9
MASSACHUSETTS	25000	X	6,593,587	15.9	11.0	4.3	500	1,901	958,910	1,060,890	87.8
Barnstable, MA	25001	3	221,151	13.0	9.6	5.4	23	60	27,594	30,787	89.3
Berkshire, MA	25003	3	129,288	14.8	12.6	4.1	42	50	18,138	19,622	89.4
Bristol, MA	25005	1	547,433	16.5	13.1	4.4	30	165	86,477	91,723	90.5
Dukes, MA	25007	7	15,974	13.4	10.5	10.3	9	7	2,277	...	...
Essex, MA	25009	1	742,582	17.0	10.9	4.7	52	225	113,593	129,721	86.8
Franklin, MA	25011	2	71,778	14.5	13.1	4.5	35	40	9,768	10,623	87.8
Hampden, MA	25013	2	471,081	17.4	21.5	3.6	24	146	75,562	81,480	91.8
Hampshire, MA	25015	2	156,044	13.1	8.6	4.7	30	54	20,155	19,095	92.1
Middlesex, MA	25017	1	1,505,006	15.4	7.2	4.5	76	383	213,121	231,854	88.3
Nantucket, MA	25019	7	11,322	13.8	5.1	9.2	1	3	1,279	...	...
Norfolk, MA	25021	1	666,303	16.7	5.2	3.9	36	188	101,575	109,929	84.2
Plymouth, MA	25023	1	498,344	18.1	7.3	4.7	35	145	81,983	90,001	88.9
Suffolk, MA	25025	1	753,580	12.1	23.7	3.6	21	179	75,124	102,426	81.7
Worcester, MA	25027	2	803,701	17.4	8.5	4.2	86	256	132,264	138,628	89.6
MICHIGAN	26000	X	9,969,727	17.4	17.8	6.8	846	4,225	1,659,921	1,827,303	90.0
Alcona, MI	26001	9	11,091	12.6	23.5	10.2	1	3	996	...	...
Alger, MI	26003	9	9,286	13.6	17.4	9.1	4	5	1,206	...	...
Allegan, MI	26005	4	113,449	18.9	12.7	8.0	12	49	15,716	21,220	84.9
Alpena, MI	26007	7	29,289	15.4	21.6	6.8	3	16	4,755	4,711	93.8
Antrim, MI	26009	9	23,834	15.9	18.4	11.5	7	14	4,222	3,837	93.5
Arenac, MI	26011	8	16,092	14.6	23.3	8.9	3	8	2,535	...	...
Baraga, MI	26013	9	8,604	14.8	20.4	11.1	3	7	1,292	...	...
Barry, MI	26015	2	58,434	18.2	10.7	7.7	4	20	7,839	11,000	93.0
Bay, MI	26017	3	107,434	16.1	16.3	6.6	7	42	15,867	17,794	87.6
Benzie, MI	26019	9	17,227	15.8	14.4	13.2	2	8	2,399	...	...
Berrien, MI	26021	3	160,472	17.4	24.6	7.9	21	88	27,012	28,791	86.5
Branch, MI	26023	6	44,737	17.1	18.4	8.5	6	24	8,215	8,024	89.2
Calhoun, MI	26025	3	135,616	17.2	20.0	6.0	15	69	23,085	24,714	91.8
Cass, MI	26027	2	49,925	17.2	17.3	6.8	5	24	7,685	9,003	91.1
Charlevoix, MI	26029	7	25,796	16.5	15.8	9.0	8	21	4,470	4,430	92.6
Cheboygan, MI	26031	7	26,106	15.4	24.4	9.1	4	16	3,595	4,234	90.3
Chippewa, MI	26033	5	38,731	13.0	20.4	8.6	9	23	5,491	5,671	94.4
Clare, MI	26035	7	30,104	15.3	27.8	6.8	4	19	4,934	5,066	94.8
Clinton, MI	26037	2	69,893	18.8	7.6	7.6	7	32	10,537	13,070	90.5
Crawford, MI	26039	7	14,203	14.9	24.7	7.3	1	6	1,821	...	...
Delta, MI	26041	5	36,918	15.1	15.4	6.8	5	18	5,140	6,073	93.7
Dickinson, MI	26043	5	26,691	16.3	12.9	6.8	5	17	4,366	4,737	97.0
Eaton, MI	26045	2	106,077	17.1	9.8	6.2	11	52	19,631	18,762	90.1
Emmet, MI	26047	7	33,649	16.4	12.4	9.3	6	17	5,593	5,576	91.1
Genesee, MI	26049	2	424,043	18.3	20.6	6.4	32	185	78,429	83,395	93.6
Gladwin, MI	26051	6	25,724	15.1	27.0	8.2	3	10	3,481	4,043	91.7
Gogebic, MI	26053	7	15,936	12.5	23.8	6.2	4	8	1,974	...	...
Grand Traverse, MI	26055	5	86,333	15.8	10.6	8.2	7	38	13,643	14,473	87.8
Gratiot, MI	26057	6	41,948	15.8	17.3	6.1	7	29	7,462	7,763	95.3
Hillsdale, MI	26059	6	45,650	17.3	18.9	7.3	11	32	7,325	8,343	89.5
Houghton, MI	26061	5	35,333	14.9	18.2	8.4	10	22	5,509	5,120	98.2
Huron, MI	26063	7	32,236	15.7	18.4	8.0	16	30	5,060	5,278	93.3
Ingham, MI	26065	2	277,633	14.9	18.5	7.1	23	168	43,248	44,061	93.0
Ionia, MI	26067	2	62,574	17.8	14.8	7.7	11	38	11,639	12,010	92.2
Iosco, MI	26069	7	25,817	13.7	27.1	6.8	6	21	4,947	3,956	94.0
Iron, MI	26071	7	11,633	13.6	20.2	7.4	2	5	1,561	...	...
Isabella, MI	26073	5	67,176	12.6	19.6	7.5	5	22	6,646	9,060	88.7
Jackson, MI	26075	3	159,828	16.8	17.0	6.5	16	69	26,110	29,485	92.5
Kalamazoo, MI	26077	2	248,407	15.8	15.4	6.7	13	91	35,577	41,499	90.1
Kalkaska, MI	26079	7	16,891	16.0	22.3	8.3	3	11	2,453	...	...
Kent, MI	26081	2	608,315	18.3	16.4	7.4	38	282	110,208	117,321	84.5
Keweenaw, MI	26083	9	2,305	12.3	24.5	18.6	1	1	5	...	...
Lake, MI	26085	8	10,926	13.4	33.9	7.1	1	4	581	...	...
Lapeer, MI	26087	1	89,974	18.4	11.6	7.5	8	40	16,404	17,083	91.9
Leelanau, MI	26089	9	21,899	15.0	11.1	13.4	4	7	2,292	3,356	83.8
Lenawee, MI	26091	4	99,837	17.2	11.8	6.4	13	50	17,465	17,632	91.1
Livingston, MI	26093	1	183,198	19.3	5.8	7.1	8	54	30,067	34,471	92.2
Luce, MI	26095	7	6,518	14.0	24.7	7.5	1	4	928	...	...
Mackinac, MI	26097	7	10,591	14.4	18.6	9.4	6	12	1,462	...	...
Macomb, MI	26099	1	831,427	17.1	11.2	6.5	35	262	137,045	144,624	91.1
Manistee, MI	26101	7	24,439	14.6	18.9	7.4	6	17	3,352	3,649	88.4
Marquette, MI	26103	5	65,703	13.2	14.5	6.6	10	31	8,554	9,308	93.3
Mason, MI	26105	7	28,637	15.6	22.6	7.4	5	19	4,534	4,600	93.1
Mecosta, MI	26107	6	41,775	14.5	23.9	8.7	5	28	6,864	5,786	89.2

[1]County type codes are from the Economic Research Service of the United States Department of Agriculture. See notes and definitions for more information.
... Not available

Table C-1. Population, School, and Student Characteristics by County—*Continued*

County	State/County Code	Characteristics of students, 2008-2009				Number of graduates, 2006-2007	Staff and students, 2008-2009			
		Percent with IEP[2]	Percent eligible for free or reduced lunch	Percent minority	Percent English Language Learners		Total staff	Number of teachers	Student/teacher ratio	Central admin. Staff
		10	11	12	13	14	15	16	17	18
MASSACHUSETTS	25000	17.6	30.7	30.1	5.1	64,762	123,626	70,395	13.6	5,792
Barnstable, MA	25001	16.2	20.6	12.8	1.7	2,292	3,895	2,233	12.4	167
Berkshire, MA	25003	17.1	33.0	13.4	1.7	1,346	2,929	1,537	11.8	154
Bristol, MA	25005	16.9	34.7	20.5	2.0	5,914	10,196	5,927	14.6	455
Dukes, MA	25007	21.6	14.1	19.5	4.3	213	490	265	8.6	17
Essex, MA	25009	17.6	34.1	32.0	6.7	7,768	14,161	8,257	13.8	574
Franklin, MA	25011	19.3	35.2	11.4	0.9	680	1,668	798	12.2	81
Hampden, MA	25013	20.4	48.3	45.7	7.4	4,514	10,093	5,761	13.1	437
Hampshire, MA	25015	18.3	21.7	16.7	1.8	1,577	3,020	1,611	12.5	160
Middlesex, MA	25017	17.5	20.4	27.4	5.5	14,840	27,929	15,842	13.5	1,234
Nantucket, MA	25019	13.1	5.0	26.8	4.2	96	225	122	10.5	13
Norfolk, MA	25021	16.9	13.8	20.7	2.8	7,114	12,766	7,309	13.9	539
Plymouth, MA	25023	15.5	23.6	18.0	2.5	5,197	9,561	5,655	14.5	408
Suffolk, MA	25025	19.4	72.4	82.5	10.5	4,276	10,273	5,830	12.9	863
Worcester, MA	25027	17.2	29.1	24.4	6.2	8,935	16,421	9,249	14.3	693
MICHIGAN	26000	14.0	41.8	28.2	3.7	112,453	208,052	94,752	17.5	4,567
Alcona, MI	26001	15.2	50.9	2.3	...	70	107	55	18.1	5
Alger, MI	26003	18.3	43.7	15.5	...	100	167	81	14.9	15
Allegan, MI	26005	12.3	38.1	10.6	2.3	1,038	2,005	877	17.9	53
Alpena, MI	26007	13.4	44.5	2.0	...	377	615	261	18.2	18
Antrim, MI	26009	33.8	48.1	5.4	0.2	323	501	244	17.3	11
Arenac, MI	26011	13.6	54.3	3.1	...	195	301	132	19.2	10
Baraga, MI	26013	13.1	46.2	33.0	23.4	76	161	87	14.9	7
Barry, MI	26015	12.4	36.3	5.6	0.7	572	875	412	19.0	20
Bay, MI	26017	16.7	45.7	10.0	1.4	1,207	1,989	856	18.5	65
Benzie, MI	26019	13.3	54.2	8.5	...	181	264	133	18.0	8
Berrien, MI	26021	14.2	50.2	31.8	2.1	1,821	3,547	1,663	16.2	94
Branch, MI	26023	13.2	50.3	8.2	5.1	520	1,014	462	17.0	23
Calhoun, MI	26025	15.3	49.0	25.4	2.1	1,484	3,000	1,451	15.9	72
Cass, MI	26027	12.9	47.5	16.5	2.8	440	916	392	19.6	38
Charlevoix, MI	26029	14.6	37.1	7.2	0.2	364	685	308	14.5	23
Cheboygan, MI	26031	14.1	55.9	5.3	...	299	516	235	15.3	18
Chippewa, MI	26033	15.5	49.7	38.4	0.1	385	833	352	15.6	39
Clare, MI	26035	16.3	59.2	3.4	...	350	656	299	16.5	20
Clinton, MI	26037	11.7	21.6	6.8	0.1	813	1,281	574	18.4	40
Crawford, MI	26039	18.7	55.3	3.3	...	146	204	109	16.7	4
Delta, MI	26041	15.6	40.0	5.8	...	440	640	289	17.8	28
Dickinson, MI	26043	14.9	33.7	2.7	0.1	362	560	280	15.6	22
Eaton, MI	26045	15.2	33.4	13.7	0.5	1,425	2,515	1,148	17.1	78
Emmet, MI	26047	11.1	34.6	9.4	...	418	639	340	16.5	16
Genesee, MI	26049	14.0	47.7	32.5	0.9	4,975	10,398	4,292	18.3	207
Gladwin, MI	26051	17.8	53.2	3.9	...	263	414	183	19.0	6
Gogebic, MI	26053	13.4	52.6	6.5	...	179	234	135	14.6	9
Grand Traverse, MI	26055	14.3	36.8	6.3	1.6	978	2,150	865	15.8	48
Gratiot, MI	26057	14.5	43.0	7.9	0.7	646	1,106	462	16.2	23
Hillsdale, MI	26059	16.0	49.0	4.1	0.1	501	912	434	16.9	25
Houghton, MI	26061	10.1	47.5	2.9	...	407	642	338	16.3	23
Huron, MI	26063	15.1	47.4	3.9	...	542	665	299	16.9	32
Ingham, MI	26065	16.3	40.6	36.1	2.4	2,859	5,683	2,554	16.9	141
Ionia, MI	26067	17.1	43.6	5.8	1.5	772	1,572	676	17.2	45
Iosco, MI	26069	15.7	63.3	4.5	0.1	373	658	282	17.5	29
Iron, MI	26071	15.6	48.2	3.9	0.1	124	176	94	16.6	1
Isabella, MI	26073	18.1	38.4	14.9	...	520	855	397	16.7	26
Jackson, MI	26075	14.9	47.4	17.0	0.5	1,720	3,187	1,563	16.7	62
Kalamazoo, MI	26077	12.5	41.8	28.8	3.1	2,258	4,767	2,140	16.6	84
Kalkaska, MI	26079	14.6	61.7	3.6	...	201	248	133	18.4	6
Kent, MI	26081	14.2	42.2	31.3	7.5	6,920	13,471	6,370	17.3	233
Keweenaw, MI	26083	...	69.4	...	...		3	1	5.0	...
Lake, MI	26085	18.9	90.0	30.4	...	38	73	41	14.2	5
Lapeer, MI	26087	11.8	34.4	7.0	1.4	1,145	1,912	861	19.1	43
Leelanau, MI	26089	14.3	30.9	18.1	3.6	205	314	152	15.1	12
Lenawee, MI	26091	14.9	37.3	15.4	1.1	1,275	2,321	1,065	16.4	83
Livingston, MI	26093	15.2	16.5	4.3	0.2	2,189	3,447	1,639	18.3	60
Luce, MI	26095	21.4	47.5	9.2	...	82	109	63	14.7	5
Mackinac, MI	26097	11.8	45.2	46.4	...	118	192	100	14.6	9
Macomb, MI	26099	13.1	32.5	20.5	3.8	9,389	15,057	7,158	19.1	288
Manistee, MI	26101	14.4	51.4	10.2	...	279	444	201	16.7	11
Marquette, MI	26103	17.5	35.1	6.8	0.1	749	1,086	517	16.5	48
Mason, MI	26105	15.6	47.8	6.8	...	378	657	280	16.2	22
Mecosta, MI	26107	19.8	55.3	9.3	...	473	970	415	16.5	29

[2]IEP= Individual Education Program. See notes and definitions for more information

... Not available

Table C-1. Population, School, and Student Characteristics by County—*Continued*

County	State/County Code	Revenues, 2007-2008				Current expenditures, 2007-2008			Resident population 16 to 19 years, 2006-2008			
		Total revenue ($1,000's)	Percentage of revenue from			Amount ($1,000's)	Amount per student	Percent for instruction	Total population 16 to 19 years	Percent enrolled in school	Percent high school graduates, not enrolled in school	Percent not enrolled, not grads, not employed or not in labor force
			Federal gov't	State gov't	Local gov't							
		19	20	21	22	23	24	25	26	27	28	29
MASSACHUSETTS	25000	14,633,578	5.1	41.8	53.1	13,308,358	14,193	63.7	374,694	88.5	6.8	3.1
Barnstable, MA	25001	447,211	3.8	29.4	66.8	410,515	15,463	64.9	9,905	90.9	7.0	1.1
Berkshire, MA	25003	301,159	6.0	46.0	48.0	269,859	14,790	62.7	7,836	88.0	7.8	2.7
Bristol, MA	25005	1,187,411	5.7	55.0	39.3	1,074,571	12,420	63.4	30,963	82.3	8.2	5.2
Dukes, MA	25007	57,706	2.7	25.9	71.4	51,487	24,138	65.7	...	...	...	...
Essex, MA	25009	1,694,396	5.1	45.5	49.4	1,523,866	13,605	64.9	40,561	87.5	7.4	3.3
Franklin, MA	25011	187,053	4.8	47.7	47.5	154,500	15,809	62.0	3,750	83.3	10.4	2.1
Hampden, MA	25013	1,113,353	8.0	59.4	32.5	1,029,997	14,178	62.6	29,375	82.4	8.8	6.1
Hampshire, MA	25015	297,857	4.3	42.1	53.6	270,609	13,673	62.6	15,064	95.9	2.2	0.8
Middlesex, MA	25017	3,370,949	3.9	33.0	63.0	3,078,164	14,807	64.2	78,547	91.3	5.6	1.9
Nantucket, MA	25019	31,389	2.2	15.3	82.6	28,759	22,208	62.8	...	...	...	...
Norfolk, MA	25021	1,467,863	3.6	29.9	66.5	1,349,283	13,535	64.1	35,616	90.5	7.3	1.9
Plymouth, MA	25023	1,091,948	4.6	44.2	51.2	1,014,031	12,462	62.8	27,364	88.5	6.6	3.0
Suffolk, MA	25025	1,509,937	7.1	33.8	59.1	1,397,604	20,106	60.7	47,391	89.8	5.4	3.8
Worcester, MA	25027	1,875,346	5.2	52.2	42.6	1,655,113	12,705	65.6	46,780	87.7	7.8	3.2
MICHIGAN	26000	20,580,072	7.3	54.8	37.8	17,018,115	10,146	56.8	601,051	86.1	8.2	4.2
Alcona, MI	26001	9,934	5.6	28.0	66.4	9,207	9,235	63.0	...	...	...	...
Alger, MI	26003	13,359	4.9	54.9	40.2	12,384	9,660	59.5	...	...	...	...
Allegan, MI	26005	179,734	6.5	55.5	38.0	145,689	9,307	58.1	6,333	83.2	9.7	5.4
Alpena, MI	26007	53,422	10.4	56.2	33.4	49,250	10,186	53.3	...	...	...	...
Antrim, MI	26009	44,244	5.0	34.2	60.8	37,403	8,620	61.4	1,133	75.9	13.9	8.8
Arenac, MI	26011	25,958	6.0	61.7	32.3	23,296	8,814	59.1	...	...	...	...
Baraga, MI	26013	14,506	12.9	58.9	28.2	12,400	9,268	61.6	...	...	...	...
Barry, MI	26015	82,305	5.3	64.0	30.7	68,273	8,611	62.8	...	...	...	...
Bay, MI	26017	183,985	8.2	58.3	33.5	156,175	9,842	55.9	5,687	82.4	11.4	3.6
Benzie, MI	26019	23,481	5.1	37.1	57.8	21,034	8,350	61.2	...	...	...	...
Berrien, MI	26021	301,498	10.0	56.2	33.8	269,608	9,971	56.7	9,261	79.5	11.8	4.2
Branch, MI	26023	84,794	9.6	57.9	32.5	76,611	10,370	61.3	...	...	...	...
Calhoun, MI	26025	291,269	10.7	58.7	30.6	243,772	10,646	54.2	8,078	82.8	8.7	5.0
Cass, MI	26027	78,149	8.2	63.3	28.6	66,866	8,761	53.6	2,855	82.8	9.8	4.0
Charlevoix, MI	26029	73,408	6.5	27.1	66.3	58,471	13,346	50.9	...	...	...	...
Cheboygan, MI	26031	46,257	9.8	43.8	46.4	38,737	10,796	56.3	...	...	...	...
Chippewa, MI	26033	69,563	20.7	51.0	28.3	60,498	10,984	55.2	...	...	...	...
Clare, MI	26035	57,097	12.5	52.9	34.6	51,418	10,290	56.7	1,562	81.5	11.8	4.0
Clinton, MI	26037	120,240	6.4	61.4	32.1	95,687	9,316	57.1	...	...	...	...
Crawford, MI	26039	18,414	6.5	49.4	44.1	16,327	8,526	58.1	...	...	...	...
Delta, MI	26041	59,751	9.9	56.0	34.0	52,738	10,232	56.3	...	...	...	...
Dickinson, MI	26043	52,056	9.0	52.6	38.4	44,482	9,958	61.1	...	...	...	...
Eaton, MI	26045	231,270	5.6	57.6	36.8	187,017	9,358	58.5	6,170	85.8	9.1	4.2
Emmet, MI	26047	62,822	3.1	21.8	75.1	51,175	8,947	65.9	...	...	...	...
Genesee, MI	26049	926,212	10.1	63.5	26.4	814,187	9,800	56.3	24,780	82.9	9.3	6.4
Gladwin, MI	26051	32,347	7.6	62.3	30.0	28,676	8,198	61.2	...	...	...	...
Gogebic, MI	26053	21,155	10.2	54.8	35.0	19,573	9,618	63.7	...	...	...	...
Grand Traverse, MI	26055	190,094	9.9	40.9	49.3	153,660	11,547	49.8	4,362	84.4	9.6	3.5
Gratiot, MI	26057	100,793	13.8	58.8	27.3	76,203	10,197	57.9	...	...	...	...
Hillsdale, MI	26059	77,043	6.7	65.7	27.6	68,500	9,725	61.4	...	...	...	...
Houghton, MI	26061	60,407	8.7	61.6	29.7	52,287	9,895	58.2	...	...	...	...
Huron, MI	26063	70,887	6.7	50.4	42.9	59,960	10,243	58.4	...	...	...	...
Ingham, MI	26065	578,098	7.7	53.4	38.9	476,818	10,897	54.2	22,760	93.7	3.6	2.5
Ionia, MI	26067	141,170	7.7	60.5	31.8	113,256	9,735	56.8	3,413	90.0	5.9	2.7
Iosco, MI	26069	53,586	10.2	47.3	42.5	47,319	9,333	60.0	...	...	...	...
Iron, MI	26071	16,680	7.2	51.1	41.7	15,254	9,206	63.2	...	...	...	...
Isabella, MI	26073	72,587	3.5	58.8	37.7	60,713	8,636	59.2	...	...	...	...
Jackson, MI	26075	311,768	6.9	58.3	34.8	266,620	10,171	57.8	9,431	85.2	7.6	6.4
Kalamazoo, MI	26077	434,027	8.0	49.9	42.1	349,050	9,941	56.8	16,702	91.0	6.1	1.8
Kalkaska, MI	26079	23,807	8.0	50.1	41.9	21,144	8,361	60.1	...	...	...	...
Kent, MI	26081	1,461,599	6.1	50.7	43.2	1,106,371	9,968	57.2	35,266	85.4	8.7	4.3
Keweenaw, MI	26083	122	13.1	...	86.9	134	44,667	54.5	...	...	...	...
Lake, MI	26085	17,027	6.4	57.5	36.0	7,277	11,852	58.2	...	...	...	...
Lapeer, MI	26087	155,441	4.9	65.5	29.6	132,147	8,803	59.2	5,439	80.4	11.1	7.7
Leelanau, MI	26089	32,606	10.9	17.9	71.2	25,107	10,621	60.5	...	...	...	...
Lenawee, MI	26091	209,637	6.1	58.7	35.2	177,962	10,082	57.9	6,294	88.3	6.1	4.1
Livingston, MI	26093	350,692	4.5	55.7	39.8	273,415	9,083	58.2	10,637	85.6	9.9	2.8
Luce, MI	26095	9,654	6.9	52.5	40.6	9,294	9,148	64.9	...	...	...	...
Mackinac, MI	26097	18,018	8.6	28.8	62.5	15,249	10,026	59.3	...	...	...	...
Macomb, MI	26099	1,644,893	6.0	57.2	36.8	1,349,220	9,939	57.4	42,883	87.7	7.3	3.7
Manistee, MI	26101	41,116	7.7	44.0	48.3	35,431	10,324	55.9	...	...	...	...
Marquette, MI	26103	98,753	10.5	55.0	34.5	86,121	10,002	55.6	...	...	...	...
Mason, MI	26105	58,218	7.5	39.9	52.7	51,099	11,174	59.9	...	...	...	...
Mecosta, MI	26107	86,101	8.0	52.6	39.4	73,973	10,982	57.3	...	...	...	...

[3]May be of any race

Table C-1. Population, School, and Student Characteristics by County—*Continued*

County	State/County Code	High school graduates, 2006-2008			College enrollment, 2006-2008		College graduates, 2006-2008 (percent)						
		Population 25 years and over	High school diploma or less (percent)	High school diploma or more (percent)	Number	Percent public	Bachelor's degree or more	+/- U.S. percent with Bachelor's degree or more	Non-Hispanic White	Black or African American	American Indian and Alaska Native	Asian, Hawaiian, and Pacific Islander	Hispanic or Latino[3]
	29	30	31	32	33	34	35	36	37	38	39	40	41
MASSACHUSETTS	25000	4,373,025	39.2	88.4	535,203	46.1	37.7	10.3	39.6	21.9	21.5	56.5	15.7
Barnstable, MA	25001	166,181	31.4	94.7	12,709	66.4	40.5	13.1	41.3	22.5	...	44.3	30.0
Berkshire, MA	25003	91,197	44.1	90.2	9,437	55.0	29.3	1.9	29.4	18.7	...	46.7	23.2
Bristol, MA	25005	370,700	51.3	79.4	35,229	65.2	24.1	-3.3	24.5	23.6	28.8	42.9	14.0
Dukes, MA	25007	...	...	...	...	...	...	...	...	...	...	...	...
Essex, MA	25009	493,656	39.4	87.8	49,519	56.1	35.9	8.5	39.2	19.9	24.2	49.4	10.8
Franklin, MA	25011	51,009	41.4	90.3	5,626	78.1	31.6	4.2	31.6	39.4	...	...	21.7
Hampden, MA	25013	300,812	50.2	83.8	34,258	59.3	23.8	-3.6	26.8	15.6	...	38.8	9.2
Hampshire, MA	25015	95,525	32.4	91.9	34,142	70.1	42.4	15.0	42.2	50.5	...	66.6	30.1
Middlesex, MA	25017	1,009,411	32.0	91.3	131,178	34.1	48.5	21.1	49.1	32.1	21.7	64.9	26.8
Nantucket, MA	25019	...	...	...	...	...	...	...	...	...	...	...	...
Norfolk, MA	25021	449,469	30.3	93.0	47,583	35.3	47.5	20.1	47.5	36.6	...	57.6	33.9
Plymouth, MA	25023	326,870	40.1	91.5	29,886	63.4	31.8	4.4	33.4	14.7	21.2	47.4	14.4
Suffolk, MA	25025	480,287	44.4	82.3	88,849	25.5	37.7	10.3	50.1	17.3	15.1	43.3	13.7
Worcester, MA	25027	520,015	43.0	88.4	56,219	53.4	31.8	4.4	32.3	21.0	34.2	61.7	13.7
MICHIGAN	26000	6,637,533	44.4	87.6	762,766	82.1	24.7	-2.7	25.7	14.2	12.6	62.1	14.0
Alcona, MI	26001	...	...	...	...	...	...	...	...	...	...	...	...
Alger, MI	26003	...	...	...	...	...	...	...	...	...	...	...	...
Allegan, MI	26005	74,395	50.9	87.3	5,642	80.8	19.6	-7.8	20.3	16.7	...	...	4.4
Alpena, MI	26007	20,981	47.0	87.9	1,916	87.0	15.6	-11.8	14.9	...	...	...	...
Antrim, MI	26009	17,330	50.0	88.6	855	81.3	21.7	-5.7	22.1	...	...	...	...
Arenac, MI	26011	...	...	...	...	...	...	...	...	...	...	...	...
Baraga, MI	26013	...	...	...	...	...	...	...	...	...	...	...	...
Barry, MI	26015	39,973	50.4	90.0	3,268	87.4	17.2	-10.2	17.5	...	...	...	3.3
Bay, MI	26017	74,403	49.2	87.2	6,634	85.8	18.0	-9.4	18.1	12.7	...	...	13.5
Benzie, MI	26019	...	...	...	...	...	...	...	...	...	...	...	...
Berrien, MI	26021	106,759	46.3	86.2	8,866	67.3	23.1	-4.3	24.5	11.1	27.0	63.5	9.7
Branch, MI	26023	31,805	55.3	86.6	2,001	79.7	13.6	-13.8	14.2	...	...	...	4.7
Calhoun, MI	26025	91,024	48.4	86.4	8,405	69.0	19.2	-8.2	20.1	11.8	...	31.1	14.1
Cass, MI	26027	34,981	53.8	85.2	2,400	84.5	15.4	-12.0	16.1	6.1	5.0	...	12.2
Charlevoix, MI	26029	18,247	45.1	91.4	638	90.4	24.2	-3.2	24.8	...	...	...	...
Cheboygan, MI	26031	19,179	51.6	88.9	949	84.7	17.7	-9.7	18.2	...	1.4	...	...
Chippewa, MI	26033	26,780	51.5	88.0	3,564	96.7	18.3	-9.1	21.5	...	8.0	...	...
Clare, MI	26035	21,565	59.4	81.2	976	91.5	9.4	-18.0	9.5	...	...	...	...
Clinton, MI	26037	46,267	39.5	93.3	4,179	87.8	27.1	-0.3	27.6	...	...	...	17.8
Crawford, MI	26039	...	...	...	...	...	...	...	...	...	...	...	...
Delta, MI	26041	26,257	48.8	89.7	2,119	96.8	17.2	-10.2	17.2	...	9.9	...	...
Dickinson, MI	26043	18,931	53.2	90.1	1,023	85.7	16.8	-10.6	16.7	...	...	...	...
Eaton, MI	26045	71,993	38.5	92.4	8,315	78.6	23.8	-3.6	23.5	27.4	...	38.0	19.1
Emmet, MI	26047	23,079	37.3	92.9	2,084	91.4	30.2	2.8	31.1	...	9.5	...	...
Genesee, MI	26049	285,461	47.1	88.4	29,365	83.0	18.7	-8.7	19.7	12.7	11.4	60.5	13.5
Gladwin, MI	26051	19,007	57.5	83.8	848	80.1	9.9	-17.5	9.8	...	...	...	...
Gogebic, MI	26053	...	...	...	...	...	...	...	...	...	...	...	...
Grand Traverse, MI	26055	59,088	36.9	92.1	4,692	90.8	27.7	0.3	28.4	...	...	16.9	...
Gratiot, MI	26057	27,536	55.1	86.0	3,403	41.1	14.1	-13.3	14.6	...	...	...	9.7
Hillsdale, MI	26059	31,169	55.7	85.8	2,828	47.7	14.2	-13.2	14.4	...	...	...	...
Houghton, MI	26061	20,988	48.9	89.6	6,378	87.3	23.6	-3.8	23.1	...	...	...	...
Huron, MI	26063	23,975	59.1	83.3	1,298	87.1	13.2	-14.2	13.2	...	...	...	3.6
Ingham, MI	26065	165,221	34.5	90.6	51,373	93.2	35.1	7.7	36.1	24.9	18.1	64.4	14.1
Ionia, MI	26067	41,800	53.3	86.2	3,419	81.1	13.1	-14.3	13.9	...	...	...	1.8
Iosco, MI	26069	19,282	55.6	83.8	940	76.9	14.7	-12.7	14.3	...	...	...	...
Iron, MI	26071	...	...	...	...	...	...	...	...	...	...	...	...
Isabella, MI	26073	34,278	43.4	89.5	1,8612	97.3	27.8	0.4	27.5	40.2	6.6	...	11.6
Jackson, MI	26075	108,989	49.6	88.1	9,521	72.1	16.9	-10.5	17.4	8.4	...	...	9.4
Kalamazoo, MI	26077	152,189	34.1	91.7	32,326	90.0	33.5	6.1	34.7	17.9	16.9	62.0	24.1
Kalkaska, MI	26079	...	...	...	...	...	...	...	...	...	...	...	...
Kent, MI	26081	381,230	39.8	87.5	42,385	67.6	29.6	2.2	32.9	11.6	14.0	36.7	10.6
Keweenaw, MI	26083	...	...	...	...	...	...	...	...	...	...	...	...
Lake, MI	26085	...	...	...	...	...	...	...	...	...	...	...	...
Lapeer, MI	26087	61,716	49.6	88.9	5,779	82.9	16.0	-11.4	16.5	...	...	...	2.9
Leelanau, MI	26089	15,826	29.0	91.5	998	86.9	39.7	12.3	42.2	...	...	...	...
Lenawee, MI	26091	67,708	49.3	86.7	6,115	55.9	18.9	-8.5	19.6	...	...	...	6.6
Livingston, MI	26093	121,447	34.3	93.4	13,007	86.5	30.8	3.4	30.7	46.8	21.2	47.0	20.7
Luce, MI	26095	...	...	...	...	...	...	...	...	...	...	...	...
Mackinac, MI	26097	...	...	...	...	...	...	...	...	...	...	...	...
Macomb, MI	26099	567,924	45.1	87.2	58,385	80.3	21.6	-5.8	20.9	16.7	18.3	52.6	18.6
Manistee, MI	26101	18,076	55.1	85.6	631	75.0	15.5	-11.9	16.4	...	...	...	1.2
Marquette, MI	26103	43,608	42.9	91.3	7,920	96.2	28.6	1.2	29.4	...	...	...	...
Mason, MI	26105	20,390	49.1	87.7	1,212	90.6	19.2	-8.2	19.9	...	...	...	4.5
Mecosta, MI	26107	25,350	50.5	86.4	8,168	97.6	18.8	-8.6	19.6	...	...	...	...

[3]May be of any race
... Not available

Table C-1. Population, School, and Student Characteristics by County—*Continued*

County	State/ County Code	County Type[1]	Population, 2009 Total	Population, 2009 Percent 5–17 years	Percent of related children 5-17 years in poverty, 2008	Percent of children under 19 years with no health insurance, 2007	Number of Schools and Students, 2008-2009 School Districts	Schools	Students	Resident enrollment, 2006-2008 K–12 enrollment Number	Resident enrollment, 2006-2008 K–12 enrollment Percent public
			1	2	3	4	5	6	7	8	9
Menominee, MI	26109	7	23,969	15.7	16.4	7.1	7	20	4,272	4,023	96.6
Midland, MI	26111	4	82,548	18.0	10.9	6.5	8	40	14,032	14,636	91.8
Missaukee, MI	26113	9	14,838	17.8	20.8	12.6	2	7	2,240	...	...
Monroe, MI	26115	3	152,721	18.0	12.2	5.7	12	59	25,028	27,740	88.0
Montcalm, MI	26117	6	62,733	17.3	20.2	7.2	7	33	10,560	12,228	93.2
Montmorency, MI	26119	9	10,094	12.5	29.8	10.0	2	3	897	...	...
Muskegon, MI	26121	3	173,951	17.8	20.9	5.4	16	82	31,932	33,302	94.0
Newaygo, MI	26123	2	48,686	18.7	19.2	7.9	7	32	9,313	9,550	89.9
Oakland, MI	26125	1	1,205,508	17.5	9.4	6.3	44	387	198,599	216,054	86.3
Oceana, MI	26127	8	27,577	18.3	27.5	12.0	5	21	3,742	5,062	91.8
Ogemaw, MI	26129	9	21,234	14.3	26.0	8.6	1	7	2,427	3,341	88.1
Ontonagon, MI	26131	9	6,569	12.5	21.5	9.7	3	6	863	...	...
Osceola, MI	26133	7	22,703	17.8	23.5	7.7	4	17	4,701	4,142	87.2
Oscoda, MI	26135	9	8,707	14.1	28.7	9.7	2	4	999	...	...
Otsego, MI	26137	7	23,412	17.1	13.5	8.1	3	10	4,305	4,168	88.9
Ottawa, MI	26139	3	261,957	18.9	8.1	7.4	16	96	44,018	49,123	84.2
Presque Isle, MI	26141	7	13,436	13.3	19.4	9.1	4	10	1,674	...	...
Roscommon, MI	26143	7	24,682	12.7	29.1	6.8	3	13	3,444	3,670	94.9
Saginaw, MI	26145	3	200,050	17.6	23.3	6.7	21	96	34,923	37,633	90.3
St. Clair, MI	26147	1	167,562	17.9	12.8	6.8	19	83	32,481	30,082	92.5
St. Joseph, MI	26149	4	61,723	18.3	18.8	8.4	10	37	11,810	11,555	93.0
Sanilac, MI	26151	6	42,064	17.7	19.8	8.2	8	30	7,734	7,766	93.0
Schoolcraft, MI	26153	7	8,127	15.3	20.8	7.4	2	4	1,311	...	...
Shiawassee, MI	26155	4	70,006	17.8	15.3	7.5	9	41	13,957	12,950	93.1
Tuscola, MI	26157	6	55,395	17.8	18.5	7.9	10	36	10,920	10,216	92.1
Van Buren, MI	26159	2	78,227	18.6	19.4	7.5	13	51	17,783	15,031	91.8
Washtenaw, MI	26161	2	347,563	14.9	11.5	7.2	20	112	47,970	53,254	88.1
Wayne, MI	26163	1	1,925,848	18.7	28.8	5.9	120	681	328,975	400,345	90.9
Wexford, MI	26165	7	31,553	16.7	22.6	6.8	5	19	5,784	5,451	92.6
MINNESOTA	27000	X	5,266,214	17.0	9.9	6.2	564	2,755	836,048	904,627	88.5
Aitkin, MN	27001	8	15,646	13.0	19.5	9.3	4	10	2,024	...	...
Anoka, MN	27003	1	331,582	18.7	6.3	5.5	11	114	64,376	63,046	91.0
Becker, MN	27005	6	32,076	17.1	16.1	6.6	5	28	4,454	5,357	93.5
Beltrami, MN	27007	7	44,350	17.3	22.8	7.4	9	34	7,503	8,084	95.3
Benton, MN	27009	3	40,193	17.1	10.1	5.6	3	9	5,433	6,822	89.5
Big Stone, MN	27011	9	5,251	14.9	13.8	9.1	2	6	866	...	...
Blue Earth, MN	27013	5	61,010	13.2	10.7	6.4	5	31	9,973	8,322	89.9
Brown, MN	27015	7	25,603	16.3	8.0	5.8	5	15	3,536	4,067	67.3
Carlton, MN	27017	2	34,327	17.3	10.4	6.3	8	27	6,423	6,104	87.5
Carver, MN	27019	1	92,107	21.3	3.5	5.3	7	50	15,308	18,828	81.5
Cass, MN	27021	9	28,534	15.4	21.2	9.1	8	27	4,149	4,572	97.0
Chippewa, MN	27023	7	12,321	17.3	10.5	7.3	3	12	2,230	...	...
Chisago, MN	27025	1	50,625	19.8	6.4	6.8	5	21	8,358	9,366	92.6
Clay, MN	27027	3	56,763	15.7	10.9	5.7	5	22	8,845	8,341	93.0
Clearwater, MN	27029	8	8,242	16.9	21.6	12.4	2	5	1,478	...	...
Cook, MN	27031	9	5,472	12.4	10.2	13.4	4	7	643	...	...
Cottonwood, MN	27033	7	11,116	18.5	13.6	7.4	3	9	1,964	...	...
Crow Wing, MN	27035	5	62,723	16.1	12.6	7.0	6	25	9,721	9,974	94.8
Dakota, MN	27037	1	396,500	18.8	4.7	5.1	17	164	75,301	76,677	89.5
Dodge, MN	27039	3	19,772	20.7	6.3	8.0	3	10	4,077	...	...
Douglas, MN	27041	7	36,390	14.8	9.5	7.0	7	28	5,299	5,414	92.9
Faribault, MN	27043	7	14,506	16.6	12.5	7.8	3	9	2,022	...	...
Fillmore, MN	27045	8	20,838	17.1	12.6	9.9	5	14	2,636	3,254	88.8
Freeborn, MN	27047	7	31,002	15.6	12.1	7.3	3	15	4,085	5,106	94.7
Goodhue, MN	27049	4	45,836	17.4	7.7	6.1	9	29	8,171	7,754	92.7
Grant, MN	27051	9	5,835	15.3	12.4	10.2	3	7	1,154	...	...
Hennepin, MN	27053	1	1,156,212	15.6	11.0	5.8	71	589	155,675	186,925	86.7
Houston, MN	27055	3	19,244	16.6	8.9	6.5	6	17	4,066	...	...
Hubbard, MN	27057	7	18,644	15.0	16.3	9.6	3	9	2,403	...	...
Isanti, MN	27059	1	39,442	18.5	8.3	7.4	5	27	6,292	6,969	89.2
Itasca, MN	27061	6	44,727	15.9	15.4	6.6	6	30	6,615	7,073	88.5
Jackson, MN	27063	7	10,786	15.5	10.2	7.5	2	6	1,497	...	...
Kanabec, MN	27065	6	15,899	17.7	14.7	6.1	2	6	2,506	...	...
Kandiyohi, MN	27067	4	41,123	16.8	11.8	7.5	4	18	5,689	6,825	91.1
Kittson, MN	27069	9	4,374	16.8	11.6	8.2	3	7	739	...	...
Koochiching, MN	27071	7	13,128	15.7	16.0	6.6	3	9	2,010	...	...
Lac qui Parle, MN	27073	9	7,110	16.0	9.4	9.7	3	7	1,506	...	...
Lake, MN	27075	6	10,610	13.6	10.3	7.4	1	5	1,442	...	...
Lake of the Woods, MN	27077	9	3,880	14.0	16.5	10.7	1	2	537	...	...
Le Sueur, MN	27079	6	28,059	18.0	8.7	7.7	5	19	4,364	5,028	90.9

[1]County type codes are from the Economic Research Service of the United States Department of Agriculture. See notes and definitions for more information.
... Not available

Table C-1.   Population, School, and Student Characteristics by County—*Continued*

County	State/County Code	Characteristics of students, 2008-2009				Number of graduates, 2006-2007	Staff and students, 2008-2009			
		Percent with IEP[2]	Percent eligible for free or reduced lunch	Percent minority	Percent English Language Learners		Total staff	Number of teachers	Student/teacher ratio	Central admin. Staff
		10	11	12	13	14	15	16	17	18
Menominee, MI	26109	13.4	42.9	7.3	0.3	298	537	249	17.2	15
Midland, MI	26111	14.8	28.3	6.9	0.4	1,024	1,715	770	18.2	28
Missaukee, MI	26113	10.5	52.9	4.4	...	179	252	123	18.2	4
Monroe, MI	26115	16.3	30.4	8.7	0.8	1,749	3,232	1,393	18.0	66
Montcalm, MI	26117	15.8	50.6	4.8	1.1	699	1,330	596	17.7	37
Montmorency, MI	26119	14.5	62.7	2.8	...	88	106	52	17.3	5
Muskegon, MI	26121	16.4	54.0	27.9	1.0	1,970	4,009	1,812	17.6	114
Newaygo, MI	26123	14.2	48.6	13.1	1.1	627	1,233	536	17.4	28
Oakland, MI	26125	12.0	25.9	31.6	5.7	14,304	24,836	11,449	17.3	428
Oceana, MI	26127	24.2	61.7	30.4	12.7	260	584	232	16.1	14
Ogemaw, MI	26129	13.8	61.9	3.9	...	201	286	134	18.1	3
Ontonagon, MI	26131	17.7	45.7	4.5	...	81	129	60	14.4	8
Osceola, MI	26133	16.5	57.2	5.4	...	410	518	269	17.5	14
Oscoda, MI	26135	17.6	59.0	2.6	...	85	125	59	16.9	1
Otsego, MI	26137	12.7	43.5	3.5	...	318	483	249	17.3	12
Ottawa, MI	26139	13.2	31.0	19.5	5.9	2,968	5,404	2,507	17.6	110
Presque Isle, MI	26141	10.3	50.7	1.7	...	164	197	98	17.1	5
Roscommon, MI	26143	18.1	60.6	4.4	...	271	468	199	17.3	16
Saginaw, MI	26145	17.4	51.1	41.2	1.6	2,045	4,559	2,064	16.9	117
St. Clair, MI	26147	13.6	36.8	9.4	0.3	2,165	3,943	1,809	18.0	105
St. Joseph, MI	26149	12.9	52.0	14.3	7.4	797	1,456	684	17.3	41
Sanilac, MI	26151	12.9	48.4	4.1	...	672	985	433	17.9	31
Schoolcraft, MI	26153	13.3	52.0	20.3	...	90	145	76	17.3	7
Shiawassee, MI	26155	14.3	37.1	3.0	...	977	1,755	790	17.7	47
Tuscola, MI	26157	16.4	51.1	7.7	...	797	1,493	620	17.6	42
Van Buren, MI	26159	11.9	47.1	19.9	8.8	1,154	2,556	1,087	16.4	62
Washtenaw, MI	26161	14.4	24.6	30.3	4.1	3,323	7,539	2,834	16.9	138
Wayne, MI	26163	13.6	55.9	55.7	6.2	20,335	39,700	18,463	17.8	711
Wexford, MI	26165	15.4	56.1	4.4	...	438	768	359	16.1	23
MINNESOTA	27000	14.4	32.7	24.3	7.4	59,453	109,212	53,081	15.8	4315
Aitkin, MN	27001	15.4	47.9	8.6	0.1	141	308	148	13.7	19
Anoka, MN	27003	13.4	27.5	20.4	6.4	4,357	7,724	3,907	16.5	246
Becker, MN	27005	21.2	39.0	18.1	0.4	336	646	317	14.1	31
Beltrami, MN	27007	18.5	55.9	35.5	0.1	487	1,331	599	12.5	58
Benton, MN	27009	16.8	30.7	7.8	0.3	390	647	306	17.8	22
Big Stone, MN	27011	14.4	43.5	4.0	0.2	85	156	72	12.0	8
Blue Earth, MN	27013	17.4	32.4	13.4	2.6	742	1,423	667	15.0	50
Brown, MN	27015	14.7	30.6	10.8	2.8	349	505	257	13.8	23
Carlton, MN	27017	14.2	30.5	12.5	0.1	454	778	386	16.6	41
Carver, MN	27019	13.1	13.8	11.5	4.0	1,117	1,925	1,001	15.3	86
Cass, MN	27021	21.6	60.2	32.3	0.2	380	718	346	12.0	34
Chippewa, MN	27023	16.5	35.9	9.7	2.7	185	337	155	14.4	13
Chisago, MN	27025	10.9	22.6	4.8	1.1	600	932	458	18.2	60
Clay, MN	27027	14.2	28.2	13.0	5.0	605	1,106	557	15.9	40
Clearwater, MN	27029	17.2	48.8	23.1	0.1	88	209	109	13.6	9
Cook, MN	27031	15.6	37.4	20.2	0.5	47	108	47	13.7	9
Cottonwood, MN	27033	18.2	41.6	20.6	10.3	117	326	156	12.6	16
Crow Wing, MN	27035	16.7	39.1	3.9	...	724	1,147	538	18.1	45
Dakota, MN	27037	14.7	19.9	21.7	5.7	5,394	8,971	4,553	16.5	339
Dodge, MN	27039	10.4	21.4	8.9	3.0	271	463	255	16.0	17
Douglas, MN	27041	17.5	29.1	3.7	0.1	468	766	363	14.6	26
Faribault, MN	27043	20.0	40.1	11.4	3.4	183	309	137	14.8	16
Fillmore, MN	27045	12.4	31.5	2.3	...	243	381	199	13.2	19
Freeborn, MN	27047	19.3	40.2	16.7	5.2	390	544	269	15.2	25
Goodhue, MN	27049	12.0	21.0	9.4	1.6	534	1023	507	16.1	46
Grant, MN	27051	15.4	36.7	5.0	...	102	176	93	12.4	11
Hennepin, MN	27053	13.3	36.6	42.9	12.0	9,735	20,980	9,708	16.0	792
Houston, MN	27055	9.1	23.7	4.1	...	314	493	262	15.5	23
Hubbard, MN	27057	19.4	50.9	10.0	0.4	188	329	172	14.0	15
Isanti, MN	27059	11.0	31.4	6.4	1.3	445	725	342	18.4	29
Itasca, MN	27061	15.5	42.6	12.6	...	587	822	394	16.8	41
Jackson, MN	27063	16.1	31.6	8.1	3.5	138	211	102	14.7	9
Kanabec, MN	27065	12.7	43.0	6.1	0.1	175	314	162	15.5	10
Kandiyohi, MN	27067	11.7	41.4	26.5	9.9	432	776	397	14.3	22
Kittson, MN	27069	18.7	38.5	3.3	...	66	144	71	10.4	8
Koochiching, MN	27071	15.2	38.1	11.2	0.1	144	289	139	14.5	10
Lac qui Parle, MN	27073	16.1	36.3	7.7	2.1	133	249	109	13.8	7
Lake, MN	27075	15.7	30.2	2.9	...	139	190	94	15.3	7
Lake of the Woods, MN	27077	15.8	43.3	6.7	...	51	80	36	14.9	4
Le Sueur, MN	27079	17.4	25.9	12.1	5.5	317	571	294	14.8	19

[2]IEP= Individual Education Program. See notes and definitions for more information
... Not available

Table C-1. Population, School, and Student Characteristics by County—*Continued*

County	State/County Code	Total revenue ($1,000's)	Percentage of revenue from Federal gov't	State gov't	Local gov't	Amount ($1,000's)	Amount per student	Percent for instruction	Total population 16 to 19 years	Percent enrolled in school	Percent high school graduates, not enrolled in school	Percent not enrolled, not grads, not employed or not in labor force
		19	20	21	22	23	24	25	26	27	28	29
Menominee, MI	26109	44,971	11.0	63.3	25.7	39,182	9,291	61.5	...	...	...	...
Midland, MI	26111	160,895	5.0	52.3	42.7	147,312	10,392	56.7	...	...	...	...
Missaukee, MI	26113	20,163	5.9	64.6	29.6	18,462	8,392	61.8	...	...	...	...
Monroe, MI	26115	283,731	5.0	54.6	40.4	238,949	9,686	56.4	8,795	86.0	8.2	4.2
Montcalm, MI	26117	116,212	7.2	64.1	28.7	99,130	9,463	56.8	3,616	82.2	10.4	5.2
Montmorency, MI	26119	9,978	6.9	39.2	53.9	8,251	8,750	59.4	...	...	...	...
Muskegon, MI	26121	395,946	11.0	57.8	31.2	319,867	9,648	56.4	10,062	84.3	9.1	4.7
Newaygo, MI	26123	107,121	7.9	62.3	29.8	90,936	9,640	61.2	2,769	80.8	11.7	6.0
Oakland, MI	26125	2,866,444	4.4	45.5	50.2	2,215,543	11,037	56.7	65,635	88.7	7.6	2.4
Oceana, MI	26127	40,667	12.6	54.9	32.6	35,408	9,070	59.8	1,714	77.5	11.6	6.2
Ogemaw, MI	26129	23,841	8.9	52.6	38.4	22,423	8,856	60.1	...	...	...	...
Ontonagon, MI	26131	10,306	7.5	47.9	44.5	8,667	10,113	58.5	...	...	...	...
Osceola, MI	26133	45,682	8.3	63.9	27.8	42,998	8,860	62.5	1,320	82.0	13.1	2.7
Oscoda, MI	26135	10,468	9.6	40.6	49.8	9,291	8,917	62.0	...	...	...	...
Otsego, MI	26137	43,230	4.7	39.9	55.4	36,460	8,254	63.4	...	...	...	...
Ottawa, MI	26139	548,497	4.8	50.3	44.9	415,773	9,507	60.9	18,487	90.0	7.3	1.4
Presque Isle, MI	26141	16,928	9.3	48.4	42.3	15,275	8,739	62.3	...	...	...	...
Roscommon, MI	26143	42,385	13.9	33.5	52.6	39,393	11,349	59.5	...	...	...	...
Saginaw, MI	26145	378,801	12.1	63.7	24.2	337,040	9,913	55.8	12,836	83.5	8.0	7.3
St. Clair, MI	26147	370,284	5.2	56.4	38.4	314,412	9,547	59.2	9,506	84.4	10.5	3.3
St. Joseph, MI	26149	124,897	7.0	60.9	32.1	106,003	8,932	58.0	3,528	83.6	8.1	4.2
Sanilac, MI	26151	80,620	7.9	66.3	25.8	70,656	8,959	60.4	2,444	82.2	12.5	4.2
Schoolcraft, MI	26153	13,336	9.0	43.6	47.5	11,782	8,470	59.5	...	...	...	...
Shiawassee, MI	26155	148,676	5.9	70.6	23.5	131,047	9,295	59.8	3,846	79.0	12.7	7.5
Tuscola, MI	26157	113,694	7.8	69.9	22.3	100,024	10,063	59.3	3,554	81.0	12.7	4.4
Van Buren, MI	26159	214,767	7.5	56.3	36.3	181,973	10,351	57.7	4,238	82.4	10.8	5.7
Washtenaw, MI	26161	711,365	3.9	43.6	52.5	526,398	10,963	54.9	...	...	...	...
Wayne, MI	26163	4,093,714	9.4	60.8	29.8	3,559,565	10,466	55.3	120,925	83.0	9.2	6.2
Wexford, MI	26165	70,399	8.1	52.9	39.0	61,357	11,069	54.7	...	...	...	...
MINNESOTA	27000	10,439,643	5.7	65.0	29.3	8,461,613	10,125	63.8	297,893	88.7	8.0	2.0
Aitkin, MN	27001	24,938	6.3	69.0	24.8	20,182	9,675	61.2	...	...	...	...
Anoka, MN	27003	726,018	4.2	70.0	25.8	613,431	9,436	66.4	18,344	84.9	10.7	2.5
Becker, MN	27005	47,260	8.8	73.4	17.7	39,980	9,113	65.1	1,721	84.0	11.6	2.8
Beltrami, MN	27007	106,623	16.5	65.3	18.1	96,543	12,819	66.1	...	...	...	...
Benton, MN	27009	66,526	3.2	61.3	35.6	46,855	8,607	58.0	...	...	...	...
Big Stone, MN	27011	11,386	4.7	69.9	25.3	9,384	10,700	62.9	...	...	...	...
Blue Earth, MN	27013	104,769	4.5	71.5	24.0	91,400	9,183	66.2	...	...	...	...
Brown, MN	27015	42,492	7.4	67.6	25.0	35,555	10,104	68.3	...	...	...	...
Carlton, MN	27017	68,543	7.3	72.4	20.3	54,849	8,751	66.7	...	...	...	...
Carver, MN	27019	203,213	2.8	54.7	42.5	145,279	9,808	65.5	...	...	...	...
Cass, MN	27021	60,764	13.7	64.5	21.8	50,222	11,876	61.7	...	...	...	...
Chippewa, MN	27023	27,708	6.1	69.5	24.4	23,094	10,817	64.1	...	...	...	...
Chisago, MN	27025	90,242	4.5	67.4	28.0	72,295	8,527	62.8	...	...	...	...
Clay, MN	27027	94,597	4.8	74.9	20.4	78,730	8,987	65.5	...	...	...	...
Clearwater, MN	27029	17,901	7.1	70.4	22.5	14,240	9,368	62.4	...	...	...	...
Cook, MN	27031	8,868	7.0	63.5	29.5	7,015	10,393	61.0	...	...	...	...
Cottonwood, MN	27033	22,690	4.5	73.8	21.7	19,061	9,478	63.2	...	...	...	...
Crow Wing, MN	27035	116,427	5.9	67.2	26.8	92,793	9,204	66.6	3,227	81.7	11.4	5.7
Dakota, MN	27037	901,786	3.6	64.0	32.4	707,829	9,437	67.3	21,404	90.4	7.4	1.7
Dodge, MN	27039	38,640	2.2	74.6	23.2	30,890	7,608	63.3	...	...	...	...
Douglas, MN	27041	58,231	4.9	69.2	25.8	48,667	9,258	67.8	...	...	...	...
Faribault, MN	27043	22,376	7.2	74.2	18.6	20,414	9,730	67.1	...	...	...	...
Fillmore, MN	27045	31,209	6.2	68.2	25.6	24,756	9,088	64.8	...	...	...	...
Freeborn, MN	27047	46,552	5.4	75.6	19.0	40,380	9,765	65.4	...	...	...	...
Goodhue, MN	27049	90,470	3.6	65.3	31.0	71,682	8,705	66.0	...	...	...	...
Grant, MN	27051	12,823	4.4	75.0	20.6	10,802	9,085	61.0	...	...	...	...
Hennepin, MN	27053	2,215,599	5.9	60.0	34.1	1,702,995	11,127	64.1	59,332	90.2	6.6	1.7
Houston, MN	27055	40,810	2.4	78.0	19.7	35,595	8,941	64.3	...	...	...	...
Hubbard, MN	27057	30,124	6.1	63.8	30.1	23,180	9,531	65.6	...	...	...	...
Isanti, MN	27059	62,913	6.6	73.0	20.4	48,647	8,022	65.2	2,020	86.4	10.9	1.9
Itasca, MN	27061	79,650	7.6	66.5	25.8	65,090	9,807	65.6	2,432	87.0	11.7	1.1
Jackson, MN	27063	16,558	3.3	69.7	27.0	12,797	8,203	64.8	...	...	...	...
Kanabec, MN	27065	24,904	6.0	76.5	17.5	21,085	8,141	68.6	...	...	...	...
Kandiyohi, MN	27067	64,771	5.5	73.9	20.6	55,947	9,706	66.5	...	...	...	...
Kittson, MN	27069	10,385	4.0	73.3	22.7	9,530	12,606	61.4	...	...	...	...
Koochiching, MN	27071	25,328	5.6	74.9	19.5	22,151	10,805	65.2	...	...	...	...
Lac qui Parle, MN	27073	18,520	5.0	74.8	20.2	15,557	9,947	64.9	...	...	...	...
Lake, MN	27075	18,577	3.9	62.3	33.8	13,963	9,217	64.2	...	...	...	...
Lake of the Woods, MN	27077	7,838	3.0	63.1	33.9	5,693	10,351	55.0	...	...	...	...
Le Sueur, MN	27079	46,271	4.1	70.2	25.7	37,928	8,371	64.0	...	...	...	...

³May be of any race

Table C-1. Population, School, and Student Characteristics by County—*Continued*

County	State/County Code	High school graduates, 2006-2008			College enrollment, 2006-2008		College graduates, 2006-2008 (percent)						
		Population 25 years and over	High school diploma or less (percent)	High school diploma or more (percent)	Number	Percent public	Bachelor's degree or more	+/- U.S. percent with Bachelor's degree or more	Non-Hispanic White	Black or African American	American Indian and Alaska Native	Asian, Hawaiian, and Pacific Islander	Hispanic or Latino[3]
		30	31	32	33	34	35	36	37	38	39	40	41
Menominee, MI	26109	17,240	55.4	88.7	856	97.2	13.5	-13.9	13.7	...	2.2	...	...
Midland, MI	26111	54,799	38.4	91.6	7,290	64.1	32.8	5.4	32.3	...	...	...	23.2
Missaukee, MI	26113	...	...	...	...	...	...	...	...	...	...	...	...
Monroe, MI	26115	102,549	51.6	87.2	8,987	85.5	16.0	-11.4	16.0	6.5	...	...	13.7
Montcalm, MI	26117	41,928	55.3	83.5	3,139	87.2	12.8	-14.6	13.2	...	...	...	2.2
Montmorency, MI	26119	...	...	...	...	...	...	...	...	...	...	...	...
Muskegon, MI	26121	114,445	48.4	87.3	9,649	73.3	16.3	-11.1	17.9	7.8	10.7	...	5.3
Newaygo, MI	26123	32,310	57.7	84.3	1,994	71.8	13.3	-14.1	13.8	7.8	1.0	...	1.4
Oakland, MI	26125	815,509	29.9	92.0	86,192	78.1	42.1	14.7	42.0	30.8	24.5	75.9	26.3
Oceana, MI	26127	18,252	55.7	83.5	1,211	85.1	14.4	-13.0	15.8	...	...	...	2.1
Ogemaw, MI	26129	15,234	61.0	80.5	1,376	85.0	10.1	-17.3	10.1	...	...	...	...
Ontonagon, MI	26131	...	...	...	...	...	...	...	...	...	...	...	...
Osceola, MI	26133	15,664	58.9	83.9	958	78.9	11.5	-15.9	11.5	...	...	...	...
Oscoda, MI	26135	...	...	...	...	...	...	...	...	...	...	...	...
Otsego, MI	26137	16,604	50.9	89.4	753	79.2	18.5	-8.9	18.7	...	...	...	...
Ottawa, MI	26139	159,320	42.1	90.4	23,254	76.1	27.8	0.4	29.3	8.6	...	30.6	10.6
Presque Isle, MI	26141	...	...	...	...	...	...	...	...	...	...	...	...
Roscommon, MI	26143	18,974	54.4	84.5	1,055	85.0	13.3	-14.1	13.5	...	...	...	...
Saginaw, MI	26145	133,299	49.4	86.9	14,239	89.4	18.8	-8.6	20.3	11.1	20.1	...	10.1
St. Clair, MI	26147	114,988	49.9	87.2	10,044	78.6	14.8	-12.6	15.0	6.6	...	43.3	9.2
St. Joseph, MI	26149	40,952	57.2	84.6	2,541	85.8	12.7	-14.7	12.6	12.2	...	...	13.4
Sanilac, MI	26151	29,505	60.7	84.9	2,011	81.9	10.6	-16.8	10.9	...	...	...	4.1
Schoolcraft, MI	26153	...	...	...	...	...	...	...	...	...	...	...	...
Shiawassee, MI	26155	48,359	49.9	87.4	3,792	68.2	16.1	-11.3	15.9	...	...	...	16.0
Tuscola, MI	26157	38,297	56.2	84.6	2,868	79.0	12.4	-15.0	12.6	...	...	...	8.6
Van Buren, MI	26159	51,397	49.4	84.5	3,509	86.2	19.7	-7.7	21.0	9.7	...	...	10.5
Washtenaw, MI	26161	214,620	23.6	93.4	66,547	92.9	51.3	23.9	52.4	25.6	25.4	81.5	41.6
Wayne, MI	26163	1,286,737	50.7	82.6	128,900	79.5	19.5	-7.9	24.2	11.2	12.7	56.4	12.7
Wexford, MI	26165	21,608	52.8	87.6	1,399	81.4	15.7	-11.7	15.8	...	...	...	...
MINNESOTA	27000	3,418,723	37.0	91.1	352,787	71.0	31.1	3.7	31.9	19.8	11.3	40.8	15.7
Aitkin, MN	27001	...	...	...	...	...	...	...	...	...	...	...	...
Anoka, MN	27003	212,267	38.9	92.2	17,925	72.5	24.9	-2.5	24.7	17.8	19.1	41.2	15.1
Becker, MN	27005	21,804	42.8	89.9	1,242	87.8	22.2	-5.2	23.1	...	12.1	...	...
Beltrami, MN	27007	26,088	38.7	88.5	4,749	89.5	28.5	1.1	31.7	...	13.0	...	...
Benton, MN	27009	25,605	44.4	89.8	2,778	83.1	20.5	-6.9	20.7	...	...	...	...
Big Stone, MN	27011	...	...	...	...	...	...	...	...	...	...	...	...
Blue Earth, MN	27013	35,721	35.6	93.2	10,580	91.2	29.9	2.5	30.1	...	...	31.4	14.6
Brown, MN	27015	17,689	52.6	86.9	1,820	40.1	18.9	-8.5	19.4	...	...	...	...
Carlton, MN	27017	22,784	43.2	90.2	1,587	78.6	21.9	-5.5	22.7	...	5.9	...	...
Carver, MN	27019	55,166	29.5	93.4	4,231	72.3	40.9	13.5	42.0	...	...	31.8	6.3
Cass, MN	27021	20,562	46.7	89.9	717	91.9	20.2	-7.2	20.7	...	17.4	...	16.2
Chippewa, MN	27023	...	...	...	...	...	...	...	...	...	...	...	...
Chisago, MN	27025	32,603	46.8	90.9	2,100	75.5	16.2	-11.2	16.8	...	...	...	8.4
Clay, MN	27027	32,524	35.8	91.9	8,065	66.3	32.6	5.2	33.2	...	...	...	9.4
Clearwater, MN	27029	...	...	...	...	...	...	...	...	...	...	...	...
Cook, MN	27031	...	...	...	...	...	...	...	...	...	...	...	...
Cottonwood, MN	27033	...	...	...	...	...	...	...	...	...	...	...	...
Crow Wing, MN	27035	42,589	40.7	91.1	2,286	88.5	21.8	-5.6	22.0	...	...	...	...
Dakota, MN	27037	252,218	28.8	94.4	23,109	68.4	38.7	11.3	39.7	25.5	9.7	45.2	19.3
Dodge, MN	27039	...	...	...	...	...	...	...	...	...	...	...	...
Douglas, MN	27041	25,193	40.7	90.4	1,560	91.2	20.0	-7.4	20.0	...	...	...	...
Faribault, MN	27043	...	...	...	...	...	...	...	...	...	...	...	...
Fillmore, MN	27045	14,356	49.9	85.9	785	81.5	19.8	-7.6	19.6	...	...	...	...
Freeborn, MN	27047	22,215	53.0	86.2	1,056	73.5	14.8	-12.6	15.0	...	...	...	2.0
Goodhue, MN	27049	31,096	44.5	90.3	1,833	72.2	22.2	-5.2	22.5	...	...	...	...
Grant, MN	27051	...	...	...	...	...	...	...	...	...	...	...	...
Hennepin, MN	27053	765,210	28.5	92.2	85,343	71.2	43.0	15.6	47.0	19.6	12.2	45.6	17.8
Houston, MN	27055	...	...	...	...	...	...	...	...	...	...	...	...
Hubbard, MN	27057	...	...	...	...	...	...	...	...	...	...	...	...
Isanti, MN	27059	25,772	47.7	90.1	1,924	86.9	16.7	-10.7	16.4	...	...	...	27.4
Itasca, MN	27061	31,081	41.4	91.8	1,642	87.0	19.9	-7.5	20.8	...	5.6	...	...
Jackson, MN	27063	...	...	...	...	...	...	...	...	...	...	...	...
Kanabec, MN	27065	...	...	...	...	...	...	...	...	...	...	...	...
Kandiyohi, MN	27067	27,123	43.2	87.8	1,903	89.1	21.7	-5.7	23.0	...	...	...	3.4
Kittson, MN	27069	...	...	...	...	...	...	...	...	...	...	...	...
Koochiching, MN	27071	...	...	...	...	...	...	...	...	...	...	...	...
Lac qui Parle, MN	27073	...	...	...	...	...	...	...	...	...	...	...	...
Lake, MN	27075	...	...	...	...	...	...	...	...	...	...	...	...
Lake of the Woods, MN	27077	...	...	...	...	...	...	...	...	...	...	...	...
Le Sueur, MN	27079	18,694	49.3	89.0	1,217	79.1	19.2	-8.2	19.6	...	...	...	9.0

[3]May be of any race
... Not available

Table C-1. Population, School, and Student Characteristics by County—*Continued*

County	State/County Code	County Type[1]	Population, 2009		Percent of related children 5-17 years in poverty, 2008	Percent of children under 19 years with no health insurance, 2007	Number of Schools and Students, 2008-2009			Resident enrollment, 2006-2008	
			Total	Percent 5–17 years			School Districts	Schools	Students	K–12 enrollment	
										Number	Percent public
			1	2	3	4	5	6	7	8	9
Lincoln, MN	27081	9	5,723	16.2	11.6	11.9	4	7	987	...	...
Lyon, MN	27083	7	25,074	16.9	10.0	7.2	8	23	4,246	4,206	85.5
McLeod, MN	27085	6	36,939	18.4	6.9	6.6	7	22	5,635	6,748	86.5
Mahnomen, MN	27087	8	5,025	20.1	33.1	7.1	3	8	1,342	...	...
Marshall, MN	27089	8	9,184	16.9	10.6	11.2	5	10	1,414	...	...
Martin, MN	27091	7	20,245	16.3	12.8	6.7	5	19	3,224	3,504	86.3
Meeker, MN	27093	6	23,154	17.9	9.4	7.2	3	14	3,488	4,079	96.3
Mille Lacs, MN	27095	6	26,383	17.5	12.8	7.3	4	19	6,667	4,495	91.1
Morrison, MN	27097	6	32,883	17.7	13.1	6.9	6	21	5,144	5,654	90.6
Mower, MN	27099	4	38,215	17.9	13.2	6.6	5	24	5,805	6,657	92.6
Murray, MN	27101	9	8,416	16.0	9.0	12.0	2	6	1,133	...	...
Nicollet, MN	27103	5	32,224	15.2	7.7	5.4	6	17	2,272	5,180	87.6
Nobles, MN	27105	7	20,558	19.0	13.2	10.9	7	17	3,785	3,375	92.7
Norman, MN	27107	8	6,455	18.8	12.6	8.2	3	8	1,193	...	...
Olmsted, MN	27109	3	143,962	17.1	8.0	5.4	10	64	22,212	24,259	84.8
Otter Tail, MN	27111	6	56,588	15.5	12.9	7.7	10	32	7,830	9,222	93.5
Pennington, MN	27113	6	13,842	16.0	12.0	6.1	3	8	2,196	...	...
Pine, MN	27115	6	28,368	15.7	15.8	7.0	5	15	3,909	4,680	93.6
Pipestone, MN	27117	6	9,353	17.6	11.8	7.2	1	5	1,167	...	...
Polk, MN	27119	3	30,776	16.9	13.1	6.3	8	21	5,118	5,133	91.7
Pope, MN	27121	8	10,869	15.1	12.0	9.0	3	9	1,332	...	...
Ramsey, MN	27123	1	506,278	15.9	17.8	5.6	43	280	83,115	87,023	83.9
Red Lake, MN	27125	8	4,188	16.1	12.3	10.0	4	6	739	...	...
Redwood, MN	27127	7	15,464	18.0	10.4	7.9	7	16	2,728	...	...
Renville, MN	27129	9	15,718	17.7	12.6	10.4	4	7	2,050	...	...
Rice, MN	27131	4	62,723	16.9	8.3	7.7	6	27	8,394	10,064	88.3
Rock, MN	27133	6	9,483	18.1	9.5	7.8	2	7	1,556	...	...
Roseau, MN	27135	7	15,911	19.5	7.9	7.8	4	13	3,129	...	...
St. Louis, MN	27137	2	197,767	14.0	12.8	4.8	21	109	25,553	28,270	90.2
Scott, MN	27139	1	131,939	20.6	4.5	6.2	8	51	20,657	26,027	84.7
Sherburne, MN	27141	1	87,832	20.8	5.0	6.1	4	38	19,205	16,859	92.0
Sibley, MN	27143	8	14,925	17.9	11.0	12.8	5	10	2,271	...	...
Stearns, MN	27145	3	148,955	16.1	8.1	6.1	15	55	23,008	23,446	84.5
Steele, MN	27147	5	36,775	19.0	8.1	6.8	4	20	6,497	6,790	91.5
Stevens, MN	27149	7	9,629	13.8	6.5	7.2	4	7	1,369	...	...
Swift, MN	27151	7	10,823	14.9	9.6	6.7	2	8	1,522	...	...
Todd, MN	27153	6	23,869	17.6	16.5	6.7	7	20	3,933	3,945	86.9
Traverse, MN	27155	9	3,573	16.4	13.7	10.4	2	4	530	...	...
Wabasha, MN	27157	3	21,884	16.9	8.3	7.5	3	8	3,588	3,783	94.1
Wadena, MN	27159	7	13,269	16.6	18.2	5.7	4	8	2,850	...	...
Waseca, MN	27161	7	18,771	17.6	9.6	6.6	4	18	3,589	...	...
Washington, MN	27163	1	231,958	19.7	3.9	5.7	12	80	38,304	44,973	90.0
Watonwan, MN	27165	7	10,912	18.8	12.1	11.3	3	7	1,976	...	...
Wilkin, MN	27167	6	6,264	17.7	9.1	6.3	3	7	1,167	...	...
Winona, MN	27169	4	49,436	13.7	10.2	6.4	7	29	5,722	7,227	79.8
Wright, MN	27171	1	121,907	20.4	5.1	6.5	13	64	25,452	22,729	91.7
Yellow Medicine, MN	27173	9	9,867	16.3	9.7	6.9	5	8	1,675	...	...
MISSISSIPPI	28000	X	2,951,996	18.5	27.8	13.5	164	1,089	491,962	555,070	89.2
Adams, MS	28001	5	30,722	17.4	34.8	11.3	1	8	3,988	5,805	78.2
Alcorn, MS	28003	7	35,822	16.9	26.6	11.7	2	17	5,689	6,403	95.2
Amite, MS	28005	8	13,038	15.9	32.4	15.8	1	4	1,274	...	...
Attala, MS	28007	6	19,755	17.5	34.7	9.9	2	11	3,421	...	...
Benton, MS	28009	8	7,981	18.0	31.3	10.4	1	5	1,347	...	...
Bolivar, MS	28011	5	36,766	18.1	50.2	11.1	6	24	6,615	7,410	92.8
Calhoun, MS	28013	7	14,422	16.8	28.4	10.5	1	8	2,556	...	...
Carroll, MS	28015	9	10,278	14.5	24.2	15.2	1	3	939	...	...
Chickasaw, MS	28017	7	18,683	19.7	28.7	13.9	3	9	3,259	...	...
Choctaw, MS	28019	9	9,023	18.5	34.4	15.7	1	6	1,590	...	...
Claiborne, MS	28021	6	10,755	16.8	46.7	16.2	1	4	1,761	...	...
Clarke, MS	28023	9	17,207	18.2	31.3	15.1	2	9	2,935	...	...
Clay, MS	28025	7	20,722	18.5	34.4	11.5	2	9	3,532	3,878	84.0
Coahoma, MS	28027	5	26,936	21.8	43.9	10.2	3	17	5,332	5,767	92.0
Copiah, MS	28029	2	29,094	17.9	33.0	11.5	2	7	4,495	5,630	85.3
Covington, MS	28031	8	20,544	18.9	35.2	19.4	1	11	3,241	4,049	94.9
De Soto, MS	28033	1	158,719	21.1	12.4	16.2	1	35	30,616	30,968	89.1
Forrest, MS	28035	3	81,078	16.3	31.6	14.7	4	22	11,450	13,752	92.1
Franklin, MS	28037	9	8,324	17.8	30.1	18.4	1	5	1,475	...	...
George, MS	28039	3	22,681	20.9	22.0	19.3	1	8	4,210	4,597	97.9
Greene, MS	28041	8	14,352	15.7	23.4	17.3	1	6	2,036	...	...
Grenada, MS	28043	7	23,046	18.5	28.0	10.0	1	6	4,438	4,195	90.1

[1]County type codes are from the Economic Research Service of the United States Department of Agriculture. See notes and definitions for more information.
... Not available

Table C-1. Population, School, and Student Characteristics by County—*Continued*

County	State/County Code	Characteristics of students, 2008-2009				Number of graduates, 2006-2007	Staff and students, 2008-2009			
		Percent with IEP[2]	Percent eligible for free or reduced lunch	Percent minority	Percent English Language Learners		Total staff	Number of teachers	Student/teacher ratio	Central admin. Staff
		10	11	12	13	14	15	16	17	18
Lincoln, MN	27081	17.4	38.0	3.0	0.7	85	152	82	12.0	8
Lyon, MN	27083	13.2	34.2	16.6	8.7	429	767	339	12.5	65
McLeod, MN	27085	13.0	31.5	10.6	3.5	469	662	340	16.6	29
Mahnomen, MN	27087	21.0	66.8	71.2	...	75	211	115	11.7	8
Marshall, MN	27089	15.3	43.9	9.1	1.8	113	259	117	12.1	13
Martin, MN	27091	16.7	38.3	7.9	2.5	263	534	225	14.3	18
Meeker, MN	27093	15.7	35.0	6.3	0.9	267	464	239	14.6	19
Mille Lacs, MN	27095	15.0	34.8	7.9	0.3	467	841	433	15.4	30
Morrison, MN	27097	14.4	40.9	4.0	0.5	455	704	345	14.9	38
Mower, MN	27099	14.7	44.6	21.5	8.0	400	837	411	14.1	31
Murray, MN	27101	17.7	32.0	6.1	2.6	106	171	83	13.7	10
Nicollet, MN	27103	19.3	29.2	11.1	2.8	181	381	164	13.9	24
Nobles, MN	27105	16.1	49.7	38.1	7.9	229	586	289	13.1	22
Norman, MN	27107	17.1	47.2	15.2	1.7	100	211	99	12.1	7
Olmsted, MN	27109	11.3	27.3	22.7	10.4	1,656	2,533	1,336	16.6	97
Otter Tail, MN	27111	16.0	36.8	8.9	3.5	669	1,023	508	15.4	39
Pennington, MN	27113	16.4	34.8	10.3	1.2	166	324	156	14.1	15
Pine, MN	27115	11.1	44.8	8.4	0.6	319	536	281	13.9	25
Pipestone, MN	27117	16.7	42.4	9.3	3.6	123	166	79	14.8	6
Polk, MN	27119	15.2	36.4	13.3	2.0	402	783	370	13.8	41
Pope, MN	27121	21.0	36.0	3.5	0.1	107	226	97	13.7	10
Ramsey, MN	27123	15.7	52.8	55.2	24.0	5,625	11,719	5,307	15.7	427
Red Lake, MN	27125	14.1	50.3	10.0	0.3	57	141	66	11.2	9
Redwood, MN	27127	14.8	36.9	19.6	0.8	191	404	207	13.2	18
Renville, MN	27129	15.2	39.3	19.3	8.3	147	293	145	14.1	9
Rice, MN	27131	16.0	31.1	20.1	9.4	636	1,184	540	15.5	52
Rock, MN	27133	15.4	29.7	5.9	1.8	115	220	113	13.8	6
Roseau, MN	27135	15.1	30.6	8.6	0.5	279	451	211	14.8	17
St. Louis, MN	27137	15.3	36.7	11.2	0.1	2,020	3,409	1,647	15.5	147
Scott, MN	27139	14.7	18.6	17.6	5.5	1,130	2,497	1,241	16.6	99
Sherburne, MN	27141	14.2	22.3	9.8	2.2	1,114	1,936	1,009	19.0	74
Sibley, MN	27143	13.7	38.6	21.1	8.7	202	317	166	13.7	10
Stearns, MN	27145	16.9	31.7	12.3	5.7	1,795	2,999	1,465	15.7	103
Steele, MN	27147	12.0	30.3	15.1	6.0	468	774	397	16.4	32
Stevens, MN	27149	19.6	27.2	6.9	1.9	101	211	103	13.3	12
Swift, MN	27151	14.9	33.0	8.0	1.3	136	230	114	13.4	10
Todd, MN	27153	17.4	53.7	11.1	5.2	359	643	298	13.2	59
Traverse, MN	27155	11.9	34.0	12.7	0.8	47	86	47	11.3	5
Wabasha, MN	27157	13.5	21.3	6.0	1.8	380	406	235	15.3	15
Wadena, MN	27159	15.0	54.0	5.3	0.1	220	393	202	14.1	18
Waseca, MN	27161	16.1	30.7	10.2	...	259	536	248	14.5	17
Washington, MN	27163	12.2	15.4	17.2	2.4	2,832	4,268	2,186	17.5	164
Watonwan, MN	27165	16.4	48.7	39.8	13.9	158	289	142	13.9	9
Wilkin, MN	27167	17.7	37.4	7.4	2.8	122	177	93	12.5	9
Winona, MN	27169	15.4	31.4	11.4	2.6	462	902	430	13.3	36
Wright, MN	27171	13.2	19.6	6.7	1.9	1,714	2,943	1,543	16.5	96
Yellow Medicine, MN	27173	20.6	43.5	16.2	3.5	150	285	136	12.3	10
MISSISSIPPI	28000	...	68.3	53.7	1.3	26,232	72,040	33,356	14.7	3,071
Adams, MS	28001	...	92.6	91.8	0.6	207	666	292	13.7	35
Alcorn, MS	28003	...	57.9	19.0	1.0	312	770	408	13.9	21
Amite, MS	28005	...	99.3	83.9	...	73	236	89	14.3	10
Attala, MS	28007	...	71.3	55.5	0.3	182	521	235	14.6	23
Benton, MS	28009	...	86.5	44.2	2.0	66	218	105	12.8	9
Bolivar, MS	28011	...	90.2	85.6	0.7	437	1,097	482	13.7	64
Calhoun, MS	28013	...	78.1	45.3	5.3	140	371	155	16.5	12
Carroll, MS	28015	...	92.0	70.8	0.4	47	152	79	11.9	8
Chickasaw, MS	28017	...	77.0	59.9	2.3	176	486	236	13.8	20
Choctaw, MS	28019	...	84.1	33.4	...	89	289	131	12.1	12
Claiborne, MS	28021	...	99.5	99.8	...	132	260	104	16.9	15
Clarke, MS	28023	...	64.8	37.6	0.1	180	475	223	13.2	27
Clay, MS	28025	...	85.1	81.9	0.6	181	513	225	15.7	25
Coahoma, MS	28027	...	96.9	96.4	0.8	278	871	368	14.5	50
Copiah, MS	28029	...	80.7	73.7	0.9	241	625	274	16.4	32
Covington, MS	28031	...	80.8	55.6	0.6	188	505	232	14.0	16
De Soto, MS	28033	...	43.8	36.1	3.0	1,341	3,718	1,723	17.8	88
Forrest, MS	28035	...	71.3	53.6	1.9	572	1,817	851	13.5	95
Franklin, MS	28037	...	70.3	46.4	0.1	93	257	123	12.0	12
George, MS	28039	...	63.0	11.7	0.5	183	602	266	15.8	19
Greene, MS	28041	...	73.7	18.8	0.1	96	327	151	13.5	14
Grenada, MS	28043	...	63.8	50.1	0.1	228	638	266	16.7	25

[2]IEP= Individual Education Program. See notes and definitions for more information
... Not available

Table C-1. Population, School, and Student Characteristics by County—*Continued*

County	State/County Code	Revenues, 2007-2008 Total revenue ($1,000's)	Percentage of revenue from Federal gov't	State gov't	Local gov't	Current expenditures, 2007-2008 Amount ($1,000's)	Amount per student	Percent for instruction	Resident population 16 to 19 years, 2006-2008 Total population 16 to 19 years	Percent enrolled in school	Percent high school graduates, not enrolled in school	Percent not enrolled, not grads, not employed or not in labor force
		19	20	21	22	23	24	25	26	27	28	29
Lincoln, MN	27081	12,705	4.5	71.0	24.5	9,929	9,297	59.2	...	...	...	...
Lyon, MN	27083	73,697	14.3	50.9	34.8	144,367	33,945	25.1	...	...	...	...
McLeod, MN	27085	57,451	4.3	74.4	21.3	47,217	8,282	61.6	...	...	...	...
Mahnomen, MN	27087	19,310	19.2	67.6	13.3	15,967	11,088	62.5	...	...	...	...
Marshall, MN	27089	20,022	8.9	70.5	20.6	18,290	12,926	63.7	...	...	...	...
Martin, MN	27091	40,910	6.3	67.1	26.6	37,053	11,397	67.5	...	...	...	...
Meeker, MN	27093	37,104	4.0	72.9	23.1	30,518	8,680	61.9	...	...	...	...
Mille Lacs, MN	27095	68,806	5.3	74.8	19.9	56,557	8,281	64.1	1,405	77.8	12.1	2.2
Morrison, MN	27097	56,310	6.2	72.9	21.0	46,996	9,143	65.3	1,802	82.9	14.1	2.1
Mower, MN	27099	67,289	6.3	74.0	19.7	56,339	9,672	65.8	...	...	...	...
Murray, MN	27101	14,177	3.9	74.1	22.0	11,725	10,125	64.5	...	...	...	...
Nicollet, MN	27103	36,543	8.2	56.6	35.2	30,478	13,403	64.2	...	...	...	...
Nobles, MN	27105	41,097	6.4	74.6	19.0	33,046	9,482	64.9	...	...	...	...
Norman, MN	27107	14,088	4.1	79.8	16.1	12,421	10,377	64.1	...	...	...	...
Olmsted, MN	27109	245,898	6.1	67.5	26.4	199,448	9,041	63.3	7,104	89.9	6.6	2.0
Otter Tail, MN	27111	131,158	4.3	46.6	49.1	114,153	14,499	41.6	3,229	84.4	11.6	1.7
Pennington, MN	27113	79,787	3.2	23.4	73.4	74,129	33,989	16.9	...	...	...	...
Pine, MN	27115	42,669	5.9	72.2	21.9	35,345	8,935	65.5	...	...	...	...
Pipestone, MN	27117	16,991	4.3	73.7	22.0	13,837	9,426	59.6	...	...	...	...
Polk, MN	27119	59,098	7.6	73.3	19.1	51,178	9,878	65.5	...	...	...	...
Pope, MN	27121	17,398	5.8	68.4	25.8	14,570	10,737	69.9	...	...	...	...
Ramsey, MN	27123	1,171,338	7.8	65.8	26.4	953,910	11,293	64.7	30,691	90.1	6.3	2.3
Red Lake, MN	27125	9,640	5.8	73.1	21.1	8,593	12,086	61.7	...	...	...	...
Redwood, MN	27127	30,138	5.3	73.5	21.2	25,262	9,243	62.0	...	...	...	...
Renville, MN	27129	22,127	6.3	75.2	18.5	18,590	8,882	63.5	...	...	...	...
Rice, MN	27131	97,450	4.6	66.4	29.1	72,510	8,589	65.5	...	...	...	...
Rock, MN	27133	16,861	4.4	74.8	20.8	13,779	8,838	65.4	...	...	...	...
Roseau, MN	27135	36,174	4.9	75.2	19.9	29,955	9,237	62.8	...	...	...	...
St. Louis, MN	27137	315,078	8.9	68.6	22.5	270,419	10,404	65.8	13,579	88.1	9.4	1.7
Scott, MN	27139	231,610	3.9	62.5	33.7	172,149	8,583	66.0	6,468	87.4	9.4	1.6
Sherburne, MN	27141	204,726	2.4	66.5	31.1	157,428	8,307	64.3	4,747	81.1	14.9	2.3
Sibley, MN	27143	23,719	4.6	77.2	18.2	20,370	8,887	65.8	...	...	...	...
Stearns, MN	27145	264,263	6.1	69.8	24.2	215,241	9,315	66.2	11,088	93.0	5.4	1.2
Steele, MN	27147	68,513	5.0	71.6	23.4	57,410	8,834	65.0	...	...	...	...
Stevens, MN	27149	18,190	5.8	61.5	32.7	12,967	9,619	64.9	...	...	...	...
Swift, MN	27151	16,868	4.2	76.4	19.5	14,681	9,614	64.8	...	...	...	...
Todd, MN	27153	56,774	10.0	64.6	25.3	46,919	11,896	63.6	...	...	...	...
Traverse, MN	27155	6,885	7.3	71.9	20.8	6,133	11,192	65.3	...	...	...	...
Wabasha, MN	27157	34,486	2.7	73.0	24.3	29,154	8,250	64.1	...	...	...	...
Wadena, MN	27159	30,349	6.0	78.7	15.3	24,485	8,558	63.2	...	...	...	...
Waseca, MN	27161	41,258	7.1	69.2	23.7	35,194	9,886	67.7	...	...	...	...
Washington, MN	27163	469,323	3.0	61.6	35.4	364,600	9,410	65.5	12,611	93.6	4.9	1.0
Watonwan, MN	27165	21,814	4.9	75.2	19.9	18,775	9,416	61.6	...	...	...	...
Wilkin, MN	27167	12,248	5.5	77.1	17.4	11,168	10,134	63.5	...	...	...	...
Winona, MN	27169	74,995	8.0	63.6	28.5	62,599	10,843	67.4	...	...	...	...
Wright, MN	27171	283,799	3.9	64.4	31.6	209,683	8,489	67.4	5,887	86.8	10.0	1.7
Yellow Medicine, MN	27173	22,829	10.1	66.8	23.1	19,590	11,298	68.7	...	...	...	...
MISSISSIPPI	28000	4,449,009	15.9	53.7	30.4	3,897,577	7,901	58.7	185,677	81.5	9.7	6.1
Adams, MS	28001	39,432	21.2	49.5	29.3	37,350	9,059	55.7	...	...	...	...
Alcorn, MS	28003	50,053	13.2	61.8	25.0	45,990	7,987	64.0	...	...	...	...
Amite, MS	28005	13,927	22.5	43.9	33.7	11,318	8,990	56.7	...	...	...	...
Attala, MS	28007	28,489	14.1	58.7	27.2	26,207	7,590	60.6	...	...	...	...
Benton, MS	28009	10,577	17.2	65.2	17.6	10,816	8,120	58.5	...	...	...	...
Bolivar, MS	28011	65,414	23.2	54.0	22.7	60,637	8,841	56.0	...	...	...	...
Calhoun, MS	28013	20,541	14.5	67.4	18.1	18,569	7,115	60.8	...	...	...	...
Carroll, MS	28015	9,841	18.8	51.8	29.4	8,824	9,387	56.8	...	...	...	...
Chickasaw, MS	28017	27,537	16.2	65.9	17.9	26,152	8,059	60.4	...	...	...	...
Choctaw, MS	28019	16,546	17.3	49.9	32.8	15,423	9,148	60.5	...	...	...	...
Claiborne, MS	28021	16,555	17.1	51.1	31.8	15,431	8,587	57.2	...	...	...	...
Clarke, MS	28023	26,726	14.0	56.7	29.3	24,814	8,154	57.2	...	...	...	...
Clay, MS	28025	32,082	19.1	56.3	24.6	28,228	7,837	56.7	...	...	...	...
Coahoma, MS	28027	49,653	23.6	55.4	21.1	43,602	7,926	55.9	...	...	...	...
Copiah, MS	28029	34,891	18.0	60.9	21.1	33,117	7,247	56.3	...	...	...	...
Covington, MS	28031	30,780	14.2	51.8	34.0	26,357	8,070	59.4	...	...	...	...
De Soto, MS	28033	232,190	7.6	57.9	34.4	185,578	6,210	59.4	8,047	82.3	12.3	2.6
Forrest, MS	28035	111,053	14.8	50.8	34.4	99,348	8,651	57.5	...	...	...	...
Franklin, MS	28037	14,801	18.9	55.5	25.5	14,143	9,767	60.1	...	...	...	...
George, MS	28039	31,217	12.9	69.6	17.4	28,078	6,536	64.5	...	...	...	...
Greene, MS	28041	16,753	17.9	60.2	21.9	17,125	8,198	57.9	...	...	...	...
Grenada, MS	28043	35,031	14.0	62.5	23.5	31,399	6,845	60.5	...	...	...	...

[3]May be of any race

Table C-1. Population, School, and Student Characteristics by County—*Continued*

County	State/County Code	High school graduates, 2006-2008			College enrollment, 2006-2008		College graduates, 2006-2008 (percent)						
		Population 25 years and over	High school diploma or less (percent)	High school diploma or more (percent)	Number	Percent public	Bachelor's degree or more	+/- U.S. percent with Bachelor's degree or more	Non-Hispanic White	Black or African American	American Indian and Alaska Native	Asian, Hawaiian, and Pacific Islander	Hispanic or Latino[3]
		30	31	32	33	34	35	36	37	38	39	40	41
Lincoln, MN	27081	...	...	...	...	...	...	...	...	...	...	...	...
Lyon, MN	27083	15,416	43.2	87.7	2,728	95.3	26.8	-0.6	28.0	...	...	...	...
McLeod, MN	27085	24,491	47.2	89.7	1,779	75.8	18.2	-9.2	18.3	...	...	...	...
Mahnomen, MN	27087	...	...	...	...	...	...	...	...	...	...	...	...
Marshall, MN	27089	...	...	...	...	...	...	...	...	...	...	...	...
Martin, MN	27091	14,457	47.7	85.1	733	73.7	18.9	-8.5	19.2	...	...	...	...
Meeker, MN	27093	15,547	52.4	86.7	1,090	79.4	13.9	-13.5	14.2	...	...	...	...
Mille Lacs, MN	27095	17,821	53.1	86.7	1,126	77.3	13.3	-14.1	13.6	...	3.6	...	...
Morrison, MN	27097	21,940	54.5	85.5	993	85.7	14.1	-13.3	14.3	...	...	...	...
Mower, MN	27099	25,258	47.9	86.2	1,511	83.7	16.5	-10.9	17.0	...	...	...	9.2
Murray, MN	27101	...	...	...	...	...	...	...	...	...	...	...	...
Nicollet, MN	27103	19,317	35.8	91.7	3,641	33.1	33.4	6.0	33.3	...	...	...	19.3
Nobles, MN	27105	13,221	55.1	78.1	1,123	94.9	16.8	-10.6	19.1	...	...	...	...
Norman, MN	27107	...	...	...	...	...	...	...	...	...	...	...	...
Olmsted, MN	27109	92,138	30.1	93.8	8,891	74.1	38.9	11.5	39.7	19.5	...	47.9	20.1
Otter Tail, MN	27111	39,787	46.6	87.6	1,719	87.6	19.3	-8.1	19.4	...	...	...	...
Pennington, MN	27113	...	...	...	...	...	...	...	...	...	...	...	...
Pine, MN	27115	19,539	54.9	87.0	903	75.2	12.4	-15.0	12.6	...	3.1	...	...
Pipestone, MN	27117	...	...	...	...	...	...	...	...	...	...	...	...
Polk, MN	27119	20,297	46.9	86.2	1,947	88.9	19.1	-8.3	19.9	...	...	...	1.0
Pope, MN	27121	...	...	...	...	...	...	...	...	...	...	...	...
Ramsey, MN	27123	325,920	33.9	90.3	43,885	53.8	38.7	11.3	42.9	18.4	18.4	30.2	17.8
Red Lake, MN	27125	...	...	...	...	...	...	...	...	...	...	...	...
Redwood, MN	27127	...	...	...	...	...	...	...	...	...	...	...	...
Renville, MN	27129	...	...	...	...	...	...	...	...	...	...	...	...
Rice, MN	27131	37,793	44.2	89.1	6,538	32.9	26.3	-1.1	27.3	...	...	...	10.0
Rock, MN	27133	...	...	...	...	...	...	...	...	...	...	...	...
Roseau, MN	27135	...	...	...	...	...	...	...	...	...	...	...	...
St. Louis, MN	27137	131,541	39.0	91.6	19,284	83.4	25.3	-2.1	25.6	8.7	12.1	49.0	24.2
Scott, MN	27139	78,205	30.8	93.6	6,908	60.9	35.8	8.4	35.9	31.2	16.6	48.7	19.4
Sherburne, MN	27141	53,254	38.2	93.0	5,288	69.5	23.1	-4.3	23.5	...	...	24.6	...
Sibley, MN	27143	...	...	...	...	...	...	...	...	...	...	...	...
Stearns, MN	27145	89,393	42.1	90.4	18,879	71.4	23.8	-3.6	23.7	8.4	...	41.5	15.8
Steele, MN	27147	23,992	48.9	88.8	1,583	68.1	20.5	-6.9	21.2	...	...	...	18.5
Stevens, MN	27149	...	...	...	...	...	...	...	...	...	...	...	...
Swift, MN	27151	...	...	...	...	...	...	...	...	...	...	...	...
Todd, MN	27153	15,919	52.1	85.6	517	83.9	12.7	-14.7	12.9	...	...	...	...
Traverse, MN	27155	...	...	...	...	...	...	...	...	...	...	...	...
Wabasha, MN	27157	14,828	51.1	89.7	943	78.0	17.2	-10.2	17.2	...	...	...	...
Wadena, MN	27159	...	...	...	...	...	...	...	...	...	...	...	...
Waseca, MN	27161	...	...	...	...	...	...	...	...	...	...	...	...
Washington, MN	27163	145,870	27.7	95.7	14,687	71.0	40.2	12.8	40.4	37.7	...	50.1	32.9
Watonwan, MN	27165	...	...	...	...	...	...	...	...	...	...	...	...
Wilkin, MN	27167	...	...	...	...	...	...	...	...	...	...	...	...
Winona, MN	27169	29,928	40.7	87.9	8,215	72.0	25.4	-2.0	25.1	...	...	...	...
Wright, MN	27171	73,640	41.5	93.3	4,586	72.5	23.2	-4.2	23.5	...	...	40.2	9.9
Yellow Medicine, MN	27173	...	...	...	...	...	...	...	...	...	...	...	...
MISSISSIPPI	28000	1,845,409	52.4	78.8	188,634	86.5	19.0	-8.4	22.6	12.0	9.0	41.7	12.3
Adams, MS	28001	20,909	52.4	80.4	1,283	86.2	20.1	-7.3	25.3	14.8	...	...	...
Alcorn, MS	28003	24,269	61.1	78.3	1,115	87.0	15.3	-12.1	16.0	7.0	...	...	...
Amite, MS	28005	...	...	...	...	...	...	...	...	...	...	...	...
Attala, MS	28007	...	...	...	...	...	...	...	...	...	...	...	...
Benton, MS	28009	...	...	...	...	...	...	...	...	...	...	...	...
Bolivar, MS	28011	21,829	56.7	69.5	3,592	81.2	21.1	-6.3	34.6	13.4	...	...	...
Calhoun, MS	28013	...	...	...	...	...	...	...	...	...	...	...	...
Carroll, MS	28015	...	...	...	...	...	...	...	...	...	...	...	...
Chickasaw, MS	28017	...	...	...	...	...	...	...	...	...	...	...	...
Choctaw, MS	28019	...	...	...	...	...	...	...	...	...	...	...	...
Claiborne, MS	28021	...	...	...	...	...	...	...	...	...	...	...	...
Clarke, MS	28023	...	...	...	...	...	...	...	...	...	...	...	...
Clay, MS	28025	13,768	58.2	76.4	779	100.0	16.7	-10.7	23.2	10.7	...	...	...
Coahoma, MS	28027	16,241	57.7	75.0	1,800	99.4	14.5	-12.9	20.1	10.8	...	...	...
Copiah, MS	28029	18,146	55.9	76.3	2,485	95.2	15.4	-12.0	21.1	8.8	...	...	...
Covington, MS	28031	12,801	58.0	79.5	1,228	70.8	16.4	-11.0	21.5	6.9	...	...	...
De Soto, MS	28033	93,245	44.5	87.1	8,304	83.6	20.7	-6.7	22.0	16.3	...	44.7	5.5
Forrest, MS	28035	45,415	42.2	86.0	11,952	90.6	26.9	-0.5	29.8	19.5	...	...	...
Franklin, MS	28037	...	...	...	...	...	...	...	...	...	...	...	...
George, MS	28039	13,690	63.4	79.7	449	72.6	12.0	-15.4	13.2	2.6	...	...	...
Greene, MS	28041	...	...	...	...	...	...	...	...	...	...	...	...
Grenada, MS	28043	15,282	60.6	69.5	1,062	90.3	18.6	-8.8	23.3	7.5	...	...	...

[3]May be of any race
... Not available

Table C-1. Population, School, and Student Characteristics by County—*Continued*

County	State/ County Code	County Type[1]	Population, 2009 Total	Population, 2009 Percent 5–17 years	Percent of related children 5-17 years in poverty, 2008	Percent of children under 19 years with no health insurance, 2007	Number of Schools and Students, 2008-2009 School Districts	Number of Schools and Students, 2008-2009 Schools	Number of Schools and Students, 2008-2009 Students	Resident enrollment, 2006-2008 K–12 enrollment Number	Resident enrollment, 2006-2008 K–12 enrollment Percent public
			1	2	3	4	5	6	7	8	9
Hancock, MS	28045	3	40,962	17.1	25.0	9.9	2	13	6,005	7,376	84.8
Harrison, MS	28047	3	181,191	17.5	21.8	15.3	7	55	27,787	32,943	87.3
Hinds, MS	28049	2	247,631	19.4	30.9	13.9	7	87	42,407	50,132	87.5
Holmes, MS	28051	6	20,290	20.3	41.7	8.6	2	12	3,864	4,182	89.2
Humphreys, MS	28053	7	9,809	19.8	56.6	7.5	1	5	1,848	...	...
Issaquena, MS	28055	9	1,612	11.1	53.9	13.7	...	...	...	...	...
Itawamba, MS	28057	7	23,000	16.9	19.3	13.5	1	8	3,588	...	...
Jackson, MS	28059	3	132,922	18.8	18.8	12.0	4	51	24,586	24,671	93.6
Jasper, MS	28061	9	17,940	18.7	27.8	13.5	2	8	2,757	...	...
Jefferson, MS	28063	7	8,928	17.2	40.4	13.1	1	6	1,474	...	...
Jefferson Davis, MS	28065	8	12,543	17.7	40.3	14.4	1	5	1,809	...	...
Jones, MS	28067	4	67,776	17.7	32.9	12.2	3	24	11,229	10,899	92.3
Kemper, MS	28069	9	9,833	17.1	32.7	15.2	1	4	1,229	...	...
Lafayette, MS	28071	6	43,975	13.2	18.2	17.9	3	13	5,820	5,765	96.1
Lamar, MS	28073	3	49,980	19.5	18.1	16.2	2	17	9,013	9,092	88.1
Lauderdale, MS	28075	5	79,099	18.2	28.6	13.5	3	24	13,256	14,859	90.9
Lawrence, MS	28077	8	13,308	18.3	26.6	15.9	1	6	2,231	...	...
Leake, MS	28079	6	23,132	22.6	33.1	11.4	1	8	3,268	5,198	94.2
Lee, MS	28081	5	81,913	19.1	24.1	12.2	4	36	16,480	15,260	94.7
Leflore, MS	28083	5	34,563	18.9	55.6	9.2	2	16	5,756	7,286	84.6
Lincoln, MS	28085	6	34,830	18.3	25.1	12.5	3	12	6,247	6,172	90.3
Lowndes, MS	28087	5	59,658	18.9	29.6	14.8	3	22	10,037	11,243	87.8
Madison, MS	28089	2	93,097	19.5	15.7	12.5	2	28	14,842	19,089	78.4
Marion, MS	28091	6	25,732	19.4	39.1	14.2	2	11	4,322	4,888	88.4
Marshall, MS	28093	1	36,900	17.2	33.8	15.7	2	14	4,920	7,172	83.8
Monroe, MS	28095	7	36,905	17.7	25.7	11.7	3	17	5,704	6,554	97.1
Montgomery, MS	28097	7	11,129	17.6	34.2	10.4	2	5	1,666	...	...
Neshoba, MS	28099	7	30,302	20.1	27.3	13.4	2	6	4,340	5,809	98.6
Newton, MS	28101	7	22,568	18.2	26.5	15.2	3	11	3,840	4,298	91.4
Noxubee, MS	28103	7	11,631	19.6	40.4	10.7	1	6	1,972	...	...
Oktibbeha, MS	28105	5	44,544	12.9	32.3	15.5	2	13	5,067	6,549	84.6
Panola, MS	28107	6	35,245	19.6	36.1	14.6	2	15	6,285	7,149	90.3
Pearl River, MS	28109	6	57,860	18.2	26.0	14.7	3	20	9,004	10,015	86.8
Perry, MS	28111	3	12,035	18.9	29.8	16.3	2	8	2,055	...	...
Pike, MS	28113	7	39,834	19.7	34.8	12.5	3	17	7,133	7,836	87.2
Pontotoc, MS	28115	7	29,248	19.2	20.4	11.7	2	11	5,602	5,539	97.0
Prentiss, MS	28117	7	25,709	16.9	22.7	12.1	2	11	3,565	...	...
Quitman, MS	28119	6	8,391	19.6	40.7	9.0	1	4	1,328	...	...
Rankin, MS	28121	2	143,124	18.0	15.2	14.3	4	32	22,114	25,782	87.3
Scott, MS	28123	6	29,341	18.9	29.8	16.8	2	11	5,314	5,240	93.9
Sharkey, MS	28125	9	5,420	20.6	51.7	17.1	1	4	1,146	...	...
Simpson, MS	28127	2	27,920	18.9	28.6	13.8	1	9	4,262	5,142	82.0
Smith, MS	28129	8	15,826	19.8	24.7	15.2	1	6	3,025	...	...
Stone, MS	28131	3	16,619	17.8	24.1	16.2	1	4	2,805	...	...
Sunflower, MS	28133	5	29,610	17.6	45.6	9.2	3	17	4,706	6,210	81.9
Tallahatchie, MS	28135	7	12,638	17.6	41.0	11.5	2	7	2,292	...	...
Tate, MS	28137	1	27,337	18.4	20.4	15.3	2	12	4,928	5,046	81.3
Tippah, MS	28139	7	21,661	17.9	23.7	11.8	2	10	4,029	3,775	98.5
Tishomingo, MS	28141	8	19,034	16.5	22.8	14.4	1	8	3,273	...	...
Tunica, MS	28143	1	10,436	20.9	36.7	8.6	1	7	2,257	...	...
Union, MS	28145	7	27,263	18.6	19.8	12.1	2	9	4,891	5,084	95.4
Walthall, MS	28147	9	15,291	18.3	37.3	16.6	1	7	2,524	...	...
Warren, MS	28149	4	48,115	19.9	29.3	12.5	1	16	9,058	9,451	87.1
Washington, MS	28151	5	54,616	20.6	48.0	9.7	4	28	10,717	12,288	91.8
Wayne, MS	28153	7	20,654	19.3	29.7	13.3	1	8	3,755	4,151	92.8
Webster, MS	28155	9	9,852	17.4	30.6	12.6	1	5	1,806	...	...
Wilkinson, MS	28157	8	10,143	17.7	36.4	15.9	1	5	1,339	...	...
Winston, MS	28159	7	19,309	17.6	28.4	15.0	1	7	2,720	...	...
Yalobusha, MS	28161	7	13,773	17.4	31.9	10.6	2	4	1,938	...	...
Yazoo, MS	28163	6	27,981	17.4	41.4	12.1	2	10	4,528	5,683	83.5
MISSOURI	29000	X	5,987,580	17.2	16.6	8.7	560	2,444	917,871	1,029,925	86.2
Adair, MO	29001	7	25,135	13.1	19.9	8.8	3	9	3,071	3,225	93.6
Andrew, MO	29003	3	17,052	18.3	10.9	12.3	3	10	2,890	...	...
Atchison, MO	29005	9	6,036	17.4	15.6	13.5	3	6	929	...	...
Audrain, MO	29007	6	25,556	17.3	22.6	11.0	3	10	3,485	4,754	83.4
Barry, MO	29009	6	35,881	18.8	25.6	10.8	6	19	6,372	6,672	95.3
Barton, MO	29011	6	12,386	18.8	21.2	10.0	3	10	2,131	...	...
Bates, MO	29013	1	16,761	18.0	21.2	10.3	4	8	2,348	...	...
Benton, MO	29015	9	18,461	13.7	27.7	11.0	3	10	2,638	...	...
Bollinger, MO	29017	9	11,841	16.9	21.8	12.9	4	9	1,953	...	...

[1]County type codes are from the Economic Research Service of the United States Department of Agriculture. See notes and definitions for more information.
... Not available

Table C-1. Population, School, and Student Characteristics by County—*Continued*

County	State/County Code	Characteristics of students, 2008-2009				Number of graduates, 2006-2007	Staff and students, 2008-2009			
		Percent with IEP[2]	Percent eligible for free or reduced lunch	Percent minority	Percent English Language Learners		Total staff	Number of teachers	Student/teacher ratio	Central admin. Staff
		10	11	12	13	14	15	16	17	18
Hancock, MS	28045	...	73.4	12.4	0.7	308	858	416	14.4	46
Harrison, MS	28047	0.1	61.2	39.7	1.7	1,510	4,012	1,879	14.8	174
Hinds, MS	28049	0.3	77.2	88.6	0.6	2,150	6,310	2,750	15.4	247
Holmes, MS	28051	...	98.6	99.3	...	207	579	218	17.7	26
Humphreys, MS	28053	...	96.5	97.7	0.9	84	261	108	17.1	15
Issaquena, MS	28055	...	...	...	...	...	...	...	...	...
Itawamba, MS	28057	...	57.7	9.3	0.2	226	552	279	12.9	14
Jackson, MS	28059	...	56.5	35.2	3.4	1,449	3,797	1,752	14.0	172
Jasper, MS	28061	...	86.9	79.4	0.5	164	435	188	14.7	29
Jefferson, MS	28063	...	97.9	99.7	...	112	257	105	14.0	15
Jefferson Davis, MS	28065	...	92.2	88.8	0.1	121	284	121	15.0	14
Jones, MS	28067	...	71.0	43.8	2.3	577	1,670	796	14.1	63
Kemper, MS	28069	...	94.8	98.4	...	67	203	92	13.4	14
Lafayette, MS	28071	...	52.9	42.1	2.1	311	901	433	13.4	42
Lamar, MS	28073	...	49.3	26.9	2.0	509	1,329	626	14.4	50
Lauderdale, MS	28075	...	68.0	63.0	0.8	683	1,852	910	14.6	69
Lawrence, MS	28077	...	69.6	44.2	0.5	134	352	178	12.5	19
Leake, MS	28079	...	78.4	63.7	3.9	167	479	221	14.8	20
Lee, MS	28081	...	58.9	40.7	1.3	785	2,428	1,200	13.7	98
Leflore, MS	28083	...	95.8	95.6	1.4	304	908	397	14.5	49
Lincoln, MS	28085	...	59.7	38.5	0.5	351	912	401	15.6	43
Lowndes, MS	28087	...	65.0	62.5	0.6	729	1,510	710	14.1	62
Madison, MS	28089	...	47.3	56.0	1.5	771	1,815	935	15.9	74
Marion, MS	28091	...	80.3	48.3	0.6	195	658	304	14.2	35
Marshall, MS	28093	...	88.9	75.6	3.5	293	685	325	15.1	29
Monroe, MS	28095	...	65.9	40.8	0.2	365	867	415	13.7	34
Montgomery, MS	28097	...	76.2	64.7	0.1	89	255	102	16.3	16
Neshoba, MS	28099	...	64.9	41.6	...	232	599	288	15.1	26
Newton, MS	28101	...	57.7	44.1	0.4	154	591	275	14.0	30
Noxubee, MS	28103	...	99.2	99.4	0.5	158	331	137	14.4	13
Oktibbeha, MS	28105	...	69.1	68.7	0.5	271	810	360	14.1	43
Panola, MS	28107	...	80.3	68.6	0.4	330	939	416	15.1	36
Pearl River, MS	28109	...	64.7	20.8	1.0	463	1,402	600	15.0	69
Perry, MS	28111	...	73.3	31.3	...	114	325	156	13.2	12
Pike, MS	28113	...	78.7	68.6	0.3	339	1,081	484	14.7	54
Pontotoc, MS	28115	...	57.9	23.0	4.0	305	781	404	13.9	26
Prentiss, MS	28117	...	61.5	17.9	0.1	272	516	285	12.5	19
Quitman, MS	28119	...	99.3	97.4	...	71	257	105	12.6	16
Rankin, MS	28121	...	41.9	27.6	2.0	1,053	2,818	1,542	14.3	111
Scott, MS	28123	...	75.3	53.5	3.9	300	719	326	16.3	29
Sharkey, MS	28125	...	95.3	97.6	...	79	180	76	15.1	14
Simpson, MS	28127	...	76.2	54.2	0.5	241	572	282	15.1	25
Smith, MS	28129	...	65.1	33.1	0.2	207	426	205	14.8	18
Stone, MS	28131	...	59.9	26.1	0.2	130	425	191	14.7	18
Sunflower, MS	28133	...	90.3	93.3	0.6	282	772	330	14.3	46
Tallahatchie, MS	28135	...	91.8	83.2	0.1	136	377	165	13.9	16
Tate, MS	28137	...	65.8	42.8	1.4	258	655	286	17.2	26
Tippah, MS	28139	...	67.6	28.0	2.7	216	541	285	14.1	15
Tishomingo, MS	28141	...	60.7	7.0	1.7	179	479	225	14.5	13
Tunica, MS	28143	...	96.7	98.8	0.5	103	405	166	13.6	25
Union, MS	28145	...	59.3	24.3	2.6	285	696	337	14.5	24
Walthall, MS	28147	...	77.1	65.3	0.4	166	357	160	15.8	13
Warren, MS	28149	...	71.4	63.8	0.5	393	1,319	570	15.9	50
Washington, MS	28151	...	94.0	89.9	0.2	529	1,638	711	15.1	68
Wayne, MS	28153	...	80.5	56.4	0.3	214	582	272	13.8	21
Webster, MS	28155	...	62.3	30.9	...	102	257	120	15.1	11
Wilkinson, MS	28157	...	86.6	99.6	...	60	228	98	13.7	15
Winston, MS	28159	...	79.4	67.0	...	163	426	192	14.2	15
Yalobusha, MS	28161	...	79.8	57.6	0.1	98	287	140	13.8	20
Yazoo, MS	28163	...	90.4	81.1	0.2	226	669	290	15.6	42
MISSOURI	29000	14.5	38.7	24.0	1.8	60,275	132,201	67,653	13.6	10,107
Adair, MO	29001	18.9	41.4	5.8	0.8	230	502	257	11.9	46
Andrew, MO	29003	13.0	29.5	3.5	...	181	377	220	13.1	26
Atchison, MO	29005	15.4	41.2	2.4	...	74	100	60	15.5	9
Audrain, MO	29007	12.9	46.3	13.1	1.3	235	541	270	12.9	44
Barry, MO	29009	11.0	54.9	17.8	9.1	402	874	461	13.8	63
Barton, MO	29011	14.2	50.9	5.2	0.3	145	294	163	13.1	25
Bates, MO	29013	11.7	43.6	4.1	...	194	307	189	12.4	25
Benton, MO	29015	16.1	57.5	3.1	0.2	200	359	197	13.4	23
Bollinger, MO	29017	12.3	50.5	1.2	...	128	259	143	13.7	21

[2]IEP= Individual Education Program. See notes and definitions for more information
... Not available

Table C-1. Population, School, and Student Characteristics by County—*Continued*

County	State/County Code	Revenues, 2007-2008				Current expenditures, 2007-2008			Resident population 16 to 19 years, 2006-2008			
		Total revenue ($1,000's)	Percentage of revenue from			Amount ($1,000's)	Amount per student	Percent for instruc-tion	Total population 16 to 19 years	Percent en-rolled in school	Percent high school graduates, not enrolled in school	Percent not enrolled, not grads, not employed or not in labor force
			Federal gov't	State gov't	Local gov't							
		19	20	21	22	23	24	25	26	27	28	29
Hancock, MS	28045	98,581	36.8	29.6	33.6	54,259	9,075	54.8	...	...	...	...
Harrison, MS	28047	327,811	25.4	40.8	33.8	253,383	9,128	56.2	10,871	72.8	14.8	7.6
Hinds, MS	28049	368,061	14.5	52.0	33.6	337,977	7,890	57.0	16,773	84.0	7.2	5.4
Holmes, MS	28051	33,952	24.6	58.3	17.0	30,570	7,595	51.8	...	...	...	...
Humphreys, MS	28053	16,662	29.8	52.9	17.2	14,026	7,606	49.0	...	...	...	...
Issaquena, MS	28055	...	...	...	...	...	...	...	...	...	...	...
Itawamba, MS	28057	28,669	11.5	66.3	22.2	26,959	7,350	63.8	...	...	...	...
Jackson, MS	28059	228,976	13.1	50.5	36.4	212,762	8,720	55.5	7,834	75.1	12.7	9.2
Jasper, MS	28061	24,839	16.6	57.8	25.6	23,146	8,228	52.1	...	...	...	...
Jefferson, MS	28063	12,712	19.7	59.9	20.4	12,079	8,394	53.3	...	...	...	...
Jefferson Davis, MS	28065	23,714	15.3	45.6	39.1	14,888	7,710	53.5	...	...	...	...
Jones, MS	28067	105,433	13.0	51.5	35.5	91,510	8,209	58.5	3,846	65.3	22.5	6.1
Kemper, MS	28069	11,041	22.7	58.5	18.8	10,733	8,250	56.2	...	...	...	...
Lafayette, MS	28071	57,422	9.3	47.4	43.2	49,816	8,539	62.3	...	...	...	...
Lamar, MS	28073	83,747	11.1	51.2	37.7	71,489	8,190	59.6	...	...	...	...
Lauderdale, MS	28075	109,376	13.8	57.0	29.3	101,334	7,684	62.8	...	...	...	...
Lawrence, MS	28077	19,965	15.4	56.1	28.5	18,805	8,365	61.5	...	...	...	...
Leake, MS	28079	25,443	17.5	62.7	19.8	23,330	7,074	57.0	...	...	...	...
Lee, MS	28081	147,310	10.7	54.1	35.2	130,981	8,064	61.5	...	...	...	...
Leflore, MS	28083	52,634	22.8	57.7	19.5	49,238	8,362	58.1	...	...	...	...
Lincoln, MS	28085	53,111	11.9	53.8	34.3	42,552	6,994	61.0	...	...	...	...
Lowndes, MS	28087	92,909	13.6	51.1	35.3	81,095	8,153	58.1	...	...	...	...
Madison, MS	28089	137,209	9.5	44.1	46.5	104,864	7,176	60.3	5,147	90.0	7.2	2.0
Marion, MS	28091	40,632	15.3	57.7	27.0	35,699	8,031	58.9	...	...	...	...
Marshall, MS	28093	41,509	19.9	62.3	17.8	36,789	7,229	58.9	...	...	...	...
Monroe, MS	28095	48,721	14.4	60.9	24.7	46,750	8,119	60.9	...	...	...	...
Montgomery, MS	28097	16,916	20.5	59.2	20.3	15,824	9,079	61.1	...	...	...	...
Neshoba, MS	28099	33,170	18.8	61.4	19.8	29,351	6,839	65.6	...	...	...	...
Newton, MS	28101	32,873	13.4	63.0	23.6	29,676	7,615	57.9	...	...	...	...
Noxubee, MS	28103	20,220	23.4	53.8	22.8	18,381	8,880	53.0	...	...	...	...
Oktibbeha, MS	28105	54,585	17.7	47.3	35.0	45,921	9,281	58.4	...	...	...	...
Panola, MS	28107	54,737	16.5	58.5	24.9	49,827	7,804	59.3	...	...	...	...
Pearl River, MS	28109	76,587	14.8	58.7	26.5	70,863	7,773	59.1	...	...	...	...
Perry, MS	28111	18,619	20.4	58.5	21.1	17,654	8,463	59.2	...	...	...	...
Pike, MS	28113	63,399	18.3	57.2	24.5	56,777	7,949	58.1	...	...	...	...
Pontotoc, MS	28115	43,023	10.8	67.7	21.5	39,287	7,079	65.7	...	...	...	...
Prentiss, MS	28117	32,928	12.6	62.4	25.0	29,806	8,361	64.0	...	...	...	...
Quitman, MS	28119	13,460	23.7	57.7	18.6	13,278	9,351	53.1	...	...	...	...
Rankin, MS	28121	182,195	7.9	52.2	39.8	158,372	7,307	61.3	6,747	86.5	7.3	4.7
Scott, MS	28123	40,518	15.8	66.5	17.8	37,441	7,011	61.1	2,243	60.3	11.3	12.1
Sharkey, MS	28125	11,709	28.6	48.5	22.9	10,372	8,805	50.2	...	...	...	...
Simpson, MS	28127	33,003	16.0	64.2	19.9	28,994	6,762	60.7	...	...	...	...
Smith, MS	28129	24,543	13.0	64.9	22.0	21,817	7,100	60.2	...	...	...	...
Stone, MS	28131	22,431	12.9	59.8	27.3	21,089	7,295	59.9	...	...	...	...
Sunflower, MS	28133	41,366	20.3	60.4	19.3	39,810	8,154	56.9	...	...	...	...
Tallahatchie, MS	28135	22,649	21.9	57.8	20.3	21,388	9,074	56.6	...	...	...	...
Tate, MS	28137	37,587	11.8	65.3	22.9	33,501	6,843	58.7	...	...	...	...
Tippah, MS	28139	31,910	12.8	69.7	17.5	30,023	7,397	62.3	...	...	...	...
Tishomingo, MS	28141	27,459	15.3	61.7	22.9	26,750	8,121	57.7	...	...	...	...
Tunica, MS	28143	25,152	13.3	38.4	48.3	23,410	10,286	52.4	...	...	...	...
Union, MS	28145	41,044	11.3	64.4	24.3	36,314	7,457	63.1	...	...	...	...
Walthall, MS	28147	22,086	18.5	58.7	22.7	19,167	7,540	64.2	...	...	...	...
Warren, MS	28149	77,050	13.4	50.9	35.7	70,276	7,812	57.8	...	...	...	...
Washington, MS	28151	95,968	23.8	55.3	21.0	90,525	8,393	57.5	...	...	...	...
Wayne, MS	28153	39,326	14.2	47.5	38.3	29,120	7,568	63.5	...	...	...	...
Webster, MS	28155	15,262	13.2	62.1	24.6	13,678	7,487	61.8	...	...	...	...
Wilkinson, MS	28157	12,856	20.1	56.0	23.9	11,799	8,606	55.6	...	...	...	...
Winston, MS	28159	24,544	15.8	58.5	25.7	22,743	8,160	59.5	...	...	...	...
Yalobusha, MS	28161	16,794	18.9	63.3	17.8	15,858	8,054	62.8	...	...	...	...
Yazoo, MS	28163	38,512	21.6	57.7	20.7	34,945	7,690	58.0	...	...	...	...
MISSOURI	29000	9,491,504	7.8	30.8	61.4	8,448,553	9,254	60.1	334,726	83.3	9.9	4.6
Adair, MO	29001	29,916	8.5	38.3	53.2	26,321	8,306	63.3	...	...	...	...
Andrew, MO	29003	24,925	5.5	43.5	51.0	23,738	8,248	62.2	...	...	...	...
Atchison, MO	29005	8,925	7.9	36.0	56.1	8,787	9,448	61.9	...	...	...	...
Audrain, MO	29007	28,751	9.9	36.1	54.0	27,027	7,749	61.4	...	...	...	...
Barry, MO	29009	57,800	11.9	41.0	47.1	51,265	7,450	63.4	...	...	...	...
Barton, MO	29011	17,420	9.0	39.7	51.2	15,709	7,137	61.7	...	...	...	...
Bates, MO	29013	23,624	8.2	43.7	48.1	21,979	8,177	61.2	...	...	...	...
Benton, MO	29015	21,989	11.1	37.2	51.7	20,592	7,672	62.7	...	...	...	...
Bollinger, MO	29017	14,679	10.5	48.9	40.6	13,760	6,939	59.0	...	...	...	...

[3]May be of any race

Table C-1. Population, School, and Student Characteristics by County—*Continued*

County	State/County Code	High school graduates, 2006-2008			College enrollment, 2006-2008		College graduates, 2006-2008 (percent)						
		Population 25 years and over	High school diploma or less (percent)	High school diploma or more (percent)	Number	Percent public	Bachelor's degree or more	+/- U.S. percent with Bachelor's degree or more	Non-Hispanic White	Black or African American	American Indian and Alaska Native	Asian, Hawaiian, and Pacific Islander	Hispanic or Latino[3]
		30	31	32	33	34	35	36	37	38	39	40	41
Hancock, MS	28045	27,095	54.3	80.5	1,478	92.8	20.6	-6.8	20.8	...	...	...	...
Harrison, MS	28047	113,105	46.4	82.1	10,224	89.7	19.1	-8.3	21.7	10.8	...	17.9	16.2
Hinds, MS	28049	152,056	40.6	83.6	22,243	75.9	27.5	0.1	40.0	19.0	...	...	27.6
Holmes, MS	28051	11,864	68.5	65.3	1,684	89.4	11.5	-15.9	16.3	10.0	...	...	...
Humphreys, MS	28053	...	...	...	...	...	...	...	...	...	...	...	...
Issaquena, MS	28055	...	...	...	...	...	...	...	...	...	...	...	...
Itawamba, MS	28057	15,228	67.5	67.4	...	...	10.8	-16.6	11.0	...	...	...	...
Jackson, MS	28059	83,982	49.6	84.0	6,020	82.8	18.0	-9.4	20.7	9.4	...	15.3	8.5
Jasper, MS	28061	...	...	...	...	...	...	...	...	...	...	...	...
Jefferson, MS	28063	...	...	...	...	...	...	...	...	...	...	...	...
Jefferson Davis, MS	28065	...	...	...	...	...	...	...	...	...	...	...	...
Jones, MS	28067	42,953	57.9	76.8	3,429	89.0	14.6	-12.8	17.2	8.8	...	...	2.6
Kemper, MS	28069	...	...	...	...	...	...	...	...	...	...	...	...
Lafayette, MS	28071	23,252	35.2	83.6	12,020	94.9	37.3	9.9	44.9	14.1	...	...	...
Lamar, MS	28073	29,086	39.2	83.3	4,455	91.8	30.3	2.9	31.1	25.8	...	...	...
Lauderdale, MS	28075	49,485	50.0	80.8	4,086	91.9	18.5	-8.9	23.9	10.0	...	...	...
Lawrence, MS	28077	...	...	...	...	...	...	...	...	...	...	...	...
Leake, MS	28079	13,566	63.8	74.8	628	72.6	8.8	-18.6	12.0	4.5	...	...	...
Lee, MS	28081	51,580	47.6	81.1	4,847	90.3	20.3	-7.1	24.0	8.6	...	...	...
Leflore, MS	28083	20,784	59.7	69.1	3,695	87.1	17.4	-10.0	30.1	10.5	...	...	...
Lincoln, MS	28085	22,896	57.2	80.5	1,390	68.6	14.8	-12.6	17.2	9.3	...	...	...
Lowndes, MS	28087	37,215	51.7	79.7	3,855	92.4	18.9	-8.5	25.9	8.6	...	...	...
Madison, MS	28089	55,405	30.5	87.9	5,691	77.5	42.7	15.3	53.3	22.2	...	...	16.9
Marion, MS	28091	16,444	64.7	74.0	965	92.1	11.9	-15.5	13.1	9.9	...	...	...
Marshall, MS	28093	23,665	68.6	67.1	1,327	64.2	10.5	-16.9	13.1	6.7	...	...	...
Monroe, MS	28095	24,952	63.1	71.4	1,545	88.3	11.8	-15.6	14.9	4.7	...	...	...
Montgomery, MS	28097	...	...	...	...	...	...	...	...	...	...	...	...
Neshoba, MS	28099	18,971	62.5	72.4	1,078	88.2	11.8	-15.6	12.4	10.8	7.1	...	...
Newton, MS	28101	13,800	57.3	78.3	1,949	95.5	10.8	-16.6	13.3	4.3	...	...	...
Noxubee, MS	28103	...	...	...	...	...	...	...	...	...	...	...	...
Oktibbeha, MS	28105	22,117	38.2	83.9	12,050	96.6	37.4	10.0	48.4	14.0	...	...	...
Panola, MS	28107	22,323	59.9	74.2	1,157	91.1	12.6	-14.8	17.6	6.3	...	...	...
Pearl River, MS	28109	37,344	53.4	78.0	2,182	89.7	15.7	-11.7	15.5	20.5	...	...	5.8
Perry, MS	28111	...	...	...	...	...	...	...	...	...	...	...	...
Pike, MS	28113	25,085	55.3	79.4	2,302	80.6	15.4	-12.0	19.9	10.2	...	...	...
Pontotoc, MS	28115	18,592	64.6	75.5	1,043	89.7	10.5	-16.9	11.3	3.9	...	...	...
Prentiss, MS	28117	16,570	59.8	73.0	...	...	12.0	-15.4	11.7	7.2	...	...	...
Quitman, MS	28119	...	...	...	...	...	...	...	...	...	...	...	...
Rankin, MS	28121	89,427	39.8	87.3	7,952	70.1	28.5	1.1	30.6	18.2	...	71.2	12.4
Scott, MS	28123	17,853	69.2	68.2	1,049	96.5	8.4	-19.0	10.9	5.2	...	...	1.6
Sharkey, MS	28125	...	...	...	...	...	...	...	...	...	...	...	...
Simpson, MS	28127	18,255	61.2	76.6	1,076	79.9	13.3	-14.1	17.1	4.2	...	...	...
Smith, MS	28129	...	...	...	...	...	...	...	...	...	...	...	...
Stone, MS	28131	...	...	...	...	...	...	...	...	...	...	...	...
Sunflower, MS	28133	18,753	60.7	70.1	2,504	80.6	13.9	-13.5	21.9	10.3	...	...	...
Tallahatchie, MS	28135	...	...	...	...	...	...	...	...	...	...	...	...
Tate, MS	28137	16,783	56.5	77.8	1,981	87.8	13.1	-14.3	14.7	9.6	...	...	...
Tippah, MS	28139	14,302	65.4	67.7	568	74.1	10.0	-17.4	12.0	2.0	...	...	...
Tishomingo, MS	28141	...	...	...	...	...	...	...	...	...	...	...	...
Tunica, MS	28143	...	...	...	...	...	...	...	...	...	...	...	...
Union, MS	28145	17,718	63.2	72.7	990	74.8	11.5	-15.9	11.9	7.8	...	...	...
Walthall, MS	28147	...	...	...	...	...	...	...	...	...	...	...	...
Warren, MS	28149	31,006	45.8	81.6	2,395	90.2	22.8	-4.6	31.3	11.9	...	...	23.0
Washington, MS	28151	34,180	57.7	71.2	1,749	79.1	17.8	-9.6	25.3	12.7	...	...	...
Wayne, MS	28153	13,834	63.2	74.5	628	86.9	9.7	-17.7	11.8	5.8	...	...	...
Webster, MS	28155	...	...	...	...	...	...	...	...	...	...	...	...
Wilkinson, MS	28157	...	...	...	...	...	...	...	...	...	...	...	...
Winston, MS	28159	...	...	...	...	...	...	...	...	...	...	...	...
Yalobusha, MS	28161	...	...	...	...	...	...	...	...	...	...	...	...
Yazoo, MS	28163	18,752	59.5	75.3	875	66.9	12.0	-15.4	17.5	7.8	...	...	...
MISSOURI	29000	3,886,568	47.5	85.6	376,488	70.0	24.5	-2.9	25.5	14.8	17.8	51.3	16.8
Adair, MO	29001	13,190	49.6	88.0	6,522	92.3	26.9	-0.5	27.3	...	...	...	...
Andrew, MO	29003	...	...	...	...	...	...	...	...	...	...	...	...
Atchison, MO	29005	...	...	...	...	...	...	...	...	...	...	...	...
Audrain, MO	29007	17,904	67.3	79.8	1,044	81.5	12.1	-15.3	12.2	14.3	...	...	...
Barry, MO	29009	24,115	62.5	79.3	1,214	80.0	12.6	-14.8	13.3	...	...	...	4.8
Barton, MO	29011	...	...	...	...	...	...	...	...	...	...	...	...
Bates, MO	29013	...	...	...	...	...	...	...	...	...	...	...	...
Benton, MO	29015	...	...	...	...	...	...	...	...	...	...	...	...
Bollinger, MO	29017	...	...	...	...	...	...	...	...	...	...	...	...

[3]May be of any race
... Not available

Table C-1. Population, School, and Student Characteristics by County—*Continued*

County	State/County Code	County Type[1]	Population, 2009 Total	Population, 2009 Percent 5–17 years	Percent of related children 5-17 years in poverty, 2008	Percent of children under 19 years with no health insurance, 2007	Number of Schools and Students, 2008-2009 School Districts	Number of Schools and Students, 2008-2009 Schools	Number of Schools and Students, 2008-2009 Students	Resident enrollment, 2006-2008 K–12 enrollment Number	Resident enrollment, 2006-2008 K–12 enrollment Percent public
			1	2	3	4	5	6	7	8	9
Boone, MO	29019	3	156,377	14.7	13.7	9.9	6	49	22,413	23,620	90.6
Buchanan, MO	29021	3	89,856	16.4	19.8	7.0	3	32	12,815	15,516	85.0
Butler, MO	29023	7	41,471	16.8	27.7	6.8	3	16	6,596	6,901	91.3
Caldwell, MO	29025	1	9,160	19.5	17.3	13.5	7	11	1,030	...	...
Callaway, MO	29027	3	43,727	16.7	13.0	11.1	5	17	5,216	7,985	93.5
Camden, MO	29029	7	40,705	13.8	19.5	14.5	4	15	5,398	5,852	93.7
Cape Girardeau, MO	29031	5	73,957	15.6	14.8	8.4	5	23	9,659	11,374	80.6
Carroll, MO	29033	6	9,535	17.9	18.5	10.5	5	13	1,645	...	...
Carter, MO	29035	9	5,870	18.2	38.7	11.2	2	5	1,335	...	...
Cass, MO	29037	1	100,184	19.8	9.0	9.8	10	45	18,426	18,627	92.5
Cedar, MO	29039	6	13,544	17.4	33.6	9.6	2	6	2,311	...	...
Chariton, MO	29041	9	7,594	16.0	16.6	13.9	4	8	1,130	...	...
Christian, MO	29043	2	77,455	19.4	12.7	11.6	7	30	14,048	13,608	91.3
Clark, MO	29045	9	7,127	17.4	22.4	16.7	3	6	1,110	...	...
Clay, MO	29047	1	228,358	18.0	7.7	8.4	6	68	37,328	38,836	90.8
Clinton, MO	29049	1	21,002	18.2	12.1	11.9	4	13	4,250	3,616	94.1
Cole, MO	29051	3	75,018	16.7	11.1	9.9	7	121	12,601	13,040	80.5
Cooper, MO	29053	6	17,298	16.3	14.5	9.7	6	15	2,541	...	...
Crawford, MO	29055	6	23,915	18.2	23.1	9.5	4	11	3,831	4,582	91.5
Dade, MO	29057	8	7,316	16.5	24.7	11.5	10	20	2,971	...	...
Dallas, MO	29059	2	16,637	18.3	26.2	8.8	1	5	1,826	...	...
Daviess, MO	29061	8	8,078	19.7	22.5	17.5	6	13	1,986	...	...
De Kalb, MO	29063	3	12,112	13.1	13.0	11.8	4	8	1,145	...	...
Dent, MO	29065	7	15,042	17.0	25.3	7.5	5	8	2,329	...	...
Douglas, MO	29067	6	13,608	16.9	30.1	7.2	3	5	1,669	...	...
Dunklin, MO	29069	7	31,039	18.2	35.2	6.0	7	20	6,003	5,568	95.3
Franklin, MO	29071	1	101,263	18.2	10.6	10.3	10	43	16,734	18,406	84.4
Gasconade, MO	29073	6	15,096	16.1	15.0	12.8	2	7	3,001	...	...
Gentry, MO	29075	8	6,108	17.0	18.5	16.0	3	7	1,140	...	...
Greene, MO	29077	2	269,630	14.8	18.7	7.5	8	80	36,352	39,391	91.6
Grundy, MO	29079	7	10,047	16.4	22.2	9.0	5	8	1,542	...	...
Harrison, MO	29081	7	8,769	17.1	21.7	10.9	5	12	1,483	...	...
Henry, MO	29083	6	22,176	16.4	21.6	8.4	8	15	3,334	3,791	88.4
Hickory, MO	29085	8	8,903	12.6	33.8	11.3	3	7	984	...	...
Holt, MO	29087	8	4,868	15.5	20.4	13.7	3	6	673	...	...
Howard, MO	29089	3	9,857	15.3	16.7	11.1	3	7	1,487	...	...
Howell, MO	29091	7	38,921	17.6	26.5	8.4	8	17	6,867	6,756	94.3
Iron, MO	29093	6	9,943	17.6	30.2	8.6	3	7	1,536	...	...
Jackson, MO	29095	1	705,708	17.2	17.5	8.9	30	250	106,020	117,830	86.6
Jasper, MO	29097	3	118,179	17.9	23.5	8.5	7	50	20,656	20,828	93.5
Jefferson, MO	29099	1	219,046	17.9	9.3	10.1	12	61	35,514	40,122	90.8
Johnson, MO	29101	4	52,657	15.5	14.3	13.1	7	28	7,743	8,675	94.5
Knox, MO	29103	9	3,981	17.0	25.6	16.3	1	2	554	...	...
Laclede, MO	29105	6	35,432	17.9	24.3	8.3	4	13	6,104	6,063	91.3
Lafayette, MO	29107	1	32,572	17.8	14.4	10.0	6	18	5,571	5,428	87.3
Lawrence, MO	29109	6	37,648	19.5	19.9	10.8	6	19	6,056	6,765	92.8
Lewis, MO	29111	9	9,791	16.4	22.0	15.2	2	4	1,552	...	...
Lincoln, MO	29113	1	53,311	19.9	12.0	11.3	4	18	8,784	10,211	89.1
Linn, MO	29115	7	12,606	17.9	21.1	9.3	5	13	2,459	...	...
Livingston, MO	29117	6	14,235	16.3	19.2	9.8	3	10	2,236	...	...
McDonald, MO	29119	2	23,063	20.2	26.4	13.0	1	10	3,785	4,668	92.9
Macon, MO	29121	7	15,359	17.4	20.0	11.6	6	14	2,382	...	...
Madison, MO	29123	7	12,341	17.4	24.7	8.2	2	6	2,110	...	...
Maries, MO	29125	8	8,821	17.3	22.4	13.2	2	5	1,331	...	...
Marion, MO	29127	5	28,449	17.6	20.8	8.6	3	13	4,987	5,043	89.9
Mercer, MO	29129	9	3,475	17.0	17.5	13.9	2	4	574	...	...
Miller, MO	29131	6	24,778	18.0	23.3	12.6	5	15	5,135	4,483	95.5
Mississippi, MO	29133	7	13,266	17.6	35.9	6.9	2	8	2,253	...	...
Moniteau, MO	29135	3	15,132	17.8	15.7	12.9	6	10	2,407	...	...
Monroe, MO	29137	9	8,993	17.4	17.5	14.0	5	10	1,619	...	...
Montgomery, MO	29139	8	11,698	16.6	20.2	14.2	2	7	1,828	...	...
Morgan, MO	29141	8	20,527	16.5	29.4	15.0	2	7	2,220	3,023	76.2
New Madrid, MO	29143	7	17,480	17.2	29.4	6.1	4	13	2,962	...	...
Newton, MO	29145	3	56,121	18.8	18.1	9.7	6	20	8,786	10,325	88.2
Nodaway, MO	29147	6	22,130	12.3	13.0	10.1	7	17	2,759	3,006	91.6
Oregon, MO	29149	9	10,291	17.9	33.1	7.1	3	6	1,751	...	...
Osage, MO	29151	3	13,561	17.8	10.9	13.7	3	6	1,671	...	...
Ozark, MO	29153	9	9,315	15.0	34.1	11.1	5	9	1,648	...	...
Pemiscot, MO	29155	7	18,193	20.1	40.7	4.4	8	19	3,893	...	...
Perry, MO	29157	7	18,847	17.9	13.5	11.0	2	6	2,503	...	...

[1]County type codes are from the Economic Research Service of the United States Department of Agriculture. See notes and definitions for more information.
... Not available

Table C-1. Population, School, and Student Characteristics by County—*Continued*

County	State/ County Code	Characteristics of students, 2008-2009				Number of graduates, 2006-2007	Staff and students, 2008-2009			
		Percent with IEP[2]	Percent eligible for free or reduced lunch	Percent minority	Percent English Language Learners		Total staff	Number of teachers	Student/ teacher ratio	Central admin. Staff
		10	11	12	13	14	15	16	17	18
Boone, MO	29019	14.0	32.4	26.1	2.4	1,587	3,127	1,690	13.3	193
Buchanan, MO	29021	13.3	51.3	15.5	2.3	931	1,980	954	13.4	102
Butler, MO	29023	15.9	54.4	12.2	0.2	363	872	458	14.4	62
Caldwell, MO	29025	18.9	44.5	3.6	...	144	186	111	9.3	25
Callaway, MO	29027	13.0	41.8	9.0	0.1	382	812	420	12.4	51
Camden, MO	29029	12.3	47.2	4.7	1.1	398	764	411	13.1	75
Cape Girardeau, MO	29031	14.2	39.4	17.6	0.6	647	1,401	732	13.2	101
Carroll, MO	29033	15.0	46.6	5.2	0.1	141	261	155	10.6	26
Carter, MO	29035	16.5	60.4	1.4	...	99	179	108	12.4	18
Cass, MO	29037	11.1	29.5	11.9	0.9	1,161	2,229	1,234	14.9	188
Cedar, MO	29039	14.5	51.2	2.4	...	150	340	179	12.9	22
Chariton, MO	29041	15.0	40.6	4.2	...	102	197	104	10.9	15
Christian, MO	29043	12.0	33.8	5.2	0.6	803	1,676	986	14.2	109
Clark, MO	29045	12.2	41.5	1.5	...	75	150	92	12.1	10
Clay, MO	29047	11.1	28.1	20.0	2.7	2,553	5,889	2,554	14.6	397
Clinton, MO	29049	14.3	26.0	6.1	...	264	547	315	13.5	45
Cole, MO	29051	28.0	36.6	20.5	1.0	845	2,164	1,050	12.0	189
Cooper, MO	29053	14.2	42.2	10.6	0.1	204	386	228	11.1	32
Crawford, MO	29055	13.3	51.0	2.7	0.3	241	551	294	13.0	43
Dade, MO	29057	12.2	53.0	4.6	0.4	98	458	275	10.8	42
Dallas, MO	29059	12.2	59.0	2.3	0.1	198	309	147	12.4	20
Daviess, MO	29061	16.6	44.0	2.2	0.1	85	326	196	10.1	31
De Kalb, MO	29063	10.9	37.5	2.5	...	88	158	104	11.0	12
Dent, MO	29065	16.8	46.5	4.5	...	151	354	165	14.1	25
Douglas, MO	29067	15.2	64.6	1.5	...	105	242	135	12.4	16
Dunklin, MO	29069	14.9	62.1	25.6	2.2	349	795	456	13.2	70
Franklin, MO	29071	18.9	35.5	3.5	0.5	1,156	2,248	1,185	14.1	178
Gasconade, MO	29073	13.8	40.0	2.0	...	234	428	230	13.0	35
Gentry, MO	29075	16.1	42.2	3.4	...	81	173	105	10.9	13
Greene, MO	29077	12.2	41.5	10.4	1.2	2,247	4,898	2,406	15.1	269
Grundy, MO	29079	17.5	47.9	3.8	0.6	110	291	142	10.9	28
Harrison, MO	29081	14.8	49.4	2.0	0.2	106	241	145	10.2	22
Henry, MO	29083	14.4	50.5	4.5	...	243	520	291	11.5	46
Hickory, MO	29085	10.7	66.8	2.3	...	97	169	89	11.1	15
Holt, MO	29087	15.0	42.9	2.8	...	42	118	73	9.2	10
Howard, MO	29089	15.6	42.7	9.1	...	100	229	123	12.1	19
Howell, MO	29091	14.6	47.9	3.2	1.0	443	1,025	529	13.0	77
Iron, MO	29093	18.9	56.9	3.9	...	150	193	104	14.8	19
Jackson, MO	29095	11.5	46.5	48.7	4.0	6,469	16,437	7,694	13.8	1116
Jasper, MO	29097	13.5	48.2	14.9	3.0	1,085	2,830	1,429	14.5	172
Jefferson, MO	29099	15.6	31.2	3.6	0.3	2,427	4,271	2,302	15.4	320
Johnson, MO	29101	14.5	37.4	11.5	0.8	547	1,164	614	12.6	82
Knox, MO	29103	10.6	58.5	3.2	...	38	107	49	11.3	6
Laclede, MO	29105	13.0	47.8	4.6	0.4	403	865	409	14.9	66
Lafayette, MO	29107	13.8	34.8	7.1	0.7	440	729	437	12.7	56
Lawrence, MO	29109	12.7	51.5	10.5	1.4	351	819	445	13.6	67
Lewis, MO	29111	17.5	40.1	5.6	0.2	104	221	126	12.3	19
Lincoln, MO	29113	13.0	36.9	6.6	0.9	583	1,017	536	16.4	78
Linn, MO	29115	17.0	39.5	3.7	0.3	189	395	225	10.9	34
Livingston, MO	29117	17.3	43.5	4.7	0.2	156	346	165	13.6	23
McDonald, MO	29119	14.0	60.5	22.3	6.3	214	484	281	13.5	32
Macon, MO	29121	15.8	46.0	6.8	0.3	159	389	212	11.2	32
Madison, MO	29123	13.5	49.6	2.7	0.7	152	315	158	13.4	22
Maries, MO	29125	17.9	45.8	1.1	0.2	96	168	104	12.8	16
Marion, MO	29127	15.6	45.5	9.6	0.3	374	740	413	12.1	57
Mercer, MO	29129	17.2	44.9	2.3	...	41	101	62	9.3	13
Miller, MO	29131	13.9	46.7	2.5	0.4	373	985	390	13.2	60
Mississippi, MO	29133	14.4	62.1	29.4	...	115	290	145	15.5	20
Moniteau, MO	29135	13.8	40.8	8.6	4.4	139	335	184	13.1	24
Monroe, MO	29137	14.4	40.0	7.8	0.2	109	273	150	10.8	25
Montgomery, MO	29139	11.7	46.0	5.4	...	139	255	148	12.4	23
Morgan, MO	29141	13.3	59.9	4.0	...	156	318	153	14.5	28
New Madrid, MO	29143	15.5	56.7	24.9	...	189	474	252	11.8	39
Newton, MO	29145	14.5	50.3	16.3	3.4	555	1,132	608	14.5	81
Nodaway, MO	29147	14.2	32.4	3.4	0.5	245	483	265	10.4	44
Oregon, MO	29149	15.4	60.5	3.2	...	151	264	142	12.3	17
Osage, MO	29151	12.2	30.2	1.2	0.2	155	223	129	13.0	21
Ozark, MO	29153	13.8	55.7	1.2	0.1	110	293	146	11.3	29
Pemiscot, MO	29155	16.4	65.6	39.5	0.2	252	496	283	13.8	56
Perry, MO	29157	17.9	44.0	2.2	0.8	159	336	185	13.5	30

[2]IEP= Individual Education Program. See notes and definitions for more information
... Not available

Table C-1. Population, School, and Student Characteristics by County—*Continued*

County	State/County Code	Revenues, 2007-2008				Current expenditures, 2007-2008			Resident population 16 to 19 years, 2006-2008			
		Total revenue ($1,000's)	Percentage of revenue from			Amount ($1,000's)	Amount per student	Percent for instruc-tion	Total population 16 to 19 years	Percent en-rolled in school	Percent high school graduates, not enrolled in school	Percent not enrolled, not grads, not employed or not in labor force
			Federal gov't	State gov't	Local gov't							
	19	20	21	22	23	24	25	26	27	28	29	
Boone, MO	29019	225,518	6.7	30.8	62.5	208,717	9,362	62.8	12,488	93.4	3.4	2.2
Buchanan, MO	29021	122,018	10.2	36.4	53.3	107,647	8,397	60.6	5,101	75.1	18.6	5.2
Butler, MO	29023	51,259	13.4	40.8	45.8	49,915	7,599	62.6	...	...	...	...
Caldwell, MO	29025	17,200	7.6	47.8	44.6	15,541	8,875	60.9	...	...	...	...
Callaway, MO	29027	46,408	7.7	35.8	56.5	42,457	8,086	59.5	...	...	...	...
Camden, MO	29029	53,952	7.2	17.4	75.3	45,791	8,638	59.3	...	...	...	...
Cape Girardeau, MO	29031	88,225	7.9	26.8	65.3	75,033	7,757	61.9	...	...	...	...
Carroll, MO	29033	16,534	8.3	38.8	52.9	14,706	8,530	59.8	...	...	...	...
Carter, MO	29035	10,968	13.1	52.4	34.5	10,707	8,180	63.1	...	...	...	...
Cass, MO	29037	176,258	5.0	40.1	54.8	153,233	8,435	57.5	...	...	...	...
Cedar, MO	29039	19,379	12.3	40.4	47.2	17,529	7,552	62.9	...	...	...	...
Chariton, MO	29041	11,021	7.5	28.2	64.3	10,039	8,829	60.8	...	...	...	...
Christian, MO	29043	108,326	5.9	42.4	51.7	96,003	7,079	63.5	3,924	87.5	9.5	1.5
Clark, MO	29045	9,686	9.0	38.0	53.0	8,661	7,789	63.0	...	...	...	...
Clay, MO	29047	395,473	4.1	24.5	71.4	329,427	9,041	59.3	...	...	...	...
Clinton, MO	29049	40,317	5.4	44.3	50.3	36,998	8,661	65.8	...	...	...	...
Cole, MO	29051	97,090	7.5	19.3	73.2	85,138	8,052	63.6	...	...	...	...
Cooper, MO	29053	24,503	7.1	36.5	56.4	23,136	8,981	61.9	...	...	...	...
Crawford, MO	29055	29,121	9.3	41.7	49.0	26,004	7,505	62.5	...	...	...	...
Dade, MO	29057	10,799	9.3	43.1	47.6	10,431	9,086	59.9	...	...	...	...
Dallas, MO	29059	22,865	10.4	49.4	40.2	21,835	8,344	60.5	...	...	...	...
Daviess, MO	29061	12,871	8.3	46.4	45.4	12,402	9,735	61.6	...	...	...	...
De Kalb, MO	29063	10,671	6.8	48.0	45.2	11,337	9,624	61.1	...	...	...	...
Dent, MO	29065	20,211	10.4	41.4	48.2	17,457	7,670	63.7	...	...	...	...
Douglas, MO	29067	13,993	17.9	45.4	36.7	12,730	8,062	62.3	...	...	...	...
Dunklin, MO	29069	49,970	15.3	45.2	39.5	46,880	7,850	63.1	...	...	...	...
Franklin, MO	29071	154,756	6.5	29.4	64.1	135,411	8,012	61.2	5,253	84.5	7.1	7.1
Gasconade, MO	29073	27,036	7.1	33.3	59.5	24,653	8,051	61.5	...	...	...	...
Gentry, MO	29075	12,113	7.4	43.0	49.6	11,299	9,551	63.2	...	...	...	...
Greene, MO	29077	308,653	9.0	24.3	66.8	277,773	7,734	60.1	15,227	89.2	6.5	2.6
Grundy, MO	29079	15,387	8.3	42.2	49.5	13,606	8,622	63.4	...	...	...	...
Harrison, MO	29081	13,943	11.2	40.7	48.0	13,851	9,197	62.8	...	...	...	...
Henry, MO	29083	31,156	11.0	35.1	53.8	28,444	8,053	63.7	...	...	...	...
Hickory, MO	29085	10,167	12.4	38.9	48.7	9,369	9,026	59.2	...	...	...	...
Holt, MO	29087	7,110	8.1	26.9	65.0	6,964	10,211	58.9	...	...	...	...
Howard, MO	29089	12,388	9.4	39.1	51.5	11,710	8,535	60.9	...	...	...	...
Howell, MO	29091	61,063	13.5	44.2	42.3	54,675	7,993	65.1	...	...	...	...
Iron, MO	29093	19,713	11.3	37.4	51.3	18,803	8,832	59.1	...	...	...	...
Jackson, MO	29095	1,252,227	7.8	34.3	57.9	1,130,084	10,487	57.4	34,834	79.8	12.3	5.5
Jasper, MO	29097	173,690	9.7	35.1	55.2	149,809	7,361	64.3	6,448	81.5	11.9	3.3
Jefferson, MO	29099	329,595	6.4	40.2	53.4	302,775	8,512	63.5	11,779	86.4	9.4	3.0
Johnson, MO	29101	70,862	16.8	38.4	44.8	65,153	8,431	61.0	...	...	...	...
Knox, MO	29103	5,559	9.7	31.3	59.0	4,974	8,835	54.9	...	...	...	...
Laclede, MO	29105	47,350	9.9	43.8	46.3	44,698	7,264	64.0	...	...	...	...
Lafayette, MO	29107	53,013	7.2	41.5	51.3	49,960	8,963	65.3	...	...	...	...
Lawrence, MO	29109	52,325	11.3	44.8	43.9	47,770	7,746	64.2	...	...	...	...
Lewis, MO	29111	13,346	8.2	46.0	45.9	12,350	7,787	63.9	...	...	...	...
Lincoln, MO	29113	69,430	6.9	40.6	52.5	62,943	7,144	60.9	...	...	...	...
Linn, MO	29115	23,025	7.5	48.6	43.9	22,501	8,968	63.6	...	...	...	...
Livingston, MO	29117	22,253	9.8	42.7	47.5	21,401	9,558	66.8	...	...	...	...
McDonald, MO	29119	36,704	9.7	40.6	49.7	30,970	8,332	66.2	...	...	...	...
Macon, MO	29121	21,947	8.9	43.7	47.4	20,428	8,598	61.4	...	...	...	...
Madison, MO	29123	15,279	10.4	48.1	41.5	16,135	7,640	64.6	...	...	...	...
Maries, MO	29125	10,794	9.0	38.1	52.9	11,001	7,892	60.3	...	...	...	...
Marion, MO	29127	41,465	10.1	37.6	52.3	39,161	7,846	64.5	...	...	...	...
Mercer, MO	29129	6,582	9.9	31.6	58.5	5,955	9,349	58.7	...	...	...	...
Miller, MO	29131	47,370	9.5	28.3	62.2	41,982	8,166	61.4	...	...	...	...
Mississippi, MO	29133	17,286	15.4	45.5	39.1	18,046	7,898	62.1	...	...	...	...
Moniteau, MO	29135	20,680	7.9	39.9	52.1	18,944	7,838	62.3	...	...	...	...
Monroe, MO	29137	15,640	8.6	38.1	53.2	14,089	8,263	60.8	...	...	...	...
Montgomery, MO	29139	15,852	11.0	34.6	54.4	15,337	8,413	63.4	...	...	...	...
Morgan, MO	29141	18,930	12.0	21.9	66.1	17,677	7,895	66.1	...	...	...	...
New Madrid, MO	29143	28,400	12.0	30.9	57.1	26,974	9,046	59.4	...	...	...	...
Newton, MO	29145	65,563	11.6	46.6	41.8	60,922	6,862	62.2	...	...	...	...
Nodaway, MO	29147	30,892	6.8	31.5	61.8	28,250	10,322	60.9	...	...	...	...
Oregon, MO	29149	16,556	12.7	48.9	38.4	15,752	7,763	66.2	...	...	...	...
Osage, MO	29151	14,099	6.8	35.4	57.8	13,538	8,362	59.2	...	...	...	...
Ozark, MO	29153	14,827	12.5	43.0	44.5	14,003	8,649	60.9	...	...	...	...
Pemiscot, MO	29155	41,971	13.7	47.1	39.3	40,962	9,909	64.1	...	...	...	...
Perry, MO	29157	20,084	8.7	25.5	65.8	18,908	7,842	56.8	...	...	...	...

[3]May be of any race

Table C-1. Population, School, and Student Characteristics by County—*Continued*

County	State/ County Code	High school graduates, 2006-2008			College enrollment, 2006-2008		College graduates, 2006-2008 (percent)						
		Population 25 years and over	High school diploma or less (percent)	High school diploma or more (percent)	Number	Percent public	Bachelor's degree or more	+/- U.S. percent with Bachelor's degree or more	Non-Hispanic White	Black or African American	American Indian and Alaska Native	Asian, Hawaiian, and Pacific Islander	Hispanic or Latino[3]
		30	31	32	33	34	35	36	37	38	39	40	41
Boone, MO	29019	90,009	31.5	92.2	27,720	88.9	44.7	17.3	46.1	16.2	...	81.6	33.0
Buchanan, MO	29021	59,091	55.4	85.9	4,886	88.1	17.3	-10.1	17.7	9.1	...	...	6.5
Butler, MO	29023	28,169	60.4	76.4	1,900	89.5	13.7	-13.7	14.0	4.0	...	...	...
Caldwell, MO	29025	...	...	...	...	...	...	...	...	...	...	...	...
Callaway, MO	29027	28,094	52.7	86.7	2,493	40.0	21.3	-6.1	21.9	13.0	...	...	...
Camden, MO	29029	29,333	48.1	89.7	1,612	43.3	20.2	-7.2	19.9	...	...	...	...
Cape Girardeau, MO	29031	47,104	49.5	85.6	8,177	92.6	26.4	-1.0	26.9	9.8	...	...	9.2
Carroll, MO	29033	...	...	...	...	...	...	...	...	...	...	...	...
Carter, MO	29035	...	...	...	...	...	...	...	...	...	...	...	...
Cass, MO	29037	62,875	46.6	91.9	5,025	75.4	20.8	-6.6	20.6	23.8	...	...	20.4
Cedar, MO	29039	...	...	...	...	...	...	...	...	...	...	...	...
Chariton, MO	29041	...	...	...	...	...	...	...	...	...	...	...	...
Christian, MO	29043	47,434	41.3	91.5	4,270	81.7	26.4	-1.0	26.9	...	...	...	13.1
Clark, MO	29045	...	...	...	...	...	...	...	...	...	...	...	...
Clay, MO	29047	138,634	40.0	90.6	12,271	65.3	29.3	1.9	30.1	22.6	...	24.9	21.8
Clinton, MO	29049	13,910	51.2	90.5	756	81.6	18.3	-9.1	18.5	...	...	...	...
Cole, MO	29051	48,235	42.8	88.7	5,591	87.9	30.0	2.6	30.0	23.8	...	...	20.5
Cooper, MO	29053	...	...	...	...	...	...	...	...	...	...	...	...
Crawford, MO	29055	16,046	65.0	76.1	701	88.7	9.9	-17.5	9.7	...	...	...	...
Dade, MO	29057	...	...	...	...	...	...	...	...	...	...	...	...
Dallas, MO	29059	...	...	...	...	...	...	...	...	...	...	...	...
Daviess, MO	29061	...	...	...	...	...	...	...	...	...	...	...	...
De Kalb, MO	29063	...	...	...	...	...	...	...	...	...	...	...	...
Dent, MO	29065	...	...	...	...	...	...	...	...	...	...	...	...
Douglas, MO	29067	...	...	...	...	...	...	...	...	...	...	...	...
Dunklin, MO	29069	21,281	69.6	68.7	694	92.7	11.5	-15.9	12.6	3.1	...	...	...
Franklin, MO	29071	66,580	51.2	85.0	4,464	74.2	16.5	-10.9	16.4	...	...	43.7	30.6
Gasconade, MO	29073	...	...	...	...	...	...	...	...	...	...	...	...
Gentry, MO	29075	...	...	...	...	...	...	...	...	...	...	...	...
Greene, MO	29077	171,482	42.0	88.0	27,291	74.5	27.4	...	27.6	13.2	25.9	54.1	23.2
Grundy, MO	29079	...	...	...	...	...	...	...	...	...	...	...	...
Harrison, MO	29081	...	...	...	...	...	...	...	...	...	...	...	...
Henry, MO	29083	15,796	59.7	84.3	521	89.1	15.7	-11.7	16.1	...	...	...	...
Hickory, MO	29085	...	...	...	...	...	...	...	...	...	...	...	...
Holt, MO	29087	...	...	...	...	...	...	...	...	...	...	...	...
Howard, MO	29089	...	...	...	...	...	...	...	...	...	...	...	...
Howell, MO	29091	26,062	61.7	80.7	1,508	87.4	12.3	-15.1	12.4	...	...	...	...
Iron, MO	29093	...	...	...	...	...	...	...	...	...	...	...	...
Jackson, MO	29095	441,228	43.1	87.3	36,598	70.4	26.5	-0.9	31.4	13.6	20.6	40.1	10.8
Jasper, MO	29097	74,291	53.5	81.2	5,716	80.6	18.4	-9.0	19.2	2.8	22.3	43.5	4.4
Jefferson, MO	29099	142,610	49.9	84.5	11,660	74.7	15.7	-11.7	15.5	...	...	44.5	17.6
Johnson, MO	29101	30,176	43.7	89.0	7,910	94.3	23.5	-3.9	23.2	26.9	...	...	...
Knox, MO	29103	...	...	...	...	...	...	...	...	...	...	...	...
Laclede, MO	29105	23,736	61.4	79.3	1,401	77.0	11.7	-15.7	11.5	...	...	...	...
Lafayette, MO	29107	22,406	56.2	86.2	1,312	78.3	15.9	-11.5	16.4	...	...	...	...
Lawrence, MO	29109	25,118	63.1	76.9	1,059	80.6	12.4	-15.0	12.2	...	...	...	...
Lewis, MO	29111	...	...	...	...	...	...	...	...	...	...	...	...
Lincoln, MO	29113	31,624	63.0	80.7	1,459	54.4	10.6	-16.8	10.2	...	...	...	12.9
Linn, MO	29115	...	...	...	...	...	...	...	...	...	...	...	...
Livingston, MO	29117	...	...	...	...	...	...	...	...	...	...	...	...
McDonald, MO	29119	14,388	64.5	74.4	448	87.5	8.4	-19.0	8.7	...	...	...	4.6
Macon, MO	29121	...	...	...	...	...	...	...	...	...	...	...	...
Madison, MO	29123	...	...	...	...	...	...	...	...	...	...	...	...
Maries, MO	29125	...	...	...	...	...	...	...	...	...	...	...	...
Marion, MO	29127	18,812	58.7	83.3	1,285	51.1	18.4	-9.0	18.9	12.9	...	...	...
Mercer, MO	29129	...	...	...	...	...	...	...	...	...	...	...	...
Miller, MO	29131	16,962	65.2	81.9	723	89.6	10.7	-16.7	10.8	...	...	...	...
Mississippi, MO	29133	...	...	...	...	...	...	...	...	...	...	...	...
Moniteau, MO	29135	...	...	...	...	...	...	...	...	...	...	...	...
Monroe, MO	29137	...	...	...	...	...	...	...	...	...	...	...	...
Montgomery, MO	29139	...	...	...	...	...	...	...	...	...	...	...	...
Morgan, MO	29141	14,634	60.0	79.3	638	59.6	14.6	-12.8	14.7	...	...	...	...
New Madrid, MO	29143	...	...	...	...	...	...	...	...	...	...	...	...
Newton, MO	29145	36,870	51.0	84.2	2,472	70.8	18.3	-9.1	18.6	...	19.5	...	6.8
Nodaway, MO	29147	12,500	48.6	88.0	4,560	94.5	23.8	-3.6	23.8	...	...	...	...
Oregon, MO	29149	...	...	...	...	...	...	...	...	...	...	...	...
Osage, MO	29151	...	...	...	...	...	...	...	...	...	...	...	...
Ozark, MO	29153	...	...	...	...	...	...	...	...	...	...	...	...
Pemiscot, MO	29155	...	...	...	...	...	...	...	...	...	...	...	...
Perry, MO	29157	...	...	...	...	...	...	...	...	...	...	...	...

[3]May be of any race
... Not available

Table C-1. Population, School, and Student Characteristics by County—*Continued*

County	State/ County Code	County Type[1]	Population, 2009 Total	Population, 2009 Percent 5–17 years	Percent of related children 5-17 years in poverty, 2008	Percent of children under 19 years with no health insurance, 2007	Number of Schools and Students, 2008-2009 School Districts	Number of Schools and Students, 2008-2009 Schools	Number of Schools and Students, 2008-2009 Students	Resident enrollment, 2006-2008 K–12 enrollment Number	Resident enrollment, 2006-2008 K–12 enrollment Percent public
			1	2	3	4	5	6	7	8	9
Pettis, MO	29159	4	41,421	18.1	20.1	9.9	7	18	6,444	7,531	89.5
Phelps, MO	29161	5	42,248	16.4	20.3	10.6	4	14	6,396	6,793	84.9
Pike, MO	29163	6	18,406	16.0	18.3	11.4	4	11	2,742	...	...
Platte, MO	29165	1	90,688	18.0	6.6	8.8	4	31	14,774	14,742	84.3
Polk, MO	29167	2	30,626	17.7	21.7	9.5	6	18	5,372	4,824	90.1
Pulaski, MO	29169	5	46,457	17.8	14.0	14.9	6	21	8,663	8,835	95.8
Putnam, MO	29171	9	4,759	16.6	25.1	13.7	1	3	795	...	...
Ralls, MO	29173	9	9,634	16.3	12.1	12.1	1	4	759	...	...
Randolph, MO	29175	6	25,501	16.6	21.9	8.7	5	15	3,894	4,686	92.1
Ray, MO	29177	1	23,358	18.4	11.2	9.8	5	13	3,713	4,171	93.0
Reynolds, MO	29179	9	6,202	16.2	32.9	9.3	4	8	1,152	...	...
Ripley, MO	29181	9	13,395	17.6	35.5	9.5	4	8	2,389	...	...
St. Charles, MO	29183	1	355,367	18.6	5.5	7.1	5	74	57,672	66,397	81.6
St. Clair, MO	29185	8	9,276	15.3	29.9	9.7	4	6	1,028	...	...
Ste. Genevieve, MO	29186	6	17,542	18.0	11.8	10.1	1	4	2,023	...	...
St. Francois, MO	29187	4	63,884	15.9	20.2	7.6	5	25	10,738	10,748	91.1
St. Louis, MO	29189	1	992,408	17.4	9.9	6.4	24	266	148,819	173,790	77.1
Saline, MO	29195	6	22,821	17.2	23.7	10.0	7	16	3,704	4,099	93.5
Schuyler, MO	29197	9	4,144	17.4	29.6	13.7	1	3	678	...	...
Scotland, MO	29199	9	4,803	19.3	18.5	20.0	2	3	748	...	...
Scott, MO	29201	5	40,855	18.1	23.6	8.3	7	22	6,951	7,938	91.4
Shannon, MO	29203	9	8,361	17.7	39.5	10.2	2	4	843	...	...
Shelby, MO	29205	9	6,325	18.4	21.5	15.5	2	6	1,122	...	...
Stoddard, MO	29207	7	29,069	17.0	23.0	8.0	7	20	5,270	4,894	97.8
Stone, MO	29209	8	31,424	15.1	24.3	14.8	5	18	4,431	...	...
Sullivan, MO	29211	9	6,835	18.0	22.1	15.3	3	7	1,164	...	...
Taney, MO	29213	6	48,023	16.3	22.2	11.4	7	19	7,650	7,400	94.0
Texas, MO	29215	9	24,563	16.3	29.6	10.2	7	15	3,987	4,049	94.2
Vernon, MO	29217	7	20,166	18.5	26.4	9.9	4	13	3,226	3,717	84.7
Warren, MO	29219	1	31,485	17.8	13.1	11.6	2	8	4,552	5,320	80.8
Washington, MO	29221	1	24,400	16.9	30.4	7.9	4	13	3,887	4,253	94.7
Wayne, MO	29223	9	12,392	16.0	34.6	7.9	2	7	1,829	...	...
Webster, MO	29225	2	36,552	19.9	23.4	14.2	5	17	7,256	5,904	91.2
Worth, MO	29227	9	2,014	15.1	21.0	14.3	1	2	385	...	...
Wright, MO	29229	6	17,908	18.6	33.7	7.6	5	15	3,674	...	...
St. Louis city, MO	29510	1	356,587	15.2	34.3	5.3	12	116	36,726	62,355	75.1
MONTANA	30000	X	974,989	16.1	16.9	12.2	513	833	141,899	158,694	91.5
Beaverhead, MT	30001	7	8,976	15.0	19.9	12.6	10	12	1,181	...	...
Big Horn, MT	30003	6	13,015	23.0	29.0	10.7	9	15	2,188	...	...
Blaine, MT	30005	9	6,485	20.6	31.3	13.3	13	17	1,118	...	...
Broadwater, MT	30007	9	4,793	15.4	14.7	13.4	2	3	735	...	...
Carbon, MT	30009	3	9,756	15.7	13.5	16.8	11	20	1,365	...	...
Carter, MT	30011	9	1,202	13.2	15.6	15.0	5	6	133	...	...
Cascade, MT	30013	3	82,178	16.1	16.4	11.1	16	42	11,804	14,491	89.9
Chouteau, MT	30015	8	5,167	16.9	16.9	20.5	12	15	653	...	...
Custer, MT	30017	7	11,189	16.7	20.5	10.0	12	13	1,738	...	...
Daniels, MT	30019	9	1,703	15.3	15.4	18.4	3	6	266	...	...
Dawson, MT	30021	7	8,558	15.0	14.1	13.6	9	10	1,301	...	...
Deer Lodge, MT	30023	7	8,792	14.3	21.4	9.2	3	4	1,135	...	...
Fallon, MT	30025	9	2,725	16.1	14.2	22.6	3	7	473	...	...
Fergus, MT	30027	7	11,208	15.7	18.0	12.3	16	24	1,714	...	...
Flathead, MT	30029	5	89,624	16.9	16.9	13.0	25	49	13,571	14,260	91.9
Gallatin, MT	30031	5	90,343	13.7	9.4	15.9	23	43	10,751	12,184	82.9
Garfield, MT	30033	9	1,173	17.3	26.8	11.7	10	9	171	...	...
Glacier, MT	30035	7	13,550	22.1	31.5	10.1	7	15	2,635	...	...
Golden Valley, MT	30037	8	1,057	20.9	27.6	13.7	3	6	164	...	...
Granite, MT	30039	8	2,879	13.0	20.9	16.5	5	7	391	...	...
Hill, MT	30041	7	16,632	17.8	22.2	11.3	12	17	3,003	...	...
Jefferson, MT	30043	9	11,470	18.1	10.4	15.4	10	13	1,648	...	...
Judith Basin, MT	30045	8	2,051	16.0	21.8	15.1	6	10	313	...	...
Lake, MT	30047	6	28,605	18.1	27.9	15.5	13	21	4,223	5,226	91.9
Lewis and Clark, MT	30049	5	61,942	16.2	10.6	9.9	16	31	9,601	10,035	92.3
Liberty, MT	30051	9	1,748	14.8	20.5	21.2	4	6	247	...	...
Lincoln, MT	30053	7	18,717	14.9	27.9	12.3	11	13	2,719	...	...
McCone, MT	30055	9	1,624	17.7	15.3	11.3	4	6	260	...	...
Madison, MT	30057	9	7,457	13.7	15.3	17.7	7	13	938	...	...
Meagher, MT	30059	9	1,908	14.6	26.5	19.4	4	4	249	...	...
Mineral, MT	30061	8	3,833	13.7	26.2	12.6	4	9	669	...	...
Missoula, MT	30063	3	108,623	13.6	15.6	10.2	16	40	13,111	16,020	90.3
Musselshell, MT	30065	8	4,600	15.0	29.1	12.0	5	6	660	...	...

[1]County type codes are from the Economic Research Service of the United States Department of Agriculture. See notes and definitions for more information.
... Not available

Table C-1. Population, School, and Student Characteristics by County—*Continued*

County	State/ County Code	Characteristics of students, 2008-2009				Number of graduates, 2006-2007	Staff and students, 2008-2009			
		Percent with IEP[2]	Percent eligible for free or reduced lunch	Percent minority	Percent English Language Learners		Total staff	Number of teachers	Student/ teacher ratio	Central admin. Staff
		10	11	12	13	14	15	16	17	18
Pettis, MO	29159	13.1	55.5	16.4	8.1	433	911	502	12.8	57
Phelps, MO	29161	14.4	45.0	8.2	0.3	462	893	449	14.2	86
Pike, MO	29163	11.7	41.8	8.5	0.4	193	359	207	13.2	29
Platte, MO	29165	11.5	20.8	19.2	2.4	946	1,892	1,028	14.4	149
Polk, MO	29167	16.8	51.3	3.3	0.8	357	705	379	14.2	49
Pulaski, MO	29169	13.8	42.1	27.0	0.6	523	1,161	583	14.9	92
Putnam, MO	29171	14.3	40.0	1.4	0.1	51	107	64	12.4	6
Ralls, MO	29173	14.4	39.4	4.0	...	63	109	60	12.7	7
Randolph, MO	29175	17.7	51.6	8.6	...	240	545	307	12.7	48
Ray, MO	29177	11.0	31.8	4.3	0.1	233	468	284	13.1	37
Reynolds, MO	29179	15.0	60.0	3.1	...	86	211	104	11.1	20
Ripley, MO	29181	13.1	63.9	2.3	...	142	331	182	13.1	24
St. Charles, MO	29183	14.4	15.6	12.0	0.9	3,766	7,021	3,676	15.7	597
St. Clair, MO	29185	13.5	49.7	3.5	...	95	157	88	11.7	16
Ste. Genevieve, MO	29186	16.2	40.9	3.1	...	159	255	139	14.6	20
St. Francois, MO	29187	15.8	48.1	3.4	0.2	684	1,427	727	14.8	109
St. Louis, MO	29189	17.5	32.3	45.2	2.0	10,578	24,106	11,588	12.8	2162
Saline, MO	29195	18.4	48.6	22.0	2.2	268	504	275	13.5	40
Schuyler, MO	29197	18.0	55.5	2.1	...	67	102	62	10.9	7
Scotland, MO	29199	11.2	40.2	0.7	...	51	101	53	14.1	8
Scott, MO	29201	12.7	54.1	22.8	0.1	441	947	515	13.5	94
Shannon, MO	29203	13.6	64.6	3.2	...	45	120	69	12.2	9
Shelby, MO	29205	14.7	40.3	0.8	...	88	168	92	12.2	13
Stoddard, MO	29207	15.3	51.0	2.7	0.1	399	745	400	13.2	54
Stone, MO	29209	15.3	52.2	3.6	0.2	286	638	350	12.7	52
Sullivan, MO	29211	12.6	61.4	25.4	7.5	80	190	106	11.0	14
Taney, MO	29213	11.4	51.5	10.5	1.9	430	1,093	521	14.7	86
Texas, MO	29215	13.7	52.2	2.6	...	270	517	286	13.9	40
Vernon, MO	29217	14.2	48.6	3.7	0.3	222	477	265	12.2	38
Warren, MO	29219	12.7	40.6	9.4	1.4	297	647	305	14.9	47
Washington, MO	29221	15.7	56.3	3.4	...	242	531	277	14.0	41
Wayne, MO	29223	14.9	64.3	2.5	0.1	158	297	142	12.9	23
Webster, MO	29225	13.1	43.2	4.0	0.3	449	962	503	14.4	64
Worth, MO	29227	13.8	47.3	...	...	34	55	34	11.3	3
Wright, MO	29229	14.1	57.5	3.1	...	249	558	292	12.6	41
St. Louis city, MO	29510	15.6	22.2	87.9	4.2	1,551	4,842	2,971	12.4	293
MONTANA	30000	12.4	36.7	16.3	3.2	10,119	15,043	10,465	13.6	168
Beaverhead, MT	30001	14.4	27.0	5.5	1.9	94	132	86	13.7	3
Big Horn, MT	30003	12.0	75.5	82.7	40.8	145	296	187	11.7	4
Blaine, MT	30005	15.5	60.9	58.4	13.0	97	184	126	8.9	4
Broadwater, MT	30007	10.1	38.4	7.2	...	38	75	53	13.9	1
Carbon, MT	30009	14.4	27.0	4.9	...	102	180	137	10.0	3
Carter, MT	30011	12.8	31.6	1.5	...	14	23	21	6.3	...
Cascade, MT	30013	11.5	35.7	17.2	3.5	867	1,162	857	13.8	6
Chouteau, MT	30015	11.8	42.6	4.0	...	62	89	67	9.7	2
Custer, MT	30017	13.4	29.2	7.3	...	124	208	129	13.5	1
Daniels, MT	30019	22.6	25.9	10.9	...	25	34	27	9.9	1
Dawson, MT	30021	14.6	25.2	4.9	...	91	167	107	12.2	2
Deer Lodge, MT	30023	15.2	48.4	7.8	...	104	112	77	14.7	1
Fallon, MT	30025	12.1	23.9	3.4	...	42	70	53	8.9	2
Fergus, MT	30027	15.5	34.8	5.6	0.1	131	223	153	11.2	4
Flathead, MT	30029	10.8	34.0	5.8	0.6	1,002	1,322	888	15.3	9
Gallatin, MT	30031	9.3	19.6	7.6	1.0	726	966	684	15.7	8
Garfield, MT	30033	11.1	27.3	0.6	...	18	26	23	7.4	...
Glacier, MT	30035	15.4	70.2	81.2	33.3	167	336	211	12.5	2
Golden Valley, MT	30037	19.5	59.8	3.7	15.9	9	29	24	6.8	1
Granite, MT	30039	21.0	37.9	2.6	...	43	47	39	10.0	1
Hill, MT	30041	14.3	52.9	45.0	9.9	221	333	220	13.7	5
Jefferson, MT	30043	11.4	25.4	5.3	...	82	159	124	13.3	4
Judith Basin, MT	30045	10.5	43.8	4.8	6.1	39	52	42	7.5	1
Lake, MT	30047	12.6	53.7	48.3	4.0	244	478	312	13.5	5
Lewis and Clark, MT	30049	11.9	30.3	9.3	0.2	650	885	619	15.5	7
Liberty, MT	30051	19.4	19.0	3.6	...	24	33	25	9.9	1
Lincoln, MT	30053	8.8	50.5	6.6	0.2	267	281	196	13.9	4
McCone, MT	30055	13.1	34.6	3.5	...	25	31	22	11.8	1
Madison, MT	30057	11.4	31.3	5.9	...	75	105	83	11.3	2
Meagher, MT	30059	8.4	52.6	2.0	6.8	21	35	27	9.2	1
Mineral, MT	30061	21.1	55.0	8.2	...	58	82	63	10.6	2
Missoula, MT	30063	13.5	34.8	9.4	3.2	883	1,266	861	15.2	10
Musselshell, MT	30065	18.3	44.4	7.4	...	40	77	50	13.2	1

[2]IEP= Individual Education Program. See notes and definitions for more information
... Not available

Table C-1. Population, School, and Student Characteristics by County—*Continued*

County	State/County Code	Revenues, 2007-2008				Current expenditures, 2007-2008			Resident population 16 to 19 years, 2006-2008			
		Total revenue ($1,000's)	Percentage of revenue from			Amount ($1,000's)	Amount per student	Percent for instruction	Total population 16 to 19 years	Percent enrolled in school	Percent high school graduates, not enrolled in school	Percent not enrolled, not grads, not employed or not in labor force
			Federal gov't	State gov't	Local gov't							
	19		20	21	22	23	24	25	26	27	28	29
Pettis, MO	29159	54,753	10.6	36.8	52.6	47,156	7,333	63.8	...	...	...	...
Phelps, MO	29161	61,411	9.5	42.0	48.5	51,672	8,035	61.9	...	...	...	...
Pike, MO	29163	25,380	9.5	35.2	55.3	23,681	8,491	62.3	...	...	...	...
Platte, MO	29165	160,757	3.4	15.9	80.6	134,606	9,387	60.0	4,240	84.8	9.1	2.8
Polk, MO	29167	48,890	12.7	45.7	41.6	46,617	8,557	62.3	...	...	...	...
Pulaski, MO	29169	79,426	28.4	41.3	30.2	70,008	8,071	61.5	...	...	...	...
Putnam, MO	29171	7,086	8.6	39.4	52.1	6,943	8,789	63.2	...	...	...	...
Ralls, MO	29173	6,409	7.9	34.9	57.2	5,476	6,736	61.0	...	...	...	...
Randolph, MO	29175	35,115	9.5	36.3	54.2	32,873	8,260	61.9	...	...	...	...
Ray, MO	29177	33,451	5.8	44.2	50.0	30,469	8,063	60.4	...	...	...	...
Reynolds, MO	29179	15,372	10.9	27.9	61.3	11,045	9,800	56.7	...	...	...	...
Ripley, MO	29181	18,134	14.5	52.0	33.5	16,831	7,227	64.4	...	...	...	...
St. Charles, MO	29183	556,773	3.6	21.4	75.0	483,218	8,191	61.2	19,093	87.4	9.1	1.8
St. Clair, MO	29185	9,097	9.9	42.8	47.3	8,657	8,614	59.4	...	...	...	...
Ste. Genevieve, MO	29186	18,254	9.8	16.7	73.5	17,209	8,605	62.1	...	...	...	...
St. Francois, MO	29187	91,837	9.4	44.7	45.9	83,235	7,866	60.8	...	...	...	...
St. Louis, MO	29189	2,023,869	4.8	17.9	77.3	1,737,465	11,897	60.0	56,735	86.8	7.1	4.5
Saline, MO	29195	33,586	10.4	43.5	46.0	32,300	8,883	64.1	...	...	...	...
Schuyler, MO	29197	6,538	8.9	47.1	44.0	6,316	9,010	57.3	...	...	...	...
Scotland, MO	29199	6,366	10.1	40.3	49.5	6,185	7,580	65.8	...	...	...	...
Scott, MO	29201	55,707	11.6	43.0	45.3	53,518	7,526	63.2	...	...	...	...
Shannon, MO	29203	7,384	14.2	48.8	37.0	7,479	8,697	59.9	...	...	...	...
Shelby, MO	29205	11,103	8.0	38.6	53.4	10,537	9,243	65.4	...	...	...	...
Stoddard, MO	29207	42,119	9.8	40.3	49.9	39,488	7,487	63.2	1,745	70.5	13.1	7.6
Stone, MO	29209	42,396	9.4	31.6	59.0	36,636	8,187	59.1	...	...	...	...
Sullivan, MO	29211	11,322	10.6	47.7	41.7	10,180	9,017	62.4	...	...	...	...
Taney, MO	29213	69,639	7.7	23.6	68.6	56,484	7,596	59.9	...	...	...	...
Texas, MO	29215	34,025	15.2	47.4	37.4	31,510	7,834	61.9	...	...	...	...
Vernon, MO	29217	28,527	10.6	45.7	43.7	27,246	8,467	64.1	...	...	...	...
Warren, MO	29219	39,881	7.0	31.6	61.4	33,792	7,488	57.4	...	...	...	...
Washington, MO	29221	33,099	11.2	50.7	38.0	29,235	7,485	56.7	...	...	...	...
Wayne, MO	29223	15,850	13.8	46.5	39.7	14,302	7,660	60.8	...	...	...	...
Webster, MO	29225	54,611	9.5	42.1	48.3	51,178	7,333	65.0	...	...	...	...
Worth, MO	29227	4,012	19.2	40.3	40.5	3,360	8,215	59.9	...	...	...	...
Wright, MO	29229	31,927	14.0	47.9	38.1	31,106	8,708	63.4	...	...	...	...
St. Louis city, MO	29510	517,652	14.0	36.1	49.9	471,598	13,452	49.5	20,533	80.4	10.0	7.5
MONTANA	30000	1,562,815	11.9	49.0	39.1	1,379,315	9,666	60.3	56,650	80.1	11.8	4.3
Beaverhead, MT	30001	13,184	6.1	51.9	42.0	12,204	10,238	65.8	...	...	...	...
Big Horn, MT	30003	33,066	37.2	39.0	23.8	29,038	13,284	53.7	...	...	...	...
Blaine, MT	30005	20,452	34.5	46.9	18.6	18,608	15,079	55.1	...	...	...	...
Broadwater, MT	30007	6,096	8.3	52.9	38.8	5,376	7,713	65.4	...	...	...	...
Carbon, MT	30009	18,629	4.7	50.1	45.1	15,121	10,619	64.0	...	...	...	...
Carter, MT	30011	2,503	6.7	52.6	40.8	2,202	15,507	56.8	...	...	...	...
Cascade, MT	30013	112,639	11.5	49.0	39.5	100,311	8,456	61.8	4,475	76.6	17.4	4.3
Chouteau, MT	30015	10,085	4.3	44.5	51.3	9,402	14,442	53.7	...	...	...	...
Custer, MT	30017	15,821	9.7	55.0	35.3	14,489	8,242	63.6	...	...	...	...
Daniels, MT	30019	4,039	4.1	56.9	39.0	3,484	13,452	56.1	...	...	...	...
Dawson, MT	30021	14,575	9.0	55.2	35.9	13,821	10,567	56.7	...	...	...	...
Deer Lodge, MT	30023	11,815	10.8	56.5	32.7	11,027	8,972	57.9	...	...	...	...
Fallon, MT	30025	15,037	1.1	83.3	15.7	7,154	15,723	59.4	...	...	...	...
Fergus, MT	30027	21,760	9.1	50.5	40.4	19,991	11,057	55.1	...	...	...	...
Flathead, MT	30029	129,182	7.8	46.2	46.0	116,116	8,539	62.3	4,478	78.4	11.5	7.1
Gallatin, MT	30031	104,344	6.3	41.7	52.0	88,812	8,334	60.8	...	...	...	...
Garfield, MT	30033	2,541	9.6	57.7	32.8	2,307	12,817	59.2	...	...	...	...
Glacier, MT	30035	39,312	35.6	42.2	22.1	34,478	12,666	56.1	...	...	...	...
Golden Valley, MT	30037	2,987	5.1	49.0	45.9	2,558	13,606	59.4	...	...	...	...
Granite, MT	30039	5,327	8.2	46.0	45.8	4,555	11,137	60.0	...	...	...	...
Hill, MT	30041	38,757	27.6	45.8	26.6	35,633	11,799	53.5	...	...	...	...
Jefferson, MT	30043	15,953	5.5	56.4	38.1	14,358	8,572	64.6	...	...	...	...
Judith Basin, MT	30045	5,531	7.7	47.3	45.0	4,745	15,160	61.0	...	...	...	...
Lake, MT	30047	49,456	21.3	46.2	32.4	41,449	9,813	64.2	...	...	...	...
Lewis and Clark, MT	30049	89,126	7.5	49.4	43.1	80,866	8,606	62.6	4,123	83.6	6.8	3.2
Liberty, MT	30051	3,806	4.4	53.3	42.3	3,307	13,553	56.2	...	...	...	...
Lincoln, MT	30053	28,396	13.3	52.2	34.5	25,550	9,400	60.5	...	...	...	...
McCone, MT	30055	3,218	5.2	49.8	45.0	2,912	11,510	59.3	...	...	...	...
Madison, MT	30057	15,601	5.2	34.8	60.0	11,836	12,227	59.7	...	...	...	...
Meagher, MT	30059	3,068	8.2	47.8	43.9	2,791	11,032	59.1	...	...	...	...
Mineral, MT	30061	9,415	8.2	48.6	43.1	7,938	11,212	62.6	...	...	...	...
Missoula, MT	30063	132,465	9.1	46.3	44.6	121,773	9,229	61.0	6,400	83.5	10.3	2.1
Musselshell, MT	30065	7,280	8.7	55.5	35.8	6,362	9,894	61.2	...	...	...	...

³May be of any race
... Not available

Table C-1. Population, School, and Student Characteristics by County—*Continued*

County	State/County Code	High school graduates, 2006-2008		College enrollment, 2006-2008		College graduates, 2006-2008 (percent)						
		Population 25 years and over	High school diploma or less (percent)	High school diploma or more (percent)	Number	Percent public	Bachelor's degree or more	+/- U.S. percent with Bachelor's degree or more	Non-Hispanic White	Black or African American	American Indian and Alaska Native	Asian, Hawaiian, and Pacific Islander	Hispanic or Latino[3]
		30	31	32	33	34	35	36	37	38	39	40	41
Pettis, MO	29159	26,818	53.1	82.0	2,249	92.0	16.5	-10.9	16.5	18.6	...	...	10.8
Phelps, MO	29161	26,960	48.3	83.8	5,590	91.2	23.6	-3.8	22.3	...	...	...	...
Pike, MO	29163												
Platte, MO	29165	56,888	30.9	94.9	5,675	63.8	36.0	8.6	36.8	26.5	...	49.3	21.3
Polk, MO	29167	18,975	57.3	80.1	3,061	33.7	15.0	-12.4	15.8	...	...	...	...
Pulaski, MO	29169	23,558	52.7	85.0	3,543	76.2	15.7	-11.7	15.6	16.3	...	8.8	19.5
Putnam, MO	29171												
Ralls, MO	29173												
Randolph, MO	29175	17,527	60.1	81.5	1,094	68.5	10.4	-17.0	11.5	1.5	...	...	...
Ray, MO	29177	15,781	59.5	87.3	959	69.6	12.6	-14.8	12.7	...	...	...	...
Reynolds, MO	29179												
Ripley, MO	29181												
St. Charles, MO	29183	220,928	35.6	91.8	22,571	59.2	32.7	5.3	32.4	30.5	...	61.2	27.1
St. Clair, MO	29185												
Ste. Genevieve, MO	29186												
St. Francois, MO	29187	43,231	57.2	77.8	2,619	80.1	13.9	-13.5	14.2	...	...	...	...
St. Louis, MO	29189	669,418	33.6	90.3	72,183	57.9	38.4	11.0	42.6	18.1	29.1	64.7	31.8
Saline, MO	29195	14,730	58.1	79.5	1,953	41.6	19.7	-7.7	20.4	23.4	...	...	11.0
Schuyler, MO	29197												
Scotland, MO	29199												
Scott, MO	29201	26,911	68.5	74.4	1,494	82.0	13.3	-14.1	14.4	1.7	...	...	...
Shannon, MO	29203												
Shelby, MO	29205												
Stoddard, MO	29207	20,651	67.4	74.9	716	83.5	12.8	-14.6	13.1	...	...	...	...
Stone, MO	29209	22,925	54.9	82.1	...	...	16.3	-11.1	17.2	...	...	...	...
Sullivan, MO	29211												
Taney, MO	29213	30,922	49.1	87.3	2,164	30.0	20.4	-7.0	21.0	...	...	...	12.9
Texas, MO	29215	17,074	66.4	77.0	883	66.9	10.5	-16.9	10.9	...	...	...	...
Vernon, MO	29217	13,256	62.8	82.2	800	81.8	15.0	-12.4	15.1	...	...	...	...
Warren, MO	29219	20,128	57.0	81.4	1,220	56.9	16.6	-10.8	16.7	...	...	...	...
Washington, MO	29221	16,278	76.1	71.3	511	95.5	5.8	-21.6	6.0	...	...	...	...
Wayne, MO	29223												
Webster, MO	29225	23,367	60.8	80.3	1,302	74.3	14.2	-13.2	14.6	...	...	...	...
Worth, MO	29227												
Wright, MO	29229												
St. Louis city, MO	29510	232,408	49.3	78.9	26,469	49.7	24.8	-2.6	35.3	12.2	26.4	38.4	23.4
MONTANA	30000	640,386	41.5	90.5	60,618	87.2	27.1	-0.3	28.3	23.8	11.3	38.4	16.7
Beaverhead, MT	30001												
Big Horn, MT	30003												
Blaine, MT	30005												
Broadwater, MT	30007												
Carbon, MT	30009												
Carter, MT	30011												
Cascade, MT	30013	55,056	41.0	91.0	4,387	78.4	23.2	-4.2	24.2	...	6.4	...	12.8
Chouteau, MT	30015												
Custer, MT	30017												
Daniels, MT	30019												
Dawson, MT	30021												
Deer Lodge, MT	30023												
Fallon, MT	30025												
Fergus, MT	30027												
Flathead, MT	30029	59,220	42.5	91.0	2,465	78.3	26.3	-1.1	27.2	...	...	...	...
Gallatin, MT	30031	54,403	25.6	95.7	12,526	96.0	45.3	17.9	45.5	...	...	...	20.9
Garfield, MT	30033												
Glacier, MT	30035												
Golden Valley, MT	30037												
Granite, MT	30039												
Hill, MT	30041												
Jefferson, MT	30043												
Judith Basin, MT	30045												
Lake, MT	30047	18,793	41.8	89.5	1,165	82.8	22.4	-5.0	24.5	...	12.2	...	...
Lewis and Clark, MT	30049	40,579	34.0	93.9	3,466	55.9	32.6	5.2	33.0	...	...	...	...
Liberty, MT	30051												
Lincoln, MT	30053												
McCone, MT	30055												
Madison, MT	30057												
Meagher, MT	30059												
Mineral, MT	30061												
Missoula, MT	30063	68,367	33.2	92.9	14,201	92.4	38.6	11.2	38.9	...	20.0	...	...
Musselshell, MT	30065												

[3]May be of any race
... Not available

Table C-1. Population, School, and Student Characteristics by County—*Continued*

County	State/County Code	County Type[1]	Population, 2009		Percent of related children 5-17 years in poverty, 2008	Percent of children under 19 years with no health insurance, 2007	Number of Schools and Students, 2008-2009			Resident enrollment, 2006-2008	
			Total	Percent 5–17 years			School Districts	Schools	Students	K–12 enrollment	
										Number	Percent public
			1	2	3	4	5	6	7	8	9
Park, MT	30067	7	15,941	14.9	14.1	16.4	12	16	2,107	...	...
Petroleum, MT	30069	9	440	13.4	17.1	23.3	2	3	99	...	...
Phillips, MT	30071	9	3,944	17.1	22.4	16.9	8	15	744	...	...
Pondera, MT	30073	7	5,814	18.8	22.6	12.3	10	15	991	...	...
Powder River, MT	30075	9	1,664	16.3	15.4	17.6	6	5	317	...	...
Powell, MT	30077	7	7,089	13.2	19.0	10.7	10	9	867	...	...
Prairie, MT	30079	9	1,108	11.8	16.9	16.2	2	3	127	...	...
Ravalli, MT	30081	6	40,431	16.6	18.1	14.8	10	23	5,853	6,708	87.7
Richland, MT	30083	7	9,313	17.8	12.6	13.4	12	14	1,648	...	...
Roosevelt, MT	30085	7	10,303	22.1	38.0	10.8	14	22	2,233	...	...
Rosebud, MT	30087	9	9,258	22.5	31.9	12.8	11	15	1,779	...	...
Sanders, MT	30089	8	11,096	15.1	26.3	15.8	14	17	1,490	...	...
Sheridan, MT	30091	9	3,243	14.0	13.2	22.3	5	9	479	...	...
Silver Bow, MT	30093	5	32,949	15.9	17.9	8.0	7	12	4,569	5,295	93.1
Stillwater, MT	30095	8	8,786	16.9	11.0	12.1	15	18	1,413	...	...
Sweet Grass, MT	30097	9	3,667	17.9	12.5	16.8	6	6	584	...	...
Teton, MT	30099	8	6,088	18.0	14.6	21.8	13	18	1,147	...	...
Toole, MT	30101	7	5,151	16.4	13.3	13.7	6	11	829	...	...
Treasure, MT	30103	8	612	13.7	18.0	19.9	2	3	112	...	...
Valley, MT	30105	7	6,771	17.5	19.9	13.1	9	17	1,238	...	...
Wheatland, MT	30107	9	2,044	18.4	31.6	21.0	6	7	363	...	...
Wibaux, MT	30109	9	897	15.3	17.5	17.9	2	3	148	...	...
Yellowstone, MT	30111	3	144,797	16.8	12.5	9.5	22	60	21,634	23,509	93.3
NEBRASKA	31000	X	1,796,619	17.6	11.7	9.0	296	1,158	292,590	316,729	86.8
Adams, NE	31001	5	33,324	17.1	11.0	9.7	6	27	4,799	5,708	86.7
Antelope, NE	31003	9	6,652	16.7	17.5	14.3	4	13	1,093	...	...
Arthur, NE	31005	9	339	15.9	16.4	19.3	1	3	91	...	...
Banner, NE	31007	9	647	17.0	22.2	12.9	1	2	167	...	...
Blaine, NE	31009	9	458	16.4	27.3	5.9	1	2	124	...	...
Boone, NE	31011	9	5,427	17.8	10.6	14.1	3	7	904	...	...
Box Butte, NE	31013	7	10,891	18.7	12.5	10.1	2	11	1,962	...	...
Boyd, NE	31015	9	2,063	15.4	19.8	11.8	2	5	350	...	...
Brown, NE	31017	9	3,062	16.2	16.5	12.2	2	3	500	...	...
Buffalo, NE	31019	5	45,814	16.4	10.7	9.2	11	31	7,413	7,265	88.7
Burt, NE	31021	8	6,922	17.0	13.5	13.9	3	8	1,347	...	...
Butler, NE	31023	6	8,400	19.7	9.7	10.0	3	8	1,157	...	...
Cass, NE	31025	2	25,485	19.0	7.7	10.0	5	14	3,774	4,944	89.4
Cedar, NE	31027	9	8,362	18.5	10.6	19.7	5	13	1,200	...	...
Chase, NE	31029	9	3,625	15.4	13.1	12.1	2	6	756	...	...
Cherry, NE	31031	7	5,474	17.2	18.6	8.2	2	16	789	...	...
Cheyenne, NE	31033	7	9,720	17.2	10.7	8.2	3	11	1,700	...	...
Clay, NE	31035	9	6,205	18.1	10.9	16.2	4	10	1,489	...	...
Colfax, NE	31037	7	10,332	21.7	12.8	17.6	4	13	2,253	...	...
Cuming, NE	31039	7	9,132	18.7	10.1	16.1	3	9	1,536	...	...
Custer, NE	31041	7	10,784	17.4	16.2	9.4	6	18	1,839	...	...
Dakota, NE	31043	3	20,651	21.8	15.0	14.1	3	16	4,092	4,050	87.7
Dawes, NE	31045	7	8,735	13.9	16.3	10.3	3	12	1,299	...	...
Dawson, NE	31047	7	25,076	21.7	14.1	14.9	5	24	5,232	5,370	96.8
Deuel, NE	31049	9	1,839	14.5	17.6	12.2	1	3	255	...	...
Dixon, NE	31051	3	6,289	17.4	11.7	13.5	4	10	1,172	...	...
Dodge, NE	31053	4	35,640	16.9	11.3	9.4	6	24	6,037	6,116	91.0
Douglas, NE	31055	2	510,199	17.9	12.8	6.7	15	184	86,086	91,876	81.6
Dundy, NE	31057	9	1,957	17.4	17.8	11.5	2	7	831	...	...
Fillmore, NE	31059	9	5,962	18.4	10.7	13.5	5	12	1,381	...	...
Franklin, NE	31061	9	3,089	15.1	15.0	12.2	1	2	352	...	...
Frontier, NE	31063	9	2,516	15.1	15.4	14.4	3	6	583	...	...
Furnas, NE	31065	9	4,556	17.6	18.2	12.1	3	9	1,175	...	...
Gage, NE	31067	6	22,653	16.0	12.0	8.7	5	13	3,174	3,676	93.8
Garden, NE	31069	9	1,739	11.7	23.2	7.1	1	3	294	...	...
Garfield, NE	31071	9	1,709	14.7	16.7	14.5	1	4	373	...	...
Gosper, NE	31073	9	1,844	17.3	12.7	17.4	1	2	251	...	...
Grant, NE	31075	9	560	15.9	13.6	15.2	1	4	121	...	...
Greeley, NE	31077	9	2,251	17.7	22.5	11.9	3	8	479	...	...
Hall, NE	31079	5	57,487	19.6	13.9	11.9	4	33	11,033	10,891	93.3
Hamilton, NE	31081	7	9,280	20.1	8.5	10.4	3	7	1,672	...	...
Harlan, NE	31083	9	3,234	16.0	14.9	14.6	1	2	314	...	...
Hayes, NE	31085	9	959	16.7	19.4	8.5	1	1	159	...	...
Hitchcock, NE	31087	9	2,806	14.9	19.4	11.9	2	4	234	...	...
Holt, NE	31089	7	10,011	17.4	15.7	9.9	5	17	1,628	...	...
Hooker, NE	31091	9	723	12.2	11.1	17.6	1	2	183	...	...

[1]County type codes are from the Economic Research Service of the United States Department of Agriculture. See notes and definitions for more information.
... Not available

Table C-1. Population, School, and Student Characteristics by County—*Continued*

County	State/County Code	Characteristics of students, 2008-2009				Number of graduates, 2006-2007	Staff and students, 2008-2009			
		Percent with IEP[2]	Percent eligible for free or reduced lunch	Percent minority	Percent English Language Learners		Total staff	Number of teachers	Student/teacher ratio	Central admin. Staff
		10	11	12	13	14	15	16	17	18
Park, MT	30067	12.6	28.2	3.9	...	158	228	159	13.3	4
Petroleum, MT	30069	10.1	68.7	3.0	...	5	14	11	9.0	...
Phillips, MT	30071	12.5	55.2	20.3	2.8	59	106	79	9.4	3
Pondera, MT	30073	12.8	43.2	25.3	4.9	88	134	89	11.1	3
Powder River, MT	30075	12.0	31.5	7.9	...	26	42	30	10.6	1
Powell, MT	30077	23.2	32.2	5.2	...	52	118	78	11.1	3
Prairie, MT	30079	13.4	50.4	10.2	...	17	20	16	7.9	...
Ravalli, MT	30081	13.0	37.3	5.3	0.1	421	631	408	14.3	8
Richland, MT	30083	7.7	41.0	7.7	...	147	194	131	12.6	3
Roosevelt, MT	30085	16.7	73.4	76.3	18.0	125	383	240	9.3	6
Rosebud, MT	30087	16.6	50.7	49.0	15.2	106	248	156	11.4	5
Sanders, MT	30089	10.8	59.3	15.0	1.6	139	177	129	11.6	4
Sheridan, MT	30091	20.7	35.9	13.4	...	43	80	60	8.0	2
Silver Bow, MT	30093	11.8	43.2	9.2	...	314	370	290	15.8	2
Stillwater, MT	30095	11.4	18.0	5.4	0.1	97	179	124	11.4	5
Sweet Grass, MT	30097	11.0	19.7	3.8	...	49	63	43	13.6	1
Teton, MT	30099	10.8	32.7	5.2	3.9	94	153	115	10.0	3
Toole, MT	30101	13.3	33.9	8.0	1.6	59	96	70	11.8	2
Treasure, MT	30103	8.0	47.3	14.3	...	10	17	15	7.5	1
Valley, MT	30105	14.1	43.9	21.0	...	93	176	126	9.8	2
Wheatland, MT	30107	12.1	47.4	5.0	19.6	42	58	43	8.4	2
Wibaux, MT	30109	9.5	35.1	4.1	...	17	22	17	8.7	1
Yellowstone, MT	30111	12.2	31.0	15.5	0.6	1,428	2,044	1,450	14.9	14
NEBRASKA	31000	15.1	38.4	25.4	6.3	19,991	45,235	22,055	13.3	1,608
Adams, NE	31001	18.9	42.0	17.8	6.6	311	816	373	12.9	39
Antelope, NE	31003	17.1	43.8	4.4	1.2	108	294	115	9.5	21
Arthur, NE	31005	13.2	...	5.5	3.3	6	20	12	7.6	2
Banner, NE	31007	9.0	46.1	18.6	1.8	18	43	19	8.8	3
Blaine, NE	31009	18.5	50.0	...	...	...	30	17	7.3	2
Boone, NE	31011	13.6	32.7	3.5	...	97	169	90	10.0	6
Box Butte, NE	31013	15.3	40.2	26.5	3.3	134	331	146	13.4	10
Boyd, NE	31015	17.7	44.9	4.6	...	52	78	37	9.5	1
Brown, NE	31017	13.8	40.2	5.6	0.8	48	89	40	12.5	7
Buffalo, NE	31019	14.9	37.0	15.8	4.2	530	1,091	541	13.7	51
Burt, NE	31021	15.5	32.5	6.8	...	68	200	106	12.7	7
Butler, NE	31023	17.0	40.3	6.1	2.8	84	202	102	11.3	7
Cass, NE	31025	15.4	26.6	5.7	0.5	245	596	289	13.1	16
Cedar, NE	31027	15.9	34.7	2.5	...	133	240	119	10.1	9
Chase, NE	31029	9.9	36.4	15.3	7.8	70	144	72	10.5	5
Cherry, NE	31031	11.4	35.8	12.2	...	72	155	87	9.1	7
Cheyenne, NE	31033	13.9	32.9	11.8	1.1	120	333	143	11.9	8
Clay, NE	31035	18.5	36.5	15.8	3.2	139	266	136	10.9	7
Colfax, NE	31037	10.0	53.8	54.6	18.9	179	363	178	12.7	8
Cuming, NE	31039	17.6	42.7	21.4	5.9	127	247	125	12.3	5
Custer, NE	31041	17.0	38.6	4.6	0.2	153	344	167	11.0	12
Dakota, NE	31043	14.0	53.9	60.5	22.6	220	631	328	12.5	25
Dawes, NE	31045	10.7	42.8	17.5	0.5	234	228	120	10.8	9
Dawson, NE	31047	15.1	59.1	49.8	18.2	326	736	387	13.5	21
Deuel, NE	31049	15.7	43.1	3.5	...	37	58	24	10.6	3
Dixon, NE	31051	15.3	36.8	9.6	1.5	98	188	98	12.0	7
Dodge, NE	31053	18.5	42.2	17.5	5.0	404	913	433	13.9	31
Douglas, NE	31055	14.6	40.5	39.0	8.2	5,089	12,704	6,031	14.3	420
Dundy, NE	31057	16.5	42.1	9.2	2.2	26	168	87	9.6	4
Fillmore, NE	31059	22.6	35.8	17.3	...	100	230	121	11.4	6
Franklin, NE	31061	13.1	42.8	2.3	...	35	57	30	11.7	1
Frontier, NE	31063	16.3	35.0	4.5	0.2	52	109	64	9.1	5
Furnas, NE	31065	16.3	45.0	5.7	0.4	89	204	99	11.9	10
Gage, NE	31067	18.5	34.3	5.0	0.3	236	512	254	12.5	30
Garden, NE	31069	12.6	60.5	9.5	...	33	56	26	11.3	7
Garfield, NE	31071	13.9	36.5	2.9	...	22	61	35	10.7	2
Gosper, NE	31073	26.7	24.7	6.4	...	16	49	22	11.4	2
Grant, NE	31075	16.5	38.8	...	...	16	33	18	6.7	1
Greeley, NE	31077	21.3	60.6	5.6	0.6	29	119	61	7.9	3
Hall, NE	31079	12.8	52.9	38.0	22.3	691	1,525	794	13.9	56
Hamilton, NE	31081	16.4	25.5	3.9	0.1	129	258	128	13.1	8
Harlan, NE	31083	19.1	42.0	4.8	...	27	57	28	11.2	2
Hayes, NE	31085	11.3	45.9	7.5	1.3	18	45	22	7.2	2
Hitchcock, NE	31087	16.2	56.8	4.1	...	21	74	25	9.4	8
Holt, NE	31089	18.4	44.8	8.1	3.6	165	272	160	10.2	11
Hooker, NE	31091	13.7	49.2	0.5	...	15	42	21	8.7	2

[2]IEP= Individual Education Program. See notes and definitions for more information
... Not available

Table C-1. Population, School, and Student Characteristics by County—*Continued*

County	State/County Code	Revenues, 2007-2008					Current expenditures, 2007-2008			Resident population 16 to 19 years, 2006-2008			
		Total revenue ($1,000's)	Percentage of revenue from				Amount ($1,000's)	Amount per student	Percent for instruc-tion	Total population 16 to 19 years	Percent en-rolled in school	Percent high school graduates, not enrolled in school	Percent not enrolled, not grads, not employed or not in labor force
			Federal gov't	State gov't	Local gov't								
	19		20	21	22		23	24	25	26	27	28	29

Park, MT	30067	22,221	10.3	49.2	40.5		20,916	10,061	57.3	...	...	...	...
Petroleum, MT	30069	1,361	8.2	56.2	35.6		1,288	13,558	50.9	...	...	...	...
Phillips, MT	30071	12,449	7.7	58.7	33.6		10,017	12,942	60.1	...	...	...	...
Pondera, MT	30073	13,478	18.9	49.5	31.6		11,672	11,376	54.7	...	...	...	...
Powder River, MT	30075	3,899	6.1	60.5	33.4		3,618	10,548	55.3	...	...	...	...
Powell, MT	30077	11,685	15.2	49.1	35.6		10,656	11,827	60.8	...	...	...	...
Prairie, MT	30079	2,043	15.1	48.7	36.2		2,010	16,891	55.4	...	...	...	...
Ravalli, MT	30081	55,223	9.3	53.3	37.4		49,168	8,210	61.7	...	...	...	...
Richland, MT	30083	36,297	3.2	78.1	18.7		19,232	11,642	59.6	...	...	...	...
Roosevelt, MT	30085	37,927	33.0	42.5	24.4		35,755	15,438	56.4	...	...	...	...
Rosebud, MT	30087	29,445	23.2	39.9	36.8		24,870	14,376	53.1	...	...	...	...
Sanders, MT	30089	19,743	12.3	49.1	38.6		17,645	11,399	59.0	...	...	...	...
Sheridan, MT	30091	10,272	6.0	64.1	29.9		8,234	16,468	58.2	...	...	...	...
Silver Bow, MT	30093	44,163	10.0	50.7	39.3		37,638	8,172	58.4	...	...	...	...
Stillwater, MT	30095	17,244	6.1	46.1	47.8		15,342	10,458	59.8	...	...	...	...
Sweet Grass, MT	30097	6,367	5.9	46.0	48.1		5,792	9,686	65.1	...	...	...	...
Teton, MT	30099	14,608	6.3	53.1	40.6		13,008	10,706	63.2	...	...	...	...
Toole, MT	30101	10,002	7.0	56.3	36.7		8,608	10,760	60.4	...	...	...	...
Treasure, MT	30103	1,725	4.8	49.2	46.0		1,606	12,450	63.4	...	...	...	...
Valley, MT	30105	17,029	15.4	43.3	41.3		14,635	11,879	57.9	...	...	...	...
Wheatland, MT	30107	4,941	10.8	45.4	43.8		4,689	13,171	62.0	...	...	...	...
Wibaux, MT	30109	2,336	4.5	69.5	25.9		1,983	13,676	60.1	...	...	...	...
Yellowstone, MT	30111	202,891	8.5	50.3	41.2		19,0359	8,852	62.0	7,031	81.0	11.9	3.8
NEBRASKA	31000	3,383,157	9.5	32.3	58.2		2,78,6052	9,577	64.0	105,506	87.3	8.1	2.6
Adams, NE	31001	62,065	8.8	33.2	58.0		52,970	11,145	68.1	...	...	...	...
Antelope, NE	31003	21,678	11.1	20.9	68.0		18,070	16,935	67.5	...	...	...	...
Arthur, NE	31005	1,625	1.5	36.4	62.1		1,430	15,213	65.7	...	...	...	...
Banner, NE	31007	2,716	5.0	39.2	55.8		2,302	13,306	61.2	...	...	...	...
Blaine, NE	31009	2,075	8.4	9.3	82.3		1,806	15,050	62.1	...	...	...	...
Boone, NE	31011	11,266	6.7	13.1	80.2		10,409	11,225	68.3	...	...	...	...
Box Butte, NE	31013	21,943	9.9	43.8	46.3		19,245	9,270	66.3	...	...	...	...
Boyd, NE	31015	5,936	8.9	35.6	55.5		4,753	13,277	65.0	...	...	...	...
Brown, NE	31017	10,324	6.1	33.4	60.5		8,010	16,020	64.1	...	...	...	...
Buffalo, NE	31019	86,305	9.2	32.7	58.1		70,957	9,857	63.1	...	...	...	...
Burt, NE	31021	13,617	7.3	23.0	69.7		12,596	9,351	65.6	...	...	...	...
Butler, NE	31023	13,165	7.2	15.0	77.8		11,663	9,735	63.2	...	...	...	...
Cass, NE	31025	42,675	9.6	29.9	60.6		34,319	8,919	64.2	...	...	...	...
Cedar, NE	31027	15,827	7.8	18.8	73.3		14,689	11,667	66.3	...	...	...	...
Chase, NE	31029	10,325	4.6	25.4	70.0		8,383	11,437	64.6	...	...	...	...
Cherry, NE	31031	12,823	6.7	33.2	60.2		10,221	12,096	68.9	...	...	...	...
Cheyenne, NE	31033	20,945	8.7	35.0	56.3		16,694	9,594	63.1	...	...	...	...
Clay, NE	31035	19,727	10.6	24.8	64.6		17,127	11,136	64.7	...	...	...	...
Colfax, NE	31037	23,196	6.9	34.7	58.4		19,789	8,826	68.7	...	...	...	...
Cuming, NE	31039	17,751	10.1	16.8	73.1		14,496	9,475	65.3	...	...	...	...
Custer, NE	31041	25,128	6.0	27.8	66.3		21,700	11,943	67.9	...	...	...	...
Dakota, NE	31043	44,201	12.9	54.8	32.3		36,439	8,986	66.0	...	...	...	...
Dawes, NE	31045	14,720	10.1	45.4	44.4		11,855	10,141	64.0	...	...	...	...
Dawson, NE	31047	56,036	12.5	47.6	39.9		46,211	8,691	68.2	...	...	...	...
Deuel, NE	31049	6,313	5.1	21.5	73.4		5,432	14,000	60.4	...	...	...	...
Dixon, NE	31051	12,312	7.6	36.4	56.0		11,056	9,490	66.2	...	...	...	...
Dodge, NE	31053	67,161	9.2	34.1	56.7		55,778	9,216	62.6	...	...	...	...
Douglas, NE	31055	942,021	11.1	32.9	56.0		757,765	8,870	60.4	28,476	86.3	8.7	3.1
Dundy, NE	31057	13,912	19.6	41.5	38.9		11,345	13,852	59.3	...	...	...	...
Fillmore, NE	31059	13,087	5.5	18.4	76.0		11,702	11,252	63.5	...	...	...	...
Franklin, NE	31061	4,203	8.7	41.6	49.8		3,419	11,065	68.1	...	...	...	...
Frontier, NE	31063	8,709	6.8	34.7	58.5		7,351	12,011	61.1	...	...	...	...
Furnas, NE	31065	16,558	8.6	42.9	48.5		12,863	11,146	63.5	...	...	...	...
Gage, NE	31067	42,461	8.7	33.8	57.5		34,651	10,688	65.7	...	...	...	...
Garden, NE	31069	4,871	7.6	12.2	80.3		3,709	13,390	68.5	...	...	...	...
Garfield, NE	31071	4,039	8.5	43.0	48.5		3,736	10,264	64.2	...	...	...	...
Gosper, NE	31073	3,086	5.1	16.0	78.9		2,776	10,397	63.9	...	...	...	...
Grant, NE	31075	2,306	5.6	8.5	85.9		2,619	20,302	54.4	...	...	...	...
Greeley, NE	31077	7,186	10.1	28.8	61.1		6,270	14,186	63.0	...	...	...	...
Hall, NE	31079	133,517	9.7	38.2	52.1		108,122	9,486	71.7	...	...	...	...
Hamilton, NE	31081	17,966	6.2	28.4	65.4		15,471	9,203	67.8	...	...	...	...
Harlan, NE	31083	3,704	13.5	34.3	52.2		3,212	9,944	68.0	...	...	...	...
Hayes, NE	31085	3,120	5.7	33.1	61.3		2,589	16,283	57.0	...	...	...	...
Hitchcock, NE	31087	5,928	10.8	20.6	68.5		5,365	22,542	63.7	...	...	...	...
Holt, NE	31089	22,237	8.5	29.5	62.0		19,240	12,116	65.5	...	...	...	...
Hooker, NE	31091	2,873	5.5	20.3	74.2		2,297	11,964	61.6	...	...	...	...

... Not available

Table C-1. Population, School, and Student Characteristics by County—*Continued*

County	State/County Code	High school graduates, 2006-2008			College enrollment, 2006-2008		College graduates, 2006-2008 (percent)						
		Population 25 years and over	High school diploma or less (percent)	High school diploma or more (percent)	Number	Percent public	Bachelor's degree or more	+/- U.S. percent with Bachelor's degree or more	Non-Hispanic White	Black or African American	American Indian and Alaska Native	Asian, Hawaiian, and Pacific Islander	Hispanic or Latino[3]
		30	31	32	33	34	35	36	37	38	39	40	41
Park, MT	30067	...	...	...	...	...	...	...	...	...	...	...	...
Petroleum, MT	30069	...	...	...	...	...	...	...	...	...	...	...	...
Phillips, MT	30071	...	...	...	...	...	...	...	...	...	...	...	...
Pondera, MT	30073	...	...	...	...	...	...	...	...	...	...	...	...
Powder River, MT	30075	...	...	...	...	...	...	...	...	...	...	...	...
Powell, MT	30077	...	...	...	...	...	...	...	...	...	...	...	...
Prairie, MT	30079	...	...	...	...	...	...	...	...	...	...	...	...
Ravalli, MT	30081	28,028	46.2	89.3	1,604	95.1	22.9	-4.5	23.3	...	...	...	...
Richland, MT	30083	...	...	...	...	...	...	...	...	...	...	...	...
Roosevelt, MT	30085	...	...	...	...	...	...	...	...	...	...	...	...
Rosebud, MT	30087	...	...	...	...	...	...	...	...	...	...	...	...
Sanders, MT	30089	...	...	...	...	...	...	...	...	...	...	...	...
Sheridan, MT	30091	...	...	...	...	...	...	...	...	...	...	...	...
Silver Bow, MT	30093	22,340	49.4	90.7	2,044	97.6	22.5	-4.9	23.0	...	...	...	15.4
Stillwater, MT	30095	...	...	...	...	...	...	...	...	...	...	...	...
Sweet Grass, MT	30097	...	...	...	...	...	...	...	...	...	...	...	...
Teton, MT	30099	...	...	...	...	...	...	...	...	...	...	...	...
Toole, MT	30101	...	...	...	...	...	...	...	...	...	...	...	...
Treasure, MT	30103	...	...	...	...	...	...	...	...	...	...	...	...
Valley, MT	30105	...	...	...	...	...	...	...	...	...	...	...	...
Wheatland, MT	30107	...	...	...	...	...	...	...	...	...	...	...	...
Wibaux, MT	30109	...	...	...	...	...	...	...	...	...	...	...	...
Yellowstone, MT	30111	93,502	40.3	90.7	7,670	82.4	27.6	0.2	28.8	...	17.4	29.2	11.6
NEBRASKA	31000	1,139,886	40.5	89.8	132,891	78.1	27.3	-0.1	28.6	16.7	11.0	48.3	9.4
Adams, NE	31001	21,028	43.3	89.1	2,524	50.2	22.1	-5.3	23.5	...	...	...	...
Antelope, NE	31003	...	...	...	...	...	...	...	...	...	...	...	...
Arthur, NE	31005	...	...	...	...	...	...	...	...	...	...	...	...
Banner, NE	31007	...	...	...	...	...	...	...	...	...	...	...	...
Blaine, NE	31009	...	...	...	...	...	...	...	...	...	...	...	...
Boone, NE	31011	...	...	...	...	...	...	...	...	...	...	...	...
Box Butte, NE	31013	...	...	...	...	...	...	...	...	...	...	...	...
Boyd, NE	31015	...	...	...	...	...	...	...	...	...	...	...	...
Brown, NE	31017	...	...	...	...	...	...	...	...	...	...	...	...
Buffalo, NE	31019	26,380	36.2	92.3	5,516	95.2	32.7	5.3	33.7	...	...	...	12.1
Burt, NE	31021	...	...	...	...	...	...	...	...	...	...	...	...
Butler, NE	31023	...	...	...	...	...	...	...	...	...	...	...	...
Cass, NE	31025	16,987	37.6	93.7	1,122	74.7	24.8	-2.6	25.3	...	...	...	...
Cedar, NE	31027	...	...	...	...	...	...	...	...	...	...	...	...
Chase, NE	31029	...	...	...	...	...	...	...	...	...	...	...	...
Cherry, NE	31031	...	...	...	...	...	...	...	...	...	...	...	...
Cheyenne, NE	31033	...	...	...	...	...	...	...	...	...	...	...	...
Clay, NE	31035	...	...	...	...	...	...	...	...	...	...	...	...
Colfax, NE	31037	...	...	...	...	...	...	...	...	...	...	...	...
Cuming, NE	31039	...	...	...	...	...	...	...	...	...	...	...	...
Custer, NE	31041	...	...	...	...	...	...	...	...	...	...	...	...
Dakota, NE	31043	12,312	60.2	76.0	650	86.0	11.9	-15.5	14.9	...	...	...	3.1
Dawes, NE	31045	...	...	...	...	...	...	...	...	...	...	...	...
Dawson, NE	31047	15,360	61.4	73.5	718	85.1	13.5	-13.9	17.3	...	...	...	1.6
Deuel, NE	31049	...	...	...	...	...	...	...	...	...	...	...	...
Dixon, NE	31051	...	...	...	...	...	...	...	...	...	...	...	...
Dodge, NE	31053	23,932	53.9	85.3	2,415	45.1	16.9	-10.5	17.4	...	...	...	...
Douglas, NE	31055	313,878	34.9	89.9	38,949	72.1	35.4	8.0	39.4	15.7	17.8	65.9	10.6
Dundy, NE	31057	...	...	...	...	...	...	...	...	...	...	...	...
Fillmore, NE	31059	...	...	...	...	...	...	...	...	...	...	...	...
Franklin, NE	31061	...	...	...	...	...	...	...	...	...	...	...	...
Frontier, NE	31063	...	...	...	...	...	...	...	...	...	...	...	...
Furnas, NE	31065	...	...	...	...	...	...	...	...	...	...	...	...
Gage, NE	31067	16,078	51.0	90.3	1,226	91.3	17.5	-9.9	17.9	...	...	...	...
Garden, NE	31069	...	...	...	...	...	...	...	...	...	...	...	...
Garfield, NE	31071	...	...	...	...	...	...	...	...	...	...	...	...
Gosper, NE	31073	...	...	...	...	...	...	...	...	...	...	...	...
Grant, NE	31075	...	...	...	...	...	...	...	...	...	...	...	...
Greeley, NE	31077	...	...	...	...	...	...	...	...	...	...	...	...
Hall, NE	31079	35,911	52.4	84.1	1,617	87.3	16.2	-11.2	18.2	...	...	...	3.8
Hamilton, NE	31081	...	...	...	...	...	...	...	...	...	...	...	...
Harlan, NE	31083	...	...	...	...	...	...	...	...	...	...	...	...
Hayes, NE	31085	...	...	...	...	...	...	...	...	...	...	...	...
Hitchcock, NE	31087	...	...	...	...	...	...	...	...	...	...	...	...
Holt, NE	31089	...	...	...	...	...	...	...	...	...	...	...	...
Hooker, NE	31091	...	...	...	...	...	...	...	...	...	...	...	...

[3]May be of any race
... Not available

Table C-1. Population, School, and Student Characteristics by County—*Continued*

County	State/County Code	County Type¹	Population, 2009 Total	Population, 2009 Percent 5–17 years	Percent of related children 5-17 years in poverty, 2008	Percent of children under 19 years with no health insurance, 2007	Number of Schools and Students, 2008-2009 School Districts	Schools	Students	Resident enrollment, 2006-2008 K–12 enrollment Number	Percent public
			1	2	3	4	5	6	7	8	9
Howard, NE	31093	9	6,443	18.4	14.0	11.9	3	8	1,319	...	...
Jefferson, NE	31095	7	7,238	15.7	13.1	10.4	2	6	1,096	...	...
Johnson, NE	31097	8	5,077	12.5	11.3	16.2	2	7	763	...	...
Kearney, NE	31099	7	6,460	17.3	9.9	9.6	3	11	1,330	...	...
Keith, NE	31101	7	7,760	16.0	15.0	9.5	4	9	1,366	...	...
Keya Paha, NE	31103	9	802	18.0	35.8	7.3	1	3	96	...	...
Kimball, NE	31105	6	3,576	16.1	16.8	10.2	1	3	591	...	...
Knox, NE	31107	9	8,378	17.6	18.1	14.7	6	12	1,558	...	...
Lancaster, NE	31109	2	281,531	15.6	9.5	8.0	11	83	38,995	44,155	84.4
Lincoln, NE	31111	5	35,670	18.0	12.5	8.1	6	24	5,761	6,603	89.1
Logan, NE	31113	9	732	14.3	19.1	20.5	2	6	247	...	...
Loup, NE	31115	9	661	18.5	21.8	10.4	1	2	123	...	...
McPherson, NE	31117	9	488	17.4	21.0	7.5	...	...	...	...	...
Madison, NE	31119	5	34,505	17.3	13.5	11.2	7	31	5,506	5,892	80.4
Merrick, NE	31121	7	7,666	18.8	11.2	11.6	2	5	1,029	...	...
Morrill, NE	31123	9	4,911	17.5	18.7	10.5	2	5	955	...	...
Nance, NE	31125	9	3,460	18.0	17.2	13.6	2	5	866	...	...
Nemaha, NE	31127	7	6,856	15.8	11.8	8.8	3	9	1,148	...	...
Nuckolls, NE	31129	9	4,334	15.3	19.8	13.0	1	3	454	...	...
Otoe, NE	31131	6	15,214	17.8	9.7	9.8	3	9	2,630	...	...
Pawnee, NE	31133	9	2,614	16.0	16.6	13.7	2	4	481	...	...
Perkins, NE	31135	9	2,769	17.6	15.1	14.2	1	3	377	...	...
Phelps, NE	31137	7	9,032	18.3	11.0	9.9	4	14	1,633	...	...
Pierce, NE	31139	9	7,184	18.8	10.0	17.1	3	7	1,298	...	...
Platte, NE	31141	5	32,515	18.9	8.3	11.3	4	15	4,812	5,960	75.2
Polk, NE	31143	9	5,079	18.3	9.2	15.1	4	12	1,262	...	...
Red Willow, NE	31145	7	10,651	17.0	12.6	9.9	2	8	1,813	...	...
Richardson, NE	31147	7	8,125	16.6	13.8	9.5	3	10	1,350	...	...
Rock, NE	31149	9	1,509	13.7	35.4	14.6	1	5	190	...	...
Saline, NE	31151	6	13,872	17.6	9.8	11.5	4	9	2,855	...	...
Sarpy, NE	31153	2	153,504	19.5	6.0	7.6	7	51	23,037	29,516	90.1
Saunders, NE	31155	2	20,057	18.7	6.7	10.7	6	15	2,812	3,659	81.1
Scotts Bluff, NE	31157	5	36,865	17.6	18.7	9.1	7	27	6,337	6,437	93.7
Seward, NE	31159	2	16,481	17.3	6.8	11.0	4	8	2,587	...	...
Sheridan, NE	31161	9	5,264	18.0	22.4	13.5	2	17	960	...	...
Sherman, NE	31163	9	2,881	17.3	17.1	12.1	2	4	489	...	...
Sioux, NE	31165	9	1,281	14.3	21.7	8.5	1	6	102	...	...
Stanton, NE	31167	9	6,311	18.3	10.3	10.3	1	2	449	...	...
Thayer, NE	31169	9	5,003	15.7	14.5	14.3	3	9	800	...	...
Thomas, NE	31171	9	565	15.0	21.7	10.7	1	4	111	...	...
Thurston, NE	31173	8	7,306	24.4	39.7	12.3	3	6	1,110	...	...
Valley, NE	31175	9	4,108	16.2	18.6	11.2	2	7	641	...	...
Washington, NE	31177	2	19,718	19.0	6.3	9.3	3	11	3,553	...	...
Wayne, NE	31179	6	9,249	12.9	10.0	9.9	4	8	1,507	...	...
Webster, NE	31181	9	3,431	16.7	13.9	13.3	2	4	634	...	...
Wheeler, NE	31183	9	763	17.6	26.6	7.6	1	2	108	...	...
York, NE	31185	7	13,837	16.8	10.6	9.8	4	9	1,796	...	...
NEVADA	32000	X	2,643,085	18.1	13.2	15.8	18	625	433,371	454,420	94.8
Churchill, NV	32001	6	24,897	19.8	13.1	13.9	1	8	4,352	4,875	94.7
Clark, NV	32003	1	1,902,834	18.3	13.0	16.4	1	351	312,761	326,753	95.1
Douglas, NV	32005	4	45,464	14.6	10.1	13.4	1	14	6,566	6,789	93.5
Elko, NV	32007	5	47,896	21.2	8.8	14.8	1	31	9,591	9,383	97.7
Esmeralda, NV	32009	9	626	9.3	14.4	15.0	1	3	67	...	...
Eureka, NV	32011	9	1,707	20.2	12.8	13.4	1	3	254	...	...
Humboldt, NV	32013	7	18,260	20.8	11.3	14.9	1	13	3,330	...	...
Lander, NV	32015	7	5,159	22.0	10.7	11.6	1	7	1,193	...	...
Lincoln, NV	32017	8	4,794	20.1	15.0	21.3	1	9	991	...	...
Lyon, NV	32019	6	52,641	18.5	12.4	13.4	1	17	8,919	10,232	95.4
Mineral, NV	32021	7	4,662	14.7	23.1	7.3	1	3	561	...	...
Nye, NV	32023	6	44,234	15.8	19.6	9.7	1	26	6,352	7,156	97.8
Pershing, NV	32027	8	6,286	16.3	18.4	22.5	1	4	712	...	...
Storey, NV	32029	2	4,441	16.0	6.6	15.7	1	4	435	...	...
Washoe, NV	32031	2	414,820	17.1	14.5	13.9	1	104	6,5421	69,317	92.3
White Pine, NV	32033	7	9,188	15.7	14.2	12.2	1	8	1417	...	...
Carson City city, NV	32510	3	55,176	16.5	13.5	16.9	2	20	10,449	9,434	96.3

¹County type codes are from the Economic Research Service of the United States Department of Agriculture. See notes and definitions for more information.
... Not available

Table C-1. Population, School, and Student Characteristics by County—*Continued*

County	State/County Code	Characteristics of students, 2008-2009				Number of graduates, 2006-2007	Staff and students, 2008-2009			
		Percent with IEP[2]	Percent eligible for free or reduced lunch	Percent minority	Percent English Language Learners		Total staff	Number of teachers	Student/teacher ratio	Central admin. Staff
		10	11	12	13	14	15	16	17	18
Howard, NE	31093	13.0	35.4	4.1	0.1	63	210	111	11.9	7
Jefferson, NE	31095	23.7	44.4	5.8	1.0	103	167	87	12.6	7
Johnson, NE	31097	14.2	32.6	14.9	5.8	69	128	69	11.1	3
Kearney, NE	31099	21.9	25.4	6.1	0.7	114	223	107	12.4	9
Keith, NE	31101	13.0	35.2	14.4	...	108	275	113	12.1	23
Keya Paha, NE	31103	2.1	53.8	...	...	...	22	13	7.4	1
Kimball, NE	31105	11.2	33.1	12.6	...	38	113	50	11.8	5
Knox, NE	31107	14.9	44.0	18.5	...	139	266	147	10.6	11
Lancaster, NE	31109	15.6	36.2	21.2	7.2	2,407	5,606	2,841	13.7	139
Lincoln, NE	31111	16.9	33.9	12.8	0.9	377	862	424	13.6	35
Logan, NE	31113	17.8	26.3	8.4	...	16	60	31	8.0	3
Loup, NE	31115	21.1	57.7	5.7	...	8	27	14	8.8	2
McPherson, NE	31117	...	...	2.7	...	12	...	...	...	...
Madison, NE	31119	16.9	39.7	26.5	4.4	415	892	427	12.9	38
Merrick, NE	31121	14.6	42.7	6.6	...	70	149	81	12.7	5
Morrill, NE	31123	10.7	53.5	20.8	5.0	77	142	79	12.1	8
Nance, NE	31125	10.9	35.3	4.4	...	73	133	67	12.9	3
Nemaha, NE	31127	15.0	36.1	8.4	1.0	82	236	95	12.1	17
Nuckolls, NE	31129	20.9	40.9	3.9	...	...	74	35	13.0	2
Otoe, NE	31131	16.8	32.8	11.3	2.8	190	394	193	13.6	11
Pawnee, NE	31133	17.7	53.8	3.9	0.8	43	90	49	9.8	1
Perkins, NE	31135	16.2	31.3	8.5	...	38	84	40	9.4	2
Phelps, NE	31137	19.1	30.1	6.7	2.4	103	273	133	12.3	19
Pierce, NE	31139	16.6	26.7	2.7	...	130	207	109	11.9	7
Platte, NE	31141	15.6	38.5	28.9	13.7	354	704	317	15.2	36
Polk, NE	31143	14.7	32.0	5.0	1.2	111	217	108	11.7	7
Red Willow, NE	31145	18.3	35.6	6.6	1.5	152	288	139	13.0	8
Richardson, NE	31147	19.8	47.4	7.9	...	117	248	126	10.7	6
Rock, NE	31149	12.1	37.3	3.6	...	21	49	28	6.8	2
Saline, NE	31151	13.8	36.1	30.9	12.3	230	421	200	14.3	15
Sarpy, NE	31153	12.6	26.7	22.5	1.2	1,603	3,285	1,581	14.6	103
Saunders, NE	31155	15.0	27.0	5.5	0.3	251	420	222	12.7	14
Scotts Bluff, NE	31157	11.2	49.5	35.9	3.0	388	1,003	456	13.9	50
Seward, NE	31159	12.6	21.3	5.3	0.5	220	441	181	14.3	28
Sheridan, NE	31161	12.7	48.7	26.2	0.1	79	213	103	9.3	9
Sherman, NE	31163	15.1	52.8	5.3	...	37	86	45	10.9	3
Sioux, NE	31165	7.8	25.0	3.6	...	8	30	20	5.1	3
Stanton, NE	31167	17.8	37.8	8.1	...	29	64	38	11.8	3
Thayer, NE	31169	21.3	33.8	4.8	0.1	73	141	80	10.0	5
Thomas, NE	31171	12.6	41.6	0.6	...	20	34	16	6.9	2
Thurston, NE	31173	22.4	68.7	73.3	9.0	88	205	104	10.7	11
Valley, NE	31175	13.6	34.9	5.8	...	70	133	64	10.0	4
Washington, NE	31177	13.0	17.3	4.5	1.4	261	501	241	14.7	16
Wayne, NE	31179	13.1	32.3	17.7	4.6	124	276	124	12.2	9
Webster, NE	31181	16.7	38.3	5.1	...	56	91	51	12.4	3
Wheeler, NE	31183	12.0	49.1	...	...	21	26	16	6.8	3
York, NE	31185	21.3	33.5	11.2	1.4	181	352	153	11.7	10
NEVADA	32000	11.1	39.0	57.7	17.5	18,632	25,383	21,991	19.7	25
Churchill, NV	32001	15.0	40.1	30.0	6.2	288	269	239	18.2	...
Clark, NV	32003	10.4	40.3	64.6	19.1	12,433	17,823	15,348	20.4	11
Douglas, NV	32005	11.8	26.2	23.5	4.4	451	411	363	18.1	...
Elko, NV	32007	11.5	33.0	36.1	11.0	550	651	564	17.0	...
Esmeralda, NV	32009	11.9	62.7	35.8	22.4	...	6	6	11.2	...
Eureka, NV	32011	7.9	24.4	20.1	0.8	17	30	25	10.2	...
Humboldt, NV	32013	13.1	32.0	36.5	9.1	204	227	206	16.2	...
Lander, NV	32015	9.6	22.0	32.7	7.0	79	66	56	21.3	...
Lincoln, NV	32017	9.9	35.1	19.1	0.1	81	87	79	12.5	...
Lyon, NV	32019	...	98.2	88.9	...	429	622	523	17.1	...
Mineral, NV	32021	16.0	48.5	38.7	...	28	36	32	17.5	...
Nye, NV	32023	16.9	47.7	31.2	6.1	284	429	384	16.5	...
Pershing, NV	32027	16.6	62.4	40.2	8.7	60	65	56	12.7	1
Storey, NV	32029	20.0	5.1	12.9	...	30	41	34	12.8	...
Washoe, NV	32031	13.1	36.0	45.7	18.2	3,110	3,903	3,461	18.9	7
White Pine, NV	32033	15.2	31.7	21.0	2.3	96	101	85	16.7	...
Carson City city, NV	32510	11.9	35.6	40.4	11.7	492	617	533	19.6	6

[2]IEP= Individual Education Program. See notes and definitions for more information
... Not available

Table C-1. Population, School, and Student Characteristics by County—*Continued*

County	State/County Code	Revenues, 2007-2008				Current expenditures, 2007-2008			Resident population 16 to 19 years, 2006-2008			
		Total revenue ($1,000's)	Percentage of revenue from			Amount ($1,000's)	Amount per student	Percent for instruction	Total population 16 to 19 years	Percent enrolled in school	Percent high school graduates, not enrolled in school	Percent not enrolled, not grads, not employed or not in labor force
			Federal gov't	State gov't	Local gov't							
		19	20	21	22	23	24	25	26	27	28	29
Howard, NE	31093	8,224	9.2	43.6	47.2	6,632	8,580	61.5	...	...	...	...
Jefferson, NE	31095	12,220	8.8	27.4	63.8	10,854	9,665	67.0	...	...	...	...
Johnson, NE	31097	11,649	4.5	22.5	73.0	8,177	10,788	64.1	...	...	...	...
Kearney, NE	31099	15,653	6.5	17.5	76.0	13,393	9,621	61.0	...	...	...	...
Keith, NE	31101	21,593	13.6	24.3	62.1	19,096	15,500	63.2	...	...	...	...
Keya Paha, NE	31103	2,418	11.2	10.3	78.6	1,568	15,373	62.2	...	...	...	...
Kimball, NE	31105	6,979	6.3	31.1	62.5	6,208	10,576	71.2	...	...	...	...
Knox, NE	31107	20,830	18.8	31.7	49.4	17,501	11,211	61.3	...	...	...	...
Lancaster, NE	31109	433,741	7.3	25.0	67.6	341,272	8,909	65.1	17,395	90.7	6.0	1.7
Lincoln, NE	31111	61,031	7.4	39.8	52.8	51,063	8,828	65.1	...	...	...	...
Logan, NE	31113	4,265	6.2	34.6	59.2	3,556	12,838	66.5	...	...	...	...
Loup, NE	31115	1,693	9.6	19.4	71.0	1,434	12,362	57.2	...	...	...	...
McPherson, NE	31117	...				...			...	...	...	...
Madison, NE	31119	59,943	8.5	29.0	62.5	52,609	9,560	66.6	...	...	...	...
Merrick, NE	31121	11,170	7.8	30.3	61.9	8,986	8,750	64.9	...	...	...	...
Morrill, NE	31123	13,106	11.6	52.7	35.8	10,456	11,088	63.7	...	...	...	...
Nance, NE	31125	9,765	7.4	23.8	68.8	8,322	9,711	62.3	...	...	...	...
Nemaha, NE	31127	17,843	8.1	34.9	56.9	15,513	12,874	52.3	...	...	...	...
Nuckolls, NE	31129	6,103	10.6	45.6	43.8	4,879	10,561	66.0	...	...	...	...
Otoe, NE	31131	27,792	6.5	30.6	62.9	23,357	8,888	66.7	...	...	...	...
Pawnee, NE	31133	6,145	8.7	35.9	55.4	5,185	10,825	65.8	...	...	...	...
Perkins, NE	31135	6,141	4.7	26.7	68.6	4,913	12,597	67.8	...	...	...	...
Phelps, NE	31137	23,222	8.1	21.3	70.6	19,058	11,837	67.0	...	...	...	...
Pierce, NE	31139	15,071	7.3	27.1	65.6	13,319	9,903	66.6	...	...	...	...
Platte, NE	31141	54,097	9.7	29.5	60.8	45,479	9,932	68.3	...	...	...	...
Polk, NE	31143	15,050	5.9	14.1	80.1	12,694	10,027	62.5	...	...	...	...
Red Willow, NE	31145	22,215	7.5	42.7	49.8	17,248	9,283	65.2	...	...	...	...
Richardson, NE	31147	16,877	8.8	34.7	56.5	14,766	10,739	63.8	...	...	...	...
Rock, NE	31149	3,109	10.5	9.9	79.5	3,021	15,492	69.3	...	...	...	...
Saline, NE	31151	35,719	8.5	30.7	60.8	28,892	9,195	64.5	...	...	...	...
Sarpy, NE	31153	247,979	9.3	38.2	52.5	209,510	9,327	65.5	8,348	83.0	12.0	2.0
Saunders, NE	31155	33,217	9.5	29.7	60.7	26,678	9,400	65.2	...	...	...	...
Scotts Bluff, NE	31157	69,635	13.4	42.2	44.4	61,136	9,553	65.7	...	...	...	...
Seward, NE	31159	34,990	7.4	23.2	69.3	30,106	11,456	60.8	...	...	...	...
Sheridan, NE	31161	12,968	12.6	40.5	46.9	12,962	13,390	64.7	...	...	...	...
Sherman, NE	31163	6,671	11.6	29.4	59.0	5,239	10,153	64.6	...	...	...	...
Sioux, NE	31165	2,025	3.8	9.4	86.8	2,081	18,918	67.0	...	...	...	...
Stanton, NE	31167	4,965	6.8	37.1	56.1	4,219	9,545	63.6	...	...	...	...
Thayer, NE	31169	12,002	5.0	21.4	73.6	10,763	13,222	64.4	...	...	...	...
Thomas, NE	31171	1,867	5.6	21.1	73.3	1,676	13,302	59.7	...	...	...	...
Thurston, NE	31173	19,081	23.1	42.5	34.4	14,784	13,613	65.2	...	...	...	...
Valley, NE	31175	8,452	6.4	38.8	54.8	7,472	11,639	61.8	...	...	...	...
Washington, NE	31177	35,236	5.1	30.4	64.5	29,175	8,015	62.7	...	...	...	...
Wayne, NE	31179	24,184	8.9	26.5	64.6	21,243	13,794	66.4	...	...	...	...
Webster, NE	31181	8,240	6.5	44.7	48.8	6,095	9,509	65.0	...	...	...	...
Wheeler, NE	31183	2,064	10.0	10.5	79.5	1,953	16,008	59.0	...	...	...	...
York, NE	31185	22,218	7.5	27.1	65.4	18,607	9,887	64.7	...	...	...	...
NEVADA	32000	4,338,601	6.5	31.0	62.5	3,552,323	8,285	59.0	128,454	75.0	14.7	6.2
Churchill, NV	32001	48,275	9.4	52.1	38.5	44,442	10,091	55.9	...	...	...	...
Clark, NV	32003	3,111,868	6.3	27.4	66.3	2,486,063	8,044	58.8	86,733	74.0	14.7	6.5
Douglas, NV	32005	73,994	4.9	35.3	59.8	67,315	9,889	58.9	...	...	...	...
Elko, NV	32007	102,331	7.0	43.5	49.5	91,634	9,396	63.8	...	...	...	...
Esmeralda, NV	32009	1,871	12.2	42.2	45.6	1,797	23,338	52.2	...	...	...	...
Eureka, NV	32011	11,189	3.6	1.8	94.5	5,788	23,528	49.4	...	...	...	...
Humboldt, NV	32013	35,035	6.5	41.8	51.7	32,739	9,209	62.6	...	...	...	...
Lander, NV	32015	12,445	8.0	47.5	44.5	11,254	8,758	57.8	...	...	...	...
Lincoln, NV	32017	14,287	8.1	70.2	21.7	13,671	14,467	63.0	...	...	...	...
Lyon, NV	32019	92,852	4.6	61.5	33.9	79,596	8,588	57.0	...	...	...	...
Mineral, NV	32021	8,770	16.1	58.9	25.0	7,144	11,673	57.0	...	...	...	...
Nye, NV	32023	78,595	6.8	46.9	46.3	65,486	10,189	57.7	...	...	...	...
Pershing, NV	32027	12,678	8.7	58.2	33.0	10,296	14,280	62.7	...	...	...	...
Storey, NV	32029	7,591	5.7	23.4	70.9	6,698	15,686	52.1	...	...	...	...
Washoe, NV	32031	618,949	7.3	33.7	59.0	537,291	8,183	59.5	21,390	77.7	12.5	5.5
White Pine, NV	32033	18,298	5.9	52.7	41.4	16,242	11,438	52.3	...	...	...	...
Carson City city, NV	32510	89,573	6.5	41.6	51.9	74,867	9,225	60.7	...	...	...	...

... Not available

Table C-1. Population, School, and Student Characteristics by County—*Continued*

County	State/County Code	High school graduates, 2006-2008			College enrollment, 2006-2008		College graduates, 2006-2008 (percent)						
		Population 25 years and over	High school diploma or less (percent)	High school diploma or more (percent)	Number	Percent public	Bachelor's degree or more	+/- U.S. percent with Bachelor's degree or more	Non-Hispanic White	Black or African American	American Indian and Alaska Native	Asian, Hawaiian, and Pacific Islander	Hispanic or Latino[3]
		30	31	32	33	34	35	36	37	38	39	40	41
Howard, NE	31093	...	...	...	...	...	...	...	...	...	...	...	...
Jefferson, NE	31095	...	...	...	...	...	...	...	...	...	...	...	...
Johnson, NE	31097	...	...	...	...	...	...	...	...	...	...	...	...
Kearney, NE	31099	...	...	...	...	...	...	...	...	...	...	...	...
Keith, NE	31101	...	...	...	...	...	...	...	...	...	...	...	...
Keya Paha, NE	31103	...	...	...	...	...	...	...	...	...	...	...	...
Kimball, NE	31105	...	...	...	...	...	...	...	...	...	...	...	...
Knox, NE	31107	...	...	...	...	...	...	...	...	...	...	...	...
Lancaster, NE	31109	171,433	30.6	93.1	36,179	83.3	35.9	8.5	37.1	17.6	16.8	44.8	19.7
Lincoln, NE	31111	23,904	42.0	91.0	1,125	88.8	19.0	-8.4	19.3	...	...	...	18.0
Logan, NE	31113	...	...	...	...	...	...	...	...	...	...	...	...
Loup, NE	31115	...	...	...	...	...	...	...	...	...	...	...	...
McPherson, NE	31117	...	...	...	...	...	...	...	...	...	...	...	...
Madison, NE	31119	21,974	46.1	86.3	2,376	92.3	18.5	-8.9	19.7	...	...	...	4.5
Merrick, NE	31121	...	...	...	...	...	...	...	...	...	...	...	...
Morrill, NE	31123	...	...	...	...	...	...	...	...	...	...	...	...
Nance, NE	31125	...	...	...	...	...	...	...	...	...	...	...	...
Nemaha, NE	31127	...	...	...	...	...	...	...	...	...	...	...	...
Nuckolls, NE	31129	...	...	...	...	...	...	...	...	...	...	...	...
Otoe, NE	31131	...	...	...	...	...	...	...	...	...	...	...	...
Pawnee, NE	31133	...	...	...	...	...	...	...	...	...	...	...	...
Perkins, NE	31135	...	...	...	...	...	...	...	...	...	...	...	...
Phelps, NE	31137	...	...	...	...	...	...	...	...	...	...	...	...
Pierce, NE	31139	...	...	...	...	...	...	...	...	...	...	...	...
Platte, NE	31141	20,569	48.4	90.2	1,674	86.9	18.9	-8.5	19.9	...	...	...	4.6
Polk, NE	31143	...	...	...	...	...	...	...	...	...	...	...	...
Red Willow, NE	31145	...	...	...	...	...	...	...	...	...	...	...	...
Richardson, NE	31147	...	...	...	...	...	...	...	...	...	...	...	...
Rock, NE	31149	...	...	...	...	...	...	...	...	...	...	...	...
Saline, NE	31151	...	...	...	...	...	...	...	...	...	...	...	...
Sarpy, NE	31153	89,016	29.5	94.5	12,353	76.5	34.6	7.2	35.7	28.4	...	32.7	20.9
Saunders, NE	31155	13,398	43.3	91.9	824	78.9	22.8	-4.6	23.2	...	...	...	...
Scotts Bluff, NE	31157	24,238	47.7	85.4	1,634	86.5	19.2	-8.2	22.0	...	...	...	3.2
Seward, NE	31159	...	...	...	...	...	...	...	...	...	...	...	...
Sheridan, NE	31161	...	...	...	...	...	...	...	...	...	...	...	...
Sherman, NE	31163	...	...	...	...	...	...	...	...	...	...	...	...
Sioux, NE	31165	...	...	...	...	...	...	...	...	...	...	...	...
Stanton, NE	31167	...	...	...	...	...	...	...	...	...	...	...	...
Thayer, NE	31169	...	...	...	...	...	...	...	...	...	...	...	...
Thomas, NE	31171	...	...	...	...	...	...	...	...	...	...	...	...
Thurston, NE	31173	...	...	...	...	...	...	...	...	...	...	...	...
Valley, NE	31175	...	...	...	...	...	...	...	...	...	...	...	...
Washington, NE	31177	...	...	...	...	...	...	...	...	...	...	...	...
Wayne, NE	31179	...	...	...	...	...	...	...	...	...	...	...	...
Webster, NE	31181	...	...	...	...	...	...	...	...	...	...	...	...
Wheeler, NE	31183	...	...	...	...	...	...	...	...	...	...	...	...
York, NE	31185	...	...	...	...	...	...	...	...	...	...	...	...
NEVADA	32000	1,676,453	46.7	83.7	127,016	81.8	21.4	-6.0	24.7	15.3	11.3	35.3	8.3
Churchill, NV	32001	15,762	47.9	87.7	854	89.6	16.9	-10.5	17.8	...	6.6	...	13.9
Clark, NV	32003	1,196,436	47.6	83.0	85,911	78.9	21.1	-6.3	25.0	15.2	14.6	34.3	8.3
Douglas, NV	32005	33,305	35.6	90.9	2,230	75.0	24.1	-3.3	25.6	...	26.7	...	4.6
Elko, NV	32007	28,851	48.6	85.9	1,925	93.0	17.2	-10.2	19.1	...	8.8	...	9.4
Esmeralda, NV	32009	...	...	...	...	...	...	...	...	...	...	...	...
Eureka, NV	32011	...	...	...	...	...	...	...	...	...	...	...	...
Humboldt, NV	32013	...	...	...	...	...	...	...	...	...	...	...	...
Lander, NV	32015	...	...	...	...	...	...	...	...	...	...	...	...
Lincoln, NV	32017	...	...	...	...	...	...	...	...	...	...	...	...
Lyon, NV	32019	31,340	55.4	88.0	2,802	79.0	10.4	-17.0	11.3	...	...	...	3.0
Mineral, NV	32021	...	...	...	...	...	...	...	...	...	...	...	...
Nye, NV	32023	30,194	61.2	77.1	1,163	96.6	9.6	-17.8	10.5	...	4.0	...	2.2
Pershing, NV	32027	...	...	...	...	...	...	...	...	...	...	...	...
Storey, NV	32029	...	...	...	...	...	...	...	...	...	...	...	...
Washoe, NV	32031	267,559	39.7	85.6	27,288	88.4	26.8	-0.6	29.9	18.8	10.7	46.0	9.0
White Pine, NV	32033	...	...	...	...	...	...	...	...	...	...	...	...
Carson City city, NV	32510	37,109	45.9	86.5	3,077	91.9	21.9	-5.5	24.0	...	4.2	34.1	10.4

[3]May be of any race
... Not available

Table C-1.   Population, School, and Student Characteristics by County—*Continued*

County	State/County Code	County Type[1]	Population, 2009 Total	Population, 2009 Percent 5–17 years	Percent of related children 5-17 years in poverty, 2008	Percent of children under 19 years with no health insurance, 2007	Number of Schools and Students, 2008-2009 School Districts	Number of Schools and Students, 2008-2009 Schools	Number of Schools and Students, 2008-2009 Students	Resident enrollment, 2006-2008 K–12 enrollment Number	Resident enrollment, 2006-2008 K–12 enrollment Percent public
			1	2	3	4	5	6	7	8	9
NEW HAMPSHIRE	33000	X	1,324,575	16.2	7.8	7.0	277	497	197,934	222,459	89.0
Belknap, NH	33001	4	61,358	15.4	9.7	7.3	19	26	10,105	9,923	92.3
Carroll, NH	33003	8	47,860	14.1	11.9	13.1	20	26	7,442	7,088	91.8
Cheshire, NH	33005	4	77,045	14.4	9.1	8.1	16	31	9,141	11,620	92.0
Coos, NH	33007	7	31,487	14.5	16.5	7.9	21	28	4,653	4,772	93.2
Grafton, NH	33009	5	86,291	13.6	9.8	7.6	41	54	11,739	12,248	90.5
Hillsborough, NH	33011	2	405,906	17.2	7.6	6.9	39	114	59,845	72,950	88.1
Merrimack, NH	33013	4	149,071	16.3	7.8	6.7	33	62	24,361	24,550	88.2
Rockingham, NH	33015	1	299,276	17.2	4.7	6.3	55	93	49,150	53,071	88.0
Strafford, NH	33017	1	123,589	14.9	9.7	6.6	16	32	14,917	19,446	87.5
Sullivan, NH	33019	7	42,692	15.5	11.5	7.3	17	31	6,581	6,791	93.8
NEW JERSEY	34000	X	8,707,739	17.1	11.0	11.1	688	2615	1,381,420	1,514,381	87.3
Atlantic, NJ	34001	2	271,712	16.8	15.5	11.9	30	81	47,132	45,933	90.1
Bergen, NJ	34003	1	895,250	16.8	5.0	12.1	81	282	134,979	148,626	86.6
Burlington, NJ	34005	1	446,108	17.1	6.1	9.3	42	135	73,362	78,461	89.8
Camden, NJ	34007	1	517,879	17.6	14.7	9.1	50	169	83,960	94,651	87.1
Cape May, NJ	34009	3	96,091	14.3	12.9	14.1	20	32	13,668	14,874	86.3
Cumberland, NJ	34011	3	157,745	17.1	18.7	11.1	17	54	26,735	27,013	90.7
Essex, NJ	34013	1	769,644	17.8	18.1	12.1	40	243	125,021	141,877	86.8
Gloucester, NJ	34015	1	289,920	17.8	7.3	8.6	29	84	49,781	49,914	88.2
Hudson, NJ	34017	1	597,924	14.0	24.0	12.0	23	118	79,681	92,286	87.4
Hunterdon, NJ	34019	1	130,034	18.6	2.6	10.0	31	51	22,989	23,672	90.6
Mercer, NJ	34021	2	366,222	16.6	11.1	10.3	23	218	62,999	62,845	87.7
Middlesex, NJ	34023	1	790,738	16.7	7.4	13.3	27	172	109,808	131,460	89.9
Monmouth, NJ	34025	1	644,105	18.2	7.3	8.7	62	204	116,694	118,366	87.0
Morris, NJ	34027	1	488,518	18.1	3.8	9.4	42	154	80,286	87,265	87.3
Ocean, NJ	34029	1	573,678	16.2	12.5	9.8	30	112	76,133	92,592	78.4
Passaic, NJ	34031	1	491,778	17.7	19.7	12.3	24	139	79,541	91,625	85.1
Salem, NJ	34033	1	66,342	17.8	13.5	10.5	16	31	12,004	11,549	88.4
Somerset, NJ	34035	1	326,869	18.5	4.0	8.9	20	79	54,936	59,946	87.9
Sussex, NJ	34037	1	151,118	18.3	4.1	10.3	28	48	25,834	28,452	88.1
Union, NJ	34039	1	526,426	17.6	10.6	15.5	27	166	87,352	93,504	89.1
Warren, NJ	34041	2	109,638	17.6	7.6	10.4	26	43	18,525	19,470	92.6
NEW MEXICO	35000	X	2,009,671	17.8	22.0	18.1	99	867	330,245	358,829	91.4
Bernalillo, NM	35001	2	642,527	16.7	17.6	13.8	6	180	97,074	107,452	87.2
Catron, NM	35003	9	3,443	11.4	36.8	19.4	2	6	351	...	...
Chaves, NM	35005	5	63,622	19.3	27.2	18.4	4	31	11,426	11,784	92.6
Cibola, NM	35006	6	27,036	18.2	30.1	12.4	1	12	3,608	5,912	90.4
Colfax, NM	35007	7	12,737	16.4	24.3	16.7	4	19	2,165	...	...
Curry, NM	35009	5	44,407	19.5	25.2	21.1	4	28	9,141	9,326	97.6
De Baca, NM	35011	9	1,819	15.7	27.5	21.8	1	3	331	...	...
Dona Ana, NM	35013	3	206,419	18.9	31.4	22.6	3	65	39,583	38,049	96.2
Eddy, NM	35015	5	52,706	19.6	19.1	15.5	3	28	10,259	9,984	95.4
Grant, NM	35017	7	29,903	16.0	24.6	15.2	2	15	4,698	4,527	92.6
Guadalupe, NM	35019	7	4,241	14.2	29.4	14.3	2	7	737	...	...
Harding, NM	35021	9	663	13.0	18.8	14.2	2	4	94	...	...
Hidalgo, NM	35023	7	5,057	18.5	28.7	17.3	2	8	939	...	...
Lea, NM	35025	5	60,232	20.9	18.3	23.1	5	36	12,588	11,179	96.4
Lincoln, NM	35027	7	21,016	14.6	23.8	23.6	5	16	3,218	3,360	97.0
Los Alamos, NM	35028	6	18,074	18.1	2.2	8.2	1	7	3,387	...	...
Luna, NM	35029	6	27,044	19.6	39.5	22.3	1	14	5,440	5,650	97.3
McKinley, NM	35031	4	70,513	22.5	36.6	17.6	2	43	14,073	17,201	95.1
Mora, NM	35033	8	4,935	16.8	30.7	14.6	2	6	678	...	...
Otero, NM	35035	4	63,201	17.0	25.0	26.3	3	24	7,626	12,038	94.3
Quay, NM	35037	7	8,917	15.1	33.6	13.0	4	12	1,550	...	...
Rio Arriba, NM	35039	6	40,678	18.0	21.7	17.0	5	35	6,305	7,177	82.2
Roosevelt, NM	35041	7	18,817	17.6	28.3	17.6	4	14	3,401	...	...
Sandoval, NM	35043	2	125,988	19.3	12.4	16.4	4	38	20,637	22,383	89.9
San Juan, NM	35045	3	124,131	20.0	19.0	23.1	4	50	23,637	23,402	95.7
San Miguel, NM	35047	6	28,323	16.4	31.6	12.7	3	22	4,430	4,756	92.7
Santa Fe, NM	35049	3	147,532	14.9	16.1	24.6	7	53	16,112	22,708	83.1
Sierra, NM	35051	6	12,886	12.9	34.7	12.2	1	6	1,501	...	...
Socorro, NM	35053	6	18,092	16.9	35.7	18.7	2	11	2,359	...	...
Taos, NM	35055	7	31,507	15.1	26.0	20.0	3	21	4,128	4,644	93.6
Torrance, NM	35057	2	16,475	18.2	26.5	14.3	3	17	4,707	...	...
Union, NM	35059	9	3,817	18.2	27.8	20.8	2	7	683	...	...
Valencia, NM	35061	2	72,913	18.9	20.1	17.9	2	29	13,379	14,040	94.7

[1]County type codes are from the Economic Research Service of the United States Department of Agriculture. See notes and definitions for more information.
... Not available

Table C-1. Population, School, and Student Characteristics by County—*Continued*

County	State/ County Code	Characteristics of students, 2008-2009				Number of graduates, 2006-2007	Staff and students, 2008-2009			
		Percent with IEP[2]	Percent eligible for free or reduced lunch	Percent minority	Percent English Language Learners		Total staff	Number of teachers	Student/ teacher ratio	Central admin. Staff
		10	11	12	13	14	15	16	17	18
NEW HAMPSHIRE	33000	15.2	20.5	8.1	1.8	14,550	32,845	15,660	12.6	1,414
Belknap, NH	33001	14.5	25.8	3.9	1.1	697	1,759	832	12.1	69
Carroll, NH	33003	15.5	27.4	3.1	0.4	480	1,449	651	11.4	88
Cheshire, NH	33005	20.5	25.5	4.0	0.5	711	1,814	814	11.2	89
Coos, NH	33007	14.9	37.2	4.0	0.2	384	906	417	11.2	41
Grafton, NH	33009	...	21.4	1.4	...	1,028	2,369	1,118	10.5	110
Hillsborough, NH	33011	14.7	21.5	14.0	3.6	4,509	8,823	4,399	13.6	462
Merrimack, NH	33013	14.3	19.6	5.7	1.4	1,673	4,082	1,820	13.4	141
Rockingham, NH	33015	15.1	11.1	5.2	0.8	3,692	8,007	3,906	12.6	242
Strafford, NH	33017	17.0	25.9	7.3	1.6	996	2,421	1,148	13.0	113
Sullivan, NH	33019	15.0	30.5	3.0	0.4	380	1,216	555	11.9	60
NEW JERSEY	34000	16.6	30.0	45.9	3.9	92,791	168,765	114,712	12.0	1,467
Atlantic, NJ	34001	17.0	41.3	50.7	4.5	3,178	5,927	4,131	11.4	64
Bergen, NJ	34003	16.5	14.8	39.9	3.8	9,360	16,453	11,012	12.3	170
Burlington, NJ	34005	19.0	18.7	33.2	1.1	5,393	9,377	6,048	12.1	93
Camden, NJ	34007	18.3	37.7	49.4	2.6	5,871	9,942	7,082	11.9	88
Cape May, NJ	34009	22.7	26.8	18.9	1.8	1,087	1,885	1,310	10.4	28
Cumberland, NJ	34011	16.7	58.7	61.8	5.3	1,578	3,597	2,368	11.3	30
Essex, NJ	34013	14.2	49.7	71.7	4.4	7,645	14,996	9,978	12.5	96
Gloucester, NJ	34015	18.9	20.9	22.7	0.8	3,472	6,074	3,937	12.6	57
Hudson, NJ	34017	13.9	67.4	82.0	9.7	4,764	10,271	7,000	11.4	62
Hunterdon, NJ	34019	14.8	4.5	11.3	0.9	1,607	3,047	2,049	11.2	56
Mercer, NJ	34021	20.3	30.0	54.9	3.7	3,914	8,233	5,198	12.1	66
Middlesex, NJ	34023	15.2	26.2	59.1	4.6	7,563	12,925	8,918	12.3	75
Monmouth, NJ	34025	16.6	16.4	25.9	2.0	8,427	14,013	9,609	12.1	138
Morris, NJ	34027	17.0	9.4	25.3	2.2	5,603	9,740	6,607	12.2	89
Ocean, NJ	34029	19.2	20.5	19.3	1.8	5,333	8,330	5,947	12.8	67
Passaic, NJ	34031	16.2	51.9	64.9	10.7	4,603	9,669	6,630	12.0	53
Salem, NJ	34033	16.5	33.3	31.6	1.2	766	1,566	1,043	11.5	25
Somerset, NJ	34035	15.8	13.4	40.0	2.6	3,670	6,456	4,669	11.8	45
Sussex, NJ	34037	15.0	10.0	10.4	0.4	2,143	3,182	2,189	11.8	50
Union, NJ	34039	15.0	39.7	60.3	5.8	5,464	10,741	7,406	11.8	70
Warren, NJ	34041	17.1	18.0	15.0	1.3	1,350	2,342	1,583	11.7	46
NEW MEXICO	35000	13.9	61.7	71.1	...	15,624	47,841	22,822	14.5	911
Bernalillo, NM	35001	13.4	52.7	69.3	...	3,831	13,423	6,612	14.7	337
Catron, NM	35003	13.4	67.8	33.9	...	25	79	41	8.6	3
Chaves, NM	35005	15.4	59.4	69.9	...	596	1,445	744	15.4	28
Cibola, NM	35006	13.9	69.9	81.8	...	248	606	280	12.9	11
Colfax, NM	35007	17.3	59.5	57.0	...	118	346	167	13.0	8
Curry, NM	35009	12.7	64.5	60.4	...	472	1,238	586	15.6	22
De Baca, NM	35011	17.8	54.4	51.7	...	26	65	29	11.4	2
Dona Ana, NM	35013	13.4	70.4	83.4	...	1,851	5,723	2,751	14.4	70
Eddy, NM	35015	15.6	53.7	55.8	...	536	1,311	666	15.4	20
Grant, NM	35017	12.9	65.8	67.4	...	271	665	329	14.3	18
Guadalupe, NM	35019	11.7	90.1	94.7	...	58	152	70	10.5	7
Harding, NM	35021	16.0	46.8	37.2	...	9	34	18	5.2	3
Hidalgo, NM	35023	17.7	63.6	80.6	...	43	182	72	13.0	7
Lea, NM	35025	12.8	58.5	67.6	...	597	1,575	790	15.9	19
Lincoln, NM	35027	12.6	63.1	57.2	...	192	455	233	13.8	9
Los Alamos, NM	35028	17.9	...	27.3	...	288	682	263	12.9	19
Luna, NM	35029	11.3	97.5	82.9	...	253	774	331	16.4	9
McKinley, NM	35031	11.4	80.7	94.6	...	756	2,453	1,052	13.4	40
Mora, NM	35033	19.6	97.1	93.4	...	69	139	58	11.7	6
Otero, NM	35035	15.5	66.0	56.2	...	506	1,201	535	14.3	22
Quay, NM	35037	16.4	89.6	56.2	...	98	271	128	12.1	7
Rio Arriba, NM	35039	12.1	94.9	96.0	...	272	1,029	466	13.5	24
Roosevelt, NM	35041	16.2	61.9	54.1	...	176	484	256	13.3	10
Sandoval, NM	35043	13.4	47.5	60.9	...	906	2,811	1,417	14.6	22
San Juan, NM	35045	14.8	62.7	65.9	...	1,218	3,495	1,609	14.7	59
San Miguel, NM	35047	15.1	78.8	92.4	...	286	776	340	13.0	19
Santa Fe, NM	35049	15.1	63.1	80.0	...	578	2,205	1,135	14.2	38
Sierra, NM	35051	17.7	72.2	51.7	...	79	256	104	14.4	5
Socorro, NM	35053	16.2	54.6	63.9	...	130	396	189	12.5	11
Taos, NM	35055	16.8	84.3	84.0	...	193	620	300	13.8	17
Torrance, NM	35057	13.4	71.3	51.0	...	308	732	318	14.8	8
Union, NM	35059	14.8	62.1	53.4	...	44	127	59	11.6	5
Valencia, NM	35061	15.8	71.4	74.7	...	591	2,093	877	15.3	28

[2]IEP= Individual Education Program. See notes and definitions for more information
... Not available

Table C-1. Population, School, and Student Characteristics by County—*Continued*

County	State/County Code	Revenues, 2007-2008				Current expenditures, 2007-2008			Resident population 16 to 19 years, 2006-2008			
		Total revenue ($1,000's)	Percentage of revenue from			Amount ($1,000's)	Amount per student	Percent for instruction	Total population 16 to 19 years	Percent enrolled in school	Percent high school graduates, not enrolled in school	Percent not enrolled, not grads, not employed or not in labor force
			Federal gov't	State gov't	Local gov't							
		19	20	21	22	23	24	25	26	27	28	29
NEW HAMPSHIRE	33000	2,715,463	5.0	37.1	57.9	2,346,059	11,990	63.7	75,929	88.5	7.7	2.2
Belknap, NH	33001	135,268	5.6	35.2	59.2	116,038	12,697	61.6	...	...	...	...
Carroll, NH	33003	126,861	4.6	37.0	58.5	101,415	13,841	63.8	...	...	...	...
Cheshire, NH	33005	148,749	5.2	37.7	57.1	129,919	13,584	61.4	...	...	...	...
Coos, NH	33007	71,652	8.1	47.5	44.4	62,899	12,810	59.6	...	...	...	...
Grafton, NH	33009	201,820	4.3	32.4	63.3	179,853	14,877	63.8	...	...	...	...
Hillsborough, NH	33011	729,422	6.3	38.5	55.3	659,116	10,746	65.1	21,349	86.0	9.1	2.8
Merrimack, NH	33013	339,774	4.2	38.4	57.5	283,432	11,771	62.7	8,198	87.7	9.0	1.8
Rockingham, NH	33015	679,376	3.3	34.8	61.8	570,658	12,145	63.5	16,121	89.8	6.3	3.1
Strafford, NH	33017	183,742	6.3	36.6	57.1	158,644	11,435	64.7	...	...	...	...
Sullivan, NH	33019	98,799	6.1	44.0	49.9	84,085	13,211	65.1	...	...	...	...
NEW JERSEY	34000	26,151,514	3.8	40.1	56.1	23,405,959	17,079	59.2	469,374	87.4	8.2	2.9
Atlantic, NJ	34001	885,187	4.8	39.4	55.7	767,626	16,511	59.9	15,057	89.4	5.8	2.5
Bergen, NJ	34003	2,575,917	2.6	18.9	78.6	2,264,058	17,100	59.6	45,487	91.4	5.7	1.9
Burlington, NJ	34005	1,362,375	3.7	37.6	58.7	1,195,266	16,232	59.0	22,865	86.9	9.5	2.7
Camden, NJ	34007	1,635,253	4.6	53.3	42.0	1,427,534	16,871	59.5	29,414	83.6	9.4	4.2
Cape May, NJ	34009	305,428	4.2	31.4	64.4	253,289	18,307	59.4	...	...	...	...
Cumberland, NJ	34011	508,292	5.7	77.6	16.7	472,483	17,945	59.9	8,547	78.2	15.2	6.1
Essex, NJ	34013	2,812,587	4.8	56.6	38.6	2,554,122	20,519	58.1	44,063	83.8	9.6	5.5
Gloucester, NJ	34015	800,636	3.5	41.4	55.1	722,896	14,562	58.0	16,481	89.9	6.9	2.2
Hudson, NJ	34017	1,600,918	6.3	65.9	27.8	1,508,533	18,865	61.7	29,156	84.2	11.1	3.0
Hunterdon, NJ	34019	455,083	1.7	18.4	79.9	408,356	17,677	54.9	...	...	...	...
Mercer, NJ	34021	1,221,984	3.3	41.4	55.3	1,063,599	17,841	58.4	23,051	88.0	6.7	3.1
Middlesex, NJ	34023	1,929,775	3.5	32.6	64.0	1,719,704	15,913	59.8	44,753	90.4	6.8	1.5
Monmouth, NJ	34025	2,115,153	2.9	33.0	64.0	1,883,795	16,221	59.2	35,804	91.2	6.4	1.6
Morris, NJ	34027	1,463,035	2.0	19.8	78.2	1,331,431	16,610	58.0	26,075	90.6	7.2	0.8
Ocean, NJ	34029	1,242,928	3.5	35.2	61.2	1,091,235	14,414	59.4	26,588	83.6	10.1	3.4
Passaic, NJ	34031	1,544,216	5.5	55.8	38.7	1,431,634	18,031	59.5	28,028	82.6	10.8	4.9
Salem, NJ	34033	212,474	5.1	48.2	46.7	186,427	15,478	57.8	3,560	83.4	13.4	0.9
Somerset, NJ	34035	974,716	2.2	19.0	78.8	869,698	15,969	58.5	15,519	93.3	4.5	1.5
Sussex, NJ	34037	480,082	2.4	34.2	63.4	442,675	16,698	57.4	8,635	88.6	6.6	3.0
Union, NJ	34039	1,691,641	4.2	41.1	54.6	1,519,980	17,833	60.8	28,758	84.6	9.4	4.2
Warren, NJ	34041	333,834	3.0	40.5	56.5	291,618	15,645	59.8	5,865	88.7	8.7	2.0
NEW MEXICO	35000	3,569,311	13.1	71.2	15.7	2,983,848	9,068	58.1	117,789	80.6	10.1	5.5
Bernalillo, NM	35001	999,503	8.8	74.3	16.9	802,455	8,362	59.5	33,647	81.8	8.6	5.2
Catron, NM	35003	6,452	13.5	78.8	7.7	6,077	16,249	49.8	...	...	...	...
Chaves, NM	35005	114,438	12.2	79.0	8.8	99,153	8,775	57.8	4,253	75.5	15.5	4.7
Cibola, NM	35006	41,665	24.4	67.3	8.2	38,789	10,235	57.8	...	...	...	...
Colfax, NM	35007	29,249	7.2	79.4	13.4	24,346	10,859	57.4	...	...	...	...
Curry, NM	35009	79,369	11.4	80.8	7.7	74,399	8,161	58.9	...	...	...	...
De Baca, NM	35011	5,523	6.7	77.4	15.9	4,885	15,459	51.0	...	...	...	...
Dona Ana, NM	35013	392,877	11.7	76.0	12.3	347,760	8,723	60.2	13,878	83.1	7.7	7.3
Eddy, NM	35015	116,738	8.4	71.4	20.2	96,635	9,468	59.8	...	...	...	...
Grant, NM	35017	51,109	9.6	80.1	10.3	46,055	9,982	56.5	...	...	...	...
Guadalupe, NM	35019	11,911	8.7	75.6	15.7	10,392	13,656	47.5	...	...	...	...
Harding, NM	35021	3,584	1.5	81.2	17.3	3,041	25,991	47.9	...	...	...	...
Hidalgo, NM	35023	13,517	8.7	76.4	14.9	12,383	12,926	49.2	...	...	...	...
Lea, NM	35025	126,464	7.8	71.8	20.4	103,416	8,374	60.9	...	...	...	...
Lincoln, NM	35027	42,008	9.6	73.4	17.0	34,456	10,605	57.6	...	...	...	...
Los Alamos, NM	35028	44,347	21.5	64.2	14.2	38,803	11,182	57.2	...	...	...	...
Luna, NM	35029	5,3501	16.0	75.2	8.8	47,944	8,642	56.9	...	...	...	...
McKinley, NM	35031	170,067	45.4	48.0	6.6	145,609	10,557	54.1	...	...	...	...
Mora, NM	35033	12,654	22.0	71.9	6.1	11,422	15,842	49.4	...	...	...	...
Otero, NM	35035	78,598	13.5	75.3	11.2	70,771	9,056	56.9	...	...	...	...
Quay, NM	35037	20,338	12.7	79.1	8.2	18,015	11,460	54.2	...	...	...	...
Rio Arriba, NM	35039	88,481	16.2	65.9	17.9	74,924	11,481	50.0	...	...	...	...
Roosevelt, NM	35041	37,643	10.2	79.1	10.6	34,284	10,057	57.3	...	...	...	...
Sandoval, NM	35043	232,407	9.4	64.6	25.9	175,608	8,675	60.2	6,393	84.4	9.4	3.6
San Juan, NM	35045	263,143	21.8	61.0	17.2	215,736	9,218	59.3	7,688	71.0	17.5	8.7
San Miguel, NM	35047	59,527	12.7	78.5	8.8	54,425	11,735	54.1	...	...	...	...
Santa Fe, NM	35049	179,474	9.2	62.1	28.7	132,771	8,518	57.4	7,228	80.3	9.7	3.8
Sierra, NM	35051	16,777	13.1	74.2	12.7	14,420	9,904	56.7	...	...	...	...
Socorro, NM	35053	30,082	15.9	70.9	13.2	26,243	10,935	56.3	...	...	...	...
Taos, NM	35055	48,613	11.4	77.0	11.6	43,956	10,421	54.9	...	...	...	...
Torrance, NM	35057	52,072	9.7	78.9	11.4	45,798	9,228	54.5	...	...	...	...
Union, NM	35059	10,263	7.4	78.9	13.6	8,625	13,435	50.9	...	...	...	...
Valencia, NM	35061	136,917	10.9	77.4	11.8	120,252	8,965	55.4	4,764	78.9	7.9	7.2

... Not available

Table C-1. Population, School, and Student Characteristics by County—*Continued*

County	State/County Code	Population 25 years and over	High school diploma or less (percent)	High school diploma or more (percent)	College enrollment, 2006-2008 Number	Percent public	Bachelor's degree or more	+/- U.S. percent with Bachelor's degree or more	Non-Hispanic White	Black or African American	American Indian and Alaska Native	Asian, Hawaiian, and Pacific Islander	Hispanic or Latino[3]
		30	31	32	33	34	35	36	37	38	39	40	41
NEW HAMPSHIRE	33000	895,988	39.8	90.5	88,362	61.1	32.6	5.2	32.2	29.6	28.7	59.5	28.1
Belknap, NH	33001	44,244	46.6	89.0	2,147	64.6	25.0	-2.4	24.8	...	...	...	...
Carroll, NH	33003	34,964	42.3	90.2	1,667	73.8	28.9	1.5	29.2	...	...	...	...
Cheshire, NH	33005	51,911	45.3	88.6	8,008	71.4	29.7	2.3	29.8	...	...	...	...
Coos, NH	33007	23,703	57.1	84.4	1,108	82.3	16.5	-10.9	16.5	...	...	...	...
Grafton, NH	33009	57,093	40.2	90.4	10,684	45.4	36.1	8.7	35.6	...	...	...	58.1
Hillsborough, NH	33011	270,190	37.9	90.5	23,096	49.2	34.5	7.1	34.0	30.1	...	65.8	22.8
Merrimack, NH	33013	101,407	38.8	90.3	10,041	48.4	32.2	4.8	32.0	...	...	70.7	25.8
Rockingham, NH	33015	204,166	34.4	93.1	15,270	61.7	36.4	9.0	36.1	39.7	...	52.4	37.2
Strafford, NH	33017	77,873	43.1	88.3	14,837	89.0	29.0	1.6	28.8	...	...	42.4	43.9
Sullivan, NH	33019	30,437	51.7	88.8	1,504	68.2	25.9	-1.5	25.6	...	...	...	...
NEW JERSEY	34000	5,836,774	43.5	86.9	560,235	66.3	34.0	6.6	36.7	20.2	17.1	66.4	15.5
Atlantic, NJ	34001	181,944	51.4	84.4	21,037	86.3	23.2	-4.2	27.0	13.9	...	30.1	9.1
Bergen, NJ	34003	622,539	34.6	90.7	57,280	58.3	44.3	16.9	43.8	35.8	...	67.0	25.6
Burlington, NJ	34005	304,727	39.9	90.6	28,449	70.7	32.8	5.4	34.2	23.9	...	56.5	18.6
Camden, NJ	34007	340,850	48.7	84.7	31,739	72.1	27.1	-0.3	30.2	16.2	11.2	51.0	10.6
Cape May, NJ	34009	70,494	48.1	88.5	3,394	72.7	27.2	-0.2	28.0	15.2	...	...	14.3
Cumberland, NJ	34011	103,810	65.6	74.6	6,983	87.8	12.5	-14.9	17.1	4.7	8.3	34.9	4.6
Essex, NJ	34013	502,746	47.8	80.8	50,910	62.4	31.7	4.3	48.5	18.1	8.7	67.8	13.7
Gloucester, NJ	34015	188,777	47.2	89.1	22,472	79.0	26.3	-1.1	25.4	26.5	...	62.0	23.1
Hudson, NJ	34017	409,379	49.2	79.3	37,699	58.4	32.3	4.9	42.5	20.8	17.9	61.6	16.1
Hunterdon, NJ	34019	88,670	29.4	94.2	7,429	61.6	47.7	20.3	47.5	20.7	...	84.7	33.5
Mercer, NJ	34021	240,154	39.8	86.3	33,212	58.5	38.1	10.7	44.0	15.2	...	77.0	13.6
Middlesex, NJ	34023	524,919	41.3	87.6	61,036	79.8	37.6	10.2	33.2	30.4	29.2	72.4	15.1
Monmouth, NJ	34025	432,340	36.8	91.1	41,347	58.3	38.7	11.3	40.3	21.8	1 4	66.0	17.5
Morris, NJ	34027	331,113	31.9	92.5	30,354	55.6	47.5	20.1	48.6	30.2	...	73.4	21.5
Ocean, NJ	34029	393,029	49.2	88.6	28,787	54.9	24.5	-2.9	24.5	22.1	...	55.0	15.5
Passaic, NJ	34031	316,260	55.1	81.0	28,765	70.8	23.6	-3.8	30.4	10.8	...	60.0	11.0
Salem, NJ	34033	45,028	53.4	85.8	4,147	79.8	17.0	-10.4	18.6	7.5	...	...	8.2
Somerset, NJ	34035	217,847	30.3	92.8	18,967	63.4	49.2	21.8	50.2	35.9	...	78.2	18.9
Sussex, NJ	34037	101,526	42.1	93.0	9,479	69.4	30.2	2.8	30.2	33.8	...	46.8	24.4
Union, NJ	34039	346,152	48.7	84.0	30,275	69.6	30.5	3.1	40.1	20.1	...	62.4	12.0
Warren, NJ	34041	74,471	46.3	89.0	6,474	57.1	28.5	1.1	27.2	47.7	...	68.4	19.8
NEW MEXICO	35000	1,258,320	45.4	82.0	145,136	87.1	24.9	-2.5	37.0	26.0	9.0	45.4	12.5
Bernalillo, NM	35001	409,400	38.9	85.7	56,214	87.9	31.3	3.9	44.9	28.5	15.8	44.5	15.1
Catron, NM	35003	...	...	...	...	...	...	...	...	...	...	...	...
Chaves, NM	35005	39,167	55.2	74.1	3,276	81.1	15.1	-12.3	21.3	...	...	11.4	7.8
Cibola, NM	35006	17,115	63.2	74.4	859	87.4	10.2	-17.2	17.3	...	8.3	...	5.6
Colfax, NM	35007	...	...	...	...	...	...	...	...	...	...	...	...
Curry, NM	35009	26,826	48.3	82.0	2,645	76.9	18.0	-9.4	24.2	19.1	...	23.0	5.3
De Baca, NM	35011	...	...	...	...	...	...	...	...	...	...	...	...
Dona Ana, NM	35013	116,733	47.1	74.7	23,182	95.7	25.0	-2.4	44.6	29.6	25.3	66.0	11.6
Eddy, NM	35015	32,987	56.1	78.2	2,256	88.2	14.9	-12.5	19.3	...	...	...	8.3
Grant, NM	35017	19,870	42.0	85.2	2,468	90.9	23.7	-3.7	32.9	...	...	...	11.4
Guadalupe, NM	35019	...	...	...	...	...	...	...	...	...	...	...	...
Harding, NM	35021	...	...	...	...	...	...	...	...	...	...	...	...
Hidalgo, NM	35023	...	...	...	...	...	...	...	...	...	...	...	...
Lea, NM	35025	35,115	57.9	71.6	2,687	73.0	13.0	-14.4	21.2	3.7	...	...	3.1
Lincoln, NM	35027	14,911	41.8	87.9	899	97.4	23.8	-3.6	29.8	...	...	...	5.5
Los Alamos, NM	35028	...	...	...	...	...	...	...	...	...	...	...	...
Luna, NM	35029	17,042	62.1	68.8	1,055	97.8	12.8	-14.6	21.5	...	...	...	4.4
McKinley, NM	35031	39,161	66.6	69.2	3,759	90.8	11.3	-16.1	41.5	...	4.1	...	6.7
Mora, NM	35033	...	...	...	...	...	...	...	...	...	...	...	...
Otero, NM	35035	40,332	45.0	84.5	4,194	92.8	15.6	-11.8	20.6	15.6	9.1	...	7.0
Quay, NM	35037	...	...	...	...	...	...	...	...	...	...	...	...
Rio Arriba, NM	35039	25,927	56.2	79.2	1,973	82.0	16.2	-11.2	33.9	...	10.2	...	12.7
Roosevelt, NM	35041	...	...	...	...	...	...	...	...	...	...	...	...
Sandoval, NM	35043	75,696	37.9	89.6	7,627	83.3	28.0	0.6	36.3	36.6	11.5	30.3	16.9
San Juan, NM	35045	74,727	51.8	81.0	5,383	81.2	14.7	-12.7	19.4	...	6.9	...	11.1
San Miguel, NM	35047	18,649	49.3	78.0	3,117	89.7	24.7	-2.7	44.9	...	...	...	17.9
Santa Fe, NM	35049	99,889	37.1	84.7	8,784	68.6	38.1	10.7	57.9	...	17.9	39.9	17.3
Sierra, NM	35051	...	...	...	...	...	...	...	...	...	...	...	...
Socorro, NM	35053	...	...	...	...	...	...	...	...	...	...	...	...
Taos, NM	35055	22,277	42.9	89.0	1,273	94.1	26.9	-0.5	48.4	...	4.7	...	11.9
Torrance, NM	35057	...	...	...	...	...	...	...	...	...	...	...	...
Union, NM	35059	...	...	...	...	...	...	...	...	...	...	...	...
Valencia, NM	35061	45,192	52.1	80.9	4,383	77.8	14.8	-12.6	20.8	...	...	8.6	9.2

[3]May be of any race
... Not available

Table C-1. Population, School, and Student Characteristics by County—*Continued*

County	State/County Code	County Type[1]	Population, 2009 Total	Population, 2009 Percent 5–17 years	Percent of related children 5-17 years in poverty, 2008	Percent of children under 19 years with no health insurance, 2007	Number of Schools and Students, 2008-2009 School Districts	Number of Schools and Students, 2008-2009 Schools	Number of Schools and Students, 2008-2009 Students	Resident enrollment, 2006-2008 K–12 enrollment Number	Resident enrollment, 2006-2008 K–12 enrollment Percent public
			1	2	3	4	5	6	7	8	9
NEW YORK	36000	X	19,541,453	16.4	18.3	8.6	891	4717	2,740,805	3,318,991	85.1
Albany, NY	36001	2	298,284	14.9	13.2	8.2	26	81	41,742	45,413	86.4
Allegany, NY	36003	7	49,157	15.6	20.8	9.4	12	22	7,620	7,868	90.4
Bronx, NY	36005	1	1,397,287	19.9	39.9	6.0	29	372	208,465	294,238	85.8
Broome, NY	36007	2	194,630	15.1	17.9	9.7	12	55	29,368	30,071	94.4
Cattaraugus, NY	36009	4	79,689	16.9	20.6	12.8	14	39	14,679	13,468	92.6
Cayuga, NY	36011	4	79,526	15.9	15.6	9.4	8	25	10,303	13,443	92.4
Chautauqua, NY	36013	4	133,503	16.1	22.7	8.6	18	54	21,512	22,013	94.0
Chemung, NY	36015	3	88,331	16.2	21.2	7.4	3	23	12,472	14,595	89.8
Chenango, NY	36017	6	50,620	17.2	20.0	9.6	9	25	8,760	8,858	96.1
Clinton, NY	36019	5	81,618	14.0	16.2	9.8	9	30	11,975	12,038	96.2
Columbia, NY	36021	6	61,618	15.7	13.5	12.1	7	19	8,253	9,632	88.3
Cortland, NY	36023	4	47,996	15.4	16.6	8.2	5	18	7,001	7,730	95.5
Delaware, NY	36025	6	45,514	14.6	20.8	10.4	14	22	6,865	7,164	93.9
Dutchess, NY	36027	2	293,562	17.2	9.2	10.1	14	82	46,287	51,896	90.6
Erie, NY	36029	1	909,247	16.2	16.9	8.7	46	229	134,505	153,316	86.4
Essex, NY	36031	6	37,686	13.7	14.9	12.9	11	15	4,208	5,667	86.9
Franklin, NY	36033	5	50,274	13.9	19.7	10.0	8	22	8,265	7,397	94.1
Fulton, NY	36035	4	55,053	16.2	19.4	7.5	7	22	9,294	8,886	97.4
Genesee, NY	36037	4	57,868	16.4	11.9	10.4	10	23	9,511	10,229	93.7
Greene, NY	36039	6	48,947	15.2	14.7	11.0	6	17	7,064	7,256	86.5
Hamilton, NY	36041	8	4,923	13.1	12.7	21.2	7	7	552	...	...
Herkimer, NY	36043	2	62,236	16.5	19.7	8.6	12	27	10,528	10,249	96.3
Jefferson, NY	36045	4	118,719	17.0	19.7	14.2	12	39	18,679	21,324	94.0
Kings, NY	36047	1	2,567,098	17.0	29.8	8.1	38	484	299,305	470,019	76.0
Lewis, NY	36049	6	26,157	16.9	19.1	10.8	5	14	4,439	4,662	94.7
Livingston, NY	36051	1	62,871	14.7	11.0	9.7	8	24	8,849	9,535	93.5
Madison, NY	36053	2	69,954	16.1	14.2	8.8	10	29	11,108	10,948	92.9
Monroe, NY	36055	1	733,703	16.6	16.0	6.6	25	188	115,397	127,778	90.7
Montgomery, NY	36057	4	48,616	17.1	22.0	7.7	6	17	7,692	8,043	92.4
Nassau, NY	36059	1	1,357,429	17.6	5.8	8.0	58	316	206,981	237,926	86.6
New York, NY	36061	1	1,629,054	10.2	24.2	6.6	36	362	177,410	182,594	71.4
Niagara, NY	36063	1	214,557	16.2	15.5	9.3	11	58	32,346	35,913	90.7
Oneida, NY	36065	2	231,044	15.9	19.3	8.9	18	75	35,211	37,896	93.5
Onondaga, NY	36067	2	454,753	16.9	13.4	8.2	21	124	74,824	78,713	93.3
Ontario, NY	36069	1	105,650	16.8	11.2	11.2	9	32	17,654	17,435	95.9
Orange, NY	36071	2	383,532	20.1	12.8	11.1	18	88	65,047	75,705	85.4
Orleans, NY	36073	1	42,051	17.0	16.1	9.8	6	14	7,155	7,838	96.2
Oswego, NY	36075	2	121,377	17.1	17.3	8.3	10	43	22,657	20,899	95.9
Otsego, NY	36077	6	61,602	14.3	19.0	11.8	12	23	8,376	8,728	97.8
Putnam, NY	36079	1	99,265	18.5	3.9	11.3	6	22	16,395	18,864	90.2
Queens, NY	36081	1	2,306,712	15.0	17.1	10.1	12	305	260,648	358,642	81.4
Rensselaer, NY	36083	2	155,541	15.8	11.2	7.8	14	44	20,891	25,479	93.1
Richmond, NY	36085	1	491,730	17.1	13.8	7.4	1	64	58,211	86,739	76.0
Rockland, NY	36087	1	300,173	20.0	17.3	9.0	9	67	41,416	58,590	69.1
St. Lawrence, NY	36089	5	109,715	15.1	20.0	8.9	18	42	16,147	16,198	92.9
Saratoga, NY	36091	2	220,069	16.5	7.4	9.3	11	49	32,192	36,444	93.6
Schenectady, NY	36093	2	152,169	16.7	16.4	8.1	7	50	26,733	25,160	93.7
Schoharie, NY	36095	2	31,529	15.7	15.0	9.3	6	13	5,049	5,017	93.9
Schuyler, NY	36097	6	18,720	15.8	17.2	10.1	3	7	2,396	...	...
Seneca, NY	36099	6	34,049	15.4	15.6	10.3	4	14	4,661	5,302	91.0
Steuben, NY	36101	4	96,552	17.1	16.7	8.4	13	43	16,793	16,742	94.7
Suffolk, NY	36103	1	1,518,475	18.1	6.0	9.6	73	351	257,236	279,798	93.0
Sullivan, NY	36105	4	75,828	16.6	20.5	12.6	9	22	10,380	13,929	87.3
Tioga, NY	36107	2	50,064	17.4	12.2	8.6	6	21	8,220	9,012	93.8
Tompkins, NY	36109	3	101,779	11.9	13.6	10.8	8	31	12,022	11,875	90.8
Ulster, NY	36111	3	181,440	15.1	13.1	12.1	11	53	26,227	28,678	92.6
Warren, NY	36113	3	66,021	15.0	13.8	9.9	9	21	10,179	10,225	94.8
Washington, NY	36115	3	62,753	15.4	14.8	10.0	12	23	9,652	10,595	90.6
Wayne, NY	36117	1	91,291	17.9	12.7	10.3	12	40	15,910	16,576	92.3
Westchester, NY	36119	1	955,962	17.8	10.1	8.8	50	258	149,474	173,271	86.0
Wyoming, NY	36121	6	41,398	15.6	13.2	12.3	5	13	4,936	6,463	93.3
Yates, NY	36123	6	24,482	17.6	19.9	12.9	2	5	2,678	3,968	74.7

[1]County type codes are from the Economic Research Service of the United States Department of Agriculture. See notes and definitions for more information.
... Not available

Table C-1. Population, School, and Student Characteristics by County—*Continued*

County	State/ County Code	Characteristics of students, 2008-2009				Number of graduates, 2006-2007	Staff and students, 2008-2009			
		Percent with IEP[2]	Percent eligible for free or reduced lunch	Percent minority	Percent English Language Learners		Total staff	Number of teachers	Student/ teacher ratio	Central admin. Staff
		10	11	12	13	14	15	16	17	18
NEW YORK	36000	16.2	44.7	48.7	6.7	168,329	428,131	217,941	12.6	26,235
Albany, NY	36001	18.2	30.3	31.5	2.1	2,676	7,399	3,505	11.9	533
Allegany, NY	36003	15.1	43.2	2.9	...	558	1,451	672	11.3	90
Bronx, NY	36005	20.7	82.0	96.0	15.7	8,234	18,958	15,580	13.4	124
Broome, NY	36007	16.4	36.6	15.3	1.6	2,030	5,675	2,639	11.1	355
Cattaraugus, NY	36009	15.4	40.6	11.1	0.1	982	2,793	1,425	10.3	187
Cayuga, NY	36011	14.4	30.8	7.8	0.2	703	1,775	959	10.7	108
Chautauqua, NY	36013	13.2	42.5	13.7	2.1	1,525	3,914	1,884	11.4	233
Chemung, NY	36015	15.3	39.8	14.8	0.2	787	2,138	944	13.2	136
Chenango, NY	36017	15.8	46.9	4.1	0.1	702	1,945	902	9.7	120
Clinton, NY	36019	19.8	36.4	7.6	0.1	864	2,393	1,184	10.1	138
Columbia, NY	36021	18.1	31.8	16.5	2.1	582	1,632	748	11.0	136
Cortland, NY	36023	16.6	36.4	5.3	0.1	464	1,293	600	11.7	87
Delaware, NY	36025	17.2	46.5	5.9	0.6	571	1,609	752	9.1	110
Dutchess, NY	36027	16.6	22.2	27.5	2.3	3,090	7,186	3,454	13.4	502
Erie, NY	36029	16.9	40.4	30.0	2.7	8,659	20,846	11,139	12.1	1,398
Essex, NY	36031	16.0	40.9	3.1	...	342	944	451	9.3	71
Franklin, NY	36033	16.9	44.8	15.6	0.1	538	1,744	780	10.6	106
Fulton, NY	36035	16.5	40.2	5.7	0.2	565	1,468	701	13.3	89
Genesee, NY	36037	14.0	33.0	8.5	0.8	712	1,826	888	10.7	107
Greene, NY	36039	15.6	29.8	10.4	0.6	491	1,282	622	11.4	84
Hamilton, NY	36041	10.1	25.5	0.5	...	37	188	90	6.1	19
Herkimer, NY	36043	14.5	40.3	3.2	0.2	709	1,779	933	11.3	112
Jefferson, NY	36045	14.5	36.1	14.0	1.2	1,092	3,012	1,508	12.4	184
Kings, NY	36047	17.5	73.4	85.8	10.7	14,000	25,576	21,292	14.1	118
Lewis, NY	36049	14.9	42.9	2.9	...	337	729	348	12.8	48
Livingston, NY	36051	12.4	29.3	5.3	0.8	673	1,620	798	11.1	104
Madison, NY	36053	13.9	28.7	4.0	0.1	801	1,838	886	12.5	124
Monroe, NY	36055	14.9	38.1	37.1	3.7	7,662	21,130	9,814	11.8	1,504
Montgomery, NY	36057	17.1	38.8	20.4	2.0	475	1,252	685	11.2	84
Nassau, NY	36059	14.9	15.9	39.1	5.4	14,473	34,888	17,599	11.8	2,984
New York, NY	36061	14.4	68.2	87.2	11.5	11,389	64,868	15,664	11.3	4,252
Niagara, NY	36063	15.5	36.4	18.0	0.6	2,291	4,852	2,432	13.3	345
Oneida, NY	36065	15.9	43.3	17.9	3.6	2,477	5,596	2,606	13.5	389
Onondaga, NY	36067	16.6	35.0	27.4	2.7	4,727	12,852	6,011	12.4	785
Ontario, NY	36069	13.8	24.7	9.8	0.8	1,252	3,184	1,488	11.9	197
Orange, NY	36071	15.2	31.9	37.8	4.7	4,673	10,172	5,047	12.9	792
Orleans, NY	36073	13.3	39.2	12.7	1.2	534	1,389	767	9.3	93
Oswego, NY	36075	15.4	41.1	4.2	0.2	1,463	4,126	1,895	12.0	254
Otsego, NY	36077	16.0	39.3	6.6	0.3	612	1,611	737	11.4	98
Putnam, NY	36079	16.2	7.4	14.3	2.2	1,247	2,743	1,228	13.4	186
Queens, NY	36081	15.5	64.6	85.9	13.1	13,302	20,400	17,134	15.2	86
Rensselaer, NY	36083	20.5	31.3	16.3	0.6	1,536	3,671	1,853	11.3	250
Richmond, NY	36085	21.6	47.5	46.4	5.2	3,179	4,633	3,857	15.1	11
Rockland, NY	36087	16.6	22.0	44.1	6.2	3,058	6,985	3,385	12.2	540
St. Lawrence, NY	36089	14.9	41.9	5.2	0.2	1,076	2,787	1,415	11.4	164
Saratoga, NY	36091	13.4	15.7	6.4	0.3	2,079	5,121	2,461	13.1	379
Schenectady, NY	36093	15.4	32.6	31.0	1.3	1,710	4,290	1,966	13.6	247
Schoharie, NY	36095	14.4	37.9	4.0	0.2	345	988	454	11.1	67
Schuyler, NY	36097	13.7	35.8	3.5	0.1	170	411	208	11.5	37
Seneca, NY	36099	17.5	37.2	7.1	0.1	322	891	406	11.5	57
Steuben, NY	36101	15.4	46.3	4.9	0.4	1,210	3,283	1,599	10.5	199
Suffolk, NY	36103	14.7	20.9	30.2	5.8	17,927	39,828	20,326	12.7	3,498
Sullivan, NY	36105	14.9	47.8	29.8	3.4	675	2,034	1,008	10.3	155
Tioga, NY	36107	14.3	35.4	3.8	0.2	592	1,386	643	12.8	82
Tompkins, NY	36109	19.6	33.4	17.8	2.2	821	2,486	1,154	10.4	155
Ulster, NY	36111	17.6	30.6	21.3	1.6	1,884	4,183	2,039	12.9	326
Warren, NY	36113	16.0	25.8	5.0	0.1	749	1,807	874	11.6	158
Washington, NY	36115	16.1	35.1	2.9	0.3	666	2,087	1,059	9.1	124
Wayne, NY	36117	15.2	36.4	10.7	1.1	1,182	3,548	1,675	9.5	255
Westchester, NY	36119	14.5	28.7	46.6	7.8	9,282	24,264	12,086	12.4	1,957
Wyoming, NY	36121	13.2	31.7	2.1	0.2	373	808	441	11.2	58
Yates, NY	36123	17.9	45.0	3.6	0.4	192	565	244	11.0	44

[2]IEP= Individual Education Program. See notes and definitions for more information
... Not available

Table C-1. Population, School, and Student Characteristics by County—*Continued*

County	State/ County Code	Total revenue ($1,000's)	Federal gov't	State gov't	Local gov't	Amount ($1,000's)	Amount per student	Percent for instruc-tion	Total population 16 to 19 years	Percent en-rolled in school	Percent high school graduates, not enrolled in school	Percent not enrolled, not grads, not employed or not in labor force
			19	20	21	22	23	24	25	26	27	28	29
		19	20	21	22	23	24	25	26	27	28	29
NEW YORK	36000	53,278,133	5.9	45.1	49.0	48,182,476	17,646	69.6	113,8097	87.2	7.4	3.8
Albany, NY	36001	791,842	4.0	36.2	59.8	636,979	15,868	65.9	20,695	88.8	7.6	2.4
Allegany, NY	36003	145,170	7.0	71.6	21.4	123,682	16,240	63.1	4,830	93.2	3.4	3.0
Bronx, NY	36005	(6)	(6)	(6)	(6)	(6)	(6)	(6)	91,452	82.1	7.9	8.0
Broome, NY	36007	491,038	5.3	57.5	37.2	440,174	14,849	65.9	13,738	90.3	4.4	2.7
Cattaraugus, NY	36009	259,570	6.0	68.4	25.5	223,668	15,035	64.3	5,172	82.8	9.9	3.8
Cayuga, NY	36011	173,015	4.9	62.7	32.4	151,132	14,275	65.2	4,339	78.1	12.4	5.2
Chautauqua, NY	36013	368,929	6.7	64.0	29.3	314,251	14,494	66.5	8,968	85.1	8.0	4.5
Chemung, NY	36015	202,633	6.0	63.2	30.7	175,964	13,985	63.4	5,192	88.7	9.1	1.1
Chenango, NY	36017	162,001	5.6	71.2	23.2	139,801	15,523	62.2	3,083	85.3	6.5	4.7
Clinton, NY	36019	222,704	4.7	59.2	36.0	197,429	16,035	68.1	...	...	...	...
Columbia, NY	36021	165,989	5.2	41.1	53.6	152,063	17,781	63.9	3,767	81.3	9.0	7.7
Cortland, NY	36023	114,349	5.8	65.6	28.6	104,236	14,650	65.4	...	...	...	...
Delaware, NY	36025	150,100	5.2	54.4	40.4	127,257	18,459	62.2	...	...	...	...
Dutchess, NY	36027	787,930	3.1	39.9	57.0	720,948	15,431	64.0	19,573	93.2	4.0	2.0
Erie, NY	36029	2,270,376	6.1	56.1	37.9	1,905,234	14,657	65.6	54,408	87.5	7.9	2.9
Essex, NY	36031	94,021	5.6	41.7	52.8	84,465	19,869	65.3	...	...	...	...
Franklin, NY	36033	151,159	6.4	66.5	27.1	135,239	16,395	65.0	...	...	...	...
Fulton, NY	36035	145,069	6.7	64.9	28.4	127,327	13,359	67.5	...	...	...	...
Genesee, NY	36037	164,793	4.5	62.8	32.7	142,703	14,837	63.3	...	...	...	...
Greene, NY	36039	135,701	4.4	44.1	51.5	116,056	15,931	62.3	2,623	71.0	11.5	12.4
Hamilton, NY	36041	19,532	2.0	17.4	80.6	16,632	30,686	60.7	...	...	...	...
Herkimer, NY	36043	170,277	5.1	66.4	28.5	145,993	13,567	65.6	3,643	82.9	8.8	6.4
Jefferson, NY	36045	269,614	10.3	65.4	24.3	238,843	12,818	64.9	6,252	78.3	13.7	5.6
Kings, NY	36047	(6)	(6)	(6)	(6)	(6)	(6)	(6)	146,821	83.8	9.3	5.3
Lewis, NY	36049	78,682	4.5	67.1	28.4	65,118	14,850	63.7	...	...	...	...
Livingston, NY	36051	155,105	4.0	62.7	33.3	126,478	14,006	63.4	...	...	...	...
Madison, NY	36053	181,681	4.8	61.0	34.2	159,912	13,905	63.5	...	...	...	...
Monroe, NY	36055	1,984,923	5.6	51.9	42.5	1,749,521	15,106	61.2	50,201	88.4	7.6	3.1
Montgomery, NY	36057	126,256	6.5	64.3	29.3	110,255	14,203	66.4	2,682	78.7	10.5	5.8
Nassau, NY	36059	4,759,954	2.1	25.9	72.0	4,317,744	20,778	65.6	79,851	91.9	4.8	2.6
New York, NY	36061	19,885,6936	9.06	46.96	44.16	18,544,5276	18,7336	76.56	63,554	88.9	4.8	4.7
Niagara, NY	36063	536,768	5.2	61.6	33.1	470,059	14,478	65.8	12,734	84.0	12.5	2.3
Oneida, NY	36065	572,112	5.9	64.5	29.6	504,162	14,342	65.9	13,814	87.2	8.0	3.4
Onondaga, NY	36067	1,238,065	5.7	55.5	38.8	1,101,781	14,809	65.8	28,922	90.3	5.5	2.4
Ontario, NY	36069	296,145	4.8	51.9	43.3	251,749	14,235	64.6	6,347	91.1	5.5	2.1
Orange, NY	36071	1,210,398	4.7	46.3	49.0	1,089,447	16,589	66.5	25,061	86.3	7.8	3.5
Orleans, NY	36073	117,849	5.7	68.4	25.9	101,033	13,789	67.5	2,661	85.0	7.1	3.3
Oswego, NY	36075	372,041	6.0	60.1	33.9	340,212	14,691	63.6	8,555	87.8	8.2	2.7
Otsego, NY	36077	151,799	5.0	60.2	34.8	131,923	15,342	64.4	...	...	...	...
Putnam, NY	36079	356,155	1.6	31.2	67.2	327,020	19,726	66.9	...	...	...	...
Queens, NY	36081	(6)	(6)	(6)	(6)	(6)	(6)	(6)	112,317	86.0	8.6	3.2
Rensselaer, NY	36083	377,506	4.6	54.0	41.5	328,976	15,619	64.2	9,893	88.4	4.4	3.3
Richmond, NY	36085	(6)	(6)	(6)	(6)	(6)	(6)	(6)	28,225	87.4	7.9	2.9
Rockland, NY	36087	938,674	3.7	28.1	68.2	849,606	20,375	65.4	19,163	89.7	6.7	2.9
St. Lawrence, NY	36089	288,447	5.1	68.7	26.2	251,277	15,381	65.0	9,505	91.6	4.4	2.9
Saratoga, NY	36091	506,695	3.0	44.7	52.3	437,283	13,522	64.2	12,018	86.4	7.3	4.0
Schenectady, NY	36093	422,696	5.2	50.5	44.4	369,077	14,006	67.9	8,722	86.2	7.1	3.2
Schoharie, NY	36095	100,369	3.8	59.3	36.9	85,627	16,809	64.1	...	...	...	...
Schuyler, NY	36097	43,992	4.6	66.1	29.3	36,960	14,994	63.1	...	...	...	...
Seneca, NY	36099	89,276	4.6	62.0	33.4	72,475	15,115	63.3	1,846	75.5	11.8	5.6
Steuben, NY	36101	288,231	5.3	64.7	30.1	250,863	14,634	64.5	5,289	86.9	8.7	3.2
Suffolk, NY	36103	5,312,676	2.5	38.3	59.1	4,806,379	18,620	66.1	88,871	88.9	7.0	2.5
Sullivan, NY	36105	249,987	4.7	45.6	49.7	218,857	20,420	65.1	4,557	85.3	10.4	3.7
Tioga, NY	36107	134,915	4.6	66.8	28.6	117,318	14,138	62.5	...	...	...	...
Tompkins, NY	36109	219,981	4.2	43.4	52.4	196,099	16,119	64.3	...	...	...	...
Ulster, NY	36111	529,205	3.5	41.3	55.1	482,313	18,027	67.2	10,860	87.9	8.4	2.1
Warren, NY	36113	181,155	4.2	43.3	52.4	162,688	15,729	67.0	...	...	...	...
Washington, NY	36115	169,143	4.9	62.0	33.1	148,847	15,118	65.8	3,727	77.8	17.9	3.7
Wayne, NY	36117	284,336	5.2	59.5	35.4	240,460	14,676	63.0	5,120	82.1	9.1	5.2
Westchester, NY	36119	3,530,863	3.2	28.2	68.7	3,204,560	21,510	65.2	53,496	90.5	5.8	2.5
Wyoming, NY	36121	84,314	4.3	67.3	28.4	70,509	14,395	63.3	2,153	77.3	13.8	6.0
Yates, NY	36123	46,234	7.4	53.0	39.6	41,285	14,958	63.9	...	...	...	...

6Bronx, Kings, Queens, and Richmond counties are included with New York county
... Not available

Table C-1. Population, School, and Student Characteristics by County—*Continued*

County	State/County Code	High school graduates, 2006-2008			College enrollment, 2006-2008		College graduates, 2006-2008 (percent)						
		Population 25 years and over	High school diploma or less (percent)	High school diploma or more (percent)	Number	Percent public	Bachelor's degree or more	+/- U.S. percent with Bachelor's degree or more	Non-Hispanic White	Black or African American	American Indian and Alaska Native	Asian, Hawaiian, and Pacific Islander	Hispanic or Latino[3]
		30	31	32	33	34	35	36	37	38	39	40	41
NEW YORK	36000	12,998,952	44.9	84.1	1,480,468	57.2	31.6	4.2	36.5	19.8	15.0	45.0	15.2
Albany, NY	36001	198,595	36.7	90.8	32,477	66.6	37.2	9.8	38.3	19.5	...	71.1	25.0
Allegany, NY	36003	30,680	52.1	87.7	6,241	44.5	18.7	-8.7	17.6	...	...	...	...
Bronx, NY	36005	844,075	60.2	68.6	95,017	56.8	17.2	-10.2	29.7	18.0	7.7	35.0	11.1
Broome, NY	36007	130,363	45.5	88.3	20,258	91.5	25.0	-2.4	24.5	18.4	...	59.0	28.2
Cattaraugus, NY	36009	53,339	54.7	87.7	5,652	47.9	17.6	-9.8	17.8	20.2	6.3	49.9	12.4
Cayuga, NY	36011	55,277	52.2	85.4	3,259	67.1	18.0	-9.4	19.0	1.2	...	...	6.0
Chautauqua, NY	36013	89,155	53.0	85.1	9,433	88.2	18.7	-8.7	19.3	10.5	...	...	5.7
Chemung, NY	36015	59,742	51.0	86.7	6,568	47.9	21.0	-6.4	21.4	12.3	...	...	11.5
Chenango, NY	36017	35,397	54.4	84.0	2,109	69.7	17.1	-10.3	17.3	...	...	...	4.7
Clinton, NY	36019	55,258	52.4	84.1	8,493	92.0	21.8	-5.6	22.5	5.3	...	...	14.4
Columbia, NY	36021	44,271	45.4	87.3	3,264	67.6	27.9	0.5	29.2	7.2	...	31.1	10.9
Cortland, NY	36023	30,004	49.5	88.1	6,478	89.5	24.1	-3.3	23.5	...	...	...	...
Delaware, NY	36025	32,376	54.0	86.8	2,340	88.1	18.5	-8.9	18.0	...	...	...	19.1
Dutchess, NY	36027	193,044	41.2	88.7	26,699	42.6	31.8	4.4	33.1	18.9	...	63.0	20.4
Erie, NY	36029	615,697	42.5	88.1	77,539	74.5	28.4	1.0	30.1	13.0	10.4	73.0	14.9
Essex, NY	36031	27,430	47.9	87.7	1,931	70.6	26.0	-1.4	27.2	...	...	...	...
Franklin, NY	36033	35,175	56.5	83.1	2,237	47.7	17.3	-10.1	18.9	...	16.9	...	4.9
Fulton, NY	36035	38,654	58.2	82.2	2,063	81.2	14.5	-12.9	14.6	...	...	...	10.6
Genesee, NY	36037	39,547	49.1	89.3	2,811	84.2	18.3	-9.1	18.3	17.4	7.0	...	...
Greene, NY	36039	33,929	52.0	85.3	1,947	72.7	19.9	-7.5	20.7	...	...	...	7.5
Hamilton, NY	36041	...	...	...	...	...	...	...	...	...	...	...	...
Herkimer, NY	36043	42,993	51.6	85.7	3,375	76.2	17.7	-9.7	17.6	...	...	...	...
Jefferson, NY	36045	74,824	50.0	88.3	6,941	81.2	18.7	8.7	19.0	11.6	...	...	17.1
Kings, NY	36047	1,640,223	52.7	77.0	180,912	58.7	27.8	0.4	42.2	18.8	21.3	26.9	12.3
Lewis, NY	36049	17,865	61.6	86.1	969	83.1	14.3	-13.1	14.1	...	...	...	...
Livingston, NY	36051	40,514	47.6	87.9	8,396	86.1	22.4	-5.0	23.0	9.7	...	...	13.9
Madison, NY	36053	44,726	47.4	87.7	7,738	48.6	21.3	-6.1	21.3	...	...	...	...
Monroe, NY	36055	478,385	38.5	88.2	67,431	47.7	33.9	6.5	37.3	13.6	29.8	52.8	15.8
Montgomery, NY	36057	33,509	56.2	82.4	2,216	75.0	15.6	-11.8	16.1	...	...	...	10.2
Nassau, NY	36059	910,709	36.8	89.5	105,669	50.9	40.5	13.1	42.8	31.0	33.4	61.9	19.5
New York, NY	36061	1,208,021	29.4	84.2	131,244	35.0	56.4	29.0	79.5	23.6	19.8	53.0	19.7
Niagara, NY	36063	146,203	49.2	87.4	13,981	62.9	19.8	-7.6	20.4	9.0	9.7	34.6	20.0
Oneida, NY	36065	157,744	49.5	85.4	15,375	58.0	20.8	-6.6	22.0	5.8	14.0	34.1	6.9
Onondaga, NY	36067	297,159	39.4	88.9	41,296	41.5	31.9	4.5	33.2	16.0	7.7	56.4	22.1
Ontario, NY	36069	70,432	38.1	90.5	7,612	51.9	29.8	2.4	30.6	7.2	...	34.9	13.4
Orange, NY	36071	234,146	44.7	86.8	28,275	67.3	26.5	-0.9	28.7	17.2	11.0	56.0	14.8
Orleans, NY	36073	28,723	58.2	83.7	1,780	84.6	13.9	-13.5	14.4	3.4	...	...	15.3
Oswego, NY	36075	78,245	56.6	86.2	12,244	88.0	15.5	-11.9	15.3	...	...	...	...
Otsego, NY	36077	39,756	48.6	87.8	8,425	64.7	25.7	-1.7	25.5	...	...	...	...
Putnam, NY	36079	66,836	35.5	93.7	5,411	52.8	38.2	10.8	39.6	31.0	...	70.5	21.4
Queens, NY	36081	1,579,499	50.7	79.6	164,435	64.3	28.3	0.9	34.5	21.0	18.3	39.8	15.8
Rensselaer, NY	36083	103,201	44.0	88.8	13,215	42.9	26.2	-1.2	26.1	18.8	...	70.8	15.3
Richmond, NY	36085	322,336	48.0	87.4	33,559	58.9	27.4	...	28.2	21.7	5.2	44.6	15.8
Rockland, NY	36087	188,012	35.2	88.7	23,052	44.1	40.9	13.5	44.0	29.9	...	62.6	21.6
St. Lawrence, NY	36089	69,301	54.0	85.4	14,370	46.1	18.1	-9.3	18.3	6.4	3.7	...	15.4
Saratoga, NY	36091	148,314	38.4	91.4	12,709	53.4	33.9	6.5	33.9	22.7	...	59.3	32.4
Schenectady, NY	36093	101,761	41.6	89.7	10,866	50.0	30.5	3.1	32.2	9.5	...	52.4	16.8
Schoharie, NY	36095	21,489	56.9	84.9	2,776	93.9	19.0	-8.4	18.9	...	...	...	...
Schuyler, NY	36097	...	...	...	...	...	...	...	...	...	...	...	...
Seneca, NY	36099	23,744	54.0	81.7	1,617	49.1	18.4	-9.0	19.4	...	...	...	7.2
Steuben, NY	36101	66,718	50.7	87.4	4,349	75.8	18.9	-8.5	17.9	25.3	...	...	25.3
Suffolk, NY	36103	1,001,255	42.1	89.1	104,531	65.7	31.3	3.9	33.5	20.4	12.6	55.3	15.2
Sullivan, NY	36105	52,380	50.1	85.4	3,325	60.7	21.1	-6.3	23.2	4.3	...	...	11.7
Tioga, NY	36107	34,451	49.9	87.5	2,613	80.1	22.3	-5.1	22.3	...	...	...	...
Tompkins, NY	36109	57,154	26.5	93.3	30,589	26.2	52.7	25.3	49.5	33.1	...	89.8	57.1
Ulster, NY	36111	124,712	42.5	87.9	13,893	80.3	29.7	2.3	31.3	13.5	...	46.5	15.9
Warren, NY	36113	46,725	44.6	89.2	3,233	63.2	26.2	-1.2	26.2	...	...	...	...
Washington, NY	36115	43,686	54.5	85.9	3,006	78.6	17.4	-10.0	17.7	...	...	...	14.2
Wayne, NY	36117	62,021	48.6	86.3	3,760	73.5	21.2	-6.2	22.2	2.0	...	...	11.8
Westchester, NY	36119	636,639	36.4	87.4	63,970	47.9	44.7	17.3	53.1	25.9	15.1	70.3	18.3
Wyoming, NY	36121	29,470	57.4	84.8	1,447	81.1	14.4	-13.0	15.5	...	...	...	...
Yates, NY	36123	15,938	56.4	82.5	2,109	29.7	20.8	-6.6	21.0	...	...	...	...

[3]May be of any race
... Not available

Table C-1. Population, School, and Student Characteristics by County—*Continued*

County	State/County Code	County Type[1]	Population, 2009 Total	Population, 2009 Percent 5–17 years	Percent of related children 5–17 years in poverty, 2008	Percent of children under 19 years with no health insurance, 2007	Number of Schools and Students, 2008-2009 School Districts	Number of Schools and Students, 2008-2009 Schools	Number of Schools and Students, 2008-2009 Students	Resident enrollment, 2006-2008 K–12 enrollment Number	Resident enrollment, 2006-2008 K–12 enrollment Percent public
			1	2	3	4	5	6	7	8	9
NORTH CAROLINA	37000	X	9,380,884	17.2	18.2	12.3	233	2583	1,488,645	1,580,036	91.0
Alamance, NC	37001	3	150,358	17.5	20.2	12.8	4	38	23,653	25,244	92.5
Alexander, NC	37003	2	36,777	16.6	16.1	12.5	1	10	5,626	6,559	95.8
Alleghany, NC	37005	9	10,964	14.3	25.1	15.2	1	4	1,618	...	...
Anson, NC	37007	1	25,056	16.4	28.9	8.3	1	11	4,046	4,328	100.0
Ashe, NC	37009	9	25,812	14.1	22.8	13.8	2	5	3,533	...	...
Avery, NC	37011	8	17,932	13.5	20.7	18.8	2	10	2,435	...	...
Beaufort, NC	37013	6	46,414	15.9	27.5	10.8	2	15	7,977	7,635	93.4
Bertie, NC	37015	9	19,345	16.5	29.5	9.8	1	8	3,113	...	...
Bladen, NC	37017	6	32,343	17.4	29.9	8.2	1	14	5,380	5,778	94.8
Brunswick, NC	37019	2	107,062	13.0	20.2	14.5	3	18	12,710	15,615	92.2
Buncombe, NC	37021	2	231,452	14.7	17.4	11.5	5	53	30,461	34,797	86.9
Burke, NC	37023	2	89,548	16.6	19.2	10.6	2	31	15,649	15,699	95.1
Cabarrus, NC	37025	1	172,223	19.8	11.6	12.7	3	44	33,600	30,377	93.2
Caldwell, NC	37027	2	79,914	16.7	19.6	8.4	1	26	13,092	13,277	93.2
Camden, NC	37029	8	9,730	20.0	9.5	18.6	1	5	1,907	...	...
Carteret, NC	37031	4	64,423	14.0	17.8	13.8	3	19	8,744	9,012	92.2
Caswell, NC	37033	8	23,004	16.1	21.9	11.5	1	6	3,444	3,816	89.9
Catawba, NC	37035	2	159,125	17.4	19.3	12.1	3	46	25,388	26,683	90.9
Chatham, NC	37037	2	64,772	15.8	14.9	18.9	3	18	8,513	10,244	87.8
Cherokee, NC	37039	9	26,307	14.6	25.5	13.6	2	15	3,889	3,663	94.2
Chowan, NC	37041	7	14,784	16.9	27.2	10.5	1	4	2,448	...	...
Clay, NC	37043	9	10,333	13.8	19.8	16.8	1	3	1,470	...	...
Cleveland, NC	37045	4	99,274	17.9	23.7	9.3	2	29	16,999	17,611	97.9
Columbus, NC	37047	6	54,221	17.8	30.2	8.3	3	26	9,974	9,202	95.4
Craven, NC	37049	5	98,529	15.1	21.6	15.1	1	24	14,809	16,228	91.4
Cumberland, NC	37051	2	315,207	18.0	20.8	11.1	3	102	54,501	61,968	91.1
Currituck, NC	37053	1	24,216	18.3	13.5	18.8	1	10	4,054	4,324	91.8
Dare, NC	37055	5	34,296	14.3	13.8	18.1	1	11	4,931	5,128	98.5
Davidson, NC	37057	4	158,582	17.6	17.8	11.5	3	43	26,799	27,707	93.1
Davie, NC	37059	2	41,420	17.9	12.8	15.6	1	12	6,655	7,344	92.0
Duplin, NC	37061	6	53,177	18.1	28.2	16.0	1	16	8,967	9,849	95.1
Durham, NC	37063	2	269,706	15.4	16.5	12.7	12	60	35,586	4,116	86.8
Edgecombe, NC	37065	3	51,853	19.0	32.9	6.8	1	15	8,067	10,290	94.1
Forsyth, NC	37067	2	359,638	17.4	19.0	11.5	7	83	54,881	57,884	90.9
Franklin, NC	37069	2	60,088	17.6	17.6	14.1	2	16	8,635	10,096	92.1
Gaston, NC	37071	1	208,958	17.4	18.7	9.1	3	57	33,677	35,262	90.9
Gates, NC	37073	8	11,768	18.8	18.1	16.8	1	5	2,004	...	...
Graham, NC	37075	9	8,001	15.3	29.0	16.4	1	3	1,231	...	...
Granville, NC	37077	6	57,639	16.9	13.9	11.7	1	21	9,295	10,855	92.0
Greene, NC	37079	3	20,658	16.4	25.4	17.0	1	5	3,343	3,545	89.2
Guilford, NC	37081	2	480,362	17.0	17.6	11.1	6	125	74,627	78,354	90.6
Halifax, NC	37083	4	54,582	17.1	30.4	8.4	4	27	8,952	10,498	93.0
Harnett, NC	37085	4	115,761	19.6	18.6	15.0	2	27	18,961	21,920	93.9
Haywood, NC	37087	2	57,109	14.8	20.4	10.9	1	16	7,962	8,102	89.5
Henderson, NC	37089	2	103,669	14.8	18.3	16.1	2	23	13,525	15,197	91.0
Hertford, NC	37091	7	23,283	15.5	26.9	9.0	1	7	3,351	3,976	92.0
Hoke, NC	37093	2	45,148	19.5	24.6	12.2	1	13	7,941	8,738	89.8
Hyde, NC	37095	9	5,211	12.5	27.1	12.1	1	5	657	...	...
Iredell, NC	37097	4	158,153	19.0	12.9	13.6	6	47	28,799	27,497	92.2
Jackson, NC	37099	6	36,891	13.0	20.7	12.9	2	10	3,898	4,468	97.2
Johnston, NC	37101	2	168,525	19.9	15.2	16.6	2	43	31,723	30,137	95.9
Jones, NC	37103	8	10,071	16.0	23.0	14.2	1	6	1,436	...	...
Lee, NC	37105	4	60,477	18.3	19.6	16.4	2	16	9,948	11,061	95.7
Lenoir, NC	37107	4	56,387	18.0	25.4	9.2	3	22	9,877	9,933	95.6
Lincoln, NC	37109	4	76,043	18.0	17.0	14.7	2	25	13,382	13,228	97.0
McDowell, NC	37111	6	43,988	15.9	19.6	10.4	1	12	6,583	6,906	96.7
Macon, NC	37113	7	33,233	14.0	21.8	16.7	1	11	4,435	4,272	92.7
Madison, NC	37115	2	20,442	15.3	21.9	12.4	1	6	2,635	2,876	85.3
Martin, NC	37117	6	23,337	16.8	30.2	8.7	1	12	3,993	4,245	96.2
Mecklenburg, NC	37119	1	913,639	17.9	13.0	12.7	13	179	139,864	157,266	85.1
Mitchell, NC	37121	9	15,634	14.9	23.5	12.4	1	8	2,154	...	...
Montgomery, NC	37123	6	27,745	17.4	25.6	14.8	1	11	4,545	5,073	89.9
Moore, NC	37125	4	87,158	16.0	16.3	13.0	3	24	12,809	13,721	93.1
Nash, NC	37127	3	94,743	17.8	18.8	11.0	2	29	19,016	17,052	93.0
New Hanover, NC	37129	2	195,085	14.1	17.3	10.6	3	41	24,582	28,648	90.0
Northampton, NC	37131	9	20,136	15.4	35.6	10.8	2	12	3,997	3,463	86.6
Onslow, NC	37133	3	173,064	14.5	18.8	18.2	1	34	24,021	28,734	90.9
Orange, NC	37135	2	129,083	15.0	11.1	13.1	4	33	19,062	16,779	87.5
Pamlico, NC	37137	9	12,422	13.0	24.6	16.1	2	5	1,832	...	...

[1]County type codes are from the Economic Research Service of the United States Department of Agriculture. See notes and definitions for more information.
... Not available

Table C-1. Population, School, and Student Characteristics by County—*Continued*

County	State/County Code	Characteristics of students, 2008-2009				Number of graduates, 2006-2007	Staff and students, 2008-2009			
		Percent with IEP[2]	Percent eligible for free or reduced lunch	Percent minority	Percent English Language Learners		Total staff	Number of teachers	Student/teacher ratio	Central admin. Staff
		10	11	12	13	14	15	16	17	18
NORTH CAROLINA	37000	12.6	33.9	45.6	7.6	76,005	199,835	101,656	14.6	6,788
Alamance, NC	37001	13.2	43.9	44.2	12.1	1,310	2,981	1,618	14.6	76
Alexander, NC	37003	13.6	42.8	15.5	5.1	358	785	351	16.0	30
Alleghany, NC	37005	14.8	55.5	16.1	8.9	97	279	135	12.0	16
Anson, NC	37007	17.3	68.3	66.6	2.3	221	577	284	14.2	29
Ashe, NC	37009	14.9	37.4	8.1	3.9	254	553	256	13.8	19
Avery, NC	37011	12.9	53.5	9.0	5.1	171	394	189	12.9	20
Beaufort, NC	37013	14.3	54.4	47.0	5.5	368	996	527	15.1	42
Bertie, NC	37015	12.6	...	88.6	1.0	209	479	215	14.5	29
Bladen, NC	37017	11.5	66.0	58.1	5.3	271	803	374	14.4	32
Brunswick, NC	37019	10.8	50.6	31.0	4.4	637	1,680	821	15.5	70
Buncombe, NC	37021	13.1	41.7	23.9	7.0	1,669	4,381	2,069	14.7	143
Burke, NC	37023	15.7	48.1	24.3	7.6	763	2,031	1,055	14.8	66
Cabarrus, NC	37025	13.3	35.7	37.3	8.6	1,529	4,396	2,355	14.3	125
Caldwell, NC	37027	10.6	49.1	16.2	3.5	722	1,789	900	14.5	50
Camden, NC	37029	12.7	26.3	19.0	0.5	89	295	135	14.1	20
Carteret, NC	37031	14.6	35.4	16.4	2.1	510	1,198	688	12.7	34
Caswell, NC	37033	12.2	57.2	47.4	1.8	173	488	229	15.0	24
Catawba, NC	37035	11.8	44.0	33.2	11.5	1,487	3,250	1,665	15.2	114
Chatham, NC	37037	14.1	38.0	41.5	16.5	472	1,253	640	13.3	60
Cherokee, NC	37039	13.1	57.2	8.4	0.3	182	586	289	13.5	19
Chowan, NC	37041	13.6	55.1	48.5	1.4	159	391	173	14.2	29
Clay, NC	37043	13.1	50.6	4.5	1.0	92	206	105	14.0	11
Cleveland, NC	37045	12.2	51.7	34.0	1.8	982	2,358	1,183	14.4	86
Columbus, NC	37047	10.5	16.6	50.1	3.4	549	1,290	635	15.7	53
Craven, NC	37049	10.7	48.5	44.2	4.2	788	1,895	1,001	14.8	61
Cumberland, NC	37051	13.5	51.5	63.3	2.4	3,009	7,617	3,746	14.5	204
Currituck, NC	37053	10.7	31.1	13.5	0.8	214	593	271	15.0	34
Dare, NC	37055	11.1	27.6	14.7	5.2	340	782	405	12.2	37
Davidson, NC	37057	11.1	18.2	24.7	5.6	1,375	3,364	1,673	16.0	110
Davie, NC	37059	12.4	26.1	20.1	4.5	318	917	453	14.7	35
Duplin, NC	37061	10.2	62.7	60.0	20.0	445	1,254	621	14.4	43
Durham, NC	37063	13.0	44.6	77.1	14.7	1,675	4,840	2,540	14.0	193
Edgecombe, NC	37065	10.2	54.8	69.6	3.7	408	1,000	468	17.2	38
Forsyth, NC	37067	12.6	45.3	55.0	12.8	2,754	7,459	4,007	13.7	184
Franklin, NC	37069	9.9	44.8	47.4	5.7	388	1,094	585	14.8	38
Gaston, NC	37071	11.0	8.4	31.8	5.0	1,814	4,058	2,057	16.4	136
Gates, NC	37073	17.2	43.7	40.9	0.6	149	352	155	12.9	18
Graham, NC	37075	12.4	57.2	16.2	0.6	80	211	90	13.7	12
Granville, NC	37077	9.3	45.4	47.2	6.0	410	1,158	593	15.7	44
Greene, NC	37079	13.8	...	67.4	16.5	167	515	239	14.0	25
Guilford, NC	37081	14.1	45.7	60.0	8.2	4,238	10,533	5,187	14.4	339
Halifax, NC	37083	11.0	68.9	72.1	1.3	336	1,295	618	14.5	65
Harnett, NC	37085	13.2	49.8	46.5	7.5	858	2,411	1,297	14.6	52
Haywood, NC	37087	15.0	...	8.3	2.3	475	1,131	568	14.0	40
Henderson, NC	37089	11.9	44.1	25.7	10.7	761	1,761	929	14.6	68
Hertford, NC	37091	15.8	23.2	84.8	1.2	205	540	240	14.0	27
Hoke, NC	37093	12.8	61.9	71.1	7.5	278	1,096	536	14.8	49
Hyde, NC	37095	15.2	54.6	51.1	7.0	42	153	73	9.0	16
Iredell, NC	37097	11.5	32.9	27.1	4.2	1,410	3,498	1,832	15.7	106
Jackson, NC	37099	15.8	41.4	21.9	3.7	201	553	274	14.2	26
Johnston, NC	37101	15.2	...	38.8	9.6	1,310	4,085	2,219	14.3	96
Jones, NC	37103	13.1	...	59.6	0.8	76	236	107	13.4	16
Lee, NC	37105	10.7	56.0	54.2	16.2	471	1,311	650	15.3	48
Lenoir, NC	37107	13.3	54.8	60.1	5.1	511	1,250	643	15.4	43
Lincoln, NC	37109	12.5	38.6	18.8	4.6	753	1,618	872	15.3	58
McDowell, NC	37111	13.9	52.1	15.0	7.3	352	936	466	14.1	37
Macon, NC	37113	16.6	48.9	13.7	7.8	229	653	321	13.8	29
Madison, NC	37115	15.1	52.3	4.5	1.5	166	363	192	13.7	18
Martin, NC	37117	12.8	57.2	55.4	0.9	244	646	310	12.9	20
Mecklenburg, NC	37119	10.9	44.9	65.4	13.0	5,987	18,692	9,567	14.6	680
Mitchell, NC	37121	15.8	53.9	6.7	3.9	121	375	168	12.8	18
Montgomery, NC	37123	12.6	59.3	50.5	17.9	255	702	321	14.2	23
Moore, NC	37125	12.0	38.6	34.4	5.2	712	1,748	848	15.1	64
Nash, NC	37127	11.0	6.7	63.3	4.6	1,053	2,433	1,212	15.7	55
New Hanover, NC	37129	12.1	37.2	36.1	4.3	1,388	3,620	1,674	14.7	139
Northampton, NC	37131	9.4	75.8	83.8	1.2	202	533	256	15.6	23
Onslow, NC	37133	11.2	37.0	39.2	1.5	1,204	3,256	1,565	15.3	91
Orange, NC	37135	11.1	24.4	39.0	8.2	1,160	2,951	1,519	12.5	121
Pamlico, NC	37137	17.4	44.1	30.6	2.2	124	281	144	12.7	20

[2]IEP= Individual Education Program. See notes and definitions for more information
... Not available

Table C-1.   Population, School, and Student Characteristics by County—*Continued*

County	State/County Code	Revenues, 2007-2008 Total revenue ($1,000's)	Percentage of revenue from Federal gov't	State gov't	Local gov't	Current expenditures, 2007-2008 Amount ($1,000's)	Amount per student	Percent for instruction	Resident population 16 to 19 years, 2006-2008 Total population 16 to 19 years	Percent enrolled in school	Percent high school graduates, not enrolled in school	Percent not enrolled, not grads, not employed or not in labor force
		19	20	21	22	23	24	25	26	27	28	29
NORTH CAROLINA	37000	13,882,032	9.0	58.9	32.0	11,671,831	8,100	63.1	50,4173	82.2	10.2	4.9
Alamance, NC	37001	190,397	8.4	65.7	25.8	171,920	7,286	65.0	8,402	84.8	9.0	4.8
Alexander, NC	37003	47,403	8.2	70.1	21.7	40,842	7,282	61.9	...	...	...	...
Alleghany, NC	37005	18,335	11.4	64.9	23.7	15,951	10,140	58.6	...	...	...	...
Anson, NC	37007	41,328	15.0	68.6	16.4	37,142	9,339	58.1	...	...	...	...
Ashe, NC	37009	35,441	11.1	62.8	26.1	28,913	8,949	61.1	...	...	...	...
Avery, NC	37011	28,049	9.5	59.6	30.9	23,265	9,989	58.6	...	...	...	...
Beaufort, NC	37013	72,890	11.7	63.9	24.4	61,535	8,347	62.5	...	...	...	...
Bertie, NC	37015	34,121	18.6	65.5	15.9	27,805	9,250	54.6	...	...	...	...
Bladen, NC	37017	53,037	17.0	64.9	18.1	45,630	8,682	60.5	...	...	...	...
Brunswick, NC	37019	128,516	7.6	54.6	37.8	102,975	8,323	60.7	...	...	...	...
Buncombe, NC.....................	37021	298,764	8.8	56.5	34.8	251,168	8,387	62.0	11,052	82.2	9.4	4.4
Burke, NC	37023	123,365	12.0	65.2	22.8	111,643	7,926	62.5	5,433	80.3	7.1	9.3
Cabarrus, NC	37025	299,119	7.1	55.9	37.0	241,114	7,419	64.7	7,869	78.3	13.9	4.3
Caldwell, NC	37027	110,921	10.0	68.0	21.9	98,457	7,596	66.2	4,181	84.0	5.6	9.6
Camden, NC	37029	18,027	4.3	76.0	19.7	16,519	8,736	59.3	...	...	...	...
Carteret, NC	37031	89,728	7.0	54.9	38.1	74,230	8,823	64.6	...	...	...	...
Caswell, NC	37033	31,581	9.8	73.6	16.5	28,071	8,892	63.3	...	...	...	...
Catawba, NC	37035	226,357	7.8	60.5	31.7	189,911	7,756	65.6	7,926	85.9	8.3	2.5
Chatham, NC	37037	88,024	7.3	51.1	41.7	73,577	9,216	61.8	...	...	...	...
Cherokee, NC......................	37039	38,719	10.1	65.9	24.1	33,104	8,835	59.9	...	...	...	...
Chowan, NC	37041	26,767	9.8	66.1	24.1	23,228	9,626	61.3	...	...	...	...
Clay, NC	37043	14,088	7.2	77.4	15.4	12,392	9,172	66.9	...	...	...	...
Cleveland, NC	37045	147,736	10.5	67.4	22.1	134,806	8,085	63.7	6,077	84.9	9.1	4.5
Columbus, NC......................	37047	87,242	13.3	73.1	13.6	77,053	8,181	61.0	...	...	...	...
Craven, NC	37049	139,834	11.5	57.9	30.7	110,777	7,626	63.3	4,654	64.7	21.6	6.0
Cumberland, NC	37051	459,970	13.2	62.9	23.9	402,488	7,653	62.3	19,645	78.6	12.7	5.6
Currituck, NC	37053	40,416	5.8	59.8	34.4	34,740	8,633	59.1	...	...	...	...
Dare, NC	37055	74,723	3.4	37.3	59.3	50,514	10,652	59.0	...	...	...	...
Davidson, NC.......................	37057	226,428	9.1	62.7	28.2	188,792	7,214	63.9	8,058	77.7	12.4	5.8
Davie, NC	37059	59,988	6.7	61.1	32.1	50,341	7,534	63.2	...	...	...	...
Duplin, NC...........................	37061	78,005	12.8	70.6	16.7	71,264	8,047	62.3	...	...	...	...
Durham, NC	37063	368,953	8.7	52.8	38.5	311,303	9,018	60.9	13,851	85.3	5.9	7.0
Edgecombe, NC	37065	64,587	11.9	71.1	16.9	56,654	7,698	59.7	2,961	73.6	14.8	3.7
Forsyth, NC	37067	521,453	8.9	58.7	32.4	458,414	8,664	66.0	18,575	87.4	6.8	3.1
Franklin, NC	37069	79,179	10.2	62.1	27.7	67,088	7,794	62.6	...	...	...	...
Gaston, NC..........................	37071	268,363	10.4	64.3	25.3	235,967	7,147	63.8	10,131	73.6	9.8	10.1
Gates, NC............................	37073	21,968	8.0	69.1	22.9	18,717	9,530	58.6	...	...	...	...
Graham, NC	37075	13,958	12.3	73.4	14.4	11,960	10,179	55.3	...	...	...	...
Granville, NC.......................	37077	73,490	8.8	69.7	21.5	66,906	7,599	61.7	...	...	...	...
Greene, NC	37079	32,372	14.3	72.9	12.8	30,124	9,165	59.9	...	...	...	...
Guilford, NC	37081	724,425	9.3	53.7	37.0	616,169	8,530	61.5	28,318	87.5	6.9	4.4
Halifax, NC	37083	88,279	14.5	66.5	19.1	78,900	9,231	58.4	3,253	73.1	18.4	7.7
Harnett, NC	37085	168,320	9.6	62.7	27.7	137,341	7,482	66.6	7,145	84.3	10.1	4.3
Haywood, NC	37087	77,929	8.7	57.4	34.0	65,292	8,393	61.3	...	...	...	...
Henderson, NC....................	37089	116,448	8.7	61.3	30.0	99,931	7,650	66.3	...	...	...	...
Hertford, NC	37091	36,480	13.9	68.5	17.6	31,960	9,907	59.6	...	...	...	...
Hoke, NC.............................	37093	65,598	13.6	71.5	14.9	60,493	8,149	61.2	...	...	...	...
Hyde, NC	37095	11,062	10.6	70.1	19.4	10,011	15,865	53.2	...	...	...	...
Iredell, NC	37097	253,123	6.9	58.9	34.1	215,364	7,616	64.4	7,616	85.6	11.6	2.4
Jackson, NC	37099	40,094	9.2	58.9	32.0	33,802	8,905	63.3	...	...	...	...
Johnston, NC.......................	37101	288,264	7.5	60.7	31.8	232,894	7,671	66.8	7,667	80.8	7.6	7.8
Jones, NC	37103	15,025	12.4	74.2	13.5	13,754	11,182	55.7	...	...	...	...
Lee, NC	37105	85,437	9.5	63.3	27.1	73,983	7,789	64.7	3,375	78.8	11.3	7.2
Lenoir, NC	37107	88,965	12.7	70.5	16.8	85,182	8,512	63.6	...	...	...	...
Lincoln, NC	37109	115,851	6.7	60.5	32.8	96,001	7,363	62.1	...	...	...	...
McDowell, NC	37111	56,378	10.1	69.2	20.7	51,711	7,908	63.2	...	...	...	...
Macon, NC	37113	39,152	10.0	65.9	24.1	36,051	8,345	60.7	...	...	...	...
Madison, NC........................	37115	25,770	13.2	68.9	17.9	22,748	8,831	59.0	...	...	...	...
Martin, NC...........................	37117	41,648	14.9	66.2	18.9	38,366	9,522	60.5	...	...	...	...
Mecklenburg, NC.................	37119	1,383,444	7.8	51.4	40.8	109,9556	8,135	62.6	45,631	84.5	9.5	3.4
Mitchell, NC	37121	21,076	8.2	75.3	16.5	19,339	8,974	59.2	...	...	...	...
Montgomery, NC	37123	43,287	12.3	65.0	22.6	39,424	8,861	63.4	...	...	...	...
Moore, NC	37125	116,900	7.7	59.2	33.2	99,003	7,786	63.8	...	...	...	...
Nash, NC.............................	37127	158,840	11.8	68.2	20.0	146,690	7,901	62.5	...	...	...	...
New Hanover, NC	37129	248,535	8.4	53.1	38.5	218,173	9,039	58.9	10,482	89.5	5.2	3.8
Northampton, NC	37131	37,214	12.2	67.0	20.8	33,230	10,051	60.0	...	...	...	...
Onslow, NC	37133	202,887	11.7	60.9	27.4	173,282	7,446	63.2	11,813	38.9	57.3	1.8
Orange, NC	37135	232,975	4.2	43.7	52.1	188,881	9,922	64.7	...	...	...	...
Pamlico, NC	37137	22,055	9.1	69.3	21.7	18,586	10,195	58.7	...	...	...	...

... Not available

Table C-1. Population, School, and Student Characteristics by County—*Continued*

County	State/County Code	High school graduates, 2006-2008 Population 25 years and over	High school diploma or less (percent)	High school diploma or more (percent)	College enrollment, 2006-2008 Number	Percent public	College graduates, 2006-2008 (percent) Bachelor's degree or more	+/- U.S. percent with Bachelor's degree or more	Non-His-panic White	Black or African Ameri-can	Ameri-can Indian and Alaska Native	Asian, Hawai-ian, and Pacific Islander	His-panic or Latino[3]
		30	31	32	33	34	35	36	37	38	39	40	41
NORTH CAROLINA	37000	5,964,892	46.0	82.9	605,708	78.3	25.6	-1.8	28.8	16.0	10.8	50.3	11.6
Alamance, NC	37001	96,050	51.2	79.8	9,430	53.7	19.8	-7.6	23.8	8.6	...	53.6	4.1
Alexander, NC	37003	24,725	62.9	74.5	1,593	69.4	13.2	-14.2	13.4	...	...	...	...
Alleghany, NC	37005	...	...	...	...	...	...	...	...	...	...	...	...
Anson, NC	37007	17,317	67.8	79.4	863	83.4	7.5	-19.9	11.6	2.9	...	...	...
Ashe, NC	37009	18,840	59.3	74.0	...	...	14.8	-12.6	15.3	...	...	...	...
Avery, NC	37011	...	...	...	...	...	...	...	...	...	...	...	...
Beaufort, NC	37013	31,841	55.7	82.5	2,117	89.8	18.4	-9.0	23.5	4.9	...	...	12.1
Bertie, NC	37015	...	...	...	...	...	...	...	...	...	...	...	...
Bladen, NC	37017	21,720	56.7	75.9	2,113	76.6	10.5	-16.9	14.1	5.0	2.1	...	...
Brunswick, NC	37019	70,123	50.4	83.3	2,667	75.7	20.2	-7.2	22.0	7.4	...	...	9.3
Buncombe, NC	37021	158,436	39.5	86.9	13,024	76.2	31.6	4.2	33.4	14.0	...	41.3	10.4
Burke, NC	37023	61,464	58.4	75.5	4,845	86.6	14.4	-13.0	14.9	15.0	...	13.0	4.7
Cabarrus, NC	37025	105,490	44.8	84.6	8,256	82.4	22.5	-4.9	23.5	19.0	...	48.0	10.8
Caldwell, NC	37027	55,990	60.9	71.8	4,462	85.7	12.0	-15.4	12.5	6.0	...	...	8.2
Camden, NC	37029	...	...	...	...	...	...	...	...	...	...	...	...
Carteret, NC	37031	46,147	44.0	87.1	2,468	86.1	23.3	-4.1	25.2	6.1	...	...	4.8
Caswell, NC	37033	16,838	63.4	77.2	1,386	92.5	9.4	-18.0	11.0	6.9	...	...	...
Catawba, NC	37035	105,840	53.2	79.6	7,681	71.7	19.0	-8.4	20.7	11.4	...	19.7	6.6
Chatham, NC	37037	42,541	43.6	83.5	3,190	92.7	33.2	5.8	39.4	10.6	...	...	9.0
Cherokee, NC	37039	19,614	53.1	79.8	805	87.1	15.3	-12.1	15.8	...	...	...	...
Chowan, NC	37041	...	...	...	...	...	...	...	...	...	...	...	...
Clay, NC	37043	...	...	...	...	...	...	...	...	...	...	...	...
Cleveland, NC	37045	66,671	56.1	77.7	6,294	67.9	14.9	-12.5	16.7	7.7	...	...	2.5
Columbus, NC	37047	36,321	55.4	76.9	2,106	89.8	11.8	-15.6	14.7	6.0	7.6	...	9.8
Craven, NC	37049	61,782	39.9	88.1	4,825	87.1	21.1	-6.3	24.9	9.4	...	27.6	9.8
Cumberland, NC	37051	185,586	40.1	88.8	25,106	82.6	21.6	-5.8	23.4	19.0	9.4	28.4	16.9
Currituck, NC	37053	16,306	50.9	82.4	1,429	81.7	16.5	-10.9	16.8	15.0	...	...	...
Dare, NC	37055	24,427	37.7	93.4	972	59.7	31.4	4.0	32.5	...	...	...	19.4
Davidson, NC	37057	107,810	58.0	77.6	6,500	83.7	15.2	-12.2	16.4	8.8	...	12.5	4.5
Davie, NC	37059	27,634	48.4	84.0	1,841	72.4	22.0	-5.4	22.6	24.7	...	...	7.2
Duplin, NC	37061	34,830	64.0	66.0	2,519	85.6	9.2	-18.2	12.4	6.7	...	...	2.7
Durham, NC	37063	165,278	34.5	85.8	27,669	51.5	42.3	14.9	55.0	28.3	...	79.6	12.3
Edgecombe, NC	37065	34,865	65.9	73.3	2,416	87.2	10.2	-17.2	14.8	6.7	...	...	...
Forsyth, NC	37067	222,830	42.4	86.1	25,800	55.8	31.0	3.6	35.9	22.0	17.2	61.1	11.6
Franklin, NC	37069	37,891	58.9	80.1	3,189	48.4	13.9	-13.5	15.9	10.3	...	...	4.8
Gaston, NC	37071	137,431	52.8	77.8	9,182	78.6	17.9	-9.5	18.6	12.4	7.2	45.9	13.0
Gates, NC	37073	...	...	...	...	...	...	...	...	...	...	...	...
Graham, NC	37075	...	...	...	...	...	...	...	...	...	...	...	...
Granville, NC	37077	36,595	54.5	80.1	2,889	87.9	13.2	-14.2	16.2	8.9	...	...	7.9
Greene, NC	37079	14,185	61.0	70.7	1,668	93.3	6.4	-21.0	10.6	2.6	...	...	...
Guilford, NC	37081	304,097	40.6	86.2	40,642	81.5	32.1	4.7	38.2	21.8	7.9	35.6	11.9
Halifax, NC	37083	37,246	63.2	72.6	2,189	81.1	11.7	-15.7	14.9	8.7	7.1	...	...
Harnett, NC	37085	68,717	52.0	79.9	8,488	55.2	15.2	-12.2	16.8	10.9	7.5	23.0	9.1
Haywood, NC	37087	41,389	48.5	82.4	2,217	76.0	18.7	-8.7	19.2	...	...	...	...
Henderson, NC	37089	71,830	41.2	87.1	3,782	88.2	26.9	-0.5	28.3	11.4	...	33.6	11.2
Hertford, NC	37091	15,234	58.7	74.2	1,756	70.2	15.0	-12.4	18.4	12.2	...	...	...
Hoke, NC	37093	24,850	52.1	79.4	3,121	86.7	14.3	-13.1	16.3	16.3	2.6	...	6.7
Hyde, NC	37095	...	...	...	...	...	...	...	...	...	...	...	...
Iredell, NC	37097	100,591	48.0	84.5	7,367	76.5	21.2	-6.2	22.3	9.4	...	43.1	25.3
Jackson, NC	37099	23,316	45.9	84.2	6,688	97.6	24.8	-2.6	26.2	...	9.5	...	...
Johnston, NC	37101	102,142	50.8	79.2	7,219	79.0	18.3	-9.1	20.1	14.4	...	31.1	7.6
Jones, NC	37103	...	...	...	...	...	...	...	...	...	...	...	...
Lee, NC	37105	37,769	53.3	77.7	2,450	81.5	15.7	-11.7	19.9	6.9	...	...	2.7
Lenoir, NC	37107	38,651	55.8	74.3	3,042	91.8	13.5	-13.9	18.0	7.5	...	...	3.2
Lincoln, NC	37109	49,700	55.2	75.2	3,531	83.1	16.8	-10.6	18.2	5.5	...	...	8.1
McDowell, NC	37111	30,701	58.6	78.2	1,805	94.3	12.6	-14.8	12.9	2.4	...	...	...
Macon, NC	37113	23,788	52.2	80.7	1,281	90.6	19.4	-8.0	19.8	...	...	...	...
Madison, NC	37115	14,022	55.7	78.2	1,922	50.1	21.3	-6.1	21.9	...	...	...	...
Martin, NC	37117	16,251	58.3	77.6	1,187	88.0	12.5	-14.9	14.3	10.0	...	...	...
Mecklenburg, NC	37119	556,852	31.8	88.9	56,247	76.2	40.4	13.0	51.0	23.4	18.7	50.2	16.0
Mitchell, NC	37121	...	...	...	...	...	...	...	...	...	...	...	...
Montgomery, NC	37123	17,886	60.5	72.8	1,201	79.4	13.6	-13.8	16.0	10.8	...	...	...
Moore, NC	37125	58,925	42.3	87.5	4,727	77.7	27.2	-0.2	30.6	8.3	...	...	19.1
Nash, NC	37127	61,899	53.5	81.9	5,556	81.4	18.9	-8.5	24.0	10.7	...	34.9	5.6
New Hanover, NC	37129	127,670	33.7	88.3	17,846	91.5	36.3	8.9	41.3	11.0	...	46.1	14.6
Northampton, NC	37131	14,152	67.8	68.7	1,203	83.8	13.4	-14.0	15.9	11.4	...	...	...
Onslow, NC	37133	85,066	43.3	88.1	8,429	86.2	17.5	-9.9	17.9	17.2	...	22.0	12.5
Orange, NC	37135	76,320	26.9	89.6	24,829	92.8	55.4	28.0	61.2	26.5	...	70.6	26.6
Pamlico, NC	37137	...	...	...	...	...	...	...	...	...	...	...	...

[3]May be of any race
... Not available

Table C-1. Population, School, and Student Characteristics by County—*Continued*

County	State/ County Code	County Type[1]	Population, 2009		Percent of related children 5-17 years in poverty, 2008	Percent of children under 19 years with no health insurance, 2007	Number of Schools and Students, 2008-2009			Resident enrollment, 2006-2008 K–12 enrollment	
			Total	Percent 5–17 years			School Districts	Schools	Students	Number	Percent public
			1	2	3	4	5	6	7	8	9
Pasquotank, NC	37139	7	41,578	16.3	22.7	12.5	1	12	6,383	7,252	94.3
Pender, NC	37141	2	52,378	16.3	18.9	16.2	1	16	8,256	8,668	97.3
Perquimans, NC	37143	9	12,734	14.4	28.4	14.2	1	4	1,768	...	...
Person, NC	37145	2	37,667	16.8	16.9	9.4	3	12	6,100	6,620	90.7
Pitt, NC	37147	3	159,057	16.0	22.3	10.4	1	37	23,487	25,692	88.0
Polk, NC	37149	8	19,255	14.2	16.6	14.4	1	7	2,620	...	...
Randolph, NC	37151	2	142,151	17.9	18.7	12.7	2	39	23,930	25,208	92.7
Richmond, NC	37153	4	45,970	17.6	28.3	8.5	1	20	7,895	8,570	91.8
Robeson, NC	37155	4	129,559	19.4	39.1	8.9	2	44	24,723	25,890	97.2
Rockingham, NC	37157	2	92,252	16.7	20.3	9.7	2	27	14,530	15,388	96.3
Rowan, NC	37159	4	140,798	17.0	19.6	11.5	1	35	21,125	23,157	94.2
Rutherford, NC	37161	4	63,415	16.9	19.9	8.8	2	19	10,491	11,402	89.3
Sampson, NC	37163	6	63,713	19.0	28.2	12.4	2	24	11,724	11,810	97.7
Scotland, NC	37165	6	36,292	18.2	34.1	7.8	1	22	6,981	7,454	96.8
Stanly, NC	37167	6	59,794	17.1	16.7	11.6	2	25	9,918	10,308	93.0
Stokes, NC	37169	2	46,150	16.9	16.9	10.4	1	18	7,431	7,794	93.5
Surry, NC	37171	4	72,496	17.4	20.3	12.4	3	22	11,038	12,537	94.0
Swain, NC	37173	8	13,404	16.3	23.1	16.8	3	9	2,142	...	...
Transylvania, NC	37175	6	30,203	14.0	20.4	13.0	3	10	3,936	4,386	84.8
Tyrrell, NC	37177	9	4,078	12.9	37.5	17.5	1	3	624	...	...
Union, NC	37179	1	198,645	22.2	10.3	15.2	2	53	39,431	36,317	88.2
Vance, NC	37181	4	43,056	18.5	30.4	9.0	2	17	8,490	8,065	89.1
Wake, NC	37183	2	897,214	18.6	10.3	11.8	20	206	144,709	149,883	87.6
Warren, NC	37185	8	19,425	14.4	29.2	12.9	1	8	2,752	...	...
Washington, NC	37187	7	12,851	17.9	34.6	8.8	1	5	2,093	...	...
Watauga, NC	37189	6	45,479	9.9	14.5	14.5	2	10	4,663	4,599	90.5
Wayne, NC	37191	3	113,811	18.0	24.2	11.0	2	34	19,779	20,881	93.0
Wilkes, NC	37193	6	66,555	16.3	25.2	10.3	3	26	11,805	10,799	94.5
Wilson, NC	37195	4	78,353	17.7	24.6	10.0	3	26	13,476	14,226	94.3
Yadkin, NC	37197	2	37,713	17.0	16.4	14.7	1	14	6,202	6,623	96.8
Yancey, NC	37199	8	18,548	14.8	24.1	14.3	1	9	2,472	...	...
NORTH DAKOTA	38000	X	646,844	15.5	11.9	8.1	229	529	94,728	101,436	92.0
Adams, ND	38001	9	2,236	13.6	12.0	9.1	1	2	281	...	...
Barnes, ND	38003	6	10,753	15.2	9.4	8.1	4	11	1,395	...	...
Benson, ND	38005	9	6,910	22.7	34.8	8.8	6	9	831	...	...
Billings, ND	38007	9	827	13.4	16.8	14.6	1	2	42	...	...
Bottineau, ND	38009	9	6,352	14.1	11.5	14.8	4	7	872	...	...
Bowman, ND	38011	9	3,028	15.8	10.9	13.1	2	5	572	...	...
Burke, ND	38013	9	1,839	14.2	11.4	15.0	3	6	250	...	...
Burleigh, ND	38015	3	79,822	15.5	8.7	6.0	11	33	11,133	12,467	87.7
Cass, ND	38017	3	143,339	14.7	8.0	6.5	11	50	19,588	20,853	90.9
Cavalier, ND	38019	9	3,699	15.1	13.9	15.0	2	5	487	...	...
Dickey, ND	38021	9	5,217	15.6	13.7	11.1	2	5	849	...	...
Divide, ND	38023	9	1,961	13.1	14.6	17.1	2	3	229	...	...
Dunn, ND	38025	9	3,365	17.7	15.7	10.3	3	5	441	...	...
Eddy, ND	38027	9	2,288	15.4	13.5	10.9	2	3	357	...	...
Emmons, ND	38029	8	3,398	16.6	17.9	8.3	5	8	629	...	...
Foster, ND	38031	9	3,259	16.2	8.6	12.6	1	2	576	...	...
Golden Valley, ND	38033	9	1,621	19.9	17.9	17.2	2	3	307	...	...
Grand Forks, ND	38035	3	66,414	13.2	11.9	7.4	10	33	8,601	9,513	92.9
Grant, ND	38037	8	2,337	14.5	29.0	7.7	2	3	264	...	...
Griggs, ND	38039	9	2,346	13.0	10.6	15.3	2	4	392	...	...
Hettinger, ND	38041	9	2,343	13.2	13.5	12.5	3	6	364	...	...
Kidder, ND	38043	8	2,201	15.6	21.5	8.3	2	5	402	...	...
La Moure, ND	38045	9	3,908	15.5	13.4	15.4	5	11	755	...	...
Logan, ND	38047	9	1,886	14.8	16.9	12.5	3	5	320	...	...
McHenry, ND	38049	9	5,173	16.6	17.0	8.1	4	10	888	...	...
McIntosh, ND	38051	9	2,582	12.0	16.4	8.5	3	6	377	...	...
McKenzie, ND	38053	9	5,799	18.4	17.7	12.9	4	7	778	...	...
McLean, ND	38055	8	8,310	14.9	14.2	10.8	7	14	1,475	...	...
Mercer, ND	38057	6	7,873	16.2	6.5	8.2	3	7	1,355	...	...
Morton, ND	38059	3	26,464	17.2	11.3	6.9	12	24	4,092	4,587	87.6
Mountrail, ND	38061	9	6,791	19.4	18.9	15.5	3	7	1,396	...	...
Nelson, ND	38063	8	3,129	13.6	12.7	13.0	2	4	470	...	...
Oliver, ND	38065	8	1,643	15.2	14.2	9.8	1	3	210	...	...
Pembina, ND	38067	9	7,392	15.4	9.5	11.9	5	12	1,109	...	...
Pierce, ND	38069	7	3,990	16.1	14.1	7.9	2	4	613	...	...
Ramsey, ND	38071	7	11,240	16.3	15.3	6.8	6	12	1,857	...	...
Ransom, ND	38073	8	5,500	17.4	9.7	10.8	3	6	983	...	...
Renville, ND	38075	9	2,227	16.0	8.5	17.1	2	5	582	...	...

[1]County type codes are from the Economic Research Service of the United States Department of Agriculture. See notes and definitions for more information.
... Not available

Table C-1. Population, School, and Student Characteristics by County—*Continued*

County	State/County Code	Characteristics of students, 2008-2009				Number of graduates, 2006-2007	Staff and students, 2008-2009			
		Percent with IEP[2]	Percent eligible for free or reduced lunch	Percent minority	Percent English Language Learners		Total staff	Number of teachers	Student/ teacher ratio	Central admin. Staff
		10	11	12	13	14	15	16	17	18
Pasquotank, NC	37139	13.7	51.4	52.5	1.4	322	917	459	13.9	36
Pender, NC	37141	11.6	49.7	32.3	5.9	420	1,036	554	14.9	42
Perquimans, NC	37143	12.2	...	35.8	0.9	113	319	133	13.3	18
Person, NC	37145	14.8	42.3	41.6	3.6	313	791	422	14.5	23
Pitt, NC	37147	12.3	...	60.7	4.7	1,088	3,170	1,633	14.4	81
Polk, NC	37149	14.5	48.8	20.0	4.7	152	425	199	13.2	33
Randolph, NC	37151	10.6	44.1	26.7	10.5	1,209	3,156	1,584	15.1	101
Richmond, NC	37153	11.5	66.3	53.8	4.0	418	1,199	548	14.4	36
Robeson, NC	37155	16.4	...	82.8	5.9	1,098	3,263	1,557	15.9	74
Rockingham, NC	37157	13.9	35.3	34.6	5.1	751	1,907	997	14.6	60
Rowan, NC	37159	12.4	3.1	35.0	7.4	1,251	2,867	1,438	14.7	91
Rutherford, NC	37161	13.1	52.4	21.6	2.8	560	1,493	720	14.6	47
Sampson, NC	37163	11.1	18.7	56.6	13.7	559	1,539	782	15.0	47
Scotland, NC	37165	14.2	65.0	65.7	1.2	362	1,153	554	12.6	44
Stanly, NC	37167	15.9	46.1	25.4	5.4	686	1,362	731	13.6	37
Stokes, NC	37169	15.6	37.4	10.1	1.9	438	994	498	14.9	27
Surry, NC	37171	14.4	49.6	22.5	9.7	686	1,455	754	14.6	49
Swain, NC	37173	17.3	...	23.6	1.4	99	326	158	13.6	18
Transylvania, NC	37175	11.5	45.0	14.1	1.7	229	557	295	13.3	19
Tyrrell, NC	37177	13.0	67.6	54.8	9.0	55	143	53	11.8	13
Union, NC	37179	9.8	...	30.2	5.0	1,829	5,264	2,672	14.8	158
Vance, NC	37181	12.3	...	72.3	6.1	432	1,142	573	14.8	50
Wake, NC	37183	13.7	0.3	47.7	9.9	6,985	17,442	9,636	15.0	577
Warren, NC	37185	15.0	71.2	82.7	2.6	171	450	194	14.2	25
Washington, NC	37187	15.1	71.2	78.2	2.1	125	370	175	12.0	19
Watauga, NC	37189	16.3	31.1	8.4	2.9	303	683	361	12.9	31
Wayne, NC	37191	14.1	51.3	55.8	7.6	1,053	2,682	1,368	14.5	64
Wilkes, NC	37193	12.0	55.3	16.1	6.3	510	1,610	773	15.3	72
Wilson, NC	37195	9.2	56.5	64.5	7.0	543	1,644	854	15.8	58
Yadkin, NC	37197	14.7	42.9	22.6	9.8	349	837	403	15.4	27
Yancey, NC	37199	15.2	2.5	11.2	7.0	166	437	175	14.1	19
NORTH DAKOTA	38000	14.0	31.6	14.7	3.7	7,098	15,629	8,179	11.6	620
Adams, ND	38001	12.1	27.8	4.6	...	32	52	28	10.0	4
Barnes, ND	38003	15.3	37.7	4.0	0.1	121	284	168	8.3	10
Benson, ND	38005	21.8	67.1	65.9	...	72	175	84	9.9	9
Billings, ND	38007	16.7	26.2	...	...	...	24	12	3.5	3
Bottineau, ND	38009	14.2	35.9	7.0	...	79	174	83	10.5	9
Bowman, ND	38011	10.8	21.9	5.4	2.6	61	95	57	10.0	5
Burke, ND	38013	21.2	25.2	4.8	0.4	23	70	41	6.1	4
Burleigh, ND	38015	12.3	23.2	10.9	2.0	749	1,468	781	14.3	34
Cass, ND	38017	12.4	24.1	12.5	6.5	1,320	2,693	1,445	13.6	81
Cavalier, ND	38019	14.2	34.1	3.9	...	60	77	45	10.8	4
Dickey, ND	38021	9.4	26.4	7.3	4.2	53	110	65	13.1	7
Divide, ND	38023	10.5	28.4	1.7	...	20	49	26	8.8	2
Dunn, ND	38025	12.2	32.9	23.1	3.2	34	108	57	7.7	6
Eddy, ND	38027	15.1	32.5	11.2	...	31	60	31	11.5	5
Emmons, ND	38029	9.1	39.4	0.8	...	54	110	54	11.6	6
Foster, ND	38031	10.4	26.9	3.3	0.3	45	68	40	14.4	2
Golden Valley, ND	38033	14.0	42.0	7.8	0.3	19	78	33	9.3	3
Grand Forks, ND	38035	15.6	33.5	14.8	3.6	663	1,445	745	11.5	47
Grant, ND	38037	20.8	47.0	5.3	...	29	62	31	8.5	4
Griggs, ND	38039	15.6	43.9	2.1	...	32	68	38	10.3	4
Hettinger, ND	38041	8.2	30.5	2.7	...	44	80	39	9.3	4
Kidder, ND	38043	13.9	40.3	8.2	0.2	30	72	41	9.8	3
La Moure, ND	38045	13.0	42.8	3.9	5.2	74	159	91	8.3	10
Logan, ND	38047	10.0	31.3	3.4	...	33	61	37	8.6	5
McHenry, ND	38049	14.1	44.7	2.4	0.1	90	169	95	9.3	8
McIntosh, ND	38051	9.5	32.9	3.7	1.3	36	80	47	8.0	4
McKenzie, ND	38053	8.4	31.2	28.0	0.4	59	165	77	10.1	11
McLean, ND	38055	12.7	35.9	14.7	2.6	125	300	157	9.4	15
Mercer, ND	38057	13.9	17.4	6.1	0.2	123	211	102	13.3	9
Morton, ND	38059	14.7	30.2	10.0	0.3	312	670	326	12.6	28
Mountrail, ND	38061	15.9	50.2	63.0	0.4	83	237	117	11.9	11
Nelson, ND	38063	19.6	40.4	5.1	0.6	41	97	55	8.5	3
Oliver, ND	38065	11.4	23.3	6.2	...	24	43	25	8.4	3
Pembina, ND	38067	17.9	35.6	13.9	6.3	94	211	121	9.2	10
Pierce, ND	38069	12.9	34.4	6.7	0.3	49	94	56	10.9	4
Ramsey, ND	38071	18.5	40.8	26.2	0.1	151	389	175	10.6	24
Ransom, ND	38073	17.7	34.5	3.4	0.2	75	134	76	12.9	6
Renville, ND	38075	16.2	31.4	6.2	...	43	96	56	10.4	5

[2]IEP= Individual Education Program. See notes and definitions for more information
... Not available

Table C-1. Population, School, and Student Characteristics by County—*Continued*

County	State/County Code	Revenues, 2007-2008				Current expenditures, 2007-2008			Resident population 16 to 19 years, 2006-2008			
		Total revenue ($1,000's)	Percentage of revenue from			Amount ($1,000's)	Amount per student	Percent for instruction	Total population 16 to 19 years	Percent enrolled in school	Percent high school graduates, not enrolled in school	Percent not enrolled, not grads, not employed or not in labor force
			Federal gov't	State gov't	Local gov't							
	19		20	21	22	23	24	25	26	27	28	29
Pasquotank, NC	37139	61,532	11.7	60.2	28.1	53,337	8,764	63.0	...	...	...	...
Pender, NC	37141	72,645	8.7	60.1	31.1	59,661	7,548	60.8	...	...	...	...
Perquimans, NC	37143	19,439	14.3	66.8	18.9	17,184	9,962	56.3	...	...	...	...
Person, NC	37145	51,993	8.6	68.5	22.9	47,708	7,757	65.9	...	...	...	...
Pitt, NC	37147	201,755	10.0	64.4	25.6	180,392	7,986	65.3	11,712	92.3	2.6	2.5
Polk, NC	37149	28,023	7.6	58.9	33.5	24,614	10,055	58.9	...	...	...	...
Randolph, NC	37151	194,313	8.9	65.4	25.8	172,655	7,411	64.4	6,845	76.4	11.3	10.2
Richmond, NC	37153	71,293	10.9	73.4	15.7	67,324	8,538	63.7	...	...	...	...
Robeson, NC	37155	223,631	17.2	72.6	10.3	199,664	8,413	64.0	7,975	77.9	7.3	11.4
Rockingham, NC	37157	125,995	10.8	66.6	22.6	113,421	7,958	62.2	4,209	77.9	9.6	7.6
Rowan, NC	37159	192,248	9.9	61.4	28.7	163,010	7,882	62.9	7,271	76.2	11.9	7.9
Rutherford, NC	37161	86,370	10.1	65.8	24.0	76,938	8,099	62.1	...	...	...	...
Sampson, NC	37163	137,997	8.9	44.7	46.5	88,929	7,864	62.8	3,578	80.3	8.7	5.3
Scotland, NC	37165	73,760	16.4	63.8	19.8	65,092	9,594	61.2	...	...	...	...
Stanly, NC	37167	84,785	9.3	69.8	21.0	76,864	7,952	65.3	...	...	...	...
Stokes, NC	37169	63,930	8.5	67.3	24.2	57,826	7,987	61.6	...	...	...	...
Surry, NC	37171	115,859	10.7	62.5	26.8	97,521	8,170	62.9	...	...	...	...
Swain, NC	37173	21,941	18.0	67.8	14.2	19,493	9,612	57.0	...	...	...	...
Transylvania, NC	37175	36,620	9.9	60.1	30.1	33,831	8,602	64.1	...	...	...	...
Tyrrell, NC	37177	9,243	10.8	78.3	10.9	8,144	14,213	52.9	...	...	...	...
Union, NC	37179	482,007	3.8	39.4	56.8	283,491	7,561	63.8	10,303	82.4	11.1	4.4
Vance, NC	37181	76,549	13.2	69.8	17.1	70,847	8,760	64.5	...	...	...	...
Wake, NC	37183	1,304,595	5.4	55.0	39.6	1,075,437	7,739	64.7	45,987	90.8	4.6	3.1
Warren, NC	37185	30,545	13.7	68.3	18.0	26,857	9,962	60.1	...	...	...	...
Washington, NC	37187	24,188	19.3	68.8	11.8	21,458	10,483	62.4	...	...	...	...
Watauga, NC	37189	54,148	5.2	50.4	44.4	42,669	9,176	63.6	...	...	...	...
Wayne, NC	37191	166,059	12.3	71.5	16.2	154,634	8,036	68.0	6,395	84.1	12.0	2.4
Wilkes, NC	37193	92,729	9.8	63.8	26.4	79,439	7,810	60.5	3,015	65.4	22.9	5.4
Wilson, NC	37195	116,292	12.3	61.8	25.9	100,170	7,591	63.3	4,387	81.7	8.1	5.6
Yadkin, NC	37197	57,521	7.9	63.2	28.9	47,591	7,824	62.5	...	...	...	...
Yancey, NC	37199	24,924	11.0	70.6	18.3	22,213	9,134	59.8	...	...	...	...
NORTH DAKOTA	38000	1,104,803	13.2	34.7	52.1	918,739	9,675	60.1	39,906	85.6	10.1	3.2
Adams, ND	38001	3,390	5.4	37.7	56.8	2,852	9,200	56.1	...	...	...	...
Barnes, ND	38003	16,957	8.4	37.3	54.2	15,583	11,292	63.7	...	...	...	...
Benson, ND	38005	12,793	44.8	33.3	21.9	10,881	13,400	64.2	...	...	...	...
Billings, ND	38007	2,440	15.5	4.6	79.9	1,618	35,174	44.5	...	...	...	...
Bottineau, ND	38009	11,759	16.1	30.3	53.6	10,673	12,691	54.7	...	...	...	...
Bowman, ND	38011	7,175	4.9	34.1	60.9	5,827	9,843	61.5	...	...	...	...
Burke, ND	38013	4,033	5.4	28.4	66.2	3,452	14,090	61.1	...	...	...	...
Burleigh, ND	38015	108,111	11.0	36.5	52.5	92,834	8,438	65.1	...	...	...	...
Cass, ND	38017	213,221	6.6	30.4	63.0	174,147	9,052	62.3	...	...	...	...
Cavalier, ND	38019	5,994	6.0	30.6	63.4	5,346	10,068	48.7	...	...	...	...
Dickey, ND	38021	8,156	5.6	38.7	55.7	6,300	7,351	50.8	...	...	...	...
Divide, ND	38023	3,633	10.4	32.5	57.1	3,140	13,362	50.4	...	...	...	...
Dunn, ND	38025	7,075	24.6	26.8	48.6	6,197	14,378	52.8	...	...	...	...
Eddy, ND	38027	4,871	15.2	37.8	47.0	4,021	10,232	56.0	...	...	...	...
Emmons, ND	38029	6,730	9.5	40.8	49.7	6,036	9,767	54.4	...	...	...	...
Foster, ND	38031	5,716	5.8	41.1	53.1	4,531	7,719	60.4	...	...	...	...
Golden Valley, ND	38033	4,768	13.7	33.3	53.0	4,087	12,975	57.6	...	...	...	...
Grand Forks, ND	38035	104,717	13.6	31.1	55.4	80,697	9,161	62.3	...	...	...	...
Grant, ND	38037	3,761	10.8	38.3	50.9	3,120	10,909	49.5	...	...	...	...
Griggs, ND	38039	5,276	6.8	32.9	60.2	4,560	11,176	52.9	...	...	...	...
Hettinger, ND	38041	6,209	7.2	34.1	58.6	4,589	11,797	49.5	...	...	...	...
Kidder, ND	38043	5,080	10.8	31.5	57.7	3,978	9,970	54.6	...	...	...	...
La Moure, ND	38045	10,989	8.8	31.5	59.8	9,492	11,850	52.6	...	...	...	...
Logan, ND	38047	4,527	13.1	39.0	47.9	3,751	11,401	53.8	...	...	...	...
McHenry, ND	38049	10,555	10.2	36.0	53.8	9,277	10,206	59.1	...	...	...	...
McIntosh, ND	38051	5,004	7.4	36.6	56.1	4,411	11,000	56.3	...	...	...	...
McKenzie, ND	38053	12,318	34.6	25.2	40.3	12,176	15,937	48.0	...	...	...	...
McLean, ND	38055	16,271	7.7	39.4	52.9	14,704	9,969	53.6	...	...	...	...
Mercer, ND	38057	14,937	6.0	39.3	54.7	13,066	9,629	53.1	...	...	...	...
Morton, ND	38059	41,210	9.5	42.9	47.6	35,096	8,685	58.7	...	...	...	...
Mountrail, ND	38061	16,207	27.3	34.5	38.2	13,007	9,304	55.1	...	...	...	...
Nelson, ND	38063	5,984	7.8	34.0	58.2	5,157	10,439	56.2	...	...	...	...
Oliver, ND	38065	3,163	4.4	37.1	58.6	2,883	12,165	57.3	...	...	...	...
Pembina, ND	38067	14,645	8.1	32.5	59.5	11,958	10,091	57.5	...	...	...	...
Pierce, ND	38069	5,834	6.7	38.7	54.5	5,244	8,311	57.1	...	...	...	...
Ramsey, ND	38071	23,771	12.9	44.5	42.6	19,949	10,583	55.2	...	...	...	...
Ransom, ND	38073	9,676	4.3	41.4	54.4	7,835	7,742	52.1	...	...	...	...
Renville, ND	38075	7,297	10.9	35.5	53.6	5,919	10,188	57.5	...	...	...	...

... Not available

Table C-1. Population, School, and Student Characteristics by County—*Continued*

County	State/County Code	High school graduates, 2006-2008			College enrollment, 2006-2008		College graduates, 2006-2008 (percent)						
		Population 25 years and over	High school diploma or less (percent)	High school diploma or more (percent)	Number	Percent public	Bachelor's degree or more	+/- U.S. percent with Bachelor's degree or more	Non-Hispanic White	Black or African American	American Indian and Alaska Native	Asian, Hawaiian, and Pacific Islander	Hispanic or Latino[3]
		30	31	32	33	34	35	36	37	38	39	40	41
Pasquotank, NC	37139	25,404	49.5	80.7	3,676	89.0	18.3	-9.1	19.6	15.5	...	...	...
Pender, NC	37141	34,554	57.2	81.1	2,203	67.7	16.2	-11.2	18.9	7.6	...	...	2.3
Perquimans, NC	37143	...	...	...	...	...	...	...	...	...	...	...	...
Person, NC	37145	25,688	58.9	80.8	2,751	88.5	14.5	-12.9	15.1	10.8	...	...	...
Pitt, NC	37147	91,055	41.3	85.8	23,801	93.2	29.0	1.6	36.8	13.1	...	...	20.7
Polk, NC	37149	...	...	...	...	...	...	...	...	...	...	...	...
Randolph, NC	37151	95,328	60.8	74.6	4,880	84.4	12.4	-15.0	12.8	14.5	...	26.8	5.3
Richmond, NC	37153	29,940	61.7	75.4	2,161	88.5	10.8	-16.6	12.2	8.4	...	...	1.1
Robeson, NC	37155	79,564	65.1	68.6	7,606	95.4	12.5	-14.9	18.2	9.1	10.5	57.2	3.5
Rockingham, NC	37157	65,220	61.2	74.9	3,506	88.8	11.5	-15.9	13.1	5.0	...	...	4.1
Rowan, NC	37159	92,888	56.7	78.0	7,675	60.4	15.9	-11.5	16.6	13.0	...	...	8.6
Rutherford, NC	37161	43,660	55.1	79.9	2,885	89.4	14.5	-12.9	15.3	5.5	...	...	12.6
Sampson, NC	37163	41,794	62.4	74.0	3,747	85.0	11.2	-16.2	15.1	6.4	7.4	...	2.6
Scotland, NC	37165	23,249	58.1	76.8	2,294	50.1	15.0	-12.4	20.3	7.7	8.0	...	...
Stanly, NC	37167	39,874	57.4	80.8	3,474	67.0	15.1	-12.3	16.1	10.6	...	...	3.1
Stokes, NC	37169	32,420	65.9	75.6	1,864	82.2	9.4	-18.0	8.9	22.8	...	...	...
Surry, NC	37171	50,419	58.9	73.4	2,991	95.9	12.9	-14.5	13.9	7.0	...	...	4.2
Swain, NC	37173	...	...	...	...	...	...	...	...	...	...	...	...
Transylvania, NC	37175	21,682	44.1	87.0	1,483	71.5	28.1	0.7	29.4	...	...	...	...
Tyrrell, NC	37177	...	...	...	...	...	...	...	...	...	...	...	...
Union, NC	37179	115,449	44.1	84.5	8,814	72.7	26.8	-0.6	28.2	19.6	...	52.1	19.1
Vance, NC	37181	27,889	62.7	72.7	1,782	90.0	11.4	-16.0	17.0	6.5	...	...	0.6
Wake, NC	37183	529,932	27.2	91.1	69,863	76.6	47.0	19.6	54.3	26.9	23.3	66.6	18.0
Warren, NC	37185	...	...	...	...	...	...	...	...	...	...	...	...
Washington, NC	37187	...	...	...	...	...	...	...	...	...	...	...	...
Watauga, NC	37189	25,313	38.1	84.6	12,826	98.9	35.3	7.9	35.4	...	...	...	...
Wayne, NC	37191	73,922	52.1	80.7	7,048	70.3	15.8	-11.6	18.8	10.1	...	31.5	7.2
Wilkes, NC	37193	47,032	63.0	69.9	2,306	88.2	11.0	-16.4	11.3	2.6	...	...	...
Wilson, NC	37195	50,895	56.5	76.3	5,097	70.1	17.6	-9.8	23.6	8.8	...	...	12.4
Yadkin, NC	37197	26,163	64.6	75.7	1,310	91.2	10.2	-17.2	11.0	1.7	...	...	1.4
Yancey, NC	37199	...	...	...	...	...	...	...	...	...	...	...	...
NORTH DAKOTA	38000	413,437	39.8	89.0	56,357	87.9	26.1	-1.3	26.6	14.9	14.0	58.1	13.8
Adams, ND	38001	...	...	...	...	...	...	...	...	...	...	...	...
Barnes, ND	38003	...	...	...	...	...	...	...	...	...	...	...	...
Benson, ND	38005	...	...	...	...	...	...	...	...	...	...	...	...
Billings, ND	38007	...	...	...	...	...	...	...	...	...	...	...	...
Bottineau, ND	38009	...	...	...	...	...	...	...	...	...	...	...	...
Bowman, ND	38011	...	...	...	...	...	...	...	...	...	...	...	...
Burke, ND	38013	...	...	...	...	...	...	...	...	...	...	...	...
Burleigh, ND	38015	50,751	32.9	91.3	6,240	62.7	31.4	4.0	31.6	...	17.4	...	...
Cass, ND	38017	85,150	29.4	94.0	17,625	93.1	36.0	8.6	36.5	11.0	30.2	68.7	11.2
Cavalier, ND	38019	...	...	...	...	...	...	...	...	...	...	...	...
Dickey, ND	38021	...	...	...	...	...	...	...	...	...	...	...	...
Divide, ND	38023	...	...	...	...	...	...	...	...	...	...	...	...
Dunn, ND	38025	...	...	...	...	...	...	...	...	...	...	...	...
Eddy, ND	38027	...	...	...	...	...	...	...	...	...	...	...	...
Emmons, ND	38029	...	...	...	...	...	...	...	...	...	...	...	...
Foster, ND	38031	...	...	...	...	...	...	...	...	...	...	...	...
Golden Valley, ND	38033	...	...	...	...	...	...	...	...	...	...	...	...
Grand Forks, ND	38035	37,336	32.3	91.8	13,282	96.0	34.9	7.5	35.5	...	...	...	9.3
Grant, ND	38037	...	...	...	...	...	...	...	...	...	...	...	...
Griggs, ND	38039	...	...	...	...	...	...	...	...	...	...	...	...
Hettinger, ND	38041	...	...	...	...	...	...	...	...	...	...	...	...
Kidder, ND	38043	...	...	...	...	...	...	...	...	...	...	...	...
La Moure, ND	38045	...	...	...	...	...	...	...	...	...	...	...	...
Logan, ND	38047	...	...	...	...	...	...	...	...	...	...	...	...
McHenry, ND	38049	...	...	...	...	...	...	...	...	...	...	...	...
McIntosh, ND	38051	...	...	...	...	...	...	...	...	...	...	...	...
McKenzie, ND	38053	...	...	...	...	...	...	...	...	...	...	...	...
McLean, ND	38055	...	...	...	...	...	...	...	...	...	...	...	...
Mercer, ND	38057	...	...	...	...	...	...	...	...	...	...	...	...
Morton, ND	38059	17,175	48.5	86.2	1,198	74.4	21.8	-5.6	21.9	...	...	...	...
Mountrail, ND	38061	...	...	...	...	...	...	...	...	...	...	...	...
Nelson, ND	38063	...	...	...	...	...	...	...	...	...	...	...	...
Oliver, ND	38065	...	...	...	...	...	...	...	...	...	...	...	...
Pembina, ND	38067	...	...	...	...	...	...	...	...	...	...	...	...
Pierce, ND	38069	...	...	...	...	...	...	...	...	...	...	...	...
Ramsey, ND	38071	...	...	...	...	...	...	...	...	...	...	...	...
Ransom, ND	38073	...	...	...	...	...	...	...	...	...	...	...	...
Renville, ND	38075	...	...	...	...	...	...	...	...	...	...	...	...

[3]May be of any race
... Not available

Table C-1. Population, School, and Student Characteristics by County—*Continued*

County	State/County Code	County Type[1]	Population, 2009 Total	Population, 2009 Percent 5–17 years	Percent of related children 5–17 years in poverty, 2008	Percent of children under 19 years with no health insurance, 2007	Number of Schools and Students, 2008-2009 School Districts	Number of Schools and Students, 2008-2009 Schools	Number of Schools and Students, 2008-2009 Students	Resident enrollment, 2006-2008 K–12 enrollment Number	Resident enrollment, 2006-2008 K–12 enrollment Percent public
			1	2	3	4	5	6	7	8	9
Richland, ND	38077	6	16,067	16.7	8.1	8.1	9	17	2,375	...	...
Rolette, ND	38079	9	13,797	23.2	31.2	12.1	7	14	2,912	...	...
Sargent, ND	38081	9	3,951	17.6	6.1	11.4	3	7	743	...	...
Sheridan, ND	38083	9	1,228	12.0	22.1	8.8	2	4	138	...	...
Sioux, ND	38085	8	4,203	23.6	50.7	5.9	4	6	358	...	...
Slope, ND	38087	9	649	12.8	9.0	9.5	2	2	14	...	...
Stark, ND	38089	7	22,847	15.4	10.7	7.1	6	17	3,210	3,636	82.6
Steele, ND	38091	8	1,747	16.5	9.2	16.0	2	3	278	...	...
Stutsman, ND	38093	7	20,463	14.7	11.5	6.5	7	18	2,649	3,015	93.2
Towner, ND	38095	9	2,209	14.4	11.2	12.5	2	4	307	...	...
Traill, ND	38097	8	7,868	16.2	7.5	12.2	5	10	1,401	...	...
Walsh, ND	38099	6	10,798	16.3	11.9	9.1	10	17	1,937	...	...
Ward, ND	38101	5	57,012	15.6	10.7	7.4	11	36	8,554	9,761	88.8
Wells, ND	38103	9	4,092	14.1	11.4	12.3	4	6	572	...	...
Williams, ND	38105	7	20,451	16.5	11.3	9.7	7	19	3,119	...	...
OHIO	39000	X	11,542,645	17.1	16.2	7.1	1,068	3,968	1,817,163	2,021,878	86.9
Adams, OH	39001	6	28,043	17.8	29.6	6.5	2	10	5,026	4,919	94.9
Allen, OH	39003	3	104,357	17.7	18.8	7.0	15	41	16,235	18,349	87.1
Ashland, OH	39005	4	55,044	17.8	14.3	9.2	8	25	10,172	8,461	80.0
Ashtabula, OH	39007	4	100,767	17.4	21.1	7.2	9	39	16,262	17,920	92.0
Athens, OH	39009	4	63,026	11.7	27.2	8.6	7	21	8,119	7,776	98.7
Auglaize, OH	39011	4	46,699	18.0	8.2	7.8	7	19	8,358	8,771	94.3
Belmont, OH	39013	3	68,066	14.6	19.9	7.1	9	26	9,028	9,747	90.4
Brown, OH	39015	1	44,003	18.1	17.9	7.1	7	17	8,209	8,357	96.7
Butler, OH	39017	1	363,184	17.7	12.1	7.5	17	93	60,315	63,285	88.5
Carroll, OH	39019	2	28,539	17.3	18.3	9.0	3	13	3,920	4,687	91.2
Champaign, OH	39021	6	39,713	18.7	14.3	8.0	8	18	8,098	7,327	96.2
Clark, OH	39023	3	139,671	17.1	20.0	6.0	12	49	22,855	24,273	90.4
Clermont, OH	39025	1	196,364	18.4	9.3	7.0	11	47	28,717	36,146	85.8
Clinton, OH	39027	6	43,058	17.8	13.5	6.5	5	16	8,494	7,726	94.8
Columbiana, OH	39029	4	107,722	16.0	18.1	7.0	15	39	16,986	18,129	95.0
Coshocton, OH	39031	6	35,767	17.5	17.1	8.0	5	15	5,533	6,638	94.2
Crawford, OH	39033	4	43,403	17.2	16.7	7.4	6	23	7,515	7,443	92.2
Cuyahoga, OH	39035	1	1,275,709	16.8	21.2	4.9	95	373	186,508	231,283	79.8
Darke, OH	39037	6	51,814	17.8	11.8	8.9	9	24	9,153	9,305	91.6
Defiance, OH	39039	4	38,432	17.4	11.9	7.9	5	19	6,828	6,783	92.5
Delaware, OH	39041	1	168,708	20.3	4.4	6.1	6	43	24,543	31,542	86.1
Erie, OH	39043	3	76,963	16.4	14.0	7.4	9	31	12,983	12,905	90.3
Fairfield, OH	39045	1	143,712	19.1	9.3	6.9	12	46	25,236	25,824	90.1
Fayette, OH	39047	6	28,117	17.3	17.8	6.2	2	17	4,823	4,941	97.8
Franklin, OH	39049	1	1,150,122	16.4	16.8	8.0	84	402	191,780	199,261	89.0
Fulton, OH	39051	2	42,402	18.9	9.0	8.4	8	23	8,554	8,209	93.8
Gallia, OH	39053	6	30,694	16.5	28.6	5.7	4	13	4,838	5,515	93.5
Geauga, OH	39055	1	99,060	19.5	7.9	13.5	8	27	12,606	16,822	81.4
Greene, OH	39057	2	159,823	15.9	11.3	6.4	11	37	23,251	25,437	84.1
Guernsey, OH	39059	6	40,054	17.8	23.2	7.5	4	15	5,794	7,407	95.2
Hamilton, OH	39061	1	855,062	16.8	18.3	7.4	52	226	115,959	154,020	77.8
Hancock, OH	39063	4	74,538	17.0	10.4	8.0	12	45	14,750	12,640	91.9
Hardin, OH	39065	6	31,818	16.1	16.3	8.0	6	16	4,721	5,192	96.7
Harrison, OH	39067	6	15,268	15.9	21.1	8.1	1	6	1,859	...	...
Henry, OH	39069	6	28,648	18.7	10.8	10.0	5	15	4,993	5,305	88.2
Highland, OH	39071	6	42,178	18.3	19.0	7.4	5	19	8,041	7,846	96.8
Hocking, OH	39073	6	28,912	17.4	19.6	7.5	1	9	4,117	5,013	93.9
Holmes, OH	39075	7	41,854	24.0	16.5	16.7	2	17	4,487	7,879	71.0
Huron, OH	39077	4	59,849	19.5	17.3	8.6	8	34	12,458	11,641	92.3
Jackson, OH	39079	7	33,440	17.4	27.0	6.3	4	12	5,608	5,670	97.7
Jefferson, OH	39081	3	67,691	14.9	21.5	6.3	7	29	10,148	10,119	85.5
Knox, OH	39083	4	59,637	17.5	16.5	8.6	7	21	8,661	9,498	91.1
Lake, OH	39085	1	236,775	16.5	10.3	7.2	12	62	34,339	39,249	87.8
Lawrence, OH	39087	2	62,744	16.5	24.1	6.2	9	24	10,655	10,689	96.9
Licking, OH	39089	1	158,488	17.9	12.1	7.4	16	58	27,350	27,521	90.6
Logan, OH	39091	4	46,582	18.1	13.8	7.7	6	15	7,328	8,564	94.6
Lorain, OH	39093	1	305,707	17.8	15.0	6.8	28	111	48,288	54,240	87.1
Lucas, OH	39095	2	463,493	17.1	22.8	5.3	49	162	73,734	81,359	82.3
Madison, OH	39097	1	42,539	16.7	12.8	8.1	7	18	7,318	7,196	86.0
Mahoning, OH	39099	2	236,735	16.3	22.4	5.8	32	89	36,781	40,390	88.8
Marion, OH	39101	4	65,655	16.3	20.9	6.3	11	27	12,327	11,573	94.1
Medina, OH	39103	1	174,035	19.0	5.8	8.4	10	43	29,196	31,644	88.2
Meigs, OH	39105	6	22,838	16.2	26.9	7.7	3	8	3,618	3,515	89.8
Mercer, OH	39107	7	40,666	19.3	7.3	9.9	7	22	8,746	7,891	95.4

[1]County type codes are from the Economic Research Service of the United States Department of Agriculture. See notes and definitions for more information.
... Not available

Table C-1. Population, School, and Student Characteristics by County—*Continued*

County	State/County Code	Characteristics of students, 2008-2009				Number of graduates, 2006-2007	Staff and students, 2008-2009			
		Percent with IEP[2]	Percent eligible for free or reduced lunch	Percent minority	Percent English Language Learners		Total staff	Number of teachers	Student/ teacher ratio	Central admin. Staff
		10	11	12	13	14	15	16	17	18
Richland, ND	38077	18.5	29.9	8.7	1.3	182	488	238	10.0	20
Rolette, ND	38079	7.8	69.2	87.0	32.3	165	662	330	8.8	36
Sargent, ND	38081	18.7	33.0	2.7	5.5	62	114	70	10.6	5
Sheridan, ND	38083	13.8	48.6	2.9	...	14	46	24	5.8	2
Sioux, ND	38085	17.3	73.7	98.0	45.3	9	123	63	5.7	8
Slope, ND	38087	28.6	...	...	...	...	7	3	4.7	1
Stark, ND	38089	14.6	29.9	4.6	...	292	483	249	12.9	22
Steele, ND	38091	12.9	25.2	1.4	...	39	47	30	9.3	2
Stutsman, ND	38093	14.4	36.6	4.8	0.4	229	456	248	10.7	18
Towner, ND	38095	10.7	33.2	9.8	0.7	28	59	34	9.0	6
Traill, ND	38097	13.8	25.4	8.6	1.2	134	213	117	12.0	10
Walsh, ND	38099	15.9	38.9	19.5	11.3	147	377	206	9.4	21
Ward, ND	38101	15.2	30.8	10.7	0.2	535	1,378	684	12.5	30
Wells, ND	38103	16.6	32.3	3.3	0.3	83	112	50	11.4	8
Williams, ND	38105	17.2	29.6	13.9	1.3	196	512	268	11.6	21
OHIO	39000	14.6	36.4	20.7	2.0	117,649	244,723	112,844	16.1	16,274
Adams, OH	39001	17.2	52.9	0.7	...	349	664	313	16.1	24
Allen, OH	39003	13.6	44.0	18.4	0.4	1,070	2,173	1,081	15.0	166
Ashland, OH	39005	14.0	35.5	2.7	0.1	749	1,266	645	15.8	52
Ashtabula, OH	39007	16.5	50.0	7.6	2.0	1,099	2,170	1050	15.5	88
Athens, OH	39009	18.7	43.8	4.1	0.6	547	1,407	594	13.7	118
Auglaize, OH	39011	14.7	25.4	1.6	0.4	661	1,088	538	15.5	67
Belmont, OH	39013	15.7	38.8	3.2	...	698	1,255	628	14.4	64
Brown, OH	39015	12.8	40.9	1.2	...	489	1,058	484	17.0	60
Butler, OH	39017	13.1	30.6	15.7	3.5	3,609	7,217	3,410	17.7	395
Carroll, OH	39019	16.6	38.3	1.0	...	289	449	217	18.1	40
Champaign, OH	39021	17.2	33.4	3.1	0.1	517	1,105	555	14.6	83
Clark, OH	39023	12.5	44.7	13.5	1.1	1,430	2,795	1,344	17.0	132
Clermont, OH	39025	14.3	28.1	2.8	0.5	1,909	3,275	1,633	17.6	156
Clinton, OH	39027	13.4	36.3	3.7	0.5	567	1,076	490	17.3	89
Columbiana, OH	39029	16.5	43.4	3.1	...	1,170	2,064	1,086	15.6	138
Coshocton, OH	39031	20.2	46.4	2.1	...	458	743	370	15.0	55
Crawford, OH	39033	18.7	43.3	2.0	0.5	498	982	465	16.2	47
Cuyahoga, OH	39035	15.8	40.6	49.4	3.0	11,141	27,954	12,076	15.4	1,864
Darke, OH	39037	13.3	24.8	1.7	0.4	664	1,118	567	16.1	72
Defiance, OH	39039	15.8	29.8	10.8	0.2	475	837	431	15.8	51
Delaware, OH	39041	11.5	13.5	11.9	1.7	1,265	2,890	1,493	16.4	130
Erie, OH	39043	15.2	39.2	13.1	0.3	943	2,035	943	13.8	141
Fairfield, OH	39045	11.6	27.0	10.6	1.3	1,661	2,736	1,434	17.6	140
Fayette, OH	39047	16.0	37.5	4.2	0.4	326	596	302	16.0	29
Franklin, OH	39049	14.0	41.9	38.8	7.0	11,188	24,365	11,270	17.0	1,950
Fulton, OH	39051	13.4	30.0	8.6	1.4	705	1,498	641	13.3	105
Gallia, OH	39053	21.5	48.3	4.3	0.1	311	658	350	13.8	34
Geauga, OH	39055	12.7	13.8	2.8	0.7	1,028	1,708	754	16.7	91
Greene, OH	39057	13.9	25.2	11.0	1.2	1,713	2,969	1,413	16.5	184
Guernsey, OH	39059	17.6	53.8	3.1	0.1	405	1,009	398	14.6	86
Hamilton, OH	39061	16.1	38.9	42.4	2.2	7,470	15,987	6,688	17.3	1,181
Hancock, OH	39063	15.3	27.8	6.6	1.1	885	2,070	985	15.0	120
Hardin, OH	39065	14.0	36.7	2.0	...	339	627	318	14.8	37
Harrison, OH	39067	20.0	52.1	2.9	...	155	253	115	16.2	10
Henry, OH	39069	9.5	30.0	8.0	0.9	380	874	436	11.5	29
Highland, OH	39071	12.7	36.1	1.7	0.1	514	943	454	17.7	53
Hocking, OH	39073	16.7	52.8	1.2	...	306	533	237	17.4	36
Holmes, OH	39075	14.7	37.2	1.1	20.2	267	616	293	15.3	16
Huron, OH	39077	14.8	37.4	7.7	0.9	819	1,500	749	16.6	74
Jackson, OH	39079	16.5	51.3	1.2	...	368	699	366	15.3	35
Jefferson, OH	39081	16.2	51.3	8.9	...	749	1,603	841	12.1	78
Knox, OH	39083	16.1	36.1	2.1	0.2	618	1,239	591	14.7	85
Lake, OH	39085	13.0	25.8	9.4	4.2	2,549	4,506	2,055	16.7	294
Lawrence, OH	39087	15.1	51.0	3.2	...	723	1,468	710	15.0	64
Licking, OH	39089	13.3	31.3	7.1	1.4	1,687	3,345	1,656	16.5	209
Logan, OH	39091	16.0	34.3	3.6	0.4	535	1,190	591	12.4	78
Lorain, OH	39093	14.0	34.9	21.7	1.1	2,854	6,293	2,914	16.6	506
Lucas, OH	39095	15.0	39.9	34.0	1.1	3,897	9,126	4,374	16.9	736
Madison, OH	39097	13.1	27.7	3.6	0.9	486	941	447	16.4	48
Mahoning, OH	39099	15.8	44.9	27.2	1.0	2,498	5,286	2,395	15.4	506
Marion, OH	39101	17.5	39.8	7.4	0.8	766	1,528	770	16.0	88
Medina, OH	39103	11.9	15.0	3.3	0.4	2,089	3,477	1,611	18.1	187
Meigs, OH	39105	14.0	55.1	1.7	...	234	467	245	14.8	23
Mercer, OH	39107	14.3	20.5	1.9	0.3	685	1,152	558	15.7	79

[2]IEP= Individual Education Program. See notes and definitions for more information
... Not available

Table C-1. Population, School, and Student Characteristics by County—*Continued*

County	State/County Code	Revenues, 2007-2008				Current expenditures, 2007-2008			Resident population 16 to 19 years, 2006-2008			
		Total revenue ($1,000's)	Percentage of revenue from			Amount ($1,000's)	Amount per student	Percent for instruction	Total population 16 to 19 years	Percent enrolled in school	Percent high school graduates, not enrolled in school	Percent not enrolled, not grads, not employed or not in labor force
			Federal gov't	State gov't	Local gov't							
	19	20	21	22	23	24	25	26	27	28	29
Richland, ND	38077	29,113	8.3	36.4	55.3	25,299	10,318	61.2	...	...	...	...
Rolette, ND	38079	36,384	49.2	38.5	12.3	33,819	11,578	61.5	...	...	...	...
Sargent, ND	38081	7,744	5.1	44.9	50.0	6,287	8,272	54.5	...	...	...	...
Sheridan, ND	38083	1,988	6.6	31.7	61.6	1,746	13,227	60.5	...	...	...	...
Sioux, ND	38085	7,421	59.1	28.1	12.8	6,655	18,233	60.2	...	...	...	...
Slope, ND	38087	458	27.5	3.7	68.8	282	17,625	65.2	...	...	...	...
Stark, ND	38089	33,182	11.8	44.4	43.8	27,091	8,382	63.5	...	...	...	...
Steele, ND	38091	3,644	4.4	33.5	62.1	2,864	10,049	53.6	...	...	...	...
Stutsman, ND	38093	31,679	10.8	37.7	51.5	25,836	9,760	60.4	...	...	...	...
Towner, ND	38095	4,762	7.8	29.7	62.5	3,780	12,558	58.4	...	...	...	...
Traill, ND	38097	17,455	7.7	32.9	59.4	14,327	9,901	59.5	...	...	...	...
Walsh, ND	38099	24,840	14.5	40.1	45.4	21,188	10,706	61.0	...	...	...	...
Ward, ND	38101	104,140	18.8	32.3	48.9	81,443	9,546	60.3	...	...	...	...
Wells, ND	38103	7,691	13.3	32.9	53.9	6,667	11,149	54.3	...	...	...	...
Williams, ND	38105	38,911	13.6	37.4	49.0	32,347	10,722	62.7	...	...	...	...
OHIO	39000	23,430,610	6.8	44.2	49.0	18,955,601	10,389	57.3	653,411	86.6	8.2	3.5
Adams, OH	39001	85,263	6.1	67.0	26.9	48,448	9,647	58.7	...	...	...	...
Allen, OH	39003	190,729	8.0	48.0	44.0	152,881	9,304	57.2	6,484	89.2	7.2	3.1
Ashland, OH	39005	103,995	6.2	46.3	47.5	90,831	8,875	60.4	...	...	...	...
Ashtabula, OH	39007	208,349	7.3	56.2	36.5	158,739	9,615	58.3	4,812	84.2	9.4	3.8
Athens, OH	39009	120,081	10.6	49.9	39.5	94,934	11,668	53.1	...	...	...	...
Auglaize, OH	39011	117,240	4.8	55.2	40.0	78,241	9,223	60.4	...	...	...	...
Belmont, OH	39013	97,399	8.9	53.8	37.3	85,069	9,604	59.3	...	...	...	...
Brown, OH	39015	118,776	4.9	68.0	27.2	75,784	9,212	56.7	...	...	...	...
Butler, OH	39017	702,358	6.0	44.3	49.6	565,427	9,445	54.4	22,322	89.9	6.1	2.8
Carroll, OH	39019	35,877	8.9	51.8	39.3	32,154	8,120	57.5	...	...	...	...
Champaign, OH	39021	87,988	4.8	49.6	45.6	75,973	9,505	56.8	...	...	...	...
Clark, OH	39023	277,510	8.2	54.4	37.4	214,152	9,226	56.3	7,358	85.2	8.7	4.4
Clermont, OH	39025	361,278	4.4	34.6	61.0	264,256	9,080	55.7	10,292	84.8	9.8	3.6
Clinton, OH	39027	104,021	5.2	56.0	38.8	72,684	8,550	53.6	...	...	...	...
Columbiana, OH	39029	195,525	7.0	58.3	34.7	153,551	9,059	59.1	5,521	82.4	10.8	5.0
Coshocton, OH	39031	58,003	8.8	52.5	38.7	50,300	8,831	59.6	...	...	...	...
Crawford, OH	39033	108,717	6.2	60.9	32.9	66,197	8,678	58.9	2,351	83.9	14.8	0.7
Cuyahoga, OH	39035	2,847,299	7.6	39.8	52.6	2,403,328	12,691	58.8	73,355	86.6	6.9	5.2
Darke, OH	39037	103,884	6.2	52.5	41.4	79,058	8,570	58.8	...	...	...	...
Defiance, OH	39039	80,836	4.5	53.7	41.8	57,010	8,321	60.9	...	...	...	...
Delaware, OH	39041	282,690	3.0	20.7	76.3	236,665	10,202	58.5	...	...	...	...
Erie, OH	39043	190,692	6.5	34.8	58.7	165,385	12,626	53.8	...	...	...	...
Fairfield, OH	39045	289,386	4.0	44.5	51.5	216,313	8,687	58.1	8,035	81.8	12.8	1.8
Fayette, OH	39047	74,136	4.2	60.7	35.1	42,611	8,654	57.4	...	...	...	...
Franklin, OH	39049	2,526,503	8.6	37.1	54.3	2,181,722	11,479	58.3	62,580	87.6	8.2	2.6
Fulton, OH	39051	140,771	6.8	40.5	52.7	101,990	11,783	53.8	...	...	...	...
Gallia, OH	39053	88,098	7.8	51.6	40.6	54,786	11,280	57.9	...	...	...	...
Geauga, OH	39055	158,689	3.4	27.3	69.4	132,744	10,437	53.7	5,462	79.2	3.4	4.6
Greene, OH	39057	268,843	5.6	34.9	59.4	231,280	10,016	56.8	12,260	92.3	5.3	2.0
Guernsey, OH	39059	64,974	9.0	51.3	39.7	56,206	9,619	54.5	...	...	...	...
Hamilton, OH	39061	1,649,853	7.9	35.9	56.2	1,369,412	11,711	56.8	51,886	87.2	7.7	3.6
Hancock, OH	39063	137,965	5.0	41.1	53.9	115,755	9,031	59.0	...	...	...	...
Hardin, OH	39065	55,445	6.0	56.4	37.6	41,666	8,768	60.1	...	...	...	...
Harrison, OH	39067	19,459	9.8	61.2	29.0	18,316	9,190	55.6	...	...	...	...
Henry, OH	39069	71,228	4.8	45.1	50.1	57,412	11,257	59.1	...	...	...	...
Highland, OH	39071	94,518	6.0	64.8	29.2	66,002	8,167	58.2	...	...	...	...
Hocking, OH	39073	63,462	5.2	69.0	25.9	34,889	8,448	54.4	...	...	...	...
Holmes, OH	39075	43,565	10.2	42.4	47.4	38,522	8,494	60.2	...	...	...	...
Huron, OH	39077	126,312	6.7	52.4	40.9	104,382	8,204	60.6	2,902	76.6	14.2	7.9
Jackson, OH	39079	57,137	8.7	60.2	31.2	50,091	8,859	59.1	...	...	...	...
Jefferson, OH	39081	117,353	8.7	47.3	44.0	102,841	9,959	52.0	4,157	89.5	6.6	3.3
Knox, OH	39083	116,967	5.7	55.4	38.8	86,325	9,914	59.5	...	...	...	...
Lake, OH	39085	460,367	4.4	36.5	59.1	367,003	10,614	56.3	12,347	88.6	8.0	1.2
Lawrence, OH	39087	147,218	8.8	66.8	24.4	107,068	10,064	56.8	...	...	...	...
Licking, OH	39089	318,697	5.2	40.4	54.4	254,496	9,345	55.4	8,721	88.6	8.0	2.1
Logan, OH	39091	93,558	5.7	41.9	52.4	78,714	10,675	58.0	...	...	...	...
Lorain, OH	39093	554,293	7.2	45.2	47.6	449,913	9,321	57.1	16,617	88.2	7.9	3.4
Lucas, OH	39095	970,841	6.7	52.2	41.1	758,647	10,404	54.2	26,561	85.7	7.6	5.1
Madison, OH	39097	87,351	4.8	38.5	56.7	71,887	9,913	55.7	...	...	...	...
Mahoning, OH	39099	553,915	8.8	55.4	35.8	386,512	10,254	53.5	13,026	87.7	6.4	4.6
Marion, OH	39101	136,005	8.9	54.0	37.1	113,329	9,184	59.8	...	...	...	...
Medina, OH	39103	313,238	3.4	36.1	60.5	264,671	9,111	58.7	8,687	87.6	9.9	1.8
Meigs, OH	39105	38,530	13.0	64.0	23.0	34,000	9,521	56.4	...	...	...	...
Mercer, OH	39107	97,326	7.0	46.1	46.9	84,017	9,498	64.1	...	...	...	...

... Not available

Table C-1. Population, School, and Student Characteristics by County—*Continued*

County	State/County Code	High school graduates, 2006-2008			College enrollment, 2006-2008		College graduates, 2006-2008 (percent)						
		Population 25 years and over	High school diploma or less (percent)	High school diploma or more (percent)	Number	Percent public	Bachelor's degree or more	+/- U.S. percent with Bachelor's degree or more	Non-Hispanic White	Black or African American	American Indian and Alaska Native	Asian, Hawaiian, and Pacific Islander	Hispanic or Latino[3]
		30	31	32	33	34	35	36	37	38	39	40	41
Richland, ND	38077	...	...	...	...	...	...	...	...	...	...	...	...
Rolette, ND	38079	...	...	...	...	...	...	...	...	...	...	...	...
Sargent, ND	38081	...	...	...	...	...	...	...	...	...	...	...	...
Sheridan, ND	38083	...	...	...	...	...	...	...	...	...	...	...	...
Sioux, ND	38085	...	...	...	...	...	...	...	...	...	...	...	...
Slope, ND	38087	...	...	...	...	...	...	...	...	...	...	...	...
Stark, ND	38089	14,320	44.5	85.7	2,444	94.8	21.6	-5.8	21.7	...	...	...	...
Steele, ND	38091	...	...	...	...	...	...	...	...	...	...	...	...
Stutsman, ND	38093	14,067	51.2	84.5	1,388	25.9	21.6	-5.8	21.3	...	...	...	...
Towner, ND	38095	...	...	...	...	...	...	...	...	...	...	...	...
Traill, ND	38097	...	...	...	...	...	...	...	...	...	...	...	...
Walsh, ND	38099	...	...	...	...	...	...	...	...	...	...	...	...
Ward, ND	38101	34,268	37.0	92.2	4,213	93.1	26.5	-0.9	26.8	...	...	...	...
Wells, ND	38103	...	...	...	...	...	...	...	...	...	...	...	...
Williams, ND	38105	...	...	...	...	...	...	...	...	...	...	...	...
OHIO	39000	7,636,835	49.3	87.0	785,787	73.9	23.8	-3.6	24.4	14.3	15.0	60.6	16.7
Adams, OH	39001	19,047	72.4	75.2	837	95.7	10.9	-16.5	10.9	...	...	...	...
Allen, OH	39003	69,087	55.9	87.5	6,702	61.3	15.2	-12.2	16.0	6.9	...	57.2	6.8
Ashland, OH	39005	35,915	58.8	84.1	4,037	36.2	17.9	-9.5	17.5	...	...	...	...
Ashtabula, OH	39007	69,925	63.0	83.3	4,529	77.8	12.8	-14.6	12.8	11.0	...	...	6.8
Athens, OH	39009	32,399	49.3	85.1	19,698	97.0	27.0	-0.4	24.9	...	...	...	...
Auglaize, OH	39011	30,903	58.9	89.8	1,606	85.1	14.4	-13.0	13.7	...	...	...	...
Belmont, OH	39013	49,025	58.4	87.5	2,901	83.0	14.1	-13.3	14.5	3.8	...	...	...
Brown, OH	39015	29,395	67.8	80.2	1,894	84.8	9.6	-17.8	9.8	...	...	...	...
Butler, OH	39017	226,832	49.3	86.4	32,274	87.6	25.3	-2.1	25.0	20.6	...	51.8	28.9
Carroll, OH	39019	19,985	66.1	84.2	1,025	66.2	11.7	-15.7	11.5	...	...	...	...
Champaign, OH	39021	26,655	62.9	89.1	1,553	68.4	13.2	-14.2	12.9	...	...	...	...
Clark, OH	39023	95,225	54.9	85.0	8,097	55.1	16.1	-11.3	16.2	13.3	...	49.4	16.7
Clermont, OH	39025	127,321	48.9	87.0	9,732	82.6	24.3	-3.1	24.2	34.5	...	43.0	18.2
Clinton, OH	39027	28,135	58.6	85.8	2,091	51.4	13.4	-14.0	13.7	...	...	...	...
Columbiana, OH	39029	75,805	62.1	85.2	3,974	85.5	12.4	-15.0	12.6	5.2	...	...	...
Coshocton, OH	39031	24,641	65.3	86.0	1,278	77.6	11.9	-15.5	11.8	...	...	...	...
Crawford, OH	39033	31,001	65.5	85.2	1,453	74.4	10.4	-17.0	10.2	...	...	...	...
Cuyahoga, OH	39035	879,390	44.8	85.9	85,290	62.8	27.8	0.4	32.9	12.9	20.3	65.8	15.9
Darke, OH	39037	35,374	64.0	84.2	2,059	79.9	10.8	-16.6	10.5	...	...	...	...
Defiance, OH	39039	26,136	59.9	87.6	2,386	58.9	15.5	-11.9	15.7	...	...	...	15.6
Delaware, OH	39041	101,866	25.3	95.2	11,005	55.2	49.2	21.8	48.4	45.5	...	79.4	33.8
Erie, OH	39043	54,092	51.6	89.3	3,492	75.9	19.4	-8.0	20.1	13.4	...	...	...
Fairfield, OH	39045	93,343	47.1	91.4	7,533	77.8	23.0	-4.4	22.6	27.6	...	42.5	23.6
Fayette, OH	39047	19,304	66.8	80.8	930	85.7	11.7	-15.7	11.9	...	...	...	...
Franklin, OH	39049	714,489	38.8	88.5	100,510	77.5	35.2	7.8	38.6	17.2	17.8	65.7	19.5
Fulton, OH	39051	28,133	55.8	89.2	2,074	81.0	14.6	-12.8	15.1	...	...	...	4.5
Gallia, OH	39053	20,765	62.7	81.2	1,919	71.3	13.7	-13.7	14.2	...	...	...	...
Geauga, OH	39055	63,594	39.8	88.6	4,806	65.3	32.5	5.1	32.2	32.5	...	...	...
Greene, OH	39057	100,301	37.2	91.0	21,944	74.0	33.5	6.1	32.5	37.8	...	57.6	43.7
Guernsey, OH	39059	27,425	64.2	82.9	1,073	68.8	10.9	-16.5	11.0	...	...	...	...
Hamilton, OH	39061	558,840	42.8	86.5	62,377	70.4	31.5	4.1	35.9	14.4	12.1	67.9	26.2
Hancock, OH	39063	48,887	48.5	90.1	5,532	46.7	23.2	-4.2	23.5	...	...	43.0	6.2
Hardin, OH	39065	19,559	65.9	86.4	4,283	12.7	13.1	-14.3	13.3	...	...	...	...
Harrison, OH	39067	...	...	...	...	...	...	...	...	...	...	...	...
Henry, OH	39069	19,424	62.0	82.2	1,507	85.1	11.8	-15.6	11.9	...	...	...	2.8
Highland, OH	39071	28,302	65.1	80.8	1,209	91.0	9.7	-17.7	9.6	...	...	...	...
Hocking, OH	39073	19,843	60.1	84.4	1,458	82.1	10.3	-17.1	9.9	...	...	...	...
Holmes, OH	39075	24,405	78.9	55.1	632	60.8	8.0	-19.4	8.0	...	...	...	...
Huron, OH	39077	39,352	65.4	85.5	2,084	74.1	11.0	-16.4	11.3	...	...	...	3.5
Jackson, OH	39079	22,807	66.8	76.7	1,096	82.1	11.6	-15.8	12.0	...	...	...	...
Jefferson, OH	39081	48,828	57.7	86.8	4,370	51.2	15.2	-12.2	15.2	7.4	...	...	...
Knox, OH	39083	38,355	58.0	87.2	5,349	30.7	17.6	-9.8	17.4	...	...	...	...
Lake, OH	39085	162,496	45.3	90.6	14,494	72.3	24.6	-2.8	24.8	10.5	...	49.4	11.2
Lawrence, OH	39087	43,198	60.6	81.6	2,915	92.6	12.4	-15.0	12.6	10.2	...	...	...
Licking, OH	39089	103,637	51.5	88.1	10,545	61.7	21.8	-5.6	21.5	24.8	...	59.3	...
Logan, OH	39091	31,317	61.2	86.2	1,467	83.0	14.2	-13.2	14.2	...	...	...	...
Lorain, OH	39093	202,329	48.8	87.9	19,599	67.5	19.9	-7.5	21.2	9.6	...	46.4	10.3
Lucas, OH	39095	286,282	46.5	86.6	35,569	85.8	22.7	-4.7	24.6	12.9	19.1	59.4	10.8
Madison, OH	39097	28,164	59.1	85.1	1,765	71.6	15.5	-11.9	16.6	2.7	...	...	...
Mahoning, OH	39099	165,986	52.9	87.1	14,690	85.0	20.8	-6.6	22.6	9.4	...	62.8	11.8
Marion, OH	39101	45,350	63.4	82.2	2,503	82.4	11.2	-16.2	11.9	2.8	...	...	3.0
Medina, OH	39103	113,517	41.7	91.8	10,609	74.4	28.6	1.2	28.6	25.9	...	45.2	15.6
Meigs, OH	39105	15,906	66.8	83.0	905	70.9	9.9	-17.5	9.8	...	...	...	...
Mercer, OH	39107	26,527	61.1	88.6	1,592	80.0	14.1	-13.3	14.2	...	...	...	...

[3]May be of any race
... Not available

Table C-1. Population, School, and Student Characteristics by County—*Continued*

County	State/ County Code	County Type[1]	Population, 2009		Percent of related children 5-17 years in poverty, 2008	Percent of children under 19 years with no health insurance, 2007	Number of Schools and Students, 2008-2009			Resident enrollment, 2006-2008	
			Total	Percent 5–17 years			School Districts	Schools	Students	K–12 enrollment	
										Number	Percent public
			1	2	3	4	5	6	7	8	9
Miami, OH	39109	2	101,256	17.4	10.7	7.7	10	38	16,549	17,748	86.3
Monroe, OH	39111	8	14,058	15.5	21.7	9.3	1	10	2,634	...	...
Montgomery, OH	39113	2	532,562	16.4	17.1	6.6	53	174	80,123	93,485	86.1
Morgan, OH	39115	6	14,288	17.3	26.2	6.9	1	5	2,166	...	...
Morrow, OH	39117	1	34,642	18.5	15.6	9.7	6	17	5,743	6,156	86.2
Muskingum, OH	39119	4	84,884	17.1	22.1	6.8	11	39	15,945	15,191	93.4
Noble, OH	39121	6	14,311	13.7	18.2	9.5	2	4	2,062	...	...
Ottawa, OH	39123	2	40,945	15.7	10.7	8.1	7	20	5,941	6,238	93.9
Paulding, OH	39125	6	18,994	17.5	13.3	10.5	5	13	3,861	...	...
Perry, OH	39127	6	35,359	19.0	21.4	7.4	6	16	6,608	6,526	89.0
Pickaway, OH	39129	1	54,734	17.1	15.0	7.1	5	20	10,085	10,253	93.2
Pike, OH	39131	7	27,722	17.8	25.8	6.0	5	14	5,432	5,260	97.2
Portage, OH	39133	2	157,530	15.7	10.7	7.2	15	59	25,103	25,076	92.6
Preble, OH	39135	2	41,422	17.3	11.6	8.0	7	17	7,036	7,100	91.5
Putnam, OH	39137	6	34,377	19.6	7.2	10.1	9	22	5,997	6,787	86.4
Richland, OH	39139	3	124,490	16.5	17.8	7.0	15	47	17,350	21,943	86.7
Ross, OH	39141	4	75,972	16.0	19.8	7.0	9	27	12,046	12,713	97.7
Sandusky, OH	39143	4	60,071	17.7	11.9	7.9	5	22	9,039	10,750	88.0
Scioto, OH	39145	4	76,334	16.3	28.5	5.2	14	32	13,035	13,019	92.6
Seneca, OH	39147	4	56,152	17.1	12.7	8.6	9	22	6,041	9,972	87.0
Shelby, OH	39149	4	48,990	19.8	10.9	7.7	9	23	9,193	9,518	92.0
Stark, OH	39151	2	379,466	16.9	15.9	6.6	27	123	61,406	65,181	89.4
Summit, OH	39153	2	542,405	16.8	15.9	6.0	32	165	80,151	96,401	85.3
Trumbull, OH	39155	2	210,157	16.3	20.1	7.0	27	75	32,936	35,794	90.9
Tuscarawas, OH	39157	4	91,137	17.1	14.2	9.8	13	46	16,452	15,273	92.3
Union, OH	39159	1	48,903	19.1	7.5	7.6	3	17	7,792	9,157	94.1
Van Wert, OH	39161	6	28,496	17.4	10.6	9.5	5	17	5,187	5,079	90.0
Vinton, OH	39163	9	13,228	18.4	29.7	7.0	1	5	2,506	...	...
Warren, OH	39165	1	210,734	19.6	5.6	7.7	11	52	36,612	39,061	86.3
Washington, OH	39167	3	61,048	15.5	19.8	7.8	7	28	9,402	10,078	93.6
Wayne, OH	39169	4	114,222	18.3	14.7	10.9	13	50	17,142	19,684	82.6
Williams, OH	39171	7	37,816	17.0	11.0	8.8	7	19	6,505	6,638	93.2
Wood, OH	39173	2	125,380	15.8	8.0	7.3	12	52	19,252	19,353	88.3
Wyandot, OH	39175	7	22,394	17.4	9.8	9.1	3	9	3,610	3,964	95.4
OKLAHOMA	40000	X	3,687,050	17.5	19.7	12.2	583	1,806	645,108	643,055	92.5
Adair, OK	40001	6	21,857	21.0	31.4	8.5	12	18	4,869	4,643	95.7
Alfalfa, OK	40003	9	5,481	12.1	19.2	24.3	4	8	832	...	...
Atoka, OK	40005	7	14,498	16.7	22.9	11.9	8	12	2,340	...	...
Beaver, OK	40007	9	5,270	18.6	15.4	29.5	4	8	1,107	...	...
Beckham, OK	40009	7	21,116	17.3	19.9	13.5	5	13	3,834	3,770	95.2
Blaine, OK	40011	6	12,609	14.0	22.0	16.9	4	11	1,860	...	...
Bryan, OK	40013	6	40,783	16.5	26.4	10.0	9	24	7,075	6,796	92.0
Caddo, OK	40015	6	30,393	18.8	27.4	13.9	12	31	5,881	5,534	96.4
Canadian, OK	40017	1	109,668	18.7	9.9	13.1	11	42	21,634	19,056	93.5
Carter, OK	40019	5	48,326	18.4	22.1	11.6	10	29	9,174	8,897	98.5
Cherokee, OK	40021	6	46,029	17.1	30.7	12.0	12	18	7,542	7,384	97.6
Choctaw, OK	40023	7	14,872	17.3	33.6	7.5	8	14	2,682	...	...
Cimarron, OK	40025	9	2,630	19.7	21.4	26.8	3	6	440	...	...
Cleveland, OK	40027	1	244,589	15.9	11.9	11.9	7	66	40,686	38,655	91.6
Coal, OK	40029	9	5,856	19.7	28.5	15.5	3	6	1,270	...	...
Comanche, OK	40031	3	113,228	18.1	21.0	14.5	11	56	21,841	22,863	95.3
Cotton, OK	40033	6	6,281	18.3	18.8	12.0	3	7	1,219	...	...
Craig, OK	40035	6	15,158	16.3	23.9	9.1	5	15	3,065	...	...
Creek, OK	40037	2	70,244	18.5	16.7	13.0	16	39	13,068	12,723	92.3
Custer, OK	40039	7	26,717	15.8	20.9	13.7	4	16	4,766	4,183	92.0
Delaware, OK	40041	6	40,555	16.3	28.5	12.4	10	19	6,901	7,210	92.7
Dewey, OK	40043	9	4,404	17.6	18.7	23.3	4	9	978	...	...
Ellis, OK	40045	9	3,925	17.2	18.4	24.5	4	8	798	...	...
Garfield, OK	40047	5	58,928	17.0	22.0	13.6	10	33	10,032	10,067	91.1
Garvin, OK	40049	6	27,113	17.4	19.3	11.2	8	22	5,310	4,786	98.9
Grady, OK	40051	1	51,649	18.5	17.1	11.8	12	31	7,753	9,327	93.4
Grant, OK	40053	9	4,317	16.3	17.8	18.6	4	8	833	...	...
Greer, OK	40055	7	5,830	14.4	28.7	8.5	3	7	1,053	...	...
Harmon, OK	40057	9	2,843	16.6	42.7	15.4	1	3	540	...	...
Harper, OK	40059	9	3,377	16.5	17.3	23.9	2	4	729	...	...
Haskell, OK	40061	6	12,393	19.0	27.0	9.7	6	10	2,326	...	...
Hughes, OK	40063	7	13,819	16.8	29.8	13.7	7	15	2,380	...	...
Jackson, OK	40065	5	25,369	18.7	20.7	14.4	7	19	5,215	5,428	99.5
Jefferson, OK	40067	8	6,319	18.3	29.0	13.9	4	9	1,190	...	...
Johnston, OK	40069	7	10,468	17.7	27.8	8.4	7	13	1,899	...	...

[1]County type codes are from the Economic Research Service of the United States Department of Agriculture. See notes and definitions for more information.
... Not available

Table C-1.   Population, School, and Student Characteristics by County—*Continued*

County	State/ County Code	Characteristics of students, 2008-2009				Number of graduates, 2006-2007	Staff and students, 2008-2009			
		Percent with IEP[2]	Percent eligible for free or reduced lunch	Percent minority	Percent English Language Learners		Total staff	Number of teachers	Student/ teacher ratio	Central admin. Staff
		10	11	12	13	14	15	16	17	18
Miami, OH	39109	12.4	28.7	4.8	0.9	1,257	2,193	1,056	15.7	128
Monroe, OH	39111	19.4	52.6	0.7	...	209	337	193	13.6	17
Montgomery, OH	39113	15.2	42.9	32.6	1.6	4,889	11,536	5,238	15.3	806
Morgan, OH	39115	15.0	51.6	4.6	0.1	148	296	161	13.5	13
Morrow, OH	39117	16.1	32.2	1.6	0.1	381	724	373	15.4	37
Muskingum, OH	39119	15.1	45.0	5.5	...	980	2,133	978	16.3	162
Noble, OH	39121	14.6	37.1	0.3	0.1	158	238	112	18.4	16
Ottawa, OH	39123	15.2	30.1	4.9	...	469	896	372	16.0	47
Paulding, OH	39125	16.4	36.0	3.1	...	253	582	272	14.2	42
Perry, OH	39127	16.4	46.8	0.6	...	440	995	443	14.9	67
Pickaway, OH	39129	14.0	31.1	2.1	0.1	622	1,210	592	17.0	54
Pike, OH	39131	14.3	47.5	2.9	...	312	752	346	15.7	55
Portage, OH	39133	13.7	29.3	6.5	0.3	1,688	3,453	1,600	15.7	226
Preble, OH	39135	10.9	31.3	1.2	0.3	474	913	424	16.6	62
Putnam, OH	39137	14.3	19.6	6.7	1.0	609	791	414	14.5	55
Richland, OH	39139	14.9	45.8	12.3	0.2	1,210	2,621	1,245	13.9	166
Ross, OH	39141	11.9	36.9	4.1	...	691	1,641	803	15.0	123
Sandusky, OH	39143	14.8	40.3	14.3	3.8	672	1,111	596	15.2	57
Scioto, OH	39145	14.2	58.6	3.4	...	744	1,743	872	14.9	98
Seneca, OH	39147	16.2	36.2	5.4	0.3	499	1,006	448	13.5	101
Shelby, OH	39149	16.1	29.0	3.8	1.4	614	1,191	526	17.5	75
Stark, OH	39151	14.4	40.4	12.6	0.6	4,228	8,009	3,516	17.5	510
Summit, OH	39153	14.4	37.9	24.5	1.7	5,286	12,822	5,082	15.8	858
Trumbull, OH	39155	13.8	35.3	12.9	0.2	2,454	4,460	2,094	15.7	330
Tuscarawas, OH	39157	17.0	34.7	2.0	0.5	1,125	2,126	1,030	16.0	155
Union, OH	39159	15.3	19.1	5.6	0.3	497	906	447	17.4	45
Van Wert, OH	39161	17.2	30.1	3.6	...	353	731	379	13.7	34
Vinton, OH	39163	18.7	61.4	0.5	0.2	160	330	161	15.6	16
Warren, OH	39165	11.9	12.2	8.3	1.6	2,102	4,474	2,018	18.1	258
Washington, OH	39167	15.8	37.6	2.0	...	739	1,138	556	16.9	66
Wayne, OH	39169	13.0	33.0	4.3	2.3	1,221	2,320	1,130	15.2	112
Williams, OH	39171	13.5	25.8	4.3	0.6	487	825	417	15.6	56
Wood, OH	39173	13.0	25.2	7.3	0.5	1,579	2,924	1,368	14.1	181
Wyandot, OH	39175	16.3	29.3	3.0	0.9	292	413	211	17.1	24
OKLAHOMA	40000	...	56.1	42.7	...	3,7046	83,055	42,153	15.3	3,785
Adair, OK	40001	...	76.4	72.6	...	226	749	351	13.9	28
Alfalfa, OK	40003	...	47.8	8.6	...	75	158	82	10.1	9
Atoka, OK	40005	...	72.2	49.2	...	152	365	175	13.4	15
Beaver, OK	40007	...	51.5	30.8	...	50	201	104	10.6	12
Beckham, OK	40009	...	47.4	23.7	...	216	449	263	14.6	19
Blaine, OK	40011	...	64.1	38.3	...	130	294	150	12.4	17
Bryan, OK	40013	...	70.4	44.6	...	427	994	487	14.5	51
Caddo, OK	40015	...	69.2	53.0	...	352	895	443	13.3	45
Canadian, OK	40017	...	36.2	24.9	...	1,258	2,483	1,293	16.7	99
Carter, OK	40019	...	62.2	37.1	...	503	1,225	610	15.0	64
Cherokee, OK	40021	...	71.5	70.4	...	340	990	505	14.9	35
Choctaw, OK	40023	...	75.6	50.3	...	169	381	189	14.2	25
Cimarron, OK	40025	...	63.2	35.0	...	44	92	50	8.8	7
Cleveland, OK	40027	...	42.0	30.0	...	2,334	4,733	2,519	16.2	223
Coal, OK	40029	...	68.2	47.2	...	78	195	96	13.2	8
Comanche, OK	40031	...	54.1	47.8	...	1,310	3,049	1,469	14.9	135
Cotton, OK	40033	...	51.7	32.6	...	71	170	90	13.5	11
Craig, OK	40035	...	63.7	52.9	...	227	436	225	13.6	29
Creek, OK	40037	...	58.9	32.2	...	799	1,605	840	15.6	93
Custer, OK	40039	...	59.6	36.0	...	279	623	320	14.9	30
Delaware, OK	40041	...	66.9	55.5	...	418	931	468	14.7	37
Dewey, OK	40043	...	48.7	16.9	...	68	176	93	10.5	16
Ellis, OK	40045	...	54.3	14.3	...	46	128	68	11.7	11
Garfield, OK	40047	...	57.5	27.5	...	566	1,314	683	14.7	56
Garvin, OK	40049	...	57.1	34.5	...	331	716	374	14.2	32
Grady, OK	40051	...	48.4	20.0	...	483	966	520	14.9	40
Grant, OK	40053	...	46.7	12.6	...	62	148	80	10.4	10
Greer, OK	40055	...	53.8	25.7	...	63	142	80	13.2	9
Harmon, OK	40057	...	80.6	51.5	...	36	86	46	11.7	4
Harper, OK	40059	...	50.2	26.3	...	53	112	56	13.0	5
Haskell, OK	40061	...	70.2	40.8	...	138	303	164	14.2	13
Hughes, OK	40063	...	76.5	43.9	...	133	349	168	14.2	22
Jackson, OK	40065	...	55.1	42.7	...	334	673	380	13.7	31
Jefferson, OK	40067	...	63.5	28.3	...	81	186	98	12.1	15
Johnston, OK	40069	...	70.5	41.0	...	103	269	144	13.2	16

[2]IEP= Individual Education Program. See notes and definitions for more information

... Not available

Table C-1. Population, School, and Student Characteristics by County—*Continued*

County	State/County Code	Revenues, 2007-2008 Total revenue ($1,000's)	Percentage of revenue from Federal gov't	State gov't	Local gov't	Current expenditures, 2007-2008 Amount ($1,000's)	Amount per student	Percent for instruction	Resident population 16 to 19 years, 2006-2008 Total population 16 to 19 years	Percent enrolled in school	Percent high school graduates, not enrolled in school	Percent not enrolled, not grads, not employed or not in labor force
		19	20	21	22	23	24	25	26	27	28	29
Miami, OH........................	39109	196,045	5.0	39.5	55.5	165,930	10,079	59.5	5,179	89.1	8.8	1.8
Monroe, OH......................	39111	26,781	9.3	57.4	33.3	24,040	9,014	58.3	...	...	...	...
Montgomery, OH................	39113	109,4051	6.9	46.8	46.3	876,375	10,802	55.8	30,294	86.2	7.4	5.0
Morgan, OH......................	39115	30,600	8.3	70.4	21.4	20,602	9,547	57.8	...	...	...	...
Morrow, OH......................	39117	64,055	7.1	57.8	35.1	48,867	8,298	58.5	...	...	...	...
Muskingum, OH................	39119	208,690	8.1	57.7	34.2	158,152	9,790	55.4	4,738	84.5	9.2	4.1
Noble, OH	39121	17,994	8.6	57.8	33.6	16,761	7,993	55.5	...	...	...	...
Ottawa, OH......................	39123	71,700	4.2	35.5	60.3	62,143	10,295	59.3	...	...	...	...
Paulding, OH....................	39125	44,855	7.6	46.9	45.5	38,448	11,109	54.3	...	...	...	...
Perry, OH	39127	74,947	10.0	60.4	29.7	65,296	9,978	52.8	...	...	...	...
Pickaway, OH...................	39129	119,565	5.2	55.0	39.8	89,504	8,833	56.6	...	...	...	...
Pike, OH..........................	39131	74,699	10.3	62.2	27.5	59,700	10,765	49.7	...	...	...	...
Portage, OH.....................	39133	285,600	4.9	42.3	52.8	237,146	9,723	57.9	...	...	...	...
Preble, OH.......................	39135	78,949	5.0	41.8	53.2	63,854	8,936	56.0	...	...	...	...
Putnam, OH......................	39137	77,101	6.0	51.8	42.1	59,018	8,988	60.0	...	...	...	...
Richland, OH....................	39139	241,947	7.7	45.4	46.9	196,304	11,168	55.4	6,634	82.8	7.6	4.7
Ross, OH.........................	39141	152,244	7.3	56.1	36.6	130,475	10,779	62.4	3,734	76.0	17.7	6.3
Sandusky, OH..................	39143	107,874	7.0	44.8	48.2	91,016	10,033	62.8	...	...	...	...
Scioto, OH.......................	39145	168,336	10.2	62.7	27.1	128,986	10,050	54.9	4,096	88.4	7.8	3.8
Seneca, OH	39147	72,776	6.2	42.7	51.2	59,195	9,668	54.9	...	...	...	...
Shelby, OH	39149	108,712	5.0	50.0	44.9	81,587	8,923	56.1	...	...	...	...
Stark, OH.........................	39151	698,598	6.9	47.3	45.8	579,938	9,324	57.9	21,082	87.2	8.9	3.2
Summit, OH......................	39153	1,043,341	6.9	41.3	51.8	867,799	10,545	59.6	28,437	88.2	8.3	2.9
Trumbull, OH....................	39155	442,101	5.9	54.0	40.0	335,866	10,083	57.2	11,351	82.0	11.9	4.2
Tuscarawas, OH................	39157	187,067	6.8	50.5	42.7	147,878	9,081	57.6	4,292	80.9	11.1	4.4
Union, OH	39159	102,657	3.1	48.3	48.6	73,104	9,340	57.3	...	...	...	...
Van Wert, OH....................	39161	73,216	4.9	49.6	45.5	51,910	9,994	62.0	...	...	...	...
Vinton, OH	39163	32,457	8.6	73.5	17.9	23,070	9,036	50.8	...	...	...	...
Warren, OH......................	39165	405,254	3.0	35.3	61.7	332,692	9,327	54.8	10,090	83.8	10.5	3.5
Washington, OH................	39167	100,192	8.5	44.8	46.7	87,246	9,083	57.4	...	...	...	...
Wayne, OH.......................	39169	210,616	6.6	42.4	51.0	168,822	9,723	57.4	6,754	76.6	9.5	6.7
Williams, OH....................	39171	79,897	4.2	50.9	44.9	54,363	8,099	61.4	...	...	...	...
Wood, OH	39173	286,532	4.6	35.3	60.1	235,231	10,984	59.6	...	...	...	...
Wyandot, OH....................	39175	36,209	4.9	43.7	51.4	29,246	7,939	59.9	...	...	...	...
OKLAHOMA...................	40000	5,780,151	11.1	51.2	37.7	4,931,406	7,685	56.2	206,679	81.7	10.8	4.5
Adair, OK.........................	40001	62,619	18.2	53.8	28.0	49,617	10,147	53.1	...	...	...	...
Alfalfa, OK.......................	40003	9,295	7.9	48.7	43.4	8,785	10,433	57.5	...	...	...	...
Atoka, OK........................	40005	48,614	8.5	47.5	44.1	29,400	12,861	48.9	...	...	...	...
Beaver, OK.......................	40007	12,811	6.0	46.5	47.4	12,086	10,648	54.1	...	...	...	...
Beckham, OK....................	40009	39,011	8.6	50.1	41.2	29,108	7,684	56.9	...	...	...	...
Blaine, OK.......................	40011	20,222	17.4	54.2	28.3	19,537	10,060	55.7	...	...	...	...
Bryan, OK........................	40013	62,981	14.4	60.0	25.6	60,065	8,438	56.2	...	...	...	...
Caddo, OK........................	40015	63,033	19.2	56.2	24.6	53,092	8,964	56.1	...	...	...	...
Canadian, OK....................	40017	181,770	7.5	49.1	43.5	147,465	6,953	57.0	6,089	82.6	8.7	2.4
Carter, OK.......................	40019	83,732	10.6	52.3	37.2	71,541	7,847	56.9	...	...	...	...
Cherokee, OK...................	40021	67,430	20.0	59.5	20.6	61,736	8,164	58.1	...	...	...	...
Choctaw, OK.....................	40023	23,009	16.0	66.5	17.6	23,022	8,381	53.7	...	...	...	...
Cimarron, OK....................	40025	5,421	9.5	53.2	37.3	5,362	12,186	54.0	...	...	...	...
Cleveland, OK...................	40027	338,791	6.7	48.6	44.7	270,405	6,755	59.1	15,286	88.0	7.7	2.5
Coal, OK..........................	40029	14,387	15.1	57.9	27.0	12,481	9,882	55.3	...	...	...	...
Comanche, OK..................	40031	177,604	16.4	58.8	24.7	164,002	7,512	55.7	8,407	69.9	25.4	2.0
Cotton, OK.......................	40033	10,252	15.5	61.1	23.5	9,757	8,064	59.6	...	...	...	...
Craig, OK	40035	27,132	14.1	56.4	29.4	25,574	8,065	59.2	...	...	...	...
Creek, OK........................	40037	119,068	9.7	57.5	32.8	95,295	7,166	58.2	...	...	...	...
Custer, OK.......................	40039	41,327	9.2	52.5	38.2	35,225	7,512	56.6	...	...	...	...
Delaware, OK....................	40041	74,004	12.0	47.0	40.9	59,633	8,759	54.8	...	...	...	...
Dewey, OK........................	40043	11,740	7.4	58.1	34.4	10,938	11,799	56.0	...	...	...	...
Ellis, OK..........................	40045	8,832	8.0	55.1	36.9	8,162	10,437	50.9	...	...	...	...
Garfield, OK.....................	40047	89,977	9.1	53.3	37.6	74,832	7,708	59.0	...	...	...	...
Garvin, OK.......................	40049	45,542	12.1	58.1	29.8	41,779	7,711	57.4	...	...	...	...
Grady, OK........................	40051	57,696	9.4	60.3	30.3	53,006	7,036	58.2	...	...	...	...
Grant, OK	40053	9,588	7.5	42.2	50.3	9,313	11,047	56.6	...	...	...	...
Greer, OK	40055	8,418	9.6	69.1	21.3	8,193	8,318	58.6	...	...	...	...
Harmon, OK	40057	5,144	10.0	69.0	21.0	4,999	9,397	65.4	...	...	...	...
Harper, OK.......................	40059	7,426	6.6	48.1	45.4	6,912	9,353	56.0	...	...	...	...
Haskell, OK......................	40061	19,377	15.3	64.0	20.7	18,568	7,905	58.6	...	...	...	...
Hughes, OK	40063	24,424	14.4	56.3	29.3	20,966	8,802	54.2	...	...	...	...
Jackson, OK.....................	40065	45,099	15.7	62.9	21.4	40,258	7,875	60.8	...	...	...	...
Jefferson, OK....................	40067	12,245	13.5	66.1	20.5	11,498	9,678	56.6	...	...	...	...
Johnston, OK....................	40069	16,660	16.6	59.0	24.4	16,117	8,577	57.2	...	...	...	...

... Not available

Table C-1. Population, School, and Student Characteristics by County—*Continued*

County	State/ County Code	Population 25 years and over	High school diploma or less (percent)	High school diploma or more (percent)	College enrollment, 2006-2008 Number	College enrollment, 2006-2008 Percent public	Bachelor's degree or more	+/- U.S. percent with Bachelor's degree or more	Non-Hispanic White	Black or African American	American Indian and Alaska Native	Asian, Hawaiian, and Pacific Islander	Hispanic or Latino[3]
		30	31	32	33	34	35	36	37	38	39	40	41
Miami, OH	39109	69,222	52.1	87.5	5,247	78.9	20.9	-6.5	20.8	13.3	...	47.2	...
Monroe, OH	39111	...	...	...	...	...	...	...	...	...	...	...	...
Montgomery, OH	39113	358,810	43.6	87.5	43,131	66.4	24.4	-3.0	25.3	18.1	...	45.7	24.9
Morgan, OH	39115	...	...	...	...	...	...	...	...	...	...	...	...
Morrow, OH	39117	23,308	61.2	84.4	1,666	78.8	13.4	-14.0	13.8	...	...	...	...
Muskingum, OH	39119	57,427	59.8	85.2	5,282	72.1	14.0	-13.4	14.4	8.1	...	...	...
Noble, OH	39121	...	...	...	...	...	...	...	...	...	...	...	...
Ottawa, OH	39123	29,383	46.9	89.0	1,939	76.8	19.1	-8.3	19.9	...	...	...	3.3
Paulding, OH	39125	...	...	...	...	...	...	...	...	...	...	...	...
Perry, OH	39127	23,242	67.7	84.0	1,414	85.7	9.8	-17.6	9.1	...	...	...	...
Pickaway, OH	39129	36,341	64.4	81.5	2,337	79.3	12.4	-15.0	13.1	...	...	...	...
Pike, OH	39131	18,715	66.6	78.8	1,143	91.5	11.9	-15.5	11.9	...	...	...	...
Portage, OH	39133	99,637	50.4	89.6	19,488	89.3	24.2	-3.2	23.5	23.7	...	72.0	29.2
Preble, OH	39135	28,801	62.8	84.4	1,797	74.0	11.5	-15.9	11.3	...	...	...	...
Putnam, OH	39137	22,061	57.6	90.4	1,658	64.2	16.2	-11.2	16.7	...	...	...	1.2
Richland, OH	39139	86,378	57.7	83.5	5,690	70.2	15.0	-12.4	15.3	8.2	...	...	10.3
Ross, OH	39141	52,645	63.0	81.3	3,419	87.2	13.0	-14.4	13.6	3.8	...	...	...
Sandusky, OH	39143	41,121	58.8	86.6	2,923	75.1	12.8	-14.6	13.3	4.7	...	...	5.6
Scioto, OH	39145	51,779	59.8	81.8	3,947	93.1	11.7	-15.7	12.0	2.8	...	...	...
Seneca, OH	39147	37,521	56.5	88.0	4,702	39.3	15.1	-12.3	15.4	...	...	...	7.2
Shelby, OH	39149	31,849	59.4	85.8	2,205	77.6	14.6	-12.8	14.5	...	...	...	...
Stark, OH	39151	259,283	53.9	87.5	23,587	66.0	20.2	-7.2	20.6	9.8	15.0	70.2	16.9
Summit, OH	39153	367,108	43.5	89.6	34,498	86.0	29.3	1.9	30.9	14.6	17.9	49.7	31.4
Trumbull, OH	39155	148,897	60.4	86.1	8,890	85.2	16.0	-11.4	16.4	7.6	...	...	20.1
Tuscarawas, OH	39157	63,109	66.0	83.4	4,066	74.3	13.0	-14.4	12.8	...	...	...	...
Union, OH	39159	31,189	48.4	89.9	2,173	67.2	24.6	-2.8	24.1	...	...	...	...
Van Wert, OH	39161	19,688	60.8	90.7	1,007	71.1	14.8	-12.6	14.9	...	...	...	...
Vinton, OH	39163	...	...	...	...	...	...	...	...	...	...	...	...
Warren, OH	39165	133,066	38.2	87.5	10,844	75.3	35.0	7.6	33.9	24.1	...	78.5	28.8
Washington, OH	39167	42,599	57.3	87.5	4,147	64.0	16.3	-11.1	16.3	...	...	...	...
Wayne, OH	39169	73,948	59.7	84.0	5,861	58.3	18.3	-9.1	18.2	8.8	...	...	20.1
Williams, OH	39171	26,494	58.8	88.2	1,096	79.3	12.2	-15.2	12.2	...	...	...	...
Wood, OH	39173	75,425	41.5	92.2	21,663	93.2	30.5	3.1	30.2	...	...	65.1	24.3
Wyandot, OH	39175	15,510	61.1	86.6	894	67.1	14.4	-13.0	14.2	...	...	...	...
OKLAHOMA	40000	2,336,187	48.1	84.9	228,432	81.6	22.4	-5.0	24.3	15.9	14.2	41.0	9.4
Adair, OK	40001	13,325	69.6	75.0	619	61.2	11.3	-16.1	13.5	...	6.6	...	...
Alfalfa, OK	40003	...	...	...	...	...	...	...	...	...	...	...	...
Atoka, OK	40005	...	...	...	...	...	...	...	...	...	...	...	...
Beaver, OK	40007	...	...	...	...	...	...	...	...	...	...	...	...
Beckham, OK	40009	12,649	55.3	80.3	481	100.0	16.8	-10.6	17.7	...	...	...	...
Blaine, OK	40011	...	...	...	...	...	...	...	...	...	...	...	...
Bryan, OK	40013	25,425	50.9	84.5	3,399	67.5	20.4	-7.0	20.2	...	20.2	...	18.4
Caddo, OK	40015	18,800	61.7	81.4	1,755	56.8	13.0	-14.4	14.4	9.5	10.8	...	3.5
Canadian, OK	40017	66,598	40.1	89.6	5,994	88.3	24.6	-2.8	26.0	12.7	14.8	32.2	6.7
Carter, OK	40019	31,891	59.7	80.7	1,255	63.3	17.3	-10.1	17.7	9.4	19.1	...	12.4
Cherokee, OK	40021	27,057	51.0	84.3	5,068	77.2	22.5	-4.9	25.0	...	18.9	...	...
Choctaw, OK	40023	...	...	...	...	...	...	...	...	...	...	...	...
Cimarron, OK	40025	...	...	...	...	...	...	...	...	...	...	...	...
Cleveland, OK	40027	147,384	36.5	90.3	31,854	94.2	30.7	3.3	30.3	33.8	21.6	53.8	25.0
Coal, OK	40029	...	...	...	...	...	...	...	...	...	...	...	...
Comanche, OK	40031	67,115	47.5	88.7	6,622	87.2	20.5	-6.9	23.5	15.3	13.9	13.0	14.8
Cotton, OK	40033	...	...	...	...	...	...	...	...	...	...	...	...
Craig, OK	40035	...	...	...	...	...	...	...	...	...	...	...	...
Creek, OK	40037	46,216	57.7	82.2	3,584	76.4	13.6	-13.8	14.2	10.5	6.8	...	10.5
Custer, OK	40039	15,391	45.3	84.6	3,261	98.6	24.1	-3.3	27.7	...	...	...	...
Delaware, OK	40041	27,832	61.5	82.0	878	86.0	13.1	-14.3	13.8	...	10.2	...	...
Dewey, OK	40043	...	...	...	...	...	...	...	...	...	...	...	...
Ellis, OK	40045	...	...	...	...	...	...	...	...	...	...	...	...
Garfield, OK	40047	38,697	51.5	85.8	1,868	80.2	22.1	-5.3	23.1	21.0	21.8	...	6.5
Garvin, OK	40049	18,689	66.0	78.2	792	43.8	15.2	-12.2	14.7	16.6	20.2	...	...
Grady, OK	40051	32,702	52.8	86.2	3,207	93.4	18.2	-9.2	18.3	3.4	31.0	...	13.5
Grant, OK	40053	...	...	...	...	...	...	...	...	...	...	...	...
Greer, OK	40055	...	...	...	...	...	...	...	...	...	...	...	...
Harmon, OK	40057	...	...	...	...	...	...	...	...	...	...	...	...
Harper, OK	40059	...	...	...	...	...	...	...	...	...	...	...	...
Haskell, OK	40061	...	...	...	...	...	...	...	...	...	...	...	...
Hughes, OK	40063	...	...	...	...	...	...	...	...	...	...	...	...
Jackson, OK	40065	15,866	47.2	81.8	1,072	89.5	19.2	-8.2	23.0	6.6	...	...	6.6
Jefferson, OK	40067	...	...	...	...	...	...	...	...	...	...	...	...
Johnston, OK	40069	...	...	...	...	...	...	...	...	...	...	...	...

[3]May be of any race
... Not available

Table C-1. Population, School, and Student Characteristics by County—*Continued*

County	State/ County Code	County Type[1]	Population, 2009		Percent of related children 5-17 years in poverty, 2008	Percent of children under 19 years with no health insurance, 2007	Number of Schools and Students, 2008-2009			Resident enrollment, 2006-2008 K–12 enrollment	
			Total	Percent 5–17 years			School Districts	Schools	Students	Number	Percent public
			1	2	3	4	5	6	7	8	9
Kay, OK	40071	5	46,110	18.4	24.5	11.8	9	26	8,586	8,369	89.5
Kingfisher, OK	40073	6	14,384	19.0	13.2	20.9	7	15	3,271	...	...
Kiowa, OK	40075	6	9,101	16.8	25.8	9.1	4	10	1,694	...	...
Latimer, OK	40077	7	10,621	17.8	20.6	9.8	5	10	1,734	...	...
Le Flore, OK	40079	2	49,915	18.2	24.6	11.4	18	37	10,026	9,236	96.0
Lincoln, OK	40081	1	32,199	18.6	19.2	14.5	8	22	5,622	6,015	95.9
Logan, OK	40083	1	39,301	17.8	16.0	12.9	4	13	4,539	8,061	90.3
Love, OK	40085	9	9,124	17.5	19.0	15.4	4	8	1,629	...	...
McClain, OK	40087	1	33,168	18.8	12.5	17.5	9	25	8,054	...	...
McCurtain, OK	40089	7	33,370	19.3	31.9	9.2	15	31	7,137	6,413	95.3
McIntosh, OK	40091	6	19,801	15.5	28.9	11.1	5	11	3,015	...	...
Major, OK	40093	9	7,189	17.2	12.9	23.5	3	5	1,031	...	...
Marshall, OK	40095	6	15,014	17.3	23.9	14.4	2	6	2,844	...	...
Mayes, OK	40097	6	40,065	18.0	22.4	11.7	9	24	7,406	6,893	97.3
Murray, OK	40099	7	12,960	17.4	19.5	12.3	3	9	2,476	...	...
Muskogee, OK	40101	4	71,412	17.9	28.1	12.0	16	41	14,108	13,137	97.3
Noble, OK	40103	6	10,950	17.7	17.4	10.0	4	10	2,191	...	...
Nowata, OK	40105	6	10,528	18.2	22.0	11.6	3	8	2,053	...	...
Okfuskee, OK	40107	6	10,924	16.2	29.9	9.4	7	14	2,118	...	...
Oklahoma, OK	40109	1	716,704	17.3	21.1	11.3	19	213	114,937	124,576	90.3
Okmulgee, OK	40111	2	39,292	17.9	27.6	9.1	10	22	7,152	6,912	98.6
Osage, OK	40113	2	45,051	18.0	17.5	12.0	11	22	3,554	8,562	92.6
Ottawa, OK	40115	6	31,629	17.2	25.5	10.8	9	23	6,012	5,814	94.2
Pawnee, OK	40117	2	16,419	17.8	20.5	12.4	4	11	3,087	...	...
Payne, OK	40119	4	79,727	13.3	15.8	15.0	8	28	10,234	10,447	95.5
Pittsburg, OK	40121	5	45,211	15.9	20.4	10.6	15	33	8,076	7,553	91.5
Pontotoc, OK	40123	7	37,422	16.6	24.6	11.7	9	24	6,887	6,109	98.5
Pottawatomie, OK	40125	4	70,274	17.8	21.6	10.7	16	38	13,251	11,973	94.2
Pushmataha, OK	40127	9	11,812	17.1	33.1	11.0	7	13	2,248	...	...
Roger Mills, OK	40129	9	3,407	18.7	17.2	25.2	4	8	746	...	...
Rogers, OK	40131	2	85,654	19.6	10.8	10.9	9	33	14,410	15,932	89.8
Seminole, OK	40133	7	24,296	18.8	32.7	8.6	11	24	5,131	4,733	98.8
Sequoyah, OK	40135	2	41,433	19.2	28.3	9.0	12	25	8,926	7,757	95.0
Stephens, OK	40137	4	43,487	17.3	17.1	11.8	9	24	8,183	7,402	95.0
Texas, OK	40139	7	21,135	21.1	15.0	29.5	10	24	4,035	4,042	98.1
Tillman, OK	40141	6	7,796	19.2	31.0	11.6	5	10	1,587	...	...
Tulsa, OK	40143	2	601,961	17.9	17.0	12.1	16	187	111,961	104,915	86.9
Wagoner, OK	40145	2	70,394	19.0	12.9	12.2	4	17	6,746	12,807	92.9
Washington, OK	40147	4	50,706	16.9	16.5	11.6	5	20	8,182	8,422	95.4
Washita, OK	40149	7	11,813	17.7	19.9	16.2	6	11	2,209	...	...
Woods, OK	40151	7	8,418	13.2	18.8	13.2	4	9	1,271	...	...
Woodward, OK	40153	7	19,959	17.6	15.4	15.2	5	13	3,627	...	...
OREGON	41000	X	3,825,657	16.3	15.7	12.8	221	1,318	563,295	618,698	90.2
Baker, OR	41001	7	16,082	14.8	22.3	11.4	4	11	2,208	...	...
Benton, OR	41003	3	82,605	14.0	11.0	12.7	4	23	9,030	10,877	88.3
Clackamas, OR	41005	1	386,143	17.8	9.8	12.6	11	115	58,897	64,576	89.1
Clatsop, OR	41007	4	37,243	15.0	17.7	15.7	5	15	5,020	6,015	96.5
Columbia, OR	41009	1	49,592	18.2	11.9	10.5	5	23	8,579	9,046	95.0
Coos, OR	41011	5	62,795	13.9	22.3	10.4	7	26	8,456	9,249	93.5
Crook, OR	41013	6	22,566	17.5	16.1	12.6	1	8	3,208	3,967	92.1
Curry, OR	41015	7	21,148	12.3	18.4	12.4	3	10	2,560	...	...
Deschutes, OR	41017	3	158,629	16.4	14.3	13.5	4	47	24,700	23,184	90.3
Douglas, OR	41019	4	103,205	15.3	18.8	9.2	15	50	15,170	15,698	90.2
Gilliam, OR	41021	9	1,645	12.9	17.1	14.1	3	4	233	...	...
Grant, OR	41023	9	6,795	15.1	18.6	15.9	6	9	1,033	...	...
Harney, OR	41025	7	6,756	16.4	22.9	10.6	11	14	1,187	...	...
Hood River, OR	41027	6	21,883	19.1	17.8	23.0	1	10	3,973	4,161	96.1
Jackson, OR	41029	3	201,286	16.0	20.8	14.1	10	63	28,571	31,040	90.2
Jefferson, OR	41031	6	19,959	19.2	23.3	17.2	5	13	3,681	3,964	92.1
Josephine, OR	41033	4	81,026	15.1	27.0	10.5	2	24	11,136	12,326	90.4
Klamath, OR	41035	5	66,247	16.8	21.7	13.8	2	33	10,069	11,421	91.4
Lake, OR	41037	7	7,089	15.6	22.9	11.3	6	8	1,103	...	...
Lane, OR	41039	2	351,109	14.5	14.7	12.7	17	130	46,662	50,744	92.4
Lincoln, OR	41041	4	46,293	13.1	23.6	12.7	1	17	5,373	6,396	93.6
Linn, OR	41043	4	116,584	17.3	17.0	10.1	8	52	21,325	19,454	91.4
Malheur, OR	41045	6	30,745	18.2	25.6	14.3	11	23	5,207	6,573	94.1
Marion, OR	41047	2	317,981	18.6	19.8	14.5	15	135	59,949	58,450	90.5
Morrow, OR	41049	6	11,533	21.5	17.7	20.7	2	9	2,412	...	...
Multnomah, OR	41051	1	726,855	14.2	17.1	10.2	9	173	91,058	109,013	87.2
Polk, OR	41053	2	78,122	17.4	13.2	12.3	5	19	7,711	12,498	93.5

[1]County type codes are from the Economic Research Service of the United States Department of Agriculture. See notes and definitions for more information.
... Not available

Table C-1. Population, School, and Student Characteristics by County—*Continued*

County	State/ County Code	Characteristics of students, 2008-2009				Number of graduates, 2006-2007	Staff and students, 2008-2009			
		Percent with IEP[2]	Percent eligible for free or reduced lunch	Percent minority	Percent English Language Learners		Total staff	Number of teachers	Student/ teacher ratio	Central admin. Staff
		10	11	12	13	14	15	16	17	18
Kay, OK	40071	...	61.4	33.9	...	555	1,163	563	15.3	53
Kingfisher, OK	40073	...	56.3	26.4	...	220	418	229	14.3	19
Kiowa, OK	40075	...	61.3	30.4	...	128	255	129	13.1	17
Latimer, OK	40077	...	56.6	41.0	...	119	251	132	13.1	14
Le Flore, OK	40079	...	67.0	43.2	...	574	1,288	692	14.5	66
Lincoln, OK	40081	...	58.2	22.9	...	402	695	381	14.8	36
Logan, OK	40083	...	61.1	27.9	...	251	589	304	14.9	32
Love, OK	40085	...	64.6	37.1	...	93	221	109	14.9	15
McClain, OK	40087	...	38.7	28.0	...	481	937	515	15.6	34
McCurtain, OK	40089	...	73.5	45.7	...	439	1,062	532	13.4	49
McIntosh, OK	40091	...	76.3	47.9	...	174	400	205	14.7	20
Major, OK	40093	...	49.0	19.1	...	90	144	81	12.7	9
Marshall, OK	40095	...	69.7	56.1	...	151	352	183	15.5	16
Mayes, OK	40097	...	61.4	54.6	...	452	926	491	15.1	31
Murray, OK	40099	6.4	47.8	35.9	...	145	253	147	16.8	13
Muskogee, OK	40101	0.6	62.8	57.5	...	753	1,722	887	15.9	82
Noble, OK	40103	...	56.3	26.3	...	169	321	164	13.4	19
Nowata, OK	40105	...	57.2	49.6	...	119	278	147	14.0	13
Okfuskee, OK	40107	...	67.3	48.8	...	113	310	157	13.5	19
Oklahoma, OK	40109	...	59.7	53.5	...	6,203	13,487	7,083	16.2	495
Okmulgee, OK	40111	...	67.1	50.6	...	426	959	491	14.6	47
Osage, OK	40113	...	53.4	48.0	...	372	540	270	13.2	28
Ottawa, OK	40115	...	67.6	48.5	...	339	789	412	14.6	35
Pawnee, OK	40117	...	60.2	27.6	...	169	407	216	14.3	18
Payne, OK	40119	...	47.7	26.4	...	601	1,378	664	15.4	70
Pittsburg, OK	40121	...	62.4	44.3	...	488	1,095	547	14.8	54
Pontotoc, OK	40123	...	61.2	47.4	...	370	1,024	508	13.6	48
Pottawatomie, OK	40125	...	59.8	36.4	...	713	1,648	874	15.2	71
Pushmataha, OK	40127	...	70.2	42.8	...	127	345	173	13.0	25
Roger Mills, OK	40129	...	42.9	20.9	...	44	166	79	9.4	16
Rogers, OK	40131	...	41.5	39.7	...	890	1,773	928	15.5	74
Seminole, OK	40133	...	71.1	45.5	...	304	744	367	14.0	42
Sequoyah, OK	40135	...	71.5	52.3	...	508	1,144	587	15.2	40
Stephens, OK	40137	...	49.1	24.5	...	518	1,055	541	15.1	46
Texas, OK	40139	...	60.5	56.1	...	186	583	305	13.2	34
Tillman, OK	40141	...	75.6	51.5	...	110	237	121	13.1	11
Tulsa, OK	40143	...	51.1	46.2	...	6,006	14,546	6,789	16.5	677
Wagoner, OK	40145	...	52.7	40.6	...	316	868	433	15.6	36
Washington, OK	40147	...	44.6	31.9	...	564	1,119	526	15.6	51
Washita, OK	40149	...	61.6	21.9	...	118	295	162	13.6	11
Woods, OK	40151	...	41.3	13.1	...	83	218	109	11.7	15
Woodward, OK	40153	...	44.2	19.4	...	208	468	244	14.9	19
OREGON	41000	14.1	46.0	26.9	11.2	33,422	64,690	30,063	18.7	3,893
Baker, OR	41001	15.4	54.3	8.5	1.4	173	288	126	17.5	15
Benton, OR	41003	12.3	34.5	17.3	6.9	681	966	453	19.9	33
Clackamas, OR	41005	13.0	31.4	17.4	8.4	3,677	6,299	3,018	19.5	183
Clatsop, OR	41007	14.9	46.0	14.6	5.4	366	659	305	16.5	34
Columbia, OR	41009	13.3	34.8	8.3	1.4	584	878	445	19.3	41
Coos, OR	41011	17.2	53.5	18.4	1.4	598	1,041	436	19.4	54
Crook, OR	41013	15.0	56.2	14.0	4.3	201	377	177	18.1	10
Curry, OR	41015	13.6	53.6	15.3	1.3	180	314	139	18.4	26
Deschutes, OR	41017	14.2	40.6	13.8	4.7	1,335	2,688	1,254	19.7	103
Douglas, OR	41019	14.0	53.9	8.0	1.0	910	1,916	859	17.7	111
Gilliam, OR	41021	17.2	42.9	10.3	...	27	62	25	9.3	5
Grant, OR	41023	15.9	43.9	5.0	...	84	189	86	12.0	25
Harney, OR	41025	16.1	58.9	8.5	0.9	89	185	91	13.0	10
Hood River, OR	41027	15.8	56.9	46.3	26.8	260	509	244	16.3	20
Jackson, OR	41029	12.6	48.7	20.7	8.5	1,610	3,020	1,384	20.6	160
Jefferson, OR	41031	13.9	75.6	60.5	30.9	211	452	214	17.2	21
Josephine, OR	41033	11.9	54.6	12.6	1.2	705	1,176	513	21.7	36
Klamath, OR	41035	16.0	61.9	23.9	6.7	537	1,209	530	19.0	82
Lake, OR	41037	13.3	50.0	18.8	6.7	75	170	74	14.9	18
Lane, OR	41039	17.2	43.3	17.4	3.8	3,054	5,518	2,379	19.6	362
Lincoln, OR	41041	15.3	58.4	23.4	7.0	432	558	271	19.8	27
Linn, OR	41043	12.5	42.2	14.1	3.1	1,052	2,396	1,040	20.5	162
Malheur, OR	41045	12.7	66.9	46.0	22.7	295	806	346	15.0	39
Marion, OR	41047	15.1	60.2	40.5	20.6	3,254	7,231	3,262	18.4	1,028
Morrow, OR	41049	13.8	67.6	44.9	22.1	142	308	145	16.6	10
Multnomah, OR	41051	14.3	51.2	40.3	16.2	4,769	10,538	4,956	18.4	235
Polk, OR	41053	15.1	42.2	24.0	9.1	446	860	396	19.5	41

[2]IEP= Individual Education Program. See notes and definitions for more information
... Not available

Table C-1. Population, School, and Student Characteristics by County—*Continued*

County	State/ County Code	Revenues, 2007-2008				Current expenditures, 2007-2008			Resident population 16 to 19 years, 2006-2008			
		Total revenue ($1,000's)	Percentage of revenue from			Amount ($1,000's)	Amount per student	Percent for instruc-tion	Total population 16 to 19 years	Percent en-rolled in school	Percent high school graduates, not enrolled in school	Percent not enrolled, not grads, not employed or not in labor force
			Federal gov't	State gov't	Local gov't							
	19	20	21	22	23	24	25	26	27	28	29	

County	State/ County Code	19	20	21	22	23	24	25	26	27	28	29
Kay, OK	40071	79,575	10.3	48.7	41.0	67,001	7,803	54.4	...	...	...	...
Kingfisher, OK	40073	31,400	12.5	45.7	41.9	26,928	8,339	57.7	...	...	...	...
Kiowa, OK	40075	15,345	13.1	59.2	27.7	15,390	9,048	55.8	...	...	...	...
Latimer, OK	40077	17,114	14.2	62.1	23.7	15,163	8,586	54.0	...	...	...	...
Le Flore, OK	40079	81,408	16.6	63.8	19.6	77,701	7,786	59.8	...	...	...	...
Lincoln, OK	40081	44,704	12.3	60.3	27.3	42,281	7,423	58.0	...	...	...	...
Logan, OK	40083	37,030	12.0	55.5	32.5	34,593	7,650	53.4	...	...	...	...
Love, OK	40085	14,008	11.0	59.7	29.3	12,477	7,631	55.6	...	...	...	...
McClain, OK	40087	68,159	7.4	56.3	36.3	60,841	7,516	56.0	...	...	...	...
McCurtain, OK	40089	61,452	16.4	62.0	21.6	58,864	8,186	56.2	...	...	...	...
McIntosh, OK	40091	24,777	18.7	57.0	24.3	23,135	7,967	57.5	...	...	...	...
Major, OK	40093	14,734	8.0	50.8	41.2	10,417	10,104	57.0	...	...	...	...
Marshall, OK	40095	22,623	15.5	59.4	25.1	21,755	7,494	57.4	...	...	...	...
Mayes, OK	40097	60,663	15.1	59.6	25.3	56,736	7,486	58.2	...	...	...	...
Murray, OK	40099	16,488	12.3	65.4	22.3	15,609	6,772	59.0	...	...	...	...
Muskogee, OK	40101	111,709	13.4	56.0	30.5	104,426	7,489	57.7	...	...	...	...
Noble, OK	40103	20,843	12.2	41.2	46.7	18,607	8,255	55.2	...	...	...	...
Nowata, OK	40105	17,231	13.1	62.5	24.4	16,116	7,820	56.9	...	...	...	...
Okfuskee, OK	40107	19,467	17.2	61.2	21.6	18,975	8,311	56.4	...	...	...	...
Oklahoma, OK	40109	1,048,281	10.2	43.6	46.2	855,147	7,488	56.1	36,001	81.0	9.4	6.0
Okmulgee, OK	40111	62,971	15.7	61.3	22.9	54,932	7,641	56.6	...	...	...	...
Osage, OK	40113	51,436	11.5	60.3	28.2	48,197	7,697	55.4	...	...	...	...
Ottawa, OK	40115	49,729	15.5	64.7	19.8	46,376	7,538	57.8	...	...	...	...
Pawnee, OK	40117	25,935	13.0	62.8	24.2	24,151	7,874	56.6	...	...	...	...
Payne, OK	40119	97,527	7.6	49.1	43.3	78,068	7,665	55.7	...	...	...	...
Pittsburg, OK	40121	67,323	14.9	57.2	27.8	63,329	8,159	56.7	...	...	...	...
Pontotoc, OK	40123	64,487	14.7	58.7	26.6	57,379	8,410	58.4	...	...	...	...
Pottawatomie, OK	40125	112,266	13.7	59.3	27.0	97,683	7,624	57.5	4,291	83.7	12.1	2.4
Pushmataha, OK	40127	21,680	16.9	67.1	16.0	20,079	8,803	57.1	...	...	...	...
Roger Mills, OK	40129	15,101	8.6	44.8	46.6	11,238	16,193	47.6	...	...	...	...
Rogers, OK	40131	107,453	9.0	54.1	36.9	97,149	6,785	58.1	...	...	...	...
Seminole, OK	40133	46,365	17.1	60.9	21.9	42,766	7,787	55.5	...	...	...	...
Sequoyah, OK	40135	68,171	15.5	68.2	16.3	65,787	7,470	57.1	...	...	...	...
Stephens, OK	40137	71,351	8.8	56.8	34.4	61,623	7,508	56.1	...	...	...	...
Texas, OK	40139	37,024	11.5	53.9	34.6	34,326	8,616	52.4	...	...	...	...
Tillman, OK	40141	34,442	9.0	50.2	40.8	20,917	12,443	51.5	...	...	...	...
Tulsa, OK	40143	1,004,821	9.1	42.3	48.5	820,650	7,562	53.9	30,533	82.1	9.8	4.9
Wagoner, OK	40145	49,667	10.5	63.2	26.3	44,589	6,709	60.2	4,067	83.4	8.4	4.2
Washington, OK	40147	76,265	7.9	51.1	41.0	65,317	7,867	55.0	...	...	...	...
Washita, OK	40149	18,729	10.0	60.3	29.7	16,771	7,661	57.5	...	...	...	...
Woods, OK	40151	12,487	7.3	42.7	49.9	11,535	9,155	53.5	...	...	...	...
Woodward, OK	40153	33,229	9.1	51.5	39.4	27,653	7,912	55.6	...	...	...	...
OREGON	41000	6,107,684	8.4	52.4	39.2	5,469,985	9,722	58.8	195,875	81.6	11.5	4.2
Baker, OR	41001	23,292	9.7	60.7	29.6	24,223	10,559	55.7	...	...	...	...
Benton, OR	41003	92,791	6.1	44.9	49.1	83,186	9,178	58.6	...	...	...	...
Clackamas, OR	41005	626,192	5.3	49.5	45.2	522,911	8,901	59.1	20,074	84.3	10.6	2.0
Clatsop, OR	41007	56,597	6.0	41.8	52.2	50,175	9,807	59.6	...	...	...	...
Columbia, OR	41009	79,300	5.9	53.6	40.5	73,150	8,468	58.7	...	...	...	...
Coos, OR	41011	96,544	8.8	52.7	38.5	94,285	11,398	54.2	3,228	75.5	13.7	1.1
Crook, OR	41013	30,182	11.0	49.8	39.2	29,692	9,144	58.5	...	...	...	...
Curry, OR	41015	29,128	10.9	44.5	44.7	25,381	9,574	59.8	...	...	...	...
Deschutes, OR	41017	265,901	6.7	42.6	50.7	223,814	9,188	59.2	7,033	72.8	19.0	5.2
Douglas, OR	41019	161,302	12.8	56.7	30.4	154,118	9,937	54.3	5,078	80.5	10.5	7.4
Gilliam, OR	41021	6,928	5.4	36.3	58.2	6,346	25,384	49.3	...	...	...	...
Grant, OR	41023	17,273	18.5	46.0	35.5	14,628	13,813	54.5	...	...	...	...
Harney, OR	41025	17,016	12.5	60.9	26.7	16,437	13,108	48.6	...	...	...	...
Hood River, OR	41027	47,036	9.8	56.0	34.2	42,471	10,709	65.3	...	...	...	...
Jackson, OR	41029	313,244	8.3	52.3	39.4	272,683	9,521	57.8	10,742	75.1	16.2	6.3
Jefferson, OR	41031	47,955	17.0	57.2	25.8	41,720	11,017	52.8	...	...	...	...
Josephine, OR	41033	107,505	9.5	57.4	33.0	100,427	8,877	60.2	4,170	79.5	12.8	6.3
Klamath, OR	41035	99,718	13.7	61.7	24.6	102,815	9,868	58.6	3,576	72.8	12.0	5.2
Lake, OR	41037	14,639	15.5	57.1	27.5	13,557	12,061	50.1	...	...	...	...
Lane, OR	41039	510,651	10.1	50.8	39.1	475,539	10,024	59.2	18,747	83.8	10.1	4.3
Lincoln, OR	41041	58,504	13.0	29.7	57.4	53,559	9,858	61.1	...	...	...	...
Linn, OR	41043	213,020	8.7	58.8	32.4	185,931	9,100	58.8	6,094	79.3	11.5	5.8
Malheur, OR	41045	62,160	12.6	70.8	16.7	57,782	10,802	59.7	...	...	...	...
Marion, OR	41047	659,505	9.0	63.2	27.8	576,346	9,845	61.4	17,224	77.2	13.3	4.9
Morrow, OR	41049	24,900	6.7	57.3	36.0	24,377	10,230	58.2	...	...	...	...
Multnomah, OR	41051	1,029,787	9.1	47.7	43.2	972,714	10,650	58.2	33,111	83.7	10.2	3.3
Polk, OR	41053	73,931	7.8	63.2	29.0	66,898	8,664	61.0	...	...	...	...

... Not available

Table C-1. Population, School, and Student Characteristics by County—*Continued*

County	State/County Code	High school graduates, 2006-2008			College enrollment, 2006-2008		College graduates, 2006-2008 (percent)						
		Population 25 years and over	High school diploma or less (percent)	High school diploma or more (percent)	Number	Percent public	Bachelor's degree or more	+/- U.S. percent with Bachelor's degree or more	Non-Hispanic White	Black or African American	American Indian and Alaska Native	Asian, Hawaiian, and Pacific Islander	Hispanic or Latino[3]
		30	31	32	33	34	35	36	37	38	39	40	41
Kay, OK	40071	30,007	52.4	85.7	2,114	92.7	19.1	-8.3	20.3	...	12.2	...	6.8
Kingfisher, OK	40073	...	...	...	...	...	...	...	...	...	...	...	...
Kiowa, OK	40075	...	...	...	...	...	...	...	...	...	...	...	...
Latimer, OK	40077	...	...	...	...	...	...	...	...	...	...	...	...
Le Flore, OK	40079	32,694	59.5	77.4	1,690	89.6	11.1	-16.3	12.1	8.9	7.2	...	...
Lincoln, OK	40081	21,246	58.5	84.5	915	82.3	13.5	-13.9	14.2	11.0	9.3	...	...
Logan, OK	40083	23,246	50.4	87.2	1,898	86.6	20.2	-7.2	20.5	18.3	17.8	...	...
Love, OK	40085	...	...	...	...	...	...	...	...	...	...	...	...
McClain, OK	40087	20,331	51.5	87.3	...	...	17.4	-10.0	17.3	...	25.4	...	4.0
McCurtain, OK	40089	22,089	65.0	77.1	1,024	86.5	11.5	-15.9	12.8	8.6	4.7	...	...
McIntosh, OK	40091	...	...	...	...	...	...	...	...	...	...	...	...
Major, OK	40093	...	...	...	...	...	...	...	...	...	...	...	...
Marshall, OK	40095	...	...	...	...	...	...	...	...	...	...	...	...
Mayes, OK	40097	26,562	58.1	85.0	1,314	88.8	11.3	-16.1	13.0	...	8.9	...	2.2
Murray, OK	40099	...	...	...	...	...	...	...	...	...	...	...	...
Muskogee, OK	40101	46,856	54.0	81.0	2,924	82.3	16.8	-10.6	18.0	13.0	20.1	...	2.3
Noble, OK	40103	...	...	...	...	...	...	...	...	...	...	...	...
Nowata, OK	40105	...	...	...	...	...	...	...	...	...	...	...	...
Okfuskee, OK	40107	...	...	...	...	...	...	...	...	...	...	...	...
Oklahoma, OK	40109	450,233	41.1	85.1	44,380	76.8	28.1	0.7	32.6	17.0	16.2	45.1	7.7
Okmulgee, OK	40111	25,489	56.1	83.2	2,343	93.2	14.0	-13.4	14.9	11.1	12.2	...	...
Osage, OK	40113	30,745	52.7	86.2	1,897	64.5	17.4	-10.0	18.4	22.0	10.8	...	...
Ottawa, OK	40115	21,285	54.5	81.9	1,607	92.0	13.8	-13.6	14.3	...	14.2	...	3.1
Pawnee, OK	40117	...	...	...	...	...	...	...	...	...	...	...	...
Payne, OK	40119	44,055	40.0	88.5	19,167	96.4	33.2	5.8	32.8	20.4	19.1	...	29.8
Pittsburg, OK	40121	31,002	56.4	82.4	1,534	80.0	16.1	-11.3	16.1	24.3	14.2	...	7.2
Pontotoc, OK	40123	23,184	47.1	84.1	3,270	89.7	24.9	-2.5	25.7	...	20.6	...	...
Pottawatomie, OK	40125	44,567	54.3	82.4	5,339	55.9	16.4	-11.0	17.2	17.4	13.0	...	7.2
Pushmataha, OK	40127	...	...	...	...	...	...	...	...	...	...	...	...
Roger Mills, OK	40129	...	...	...	...	...	...	...	...	...	...	...	...
Rogers, OK	40131	54,337	47.2	89.0	4,775	89.4	19.9	-7.5	21.3	...	15.1	...	3.8
Seminole, OK	40133	15,449	61.9	78.2	1,146	90.7	13.7	-13.7	15.3	16.0	5.6	...	16.4
Sequoyah, OK	40135	26,484	61.2	79.2	1,896	98.5	11.8	-15.6	12.9	...	9.1	...	...
Stephens, OK	40137	29,283	57.3	84.3	1,296	95.6	15.6	-11.8	16.7	8.4	8.4	...	2.1
Texas, OK	40139	11,953	61.6	66.8	1,018	81.0	16.4	-11.0	25.6	...	...	...	2.7
Tillman, OK	40141	...	...	...	...	...	...	...	...	...	...	...	...
Tulsa, OK	40143	377,796	40.1	87.6	34,517	64.9	29.0	1.6	32.6	15.1	20.9	43.2	12.1
Wagoner, OK	40145	43,532	45.3	87.7	3,456	84.6	20.5	-6.9	21.9	22.3	9.7	...	11.4
Washington, OK	40147	33,822	45.7	87.6	2,127	60.0	26.6	-0.8	28.3	22.4	12.8	...	5.0
Washita, OK	40149	...	...	...	...	...	...	...	...	...	...	...	...
Woods, OK	40151	...	...	...	...	...	...	...	...	...	...	...	...
Woodward, OK	40153	...	...	...	...	...	...	...	...	...	...	...	...
OREGON	41000	2,538,321	38.4	88.1	239,925	78.3	28.0	0.6	29.3	19.7	8.8	44.2	10.4
Baker, OR	41001	...	...	...	...	...	...	...	...	...	...	...	...
Benton, OR	41003	49,514	22.4	94.5	17,170	96.8	48.3	20.9	48.0	...	...	68.7	35.1
Clackamas, OR	41005	258,064	33.6	91.3	23,859	78.2	30.9	3.5	31.5	16.9	7.0	47.9	14.9
Clatsop, OR	41007	25,996	41.2	88.5	1,836	86.3	20.3	-7.1	20.8	...	...	...	6.9
Columbia, OR	41009	33,390	46.8	88.4	2,364	76.1	16.3	-11.1	15.2	...	...	...	26.6
Coos, OR	41011	46,374	48.6	85.6	2,413	86.6	17.6	-9.8	18.3	...	8.2	37.1	1.1
Crook, OR	41013	15,887	52.4	87.2	283	86.2	15.0	-12.4	14.9	...	...	...	17.5
Curry, OR	41015	16,813	48.2	90.2	...	...	16.9	-10.5	16.0	...	...	...	...
Deschutes, OR	41017	107,097	34.9	92.5	5,804	85.9	28.4	1.0	28.7	...	...	53.3	12.0
Douglas, OR	41019	74,595	50.1	86.2	3,930	88.7	14.1	-13.3	14.3	...	3.8	42.0	4.4
Gilliam, OR	41021	...	...	...	...	...	...	...	...	...	...	...	...
Grant, OR	41023	...	...	...	...	...	...	...	...	...	...	...	...
Harney, OR	41025	...	...	...	...	...	...	...	...	...	...	...	...
Hood River, OR	41027	14,220	43.3	82.5	653	77.5	26.6	-0.8	31.9	...	...	...	4.5
Jackson, OR	41029	138,194	41.5	88.1	10,867	91.2	24.0	-3.4	24.6	32.8	6.8	50.6	9.6
Jefferson, OR	41031	13,065	56.7	80.5	414	84.1	14.1	-13.3	15.8	...	10.8	...	6.4
Josephine, OR	41033	58,875	48.3	85.1	3,097	81.7	15.7	-11.7	16.1	...	...	...	4.6
Klamath, OR	41035	44,457	48.4	86.6	3,950	94.9	17.4	-10.0	18.5	...	7.7	...	3.5
Lake, OR	41037	...	...	...	...	...	...	...	...	...	...	...	...
Lane, OR	41039	233,858	36.7	89.7	33,666	83.8	27.9	0.5	27.7	42.8	6.4	64.4	17.4
Lincoln, OR	41041	33,789	38.8	89.9	1,537	82.6	23.0	-4.4	24.3	...	9.3	...	7.0
Linn, OR	41043	76,622	47.8	84.9	5,152	91.8	15.2	-12.2	15.5	...	15.4	20.3	7.5
Malheur, OR	41045	19,992	55.3	77.0	1,416	87.6	14.0	-13.4	17.6	...	...	...	3.3
Marion, OR	41047	198,890	45.7	81.5	16,738	66.2	20.7	-6.7	23.9	14.7	3.8	25.4	6.5
Morrow, OR	41049	...	...	...	...	...	...	...	...	...	...	...	...
Multnomah, OR	41051	483,141	33.2	88.8	51,815	68.9	36.3	8.9	40.2	17.1	14.9	32.9	14.6
Polk, OR	41053	48,892	39.1	89.1	6,961	84.0	26.9	-0.5	29.0	...	...	...	10.1

[3]May be of any race
... Not available

Table C-1. Population, School, and Student Characteristics by County—*Continued*

County	State/ County Code	County Type[1]	Population, 2009		Percent of related children 5-17 years in poverty, 2008	Percent of children under 19 years with no health insurance, 2007	Number of Schools and Students, 2008-2009			Resident enrollment, 2006-2008	
			Total	Percent 5–17 years			School Districts	Schools	Students	K–12 enrollment	
										Number	Percent public
			1	2	3	4	5	6	7	8	9
Sherman, OR	41055	9	1,711	14.1	23.6	18.8	1	3	275	...	...
Tillamook, OR	41057	6	24,889	14.2	20.4	17.4	3	12	3,301	3,840	94.6
Umatilla, OR	41059	5	73,347	19.4	18.7	15.5	11	36	13,551	14,000	95.8
Union, OR	41061	7	25,038	16.1	17.4	12.3	7	15	3,830	4,100	86.3
Wallowa, OR	41063	9	6,889	14.6	18.0	20.9	5	9	871	...	...
Wasco, OR	41065	6	24,149	16.8	21.9	17.5	4	9	3,450	3,799	93.0
Washington, OR	41067	1	537,318	18.1	10.2	14.1	8	131	83,621	94,679	88.7
Wheeler, OR	41069	9	1,363	13.6	27.7	13.6	3	4	198	...	...
Yamhill, OR	41071	1	99,037	18.1	13.6	14.4	6	35	15,687	16,677	92.7
PENNSYLVANIA	42000	X	12,604,767	16.1	15.1	7.1	790	3280	1,769,789	2,040,241	85.0
Adams, PA	42001	4	102,323	16.7	9.1	9.4	7	26	14,313	16,374	87.1
Allegheny, PA	42003	1	1,218,494	14.6	14.9	5.4	75	313	150,615	188,457	84.7
Armstrong, PA	42005	1	67,851	15.3	15.1	8.8	3	15	6,992	10,628	94.0
Beaver, PA	42007	1	171,673	15.1	14.9	6.3	20	61	31,976	27,227	93.0
Bedford, PA	42009	6	49,579	16.0	16.1	10.2	6	22	7,828	7,701	93.9
Berks, PA	42011	2	407,125	17.4	14.9	8.5	21	114	70,160	68,338	90.8
Blair, PA	42013	3	126,122	15.3	18.8	7.3	10	38	18,341	19,101	89.4
Bradford, PA	42015	6	61,131	16.8	21.1	10.5	7	23	8,648	10,614	94.1
Bucks, PA	42017	1	626,015	17.1	5.5	7.3	22	141	91,576	106,779	81.3
Butler, PA	42019	1	184,694	16.8	8.9	7.4	10	55	33,159	31,367	89.6
Cambria, PA	42021	3	143,998	14.5	19.4	6.2	16	41	19,189	20,841	88.6
Cameron, PA	42023	7	5,163	15.3	16.1	7.0	1	2	787	...	...
Carbon, PA	42025	2	63,865	15.6	14.9	6.8	6	21	9,532	9,309	92.4
Centre, PA	42027	3	146,212	11.5	11.2	10.3	9	31	13,717	17,167	92.8
Chester, PA	42029	1	498,894	18.0	5.9	7.1	32	108	80,148	85,639	81.0
Clarion, PA	42031	6	39,474	14.4	17.5	8.4	8	16	5,875	5,768	93.0
Clearfield, PA	42033	4	82,324	14.7	20.7	7.1	11	32	12,484	12,271	89.6
Clinton, PA	42035	6	36,797	14.7	19.5	7.4	3	14	3,874	5,184	90.9
Columbia, PA	42037	4	65,111	13.9	15.2	6.7	7	17	7,440	9,018	95.3
Crawford, PA	42039	4	88,521	16.5	24.0	9.4	5	28	12,591	14,448	88.3
Cumberland, PA	42041	2	232,483	14.9	7.7	7.5	11	48	28,032	33,875	89.4
Dauphin, PA	42043	2	258,934	16.3	16.2	8.3	14	75	37,777	43,206	86.5
Delaware, PA	42045	1	558,028	17.1	12.2	5.6	22	113	72,892	99,051	77.8
Elk, PA	42047	7	32,011	15.8	11.0	7.6	3	10	4,064	5,200	76.8
Erie, PA	42049	2	280,291	16.6	19.1	6.5	21	83	41,148	47,439	85.6
Fayette, PA	42051	1	142,605	15.2	31.7	5.9	8	46	18,913	22,022	94.1
Forest, PA	42053	9	6,775	12.4	26.3	12.7	3	6	1,228	...	...
Franklin, PA	42055	4	144,994	16.4	10.9	10.5	11	48	22,766	22,641	84.4
Fulton, PA	42057	8	14,852	16.4	16.4	11.8	4	8	2,364	...	...
Greene, PA	42059	6	39,245	14.5	20.5	6.4	6	15	5,608	6,116	97.7
Huntingdon, PA	42061	6	45,395	14.4	15.0	8.1	7	21	6,261	6,516	90.7
Indiana, PA	42063	4	87,450	13.7	16.9	8.3	11	27	12,064	11,246	90.7
Jefferson, PA	42065	7	44,634	15.7	18.4	8.3	4	16	5,682	7,015	90.4
Juniata, PA	42067	6	23,118	17.2	14.2	15.5	1	12	3,101	3,653	81.9
Lackawanna, PA	42069	2	208,801	15.2	17.0	5.4	14	52	28,434	32,014	84.8
Lancaster, PA	42071	2	507,766	17.8	12.4	12.2	21	122	68,859	85,144	78.4
Lawrence, PA	42073	4	90,160	15.9	18.7	7.4	10	30	14,040	14,550	94.2
Lebanon, PA	42075	3	130,506	16.4	11.4	8.3	7	35	18,893	20,922	88.2
Lehigh, PA	42077	2	343,519	17.0	13.7	6.7	14	69	50,423	58,210	87.9
Luzerne, PA	42079	2	312,845	15.0	16.9	5.7	18	74	45,492	47,469	87.2
Lycoming, PA	42081	3	116,840	15.2	17.0	7.3	11	37	16,704	18,163	93.8
McKean, PA	42083	7	43,196	15.7	22.1	7.6	7	15	6,724	7,253	91.0
Mercer, PA	42085	2	116,071	16.2	20.0	7.3	15	41	17,348	18,269	90.7
Mifflin, PA	42087	4	45,937	16.6	17.6	8.6	3	14	5,656	7,108	80.9
Monroe, PA	42089	4	166,355	18.6	11.5	8.4	7	43	32,180	31,722	89.4
Montgomery, PA	42091	1	782,339	16.6	6.6	6.3	34	162	107,750	132,714	78.9
Montour, PA	42093	6	17,715	15.8	12.8	7.7	3	8	2,487	...	...
Northampton, PA	42095	2	298,990	16.3	10.0	6.7	13	62	45,574	47,379	87.8
Northumberland, PA	42097	4	91,311	14.6	17.1	6.0	9	26	12,307	13,382	88.0
Perry, PA	42099	2	45,502	17.0	12.3	11.2	5	16	6,805	7,459	91.3
Philadelphia, PA	42101	1	1,547,297	16.3	30.8	5.1	71	337	191,736	260,126	77.1
Pike, PA	42103	1	60,529	17.8	10.7	11.6	2	13	9,630	11,350	95.6
Potter, PA	42105	9	16,714	16.5	18.1	9.4	5	10	2,581	...	...
Schuylkill, PA	42107	4	146,952	14.5	14.9	6.1	14	38	19,153	21,282	90.0
Snyder, PA	42109	7	38,519	15.8	14.6	9.2	2	11	4,957	5,688	87.1
Somerset, PA	42111	4	76,953	14.5	18.8	9.1	13	35	10,537	11,753	91.5
Sullivan, PA	42113	8	6,140	14.1	18.7	16.2	1	3	668	...	...
Susquehanna, PA	42115	6	40,646	16.7	17.1	10.5	7	15	7,196	7,009	92.4
Tioga, PA	42117	6	40,875	15.2	18.8	9.1	3	16	5,880	6,453	95.7

[1]County type codes are from the Economic Research Service of the United States Department of Agriculture. See notes and definitions for more information.
... Not available

Table C-1.   Population, School, and Student Characteristics by County—*Continued*

County	State/ County Code	Characteristics of students, 2008-2009				Number of graduates, 2006-2007	Staff and students, 2008-2009			
		Percent with IEP[2]	Percent elligible for free or reduced lunch	Percent minority	Percent English Language Learners		Total staff	Number of teachers	Student/ teacher ratio	Central admin. Staff
		10	11	12	13	14	15	16	17	18
Sherman, OR	41055	18.9	52.0	11.6	3.6	16	46	25	11.0	2
Tillamook, OR	41057	15.0	57.0	21.5	10.6	271	470	205	16.1	28
Umatilla, OR	41059	12.3	59.1	38.5	16.0	849	1,714	765	17.7	82
Union, OR	41061	16.4	41.7	9.0	2.0	325	443	225	17.0	32
Wallowa, OR	41063	15.7	45.7	3.8	...	75	134	65	13.4	11
Wasco, OR	41065	16.3	46.3	29.1	15.1	215	496	211	16.4	28
Washington, OR	41067	12.8	34.7	34.0	14.7	4,889	9,079	4,541	18.4	754
Wheeler, OR	41069	14.1	58.6	7.1	4.0	24	51	25	7.9	5
Yamhill, OR	41071	13.6	45.6	24.9	13.0	1,011	1,646	835	18.8	61
PENNSYLVANIA	42000	16.7	33.4	26.0	2.6	128,603	251,847	129,660	13.6	9,744
Adams, PA	42001	13.6	25.7	13.7	2.9	1,041	3,323	1,457	9.8	176
Allegheny, PA	42003	17.4	30.9	26.1	0.8	12,342	22,587	11,754	12.8	824
Armstrong, PA	42005	17.7	36.3	1.8	0.1	629	892	541	12.9	36
Beaver, PA	42007	14.0	26.1	12.4	0.1	2,523	3,760	1,913	16.7	161
Bedford, PA	42009	16.8	40.2	1.9	0.2	629	1,041	552	14.2	47
Berks, PA	42011	16.9	34.9	32.4	6.2	4,554	10,308	4,990	14.1	515
Blair, PA	42013	19.1	42.9	4.6	0.2	1,369	2,974	1,446	12.7	185
Bradford, PA	42015	17.0	39.9	3.1	0.1	778	1,185	627	13.8	53
Bucks, PA	42017	17.5	14.3	14.2	1.8	7,156	13,243	6,576	13.9	459
Butler, PA	42019	13.6	18.6	3.0	0.3	2,201	3,817	2,202	15.1	138
Cambria, PA	42021	17.0	42.7	7.1	0.3	1,549	2,375	1,338	14.3	100
Cameron, PA	42023	22.7	45.5	2.3	0.5	71	119	60	13.1	4
Carbon, PA	42025	17.6	35.1	9.4	0.4	687	1,260	661	14.4	56
Centre, PA	42027	14.7	23.8	6.7	1.7	1,216	2,317	1,092	12.6	87
Chester, PA	42029	16.5	12.1	21.0	3.3	5,494	11,393	5,695	14.1	520
Clarion, PA	42031	17.8	35.9	2.4	...	457	1,065	528	11.1	32
Clearfield, PA	42033	18.5	43.4	1.5	0.1	918	1,886	909	13.7	96
Clinton, PA	42035	23.2	51.0	2.3	0.1	364	650	386	10.0	23
Columbia, PA	42037	16.8	30.7	4.4	0.5	643	1,067	579	12.8	53
Crawford, PA	42039	17.1	41.1	5.2	0.3	932	1,703	950	13.3	79
Cumberland, PA	42041	15.5	16.9	12.9	1.1	1,895	4,176	2,194	12.8	164
Dauphin, PA	42043	16.9	35.7	41.6	3.2	2,620	5,510	2,979	12.7	190
Delaware, PA	42045	19.3	27.3	37.9	2.3	5,260	11,511	5,379	13.6	522
Elk, PA	42047	18.8	35.9	2.4	0.1	366	523	274	14.8	19
Erie, PA	42049	18.4	45.1	18.0	2.2	2,899	5,612	2,935	14.0	195
Fayette, PA	42051	17.3	53.0	8.4	0.1	1,327	2,287	1,310	14.4	89
Forest, PA	42053	25.2	39.9	1.4	...	116	187	111	11.1	8
Franklin, PA	42055	15.5	29.8	12.7	2.1	1,577	2,861	1,524	14.9	94
Fulton, PA	42057	15.2	39.9	2.5	...	174	345	189	12.5	12
Greene, PA	42059	20.8	42.9	2.3	0.1	434	861	526	10.7	27
Huntingdon, PA	42061	19.2	41.8	4.2	0.1	505	855	497	12.6	47
Indiana, PA	42063	19.9	38.5	3.9	0.5	906	1,858	977	12.3	94
Jefferson, PA	42065	18.0	42.7	1.4	0.1	546	826	421	13.5	35
Juniata, PA	42067	13.4	33.4	6.3	1.2	213	365	215	14.4	12
Lackawanna, PA	42069	17.8	38.4	13.8	0.4	2,156	3,775	2,166	13.1	103
Lancaster, PA	42071	16.8	29.8	24.0	5.1	5,151	10,095	5,051	13.6	506
Lawrence, PA	42073	15.0	36.1	11.3	0.2	1,084	1,831	978	14.4	84
Lebanon, PA	42075	15.4	29.5	20.0	4.6	1,275	2,393	1,295	14.6	89
Lehigh, PA	42077	15.8	39.4	40.0	5.9	3,629	7,501	3,509	14.4	271
Luzerne, PA	42079	16.4	41.6	16.7	3.5	3,372	5,673	3,134	14.5	213
Lycoming, PA	42081	17.5	38.5	10.0	0.3	1,270	2,492	1,352	12.4	139
McKean, PA	42083	15.7	40.5	3.1	0.1	523	1,129	618	10.9	70
Mercer, PA	42085	...	58.6	4.3	...	1,406	2,794	1,335	13.0	122
Mifflin, PA	42087	16.5	39.9	5.0	0.4	440	805	494	11.4	26
Monroe, PA	42089	16.8	36.8	39.2	2.6	2,322	5,063	2,679	12.0	129
Montgomery, PA	42091	16.3	14.8	25.1	2.4	8,044	16,298	8,237	13.1	639
Montour, PA	42093	17.2	28.5	10.6	2.3	196	418	249	10.0	11
Northampton, PA	42095	15.3	25.4	25.9	4.1	3,469	7,078	3,631	12.6	267
Northumberland, PA	42097	15.5	40.5	6.5	1.3	985	2,381	1,015	12.1	93
Perry, PA	42099	19.5	27.0	3.9	0.2	523	1,172	682	10.0	65
Philadelphia, PA	42101	15.5	63.5	84.4	6.7	10,308	24,530	12,305	15.6	550
Pike, PA	42103	16.2	31.2	19.9	0.4	454	1,251	631	15.3	27
Potter, PA	42105	15.7	45.0	3.1	0.3	201	373	197	13.1	19
Schuylkill, PA	42107	19.7	36.8	6.0	0.7	1,429	2,784	1,493	12.8	126
Snyder, PA	42109	15.6	33.1	6.0	1.1	399	700	370	13.4	19
Somerset, PA	42111	17.1	38.4	1.9	0.3	863	1,512	799	13.2	73
Sullivan, PA	42113	16.5	32.8	2.1	...	62	116	48	13.9	6
Susquehanna, PA	42115	20.6	41.1	3.4	0.4	638	1,076	583	12.3	45
Tioga, PA	42117	16.2	44.1	3.0	0.2	496	872	504	11.7	34

[2]IEP= Individual Education Program. See notes and definitions for more information
... Not available

Table C-1. Population, School, and Student Characteristics by County—*Continued*

County	State/ County Code	Revenues, 2007-2008				Current expenditures, 2007-2008			Resident population 16 to 19 years, 2006-2008			
		Total revenue ($1,000's)	Percentage of revenue from			Amount ($1,000's)	Amount per student	Percent for instruc- tion	Total population 16 to 19 years	Percent en- rolled in school	Percent high school graduates, not enrolled in school	Percent not enrolled, not grads, not employed or not in labor force
			Federal gov't	State gov't	Local gov't							
	19		20	21	22	23	24	25	26	27	28	29
Sherman, OR	41055	4,154	4.1	65.0	30.8	4,006	14,782	51.0	...	...	...	...
Tillamook, OR	41057	44,299	8.7	33.5	57.8	37,330	11,295	58.3	...	...	...	...
Umatilla, OR	41059	151,762	10.7	62.9	26.4	136,912	10,126	59.4	3,972	79.3	12.7	5.9
Union, OR	41061	40,827	7.1	63.7	29.2	38,556	10,054	58.7	...	...	...	...
Wallowa, OR	41063	14,823	9.3	49.5	41.2	12,672	14,351	58.2	...	...	...	...
Wasco, OR	41065	42,589	9.7	55.8	34.6	39,251	11,148	57.3	...	...	...	...
Washington, OR	41067	884,675	6.3	49.3	44.3	760,289	9,154	58.5	25,459	81.6	11.6	4.9
Wheeler, OR	41069	4,120	13.4	63.3	23.3	3,971	18,643	50.8	...	...	...	...
Yamhill, OR	41071	155,434	6.8	58.3	34.9	131,833	8,409	61.8	5,561	85.9	9.4	3.6
PENNSYLVANIA	42000	27,175,803	7.1	33.4	59.5	21,569,651	12,078	59.3	729,794	86.6	8.0	3.5
Adams, PA	42001	278,261	10.8	30.6	58.6	254,349	17,682	57.8	6,354	90.4	6.5	1.2
Allegheny, PA	42003	2,713,069	6.8	29.2	64.0	2,106,628	13,449	58.5	69,323	88.4	7.7	2.5
Armstrong, PA	42005	103,933	4.2	47.5	48.3	88,170	13,160	60.1	3,156	84.2	9.4	3.7
Beaver, PA	42007	415,570	6.3	39.2	54.4	343,138	10,520	60.2	9,154	84.8	10.7	3.0
Bedford, PA	42009	93,407	7.3	56.0	36.6	78,356	9,841	58.5	2,391	81.3	12.0	4.1
Berks, PA	42011	1,042,225	8.5	33.9	57.6	857,232	12,202	54.3	24,120	86.8	7.6	3.2
Blair, PA	42013	260,431	12.1	48.6	39.3	221,815	12,043	56.0	6,663	87.9	8.5	2.7
Bradford, PA	42015	117,423	5.6	54.8	39.6	98,314	11,022	62.6	3,199	85.8	9.8	3.6
Bucks, PA	42017	1,571,166	3.9	19.5	76.6	1,286,059	14,100	63.4	34,528	84.1	7.3	7.6
Butler, PA	42019	343,269	3.7	38.6	57.7	273,482	9,372	63.0	10,536	90.3	6.7	1.5
Cambria, PA	42021	241,734	6.5	56.0	37.5	195,116	10,178	60.5	8,295	89.9	7.8	1.7
Cameron, PA	42023	11,254	2.2	62.8	34.9	8,662	10,538	60.6	...	...	...	...
Carbon, PA	42025	124,092	4.7	31.6	63.7	95,597	10,505	61.9	2,780	78.3	10.6	7.3
Centre, PA	42027	201,458	3.4	25.8	70.8	163,375	11,750	61.3	19,140	92.6	5.3	0.9
Chester, PA	42029	1,330,588	4.1	17.5	78.4	1,047,412	14,034	57.0	28,410	90.5	5.6	2.0
Clarion, PA	42031	105,082	11.3	54.7	34.0	91,768	15,241	53.8	...	...	...	...
Clearfield, PA	42033	179,603	9.3	51.2	39.6	151,932	11,945	57.4	3,913	73.3	17.4	8.1
Clinton, PA	42035	65,505	4.7	49.0	46.3	55,250	11,597	65.7	...	...	...	...
Columbia, PA	42037	92,611	5.0	39.0	56.0	74,237	10,834	61.5	5,298	92.0	5.2	1.5
Crawford, PA	42039	164,777	6.0	51.7	42.3	133,179	10,377	60.6	5,333	84.3	7.9	5.3
Cumberland, PA	42041	421,071	7.8	26.0	66.2	343,951	12,665	53.5	14,253	91.6	5.8	1.2
Dauphin, PA	42043	562,165	4.7	32.3	63.0	422,619	11,354	61.5	12,712	82.6	10.4	4.3
Delaware, PA	42045	1,209,660	6.1	25.0	68.8	986,456	13,240	60.9	37,710	90.7	5.8	2.8
Elk, PA	42047	47,174	4.6	49.9	45.5	41,276	10,035	60.6	...	...	...	...
Erie, PA	42049	581,919	9.8	42.2	48.0	461,124	11,091	58.5	17,758	87.5	8.4	3.3
Fayette, PA	42051	233,735	7.6	60.0	32.4	197,254	10,565	60.4	6,710	80.0	8.6	8.5
Forest, PA	42053	18,191	10.7	49.9	39.4	16,355	12,960	56.0	...	...	...	...
Franklin, PA	42055	275,906	3.8	32.7	63.4	210,181	9,242	64.1	6,385	78.4	11.2	3.4
Fulton, PA	42057	32,244	6.8	55.4	37.7	26,002	10,798	60.5	...	...	...	...
Greene, PA	42059	87,686	6.7	46.4	46.9	66,420	11,910	58.7	...	...	...	...
Huntingdon, PA	42061	70,137	7.2	56.4	36.4	60,279	9,861	59.5	...	...	...	...
Indiana, PA	42063	199,061	8.5	49.3	42.2	171,131	13,886	58.9	6,957	87.8	4.9	5.6
Jefferson, PA	42065	79,334	6.4	55.3	38.3	62,784	11,650	59.3	2,202	85.7	9.1	4.4
Juniata, PA	42067	30,941	5.5	49.6	44.8	27,403	8,601	58.2	1,131	60.8	18.9	10.2
Lackawanna, PA	42069	369,506	9.0	37.0	54.0	315,451	11,022	61.1	12,698	91.0	5.9	2.0
Lancaster, PA	42071	1,106,962	9.0	25.2	65.7	832,878	11,906	59.0	28,913	80.5	6.9	4.4
Lawrence, PA	42073	170,955	4.9	54.9	40.2	137,285	10,044	64.1	5,057	83.1	8.5	5.3
Lebanon, PA	42075	230,385	6.0	36.6	57.4	184,107	9,712	62.5	6,584	81.8	9.0	6.6
Lehigh, PA	42077	742,603	6.7	28.0	65.4	578,100	11,353	58.2	18,593	86.7	7.8	4.1
Luzerne, PA	42079	570,962	7.6	40.2	52.2	482,954	10,547	61.5	16,882	87.3	8.9	2.1
Lycoming, PA	42081	237,236	8.5	44.4	47.0	200,111	11,814	60.1	7,105	87.3	8.0	3.8
McKean, PA	42083	110,594	10.3	53.1	36.6	93,160	13,362	59.3	...	...	...	...
Mercer, PA	42085	287,913	12.9	42.8	44.3	234,131	13,174	61.6	7,508	90.4	4.0	4.4
Mifflin, PA	42087	99,029	20.3	46.6	33.1	96,430	16,736	46.7	1,982	59.7	15.6	14.8
Monroe, PA	42089	485,726	3.4	25.2	71.4	394,056	12,111	61.7	...	...	...	...
Montgomery, PA	42091	1,924,955	4.2	16.0	79.9	1,616,314	14,608	60.7	42,049	91.6	5.2	2.0
Montour, PA	42093	31,687	5.6	37.2	57.1	26,580	11,024	65.7	...	...	...	...
Northampton, PA	42095	691,276	6.0	23.9	70.1	543,803	11,816	57.9	17,997	88.1	8.7	2.5
Northumberland, PA	42097	200,312	15.2	43.6	41.2	180,594	14,262	54.1	4,451	80.3	9.3	5.8
Perry, PA	42099	90,572	3.9	45.6	50.5	67,346	9,837	59.1	2,245	77.9	13.5	4.9
Philadelphia, PA	42101	3,296,323	11.9	45.0	43.0	2,306,187	11,423	56.1	94,841	82.2	11.1	5.5
Pike, PA	42103	126,934	4.2	25.8	70.1	105,584	10,731	65.9	3,387	85.1	10.8	1.9
Potter, PA	42105	39,202	4.1	55.3	40.6	30,211	11,298	57.8	...	...	...	...
Schuylkill, PA	42107	269,813	7.3	43.1	49.6	216,098	11,124	58.2	6,660	83.4	8.6	4.6
Snyder, PA	42109	60,804	5.3	40.4	54.3	49,424	9,928	61.9	...	...	...	...
Somerset, PA	42111	141,899	6.1	54.9	39.0	112,049	10,444	60.0	3,439	84.5	9.9	2.0
Sullivan, PA	42113	12,206	3.6	34.6	61.7	10,457	15,561	58.4	...	...	...	...
Susquehanna, PA	42115	105,130	5.3	51.5	43.2	86,085	11,490	60.8	2,239	86.3	9.3	2.3
Tioga, PA	42117	77,819	6.7	51.7	41.6	66,321	10,826	62.1	...	...	...	...
Union, PA	42119	53,336	4.5	33.1	62.4	44,495	10,706	63.0	...	...	...	...

... Not available

Table C-1. Population, School, and Student Characteristics by County—*Continued*

County	State/County Code	High school graduates, 2006-2008			College enrollment, 2006-2008		College graduates, 2006-2008 (percent)						
		Population 25 years and over	High school diploma or less (percent)	High school diploma or more (percent)	Number	Percent public	Bachelor's degree or more	+/- U.S. percent with Bachelor's degree or more	Non-Hispanic White	Black or African American	American Indian and Alaska Native	Asian, Hawaiian, and Pacific Islander	Hispanic or Latino[3]
		30	31	32	33	34	35	36	37	38	39	40	41
Sherman, OR	41055	...	...	...	...	...	...	...	...	...	...	...	...
Tillamook, OR	41057	18,380	48.2	88.4	511	84.1	18.0	-9.4	18.8	...	...	...	...
Umatilla, OR	41059	47,446	49.9	81.6	2,911	86.3	15.4	-12.0	18.1	...	4.8	...	3.8
Union, OR	41061	16,126	46.4	90.0	1,927	90.2	20.1	-7.3	20.8	...	...	...	...
Wallowa, OR	41063	...	...	...	...	...	...	...	...	...	...	...	...
Wasco, OR	41065	16,327	48.5	82.6	717	78.7	21.4	-6.0	23.5	...	7.1	...	6.2
Washington, OR	41067	343,780	29.7	89.8	31,842	74.2	37.9	10.5	40.3	27.9	6.0	54.9	10.1
Wheeler, OR	41069	...	...	...	...	...	...	...	...	...	...	...	...
Yamhill, OR	41071	62,140	45.4	84.5	6,353	45.1	22.8	-4.6	25.4	...	1.7	38.0	4.5
PENNSYLVANIA	42000	8,439,935	51.3	86.8	847,590	58.6	25.9	-1.5	26.9	14.9	17.9	53.3	13.4
Adams, PA	42001	67,944	59.0	84.1	7,820	42.7	18.9	-8.5	19.2	...	...	...	8.9
Allegheny, PA	42003	845,829	41.3	91.3	98,146	59.9	33.5	6.1	34.7	16.5	23.3	73.6	40.3
Armstrong, PA	42005	50,178	64.8	86.5	2,546	85.3	14.2	-13.2	13.8	...	...	...	...
Beaver, PA	42007	123,468	54.4	89.0	8,159	65.3	19.0	-8.4	19.5	7.7	...	25.9	14.5
Bedford, PA	42009	35,553	67.5	83.8	1,468	81.3	12.8	-14.6	12.7	...	...	...	...
Berks, PA	42011	267,811	55.7	82.4	26,492	69.5	21.9	-5.5	23.3	17.4	...	40.1	8.0
Blair, PA	42013	88,006	59.7	85.8	6,406	76.2	17.5	-9.9	17.3	22.8	...	...	11.1
Bradford, PA	42015	42,853	64.1	84.5	2,070	70.1	15.2	-12.2	15.0	...	...	...	...
Bucks, PA	42017	424,492	40.1	90.9	33,636	59.7	34.5	7.1	34.6	18.7	...	60.4	18.5
Butler, PA	42019	123,038	46.1	91.3	12,833	79.1	29.0	1.6	28.7	25.4	...	...	20.4
Cambria, PA	42021	102,630	61.9	86.7	9,472	68.8	16.6	-10.8	16.9	9.7	...	39.7	8.2
Cameron, PA	42023	...	...	...	...	...	...	...	...	...	...	...	...
Carbon, PA	42025	45,319	62.1	86.8	2,981	67.7	13.3	-14.1	12.1	...	...	...	25.9
Centre, PA	42027	79,926	39.7	92.6	39,337	95.3	40.7	13.3	38.0	26.5	...	51.1	...
Chester, PA	42029	320,415	32.5	92.4	36,227	61.6	47.3	19.9	49.0	23.1	...	75.7	17.0
Clarion, PA	42031	26,431	64.7	86.4	4,484	91.9	16.1	-11.3	15.9	...	...	...	...
Clearfield, PA	42033	59,553	66.7	85.6	2,855	69.7	12.2	-15.2	12.2	...	...	...	...
Clinton, PA	42035	24,871	62.8	83.9	4,637	89.3	16.3	-11.1	15.8	...	...	...	...
Columbia, PA	42037	43,016	62.7	85.4	8,111	93.5	17.4	-10.0	17.0	...	...	...	10.3
Crawford, PA	42039	60,506	62.8	85.1	4,722	44.9	17.5	-9.9	17.4	5.2	...	...	...
Cumberland, PA	42041	155,680	45.7	90.3	19,274	65.7	31.6	4.2	31.4	19.3	...	64.0	26.2
Dauphin, PA	42043	176,044	50.4	88.1	12,792	75.3	26.1	-1.3	28.7	11.3	...	51.0	13.6
Delaware, PA	42045	360,555	42.1	90.1	47,777	42.6	34.2	6.8	36.6	18.4	...	52.8	25.3
Elk, PA	42047	23,382	62.5	89.9	1,302	82.3	16.5	-10.9	16.5	...	...	...	...
Erie, PA	42049	183,502	54.7	88.6	22,812	52.1	23.1	-4.3	24.2	5.8	...	45.4	14.8
Fayette, PA	42051	103,373	66.9	81.6	5,168	78.2	13.6	-13.8	13.6	11.5	...	...	5.3
Forest, PA	42053	...	...	...	...	...	...	...	...	...	...	...	...
Franklin, PA	42055	98,526	60.5	83.4	6,073	71.4	17.1	-10.3	17.2	12.7	...	35.8	15.9
Fulton, PA	42057	...	...	...	...	...	...	...	...	...	...	...	...
Greene, PA	42059	27,508	62.1	83.9	2,150	40.6	15.5	-11.9	15.7	...	...	...	...
Huntingdon, PA	42061	32,254	66.2	85.7	2,654	37.4	13.8	-13.6	14.4	6.5	...	...	...
Indiana, PA	42063	55,867	60.8	85.4	11,428	89.4	19.4	-8.0	19.2	17.9	...	...	...
Jefferson, PA	42065	32,110	69.8	86.4	1,413	69.5	11.9	-15.5	11.6	...	...	...	...
Juniata, PA	42067	16,142	73.8	77.5	477	67.9	9.8	-17.6	9.8	...	...	...	...
Lackawanna, PA	42069	144,934	52.8	87.3	14,911	30.9	22.4	-5.0	22.6	17.9	...	47.4	5.1
Lancaster, PA	42071	329,089	57.6	81.0	27,407	61.5	23.1	-4.3	23.8	16.7	...	35.0	9.3
Lawrence, PA	42073	63,228	59.2	85.9	4,766	48.7	18.1	-9.3	18.4	6.4	...	...	...
Lebanon, PA	42075	88,496	61.8	83.9	5,790	50.8	18.0	-9.4	18.5	11.6	...	36.6	6.6
Lehigh, PA	42077	228,972	48.9	85.4	19,803	55.4	26.7	-0.7	28.7	11.4	...	61.7	7.8
Luzerne, PA	42079	220,772	55.8	86.6	19,611	52.0	19.7	-7.7	19.9	10.9	...	57.5	9.4
Lycoming, PA	42081	79,996	55.7	84.4	7,859	70.8	18.7	-8.7	18.5	20.6	...	53.9	...
McKean, PA	42083	30,703	62.8	85.7	1,749	81.5	16.4	-11.0	16.6	...	...	...	...
Mercer, PA	42085	80,840	60.4	86.2	7,605	38.2	18.1	-9.3	18.4	7.6	...	...	...
Mifflin, PA	42087	32,327	74.2	79.9	922	79.9	10.8	-16.6	10.4	...	...	...	...
Monroe, PA	42089	107,339	50.7	88.6	11,315	79.7	22.8	-4.6	23.1	17.0	...	56.4	13.6
Montgomery, PA	42091	530,839	34.8	92.1	51,698	47.3	43.4	16.0	44.1	30.2	21.7	60.4	26.8
Montour, PA	42093	...	...	...	...	...	...	...	...	...	...	...	...
Northampton, PA	42095	198,081	49.4	86.6	22,977	43.4	26.2	-1.2	26.5	24.0	...	59.8	13.9
Northumberland, PA	42097	65,892	66.9	84.5	2,865	69.0	14.0	-13.4	14.0	16.0	...	...	4.3
Perry, PA	42099	31,284	65.2	86.4	1,773	79.0	13.7	-13.7	13.7	...	...	...	...
Philadelphia, PA	42101	926,082	57.9	78.5	117,808	42.3	21.1	-6.3	29.6	12.2	12.4	34.5	10.2
Pike, PA	42103	40,807	49.2	91.0	2,201	69.2	22.5	-4.9	22.3	28.5	...	...	16.7
Potter, PA	42105	...	...	...	...	...	...	...	...	...	...	...	...
Schuylkill, PA	42107	107,281	64.8	82.6	5,574	68.1	13.9	-13.5	14.0	8.3	...	45.7	1.3
Snyder, PA	42109	24,995	65.6	81.8	3,036	25.0	15.0	-12.4	15.2	...	...	...	...
Somerset, PA	42111	56,783	66.6	81.7	2,894	76.3	14.5	-12.9	14.4	...	...	...	...
Sullivan, PA	42113	...	...	...	...	...	...	...	...	...	...	...	...
Susquehanna, PA	42115	28,910	60.1	86.2	1,248	58.5	14.7	-12.7	14.6	...	...	...	6.4
Tioga, PA	42117	27,728	58.0	85.5	2,983	77.7	18.0	-9.4	17.9	...	...	...	...
Union, PA	42119	29,619	56.7	81.5	5,286	11.0	22.4	-5.0	25.4	...	...	...	...

[3]May be of any race
... Not available

Table C-1. Population, School, and Student Characteristics by County—*Continued*

County	State/County Code	County Type[1]	Population, 2009		Percent of related children 5-17 years in poverty, 2008	Percent of children under 19 years with no health insurance, 2007	Number of Schools and Students, 2008-2009			Resident enrollment, 2006-2008	
			Total	Percent 5–17 years			School Districts	Schools	Students	K–12 enrollment	
										Number	Percent public
			1	2	3	4	5	6	7	8	9
Union, PA	42119	4	43,560	13.2	13.1	10.3	3	12	4,070	5,701	86.7
Venango, PA	42121	4	54,183	16.0	22.1	7.1	5	21	6,642	9,103	91.8
Warren, PA	42123	6	40,638	15.8	17.4	8.6	3	14	5,483	6,366	87.0
Washington, PA	42125	1	207,389	15.4	11.9	7.2	17	57	29,137	32,184	90.2
Wayne, PA	42127	6	51,337	15.6	15.7	11.0	2	11	5,415	8,256	90.7
Westmoreland, PA	42129	1	362,251	15.0	11.8	6.8	22	102	51,672	54,116	91.7
Wyoming, PA	42131	2	27,808	16.9	15.8	8.4	3	13	5,507	4,763	94.8
York, PA	42133	2	428,937	16.9	8.4	6.7	21	120	68,704	69,353	90.5
RHODE ISLAND	44000	X	1,053,209	15.8	14.8	7.2	53	332	145,342	169,547	86.4
Bristol, RI	44001	1	49,542	15.5	6.0	5.0	2	14	6,894	7,582	80.5
Kent, RI	44003	1	168,752	15.6	8.6	4.9	6	53	24,108	26,738	88.8
Newport, RI	44005	1	80,300	14.5	9.1	6.3	6	27	10,184	12,164	83.7
Providence, RI	44007	1	627,690	16.1	19.1	8.0	31	199	87,233	102,661	86.5
Washington, RI	44009	1	126,925	15.5	7.7	6.9	8	39	16,923	20,402	87.0
SOUTH CAROLINA	45000	X	4,561,242	16.9	19.6	12.0	103	1,219	718,113	773,394	89.3
Abbeville, SC	45001	6	25,098	16.7	20.3	9.6	1	10	3,297	4,546	94.2
Aiken, SC	45003	2	156,017	16.9	22.1	11.1	1	41	24,687	27,430	89.7
Allendale, SC	45005	6	10,195	17.0	44.8	8.1	1	4	1,577	…	…
Anderson, SC	45007	3	184,901	17.6	17.8	10.2	6	50	31,130	30,858	92.5
Bamberg, SC	45009	7	15,005	16.3	33.1	9.2	2	8	2,409	…	…
Barnwell, SC	45011	6	22,688	18.6	27.8	9.7	4	11	4,352	4,126	93.0
Beaufort, SC	45013	5	155,215	14.3	16.5	21.6	1	28	19,353	24,350	82.5
Berkeley, SC	45015	2	173,498	17.6	18.7	14.6	1	36	28,957	32,083	86.3
Calhoun, SC	45017	2	14,621	15.7	21.8	14.4	1	4	1,695	…	…
Charleston, SC	45019	2	355,276	14.3	19.4	12.0	1	81	42,303	56,381	83.5
Cherokee, SC	45021	4	54,714	18.0	21.6	10.1	1	19	9,360	9,848	96.7
Chester, SC	45023	6	32,410	17.3	22.6	8.7	1	13	5,746	6,018	89.3
Chesterfield, SC	45025	6	43,037	18.2	25.0	9.0	1	16	7,989	7,965	90.6
Clarendon, SC	45027	6	32,988	15.9	31.3	9.9	4	14	5,373	5,947	80.8
Colleton, SC	45029	6	39,246	17.7	29.0	10.9	1	12	6,276	7,608	87.3
Darlington, SC	45031	3	66,445	17.9	31.2	9.1	1	23	11,039	13,195	86.8
Dillon, SC	45033	6	30,912	19.9	31.7	7.8	4	14	6,078	5,850	91.5
Dorchester, SC	45035	2	130,417	19.5	12.3	14.1	3	26	24,101	24,171	83.9
Edgefield, SC	45037	2	25,752	15.9	20.9	14.6	1	9	4,051	4,508	84.6
Fairfield, SC	45039	2	23,343	16.9	25.5	9.6	1	9	3,382	4,439	89.2
Florence, SC	45041	3	134,208	17.9	22.6	9.2	5	40	23,111	24,078	90.9
Georgetown, SC	45043	4	60,703	16.0	25.6	13.7	1	18	10,074	10,299	93.8
Greenville, SC	45045	2	451,428	17.4	16.1	11.7	1	94	70,441	74,849	85.6
Greenwood, SC	45047	4	69,671	17.4	21.4	10.6	4	23	12,060	12,375	91.9
Hampton, SC	45049	6	21,014	18.1	27.3	10.7	2	10	3,921	4,103	91.6
Horry, SC	45051	3	263,868	14.4	21.1	15.6	1	48	37,948	36,299	95.1
Jasper, SC	45053	6	23,221	17.3	27.8	17.9	2	6	3,368	4,464	76.6
Kershaw, SC	45055	2	60,042	18.1	18.3	12.5	1	19	10,505	10,743	93.4
Lancaster, SC	45057	4	77,767	17.2	19.4	10.8	1	20	11,808	13,764	94.4
Laurens, SC	45059	2	70,045	16.5	22.5	8.8	2	18	9,259	12,099	92.8
Lee, SC	45061	6	19,722	16.0	31.8	8.4	1	9	2,526	…	…
Lexington, SC	45063	2	255,607	18.0	12.8	13.0	4	52	36,319	43,693	94.2
McCormick, SC	45065	8	10,140	10.6	28.4	12.4	1	3	894	…	…
Marion, SC	45067	6	33,468	17.9	36.4	8.3	4	12	5,583	6,420	93.1
Marlboro, SC	45069	6	28,783	16.3	32.6	6.4	1	9	4,597	5,312	91.3
Newberry, SC	45071	6	38,763	16.5	21.2	13.5	1	14	5,983	6,434	90.3
Oconee, SC	45073	6	71,514	15.5	20.6	10.3	1	21	10,645	11,180	92.9
Orangeburg, SC	45075	4	90,112	16.6	27.1	11.0	5	30	14,340	15,143	83.4
Pickens, SC	45077	2	118,144	15.4	15.9	11.5	1	25	16,647	17,497	88.9
Richland, SC	45079	2	372,023	17.0	16.7	11.3	6	124	69,142	63,691	89.4
Saluda, SC	45081	2	19,094	16.1	22.6	14.0	1	5	2,100	…	…
Spartanburg, SC	45083	2	286,822	17.6	18.1	12.6	11	83	47,243	47,369	93.0
Sumter, SC	45085	3	104,495	18.1	24.9	10.1	3	28	17,566	19,847	85.4
Union, SC	45087	6	27,362	16.9	23.9	7.8	1	10	4,629	4,768	94.8
Williamsburg, SC	45089	6	34,445	16.5	41.0	8.4	1	15	5,409	6,566	87.7
York, SC	45091	1	227,003	18.4	13.0	12.3	4	55	38,840	37,722	92.3

[1]County type codes are from the Economic Research Service of the United States Department of Agriculture. See notes and definitions for more information.
… Not available

Table C-1. Population, School, and Student Characteristics by County—*Continued*

County	State/ County Code	Characteristics of students, 2008-2009				Number of graduates, 2006-2007	Staff and students, 2008-2009			
		Percent with IEP[2]	Percent eligible for free or reduced lunch	Percent minority	Percent English Language Learners		Total staff	Number of teachers	Student/ teacher ratio	Central admin. Staff
		10	11	12	13	14	15	16	17	18
Union, PA	42119	15.8	27.4	7.5	1.0	328	608	329	12.4	28
Venango, PA	42121	24.7	43.3	4.2	0.3	519	942	515	12.9	33
Warren, PA	42123	19.3	31.9	2.3	0.1	444	834	457	12.0	38
Washington, PA	42125	16.2	28.1	6.8	0.3	2,298	4,264	2,210	13.2	141
Wayne, PA	42127	15.6	40.2	5.1	0.3	733	712	398	13.6	25
Westmoreland, PA	42129	14.4	27.5	6.1	0.2	4,094	6,341	3,591	14.4	257
Wyoming, PA	42131	17.5	40.6	2.5	0.3	309	741	417	13.2	28
York, PA	42133	16.6	27.4	18.2	3.1	4,792	8,551	4,610	14.9	324
RHODE ISLAND	44000	19.0	39.8	31.4	...	10,387	18,214	11,325	12.8	500
Bristol, RI	44001	14.7	15.2	5.9	...	541	698	511	13.5	19
Kent, RI	44003	19.3	24.2	9.0	...	1,686	2,953	1,979	12.2	89
Newport, RI	44005	19.7	23.6	17.0	...	705	1,266	833	12.2	39
Providence, RI	44007	19.7	52.2	45.9	...	6,158	10,879	6,623	13.2	293
Washington, RI	44009	16.2	18.6	8.0	...	1,297	2,418	1,379	12.3	60
SOUTH CAROLINA	45000	14.1	52.5	46.0	4.4	35,108	67,395	47,552	15.1	1216
Abbeville, SC	45001	17.3	62.8	41.8	1.9	220	381	254	13.0	8
Aiken, SC	45003	11.7	53.2	40.8	4.2	1,291	2,297	1,553	15.9	18
Allendale, SC	45005	12.6	85.5	98.1	1.3	63	162	92	17.1	10
Anderson, SC	45007	15.5	45.6	26.6	2.5	1,526	2,714	1,953	15.9	71
Bamberg, SC	45009	16.2	70.2	72.9	1.1	175	265	172	14.0	9
Barnwell, SC	45011	17.2	67.7	56.3	0.4	278	464	311	14.0	8
Beaufort, SC	45013	11.2	50.1	55.0	13.4	936	1,679	1,366	14.2	18
Berkeley, SC	45015	14.3	51.9	44.1	5.1	1,295	2,586	1,781	16.3	48
Calhoun, SC	45017	14.3	87.3	85.4	2.0	91	190	120	14.1	6
Charleston, SC	45019	11.3	49.6	56.7	4.6	2,088	4,422	3,211	13.2	37
Cherokee, SC	45021	10.5	62.4	32.1	3.7	450	890	631	14.8	13
Chester, SC	45023	12.6	61.0	50.4	0.7	260	596	422	13.6	6
Chesterfield, SC	45025	11.6	62.6	44.9	2.2	419	705	521	15.3	8
Clarendon, SC	45027	17.0	70.8	66.7	2.4	309	569	341	15.8	22
Colleton, SC	45029	16.0	75.0	59.2	2.4	245	633	386	16.3	6
Darlington, SC	45031	17.2	66.7	59.6	0.8	530	1,178	739	14.9	29
Dillon, SC	45033	11.6	79.9	63.9	2.1	287	536	365	16.7	11
Dorchester, SC	45035	12.3	37.2	41.7	2.0	1,011	1,956	1,531	15.7	18
Edgefield, SC	45037	16.7	63.0	51.8	1.3	182	418	295	13.7	7
Fairfield, SC	45039	18.2	82.0	88.0	1.4	168	408	255	13.3	16
Florence, SC	45041	17.0	62.5	57.3	1.5	1,130	2,335	1,513	15.3	53
Georgetown, SC	45043	12.7	58.2	48.8	2.3	552	905	694	14.5	24
Greenville, SC	45045	14.8	42.0	39.3	8.4	3,229	6,132	4,542	15.5	25
Greenwood, SC	45047	13.3	55.5	46.0	6.2	639	1,345	820	14.7	72
Hampton, SC	45049	14.6	71.5	67.6	1.4	179	451	265	14.8	34
Horry, SC	45051	16.4	58.0	32.9	5.5	1,661	3,834	2,560	14.8	32
Jasper, SC	45053	13.1	78.3	86.2	18.3	138	349	239	14.1	8
Kershaw, SC	45055	12.8	47.9	36.0	2.1	537	975	669	15.7	11
Lancaster, SC	45057	12.9	49.1	36.9	3.5	648	1,079	707	16.7	21
Laurens, SC	45059	18.5	64.1	38.2	4.3	417	973	568	16.3	55
Lee, SC	45061	15.7	84.2	95.4	1.7	123	276	183	13.8	6
Lexington, SC	45063	13.5	39.5	28.8	4.2	1,900	3,140	2,181	16.7	118
McCormick, SC	45065	11.6	74.4	81.1	...	44	120	68	13.1	7
Marion, SC	45067	17.9	81.7	76.6	0.8	311	563	344	16.2	12
Marlboro, SC	45069	16.5	84.4	68.3	0.3	237	452	314	14.6	8
Newberry, SC	45071	16.9	64.0	55.0	8.0	283	633	429	13.9	17
Oconee, SC	45073	16.1	54.8	20.1	4.4	580	1,197	845	12.6	25
Orangeburg, SC	45075	16.4	78.5	80.0	0.9	807	1,477	1,006	14.3	24
Pickens, SC	45077	12.8	42.6	15.1	3.1	828	1,560	1,153	14.4	21
Richland, SC	45079	13.7	46.6	67.3	3.2	3,322	6,002	4,729	14.6	78
Saluda, SC	45081	12.4	68.2	54.9	15.5	98	235	144	14.6	18
Spartanburg, SC	45083	14.4	50.0	37.0	7.4	2,245	4,231	3,148	15.0	70
Sumter, SC	45085	13.7	67.8	66.0	1.2	915	1,697	1,033	17.0	50
Union, SC	45087	19.0	61.4	40.0	0.6	246	488	327	14.2	7
Williamsburg, SC	45089	19.6	87.3	92.6	...	281	536	308	17.6	6
York, SC	45091	12.4	37.0	32.3	3.2	1,934	3,365	2,468	15.7	46

[2]IEP= Individual Education Program. See notes and definitions for more information
... Not available

Table C-1. Population, School, and Student Characteristics by County—*Continued*

County	State/ County Code	Revenues, 2007-2008				Current expenditures, 2007-2008			Resident population 16 to 19 years, 2006-2008			
		Total revenue ($1,000's)	Percentage of revenue from			Amount ($1,000's)	Amount per student	Percent for instruc- tion	Total population 16 to 19 years	Percent en- rolled in school	Percent high school graduates, not enrolled in school	Percent not enrolled, not grads, not employed or not in labor force
			Federal gov't	State gov't	Local gov't							
		19	20	21	22	23	24	25	26	27	28	29
Venango, PA	42121	98,049	6.3	52.9	40.8	75,690	10,930	59.3	2,724	80.0	11.0	5.8
Warren, PA	42123	70,849	6.9	53.0	40.1	60,943	10,908	62.8	2,133	78.6	15.8	3.2
Washington, PA	42125	425,008	8.1	39.6	52.3	346,113	11,750	58.3	11,259	89.6	7.6	2.2
Wayne, PA	42127	81,763	5.5	31.5	63.0	66,619	11,837	62.8	...	...	...	...
Westmoreland, PA	42129	678,113	5.3	39.3	55.4	542,912	10,383	60.6	18,860	89.6	7.4	1.8
Wyoming, PA	42131	75,403	5.7	47.9	46.4	65,365	11,536	62.3	1,683	83.8	12.1	2.3
York, PA	42133	907,797	3.7	29.6	66.7	684,492	10,291	63.2	21,211	82.6	10.8	3.5
RHODE ISLAND	44000	2,202,273	7.6	38.8	53.6	2,069,904	14,202	60.0	65,453	87.0	6.9	3.6
Bristol, RI	44001	101,135	4.3	29.4	66.3	92,296	13,324	64.5	...	...	...	...
Kent, RI	44003	375,099	4.8	29.1	66.1	358,183	14,853	62.2	8,608	84.8	10.8	2.2
Newport, RI	44005	166,711	7.2	26.4	66.3	146,585	14,089	63.8	...	...	...	...
Providence, RI	44007	1,280,531	9.5	47.5	43.1	1,210,097	13,891	58.7	39,916	84.7	7.7	4.7
Washington, RI	44009	278,797	4.1	22.8	73.0	262,743	15,286	59.6	...	...	...	...
SOUTH CAROLINA	45000	7,743,317	9.0	50.6	40.5	6,560,155	9,231	57.1	262,482	80.7	11.9	4.8
Abbeville, SC	45001	36,097	9.9	61.9	28.2	33,088	9,365	57.6	...	...	...	...
Aiken, SC	45003	224,216	10.2	58.4	31.4	202,189	8,151	61.1	8,354	82.3	11.9	4.1
Allendale, SC	45005	20,240	15.0	57.8	27.2	20,368	12,442	45.6	...	...	...	...
Anderson, SC	45007	297,896	8.2	56.1	35.7	262,947	8,524	58.7	9,579	76.1	11.3	7.2
Bamberg, SC	45009	28,670	12.6	62.0	25.5	24,982	10,073	54.3	...	...	...	...
Barnwell, SC	45011	47,134	11.0	61.4	27.6	42,549	9,721	56.3	...	...	...	...
Beaufort, SC	45013	249,942	7.4	30.3	62.3	193,511	9,913	57.5	8,207	69.2	25.8	2.4
Berkeley, SC	45015	287,351	9.4	53.6	37.1	240,185	8,437	54.8	10,667	67.6	23.4	1.1
Calhoun, SC	45017	25,625	11.2	45.9	42.9	20,091	11,708	51.4	...	...	...	...
Charleston, SC	45019	527,501	9.2	38.3	52.5	435,331	10,312	57.0	20,383	81.8	12.9	2.0
Cherokee, SC	45021	97,561	10.3	51.6	38.2	82,969	8,859	56.6	...	...	...	...
Chester, SC	45023	65,837	10.4	53.3	36.3	59,134	10,028	56.4	...	...	...	...
Chesterfield, SC	45025	77,839	10.9	58.7	30.4	68,545	8,523	58.3	...	...	...	...
Clarendon, SC	45027	55,633	15.4	59.6	24.9	49,258	9,005	56.0	...	...	...	...
Colleton, SC	45029	72,613	13.2	49.1	37.7	59,809	9,379	54.9	...	...	...	...
Darlington, SC	45031	120,762	11.5	51.7	36.8	99,984	8,906	57.0	...	...	...	...
Dillon, SC	45033	55,061	15.7	62.8	21.5	52,046	8,510	52.3	...	...	...	...
Dorchester, SC	45035	222,465	6.6	59.7	33.6	195,600	8,317	58.9	7,842	80.6	12.1	3.9
Edgefield, SC	45037	42,392	9.5	57.6	32.9	38,685	9,528	60.7	...	...	...	...
Fairfield, SC	45039	47,778	10.0	44.0	46.0	43,909	12,542	51.7	...	...	...	...
Florence, SC	45041	233,969	12.6	57.3	30.1	209,059	9,083	57.4	7,712	84.7	6.0	7.3
Georgetown, SC	45043	119,810	9.7	44.0	46.3	99,957	9,721	56.4	...	...	...	...
Greenville, SC	45045	684,420	8.0	53.7	38.2	564,693	8,132	57.1	23,458	85.7	7.5	3.2
Greenwood, SC	45047	129,941	8.6	48.4	43.0	106,700	8,804	57.1	...	...	...	...
Hampton, SC	45049	42,670	13.4	61.7	25.0	40,067	9,913	54.0	...	...	...	...
Horry, SC	45051	444,197	7.5	37.8	54.7	357,255	9,604	59.0	11,030	75.8	14.9	4.4
Jasper, SC	45053	43,172	10.8	45.6	43.5	37,743	11,310	52.3	...	...	...	...
Kershaw, SC	45055	106,770	8.2	56.4	35.4	88,020	8,356	58.2	...	...	...	...
Lancaster, SC	45057	114,996	12.1	55.2	32.8	102,416	8,888	59.7	...	...	...	...
Laurens, SC	45059	88,120	13.0	59.3	27.6	82,409	8,781	53.2	3,958	78.5	10.1	7.0
Lee, SC	45061	33,229	12.8	65.4	21.8	27,340	10,747	51.6	...	...	...	...
Lexington, SC	45063	390,229	6.6	55.4	38.0	331,540	9,269	57.6	12,735	84.6	12.0	1.8
McCormick, SC	45065	15,259	12.6	51.2	36.2	11,018	11,976	48.2	...	...	...	...
Marion, SC	45067	61,281	16.7	59.3	23.9	55,322	9,566	56.4	...	...	...	...
Marlboro, SC	45069	51,223	17.4	60.1	22.5	45,918	9,669	53.3	...	...	...	...
Newberry, SC	45071	72,157	10.3	51.9	37.8	60,347	10,073	55.2	...	...	...	...
Oconee, SC	45073	124,475	7.9	42.2	50.0	114,693	10,687	49.9	...	...	...	...
Orangeburg, SC	45075	171,832	11.7	50.6	37.6	154,527	10,620	54.8	...	...	...	...
Pickens, SC	45077	174,812	6.7	49.1	44.2	131,055	7,867	58.7	9,955	90.6	4.5	3.9
Richland, SC	45079	825,248	7.0	46.5	46.5	701,806	10,784	57.7	29,304	80.6	15.3	2.9
Saluda, SC	45081	21,655	10.3	61.6	28.1	18,661	8,757	51.5	...	...	...	...
Spartanburg, SC	45083	492,206	7.6	53.3	39.0	413,422	8,946	58.9	15,263	82.8	8.3	6.9
Sumter, SC	45085	170,102	13.4	57.9	28.7	148,503	8,380	56.2	6,194	82.8	12.7	4.0
Union, SC	45087	46,777	10.5	63.0	26.4	41,607	8,851	57.9	...	...	...	...
Williamsburg, SC	45089	64,156	17.4	54.5	28.2	54,398	9,810	52.5	...	...	...	...
York, SC	45091	417,998	5.5	51.1	43.4	336,499	8,964	57.7	11,885	84.7	6.9	6.2

... Not available

Table C-1. Population, School, and Student Characteristics by County—*Continued*

County	State/County Code	High school graduates, 2006-2008			College enrollment, 2006-2008		College graduates, 2006-2008 (percent)						
		Population 25 years and over	High school diploma or less (percent)	High school diploma or more (percent)	Number	Percent public	Bachelor's degree or more	+/- U.S. percent with Bachelor's degree or more	Non-Hispanic White	Black or African American	American Indian and Alaska Native	Asian, Hawaiian, and Pacific Islander	Hispanic or Latino[3]
		30	31	32	33	34	35	36	37	38	39	40	41
Venango, PA	42121	38,791	63.0	86.4	1,613	71.9	13.5	-13.9	13.4	...	...	...	...
Warren, PA	42123	29,523	60.6	87.8	954	63.8	16.2	-11.2	16.0	...	...	...	...
Washington, PA	42125	144,775	51.7	88.7	11,843	68.9	24.5	-2.9	24.6	13.2	...	62.8	32.5
Wayne, PA	42127	37,439	55.8	84.2	2,413	43.8	19.5	-7.9	19.1	20.7	...	...	12.8
Westmoreland, PA	42129	261,320	49.9	91.2	19,013	62.6	24.0	-3.4	23.8	19.8	...	77.6	25.8
Wyoming, PA	42131	19,053	58.5	89.3	1,347	44.9	16.8	-10.6	16.9	...	...	...	...
York, PA	42133	289,204	54.9	86.0	20,608	63.4	21.9	-5.5	22.4	16.3	...	36.4	10.2
RHODE ISLAND	44000	708,457	45.8	83.0	96,080	55.2	29.8	2.4	31.9	18.9	10.9	45.7	12.8
Bristol, RI	44001	34,146	37.3	85.2	5,296	40.1	40.4	13.0	40.2	...	...	...	...
Kent, RI	44003	119,092	42.6	89.3	10,562	67.2	29.2	1.8	28.8	32.0	...	55.0	26.8
Newport, RI	44005	57,997	34.5	89.8	7,093	49.7	41.4	14.0	42.3	16.2	...	...	45.2
Providence, RI	44007	412,847	51.7	78.2	58,298	48.4	25.1	-2.3	27.9	18.0	14.2	41.6	10.8
Washington, RI	44009	84,375	32.8	92.3	14,831	81.4	41.2	13.8	41.7	...	...	50.8	40.3
SOUTH CAROLINA	45000	2,908,381	49.9	82.1	266,841	77.3	23.2	-4.2	27.5	12.1	11.9	45.8	12.1
Abbeville, SC	45001	17,104	57.3	78.1	1,602	52.4	16.2	-11.2	18.4	9.0	...	...	...
Aiken, SC	45003	102,618	50.3	82.0	8,330	88.0	22.3	-5.1	26.5	9.2	...	...	7.0
Allendale, SC	45005	...	...	...	...	...	...	...	...	...	...	...	...
Anderson, SC	45007	122,332	54.6	79.3	8,537	66.6	17.5	-9.9	19.2	7.6	...	24.1	14.1
Bamberg, SC	45009	...	...	...	...	...	...	...	...	...	...	...	...
Barnwell, SC	45011	15,042	62.9	77.7	1,072	86.8	14.1	-13.3	17.5	9.1	...	...	...
Beaufort, SC	45013	97,110	34.4	90.2	6,194	83.0	36.9	9.5	44.5	15.9	...	39.9	11.3
Berkeley, SC	45015	103,088	51.9	86.5	8,558	76.6	17.6	-9.8	19.4	12.8	...	25.8	13.7
Calhoun, SC	45017	...	...	...	...	...	...	...	...	...	...	...	...
Charleston, SC	45019	225,948	37.5	87.5	27,694	84.5	36.5	9.1	47.6	12.6	28.6	44.9	16.1
Cherokee, SC	45021	36,769	67.1	74.7	2,437	73.5	11.8	-15.6	12.9	7.9	...	...	5.1
Chester, SC	45023	21,951	65.7	72.5	1,194	84.2	10.1	-17.3	11.7	6.7	...	...	...
Chesterfield, SC	45025	28,933	66.5	72.4	1,475	76.0	11.3	-16.1	13.4	6.4	...	...	...
Clarendon, SC	45027	21,796	67.0	75.0	1,155	65.7	12.0	-15.4	17.4	6.3	...	...	...
Colleton, SC	45029	25,538	65.1	77.6	1,674	83.8	12.5	-14.9	15.9	6.9	...	...	...
Darlington, SC	45031	44,832	61.2	75.7	3,171	71.0	16.3	-11.1	20.6	9.6	...	...	...
Dillon, SC	45033	19,743	71.1	63.3	995	95.5	10.2	-17.2	13.9	5.7	...	...	...
Dorchester, SC	45035	78,680	44.3	87.6	7,213	71.2	21.5	-5.9	25.3	9.9	...	36.1	7.9
Edgefield, SC	45037	17,319	58.9	78.9	1,145	89.0	15.3	-12.1	20.2	8.2	...	...	...
Fairfield, SC	45039	15,598	65.7	73.5	792	60.7	13.9	-13.5	18.8	9.4	...	...	...
Florence, SC	45041	86,487	53.8	79.8	7,652	80.6	20.4	-7.0	24.2	13.7	...	55.7	16.9
Georgetown, SC	45043	41,561	48.8	83.5	2,631	76.6	22.9	-4.5	30.5	6.4	...	...	6.5
Greenville, SC	45045	284,118	45.4	82.8	25,228	58.6	28.8	1.4	33.2	12.8	19.2	52.3	12.6
Greenwood, SC	45047	44,861	53.8	79.4	4,543	91.5	22.5	-4.9	27.3	10.4	...	...	14.7
Hampton, SC	45049	13,443	65.8	77.3	1,064	88.5	10.3	-17.1	14.5	6.0	...	...	...
Horry, SC	45051	175,713	49.7	85.4	10,240	84.4	20.7	-6.7	22.6	10.6	9.9	27.8	10.8
Jasper, SC	45053	13,927	66.8	73.1	560	90.4	8.9	-18.5	14.6	4.6	...	...	6.4
Kershaw, SC	45055	38,584	54.7	81.7	2,594	78.8	19.9	-7.5	22.2	13.5	...	...	6.3
Lancaster, SC	45057	49,186	65.0	74.6	2,476	82.6	12.6	-14.8	15.1	4.5	...	...	14.1
Laurens, SC	45059	46,971	61.3	72.6	3,421	56.3	15.2	-12.2	18.0	8.2	...	...	...
Lee, SC	45061	...	...	...	...	...	...	...	...	...	...	...	...
Lexington, SC	45063	161,743	42.5	88.0	13,079	86.7	26.6	-0.8	27.7	19.2	...	63.5	13.5
McCormick, SC	45065	...	...	...	...	...	...	...	...	...	...	...	...
Marion, SC	45067	22,574	67.9	76.1	1,097	80.7	12.8	-14.6	18.3	7.6	...	...	...
Marlboro, SC	45069	19,787	71.0	69.9	732	88.3	8.5	-18.9	14.0	3.7	6.6	...	...
Newberry, SC	45071	25,099	57.4	75.5	1,708	71.7	18.6	-8.8	24.6	7.2	...	...	14.1
Oconee, SC	45073	50,230	52.0	80.1	3,501	87.2	20.5	-6.9	21.3	9.3	...	...	14.1
Orangeburg, SC	45075	57,329	60.9	76.9	8,028	73.3	15.8	-11.6	17.7	14.1	...	...	...
Pickens, SC	45077	72,799	51.9	80.5	17,885	95.4	21.6	-5.8	21.7	9.4	...	...	13.1
Richland, SC	45079	220,819	35.3	88.4	37,913	74.4	36.5	9.1	48.5	22.2	18.1	58.8	20.5
Saluda, SC	45081	...	...	...	...	...	...	...	...	...	...	...	...
Spartanburg, SC	45083	184,791	53.2	78.5	14,924	64.5	19.9	-7.5	22.2	12.3	...	28.8	8.3
Sumter, SC	45085	66,199	53.2	81.1	5,437	75.8	18.0	-9.4	23.6	10.2	...	55.7	12.1
Union, SC	45087	19,413	60.2	74.6	1,272	84.7	12.9	-14.5	14.9	8.6	...	...	...
Williamsburg, SC	45089	22,059	70.4	76.4	1,099	93.5	10.4	-17.0	17.2	6.7	...	...	...
York, SC	45091	135,921	44.2	84.9	12,518	81.3	25.6	-1.8	28.4	13.4	6.0	49.2	15.4

[3]May be of any race

... Not available

Table C-1. Population, School, and Student Characteristics by County—*Continued*

County	State/ County Code	County Type[1]	Population, 2009		Percent of related children 5–17 years in poverty, 2008	Percent of children under 19 years with no health insurance, 2007	Number of Schools and Students, 2008-2009			Resident enrollment, 2006-2008	
			Total	Percent 5–17 years			School Districts	Schools	Students	K–12 enrollment	
										Number	Percent public
			1	2	3	4	5	6	7	8	9
SOUTH DAKOTA	46000	X	812,383	17.2	15.6	8.9	169	728	126,624	138,055	91.3
Aurora, SD	46003	9	2,868	19.9	15.6	13.0	3	11	560	...	...
Beadle, SD	46005	7	16,266	16.9	15.0	8.7	2	13	2,475	...	...
Bennett, SD	46007	9	3,348	24.6	43.4	10.9	1	3	556	...	...
Bon Homme, SD	46009	9	6,995	14.3	14.8	12.0	3	13	1,092	...	...
Brookings, SD	46011	7	30,056	12.8	8.2	8.8	5	21	4,144	3,441	94.6
Brown, SD	46013	5	35,204	15.8	10.5	7.4	7	25	5,058	5,468	89.1
Brule, SD	46015	9	5,275	20.6	17.3	14.3	2	8	1,153	...	...
Buffalo, SD	46017	9	2,067	25.2	50.0	5.2	...	...	...	...	...
Butte, SD	46019	6	9,577	17.8	19.1	11.4	2	8	1,737	...	...
Campbell, SD	46021	9	1,344	15.0	10.1	12.8	1	3	133	...	...
Charles Mix, SD	46023	9	8,984	21.2	29.5	11.4	3	15	1,679	...	...
Clark, SD	46025	9	3,431	16.4	17.0	15.2	2	11	594	...	...
Clay, SD	46027	6	13,490	11.5	15.3	9.6	1	4	1,278	...	...
Codington, SD	46029	7	26,168	17.5	9.6	8.6	5	19	4,539	4,571	87.1
Corson, SD	46031	9	4,093	22.7	46.4	10.8	3	8	934	...	...
Custer, SD	46033	8	7,924	15.8	16.6	15.0	3	10	1,004	...	...
Davison, SD	46035	7	18,929	16.1	12.8	8.0	3	14	2,960	...	...
Day, SD	46037	9	5,509	16.6	20.0	12.7	3	9	793	...	...
Deuel, SD	46039	9	4,203	16.8	11.6	11.2	1	3	526	...	...
Dewey, SD	46041	9	5,969	24.2	38.2	11.6	3	12	638	...	...
Douglas, SD	46043	9	2,933	17.0	16.3	14.9	2	6	339	...	...
Edmunds, SD	46045	9	3,935	17.8	13.7	12.8	3	12	675	...	...
Fall River, SD	46047	7	7,241	15.0	21.7	6.4	3	8	1,208	...	...
Faulk, SD	46049	9	2,210	16.0	15.9	17.2	1	7	328	...	...
Grant, SD	46051	7	7,068	17.1	10.4	9.3	3	9	1,192	...	...
Gregory, SD	46053	9	4,003	15.7	24.5	14.5	3	8	723	...	...
Haakon, SD	46055	8	1,777	17.0	15.4	13.6	1	5	294	...	...
Hamlin, SD	46057	9	5,754	20.1	14.1	16.4	3	10	1,224	...	...
Hand, SD	46059	9	3,238	15.3	12.8	12.7	1	4	474	...	...
Hanson, SD	46061	8	3,553	20.6	11.7	19.0	2	9	579	...	...
Harding, SD	46063	9	1,123	15.0	19.4	11.4	1	5	226	...	...
Hughes, SD	46065	7	16,969	17.9	10.6	9.1	3	6	2,681	...	...
Hutchinson, SD	46067	8	7,124	18.2	13.4	13.2	4	22	1,523	...	...
Hyde, SD	46069	9	1,393	18.0	17.0	9.0	1	4	311	...	...
Jackson, SD	46071	8	2,658	21.9	49.1	7.4	1	5	405	...	...
Jerauld, SD	46073	9	1,953	14.3	21.1	7.9	1	6	306	...	...
Jones, SD	46075	9	1,037	16.4	29.2	15.1	1	3	177	...	...
Kingsbury, SD	46077	9	5,308	15.9	11.6	13.0	4	14	965	...	...
Lake, SD	46079	6	11,994	14.3	10.8	8.2	4	16	2,139	...	...
Lawrence, SD	46081	6	23,498	13.9	14.6	9.3	2	8	2,878	3,668	97.1
Lincoln, SD	46083	3	41,218	19.4	4.0	9.3	4	16	4,989	7,637	92.8
Lyman, SD	46085	9	3,891	22.3	29.7	12.3	1	4	418	...	...
McCook, SD	46087	3	5,619	18.7	9.2	14.3	4	14	1,001	...	...
McPherson, SD	46089	9	2,439	15.5	18.2	14.7	2	9	439	...	...
Marshall, SD	46091	9	4,160	17.6	16.3	16.7	2	9	709	...	...
Meade, SD	46093	3	23,916	16.6	13.4	11.4	2	16	2,753	4,315	93.6
Mellette, SD	46095	9	2,042	20.9	46.7	9.6	2	7	419	...	...
Miner, SD	46097	8	2,420	16.5	13.4	10.4	2	5	389	...	...
Minnehaha, SD	46099	3	183,048	16.6	9.1	6.4	8	73	29,011	31,165	89.5
Moody, SD	46101	8	6,375	17.9	11.5	12.7	2	7	941	...	...
Pennington, SD	46103	3	100,850	17.0	17.2	8.5	5	45	16,956	17,070	89.2
Perkins, SD	46105	9	2,869	16.2	22.0	9.8	3	7	420	...	...
Potter, SD	46107	9	2,053	13.8	16.9	16.6	2	6	371	...	...
Roberts, SD	46109	9	9,933	19.7	24.5	10.6	4	15	1,608	...	...
Sanborn, SD	46111	9	2,432	17.4	20.4	11.4	2	6	397	...	...
Shannon, SD	46113	7	13,727	27.4	50.6	9.6	1	8	1,424	...	...
Spink, SD	46115	7	6,554	16.9	12.8	10.4	4	19	1,350	...	...
Stanley, SD	46117	9	2,792	18.6	13.7	11.1	1	6	481	...	...
Sully, SD	46119	9	1,348	17.7	12.8	18.0	1	4	307	...	...
Todd, SD	46121	9	10,095	27.5	46.5	5.7	1	12	1,940	...	...
Tripp, SD	46123	7	5,541	17.9	23.8	8.8	2	8	1,011	...	...
Turner, SD	46125	3	8,237	17.0	8.1	11.0	6	18	1,592	...	...
Union, SD	46127	3	14,589	18.6	5.9	7.4	4	14	2,834	...	...
Walworth, SD	46129	7	5,228	16.1	21.6	9.2	2	11	859	...	...
Yankton, SD	46135	7	21,986	16.5	11.0	7.7	2	9	3,164	3,098	89.4
Ziebach, SD	46137	9	2,552	23.0	52.9	5.9	1	3	341	...	...

[1]County type codes are from the Economic Research Service of the United States Department of Agriculture. See notes and definitions for more information.
... Not available

Table C-1. Population, School, and Student Characteristics by County—*Continued*

County	State/ County Code	Characteristics of students, 2008-2009				Number of graduates, 2006-2007	Staff and students, 2008-2009			
		Percent with IEP[2]	Percent eligible for free or reduced lunch	Percent minority	Percent English Language Learners		Total staff	Number of teachers	Student/ teacher ratio	Central admin. Staff
		10	11	12	13	14	15	16	17	18
SOUTH DAKOTA........................	46000	14.0	34.7	18.7	2.8	8,346	18,384	9,242	13.7	1,030
Aurora, SD	46003	15.4	38.2	12.5	1.3	37	103	49	11.4	9
Beadle, SD.................................	46005	13.6	40.6	17.9	7.4	153	352	157	15.8	19
Bennett, SD................................	46007	13.8	65.8	70.5	1.6	30	98	46	12.1	7
Bon Homme, SD..........................	46009	14.4	35.3	4.7	2.2	106	172	87	12.6	12
Brookings, SD.............................	46011	12.6	20.9	8.1	1.2	286	523	291	14.2	25
Brown, SD..................................	46013	15.4	26.5	9.3	0.3	331	750	377	13.4	31
Brule, SD...................................	46015	15.8	43.2	28.1	1.3	67	188	108	10.7	11
Buffalo, SD.................................	46017	...	...	...	...	...	...	...	...	...
Butte, SD...................................	46019	14.3	42.3	7.5	0.1	124	264	120	14.5	15
Campbell, SD..............................	46021	11.3	25.1	1.2	...	20	30	14	9.5	3
Charles Mix, SD	46023	15.0	55.3	46.3	4.2	95	290	142	11.8	21
Clark, SD....................................	46025	10.4	44.2	4.4	5.7	51	111	52	11.4	7
Clay, SD....................................	46027	14.2	31.5	16.7	0.6	91	169	94	13.6	10
Codington, SD............................	46029	13.8	29.7	7.1	0.4	337	675	310	14.6	38
Corson, SD.................................	46031	15.4	82.1	86.6	8.2	40	191	85	11.0	16
Custer, SD..................................	46033	16.6	32.1	15.9	0.9	73	198	94	10.7	14
Davison, SD	46035	14.7	32.2	9.2	1.6	215	433	220	13.5	25
Day, SD......................................	46037	12.5	49.9	13.6	0.1	72	171	70	11.3	8
Deuel, SD...................................	46039	12.5	27.8	3.3	...	41	78	38	13.8	5
Dewey, SD..................................	46041	42.5	33.6	70.6	0.3	30	195	90	7.1	18
Douglas, SD................................	46043	9.7	36.2	4.5	...	30	67	35	9.7	3
Edmunds, SD..............................	46045	11.1	34.7	4.5	6.1	47	112	63	10.7	7
Fall River, SD	46047	12.9	45.9	25.3	0.6	75	182	90	13.4	15
Faulk, SD...................................	46049	16.2	36.4	0.6	11.9	23	50	28	11.7	2
Grant, SD	46051	13.4	29.2	4.4	1.3	83	182	92	13.0	13
Gregory, SD................................	46053	13.3	58.2	18.0	0.3	57	153	65	11.1	12
Haakon, SD.................................	46055	11.9	25.5	7.4	...	31	52	25	11.8	3
Hamlin, SD.................................	46057	11.5	39.0	4.6	1.5	81	169	85	14.4	12
Hand, SD	46059	14.6	34.4	0.4	2.5	35	87	43	11.0	4
Hanson, SD.................................	46061	11.1	33.4	2.0	5.9	37	85	49	11.8	6
Harding, SD................................	46063	7.1	31.0	1.3	...	23	38	25	9.0	4
Hughes, SD.................................	46065	10.5	26.6	21.1	0.9	197	337	161	16.7	14
Hutchinson, SD...........................	46067	13.5	33.7	5.4	5.8	113	246	139	11.0	17
Hyde, SD....................................	46069	11.9	42.4	14.1	0.6	10	61	27	11.5	5
Jackson, SD	46071	12.8	44.8	52.8	0.2	22	72	41	9.9	6
Jerauld, SD	46073	9.8	39.9	3.9	6.9	33	63	26	11.8	5
Jones, SD...................................	46075	8.5	51.4	16.9	1.7	13	34	20	8.9	3
Kingsbury, SD.............................	46077	14.3	27.8	4.2	0.9	76	172	93	10.4	18
Lake, SD....................................	46079	9.9	23.5	5.8	1.7	138	273	157	13.6	21
Lawrence, SD	46081	14.0	27.7	9.5	0.6	267	407	218	13.2	16
Lincoln, SD	46083	13.7	16.1	4.0	0.3	250	646	339	14.7	31
Lyman, SD..................................	46085	16.7	46.6	38.2	...	33	86	40	10.5	3
McCook, SD	46087	15.8	33.0	5.4	2.3	81	164	89	11.2	14
McPherson, SD............................	46089	12.5	49.5	2.4	10.0	33	81	46	9.5	7
Marshall, SD...............................	46091	12.0	41.0	6.9	3.2	59	112	57	12.4	9
Meade, SD..................................	46093	13.3	35.5	7.8	0.1	214	371	210	13.1	13
Mellette, SD................................	46095	21.2	88.1	78.3	2.4	23	96	46	9.1	6
Miner, SD...................................	46097	16.7	35.7	5.1	0.5	38	81	34	11.4	6
Minnehaha, SD	46099	13.6	31.1	18.7	4.4	1,646	3,494	1,841	15.8	102
Moody, SD	46101	14.2	34.9	33.5	8.7	78	141	72	13.1	10
Pennington, SD...........................	46103	13.7	34.5	23.8	0.6	1,097	2,209	1,090	15.6	139
Perkins, SD.................................	46105	14.3	35.5	2.9	...	30	84	41	10.2	6
Potter, SD	46107	13.2	29.6	4.3	...	38	75	40	9.3	6
Roberts, SD.................................	46109	18.3	49.9	43.2	1.6	96	297	136	11.8	19
Sanborn, SD................................	46111	10.1	44.1	3.5	4.3	39	80	41	9.7	6
Shannon, SD...............................	46113	17.8	83.6	99.5	29.2	...	361	100	14.2	21
Spink, SD...................................	46115	17.6	36.2	3.1	3.0	95	210	119	11.3	12
Stanley, SD.................................	46117	13.7	34.5	17.9	...	36	72	40	12.0	5
Sully, SD....................................	46119	13.7	14.6	7.7	...	26	52	30	10.2	6
Todd, SD....................................	46121	16.9	97.4	96.6	28.1	68	459	177	11.0	40
Tripp, SD....................................	46123	8.7	44.6	24.0	0.1	79	153	84	12.0	12
Turner, SD	46125	16.3	25.8	4.8	...	117	254	141	11.3	23
Union, SD	46127	12.4	18.7	6.8	0.2	179	363	205	13.8	22
Walworth, SD..............................	46129	15.1	37.3	24.4	...	48	142	74	11.6	12
Yankton, SD................................	46135	15.5	33.5	9.0	0.4	269	408	197	16.1	17
Ziebach, SD................................	46137	10.0	76.0	85.7	1.5	84	65	32	10.7	5

[2]IEP= Individual Education Program. See notes and definitions for more information
... Not available

Table C-1. Population, School, and Student Characteristics by County—*Continued*

County	State/County Code	Revenues, 2007-2008				Current expenditures, 2007-2008			Resident population 16 to 19 years, 2006-2008			
		Total revenue ($1,000's)	Percentage of revenue from			Amount ($1,000's)	Amount per student	Percent for instruction	Total population 16 to 19 years	Percent enrolled in school	Percent high school graduates, not enrolled in school	Percent not enrolled, not grads, not employed or not in labor force
			Federal gov't	State gov't	Local gov't							
	19	20	21	22	23	24	25	26	27	28	29
SOUTH DAKOTA	46000	1,190,917	15.2	33.1	51.7	1,010,472	8,309	60.4	48215	84.7	9.2	3.6
Aurora, SD	46003	6,185	11.8	36.7	51.5	5,321	10,021	65.0	...	...	...	...
Beadle, SD	46005	21,762	11.8	37.7	50.5	18,364	7,828	58.2	...	...	...	...
Bennett, SD	46007	5,920	35.4	39.0	25.7	4,929	8,881	62.0	...	...	...	...
Bon Homme, SD	46009	11,004	13.9	42.0	44.1	9,918	8,777	55.8	...	...	...	...
Brookings, SD	46011	36,082	6.6	34.1	59.3	30,941	7,839	61.5	...	...	...	...
Brown, SD	46013	45,021	8.0	33.4	58.6	36,448	7,332	59.8	...	...	...	...
Brule, SD	46015	12,898	20.0	36.9	43.1	10,433	8,709	62.3	...	...	...	...
Buffalo, SD	46017	...	...	...	...	...	...	...	...	...	...	...
Butte, SD	46019	14,440	13.5	47.3	39.3	12,469	7,631	61.6	...	...	...	...
Campbell, SD	46021	2,415	14.8	38.4	46.7	2,249	12,290	60.6	...	...	...	...
Charles Mix, SD	46023	23,537	44.2	27.3	28.5	16,628	9,718	60.0	...	...	...	...
Clark, SD	46025	5,910	9.9	32.5	57.5	5,181	8,621	62.1	...	...	...	...
Clay, SD	46027	11,656	9.7	37.2	53.1	9,906	7,573	58.3	...	...	...	...
Codington, SD	46029	37,613	7.4	40.4	52.1	30,819	7,033	64.1	...	...	...	...
Corson, SD	46031	13,278	52.8	36.5	10.7	11,805	14,414	58.0	...	...	...	...
Custer, SD	46033	10,711	18.3	13.7	68.0	9,408	9,739	59.1	...	...	...	...
Davison, SD	46035	26,016	11.0	39.3	49.7	22,665	7,778	61.4	...	...	...	...
Day, SD	46037	8,021	14.6	33.7	51.7	6,874	8,636	56.1	...	...	...	...
Deuel, SD	46039	4,688	6.4	36.3	57.3	3,945	7,735	57.4	...	...	...	...
Dewey, SD	46041	5,673	49.4	31.6	19.0	4,842	14,584	56.3	...	...	...	...
Douglas, SD	46043	3,708	9.1	35.7	55.2	3,229	9,147	56.1	...	...	...	...
Edmunds, SD	46045	6,375	9.6	27.7	62.8	5,644	8,578	57.7	...	...	...	...
Fall River, SD	46047	11,115	20.6	32.0	47.4	9,617	8,743	58.3	...	...	...	...
Faulk, SD	46049	3,077	9.9	31.9	58.2	2,851	8,361	57.3	...	...	...	...
Grant, SD	46051	11,211	7.8	32.9	59.3	9,885	8,265	57.7	...	...	...	...
Gregory, SD	46053	8,321	23.6	34.0	42.5	7,141	9,987	58.2	...	...	...	...
Haakon, SD	46055	2,651	8.9	32.2	58.9	2,289	8,088	62.6	...	...	...	...
Hamlin, SD	46057	11,359	7.6	39.6	52.8	9,355	7,700	58.3	...	...	...	...
Hand, SD	46059	4,700	7.3	28.0	64.7	4,551	9,048	62.3	...	...	...	...
Hanson, SD	46061	5,247	7.7	43.8	48.6	4,719	8,596	60.4	...	...	...	...
Harding, SD	46063	2,905	12.6	15.1	72.3	2,726	12,620	58.5	...	...	...	...
Hughes, SD	46065	22,642	11.5	38.6	49.8	18,928	7,280	62.1	...	...	...	...
Hutchinson, SD	46067	16,845	10.4	35.5	54.1	13,916	9,234	62.9	...	...	...	...
Hyde, SD	46069	3,014	10.1	22.5	67.5	2,310	7,778	59.9	...	...	...	...
Jackson, SD	46071	4,494	32.8	34.3	32.8	4,014	10,591	58.3	...	...	...	...
Jerauld, SD	46073	3,142	10.4	23.8	65.8	3,001	11,033	61.9	...	...	...	...
Jones, SD	46075	2,025	13.2	25.8	60.9	1,811	10,529	59.1	...	...	...	...
Kingsbury, SD	46077	10,309	7.9	35.7	56.4	9,100	9,211	56.7	...	...	...	...
Lake, SD	46079	17,673	8.7	34.5	56.7	15,585	7,871	61.4	...	...	...	...
Lawrence, SD	46081	26,518	8.8	18.7	72.5	22,269	7,914	61.6	...	...	...	...
Lincoln, SD	46083	42,286	4.6	31.0	64.4	31,784	6,846	59.4	...	...	...	...
Lyman, SD	46085	4,994	25.1	23.8	51.1	4,169	11,147	52.2	...	...	...	...
McCook, SD	46087	11,007	7.2	36.8	56.0	8,824	8,754	58.0	...	...	...	...
McPherson, SD	46089	4,860	9.3	31.8	58.9	4,241	10,170	59.1	...	...	...	...
Marshall, SD	46091	6,513	9.0	33.2	57.8	5,582	7,615	58.5	...	...	...	...
Meade, SD	46093	24,870	9.8	33.6	56.6	20,916	7,578	61.2	...	...	...	...
Mellette, SD	46095	5,875	45.5	32.4	22.0	5,162	12,714	61.7	...	...	...	...
Miner, SD	46097	3,911	7.5	30.7	61.9	3,429	9,472	53.4	...	...	...	...
Minnehaha, SD	46099	244,630	9.6	33.1	57.2	205,406	7,633	62.4	9,263	84.9	10.7	1.7
Moody, SD	46101	9,101	13.2	38.7	48.1	7,524	8,511	56.3	...	...	...	...
Pennington, SD	46103	147,749	16.5	28.8	54.6	135,233	8,167	61.0	4,946	79.7	12.7	3.1
Perkins, SD	46105	5,025	11.9	39.1	49.0	4,649	10,614	53.8	...	...	...	...
Potter, SD	46107	4,327	7.9	31.5	60.6	3,886	9,788	62.6	...	...	...	...
Roberts, SD	46109	17,385	23.8	35.0	41.1	14,954	10,860	57.3	...	...	...	...
Sanborn, SD	46111	4,676	11.8	29.3	58.9	3,680	9,246	59.8	...	...	...	...
Shannon, SD	46113	21,356	63.3	30.5	6.1	17,791	15,606	56.6	...	...	...	...
Spink, SD	46115	11,997	10.8	40.5	48.7	11,009	8,495	60.2	...	...	...	...
Stanley, SD	46117	4,604	15.5	24.9	59.5	4,497	9,122	59.4	...	...	...	...
Sully, SD	46119	3,235	6.0	13.1	80.8	3,049	9,867	56.9	...	...	...	...
Todd, SD	46121	31,231	57.8	33.8	8.4	25,808	13,331	53.3	...	...	...	...
Tripp, SD	46123	9,331	14.3	36.3	49.4	8,331	8,390	57.7	...	...	...	...
Turner, SD	46125	16,290	6.9	38.3	54.9	13,708	8,770	57.5	...	...	...	...
Union, SD	46127	28,707	5.3	24.1	70.5	21,143	7,857	58.4	...	...	...	...
Walworth, SD	46129	7,918	12.0	41.2	46.8	6,824	8,584	59.4	...	...	...	...
Yankton, SD	46135	27,760	8.6	42.6	48.9	23,568	7,487	62.4	...	...	...	...
Ziebach, SD	46137	10,521	54.2	34.2	11.6	9,129	15,089	64.1	...	...	...	...

... Not available

Table C-1. Population, School, and Student Characteristics by County—*Continued*

County	State/County Code	High school graduates, 2006-2008			College enrollment, 2006-2008		College graduates, 2006-2008 (percent)						
		Population 25 years and over	High school diploma or less (percent)	High school diploma or more (percent)	Number	Percent public	Bachelor's degree or more	+/- U.S. percent with Bachelor's degree or more	Non-Hispanic White	Black or African American	American Indian and Alaska Native	Asian, Hawaiian, and Pacific Islander	Hispanic or Latino[3]
		30	31	32	33	34	35	36	37	38	39	40	41
SOUTH DAKOTA	46000	516,633	44.5	88.9	51,257	80.6	24.8	-2.6	25.9	15.9	10.5	45.3	13.6
Aurora, SD	46003	...	...	...	...	...	...	...	...	...	...	...	...
Beadle, SD	46005	...	...	...	...	...	...	...	...	...	...	...	...
Bennett, SD	46007	...	...	...	...	...	...	...	...	...	...	...	...
Bon Homme, SD	46009	...	...	...	...	...	...	...	...	...	...	...	...
Brookings, SD	46011	15,941	38.4	92.1	7,615	96.8	36.1	8.7	34.9	...	...	...	...
Brown, SD	46013	23,225	44.5	89.1	2,490	84.2	21.9	-5.5	22.3	...	...	...	...
Brule, SD	46015	...	...	...	...	...	...	...	...	...	...	...	...
Buffalo, SD	46017	...	...	...	...	...	...	...	...	...	...	...	...
Butte, SD	46019	...	...	...	...	...	...	...	...	...	...	...	...
Campbell, SD	46021	...	...	...	...	...	...	...	...	...	...	...	...
Charles Mix, SD	46023	...	...	...	...	...	...	...	...	...	...	...	...
Clark, SD	46025	...	...	...	...	...	...	...	...	...	...	...	...
Clay, SD	46027	...	...	...	...	...	...	...	...	...	...	...	...
Codington, SD	46029	17,509	53.4	87.7	1,101	87.2	21.3	-6.1	21.9	...	...	...	...
Corson, SD	46031	...	...	...	...	...	...	...	...	...	...	...	...
Custer, SD	46033	...	...	...	...	...	...	...	...	...	...	...	...
Davison, SD	46035	...	...	...	...	...	...	...	...	...	...	...	...
Day, SD	46037	...	...	...	...	...	...	...	...	...	...	...	...
Deuel, SD	46039	...	...	...	...	...	...	...	...	...	...	...	...
Dewey, SD	46041	...	...	...	...	...	...	...	...	...	...	...	...
Douglas, SD	46043	...	...	...	...	...	...	...	...	...	...	...	...
Edmunds, SD	46045	...	...	...	...	...	...	...	...	...	...	...	...
Fall River, SD	46047	...	...	...	...	...	...	...	...	...	...	...	...
Faulk, SD	46049	...	...	...	...	...	...	...	...	...	...	...	...
Grant, SD	46051	...	...	...	...	...	...	...	...	...	...	...	...
Gregory, SD	46053	...	...	...	...	...	...	...	...	...	...	...	...
Haakon, SD	46055	...	...	...	...	...	...	...	...	...	...	...	...
Hamlin, SD	46057	...	...	...	...	...	...	...	...	...	...	...	...
Hand, SD	46059	...	...	...	...	...	...	...	...	...	...	...	...
Hanson, SD	46061	...	...	...	...	...	...	...	...	...	...	...	...
Harding, SD	46063	...	...	...	...	...	...	...	...	...	...	...	...
Hughes, SD	46065	...	...	...	...	...	...	...	...	...	...	...	...
Hutchinson, SD	46067	...	...	...	...	...	...	...	...	...	...	...	...
Hyde, SD	46069	...	...	...	...	...	...	...	...	...	...	...	...
Jackson, SD	46071	...	...	...	...	...	...	...	...	...	...	...	...
Jerauld, SD	46073	...	...	...	...	...	...	...	...	...	...	...	...
Jones, SD	46075	...	...	...	...	...	...	...	...	...	...	...	...
Kingsbury, SD	46077	...	...	...	...	...	...	...	...	...	...	...	...
Lake, SD	46079	...	...	...	...	...	...	...	...	...	...	...	...
Lawrence, SD	46081	15,033	40.5	92.0	2,283	95.5	31.2	3.8	31.0	...	...	...	...
Lincoln, SD	46083	21,406	35.3	94.9	2,341	61.4	32.4	5.0	32.4	...	...	...	...
Lyman, SD	46085	...	...	...	...	...	...	...	...	...	...	...	...
McCook, SD	46087	...	...	...	...	...	...	...	...	...	...	...	...
McPherson, SD	46089	...	...	...	...	...	...	...	...	...	...	...	...
Marshall, SD	46091	...	...	...	...	...	...	...	...	...	...	...	...
Meade, SD	46093	15,750	41.6	93.9	1,249	81.4	23.6	-3.8	23.5	...	...	...	...
Mellette, SD	46095	...	...	...	...	...	...	...	...	...	...	...	...
Miner, SD	46097	...	...	...	...	...	...	...	...	...	...	...	...
Minnehaha, SD	46099	114,868	40.0	90.5	10,335	62.6	28.5	1.1	29.9	11.4	5.4	44.3	5.4
Moody, SD	46101	...	...	...	...	...	...	...	...	...	...	...	...
Pennington, SD	46103	62,558	37.6	91.1	5,912	85.3	26.9	-0.5	28.3	...	12.6	22.8	12.1
Perkins, SD	46105	...	...	...	...	...	...	...	...	...	...	...	...
Potter, SD	46107	...	...	...	...	...	...	...	...	...	...	...	...
Roberts, SD	46109	...	...	...	...	...	...	...	...	...	...	...	...
Sanborn, SD	46111	...	...	...	...	...	...	...	...	...	...	...	...
Shannon, SD	46113	...	...	...	...	...	...	...	...	...	...	...	...
Spink, SD	46115	...	...	...	...	...	...	...	...	...	...	...	...
Stanley, SD	46117	...	...	...	...	...	...	...	...	...	...	...	...
Sully, SD	46119	...	...	...	...	...	...	...	...	...	...	...	...
Todd, SD	46121	...	...	...	...	...	...	...	...	...	...	...	...
Tripp, SD	46123	...	...	...	...	...	...	...	...	...	...	...	...
Turner, SD	46125	...	...	...	...	...	...	...	...	...	...	...	...
Union, SD	46127	...	...	...	...	...	...	...	...	...	...	...	...
Walworth, SD	46129	...	...	...	...	...	...	...	...	...	...	...	...
Yankton, SD	46135	14,804	44.2	88.7	1,654	37.7	26.7	-0.7	27.2	...	...	...	...
Ziebach, SD	46137	...	...	...	...	...	...	...	...	...	...	...	...

[3]May be of any race
... Not available

Table C-1. Population, School, and Student Characteristics by County—*Continued*

County	State/County Code	County Type[1]	Population, 2009 Total	Population, 2009 Percent 5–17 years	Percent of related children 5-17 years in poverty, 2008	Percent of children under 19 years with no health insurance, 2007	Number of Schools and Students, 2008-2009 School Districts	Number of Schools and Students, 2008-2009 Schools	Number of Schools and Students, 2008-2009 Students	Resident enrollment, 2006-2008 K–12 enrollment Number	Resident enrollment, 2006-2008 K–12 enrollment Percent public
			1	2	3	4	5	6	7	8	9
TENNESSEE	47000	X	6,296,254	17.0	19.5	9.5	140	1764	971,950	1,061,003	88.2
Anderson, TN	47001	2	74,849	16.5	19.6	7.4	3	28	12,468	11,692	92.1
Bedford, TN	47003	6	45,947	18.7	20.1	13.2	1	12	7,836	8,292	95.7
Benton, TN	47005	7	16,025	15.2	26.9	8.3	1	8	2,483	...	...
Bledsoe, TN	47007	8	12,967	15.9	27.2	11.0	1	6	1,948	...	...
Blount, TN	47009	2	122,784	16.4	14.4	8.6	3	30	18,577	19,466	92.4
Bradley, TN	47011	3	97,710	16.7	17.3	8.7	2	25	15,340	15,353	90.8
Campbell, TN	47013	6	40,970	15.9	31.1	5.3	1	15	6,013	6,435	94.8
Cannon, TN	47015	1	13,860	16.9	18.5	13.2	1	7	2,322	...	...
Carroll, TN	47017	6	28,517	16.7	21.5	8.7	6	15	4,923	4,431	95.8
Carter, TN	47019	3	59,043	14.1	24.9	6.3	2	23	8,072	8,505	97.8
Cheatham, TN	47021	1	39,876	18.6	11.2	12.1	1	13	6,869	7,717	89.2
Chester, TN	47023	3	16,312	17.3	20.7	9.2	1	6	2,762	...	...
Claiborne, TN	47025	6	31,243	15.8	26.5	5.7	1	13	4,850	5,198	95.9
Clay, TN	47027	8	7,895	15.8	31.5	9.1	1	5	1,091	...	...
Cocke, TN	47029	6	36,047	15.9	31.4	6.2	2	13	5,757	5,401	98.2
Coffee, TN	47031	4	52,521	17.3	21.5	9.9	3	18	9,325	9,021	93.3
Crockett, TN	47033	8	14,492	17.6	21.4	15.5	3	7	2,855	...	...
Cumberland, TN	47035	7	54,109	13.7	23.8	9.5	1	12	7,528	8,054	91.7
Davidson, TN	47037	1	635,710	14.7	24.2	11.5	2	142	74,458	100,858	80.6
Decatur, TN	47039	9	11,525	15.3	24.6	10.7	1	4	1,674	...	...
De Kalb, TN	47041	6	18,954	16.2	25.9	11.0	1	6	2,965	...	...
Dickson, TN	47043	1	48,230	18.1	15.9	10.7	1	16	8,520	8,715	92.0
Dyer, TN	47045	5	37,811	18.1	22.0	7.3	2	12	6,989	6,604	98.0
Fayette, TN	47047	1	38,785	16.7	15.0	15.0	1	10	3,823	6,558	68.3
Fentress, TN	47049	9	17,677	17.0	30.7	12.9	2	7	3,169	...	...
Franklin, TN	47051	6	41,310	15.9	18.6	9.0	1	11	6,141	6,272	93.8
Gibson, TN	47053	4	49,468	17.6	20.3	8.0	5	20	9,065	8,190	93.5
Giles, TN	47055	6	29,082	16.7	20.4	8.8	1	8	4,446	5,225	95.1
Grainger, TN	47057	3	22,857	16.3	24.7	10.6	1	9	3,121	3,340	95.2
Greene, TN	47059	6	66,282	15.6	21.7	8.2	2	25	10,490	9,576	93.9
Grundy, TN	47061	8	14,130	17.5	35.6	7.7	1	8	2,332	...	...
Hamblen, TN	47063	3	63,033	16.6	22.4	9.5	1	18	10,101	10,363	94.5
Hamilton, TN	47065	2	337,175	15.6	17.6	8.6	1	77	41,547	53,138	79.9
Hancock, TN	47067	8	6,588	14.9	42.7	4.9	1	3	1,103	...	...
Hardeman, TN	47069	6	27,613	15.9	23.2	7.4	1	9	4,347	4,647	87.3
Hardin, TN	47071	6	26,258	16.1	27.9	7.8	1	10	3,887	4,481	95.0
Hawkins, TN	47073	3	57,784	16.2	23.4	6.6	2	18	8,487	9,480	94.4
Haywood, TN	47075	6	18,881	19.2	25.2	7.2	1	7	3,322	...	...
Henderson, TN	47077	6	27,037	17.4	18.1	10.0	2	12	4,770	4,604	88.7
Henry, TN	47079	7	31,876	15.2	23.8	9.1	2	9	4,864	4,770	96.1
Hickman, TN	47081	1	23,805	17.4	21.7	12.9	1	8	3,961	4,406	93.6
Houston, TN	47083	8	8,154	18.2	23.9	12.2	1	5	1,513	...	...
Humphreys, TN	47085	6	18,274	17.0	18.0	10.0	1	7	3,232	...	...
Jackson, TN	47087	8	10,875	14.5	26.1	8.1	1	4	1,608	...	...
Jefferson, TN	47089	3	51,722	15.9	20.4	9.3	1	12	7,589	8,065	94.7
Johnson, TN	47091	6	18,006	13.0	31.5	6.1	1	7	2,303	...	...
Knox, TN	47093	2	435,725	15.6	15.1	8.9	2	90	55,697	66,061	85.9
Lake, TN	47095	9	7,303	11.5	35.4	8.5	1	3	956	...	...
Lauderdale, TN	47097	6	26,471	17.5	25.4	7.0	1	8	4,734	4,663	97.2
Lawrence, TN	47099	6	41,314	18.2	20.2	9.6	1	13	6,914	7,371	92.5
Lewis, TN	47101	6	11,521	17.7	26.7	9.9	1	4	2,018	...	...
Lincoln, TN	47103	6	33,374	16.5	19.2	10.2	2	11	5,256	5,583	85.7
Loudon, TN	47105	2	46,725	14.8	16.7	10.6	2	12	7,454	6,954	90.9
McMinn, TN	47107	4	52,739	17.2	20.4	8.0	3	16	8,431	8,919	95.0
McNairy, TN	47109	6	25,796	17.1	23.9	7.4	1	8	4,484	4,407	87.5
Macon, TN	47111	1	22,057	18.0	22.9	10.5	1	9	3,834	...	...
Madison, TN	47113	3	97,317	17.7	19.4	9.5	2	29	13,713	17,506	78.4
Marion, TN	47115	2	28,068	16.5	22.4	7.5	2	11	4,608	4,767	85.2
Marshall, TN	47117	6	30,279	17.5	20.6	9.6	1	9	5,331	5,128	99.1
Maury, TN	47119	4	84,302	17.1	16.2	9.8	1	19	11,789	14,369	86.1
Meigs, TN	47121	8	12,108	17.9	27.1	8.5	1	4	1,867	...	...
Monroe, TN	47123	6	45,830	16.6	21.3	8.3	2	17	7,181	7,996	93.8
Montgomery, TN	47125	3	160,978	18.2	15.7	13.4	1	36	28,737	30,191	90.1
Moore, TN	47127	9	6,096	16.4	15.7	13.6	1	2	1,003	...	...
Morgan, TN	47129	6	18,738	17.7	24.5	7.7	1	8	3,418	3,176	92.7
Obion, TN	47131	7	31,431	16.8	19.7	8.8	2	11	5,501	5,135	96.6
Overton, TN	47133	7	21,060	16.3	24.3	7.4	1	9	3,448	3,251	95.0
Perry, TN	47135	8	7,826	16.0	25.6	10.2	1	4	1,177	...	...
Pickett, TN	47137	9	4,783	13.7	29.3	11.1	1	2	684	...	...

[1]County type codes are from the Economic Research Service of the United States Department of Agriculture. See notes and definitions for more information.
... Not available

Table C-1. Population, School, and Student Characteristics by County—*Continued*

County	State/ County Code	Characteristics of students, 2008-2009				Number of graduates, 2006-2007	Staff and students, 2008-2009			
		Percent with IEP[2]	Percent eligible for free or reduced lunch	Percent minority	Percent English Language Learners		Total staff	Number of teachers	Student/ teacher ratio	Central admin. Staff
		10	11	12	13	14	15	16	17	18
TENNESSEE	47000	12.2	50.0	31.7	2.8	56,926	126,833	64,923	15.0	1,005
Anderson, TN	47001	16.1	43.3	11.2	1.0	761	1,827	955	13.1	21
Bedford, TN	47003	11.7	52.6	26.2	8.6	409	1,002	502	15.6	8
Benton, TN	47005	15.6	61.9	6.2	0.4	165	367	179	13.9	2
Bledsoe, TN	47007	18.5	75.9	5.1	...	110	320	135	14.4	1
Blount, TN	47009	12.9	38.4	8.0	1.3	1,104	2,384	1,176	15.8	12
Bradley, TN	47011	9.8	48.6	13.0	1.7	795	1,706	965	15.9	11
Campbell, TN	47013	12.4	68.1	1.2	0.3	310	792	391	15.4	1
Cannon, TN	47015	14.0	50.7	4.0	0.9	143	317	162	14.3	3
Carroll, TN	47017	13.2	48.6	14.6	0.1	313	668	343	14.4	17
Carter, TN	47019	13.9	59.9	3.4	0.2	472	1,291	593	13.6	21
Cheatham, TN	47021	10.9	36.2	4.0	0.7	425	960	442	15.5	20
Chester, TN	47023	7.9	49.3	17.0	0.7	143	360	164	16.8	1
Claiborne, TN	47025	12.3	66.7	1.8	0.1	261	800	372	13.0	5
Clay, TN	47027	13.1	67.4	3.3	0.4	87	185	82	13.3	3
Cocke, TN	47029	15.3	61.8	5.6	0.5	299	761	389	14.8	5
Coffee, TN	47031	15.5	47.9	10.5	1.7	660	1,266	639	14.6	15
Crockett, TN	47033	9.9	59.0	28.7	5.5	174	377	187	15.3	6
Cumberland, TN	47035	11.3	57.7	5.0	0.8	390	1,017	481	15.7	27
Davidson, TN	47037	11.2	65.0	66.7	10.2	3,845	10,735	5,307	14.0	41
Decatur, TN	47039	21.7	53.9	7.4	0.7	104	231	120	14.0	1
De Kalb, TN	47041	13.3	55.0	9.7	3.9	149	415	200	14.8	4
Dickson, TN	47043	15.4	48.5	10.7	1.2	564	1,148	576	14.8	5
Dyer, TN	47045	9.4	60.8	24.5	0.8	418	893	423	16.5	7
Fayette, TN	47047	11.9	72.6	64.9	2.5	191	634	274	14.0	6
Fentress, TN	47049	33.6	55.1	1.2	0.2	60	355	166	19.1	4
Franklin, TN	47051	14.4	53.3	10.3	0.6	387	796	401	15.3	4
Gibson, TN	47053	13.0	53.0	27.9	0.8	503	1,151	574	15.8	29
Giles, TN	47055	9.6	50.3	16.9	0.2	279	623	308	14.4	3
Grainger, TN	47057	15.0	64.8	2.5	1.9	251	436	227	13.7	9
Greene, TN	47059	14.5	50.1	6.6	1.0	728	1,383	688	15.2	12
Grundy, TN	47061	19.2	75.3	0.3	0.1	143	379	194	12.0	2
Hamblen, TN	47063	11.0	50.9	20.8	7.0	517	1,180	644	15.7	6
Hamilton, TN	47065	11.6	50.7	40.6	2.3	2,433	5,033	2,865	14.5	34
Hancock, TN	47067	16.2	78.2	1.0	...	64	207	90	12.3	3
Hardeman, TN	47069	13.5	77.7	56.3	0.5	245	671	322	13.5	8
Hardin, TN	47071	12.5	60.5	7.9	0.3	253	587	281	13.8	4
Hawkins, TN	47073	14.0	54.5	3.9	0.5	465	1,250	580	14.6	11
Haywood, TN	47075	11.1	76.9	69.9	1.5	177	545	236	14.1	4
Henderson, TN	47077	12.6	55.4	13.6	0.4	293	657	315	15.1	7
Henry, TN	47079	13.4	55.5	14.3	0.4	260	684	330	14.7	9
Hickman, TN	47081	15.6	52.0	4.7	0.2	274	535	277	14.3	1
Houston, TN	47083	15.6	51.6	7.7	0.1	89	273	97	15.6	1
Humphreys, TN	47085	14.1	40.8	5.0	0.2	226	518	215	15.0	4
Jackson, TN	47087	15.2	71.4	1.6	0.6	106	271	120	13.4	1
Jefferson, TN	47089	11.3	51.9	6.7	2.4	465	961	484	15.7	11
Johnson, TN	47091	15.7	72.8	2.2	0.6	163	384	167	13.8	5
Knox, TN	47093	11.0	38.6	20.6	1.9	3,391	6,966	3,831	14.5	24
Lake, TN	47095	17.3	72.9	30.5	0.1	55	159	80	12.0	1
Lauderdale, TN	47097	14.5	73.1	44.0	0.8	252	652	314	15.1	6
Lawrence, TN	47099	14.0	54.9	4.6	0.3	451	971	458	15.1	5
Lewis, TN	47101	12.5	58.4	6.1	0.1	114	274	135	14.9	11
Lincoln, TN	47103	10.7	47.8	13.2	0.7	315	766	351	15.0	7
Loudon, TN	47105	10.8	49.0	13.2	4.9	431	1,184	479	15.6	22
McMinn, TN	47107	11.5	53.8	12.0	0.9	453	998	522	16.2	11
McNairy, TN	47109	10.5	52.7	9.4	0.5	292	658	329	13.6	3
Macon, TN	47111	14.0	52.5	5.4	1.7	253	529	234	16.4	14
Madison, TN	47113	14.3	67.5	63.9	2.5	881	2,012	962	14.3	13
Marion, TN	47115	11.9	60.2	6.0	0.8	245	619	307	15.0	14
Marshall, TN	47117	9.0	44.1	14.6	2.5	285	707	345	15.5	6
Maury, TN	47119	15.8	48.6	26.4	2.5	697	1,637	807	14.6	7
Meigs, TN	47121	14.9	65.9	2.9	0.1	98	268	126	14.8	6
Monroe, TN	47123	12.6	65.1	8.0	2.3	413	833	423	17.0	6
Montgomery, TN	47125	10.2	42.2	38.8	2.2	1,716	3,640	1,870	15.4	26
Moore, TN	47127	15.4	42.0	3.5	...	75	148	70	14.3	1
Morgan, TN	47129	16.6	57.9	0.9	...	210	526	251	13.6	4
Obion, TN	47131	12.4	51.7	18.4	2.1	337	757	376	14.6	7
Overton, TN	47133	13.3	62.0	2.0	0.1	210	471	218	15.8	1
Perry, TN	47135	18.2	59.1	5.9	...	82	181	88	13.4	2
Pickett, TN	47137	12.1	65.9	0.6	...	49	109	57	12.0	1

[2]IEP= Individual Education Program. See notes and definitions for more information
... Not available

Table C-1. Population, School, and Student Characteristics by County—*Continued*

County	State/County Code	Revenues, 2007-2008				Current expenditures, 2007-2008			Resident population 16 to 19 years, 2006-2008			
		Total revenue ($1,000's)	Percentage of revenue from			Amount ($1,000's)	Amount per student	Percent for instruction	Total population 16 to 19 years	Percent enrolled in school	Percent high school graduates, not enrolled in school	Percent not enrolled, not grads, not employed or not in labor force
			Federal gov't	State gov't	Local gov't							
		19	20	21	22	23	24	25	26	27	28	29
TENNESSEE	47000	8,086,152	10.4	45.9	43.7	7,455,053	7,710	63.2	331,173	82.8	10.9	3.9
Anderson, TN	47001	123,331	10.3	43.7	45.9	111,835	8,347	62.7	...	...	...	...
Bedford, TN	47003	53,312	9.9	63.3	26.9	47,175	6,120	66.4	...	...	...	...
Benton, TN	47005	21,171	12.3	56.1	31.6	17,784	6,999	66.8	...	...	...	...
Bledsoe, TN	47007	16,507	12.8	68.9	18.3	14,512	7,370	61.9	...	...	...	...
Blount, TN	47009	152,287	6.5	45.9	47.5	146,280	7,840	66.8	6,308	85.5	8.4	5.3
Bradley, TN	47011	111,448	10.0	51.5	38.6	106,092	7,008	66.1	5,779	82.6	8.2	5.2
Campbell, TN	47013	44,161	16.7	62.6	20.8	40,525	8,237	61.3	...	...	...	...
Cannon, TN	47015	17,395	10.7	66.8	22.5	16,415	7,485	65.7	...	...	...	...
Carroll, TN	47017	41,910	10.2	60.2	29.6	34,771	6,992	62.6	...	...	...	...
Carter, TN	47019	66,632	12.4	58.0	29.6	62,088	7,690	65.5	...	...	...	...
Cheatham, TN	47021	49,829	7.4	60.6	32.0	47,593	6,877	64.5	...	...	...	...
Chester, TN	47023	18,143	10.9	69.1	20.0	16,607	6,124	62.1	...	...	...	...
Claiborne, TN	47025	43,819	15.6	57.4	27.1	34,944	7,025	69.0	...	...	...	...
Clay, TN	47027	10,498	13.0	64.0	23.0	9,313	8,390	58.4	...	...	...	...
Cocke, TN	47029	44,396	14.4	58.6	27.0	40,567	7,097	62.3	...	...	...	...
Coffee, TN	47031	81,739	9.5	47.1	43.4	73,105	7,846	65.2	...	...	...	...
Crockett, TN	47033	21,692	12.5	69.2	18.3	19,122	6,745	63.2	...	...	...	...
Cumberland, TN	47035	50,696	12.6	56.1	31.3	50,150	6,559	63.1	...	...	...	...
Davidson, TN	47037	740,835	10.6	27.1	62.2	678,154	9,200	59.0	32,576	85.5	8.8	3.8
Decatur, TN	47039	13,268	11.9	63.0	25.1	10,946	6,519	67.3	...	...	...	...
De Kalb, TN	47041	20,900	12.5	62.5	25.0	19,311	8,197	63.8	...	...	...	...
Dickson, TN	47043	64,160	8.6	53.5	37.9	58,872	6,982	63.7	...	...	...	...
Dyer, TN	47045	57,014	10.5	52.2	37.3	53,315	7,746	61.7	...	...	...	...
Fayette, TN	47047	32,516	21.1	50.5	28.3	31,333	8,589	59.4	...	...	...	...
Fentress, TN	47049	19,353	13.1	65.6	21.2	17,582	7,136	64.6	...	...	...	...
Franklin, TN	47051	47,947	9.4	55.5	35.1	45,016	7,221	61.5	...	...	...	...
Gibson, TN	47053	70,521	10.9	57.3	31.7	61,464	7,196	63.2	...	...	...	...
Giles, TN	47055	35,509	9.6	55.1	35.2	34,369	7,722	62.3	...	...	...	...
Grainger, TN	47057	26,420	12.3	69.3	18.3	23,147	6,528	67.5	...	...	...	...
Greene, TN	47059	81,132	10.9	52.9	36.2	76,466	7,266	63.4	...	...	...	...
Grundy, TN	47061	20,195	16.1	67.0	16.9	17,723	7,666	66.3	...	...	...	...
Hamblen, TN	47063	74,789	10.1	48.7	41.1	69,064	6,909	68.7	...	...	...	...
Hamilton, TN	47065	360,382	11.5	32.3	56.2	344,310	8,351	64.0	18,679	84.7	8.0	5.1
Hancock, TN	47067	9,770	14.9	71.4	13.7	8,768	7,935	61.6	...	...	...	...
Hardeman, TN	47069	37,120	13.7	60.0	26.2	33,962	7,661	63.1	...	...	...	...
Hardin, TN	47071	31,931	14.0	51.1	34.9	28,330	7,292	62.4	...	...	...	...
Hawkins, TN	47073	64,953	10.6	59.8	29.6	60,401	7,073	63.7	...	...	...	...
Haywood, TN	47075	28,478	13.4	59.1	27.5	26,635	7,645	61.9	...	...	...	...
Henderson, TN	47077	35,824	11.0	60.5	28.5	31,645	6,729	67.1	...	...	...	...
Henry, TN	47079	40,964	10.5	53.8	35.7	35,143	7,231	62.3	...	...	...	...
Hickman, TN	47081	31,333	10.0	66.7	23.2	28,738	7,257	60.8	...	...	...	...
Houston, TN	47083	11,893	9.3	70.9	19.7	10,511	6,738	61.0	...	...	...	...
Humphreys, TN	47085	23,048	10.4	60.5	29.0	22,746	7,194	65.8	...	...	...	...
Jackson, TN	47087	14,432	17.3	62.2	20.6	12,953	7,642	61.4	...	...	...	...
Jefferson, TN	47089	55,988	10.3	58.1	31.6	52,758	6,940	64.2	...	...	...	...
Johnson, TN	47091	20,994	15.0	59.8	25.3	19,771	8,482	59.6	...	...	...	...
Knox, TN	47093	487,605	8.9	30.3	60.8	429,304	7,879	62.0	23,767	88.6	7.5	1.6
Lake, TN	47095	8,229	16.6	64.2	19.2	7,590	7,898	67.0	...	...	...	...
Lauderdale, TN	47097	36,033	13.6	65.6	20.8	33,190	7,215	65.9	...	...	...	...
Lawrence, TN	47099	52,791	10.3	59.2	30.6	49,733	7,125	67.6	...	...	...	...
Lewis, TN	47101	14,313	11.9	68.2	19.9	12,606	6,624	64.2	...	...	...	...
Lincoln, TN	47103	39,152	10.9	59.9	29.2	34,602	6,537	67.7	...	...	...	...
Loudon, TN	47105	60,613	8.6	49.4	42.0	52,997	7,095	70.5	...	...	...	...
McMinn, TN	47107	61,080	12.0	54.7	33.3	57,717	6,841	62.9	...	...	...	...
McNairy, TN	47109	33,803	13.3	61.1	25.6	30,165	6,735	70.3	...	...	...	...
Macon, TN	47111	27,881	11.0	64.7	24.3	23,717	6,194	68.4	...	...	...	...
Madison, TN	47113	114,986	11.7	42.3	46.0	110,861	8,016	62.0	...	...	...	...
Marion, TN	47115	35,626	10.4	56.1	33.5	32,754	7,152	61.7	...	...	...	...
Marshall, TN	47117	38,701	8.2	56.1	35.7	37,077	6,969	62.5	...	...	...	...
Maury, TN	47119	89,239	9.5	50.6	39.9	88,753	7,568	63.9	4,368	82.6	10.9	3.4
Meigs, TN	47121	14,948	13.6	66.6	19.8	13,358	6,907	67.4	...	...	...	...
Monroe, TN	47123	60,109	9.6	54.0	36.5	48,398	6,780	63.3	...	...	...	...
Montgomery, TN	47125	212,577	12.2	52.4	35.4	201,522	7,070	59.5	8,701	81.0	12.2	4.5
Moore, TN	47127	8,234	7.4	57.7	34.9	7,808	8,254	59.8	...	...	...	...
Morgan, TN	47129	26,856	13.1	68.1	18.8	25,870	7,611	66.3	...	...	...	...
Obion, TN	47131	43,449	10.3	54.7	34.9	40,793	7,394	63.1	...	...	...	...
Overton, TN	47133	26,072	11.9	65.9	22.2	23,506	6,749	62.9	...	...	...	...
Perry, TN	47135	9,385	11.3	64.3	24.5	9,197	7,867	60.2	...	...	...	...
Pickett, TN	47137	6,339	11.7	64.1	24.2	5,631	8,330	64.1	...	...	...	...

... Not available

Table C-1. Population, School, and Student Characteristics by County—*Continued*

County	State/County Code	High school graduates, 2006-2008			College enrollment, 2006-2008		College graduates, 2006-2008 (percent)						
		Population 25 years and over	High school diploma or less (percent)	High school diploma or more (percent)	Number	Percent public	Bachelor's degree or more	+/- U.S. percent with Bachelor's degree or more	Non-Hispanic White	Black or African American	American Indian and Alaska Native	Asian, Hawaiian, and Pacific Islander	Hispanic or Latino[3]
		30	31	32	33	34	35	36	37	38	39	40	41
TENNESSEE	47000	4,126,506	51.8	81.8	353,753	73.9	22.2	-5.2	23.4	15.1	16.5	49.8	11.5
Anderson, TN	47001	51,847	53.1	83.9	2,589	78.9	20.6	-6.8	20.1	9.5	...	...	...
Bedford, TN	47003	28,973	67.9	71.4	1,048	77.5	13.4	-14.0	15.9	3.3	...	...	...
Benton, TN	47005	...	...	...	...	...	...	...	...	...	...	...	...
Bledsoe, TN	47007	...	...	...	...	...	...	...	...	...	...	...	...
Blount, TN	47009	83,428	49.5	84.9	5,823	61.2	20.7	-6.7	21.2	9.4	...	...	8.6
Bradley, TN	47011	64,367	50.9	79.3	7,451	46.7	20.1	-7.3	20.3	9.1	...	...	8.6
Campbell, TN	47013	29,163	71.9	68.1	1,220	68.4	8.6	-18.8	8.3	...	...	...	...
Cannon, TN	47015	...	...	...	...	...	...	...	...	...	...	...	...
Carroll, TN	47017	20,147	65.1	76.5	1,178	48.4	14.7	-12.7	15.2	11.5	...	...	...
Carter, TN	47019	42,307	63.0	76.0	3,548	63.6	15.4	-12.0	14.7	...	...	...	...
Cheatham, TN	47021	26,295	56.4	81.7	1,455	69.2	16.6	-10.8	16.1	...	...	...	...
Chester, TN	47023	...	...	...	...	...	...	...	...	...	...	...	...
Claiborne, TN	47025	21,911	68.3	69.9	1,602	45.8	11.9	-15.5	11.1	...	...	...	...
Clay, TN	47027	...	...	...	...	...	...	...	...	...	...	...	...
Cocke, TN	47029	25,092	72.0	71.0	1,159	80.8	7.7	-19.7	7.8	...	...	...	...
Coffee, TN	47031	35,384	57.7	81.4	1,998	79.4	19.9	-7.5	20.4	18.7	...	...	...
Crockett, TN	47033	...	...	...	...	...	...	...	...	...	...	...	...
Cumberland, TN	47035	38,520	60.2	80.2	1,702	88.2	15.8	-11.6	15.4	...	...	...	...
Davidson, TN	47037	415,759	41.4	84.8	46,620	50.1	32.8	5.4	38.3	21.9	21.7	43.7	9.3
Decatur, TN	47039	...	...	...	...	...	...	...	...	...	...	...	...
De Kalb, TN	47041	...	...	...	...	...	...	...	...	...	...	...	...
Dickson, TN	47043	31,548	63.8	79.3	1,554	81.8	13.7	-13.7	14.1	4.1	...	...	...
Dyer, TN	47045	25,554	65.4	77.0	1,387	88.8	13.4	-14.0	13.9	10.9	...	...	...
Fayette, TN	47047	24,464	56.1	80.0	1,749	81.6	16.6	-10.0	20.7	6.5	...	...	...
Fentress, TN	47049	...	...	...	...	...	...	...	...	...	...	...	...
Franklin, TN	47051	27,961	60.1	80.1	2,355	32.7	15.0	-12.4	15.4	6.3	...	...	...
Gibson, TN	47053	33,563	61.1	78.1	1,558	88.5	13.7	-13.7	16.1	3.0	...	...	...
Giles, TN	47055	20,282	66.2	77.0	905	56.0	12.8	-14.6	12.6	11.9	...	...	...
Grainger, TN	47057	16,106	73.5	67.8	703	75.2	7.9	-19.5	8.0	...	...	...	...
Greene, TN	47059	46,600	67.5	74.6	2,068	60.4	12.2	-15.2	12.4	6.7	...	...	...
Grundy, TN	47061	...	...	...	...	...	...	...	...	...	...	...	...
Hamblen, TN	47063	42,466	61.6	75.4	1,853	83.8	13.8	-13.6	15.2	7.7	...	...	2.9
Hamilton, TN	47065	224,812	44.6	85.0	20,746	75.3	26.3	-1.1	29.0	14.3	6.4	57.7	15.6
Hancock, TN	47067	...	...	...	...	...	...	...	...	...	...	...	...
Hardeman, TN	47069	19,369	69.2	70.7	837	82.7	10.2	-17.2	11.3	6.7	...	...	...
Hardin, TN	47071	18,528	71.3	72.5	862	85.3	10.2	-17.2	10.3	...	...	...	...
Hawkins, TN	47073	40,484	62.5	76.2	2,301	93.3	11.5	-15.9	11.1	...	...	...	...
Haywood, TN	47075	...	...	...	...	...	...	...	...	...	...	...	...
Henderson, TN	47077	18,295	62.8	78.1	1,053	89.6	12.7	-14.7	13.3	4.0	...	...	...
Henry, TN	47079	22,609	62.4	81.1	1,152	75.5	14.5	-12.9	14.4	13.3	...	...	...
Hickman, TN	47081	16,424	69.8	72.5	829	94.6	8.0	-19.4	8.2	...	...	...	...
Houston, TN	47083	...	...	...	...	...	...	...	...	...	...	...	...
Humphreys, TN	47085	...	...	...	...	...	...	...	...	...	...	...	...
Jackson, TN	47087	...	...	...	...	...	...	...	...	...	...	...	...
Jefferson, TN	47089	33,876	57.7	76.3	3,099	38.9	13.2	-14.2	13.2	...	...	...	...
Johnson, TN	47091	...	...	...	...	...	...	...	...	...	...	...	...
Knox, TN	47093	282,604	40.3	87.6	38,358	85.9	33.4	6.0	34.2	19.5	...	68.0	24.6
Lake, TN	47095	...	...	...	...	...	...	...	...	...	...	...	...
Lauderdale, TN	47097	17,808	75.2	71.1	849	86.7	7.8	-19.6	10.1	3.5	...	...	...
Lawrence, TN	47099	27,487	66.5	72.6	1,696	86.9	10.8	-16.6	10.7	...	...	...	...
Lewis, TN	47101	...	...	...	...	...	...	...	...	...	...	...	...
Lincoln, TN	47103	22,637	60.8	77.8	1,101	91.0	14.6	-12.8	15.3	6.5	...	...	...
Loudon, TN	47105	32,765	52.7	84.5	1,474	79.2	21.6	-5.8	22.0	...	...	...	...
McMinn, TN	47107	36,535	62.9	78.7	1,720	64.2	13.9	-13.5	13.1	21.1	...	...	...
McNairy, TN	47109	17,757	69.2	74.6	1,100	77.0	9.9	-17.5	9.7	13.5	...	...	...
Macon, TN	47111	14,806	76.6	71.7	...	...	7.4	-20.0	7.7	...	...	...	...
Madison, TN	47113	62,284	45.2	84.7	6,121	54.0	24.6	-2.8	28.8	15.1	...	...	14.3
Marion, TN	47115	19,711	62.8	74.5	891	90.6	11.2	-16.2	11.3	...	...	...	...
Marshall, TN	47117	20,106	65.0	79.4	951	76.6	10.3	-17.1	10.9	2.9	...	...	...
Maury, TN	47119	53,640	54.6	82.9	3,268	76.6	15.8	-11.6	17.4	7.7	...	...	7.4
Meigs, TN	47121	...	...	...	...	...	...	...	...	...	...	...	...
Monroe, TN	47123	30,470	68.5	70.6	1,467	74.8	11.3	-16.1	11.3	...	...	...	...
Montgomery, TN	47125	93,525	40.5	90.8	11,981	85.2	22.8	-4.6	24.6	16.8	...	24.1	18.1
Moore, TN	47127	...	...	...	...	...	...	...	...	...	...	...	...
Morgan, TN	47129	14,373	75.7	73.2	456	77.6	4.3	-23.1	4.5	...	...	...	...
Obion, TN	47131	22,185	67.5	80.3	1,075	86.8	11.5	-15.9	12.5	3.3	...	...	...
Overton, TN	47133	14,708	72.2	70.5	746	96.2	10.3	-17.1	10.4	...	...	...	...
Perry, TN	47135	...	...	...	...	...	...	...	...	...	...	...	...
Pickett, TN	47137	...	...	...	...	...	...	...	...	...	...	...	...

[3]May be of any race
... Not available

Table C-1. Population, School, and Student Characteristics by County—*Continued*

County	State/County Code	County Type[1]	Population, 2009 Total	Population, 2009 Percent 5–17 years	Percent of related children 5-17 years in poverty, 2008	Percent of children under 19 years with no health insurance, 2007	Number of Schools and Students, 2008-2009 School Districts	Number of Schools and Students, 2008-2009 Schools	Number of Schools and Students, 2008-2009 Students	Resident enrollment, 2006-2008 K-12 enrollment Number	Resident enrollment, 2006-2008 K-12 enrollment Percent public
			1	2	3	4	5	6	7	8	9
Polk, TN	47139	3	15,648	16.9	22.7	10.9	1	6	2,766	...	...
Putnam, TN	47141	4	72,431	15.6	19.5	11.9	1	19	10,899	10,280	94.0
Rhea, TN	47143	6	31,516	17.1	24.2	7.9	2	7	5,073	5,080	94.4
Roane, TN	47145	4	53,508	15.4	18.6	7.8	1	18	7,556	8,010	91.9
Robertson, TN	47147	1	66,581	18.2	14.7	10.5	1	18	11,089	11,405	88.3
Rutherford, TN	47149	1	257,048	18.3	10.9	11.2	2	55	44,321	45,088	91.4
Scott, TN	47151	6	21,866	17.9	31.0	6.6	2	10	4,339	...	...
Sequatchie, TN	47153	2	13,915	17.6	25.3	11.7	1	3	2,276	...	...
Sevier, TN	47155	4	86,243	15.7	18.5	12.0	1	27	14,446	13,794	93.7
Shelby, TN	47157	1	920,232	19.3	23.9	8.4	2	251	159,402	180,631	85.4
Smith, TN	47159	1	19,201	17.8	18.1	10.0	1	10	3,319	...	...
Stewart, TN	47161	3	13,340	17.1	18.6	12.4	1	6	2,330	...	...
Sullivan, TN	47163	3	154,552	15.4	17.0	6.7	3	47	22,571	23,688	92.6
Sumner, TN	47165	1	158,759	18.6	10.6	9.5	1	43	26,738	27,846	88.0
Tipton, TN	47167	1	59,495	19.9	16.5	10.7	1	14	12,055	11,333	90.4
Trousdale, TN	47169	1	7,922	17.2	17.5	13.3	1	3	661	...	...
Unicoi, TN	47171	3	17,740	14.6	21.6	6.0	1	7	2,644	...	...
Union, TN	47173	2	19,164	16.5	27.5	10.6	1	7	3,058	...	...
Van Buren, TN	47175	9	5,480	15.5	26.7	8.8	1	2	813	...	...
Warren, TN	47177	6	40,481	17.2	24.6	10.5	1	11	6,606	6,656	88.5
Washington, TN	47179	3	120,598	14.9	15.9	7.9	2	27	16,665	17,904	91.1
Wayne, TN	47181	8	16,506	13.9	23.8	9.9	1	8	2,569	...	...
Weakley, TN	47183	7	33,459	15.0	19.9	9.2	1	11	4,833	5,250	93.4
White, TN	47185	7	25,444	16.6	24.5	7.9	1	9	4,067	4,214	92.4
Williamson, TN	47187	1	176,838	21.3	5.2	11.6	2	45	33,675	32,200	82.2
Wilson, TN	47189	1	112,377	18.3	9.6	9.9	2	25	18,098	19,183	86.9
TEXAS	48000	X	24,782,302	19.5	20.6	19.5	1276	9,283	4,752,148	4,658,414	93.1
Anderson, TX	48001	5	57,001	14.2	23.4	16.1	7	23	8,509	9,092	96.8
Andrews, TX	48003	6	14,057	21.7	16.6	20.3	1	7	3,120	...	...
Angelina, TX	48005	5	83,675	18.9	28.9	18.4	7	44	17,061	16,094	96.1
Aransas, TX	48007	2	24,826	14.8	29.9	19.1	1	5	3,039	...	...
Archer, TX	48009	3	8,912	18.7	9.8	21.3	3	7	1,807	...	...
Armstrong, TX	48011	3	2,065	17.7	13.8	22.6	1	2	325	...	...
Atascosa, TX	48013	1	44,633	21.3	25.8	19.2	5	32	8,661	8,673	95.0
Austin, TX	48015	1	27,248	18.5	13.2	22.2	3	13	5,618	5,454	84.5
Bailey, TX	48017	7	6,273	21.8	26.0	22.5	1	5	1,467	...	...
Bandera, TX	48019	1	20,560	15.7	19.1	26.1	2	6	2,859	3,268	92.7
Bastrop, TX	48021	1	74,876	19.2	16.8	23.6	5	28	14,590	14,787	91.0
Baylor, TX	48023	6	3,677	16.3	25.5	10.8	1	3	555	...	...
Bee, TX	48025	4	32,487	15.1	30.3	16.6	5	15	5,119	5,504	90.9
Bell, TX	48027	2	285,787	19.7	16.7	13.0	12	122	61,667	55,497	95.7
Bexar, TX	48029	1	1,651,448	19.6	22.0	16.2	42	514	314,401	317,584	91.9
Blanco, TX	48031	8	9,198	17.3	15.5	29.5	2	6	1,648	...	...
Borden, TX	48033	9	595	18.3	10.7	18.3	1	2	192	...	...
Bosque, TX	48035	6	17,631	16.9	18.8	18.9	7	21	2,517	...	...
Bowie, TX	48037	3	93,964	17.7	24.9	13.5	13	55	17,659	16,247	97.7
Brazoria, TX	48039	1	309,208	19.7	10.8	19.9	8	99	59,074	58,782	92.5
Brazos, TX	48041	3	179,992	14.7	20.5	20.1	4	46	25,693	25,102	93.5
Brewster, TX	48043	7	9,481	13.2	23.3	20.6	4	7	1,232	...	...
Briscoe, TX	48045	9	1,428	17.6	25.0	31.8	2	2	394	...	...
Brooks, TX	48047	6	7,377	20.5	45.0	8.8	3	6	1,629	...	...
Brown, TX	48049	5	38,088	17.2	23.4	14.4	9	35	6,880	6,712	96.1
Burleson, TX	48051	3	16,570	16.7	20.0	18.1	3	13	2,801	...	...
Burnet, TX	48053	6	45,149	15.7	17.5	24.7	2	14	7,332	7,453	93.0
Caldwell, TX	48055	1	37,810	19.0	18.0	18.5	3	15	6,244	6,879	97.2
Calhoun, TX	48057	3	20,573	19.9	21.1	17.3	1	10	4,394	3,760	96.3
Callahan, TX	48059	3	13,426	18.2	22.0	17.6	5	12	2,567	...	...
Cameron, TX	48061	2	396,371	23.9	42.9	19.2	11	162	98,311	89,957	96.1
Camp, TX	48063	6	12,793	19.8	25.5	20.5	1	5	2,356	...	...
Carson, TX	48065	3	6,110	19.0	10.7	14.1	4	8	1,313	...	...
Cass, TX	48067	6	29,203	16.9	23.7	13.5	7	21	5,647	4,793	94.5
Castro, TX	48069	6	7,130	21.9	30.1	23.7	3	6	1,664	...	...
Chambers, TX	48071	1	31,431	20.7	11.5	20.1	3	23	6,516	5,475	97.0
Cherokee, TX	48073	6	48,473	18.2	27.9	19.7	6	25	10,230	8,971	97.3
Childress, TX	48075	7	7,548	15.1	28.2	17.3	1	3	1,107	...	...
Clay, TX	48077	3	10,893	16.7	13.8	15.6	5	9	1,813	...	...
Cochran, TX	48079	9	2,927	20.7	32.2	23.2	1	10	1,305	...	...
Coke, TX	48081	8	3,311	17.4	18.0	21.2	2	12	556	...	...
Coleman, TX	48083	6	8,480	16.8	31.1	13.4	4	12	1,533	...	...
Collin, TX	48085	1	791,631	20.3	6.8	10.3	14	263	155,100	145,634	90.0

[1]County type codes are from the Economic Research Service of the United States Department of Agriculture. See notes and definitions for more information.
... Not available

Table C-1. Population, School, and Student Characteristics by County—*Continued*

County	State/ County Code	Characteristics of students, 2008-2009				Number of graduates, 2006-2007	Staff and students, 2008-2009			
		Percent with IEP[2]	Percent eligible for free or reduced lunch	Percent minority	Percent English Language Learners		Total staff	Number of teachers	Student/ teacher ratio	Central admin. Staff
		10	11	12	13	14	15	16	17	18
Polk, TN	47139	11.0	59.4	2.0	0.2	151	320	178	15.5	2
Putnam, TN	47141	13.4	47.7	12.3	3.9	647	1,432	660	16.5	9
Rhea, TN	47143	10.9	62.5	8.3	2.3	308	660	330	15.4	7
Roane, TN	47145	13.8	48.0	5.9	0.1	419	959	493	15.3	6
Robertson, TN	47147	12.6	39.1	17.8	3.8	665	1,548	707	15.7	4
Rutherford, TN	47149	9.6	34.2	30.6	4.0	2,425	4,934	2,921	15.2	45
Scott, TN	47151	9.8	73.6	0.6	...	213	636	307	14.1	9
Sequatchie, TN	47153	17.1	60.1	3.4	0.6	131	294	144	15.8	2
Sevier, TN	47155	10.9	47.7	7.2	2.2	796	2,013	964	15.0	4
Shelby, TN	47157	11.4	56.8	79.2	4.0	8,935	18,118	10,183	15.7	193
Smith, TN	47159	13.6	48.8	6.2	0.3	239	476	226	14.7	4
Stewart, TN	47161	12.4	50.6	3.4	0.3	152	354	141	16.5	3
Sullivan, TN	47163	14.4	43.6	6.1	0.5	1,472	3,188	1,530	14.8	17
Sumner, TN	47165	13.5	31.9	15.3	1.8	1,759	3,570	1,838	14.5	4
Tipton, TN	47167	11.9	49.2	27.3	0.2	794	1,483	756	15.9	4
Trousdale, TN	47169	36.6	40.7	15.1	2.0	94	205	93	7.1	3
Unicoi, TN	47171	17.2	51.0	7.3	2.6	173	345	168	15.7	7
Union, TN	47173	13.5	62.9	1.6	0.4	220	426	225	13.6	3
Van Buren, TN	47175	11.8	59.3	0.7	...	37	132	61	13.3	2
Warren, TN	47177	17.0	55.5	16.6	5.3	423	903	429	15.4	3
Washington, TN	47179	12.1	41.7	11.1	1.5	1,083	2,183	1,109	15.0	11
Wayne, TN	47181	14.2	66.5	2.4	...	192	444	210	12.2	1
Weakley, TN	47183	13.5	51.5	12.4	0.5	305	640	319	15.2	7
White, TN	47185	16.2	53.7	4.4	...	265	576	268	15.2	3
Williamson, TN	47187	9.5	11.4	14.2	1.9	1,983	4,230	2,247	15.0	23
Wilson, TN	47189	12.1	28.3	15.3	2.5	1,067	2,371	1,151	15.7	20
TEXAS	48000	9.5	48.8	66.0	15.1	241,186	649,371	327,903	14.5	27,311
Anderson, TX	48001	10.3	54.5	38.6	4.9	516	1,284	686	12.4	55
Andrews, TX	48003	9.6	28.9	64.0	8.2	206	465	226	13.8	21
Angelina, TX	48005	12.0	63.0	47.1	12.5	987	2,533	1,241	13.7	79
Aransas, TX	48007	10.2	60.4	43.6	4.3	195	505	244	12.5	21
Archer, TX	48009	9.8	32.1	11.1	3.5	128	264	152	11.9	10
Armstrong, TX	48011	14.8	34.2	9.2	1.8	25	66	39	8.3	4
Atascosa, TX	48013	9.2	66.4	73.5	3.8	489	1,355	635	13.6	63
Austin, TX	48015	11.2	43.7	47.0	9.4	362	836	433	13.0	38
Bailey, TX	48017	11.4	78.6	78.7	17.0	75	228	123	11.9	6
Bandera, TX	48019	13.4	50.3	26.2	4.3	194	448	228	12.5	15
Bastrop, TX	48021	11.1	59.9	53.5	13.1	679	1,919	992	14.7	82
Baylor, TX	48023	9.0	47.7	21.6	0.7	51	94	57	9.7	5
Bee, TX	48025	9.9	67.4	77.2	2.3	288	754	361	14.2	35
Bell, TX	48027	11.2	50.2	57.5	6.0	2,886	9,018	4,467	13.8	330
Bexar, TX	48029	11.1	46.5	79.6	9.3	15,085	42,365	20,621	15.2	1,960
Blanco, TX	48031	10.0	41.3	30.3	4.9	103	264	148	11.1	10
Borden, TX	48033	7.8	3.6	27.6	2.1	19	47	19	10.1	1
Bosque, TX	48035	12.8	53.3	30.5	7.1	182	428	228	11.0	20
Bowie, TX	48037	12.9	52.1	39.3	1.6	1,023	2,572	1,384	12.8	113
Brazoria, TX	48039	10.5	42.6	54.2	8.2	3,087	7,679	3,804	15.5	273
Brazos, TX	48041	7.6	49.6	58.6	13.3	1,310	3,631	1,801	14.3	149
Brewster, TX	48043	11.0	52.1	66.1	9.3	87	230	118	10.4	14
Briscoe, TX	48045	7.9	51.0	39.6	7.9	20	84	45	8.8	5
Brooks, TX	48047	11.2	24.7	96.8	3.2	94	297	144	11.3	17
Brown, TX	48049	11.7	54.6	33.4	1.6	445	1,033	537	12.8	27
Burleson, TX	48051	11.3	51.4	43.6	7.2	180	507	242	11.6	28
Burnet, TX	48053	12.1	53.1	32.0	7.1	469	1,124	534	13.7	31
Caldwell, TX	48055	10.5	60.4	66.1	7.3	369	900	469	13.3	36
Calhoun, TX	48057	13.0	56.5	63.9	9.5	266	622	294	14.9	16
Callahan, TX	48059	11.2	47.0	10.8	0.5	225	428	231	11.1	16
Cameron, TX	48061	9.1	19.4	96.6	25.2	4,238	14,789	6,552	15.0	605
Camp, TX	48063	15.4	69.6	53.4	11.8	141	440	217	10.9	13
Carson, TX	48065	10.5	26.3	9.6	0.8	97	233	124	10.6	13
Cass, TX	48067	12.0	55.1	27.6	1.1	368	974	484	11.7	40
Castro, TX	48069	5.9	72.5	76.4	12.6	104	297	145	11.5	14
Chambers, TX	48071	8.8	33.5	29.5	4.3	354	906	452	14.4	33
Cherokee, TX	48073	10.3	63.8	46.7	14.1	499	1,571	773	13.2	52
Childress, TX	48075	12.5	50.7	43.0	2.8	72	207	98	11.3	7
Clay, TX	48077	12.2	38.9	8.3	0.3	146	325	170	10.7	14
Cochran, TX	48079	11.0	72.2	63.4	8.9	91	279	138	9.5	10
Coke, TX	48081	12.6	52.1	31.3	5.9	42	105	62	9.0	5
Coleman, TX	48083	11.8	55.3	29.3	2.8	114	287	147	10.4	20
Collin, TX	48085	9.9	20.4	41.4	7.7	7,376	19,611	11,232	13.8	665

[2]IEP= Individual Education Program. See notes and definitions for more information

... Not available

Table C-1. Population, School, and Student Characteristics by County—*Continued*

County	State/County Code	Revenues, 2007-2008				Current expenditures, 2007-2008			Resident population 16 to 19 years, 2006-2008			
		Total revenue ($1,000's)	Percentage of revenue from			Amount ($1,000's)	Amount per student	Percent for instruction	Total population 16 to 19 years	Percent enrolled in school	Percent high school graduates, not enrolled in school	Percent not enrolled, not grads, not employed or not in labor force
			Federal gov't	State gov't	Local gov't							
		19	20	21	22	23	24	25	26	27	28	29
Polk, TN	47139	21,070	11.2	65.8	23.0	19,807	7,301	67.0	...	...	...	...
Putnam, TN	47141	83,900	10.8	47.5	41.7	76,957	6,999	62.7	4,508	78.4	12.9	8.5
Rhea, TN	47143	36,063	10.9	64.0	25.1	33,984	6,732	65.1	...	...	...	...
Roane, TN	47145	61,252	9.8	52.1	38.1	57,116	7,660	64.0	2,565	69.4	24.0	5.7
Robertson, TN	47147	77,550	8.3	57.5	34.3	72,461	6,529	70.2	3,395	79.0	12.6	3.3
Rutherford, TN	47149	326,684	6.4	49.3	44.3	306,019	7,206	65.2	14,294	87.5	8.9	1.8
Scott, TN	47151	33,267	12.4	64.7	23.0	30,485	7,222	67.2	...	...	...	...
Sequatchie, TN	47153	19,171	13.2	58.2	28.6	14,527	6,564	65.7	...	...	...	...
Sevier, TN	47155	122,660	8.2	32.3	59.5	111,626	7,774	61.8	...	...	...	...
Shelby, TN	47157	1,487,418	12.2	41.0	46.9	1,370,148	8,444	61.3	54,235	81.4	10.5	6.0
Smith, TN	47159	23,929	10.1	63.6	26.3	22,291	6,798	64.4	...	...	...	...
Stewart, TN	47161	17,674	10.1	74.0	15.9	16,329	7,219	58.3	...	...	...	...
Sullivan, TN	47163	205,454	8.8	38.9	52.4	187,431	8,229	63.3	7,314	81.9	11.0	5.2
Sumner, TN	47165	200,821	7.2	51.5	41.3	192,505	7,268	66.1	7,476	85.2	10.6	1.6
Tipton, TN	47167	85,532	10.1	65.7	24.2	80,139	6,645	67.6	3,775	76.2	17.5	2.3
Trousdale, TN	47169	10,687	9.1	66.4	24.5	9,569	7,282	67.6	...	...	...	...
Unicoi, TN	47171	20,314	12.1	60.5	27.4	18,413	7,017	60.6	...	...	...	...
Union, TN	47173	25,455	12.1	68.6	19.3	24,842	8,142	62.9	...	...	...	...
Van Buren, TN	47175	7,776	10.3	65.1	24.5	6,226	7,763	60.3	...	...	...	...
Warren, TN	47177	48,510	12.4	57.0	30.6	44,361	6,884	62.4	...	...	...	...
Washington, TN	47179	130,271	9.2	42.3	48.6	118,653	7,132	66.6	...	...	...	...
Wayne, TN	47181	21,840	16.5	66.6	16.8	20,294	7,728	72.6	...	...	...	...
Weakley, TN	47183	36,574	11.0	60.6	28.4	34,110	7,196	65.0	...	...	...	...
White, TN	47185	30,041	13.5	62.5	24.0	26,614	6,539	67.9	...	...	...	...
Williamson, TN	47187	270,838	4.3	37.3	58.4	258,508	8,008	64.4	9,064	92.5	4.6	1.9
Wilson, TN	47189	132,745	6.9	48.3	44.8	122,178	6,833	64.9	5,780	84.6	9.5	2.6
TEXAS	48000	47,040,194	9.8	43.7	46.5	38,823,720	8,312	59.8	1,404,351	81.6	11.0	4.4
Anderson, TX	48001	81,292	9.9	51.5	38.6	68,775	8,054	61.3	...	...	...	...
Andrews, TX	48003	54,079	4.2	17.9	77.9	29,225	9,623	61.2	...	...	...	...
Angelina, TX	48005	143,068	11.0	61.1	27.9	131,707	7,739	58.9	...	...	...	...
Aransas, TX	48007	41,073	9.3	25.3	65.4	30,980	9,798	57.7	...	...	...	...
Archer, TX	48009	18,096	4.4	62.3	33.3	15,346	8,526	63.6	...	...	...	...
Armstrong, TX	48011	4,382	4.5	65.4	30.1	3,740	10,506	62.0	...	...	...	...
Atascosa, TX	48013	80,207	11.2	62.9	25.9	73,462	8,526	58.4	...	...	...	...
Austin, TX	48015	56,503	7.1	41.5	51.4	50,563	8,963	59.9	...	...	...	...
Bailey, TX	48017	16,448	11.6	59.1	29.3	12,569	8,430	61.6	...	...	...	...
Bandera, TX	48019	29,558	7.0	38.8	54.2	25,468	8,794	60.7	...	...	...	...
Bastrop, TX	48021	141,380	8.5	45.7	45.9	113,542	8,011	58.3	...	...	...	...
Baylor, TX	48023	6,595	6.3	61.1	32.7	5,923	10,212	65.4	...	...	...	...
Bee, TX	48025	52,145	13.3	60.1	26.6	43,705	8,421	60.7	...	...	...	...
Bell, TX	48027	578,231	17.1	56.1	26.8	481,383	7,915	61.3	16,119	73.9	18.3	4.7
Bexar, TX	48029	3,061,693	11.2	47.7	41.2	2,575,993	8,359	59.1	94,175	78.9	13.2	5.0
Blanco, TX	48031	20,951	4.2	35.2	60.6	15,927	9,537	63.6	...	...	...	...
Borden, TX	48033	9,916	1.8	18.0	80.2	4,149	24,696	44.1	...	...	...	...
Bosque, TX	48035	28,773	8.9	48.9	42.2	23,565	9,060	61.1	...	...	...	...
Bowie, TX	48037	172,436	10.0	54.3	35.8	142,173	8,167	64.0	4,888	78.0	14.8	4.8
Brazoria, TX	48039	555,578	6.9	39.8	53.2	440,731	7,599	57.6	16,154	85.1	8.9	4.5
Brazos, TX	48041	242,189	9.8	37.2	53.0	192,115	7,774	59.8	...	...	...	...
Brewster, TX	48043	15,527	15.3	47.0	37.7	14,033	11,531	59.7	...	...	...	...
Briscoe, TX	48045	5,021	8.9	66.0	25.1	4,570	11,065	65.6	...	...	...	...
Brooks, TX	48047	23,562	13.9	40.4	45.7	20,325	11,935	58.2	...	...	...	...
Brown, TX	48049	68,436	10.2	54.8	35.0	58,143	8,513	62.0	...	...	...	...
Burleson, TX	48051	30,813	13.0	46.1	41.0	27,868	9,603	55.9	...	...	...	...
Burnet, TX	48053	78,401	6.6	28.8	64.6	62,768	8,526	57.0	...	...	...	...
Caldwell, TX	48055	67,612	11.4	61.5	27.0	60,955	8,623	60.2	...	...	...	...
Calhoun, TX	48057	60,913	5.4	17.1	77.4	37,764	8,850	59.4	...	...	...	...
Callahan, TX	48059	26,278	5.7	60.5	33.8	22,864	8,821	60.4	...	...	...	...
Cameron, TX	48061	955,634	15.7	65.2	19.1	833,556	8,506	59.2	24,722	81.2	8.6	7.7
Camp, TX	48063	23,998	10.4	55.8	33.8	21,124	8,733	67.3	...	...	...	...
Carson, TX	48065	18,748	3.1	32.3	64.6	13,278	9,939	60.2	...	...	...	...
Cass, TX	48067	57,439	12.0	56.7	31.3	49,985	8,780	63.3	...	...	...	...
Castro, TX	48069	19,169	14.6	58.6	26.8	16,045	9,666	61.4	...	...	...	...
Chambers, TX	48071	85,786	3.5	34.8	61.7	55,629	8,706	56.9	...	...	...	...
Cherokee, TX	48073	95,384	10.8	54.9	34.3	81,052	7,962	61.4	...	...	...	...
Childress, TX	48075	11,611	8.9	68.0	23.0	10,799	9,582	63.2	...	...	...	...
Clay, TX	48077	21,465	9.1	54.7	36.2	17,915	9,715	61.8	...	...	...	...
Cochran, TX	48079	24,159	9.1	43.4	47.5	18,354	13,779	59.2	...	...	...	...
Coke, TX	48081	8,650	6.3	58.3	35.4	7,287	12,165	61.5	...	...	...	...
Coleman, TX	48083	16,912	9.1	68.4	22.5	14,811	9,750	59.3	...	...	...	...
Collin, TX	48085	1,567,133	3.2	28.3	68.5	1,160,793	7,853	63.1	36,243	87.2	9.2	1.5

... Not available

Table C-1. Population, School, and Student Characteristics by County—*Continued*

County	State/County Code	High school graduates, 2006-2008			College enrollment, 2006-2008		College graduates, 2006-2008 (percent)						
		Population 25 years and over	High school diploma or less (percent)	High school diploma or more (percent)	Number	Percent public	Bachelor's degree or more	+/- U.S. percent with Bachelor's degree or more	Non-Hispanic White	Black or African American	American Indian and Alaska Native	Asian, Hawaiian, and Pacific Islander	Hispanic or Latino[3]
		30	31	32	33	34	35	36	37	38	39	40	41
Polk, TN	47139	...	...	...	...	...	...	...	...	...	...	...	...
Putnam, TN	47141	44,582	55.0	79.9	6,776	95.3	21.6	-5.8	21.3	34.5	...	...	6.1
Rhea, TN	47143	20,605	63.2	73.2	1,566	40.0	10.9	-16.5	10.6	...	...	...	...
Roane, TN	47145	38,546	55.4	79.2	1,633	86.6	16.3	-11.1	16.4	5.3	...	...	...
Robertson, TN	47147	41,931	61.3	78.9	1,998	78.3	12.7	-14.7	13.8	5.7	...	...	1.6
Rutherford, TN	47149	149,035	44.6	87.3	21,821	89.9	26.1	-1.3	28.0	19.4	...	26.5	7.9
Scott, TN	47151	14,782	72.6	73.5	...	...	9.1	-18.3	9.2	...	...	...	...
Sequatchie, TN	47153	...	...	...	...	...	...	...	...	...	...	...	...
Sevier, TN	47155	58,561	59.3	78.7	2,956	81.8	15.5	-11.9	15.4	...	...	...	14.1
Shelby, TN	47157	573,708	43.5	84.7	57,197	75.6	27.5	0.1	40.6	14.2	14.3	60.8	12.7
Smith, TN	47159	...	...	...	...	...	...	...	...	...	...	...	...
Stewart, TN	47161	...	...	...	...	...	...	...	...	...	...	...	...
Sullivan, TN	47163	110,609	52.2	81.9	7,163	78.5	19.8	-7.6	20.1	12.6	...	...	10.0
Sumner, TN	47165	101,976	47.7	85.2	7,069	77.0	22.0	-5.4	22.3	19.7	...	38.3	12.7
Tipton, TN	47167	37,157	55.2	82.6	2,436	82.8	13.4	-14.0	14.7	6.1	...	...	...
Trousdale, TN	47169	...	...	...	...	...	...	...	...	...	...	...	...
Unicoi, TN	47171	...	...	...	...	...	...	...	...	...	...	...	...
Union, TN	47173	...	...	...	...	...	...	...	...	...	...	...	...
Van Buren, TN	47175	...	...	...	...	...	...	...	...	...	...	...	...
Warren, TN	47177	27,199	67.9	73.3	1,490	93.6	11.1	-16.3	11.4	...	...	...	...
Washington, TN	47179	79,681	47.6	83.4	10,847	91.1	27.2	-0.2	27.1	23.9	...	...	23.3
Wayne, TN	47181	...	...	...	...	...	...	...	...	...	...	...	...
Weakley, TN	47183	21,737	58.8	81.9	3,830	95.7	17.9	-9.5	16.6	20.9	...	...	...
White, TN	47185	17,219	71.4	74.2	952	96.0	10.1	-17.3	10.1	...	...	...	...
Williamson, TN	47187	108,194	25.3	94.3	9,907	68.4	50.2	22.8	51.7	32.9	...	82.5	18.3
Wilson, TN	47189	70,757	47.4	86.2	5,937	58.1	23.8	-3.6	24.3	17.0	...	...	13.4
TEXAS	48000	14,807,376	47.4	79.2	1,509,946	82.2	25.1	-2.3	33.1	18.2	17.9	52.1	10.7
Anderson, TX	48001	39,634	62.7	74.3	2,682	96.1	11.8	-15.6	15.6	5.2	...	27.3	4.0
Andrews, TX	48003	...	...	...	...	...	...	...	...	...	...	...	...
Angelina, TX	48005	52,809	53.9	77.1	3,267	95.8	15.9	-11.5	19.2	7.8	...	...	3.5
Aransas, TX	48007	16,833	47.6	81.4	...	...	23.7	-3.7	28.0	...	...	...	4.0
Archer, TX	48009	...	...	...	...	...	...	...	...	...	...	...	...
Armstrong, TX	48011	...	...	...	...	...	...	...	...	...	...	...	...
Atascosa, TX	48013	26,951	62.7	74.2	1,709	87.5	10.3	-17.1	17.3	...	...	...	4.7
Austin, TX	48015	17,281	53.1	81.2	1,022	94.3	16.4	-11.0	20.8	3.5	...	...	3.2
Bailey, TX	48017	...	...	...	...	...	...	...	...	...	...	...	...
Bandera, TX	48019	13,833	44.2	88.6	640	41.1	25.3	-2.1	27.8	...	...	...	8.9
Bastrop, TX	48021	46,303	53.4	80.0	3,059	73.9	17.2	-10.2	20.1	19.4	...	...	6.5
Baylor, TX	48023	...	...	...	...	...	...	...	...	...	...	...	...
Bee, TX	48025	21,544	61.2	70.4	1,874	92.6	10.3	-17.1	21.7	3.1	...	...	3.3
Bell, TX	48027	163,179	40.6	88.0	17,108	78.1	21.7	-5.7	26.3	13.8	20.3	34.7	10.8
Bexar, TX	48029	972,570	46.7	80.6	114,750	76.2	24.3	-3.1	39.2	20.5	20.3	44.9	13.4
Blanco, TX	48031	...	...	...	...	...	...	...	...	...	...	...	...
Borden, TX	48033	...	...	...	...	...	...	...	...	...	...	...	...
Bosque, TX	48035	...	...	...	...	...	...	...	...	...	...	...	...
Bowie, TX	48037	60,699	51.3	82.9	4,937	90.4	17.3	-10.1	19.5	11.1	...	...	12.0
Brazoria, TX	48039	183,982	42.5	83.8	17,418	87.6	25.1	-2.3	26.7	29.7	27.0	61.7	11.3
Brazos, TX	48041	83,340	39.4	85.1	48,834	96.7	39.6	12.2	49.4	14.2	...	82.8	13.0
Brewster, TX	48043	...	...	...	...	...	...	...	...	...	...	...	...
Briscoe, TX	48045	...	...	...	...	...	...	...	...	...	...	...	...
Brooks, TX	48047	...	...	...	...	...	...	...	...	...	...	...	...
Brown, TX	48049	25,345	58.9	80.8	1,430	48.9	15.6	-11.8	18.2	...	...	...	5.0
Burleson, TX	48051	...	...	...	...	...	...	...	...	...	...	...	...
Burnet, TX	48053	30,629	50.2	81.3	1,037	80.3	20.1	-7.3	22.1	...	...	...	5.1
Caldwell, TX	48055	23,352	61.0	75.0	1,237	87.6	15.1	-12.3	21.5	7.4	...	...	7.8
Calhoun, TX	48057	13,275	57.5	73.9	701	88.3	12.8	-14.6	17.6	...	...	...	3.6
Callahan, TX	48059	...	...	...	...	...	...	...	...	...	...	...	...
Cameron, TX	48061	213,002	61.9	62.5	21,596	93.0	15.0	-12.4	30.5	...	34.9	56.2	11.2
Camp, TX	48063	...	...	...	...	...	...	...	...	...	...	...	...
Carson, TX	48065	...	...	...	...	...	...	...	...	...	...	...	...
Cass, TX	48067	20,418	60.1	79.9	1,002	93.4	12.4	-15.0	13.4	8.6	...	...	...
Castro, TX	48069	...	...	...	...	...	...	...	...	...	...	...	...
Chambers, TX	48071	19,171	47.4	83.5	1,242	89.9	14.9	-12.5	15.8	11.2	...	...	9.6
Cherokee, TX	48073	30,815	63.7	72.9	1,621	82.4	11.0	-16.4	14.3	3.0	...	...	3.7
Childress, TX	48075	...	...	...	...	...	...	...	...	...	...	...	...
Clay, TX	48077	...	...	...	...	...	...	...	...	...	...	...	...
Cochran, TX	48079	...	...	...	...	...	...	...	...	...	...	...	...
Coke, TX	48081	...	...	...	...	...	...	...	...	...	...	...	...
Coleman, TX	48083	...	...	...	...	...	...	...	...	...	...	...	...
Collin, TX	48085	466,989	24.0	91.9	47,073	81.6	47.4	20.0	49.3	39.2	40.8	71.4	20.9

[3]May be of any race
... Not available

Table C-1. Population, School, and Student Characteristics by County—*Continued*

County	State/County Code	County Type[1]	Population, 2009 Total	Percent 5–17 years	Percent of related children 5-17 years in poverty, 2008	Percent of children under 19 years with no health insurance, 2007	School Districts	Schools	Students	K–12 enrollment Number	Percent public
			1	2	3	4	5	6	7	8	9
Collingsworth, TX	48087	9	3,058	17.7	33.0	26.9	2	4	642	...	...
Colorado, TX	48089	6	20,650	16.7	23.8	20.6	3	14	3,401	3,537	89.7
Comal, TX	48091	1	114,525	18.2	10.8	19.9	3	46	23,709	18,343	86.3
Comanche, TX	48093	7	13,559	17.1	25.2	18.3	4	10	2,260	...	...
Concho, TX	48095	8	3,579	10.6	27.8	21.2	2	20	414	...	...
Cooke, TX	48097	6	38,650	18.2	17.1	21.2	9	22	6,445	7,334	89.9
Coryell, TX	48099	2	72,529	16.5	14.3	14.1	4	22	11,054	15,881	96.4
Cottle, TX	48101	9	1,566	17.5	30.4	20.9	1	1	256	...	...
Crane, TX	48103	6	4,165	23.6	13.3	25.1	1	3	1,025	...	...
Crockett, TX	48105	7	3,740	20.0	18.5	27.4	1	5	755	...	...
Crosby, TX	48107	3	6,109	21.0	35.8	20.5	3	10	1,247	...	...
Culberson, TX	48109	9	2,300	17.5	33.7	30.2	1	3	497	...	...
Dallam, TX	48111	7	6,293	19.5	19.6	34.6	2	6	1,766	...	...
Dallas, TX	48113	1	2,451,730	19.2	23.3	25.5	53	737	449,283	461,525	91.2
Dawson, TX	48115	7	13,657	17.0	30.6	17.2	4	8	2,518	...	...
Deaf Smith, TX	48117	6	18,353	22.4	25.8	22.8	2	9	4,325	...	...
Delta, TX	48119	1	5,410	16.2	25.6	13.8	1	3	852	...	...
Denton, TX	48121	1	658,616	19.5	6.2	17.5	14	217	110,176	117,930	92.0
De Witt, TX	48123	6	19,713	15.9	23.0	15.1	6	24	4,344	...	...
Dickens, TX	48125	8	2,439	15.0	28.7	15.2	2	2	384	...	...
Dimmit, TX	48127	6	9,772	22.1	44.6	13.4	1	6	2,382	...	...
Donley, TX	48129	8	3,664	17.0	22.2	26.1	2	4	674	...	...
Duval, TX	48131	7	12,010	19.9	32.8	9.4	4	11	2,652	...	...
Eastland, TX	48133	6	18,167	16.6	25.3	15.3	5	15	3,144	...	...
Ector, TX	48135	3	134,625	20.6	20.6	18.4	2	42	27,994	26,605	94.3
Edwards, TX	48137	9	1,863	18.0	37.5	29.0	2	5	607	...	...
Ellis, TX	48139	1	151,737	21.0	12.3	20.8	11	62	33,858	28,467	93.1
El Paso, TX	48141	2	751,296	21.6	32.5	19.9	18	274	174,364	163,943	95.4
Erath, TX	48143	7	36,184	15.7	18.6	19.8	9	23	5,834	5,904	99.7
Falls, TX	48145	6	16,782	18.2	30.7	15.6	4	15	2,613	...	...
Fannin, TX	48147	6	32,999	16.1	16.9	17.0	9	25	5,655	5,771	90.3
Fayette, TX	48149	6	22,891	16.2	15.8	19.9	5	12	3,619	3,461	95.8
Fisher, TX	48151	8	3,866	16.4	22.4	19.4	2	7	651	...	...
Floyd, TX	48153	6	6,474	20.8	29.8	20.9	2	10	1,445	...	...
Foard, TX	48155	9	1,334	17.4	21.1	22.8	1	2	239	...	...
Fort Bend, TX	48157	1	556,870	21.8	9.4	19.5	7	183	154,563	106,221	92.1
Franklin, TX	48159	8	10,841	17.4	22.8	17.5	1	4	1,507	...	...
Freestone, TX	48161	7	19,390	16.9	18.8	17.4	4	15	3,673	...	...
Frio, TX	48163	6	16,156	19.1	34.6	13.5	2	10	3,144	...	...
Gaines, TX	48165	7	15,382	22.8	27.1	27.0	3	11	3,099	...	...
Galveston, TX	48167	1	286,814	18.6	14.5	15.4	13	117	74,300	53,098	92.0
Garza, TX	48169	6	4,659	19.8	25.5	18.7	2	5	1,001	...	...
Gillespie, TX	48171	7	24,180	15.1	14.8	26.3	3	10	3,447	3,362	81.9
Glasscock, TX	48173	8	1,221	20.4	13.8	38.9	1	2	262	...	...
Goliad, TX	48175	3	7,033	17.3	18.9	19.3	1	5	1,315	...	...
Gonzales, TX	48177	6	19,610	19.3	28.2	19.3	3	14	3,808	...	...
Gray, TX	48179	6	22,074	17.3	16.9	18.1	4	10	3,819	3,463	97.8
Grayson, TX	48181	3	120,030	17.5	16.4	17.1	13	68	21,010	20,401	93.4
Gregg, TX	48183	3	119,637	18.6	17.3	21.9	9	55	23,550	21,096	91.7
Grimes, TX	48185	6	26,011	16.2	19.7	22.0	4	13	4,228	4,809	95.3
Guadalupe, TX	48187	1	121,432	19.6	13.4	18.0	4	40	21,559	22,167	94.6
Hale, TX	48189	4	35,408	20.8	23.5	19.0	5	25	7,526	7,500	95.1
Hall, TX	48191	9	3,327	19.4	35.2	28.4	1	4	561	...	...
Hamilton, TX	48193	6	8,043	16.1	21.8	18.3	3	8	1,809	...	...
Hansford, TX	48195	7	5,406	22.2	17.7	31.0	3	7	1,338	...	...
Hardeman, TX	48197	7	3,874	17.7	26.5	16.7	2	5	740	...	...
Hardin, TX	48199	2	53,424	19.1	15.4	15.0	5	26	10,867	9,764	94.3
Harris, TX	48201	1	4,070,989	20.0	20.5	21.9	65	1023	731,696	788,924	92.9
Harrison, TX	48203	4	64,795	18.3	20.5	16.8	6	31	12,650	11,273	97.0
Hartley, TX	48205	9	4,968	18.2	10.6	20.4	2	2	352	...	...
Haskell, TX	48207	6	5,002	16.1	32.5	17.7	3	6	893	...	...
Hays, TX	48209	1	155,545	17.6	12.7	19.1	6	47	27,645	23,704	90.5
Hemphill, TX	48211	9	3,463	21.8	13.7	32.7	1	4	809	...	...
Henderson, TX	48213	4	78,921	16.7	20.5	16.5	9	40	11,898	13,086	94.4
Hidalgo, TX	48215	2	741,152	24.6	44.4	17.4	23	336	201,272	169,049	98.0
Hill, TX	48217	6	35,840	17.9	20.1	19.2	12	39	6,447	6,454	92.6
Hockley, TX	48219	6	22,272	18.9	23.6	19.0	6	21	4,839	3,886	98.2
Hood, TX	48221	4	51,462	15.8	14.8	16.5	3	17	7,817	8,235	95.9
Hopkins, TX	48223	6	34,581	18.3	23.4	17.8	7	17	6,581	5,940	95.7
Houston, TX	48225	7	22,363	15.4	30.6	15.5	6	15	3,580	3,745	93.0

[1]County type codes are from the Economic Research Service of the United States Department of Agriculture. See notes and definitions for more information.
... Not available

Table C-1.   Population, School, and Student Characteristics by County—*Continued*

County	State/ County Code	Characteristics of students, 2008-2009				Number of graduates, 2006-2007	Staff and students, 2008-2009			
		Percent with IEP[2]	Percent eligible for free or reduced lunch	Percent minority	Percent English Language Learners		Total staff	Number of teachers	Student/ teacher ratio	Central admin. Staff
		10	11	12	13	14	15	16	17	18
Collingsworth, TX	48087	13.6	58.6	43.1	8.4	36	118	64	10.0	5
Colorado, TX	48089	12.8	54.7	54.5	8.1	250	523	285	11.9	17
Comal, TX	48091	8.9	33.3	37.4	5.1	1,306	3,176	1,564	15.2	149
Comanche, TX	48093	9.1	61.5	41.2	8.0	164	383	200	11.3	13
Concho, TX	48095	8.9	55.0	46.0	2.4	14	84	44	9.4	6
Cooke, TX	48097	12.3	49.2	33.6	9.9	376	955	512	12.6	37
Coryell, TX	48099	10.9	46.9	40.5	1.4	625	1,654	791	14.0	49
Cottle, TX	48101	10.5	69.9	49.2	...	22	45	25	10.2	3
Crane, TX	48103	8.1	30.6	67.9	10.0	56	163	94	10.9	10
Crockett, TX	48105	8.5	50.3	74.3	14.6	58	163	80	9.4	6
Crosby, TX	48107	13.6	60.8	76.9	3.3	85	297	142	8.8	18
Culberson, TX	48109	7.0	84.1	86.7	6.8	38	93	48	10.4	5
Dallam, TX	48111	11.8	49.5	43.5	8.2	105	313	154	11.5	10
Dallas, TX	48113	8.9	67.3	82.9	22.6	21,980	57,515	30,473	14.7	3,441
Dawson, TX	48115	12.1	40.5	72.9	6.8	144	458	219	11.5	13
Deaf Smith, TX	48117	10.8	73.4	83.5	13.5	228	637	321	13.5	18
Delta, TX	48119	13.8	59.4	22.8	1.2	70	134	69	12.3	5
Denton, TX	48121	10.1	28.2	41.0	11.3	5,728	13,920	8,020	13.7	576
De Witt, TX	48123	13.2	56.6	53.2	4.4	335	796	355	12.2	31
Dickens, TX	48125	10.7	36.5	41.7	...	37	90	44	8.7	7
Dimmit, TX	48127	9.5	78.6	93.5	6.2	104	358	161	14.8	18
Donley, TX	48129	12.2	54.7	23.0	1.3	49	131	76	8.9	8
Duval, TX	48131	8.8	53.7	95.3	5.9	162	448	210	12.6	19
Eastland, TX	48133	12.6	58.3	24.2	4.5	225	575	295	10.7	24
Ector, TX	48135	9.7	48.6	70.9	11.4	1,304	3,376	1,723	16.2	160
Edwards, TX	48137	11.7	68.1	67.9	5.1	54	133	67	9.1	5
Ellis, TX	48139	11.6	42.3	44.4	6.8	1,890	4,494	2,226	15.2	155
El Paso, TX	48141	8.9	66.4	92.8	24.1	9,057	23,457	11,639	15.0	1,092
Erath, TX	48143	8.9	48.9	34.9	9.5	356	808	418	14.0	35
Falls, TX	48145	15.5	73.5	68.9	8.1	181	495	223	11.7	21
Fannin, TX	48147	13.4	49.1	19.9	4.0	397	911	464	12.2	36
Fayette, TX	48149	9.1	47.2	42.6	9.5	265	587	292	12.4	24
Fisher, TX	48151	12.4	60.1	42.3	1.2	38	125	62	10.5	7
Floyd, TX	48153	11.2	66.4	74.4	7.6	97	286	146	9.9	9
Foard, TX	48155	16.7	69.0	23.8	1.7	21	49	24	10.0	3
Fort Bend, TX	48157	8.0	29.8	67.6	11.3	9,143	19,694	10,117	15.3	655
Franklin, TX	48159	11.9	48.2	29.2	7.4	110	213	124	12.2	6
Freestone, TX	48161	10.5	43.5	35.5	5.7	222	615	313	11.7	22
Frio, TX	48163	10.2	66.0	90.5	4.6	98	557	255	12.3	25
Gaines, TX	48165	10.4	52.0	49.8	10.5	193	569	266	11.7	20
Galveston, TX	48167	9.4	44.2	49.3	6.4	4,217	9,834	5,029	14.8	390
Garza, TX	48169	11.0	66.1	58.9	6.6	67	201	108	9.3	8
Gillespie, TX	48171	9.7	44.7	37.6	7.4	249	540	267	12.9	19
Glasscock, TX	48173	10.3	38.5	41.6	9.5	27	54	27	9.7	2
Goliad, TX	48175	11.0	47.5	52.5	2.7	107	221	111	11.8	17
Gonzales, TX	48177	8.7	69.3	70.8	11.3	196	617	289	13.2	24
Gray, TX	48179	10.3	50.1	38.2	9.1	222	602	299	12.8	25
Grayson, TX	48181	13.4	45.8	26.4	4.8	1,305	2,988	1,641	12.8	114
Gregg, TX	48183	10.4	52.3	50.1	9.1	1,385	3,496	1,684	14.0	141
Grimes, TX	48185	8.0	63.8	52.9	9.3	246	624	322	13.1	24
Guadalupe, TX	48187	10.1	40.7	54.8	4.7	1,330	2,861	1,449	14.9	124
Hale, TX	48189	12.9	68.2	76.4	6.2	440	1,009	561	13.4	36
Hall, TX	48191	12.8	63.8	59.5	10.0	51	116	55	10.2	5
Hamilton, TX	48193	10.8	42.1	16.7	5.4	141	296	166	10.9	14
Hansford, TX	48195	6.9	54.3	58.2	20.7	75	233	131	10.2	24
Hardeman, TX	48197	16.6	63.9	35.7	2.2	47	165	80	9.3	10
Hardin, TX	48199	11.1	38.1	14.1	1.1	640	1,689	809	13.4	44
Harris, TX	48201	8.2	58.1	77.7	21.2	32,505	93,812	47,118	15.5	4,223
Harrison, TX	48203	11.4	53.1	39.6	6.1	798	2,119	1,014	12.5	72
Hartley, TX	48205	8.2	52.1	43.7	22.7	17	63	36	9.8	4
Haskell, TX	48207	13.2	65.3	39.5	3.4	76	183	98	9.1	6
Hays, TX	48209	9.2	41.9	56.3	9.5	1,475	3,893	1,894	14.6	148
Hemphill, TX	48211	7.9	33.7	41.8	16.2	45	150	80	10.1	5
Henderson, TX	48213	11.6	58.2	28.7	7.9	648	1,872	890	13.4	82
Hidalgo, TX	48215	7.3	14.5	97.8	35.5	8,099	29,006	13,328	15.1	1,068
Hill, TX	48217	11.7	62.2	39.2	7.7	374	1,065	514	12.5	53
Hockley, TX	48219	11.7	55.8	60.9	3.5	293	773	424	11.4	32
Hood, TX	48221	12.2	38.4	17.2	3.9	537	1,185	582	13.4	36
Hopkins, TX	48223	10.7	54.2	32.0	7.5	401	1,010	525	12.5	36
Houston, TX	48225	11.6	60.8	47.0	4.3	198	560	285	12.6	30

[2]IEP= Individual Education Program. See notes and definitions for more information

... Not available

Table C-1. Population, School, and Student Characteristics by County—*Continued*

County	State/ County Code	Revenues, 2007-2008				Current expenditures, 2007-2008			Resident population 16 to 19 years, 2006-2008			
		Total revenue ($1,000's)	Percentage of revenue from			Amount ($1,000's)	Amount per student	Percent for instruc-tion	Total population 16 to 19 years	Percent en-rolled in school	Percent high school graduates, not enrolled in school	Percent not enrolled, not grads, not employed or not in labor force
			Federal gov't	State gov't	Local gov't							
	19		20	21	22	23	24	25	26	27	28	29
Collingsworth, TX	48087	7,824	7.2	71.8	21.1	7,061	10,666	65.3	...	...	...	...
Colorado, TX	48089	39,610	9.9	36.7	53.5	31,024	9,152	61.4	...	...	...	...
Comal, TX	48091	231,549	6.5	26.1	67.4	172,065	7,586	59.7	4,673	79.1	11.5	4.3
Comanche, TX	48093	24,324	11.0	62.6	26.3	20,041	8,813	64.5	...	...	...	...
Concho, TX	48095	1,927	5.7	43.9	50.4	1,653	10,665	56.1	...	...	...	...
Cooke, TX	48097	65,495	8.1	46.7	45.2	53,742	8,633	62.4	...	...	...	...
Coryell, TX	48099	103,121	17.3	57.2	25.5	86,846	7,930	60.3	...	...	...	...
Cottle, TX	48101	3,265	9.9	44.1	46.0	2,686	10,963	65.1	...	...	...	...
Crane, TX	48103	28,265	2.5	25.5	72.0	12,672	12,904	61.9	...	...	...	...
Crockett, TX	48105	26,769	2.0	17.5	80.4	9,776	12,680	58.7	...	...	...	...
Crosby, TX	48107	17,592	20.4	41.4	38.2	16,381	13,011	60.9	...	...	...	...
Culberson, TX	48109	7,556	11.1	36.9	52.0	6,858	12,357	59.9	...	...	...	...
Dallam, TX	48111	18,308	11.4	45.1	43.5	15,165	8,374	60.8	...	...	...	...
Dallas, TX	48113	4,471,686	10.1	38.0	51.9	3,718,423	8,338	60.9	128,923	80.1	11.1	4.0
Dawson, TX	48115	31,391	10.8	44.2	45.0	24,343	9,443	59.3	...	...	...	...
Deaf Smith, TX	48117	38,253	14.3	60.7	24.9	34,762	7,926	62.3	...	...	...	...
Delta, TX	48119	9,298	9.7	64.2	26.1	7,290	8,497	60.4	...	...	...	...
Denton, TX	48121	1,133,765	4.4	31.4	64.2	864,300	8,216	62.2	33,829	90.5	6.3	1.3
De Witt, TX	48123	47,288	13.3	55.7	31.1	40,562	9,361	60.7	...	...	...	...
Dickens, TX	48125	7,047	6.1	34.4	59.5	5,344	13,393	55.0	...	...	...	...
Dimmit, TX	48127	24,497	15.8	59.8	24.4	22,260	9,322	58.6	...	...	...	...
Donley, TX	48129	8,154	6.3	70.3	23.4	7,323	11,197	63.9	...	...	...	...
Duval, TX	48131	36,559	13.7	48.9	37.4	27,908	10,375	56.7	...	...	...	...
Eastland, TX	48133	33,163	10.6	57.4	32.0	30,229	9,661	61.1	...	...	...	...
Ector, TX	48135	222,412	10.5	46.9	42.6	202,652	7,545	60.0	8,312	78.4	10.7	5.5
Edwards, TX	48137	10,378	7.4	42.7	49.9	8,161	12,614	55.1	...	...	...	...
Ellis, TX	48139	309,620	6.0	49.1	44.9	249,985	7,634	59.8	8,688	81.4	12.8	3.3
El Paso, TX	48141	1,654,212	14.7	61.7	23.7	1,461,720	8,465	59.7	48,673	83.1	10.4	4.0
Erath, TX	48143	53,711	8.5	47.8	43.7	45,314	7,908	60.9	...	...	...	...
Falls, TX	48145	29,389	14.2	64.0	21.8	25,535	10,141	58.1	...	...	...	...
Fannin, TX	48147	56,545	10.1	61.6	28.3	49,090	8,735	60.1	...	...	...	...
Fayette, TX	48149	41,149	5.8	34.8	59.4	32,722	8,965	61.4	...	...	...	...
Fisher, TX	48151	7,393	8.7	68.5	22.8	6,820	10,381	59.9	...	...	...	...
Floyd, TX	48153	17,940	13.8	62.9	23.3	15,500	10,098	61.5	...	...	...	...
Foard, TX	48155	3,476	9.3	63.5	27.2	2,965	11,813	58.4	...	...	...	...
Fort Bend, TX	48157	1,352,632	5.0	41.7	53.3	1,150,161	7,670	62.4	30,401	85.6	9.7	2.5
Franklin, TX	48159	14,212	8.6	29.4	62.0	11,522	7,546	65.4	...	...	...	...
Freestone, TX	48161	72,027	4.5	22.5	73.0	36,078	9,839	58.9	...	...	...	...
Frio, TX	48163	24,120	14.7	57.7	27.6	20,898	9,039	56.7	...	...	...	...
Gaines, TX	48165	77,867	4.5	19.5	75.9	36,524	12,066	59.1	...	...	...	...
Galveston, TX	48167	729,903	6.8	36.3	56.9	602,103	8,035	60.1	16,474	85.5	8.0	4.7
Garza, TX	48169	12,915	6.9	35.5	57.6	10,924	10,384	61.9	...	...	...	...
Gillespie, TX	48171	41,902	6.0	27.5	66.5	30,688	8,963	59.6	...	...	...	...
Glasscock, TX	48173	10,172	1.9	8.7	89.4	3,767	13,649	57.3	...	...	...	...
Goliad, TX	48175	21,859	10.6	30.3	59.2	16,380	12,409	55.5	...	...	...	...
Gonzales, TX	48177	37,105	12.1	61.9	26.0	32,093	8,450	59.8	...	...	...	...
Gray, TX	48179	41,139	7.5	40.0	52.5	30,197	7,934	61.7	...	...	...	...
Grayson, TX	48181	205,177	8.3	49.2	42.5	180,502	8,538	61.1	6,694	85.4	8.1	4.7
Gregg, TX	48183	244,310	14.8	38.2	47.0	210,694	9,033	54.2	6,548	79.8	10.7	5.3
Grimes, TX	48185	42,345	9.4	40.9	49.8	37,948	9,061	57.0	...	...	...	...
Guadalupe, TX	48187	186,916	7.4	45.9	46.7	156,086	7,499	60.7	6,676	85.8	8.7	4.5
Hale, TX	48189	66,754	11.4	60.2	28.4	61,163	8,062	63.0	...	...	...	...
Hall, TX	48191	7,843	10.7	64.0	25.3	6,343	10,861	63.7	...	...	...	...
Hamilton, TX	48193	18,829	5.9	62.1	32.0	16,174	8,682	60.2	...	...	...	...
Hansford, TX	48195	20,167	3.7	35.9	60.5	14,849	11,556	61.0	...	...	...	...
Hardeman, TX	48197	10,837	14.3	42.8	42.9	9,055	11,729	58.8	...	...	...	...
Hardin, TX	48199	97,715	6.6	55.9	37.5	89,012	8,218	60.6	...	...	...	...
Harris, TX	48201	6,894,992	9.7	40.7	49.6	5,848,641	8,152	59.5	221,795	81.2	10.1	4.9
Harrison, TX	48203	131,778	8.5	33.2	58.4	104,219	8,420	59.7	...	...	...	...
Hartley, TX	48205	4,644	5.7	36.5	57.8	3,600	10,876	58.6	...	...	...	...
Haskell, TX	48207	12,100	10.2	65.6	24.2	10,833	12,090	61.7	...	...	...	...
Hays, TX	48209	278,668	6.0	41.3	52.7	217,936	8,197	58.6	10,972	86.2	6.8	5.8
Hemphill, TX	48211	22,034	1.3	18.7	80.0	8,061	11,227	60.2	...	...	...	...
Henderson, TX	48213	122,193	9.8	46.8	43.5	101,928	8,487	60.4	...	...	...	...
Hidalgo, TX	48215	1,954,763	15.9	64.2	19.9	1,721,781	8,794	58.5	46,471	81.8	8.8	5.9
Hill, TX	48217	66,422	9.3	57.9	32.8	56,755	8,880	58.4	...	...	...	...
Hockley, TX	48219	64,735	8.4	38.0	53.6	47,834	9,875	61.6	...	...	...	...
Hood, TX	48221	81,483	6.4	33.2	60.3	68,911	8,880	58.7	...	...	...	...
Hopkins, TX	48223	62,312	12.8	56.5	30.7	52,551	8,018	63.8	...	...	...	...
Houston, TX	48225	37,154	12.6	50.7	36.7	31,778	9,349	59.2	...	...	...	...

... Not available

Table C-1. Population, School, and Student Characteristics by County—*Continued*

County	State/County Code	High school graduates, 2006-2008		College enrollment, 2006-2008		College graduates, 2006-2008 (percent)							
		Population 25 years and over	High school diploma or less (percent)	High school diploma or more (percent)	Number	Percent public	Bachelor's degree or more	+/- U.S. percent with Bachelor's degree or more	Non-Hispanic White	Black or African American	American Indian and Alaska Native	Asian, Hawaiian, and Pacific Islander	Hispanic or Latino[3]
		30	31	32	33	34	35	36	37	38	39	40	41
Collingsworth, TX	48087	...	...	...	...	...	...	...	...	...	...	...	...
Colorado, TX	48089	13,580	60.6	76.4	908	86.7	16.8	-10.6	20.8	10.0	...	...	4.4
Comal, TX	48091	70,085	38.2	88.2	4,776	84.0	30.3	2.9	35.2	35.3	...	32.5	12.0
Comanche, TX	48093	...	...	...	...	...	...	...	...	...	...	...	...
Concho, TX	48095	...	...	...	...	...	...	...	...	...	...	...	...
Cooke, TX	48097	24,632	49.0	82.9	1,576	94.9	19.8	-7.6	21.6	...	...	...	7.9
Coryell, TX	48099	41,746	41.7	88.3	4,663	83.0	15.9	-11.5	17.6	13.7	...	6.8	11.7
Cottle, TX	48101	...	...	...	...	...	...	...	...	...	...	...	...
Crane, TX	48103	...	...	...	...	...	...	...	...	...	...	...	...
Crockett, TX	48105	...	...	...	...	...	...	...	...	...	...	...	...
Crosby, TX	48107	...	...	...	...	...	...	...	...	...	...	...	...
Culberson, TX	48109	...	...	...	...	...	...	...	...	...	...	...	...
Dallam, TX	48111	...	...	...	...	...	...	...	...	...	...	...	...
Dallas, TX	48113	1,500,439	49.1	74.6	118,041	72.3	26.4	-1.0	41.6	18.6	16.5	48.5	7.9
Dawson, TX	48115	...	...	...	...	...	...	...	...	...	...	...	...
Deaf Smith, TX	48117	...	...	...	...	...	...	...	...	...	...	...	...
Delta, TX	48119	...	...	...	...	...	...	...	...	...	...	...	...
Denton, TX	48121	378,971	30.0	90.3	56,009	89.7	38.0	10.6	41.1	37.1	34.3	54.3	17.5
De Witt, TX	48123	...	...	...	...	...	...	...	...	...	...	...	...
Dickens, TX	48125	...	...	...	...	...	...	...	...	...	...	...	...
Dimmit, TX	48127	...	...	...	...	...	...	...	...	...	...	...	...
Donley, TX	48129	...	...	...	...	...	...	...	...	...	...	...	...
Duval, TX	48131	...	...	...	...	...	...	...	...	...	...	...	...
Eastland, TX	48133	...	...	...	...	...	...	...	...	...	...	...	...
Ector, TX	48135	77,295	57.9	72.2	7,338	92.2	12.2	-15.2	16.7	15.4	...	...	5.6
Edwards, TX	48137	...	...	...	...	...	...	...	...	...	...	...	...
Ellis, TX	48139	88,459	49.3	82.2	7,475	77.0	20.1	-7.3	25.0	13.6	12.3	...	3.6
El Paso, TX	48141	421,226	53.9	70.3	59,065	89.1	18.9	-8.5	37.4	22.6	14.3	48.0	14.1
Erath, TX	48143	20,515	47.1	79.6	5,354	98.5	25.5	-1.9	28.3	...	...	...	7.3
Falls, TX	48145	...	...	...	...	...	...	...	...	...	...	...	...
Fannin, TX	48147	22,638	58.9	80.8	907	86.3	14.7	-12.7	16.3	0.3	...	...	13.2
Fayette, TX	48149	15,838	61.0	75.6	942	89.9	15.5	-11.9	17.9	1.9	...	...	5.8
Fisher, TX	48151	...	...	...	...	...	...	...	...	...	...	...	...
Floyd, TX	48153	...	...	...	...	...	...	...	...	...	...	...	...
Foard, TX	48155	...	...	...	...	...	...	...	...	...	...	...	...
Fort Bend, TX	48157	313,714	34.8	87.5	37,921	73.0	39.2	11.8	46.2	35.6	25.0	56.8	14.6
Franklin, TX	48159	...	...	...	...	...	...	...	...	...	...	...	...
Freestone, TX	48161	...	...	...	...	...	...	...	...	...	...	...	...
Frio, TX	48163	...	...	...	...	...	...	...	...	...	...	...	...
Gaines, TX	48165	...	...	...	...	...	...	...	...	...	...	...	...
Galveston, TX	48167	183,611	41.3	85.5	19,725	89.5	25.7	-1.7	29.8	14.3	26.2	59.8	12.9
Garza, TX	48169	...	...	...	...	...	...	...	...	...	...	...	...
Gillespie, TX	48171	17,251	45.9	84.7	347	87.3	26.2	-1.2	28.7	...	...	...	8.3
Glasscock, TX	48173	...	...	...	...	...	...	...	...	...	...	...	...
Goliad, TX	48175	...	...	...	...	...	...	...	...	...	...	...	...
Gonzales, TX	48177	...	...	...	...	...	...	...	...	...	...	...	...
Gray, TX	48179	14,791	59.8	78.1	667	88.5	11.1	-16.3	13.2	3.7	...	...	4.7
Grayson, TX	48181	78,541	49.2	84.1	6,938	70.1	18.4	-9.0	19.7	11.9	...	...	4.5
Gregg, TX	48183	74,469	46.0	84.0	6,315	70.2	21.9	-5.5	26.5	11.5	...	44.9	7.0
Grimes, TX	48185	17,630	67.6	73.5	770	93.4	12.4	-15.0	16.7	3.0	...	...	3.6
Guadalupe, TX	48187	71,657	48.0	82.7	7,358	69.2	22.9	-4.5	29.2	30.9	...	26.4	8.2
Hale, TX	48189	21,047	62.0	69.9	1,611	58.6	15.3	-12.1	28.7	7.7	...	...	2.3
Hall, TX	48191	...	...	...	...	...	...	...	...	...	...	...	...
Hamilton, TX	48193	...	...	...	...	...	...	...	...	...	...	...	...
Hansford, TX	48195	...	...	...	...	...	...	...	...	...	...	...	...
Hardeman, TX	48197	...	...	...	...	...	...	...	...	...	...	...	...
Hardin, TX	48199	33,936	54.7	84.4	1,879	90.7	15.6	-11.8	16.6	4.9	...	...	9.7
Harris, TX	48201	2,423,003	47.5	77.1	219,575	79.9	27.4	...	41.7	18.8	17.7	50.0	9.7
Harrison, TX	48203	40,474	53.0	83.3	3,853	55.2	15.6	-11.8	17.6	9.2	...	...	11.8
Hartley, TX	48205	...	...	...	...	...	...	...	...	...	...	...	...
Haskell, TX	48207	...	...	...	...	...	...	...	...	...	...	...	...
Hays, TX	48209	79,795	37.3	87.6	22,190	96.3	32.7	5.3	41.7	19.4	14.9	...	12.3
Hemphill, TX	48211	...	...	...	...	...	...	...	...	...	...	...	...
Henderson, TX	48213	54,057	57.9	78.7	4,085	91.0	13.7	-13.7	14.8	10.2	...	...	3.7
Hidalgo, TX	48215	376,861	65.6	59.3	38,671	93.3	14.8	-12.6	29.6	20.9	17.7	65.0	12.0
Hill, TX	48217	23,009	54.1	77.3	1,812	86.8	14.1	-13.3	16.0	16.3	...	...	2.0
Hockley, TX	48219	13,095	53.2	73.0	2,402	91.0	14.8	-12.6	22.4	...	...	...	2.3
Hood, TX	48221	34,131	42.7	85.9	1,515	83.1	23.6	-3.8	25.3	...	...	...	7.2
Hopkins, TX	48223	22,215	55.4	79.7	1,503	91.5	16.1	-11.3	18.2	8.6	...	...	3.1
Houston, TX	48225	15,763	66.5	75.9	660	67.9	10.6	-16.8	14.5	2.9	...	...	...

[3]May be of any race
... Not available

Table C-1. Population, School, and Student Characteristics by County—*Continued*

County	State/ County Code	County Type[1]	Population, 2009		Percent of related children 5-17 years in poverty, 2008	Percent of children under 19 years with no health insurance, 2007	Number of Schools and Students, 2008-2009			Resident enrollment, 2006-2008 K–12 enrollment	
			Total	Percent 5–17 years			School Districts	Schools	Students	Number	Percent public
	1	2	3	4	5	6	7	8	9
Howard, TX	48227	5	32,940	16.8	24.8	16.7	3	14	5,376	5,317	97.4
Hudspeth, TX	48229	8	3,115	19.7	44.3	36.0	3	5	752	...	...
Hunt, TX	48231	1	82,831	17.9	19.5	16.9	11	48	14,442	14,727	96.5
Hutchinson, TX	48233	6	21,538	19.4	14.2	17.1	3	15	4,268	4,103	98.1
Irion, TX	48235	3	1,741	16.4	11.2	22.0	1	2	336	...	...
Jack, TX	48237	6	8,497	16.4	16.1	21.2	3	7	1,602	...	...
Jackson, TX	48239	6	14,274	18.0	18.2	17.6	3	12	3,250	...	...
Jasper, TX	48241	6	34,370	17.6	27.3	13.6	4	16	6,193	6,228	90.5
Jeff Davis, TX	48243	9	2,258	17.5	19.7	34.6	2	4	396	...	...
Jefferson, TX	48245	2	243,237	17.5	25.7	13.5	13	96	41,859	42,811	90.7
Jim Hogg, TX	48247	6	4,997	20.3	30.9	10.4	1	3	1,129	...	...
Jim Wells, TX	48249	4	41,001	21.0	29.2	14.2	4	20	8,417	8,825	96.2
Johnson, TX	48251	1	156,997	19.8	12.5	19.9	9	73	30,599	28,393	93.2
Jones, TX	48253	3	18,961	15.1	25.9	16.8	5	14	2,768	...	...
Karnes, TX	48255	6	15,029	14.5	28.2	16.5	4	20	2,269	...	...
Kaufman, TX	48257	1	103,038	21.3	13.8	19.8	6	47	22,219	18,818	93.4
Kendall, TX	48259	1	34,053	18.9	10.7	21.5	3	16	7,520	5,817	85.9
Kenedy, TX	48261	9	369	20.1	19.2	40.2	1	1	88	...	...
Kent, TX	48263	9	703	16.6	17.2	27.5	1	1	143	...	...
Kerr, TX	48265	4	48,381	15.2	22.7	21.2	5	21	6,906	7,421	82.3
Kimble, TX	48267	7	4,539	15.1	28.1	23.4	1	3	670	...	...
King, TX	48269	9	286	21.7	14.9	16.8	1	1	95	...	...
Kinney, TX	48271	9	3,274	17.0	28.7	18.9	1	4	594	...	...
Kleberg, TX	48273	4	30,647	17.2	28.8	14.7	4	21	5,494	5,447	93.0
Knox, TX	48275	9	3,322	17.9	30.4	20.8	3	7	763	...	...
Lamar, TX	48277	4	48,965	17.8	21.4	10.8	5	26	9,034	9,092	97.2
Lamb, TX	48279	6	13,162	20.1	27.0	19.6	5	16	3,147	...	...
Lampasas, TX	48281	2	20,915	17.9	22.4	22.1	2	7	3,664	...	...
La Salle, TX	48283	6	5,810	20.2	38.6	9.6	1	6	1,197	...	...
Lavaca, TX	48285	6	18,539	17.1	17.2	15.8	6	17	2,042	...	...
Lee, TX	48287	6	16,231	19.4	15.4	22.8	4	10	3,339	...	...
Leon, TX	48289	8	16,923	16.4	22.5	21.4	5	13	3,020	...	...
Liberty, TX	48291	1	75,779	19.1	21.7	17.0	7	39	14,505	14,779	96.5
Limestone, TX	48293	6	22,287	16.8	23.8	16.9	3	13	4,045	3,239	97.4
Lipscomb, TX	48295	9	3,094	19.3	18.7	33.3	4	5	805	...	...
Live Oak, TX	48297	6	11,046	14.2	21.6	17.1	2	7	1,724	...	...
Llano, TX	48299	7	18,274	12.3	22.9	17.1	1	4	1,961	...	...
Loving, TX	48301	9	45	11.1	66.7	28.5	...	...	...	...	...
Lubbock, TX	48303	3	270,550	17.0	19.0	15.9	12	108	45,686	44,946	93.2
Lynn, TX	48305	6	5,674	20.5	29.2	21.5	4	8	1,294	...	...
McCulloch, TX	48307	7	7,980	18.5	33.9	16.5	3	7	1,651	...	...
McLennan, TX	48309	3	233,378	18.1	21.2	16.2	24	151	42,149	41,367	92.8
McMullen, TX	48311	8	810	10.4	16.7	23.6	1	2	165	...	...
Madison, TX	48313	6	13,333	14.6	24.9	21.4	2	6	2,567	...	...
Marion, TX	48315	8	10,306	14.9	31.5	14.2	1	4	1,235	...	...
Martin, TX	48317	6	4,581	22.1	21.3	22.0	2	4	942	...	...
Mason, TX	48319	9	3,965	16.2	24.5	29.3	1	3	634	...	...
Matagorda, TX	48321	4	36,978	19.8	24.6	17.2	5	28	7,286	7,479	98.5
Maverick, TX	48323	5	53,203	25.2	35.7	17.7	1	23	14,129	12,656	98.1
Medina, TX	48325	1	44,728	18.9	21.9	20.2	5	23	8,925	9,043	93.1
Menard, TX	48327	8	2,127	13.7	37.5	23.5	1	4	346	...	...
Midland, TX	48329	3	132,316	19.6	14.1	20.1	4	42	23,606	25,320	89.4
Milam, TX	48331	6	24,628	19.8	23.9	17.0	6	17	4,667	4,936	92.6
Mills, TX	48333	9	4,994	17.8	26.4	22.5	4	8	841	...	...
Mitchell, TX	48335	7	9,347	14.1	25.9	15.6	3	8	1,431	...	...
Montague, TX	48337	6	19,568	16.6	17.8	18.1	7	15	3,293	...	...
Montgomery, TX	48339	1	447,718	20.2	11.1	20.9	7	121	84,515	81,018	90.8
Moore, TX	48341	6	20,736	23.4	17.6	31.0	2	12	4,851	4,427	98.9
Morris, TX	48343	6	12,635	17.8	24.8	13.0	2	8	2,287	...	...
Motley, TX	48345	8	1,282	16.0	26.5	22.6	1	1	177	...	...
Nacogdoches, TX	48347	5	64,117	16.1	24.3	17.9	10	36	10,325	10,043	94.6
Navarro, TX	48349	4	49,440	19.3	24.3	18.5	8	28	9,627	9,461	95.9
Newton, TX	48351	8	13,667	16.3	26.7	14.6	3	10	2,185	...	...
Nolan, TX	48353	6	14,917	19.2	31.1	14.7	4	12	3,064	...	...
Nueces, TX	48355	2	323,046	19.0	23.8	13.8	18	123	61,260	62,248	94.0
Ochiltree, TX	48357	7	9,791	21.8	15.3	28.4	1	6	2,239	...	...
Oldham, TX	48359	8	2,118	29.7	18.2	30.8	4	8	826	...	...
Orange, TX	48361	2	81,816	18.7	17.4	11.9	5	27	15,152	14,968	94.4
Palo Pinto, TX	48363	6	27,567	17.7	21.1	19.3	6	13	4,926	4,977	98.3
Panola, TX	48365	6	23,310	18.0	17.6	16.9	4	9	3,904	4,076	94.8

[1]County type codes are from the Economic Research Service of the United States Department of Agriculture. See notes and definitions for more information.
... Not available

Table C-1. Population, School, and Student Characteristics by County—*Continued*

County	State/County Code	Characteristics of students, 2008-2009				Number of graduates, 2006-2007	Staff and students, 2008-2009			
		Percent with IEP[2]	Percent eligible for free or reduced lunch	Percent minority	Percent English Language Learners		Total staff	Number of teachers	Student/teacher ratio	Central admin. Staff
		10	11	12	13	14	15	16	17	18
Howard, TX	48227	11.3	51.7	55.3	1.2	304	795	375	14.3	27
Hudspeth, TX	48229	7.6	80.0	88.4	35.6	35	143	68	11.1	15
Hunt, TX	48231	11.1	52.8	32.8	7.3	874	2,228	1,128	12.8	84
Hutchinson, TX	48233	12.1	43.2	32.3	4.8	305	712	354	12.1	23
Irion, TX	48235	7.4	37.2	33.3	...	22	58	31	10.8	3
Jack, TX	48237	10.0	40.3	20.0	6.5	107	245	149	10.8	10
Jackson, TX	48239	10.3	45.0	45.2	5.4	223	475	247	13.2	14
Jasper, TX	48241	12.8	53.2	30.1	2.6	355	1,059	505	12.3	85
Jeff Davis, TX	48243	12.4	21.5	40.2	10.1	52	99	58	6.8	10
Jefferson, TX	48245	9.2	61.5	68.7	6.3	2,155	5,714	2,906	14.4	188
Jim Hogg, TX	48247	7.2	44.3	96.7	16.3	66	167	87	13.0	10
Jim Wells, TX	48249	9.6	66.3	85.2	5.3	442	1,231	594	14.2	40
Johnson, TX	48251	10.2	45.0	28.7	7.7	1,636	4,283	2,148	14.2	150
Jones, TX	48253	12.1	58.4	36.9	3.3	216	515	260	10.6	15
Karnes, TX	48255	10.7	59.7	66.9	1.1	173	433	210	10.8	35
Kaufman, TX	48257	9.6	43.6	35.1	7.4	1,174	2,870	1,494	14.9	115
Kendall, TX	48259	9.0	26.9	30.1	6.7	550	1,118	575	13.1	38
Kenedy, TX	48261	5.7	25.0	77.3	2.3	...	20	9	9.8	3
Kent, TX	48263	11.9	43.4	21.0	...	14	42	20	7.2	4
Kerr, TX	48265	9.3	53.0	45.0	5.9	392	1,049	514	13.4	39
Kimble, TX	48267	11.2	52.4	37.0	2.1	44	106	59	11.4	6
King, TX	48269	14.7	18.9	13.7	...	11	34	19	5.0	2
Kinney, TX	48271	11.1	64.0	71.2	7.6	34	107	53	11.2	3
Kleberg, TX	48273	9.0	68.1	84.1	4.2	319	876	396	13.9	46
Knox, TX	48275	10.9	64.4	49.8	7.3	52	157	84	9.1	8
Lamar, TX	48277	12.4	53.8	30.3	3.3	512	1,408	741	12.2	49
Lamb, TX	48279	12.2	67.3	70.7	10.0	180	492	262	12.0	15
Lampasas, TX	48281	11.2	50.4	30.8	3.7	238	538	252	14.5	18
La Salle, TX	48283	9.2	81.4	93.3	12.2	69	206	89	13.4	18
Lavaca, TX	48285	14.0	37.6	25.6	1.8	156	327	172	11.9	13
Lee, TX	48287	11.0	59.8	52.0	8.9	219	485	251	13.3	24
Leon, TX	48289	10.7	48.3	29.7	8.2	185	518	266	11.4	19
Liberty, TX	48291	8.2	55.0	33.9	9.3	800	2,130	1,024	14.2	82
Limestone, TX	48293	14.9	62.1	53.4	7.4	267	683	329	12.3	29
Lipscomb, TX	48295	10.4	56.4	41.0	12.9	35	172	93	8.7	9
Live Oak, TX	48297	11.4	43.2	54.3	2.5	134	304	152	11.3	17
Llano, TX	48299	10.7	52.8	16.9	3.3	99	303	152	12.9	14
Loving, TX	48301	...	...	...	...	...	...	...	...	...
Lubbock, TX	48303	11.2	55.3	58.4	2.3	2,369	5,940	3,315	13.8	255
Lynn, TX	48305	9.8	60.2	62.1	5.0	101	256	137	9.4	10
McCulloch, TX	48307	14.1	54.2	44.9	2.7	114	329	154	10.7	14
McLennan, TX	48309	11.2	58.2	54.5	8.2	2,269	6,147	3,006	14.0	216
McMullen, TX	48311	6.1	41.8	52.7	3.0	14	43	19	8.7	2
Madison, TX	48313	8.9	64.0	46.5	11.0	139	359	191	13.4	17
Marion, TX	48315	14.0	45.3	47.2	1.4	82	250	117	10.6	9
Martin, TX	48317	11.6	31.7	52.8	5.6	67	174	91	10.4	6
Mason, TX	48319	10.7	59.1	36.4	4.9	51	118	54	11.7	5
Matagorda, TX	48321	9.4	56.7	65.4	7.7	396	1,206	584	12.5	41
Maverick, TX	48323	7.6	1.0	98.9	35.5	696	1,999	883	16.0	73
Medina, TX	48325	9.0	48.2	62.3	3.4	487	1,335	645	13.8	48
Menard, TX	48327	11.0	62.7	59.5	2.9	32	78	35	9.9	3
Midland, TX	48329	7.6	44.8	63.0	8.7	1,258	2,887	1,534	15.4	102
Milam, TX	48331	11.7	58.5	47.1	5.6	296	686	366	12.8	36
Mills, TX	48333	10.8	55.6	29.3	4.9	65	201	95	8.9	10
Mitchell, TX	48335	10.7	59.3	54.8	2.6	94	291	143	10.0	7
Montague, TX	48337	12.2	44.5	16.9	4.9	211	569	292	11.3	23
Montgomery, TX	48339	9.4	37.7	35.1	9.9	4,460	10,773	5,561	15.2	332
Moore, TX	48341	9.3	59.3	72.1	25.3	250	701	378	12.8	22
Morris, TX	48343	11.1	63.4	43.9	3.2	128	422	206	11.1	17
Motley, TX	48345	5.1	64.4	27.1	1.7	10	40	19	9.3	2
Nacogdoches, TX	48347	8.6	60.2	50.8	12.4	568	1,549	788	13.1	58
Navarro, TX	48349	10.6	62.1	52.5	12.3	521	1,411	715	13.5	55
Newton, TX	48351	10.8	63.2	29.7	0.1	142	422	197	11.1	19
Nolan, TX	48353	12.6	57.6	49.4	2.3	156	572	263	11.7	24
Nueces, TX	48355	11.3	57.5	77.4	4.7	3,301	8,256	4,001	15.3	390
Ochiltree, TX	48357	6.5	53.0	62.9	22.9	123	321	168	13.3	11
Oldham, TX	48359	13.0	29.5	24.7	1.1	73	189	116	7.1	12
Orange, TX	48361	13.9	53.4	20.9	1.4	942	2,314	1,099	13.8	72
Palo Pinto, TX	48363	13.1	53.4	31.4	7.3	274	759	395	12.5	33
Panola, TX	48365	10.7	39.2	32.6	5.0	232	614	307	12.7	24

[2]IEP= Individual Education Program. See notes and definitions for more information
... Not available

Table C-1. Population, School, and Student Characteristics by County—*Continued*

County	State/County Code	Revenues, 2007-2008 Total revenue ($1,000's)	Percentage of revenue from Federal gov't	State gov't	Local gov't	Current expenditures, 2007-2008 Amount ($1,000's)	Amount per student	Percent for instruc-tion	Resident population 16 to 19 years, 2006-2008 Total population 16 to 19 years	Percent en-rolled in school	Percent high school graduates, not enrolled in school	Percent not enrolled, not grads, not employed or not in labor force
		19	20	21	22	23	24	25	26	27	28	29
Howard, TX	48227	49,934	10.7	48.1	41.2	43,814	8,191	58.5	...	...	...	...
Hudspeth, TX	48229	11,819	10.1	61.3	28.5	9,271	12,648	57.0	...	...	...	...
Hunt, TX	48231	138,881	10.6	56.4	33.1	121,865	8,361	58.7	4,771	77.3	14.4	4.5
Hutchinson, TX	48233	54,129	8.6	40.6	50.8	36,761	8,684	63.2	...	...	...	...
Irion, TX	48235	8,944	2.1	16.7	81.3	3,861	11,000	57.6	...	...	...	...
Jack, TX	48237	21,756	3.7	36.0	60.3	15,782	9,839	62.7	...	...	...	...
Jackson, TX	48239	39,657	8.8	43.0	48.2	31,132	9,053	59.9	...	...	...	...
Jasper, TX	48241	60,445	10.5	57.0	32.5	53,385	8,450	58.2	...	...	...	...
Jeff Davis, TX	48243	7,393	4.0	65.4	30.5	6,369	16124	61.3	...	...	...	...
Jefferson, TX	48245	442,308	12.3	30.7	57.0	383,437	9210	56.0	14,017	82.3	9.9	6.9
Jim Hogg, TX	48247	12,698	12.2	46.2	41.7	11,761	10,682	60.4	...	...	...	...
Jim Wells, TX	48249	80,605	12.3	62.1	25.6	71,260	8,340	59.4	...	...	...	...
Johnson, TX	48251	288,656	6.6	46.0	47.4	240,915	8,094	61.8	9,050	80.8	11.5	3.6
Jones, TX	48253	30,835	12.6	65.2	22.2	27,416	9,973	61.6	...	...	...	...
Karnes, TX	48255	25,402	16.2	61.3	22.5	23,200	10,135	59.4	...	...	...	...
Kaufman, TX	48257	200,671	7.2	48.1	44.7	166,541	7,663	58.3	5,785	78.2	12.5	6.9
Kendall, TX	48259	84,869	3.9	23.2	72.9	65,411	8,731	61.5	...	...	...	...
Kenedy, TX	48261	5,760	...	5.6	94.4	1,448	16,837	46.4	...	...	...	...
Kent, TX	48263	7,370	1.2	18.1	80.7	2,711	18,568	52.3	...	...	...	...
Kerr, TX	48265	68,004	9.6	39.0	51.4	58,423	8,421	61.7	...	...	...	...
Kimble, TX	48267	6,456	7.7	50.8	41.5	6,311	9,591	64.0	...	...	...	...
King, TX	48269	8,670	0.5	25.0	74.6	2,794	28,804	52.2	...	...	...	...
Kinney, TX	48271	6,844	8.1	67.4	24.5	5,753	9,604	64.8	...	...	...	...
Kleberg, TX	48273	59,349	12.4	52.6	35.0	51,733	9,246	57.9	...	...	...	...
Knox, TX	48275	9,408	13.4	64.7	21.9	8,886	11,661	63.4	...	...	...	...
Lamar, TX	48277	87,463	10.5	52.9	36.7	75,021	8,187	62.3	...	...	...	...
Lamb, TX	48279	33,630	11.8	60.8	27.5	29,341	9,288	62.2	...	...	...	...
Lampasas, TX	48281	40,423	9.4	48.4	42.2	29,627	7,846	60.8	...	...	...	...
La Salle, TX	48283	16,103	7.9	42.8	49.3	13,675	11,200	53.7	...	...	...	...
Lavaca, TX	48285	26,326	3.6	41.5	54.9	17,915	8,676	63.4	...	...	...	...
Lee, TX	48287	35,123	8.8	39.6	51.7	27,002	8,986	61.3	...	...	...	...
Leon, TX	48289	42,251	6.1	38.8	55.0	29,283	9,696	60.6	...	...	...	...
Liberty, TX	48291	144,758	8.2	49.5	42.3	117,981	8,048	58.6	...	...	...	...
Limestone, TX	48293	51,975	8.1	43.2	48.7	38,330	9,585	59.2	...	...	...	...
Lipscomb, TX	48295	16,242	4.1	28.4	67.6	9,970	13,153	62.3	...	...	...	...
Live Oak, TX	48297	19,452	6.3	39.1	54.7	17,494	10,048	60.3	...	...	...	...
Llano, TX	48299	35,912	4.5	13.0	82.4	16,892	8,497	59.5	...	...	...	...
Loving, TX	48301	...	...	...	...	...	...	...	...	...	...	...
Lubbock, TX	48303	429,115	12.8	45.0	42.2	370,236	8,345	59.1	18,038	87.9	6.3	4.0
Lynn, TX	48305	15,403	13.5	63.1	23.4	14,669	11,345	61.4	...	...	...	...
McCulloch, TX	48307	20,634	10.9	59.0	30.1	16,941	10,490	59.6	...	...	...	...
McLennan, TX	48309	416,186	11.6	51.7	36.7	356,261	8,612	56.4	16,508	87.9	6.6	2.9
McMullen, TX	48311	6,444	0.7	27.0	72.3	2,854	17,617	50.4	...	...	...	...
Madison, TX	48313	24,672	9.4	58.2	32.4	20,079	7,774	58.7	...	...	...	...
Marion, TX	48315	14,073	14.3	40.8	44.9	11,942	9,352	56.3	...	...	...	...
Martin, TX	48317	14,685	5.0	37.0	58.1	11,985	12,537	59.0	...	...	...	...
Mason, TX	48319	7,524	9.8	53.0	37.2	6,109	10,081	57.4	...	...	...	...
Matagorda, TX	48321	88,745	8.2	40.7	51.1	69,932	9,475	59.4	...	...	...	...
Maverick, TX	48323	137,930	15.3	68.9	15.8	119,973	8,642	60.3	...	...	...	...
Medina, TX	48325	85,496	10.5	58.8	30.7	72,816	8,247	59.4	...	...	...	...
Menard, TX	48327	4,877	23.5	49.9	26.5	5,084	14,694	48.0	...	...	...	...
Midland, TX	48329	211,921	11.7	35.9	52.4	188,289	8,088	56.7	7,647	82.2	9.8	4.2
Milam, TX	48331	48,182	7.7	53.0	39.3	39,430	8,273	62.4	...	...	...	...
Mills, TX	48333	11,644	14.6	60.9	24.5	11,617	12,808	62.9	...	...	...	...
Mitchell, TX	48335	18,605	8.4	53.3	38.3	14,579	10,217	60.2	...	...	...	...
Montague, TX	48337	34,193	9.4	51.6	39.0	30,064	9,099	62.4	...	...	...	...
Montgomery, TX	48339	742,404	6.2	43.8	49.9	608,456	7,428	60.3	23,419	80.2	13.3	3.0
Moore, TX	48341	42,247	9.6	30.8	59.5	36,930	8,042	62.6	...	...	...	...
Morris, TX	48343	24,028	10.0	39.1	50.9	22,039	9,607	60.2	...	...	...	...
Motley, TX	48345	2,808	23.8	41.3	34.9	2,565	14,410	62.3	...	...	...	...
Nacogdoches, TX	48347	101,182	11.3	50.4	38.3	82,483	7,917	60.9	...	...	...	...
Navarro, TX	48349	89,156	8.6	57.2	34.3	76,649	8,101	60.6	...	...	...	...
Newton, TX	48351	26,165	10.8	43.6	45.6	23,283	9,971	56.8	...	...	...	...
Nolan, TX	48353	41,292	11.0	38.1	50.8	29,982	9,788	58.1	...	...	...	...
Nueces, TX	48355	577,826	12.7	47.1	40.2	504,133	8,213	56.9	19,449	79.9	12.8	4.8
Ochiltree, TX	48357	19,172	12.6	39.3	48.0	17,551	8,055	63.0	...	...	...	...
Oldham, TX	48359	12,772	8.6	47.9	43.5	12,055	15,676	66.7	...	...	...	...
Orange, TX	48361	141,211	10.4	51.8	37.8	128,517	8,326	57.6	4,622	81.2	12.0	4.8
Palo Pinto, TX	48363	55,217	8.3	47.1	44.6	44,501	8,994	58.8	...	...	...	...
Panola, TX	48365	68,283	4.4	24.0	71.6	35,432	9,132	56.7	...	...	...	...

... Not available

Table C-1. Population, School, and Student Characteristics by County—*Continued*

County	State/County Code	High school graduates, 2006-2008			College enrollment, 2006-2008		College graduates, 2006-2008 (percent)						
		Population 25 years and over	High school diploma or less (percent)	High school diploma or more (percent)	Number	Percent public	Bachelor's degree or more	+/- U.S. percent with Bachelor's degree or more	Non-Hispanic White	Black or African American	American Indian and Alaska Native	Asian, Hawaiian, and Pacific Islander	Hispanic or Latino[3]
		30	31	32	33	34	35	36	37	38	39	40	41
Howard, TX	48227	21,607	58.1	70.9	1,252	88.0	10.5	-16.9	16.7	3.2	...	...	1.9
Hudspeth, TX	48229	...	...	...	...	...	...	...	...	...	...	...	...
Hunt, TX	48231	53,335	54.4	79.3	5,797	87.1	17.5	-9.9	18.7	10.4	...	...	8.3
Hutchinson, TX	48233	13,962	54.2	81.8	808	96.0	12.5	-14.9	14.7	...	...	...	1.7
Irion, TX	48235	...	...	...	...	...	...	...	...	...	...	...	...
Jack, TX	48237	...	...	...	...	...	...	...	...	...	...	...	...
Jackson, TX	48239	...	...	...	...	...	...	...	...	...	...	...	...
Jasper, TX	48241	23,097	61.4	80.5	1,051	87.5	14.3	-13.1	16.3	5.5	...	...	...
Jeff Davis, TX	48243	...	...	...	...	...	...	...	...	...	...	...	...
Jefferson, TX	48245	158,381	51.7	81.0	14,785	92.2	18.1	-9.3	24.8	9.2	9.6	40.0	7.3
Jim Hogg, TX	48247	...	...	...	...	...	...	...	...	...	...	...	...
Jim Wells, TX	48249	24,700	64.8	70.3	1,457	83.3	9.7	-17.7	20.7	...	...	...	5.9
Johnson, TX	48251	96,121	54.5	80.8	6,436	78.5	15.7	-11.7	16.7	13.2	12.2	...	7.8
Jones, TX	48253	...	...	...	...	...	...	...	...	...	...	...	...
Karnes, TX	48255	...	...	...	...	...	...	...	...	...	...	...	...
Kaufman, TX	48257	60,495	54.6	79.6	5,197	79.1	15.3	-12.1	17.6	11.9	...	...	4.3
Kendall, TX	48259	21,416	31.9	91.7	1,473	82.2	36.8	9.4	40.1	...	...	...	20.3
Kenedy, TX	48261	...	...	...	...	...	...	...	...	...	...	...	...
Kent, TX	48263	...	...	...	...	...	...	...	...	...	...	...	...
Kerr, TX	48265	33,296	44.6	85.1	1,823	33.4	24.9	-2.5	30.1	...	...	...	2.9
Kimble, TX	48267	...	...	...	...	...	...	...	...	...	...	...	...
King, TX	48269	...	...	...	...	...	...	...	...	...	...	...	...
Kinney, TX	48271	...	...	...	...	...	...	...	...	...	...	...	...
Kleberg, TX	48273	17,161	53.1	74.8	4,991	96.8	17.9	-9.5	28.0	...	...	...	13.8
Knox, TX	48275	...	...	...	...	...	...	...	...	...	...	...	...
Lamar, TX	48277	32,624	52.8	81.8	2,288	89.9	16.7	-10.7	17.5	10.8	...	...	11.8
Lamb, TX	48279	...	...	...	...	...	...	...	...	...	...	...	...
Lampasas, TX	48281	12,964	52.2	79.1	...	...	16.9	-10.5	18.5	...	...	...	5.2
La Salle, TX	48283	...	...	...	...	...	...	...	...	...	...	...	...
Lavaca, TX	48285	...	...	...	...	...	...	...	...	...	...	...	...
Lee, TX	48287	...	...	...	...	...	...	...	...	...	...	...	...
Leon, TX	48289	...	...	...	...	...	...	...	...	...	...	...	...
Liberty, TX	48291	48,697	62.3	73.0	2,464	82.4	8.6	-18.8	10.2	5.5	...	...	1.5
Limestone, TX	48293	14,935	61.6	70.3	785	93.1	12.7	-14.7	17.3	4.4	...	...	0.3
Lipscomb, TX	48295	...	...	...	...	...	...	...	...	...	...	...	...
Live Oak, TX	48297	...	...	...	...	...	...	...	...	...	...	...	...
Llano, TX	48299	...	...	...	...	...	...	...	...	...	...	...	...
Loving, TX	48301	...	...	...	...	...	...	...	...	...	...	...	...
Lubbock, TX	48303	155,364	44.2	83.4	33,201	90.6	27.9	0.5	36.3	15.3	11.0	68.4	8.8
Lynn, TX	48305	...	...	...	...	...	...	...	...	...	...	...	...
McCulloch, TX	48307	...	...	...	...	...	...	...	...	...	...	...	...
McLennan, TX	48309	135,795	49.7	79.5	25,596	47.3	19.8	-7.6	24.9	10.1	7.0	29.5	7.1
McMullen, TX	48311	...	...	...	...	...	...	...	...	...	...	...	...
Madison, TX	48313	...	...	...	...	...	...	...	...	...	...	...	...
Marion, TX	48315	...	...	...	...	...	...	...	...	...	...	...	...
Martin, TX	48317	...	...	...	...	...	...	...	...	...	...	...	...
Mason, TX	48319	...	...	...	...	...	...	...	...	...	...	...	...
Matagorda, TX	48321	23,400	57.8	74.4	871	81.4	15.0	-12.4	22.8	6.9	...	...	3.7
Maverick, TX	48323	28,203	68.3	52.5	2,878	94.9	12.7	-14.7	30.0	...	...	...	11.9
Medina, TX	48325	27,897	50.9	78.5	2,511	77.6	18.6	-8.8	25.9	...	...	...	9.6
Menard, TX	48327	...	...	...	...	...	...	...	...	...	...	...	...
Midland, TX	48329	77,559	46.3	80.4	6,490	92.7	24.3	-3.1	33.1	13.7	...	...	6.3
Milam, TX	48331	16,677	60.5	80.1	564	75.4	14.5	-12.9	18.7	3.4	...	...	2.1
Mills, TX	48333	...	...	...	...	...	...	...	...	...	...	...	...
Mitchell, TX	48335	...	...	...	...	...	...	...	...	...	...	...	...
Montague, TX	48337	...	...	...	...	...	...	...	...	...	...	...	...
Montgomery, TX	48339	261,519	42.1	85.0	19,135	84.9	28.0	0.6	30.5	18.3	15.6	60.0	13.4
Moore, TX	48341	11,679	65.3	64.3	784	89.7	10.8	-16.6	17.1	...	...	...	3.3
Morris, TX	48343	...	...	...	...	...	...	...	...	...	...	...	...
Motley, TX	48345	...	...	...	...	...	...	...	...	...	...	...	...
Nacogdoches, TX	48347	34,210	48.3	80.8	11,116	95.3	25.7	-1.7	30.4	15.5	...	...	5.7
Navarro, TX	48349	30,322	58.0	74.7	3,689	96.8	13.4	-14.0	17.0	7.1	...	...	3.6
Newton, TX	48351	...	...	...	...	...	...	...	...	...	...	...	...
Nolan, TX	48353	...	...	...	...	...	...	...	...	...	...	...	...
Nueces, TX	48355	200,565	49.1	78.0	21,537	92.4	19.5	-7.9	30.8	10.1	32.1	47.3	11.2
Ochiltree, TX	48357	...	...	...	...	...	...	...	...	...	...	...	...
Oldham, TX	48359	...	...	...	...	...	...	...	...	...	...	...	...
Orange, TX	48361	54,855	55.6	85.8	3,236	93.0	12.9	-14.5	13.6	3.9	...	...	8.6
Palo Pinto, TX	48363	18,510	58.9	75.7	687	89.2	13.2	-14.2	14.3	...	...	...	6.9
Panola, TX	48365	15,412	55.2	81.4	1,219	90.3	12.0	-15.4	12.7	9.2	...	...	...

[3]May be of any race
... Not available

Table C-1. Population, School, and Student Characteristics by County—*Continued*

County	State/County Code	County Type[1]	Population, 2009 Total	Population, 2009 Percent 5–17 years	Percent of related children 5-17 years in poverty, 2008	Percent of children under 19 years with no health insurance, 2007	Number of Schools and Students, 2008-2009 School Districts	Number of Schools and Students, 2008-2009 Schools	Number of Schools and Students, 2008-2009 Students	Resident enrollment, 2006-2008 K–12 enrollment Number	Resident enrollment, 2006-2008 K–12 enrollment Percent public
			1	2	3	4	5	6	7	8	9
Parker, TX	48367	1	114,919	19.0	12.7	18.3	9	38	19,241	19,913	91.3
Parmer, TX	48369	7	9,290	22.7	19.1	29.2	4	11	2,383	...	...
Pecos, TX	48371	7	16,248	18.6	25.8	25.1	3	12	3,037	...	...
Polk, TX	48373	6	46,530	14.7	24.8	19.6	6	17	6,944	7,460	93.6
Potter, TX	48375	3	121,816	18.8	28.4	17.7	4	65	34,552	23,762	95.1
Presidio, TX	48377	7	7,470	19.9	34.0	29.5	2	5	1,719	...	...
Rains, TX	48379	8	11,287	15.4	22.2	22.0	2	7	2,468	...	...
Randall, TX	48381	3	116,483	18.2	8.4	16.3	3	16	8,820	19,980	91.8
Reagan, TX	48383	6	3,014	22.7	11.2	36.7	1	3	807	...	...
Real, TX	48385	9	2,925	14.5	38.8	21.7	2	3	366	...	...
Red River, TX	48387	6	12,765	16.0	27.7	13.0	4	12	2,478	...	...
Reeves, TX	48389	7	11,046	19.6	34.6	14.6	2	8	2,385	...	...
Refugio, TX	48391	6	7,225	17.0	21.8	15.1	3	6	1,481	...	...
Roberts, TX	48393	9	878	16.1	11.5	24.5	1	1	162	...	...
Robertson, TX	48395	3	15,706	18.7	29.0	17.7	5	16	3,285	...	...
Rockwall, TX	48397	1	81,391	21.8	6.5	18.0	2	27	17,820	14,790	94.9
Runnels, TX	48399	6	10,170	18.8	24.1	18.2	4	18	2,118	...	...
Rusk, TX	48401	3	49,180	17.0	19.8	20.5	8	24	7,696	8,240	93.9
Sabine, TX	48403	9	10,208	14.7	25.6	14.1	3	7	2,094	...	...
San Augustine, TX	48405	9	8,574	15.5	32.3	14.2	2	7	1,326	...	...
San Jacinto, TX	48407	1	24,902	16.7	26.0	18.1	2	8	3,449	3,919	96.4
San Patricio, TX	48409	2	68,223	20.5	21.8	13.8	7	37	14,870	14,764	97.1
San Saba, TX	48411	7	5,871	20.1	33.9	19.7	3	5	979	...	...
Schleicher, TX	48413	8	2,731	18.5	23.8	34.3	1	3	625	...	...
Scurry, TX	48415	7	16,222	17.8	21.3	16.0	3	9	3,141	...	...
Shackelford, TX	48417	8	3,047	17.8	16.1	27.7	2	3	681	...	...
Shelby, TX	48419	6	26,812	19.5	30.4	19.8	6	15	5,193	4,589	97.8
Sherman, TX	48421	9	2,913	22.2	19.5	36.1	2	4	881	...	...
Smith, TX	48423	3	204,665	18.0	19.3	20.2	9	72	32,676	35,101	88.4
Somervell, TX	48425	8	8,031	19.7	13.4	24.5	2	5	1,860	...	...
Starr, TX	48427	4	62,671	25.4	48.5	14.5	3	27	16,683	15,099	99.2
Stephens, TX	48429	7	9,632	16.9	26.4	20.1	1	6	1,540	...	...
Sterling, TX	48431	8	1,259	18.0	14.9	30.7	1	7	201	...	...
Stonewall, TX	48433	8	1,354	16.7	30.9	21.2	1	2	231	...	...
Sutton, TX	48435	7	4,273	21.0	15.5	26.2	1	3	1,010	...	...
Swisher, TX	48437	6	7,424	18.3	26.3	20.5	3	8	1,464	...	...
Tarrant, TX	48439	1	1,789,900	19.8	15.2	22.7	30	522	328,844	332,581	91.6
Taylor, TX	48441	3	127,683	16.6	19.9	15.5	5	64	22,018	22,008	95.7
Terrell, TX	48443	9	969	17.6	29.7	20.3	1	3	168	...	...
Terry, TX	48445	6	12,142	18.5	31.9	18.1	3	7	2,248	...	...
Throckmorton, TX	48447	9	1,593	15.8	18.9	26.5	2	3	339	...	...
Titus, TX	48449	7	30,206	21.3	21.1	25.9	5	15	6,767	6,102	96.7
Tom Green, TX	48451	3	108,378	16.4	20.7	19.2	7	67	18,074	18,929	95.7
Travis, TX	48453	1	1,026,158	16.0	16.7	17.4	24	247	141,247	161,858	91.6
Trinity, TX	48455	8	13,897	16.1	29.2	18.6	4	10	2,280	...	...
Tyler, TX	48457	6	20,556	16.1	25.4	13.9	5	15	3,618	...	...
Upshur, TX	48459	3	38,057	18.6	20.3	16.9	7	26	7,078	6,454	87.5
Upton, TX	48461	8	3,130	19.2	20.4	29.0	2	5	695	...	...
Uvalde, TX	48463	7	26,811	20.9	34.1	20.5	5	16	6,103	5,971	95.9
Val Verde, TX	48465	5	48,165	20.0	31.1	18.6	2	15	10,352	10,321	94.1
Van Zandt, TX	48467	6	52,005	17.4	19.4	21.0	8	38	9,922	8,815	94.7
Victoria, TX	48469	3	87,790	19.3	20.0	14.8	5	33	14,951	16,907	89.7
Walker, TX	48471	4	64,119	11.2	20.8	18.4	4	14	6,893	8,764	94.7
Waller, TX	48473	1	36,530	17.5	18.9	22.4	3	18	8,576	6,390	91.5
Ward, TX	48475	6	10,528	22.1	22.0	15.0	3	10	2,128	...	...
Washington, TX	48477	6	32,893	16.3	17.1	19.9	2	11	5,284	4,861	80.4
Webb, TX	48479	3	241,438	25.1	33.2	25.4	5	90	66,225	58,060	96.6
Wharton, TX	48481	4	41,000	19.5	22.1	18.9	5	23	8,010	7,674	95.2
Wheeler, TX	48483	9	4,888	19.3	15.7	28.6	4	6	1,025	...	...
Wichita, TX	48485	3	127,616	16.8	17.0	16.6	7	57	21,626	23,425	95.8
Wilbarger, TX	48487	6	13,541	19.1	22.1	14.5	4	9	2,592	...	...
Willacy, TX	48489	6	20,395	20.7	40.9	14.4	4	15	4,484	4,641	98.7
Williamson, TX	48491	1	410,686	20.0	6.9	16.4	12	166	94,262	74,589	93.6
Wilson, TX	48493	1	40,749	19.6	14.2	19.4	4	29	8,218	7,866	94.1
Winkler, TX	48495	6	6,772	20.5	19.3	22.5	2	6	1,609	...	...
Wise, TX	48497	1	59,415	19.0	12.3	20.4	7	27	8,952	11,037	94.1
Wood, TX	48499	6	43,136	14.9	21.4	19.8	5	19	5,245	6,238	95.6
Yoakum, TX	48501	7	7,698	23.6	17.7	29.4	2	6	1,987	...	...
Young, TX	48503	6	17,792	18.5	20.4	17.9	3	10	3,457	...	...
Zapata, TX	48505	6	14,036	22.9	37.8	26.2	1	6	3,691	...	...
Zavala, TX	48507	7	11,585	21.7	47.7	12.7	2	7	2,504	...	...

[1]County type codes are from the Economic Research Service of the United States Department of Agriculture. See notes and definitions for more information.
... Not available

Table C-1. Population, School, and Student Characteristics by County—*Continued*

County	State/County Code	Characteristics of students, 2008-2009				Number of graduates, 2006-2007	Staff and students, 2008-2009			
		Percent with IEP[2]	Percent eligible for free or reduced lunch	Percent minority	Percent English Language Learners		Total staff	Number of teachers	Student/ teacher ratio	Central admin. Staff
		10	11	12	13	14	15	16	17	18
Parker, TX	48367	9.4	30.4	17.2	3.7	1,164	2,528	1,364	14.1	97
Parmer, TX	48369	7.9	61.5	72.9	17.5	142	453	231	10.3	17
Pecos, TX	48371	8.0	56.8	78.3	11.8	198	525	255	11.9	23
Polk, TX	48373	13.6	59.8	33.7	5.5	374	1,100	519	13.4	38
Potter, TX	48375	10.1	68.4	60.5	9.1	1,659	4,509	2,444	14.1	128
Presidio, TX	48377	5.9	46.4	95.9	37.6	114	315	154	11.2	17
Rains, TX	48379	12.6	49.2	15.6	4.1	109	398	204	12.1	16
Randall, TX	48381	10.1	34.0	29.9	0.9	559	1,167	563	15.7	61
Reagan, TX	48383	8.3	41.3	75.3	10.5	39	141	77	10.5	9
Real, TX	48385	38.0	63.8	37.6	3.6	14	105	49	7.5	10
Red River, TX	48387	11.3	62.0	36.7	3.8	166	495	228	10.9	19
Reeves, TX	48389	10.8	65.6	90.1	6.8	153	411	192	12.4	19
Refugio, TX	48391	13.0	52.9	64.2	1.8	103	299	144	10.3	18
Roberts, TX	48393	6.2	20.4	13.0	...	10	40	22	7.4	4
Robertson, TX	48395	12.2	62.6	54.6	6.3	192	590	280	11.7	31
Rockwall, TX	48397	8.7	23.6	29.7	6.5	928	2,349	1,171	15.2	81
Runnels, TX	48399	10.3	53.6	46.4	4.8	137	359	184	11.5	16
Rusk, TX	48401	10.5	56.7	42.8	8.2	417	1,246	617	12.5	43
Sabine, TX	48403	12.0	58.8	16.8	1.3	112	326	169	12.4	18
San Augustine, TX	48405	11.7	77.7	48.0	4.3	95	228	104	12.8	10
San Jacinto, TX	48407	11.1	62.9	29.1	3.1	187	577	277	12.5	24
San Patricio, TX	48409	10.7	57.6	67.1	3.7	898	2,288	1,043	14.3	103
San Saba, TX	48411	13.4	62.4	40.1	9.1	66	191	104	9.4	8
Schleicher, TX	48413	6.9	37.8	64.2	7.4	46	108	62	10.1	4
Scurry, TX	48415	12.1	44.5	53.4	4.4	183	436	232	13.5	24
Shackelford, TX	48417	11.9	43.0	16.6	1.5	48	117	65	10.5	5
Shelby, TX	48419	11.5	64.0	46.8	13.6	267	833	429	12.1	29
Sherman, TX	48421	7.2	55.4	53.5	16.6	41	135	73	12.1	7
Smith, TX	48423	9.8	54.8	53.6	11.6	1,646	4,526	2,306	14.2	192
Somervell, TX	48425	11.1	43.1	27.7	9.9	166	299	154	12.1	17
Starr, TX	48427	9.5	52.3	99.8	55.7	670	3,043	1,215	13.7	99
Stephens, TX	48429	10.3	57.1	38.0	8.0	85	271	133	11.6	10
Sterling, TX	48431	10.4	36.2	49.2	2.0	24	54	28	7.2	3
Stonewall, TX	48433	7.8	39.4	30.7	1.7	19	51	28	8.3	2
Sutton, TX	48435	8.1	41.5	69.0	10.3	58	177	93	10.9	7
Swisher, TX	48437	9.6	66.4	57.2	4.0	107	266	139	10.5	11
Tarrant, TX	48439	8.6	47.2	60.1	14.3	16,568	41,571	21,310	15.4	1,370
Taylor, TX	48441	13.9	50.7	43.2	2.4	1,263	3,128	1,605	13.7	85
Terrell, TX	48443	6.5	33.9	64.3	0.6	11	45	21	8.0	4
Terry, TX	48445	10.0	65.9	71.0	6.4	176	376	186	12.1	18
Throckmorton, TX	48447	10.9	54.3	20.4	0.6	25	67	38	8.9	4
Titus, TX	48449	11.8	71.4	66.6	25.6	354	1,178	539	12.6	34
Tom Green, TX	48451	11.5	49.6	54.3	4.7	1,125	2,501	1,269	14.2	90
Travis, TX	48453	10.1	52.3	67.0	20.9	6,263	18,548	9,895	14.3	799
Trinity, TX	48455	12.5	55.9	27.1	5.4	123	396	186	12.3	13
Tyler, TX	48457	12.8	53.7	17.0	1.1	207	630	308	11.7	29
Upshur, TX	48459	9.7	45.4	22.7	3.4	448	1,108	571	12.4	48
Upton, TX	48461	9.8	43.7	59.3	3.7	66	154	68	10.2	6
Uvalde, TX	48463	9.8	64.7	83.2	6.1	297	961	465	13.1	29
Val Verde, TX	48465	9.6	71.6	91.6	17.4	498	1,318	677	15.3	56
Van Zandt, TX	48467	11.5	46.5	18.6	4.3	620	1,433	741	13.4	45
Victoria, TX	48469	11.5	60.3	68.7	2.5	688	2,184	1,023	14.6	81
Walker, TX	48471	11.3	43.7	50.9	8.4	413	949	480	14.4	43
Waller, TX	48473	8.7	67.6	72.6	21.4	456	1,201	623	13.8	54
Ward, TX	48475	12.0	53.6	62.5	3.9	166	339	162	13.1	7
Washington, TX	48477	13.6	51.0	49.6	8.6	362	761	412	12.8	34
Webb, TX	48479	9.3	46.1	99.0	52.1	2,942	9,986	4,183	15.8	463
Wharton, TX	48481	9.5	59.7	65.3	7.8	503	1,262	615	13.0	44
Wheeler, TX	48483	6.4	42.6	36.5	11.9	49	209	113	9.1	12
Wichita, TX	48485	13.3	51.6	40.0	3.6	1,310	2,976	1,627	13.3	139
Wilbarger, TX	48487	13.0	63.8	52.0	3.7	150	384	198	13.1	13
Willacy, TX	48489	7.9	18.4	96.8	8.9	240	772	329	13.6	46
Williamson, TX	48491	8.5	29.4	42.1	6.1	4,581	12,590	6,687	14.1	552
Wilson, TX	48493	12.4	41.2	45.8	2.8	503	1,124	569	14.4	44
Winkler, TX	48495	8.5	36.0	62.5	8.1	78	312	141	11.4	10
Wise, TX	48497	11.2	37.6	27.8	9.6	579	1,358	709	12.6	47
Wood, TX	48499	11.0	51.2	24.2	6.1	380	826	427	12.3	33
Yoakum, TX	48501	8.0	55.1	67.5	16.7	127	310	164	12.1	12
Young, TX	48503	11.3	46.7	24.5	6.9	249	510	275	12.6	18
Zapata, TX	48505	6.9	70.2	98.1	31.6	168	572	251	14.7	24
Zavala, TX	48507	8.7	87.6	98.0	9.1	111	433	183	13.7	21

[2]IEP= Individual Education Program. See notes and definitions for more information
... Not available

Table C-1. Population, School, and Student Characteristics by County—*Continued*

County	State/County Code	Revenues, 2007-2008				Current expenditures, 2007-2008			Resident population 16 to 19 years, 2006-2008			
		Total revenue ($1,000's)	Percentage of revenue from			Amount ($1,000's)	Amount per student	Percent for instruction	Total population 16 to 19 years	Percent enrolled in school	Percent high school graduates, not enrolled in school	Percent not enrolled, not grads, not employed or not in labor force
			Federal gov't	State gov't	Local gov't							
	19		20	21	22	23	24	25	26	27	28	29
Parker, TX	48367	188,370	5.1	37.6	57.4	153,245	8,160	60.5	6,081	79.5	15.7	4.0
Parmer, TX	48369	25,658	12.3	63.8	23.9	21,834	9,022	65.4	...	...	...	...
Pecos, TX	48371	54,865	5.8	25.1	69.1	32,312	11,146	57.8	...	...	...	...
Polk, TX	48373	68,876	11.5	50.7	37.8	61,217	8,689	57.3	...	...	...	...
Potter, TX	48375	300,995	11.8	49.4	38.8	267,774	7,871	62.5	6,596	71.8	16.2	8.7
Presidio, TX	48377	25,237	12.0	69.3	18.7	17,062	9,783	60.7	...	...	...	...
Rains, TX	48379	15,228	8.2	53.0	38.8	14,105	8,637	61.8	...	...	...	...
Randall, TX	48381	100,528	24.0	33.1	42.9	75,488	8,828	49.6	...	...	...	...
Reagan, TX	48383	20,673	3.1	17.3	79.6	9,313	11,864	59.7	...	...	...	...
Real, TX	48385	6,581	6.5	61.1	32.4	5,934	16,483	61.2	...	...	...	...
Red River, TX	48387	29,838	12.9	64.1	22.9	26,126	10,213	60.6	...	...	...	...
Reeves, TX	48389	29,185	10.8	41.1	48.1	23,956	10,172	60.2	...	...	...	...
Refugio, TX	48391	22,180	6.0	39.3	54.7	16,505	11,470	62.4	...	...	...	...
Roberts, TX	48393	9,327	1.0	13.2	85.8	2,314	13,612	56.7	...	...	...	...
Robertson, TX	48395	60,969	7.4	34.8	57.7	34,418	10,370	60.1	...	...	...	...
Rockwall, TX	48397	177,456	3.7	37.9	58.3	139,037	8,080	59.5	...	...	...	...
Runnels, TX	48399	25,147	11.2	65.1	23.6	20,866	9,852	64.1	...	...	...	...
Rusk, TX	48401	90,788	7.9	35.9	56.3	65,650	8,554	61.5	...	...	...	...
Sabine, TX	48403	22,071	17.3	47.9	34.8	19,020	9,724	61.6	...	...	...	...
San Augustine, TX	48405	15,226	12.5	68.3	19.2	12,354	9,797	59.6	...	...	...	...
San Jacinto, TX	48407	33,454	10.9	52.2	37.0	31,011	8,860	57.3	...	...	...	...
San Patricio, TX	48409	147,542	13.2	51.9	34.9	128,153	8,399	58.1	...	...	...	...
San Saba, TX	48411	11,647	9.0	64.1	27.0	10,900	10,461	62.4	...	...	...	...
Schleicher, TX	48413	7,624	5.7	36.4	57.9	6,038	9,361	61.9	...	...	...	...
Scurry, TX	48415	46,301	6.3	26.0	67.7	27,422	9,065	60.2	...	...	...	...
Shackelford, TX	48417	9,030	7.5	46.3	46.2	7,351	10,826	60.5	...	...	...	...
Shelby, TX	48419	55,323	12.4	58.1	29.5	46,287	8,910	58.6	...	...	...	...
Sherman, TX	48421	10,396	7.7	30.0	62.3	7,658	9,385	65.2	...	...	...	...
Smith, TX	48423	305,995	10.3	40.8	48.9	260,213	8,035	60.7	11,308	82.5	8.1	6.9
Somervell, TX	48425	31,838	4.2	12.8	83.0	19,907	10,884	60.9	...	...	...	...
Starr, TX	48427	184,048	18.0	66.5	15.5	159,875	9,674	60.0	4,018	65.7	16.8	7.2
Stephens, TX	48429	15,902	7.9	41.9	50.2	13,651	8,602	59.0	...	...	...	...
Sterling, TX	48431	8,819	1.9	12.0	86.2	3,078	15,704	58.0	...	...	...	...
Stonewall, TX	48433	3,398	5.9	42.1	51.9	2,993	11,512	63.6	...	...	...	...
Sutton, TX	48435	23,742	3.3	26.0	70.8	10,195	10,205	60.5	...	...	...	...
Swisher, TX	48437	16,486	9.5	68.3	22.2	14,197	9,778	61.4	...	...	...	...
Tarrant, TX	48439	302,8819	7.8	39.1	53.2	2,513,861	7,789	60.6	91,583	82.0	11.1	4.0
Taylor, TX	48441	229,477	19.4	47.9	32.7	188,718	8,507	58.8	9,930	86.6	7.0	3.9
Terrell, TX	48443	13,240	1.1	7.6	91.3	3,521	23,164	53.3	...	...	...	...
Terry, TX	48445	26,064	16.5	43.4	40.1	23,120	10,194	60.9	...	...	...	...
Throckmorton, TX	48447	4,486	5.7	56.8	37.5	4,016	11,812	65.4	...	...	...	...
Titus, TX	48449	85,245	17.7	36.4	45.9	69,699	10,193	53.5	...	...	...	...
Tom Green, TX	48451	167,282	14.2	56.4	29.4	152,346	8,540	57.3	7,958	82.9	13.0	1.8
Travis, TX	48453	1,683,013	8.0	27.7	64.3	1,238,324	9,009	56.6	52,873	83.6	8.4	4.1
Trinity, TX	48455	22,833	15.4	60.3	24.3	21,335	9,593	59.8	...	...	...	...
Tyler, TX	48457	39,276	9.7	51.8	38.5	34,031	9,482	57.8	...	...	...	...
Upshur, TX	48459	68,864	9.2	52.9	37.9	60,063	8,616	61.3	...	...	...	...
Upton, TX	48461	36,671	2.5	9.6	87.9	11,218	16,644	54.4	...	...	...	...
Uvalde, TX	48463	61,059	15.0	60.4	24.6	58,313	9,547	58.2	...	...	...	...
Val Verde, TX	48465	92,497	15.9	63.7	20.4	80,902	7,726	62.4	...	...	...	...
Van Zandt, TX	48467	95,099	8.5	57.9	33.6	78,031	7,893	60.6	...	...	...	...
Victoria, TX	48469	143,851	12.6	41.5	45.9	123,193	8,322	56.7	5,246	76.4	16.6	3.7
Walker, TX	48471	76,649	15.4	47.5	37.1	64,384	9,145	49.4	...	...	...	...
Waller, TX	48473	84,917	9.7	47.2	43.1	70,708	8,447	61.0	...	...	...	...
Ward, TX	48475	28,171	5.6	26.1	68.3	18,500	8,955	60.5	...	...	...	...
Washington, TX	48477	53,606	7.3	37.7	55.0	43,035	8,270	60.6	...	...	...	...
Webb, TX	48479	660,486	12.3	62.6	25.1	530,655	8,224	58.9	16,049	82.8	8.7	5.7
Wharton, TX	48481	79,446	8.5	51.4	40.1	71,981	8,937	62.7	...	...	...	...
Wheeler, TX	48483	26,759	4.7	21.8	73.4	11,857	12,494	59.5	...	...	...	...
Wichita, TX	48485	208,015	15.7	46.5	37.8	180,753	8,307	58.7	9,323	69.2	25.8	1.8
Wilbarger, TX	48487	25,251	8.7	48.8	42.5	20,976	8,458	62.7	...	...	...	...
Willacy, TX	48489	48,836	19.7	61.7	18.6	44,647	9,911	56.4	...	...	...	...
Williamson, TX	48491	907,661	4.6	30.5	64.8	707,466	7,854	60.9	19,028	82.5	11.6	2.7
Wilson, TX	48493	77,476	6.9	54.0	39.1	62,769	7,725	59.5	...	...	...	...
Winkler, TX	48495	34,804	6.1	24.3	69.6	19,123	11,660	55.3	...	...	...	...
Wise, TX	48497	107,281	4.8	37.2	57.9	78,247	8,740	60.3	3,106	80.4	13.7	4.4
Wood, TX	48499	63,435	8.0	45.7	46.3	52,676	8,614	61.7	...	...	...	...
Yoakum, TX	48501	46,356	3.2	18.8	78.0	20,412	10,441	61.0	...	...	...	...
Young, TX	48503	35,716	9.8	53.0	37.3	27,841	8,205	64.5	...	...	...	...
Zapata, TX	48505	61,129	8.8	28.2	62.9	34,420	9,435	58.1	...	...	...	...
Zavala, TX	48507	30,869	18.5	65.3	16.2	26,787	10,460	59.1	...	...	...	...

... Not available

Table C-1. Population, School, and Student Characteristics by County—*Continued*

County	State/County Code	High school graduates, 2006-2008			College enrollment, 2006-2008		College graduates, 2006-2008 (percent)						
		Population 25 years and over	High school diploma or less (percent)	High school diploma or more (percent)	Number	Percent public	Bachelor's degree or more	+/- U.S. percent with Bachelor's degree or more	Non-Hispanic White	Black or African American	American Indian and Alaska Native	Asian, Hawaiian, and Pacific Islander	Hispanic or Latino[3]
		30	31	32	33	34	35	36	37	38	39	40	41
Parker, TX	48367	71,473	46.8	84.2	4,882	88.0	19.6	-7.8	20.7	19.4	...	...	6.8
Parmer, TX	48369	...	...	...	...	...	...	...	...	...	...	...	...
Pecos, TX	48371	...	...	...	...	...	...	...	...	...	...	...	...
Polk, TX	48373	31,887	64.1	75.6	1,217	85.4	10.9	-16.5	12.6	3.7	25.7	...	0.3
Potter, TX	48375	74,673	54.8	74.2	5,707	93.3	14.4	-13.0	19.5	13.3	6.9	7.8	4.0
Presidio, TX	48377	...	...	...	...	...	...	...	...	...	...	...	...
Rains, TX	48379	...	...	...	...	...	...	...	...	...	...	...	...
Randall, TX	48381	70,976	34.3	91.0	10,988	92.3	28.8	1.4	31.3	24.3	...	62.9	9.2
Reagan, TX	48383	...	...	...	...	...	...	...	...	...	...	...	...
Real, TX	48385	...	...	...	...	...	...	...	...	...	...	...	...
Red River, TX	48387	...	...	...	...	...	...	...	...	...	...	...	...
Reeves, TX	48389	...	...	...	...	...	...	...	...	...	...	...	...
Refugio, TX	48391	...	...	...	...	...	...	...	...	...	...	...	...
Roberts, TX	48393	...	...	...	...	...	...	...	...	...	...	...	...
Robertson, TX	48395	...	...	...	...	...	...	...	...	...	...	...	...
Rockwall, TX	48397	45,417	33.6	91.2	4,433	71.2	34.1	6.7	37.3	25.8	...		13.0
Runnels, TX	48399	...	...	...	...	...	...	...	...	...	...	...	...
Rusk, TX	48401	32,662	56.8	80.0	1,929	91.2	15.8	-11.6	19.0	7.2	...		4.8
Sabine, TX	48403	...	...	...	...	...	...	...	...	...	...	...	...
San Augustine, TX	48405	...	...	...	...	...	...	...	...	...	...	...	...
San Jacinto, TX	48407	17,038	63.1	76.6	609	54.2	10.7	-16.7	12.2	1.8	...	...	
San Patricio, TX	48409	41,388	55.8	74.5	2,718	86.3	14.3	-13.1	21.8	...	...		6.0
San Saba, TX	48411	...	...	...	...	...	...	...	...	...	...	...	...
Schleicher, TX	48413	...	...	...	...	...	...	...	...	...	...	...	...
Scurry, TX	48415	...	...	...	...	...	...	...	...	...	...	...	...
Shackelford, TX	48417	...	...	...	...	...	...	...	...	...	...	...	...
Shelby, TX	48419	17,211	67.7	73.2	1,171	96.1	14.2	-13.2	18.4	2.8	...	...	
Sherman, TX	48421	...	...	...	...	...	...	...	...	...	...	...	...
Smith, TX	48423	126,965	44.2	83.2	14,321	84.7	23.4	-4.0	28.7	13.2	...	52.5	3.8
Somervell, TX	48425	...	...	...	...	...	...	...	...	...	...	...	...
Starr, TX	48427	32,011	73.7	49.2	2,751	98.2	10.0	-17.4	...	...	...		8.4
Stephens, TX	48429	...	...	...	...	...	...	...	...	...	...	...	...
Sterling, TX	48431	...	...	...	...	...	...	...	...	...	...	...	...
Stonewall, TX	48433	...	...	...	...	...	...	...	...	...	...	...	...
Sutton, TX	48435	...	...	...	...	...	...	...	...	...	...	...	...
Swisher, TX	48437	...	...	...	...	...	...	...	...	...	...	...	...
Tarrant, TX	48439	1,068,794	41.9	83.0	104,314	73.5	28.2	0.8	35.1	21.0	24.0	41.8	9.6
Taylor, TX	48441	76,959	44.4	83.7	12,253	36.3	23.6	-3.8	27.8	16.5	...	49.2	6.9
Terrell, TX	48443	...	...	...	...	...	...	...	...	...	...	...	...
Terry, TX	48445	...	...	...	...	...	...	...	...	...	...	...	...
Throckmorton, TX	48447	...	...	...	...	...	...	...	...	...	...	...	...
Titus, TX	48449	17,592	60.7	72.7	1,799	92.7	13.5	-13.9	19.3	7.5	...	...	4.4
Tom Green, TX	48451	65,879	48.8	80.6	8,157	91.0	22.1	-5.3	28.7	25.3	...	10.6	8.1
Travis, TX	48453	611,630	32.8	85.3	89,857	87.3	42.6	15.2	55.7	23.7	24.2	64.9	17.0
Trinity, TX	48455	...	...	...	...	...	...	...	...	...	...	...	...
Tyler, TX	48457	14,326	58.6	81.7	...	...	13.8	-13.6	15.6	2.8	...	...	
Upshur, TX	48459	25,614	53.1	83.2	1,577	84.8	15.3	-12.1	16.2	9.3	...		6.9
Upton, TX	48461	...	...	...	...	...	...	...	...	...	...	...	...
Uvalde, TX	48463	15,793	57.3	70.1	1,297	95.3	14.9	-12.5	25.7	...	...		7.2
Val Verde, TX	48465	28,778	65.7	61.2	2,093	91.8	14.3	-13.1	30.9	...	...		8.9
Van Zandt, TX	48467	35,338	58.5	77.2	2,005	86.9	11.8	-15.6	12.0	11.2	...	...	4.5
Victoria, TX	48469	54,725	50.8	80.1	3,636	93.9	16.1	-11.3	22.7	10.2	...	...	5.7
Walker, TX	48471	39,884	56.2	78.2	11,651	97.8	16.6	-10.8	23.3	5.0	...	...	6.5
Waller, TX	48473	20,784	56.6	77.7	2,776	98.4	17.9	-9.5	22.4	18.6	...	...	4.7
Ward, TX	48475	...	...	...	...	...	...	...	...	...	...	...	...
Washington, TX	48477	20,628	51.9	78.2	2,768	95.5	23.4	-4.0	28.1	7.2	...	...	10.8
Webb, TX	48479	119,443	60.1	61.9	15,627	92.8	16.5	-10.9	41.3	...	...	...	14.6
Wharton, TX	48481	25,886	59.4	72.0	2,169	94.9	15.1	-12.3	23.2	6.0	...	...	3.7
Wheeler, TX	48483	...	...	...	...	...	...	...	...	...	...	...	...
Wichita, TX	48485	79,164	50.2	82.9	8,237	90.9	21.2	-6.2	24.1	11.9	30.9	28.1	9.0
Wilbarger, TX	48487	...	...	...	...	...	...	...	...	...	...	...	...
Willacy, TX	48489	12,008	72.2	53.0	527	96.2	10.8	-16.6	30.8	...	...	...	6.7
Williamson, TX	48491	232,838	32.3	90.1	19,537	78.9	35.6	8.2	39.4	22.9	13.2	62.1	17.9
Wilson, TX	48493	25,125	52.9	82.7	1,788	88.9	18.8	-8.6	23.6	...	...	...	8.3
Winkler, TX	48495	...	...	...	...	...	...	...	...	...	...	...	...
Wise, TX	48497	37,571	56.1	79.6	2,131	89.3	14.6	-12.8	15.5	...	...	...	6.5
Wood, TX	48499	28,415	55.2	80.7	3,247	37.1	14.6	-12.8	15.4	...	...	...	3.1
Yoakum, TX	48501	...	...	...	...	...	...	...	...	...	...	...	...
Young, TX	48503	...	...	...	...	...	...	...	...	...	...	...	...
Zapata, TX	48505	...	...	...	...	...	...	...	...	...	...	...	...
Zavala, TX	48507	...	...	...	...	...	...	...	...	...	...	...	...

[3]May be of any race
... Not available

Table C-1. Population, School, and Student Characteristics by County—*Continued*

County	State/County Code	County Type[1]	Population, 2009		Percent of related children 5-17 years in poverty, 2008	Percent of children under 19 years with no health insurance, 2007	Number of Schools and Students, 2008-2009			Resident enrollment, 2006-2008	
			Total	Percent 5–17 years			School Districts	Schools	Students	K–12 enrollment	
										Number	Percent public
			1	2	3	4	5	6	7	8	9
UTAH....................	49000	X	2,784,572	21.4	9.7	10.9	119	1,040	559,778	559,976	95.1
Beaver, UT............................	49001	9	6,267	23.3	10.5	17.8	1	7	1,580	...	...
Box Elder, UT........................	49003	4	49,902	23.6	8.1	9.8	1	30	11,264	11,060	98.7
Cache, UT.............................	49005	3	115,269	20.5	9.9	11.2	6	45	22,334	22,059	97.6
Carbon, UT............................	49007	7	19,989	19.0	14.4	6.9	3	12	4,109	...	...
Daggett, UT...........................	49009	8	941	14.2	7.5	17.0	1	4	180	...	...
Davis, UT..............................	49011	2	300,827	23.4	7.1	6.6	8	109	69,376	64,833	97.2
Duchesne, UT........................	49013	6	17,948	23.8	13.0	11.2	2	15	4,444	...	...
Emery, UT.............................	49015	9	10,629	22.5	11.8	10.3	1	10	2,312	...	...
Garfield, UT...........................	49017	9	4,625	19.3	14.3	14.2	1	9	951	...	...
Grand, UT.............................	49019	7	9,660	16.5	18.4	11.8	2	7	1,546	...	...
Iron, UT...............................	49021	4	45,280	19.9	17.3	11.6	4	23	9,398	8,534	93.5
Juab, UT..............................	49023	2	10,244	26.0	11.8	9.4	2	12	2,474	...	...
Kane, UT..............................	49025	6	6,601	17.3	13.6	11.1	1	10	1,201	...	...
Millard, UT............................	49027	7	12,276	23.3	15.0	11.3	2	12	3,036	...	...
Morgan, UT...........................	49029	2	8,908	24.8	4.1	15.8	1	5	2,313	...	...
Piute, UT..............................	49031	9	1,431	20.8	26.4	10.8	1	6	361	...	...
Rich, UT...............................	49033	8	2,160	22.4	12.2	23.7	1	5	455	...	...
Salt Lake, UT.........................	49035	2	1,034,989	19.9	9.9	13.1	32	295	191,513	202,499	93.1
San Juan, UT.........................	49037	7	15,049	24.6	25.2	10.6	1	13	2,975	...	...
Sanpete, UT...........................	49039	6	25,946	21.7	15.0	12.5	2	19	5,385	5,346	96.6
Sevier, UT.............................	49041	7	19,976	23.7	13.9	10.0	2	14	4,732	4,192	96.6
Summit, UT............................	49043	2	36,969	19.4	7.0	15.5	3	18	6,962	6,548	94.3
Tooele, UT............................	49045	2	58,335	24.9	7.5	10.0	2	28	13,504	12,243	98.9
Uintah, UT............................	49047	7	31,536	22.3	11.5	16.5	2	17	6,411	6,304	97.4
Utah, UT..............................	49049	2	545,307	23.5	8.1	9.3	23	164	113,533	113,944	95.3
Wasatch, UT..........................	49051	6	21,600	22.9	7.7	15.2	3	9	5,003	4,684	98.8
Washington, UT.......................	49053	3	137,473	19.7	12.9	11.0	3	48	26,776	25,348	94.8
Wayne, UT............................	49055	9	2,601	21.9	18.5	15.0	1	4	579	...	...
Weber, UT.............................	49057	2	231,834	20.2	10.6	9.3	7	90	45,071	45,741	96.2
VERMONT................	50000	X	621,760	15.1	10.6	6.4	362	330	92,446	98,572	90.2
Addison, VT...........................	50001	6	36,760	16.0	8.4	6.9	28	23	5,105	6,172	90.4
Bennington, VT.......................	50003	6	36,411	14.8	14.4	6.5	23	18	5,159	5,451	82.2
Caledonia, VT.........................	50005	7	30,252	15.8	15.5	8.1	21	15	4,982	4,878	71.3
Chittenden, VT.......................	50007	3	152,313	14.8	7.3	4.9	33	51	22,373	24,416	92.4
Essex, VT.............................	50009	9	6,394	14.8	19.5	6.3	18	6	755	...	...
Franklin, VT..........................	50011	3	48,182	17.8	10.9	6.0	21	22	8,762	9,235	96.3
Grand Isle, VT........................	50013	3	7,560	14.9	10.6	10.2	6	5	712	...	...
Lamoille, VT..........................	50015	8	25,958	14.1	11.5	9.3	13	15	3,668	3,854	93.1
Orange, VT............................	50017	9	28,896	15.5	13.2	7.5	22	23	4,693	4,706	83.1
Orleans, VT...........................	50019	7	27,301	15.6	16.6	6.9	28	22	4,279	4,251	92.5
Rutland, VT...........................	50021	5	63,014	14.2	11.7	7.5	39	33	8,955	9,367	93.2
Washington, VT.......................	50023	4	58,696	14.7	8.9	5.6	31	27	8,880	8,802	94.8
Windham, VT..........................	50025	6	43,471	14.6	12.4	6.4	34	31	6,214	6,590	87.3
Windsor, VT...........................	50027	7	56,552	14.6	9.7	6.4	44	39	7,909	8,566	88.2
VIRGINIA	51000	X	7,882,590	16.7	12.2	9.9	139	2070	1,235,795	1,307,503	89.6
Accomack, VA.........................	51001	7	38,462	15.6	26.1	13.3	1	13	5,193	6,685	88.8
Albemarle, VA.........................	51003	3	94,908	15.6	7.1	12.7	(7)	(7)	(7)	14,413	80.7
Alleghany, VA.........................	51005	6	16,242	16.1	16.2	7.8	1	7	2,896	...	...
Amelia, VA............................	51007	1	12,886	17.0	11.8	14.0	1	3	1,849	...	...
Amherst, VA...........................	51009	3	32,482	15.7	14.9	9.6	1	10	4,771	4,773	81.6
Appomattox, VA.......................	51011	3	14,552	16.3	17.4	13.1	1	4	2,247	...	...
Arlington, VA.........................	51013	1	217,483	10.2	8.2	10.1	1	31	19,599	22,792	91.8
Augusta, VA...........................	51015	4	72,020	16.3	9.5	11.6	1	21	10,999	11,279	88.4
Bath, VA..............................	51017	9	4,482	14.8	9.7	14.8	1	3	732	...	...
Bedford, VA...........................	51019	3	67,154	17.2	8.9	12.2	(8)	(8)	(8)	10,858	84.8
Bland, VA.............................	51021	8	6,791	13.6	15.2	8.7	1	4	930	...	...
Botetourt, VA.........................	51023	2	32,551	16.8	6.7	10.4	1	12	4,947	5,166	89.1
Brunswick, VA........................	51025	6	17,514	13.0	21.9	9.1	1	5	2,167	...	...
Buchanan, VA.........................	51027	9	22,860	14.7	30.3	6.7	1	11	3,399	3,411	88.7

[1]County type codes are from the Economic Research Service of the United States Department of Agriculture. See notes and definitions for more information.
[7]Albemarle county is included with Charlottesville city
[8]Bedford county is included with Bedford city
... Not available

Table C-1. Population, School, and Student Characteristics by County—*Continued*

County	State/ County Code	Characteristics of students, 2008-2009					Staff and students, 2008-2009			
		Percent with IEP[2]	Percent eligible for free or reduced lunch	Percent minority	Percent English Language Learners	Number of graduates, 2006-2007	Total staff	Number of teachers	Student/ teacher ratio	Central admin. Staff
		10	11	12	13	14	15	16	17	18
UTAH....................	49000	11.6	31.2	20.5	7.9	30,400	49,017	23,644	23.7	1187
Beaver, UT....................	49001	13.5	47.5	14.3	4.2	97	163	78	20.3	5
Box Elder, UT....................	49003	11.8	34.5	11.3	3.7	657	1084	466	24.2	17
Cache, UT....................	49005	11.8	33.3	15.8	6.3	1,411	2,113	934	23.9	44
Carbon, UT....................	49007	18.2	51.0	13.8	1.2	252	467	197	20.9	30
Daggett, UT....................	49009	9.4	15.0	6.7	...	14	34	13	13.8	3
Davis, UT....................	49011	10.2	28.9	12.5	4.0	4,132	6,269	2,894	24.0	179
Duchesne, UT....................	49013	16.1	38.7	18.4	1.5	247	469	218	20.4	15
Emery, UT....................	49015	16.8	45.8	8.7	2.4	166	257	119	19.4	8
Garfield, UT....................	49017	13.1	42.3	9.0	3.0	59	144	65	14.6	6
Grand, UT....................	49019	13.8	47.0	20.9	6.1	96	211	89	17.4	8
Iron, UT....................	49021	12.3	30.4	13.4	3.0	501	973	432	21.8	20
Juab, UT....................	49023	11.3	33.7	5.8	...	124	254	119	20.8	7
Kane, UT....................	49025	16.2	44.8	5.7	1.0	76	159	72	16.7	6
Millard, UT....................	49027	14.6	47.6	18.4	7.9	237	318	142	21.4	7
Morgan, UT....................	49029	7.5	13.8	3.2	0.6	156	202	107	21.6	6
Piute, UT....................	49031	14.4	58.2	12.7	5.0	22	56	27	13.4	3
Rich, UT....................	49033	10.1	49.7	3.7	1.8	41	62	32	14.2	3
Salt Lake, UT....................	49035	11.0	27.6	29.6	12.7	10,371	16,157	7,864	24.4	356
San Juan, UT....................	49037	11.6	67.3	56.4	21.0	227	398	158	18.8	13
Sanpete, UT....................	49039	15.6	48.7	13.4	6.9	313	662	282	19.1	15
Sevier, UT....................	49041	13.6	45.8	8.9	2.3	287	443	221	21.4	13
Summit, UT....................	49043	9.4	18.9	14.2	7.6	472	760	355	19.6	25
Tooele, UT....................	49045	12.4	35.4	15.1	5.2	542	1,156	605	22.3	13
Uintah, UT....................	49047	13.3	29.1	11.3	1.2	292	591	263	24.4	14
Utah, UT....................	49049	11.8	27.4	15.0	5.4	5,358	9,105	4,625	24.5	215
Wasatch, UT....................	49051	13.7	31.5	17.3	10.8	270	488	219	22.8	17
Washington, UT....................	49053	10.8	36.0	16.2	7.9	1,407	2,226	1,166	23.0	41
Wayne, UT....................	49055	10.2	50.1	6.7	0.9	36	70	36	16.1	4
Weber, UT....................	49057	12.9	44.3	25.4	7.5	2,537	3,726	1,850	24.4	97
VERMONT....................	50000	14.2	30.1	6.2	1.6	7,317	19,336	8,755	10.6	577
Addison, VT....................	50001	12.8	26.7	3.2	0.5	429	1,107	499	10.2	38
Bennington, VT....................	50003	17.9	32.1	3.9	0.6	450	1,119	515	10.0	59
Caledonia, VT....................	50005	13.2	30.4	8.2	0.4	486	1,090	501	9.9	52
Chittenden, VT....................	50007	12.5	22.4	10.1	4.3	1,784	4,374	1,874	11.9	134
Essex, VT....................	50009	...	41.8	1.5	0.3	40	177	83	9.1	6
Franklin, VT....................	50011	16.7	33.7	8.1	0.4	652	1,732	825	10.6	30
Grand Isle, VT....................	50013	22.9	37.0	2.5	0.6	...	144	71	10.0	5
Lamoille, VT....................	50015	12.9	32.6	4.3	0.4	307	685	306	12.0	19
Orange, VT....................	50017	11.3	35.8	3.0	0.2	348	1,046	481	9.8	32
Orleans, VT....................	50019	18.3	50.6	4.3	0.3	304	1,021	446	9.6	10
Rutland, VT....................	50021	14.4	33.8	3.6	0.5	744	1,982	896	10.0	53
Washington, VT....................	50023	11.5	26.5	5.2	1.7	718	1,727	825	10.8	47
Windham, VT....................	50025	20.0	34.0	6.3	1.0	400	1,333	612	10.2	35
Windsor, VT....................	50027	14.1	28.8	4.6	1.0	655	1,798	821	9.6	58
VIRGINIA....................	51000	13.5	33.1	40.6	7.0	78,534	203,559	71,413	17.3	6,526
Accomack, VA....................	51001	13.6	61.1	54.2	9.7	329	918	336	15.5	23
Albemarle, VA....................	51003	(7)	21.3	23.6	(7)	(7)	(7)	(7)	(7)	(7)
Alleghany, VA....................	51005	18.1	40.8	9.0	0.2	180	509	191	15.2	11
Amelia, VA....................	51007	12.2	45.3	34.1	0.8	117	267	99	18.7	7
Amherst, VA....................	51009	11.6	40.6	29.9	0.4	323	841	299	16.0	27
Appomattox, VA....................	51011	13.2	42.5	31.5	...	147	346	150	15.0	14
Arlington, VA....................	51013	14.8	32.4	50.9	26.9	1,094	3,443	1,271	15.4	223
Augusta, VA....................	51015	12.4	32.2	7.4	1.8	763	1,741	714	15.4	30
Bath, VA....................	51017	13.9	36.1	2.9	0.3	65	125	47	15.6	3
Bedford, VA....................	51019	(8)	28.9	11.0	(8)	(8)	(8)	(8)	(8)	(8)
Bland, VA....................	51021	14.0	40.4	1.0	...	68	148	59	15.8	5
Botetourt, VA....................	51023	16.5	17.2	5.1	0.3	358	848	271	18.3	15
Brunswick, VA....................	51025	12.2	73.1	80.2	1.0	132	465	157	13.8	17
Buchanan, VA....................	51027	19.7	62.4	0.2	...	226	523	231	14.7	9

[2]IEP= Individual Education Program. See notes and definitions for more information
[7]Albemarle county is included with Charlottesville city
[8]Bedford county is included with Bedford city
... Not available

Table C-1. Population, School, and Student Characteristics by County—*Continued*

County	State/ County Code	Total revenue ($1,000's)	Revenues, 2007-2008 Percentage of revenue from			Current expenditures, 2007-2008 Amount ($1,000's)	Amount per student	Percent for instruc- tion	Resident population 16 to 19 years, 2006-2008 Total population 16 to 19 years	Percent en- rolled in school	Percent high school graduates, not enrolled in school	Percent not enrolled, not grads, not employed or not in labor force
			Federal gov't	State gov't	Local gov't							
		19	20	21	22	23	24	25	26	27	28	29
UTAH	49000	4,345,154	9.0	57.4	33.6	3,333,395	5,787	64.4	170,998	81.1	13.0	2.6
Beaver, UT	49001	14,115	7.3	60.1	32.6	10,743	6,495	63.7	...	...	...	...
Box Elder, UT	49003	84,264	8.0	64.1	27.9	67,406	5,660	63.2	3,164	80.8	16.1	0.6
Cache, UT	49005	165,742	8.4	65.8	25.8	138,113	6,093	65.9	8,533	86.8	10.2	0.4
Carbon, UT	49007	41,535	13.3	49.7	37.0	31,844	6,829	62.8	...	...	...	...
Daggett, UT	49009	3,537	3.9	58.0	38.1	2,732	15,523	51.9	...	...	...	...
Davis, UT	49011	502,974	8.3	63.9	27.8	405,587	5,604	63.6	18,679	83.3	12.4	2.0
Duchesne, UT	49013	38,302	8.4	58.2	33.4	29,342	6,462	59.7	...	...	...	...
Emery, UT	49015	23,926	7.1	50.1	42.8	19,174	8,050	62.3	...	...	...	...
Garfield, UT	49017	12,366	7.9	59.9	32.2	10,251	9,653	63.1	...	...	...	...
Grand, UT	49019	13,790	6.7	54.3	39.0	10,750	6,214	64.5	...	...	...	...
Iron, UT	49021	72,825	8.9	56.7	34.4	54,179	5,649	63.2	...	...	...	...
Juab, UT	49023	22,031	6.4	61.4	32.2	16,447	6,473	64.9	...	...	...	...
Kane, UT	49025	14,606	6.1	49.9	44.0	11,358	8,798	62.7	...	...	...	...
Millard, UT	49027	29,960	8.2	49.3	42.5	24,373	7,638	62.9	...	...	...	...
Morgan, UT	49029	16,942	5.0	58.6	36.5	12,021	5,359	65.4	...	...	...	...
Piute, UT	49031	4,583	9.2	76.3	14.5	3,892	10,162	62.6	...	...	...	...
Rich, UT	49033	6,628	5.4	50.1	44.5	5,302	11,526	60.5	...	...	...	...
Salt Lake, UT	49035	1,487,946	10.2	52.7	37.1	1,129,630	5,678	63.8	57,412	78.2	13.2	3.4
San Juan, UT	49037	37,416	12.9	54.6	32.5	35,251	10,319	55.5	...	...	...	...
Sanpete, UT	49039	48,441	10.1	68.9	21.0	39,052	7,096	66.0	...	...	...	...
Sevier, UT	49041	38,215	11.2	64.5	24.4	31,039	6,173	66.2	...	...	...	...
Summit, UT	49043	106,271	2.9	33.8	63.4	56,888	7,980	62.6	...	...	...	...
Tooele, UT	49045	98,639	6.5	64.8	28.6	74,192	5,477	65.1	...	...	...	...
Uintah, UT	49047	60,765	10.2	44.8	45.0	40,809	6,304	61.8	...	...	...	...
Utah, UT	49049	793,544	8.7	62.3	28.9	608,555	5,312	67.5	38,913	84.6	12.0	1.7
Wasatch, UT	49051	49,492	5.6	41.0	53.4	32,249	6,427	68.4	...	...	...	...
Washington, UT	49053	212,106	7.3	52.4	40.3	156,684	5,828	64.8	7,190	78.2	13.3	3.3
Wayne, UT	49055	6,197	8.1	72.0	19.9	5,134	8,746	61.9	...	...	...	...
Weber, UT	49057	337,996	10.0	63.3	26.6	270,398	5,871	62.3	12,842	78.1	15.2	3.7
VERMONT	50000	1,904,181	5.0	67.8	27.2	1,343,252	15,085	62.5	37,985	87.0	9.3	2.1
Addison, VT	50001	130,075	2.9	61.6	35.5	79,925	15,385	61.3	2,869	84.9	10.5	1.7
Bennington, VT	50003	122,429	5.6	62.1	32.3	75,482	17,159	58.5	...	...	...	...
Caledonia, VT	50005	75,575	7.1	77.8	15.1	63,783	20,089	69.8	...	...	...	...
Chittenden, VT	50007	408,650	4.4	71.3	24.3	310,160	14,119	62.5	...	...	...	...
Essex, VT	50009	17,196	5.9	79.2	15.0	12,838	15,968	62.9	...	...	...	...
Franklin, VT	50011	154,594	6.2	69.1	24.7	111,135	12,936	62.8	2,437	78.9	18.4	1.1
Grand Isle, VT	50013	17,159	5.8	87.5	6.8	11,140	16,828	60.8	...	...	...	...
Lamoille, VT	50015	74,249	4.7	68.7	26.7	50,204	13,605	60.0	...	...	...	...
Orange, VT	50017	100,009	4.2	68.0	27.7	75,126	16,958	61.9	...	...	...	...
Orleans, VT	50019	88,748	7.3	61.3	31.4	62,380	14,913	60.2	...	...	...	...
Rutland, VT	50021	186,973	5.0	64.5	30.5	135,056	14,872	64.8	...	...	...	...
Washington, VT	50023	170,691	4.7	67.6	27.7	120,693	13,419	63.3	3,475	80.3	10.4	5.4
Windham, VT	50025	172,530	5.7	61.8	32.5	104,269	17,320	64.2	...	...	...	...
Windsor, VT	50027	185,303	4.2	72.1	23.7	131,061	16,486	60.0	...	...	...	...
VIRGINIA	51000	14,768,120	6.1	40.3	53.6	13,125,471	10,664	61.0	443,821	84.1	11.1	3.1
Accomack, VA	51001	56,983	11.2	55.9	32.9	51,578	9,907	61.1	...	...	...	...
Albemarle, VA	51003	(7)	(7)	(7)	(7)	(7)	(7)	(7)	...	...	...	...
Alleghany, VA	51005	32,798	6.8	57.4	35.8	29,512	10,128	58.6	...	...	...	...
Amelia, VA	51007	17,611	8.1	59.7	32.2	16,717	8,892	61.1	...	...	...	...
Amherst, VA	51009	48,234	8.3	58.3	33.4	43,156	9,059	65.0	...	...	...	...
Appomattox, VA	51011	21,000	8.8	66.0	25.2	19,944	8,608	61.2	...	...	...	...
Arlington, VA	51013	419,457	3.2	11.4	85.4	347,342	18,539	60.6	...	...	...	...
Augusta, VA	51015	117,899	7.6	52.5	39.9	101,534	9,197	65.9	...	...	...	...
Bath, VA	51017	10,374	6.5	20.4	73.1	9,966	13,341	53.8	...	...	...	...
Bedford, VA	51019	(8)	(8)	(8)	(8)	(8)	(8)	(8)	...	...	...	...
Bland, VA	51021	9,017	6.9	63.1	30.0	8,112	8,954	62.6	...	...	...	...
Botetourt, VA	51023	49,399	4.6	51.4	44.1	46,112	9,226	61.9	...	...	...	...
Brunswick, VA	51025	24,820	12.5	63.0	24.5	23,634	10,476	50.9	...	...	...	...
Buchanan, VA	51027	38,731	12.0	56.7	31.3	36,603	10,533	60.1	...	...	...	...

[7]Albemarle county is included with Charlottesville city
[8]Bedford county is included with Bedford city
... Not available

Table C-1. Population, School, and Student Characteristics by County—*Continued*

County	State/County Code	High school graduates, 2006-2008			College enrollment, 2006-2008		College graduates, 2006-2008 (percent)						
		Population 25 years and over	High school diploma or less (percent)	High school diploma or more (percent)	Number	Percent public	Bachelor's degree or more	+/- U.S. percent with Bachelor's degree or more	Non-Hispanic White	Black or African American	American Indian and Alaska Native	Asian, Hawaiian, and Pacific Islander	Hispanic or Latino[3]
		30	31	32	33	34	35	36	37	38	39	40	41
UTAH	49000	1,508,950	35.3	90.3	237,248	71.1	28.8	1.4	30.9	24.7	10.4	36.5	11.1
Beaver, UT	49001	...	...	...	...	...	...	...	...	...	...	...	...
Box Elder, UT	49003	27,609	43.7	89.8	2,696	88.3	22.0	-5.4	23.3	...	...	...	8.3
Cache, UT	49005	54,441	30.5	92.5	18,732	94.5	34.3	6.9	36.0	...	...	68.2	8.7
Carbon, UT	49007	...	...	...	...	...	...	...	...	...	...	...	...
Daggett, UT	49009	...	...	...	...	...	...	...	...	...	...	...	...
Davis, UT	49011	160,146	29.1	94.6	22,499	85.6	32.4	5.0	33.9	24.6	...	42.9	11.7
Duchesne, UT	49013	...	...	...	...	...	...	...	...	...	...	...	...
Emery, UT	49015	...	...	...	...	...	...	...	...	...	...	...	...
Garfield, UT	49017	...	...	...	...	...	...	...	...	...	...	...	...
Grand, UT	49019	...	...	...	...	...	...	...	...	...	...	...	...
Iron, UT	49021	22,081	36.0	90.5	6,271	79.9	28.8	1.4	28.7	...	...	...	6.5
Juab, UT	49023	...	...	...	...	...	...	...	...	...	...	...	...
Kane, UT	49025	...	...	...	...	...	...	...	...	...	...	...	...
Millard, UT	49027	...	...	...	...	...	...	...	...	...	...	...	...
Morgan, UT	49029	...	...	...	...	...	...	...	...	...	...	...	...
Piute, UT	49031	...	...	...	...	...	...	...	...	...	...	...	...
Rich, UT	49033	...	...	...	...	...	...	...	...	...	...	...	...
Salt Lake, UT	49035	602,507	36.5	88.6	74,001	81.6	29.6	2.2	32.7	24.4	13.8	34.8	10.7
San Juan, UT	49037	...	...	...	...	...	...	...	...	...	...	...	...
Sanpete, UT	49039	13,432	44.6	87.2	2,954	95.4	19.9	-7.5	21.3	...	...	...	7.4
Sevier, UT	49041	11,450	45.3	88.9	1,328	93.6	18.2	-9.2	18.9	...	...	...	...
Summit, UT	49043	22,860	24.8	94.5	1,584	72.0	51.0	23.6	53.4	...	...	...	9.6
Tooele, UT	49045	31,444	42.2	92.8	3,047	85.6	18.8	-8.6	19.4	...	...	...	7.7
Uintah, UT	49047	17,104	55.3	83.3	1,009	83.1	12.1	-15.3	13.6	...	1.7	...	4.5
Utah, UT	49049	246,392	25.6	92.9	73,780	41.1	34.9	7.5	36.5	26.3	24.0	42.2	17.4
Wasatch, UT	49051	12,436	33.6	91.7	1,217	85.3	30.8	3.4	32.6	...	...	...	...
Washington, UT	49053	80,133	40.0	90.6	8,164	91.2	22.1	-5.3	23.1	...	...	...	7.3
Wayne, UT	49055	...	...	...	...	...	...	...	...	...	...	...	...
Weber, UT	49057	132,605	41.6	88.3	14,786	80.3	21.7	-5.7	23.2	25.7	...	30.3	10.0
VERMONT	50000	427,462	42.1	90.4	46,030	62.0	33.1	5.7	32.9	43.0	13.7	59.1	36.8
Addison, VT	50001	23,996	45.3	90.0	3,184	25.0	32.0	4.6	31.8	...	...	...	50.5
Bennington, VT	50003	25,851	43.5	89.3	2,329	53.9	32.1	4.7	31.8	...	...	...	...
Caledonia, VT	50005	21,092	47.7	88.9	1,784	77.9	27.7	0.3	28.2	...	...	...	...
Chittenden, VT	50007	99,336	30.3	92.5	17,535	69.3	44.1	16.7	43.6	53.9	...	63.0	37.0
Essex, VT	50009	...	...	...	...	...	...	...	...	...	...	...	...
Franklin, VT	50011	32,320	53.2	87.6	2,108	81.0	19.1	-8.3	19.1	...	...	...	...
Grand Isle, VT	50013	...	...	...	...	...	...	...	...	...	...	...	...
Lamoille, VT	50015	16,865	37.9	91.8	1,913	91.2	32.6	5.2	32.6	...	...	...	...
Orange, VT	50017	20,278	46.0	89.2	1,809	65.7	28.6	1.2	28.6	...	...	...	...
Orleans, VT	50019	19,354	57.4	84.8	1,077	80.1	20.1	-7.3	20.3	...	...	...	...
Rutland, VT	50021	44,783	48.6	89.2	4,482	70.6	26.2	-1.2	25.9	...	...	...	...
Washington, VT	50023	40,988	38.5	92.3	3,780	29.1	38.5	11.1	38.7	...	...	...	26.1
Windham, VT	50025	30,986	41.7	90.8	2,773	42.0	34.7	7.3	34.8	...	...	...	...
Windsor, VT	50027	41,513	43.6	91.3	2,725	60.9	32.9	5.5	32.9	...	...	...	...
VIRGINIA	51000	5,108,315	40.9	85.7	575,498	75.6	33.2	5.8	36.5	17.7	19.2	54.7	22.7
Accomack, VA	51001	26,260	59.1	81.9	1,564	85.6	18.3	-9.1	22.8	8.9	...	...	11.3
Albemarle, VA	51003	59,864	28.7	90.7	12,638	94.2	52.2	24.8	55.7	15.9	...	77.2	25.6
Alleghany, VA	51005	...	...	...	...	...	...	...	...	...	...	...	...
Amelia, VA	51007	...	...	...	...	...	...	...	...	...	...	...	...
Amherst, VA	51009	21,780	56.5	79.4	2,529	46.9	14.6	-12.8	16.4	7.0	...	...	...
Appomattox, VA	51011	...	...	...	...	...	...	...	...	...	...	...	...
Arlington, VA	51013	152,786	18.7	90.8	15,260	55.6	68.0	40.6	79.5	34.0	...	68.5	33.7
Augusta, VA	51015	50,567	58.4	84.3	2,738	70.1	19.4	-8.0	20.5	6.0	...	...	...
Bath, VA	51017	...	...	...	...	...	...	...	...	...	...	...	...
Bedford, VA	51019	46,761	47.5	84.2	3,114	58.5	24.6	-2.8	25.0	12.9	...	...	...
Bland, VA	51021	...	...	...	...	...	...	...	...	...	...	...	...
Botetourt, VA	51023	22,948	48.5	88.3	1,601	65.2	23.2	-4.2	22.7	35.4	...	...	...
Brunswick, VA	51025	...	...	...	...	...	...	...	...	...	...	...	...
Buchanan, VA	51027	17,342	69.6	63.1	1,055	91.5	7.7	-19.7	7.4	...	...	...	...

[3]May be of any race
... Not available

Table C-1. Population, School, and Student Characteristics by County—*Continued*

County	State/County Code	County Type[1]	Population, 2009		Percent of related children 5-17 years in poverty, 2008	Percent of children under 19 years with no health insurance, 2007	Number of Schools and Students, 2008-2009			Resident enrollment, 2006-2008	
			Total	Percent 5–17 years			School Districts	Schools	Students	K–12 enrollment	
										Number	Percent public
			1	2	3	4	5	6	7	8	9
Buckingham, VA	51029	8	16,080	14.1	22.3	13.1	1	6	2,068	...	...
Campbell, VA	51031	3	52,976	16.3	14.2	10.1	1	15	8,734	8,828	87.3
Caroline, VA	51033	1	27,870	16.5	13.4	14.0	1	7	4,244	4,445	84.2
Carroll, VA	51035	6	29,034	14.6	19.4	9.0	1	10	4,076	4,322	96.4
Charles City County, VA	51036	1	7,217	13.7	14.8	15.3	1	3	859	...	...
Charlotte, VA	51037	8	12,039	16.7	24.5	10.9	1	7	2,182	...	...
Chesterfield, VA	51041	1	306,670	19.9	7.1	10.7	1	64	59,080	56,732	92.9
Clarke, VA	51043	1	14,588	16.4	7.6	10.1	1	5	2,169	...	...
Craig, VA	51045	2	4,969	16.1	15.1	12.3	1	2	702	...	...
Culpeper, VA	51047	6	46,502	18.6	10.3	13.3	1	11	7,394	7,605	88.6
Cumberland, VA	51049	1	9,757	16.2	20.6	11.0	1	3	1,550	...	...
Dickenson, VA	51051	9	16,087	14.9	27.0	7.0	1	8	2,533	...	...
Dinwiddie, VA	51053	1	26,338	16.7	13.1	9.5	1	8	4,675	4,332	92.2
Essex, VA	51057	8	11,189	15.2	19.1	10.9	1	3	1,629	...	...
Fairfax, VA	51059	1	1,037,605	17.5	5.6	9.2	1	202[9]	169,030[9]	178,676	86.1
Fauquier, VA	51061	1	68,010	18.8	6.1	11.4	1	19	11,264	12,091	85.0
Floyd, VA	51063	8	15,013	15.4	14.6	14.6	1	5	2,063	...	...
Fluvanna, VA	51065	3	25,732	16.1	7.1	13.3	1	5	3,705	3,924	88.9
Franklin, VA	51067	2	51,924	14.8	15.9	11.4	1	16	7,429	8,218	94.4
Frederick, VA	51069	3	74,972	18.8	8.7	10.9	(11)	(11)	(11)	12,957	89.7
Giles, VA	51071	3	17,358	16.2	14.2	8.2	1	6	2,581	...	...
Gloucester, VA	51073	1	39,184	17.1	11.4	13.2	1	9	6,033	6,120	92.8
Goochland, VA	51075	1	21,311	15.0	6.6	10.8	1	5	2,422	2,975	72.1
Grayson, VA	51077	9	15,793	14.0	23.2	7.7	1	11	2,058	...	...
Greene, VA	51079	3	18,421	18.1	9.9	15.7	1	6	2,852	...	...
Greensville, VA	51081	6	12,049	12.1	24.1	7.2	(12)	(12)	(12)	...	...
Halifax, VA	51083	6	35,258	16.3	21.3	7.8	1	10	6,023	6,001	93.3
Hanover, VA	51085	1	99,933	19.4	4.6	9.4	1	25	18,970	17,934	94.3
Henrico, VA	51087	1	296,415	16.9	10.3	9.3	1	71	48,991	50,584	90.7
Henry, VA	51089	4	54,888	14.7	21.1	7.8	1	15	7,563	8,604	94.5
Highland, VA	51091	9	2,338	13.0	14.8	17.8	1	2	273	...	...
Isle of Wight, VA	51093	1	35,877	17.2	9.0	9.9	1	9	5,495	5,897	77.3
James City County, VA	51095	1	63,735	16.0	7.4	10.4	2[13]	15[13]	10,539[13]	9,223	90.4
King and Queen, VA	51097	1	6,796	14.1	15.1	12.1	1	3	802	...	...
King George, VA	51099	8	23,557	19.3	7.1	12.9	1	5	4,064	4,185	82.0
King William, VA	51101	1	16,225	18.6	7.1	10.9	2	7	2,985	...	...
Lancaster, VA	51103	9	11,230	12.1	20.9	16.6	1	3	1,380	...	...
Lee, VA	51105	8	25,166	15.0	30.2	7.3	1	14	3,694	...	...
Loudoun, VA	51107	1	301,171	20.7	3.1	9.2	1	76	56,894	56,474	88.4
Louisa, VA	51109	1	33,078	15.8	12.5	12.4	1	5	4,736	5,115	92.3
Lunenburg, VA	51111	9	12,799	13.7	26.7	9.2	1	4	1,686	...	...
Madison, VA	51113	8	13,702	15.9	13.2	17.3	1	4	1,870	...	...
Mathews, VA	51115	1	8,984	14.0	12.1	15.3	1	3	1,260	...	...
Mecklenburg, VA	51117	7	31,969	14.5	22.1	9.0	1	11	4,837	4,797	96.2
Middlesex, VA	51119	8	10,731	11.9	17.5	17.4	1	3	1,286	...	...
Montgomery, VA	51121	3	91,023	11.4	14.1	11.2	1	21	9,723	10,059	92.2
Nelson, VA	51125	3	15,487	13.9	16.4	13.4	1	4	1,935	...	...
New Kent, VA	51127	1	18,112	16.6	7.1	14.8	1	4	2,784	...	...
Northampton, VA	51131	9	13,492	15.8	27.7	12.0	1	4	1,842	...	...
Northumberland, VA	51133	9	12,995	11.9	21.3	18.9	1	3	1,478	...	...
Nottoway, VA	51135	6	15,929	15.3	25.6	9.3	1	6	2,428	...	...
Orange, VA	51137	6	33,600	16.8	10.7	12.1	1	10	5,319	5,430	91.9
Page, VA	51139	6	24,070	15.6	18.2	9.3	1	9	3,687	3,575	91.5
Patrick, VA	51141	8	18,636	14.3	21.8	9.2	1	7	2,642	...	...
Pittsylvania, VA	51143	3	61,414	15.9	16.7	9.0	1	19	9,252	9,766	90.2
Powhatan, VA	51145	1	27,964	17.4	6.2	16.5	1	7	4,475	4,285	92.3
Prince Edward, VA	51147	6	22,370	12.8	24.0	9.3	1	3	2,615	3,500	88.5
Prince George, VA	51149	1	37,116	16.7	11.2	13.2	1	8	6,273	6,220	96.0
Prince William, VA	51153	1	379,166	20.4	6.8	11.4	1	83	73,917	72,985	90.7
Pulaski, VA	51155	3	35,022	14.0	17.4	6.7	1	9	4,849	4,932	99.4
Rappahannock, VA	51157	8	7,035	15.2	11.6	17.9	1	2	921	...	...
Richmond, VA	51159	9	8,961	11.9	20.1	11.0	1	3	1,213	...	...
Roanoke, VA	51161	2	91,011	17.2	6.9	8.4	1	28	14,937	15,116	90.3
Rockbridge, VA	51163	6	21,294	14.7	13.2	11.8	1	8	2,888	3,219	97.8
Rockingham, VA	51165	3	75,134	16.8	10.0	17.4	(14)	(14)	(14)	11,739	87.1

[1]County type codes are from the Economic Research Service of the United States Department of Agriculture. See notes and definitions for more information.
[9]Fairfax city is included with Fairfax county
[11]Frederick county is included with Winchester city
[12]Greensville county is included with Emporia city
[13]Williamsburg city is included with James City county
[14]Rockingham county is included with Harrisonburg city
... Not available

Table C-1. Population, School, and Student Characteristics by County—*Continued*

County	State/ County Code	Characteristics of students, 2008-2009				Number of graduates, 2006-2007	Staff and students, 2008-2009			
		Percent with IEP[2]	Percent eligible for free or reduced lunch	Percent minority	Percent English Language Learners		Total staff	Number of teachers	Student/ teacher ratio	Central admin. Staff
		10	11	12	13	14	15	16	17	18
Buckingham, VA	51029	12.3	57.1	44.2	...	138	279	131	15.8	17
Campbell, VA	51031	10.8	30.6	21.4	1.0	587	767	493	17.7	4
Caroline, VA	51033	15.0	45.0	43.2	1.5	230	776	238	17.8	16
Carroll, VA	51035	14.3	51.1	5.2	3.3	245	740	254	16.0	18
Charles City County, VA	51036	15.3	48.5	71.9	1.5	47	113	52	16.5	4
Charlotte, VA	51037	15.0	51.3	37.7	1.0	147	406	136	16.0	13
Chesterfield, VA	51041	13.0	17.0	39.5	4.0	4,169	7,876	3,195	18.5	232
Clarke, VA	51043	7.8	14.8	13.8	1.6	179	339	134	16.2	8
Craig, VA	51045	14.8	34.3	0.6	...	48	104	49	14.3	3
Culpeper, VA	51047	10.1	35.0	32.7	6.0	423	1,278	442	16.7	36
Cumberland, VA	51049	12.6	56.6	48.2	2.0	100	224	106	14.6	9
Dickenson, VA	51051	16.3	52.0	1.1	...	161	298	131	19.3	8
Dinwiddie, VA	51053	13.8	41.4	42.5	1.0	281	731	247	18.9	20
Essex, VA	51057	13.3	67.3	58.9	1.3	99	294	101	16.1	7
Fairfax, VA	51059	14.0[9]	21.6	46.9	20.2[9]	11,912[9]	32,373[9]	9,274[9]	18.2[9]	1,487[9]
Fauquier, VA	51061	11.0	20.6	21.6	3.3	798	1,951	702	16.0	18
Floyd, VA	51063	16.3	39.7	5.6	2.1	134	403	132	15.6	17
Fluvanna, VA	51065	12.6	21.0	21.3	0.7	233	652	185	20.0	14
Franklin, VA	51067	17.8	45.8	15.6	1.7	474	1,357	472	15.7	36
Frederick, VA	51069	(11)	24.3	16.6	(11)	(11)	(11)	(11)	(11)	(11)
Giles, VA	51071	14.3	40.3	3.6	0.1	183	456	158	16.3	8
Gloucester, VA	51073	12.4	27.5	13.7	0.3	398	1,073	367	16.4	23
Goochland, VA	51075	14.2	21.2	29.3	1.8	157	431	148	16.4	14
Grayson, VA	51077	14.3	55.3	6.0	1.2	142	478	128	16.1	13
Greene, VA	51079	15.5	30.1	18.0	3.6	177	538	179	15.9	13
Greensville, VA	51081	(12)	70.6	73.9	(12)	(12)	(12)	(12)	(12)	(12)
Halifax, VA	51083	18.2	58.9	49.5	0.6	372	1,386	382	15.8	36
Hanover, VA	51085	13.9	9.3	13.8	0.7	1,322	3,163	1,064	17.8	79
Henrico, VA	51087	13.8	29.9	48.1	5.5	3,019	6,461	2,654	18.5	309
Henry, VA	51089	15.5	53.9	33.1	5.8	518	975	443	17.1	2
Highland, VA	51091	17.9	52.4	1.8	1.5	25	74	19	14.4	3
Isle of Wight, VA	51093	13.0	29.6	35.5	0.7	361	956	329	16.7	18
James City County, VA	51095	14.5[13]	23.9	29.4	2.2[13]	630[13]	1,823[13]	673[13]	15.7[13]	34[13]
King and Queen, VA	51097	15.7	71.2	50.1	1.6	38	205	65	12.3	6
King George, VA	51099	11.0	24.5	29.4	0.9	222	640	197	20.6	16
King William, VA	51101	12.7	26.1	23.0	0.6	178	564	181	16.5	17
Lancaster, VA	51103	12.0	57.7	53.0	0.2	103	210	64	21.6	7
Lee, VA	51105	20.7	58.2	1.6	0.1	187	781	204	18.1	11
Loudoun, VA	51107	10.3	13.2	34.7	7.8	2,829	9,999	3,222	17.7	279
Louisa, VA	51109	16.4	41.9	24.1	0.7	277	813	294	16.1	21
Lunenburg, VA	51111	14.9	61.2	46.8	1.7	120	359	90	18.7	21
Madison, VA	51113	9.9	24.1	15.8	0.9	134	308	115	16.3	11
Mathews, VA	51115	14.5	31.0	13.0	0.5	105	292	69	18.3	10
Mecklenburg, VA	51117	14.3	55.0	50.0	0.6	344	845	330	14.7	21
Middlesex, VA	51119	14.8	36.3	28.6	0.7	115	262	84	15.3	7
Montgomery, VA	51121	12.7	34.1	12.2	2.1	629	1,764	644	15.1	47
Nelson, VA	51125	13.8	47.8	22.2	3.3	148	358	132	14.7	10
New Kent, VA	51127	14.0	15.6	19.1	0.4	171	469	157	17.7	13
Northampton, VA	51131	14.4	68.9	62.2	9.8	138	392	122	15.1	24
Northumberland, VA	51133	11.3	45.1	44.0	2.3	80	255	88	16.8	6
Nottoway, VA	51135	14.9	54.6	49.7	2.6	154	502	135	18.0	12
Orange, VA	51137	9.8	31.8	24.0	1.9	284	827	292	18.2	22
Page, VA	51139	11.4	43.8	4.7	1.1	228	679	232	15.9	16
Patrick, VA	51141	16.3	50.7	12.4	3.6	136	460	151	17.5	12
Pittsylvania, VA	51143	14.9	44.9	29.4	1.4	658	1,557	611	15.1	43
Powhatan, VA	51145	13.1	14.2	12.2	0.7	303	784	257	17.4	20
Prince Edward, VA	51147	19.6	61.6	60.8	0.4	211	507	174	15.0	15
Prince George, VA	51149	12.4	32.2	42.8	0.7	398	911	393	16.0	23
Prince William, VA	51153	11.3	30.7	54.2	17.8	4,124	10,419	3,845	19.2	328
Pulaski, VA	51155	16.0	42.0	8.6	0.5	299	985	317	15.3	21
Rappahannock, VA	51157	13.5	28.6	9.1	0.4	84	179	64	14.4	7
Richmond, VA	51159	13.1	41.2	38.5	4.1	81	182	75	16.2	8
Roanoke, VA	51161	14.8	19.4	11.9	1.9	1,135	2,650	802	18.6	58
Rockbridge, VA	51163	12.6	31.7	5.9	0.3	240	519	192	15.0	21
Rockingham, VA	51165	(14)	33.0	11.3	(14)	(14)	(14)	(14)	(14)	(14)

[2]IEP= Individual Education Program. See notes and definitions for more information
[9]Fairfax city is included with Fairfax county
[11]Frederick county is included with Winchester city
[12]Greensville county is included with Emporia city
[13]Williamsburg city is included with James City county
[14]Rockingham county is included with Harrisonburg city
... Not available

Table C-1. Population, School, and Student Characteristics by County—*Continued*

County	State/County Code	Revenues, 2007-2008				Current expenditures, 2007-2008			Resident population 16 to 19 years, 2006-2008			
		Total revenue ($1,000's)	Percentage of revenue from			Amount ($1,000's)	Amount per student	Percent for instruction	Total population 16 to 19 years	Percent enrolled in school	Percent high school graduates, not enrolled in school	Percent not enrolled, not grads, not employed or not in labor force
			Federal gov't	State gov't	Local gov't							
		19	20	21	22	23	24	25	26	27	28	29
Buckingham, VA	51029	23,728	9.3	60.1	30.6	21,329	10,137	60.5	...	...	...	...
Campbell, VA	51031	79,968	6.2	63.6	30.2	74,059	8,403	62.0	...	...	...	...
Caroline, VA	51033	53,528	5.7	42.1	52.2	36,341	8,713	61.6	...	...	...	...
Carroll, VA	51035	43,487	11.9	57.5	30.6	38,115	9,328	57.0	...	...	...	...
Charles City County, VA	51036	13,176	7.1	40.5	52.4	11,145	12,884	50.8	...	...	...	...
Charlotte, VA	51037	21,336	9.0	68.5	22.5	20,425	9,305	59.5	...	...	...	...
Chesterfield, VA	51041	609,461	4.0	47.2	48.8	532,178	9,025	62.9	18,710	89.0	7.4	1.8
Clarke, VA	51043	25,508	3.4	33.8	62.8	20,420	9,223	57.2	...	...	...	...
Craig, VA	51045	7,240	7.2	64.1	28.7	6,846	9,140	59.5	...	...	...	...
Culpeper, VA	51047	99,592	4.1	35.9	60.0	69,150	9,242	63.9	...	...	...	...
Cumberland, VA	51049	21,670	9.8	56.6	33.6	15,294	9,899	54.7	...	...	...	...
Dickenson, VA	51051	26,724	9.9	60.6	29.4	24,942	9,847	60.9	...	...	...	...
Dinwiddie, VA	51053	52,853	4.8	53.7	41.5	41,861	8,931	56.2	...	...	...	...
Essex, VA	51057	24,040	7.0	38.4	54.6	16,007	9,643	62.6	...	...	...	...
Fairfax, VA	51059	2,406,539[9,10]	3.6[9,10]	19.5[9,10]	76.9[9,10]	2,234,879[9,10]	13,330[9,10]	60.6[9,10]	53,593	92.0	5.5	1.5
Fauquier, VA	51061	137,184	3.0	28.2	68.8	119,882	10,631	65.7	...	...	...	...
Floyd, VA	51063	20,423	6.6	59.8	33.6	18,433	8,952	62.2	...	...	...	...
Fluvanna, VA	51065	36,919	4.8	51.5	43.7	34,337	9,120	68.1	...	...	...	...
Franklin, VA	51067	78,554	8.0	50.3	41.7	68,781	9,135	59.3	...	...	...	...
Frederick, VA	51069	(11)	(11)	(11)	(11)	(11)	(11)	(11)	...	...	...	...
Giles, VA	51071	25,303	6.0	62.0	32.0	22,850	8,971	63.7	...	...	...	...
Gloucester, VA	51073	64,713	5.4	49.9	44.7	57,843	9,506	57.6	...	...	...	...
Goochland, VA	51075	26,848	4.1	20.7	75.1	24,562	10,187	59.4	...	...	...	...
Grayson, VA	51077	21,990	8.3	63.6	28.1	20,468	9,705	60.8	...	...	...	...
Greene, VA	51079	30,812	5.3	52.7	42.0	27,530	9,755	66.8	...	...	...	...
Greensville, VA	51081	(12)	(12)	(12)	(12)	(12)	(12)	(12)	...	...	...	...
Halifax, VA	51083	61,580	9.1	64.8	26.0	59,742	9,792	60.8	...	...	...	...
Hanover, VA	51085	195,986	3.9	43.1	53.0	170,317	8,917	67.6	...	...	...	...
Henrico, VA	51087	474,941	5.4	46.5	48.1	420,874	8,656	60.6	14,134	86.3	10.3	2.4
Henry, VA	51089	78,457	9.9	62.6	27.5	68,624	8,935	59.4	...	...	...	...
Highland, VA	51091	4,369	7.7	46.0	46.3	4,039	14,323	59.5	...	...	...	...
Isle of Wight, VA	51093	63,342	5.4	44.8	49.8	53,479	9,833	62.7	...	...	...	...
James City County, VA	51095	138,862[13]	3.4[13]	28.4[13]	68.2[13]	116,687[13]	11,209[13]	62.1[13]	...	...	...	...
King and Queen, VA	51097	12,529	8.7	42.6	48.7	10,984	13,092	55.5	...	...	...	...
King George, VA	51099	36,485	4.2	51.3	44.5	31,211	7,850	61.5	...	...	...	...
King William, VA	51101	33,786	4.9	52.6	42.5	28,419	9,495	63.0	...	...	...	...
Lancaster, VA	51103	16,783	7.5	27.3	65.2	15,305	10,606	58.6	...	...	...	...
Lee, VA	51105	43,971	13.8	63.8	22.5	41,104	11,127	64.1	...	...	...	...
Loudoun, VA	51107	814,891	2.4	20.2	77.3	710,769	13,172	64.2	12,221	92.0	7.2	0.3
Louisa, VA	51109	49,773	5.5	37.3	57.1	45,035	9,598	60.1	...	...	...	...
Lunenburg, VA	51111	18,382	11.1	63.5	25.4	16,658	9,640	60.1	...	...	...	...
Madison, VA	51113	18,965	5.3	49.9	44.8	17,702	9,278	60.4	...	...	...	...
Mathews, VA	51115	13,691	5.4	43.9	50.7	11,965	9,275	58.8	...	...	...	...
Mecklenburg, VA	51117	46,100	9.2	63.8	27.1	42,212	8,645	63.6	...	...	...	...
Middlesex, VA	51119	14,979	6.1	34.7	59.2	12,455	9,486	55.5	...	...	...	...
Montgomery, VA	51121	104,529	6.2	50.0	43.7	92,356	9,491	61.0	...	...	...	...
Nelson, VA	51125	23,480	7.9	43.2	48.8	22,653	10,746	55.1	...	...	...	...
New Kent, VA	51127	25,287	3.9	52.9	43.1	24,473	8,800	57.7	...	...	...	...
Northampton, VA	51131	23,163	10.5	50.1	39.4	21,793	11,362	57.1	...	...	...	...
Northumberland, VA	51133	17,364	8.2	32.2	59.5	14,861	9,921	63.1	...	...	...	...
Nottoway, VA	51135	24,642	13.2	63.6	23.2	21,989	9,135	61.6	...	...	...	...
Orange, VA	51137	47,239	7.7	52.4	39.9	45,073	8,727	60.0	...	...	...	...
Page, VA	51139	43,635	6.0	54.6	39.4	34,158	9,252	63.9	...	...	...	...
Patrick, VA	51141	26,346	9.2	63.5	27.3	23,367	8,828	64.8	...	...	...	...
Pittsylvania, VA	51143	83,937	9.5	67.3	23.3	78,880	8,447	60.3	2,976	84.5	8.5	3.4
Powhatan, VA	51145	45,519	3.4	49.2	47.4	43,297	9,765	59.5	...	...	...	...
Prince Edward, VA	51147	28,416	9.1	61.4	29.5	26,436	9,916	65.0	...	...	...	...
Prince George, VA	51149	61,381	9.9	62.8	27.2	54,343	8,630	60.4	...	...	...	...
Prince William, VA	51153	878,492	3.9	41.7	54.3	757,021	10,372	57.9	19,250	85.2	9.4	2.1
Pulaski, VA	51155	45,769	9.2	62.5	28.3	44,171	8,967	58.1	...	...	...	...
Rappahannock, VA	51157	12,484	4.1	24.3	71.6	11,428	12,145	59.4	...	...	...	...
Richmond, VA	51159	13,684	5.8	51.3	42.9	12,312	10,303	60.5	...	...	...	...
Roanoke, VA	51161	159,384	4.3	46.9	48.9	134,996	8,937	65.2	...	...	...	...
Rockbridge, VA	51163	32,599	8.8	40.4	50.9	28,367	10,034	62.7	...	...	...	...
Rockingham, VA	51165	(14)	(14)	(14)	(14)	(14)	(14)	(14)	4,071	81.5	10.0	4.3

[9]Fairfax city is included with Fairfax county
[10]Falls Church city is included with Fairfax county
[11]Frederick county is included with Winchester city
[12]Greensville county is included with Emporia city
[13]Williamsburg city is included with James City county
[14]Rockingham county is included with Harrisonburg city
... Not available

Table C-1. Population, School, and Student Characteristics by County—*Continued*

County	State/County Code	High school graduates, 2006-2008			College enrollment, 2006-2008		College graduates, 2006-2008 (percent)						
		Population 25 years and over	High school diploma or less (percent)	High school diploma or more (percent)	Number	Percent public	Bachelor's degree or more	+/- U.S. percent with Bachelor's degree or more	Non-Hispanic White	Black or African American	American Indian and Alaska Native	Asian, Hawaiian, and Pacific Islander	Hispanic or Latino[3]
		30	31	32	33	34	35	36	37	38	39	40	41
Buckingham, VA	51029	...	...	...	...	...	...	...	...	...	...	...	...
Campbell, VA	51031	36,590	54.5	81.2	3,250	51.8	15.8	-11.6	17.3	4.7	...	...	...
Caroline, VA	51033	18,142	57.2	81.0	1,304	86.0	15.8	-11.6	18.4	9.4	...	...	...
Carroll, VA	51035	21,604	64.4	73.0	1,476	87.3	13.5	-13.9	13.4	...	...	...	...
Charles City County, VA	51036	...	...	...	...	...	...	...	...	...	...	...	...
Charlotte, VA	51037	...	...	...	...	...	...	...	...	...	...	...	...
Chesterfield, VA	51041	192,184	34.4	90.1	22,579	81.5	36.0	8.6	38.9	28.1	...	47.2	17.3
Clarke, VA	51043	...	...	...	...	...	...	...	...	...	...	...	...
Craig, VA	51045	...	...	...	...	...	...	...	...	...	...	...	...
Culpeper, VA	51047	30,446	53.1	81.4	2,187	72.6	20.4	-7.0	22.4	11.3	...	...	13.3
Cumberland, VA	51049	...	...	...	...	...	...	...	...	...	...	...	...
Dickenson, VA	51051	...	...	...	...	...	...	...	...	...	...	...	...
Dinwiddie, VA	51053	17,433	61.7	73.8	862	61.4	14.1	-13.3	14.7	12.0	...	...	...
Essex, VA	51057	...	...	...	...	...	...	...	...	...	...	...	...
Fairfax, VA	51059	673,883	21.5	92.3	75,360	75.5	58.8	31.4	67.3	39.0	31.5	58.6	28.3
Fauquier, VA	51061	44,516	43.2	87.3	3,618	81.0	27.1	-0.3	30.7	2.5	...	...	3.5
Floyd, VA	51063	...	...	...	...	...	...	...	...	...	...	...	...
Fluvanna, VA	51065	17,550	40.2	89.2	1,166	77.1	30.2	2.8	34.3	11.1	...	...	...
Franklin, VA	51067	35,757	58.7	78.6	2,295	45.3	14.3	-13.1	14.8	5.3	...	...	...
Frederick, VA	51069	48,792	49.3	84.3	3,812	77.9	23.1	-4.3	23.2	10.6	...	...	16.2
Giles, VA	51071	...	...	...	...	...	...	...	...	...	...	...	...
Gloucester, VA	51073	26,478	50.3	83.5	1,836	83.1	17.6	-9.8	18.1	7.3	...	...	...
Goochland, VA	51075	15,728	47.5	78.1	248	74.2	31.6	4.2	44.9	1.6	...	...	...
Grayson, VA	51077	...	...	...	...	...	...	...	...	...	...	...	...
Greene, VA	51079	...	...	...	...	...	...	...	...	...	...	...	...
Greensville, VA	51081	...	...	...	...	...	...	...	...	...	...	...	...
Halifax, VA	51083	24,822	64.7	71.7	1,818	80.7	12.5	-14.9	14.6	7.8	...	...	...
Hanover, VA	51085	65,837	40.1	89.6	6,884	65.9	30.6	3.2	31.5	17.7	...	...	31.0
Henrico, VA	51087	195,667	35.0	88.8	17,178	76.3	38.3	10.9	44.5	21.2	...	54.8	21.6
Henry, VA	51089	39,550	63.8	70.1	2,106	91.0	10.3	-17.1	11.3	8.3	...	...	...
Highland, VA	51091	...	...	...	...	...	...	...	...	...	...	...	...
Isle of Wight, VA	51093	24,044	47.4	85.9	2,390	79.7	24.3	-3.1	29.2	10.0	...	...	...
James City County, VA	51095	43,212	28.3	92.7	3,900	84.4	45.3	17.9	50.9	13.8	...	...	27.9
King and Queen, VA	51097	...	...	...	...	...	...	...	...	...	...	...	...
King George, VA	51099	14,421	43.4	90.3	1,224	84.4	27.8	0.4	32.1	10.2	...	...	...
King William, VA	51101	...	...	...	...	...	...	...	...	...	...	...	...
Lancaster, VA	51103	...	...	...	...	...	...	...	...	...	...	...	...
Lee, VA	51105	16,582	61.4	70.3	...	...	12.9	-14.5	13.3	...	...	...	...
Loudoun, VA	51107	174,439	21.3	93.4	19,587	70.3	56.3	28.9	59.7	45.2	...	63.0	30.1
Louisa, VA	51109	22,177	60.4	78.9	1,235	84.5	15.9	-11.5	17.9	4.4	...	...	...
Lunenburg, VA	51111	...	...	...	...	...	...	...	...	...	...	...	...
Madison, VA	51113	...	...	...	...	...	...	...	...	...	...	...	...
Mathews, VA	51115	...	...	...	...	...	...	...	...	...	...	...	...
Mecklenburg, VA	51117	23,112	60.5	74.6	1,039	65.0	13.2	-14.2	17.5	5.0	...	...	...
Middlesex, VA	51119	...	...	...	...	...	...	...	...	...	...	...	...
Montgomery, VA	51121	46,516	35.7	88.8	29,175	97.0	39.7	12.3	37.5	38.0	...	...	...
Nelson, VA	51125	...	...	...	...	...	...	...	...	...	...	...	...
New Kent, VA	51127	...	...	...	...	...	...	...	...	...	...	...	...
Northampton, VA	51131	...	...	...	...	...	...	...	...	...	...	...	...
Northumberland, VA	51133	...	...	...	...	...	...	...	...	...	...	...	...
Nottoway, VA	51135	...	...	...	...	...	...	...	...	...	...	...	...
Orange, VA	51137	22,900	52.3	84.4	866	83.3	18.7	-8.7	20.9	8.6	...	...	...
Page, VA	51139	17,430	73.7	69.5	752	94.7	9.8	-17.6	9.6	...	...	...	...
Patrick, VA	51141	...	...	...	...	...	...	...	...	...	...	...	...
Pittsylvania, VA	51143	43,113	60.1	76.0	2,837	66.0	12.9	-14.5	14.9	6.5	...	...	0.7
Powhatan, VA	51145	20,594	54.9	77.9	733	65.3	20.3	-7.1	25.7	2.4	...	...	...
Prince Edward, VA	51147	11,688	63.8	79.9	4,666	77.2	18.2	-9.2	24.0	10.7	...	...	...
Prince George, VA	51149	22,181	49.7	85.1	1,854	68.3	19.4	-8.0	21.6	13.1	...	...	20.1
Prince William, VA	51153	221,097	34.5	88.5	23,635	76.4	37.1	9.7	42.8	33.3	...	48.6	16.1
Pulaski, VA	51155	25,810	57.4	79.0	1,629	90.1	13.1	-14.3	12.7	11.0	...	...	...
Rappahannock, VA	51157	...	...	...	...	...	...	...	...	...	...	...	...
Richmond, VA	51159	...	...	...	...	...	...	...	...	...	...	...	...
Roanoke, VA	51161	62,691	37.2	89.3	4,257	68.5	31.8	4.4	31.9	22.4	...	39.1	33.0
Rockbridge, VA	51163	15,306	53.8	78.9	1,556	55.6	23.2	-4.2	23.9	...	...	...	...
Rockingham, VA	51165	50,010	59.8	76.7	4,291	52.4	20.8	-6.6	21.3	...	...	...	10.6

[3]May be of any race
... Not available

Table C-1. Population, School, and Student Characteristics by County—*Continued*

County	State/County Code	County Type[1]	Population, 2009 Total	Population, 2009 Percent 5–17 years	Percent of related children 5–17 years in poverty, 2008	Percent of children under 19 years with no health insurance, 2007	Number of Schools and Students, 2008-2009 School Districts	Number of Schools and Students, 2008-2009 Schools	Number of Schools and Students, 2008-2009 Students	Resident enrollment 2006-2008 K–12 enrollment Number	Resident enrollment 2006-2008 K–12 enrollment Percent public
			1	2	3	4	5	6	7	8	9
Russell, VA	51167	6	29,250	14.9	22.5	6.6	1	14	4,326	4,466	95.3
Scott, VA	51169	3	22,585	14.2	19.7	5.8	1	14	3,963	...	...
Shenandoah, VA	51171	6	41,036	15.9	13.6	12.4	1	10	6,326	6,630	90.7
Smyth, VA	51173	6	31,738	15.2	20.8	6.4	1	14	5,042	5,092	98.2
Southampton, VA	51175	6	18,483	15.0	19.2	9.9	1	6	2,850	...	...
Spotsylvania, VA	51177	1	120,977	20.9	7.6	10.4	1	33	24,116	24,420	90.4
Stafford, VA	51179	1	124,166	22.2	4.8	9.9	1	30	26,850	25,648	92.3
Surry, VA	51181	1	7,088	14.9	14.4	10.5	1	3	1,041	...	...
Sussex, VA	51183	1	12,116	12.2	21.6	9.8	1	5	1,215	...	...
Tazewell, VA	51185	7	44,907	15.1	22.5	6.8	1	17	6,856	6,644	92.5
Warren, VA	51187	1	36,713	17.1	10.6	10.7	1	8	5,434	6,233	88.4
Washington, VA	51191	3	53,018	14.5	17.0	7.7	1	17	7,514	7,284	94.6
Westmoreland, VA	51193	7	17,686	14.7	21.5	12.5	2	6	2,393	...	...
Wise, VA	51195	7	41,773	15.6	26.2	5.9	1	16	6,782	6,381	95.4
Wythe, VA	51197	6	28,868	15.0	18.1	8.4	1	13	4,419	4,062	96.2
York, VA	51199	1	61,140	20.0	4.3	13.0	1	19	12,893	11,509	93.9
Alexandria City, VA	51510	1	150,006	10.2	13.2	11.9	1	19	11,223	16,164	82.8
Bedford City, VA	51515	3	6,350	15.1	21.6	6.7	2[8]	22[8]	10,926[8]	...	...
Bristol City, VA	51520	3	17,690	14.1	35.3	5.3	1	6	2,414	...	...
Buena Vista City, VA	51530	6	6,222	14.3	14.6	5.3	1	4	1,151	...	...
Charlottesville City, VA	51540	3	42,218	10.1	19.9	9.9	2[7]	36[7]	16,870[7]	5,116	90.4
Chesapeake City, VA	51550	1	222,455	19.3	9.6	9.6	1	46	39,901	42,026	89.9
Colonial Heights City, VA	51570	1	17,823	16.7	11.6	11.4	1	5	2,902	...	...
Covington City, VA	51580	6	6,149	15.7	17.8	7.2	1	3	917	...	...
Danville City, VA	51590	3	44,400	14.7	30.7	5.4	1	17	6,556	7,092	87.0
Emporia City, VA	51595	6	5,635	17.2	25.2	6.2	2[12]	4[12]	2,726[12]	...	...
Fairfax City, VA	51600	1	24,665	13.8	6.1	16.0	1	(9)	(9)	3,443	87.0
Falls Church City, VA	51610	1	11,957	16.8	2.4	11.7	1	4	1,967	...	...
Franklin City, VA	51620	6	8,814	16.8	28.8	6.6	1	3	1,299	...	...
Fredericksburg City, VA	51630	1	23,193	12.5	20.7	10.9	1	5	2,842	2,626	88.5
Galax City, VA	51640	6	6,880	16.8	30.7	7.0	1	3	1,361	...	...
Hampton City, VA	51650	1	144,236	15.6	18.4	8.4	1	37	21,806	24,473	92.6
Harrisonburg City, VA	51660	3	45,137	10.5	20.3	15.7	2[14]	31[14]	16,457[14]	4,897	93.0
Hopewell City, VA	51670	1	23,123	18.2	22.7	7.0	1	7	4,188	4,650	97.3
Lexington City, VA	51678	6	6,901	7.4	9.4	7.9	1	2	491	...	...
Lynchburg City, VA	51680	3	73,933	13.6	22.0	6.0	1	16	8,634	9,946	81.2
Manassas City, VA	51683	1	36,514	19.5	11.5	14.2	1	9	6,566	7,166	90.8
Manassas Park City, VA	51685	1	12,042	19.5	10.0	14.4	1	4	2,464	...	...
Martinsville City, VA	51690	4	14,635	15.9	29.7	5.3	1	5	2,544	...	...
Newport News City, VA	51700	1	193,172	17.6	17.1	8.4	1	46	31,298	35,040	90.6
Norfolk City, VA	51710	1	233,333	15.4	25.7	7.9	1	54	34,341	41,351	87.5
Norton City, VA	51720	7	3,713	15.1	28.6	3.6	1	2	805	...	...
Petersburg City, VA	51730	1	32,986	16.2	29.8	5.7	1	11	4,675	5,527	94.3
Poquoson City, VA	51735	1	11,794	19.7	4.3	9.7	1	4	2,491	...	...
Portsmouth City, VA	51740	1	99,321	16.5	25.0	7.0	1	22	15,323	18,400	89.7
Radford City, VA	51750	3	16,184	8.1	15.5	6.4	1	4	1,497	...	...
Richmond City, VA	51760	1	204,451	12.9	36.4	7.2	3	149	23,776	29,931	83.3
Roanoke City, VA	51770	2	94,482	14.2	24.4	6.0	1	30	13,214	14,699	93.3
Salem City, VA	51775	2	25,462	14.9	9.8	6.2	1	6	3,930	3,330	94.7
Staunton City, VA	51790	4	23,886	13.8	19.2	7.5	2	8	2,866	3,518	87.7
Suffolk City, VA	51800	1	83,659	18.7	12.9	9.8	1	21	14,093	15,441	87.3
Virginia Beach City, VA	51810	1	433,575	17.5	9.1	11.5	1	86	71,554	81,185	90.8
Waynesboro City, VA	51820	4	22,241	16.2	21.0	9.9	1	6	3,188	3,757	97.7
Williamsburg City, VA	51830	1	12,729	7.6	29.3	8.7	(13)	(13)	(13)	...	...
Winchester City, VA	51840	3	26,322	14.2	16.8	10.0	2[11]	25[11]	16,842[11]	3,686	96.1

[1]County type codes are from the Economic Research Service of the United States Department of Agriculture. See notes and definitions for more information.
[7]Albemarle county is included with Charlottesville city
[8]Bedford county is included with Bedford city
[9]Fairfax city is included with Fairfax county
[11]Frederick county is included with Winchester city
[12]Greensville county is included with Emporia city
[13]Williamsburg city is included with James City county
[14]Rockingham county is included with Harrisonburg city
... Not available

Table C-1. Population, School, and Student Characteristics by County—*Continued*

County	State/County Code	Characteristics of students, 2008-2009					Staff and students, 2008-2009			
		Percent with IEP[2]	Percent eligible for free or reduced lunch	Percent minority	Percent English Language Learners	Number of graduates, 2006-2007	Total staff	Number of teachers	Student/teacher ratio	Central admin. Staff
		10	11	12	13	14	15	16	17	18
Russell, VA	51167	17.8	47.3	1.3	0.1	266	686	243	17.8	12
Scott, VA	51169	17.9	48.9	2.6	0.5	246	692	231	17.2	10
Shenandoah, VA	51171	12.8	33.6	14.1	5.1	396	1,132	385	16.4	21
Smyth, VA	51173	16.5	53.7	4.5	0.7	315	916	244	20.7	14
Southampton, VA	51175	16.8	42.4	46.2	...	170	525	164	17.4	15
Spotsylvania, VA	51177	11.9	23.3	30.9	3.2	1,529	2,781	1,395	17.3	104
Stafford, VA	51179	8.9	17.5	33.1	3.9	1,803	3,520	1,442	18.6	55
Surry, VA	51181	13.6	52.4	66.1	0.1	74	256	72	14.5	14
Sussex, VA	51183	16.0	76.8	78.3	2.0	91	285	93	13.1	8
Tazewell, VA	51185	14.4	48.0	4.3	0.2	409	1,005	403	17.0	21
Warren, VA	51187	11.1	29.7	12.8	2.2	368	713	321	16.9	27
Washington, VA	51191	14.7	40.2	3.6	0.6	501	1,025	451	16.7	33
Westmoreland, VA	51193	11.7	54.5	53.1	7.1	151	376	138	17.3	10
Wise, VA	51195	13.3	50.5	2.6	0.3	456	1,253	440	15.4	23
Wythe, VA	51197	10.6	41.5	6.7	0.2	273	526	254	17.4	15
York, VA	51199	9.7	15.3	27.3	1.6	988	2,212	715	18.0	27
Alexandria City, VA	51510	16.2	48.7	72.1	25.6	525	2,429	737	15.2	108
Bedford City, VA	51515	10.1[8]	51.8	21.6	0.9[8]	763[8]	1,869[8]	677[8]	16.1[8]	29[8]
Bristol City, VA	51520	15.4	55.5	12.7	0.4	127	389	156	15.5	16
Buena Vista City, VA	51530	12.6	36.1	7.8	0.1	76	224	81	14.2	5
Charlottesville City, VA	51540	13.6[7]	50.9	51.4	6.8[7]	11,547	2,998[7]	1,073[7]	15.7[7]	55[7]
Chesapeake City, VA	51550	17.6	25.6	42.1	1.2	2,966	6,296	2,156	18.5	232
Colonial Heights City, VA	51570	14.5	22.1	24.4	3.6	202	485	158	18.4	15
Covington City, VA	51580	19.4	48.7	19.8	0.3	57	172	66	13.9	7
Danville City, VA	51590	15.1	66.6	75.4	2.8	464	1,223	455	14.4	59
Emporia City, VA	51595	12.3[12]	55.6	77.4	1.9[12]	163[12]	429[12]	155[12]	17.6[12]	17[12]
Fairfax City, VA	51600	(9)	23.1	50.0	(9)	(9)	(9)	(9)	(9)	(9)
Falls Church City, VA	51610	13.1	7.3	25.5	9.2	159	419	138	14.3	17
Franklin City, VA	51620	15.6	66.8	80.3	0.1	75	254	92	14.1	9
Fredericksburg City, VA	51630	10.7	48.3	61.4	9.4	179	516	170	16.7	27
Galax City, VA	51640	10.4	54.6	32.6	16.7	66	191	67	20.3	8
Hampton City, VA	51650	13.9	45.1	69.3	1.7	1,347	3,891	1,285	17.0	129
Harrisonburg City, VA	51660	11.3[14]	57.9	51.3	15.4[14]	1,030[14]	2,807[14]	1,090[14]	15.1[14]	50[14]
Hopewell City, VA	51670	15.3	60.6	62.3	2.5	176	644	242	17.3	20
Lexington City, VA	51678	12.0	27.1	10.9	1.4	...	67	38	12.9	1
Lynchburg City, VA	51680	14.8	52.9	57.4	1.9	576	1,270	552	15.6	31
Manassas City, VA	51683	14.0	33.0	61.4	35.0	362	981	378	17.4	32
Manassas Park City, VA	51685	11.1	44.1	62.1	25.9	150	360	140	17.6	16
Martinsville City, VA	51690	11.9	65.4	66.6	5.6	200	458	141	18.0	13
Newport News City, VA	51700	13.2	49.5	67.4	2.0	1,905	4,695	1,682	18.6	77
Norfolk City, VA	51710	13.9	58.3	70.2	1.5	1,599	5,553	2,148	16.0	266
Norton City, VA	51720	13.7	48.2	13.3	0.2	36	129	36	22.4	5
Petersburg City, VA	51730	10.4	68.7	92.3	2.4	283	714	289	16.2	36
Poquoson City, VA	51735	10.7	10.6	4.7	0.4	223	337	149	16.7	14
Portsmouth City, VA	51740	13.4	54.4	76.6	0.3	782	2,298	794	19.3	84
Radford City, VA	51750	14.4	33.9	16.1	0.3	109	234	106	14.1	8
Richmond City, VA	51760	22.5	66.5	91.5	3.2	1,169	4,289	1,407	16.9	75
Roanoke City, VA	51770	13.8	59.2	53.2	6.6	583	2,527	850	15.5	108
Salem City, VA	51775	12.4	23.8	15.5	1.3	277	587	249	15.8	19
Staunton City, VA	51790	18.3	47.7	28.5	1.1	195	763	179	16.0	29
Suffolk City, VA	51800	12.1	39.6	61.5	0.2	729	2,328	804	17.5	56
Virginia Beach City, VA	51810	13.2	28.3	40.5	1.5	4,902	10,923	3,984	18.0	276
Waynesboro City, VA	51820	10.4	48.0	25.6	3.9	183	560	210	15.2	16
Williamsburg City, VA	51830	(13)	33.1	34.7	(13)	(13)	(13)	(13)	(13)	(13)
Winchester City, VA	51840	12.8[11]	40.3	32.9	6.6[11]	1,042[11]	2,726[11]	1,051[11]	16.0[11]	121[11]

[2]IEP= Individual Education Program. See notes and definitions for more information
[7]Albemarle county is included with Charlottesville city
[8]Bedford county is included with Bedford city
[9]Fairfax city is included with Fairfax county
[11]Frederick county is included with Winchester city
[12]Greensville county is included with Emporia city
[13]Williamsburg city is included with James City county
[14]Rockingham county is included with Harrisonburg city
... Not available

Table C-1. Population, School, and Student Characteristics by County—*Continued*

County	State/County Code	Revenues, 2007-2008				Current expenditures, 2007-2008			Resident population 16 to 19 years, 2006-2008			
		Total revenue ($1,000's)	Percentage of revenue from			Amount ($1,000's)	Amount per student	Percent for instruc-tion	Total population 16 to 19 years	Percent en-rolled in school	Percent high school graduates, not enrolled in school	Percent not enrolled, not grads, not employed or not in labor force
			Federal gov't	State gov't	Local gov't							
	19	19	20	21	22	23	24	25	26	27	28	29
Russell, VA	51167	42,768	14.9	65.4	19.8	38,529	8,709	60.9	...	...	...	...
Scott, VA	51169	37,805	9.4	71.7	18.9	35,995	9,008	60.0	...	...	...	...
Shenandoah, VA	51171	64,709	4.9	51.2	43.9	60,854	9,712	67.0	...	...	...	...
Smyth, VA	51173	51,468	10.2	66.1	23.6	47,006	9,279	65.0	...	...	...	...
Southampton, VA	51175	32,621	7.7	56.2	36.1	28,343	9,667	57.0	...	...	...	...
Spotsylvania, VA	51177	265,169	4.0	48.0	48.0	227,666	9,367	60.7	6,393	84.5	9.5	1.6
Stafford, VA	51179	259,533	4.9	51.1	44.0	244,616	9,202	59.9	7,502	86.9	9.8	2.1
Surry, VA	51181	16,726	6.1	17.5	76.4	14,730	14,109	57.4	...	...	...	...
Sussex, VA	51183	20,905	8.4	43.0	48.6	19,456	14,955	52.0	...	...	...	...
Tazewell, VA	51185	61,636	10.9	67.5	21.6	59,331	8,589	64.2	...	...	...	...
Warren, VA	51187	50,027	5.4	53.4	41.2	47,040	8,778	58.1	...	...	...	...
Washington, VA	51191	75,033	8.0	53.9	38.1	69,101	9,139	61.2	...	...	...	...
Westmoreland, VA	51193	26,393	11.7	52.4	35.9	24,113	9,923	58.6	...	...	...	...
Wise, VA	51195	72,413	12.7	61.7	25.6	61,867	9,054	63.4	...	...	...	...
Wythe, VA	51197	42,570	10.4	57.7	31.9	38,837	8,831	63.8	...	...	...	...
York, VA	51199	125,732	10.8	49.4	39.8	114,786	8,943	59.3	...	...	...	...
Alexandria City, VA	51510	206,451	4.6	14.1	81.2	193,671	18,323	59.6	...	...	...	...
Bedford City, VA	51515	132,209[8]	5.0[8]	41.7[8]	53.3[8]	94,158[8]	8,535[8]	59.6[8]	...	...	...	...
Bristol City, VA	51520	25,333	10.3	57.9	31.8	23,038	9,754	65.8	...	...	...	...
Buena Vista City, VA	51530	11,190	4.7	69.0	26.3	10,486	9,118	60.3	...	...	...	...
Charlottesville City, VA	51540	248,564[7]	4.9[7]	26.5[7]	68.6[7]	211,420[7]	12,529[7]	57.9[7]	...	...	...	...
Chesapeake City, VA	51550	466,334	5.3	47.5	47.2	417,893	10,447	63.0	13,553	82.4	11.9	4.0
Colonial Heights City, VA	51570	38,622	3.5	33.8	62.7	31,344	10,727	66.3	...	...	...	...
Covington City, VA	51580	11,311	7.8	50.6	41.6	10,680	11,242	66.3	...	...	...	...
Danville City, VA	51590	72,941	11.4	57.4	31.2	67,004	9,820	60.8	...	...	...	...
Emporia City, VA	51595	36,331[12]	9.4[12]	48.7[12]	41.9[12]	26,084[12]	9,873[12]	62.2[12]	...	...	...	...
Fairfax City, VA	51600	(9)	(9)	(9)	(9)	(9)	(9)	(9)	...	...	...	...
Falls Church City, VA	51610	(10)	(10)	(10)	(10)	(10)	(10)	(10)	...	...	...	...
Franklin City, VA	51620	17,709	9.9	52.8	37.3	15,722	11,543	56.2	...	...	...	...
Fredericksburg City, VA	51630	36,921	9.2	20.5	70.3	35,314	12,795	62.2	...	...	...	...
Galax City, VA	51640	16,931	7.7	62.9	29.4	11,883	8,686	63.6	...	...	...	...
Hampton City, VA	51650	236,642	9.0	58.5	32.4	222,920	9,983	58.8	9,122	85.9	9.2	3.0
Harrisonburg City, VA	51660	199,060[14]	5.9[14]	42.9[14]	51.2[14]	161,029[14]	9,832[14]	63.7[14]	...	...	...	...
Hopewell City, VA	51670	44,028	11.4	57.2	31.5	40,510	9,615	62.7	...	...	...	...
Lexington City, VA	51678	6,217	4.1	48.6	47.3	4,481	9,182	63.8	...	...	...	...
Lynchburg City, VA	51680	96,861	9.5	49.9	40.6	91,381	10,485	63.1	...	...	...	...
Manassas City, VA	51683	90,481	4.0	36.7	59.3	80,271	12,399	62.3	...	...	...	...
Manassas Park City, VA	51685	37,308	3.7	37.9	58.4	29,647	11,783	58.8	...	...	...	...
Martinsville City, VA	51690	26,885	10.8	58.6	30.6	25,424	10,153	58.6	...	...	...	...
Newport News City, VA	51700	359,855	10.9	53.0	36.1	316,526	10,032	57.5	12,021	75.3	19.4	4.2
Norfolk City, VA	51710	383,347	11.9	55.0	33.1	360,804	10,290	62.6	17,151	69.7	22.0	4.6
Norton City, VA	51720	7,929	10.0	58.0	32.0	6,704	8,307	66.3	...	...	...	...
Petersburg City, VA	51730	58,384	12.8	58.8	28.5	49,689	10,139	55.7	...	...	...	...
Poquoson City, VA	51735	22,651	4.3	54.9	40.8	21,209	8,480	60.7	...	...	...	...
Portsmouth City, VA	51740	187,994	9.4	52.4	38.2	152,946	9,928	59.0	6,201	64.8	24.1	7.2
Radford City, VA	51750	17,070	5.7	50.2	44.1	14,326	9,096	62.4	...	...	...	...
Richmond City, VA	51760	319,884	13.4	42.1	44.5	305,938	12,879	59.5	13,947	85.1	8.9	4.2
Roanoke City, VA	51770	174,832	11.9	43.7	44.4	142,593	11,019	60.3	4,278	75.7	16.5	3.7
Salem City, VA	51775	41,932	4.0	45.4	50.6	38,150	9,663	63.7	...	...	...	...
Staunton City, VA	51790	34,855	6.6	48.8	44.6	31,129	11,275	65.0	...	...	...	...
Suffolk City, VA	51800	167,564	6.6	47.1	46.2	131,156	9,351	64.1	4,150	81.6	6.4	5.9
Virginia Beach City, VA	51810	808,886	7.7	46.6	45.7	749,676	10,344	58.9	24,801	80.2	15.7	2.4
Waynesboro City, VA	51820	37,532	7.4	45.0	47.7	30,733	9,747	62.2	...	...	...	...
Williamsburg City, VA	51830	(13)	(13)	(13)	(13)	(13)	(13)	(13)	...	...	...	...
Winchester City, VA	51840	208,427[11]	4.0[11]	38.7[11]	57.3[11]	175,820[11]	10,511[11]	60.6[11]	...	...	...	...

[7]Albemarle county is included with Charlottesville city
[8]Bedford county is included with Bedford city
[9]Fairfax city is included with Fairfax county
[11]Frederick county is included with Winchester city
[12]Greensville county is included with Emporia city
[13]Williamsburg city is included with James City county
[14]Rockingham county is included with Harrisonburg city
... Not available

Table C-1. Population, School, and Student Characteristics by County—*Continued*

County	State/County Code	High school graduates, 2006-2008			College enrollment, 2006-2008		College graduates, 2006-2008 (percent)						
		Population 25 years and over	High school diploma or less (percent)	High school diploma or more (percent)	Number	Percent public	Bachelor's degree or more	+/- U.S. percent with Bachelor's degree or more	Non-Hispanic White	Black or African American	American Indian and Alaska Native	Asian, Hawaiian, and Pacific Islander	Hispanic or Latino[3]
		30	31	32	33	34	35	36	37	38	39	40	41
Russell, VA	51167	20,654	65.5	71.6	1,359	95.9	8.4	-19.0	8.6	...	...	...	...
Scott, VA	51169	16,573	66.1	72.1	...	...	9.9	-17.5	9.9	...	...	...	...
Shenandoah, VA	51171	28,640	60.3	81.6	1,323	77.5	16.2	-11.2	16.5	22.9	...	...	...
Smyth, VA	51173	23,253	62.3	74.3	1,376	74.9	11.8	-15.6	12.0	...	...	...	...
Southampton, VA	51175	...	...	...	...	...	...	...	...	...	...	...	...
Spotsylvania, VA	51177	75,858	42.9	87.7	6,707	84.6	29.5	2.1	30.3	26.4	...	55.6	17.2
Stafford, VA	51179	74,164	36.8	90.8	7,711	75.2	34.5	7.1	36.0	31.1	...	40.7	26.1
Surry, VA	51181	...	...	...	...	...	...	...	...	...	...	...	...
Sussex, VA	51183	...	...	...	...	...	...	...	...	...	...	...	...
Tazewell, VA	51185	31,509	57.7	75.0	1,832	74.5	14.0	-13.4	13.5	24.9	...	...	...
Warren, VA	51187	24,185	54.5	83.0	1,960	71.1	20.2	-7.2	19.9	20.0	...	...	...
Washington, VA	51191	37,979	52.0	79.2	3,620	50.2	20.8	-6.6	21.0	...	...	...	...
Westmoreland, VA	51193	...	...	...	...	...	...	...	...	...	...	...	...
Wise, VA	51195	28,552	65.6	68.9	2,163	95.0	11.1	-16.3	11.9	...	...	...	...
Wythe, VA	51197	20,632	56.5	75.2	720	91.5	13.8	-13.6	13.7	...	...	...	...
York, VA	51199	40,360	26.1	94.0	5,521	85.5	40.9	13.5	44.4	22.8	...	46.7	35.8
Alexandria City, VA	51510	104,301	22.0	90.8	10,181	61.5	59.9	32.5	74.2	29.4	...	60.0	30.4
Bedford City, VA	51515	...	...	...	...	...	...	...	...	...	...	...	...
Bristol City, VA	51520	...	...	...	...	...	...	...	...	...	...	...	...
Buena Vista City, VA	51530	...	...	...	...	...	...	...	...	...	...	...	...
Charlottesville City, VA	51540	23,906	35.8	83.9	10,153	97.6	46.6	19.2	56.2	11.0	...	...	...
Chesapeake City, VA	51550	140,799	40.3	88.6	15,281	76.5	26.9	-0.5	29.0	21.1	...	41.6	22.1
Colonial Heights City, VA	51570	...	...	...	...	...	...	...	...	...	...	...	...
Covington City, VA	51580	...	...	...	...	...	...	...	...	...	...	...	...
Danville City, VA	51590	31,386	55.8	74.6	2,604	75.0	14.6	-12.8	19.0	8.1	...	...	...
Emporia City, VA	51595	...	...	...	...	...	...	...	...	...	...	...	...
Fairfax City, VA	51600	16,673	24.4	91.2	1,713	80.9	51.7	24.3	55.8	47.2	...	59.2	21.1
Falls Church City, VA	51610	...	...	...	...	...	...	...	...	...	...	...	...
Franklin City, VA	51620	...	...	...	...	...	...	...	...	...	...	...	...
Fredericksburg City, VA	51630	12,944	47.5	85.1	3,220	86.8	30.9	3.5	37.6	14.3	...	...	...
Galax City, VA	51640	...	...	...	...	...	...	...	...	...	...	...	...
Hampton City, VA	51650	94,500	45.1	87.8	14,266	61.9	20.7	-6.7	23.1	17.1	...	32.5	22.2
Harrisonburg City, VA	51660	20,080	49.9	77.5	15,381	89.2	31.7	4.3	36.6	22.0	...	...	8.6
Hopewell City, VA	51670	14,682	61.6	80.3	799	78.7	12.2	-15.2	14.3	7.4	...	...	...
Lexington City, VA	51678	...	...	...	...	...	...	...	...	...	...	...	...
Lynchburg City, VA	51680	43,181	46.6	83.2	12,160	18.1	27.6	0.2	33.9	10.4	...	...	...
Manassas City, VA	51683	22,213	49.7	76.7	1,642	78.1	26.5	-0.9	33.5	25.7	...	53.9	3.4
Manassas Park City, VA	51685	...	...	...	...	...	...	...	...	...	...	...	...
Martinsville City, VA	51690	...	...	...	...	...	...	...	...	...	...	...	...
Newport News City, VA	51700	112,139	40.9	88.2	14,168	79.7	23.0	-4.4	28.0	15.9	...	32.3	15.8
Norfolk City, VA	51710	136,744	47.5	83.6	20,640	81.3	23.4	-4.0	32.8	10.6	...	39.0	20.3
Norton City, VA	51720	...	...	...	...	...	...	...	...	...	...	...	...
Petersburg City, VA	51730	21,467	61.3	72.2	1,096	81.9	15.5	-11.9	22.8	13.2	...	...	...
Poquoson City, VA	51735	...	...	...	...	...	...	...	...	...	...	...	...
Portsmouth City, VA	51740	63,636	49.3	81.3	6,645	80.9	18.9	-8.5	24.6	13.9	...	...	15.1
Radford City, VA	51750	...	...	...	...	...	...	...	...	...	...	...	...
Richmond City, VA	51760	129,862	45.3	80.0	23,176	68.9	32.2	4.8	56.3	11.8	...	64.4	11.6
Roanoke City, VA	51770	65,545	49.5	81.0	4,830	74.2	20.7	-6.7	25.1	8.8	...	12.5	16.4
Salem City, VA	51775	16,896	47.5	84.2	3,257	40.0	25.3	-2.1	25.6	25.5	...	...	...
Staunton City, VA	51790	16,669	49.8	81.0	1,504	59.6	26.8	-0.6	28.5	12.7	...	...	...
Suffolk City, VA	51800	52,416	45.7	84.0	4,347	76.0	24.0	-3.4	29.2	14.5	...	53.4	35.1
Virginia Beach City, VA	51810	282,313	33.3	92.2	32,492	75.2	31.3	3.9	34.2	20.1	...	39.8	20.2
Waynesboro City, VA	51820	14,787	58.5	79.1	694	65.6	20.2	-7.2	21.2	12.0	...	...	...
Williamsburg City, VA	51830	...	...	...	...	...	...	...	...	...	...	...	...
Winchester City, VA	51840	17,361	51.4	80.8	1,663	40.8	27.5	0.1	33.2	...	...	...	4.5

[3]May be of any race
... Not available

Table C-1. Population, School, and Student Characteristics by County—*Continued*

County	State/County Code	County Type[1]	Population, 2009 Total	Population, 2009 Percent 5–17 years	Percent of related children 5-17 years in poverty, 2008	Percent of children under 19 years with no health insurance, 2007	Number of Schools and Students, 2008-2009 School Districts	Number of Schools and Students, 2008-2009 Schools	Number of Schools and Students, 2008-2009 Students	Resident enrollment, 2006-2008 K–12 enrollment Number	Resident enrollment, 2006-2008 K–12 enrollment Percent public
			1	2	3	4	5	6	7	8	9
WASHINGTON	53000	X	6,664,195	16.8	12.5	8.2	309	2,345	1,037,018	1,108,377	90.7
Adams, WA	53001	6	17,732	24.4	25.4	14.3	5	11	4,162	...	...
Asotin, WA	53003	3	21,432	16.1	19.9	5.9	2	11	3,302	3,528	88.8
Benton, WA	53005	3	168,294	19.7	13.9	7.1	6	56	31,495	30,867	93.6
Chelan, WA	53007	3	72,372	17.9	14.8	13.2	8	36	12,868	12,819	93.7
Clallam, WA	53009	5	71,413	13.8	17.3	9.1	5	29	10,622	10,340	92.1
Clark, WA	53011	1	432,002	19.1	12.1	7.7	10	131	76,618	79,495	92.8
Columbia, WA	53013	6	4,040	15.0	19.2	5.4	2	4	541	...	...
Cowlitz, WA	53015	3	101,966	18.1	16.3	6.6	6	42	17,715	17,866	94.4
Douglas, WA	53017	3	37,565	20.1	14.8	12.1	6	21	6,865	6,838	97.3
Ferry, WA	53019	9	7,520	17.0	26.7	7.6	5	12	1,052	...	...
Franklin, WA	53021	3	77,355	23.5	21.0	22.4	5	28	15,889	15,390	90.4
Garfield, WA	53023	8	2,101	13.9	17.1	10.2	1	2	331	...	...
Grant, WA	53025	4	88,098	21.6	22.5	13.8	10	53	18,268	17,967	95.8
Grays Harbor, WA	53027	4	71,797	16.0	18.3	7.9	13	40	11,242	11,896	93.2
Island, WA	53029	4	81,054	14.1	10.9	12.0	3	24	8,712	12,994	91.4
Jefferson, WA	53031	6	29,676	11.7	16.8	9.3	5	15	2,931	3,768	89.5
King, WA	53033	1	1,916,441	14.9	8.6	7.1	20	475	239,309	282,830	86.8
Kitsap, WA	53035	3	240,862	16.5	9.6	8.8	6	79	38,098	41,573	90.8
Kittitas, WA	53037	6	39,532	13.1	13.1	9.4	6	19	5,378	5,237	96.3
Klickitat, WA	53039	6	20,554	16.8	22.3	9.2	10	20	3,258	3,468	96.8
Lewis, WA	53041	4	74,741	17.2	17.7	7.5	14	41	12,240	12,956	91.5
Lincoln, WA	53043	8	10,248	17.3	17.0	10.5	8	15	2,151	...	...
Mason, WA	53045	6	58,016	15.2	16.2	9.0	7	21	8,237	9,381	94.3
Okanogan, WA	53047	6	40,552	17.0	26.3	10.4	8	27	6,221	7,302	95.2
Pacific, WA	53049	7	21,272	13.1	21.9	8.4	6	18	2,843	3,090	96.7
Pend Oreille, WA	53051	8	12,946	17.4	23.7	7.2	3	9	1,773	...	...
Pierce, WA	53053	1	796,836	17.5	12.8	8.5	17	264	131,016	141,262	91.4
San Juan, WA	53055	9	15,484	12.0	12.1	19.6	4	14	1,636	...	...
Skagit, WA	53057	3	119,534	17.0	12.9	9.5	8	54	19,339	19,603	93.5
Skamania, WA	53059	1	10,894	17.3	13.4	11.4	4	9	1,294	...	...
Snohomish, WA	53061	1	694,571	17.7	8.1	7.9	14	239	127,545	123,674	90.3
Spokane, WA	53063	2	468,684	16.7	15.4	6.3	16	182	75,666	77,907	89.8
Stevens, WA	53065	6	42,334	18.4	20.0	7.4	12	36	6,860	7,594	90.7
Thurston, WA	53067	3	250,979	16.5	10.0	7.5	10	78	41,418	39,445	92.8
Wahkiakum, WA	53069	8	4,062	14.1	19.6	9.6	1	2	472	...	...
Walla Walla, WA	53071	4	59,059	16.5	18.6	9.1	7	28	8,784	10,068	89.5
Whatcom, WA	53073	3	200,434	15.0	13.0	8.5	7	72	26,454	31,027	89.8
Whitman, WA	53075	4	42,689	10.6	12.7	9.4	13	26	4,546	4,622	93.0
Yakima, WA	53077	3	239,054	21.7	23.6	8.5	16	102	49,867	49,858	94.7
WEST VIRGINIA	54000	X	1,819,777	15.4	20.6	8.9	57	772	282,729	282,292	93.2
Barbour, WV	54001	7	15,758	15.1	29.1	9.6	1	9	2,496	...	...
Berkeley, WV	54003	3	103,854	17.9	11.7	10.4	1	29	17,214	18,530	90.8
Boone, WV	54005	2	24,709	16.9	23.3	5.7	1	16	4,622	...	...
Braxton, WV	54007	8	14,434	15.2	26.7	9.5	1	8	2,289	...	...
Brooke, WV	54009	3	23,509	14.6	15.5	10.3	1	10	3,423	3,376	94.9
Cabell, WV	54011	2	95,214	13.9	22.9	7.7	1	29	12,522	13,952	92.1
Calhoun, WV	54013	8	7,118	15.0	29.3	8.3	1	4	1,126	...	...
Clay, WV	54015	2	10,022	16.9	31.0	6.8	1	6	2,026	...	...
Doddridge, WV	54017	9	7,202	16.4	26.1	11.7	1	3	1,206	...	...
Fayette, WV	54019	6	46,123	15.2	27.9	7.3	1	24	6,810	7,259	90.9
Gilmer, WV	54021	9	6,824	12.8	27.6	10.6	1	5	941	...	...
Grant, WV	54023	6	11,833	15.0	19.3	11.0	1	6	1,975	...	...
Greenbrier, WV	54025	7	34,527	15.1	20.3	9.8	1	13	5,248	5,479	87.3
Hampshire, WV	54027	3	22,695	17.0	20.1	15.5	2	13	3,892	4,281	91.6
Hancock, WV	54029	3	29,729	14.8	17.8	10.7	1	10	4,327	4,421	87.0
Hardy, WV	54031	8	13,611	16.1	15.8	12.0	1	6	2,353	...	...
Harrison, WV	54033	5	68,911	16.2	21.2	8.8	1	27	11,192	11,138	94.1
Jackson, WV	54035	6	28,067	16.3	20.0	9.2	1	13	5,067	4,398	95.3
Jefferson, WV	54037	1	52,750	17.2	9.3	11.4	1	15	8,398	9,531	90.2
Kanawha, WV	54039	2	191,663	15.2	19.5	7.4	2	94	29,121	29,688	92.0
Lewis, WV	54041	7	17,391	15.5	23.7	8.9	1	6	2,686	...	...
Lincoln, WV	54043	2	22,147	16.3	29.1	7.2	1	9	3,606	3,620	96.5
Logan, WV	54045	6	35,498	16.1	27.9	6.5	1	19	6,506	5,393	97.5
McDowell, WV	54047	7	22,398	15.7	42.8	4.4	1	14	3,675	3,095	99.1
Marion, WV	54049	4	56,706	14.3	21.9	10.9	1	21	8,122	8,181	94.3
Marshall, WV	54051	3	32,556	15.3	20.4	9.0	1	16	4,886	5,011	91.3
Mason, WV	54053	6	25,568	15.7	23.4	6.6	1	12	4,299	4,087	97.2
Mercer, WV	54055	5	61,921	15.2	24.8	7.1	1	25	9,538	8,935	96.9
Mineral, WV	54057	3	27,204	16.0	17.4	9.6	1	14	4,551	4,559	92.6

[1]County type codes are from the Economic Research Service of the United States Department of Agriculture. See notes and definitions for more information.
... Not available

Table C-1. Population, School, and Student Characteristics by County—*Continued*

County	State/County Code	Characteristics of students, 2008-2009				Number of graduates, 2006-2007	Staff and students, 2008-2009			
		Percent with IEP[2]	Percent eligible for free or reduced lunch	Percent minority	Percent English Language Learners		Total staff	Number of teachers	Student/teacher ratio	Central admin. Staff
		10	11	12	13	14	15	16	17	18
WASHINGTON	53000	12.1	38.2	31.9	8.0	62,894	104,610	54,427	19.1	2,854
Adams, WA	53001	8.9	73.0	72.2	31.3	212	453	240	17.3	15
Asotin, WA	53003	16.9	45.2	7.2	0.6	197	346	175	18.9	9
Benton, WA	53005	11.3	43.4	29.7	8.5	2,048	3,060	1,584	19.9	79
Chelan, WA	53007	9.9	54.4	42.0	18.3	820	1,399	702	18.3	57
Clallam, WA	53009	11.3	35.2	21.0	2.8	582	932	516	20.6	32
Clark, WA	53011	11.9	34.7	18.9	6.3	4,522	7,705	3,970	19.3	186
Columbia, WA	53013	7.8	42.9	13.3	...	33	61	34	15.9	3
Cowlitz, WA	53015	12.5	42.8	16.8	3.6	1,096	1,785	915	19.4	56
Douglas, WA	53017	11.6	56.5	43.0	19.2	450	745	387	17.7	20
Ferry, WA	53019	10.6	45.1	26.7	...	74	133	70	15.0	11
Franklin, WA	53021	11.5	66.7	72.9	34.4	596	1,665	857	18.5	52
Garfield, WA	53023	17.8	42.3	6.6	1.2	26	43	23	14.4	2
Grant, WA	53025	11.4	60.7	52.6	20.4	1,034	1,938	1,009	18.1	55
Grays Harbor, WA	53027	13.3	52.9	22.1	4.2	742	1,264	654	17.2	46
Island, WA	53029	11.4	29.1	22.5	1.9	561	804	432	20.2	24
Jefferson, WA	53031	12.6	39.5	13.1	1.0	241	313	161	18.2	15
King, WA	53033	11.4	30.3	41.5	10.3	16,266	23,878	12,564	19.0	520
Kitsap, WA	53035	13.5	28.8	19.8	1.6	2,709	4,119	2,042	18.7	108
Kittitas, WA	53037	10.6	32.7	16.4	4.5	321	512	281	19.1	25
Klickitat, WA	53039	15.4	46.7	24.7	7.6	218	384	206	15.8	18
Lewis, WA	53041	13.0	48.8	15.5	3.7	873	1,253	679	18.0	47
Lincoln, WA	53043	11.0	42.0	8.5	...	135	288	158	13.6	18
Mason, WA	53045	15.8	47.8	21.6	4.3	506	898	463	17.8	34
Okanogan, WA	53047	13.5	61.4	45.5	11.5	409	734	370	16.8	36
Pacific, WA	53049	15.2	57.9	25.0	6.8	236	356	188	15.1	17
Pend Oreille, WA	53051	12.4	53.5	11.4	...	145	199	111	16.0	11
Pierce, WA	53053	12.2	38.1	32.3	4.0	6,968	12,851	6,705	19.5	305
San Juan, WA	53055	13.0	27.7	11.8	2.0	137	192	103	15.9	11
Skagit, WA	53057	12.6	45.0	32.1	12.2	1104	2,123	1,038	18.6	62
Skamania, WA	53059	14.8	32.4	10.9	1.6	75	145	70	18.5	7
Snohomish, WA	53061	12.0	28.5	26.1	6.8	6,300	11,715	6,238	20.4	304
Spokane, WA	53063	13.4	41.9	12.1	2.3	5,004	7,792	4,121	18.4	209
Stevens, WA	53065	10.6	42.9	13.3	0.7	574	740	370	18.5	37
Thurston, WA	53067	12.5	28.8	22.7	1.9	2,532	4,229	2,089	19.8	113
Wahkiakum, WA	53069	18.0	47.7	8.9	1.7	36	48	27	17.5	2
Walla Walla, WA	53071	12.2	49.8	36.3	12.2	537	968	504	17.4	35
Whatcom, WA	53073	13.1	38.8	22.6	6.0	1,682	2,644	1,373	19.3	74
Whitman, WA	53075	10.1	31.3	14.2	1.6	349	559	293	15.5	28
Yakima, WA	53077	11.9	69.2	66.0	20.6	2,544	5,337	2,706	18.4	172
WEST VIRGINIA	54000	16.5	50.0	7.2	0.6	16,974	38,589	20,208	14.0	1,871
Barbour, WV	54001	16.9	61.4	2.4	0.1	162	333	181	13.8	12
Berkeley, WV	54003	16.4	42.3	18.6	2.0	889	2,368	1,217	14.1	123
Boone, WV	54005	18.6	51.1	1.3	...	228	671	369	12.5	33
Braxton, WV	54007	17.9	59.2	1.7	...	156	338	180	12.7	23
Brooke, WV	54009	22.3	45.0	2.3	0.1	241	467	255	13.4	35
Cabell, WV	54011	14.5	50.9	10.8	0.8	769	1,608	876	14.3	76
Calhoun, WV	54013	13.9	62.6	1.0	...	71	164	90	12.5	16
Clay, WV	54015	16.5	70.2	0.7	...	131	283	148	13.7	15
Doddridge, WV	54017	20.3	59.7	1.3	...	84	189	94	12.8	12
Fayette, WV	54019	14.0	55.9	7.1	0.1	456	938	500	13.6	52
Gilmer, WV	54021	15.9	61.2	2.9	0.2	75	136	68	13.8	12
Grant, WV	54023	19.3	51.4	2.0	0.1	127	274	148	13.3	14
Greenbrier, WV	54025	18.3	53.0	5.4	0.5	...	771	383	13.7	40
Hampshire, WV	54027	20.5	57.3	2.6	...	245	679	303	12.8	34
Hancock, WV	54029	19.8	41.5	5.1	0.1	292	560	298	14.5	31
Hardy, WV	54031	15.0	49.7	6.0	1.4	152	286	145	16.2	11
Harrison, WV	54033	17.7	46.6	4.4	1.0	666	1,533	776	14.4	76
Jackson, WV	54035	17.0	41.7	1.4	0.4	328	675	370	13.7	33
Jefferson, WV	54037	14.9	30.7	17.0	3.5	471	1,146	587	14.3	53
Kanawha, WV	54039	15.2	51.7	15.0	0.8	1,540	3,929	2,015	14.5	151
Lewis, WV	54041	18.3	51.9	1.6	0.1	162	384	193	13.9	21
Lincoln, WV	54043	20.7	66.4	0.9	...	176	498	260	13.9	21
Logan, WV	54045	12.8	50.7	3.6	...	394	841	433	15.0	38
McDowell, WV	54047	17.4	78.3	11.3	...	269	565	294	12.5	34
Marion, WV	54049	15.5	48.6	7.2	0.1	583	1,108	578	14.1	44
Marshall, WV	54051	17.9	47.6	1.9	...	389	688	350	14.0	34
Mason, WV	54053	21.6	52.5	2.0	0.2	278	601	318	13.5	30
Mercer, WV	54055	14.8	57.7	10.8	0.1	525	1,238	667	14.3	58
Mineral, WV	54057	16.8	44.6	5.2	...	317	625	321	14.2	24

[2]IEP= Individual Education Program. See notes and definitions for more information
... Not available

Table C-1. Population, School, and Student Characteristics by County—*Continued*

County	State/County Code	Revenues, 2007-2008 Total revenue ($1,000's)	Percentage of revenue from Federal gov't	State gov't	Local gov't	Current expenditures, 2007-2008 Amount ($1,000's)	Amount per student	Percent for instruction	Resident population 16 to 19 years, 2006-2008 Total population 16 to 19 years	Percent enrolled in school	Percent high school graduates, not enrolled in school	Percent not enrolled, not grads, not employed or not in labor force
		19	20	21	22	23	24	25	26	27	28	29
WASHINGTON	53000	11,195,224	8.0	61.9	30.1	9,372,620	9,103	59.3	355,181	82.3	11.1	4.1
Adams, WA	53001	43,706	10.3	71.3	18.4	37,530	9,294	60.5	...	...	...	...
Asotin, WA	53003	33,106	11.2	69.3	19.4	30,610	9,245	61.5	...	...	...	...
Benton, WA	53005	306,357	7.2	69.8	23.1	261,467	8,436	60.4	9,208	85.2	10.5	4.1
Chelan, WA	53007	140,307	12.2	61.1	26.6	125,577	9,747	55.3	...	...	...	...
Clallam, WA	53009	97,782	10.8	69.6	19.6	88,699	8,512	63.1	...	...	...	...
Clark, WA	53011	802,227	6.8	64.2	29.0	667,216	8,781	57.6	22,365	81.6	10.4	5.1
Columbia, WA	53013	6,137	10.8	69.5	19.7	5,952	10,610	57.8	...	...	...	...
Cowlitz, WA	53015	169,787	7.8	68.6	23.5	157,711	8,796	58.7	5,220	82.6	11.6	2.9
Douglas, WA	53017	72,073	8.8	71.3	19.9	63,370	9,355	61.6	...	...	...	...
Ferry, WA	53019	12,526	22.7	69.0	8.3	11,984	12,655	56.1	...	...	...	...
Franklin, WA	53021	186,492	9.5	68.6	22.0	136,733	9,022	59.4	4,152	77.5	12.9	3.8
Garfield, WA	53023	4,702	11.9	66.5	21.6	4,125	11,332	58.9	...	...	...	...
Grant, WA	53025	183,223	11.2	70.6	18.2	162,860	9,056	61.4	5,521	81.7	13.1	4.5
Grays Harbor, WA	53027	126,659	10.9	65.9	23.2	110,854	9,656	60.9	3,928	78.0	10.8	5.0
Island, WA	53029	89,954	12.7	61.7	25.6	72,402	8,261	60.1	4,081	63.5	26.4	6.6
Jefferson, WA	53031	32,932	10.8	57.5	31.7	28,470	9,550	57.7	...	...	...	...
King, WA	53033	2,906,067	6.4	55.0	38.6	2,363,620	9,199	59.5	88,514	85.8	9.1	2.8
Kitsap, WA	53035	410,460	10.1	62.4	27.5	360,925	9,343	58.2	13,867	80.9	13.6	2.6
Kittitas, WA	53037	50,948	7.6	65.6	26.7	45,152	8,962	58.9	...	...	...	...
Klickitat, WA	53039	37,926	9.1	73.3	17.7	33,723	10,364	60.7	...	...	...	...
Lewis, WA	53041	122,099	10.0	70.2	19.9	111,090	8,879	60.2	4,505	80.2	16.3	3.2
Lincoln, WA	53043	28,810	5.2	75.3	19.5	26,801	12,144	56.5	...	...	...	...
Mason, WA	53045	85,710	9.6	66.4	24.0	75,361	9,050	58.7	...	...	...	...
Okanogan, WA	53047	74,838	13.1	71.1	15.8	62,431	9,930	59.6	...	...	...	...
Pacific, WA	53049	44,188	7.5	68.7	23.8	33,984	11,358	59.1	...	...	...	...
Pend Oreille, WA	53051	18,967	13.0	71.3	15.7	17,813	10,115	59.4	...	...	...	...
Pierce, WA	53053	1,397,559	7.7	61.0	31.3	1,163,560	8,920	59.2	43,546	80.1	12.0	5.4
San Juan, WA	53055	21,834	5.5	53.7	40.8	17,951	10,717	57.0	...	...	...	...
Skagit, WA	53057	223,681	10.1	58.1	31.7	196,013	10,100	57.2	6,743	79.7	12.4	4.3
Skamania, WA	53059	14,590	43.4	46.8	9.9	13,065	10,771	59.3	...	...	...	...
Snohomish, WA	53061	1,155,774	5.2	61.4	33.3	923,877	8,656	60.8	36,944	80.3	12.5	3.9
Spokane, WA	53063	811,579	8.2	66.9	24.8	685,193	9,107	58.9	26,481	83.8	10.9	4.2
Stevens, WA	53065	73,373	12.6	75.0	12.4	64,330	9,835	60.6	2,351	79.7	17.0	2.7
Thurston, WA	53067	450,127	7.3	61.8	31.0	372,204	9,278	58.4	12,520	82.5	13.2	2.9
Wahkiakum, WA	53069	5,469	9.0	64.6	26.5	4,550	9,401	54.2	...	...	...	...
Walla Walla, WA	53071	95,741	9.5	63.1	27.4	83,601	9,454	60.1	...	...	...	...
Whatcom, WA	53073	269,490	7.4	61.7	30.9	234,971	8,899	60.9	12,696	88.3	8.2	2.2
Whitman, WA	53075	56,401	5.6	68.2	26.2	49,744	10,904	56.4	...	...	...	...
Yakima, WA	53077	531,623	15.0	68.5	16.4	467,101	9,454	59.1	14,918	74.1	13.7	9.0
WEST VIRGINIA	54000	2,965,828	10.8	58.1	31.1	2,775,676	9,852	60.1	97,348	81.9	10.1	5.4
Barbour, WV	54001	24,879	13.5	71.4	15.1	22,925	8,983	61.7	...	...	...	...
Berkeley, WV	54003	166,571	8.1	53.8	38.1	159,174	9,436	59.8	4,638	78.4	10.7	6.2
Boone, WV	54005	52,757	9.6	46.3	44.1	50,592	10,996	55.6	...	...	...	...
Braxton, WV	54007	23,242	16.6	68.2	15.1	23,522	10,267	59.4	...	...	...	...
Brooke, WV	54009	38,478	8.4	58.6	33.0	34,630	9,835	60.5	...	...	...	...
Cabell, WV	54011	139,507	9.9	52.7	37.4	121,718	9,859	60.5	5,400	82.4	5.7	7.3
Calhoun, WV	54013	10,407	12.1	71.0	17.0	10,688	9,286	58.2	...	...	...	...
Clay, WV	54015	21,954	15.6	68.3	16.1	20,634	10,130	55.9	...	...	...	...
Doddridge, WV	54017	18,231	9.4	57.8	32.8	13,807	11,189	55.3	...	...	...	...
Fayette, WV	54019	72,633	15.7	61.1	23.2	68,431	10,027	60.6	...	...	...	...
Gilmer, WV	54021	10,587	17.5	51.7	30.8	10,147	10,772	56.1	...	...	...	...
Grant, WV	54023	17,324	11.3	60.8	28.0	17,392	8,700	60.3	...	...	...	...
Greenbrier, WV	54025	56,588	13.1	59.9	27.0	52,797	10,101	63.5	...	...	...	...
Hampshire, WV	54027	34,317	12.5	62.9	24.6	33,558	8,956	59.1	...	...	...	...
Hancock, WV	54029	42,984	6.3	61.2	32.5	41,991	9,754	61.5	...	...	...	...
Hardy, WV	54031	20,026	13.0	65.7	21.4	19,927	8,444	57.9	...	...	...	...
Harrison, WV	54033	114,588	10.6	57.6	31.8	109,760	9,769	57.7	...	...	...	...
Jackson, WV	54035	50,554	10.1	58.9	31.0	48,249	9,533	57.9	...	...	...	...
Jefferson, WV	54037	97,535	4.9	40.8	54.3	79,353	9,562	61.0	...	...	...	...
Kanawha, WV	54039	301,889	11.8	52.2	36.1	279,643	9,864	60.8	9,411	81.1	10.5	3.9
Lewis, WV	54041	27,874	10.1	55.0	34.9	27,136	10,036	56.9	...	...	...	...
Lincoln, WV	54043	39,572	15.6	66.3	18.1	37,817	10,734	57.0	...	...	...	...
Logan, WV	54045	66,426	11.5	60.0	28.5	60,684	9,407	60.7	...	...	...	...
McDowell, WV	54047	59,715	11.2	67.4	21.4	42,548	11,262	58.3	...	...	...	...
Marion, WV	54049	86,031	10.3	58.9	30.8	85,214	10,500	62.9	...	...	...	...
Marshall, WV	54051	63,531	9.2	51.0	39.8	55,656	11,154	59.8	...	...	...	...
Mason, WV	54053	46,795	10.9	57.8	31.3	43,382	9,860	60.2	...	...	...	...
Mercer, WV	54055	91,392	14.1	66.3	19.6	92,511	9,754	59.7	...	...	...	...
Mineral, WV	54057	46,356	10.8	67.3	21.9	45,741	10,038	57.6	...	...	...	...

... Not available

Table C-1. Population, School, and Student Characteristics by County—*Continued*

County	State/County Code	High school graduates, 2006-2008			College enrollment, 2006-2008		College graduates, 2006-2008 (percent)						
		Population 25 years and over	High school diploma or less (percent)	High school diploma or more (percent)	Number	Percent public	Bachelor's degree or more	+/- U.S. percent with Bachelor's degree or more	Non-Hispanic White	Black or African American	American Indian and Alaska Native	Asian, Hawaiian, and Pacific Islander	Hispanic or Latino[3]
	30	30	31	32	33	34	35	36	37	38	39	40	41
WASHINGTON	53000	4,313,853	35.6	89.3	404,343	79.5	30.5	3.1	31.8	19.8	11.9	42.0	12.0
Adams, WA	53001	...	...	...	...	...	...	...	...	...	...	...	...
Asotin, WA	53003	14,705	45.5	89.7	766	96.1	18.9	-8.5	19.3	...	...	...	...
Benton, WA	53005	103,161	40.2	87.2	7,852	86.9	26.8	-0.6	29.5	17.6	20.5	38.7	6.8
Chelan, WA	53007	46,490	47.2	82.6	2,523	90.3	22.0	-5.4	24.9	...	...	...	6.4
Clallam, WA	53009	51,139	37.6	90.8	3,010	89.2	23.0	-4.4	24.3	...	8.6	32.7	2.4
Clark, WA	53011	273,327	36.6	89.9	22,410	82.4	25.5	-1.9	25.6	13.9	20.1	44.0	12.9
Columbia, WA	53013	...	...	...	...	...	...	...	...	...	...	...	...
Cowlitz, WA	53015	66,896	45.7	84.8	5,357	82.7	14.4	-13.0	14.9	...	1.0	20.2	6.3
Douglas, WA	53017	22,983	47.5	79.2	1,802	84.8	16.7	-10.7	19.9	...	...	...	1.4
Ferry, WA	53019	...	...	...	...	...	...	...	...	...	...	...	...
Franklin, WA	53021	38,853	59.0	68.8	2,870	90.6	14.2	-13.2	21.8	8.3	...	10.0	4.0
Garfield, WA	53023	...	...	...	...	...	...	...	...	...	...	...	...
Grant, WA	53025	49,515	55.9	73.5	3,409	91.8	14.6	-12.8	18.7	...	...	...	4.0
Grays Harbor, WA	53027	48,788	50.2	84.0	2,844	92.5	13.6	-13.8	14.2	...	5.1	...	6.3
Island, WA	53029	54,806	31.4	94.4	3,059	80.9	28.1	0.7	29.2	...	...	24.2	15.1
Jefferson, WA	53031	22,430	35.3	93.0	963	74.2	32.1	4.7	32.9	...	...	...	...
King, WA	53033	1,294,338	26.5	91.8	127,810	76.0	44.4	17.0	47.8	21.2	16.5	47.3	20.8
Kitsap, WA	53035	160,920	32.2	92.3	12,440	80.8	27.9	0.5	29.5	13.1	17.8	24.3	12.3
Kittitas, WA	53037	22,376	40.7	89.4	8,292	98.0	31.5	4.1	31.8	...	...	...	5.4
Klickitat, WA	53039	14,103	50.6	86.6	863	87.5	17.8	-9.6	19.6	...	...	...	3.9
Lewis, WA	53041	49,887	48.7	84.8	2,700	82.0	15.4	-12.0	15.5	...	...	...	8.2
Lincoln, WA	53043	...	...	...	...	...	...	...	...	...	...	...	...
Mason, WA	53045	38,712	47.3	86.3	3,155	76.3	18.6	-8.8	19.1	...	2.5	...	8.7
Okanogan, WA	53047	26,632	50.0	83.0	1,043	89.3	18.5	-8.9	21.4	...	10.7	...	2.4
Pacific, WA	53049	15,674	46.9	85.0	669	81.6	15.3	-12.1	16.4	...	...	...	2.3
Pend Oreille, WA	53051	...	...	...	...	...	...	...	...	...	...	...	...
Pierce, WA	53053	505,895	40.6	89.5	43,561	70.7	22.9	-4.5	24.4	17.2	9.1	23.8	11.0
San Juan, WA	53055	...	...	...	...	...	...	...	...	...	...	...	...
Skagit, WA	53057	78,002	40.8	86.2	5,234	91.1	23.1	-4.3	25.5	...	6.9	20.3	3.9
Skamania, WA	53059	...	...	...	...	...	...	...	...	...	...	...	...
Snohomish, WA	53061	445,837	35.4	91.1	34,094	79.4	27.8	0.4	27.3	25.2	10.4	44.6	14.0
Spokane, WA	53063	299,880	33.7	91.7	36,542	73.2	27.3	-0.1	27.6	18.1	14.5	39.8	18.3
Stevens, WA	53065	28,054	45.7	89.8	1,262	95.4	17.0	-10.4	17.3	...	8.8	...	...
Thurston, WA	53067	162,537	32.5	92.6	15,614	83.2	31.4	4.0	32.0	29.1	27.9	33.4	22.3
Wahkiakum, WA	53069	...	...	...	...	...	...	...	...	...	...	...	...
Walla Walla, WA	53071	36,444	40.5	86.7	5,978	52.0	23.4	-4.0	26.2	...	...	...	8.9
Whatcom, WA	53073	123,561	35.9	90.0	21,719	92.7	31.2	3.8	32.4	25.8	8.0	40.5	12.2
Whitman, WA	53075	20,677	22.0	95.8	15,425	98.0	49.0	21.6	45.1	...	...	...	...
Yakima, WA	53077	139,853	57.5	71.1	8,965	78.0	15.6	-11.8	20.5	5.7	9.9	36.6	5.6
WEST VIRGINIA	54000	1,261,678	60.0	81.5	104,960	83.8	17.0	-10.4	16.9	13.8	10.6	61.2	18.1
Barbour, WV	54001	...	...	...	...	...	...	...	...	...	...	...	...
Berkeley, WV	54003	66,495	56.1	84.6	5,079	75.9	18.3	-9.1	18.2	18.0	...	...	24.1
Boone, WV	54005	17,822	75.5	72.5	...	...	7.9	-19.5	7.8	...	...	...	...
Braxton, WV	54007	...	...	...	...	...	...	...	...	...	...	...	...
Brooke, WV	54009	16,989	59.4	86.4	1,564	64.8	15.1	-12.3	15.2	...	...	...	...
Cabell, WV	54011	63,059	50.3	85.5	9,908	89.1	22.3	-5.1	22.1	17.5	...	...	...
Calhoun, WV	54013	...	...	...	...	...	...	...	...	...	...	...	...
Clay, WV	54015	...	...	...	...	...	...	...	...	...	...	...	...
Doddridge, WV	54017	...	...	...	...	...	...	...	...	...	...	...	...
Fayette, WV	54019	32,447	71.0	76.3	2,265	86.9	10.7	-16.7	10.8	11.8	...	...	...
Gilmer, WV	54021	...	...	...	...	...	...	...	...	...	...	...	...
Grant, WV	54023	...	...	...	...	...	...	...	...	...	...	...	...
Greenbrier, WV	54025	24,713	61.8	76.5	1,376	84.6	16.8	-10.6	16.8	9.7	...	...	...
Hampshire, WV	54027	15,613	72.1	78.1	611	93.3	9.4	-18.0	9.0	...	...	...	...
Hancock, WV	54029	22,287	55.8	86.8	1,297	83.8	16.4	-11.0	16.0	...	...	...	...
Hardy, WV	54031	...	...	...	...	...	...	...	...	...	...	...	...
Harrison, WV	54033	47,504	55.8	84.4	2,518	74.4	17.3	-10.1	17.3	...	...	...	...
Jackson, WV	54035	19,875	57.9	82.7	1,270	89.6	15.6	-11.8	15.5	...	...	...	...
Jefferson, WV	54037	33,717	47.3	85.1	4,483	85.4	28.9	1.5	30.1	11.1	...	...	19.1
Kanawha, WV	54039	136,454	52.3	85.3	8,829	84.9	22.3	-5.1	22.3	17.8	...	62.9	14.1
Lewis, WV	54041	...	...	...	...	...	...	...	...	...	...	...	...
Lincoln, WV	54043	15,807	71.8	66.5	590	82.2	8.9	-18.5	8.7	...	...	...	...
Logan, WV	54045	25,464	71.4	73.4	1,057	91.7	8.5	-18.9	8.1	...	...	...	...
McDowell, WV	54047	16,618	78.3	60.0	585	90.9	6.1	-21.3	5.6	7.8	...	...	...
Marion, WV	54049	39,037	56.0	86.4	4,632	87.3	20.1	-7.3	20.1	16.8	...	...	...
Marshall, WV	54051	23,805	62.5	85.2	1,673	84.4	11.4	-16.0	11.1	...	...	...	...
Mason, WV	54053	18,271	67.2	77.8	911	86.4	12.6	-14.8	12.7	...	...	...	...
Mercer, WV	54055	43,392	61.6	77.1	3,317	80.4	17.5	-9.9	17.5	13.7	...	...	...
Mineral, WV	54057	18,425	64.4	87.5	1,374	93.2	11.8	-15.6	11.8	...	...	...	...

[3]May be of any race
... Not available

Table C-1. Population, School, and Student Characteristics by County—*Continued*

County	State/ County Code	County Type[1]	Population, 2009		Percent of related children 5–17 years in poverty, 2008	Percent of children under 19 years with no health insurance, 2007	Number of Schools and Students, 2008-2009			Resident enrollment, 2006-2008	
			Total	Percent 5–17 years			School Districts	Schools	Students	K–12 enrollment	
										Number	Percent public
			1	2	3	4	5	6	7	8	9
Mingo, WV	54059	6	26,387	16.8	28.7	6.3	1	15	4,688	4,075	96.2
Monongalia, WV	54061	3	90,080	11.6	13.1	10.9	1	21	10,294	10,966	90.8
Monroe, WV	54063	8	13,715	14.8	18.4	12.5	1	5	1,955	...	...
Morgan, WV	54065	3	16,385	15.8	13.5	17.9	1	8	2,692	...	...
Nicholas, WV	54067	6	26,213	15.2	24.3	7.8	1	16	4,083	3,994	98.5
Ohio, WV	54069	3	44,015	14.5	18.1	9.3	1	13	5,279	6,904	69.5
Pendleton, WV	54071	8	7,390	14.8	15.4	14.8	1	4	1,101	...	...
Pleasants, WV	54073	3	7,364	16.1	13.1	11.7	1	5	1,346	...	...
Pocahontas, WV	54075	9	8,418	13.7	22.0	13.0	1	5	1,209	...	...
Preston, WV	54077	3	30,247	15.6	21.4	12.2	1	12	4,559	4,664	95.8
Putnam, WV	54079	2	55,673	17.0	10.1	9.4	1	23	9,341	8,766	90.0
Raleigh, WV	54081	4	79,187	15.0	25.2	7.1	1	30	12,316	11,861	94.5
Randolph, WV	54083	7	28,390	15.0	22.6	9.2	1	16	4,425	4,263	95.0
Ritchie, WV	54085	8	10,208	16.1	21.7	12.0	1	6	1,589	...	...
Roane, WV	54087	6	14,870	15.8	28.4	7.0	1	6	2,538	...	...
Summers, WV	54089	7	13,081	12.2	30.8	7.8	1	5	1,532	...	...
Taylor, WV	54091	6	16,328	15.1	22.3	9.4	1	6	2,426	...	...
Tucker, WV	54093	9	6,812	14.8	21.3	12.9	1	3	1,127	...	...
Tyler, WV	54095	6	8,680	15.4	22.4	7.9	1	4	1,479	...	...
Upshur, WV	54097	7	23,806	15.4	24.8	8.4	1	12	3,862	3,393	97.2
Wayne, WV	54099	2	41,119	16.2	20.6	6.1	1	21	7,726	7,061	95.7
Webster, WV	54101	9	9,444	15.4	38.1	6.9	1	6	1,550	...	...
Wetzel, WV	54103	6	16,226	16.4	23.7	9.8	1	9	2,920	...	...
Wirt, WV	54105	3	5,605	15.9	26.1	11.5	1	3	954	...	...
Wood, WV	54107	3	86,888	15.8	19.0	8.2	1	28	13,481	13,407	93.7
Wyoming, WV	54109	7	23,304	16.2	28.6	7.0	1	14	4,140	3,496	95.4
WISCONSIN	55000	X	5,654,774	16.7	11.9	5.8	462	2,305	873,750	973,126	86.7
Adams, WI	55001	8	20,088	12.8	19.3	6.6	1	7	1,833	2,784	95.3
Ashland, WI	55003	7	16,181	16.9	20.4	6.0	5	15	2,866	...	...
Barron, WI	55005	6	45,591	15.7	14.9	5.9	9	35	7,909	7,133	91.7
Bayfield, WI	55007	8	14,789	14.7	16.5	10.8	4	13	1,552	...	...
Brown, WI	55009	2	247,319	17.2	8.7	5.5	10	78	42,072	43,212	87.3
Buffalo, WI	55011	8	13,425	16.8	11.7	7.1	4	11	2,233	...	...
Burnett, WI	55013	8	15,884	14.3	19.2	9.3	3	11	2,612	...	...
Calumet, WI	55015	3	44,739	19.4	5.3	5.6	6	15	4,019	8,438	87.0
Chippewa, WI	55017	3	60,609	16.7	12.5	5.6	7	23	8,837	10,075	86.9
Clark, WI	55019	8	33,426	20.5	20.3	7.5	8	21	5,178	6,085	75.6
Columbia, WI	55021	2	55,170	16.4	8.3	6.6	9	35	8,923	9,013	90.2
Crawford, WI	55023	7	16,731	16.9	15.5	5.4	4	11	2,300	...	...
Dane, WI	55025	2	491,357	14.5	8.5	5.7	18	179	67,752	73,890	92.1
Dodge, WI	55027	4	87,333	16.0	7.9	5.7	11	36	10,933	13,880	80.8
Door, WI	55029	6	27,815	13.4	9.8	7.7	5	17	3,721	3,744	88.8
Douglas, WI	55031	2	44,274	15.3	14.4	5.1	3	13	6,710	6,984	92.0
Dunn, WI	55033	6	42,968	14.7	12.6	5.7	4	16	5,983	6,319	91.0
Eau Claire, WI	55035	3	99,409	14.6	11.0	4.9	4	34	13,741	15,303	91.4
Florence, WI	55037	9	4,554	12.8	14.2	8.2	1	3	516	...	...
Fond du Lac, WI	55039	3	100,070	16.5	7.2	5.5	6	35	13,620	16,805	86.4
Forest, WI	55041	9	9,605	15.9	19.8	9.0	3	8	1,737	...	...
Grant, WI	55043	6	48,965	15.1	13.2	6.1	11	28	7,150	7,307	85.5
Green, WI	55045	6	36,110	17.6	8.8	5.8	6	23	6,040	6,273	92.1
Green Lake, WI	55047	6	18,472	16.3	12.7	7.3	4	12	3,038	...	...
Iowa, WI	55049	2	23,498	17.3	9.0	7.1	5	13	3,670	4,072	87.1
Iron, WI	55051	9	6,078	12.5	17.7	5.6	2	5	819	...	...
Jackson, WI	55053	6	19,886	15.8	16.1	6.0	3	11	3,231	...	...
Jefferson, WI	55055	4	80,833	16.5	8.4	5.8	8	37	13,561	13,048	83.0
Juneau, WI	55057	7	26,451	15.9	14.7	6.3	5	17	3,932	4,475	88.9
Kenosha, WI	55059	1	165,382	18.7	12.1	5.5	12	59	29,963	31,616	90.8
Kewaunee, WI	55061	2	20,315	17.2	7.3	6.5	3	12	3,557	3,361	82.9
La Crosse, WI	55063	3	113,679	15.1	10.9	4.5	6	39	15,977	17,779	86.1
Lafayette, WI	55065	8	15,737	17.5	14.6	9.3	7	17	2,939	...	...
Langlade, WI	55067	6	20,008	15.7	16.2	5.9	3	13	3,136	3,245	91.4
Lincoln, WI	55069	6	29,404	16.9	10.8	5.6	3	12	4,548	4,961	89.9
Manitowoc, WI	55071	4	80,583	16.5	8.8	5.1	6	30	11,691	13,601	85.1
Marathon, WI	55073	3	131,612	17.5	9.5	5.9	9	47	19,978	23,130	87.4
Marinette, WI	55075	6	41,968	14.9	13.6	5.3	8	21	6,422	6,279	89.3
Marquette, WI	55077	8	14,727	14.8	16.2	7.6	2	8	1,944	...	...
Menominee, WI	55078	8	4,513	22.4	42.8	4.8	1	3	809	...	...
Milwaukee, WI	55079	1	959,521	17.4	21.1	5.6	33	340	141,942	184,824	82.4
Monroe, WI	55081	6	43,760	18.6	18.1	6.5	4	25	6,894	7,424	84.9
Oconto, WI	55083	2	37,149	16.4	11.8	6.6	6	21	4,756	6,192	97.4

[1]County type codes are from the Economic Research Service of the United States Department of Agriculture. See notes and definitions for more information.
... Not available

Table C-1. Population, School, and Student Characteristics by County—*Continued*

County	State/ County Code	Characteristics of students, 2008-2009				Number of graduates, 2006-2007	Staff and students, 2008-2009			
		Percent with IEP[2]	Percent eligible for free or reduced lunch	Percent minority	Percent English Language Learners		Total staff	Number of teachers	Student/ teacher ratio	Central admin. Staff
		10	11	12	13	14	15	16	17	18
Mingo, WV	54059	15.6	60.1	2.8	...	258	665	342	13.7	35
Monongalia, WV	54061	15.0	37.3	10.6	2.5	641	1,372	718	14.3	70
Monroe, WV	54063	16.8	55.8	2.0	...	136	295	148	13.2	17
Morgan, WV	54065	13.1	44.3	2.4	0.7	170	353	188	14.3	23
Nicholas, WV	54067	19.8	55.7	1.1	0.1	260	612	311	13.1	30
Ohio, WV	54069	17.4	45.9	10.7	0.4	380	733	381	13.9	48
Pendleton, WV	54071	18.1	52.6	4.7	...	86	165	84	13.1	11
Pleasants, WV	54073	19.7	45.0	2.3	...	79	211	108	12.5	13
Pocahontas, WV	54075	18.1	58.7	0.5	...	96	187	92	13.1	7
Preston, WV	54077	20.0	50.0	1.1	...	278	630	347	13.1	31
Putnam, WV	54079	17.1	36.3	3.6	0.4	608	1,179	647	14.4	61
Raleigh, WV	54081	12.9	51.4	12.0	0.2	716	1,576	862	14.3	68
Randolph, WV	54083	16.6	55.0	1.9	...	297	585	321	13.8	25
Ritchie, WV	54085	17.9	53.0	1.9	...	101	236	119	13.4	12
Roane, WV	54087	17.5	60.3	1.6	...	182	339	179	14.2	18
Summers, WV	54089	15.6	61.3	5.0	0.1	89	216	111	13.8	11
Taylor, WV	54091	15.8	51.5	1.2	...	141	313	163	14.9	15
Tucker, WV	54093	14.6	58.1	3.0	...	86	159	83	13.6	12
Tyler, WV	54095	19.2	56.4	0.9	...	...	220	115	12.9	14
Upshur, WV	54097	18.6	54.4	1.7	0.1	243	513	277	13.9	19
Wayne, WV	54099	18.7	54.6	1.4	...	443	1,041	552	14.0	39
Webster, WV	54101	15.0	67.5	1.3	0.1	106	222	111	14.0	9
Wetzel, WV	54103	20.5	48.5	1.7	0.1	228	403	217	13.5	18
Wirt, WV	54105	14.3	53.9	0.6	...	67	140	77	12.4	6
Wood, WV	54107	13.9	45.4	4.2	0.3	855	1,752	925	14.6	86
Wyoming, WV	54109	20.1	55.5	1.6	...	252	582	318	13.0	26
WISCONSIN	55000	14.3	33.5	23.6	5.5	63,893	106,588	59,398	14 7	3700
Adams, WI	55001	20.9	52.0	7.9	0.2	261	275	145	12.6	9
Ashland, WI	55003	16.5	52.5	19.8	...	228	406	227	12.6	31
Barron, WI	55005	14.1	39.9	7.6	2.5	608	1,047	576	13.7	61
Bayfield, WI	55007	17.9	50.1	26.3	0.4	150	263	139	11.2	15
Brown, WI	55009	14.6	33.6	24.0	10.8	2,905	5,027	2,892	14.5	168
Buffalo, WI	55011	13.8	31.5	3.0	0.5	170	293	164	13.6	16
Burnett, WI	55013	15.5	50.1	15.4	1.3	167	305	176	14.8	17
Calumet, WI	55015	15.1	24.8	12.4	2.2	371	531	303	13.3	16
Chippewa, WI	55017	14.2	34.6	4.1	0.6	625	1,091	596	14.8	59
Clark, WI	55019	12.6	43.3	9.0	4.8	478	659	384	13.5	27
Columbia, WI	55021	13.6	23.7	7.7	2.2	676	1,278	672	13.3	63
Crawford, WI	55023	17.0	46.7	4.1	0.1	219	315	178	12.9	17
Dane, WI	55025	14.8	26.2	27.0	9.1	4,754	9,273	4,969	13.6	269
Dodge, WI	55027	15.3	27.7	9.0	3.7	887	1,360	781	14.0	53
Door, WI	55029	12.7	26.7	6.7	2.6	301	538	295	12.6	29
Douglas, WI	55031	14.2	40.1	8.8	0.4	478	849	439	15.3	28
Dunn, WI	55033	13.8	33.9	9.2	4.5	506	658	377	15.9	21
Eau Claire, WI	55035	13.3	33.7	13.6	3.9	1,079	1,582	900	15.3	51
Florence, WI	55037	13.8	37.8	5.0	0.6	48	78	41	12.6	4
Fond du Lac, WI	55039	14.3	29.6	10.7	4.0	940	1,478	894	15.2	36
Forest, WI	55041	16.3	42.0	25.4	0.1	117	258	134	13.0	11
Grant, WI	55043	17.3	36.2	4.0	0.5	644	995	568	12.6	47
Green, WI	55045	13.2	21.1	6.2	1.5	446	741	434	13.9	31
Green Lake, WI	55047	13.8	29.8	9.3	5.5	251	422	240	12.7	14
Iowa, WI	55049	14.6	24.6	3.0	0.9	311	479	275	13.3	16
Iron, WI	55051	16.2	24.7	3.7	0.4	67	108	65	12.6	6
Jackson, WI	55053	13.6	41.2	17.2	1.9	267	447	246	13.1	14
Jefferson, WI	55055	14.3	26.4	13.8	4.7	1,003	1,716	914	14.8	60
Juneau, WI	55057	13.8	44.8	5.7	1.1	303	557	324	12.1	19
Kenosha, WI	55059	13.1	36.0	31.1	7.0	1,909	3,438	1,944	15.4	88
Kewaunee, WI	55061	15.6	16.5	5.0	2.0	293	443	253	14.1	14
La Crosse, WI	55063	13.3	31.5	15.2	5.3	1,174	2,131	1,198	13.3	87
Lafayette, WI	55065	13.4	26.1	4.1	1.1	265	421	252	11.7	16
Langlade, WI	55067	17.8	44.9	5.4	1.0	302	415	244	12.9	15
Lincoln, WI	55069	13.5	32.5	7.4	0.7	430	546	301	15.1	30
Manitowoc, WI	55071	15.2	25.8	13.6	4.9	959	1,450	812	14.4	51
Marathon, WI	55073	12.4	30.2	17.4	11.1	1,634	2,392	1,363	14.7	64
Marinette, WI	55075	15.2	40.5	3.5	0.4	504	775	440	14.6	41
Marquette, WI	55077	15.1	42.9	6.2	0.9	160	267	157	12.4	8
Menominee, WI	55078	26.5	82.8	99.5	...	84	177	95	8.5	7
Milwaukee, WI	55079	16.0	56.4	63.5	7.0	8,621	17,127	8,824	16.1	453
Monroe, WI	55081	15.3	41.5	9.6	2.3	557	917	531	13.0	32
Oconto, WI	55083	17.2	32.9	5.7	0.6	393	653	374	12.7	35

[2]IEP= Individual Education Program. See notes and definitions for more information
... Not available

Table C-1. Population, School, and Student Characteristics by County—*Continued*

County	State/County Code	Total revenue ($1,000's)	Percentage of revenue from Federal gov't	State gov't	Local gov't	Amount ($1,000's)	Amount per student	Percent for instruction	Total population 16 to 19 years	Percent enrolled in school	Percent high school graduates, not enrolled in school	Percent not enrolled, not grads, not employed or not in labor force
		19	20	21	22	23	24	25	26	27	28	29
Mingo, WV	54059	51,506	14.2	54.8	31.0	48,862	10,531	58.4	...	...	...	...
Monongalia, WV	54061	115,951	9.0	47.8	43.2	100,296	9,813	60.2	9,955	94.2	3.4	2.1
Monroe, WV	54063	20,471	17.0	66.1	16.9	19,710	9,914	59.9	...	...	...	...
Morgan, WV	54065	25,686	7.7	55.4	36.9	25,325	9,314	56.1	...	...	...	...
Nicholas, WV	54067	42,795	15.8	62.9	21.3	41,420	10,068	61.5	...	...	...	...
Ohio, WV	54069	58,263	10.4	56.3	33.3	54,082	10,187	59.6	...	...	...	...
Pendleton, WV	54071	11,947	11.0	70.6	18.4	11,656	10,297	57.9	...	...	...	...
Pleasants, WV	54073	16,288	7.9	44.2	47.9	15,457	11,433	55.5	...	...	...	...
Pocahontas, WV	54075	12,565	17.0	52.0	31.0	13,311	11,046	59.0	...	...	...	...
Preston, WV	54077	42,100	11.8	69.3	19.0	42,089	9,182	64.3	...	...	...	...
Putnam, WV	54079	95,119	7.3	56.8	35.9	88,517	9,620	61.7	...	...	...	...
Raleigh, WV	54081	123,919	9.4	59.3	31.3	116,158	9,558	58.3	...	...	...	...
Randolph, WV	54083	36,940	10.2	74.5	15.3	39,502	8,949	63.7	...	...	...	...
Ritchie, WV	54085	16,373	10.8	64.0	25.2	16,872	10,565	57.7	...	...	...	...
Roane, WV	54087	24,585	16.8	71.7	11.5	23,577	9,160	59.4	...	...	...	...
Summers, WV	54089	15,973	17.9	66.7	15.4	15,014	9,581	58.3	...	...	...	...
Taylor, WV	54091	24,737	11.6	65.0	23.4	22,416	9,097	60.1	...	...	...	...
Tucker, WV	54093	12,050	14.9	57.5	27.6	11,685	10,117	58.8	...	...	...	...
Tyler, WV	54095	17,258	10.5	61.8	27.7	16,963	11,175	57.8	...	...	...	...
Upshur, WV	54097	39,268	9.6	64.0	26.4	36,720	9,461	60.3	...	...	...	...
Wayne, WV	54099	73,056	9.7	67.5	22.8	70,875	9,187	62.4	...	...	...	...
Webster, WV	54101	18,202	15.9	70.9	13.1	15,223	9,426	62.9	...	...	...	...
Wetzel, WV	54103	32,103	12.0	63.1	24.9	31,705	10,551	60.1	...	...	...	...
Wirt, WV	54105	10,182	14.3	69.6	16.1	9,793	9,822	58.1	...	...	...	...
Wood, WV	54107	138,560	9.4	59.6	31.0	134,687	9,963	62.4	4,408	75.6	15.2	7.1
Wyoming, WV	54109	47,188	10.9	57.5	31.7	44,134	10,655	62.2	...	...	...	...
WISCONSIN	55000	10,619,354	5.9	49.2	44.9	9,269,637	10,680	60.6	321,691	86.4	9.3	2.6
Adams, WI	55001	43,525	7.5	29.8	62.7	38,106	10,680	62.6	804	67.5	28.9	2.6
Ashland, WI	55003	35,906	9.4	59.7	30.8	33,626	11,733	59.0	...	...	...	...
Barron, WI	55005	98,665	5.2	48.7	46.1	83,098	10,367	59.9	2,483	81.8	13.7	0.7
Bayfield, WI	55007	26,586	14.2	23.6	62.2	22,641	13,365	55.5	...	...	...	...
Brown, WI	55009	481,181	5.3	55.9	38.8	420,680	10,397	61.7	13,811	88.5	7.5	2.7
Buffalo, WI	55011	28,268	4.5	57.6	37.9	23,572	10,389	62.1	...	...	...	...
Burnett, WI	55013	30,324	5.4	33.2	61.4	24,659	9,678	60.7	...	...	...	...
Calumet, WI	55015	50,259	2.4	54.0	43.6	37,203	9,245	57.7	...	...	...	...
Chippewa, WI	55017	104,918	4.0	56.0	40.0	85,015	9,517	60.4	3,266	80.6	16.4	2.4
Clark, WI	55019	66,350	5.1	61.1	33.8	52,889	10,153	59.0	1,938	67.8	8.2	14.3
Columbia, WI	55021	105,515	3.7	50.2	46.1	90,562	10,161	61.8	...	...	...	...
Crawford, WI	55023	30,197	5.9	60.8	33.3	24,867	10,636	62.7	...	...	...	...
Dane, WI	55025	854,464	4.0	35.6	60.4	747,845	11,387	59.9	28,399	91.0	6.5	1.7
Dodge, WI	55027	132,161	3.6	55.6	40.8	112,616	10,391	63.0	4,424	77.4	18.7	3.0
Door, WI	55029	50,045	4.3	23.5	72.2	43,463	11,441	62.3	...	...	...	...
Douglas, WI	55031	81,356	6.1	56.3	37.6	70,402	10,364	58.8	...	...	...	...
Dunn, WI	55033	69,738	4.9	55.8	39.3	59,612	10,313	62.4	...	...	...	...
Eau Claire, WI	55035	169,788	4.8	52.8	42.5	142,518	10,337	59.9	7,033	88.9	8.2	1.8
Florence, WI	55037	8,457	4.6	27.7	67.7	6,564	12,292	48.8	...	...	...	...
Fond du Lac, WI	55039	160,691	4.7	57.1	38.3	135,725	9,919	61.4	5,479	90.1	8.1	0.7
Forest, WI	55041	23,116	10.6	27.3	62.1	20,229	11,220	58.3	...	...	...	...
Grant, WI	55043	87,912	5.5	60.5	34.1	78,596	10,910	62.4	4,268	90.9	5.4	3.1
Green, WI	55045	74,100	4.3	55.6	40.1	60,689	9,944	61.1	...	...	...	...
Green Lake, WI	55047	41,426	3.4	41.2	55.4	33,569	10,586	61.0	...	...	...	...
Iowa, WI	55049	45,683	3.5	58.1	38.4	39,685	10,855	60.9	...	...	...	...
Iron, WI	55051	11,273	7.9	36.4	55.8	9,262	11,000	56.3	...	...	...	...
Jackson, WI	55053	36,426	5.6	63.5	30.9	32,015	10,235	60.5	...	...	...	...
Jefferson, WI	55055	158,282	4.3	49.8	45.9	139,137	10,436	59.0	...	...	...	...
Juneau, WI	55057	53,246	4.2	52.2	43.5	42,362	10,765	59.4	...	...	...	...
Kenosha, WI	55059	350,347	5.8	54.9	39.3	316,937	10,594	63.5	9,775	89.4	8.8	0.9
Kewaunee, WI	55061	40,052	3.9	59.4	36.7	34,562	9,569	60.1	...	...	...	...
La Crosse, WI	55063	198,978	5.2	52.7	42.1	179,397	11,198	60.8	7,490	91.7	7.5	0.3
Lafayette, WI	55065	39,141	4.6	61.4	34.0	33,285	11,256	60.8	...	...	...	...
Langlade, WI	55067	41,794	6.7	52.7	40.6	36,632	11,338	59.8	...	...	...	...
Lincoln, WI	55069	53,076	5.8	52.3	41.9	46,724	10,124	61.4	1,592	80.9	14.3	3.7
Manitowoc, WI	55071	134,187	5.0	61.3	33.7	118,049	10,068	61.6	...	...	...	...
Marathon, WI	55073	238,345	5.0	58.5	36.5	213,956	10,725	60.8	7,316	81.2	14.8	1.5
Marinette, WI	55075	77,311	4.7	48.9	46.4	65,781	10,106	60.9	...	...	...	...
Marquette, WI	55077	25,434	6.0	39.7	54.2	21,229	10,396	59.6	...	...	...	...
Menominee, WI	55078	20,073	34.8	45.6	19.5	14,728	17,146	50.7	...	...	...	...
Milwaukee, WI	55079	1,817,036	11.5	51.9	36.6	1,640,878	11,866	57.9	56,560	86.0	8.0	4.6
Monroe, WI	55081	82,005	7.4	63.8	28.8	70,130	10,054	60.6	...	...	...	...
Oconto, WI	55083	58,809	4.7	54.9	40.4	47,669	9,827	60.8	...	...	...	...

... Not available

Table C-1. Population, School, and Student Characteristics by County—*Continued*

County	State/ County Code	High school graduates, 2006-2008			College enrollment, 2006-2008		College graduates, 2006-2008 (percent)						
		Population 25 years and over	High school diploma or less (percent)	High school diploma or more (percent)	Number	Percent public	Bachelor's degree or more	+/- U.S. percent with Bachelor's degree or more	Non-Hispanic White	Black or African American	American Indian and Alaska Native	Asian, Hawaiian, and Pacific Islander	Hispanic or Latino[3]
		30	31	32	33	34	35	36	37	38	39	40	41
Mingo, WV	54059	18,663	71.8	69.8	582	80.9	8.7	-18.7	8.4	...	...	...	...
Monongalia, WV	54061	50,746	46.5	86.1	20,204	98.3	34.9	7.5	34.5	15.4	...	...	...
Monroe, WV	54063	...	...	...	...	...	...	...	...	...	...	...	...
Morgan, WV	54065	...	...	...	...	...	...	...	...	...	...	...	...
Nicholas, WV	54067	18,808	68.3	77.0	1,048	100.0	11.9	-15.5	12.0	...	...	...	...
Ohio, WV	54069	30,823	49.8	87.3	2,911	81.6	23.9	-3.5	24.4	5.0	...	...	...
Pendleton, WV	54071	...	...	...	...	...	...	...	...	...	...	...	...
Pleasants, WV	54073	...	...	...	...	...	...	...	...	...	...	...	...
Pocahontas, WV	54075	...	...	...	...	...	...	...	...	...	...	...	...
Preston, WV	54077	21,622	68.5	80.1	714	98.2	11.6	-15.8	11.8	...	...	...	...
Putnam, WV	54079	37,938	49.1	89.0	2,261	81.3	24.0	-3.4	23.9	...	...	...	...
Raleigh, WV	54081	56,409	61.5	78.0	4,069	41.2	15.3	-12.1	15.5	9.5	...	...	...
Randolph, WV	54083	20,017	66.7	80.0	1,109	40.7	15.8	-11.6	15.4	...	...	...	...
Ritchie, WV	54085	...	...	...	...	...	...	...	...	...	...	...	...
Roane, WV	54087	...	...	...	...	...	...	...	...	...	...	...	...
Summers, WV	54089	...	...	...	...	...	...	...	...	...	...	...	...
Taylor, WV	54091	...	...	...	...	...	...	...	...	...	...	...	...
Tucker, WV	54093	...	...	...	...	...	...	...	...	...	...	...	...
Tyler, WV	54095	...	...	...	...	...	...	...	...	...	...	...	...
Upshur, WV	54097	15,845	65.2	81.9	1,999	33.3	18.5	-8.9	18.1	...	...	...	...
Wayne, WV	54099	29,179	61.4	77.5	2,065	81.9	12.6	-14.8	12.7	...	...	...	...
Webster, WV	54101	...	...	...	...	...	...	...	...	...	...	...	...
Wetzel, WV	54103	...	...	...	...	...	...	...	...	...	...	...	...
Wirt, WV	54105	...	...	...	...	...	...	...	...	...	...	...	...
Wood, WV	54107	60,923	51.0	86.5	4,520	85.3	18.7	-8.7	18.4	...	...	...	...
Wyoming, WV	54109	17,152	75.3	70.8	759	89.6	8.1	-19.3	7.7	...	...	...	...
WISCONSIN	55000	3,727,936	45.4	89.0	389,054	77.5	25.5	-1.9	26.5	12.4	11.0	46.6	11.5
Adams, WI	55001	15,652	60.1	84.0	742	79.4	10.8	-16.6	11.2	...	...	...	9.2
Ashland, WI	55003	...	...	...	...	...	...	...	...	...	...	...	...
Barron, WI	55005	31,937	54.2	85.7	1,779	87.2	16.8	-10.6	17.0	...	...	...	...
Bayfield, WI	55007	...	...	...	...	...	...	...	...	...	...	...	...
Brown, WI	55009	159,064	44.8	90.1	16,683	73.0	25.9	-1.5	27.0	8.9	18.5	35.6	7.5
Buffalo, WI	55011	...	...	...	...	...	...	...	...	...	...	...	...
Burnett, WI	55013	...	...	...	...	...	...	...	...	...	...	...	...
Calumet, WI	55015	29,443	46.5	91.7	2,024	83.2	23.4	-4.0	23.7	...	...	40.4	1.5
Chippewa, WI	55017	40,569	49.3	88.0	2,766	85.5	17.3	-10.1	17.4	...	...	14.2	...
Clark, WI	55019	21,554	64.4	79.5	948	88.4	11.3	-16.1	11.2	...	...	...	7.9
Columbia, WI	55021	38,248	48.9	90.7	2,199	77.7	20.0	-7.4	20.4	...	...	...	20.1
Crawford, WI	55023	...	...	...	...	...	...	...	...	...	...	...	...
Dane, WI	55025	308,722	26.9	94.2	59,734	87.4	44.4	17.0	45.6	21.5	25.6	63.9	24.4
Dodge, WI	55027	61,339	56.4	86.1	3,767	76.3	15.3	-12.1	16.2	...	...	...	3.3
Door, WI	55029	21,208	46.3	91.4	1,040	75.6	25.4	-2.0	25.8	...	...	...	...
Douglas, WI	55031	29,945	45.7	88.8	3,201	85.5	20.8	-6.6	21.3	...	10.3	...	...
Dunn, WI	55033	25,156	47.8	90.7	7,576	92.9	24.2	-3.2	24.3	...	...	...	...
Eau Claire, WI	55035	60,235	38.7	91.1	13,092	95.0	29.5	2.1	29.6	...	...	38.0	...
Florence, WI	55037	...	...	...	...	...	...	...	...	...	...	...	...
Fond du Lac, WI	55039	66,851	53.2	87.8	6,564	60.8	17.9	-9.5	17.7	...	...	...	13.1
Forest, WI	55041	...	...	...	...	...	...	...	...	...	...	...	...
Grant, WI	55043	31,170	52.9	88.4	6,112	95.8	19.5	-7.9	19.3	...	...	...	...
Green, WI	55045	24,516	50.4	89.8	1,285	87.2	18.4	-9.0	18.5	...	...	...	...
Green Lake, WI	55047	...	...	...	...	...	...	...	...	...	...	...	...
Iowa, WI	55049	16,031	45.9	91.5	598	82.6	23.1	-4.3	23.2	...	...	...	...
Iron, WI	55051	...	...	...	...	...	...	...	...	...	...	...	...
Jackson, WI	55053	...	...	...	...	...	...	...	...	...	...	...	...
Jefferson, WI	55055	53,448	49.7	87.5	6,454	81.6	21.0	-6.4	21.5	...	...	...	7.8
Juneau, WI	55057	18,507	60.3	84.1	844	86.4	11.9	-15.5	11.8	...	...	...	...
Kenosha, WI	55059	105,073	46.0	87.8	12,347	68.9	21.9	-5.5	22.5	17.0	17.1	60.3	10.4
Kewaunee, WI	55061	14,151	55.9	90.0	1,014	84.5	13.5	-13.9	13.5	...	...	...	...
La Crosse, WI	55063	70,662	36.5	92.8	13,056	83.1	29.4	2.0	29.6	18.0	...	28.2	27.4
Lafayette, WI	55065	...	...	...	...	...	...	...	...	...	...	...	...
Langlade, WI	55067	14,513	61.8	86.1	643	91.1	11.5	-15.9	11.7	...	...	...	...
Lincoln, WI	55069	20,951	56.5	87.5	741	89.9	14.3	-13.1	14.3	...	...	...	...
Manitowoc, WI	55071	56,019	52.5	90.2	4,063	74.2	18.0	-9.4	17.9	...	...	18.4	13.7
Marathon, WI	55073	87,896	49.7	88.1	6,527	84.8	20.7	-6.7	20.7	...	...	18.9	16.1
Marinette, WI	55075	30,036	56.6	86.7	2,393	51.5	15.3	-12.1	15.1	...	...	...	...
Marquette, WI	55077	...	...	...	...	...	...	...	...	...	...	...	...
Menominee, WI	55078	...	...	...	...	...	...	...	...	...	...	...	...
Milwaukee, WI	55079	610,541	46.7	84.3	66,722	63.1	26.2	-1.2	32.6	11.7	10.4	43.5	9.7
Monroe, WI	55081	28,248	52.9	87.8	1,585	87.0	15.3	-12.1	15.3	...	1.8	...	...
Oconto, WI	55083	26,364	57.7	86.5	1,184	67.0	12.7	-14.7	12.5	...	7.3	...	...

[3]May be of any race
... Not available

Table C-1. Population, School, and Student Characteristics by County—*Continued*

County	State/ County Code	County Type[1]	Population, 2009		Percent of related children 5-17 years in poverty, 2008	Percent of children under 19 years with no health insurance, 2007	Number of Schools and Students, 2008-2009			Resident enrollment, 2006-2008 K–12 enrollment	
			Total	Percent 5–17 years			School Districts	Schools	Students	Number	Percent public
	1			2	3	4	5	6	7	8	9
Oneida, WI	55085	7	35,930	13.5	11.9	7.1	4	13	4,749	5,232	90.7
Outagamie, WI	55087	3	177,155	17.8	8.0	7.1	8	70	33,364	31,818	88.2
Ozaukee, WI	55089	1	86,311	18.1	3.4	5.5	5	27	13,578	15,314	77.6
Pepin, WI	55091	8	7,293	16.3	15.1	9.0	2	4	1,269	...	...
Pierce, WI	55093	1	40,081	15.5	6.4	6.2	6	24	7,452	6,105	89.7
Polk, WI	55095	6	44,252	16.9	10.3	7.7	8	27	7,920	7,503	96.6
Portage, WI	55097	4	69,176	14.9	9.4	5.4	4	27	9,585	10,762	82.6
Price, WI	55099	9	14,214	14.6	13.9	8.1	4	10	2,118	...	...
Racine, WI	55101	3	200,601	18.1	12.8	6.6	13	57	30,993	37,482	83.3
Richland, WI	55103	6	17,848	16.0	14.5	6.0	2	9	1,760	...	...
Rock, WI	55105	3	160,155	17.8	13.6	5.9	9	72	28,365	29,445	93.4
Rusk, WI	55107	6	14,367	16.9	20.4	4.6	4	14	2,315	...	...
St. Croix, WI	55109	1	83,351	18.5	5.4	5.2	6	27	13,498	14,984	90.7
Sauk, WI	55111	4	58,922	16.6	11.1	5.8	6	38	11,585	9,510	90.9
Sawyer, WI	55113	9	16,939	15.0	21.9	10.4	2	13	2,289	...	...
Shawano, WI	55115	6	41,166	17.0	13.1	6.6	6	18	5,712	6,999	92.6
Sheboygan, WI	55117	3	114,560	17.1	7.2	6.4	9	52	19,732	20,014	88.2
Taylor, WI	55119	6	19,222	17.0	14.7	5.3	3	10	3,101	...	...
Trempealeau, WI	55121	8	27,754	17.6	11.6	7.4	7	24	5,921	4,951	93.1
Vernon, WI	55123	6	29,324	18.6	23.6	7.7	6	20	4,178	4,979	80.8
Vilas, WI	55125	9	21,496	12.9	16.8	10.7	5	10	2,759	2,987	94.6
Walworth, WI	55127	4	100,593	16.6	10.5	7.4	16	39	16,395	16,999	90.7
Washburn, WI	55129	6	16,666	14.7	17.7	7.1	4	11	2,638	...	...
Washington, WI	55131	1	130,681	17.7	4.5	4.8	9	36	20,147	23,044	80.9
Waukesha, WI	55133	1	383,154	17.8	3.7	4.4	20	108	62,600	67,294	81.4
Waupaca, WI	55135	6	51,665	17.0	9.7	5.7	7	28	9,495	8,897	88.2
Waushara, WI	55137	8	24,606	15.0	16.1	9.4	3	10	2,914	4,009	84.8
Winnebago, WI	55139	3	163,370	15.3	7.9	4.9	6	60	23,176	25,726	89.2
Wood, WI	55141	4	73,932	16.4	8.6	5.3	6	38	13,098	12,454	91.5
WYOMING	56000	X	544,270	16.8	9.8	9.7	60	372	87,161	88,878	94.2
Albany, WY	56001	4	33,979	10.5	11.1	10.2	2	19	3,626	3,871	85.9
Big Horn, WY	56003	9	11,581	18.8	11.8	14.4	4	16	2,096	...	...
Campbell, WY	56005	5	43,967	19.4	5.3	8.0	2	21	7,985	7,591	98.0
Carbon, WY	56007	7	15,720	16.8	10.2	10.6	2	16	2,437	...	...
Converse, WY	56009	6	13,578	17.8	8.8	9.8	2	13	2,381	...	...
Crook, WY	56011	9	6,653	16.0	8.2	12.2	1	13	1,085	...	...
Fremont, WY	56013	7	38,719	17.8	15.9	12.6	8	31	6,391	7,234	94.1
Goshen, WY	56015	7	12,319	16.4	14.3	8.0	2	12	1,867	...	...
Hot Springs, WY	56017	7	4,590	14.6	13.7	7.8	2	4	665	...	...
Johnson, WY	56019	7	8,531	15.6	8.6	9.7	1	7	1,222	...	...
Laramie, WY	56021	3	88,854	16.6	10.6	7.3	7	44	13,855	15,741	93.0
Lincoln, WY	56023	7	16,995	19.8	8.8	14.1	2	13	3,279	...	...
Natrona, WY	56025	3	74,508	16.9	9.9	8.8	1	34	11,989	12,320	93.5
Niobrara, WY	56027	9	2,366	15.3	10.9	12.7	1	4	376	...	...
Park, WY	56029	7	27,976	15.1	12.3	9.8	3	15	3,952	4,190	95.6
Platte, WY	56031	7	8,196	16.4	12.3	9.5	2	13	1,294	...	...
Sheridan, WY	56033	7	29,163	15.8	9.4	9.3	4	22	4,151	4,335	94.3
Sublette, WY	56035	9	8,792	18.0	5.0	14.1	2	8	1,680	...	...
Sweetwater, WY	56037	5	41,226	19.0	6.3	9.5	2	25	7,628	6,596	97.7
Teton, WY	56039	7	20,710	11.7	5.0	14.7	3	13	2,316	...	...
Uinta, WY	56041	7	20,927	22.2	8.2	8.8	3	15	4,375	4,432	99.6
Washakie, WY	56043	7	7,911	18.9	13.1	10.6	2	6	1,400	...	...
Weston, WY	56045	7	7,009	16.1	9.1	8.9	2	8	1,111	...	...

[1]County type codes are from the Economic Research Service of the United States Department of Agriculture. See notes and definitions for more information.
... Not available

Table C-1. Population, School, and Student Characteristics by County—*Continued*

County	State/ County Code	Characteristics of students, 2008-2009				Number of graduates, 2006-2007	Staff and students, 2008-2009			
		Percent with IEP[2]	Percent eligible for free or reduced lunch	Percent minority	Percent English Language Learners		Total staff	Number of teachers	Student/ teacher ratio	Central admin. Staff
		10	11	12	13	14	15	16	17	18
Oneida, WI	55085	13.8	34.3	8.9	0.6	545	600	316	15.0	22
Outagamie, WI	55087	12.4	23.9	14.3	6.2	2,501	3,378	2,109	15.8	86
Ozaukee, WI	55089	13.0	8.6	8.7	2.3	1,181	1,431	780	17.4	49
Pepin, WI	55091	17.8	32.0	2.4	0.6	125	174	92	13.8	10
Pierce, WI	55093	11.5	21.1	5.0	0.6	342	923	497	15.0	33
Polk, WI	55095	12.6	30.4	4.6	0.7	582	1,007	558	14.2	39
Portage, WI	55097	12.5	28.8	11.8	4.9	742	1,131	613	15.6	42
Price, WI	55099	15.4	32.0	4.7	0.5	190	300	163	13.0	11
Racine, WI	55101	15.6	37.4	38.0	9.2	1,945	3,630	2,026	15.3	225
Richland, WI	55103	20.1	40.2	4.9	1.4	155	231	137	12.8	10
Rock, WI	55105	15.2	36.5	23.1	7.3	1,867	3,596	1,975	14.4	132
Rusk, WI	55107	15.0	54.8	3.7	0.3	174	303	183	12.7	18
St. Croix, WI	55109	12.6	16.3	7.0	1.7	1,193	1,540	862	15.7	54
Sauk, WI	55111	15.1	30.9	9.4	3.3	829	1,575	843	13.7	56
Sawyer, WI	55113	15.2	48.6	25.7	0.2	194	312	175	13.1	11
Shawano, WI	55115	14.9	39.4	18.4	1.3	438	740	424	13.5	30
Sheboygan, WI	55117	14.7	25.6	21.4	11.1	1,476	2,399	1,380	14.3	76
Taylor, WI	55119	13.4	35.8	3.3	0.9	268	353	210	14.8	13
Trempealeau, WI	55121	14.7	31.0	7.4	3.3	377	806	448	13.2	29
Vernon, WI	55123	15.3	37.5	2.3	0.2	320	558	317	13.2	25
Vilas, WI	55125	13.5	40.2	19.4	0.1	160	422	244	11.3	18
Walworth, WI	55127	13.4	32.3	21.8	12.6	1,098	1,900	1,139	14.4	54
Washburn, WI	55129	14.6	44.7	5.5	0.2	203	333	203	13.0	16
Washington, WI	55131	12.8	16.7	7.2	1.5	1,690	2,152	1,273	15.8	80
Waukesha, WI	55133	12.1	11.3	13.0	3.1	5,052	6,715	3,900	16.1	221
Waupaca, WI	55135	13.3	30.0	6.0	1.9	769	1,209	696	13.6	41
Waushara, WI	55137	12.5	51.3	16.6	8.2	197	373	218	13.4	11
Winnebago, WI	55139	15.6	29.9	13.4	5.4	1,652	2,768	1,589	14.6	89
Wood, WI	55141	12.8	30.3	9.2	2.8	1,083	1,552	900	14.6	53
WYOMING	56000	16.9	31.0	16.7	2.6	5,458	15,831	6,998	12.5	797
Albany, WY	56001	16.1	31.4	21.4	1.9	247	691	322	11.3	24
Big Horn, WY	56003	20.6	39.5	13.1	2.4	162	451	203	10.3	31
Campbell, WY	56005	14.7	23.7	10.2	2.5	491	1,445	590	13.5	42
Carbon, WY	56007	22.2	33.0	24.4	4.3	158	484	238	10.2	23
Converse, WY	56009	17.7	28.1	8.1	1.0	110	470	213	11.2	22
Crook, WY	56011	20.9	24.5	4.8	0.1	87	231	102	10.6	13
Fremont, WY	56013	19.9	44.8	38.9	6.4	372	1,325	554	11.5	95
Goshen, WY	56015	17.4	49.0	16.7	1.4	134	351	157	11.9	21
Hot Springs, WY	56017	18.0	39.8	6.3	0.2	48	133	56	11.9	11
Johnson, WY	56019	17.9	24.7	4.6	0.4	99	249	113	10.8	13
Laramie, WY	56021	16.0	33.4	23.5	1.2	792	2,304	1,061	13.1	113
Lincoln, WY	56023	14.8	29.7	6.3	0.5	195	573	245	13.4	26
Natrona, WY	56025	14.3	31.4	11.6	1.2	680	2,004	833	14.4	101
Niobrara, WY	56027	24.2	33.0	4.8	...	29	81	37	10.2	7
Park, WY	56029	18.5	29.4	8.1	0.5	310	701	309	12.8	35
Platte, WY	56031	17.2	26.9	10.0	2.2	103	305	149	8.7	16
Sheridan, WY	56033	16.8	29.7	9.3	0.4	279	756	367	11.3	34
Sublette, WY	56035	15.5	16.9	10.7	3.4	98	281	124	13.5	20
Sweetwater, WY	56037	17.9	23.9	20.2	5.4	390	1,305	557	13.7	50
Teton, WY	56039	12.6	14.5	26.1	12.1	166	401	196	11.8	18
Uinta, WY	56041	17.2	33.8	11.7	3.7	313	777	350	12.5	44
Washakie, WY	56043	26.1	46.0	21.8	5.5	101	290	122	11.5	17
Weston, WY	56045	23.4	26.3	6.5	...	94	225	100	11.1	19

[2]IEP= Individual Education Program. See notes and definitions for more information
... Not available

Table C-1. Population, School, and Student Characteristics by County—*Continued*

County	State/County Code	Total revenue ($1,000's)	Federal gov't	State gov't	Local gov't	Amount ($1,000's)	Amount per student	Percent for instruction	Total population 16 to 19 years	Percent enrolled in school	Percent high school graduates, not enrolled in school	Percent not enrolled, not grads, not employed or not in labor force
		19	20	21	22	23	24	25	26	27	28	29
Oneida, WI	55085	69,415	6.5	19.1	74.4	56,528	11,586	57.9	...	...	...	...
Outagamie, WI	55087	367,053	4.3	58.9	36.9	321,499	9,643	62.7	10,052	88.1	8.8	1.5
Ozaukee, WI	55089	156,826	2.5	28.6	68.9	139,998	10,455	58.8	...	...	...	...
Pepin, WI	55091	18,176	4.7	51.7	43.5	15,239	11,553	55.7	...	...	...	...
Pierce, WI	55093	52,561	3.8	49.5	46.6	43,999	10,488	59.9	...	...	...	...
Polk, WI	55095	99,633	3.7	46.2	50.0	81,335	10,209	62.0	2,282	82.9	11.1	3.1
Portage, WI	55097	106,638	4.5	56.2	39.4	97,365	10,134	62.8	...	...	...	...
Price, WI	55099	25,625	6.9	42.2	50.9	22,529	10,420	58.8	...	...	...	...
Racine, WI	55101	354,753	6.2	56.7	37.1	318,449	10,298	62.3	10,543	83.9	10.4	3.4
Richland, WI	55103	23,765	5.6	57.8	36.6	19,838	10,966	58.3	...	...	...	...
Rock, WI	55105	325,338	5.9	63.0	31.0	291,245	10,277	61.3	8,985	81.1	13.0	3.4
Rusk, WI	55107	33,830	6.1	53.0	40.9	27,194	11,426	58.5	...	...	...	...
St. Croix, WI	55109	189,018	3.0	48.3	48.7	155,190	9,423	61.1	4,128	91.8	6.7	0.7
Sauk, WI	55111	116,440	5.0	50.3	44.6	102,679	10,259	61.6	2,933	86.1	10.0	2.5
Sawyer, WI	55113	30,196	10.4	13.2	76.5	26,058	11,242	57.5	...	...	...	...
Shawano, WI	55115	69,056	6.3	59.3	34.4	61,121	10,468	59.1	2,284	83.9	10.1	2.3
Sheboygan, WI	55117	233,210	4.7	55.2	40.1	209,593	10,604	65.1	6,006	85.1	10.8	2.8
Taylor, WI	55119	35,307	5.7	60.5	33.7	31,754	10,330	60.3	...	...	...	...
Trempealeau, WI	55121	72,759	4.5	63.7	31.8	60,110	10,307	59.5	...	...	...	...
Vernon, WI	55123	52,923	6.6	58.3	35.1	44,611	10,683	58.7	16,11	73.0	15.5	8.9
Vilas, WI	55125	48,247	10.4	8.3	81.3	38,247	14,046	57.9	...	...	...	...
Walworth, WI	55127	212,128	3.6	33.0	63.5	170,025	10,421	62.9	5,881	87.9	9.3	2.4
Washburn, WI	55129	37,758	6.3	19.5	74.2	29,668	11,099	60.7	...	...	...	...
Washington, WI	55131	226,224	3.1	42.7	54.2	200,081	10,048	61.6	...	...	...	...
Waukesha, WI	55133	763,398	2.8	29.0	68.2	650,011	10,304	61.4	21,954	89.5	7.6	1.6
Waupaca, WI	55135	114,059	4.6	56.9	38.5	97,930	10,115	60.8	2,571	79.0	16.2	3.1
Waushara, WI	55137	36,065	8.3	41.4	50.3	31,151	10,503	59.5	...	...	...	...
Winnebago, WI	55139	260,660	4.8	56.5	38.7	235,365	10,185	63.4	9,359	90.9	6.2	1.6
Wood, WI	55141	151,847	4.6	59.2	36.1	139,661	10,556	62.3	...	...	...	...
WYOMING	56000	1,602,514	6.3	52.8	40.9	1,190,136	13,840	59.1	30,130	82.6	11.0	3.9
Albany, WY	56001	52,482	7.7	65.2	27.0	48,239	13,527	62.9	...	...	...	...
Big Horn, WY	56003	42,113	7.3	69.0	23.7	33,045	15,834	58.3	...	...	...	...
Campbell, WY	56005	128,360	3.9	8.2	87.9	103,322	13,615	56.5	...	...	...	...
Carbon, WY	56007	46,272	4.8	32.9	62.4	35,605	14,334	56.5	...	...	...	...
Converse, WY	56009	41,343	5.1	48.1	46.8	32,234	13,151	65.1	...	...	...	...
Crook, WY	56011	21,382	2.8	68.3	29.0	16,444	14,801	58.0	...	...	...	...
Fremont, WY	56013	153,653	16.3	64.9	18.8	111,017	17,577	59.8	...	...	...	...
Goshen, WY	56015	41,240	5.3	81.5	13.3	26,534	14,523	57.9	...	...	...	...
Hot Springs, WY	56017	15,039	6.3	40.2	53.5	10,459	16,291	53.0	...	...	...	...
Johnson, WY	56019	22,808	4.1	8.1	87.8	18,481	14,506	55.3	...	...	...	...
Laramie, WY	56021	242,264	5.5	78.6	15.9	179,852	13,124	59.2	...	...	...	...
Lincoln, WY	56023	58,781	3.4	55.8	40.8	43,090	13,320	61.7	...	...	...	...
Natrona, WY	56025	202,731	7.0	70.2	22.8	151,564	12,722	60.8	4,211	85.5	9.7	3.0
Niobrara, WY	56027	7,359	5.1	58.4	36.6	6,216	17,077	56.5	...	...	...	...
Park, WY	56029	83,287	4.8	62.0	33.1	52,712	13,396	61.2	...	...	...	...
Platte, WY	56031	25,582	6.0	69.5	24.5	21,981	16,355	61.5	...	...	...	...
Sheridan, WY	56033	69,034	5.8	57.8	36.4	57,716	13,975	60.7	...	...	...	...
Sublette, WY	56035	79,970	0.6	11.6	87.8	24,896	15,368	55.1	...	...	...	...
Sweetwater, WY	56037	110,135	5.8	17.2	76.9	90,670	12,351	55.0	...	...	...	...
Teton, WY	56039	49,606	3.7	22.6	73.6	34,094	15,019	60.9	...	...	...	...
Uinta, WY	56041	67,612	5.1	52.4	42.5	55,158	12,783	57.6	...	...	...	...
Washakie, WY	56043	23,216	7.0	67.4	25.6	21,178	14,967	63.1	...	...	...	...
Weston, WY	56045	18,245	4.2	65.1	30.7	15,629	14,786	55.5	...	...	...	...

... Not available

Table C-1. Population, School, and Student Characteristics by County—*Continued*

County	State/County Code	High school graduates, 2006-2008		College enrollment, 2006-2008		College graduates, 2006-2008 (percent)						
		Population 25 years and over	High school diploma or less (percent)	High school diploma or more (percent)	Number	Percent public	Bachelor's degree or more	+/- U.S. percent with Bachelor's degree or more	Non-Hispanic White	Black or African American	American Indian and Alaska Native	Asian, Hawaiian, and Pacific Islander	Hispanic or Latino[3]
		30	31	32	33	34	35	36	37	38	39	40	41
Oneida, WI	55085	26,539	42.7	91.5	1,419	78.8	21.2	-6.2	21.4	...	...	...	...
Outagamie, WI	55087	114,087	45.0	91.7	10,195	67.8	25.3	-2.1	25.7	2.7	10.7	35.1	12.9
Ozaukee, WI	55089	57,831	28.9	94.5	6,020	54.5	42.7	15.3	42.8	23.6	...	...	30.3
Pepin, WI	55091	...	...	...	...	...	...	...	...	...	...	...	...
Pierce, WI	55093	24,272	39.5	92.4	6,461	94.5	27.6	0.2	27.5	...	...	...	...
Polk, WI	55095	30,669	51.0	91.3	1,760	79.4	17.4	-10.0	17.5	...	11.2	...	...
Portage, WI	55097	42,574	46.1	90.2	9,572	95.5	28.0	0.6	28.4	...	...	22.6	13.2
Price, WI	55099	...	...	...	...	...	...	...	...	...	...	...	...
Racine, WI	55101	131,774	47.5	87.0	11,638	78.6	23.0	-4.4	25.9	6.9	...	60.4	6.1
Richland, WI	55103	...	...	...	...	...	...	...	...	...	...	...	...
Rock, WI	55105	106,216	51.7	87.0	7,745	67.4	19.6	-7.8	20.6	9.0	17.3	...	6.6
Rusk, WI	55107	...	...	...	...	...	...	...	...	...	...	...	...
St. Croix, WI	55109	53,205	36.0	94.3	4,023	79.9	32.0	4.6	32.0	...	...	36.3	...
Sauk, WI	55111	40,133	51.1	88.7	2,239	89.8	19.5	-7.9	19.7	...	0.9	...	14.4
Sawyer, WI	55113	...	...	...	...	...	...	...	...	...	...	...	...
Shawano, WI	55115	28,290	61.0	85.6	1,917	81.1	13.5	-13.9	13.7	...	9.4	...	...
Sheboygan, WI	55117	77,810	49.3	88.9	5,522	63.0	21.0	-6.4	21.5	...	...	20.4	10.3
Taylor, WI	55119	...	...	...	...	...	...	...	...	...	...	...	...
Trempealeau, WI	55121	19,248	56.4	85.1	1,022	86.2	17.3	-10.1	17.7	...	...	...	...
Vernon, WI	55123	19,303	52.3	85.4	944	82.3	18.5	-8.9	18.7	...	...	...	...
Vilas, WI	55125	16,992	43.5	92.0	403	63.3	25.5	-1.9	27.1	...	3.6	...	...
Walworth, WI	55127	65,525	45.8	88.7	8,792	88.8	25.3	-2.1	26.7	...	...	...	2.8
Washburn, WI	55129	...	...	...	...	...	...	...	...	...	...	...	...
Washington, WI	55131	87,158	42.9	91.6	6,687	71.0	26.0	-1.4	25.8	...	...	...	23.3
Waukesha, WI	55133	257,115	32.0	94.7	24,591	67.3	38.7	11.3	38.6	43.2	...	67.1	22.5
Waupaca, WI	55135	36,255	58.9	87.0	2,156	81.6	15.5	-11.9	15.7	...	...	...	...
Waushara, WI	55137	17,494	61.3	83.4	690	85.9	12.5	-14.9	13.1	...	...	...	1.5
Winnebago, WI	55139	108,317	46.9	89.6	14,305	92.5	24.1	-3.3	24.6	1.5	6.4	39.9	11.1
Wood, WI	55141	51,460	50.0	88.7	3,076	86.4	19.4	-8.0	18.9	...	...	...	17.4
WYOMING	56000	343,120	40.8	90.9	33,407	87.4	23.3	-4.1	24.5	8.4	8.1	45.3	9.0
Albany, WY	56001	17,464	23.6	93.1	9,001	91.5	49.5	22.1	51.3	...	...	...	16.4
Big Horn, WY	56003	...	...	...	...	...	...	...	...	...	...	...	...
Campbell, WY	56005	25,433	43.2	90.3	1,477	95.1	17.0	-10.4	17.5	...	...	...	8.5
Carbon, WY	56007	...	...	...	...	...	...	...	...	...	...	...	...
Converse, WY	56009	...	...	...	...	...	...	...	...	...	...	...	...
Crook, WY	56011	...	...	...	...	...	...	...	...	...	...	...	...
Fremont, WY	56013	24,524	42.0	88.7	1,742	88.6	22.6	-4.8	26.1	...	7.4	...	...
Goshen, WY	56015	...	...	...	...	...	...	...	...	...	...	...	...
Hot Springs, WY	56017	...	...	...	...	...	...	...	...	...	...	...	...
Johnson, WY	56019	...	...	...	...	...	...	...	...	...	...	...	...
Laramie, WY	56021	56,771	38.1	90.3	6,057	81.1	22.9	-4.5	25.4	9.7	1.8	...	8.7
Lincoln, WY	56023	...	...	...	...	...	...	...	...	...	...	...	...
Natrona, WY	56025	47,275	39.8	92.1	3,933	88.9	19.9	-7.5	20.3	...	...	...	12.9
Niobrara, WY	56027	...	...	...	...	...	...	...	...	...	...	...	...
Park, WY	56029	18,501	35.2	92.3	2,165	98.8	27.5	0.1	28.8	...	...	...	...
Platte, WY	56031	...	...	...	...	...	...	...	...	...	...	...	...
Sheridan, WY	56033	19,437	40.9	91.4	1,272	93.9	20.8	-6.6	21.1	...	...	...	...
Sublette, WY	56035	...	...	...	...	...	...	...	...	...	...	...	...
Sweetwater, WY	56037	24,645	45.7	89.5	2,011	92.0	18.0	-9.4	19.4	...	...	...	2.8
Teton, WY	56039	14,850	25.2	95.8	...	...	51.5	24.1	54.5	...	...	...	...
Uinta, WY	56041	12,657	47.0	86.4	478	86.0	16.2	-11.2	16.3	...	...	...	18.7
Washakie, WY	56043	...	...	...	...	...	...	...	...	...	...	...	...
Weston, WY	56045	...	...	...	...	...	...	...	...	...	...	...	...

[3]May be of any race
... Not available

NOTES AND DEFINITIONS: COUNTY EDUCATION STATISTICS

Part C presents 41 data items for each county, county equivalent, and independent city. The counties are presented in alphabetical order within states, which are also in alphabetical order. Independent cities, found in Maryland, Missouri, Nevada, and Virginia, are placed in alphabetical order at the end of the list of counties for those states. The District of Columbia is included as both a county and a state.

COMMON CORE OF DATA

For Items 5–7 and 10–25—National Center for Education Statistics, U.S. Department of Education. *Common Core of Data: 2008-2009 and 2007-2008.* <http://nces.ed.gov/ccd/>.

NCES uses the Common Core of Data (CCD) system to acquire and maintain statistical data from each of the 50 states, the District of Columbia, and the outlying areas. Information about staff and students is collected annually at the school, local education agency (LEA) or school district, and state levels. Information about revenues and expenditures is also collected at the state level. In addition, information about revenues and expenditures at the school district level is assembled from the Census Bureau's annual surveys of government finances.

Data are collected for a particular school year (July 1 through June 30) via survey instruments sent to the state education agencies during the subsequent school year. States have one year in which to modify the data originally submitted. This volume uses the data from the 2008-2009 school year, except for the revenue and expenditure data for counties, which is for school year 2007-2008 (fiscal year 2008). The high school graduates data also come from earlier years.

Since the CCD is a universe survey, the CCD information is not subject to sampling error.

However, nonsampling errors could come from two sources—nonreturn and inaccurate reporting. Almost all of the states submit the six CCD survey instruments each year, but submissions are sometimes incomplete or made too late for publication.

Understandably, when 51 education agencies compile and submit data for more than 97,000 public schools and almost 18,000 local school districts, misreporting can occur. This typically results from varying interpretation of NCES definitions and differences in record keeping systems. NCES attempts to minimize these errors by working closely with the Council of Chief State School Officers (CCSSO) and its Committee on Evaluation and Information Systems (CEIS).

The state education agencies report data to NCES from data collected and edited during their regular reporting cycles. NCES encourages the agencies to incorporate the NCES items they do not already collect into their own survey systems so that those items will be available for the subsequent CCD survey. Over time, this has meant fewer missing data cells in each state's response and a reduction in the need to impute data.

Data from the education agencies is subjected to a comprehensive edit by NCES. Where data are determined to be inconsistent, missing, or out of range, NCES contacts the education agencies for verification. NCES-prepared state summary forms are returned to the state education agencies for verification. States are also given an opportunity to revise their state-level aggregates from the previous survey cycle. The county-level data in this volume have not been adjusted,

The CCD data are collected at three levels—the school, the school district, and the state. In Part C, selected school and school district data items have been aggregated to the county level because the county is a widely used statistical area. School districts, and even some schools, can serve populations in different counties. In this volume, schools and school districts are assigned to the county where the school district office is located, as coded by NCES in their files. Consequently, the numbers do not necessarily represent the population of a given county. NCES has begun to include the county code in the schools data file. A few items thus represent the county of the individual schools, rather than the school district office.

The structure of school districts ranges from that of states like West Virginia and Nevada, where most counties have a single school district, to Maricopa County, Arizona, which includes 285 separate school districts. Some counties have no school districts. Hawaii has a single statewide school district whose offices are located in Honolulu County. New York City has a single school system for all five boroughs (counties). It is now divided into geographic districts within the city, allowing most of the CCD data to be tallied by county, but the fiscal data for New York county represent the entire city school system. A few other counties report no school districts. These are usually counties with very small populations or independent cities in Virginia whose school systems are run by the neighboring or surrounding county.

The CCD data files now include charter schools. Charter schools are often managed independently from the local school district. When this is the case, each charter school is considered a single district. This affects the county aggregations and should be considered in interpreting these data. Additional attention should be given to the fiscal data because some states include revenues and expenditures for charter schools, while others do not.

AMERICAN COMMUNITY SURVEY, 2006–2008

Items 8, 9, and 26–41 are from the American Community Survey, the sample survey that has replaced the long form of the decennial census. The sample data are estimates of the actual figures that would have been obtained from a complete count. Estimates derived from a sample are expected to be different from the 100-percent figures because they are subject to sampling and nonsampling errors. Sampling error in data arises from the selection of people and housing units included in the sample. Nonsampling error affects both sample and 100-percent data. It is introduced as a result of errors that may occur during the data collection and processing phases of the census.

The American Community Survey is ongoing and data are released on an annual basis. Single year data are available for geographic areas with populations of 65,000 or more. Three-year data are available for areas with populations of 20,000 or more. This book uses the 2006–2008 3-year data for the county table because about 57 percent of the counties in the United States are included in this group.

For additional information about the American Community Survey, see <http://www.census.gov/acs/www/>.

GEOGRAPHIC IDENTIFICATION
Data are presented for 3,146 counties and county equivalents. A five-digit state and county code is given for each entity. The first two digits indicate the state; the remaining three identify the county. Within each state, the counties are numbered in alphabetical order, beginning with 001, with even numbers usually omitted. Independent cities follow the counties and begin with the number 510.

These codes have been established by the U.S. government as Federal Information Processing Standards and are often referred to as "FIPS codes." They are used by U.S. government agencies and many other organizations for data presentation. They are provided in this volume for use in matching the data given here with other data sources in which counties may be identified by FIPS codes.

County equivalents. In Louisiana, the primary divisions of the state are known as parishes rather than counties. In Alaska, the county equivalents are the organized boroughs, together with the census areas that were developed for general statistical purposes by the state of Alaska and the U.S. Census Bureau. Several recent changes have occurred in Alaska's county equivalents. The changes span the years covered by the data in this book so the old and the new county equivalents are all included.

The old Skagway-Hoonah-Angoon Census Area has been divided into the Skagway Municipality and the Hoonah-Angoon Census Area.

A new Prince of Wales-Hyder Census Area was created after part of the old Prince of Wales-Outer Ketchikan Census Area was annexed by the Ketchikan Gateway Borough.

The old Wrangell-Petersburg Census Area was divided into the Wrangell City and Borough and the Petersburg Census Area.

Independent cities. Independent cities are not included in any county; data are presented separately in this volume where available.

Maryland
　　Baltimore (separate from Baltimore County)

Missouri
　　St. Louis (separate from St. Louis County)

Nevada
　　Carson City

Virginia
　　Alexandria
　　Bedford
　　Bristol
　　Buena Vista
　　Charlottesville
　　Chesapeake
　　Colonial Heights
　　Covington
　　Danville
　　Emporia
　　Fairfax
　　Falls Church
　　Franklin
　　Fredericksburg
　　Galax
　　Hampton
　　Harrisonburg
　　Hopewell
　　Lexington
　　Lynchburg
　　Manassas
　　Manassas Park
　　Martinsville
　　Newport News
　　Norfolk
　　Norton
　　Petersburg
　　Poquoson
　　Portsmouth
　　Radford
　　Richmond
　　Roanoke
　　Salem
　　Staunton
　　Suffolk
　　Virginia Beach
　　Waynesboro
　　Williamsburg
　　Winchester

County type. Table C's third column provides a county type code that identifies each county by its metropolitan/nonmetropolitan status and size. These are the "rural-urban continuum codes" developed by the

Economic Research Service of the U.S. Department of Agriculture.

The 2003 Rural-Urban Continuum Codes form a classification scheme to distinguish metropolitan counties by size and nonmetropolitan counties by degree of urbanization and proximity to metro areas. The standard Office of Management and Budget (OMB) metro and nonmetro categories have been subdivided into three metro and six nonmetro categories, resulting in a nine-part county codification. This scheme was originally developed in 1974. The codes were updated in 1983, 1993, and slightly revised in 1988. The 1988 revision was first published in 1990. This scheme allows researchers to break county data into residential groups beyond metro and nonmetro; this is particularly helpful in analyzing trends in nonmetro areas related to population density and metro influence. The 2003 Rural-Urban Continuum Codes are not directly comparable with the codes from previous years because of the new methodology used in developing the 2003 metropolitan areas.

Metropolitan counties:
1 Counties in metro areas of 1 million population or more.
2 Counties in metro areas of 250,000 to 1 million population.
3 Counties in metro areas of fewer than 250,000 population.

Nonmetropolitan counties:
4 Urban population of 20,000 or more, adjacent to a metro area.
5 Urban population of 20,000 or more, not adjacent to a metro area.
6 Urban population of 2,500 to 19,999, adjacent to a metro area.
7 Urban population of 2,500 to 19,999, not adjacent to a metro area.
8 Completely rural or less than 2,500 urban population, adjacent to a metro area.

9 Completely rural or less than 2,500 urban population, not adjacent to a metro area.

Data sources and explanations. The schools and students data in Table C have been developed by Bernan from the individual school and school district data from the CCD or generated through the "Build a Table" feature on the CCD Web site. The files used were:
   Local Education Agency Universe Survey: School Year 2008-2009, version 1a
   Public Elementary/Secondary School Universe Survey: School Year 2008-2009, version 1b
   School District Finance Survey (F-33), School Year 2007-2008 (Fiscal Year 2008), version 1a

The population, characteristics, enrollment, and attainment data in Table C have been compiled from ACS data that can be found on the Census Web site in the "American FactFinder" section.

TABLE C-1

POPULATION, ITEMS 1–2
Source: U.S. Bureau of the Census. *Population Estimates Program.* (July 2009). < http://www.census.gov/popest/counties/asrh/CC-EST2009-agesex.html >.
The population data for 2009 are U.S. Census Bureau estimates of the resident population as of July 1, 2009.

Age is defined as age at last birthday (that is, number of completed years from birth to July 1, 2009).

The Census Bureau's Population Estimates Program (PEP) produces July 1 estimates for years after the last published decennial census (2000), as well as for past decades. Existing data series such as births, deaths, federal tax returns, Medicare enrollment, and immigration, are used to update the decennial census base counts.

CHILDREN IN POVERTY, ITEM 3

Source: U.S. Bureau of the Census, Small Area Income and Poverty Estimates Program. http://www.census.gov/did/www/saipe/

The U.S. Census Bureau, with support from other Federal agencies, created the Small Area Income and Poverty Estimates (SAIPE) program to provide more current estimates of selected income and poverty statistics than those from the most recent decennial census.

Estimates are created for school districts, counties, and states. The main objective of this program is to provide updated estimates of income and poverty statistics for the administration of federal programs and the allocation of federal funds to local jurisdictions. Estimates for 2008 were released in November 2009. These estimates combine data from administrative records, intercensal population estimates, and the decennial census with direct estimates from the American Community Survey to provide consistent and reliable single-year estimates. These model-based single-year estimates are more reflective of current conditions than multi-year survey estimates.

CHILDREN WITH NO HEALTH INSURANCE, ITEM 4

Source: U.S. Bureau of the Census, Small Area Health Insurance Estimates for Counties and States. http://www.census.gov/did/www/sahie/

The Small Area Health Insurance Estimates (SAHIE) program was created to develop model-based estimates of health insurance coverage for counties and states. This developmental program builds on the work of the Small Area Income and Poverty Estimates (SAIPE) program. Data on health insurance coverage for all counties are not currently

available elsewhere. In the fall of 2009, the American Community Survey released health insurance estimates for areas with a total population size of 65,000 or more.

SCHOOL DISTRICTS, ITEM 5

Source: National Center for Education Statistics, U.S. Department of Education. *Common Core of Data, 2008-2009.* < http://nces. ed.gov/ccd/pubagency.asp>.

A school district or Local Education Agency (LEA) is a local-level education agency that exists primarily to operate public schools or to contract for public school services. A public school is controlled and operated by publicly elected or appointed officials. It derives its primary support from public funds.

The county totals in this volume include 17,885 regular and special school districts. Special districts typically offer research, administrative, or other support services to client agencies. Charter schools are often included as one agency for each school.

NUMBER OF SCHOOLS AND STUDENTS, ITEMS 6–7

Source: National Center for Education Statistics, U.S. Department of Education. *Common Core of Data, 2008-2009.* < http://nces. ed.gov/ccd/pubagency.asp>.

The county table shows the number of schools and students as reported by the LEAs in the school district file.

RESIDENT ENROLLMENT AND TYPE OF SCHOOL, ITEMS 8–9 AND 33–34

Source: U.S. Bureau of the Census. American Community Survey, 2006-2008. <http://factfinder.census.gov>..

Data on school enrollment of county residents are from the 2006-2008 American community Survey (ACS). The ACS gathers demographic, social, economic, housing and financial information about the nation's people and communities on a continuous basis, providing the detailed characteristics that have previously come from the sample long form of the decennial census. This book uses the 3-year estimates data from 2006-2008, available for geographic areas with populations of 20,000 or more, including more than half of the counties in the United States.

People were classified as enrolled in school if they reported attending a "regular" public or private school or college during the three months prior to the interview. The question included instructions to "include only nursery school or preschool, kindergarten, elementary school, and schooling which leads to a high school diploma or a college degree" as regular school or college. Respondents who did not answer the enrollment question were assigned the enrollment status and type of school of a person with the same age, sex, and race/Hispanic or Latino origin whose residence was in the same or a nearby area. All persons 3 years old and over are included.

Public and private schools. Public and private schools include people who attended school during the reference period and who indicated they were enrolled by marking one of the questionnaire categories for either "public school, public college" or "private school, private college." Schools primarily supported and controlled by a federal, state, or local government are defined as public (including tribal schools). Those primarily supported and controlled by religious organizations or other private groups are considered private, as are home schools.

STUDENTS WITH INDIVIDUAL EDUCATION PROGRAMS, ITEM 10
Source: National Center for Education Statistics, U.S. Department of Education. *Common Core of Data, 2008-2009.* <http://nces.ed.gov/ccd//>.

An Individualized Education Program (IEP) is a written instructional plan for students with disabilities designated as special education students under IDEA (Individuals with Disabilities Education Act). This includes a statement of the child's present levels of educational performance; a statement of annual goals, including short-term instructional objectives; a statement of the specific educational services to be provided and the extent to which the child will be able to participate in regular educational programs; a projected date for initiation and the anticipated duration of services; appropriate objectives, criteria and evaluation procedures; and schedules for determining, on at least an annual basis, whether instructional objectives are being achieved.

IEP counts for the counties are from the agency universe through the Build-a-Table data tool. Some agencies did not report this information.

STUDENTS WHO ARE ELIGIBLE FOR FREE OR REDUCED-PRICE LUNCH, ITEM 11
Source: National Center for Education Statistics, U.S. Department of Education. *Common Core of Data, 2008-2009* <http://nces.ed.gov/ccd//>.

The Free and Reduced-Price Lunch Program is a program under the National School Lunch Act that provides cash subsidies for free or reduced-price meals to students based on family size and income criteria. Participation in the Free and Reduced-Price Lunch Program depends on income, and eligibility is often used to estimate student needs.

The number of students eligible for free or reduced-price meals was aggregated from the school universe data file for 2008-2009, using the Build-a-Table data tool.

MINORITY STUDENTS, ITEM 12
National Center for Education Statistics, U.S. Department of Education. *Common Core of Data, 2008-2009.* <http://nces.ed.gov/ccd//>.

The percentage of a county's students belonging to a minority group was tallied from the CCD school universe. Individual schools reported the number of students who were American Indian/Alaskan Native, Asian/Pacific Islander, Hispanic, Black non-Hispanic, and White non-Hispanic. "Minority" includes all categories except White non-Hispanic.

The number of students by race and Hispanic origin is from the school universe data file, using the Build-a-Table data tool.

ENGLISH LANGUAGE LEARNERS, ITEM 13
Source: National Center for Education Statistics, U.S. Department of Education. *Common Core of Data, 2008-2009.* <http://nces.ed.gov/ccd//>.

This category contains the number of students served in appropriate programs of language assistance (e.g., English as a Second Language, High Intensity Language Training, and bilingual education). The name of this field changed from Limited-English Proficient (LEP) to English Language Learners (ELL) in the 2001–2002 school year.

ELL counts for the counties are from the agency universe through the Build-a-Table data tool. Some agencies did not report this information.

GRADUATES, ITEM 14
Source: National Center for Education Statistics, U.S. Department of Education. *Common Core of Data (CCD), "Local Education Agency (School District) Universe Dropout and Completion Data", 2006-07 v.1a.* <http://nces.ed.gov/ccd//>.

The county data are from the CCD agency universe. The number of graduates includes those who received a regular diploma, those who received a diploma from a program different from the regular school program, and those who received a certificate of attendance

or other certificate of completion in lieu of a diploma during the previous school year (2005–2006) and subsequent summer school session. Recipients of high school equivalency certificates are not included.

The counts of diploma recipients and other high school completeres are from the agency universe throught the Build-a-Table data tool.

STAFF AND TEACHERS, ITEMS 15-18
Source: National Center for Education Statistics, U.S. Department of Education. *Common Core of Data (CCD), "Local Education Agency Universe Survey", 2008-09 v.1a.* <http://nces.ed.gov/ccd//>.

The total staff of the school systems in each county is aggregated from the CCD agency universe. The number of teachers in each county is aggregated from the full-time-equivalent numbers in the CCD agency universe. The student/teacher ratio is calculated from this agency-based number and the total number of students reported by the school districts in the county.

The county data for the central administrative staff are aggregated from the CCD agency universe. Central administration staff and support include the LEA superintendents, deputies, assistant superintendents, all persons with district-wide responsibilities, and their support staffs, as well as all staff, such as curriculum coordinators, supervising instructional programs at the district or sub-district level.

The counts of staff and teachers are from the agency universe through the Build-a-Table data tool. The state totals in this section were aggregated from the counties and often will differ from the numbers in Table B, which come from the state file.

REVENUES, ITEMS 19–22
Source: National Center for Education Statistics, U.S. Department of Education.

Common Core of Data, School District Finance Survey, Fiscal Year 2008. <http://nces.ed.gov/ccd//>.

The county data are aggregated from the agencies in the Public School District Financial Survey data file for fiscal year 2008 (school year 2007-2008), using the Build-a-Table data tool. Some of these school districts have no students in membership. However, the districts have revenues and expenditures, usually because of financial arrangements with neighboring counties or regional agencies. These revenue and expenditure data are obtained by the U.S. Census Bureau through its annual surveys of government finances and are supplied to NCES by the Census Bureau. The state totals in Table C are also aggregated from the agencies in this file, sometimes resulting in different numbers from the state data in Table B.

Charter school systems' reporting requirements vary from state to state, and data are currently not reported uniformly to the State Education Agencies (SEAs). Note that some charter school data may be missing from this volume, since some charter schools are not required to submit finance data to the SEA. Only those charter schools that submit data to the SEA and whose data are maintained by the SEA are included in the CCD fiscal files.

Revenues from federal sources include direct grants-in-aid from the federal government, federal grants-in-aid through the state or an intermediate agency, and other revenue in lieu of taxes to compensate a school district for nontaxable federal institutions within a district's boundaries.

State revenues include those that can be used without restriction; those for categorical purposes; and revenues in lieu of taxation. Included are revenues from payments made by a state for the benefit of the LEA or contributions of equipment or supplies. Such revenues include the payment of a pension fund by the state on behalf of an LEA employee for services rendered and contributions of fixed assets (property, plant, and equipment), such as school buses and textbooks.

Revenues from local sources include local property and non-property tax revenues, taxes levied or assessed by an LEA, revenues from a local government to the LEA, tuition received, transportation fees, earnings on investments from LEA holdings, net revenues from food services (gross receipts less gross expenditures), net revenues from student activities (gross receipts less gross expenditures), and other revenues (textbook sales, donations, property rentals). Intermediate revenues are included in local revenue totals. Intermediate revenues come from sources that are not local or state education agencies, but operate at an intermediate level between local and state education agencies and possess independent fundraising capability (such as county or municipal agencies).

EXPENDITURES, ITEMS 23–25
Source: National Center for Education Statistics, U.S. Department of Education. *Common Core of Data, School District Finance Survey, Fiscal Year 2008.* <http://nces.ed.gov/ccd//>.

The county data are aggregated from the agencies in the Public School District Financial Survey data file for fiscal year 2008 (school year 2007-2008). Some of these school districts have no students in membership but they have revenues and expenditures, usually because of financial arrangements with neighboring counties or regional agencies. These revenue and expenditure data are obtained by the U.S. Census Bureau through its annual surveys of government finances and are supplied to NCES by the Census Bureau. The state totals in Table C are also aggregated from the agencies in this file, sometimes resulting in different numbers from the state data in Table B.

Current expenditures are defined as expenditures for the categories of instruction, support services, and non-instructional services for salaries, employee benefits, purchased services and supplies, and state-level payments made for or on behalf of school systems. This does not include expenditures for debt service, capital outlay, and property (e.g., equipment), direct costs (e.g., Head Start, adult education, community colleges, etc.), or community services expenditures.

Current expenditures per student for counties are calculated by dividing current expenditures by the number of students in fall membership. Student membership is the count of students enrolled on or about October 1 and is comparable across all counties. However, comparisons should be made with caution because counties vary greatly in type of school districts as well as contractual arrangements with regional administrative school agencies or neighboring counties. For example, a county with a small population may have a school district that operates an elementary school and pays an intergovernmental fee to a neighboring county's school district for educational services to children in middle and high school. This hypothetical county would have artificially high per student expenditures because only the elementary school children would be included in its membership count.

Current expenditures for instruction are expenditures for activities dealing directly with the interaction between students and teachers (salaries, including sabbatical leave; employee benefits; instructional staff support such as librarians and instructional specialists; and purchased instructional services).

POPULATION 16 TO 19 YEARS BY SCHOOL ENROLLMENT AND EMPLOYMENT STATUS, ITEMS 26–29

Source: U.S. Bureau of the Census. American Community Survey, 2006-2008. <http://factfinder.census.gov>.

American Community Survey data on school enrollment, educational attainment, and employment status for the population 16 to 19 years old allows for calculating the proportion of people 16 to 19 years old who are not enrolled in school and not high school graduates ("dropouts") and an unemployment rate for the "dropout" population. Data are from the 2006-2008 ACS. The ACS gathers demographic, social, economic, housing and financial information about the nation's people and communities on a continuous basis, providing the detailed characteristics that have previously come from the sample long form of the decennial census. This book uses the 3-year estimates data from 2006-2008, available for geographic areas with populations of 20,000 or more, including more than half of the counties in the United States. Even fewer counties have enough residents in the 16- to 19-year age group, resulting in missing data.

EDUCATIONAL ATTAINMENT, ITEMS 30–32 AND 35–41

Source: U.S. Bureau of the Census. American Community Survey, 2006-2008. <http://factfinder.census.gov>.

Data are from the 2006-2008 ACS. The ACS gathers demographic, social, economic, housing and financial information about the nation's people and communities on a continuous basis, providing the detailed characteristics that have previously come from the sample long form of the decennial census. This book uses the 3-year estimates data from 2006-2008, available for geographic areas with populations of 20,000 or more, including more than half of the counties in the United States.

Data on attainment are tabulated for the population age 25 years old and over. People are classified according to the highest degree or level of school completed. The order in which degrees were listed on the questionnaire suggested that doctorate degrees were "higher" than professional school degrees, which were "higher" than master's degrees. The question included instructions for people currently enrolled in school to report the level of the previous grade attended or the highest degree received. Respondents who did not report educational attainment or enrollment level were assigned the attainment of a person of the same age, race, Hispanic or Latino origin, occupation, and sex, where possible, who resided in the same area or nearby. Respondents who filled in more than one box were edited to the highest level or degree reported. The question included a response category that allowed respondents to report completing the 12th grade without receiving a high school diploma. It allowed people who received either a high school diploma or the equivalent, such as those who passed the Test of General Educational Development (G.E.D.) and did not attend college, to be reported as "high school graduate(s)."

High School diploma or less. This category includes all persons who have not received a high school diploma, as well as those high school graduates who never attended college.

High school graduate or more. This category includes people whose highest degree was a high school diploma or its equivalent, people who attended college but did not receive a degree, and people who received a college, university, or professional degree. People who reported completing the 12th grade but not receiving a diploma are not high school graduates.

Bachelor's degree or more. This category includes people whose highest degree was a bachelor's, master's, professional, or doctorate degree. Master's degrees include the traditional M.A. and M.S. degrees and field-specific degrees. Some examples of professional degrees include medicine, dentistry, chiropractic, optometry, osteopathic medicine, pharmacy, podiatry, veterinary medicine, law, and theology. Vocational and technical training, such as barber school training; business, trade, technical, and vocational schools; or other training for a specific trade are specifically excluded.

APPENDIX—GUIDE TO EDUCATIONAL RESOURCES ON THE INTERNET

The Department of Education is naturally the leader in publishing federal government education information on the Internet. This chapter includes many of the online resources made available by the Education Department, but also includes information about military education activities, federally sponsored scholarships, and some education-related social service programs. The Kids' Pages section of this chapter includes over 40 Web sites designed for a younger audience that cover a wide variety of subject areas. Subsections in this chapter are Adult Education, Curriculum, Early Childhood Education, Education Funding, Education Policy, Education Research and Statistics, Educational Technology, Elementary and Secondary Education, Higher Education, International Education, Kids' Pages, and Teaching.

Site Name: Determining the site name of an Internet source is not as easy as finding the title of a book. For the purposes of this work, several sources may have been used to identify the site name, including agency press releases referring to the site, the name given to the site in the HTML <title> tag, or the initial heading or graphic.

URL: The Web address or URL indicates the location that should be entered into your Web browser to retrieve the Web site.

Sponsors: This section identifies the lead organizations that produce the site. Sponsors are most often federal government agencies, but commercial, educational, and nonprofit organizations will be listed here as well when they host or sponsor a specific resource.

Description: The resource description explains a site's organization, principal features, menu items, and significant links. For many agencies, a brief description of the agency's mission is included to help explain the site's subject coverage. The description may mention significant publications available on the site or which sections of the site include online documents. If the site content is available in languages other than English, this is noted. The utility of the site, its ease of use, and the potential audience may be evaluated as well, usually in the last paragraph of the description.

ADULT EDUCATION

DANTES—Defense Activity for Non-Traditional Education Support
http://www.dantes.doded.mil/
Sponsor(s): Defense Department
Description: DANTES provides support for the Department of Defense's off-duty, voluntary education programs. Its Web site has information about certification programs, counselor support, distance learning, and tuition assistance. It also has a section about the Troops-to-Teachers program, which assists military personnel interested in beginning a second career as public school teacher.

Interagency Coordinating Group for Adult Literacy
http://www.ed.gov/about/bdscomm/list/icgae/edlite-index.html
Sponsor(s): Education Department
Description: This interagency group was established in 2006 to improve the investment in and outcomes of adult education. The Web site includes a database of federal funding sources for adult literacy education and a directory of foundations likely to fund adult literacy projects.

Literacy Information and Communication System (LINCS)

http://lincs.ed.gov/

Sponsor(s): National Institute for Literacy (NIFL)

Description: NIFL and its partners sponsor this Web site as a gateway to adult education and literacy resources on the Internet. The site has information about grants and funding, literacy job openings, events, discussion lists, Web sites, statistics, and resources for teachers and students. The site also features America's Literacy Directory, a database of local adult education programs that can be searched by town or ZIP code.

National Audiovisual Center (NAC)

http://www.ntis.gov/products/nac.aspx

Sponsor(s): Commerce Department — Technology Administration (TA) — National Technical Information Service (NTIS)

Description: NAC manages a catalog of over 9,000 training and education materials on video, audiocassette, CD-ROM, and other types of media. The products are available for sale. The Web site features an online "screening room," with clips from the most popular videos available for purchase. Major topics covered by the collection include language training, law enforcement, health, and safety.

Office of Vocational and Adult Education, Department of Education

http://www.ed.gov/about/offices/list/ovae/index.html

Sponsor(s): Education Department — Vocational and Adult Education Office

Description: This site provides information about the Office of Vocational and Adult Education programs, grants, events, legislation, and resources concerning the fields of adult education and vocational education. Key sections are High Schools, Career and Technical Education, Community Colleges, and Adult Literacy and Education.

USDA Graduate School

http://graduateschool.edu/

Sponsor(s): Agriculture Department (USDA) — Graduate School, USDA

Description: The USDA Graduate School is a continuing education institution that offers career-related courses to federal workers and the public. The Web site has the current course catalog and information on faculty and certification programs.

CURRICULUM

Agriculture in the Classroom

http://www.agclassroom.org/

Sponsor(s): Agriculture Department (USDA) — Cooperative State Research, Education, and Extension Service (CSREES)

Description: The USDA's Agriculture in the Classroom program coordinates state education programs designed to teach children about the role of agriculture in the economy and in society. The site includes a directory of state programs, a National Resource Directory of educational materials about agriculture, information on the national Agriculture in the Classroom conference, and the online magazine *AgroWorld* for high school educators and students.

ArtsEdge: The National Arts and Education Information Network

http://artsedge.kennedy-center.org/

Sponsor(s): Kennedy Center for the Performing Arts; National Endowment for the Arts (NEA)

Description: ArtsEdge, from the Kennedy Center, is a major arts resource for educators and students. The site includes lesson plans and content standards for grades K–12. It also highlights articles, reports, and organizations related to arts education and features an arts education advocacy section. This well-designed site should be a primary starting point for people involved in arts education.

The Kennedy Center is a federal government building, but its programs are privately funded. ArtsEdge and the John F. Kennedy Center for the Performing Arts hold the copyright to all of the content on the site.

BLM Learning Landscapes

http://www.blm.gov/wo/st/en/res/Education_
in_BLM/Learning_Landscapes.html

Sponsor(s): Interior Department — Bureau of Land Management (BLM)

Description: This BLM Web site has information and activities for students and teachers. The Teachers section has information about field programs (mostly in western states), Web sites, resources, and classroom activities. The site's Curriculum Connections correlates BLM classroom activities to National Science Education Standards and National Geography Standards. Online resources for teachers and learners cover such areas as archeology, geology, paleontology, American history, wildlife, and energy.

Census in Schools

http://www.census.gov/dmd/www/teachers
.html

Sponsor(s): Commerce Department — Economics and Statistics Administration (ESA) — Census Bureau

Description: The Census in Schools program provides K–12 teaching materials, workshops for educators, and other outreach activities. Its Web site includes teaching kits and reference materials (primarily about the decennial census).

EDSITEment

http://edsitement.neh.gov/

Sponsor(s): National Endowment for the Humanities (NEH)

Description: The EDSITEment Web site's tag line is "the best of the humanities on the Web." It provides a cataloged selection of lesson plans built around high-quality, freely accessible material available on the Internet. The lesson plans are organized into sections including Art and Culture, Literature and Language Arts, Foreign Language, and History and Social Studies. Each detailed lesson plan is labeled with the appropriate grade level, subject area, time required, and skills taught. The site is sponsored by a partnership between the National Endowment for the Humanities and the Verizon Foundation.

EDSITEment provides quality resources on a well-designed and attractive Web site.

Energy Education and Workforce Development

http://www.eere.energy.gov/education/

Sponsor(s): Energy Department — Energy Efficiency and Renewable Energy Office

Description: The Energy Education site links to numerous resources, including more than 350 lesson plans and activities on energy efficiency and renewable energy for grades K–12. It also features science projects, science contests, and links to other energy education resources. The site also links to information on education opportunities for teachers, higher education students, and energy professionals.

For Educators and Students

http://www.archives.gov/education/

Sponsor(s): National Archives and Records Administration (NARA)

Description: Also called the "Digital Classroom," this National Archives site features history lesson plans and teaching activities correlated to the National History Standards and the National Standards for Civics and Government. It focuses on teaching, with primary documents available on the Archives site. The site also links to information on teacher training, videoconferences, workshops, and other educational services from the National Archives.

GLOBE Program

http://www.globe.gov/

Sponsor(s): National Aeronautics and Space Administration (NASA)

Description: The GLOBE (Global Learning and Observations to Benefit the Environment) program is designed to promote science education at the primary and secondary school levels. GLOBE is funded by NASA and the National Science Foundation, supported by the Department of State, and implemented through a cooperative agreement between NASA; the University Corporation for Atmospheric Research in Boulder, Colo.; and Colorado State University in Fort Collins, Colo. The GLOBE program's primary objective is to involve students in taking environmental measurements. Schools in over 100 countries are participating. The data they collect is accessible to anyone and there is information on how new schools can register to be included in the program. The site also has a teacher's guide and schedule of teacher workshops. Much of the content is available in Spanish and other non-English languages.

With participating schools from all over the world, this kind of collaborative project demonstrates how the Internet can be used in a K–12 environment. In addition, this Web site is well designed and makes navigation easy even for users who are unfamiliar with the program.

Learning Page of the Library of Congress
http://lcweb2.loc.gov/ammem/ndlpedu/
Sponsor(s): Library of Congress
Description: Designed for the educational community, this Web site helps students and teachers find relevant materials within the National Digital Library collection on the Library of Congress Web pages, with particular emphasis on the American Memory project. For educators, the site has guides and information on workshops about teaching with primary sources.

NASA Education
http://education.nasa.gov/home/
Sponsor(s): National Aeronautics and Space Administration (NASA) — Education Office
Description: The NASA Education Web site provides information about the education programs that NASA offers to K–12 educators and students, as well as those offered to undergraduate and graduate students and faculty at universities. News and resources are divided into sections including Elementary and Secondary Education,

Higher Education, and Informal Education. The section on Elementary and Secondary School programs has information on Educator Astronauts and the NASA Explorer Schools program. Under the NASA Education Offices heading, the site links to the individual Web sites of NASA education programs, NASA Flight and Research Centers, and each of NASA's directorates.

National Marine Sanctuaries Education
http://sanctuaries.noaa.gov/education/
Sponsor(s): Commerce Department — National Oceanic and Atmospheric Administration (NOAA)
Description: The National Marine Sanctuaries Education Web site features lesson plans, free materials, information on workshops, and other items of interest to science or environment teachers. The site has a section specifically for teachers, but resources can also be found in other sections, such as the sections for events and references.

NIH Office of Science Education
http://science-education.nih.gov/
Sponsor(s): National Institutes of Health (NIH)
Description: The NIH Office of Science Education (OSE) develops curriculum supplements, model programs, and other resources focusing on medicine, biology, and research in order to promote public science education. This Web site serves as a portal to resources from NIH. The site features the *NIH Curriculum Supplement Series* for grades K–12, a LifeWorks site about health careers, information on science education funding programs, and many other online resources.

NOAA Education Resources
http://www.education.noaa.gov/
Sponsor(s): Commerce Department — National Oceanic and Atmospheric Administration (NOAA)
Description: The NOAA Education site has teacher training opportunity announcements and materials for teachers that cover

weather, climate change, oceans and coasts, weather satellites, and space environments. The Primarily for Students section has educational resources and other information color-coded for grade K–5, grades 6–12, and higher education students. The Cool Sites for Everyone section highlights NOAA Web sites covering a variety of topics.

NSF Classroom Resources

http://www.nsf.gov/news/classroom/
Sponsor(s): National Science Foundation (NSF)
Description: The NSF provides organized links to classroom resources on the Internet. The Web site describes its intended audience as "classroom teachers, their students, and students' families." Links are organized into science topics such as biology, computing, environment, mathematics, and physics. The linked sites are from a variety of educational organizations and institutions.

Office of English Language Acquisition

http://www.ed.gov/about/offices/list/oela/
Sponsor(s): Education Department — English Language Acquisition Office
Description: The full title of this office is the Office of English Language Acquisition, Language Enhancement, and Academic Achievement for Limited English Proficient Students (OELA). OELA administers Title III of the No Child Left Behind Act (Public Law 107-110) on Language Instruction for Limited English Proficient and Immigrant Students. It also administers a state formula grant program. The site has program information and technical assistance for those applying for Title III grants, and also links to the National Clearinghouse for English Language Acquisition and Language Instruction Educational Programs (NCELA), which is funded by the Department of Education.

USGS and Science Education

http://education.usgs.gov/
Sponsor(s): Interior Department — U.S. Geological Survey (USGS)

Description: The USGS education Web site covers topics of concern to USGS scientists, including geography, geology, biology, and water resources. Educational resources are organized for grades K–6, grades 7–12, and undergraduate education. One section aligns USGS and other Web resources with an established list of science and social science curriculum standards for California. The site also covers USGS careers, internships, and postdoctoral fellowships.

EARLY CHILDHOOD EDUCATION

Early Childhood Learning and Knowledge Center

http://eclkc.ohs.acf.hhs.gov/hslc/
Sponsor(s): Health and Human Services Department — Administration for Children and Families (ACF) — Office of Head Start (OHS)
Description: The Early Childhood Learning and Knowledge Center (ECLKC) Web site states that it is designed to provide "relevant, timely information, knowledge and learning to Head Start programs and the early childhood community in an easy-to-use format." The site has information on the Head Start Program and on topics such as early education, child health, supporting your child in Head Start, and professional development for program grantees. It includes an online directory of Head Start programs. ECLKC also provides information on Head Start regulations and policy, performance standards, and program monitoring. Some information is provided in Spanish.

This Web site duplicates some information provided on the Office of Head Start Web site, but also offers unique resources—particularly for the support of program grantees.

Head Start

http://www.acf.hhs.gov/programs/ohs/
Sponsor(s): Health and Human Services Department — Administration for Children and Families (ACF) — Office of Head Start (OHS)

Description: The Office of Head Start administers grants for local public and private non-profit and for-profit agencies that provide child development services for low-income children and their families. The Web site has information on the program and relevant laws and regulations. The site also links to research on outcomes for the Head Start (preschool) and Early Head Start (infant to three years) programs.

National Child Care Information Center (NCCIC)
http://nccic.org/
Sponsor(s): Health and Human Services Department — Administration for Children and Families (ACF) — Child Care Bureau
Description: NCCIC is a national clearinghouse and technical assistance center for parents, early education professionals, governments, researchers, and the general public. The site has background information and an extensive section of links on topics such as licensing regulations, childcare as a business, federal policy, child development, literacy, and school readiness. The State Information section has profiles of childcare in each individual state. Some information is available in Spanish.

EDUCATION FUNDING

FAFSA4caster
http://www.fafsa4caster.ed.gov/
Sponsor(s): Education Department — Federal Student Aid Office
Description: The FAFSA4caster Web site is for those planning for higher education but not yet ready to apply for financial aid. The site provides an orientation to the financial aid process and an estimate of eligibility for aid. FAFSA4caster is available in English and Spanish.

Federal Cyber Service: Scholarship for Service
http://www.sfs.opm.gov/
Sponsor(s): Office of Personnel Management (OPM)

Description: OPM's Scholarship for Service program funds the education expenses of graduate and undergraduate students in information assurance fields in exchange for an obligation to work for the federal government for an agreed-upon term. The program is designed to strengthen the federal government's expertise in information assurance (the security of computer and communication networks and the information they carry). This Web site has further details about the program and a list of participating higher education institutions.

Federal School Code Search Page
http://www.fafsa.ed.gov/FOTWWebApp/FSLookupServlet
Sponsor(s): Education Department — Federal Student Aid Office
Description: This site provides searchable access to the federal Title IV School Codes required on many financial aid forms.

Federal Student Aid Gateway
http://federalstudentaid.ed.gov/
Sponsor(s): Education Department — Federal Student Aid Office
Description: This site proves information, referrals, and Web links for students, parents, financial aid professionals, those repaying student loans, and those doing business with the Federal Student Aid Office. The site also has press releases and general information about the office.

The Federal Student Aid Gateway serves a broad audience. Other financial aid Web sites listed in this section are more specialized.

Free Application for Federal Student Aid (FAFSA)
http://www.fafsa.ed.gov/
Sponsor(s): Education Department — Federal Student Aid Office
Description: FAFSA on the Web makes it possible to apply online for federal financial aid for college. The site provides guidance on applying for aid, the application process, and deadlines.

GI Bill Website
http://www.gibill.va.gov/
Sponsor(s): Veterans Affairs Department
Description: The GI Bill site provides information on the range of education benefits for active duty and reserve servicemembers, veterans, survivors, and dependents. Information on the programs is available in the Education Benefits, Information for Benefit Recipients, and Questions and Answers sections. It includes a database of approved programs at colleges, non-college degree granting institutions, licensing and certification granting providers, and national testing providers

The site has a history of the original GI Bill—the Servicemembers' Readjustment Act of 1944—which preceded the current program.

Information for Financial Aid Professionals (IFAP)
http://ifap.ed.gov/
Sponsor(s): Education Department — Federal Student Aid Office
Description: IFAP is an electronic library for financial aid professionals that contains publications, regulations, and guidance regarding the administration of the Title IV Federal Student Aid (FSA) Programs. This site features technical documentation, online tools, worksheets, and schedules related to the programs. The site also has an RSS feed of program news.

Student Aid on the Web
http://studentaid.ed.gov/
Sponsor(s): Education Department — Federal Student Aid Office
Description: This Web site is a portal and service center for federal student aid information and programs, designed for students and their parents or advisers. It begins with information about preparing for, choosing, applying to, and attending a college. Other sections contain facts about funding a college education and repaying student loans. The site links to the Free Application for Federal Student Aid (FAFSA) online.

Tax Benefits for Education
http://www.irs.gov/publications/p970/
Sponsor(s): Treasury Department — Internal Revenue Service (IRS)
Description: This Web page has the full text of Publication 970, *Tax Benefits for Education*. The publication outlines the tax deductions and benefits available to those saving for or paying education costs.

EDUCATION POLICY

Directorate for Education and Human Resources—NSF
http://www.nsf.gov/dir/index.jsp?org=ehr
Sponsor(s): National Science Foundation (NSF)
Description: The Directorate for Education and Human Resources (EHR) provides leadership in the effort to improve science, mathematics, engineering, and technology education in the United States. Its Web site includes links to descriptions of the EHR divisions—the Division of Graduate Education (DGE); the Division of Undergraduate Education (DUE); Research on Learning in Formal and Informal Settings (DRL); and the Human Resource Development (HRD)—and the types of projects they sponsor. The Publications category includes selected full-text documents.

This site will be of assistance to science and engineering students and educators at all levels who are interested in pursuing grants or scholarships.

ED.gov—U.S. Department of Education
http://www.ed.gov/
Sponsor(s): Education Department
Description: The Department of Education Web site features current news and links to information on the No Child Left Behind program and other high-profile initiatives. The top menu of the site's home page directs users to information by audience, with sections including Students (financial aid and homework help), Parents (encouraging learning, finding schools, and college

planning), Teachers (how to become a teacher and finding teaching jobs), and Administrators (guidance on school safety, teacher recruitment, and other topics). The site also organizes its content into several information centers, including Grants and Contracts, Financial Aid, Research and Statistics, Policy, and Programs. In addition, it has an A to Z index and a site map.

The About ED section has a directory of offices, budget and appropriations information, and press releases. Publications are available through the linked ED Pubs Web site and the ERIC (Education Resources Information Center) database. Some information is available in Spanish.

The Center for the Book
http://read.gov/
Sponsor(s): Library of Congress
Description: This Web site is a companion to an advertising campaign to encourage young people to read. The site links to resources from the Library of Congress and elsewhere that promote reading, books, poetry, Braille literacy, and libraries.

No Child Left Behind
http://www2.ed.gov/nclb/landing.jhtml
Alternate URL(s): http://www.nochildleftbehind.gov/
Sponsor(s): Education Department
Description: This Department of Education Web site is dedicated to information about Public Law 107-110, better known as the No Child Left Behind Act of 2001. The law concerns educational standards and testing, teacher training and recruitment, English language instruction, school safety, and other matters. The site has an A to Z index, individual state assessments, legislative updates, and information for parents and teachers. It is also an e-mail newsletter, *The Achiever*.

Office of Innovation and Improvement (OII)
http://www.ed.gov/about/offices/list/oii/
Sponsor(s): Education Department — Innovation and Improvement Office

Description: OII administers discretionary grant programs, coordinates public school choice and supplemental educational efforts, works with the nonpublic education community, and develops guidance for the No Child Left Behind initiative. The Web site's Non-Public Education section includes a private school locator and statistics on private education in the United States. The office also has an e-mail newsletter, *The Education Innovator*.

White House Initiative on Educational Excellence for Hispanic Americans
http://www.yic.gov/
Alternate URL(s): http://www.yosipuedo.gov/
Sponsor(s): President's Advisory Commission on Educational Excellence for Hispanic Americans
Description: The White House Initiative on Educational Excellence for Hispanic Americans and the President's Advisory Commission on Educational Excellence for Hispanic Americans were established by executive order in 2001. The Education Department provides the primary support for the initiative. The Web site has information on the commission and also features a series of toolkits, or online guides, with educational tips relevant to early childhood, elementary and secondary schooling, and postsecondary education. The alternate URL listed above links to a Spanish-language version of the site.

EDUCATION RESEARCH AND STATISTICS

ERIC—Educational Resources Information Center
http://www.eric.ed.gov/
Sponsor(s): Education Department — Institute of Education Sciences
Description: ERIC is a database and information system funded by the Department of Education to provide organized access to a wide array of published and unpublished material about education. It references

education literature from 1966 to the present. The Web site describes ERIC as "the world's largest digital library of education literature."

The ERIC search interface has basic and advanced versions. Searchable fields include title, author, ERIC number, identifier, ISBN, ISSN, journal name, source institution, sponsoring agency, thesaurus descriptor, and date range. Searches can be limited by type of material cited (e.g., journal article, non-print media, or dissertation) and full-text availability. The ERIC Thesaurus is linked to the search interface; users can also browse and search the thesaurus separately. An interface called My ERIC allows for some customization once users register for a My ERIC account.

ERIC is a key resource for research in education and related fields. Although the database was previously handled by a network of academic and nonprofit clearinghouses, the Department of Education established centralized control in late 2004. Since then, new features and content have been phased in. ERIC users should check the ERIC online news for regular updates; however, there is no e-mail or RSS feed subscription for the news.

Institute of Education Sciences (IES)

http://www.ed.gov/about/offices/list/ies/
Sponsor(s): Education Department — Institute of Education Sciences
Description: IES was established in 2002 to focus on education research. It includes the National Center for Education Research (NCER), the National Center for Education Statistics (NCES), the National Center for Education Evaluation and Regional Assistance (NCEE), and the National Center for Special Education Research (NCSER). The Web site has information on IES and its grants and component programs.

International Activities Program

http://nces.ed.gov/surveys/international/
Sponsor(s): Education Department — Institute of Education Sciences — National Center for Education Statistics (NCES)

Description: NCES provides a central page for linking to the international education statistics that the agency collects. The site links to information on the Trends in International Mathematics and Science Study (TIMSS) and Program for International Student Assessment (PISA) assessments, as well as the Progress in International Reading Literacy Study (PIRLS) and Adult Literacy and Lifeskills (ALL) international comparative studies.

National Center for Education Statistics

http://nces.ed.gov/
Sponsor(s): Education Department — Institute of Education Sciences — National Center for Education Statistics (NCES)
Description: NCES collects and analyzes data concerning education in the United States and other nations. Its Web site is a primary source for education statistics for all educational levels and for data on educational assessment, libraries, and international educational outcomes. Most data on the site are drawn from major NCES statistical publications, such as *Education Statistics Quarterly*, *The Condition of Education*, and the *Digest of Education Statistics*. The site provides a variety of tools to search and report the data. The Fast Facts section highlights frequently requested information, such as data on high school dropout rates or the effects of reading to children. The site also includes a searchable directory of private and public schools, colleges, and public libraries.

For users searching for statistics related to any form of education, this site should be the first place to visit.

Research on Learning in Formal and Informal Settings

http://www.nsf.gov/div/index.jsp?div=DRL
Sponsor(s): National Science Foundation (NSF)
Description: The NSF Division of Research on Learning in Formal and Informal Settings (DRL) is concerned with teaching and learning in science, technology, engineering, and

mathematics at all age levels. The division's Web site has information on funding opportunities for research in this area, along with division news and events.

EDUCATIONAL TECHNOLOGY

Computers for Learning

http://computersforlearning.gov/

Sponsor(s): General Services Administration (GSA)

Description: The Computers for Learning Web site is designed for public, private, parochial, and home schools serving the K–12 student population, as well as other nonprofit educational organizations. The service allows these groups of students and nonprofit organizations to request donations of surplus federal computer equipment. The site includes program and eligibility information and sections on how to give and receive computers.

Minority University Space Interdisciplinary Network (MU-SPIN)

http://muspin.gsfc.nasa.gov/

Sponsor(s): National Aeronautics and Space Administration (NASA) — Goddard Space Flight Center (GSFC)

Description: MU-SPIN is designed for Historically Black Colleges and Universities (HBCUs), Hispanic Serving Institutions (HSIs), and Tribal Colleges. The program focuses on training the next generation of minority scientists and engineer through technology, research, and education programs. The Web site has information about the program and its associated events, conferences, and resources.

For minority colleges and universities, this is an important resource for high technology and computer networking information and training.

Office of Educational Technology (OET), Department of Education

http://www.ed.gov/about/offices/list/os/technology/

Sponsor(s): Education Department — Educational Technology Office

Description: OET develops national educational technology policy and works with the educational community and the Department of Education to promote national goals for educational technology. Major sections of the site are Grants Programs, Reports and Research, and Internet Safety. The site also has a directory of state government contacts for educational technology.

ELEMENTARY AND SECONDARY EDUCATION

Education Resource Organizations Directory (EROD)

http://wdcrobcolp01.ed.gov/Programs/EROD/

Sponsor(s): Education Department — Elementary and Secondary Education Office

Description: EROD is a database of approximately 3,000 state and regional organizations that provide education-related information. It includes organizations such as state literary resource centers and regional education laboratories. Each organization's entry has complete contact information and a description of its services.

Emergency Planning

http://www.ed.gov/emergencyplan/

Sponsor(s): Education Department — Office of Safe and Drug-Free Schools

Description: The Emergency Planning Web site, launched in March 2003, provides school leaders with information to plan for emergencies such as natural disasters or violent incidents. The site includes instructional webcasts, a crisis planning guide, information on pandemic flu preparedness, and links to related assistance programs from the Education Department.

Office of Elementary and Secondary Education (OESE)

http://www.ed.gov/about/offices/list/oese/

Sponsor(s): Education Department — Elementary and Secondary Education Office

Description: The OESE Web site has information on its programs, office contacts, and reports. The Laws, Regulations, and Guidance section is largely concerned with the No Child Left Behind Act. The Standards, Assessment, and Accountability and the Flexibility and Waivers sections also cover areas of No Child Left Behind. The Consolidated State Info section has information on the No Child Left Behind Consolidated State Performance Report for states reporting accomplishments and data. The site is searchable through an A to Z index.

The alphabetical index is useful in uncovering all of the information at this site. Much of the information on the site is intended for elementary and secondary education professionals and officials who need to comply with the No Child Left Behind Act or who are interested in its documents.

Office of Safe and Drug-Free Schools
http://www.ed.gov/about/offices/list/osdfs/
Sponsor(s): Education Department — Office of Safe and Drug-Free Schools
Description: OSDFS's major programs come under the categories of Health, Mental Health, Environmental Health, and Physical Education; Drug-Violence Prevention; and Character and Civic Education. Many of the programs are for the elementary and secondary level, although some programs also apply to higher education. The Web site has information on the grants that fall under these program categories and offers news, publications; it also links to related resources on the Internet.

Office of Special Education Programs (OSEP)
http://www.ed.gov/about/offices/list/osers/osep/
Sponsor(s): Education Department — Special Education and Rehabilitative Services Office — Office of Special Education Programs (OSEP)
Description: OSEP has the primary responsibility of administering programs and projects relating to the education of all children, youth, and adults with disabilities, from birth through age 21. Sections describe OSEP's Programs and Projects, Grants and Funding, Legislation and Policy, Publications and Products, and Research and Statistics. It includes extensive information on the Individuals with Disabilities Education Act (IDEA), which authorizes OSEP programs.

School District Demographics System
http://nces.ed.gov/surveys/sdds/
Sponsor(s): Education Department — Institute of Education Sciences — National Center for Education Statistics (NCES)
Description: This site presents demographic and geographic data for school districts from the decennial census and the American Community Survey. The Map Viewer application allows users to view state or individual school district maps. The School District Profiles section can be used to compare demographic information between any of the nation's school districts. Users can also download school district data from the American Community Survey in spreadsheet file format. Documentation for the data and the system can be found in the Library section.

The data from this special census tabulation can be helpful for studying school districts and for examining general demographics of children and families with children.

The Nation's Report Card
http://nces.ed.gov/nationsreportcard/
Sponsor(s): Education Department — Institute of Education Sciences — National Center for Education Statistics (NCES)
Description: This is the online home of the National Assessment of Educational Progress (NAEP), an ongoing national assessment for student achievement in grades 4, 8, and 12. It provides background information on the history and current operations of the NAEP. Current results are available in the form of state profiles. Users can also construct custom data tables and get reports at

the national level or by state, region, or major urban district. The Subject Areas section provides background and reports on assessments in mathematics, reading, science, civics, and other specific subjects.

U.S. Presidential Scholars Program

http://www.ed.gov/programs/psp/
Sponsor(s): Education Department
Description: The U.S. Presidential Scholars Program recognizes up to 141 outstanding high school graduates each year. The Web site has information on eligibility, the application process, and the current year's presidential scholars.

HIGHER EDUCATION

Air Force Institute of Technology

http://www.afit.edu/
Sponsor(s): Air Force — Air Force Institute of Technology (AFIT)
Description: A component of Air University, AFIT is the Air Force's graduate school of engineering and management and its institute for technical professional continuing education. The Web site provides information on each of AFIT's schools and centers.

Air University

http://www.au.af.mil/au/
Sponsor(s): Air Force — Air University
Description: Air University (AU), located at Maxwell Air Force Base, conducts professional military education, graduate education, and professional continuing education for officers, enlisted personnel, and civilians. This site links to each of the component schools that make up AU and to its research centers, including the USAF Counterproliferation Center, Nation Space Studies Center, and Cyberspace and Information Operations Study Center. It also provides information on the university's history and mission. The Other AU Links section links to the university's course catalogs and publications, Air University Press, and the Air University Library.

Army Logistics University

http://www.almc.army.mil/
Sponsor(s): Army — Army Logistics University (ALU)
Description: The Army Logistics University site features a course catalog, course schedule, online version of *Army Logistician*, and a link to the Army Logistics Library Web site.

Barry M. Goldwater Scholarships

http://www.act.org/goldwater/
Sponsor(s): Goldwater Scholarship and Excellence in Education Foundation
Description: Goldwater Scholarships are awarded for undergraduate education in the fields of mathematics, science, and engineering. The Goldwater Foundation was established by Congress to encourage study in these fields. The Web site has scholarship application information and lists of past awardees.

Carlisle Barracks and the U.S. Army War College

http://carlisle-www.army.mil/
Sponsor(s): Army — Carlisle Barracks
Description: Carlisle Barracks is the home of the U.S. Army War College, the Center for Strategic Leadership, the Strategic Studies Institute, the Peacekeeping and Stability Operations Institute, the Army Physical Fitness Research Institute, the Army Heritage and Education Center, and the Military History Institute. This site features information on the barracks and the resident institutions. The Web site's home page features summaries of timely studies in national defense. The site also carries the quarterly *Parameters*, the Army's senior professional journal; issues are archived online from 1996 onward.

College Navigator

http://nces.ed.gov/collegenavigator/
Sponsor(s): Education Department — Institute of Education Sciences — National Center for Education Statistics (NCES)
Description: College Navigator is a database of information on colleges, universities,

community colleges, technical colleges, and similar institutions. Prior to September 2007, it was known as the College Opportunities Online (COOL) database. The database can be searched by institution name or by location, type of school, programs offered, tuition and enrollment ranges, and other criteria. For each institution, the database typically supplies phone numbers, a URL, average costs, and basic background information. Colleges can also be compared side-by-side for such factors as estimated student expenses and graduation rates.

College Navigator is a useful reference for college-bound students as well as for those simply looking for a college's phone number or URL. Note that the site states that an institution's inclusion in the database does not constitute a recommendation by the Department of Education.

Command and General Staff College

http://www.cgsc.edu/

Sponsor(s): Army — Army Command and General Staff College

Description: The U.S. Army Command and General Staff College is focused on leadership development within the Army. This site offers information on the college, its training programs, and its organizations.

Defense Language Institute Foreign Language Center (DLIFLC)

http://www.dliflc.edu/

Sponsor(s): Defense Department — Defense Language Institute (DLI)

Description: DLIFLC is the primary foreign-language training institution within the Department of Defense. Programs are for U.S. military personnel and select agency staff. The Web site has information on the history of the center and its current language programs. The center's journal, *Applied Language Learning*, is online dating back to 1996.

The site is primarily of interest to those eligible for and interested in DLI language training.

Harry S. Truman Scholarship Foundation

http://www.truman.gov/

Sponsor(s): Truman Scholarship Foundation

Description: Truman Scholarships are awarded to outstanding undergraduate students who wish to pursue graduate study and careers in government or public service. This Web site has information about the Truman Foundation and its scholarship program, with sections for candidates, faculty, and current Truman scholars.

Marine Corps University

http://www.mcu.usmc.mil/

Sponsor(s): Marine Corps — Training and Education Command

Description: The Marine Corps University's Web site provides information about its schools, including the Expeditionary Warfare School, the Command and Staff College, the School of Advanced Warfighting, and the Marine Corps War College.

NASA Academy

http://academy.nasa.gov/

Sponsor(s): National Aeronautics and Space Administration (NASA) — Goddard Space Flight Center (GSFC)

Description: This is the central page for NASA Academy summer programs for college students in science, math, engineering, or computer science. The site has application forms and detailed program information.

The information on these pages will be of interest to college students interested in careers or further study with NASA and to the advisers of students in relevant fields of study.

NASA Office of Higher Education at Goddard Space Flight Center

http://university.gsfc.nasa.gov/

Sponsor(s): National Aeronautics and Space Administration (NASA) — Goddard Space Flight Center (GSFC)

Description: This office manages fellowships, grants, and other higher education programs at NASA's Goddard Space Flight Center in

Maryland. The programs target colleges and universities along the eastern seaboard and aerospace-oriented institutions nationwide with programs of mutual interest to Goddard. The site has information about these and other NASA-wide higher education programs.

National Defense University (NDU)
http://www.ndu.edu/
Sponsor(s): Defense Department — National Defense University (NDU)
Description: The NDU Web site provides an online course catalog and links to the university's component colleges and schools: the Joint Forces Staff College, the National War College, the Industrial College of the Armed Forces, the Information Resources Management College, and the School for National Security Executive Education. NDU Research Centers online include the Institute for National Strategic Studies and the Center for the Study of Weapons of Mass Destruction. A Professional Military Reading Lists section presents bibliographies of recommended reading from the chiefs of the armed services and others.

Naval Postgraduate School
http://www.nps.edu/
Sponsor(s): Navy — Naval Postgraduate School (NPS)
Description: NPS emphasizes education and research programs relevant to the Navy, defense, and national and international security interests. The Web site links to information from each of the NPS component schools: Business and Public Policy, Engineering and Applied Sciences, Operational and Information Sciences, and International Graduate Studies. The Research section includes archives of technical reports and abstracts from theses.

Naval War College
http://www.nwc.navy.mil/
Sponsor(s): Navy — Naval War College (NWC)

Description: The Naval War College in Newport, R.I., is open to selected mid-grade and senior military officers of the U.S. armed services and civilian government officials. Naval officers from other countries attend international programs by invitation. The Web site has information on the component colleges, the Center for Naval Warfare Studies, and the Naval War College Press. The Press section includes the full texts of studies in the Newport Papers series and the *Naval War College Review*.

NSF Division of Graduate Education
http://www.nsf.gov/div/index.jsp?div=DGE
Sponsor(s): National Science Foundation (NSF)
Description: The programs of the NSF's Division of Graduate Education promote the early career development of scientists and engineers by offering support at critical junctures of their careers. This Web site describes the division's research and teaching fellowships for graduate students in the sciences. The Publications section includes program guidelines. There is also a page to search for awards.

NSF Division of Undergraduate Education
http://www.nsf.gov/div/index.jsp?div=DUE
Sponsor(s): National Science Foundation (NSF)
Description: The NSF's Division of Undergraduate Education (DUE) focuses on improving undergraduate education in science, technology, mathematics, and engineering. The division awards funds to scholarship programs at educational institutions; they do not award scholarships directly to students. The division also funds programs for teacher education and curriculum development. The Web site has information on the programs, deadlines, and awards.

Office of Postsecondary Education (OPE)
http://www.ed.gov/about/offices/list/ope/
Sponsor(s): Education Department — Postsecondary Education Office

Description: In the Programs/Initiatives section, this Web site provides a guide to the more than 40 postsecondary-related education programs administered by the OPE. Initiatives include programs for improving educational institutions, supporting international education, funding teacher training, and reaching out to students from disadvantaged backgrounds. The Reports and Resources section of the site includes the *Federal Campus-Based Programs Data Book.* The Accreditation section of the site explains the accreditation of educational institutions and has a directory of the numerous accrediting agencies.

This is a useful site with a substantial body of information sources of interest to students, educators, and financial aid offices.

Smithsonian Office of Fellowships

http://www.si.edu/ofg/

Sponsor(s): Smithsonian Institution

Description: The Office of Fellowships has applications, lists of fellowship and internship opportunities, and announcements of current recipients. The publication *Smithsonian Opportunities for Research and Study* is available online in an HTML format.

U.S. Merchant Marine Academy

http://www.usmma.edu/

Sponsor(s): Transportation Department — Maritime Administration (MARAD)

Description: The Merchant Marine Academy Web site has information about admissions, academics, and other activities. The site also links to the Global Maritime and Transportation School (GMATS) for maritime and transportation industry professionals.

United States Air Force Academy

http://www.usafa.af.mil/

Sponsor(s): Air Force — Air Force Academy

Description: The United States Air Force Academy Web site provides information for cadets, staff, and faculty. It includes visitor information and sections on admissions, academics, and cadet life. The academy's

libraries are listed in the USAFA Organizations section.

United States Military Academy at West Point

http://www.usma.edu/

Sponsor(s): Army — United States Military Academy (USMA)

Description: The West Point Web site has information for prospective and current students, alumni, visitors, and the West Point community. Sections include Admissions, Cadet Life, and the Academic, Physical, and Military Programs. A brief section on USMA history, found in the About the Academy section, includes a timeline and list of notable graduates.

United States Naval Academy

http://www.usna.edu

Sponsor(s): Navy — United States Naval Academy (USNA)

Description: This site contains information on the Naval Academy, mainly for students, prospective students, and midshipmen. The About USNA section links to information about the academy's history and notable graduates.

White House Initiative on Historically Black Colleges and Universities

http://www.ed.gov/about/inits/list/whhbcu/edlite-index.html

Sponsor(s): Education Department — White House Initiative on Historically Black Colleges and Universities

Description: The White House Initiative on Historically Black Colleges and Universities was established by executive order in 1981. This Web site has information on the initiative's work, board of advisers and staff, and budget. It also has a list of Historically Black Colleges and Universities by state and type of institution, with URLs provided for each institution.

White House Initiative on Tribal Colleges and Universities

http://www.ed.gov/about/inits/list/whtc/edlite-index.html

Sponsor(s): Education Department — White House Initiative on Tribal Colleges and Universities

Description: The President's Board of Advisors on Tribal Colleges and Universities and the White House Initiative on Tribal Colleges and Universities were established by executive order in 2002. In addition to information on the board and its activities, this site has a directory of tribal colleges and universities.

INTERNATIONAL EDUCATION

Bureau of Educational and Cultural Affairs

http://exchanges.state.gov/

Sponsor(s): State Department — Educational and Cultural Affairs Bureau

Description: The Bureau of Educational and Cultural Affairs Web site has information about its many international exchange and education programs. For U.S. citizens, the site has information on Fulbright Scholarships, English-language teaching abroad, study abroad, and other opportunities. For the audience abroad, the site has information about studying in the United States, the Fulbright Program, and a range of programs from the high school level up to the scholar and professional level. The site covers a range of other initiatives, such as the National Security Language Initiative, the Global Cultural Initiative, and the Edward R. Murrow Journalism Initiative.

EducationUSA

http://www.educationusa.state.gov/

Sponsor(s): State Department — Educational and Cultural Affairs Bureau

Description: EducationUSA is a global network of more than 450 advising and information centers in 170 countries supported by the Department of State's Bureau of Educational and Cultural Affairs. The Web site's About Us section provides contact information for individual centers worldwide. Other sections of the site provide information about finding a school, student visas, and living in the United States. Information is available for all levels of higher education and specialized professional study. Booklets from the department's "If You Want to Study in the United States" series are available online in Arabic, Chinese, French, Russian, Spanish, and English.

Fulbright Scholar Program

http://www.cies.org/

Alternate URL(s): http://www.iie.org/en/Fulbright/

Sponsor(s): State Department — Educational and Cultural Affairs Bureau; Institute of International Education (IIE)

Description: The Fulbright Program, sponsored by the United States, is an international education program that provides grants for graduate students, scholars, professionals, teachers, and administrators from the United States and other countries. This site, geared toward U.S. and non-U.S. applicants, describes the program and links to the Fulbright Commissions around the world.

Much of the program is administered for the Department of State by the Institute of International Education (IIE), an independent nonprofit organization. The alternate URL for this entry leads to the IIE Fulbright Web site. For applicants from the United States, the relevant applications are available online.

Future State

http://www.future.state.gov/

Sponsor(s): State Department

Description: Designed as the student Web site for the Department of State, Future State is largely written for students at the secondary school level, although it has one section for students in grades K–6. The site explains the work of the department, international education opportunities available to students, and the nature of careers within the Department of State. A section for parents and educators includes lesson plans and online resources.

Future State includes a substantial amount and variety of information relating to diplomacy, U.S. diplomatic history, country information, international exchange programs, and educational outreach activities.

International Affairs Office

http://www.ed.gov/about/inits/ed/internationaled/

Sponsor(s): Education Department
Description: The International Affairs Office coordinates the Education Department's international programs and works with international agencies such as the United Nations Educational, Scientific, and Cultural Organization (UNESCO). The Web site provides a directory to Education Department programs that have an international aspect. It also describes the office's activities, such as International Education Week and the United States Network for Education Information (USNEI) program.

National Security Education Program

http://www.nsep.gov/

Sponsor(s): National Security Education Program
Description: The National Security Education Program (NSEP) is a government program that works to strengthen national security by helping educate U.S. citizens about world cultures and languages. NSEP awards the David L. Boren Scholarships and Fellowships for study relating to global security at the graduate and undergraduate levels. The site provides information on the Boren grants and features accounts of student experiences while studying abroad.

U.S. Network for Education Information (USNEI)

http://www.ed.gov/about/offices/list/ous/international/usnei/edlite-index.html

Sponsor(s): Education Department
Description: USNEI is an interagency and public-private partnership set up to provide official information for anyone researching U.S. education. It also provides U.S. citizens with authoritative information about education in other countries. The site covers all

levels of education, with topics including visas, accreditation, professional licensure, and teaching abroad (or in the United States). The site's Foreign Country Database links to Web sites for individual countries' official education agencies and organizations.

KIDS' PAGES

America's Story from America's Library

http://www.americaslibrary.gov/

Sponsor(s): Library of Congress
Description: This Library of Congress Web site is designed for children and their families. It uses digitized images from the library's collection, accompanied by text and graphics, to create educational pages about American history and culture. Sections include Explore the States, Jump Back in Time, and Meet Amazing Americans.

ATF Kids' Page

http://www.atf.gov/kids/

Sponsor(s): Justice Department — Bureau of Alcohol, Tobacco, Firearms, and Explosives
Description: Several sections of the site are designed specifically for children, such as those about Elliot Ness and ATF canines. Other menu items link to content on the main ATF Web site, such as those about ATF history and ATF special agents killed in the line of duty.

BAM! Body and Mind

http://www.bam.gov/

Sponsor(s): Health and Human Services Department — Centers for Disease Control and Prevention (CDC)
Description: BAM!, designed for children age 9 to 13, has tips on fighting stress and adopting healthy lifestyles. It contains information about fitness, nutrition, safety, and handling peer pressure.

Ben's Guide to U.S. Government for Kids

http://bensguide.gpo.gov/

Sponsor(s): Government Printing Office (GPO) — Superintendent of Documents

Description: With a cartoon version of Benjamin Franklin as a guide, this GPO site for children covers topics such as the U.S. Constitution, how laws are made, the branches of the federal government, and citizenship. It features sections for specific age groups, plus a special section for parents and educators. The major sections are About Ben, K–2, 3–5, 6–8, 9–12, and Parents and Teachers.

Ben's Guide has received numerous accolades. It is useful as a grade school or high school student's homework helper, but may also help older students refresh their basic knowledge of U.S. government and history.

BLS Career Information
http://www.bls.gov/k12/
Sponsor(s): Labor Department — Bureau of Labor Statistics (BLS)
Description: The BLS Career Information page for youth uses a graphical interface to match kids' interests with potential careers. A Teachers' Guide refers teachers to additional information available from BLS.

The site is easy and fun to use. It is most appropriate for upper elementary grades and high school students.

CIA Kids' Page
https://www.cia.gov/kids-page/index.html
Sponsor(s): Central Intelligence Agency (CIA)
Description: The CIA Kids' Page has section for students in grades K–5 and 6–12 and for parents and teachers. It also has a separate games section and links to the kids' pages at other intelligence agency Web sites. Kids' activities include learning about the CIA seal, CIA history, and working for the CIA. Parent and teacher materials include lesson plans and guidance on topics such as Internet safety and helping children avoid drug abuse.

CryptoKids™
http://www.nsa.gov/kids/
Sponsor(s): Defense Department — National Security Agency (NSA)

Description: This site has games, activities, and background information about NSA's specialty, cryptography. The Student Resources section has NSA career information for high school and college students. The site has both a Flash and text version.

DOI Just For Kids
http://www.doi.gov/public/teachandlearn_kids.cfm
Sponsor(s): Interior Department
Description: This Department of the Interior site is a portal to the various kids' pages hosted by the department's agencies and bureaus. Linked sites include Endangered Species, Astrogeology for Kids, Earthquakes for Kids, Web Rangers, and Careers in Science. The target audience age varies with the sites. Many sites include sections for teachers and field trip information.

EIA Energy Kid's Page
http://www.eia.doe.gov/kids/
Sponsor(s): Energy Department — Energy Information Administration (EIA)
Description: The Department of Energy's Information Administration provides this educational page. Sections include: Energy Facts, Fun and Games, Energy History, Classroom Activities, and Glossary. The Classroom Activities section includes materials for teachers and parents to use in working with learners from grades K–12.

Energy Department—For Students and Kids
http://www.energy.gov/forstudentsandkids.htm
Sponsor(s): Energy Department
Description: This site centralizes access to Energy Department Web sites for kids and students, including energy glossaries and agency-sponsored contests and competitions. Linked sites cover a range of topics, from the relationship between garbage and energy to the Virtual Frog Dissection Kit. The More Kids Pages link leads to a list of kids' pages at the Energy Department's national laboratories and other centers. The Scholarships

and Internships link leads to information on opportunities for undergraduate college students, graduate students, postdoctoral scholars, and faculty.

EPA Climate Change Kids Site

http://www.epa.gov/climatechange/kids/

Sponsor(s): Environmental Protection Agency (EPA)

Description: This site provides explanations of climate, weather, and the greenhouse effect. It also has games and a section for teachers. Due to the amount of text and the complicated nature of the subject, this site is best for students in the upper grades.

EPA Student Center

http://www.epa.gov/students/

Sponsor(s): Environmental Protection Agency (EPA)

Description: The EPA Student Center Web site serves as a portal to information at a variety of educational levels and offers links to a Kids' Page, a site for high schoolers, and a site for teachers. Sections include Environmental Club Projects, Environmental Youth Awards, Fun Activities, and Environmental Basics.

FBI Kids' Page

http://www.fbi.gov/fbikids.htm

Sponsor(s): Justice Department — Federal Bureau of Investigation (FBI)

Description: The FBI Web site provides pages for kids in kindergarten through fifth grade, such as the About Our Dogs section, and pages for those in grades 6–12, such as the How We Investigate section.

FCC Kids Zone

http://www.fcc.gov/cgb/kidszone/

Sponsor(s): Federal Communications Commission (FCC) — Consumer and Governmental Affairs Bureau

Description: The FCC Kids Zone has information on the history of communications technology, online games, and a section about satellites. It also has answers to questions

kids ask, such as "What is 911?" and "What is the difference between AM radio and FM radio?"

FDA Kids' Site

http://www.fda.gov/ForConsumers/ByAudience/ForKids/default.htm

Sponsor(s): Health and Human Services Department — Food and Drug Administration (FDA)

Description: The colorful FDA Web site for children presents health and safety information in several sections, including the Food Safety Quiz and All About Animals. The center box links to the Parents' Corner with information on child health and safety.

Federal Reserve Kids Page

http://www.federalreserve.gov/kids/

Sponsor(s): Federal Reserve

Description: This site has answers to twelve questions, ranging from "What is inflation?" to "What is the FOMC, and what does it do?"

The Federal Reserve has a broader education site with resources for teachers available at <http://www.federalreserveeducation.org/>.

FEMA for Kids

http://www.fema.gov/kids/

Sponsor(s): Federal Emergency Management Agency (FEMA)

Description: This FEMA site provides information and resources to help children prepare for and prevent disasters. Children can go through a series of activities and receive a Disaster Action Kid certificate. A section called the Disaster Area explains threats like floods and hurricanes. The site includes a section for parents and teachers with curriculum resources and links to further information.

Because of the sensitive nature of disaster threats, parents and teachers will probably want to review this site before sharing sections of it with young children.

FireSafety.gov
http://www.firesafety.gov/
Sponsor(s): Health and Human Services Department — Centers for Disease Control and Prevention (CDC); Consumer Product Safety Commission (CPSC); Homeland Security Department — Federal Emergency Management Agency (FEMA) — U.S. Fire Administration
Description: FireSafety.gov is the product of an interagency collaboration to increase awareness of fire dangers and fire prevention. The site features current news of product recalls and a Fire Safety Directory. The directory provides information about residential fire safety and prevention, with sections for at-risk populations such as the elderly, the visually impaired, and the hearing impaired. The Reference Materials section includes statistics, information on grants, and a database of fire-related consumer product recalls. Selected information from the site is available in Spanish.

FSAKids
www.fsa.usda.gov/fsakids/
Sponsor(s): Agriculture Department (USDA) — Farm Service Agency (FSA)
Description: The Farm Service Agency provides coloring books and games with an agricultural theme, along with recipes for kids to try. The site also has online games in Spanish. Each section of the site also has information for parents and educators.

GirlsHealth.gov
http://girlshealth.gov/
Sponsor(s): Health and Human Services Department
Description: GirlsHealth.gov is designed to help adolescent girls (ages 10 to 16) learn about the health issues and social situations that they will encounter during the teen years. Sections provide information about fitness, nutrition, the mind, relationships, and other related topics. The site also has sections for parents, caregivers, and teachers.

HHS Pages for Kids
http://www.hhs.gov/kids/
Sponsor(s): Health and Human Services Department
Description: This portal links to kids' pages offered by agencies related to the Department of Health and Human Services. They distribute information about health, avoiding cigarettes and drugs, food safety, medical science, and more. The site includes sections for parents and teachers.

Inside the Courtroom
http://www.usdoj.gov/usao/eousa/kidspage/
Sponsor(s): Justice Department — United States Attorneys
Description: This kids' page describes a typical courtroom and the jobs of the people who work in a courthouse. It also presents a fictional account of an FBI case and how it moved from investigation to prosecution.

Kidd Safety
http://www.cpsc.gov/kids/kidsafety/
Sponsor(s): Consumer Product Safety Commission (CPSC)
Description: The Kidd Safety page uses a cartoon goat named Kidd to guide users through games and information about safety. The site covers topics such as bicycle helmets, riding a scooter, and safety around the house.

Kids and Families—Social Security
http://www.ssa.gov/kids/
Sponsor(s): Social Security Administration (SSA)
Description: This SSA Web site includes a Kids' Place and a Parents' Place. The Kids' Place offers tales about saving for the future and an introduction to the Social Security card. On the main page, there is also a link to information for the families of youth with disabilities.

Kids' Corner, Endangered Species Program
http://www.endangeredspecie.com/kids.htm
Sponsor(s): Interior Department — Fish and Wildlife Service (FWS)

Description: This site features a selection of educational activities about endangered species, most designed to be used by a teacher or parent for the benefit of young learners. In the Educators' section, the Endangered Means There is Still Time activity includes slide shows, a quiz, an activity workbook, and teachers' resources. The site also links to related programs from inside and outside the government, such as the Junior Duck Stamp Program and the National Wildlife Federation's Backyard Wildlife Habitats program.

Kids in the House

http://clerkkids.house.gov/

Sponsor(s): Congress — House of Representatives — Office of the Clerk

Description: The House Clerk's Web site for kids includes material (written primarily for upper grade or high school students) on House procedures and history. It also discusses how bills are made into law. Features include a cartoon field trip to Capitol Hill, games, and a resource section for parents and teachers.

Kids Next Door

http://www.hud.gov/kids/kids.html

Sponsor(s): Housing and Urban Development (HUD)

Description: HUD's Web site for children is subtitled "Where kids can learn more about being good citizens." The page features sections including Meet Cool People, See Neat Things, and Visit Awesome Places. Within each of these sections are activities and pages such as Help the Homeless, Kids Volunteer, Safe Places to Play, and Build A Community. A section called Franklin's Fair Housing Corner provides educational materials on fair housing law that will be of interest to teachers and schools.

Kids Saving Energy

http://www.eere.energy.gov/kids/

Sponsor(s): Energy Department — Energy Efficiency and Renewable Energy Office

Description: This Department of Energy page for children includes home energy saving tips, an introduction to renewable energy technologies, games, and an energy quiz. A section for parents and teachers includes lesson plans for grades K–4, 5–8, and 9–12.

Kid's Zone, Pablo's Classroom

http://www.yesicankids.gov

Alternate URL(s): http://www.yosipuedo. gov/kidszone/kidszone3.html

Sponsor(s): President's Advisory Commission on Educational Excellence for Hispanic Americans

Description: Featuring the cartoon character Pablo the Eagle, this kids' page is part of the White House Initiative on Educational Excellence for Hispanic Americans. Reflecting the initiative's emphasis on reading skills, the site has a collection of bedtime stories with color illustrations. The site also has a Spanish-language version, which is available at the alternate URL listed above.

Kids.gov

http://www.kids.gov/

Sponsor(s): General Services Administration (GSA)

Description: Kids.gov is a portal to U.S. federal and state government Web pages designed for children. The site groups links by age group, grades K–5 and grades 6–8. Links are then organized by topic, such as careers, computers, and "fun stuff." A section for educators provides links organized in the same categories, supplemented with parent and teacher resource sites.

Kids.gov provides an easy way for children (as well as teachers and parents) to find kid-friendly information on the Web.

MyPyramid for Kids

http://www.fns.usda.gov/tn/kids-pyramid .html

Sponsor(s): Agriculture Department (USDA) — Food and Nutrition Service (FNS)

Description: The MyPyramid for Kids Web site provides nutrition education resources for teachers and parents of elementary school children. Resources include a MyPyramid for

Kids poster, coloring page, and worksheet in PDF format. Classroom materials on the site include three lesson plans. The site also has a Tips for Families color brochure and offers the MyPyramid Blast Off game, which requires Flash.

NASA Kids

http://www.nasa.gov/audience/forkids/home/
Alternate URL(s): http://www.nasa.gov/audience/forstudents/
Sponsor(s): National Aeronautics and Space Administration (NASA) — Education Office
Description: The NASA Kids page features games, stories, and activities related to space and science. It also has information on current NASA missions.
The alternate URL above links to the NASA For Students page, which has sections for students in grades K–4, 5–8, 9–12, and postsecondary levels. Both the Kids page and the For Students Page are part of a comprehensive NASA Education Web site at <http://education.nasa.gov/home/>.
This site and the central NASA education site are rich sources of material for students and teachers.

NCEH Kids' Page

http://www.cdc.gov/nceh/kids/99kidsday/
Sponsor(s): Health and Human Services Department — Centers for Disease Control and Prevention (CDC) — National Center for Environmental Health (NCEH)
Description: Designed for the young reader, the site is based on "Take Your Children to Work Day," a booklet created by NCEH for its employees' children to introduce them to the work of the agency. It includes the following sections: Asthma, Cruise Ship Inspection, Disabilities, Emergency Response, Global Health, and Lead Poisoning. The booklet is available as a PDF version that may be downloaded and printed.

NIEHS Kids' Pages

http://www.niehs.nih.gov/kids/home.htm

Sponsor(s): National Institutes of Health (NIH) — National Institute of Environmental Health Sciences (NIEHS)
Description: This Kids Page offering from the NIEHS has both a Spanish-language and a text-only version. It includes sections such as Games and Activities, Color Our World, and Sing-Along Songs. It also has a page for kids about Pandemic Flu.

NLS Kids Zone

http://www.loc.gov/nls/children/
Sponsor(s): Library of Congress — National Library Services for the Blind and Physically Handicapped (NLS)
Description: This Web site for kids is designed to be used with text-based browsers, such as Lynx, frequently used by blind readers. It recommends audio, Braille, and print/Braille books for children.

NRC: Students' Corner

http://www.nrc.gov/reading-rm/basic-ref/students.html
Sponsor(s): Nuclear Regulatory Commission (NRC)
Description: The NRC student's Web site explains everything from what nuclear energy is, to emergency planning, to radioactive waste. It also has a section for teachers' lesson plans.

NROjr.GOV

http://www.nrojr.gov/
Sponsor(s): Defense Department — National Reconnaissance Office (NRO)
Description: The NRO kids' page features games and activities with a satellite and space theme. With content including simple online coloring pages, stories, and music, it is aimed at the younger set.

Patent and Trademark Office Kids' Page

http://www.uspto.gov/go/kids/
Sponsor(s): Commerce Department — Patent and Trademark Office (PTO)
Description: The PTO Web site offers children's contests, games, and puzzles having to

do with creativity, invention, and the operations of the PTO. The site has sections designed for students in grades K–6 and 6–12, as well as information for parents, teachers, and coaches.

Peace Corps Kids' World
http://www.peacecorps.gov/kids/
Sponsor(s): Peace Corps
Description: The Peace Corps offers this kids' page, with sections including: What is the Peace Corps?; Make a Difference; Explore the World; Tell Me a Story; and Food, Friends, and Fun. This site mainly provides information about the Peace Corps program. Some resources on foreign countries are listed in the Explore the World and Food, Friends, and Fun sections.

Sci4Kids
http://www.ars.usda.gov/is/kids/
Alternate URL(s): http://www.ars.usda.gov/is/espanol/kids/
Sponsor(s): Agriculture Department (USDA) — Agricultural Research Service (ARS)
Description: Sci4Kids is designed for children between the ages of 8 and 13. With a colorful all-graphics menu, it shows how scientific research affects many areas of life. The site includes information about careers in science. The alternate URL links to the Spanish-language version of the site.

ScienceLab
http://www.osti.gov/sciencelab/
Sponsor(s): Energy Department — Scientific and Technical Information Office
Description: ScienceLab links to student resources at government and other Web sites. Major sections for students include Elementary Lab, Middle School Lab, High School Lab, and Experiments. The site also has a Teachers' Lab section and sections about science careers, competitions, and summer camps.

Smithsonian Education
http://www.smithsonianeducation.org/students/
Sponsor(s): Smithsonian Institution
Description: The Smithsonian Web site for kids and students features themed IdeaLabs called Mr. President, Walking on the Moon, and Amazing Collections. The At the Smithsonian section links to pages of interest to kids from many Smithsonian Web sites. More activities are organized under the topics of art, science and nature, history and culture, and people and places.

Much of the content will be of interest to students in the upper grades through high school and their parents. The site will be particularly useful for kids preparing to visit Smithsonian museums.

Space Place
http://spaceplace.jpl.nasa.gov/spacepl.htm
Alternate URL(s): http://spaceplace.jpl.nasa.gov/sp/kids/index.shtml
Sponsor(s): National Aeronautics and Space Administration (NASA) — Jet Propulsion Laboratory (JPL)
Description: Space Place is full of games, projects, and animations relating to earth and space science. The Teachers' Corner has classroom activity articles. The site has a Spanish-language version available; this can be linked from the top of the home page or directly accessed at the alternate URL listed above.

State Facts for Children
http://www.census.gov/schools/facts/
Sponsor(s): Commerce Department — Economics and Statistics Administration (ESA) — Census Bureau
Description: A map of the United States serves as a menu for basic Census statistics, history, and trivia concerning each of the states, Puerto Rico, and the District of Columbia.

Stop Bullying Now
http://www.stopbullyingnow.hrsa.gov/
Sponsor(s): Health and Human Services Department — Health Resources and Services Administration (HRSA)

Description: This site has extensive information and a variety of activities for kids about dealing with bullying behavior. The portion of the site for adults and educators is also available in Spanish.

This site makes extensive use of animation, sound, and features such as webcasts and podcasts. There does not appear to be a text-only version.

ToxMystery
http://toxmystery.nlm.nih.gov/
Sponsor(s): National Institutes of Health (NIH) — National Library of Medicine (NLM)
Description: ToxMystery is an interactive game designed to teach kids about dangerous household substances. The site includes sections for parents and teachers, and has a version in Spanish.

U.S. Army Corps of Engineers Education Center
http://education.usace.army.mil/
Sponsor(s): Army — Army Corps of Engineers
Description: This site provides educational information and activities about ports, waterway navigation, engineering, and related topics. Some links lead directly to Corps Web site pages that are not written for children.

Teachers and parents will need to preview and select the sections written for their students' grade level and interests.

United States Mint's Site for Kids
http://www.usmint.gov/kids/
Sponsor(s): Treasury Department — United States Mint
Description: This site is alternatively called H.I.P (History in Your Pocket)/Pocket Change. It features games and activities to teach children about the history of coins, coins around the world, and coin collecting. It also includes a section for teachers.

United We Serve
http://www.serve.gov/
Sponsor(s): Corporation for National and Community Service

Description: This United We Serve page has information for kids, youth, parents, and teachers—all focused on volunteering. The Toolkits section includes resources for teachers.

USFA Kids
http://www.usfa.fema.gov/kids/flash.shtm
Sponsor(s): Homeland Security Department — Federal Emergency Management Agency (FEMA) — U.S. Fire Administration
Description: USFA Kids has information on home fire safety, smoke alarms, and escaping from fire. It includes coloring pages and a Hazard House game. The section for parents and teachers includes lesson plans and downloadable activity sheets.

VA KIDS
http://www.va.gov/kids/
Sponsor(s): Veterans Affairs Department
Description: VA KIDS has sections for grades K–5 and 6–12 and for teachers. The grades 6–12 section includes information about volunteer and scholarship opportunities. The teacher section has resource guides and contacts for finding classroom speakers.

White House 101
http://www.whitehouse.gov/about/white-house-101/
Sponsor(s): White House
Description: The White House 101 Web site features "Facts and fun for all ages", including sections on White House history and traditions, tours of the White House, the First Family's pets, and photos and biographies of all the Presidents.

World Book @ NASA
http://www.nasa.gov/worldbook/
Sponsor(s): National Aeronautics and Space Administration (NASA)
Description: Through a partnership with World Book, the NASA Web site is offering a selection of over 40 *World Book* encyclopedia articles concerning space exploration. Entries range from "Armstrong, Neil" to "Weather."

While not strictly a kids' page, *World Book @ NASA* will certainly be a homework helper.

TEACHING

Federal Resources for Educational Excellence (FREE)

http://www.free.ed.gov/

Sponsor(s): Education Department

Description: FREE is a central finding aid for roughly 1,500 Web-based teaching and learning resources on government and government-supported sites. Resources are organized by broad topics, such as Arts and Music, History and Social Studies, and Math. The Subject Map provides a detailed breakdown of the topics. Announcements of newly added resources are available via RSS feed.

This is one of the most comprehensive finding aids for education-related U.S. government Web sites. Its primary focus is on K–12 resources.

For Teachers

http://www.loc.gov/teachers/

Sponsor(s): Library of Congress

Description: This site focuses on using the digital collections of the Library of Congress in classroom education. It serves as a portal to relevant resources on the library site and also links to professional development tools for teachers.

James Madison Graduate Fellowships

http://www.jamesmadison.com/

Sponsor(s): James Madison Memorial Fellowship Foundation

Description: James Madison Graduate Fellowships are for teachers at the secondary school level who wish to enhance their knowledge of the U.S. Constitution. The fellowships are for graduate study leading to a master's degree. This Web site has more about the program and about the James Madison Memorial Fellowship Foundation, an independent agency within the executive branch.

NCELA—National Clearinghouse for English Language Acquisition

http://www.ncela.gwu.edu/

Sponsor(s): Education Department — English Language Acquisition Office

Description: NCELA, known in full as the National Clearinghouse for English Language Acquisition and Language Instruction Educational Programs and funded by the Department of Education, is concerned with the effective education of linguistically and culturally diverse learners in the United States. The NCELA Web site provides direct access to a wealth of information on research, resources, statistics, funding, and programs to assist those working with English-language learners.

What Works Clearinghouse (WWC)

http://www.whatworks.ed.gov/

Sponsor(s): Education Department — Institute of Education Sciences

Description: WWC collects and reviews studies of the effectiveness of educational programs and practices. It is intended to be a "central and trusted source of scientific evidence of what works in education." (From the Web site.) It addition to the reports and guides, the site provides a database of education program evaluators and technical information on evaluating education programs.

INDEX